Introduction

This supplement is the first of three cumulative updating supplements to *Blackstone's Criminal Practice 2020*.

This supplement contains the complete text of the Criminal Procedure Rules 2015 as amended by the Criminal Procedure (Amendment) Rules 2016 (SI 2016 No. 120), the Criminal Procedure (Amendment No. 2) Rules 2016 (SI 2016 No. 705), the Criminal Procedure (Amendment) Rules 2017 (SI 2017 No. 144), the Criminal Procedure (Amendment No. 2) Rules 2017 (SI 2017 No. 282), the Criminal Procedure (Amendment No. 3) Rules 2017 (SI 2017 No. 755), the Criminal Procedure (Amendment No. 4) Rules 2017 (SI 2017 No. 915), the Criminal Procedure (Amendment) Rules 2018 (SI 2018 No. 132), the Criminal Procedure (Amendment No. 2) Rules 2018 (SI 2018 No. 847), the Criminal Procedure (Amendment) Rules 2019 (SI 2019 No. 143) and the Criminal Procedure (Amendment No. 2) Rules 2019 (SI 2019 No. 1119); the Criminal Practice Directions; and the Sentencing Guidelines as at 1 October 2019.

David Ormerod is currently the Criminal Law Commissioner for England and Wales, but nothing in this work should be taken as representing the views of the Law Commission unless expressly stated to do so.

Please visit the *Blackstone's Criminal Practice 2020* companion website at www.oup.com/blackstones/criminal for free online fortnightly updates, and also to receive *Blackstone's Briefing*, a free regular newsletter. If you have any queries, please contact blackstonescriminal@oup.com.

BLACKSTONE'S

CRIMINAL PRACTICE

BLACKSTONE'S

CRIMINAL PRACTICE

2020

SUPPLEMENT 1

GENERAL EDITORS
DAVID ORMEROD QC (HON)
LAW COMMISSIONER, BARRISTER, BENCHER OF MIDDLE TEMPLE,
PROFESSOR OF CRIMINAL JUSTICE,
UNIVERSITY COLLEGE LONDON

DAVID PERRY QC
BARRISTER, 6KBW COLLEGE HILL

FOUNDING EDITOR
HHJ PETER MURPHY

SUPPLEMENT EDITOR
WILLIAM HAYS
BARRISTER, 6KBW COLLEGE HILL

CONTRIBUTORS
PARAMJIT AHLUWALIA, DUNCAN ATKINSON QC, ALEX BAILIN QC, DIANE BIRCH OBE, HHJ JONATHAN COOPER, HHJ JOHANNAH CUTTS QC, ANAND DOOBAY, ANTHONY EDWARDS, RUDI FORTSON QC, DANIEL GODDEN, KATHERINE HARDCASTLE, WILLIAM HAYS, MICHAEL HIRST, LAURA C. H. HOYANO, PETER HUNGERFORD-WELCH, PAUL JARVIS, ADRIAN KEANE, MICHAEL LEREGO QC, RICHARD MCMAHON QC, VALSAMIS MITSILEGAS, TIM MOLONEY QC, REBECCA NIBLOCK, AMANDA PINTO QC, HH PETER ROOK QC, RICHARD D. TAYLOR, MARK TOPPING, MARTIN WASIK CBE

OXFORD
UNIVERSITY PRESS

Great Clarendon Street, Oxford, OX2 6DP,
United Kingdom

Oxford University Press is a department of the University of Oxford. It furthers the University's objective of excellence in research, scholarship, and education by publishing worldwide. Oxford is a registered trade mark of Oxford University Press in the UK and in certain other countries

First Edition published in 2019

Impression: 1

Published in the United States of America by Oxford University Press
198 Madison Avenue, New York, NY 10016, United States of America

British Library Cataloguing in Publication Data
Data available

ISBN 978–0–19–884920–9

Printed in Italy by
L.E.G.O. S.p.A.

Contents

Table of Cases . . . xi
Table of Statutes . . . xv
Table of Statutory Instruments . . . xxvi
Table of Practice Directions . . . xxxii
Table of Codes of Conduct . . . xxxii
Table of Guidelines . . . xxxiii
Table of Protocols and Circulars . . . xxxiii
Table of International Treaties and Conventions and other Legal Instruments . . . xxxiv
Table of European Legislation . . . xxxiv

Criminal Procedure Rules and Criminal Practice Directions . . . 1

CPD General Matters . . . 3

CrimPR Part 1 The Overriding Objective . . . 4
CPD Part 1 The Overriding Objective . . . 5
CrimPR Part 2 Understanding and Applying the Rules . . . 5
CrimPR Part 3 Case Management . . . 6
CPD Part 3 Case Management . . . 16
CrimPR Part 4 Service of Documents . . . 36
CrimPR Part 5 Forms and Court Records . . . 39
CPD Part 5 Forms and Court Records . . . 43
CrimPR Part 6 Reporting, etc. Restrictions . . . 49
CPD Part 6 Reporting, etc. Restrictions . . . 53
CrimPR Part 7 Starting a Prosecution in a Magistrates' Court . . . 56
CrimPR Part 8 Initial Details of the Prosecution Case . . . 58
CPD Part 8 Initial Details of the Prosecution Case . . . 59
CrimPR Part 9 Allocation and Sending for Trial . . . 59
CPD Part 9 Allocation and Sending for Trial . . . 66
CrimPR Part 10 The Indictment . . . 66
CPD Part 10 The Indictment . . . 69
CrimPR Part 11 Deferred Prosecution Agreements . . . 72
CrimPR Part 12 Discontinuing a Prosecution . . . 76
CrimPR Part 13 Warrants for Arrest, Detention or Imprisonment . . . 77
CrimPR Part 14 Bail and Custody Time Limits . . . 79
CPD Part 14 Bail and Custody Time Limits . . . 89
CrimPR Part 15 Disclosure . . . 94
CPD Part 15 Disclosure . . . 97
CrimPR Part 16 Written Witness Statements . . . 97
CPD Part 16 Written Witness Statements . . . 98
CrimPR Part 17 Witness Summonses, Warrants and Orders . . . 101
CPD Part 17 Witness Summonses, Warrants and Orders . . . 103
CrimPR Part 18 Measures to Assist a Witness or Defendant to Give Evidence . . . 103
CPD Part 18 Measures to Assist a Witness or Defendant to Give Evidence . . . 110
CrimPR Part 19 Expert Evidence . . . 122
CPD Part 19 Expert Evidence . . . 125
CrimPR Part 20 Hearsay Evidence . . . 128
CrimPR Part 21 Evidence of Bad Character . . . 130
CPD Part 21 Evidence of Bad Character . . . 132
CrimPR Part 22 Evidence of a Complainant's Previous Sexual Behaviour . . . 132
CPD Part 22 Evidence of a Complainant's Previous Sexual Behaviour . . . 134

CrimPR Part 23 Restriction on Cross-Examination by a Defendant 135
CPD Part 23 *Cross-Examination Advocates* 139
CrimPR Part 24 Trial and Sentence in a Magistrates' Court 141
CPD Part 24 *Trial and Sentence in a Magistrates' Court* 151
CrimPR Part 25 Trial and Sentence in the Crown Court 157
CPD Part 25 *Trial and Sentence in the Crown Court* 165
CrimPR Part 26 Jurors 166
CPD Part 26 *Jurors* 167
CrimPR Part 27 Retrial After Acquittal 180
CPD Sentencing 183
CrimPR Part 28 Sentencing Procedures in Special Cases 200
CrimPR Part 29 Road Traffic Penalties 205
CrimPR Part 30 Enforcement of Fines and Other Orders for Payment 208
CrimPR Part 31 Behaviour Orders 212
CrimPR Part 32 Breach, Revocation and Amendment of Community and Other Orders 216
CrimPR Part 33 Confiscation and Related Proceedings 217
CrimPR Part 34 Appeal to the Crown Court 238
CPD Part 34 *Appeal to the Crown Court* 242
CrimPR Part 35 Appeal to the High Court by Case Stated 243
CrimPR Part 36 Appeal to the Court of Appeal: General Rules 245
CrimPR Part 37 Appeal to the Court of Appeal against Ruling at Preparatory Hearing 249
CrimPR Part 38 Appeal to the Court of Appeal against Ruling Adverse to Prosecution 251
CrimPR Part 39 Appeal to the Court of Appeal about Conviction or Sentence 253
CPD Part 39 *Appeal to the Court of Appeal about Conviction or Sentence* 258
CrimPR Part 40 Appeal to the Court of Appeal about Reporting or Public Access Restriction 262
CrimPR Part 41 Reference to the Court of Appeal of Point of Law or Unduly Lenient Sentencing 264
CrimPR Part 42 Appeal to the Court of Appeal in Confiscation and Related Proceedings 266
CrimPR Part 43 Appeal or Reference to the Supreme Court 270
CrimPR Part 44 Request to the European Court for a Preliminary Ruling 271
CPD Part 44 *Request to the European Court for a Preliminary Ruling* 272
CrimPR Part 45 Costs 273
CPD Part 45 *Costs* 281
CrimPR Part 46 Representatives 281
CrimPR Part 47 Investigation Orders and Warrants[1] 284
CPD Part 47 *Investigation Orders and Warrants* 315
CrimPR Part 47A Investigation Orders and Warrants[2] 318
CrimPR Part 48 Contempt of Court 347
CPD Part 48 *Contempt of Court* 351
CrimPR Part 49 International Co-operation 351
CrimPR Part 50 Extradition 358
CPD Part 50 *Extradition* 373
CPD: General Application 381
CPD Listing 387

Sentencing Guidelines 403

Part A – General and Overarching Principles 404
Part 1 Allocation 422
Part 2 General Guideline: Overarching Principles 424
Part 3 Offences taken into Consideration and Totality 429
Part 4 Reduction in Sentence for a Guilty Plea 440

[1] This Part only applies in the event that the Criminal Procedure (Amendment) (EU Exit) Regulations 2019 (SI 2019 No. 908) come into force on or after 7 October 2019. Otherwise, Part 47A applies and Part 47 should be ignored.
[2] This Part only applies in the event that the Criminal Procedure (Amendment) (EU Exit) Regulations 2019 (SI 2019 No. 908) come into force before 7 October 2019. Otherwise, Part 47 applies and Part 47A should be ignored.

Part 5 Domestic Abuse . . . 446
Part 6 Overarching Principles: Assaults on Children and Cruelty to a Child . . . 449
Part 7 Overarching Principles: Sentencing Youths . . . 450
Part 8 Sentencing Children and Young People: Overarching Principles and Offence-Specific Guidelines for Sexual Offences and Robbery . . . 451
Part 9 Imposition of Community and Custodial Sentences . . . 481

Part B – Magistrates' Court Sentencing Guidelines . . . 486
Part 10 Magistrates' Court Sentencing Guidelines . . . 486

Part C – Specific Offences . . . 591
Part 11 Arson and Criminal Damage . . . 591
Part 12 Assault . . . 609
Part 13 Attempted Murder . . . 622
Part 14 Bladed Articles and Offensive Weapons . . . 625

Breach Offences . . . 636
Part 15 Breach Offences . . . 636
Part 16 Bail, Fail to Surrender to . . . 655
Part 17 Anti-social Behaviour Orders, Breach of . . . 661
Part 18 Protective Order, Breach of . . . 667
Part 19 Burglary Offences . . . 672
Part 20 Child Cruelty . . . 678
Part 21 Dangerous Dog Offences . . . 688
Part 22 Death by Driving, Causing . . . 698
Part 23 Drug Offences . . . 709
Part 24 Environmental Offences . . . 725
Part 25 Manslaughter . . . 738
Part 26 Fraud, Bribery and Money Laundering Offences . . . 750
Part 27 Intimidatory Offences . . . 777
Part 28 Corporate Manslaughter . . . 793
Part 29 Manslaughter by Reason of Provocation . . . 798
Part 30 Robbery . . . 799
Part 31 Sexual Offences . . . 807
Part 32 Terrorism Offences . . . 879
Part 33 Theft . . . 903

Index . . . 919

Table of Cases

A [2015] 2 Cr App R 12 (115), [2015] EWCA Crim 177 . . . . . PD-26
Abbas v CPS [2015] 2 Cr App R 11 (183), [2015] EWHC 579 (Admin) PD-52
Abdroikov [2007] 1 WLR 2679, [2008] 1 All ER 315, [2008] 1 Cr App R 21 (280), [2008] Crim LR 134, [2007] UKHL 37 . . . . . PD-60
Ali [1998] 2 Cr App R 123 . . . . . SG3-10
Anderson v DPP [1978] AC 964, [1978] 2 All ER 512, (1978) 67 Cr App R 185, [1978] Crim LR 568 . . . . . SG3-5
Ashes [2008] 1 All ER 113, [2008] 1 Cr App R (S) 86 (507), [2007] EWCA Crim 1848. . . . . SG3-13
Attorney General's Reference (No. 1 of 1990) [1992] QB 630, [1992] 3 WLR 9, [1992] 3 All ER 169, 95 Cr App R 296, 156 JP 693, [1993] Crim LR 37 . . . . . SG3-10
Attorney General's Reference (No. 21 of 2002) [2001] 1 Cr App R (S) 50 (173) SG22-8

B [2011] Crim LR 233, [2010] EWCA Crim 4 . . . . . PD-46
Barker [2011] Crim LR 233, [2010] EWCA Crim 4 . . . . . PD-116
Boardman [2015] EWCA Crim 175 . . . . . PD-54
BPS Advertising Ltd v London Borough of Barnet [2006] EWHC 3335 (Admin). SG10-147

C v Sevenoaks Youth Court [2009] EWHC 3088 (Admin) PD-8
Canavan [1998] 1 Cr App R 79, [1998] 1 All ER 42, 161 JP 709, [1997] Crim LR 766 . . . . PD-4, PD-26
Celaire [2003] 1 Cr App R (S) 116 (610), [2003] 4 All ER 869, [2003] Crim LR 124, [2002] EWCA Crim 2487 . . . . . SG3-10
Cliff [2004] EWCA Crim 3139 . . . . . SG10-160
Connors and Mirza [2004] 1 AC 1118, [2004] 2 Cr App R 8 (112), [2004] UKHL 2 . . . . . PD-69
Cornelius [2002] 2 Cr App R (S) 69 (297), [2002] EWCA Crim 138 . . . . . SG3-12
Costello [2011] 1 WLR 638, [2010] 3 All ER 490, [2010] 2 Cr App R (S) 94 (608), [2010] EWCA Crim 371 . . . . . SG3-10
Cox [2012] 2 Cr App R 6 (63), [2012] 176 JP 549, [2012] Crim LR 621, [2012] EWCA Crim 549 . . . . . PD-6, PD-8

D v Sheffield Youth Court (2003) 167 JP 159, [2003] EWHC 35 (Admin). SG22-12
DPP v Mullally [2006] EWHC 3448 (Admin) SG22-12
DPP v Petrie [2015] EWHC 48 (Admin). PD-55
DPP v Woods [2017] EWHC 1070 (Admin). PD-55
Delucca [2011] 1 WLR 1148, [2010] 4 All ER 290, [2011] 1 Cr App R (S) 7 (46), [2010] Crim LR 584, [2010] EWCA Crim 710. . . . . SG3-12
Dlugosz [2013] 1 Cr App R 32 (425), [2013] Crim LR 684, [2013] EWCA Crim 2. . . . . PD-47
Donovan [2012] EWCA Crim 2749 . . . . . PD-44

E [2012] Crim LR 563, [2011] EWCA Crim 3028 . . . . . PD-6
Eagles [2007] 1 Cr App R (S) 99 (612), [2006] EWCA Crim 2368. . . . . SG8-9
Ealing Magistrates' Court, ex parte Burgess [2001] 165 JP 82, [2000] Crim LR 855 . . . . . PD-19
Edwards [2012] Crim LR 563, [2011] EWCA Crim 3028. . . . . PD-46
Engen [2004] EWCA Crim 1536. . . . . SG10-136
Erskine [2010] 1 WLR 183, [2010] 1 All ER 1196, [2009] 2 Cr App R 29 (461), [2009] EWCA Crim 1425 . . . . . PD-113

F [2013] 1 WLR 2143, [2013] 2 Cr App R 13 (137), 177 JP 406 [2013], EWCA Crim 424 .... PD-46
F Howe & Son (Engineers) Ltd [1999] 2 All ER 249, [1999] 2 Cr App R (S) 37, 163 JP 359, [1999] Crim LR 238 .... PD-88
Ford [2006] 1 Cr App R (S) 36 (204), [2005] Crim LR 807, [2005] EWCA Crim 1358..... SG13-2
Friskies Petcare (UK) Ltd [2000] 2 Cr App R (S) 401 .... PD-88

Ghafoor [2003] 1 Cr App R (S) 84 (428), 166 JP 601, [2002] Crim LR 739, [2002] EWCA Crim 1857 .... SG8-8
Goodyear [2005] 1 WLR 2532, [2005] 3 All ER 117, [2005] 2 Cr App R 20 (281), [2006] 1 Cr App R (S) 6 (23), [2005] Crim LR 659, [2005] EWCA Crim 888.....PD-74, PD-75
Gray [2014] EWCA Crim 2372....PD-94, PD-96

H [2004] 2 AC 134, [2004] 2 WLR 335, [2004] 1 All ER 1269, [2004] 2 Cr App R 10 (179), [2004] UKHL 3.... F2.17, PD-44
H [2012] 1 WLR 1416, [2012] 2 All ER 340, [2012] 2 Cr App R (S) 21 (88), [2012] Crim LR 149, [2011] EWCA Crim 2753.... SG31-157
Hanif v UK [2011] ECHR 2247 .... PD-60
Hart [2007] 1 Cr App R 31 (412), [2007] 2 Cr App R (S) 34 (192), [2007] Crim LR 313, [2006] EWCA Crim 3239 .... PD-96
Hasan [2005] 2 AC 467, [2005] 2 WLR 709, [2005] 4 All ER 685, [2005] 2 Cr App R 22 (315), [2006] Crim LR 142, [2005] UKHL 22 .... SG22-12
Hashman and Harrup v United Kingdom (2000) 30 EHRR 241, [2000] Crim LR 185 ...... PD-82
Hills [2012] 1 WLR 2121, [2009] 1 Cr App R (S) 75 (441), [2008] EWCA Crim 1871..... SG3-13

Jalil [2009] 2 Cr App R (S) 40 (276), [2009] Crim LR 442, [2008] EWCA Crim 2910 ...... PD-60
James [2017] Crim LR 228, [2016] EWCA Crim 1639....PD-113
James [2018] 1 WLR 2749, [2018] Cr App R 33 (258), [2018] EWCA Crim 285 .... PD-94
Jamieson [2009] 2 Cr App R (S) 26 (199), [2008] EWCA Crim 2761.... SG3-10
Jones [2003] 1 AC 1, [2002] 2 WLR 524, [2002] 2 All ER 113, [2002] 2 Cr App R 9 (128), 166 JP 333, [2002] Crim LR 554, [2002] UKHL 5 .... PD-57

Kastercum (1972) 56 Cr App R 298, [1972] Crim LR 263 .... SG3-10
Kidd [1998] 1 Cr App R 79, [1998] 1 All ER 42, 161 JP 709, [1997] Crim LR 766.... PD-26
Kirk [2015] EWCA Crim 1764 .... PD-94

L [2011] 1 Cr App R 27 (338), [2011] EWCA Crim 65 .... PD-60
Laidlaw v Atkinson QBD CO/275/86 .... SG16-3
Lang [2006] 1 WLR 2509, [2005] EWCA Crim 2864.....E4.21, SG8-5
Lawrence (1989) 11 Cr App R (S) 580.... SG3-10
Little (14 April 1976 unreported (CA)) SG10-137
Lubemba [2015] 1 WLR 1579, [2015] 1 Cr App R 11 (137), [2014] EWCA Crim 2064..... PD-46

M [2008] EWCA Crim 3329.... SG8-8
McClelland [1951] 1 All ER 557, 35 Cr App R 22, 115 JP 179.... SG3-15
McCook [2014] EWCA Crim 734.... PD-94
Maidstone Crown Court, ex parte Waitt [1988] Crim LR 384.... PD-102
Makin [2004] EWCA Crim 1607 .... PD-69
Mason [1981] QB 881, [1980] 3 WLR 617, [1980] 3 All ER 777, 71 Cr App R 157 .... PD-60
Mayers [2009] 1 WLR 1915, [2009] 2 All ER 145, [2009] 1 Cr App R 30 (403), [2009] Crim LR 272, [2008] EWCA Crim 2989.... PD-44
Miles [2006] EWCA Crim 256 .... SG3-3

Millen (1980) 2 Cr App R (S) 357 . . . . . SG3-10
Miller [1976] Crim LR 694 . . . . . SG3-18
Mitchell [2001] 2 Cr App R (S) 29 (141), [2001] Crim LR 239 . . . . . SG3-18
Musone [2007] 1 WLR 2467, [2007] 2 Cr App R 29 (379), 171 JP 425, [2007] Crim LR 972, [2007] EWCA Crim 1237 . . . . . PD-51

Nasteska v The Former Yugoslav Republic of Macedonia (Application No. 23152/05) PD-92
Newman [2010] EWCA Crim 1566 . . . . . PD-75
Newton (1982) 77 Cr App R 13, 4 Cr App R (S) 388, [1983] Crim LR 198 . . . . . PD-74
Nolan [2017] EWCA Crim 2449 . . . . . PD-96
Northallerton Magistrates' Court, ex parte Dove [2000] 1 Cr App R (S) 136, 163 JP 657, [1999] Crim LR 760 . . . . . SG10-147

O'Brien [2007] 1 WLR 833, [2006] 4 All ER 1012, [2007] 1 Cr App R (S) 75 (442), [2006] Crim LR 1074, [2006] EWCA Crim 1741 . . . . . SG3-13
OP v Secretary of State for Justice [2014] 1944 (Admin) PD-8
Observer and Guardian v United Kingdom (1992) 14 EHRR 153 . . . . . PD-18

Pepper v Hart [1993] AC 593 . . . . . PD-115
Perkins [2013] Crim LR 533, [2013] EWCA Crim 323 . . . . . PD-78
Pickstone v Freemans PLC [1989] AC 66, [1987] 3 WLR 811, [1987] 3 All ER 756 . . . . . PD-115
Pinnell [2012] 1 WLR 17, [2011] 2 Cr App R (S) 30 (168), [2011] Crim LR 253, [2010] EWCA Crim 2848 . . . . . SG3-12
Pointon [2008] 2 Cr App R (S) 82 (472), [2008] EWCA Crim 513 . . . . . SG3-14
Porter v Magill [2002] 2 AC 357, [2001] UKHL 67 . . . . . PD-69
Poulton [2003] 4 All ER 869, [2003] 1 Cr App R (S) 116 (610), [2003] Crim LR 124, [2002] EWCA Crim 2487 . . . . . SG3-10

R [2015] EWCA Crim 1870 . . . . . PD-8
R (DPP) v South Tyneside Youth Court [2015] 2 Cr App R (S) 59 (411), [2015] EWHC 1455 (Admin) SG8-5
R (DPP) v Sunderland Magistrates' Court [2018] EWHC 229 (Admin) PD-55
R (F) v Knowsley Magistrates Court [2006] EWHC 695 (Admin) PD-55
R (Guardian News and Media Ltd) v City of Westminster Magistrates' Court [2012] 3 WLR 1343, [2012] 3 All ER 551, [2012] EWCA Civ 420 . . . . . PD-18
R (H, A and O) v Southampton Youth Court [2005] 2 Cr App R (S) 30 (171), 169 JP 37, [2005] Crim LR 395, [2004] EWHC 2912 (Admin) SG8-5
R (Jones) v South East Surry Local Justice Area [2010] EWHC 916 (Admin) PD-55
R (Kharaghan) v City of London Magistrates' Court [2018] EWHC 229 (Admin) PD-55
R (OP) v Ministry of Justice [2014] EWHC 1944 (Admin) PD-8
R (S, F and L) v Chief Constable of the British Transport Police and Southwark Crown Court [2013] EWHC 2189 (Admin) PD-102
Ralphs [2010] 2 Cr App R (S) 30 (190), [2010] Crim LR 318, [2009] EWCA Crim 2555 . . . SG3-10
Ranniman v Finland (1997) 26 EHRR 56 . . . . . PD-13
Rashid [2017] EWCA Crim 2 . . . . . PD-8
Raza (2010) 1 Cr App R (S) 56 (354), [2009] Crim LR 820, [2009] EWCA Crim 1413 . . . . . SG3-10
Reading Crown Court, ex parte Bello [1992] 3 All ER 353, 92 Cr App R 303, 155 JP 637 . . . PD-122
Rollinson (1996) 161 JP 107, CA PD-13

S [2000] 2 Cr App R (S) 18 . . . . . SG8-9
Selby [2017] Crim LR 228, [2016] EWCA Crim 1639 . . . . . PD-113

Shaw [1998] 1 Cr App R 79, [1998] 1 All ER 42, 161 JP 709, [1997] Crim LR 766 . . . . PD-26
Smith [2011] EWCA Crim 1772 . . . . SG10-171
Sofekun [2009] 1 Cr App R (S) 78 (460), [2008] EWCA Crim 2035 . . . . SG10-156
Standard Bank PLC v Via Mat International [2013] 2 All ER (Comm) 1222, [2013] EWHC Civ 490 . . . . PD-113
Stanford International Bank v SFO [2011] Ch 33, [2010] 3 WLR 941, [2010] EWCA Civ 137 . . . . PD-101
Steel v UK (1999) 28 EHRR 603 . . . . PD-82
Sullivan, Gibbs, Elener and Elener [2005] 1 Cr App R 3 (23), [2005] 1 Cr App R (S) 67 (308), [2004] EWCA Crim 1762 . . . . PD-85, PD-86
Szczerba [2002] 2 Cr App R (S) 86 (387), [2002] Crim LR 429, [2002] EWCA Crim 440 . . . . SG13-6
Szombathely City Court v Fenyvesi [2009] EWHC 231 (Admin) PD-106

Taylor [2013] UKPC 8 . . . . PD-64
Tchenquiz v Director of the Serious Fraud Office [2015] 1 WLR 838, [2014] EWCA Civ 1333 . . . . PD-113
Thompson [2011] 1 WLR 200, [2011] 2 All ER 83, [2010] 2 Cr App R 27 (259), [2010] EWCA Crim 1623 . . . . PD-58, PD-64, PD-69
Tombstone Ltd v Raja [2009] 1 WLR 1143, [2008] EWCA Civ 1441 . . . . PD-113

Underwood [2005] 1 Cr App R 13 (178), [2005] 1 Cr App R (S) 90 (478), [2004] EWCA Crim 2256 . . . . PD-74, PD-75

W and M [2010] EWCA Crim 1926 . . . . PD-46
Warton [1976] Crim LR 520 . . . . SG3-18
Watts [2011] Crim LR 68, [2010] EWCA Crim 1824 . . . . PD-46
Webb (1953) 37 Cr App R 82 . . . . SG3-3
Whittal v Kirby [1946] 2 All ER 552 (CA) SG10-183
Wickens (1958) 42 Cr App R 436 (CA) SG10-183
Wills [2012] 1 Cr App R 2 (16), [2012] Crim LR 565, [2011] EWCA Crim 1938 . . . . PD-6, PD-8, PD-46

Table of Statutes

Access to Justice Act 1999
s. 11. . . . . R-366
Administration of Justice Act 1960
s. 13. . . . . R-437, SG16-2
Administration of Justice (Miscellaneous Provisions) Act 1933
s. 2. . . . . PD-26, R-92
s. 2(1) PD-26
s. 2(2)(b) PD-27
Adoption and Children Act 2002
s. 120. . . . . SG18-5
Animal Welfare Act 2006. . . . . SG10-159
s. 4. . . . . SG10-19, SG10-157, SG10-159
s. 5. . . . . SG10-157, SG10-159
s. 6(1) SG10-157, SG10-159
s. 6(2) SG10-157, SG10-159
s. 7. . . . . SG10-159
s. 8. . . . . SG10-19, SG10-157, SG10-159
s. 9. . . . . SG10-19, SG10-157, SG10-159
s. 13(6) SG10-159
s. 32. . . . . SG15-45
s. 33. . . . . SG10-157
s. 34. . . . . SG10-159
s. 36(9) SG10-157, SG10-159
s. 43. . . . . SG10-159
Anti-social Behaviour, Crime and Policing Act 2014 . . . . PD-122
pt. 3. . . . . SG15-49
pt. 4
chap. 1. . . . . SG15-49
chap. 2. . . . . SG15-49
chap. 3. . . . . SG15-49
s. 22. . . . . SG10-155
s. 22(2) SG10-155
s. 22(3) SG10-155
s. 22(4) SG10-155
s. 22(5) SG10-155
s. 22(9) SG10-155
s. 23(1) SG10-155
s. 23(2) SG10-155
s. 23(4) SG10-155
s. 23(5) SG10-155
s. 23(6) SG10-155
s. 24(2) SG10-155
s. 24(3) SG10-155
s. 25(1) SG10-155
s. 25(2) SG10-155
s. 25(3) SG10-155
s. 25(5) SG10-155
s. 25(6) SG10-155
s. 26(2) SG10-155
s. 26(3) SG10-155
s. 26(4) SG10-155
s. 30. . . . . SG15-29
s. 31. . . . . SG10-155

Backing of Warrants (Republic of Ireland) Act 1965
s. 3. . . . . R-68
Bail Act 1976. . . . . PD-34, SG16-1, SG16-4, SG16-6
s. 5. . . . . R-79, R-284, R-445
s. 5(6A) PD-28, R-12
s. 6. . . . . PD-30, R-586, SG15-16, SG16-2
s. 6(1) PD-30, SG10-25, SG16-3, SG16-7
s. 6(2) PD-30, SG10-25, SG16-3, SG16-7
s. 6(3) PD-30
s. 6(6) SG16-4
s. 6(6)(a) SG15-17
s. 6(10)–(14) PD-30
Bankers' Books Evidence Act 1879
s. 7. . . . . R-156
s. 8. . . . . R-494
Banking and Financial Dealings Act 1971 . . . . . R-316
Bankruptcy (Scotland) Act 1985
s. 31B R-375
Biological Weapons Act 1974
s. 1. . . . . PD-126
Bribery Act 2010 . . . . SG26-36
s. 1. . . . . SG26-29, SG26-31, SG26-33
s. 2. . . . . SG26-29, SG26-31, SG26-33
s. 6. . . . . SG26-29, SG26-31, SG26-33
s. 7. . . . . SG26-33, SG26-36

Chemical Weapons Act 1996
s. 2. . . . . PD-126
Children Act 1989
s. 31(9) SG18-5
Children and Young Persons Act 1933 . . . . PD-6
s. 1(1) SG20-3
s. 34A SG8-6
s. 37. . . . . PD-45
s. 39. . . . . PD-9, PD-112
s. 44. . . . . PD-6, SG8-4
s. 49. . . . . PD-9
s. 50. . . . . SG8-7
Civil Evidence Act 1995
s. 1(2) R-302, R-317
s. 2(1) R-355
Communications Act 2003
s. 127(1) SG10-34
s. 127(2) SG10-34
s. 363. . . . . SG10-98
Company Directors Disqualification Act 1986
s. 2. . . . . SG10-161, SG24-28, SG25-20
s. 5. . . . . SG10-161
s. 13. . . . . SG15-41
Constitutional Reform Act 2005
sch. 2, pt. 1 . . . . PD-1
Contempt of Court Act 1981
s. 1. . . . . PD-22
s. 2. . . . . PD-22
s. 4. . . . . PD-22
s. 4(2) PD-45, PD-18
s. 8. . . . . PD-69
s. 9. . . . . PD-20, PD-22, R-586
s. 9(1) PD-20
s. 9(1)(b) PD-20
s. 9(3) PD-20
s. 9(4) PD-20
s. 12. . . . . PD-103, R-586
s. 12(2) PD-103
s. 12(5) R-387
Control of Pollution (Amendment) Act 1989
s. 1. . . . . SG24-17
Coroners and Justice Act 2009
s. 5. . . . . PD-102
s. 54. . . . . SG25-23
s. 55. . . . . SG25-23
s. 76. . . . . R-556, R-556A
s. 78. . . . . R-558, R-558A
s. 79. . . . . R-556, R-556A
s. 80(1) R-556, R-556A

s. 80(6) R-556, R-556A
s. 86. . . . . R-62, R-164
s. 88. . . . . R-182, R-185
s. 89. . . . . R-185
s. 91. . . . . R-164
s. 92. . . . . R-164
s. 93. . . . . R-164
s. 116. . . . . PD-26
s. 120. . . . . SG2-2, SG3-1, SG3-7, SG4-2, SG5-2, SG9-1, SG8-2, SG11-1, SG11-21, SG11-31, SG11-41, SG12-1, SG14-2, SG15-1, SG19-1, SG25-1, SG27-1, SG31-1, SG32-1
s. 122(2) SG1-1
s. 125(1) PD-29, PD-77, SG1-1, SG2-2, SG3-1, SG3-7, SG4-2, SG5-2, SG8-2, SG9-1, SG10-1, SG11-1, SG11-21, SG11-31, SG11-41, SG12-1, SG14-2, SG15-1, SG19-1, SG25-1, SG27-1, SG32-1, SG31-159
s. 125(3)–(4) SG12-2, SG15-2, SG19-2, SG20-2, SG25-2, SG27-2, SG30-2, SG31-2, SG32-2

Corporate Manslaughter and Corporate Homicide Act 2007
s. 1. . . . . SG28-2
s. 9. . . . . SG28-10
s. 9(2) SG28-10
s. 10. . . . . SG28-10
s. 10(1) SG28-10

Counter-Terrorism Act 2008
s. 30. . . . . SG13-3, SG32-100
ss. 41–53 . . . . SG32-100
s. 42. . . . . R-387, R-437
sch. 2. . . . . SG32-100

Courts Act 2003. . . . . SG10-144
s. 54A PD-69
s. 74. . . . . PD-1
sch. 2. . . . . SG13-3
sch. 5
para. 7A. SG10-144
para. 8 . . . . SG10-144
para. 9 . . . . SG10-144
para. 12 . . . . SG10-144
para. 22 . . . . R-295
para. 31 . . . . R-295
para. 37 . . . . R-295

Courts and Legal Services Act 1990
s. 115. . . . . PD-113

Crime and Courts Act 2013. . . . . SG10-126
s. 44. . . . . SG10-173
s. 45. . . . . PD-117
sch. 16
pt. 2, para 5 . . . . SG10-173
sch. 17. . . . . PD-117
pt. 2. . . . . R-91, R-102
para. 1 . . . . R-100
para. 3 . . . . R-100
para. 6 . . . . R-102

Crime and Disorder Act 1998 . . . . SG10-180
s. 1(8) SG17-4
s. 1(10) SG10-20, SG17-2, SG17-6
s. 1(11) SG17-2, SG17-7
s. 1C(9) SG17-7
s. 8. . . . . SG8-6, SG22-12
s. 9(1A) SG8-6
s. 10(4) R-387
s. 10(5) R-387
s. 29. . . . . SG12-13, SG12-15, SG12-19, SG12-21, SG12-28, SG12-30
ss. 29–32 . . . . SG10-176
s. 30. . . . . SG10-37, SG11-11, SG11-21
s. 31. . . . . SG10-72, SG10-73, SG10-74
s. 32. . . . . SG10-59, SG10-60
s. 32(1)(a) SG27-19, SG27-20
s. 32(1)(b) SG27-6
s. 37(1) SG8-4
s. 49. . . . . PD-4
ss. 50A–52. . . . . R-75
s. 51. . . . . PD-4, PD-126, R-91
s. 51(1) PD-25
s. 51(13) PD-4
s. 51A R-91
s. 51A(11) PD-4
s. 51B PD-126, SG8-5
s. 51C SG8-5
s. 52A PD-18
ss. 57A–57F. PD-15
s. 57C(6A), ... PD-15
s. 66ZB SG8-8
sch. 3. . . . . SG1-1
para. 1 . . . . PD-4
para. 2(6). PD-27
para. 4 . . . . R-156

Crime (International Co-operation) Act 2003
s. 3(3)(b) R-599
s. 3(4)(b) R-599
s. 4(1) R-600
s. 7. . . . . R-601
s. 8(1) R-601
s. 15(1) R-595, R-602, R-603
s. 21(1) R-608
s. 30(1) R-604
s. 30(3) R-604, R-605
s. 31(1) R-604
s. 31(4) R-604, R-606
s. 51(3) R-599, R-600
s. 56. . . . . R-291
s. 57. . . . . R-291
s. 59. . . . . R-291
s. 60. . . . . R-291
sch. 1. . . . . R-602
para. 6(1). R-603
sch. 2
pt. 1. . . . . R-604, R-605
pt. 2. . . . . R-606

Crime (Overseas Production Orders) Act 2019 . . . . R-578A
s. 1. . . . . R-576, R-573A
s. 3. . . . . R-574A, R-577
s. 8(4) R-576A, R-579
s. 13(3) R-576A, R-579
s. 13(4)(b) R-576A, R-579

Crime (Sentences) Act 1997
s. 28. . . . . PD-85, SG3-13
s. 28(1B) SG3-13

Criminal Appeal Act 1968
pt. 1. . . . . R-468, R-437, R-469, R-470, R-475
s. 7. . . . . R-274, R-450
s. 8. . . . . R-91
s. 11(1A) PD-35
s. 18A R-437
s. 23A PD-69
s. 29. . . . . PD-96
s. 31. . . . . PD-94, PD-96
s. 31(2) R-472, R-473
s. 81(1)(f) PD-35

Criminal Appeal Act 1995
s. 9. . . . . R-437
s. 11. . . . . R-387
s. 18A R-564, R-564A, R-568, R-568A, R-590

Criminal Attempts Act 1981
s. 1(1) SG13-7
s. 9. . . . . SG10-99, SG15-12

Criminal Damage Act 1971
s. 1. . . . . SG10-21, SG11-1
s. 1(1) SG10-37, SG11-11, SG11-21
s. 1(2) PD-126, SG11-31
s. 2. . . . . SG11-41

Criminal Justice Act 1925
s. 41. . . . . PD-9, PD-22

Criminal Justice Act 1967
s. 9. . . . PD-18, PD-37, PD-78, PD-80, PD-81, R-152

s. 10. . . . PD-18, PD-74
s. 91. . . . SG10-48, SG10-191
Criminal Justice Act 1972
s. 36. . . . R-460
s. 36(5) R-494
Criminal Justice Act 1987
s. 2. . . . PD-102, R-534, R-534A, R-539, R-539A
s. 7. . . . R-20
s. 9. . . . R-202, R-207, R-208, R-212
s. 9(11) R-418
Criminal Justice Act 1988 . . . . R-186, SG4-7
pt. VI. . . . R-380
s. 30. . . . PD-47
s. 32. . . . R-164, R-187
s. 36. . . . R-460
s. 39. . . . SG12-28
s. 40. . . . SG3-4
s. 72A(4) R-381
s. 72A(5)(a) R-381
s. 73. . . . R-380
s. 73(1A) R-380
s. 73(1C) R-380
s. 74A R-382
s. 74B R-382
s. 74C R-382
s. 75A R-384
s. 93H R-383
s. 139. . . . SG4-7, SG8-8
s. 139(1) SG14-3
s. 139AA SG4-7, SG8-8
s. 139AA(1). . . . SG14-13
s. 139A SG4-7, SG8-8
s. 139A(1) SG14-3
s. 139A(2) SG14-3
s. 152. . . . R-116
s. 159(1) R-451
s. 160. . . . SG31-86
sch. 4. . . . R-380
Criminal Justice Act 1991
s. 20A PD-86
s. 33(b) SG3-11
Criminal Justice Act 2003 . . . . R-20, SG16-2, SG17-1, SG18-7
pt. 12
chap. 5. . . . SG2-7, SG12-8, SG12-18, SG19-8, SG20-10, SG20-22, SG25-8, SG25-18, SG25-28, SG25-36, SG27-12, SG27-43, SG30-8, SG31-22, SG31-33, SG31-44, SG31-55, SG32-5, SG32-9, SG32-17, SG32-21
chap. 15. . . . SG11-6, SG11-36
s. 15(3) PD-30
s. 18A SG2-8
s. 22. . . . SG10-185
s. 29. . . . R-67, R-508
s. 44. . . . PD-69, R-20
s. 46(3) PD-69
s. 46(5) PD-69
s. 47(1) R-418
s. 51. . . . R-164
s. 52. . . . R-164
s. 58(2) R-426
s. 77. . . . R-91, R-268
s. 80(6) R-271, R-272
s. 82. . . . R-270, R-271
s. 82A PD-84
s. 84. . . . R-274
s. 87. . . . R-271
s. 88. . . . R-127, R-273
s. 89. . . . R-127, R-273
s. 98. . . . R-205
s. 100. . . . PD-45, PD-46
s. 107. . . . R-209
s. 114. . . . R-200
s. 114(1)(d) PD-55, R-201
s. 116. . . . R-182, R-201
s. 117. . . . PD-79, PD-81
s. 117(1)(c) R-201
s. 121. . . . R-201
s. 142. . . . SG8-4
s. 142(1) SG2-2, SG22-11
s. 142A SG8-4, SG8-8
s. 143. . . . SG22-4, SG31-158
s. 143(1) SG2-2, SG8-4, SG10-5, SG10-6, SG16-3, SG17-4
s. 143(2) PD-85, SG10-6, SG13-5, SG16-3, SG16-5, SG17-5, SG18-5, SG22-5
s. 143(3) PD-85
s. 144. . . . PD-85, SG2-6, SG8-3, SG8-11, SG8-12, SG10-18, SG10-18, SG10-19, SG10-34, SG10-40, SG10-41, SG10-48, SG10-54, SG10-67, SG10-75, SG10-77, SG10-79, SG10-82, SG10-98, SG10-99, SG10-101, SG10-106, SG10-110, SG10-111, SG10-112, SG10-113, SG10-114, SG10-115, SG10-116, SG10-117, SG10-118, SG10-119, SG11-5, SG11-16, SG11-26, SG11-35, SG11-45, SG12-3, SG12-7, SG12-17, SG14-8, SG14-18, SG14-27, SG15-20, SG19-7, SG19-17, SG20-8, SG20-20, SG20-31, SG21-6, SG23-7, SG24-13, SG24-14, SG24-27, SG25-7, SG25-17, SG25-27, SG25-40, SG26-8, SG26-40, SG27-11, SG27-25, SG27-42, SG28-9 SG30-7, SG31-7, SG31-21, SG31-32, SG31-43, SG31-54, SG32-8, SG32-20, SG32-32, SG32-42, SG32-52, SG32-62, SG32-72, SG32-82, SG33-6
s. 144(1) SG4-1
s. 144(2) SG4-7
s. 144(3) SG4-7
s. 145. . . . SG10-176, SG10-178
s. 146 . . . . SG10-175, SG10-176, SG10-177, SG10-178
s. 148(1) SG3-14, SG3-16, SG9-3
s. 148(2)(a) SG9-3
s. 148(2)(b) SG9-3
s. 149. . . . SG9-12
s. 150A SG3-14, SG9-3
s. 151(2) SG9-3
s. 152(2) SG8-8, SG16-6, SG17-4
s. 154(1) SG22-10, SG22-12
s. 159(5) R-494
s. 161A SG10-148
s. 161A(3) SG10-148
s. 162. . . . SG2-4, SG24-22
s. 163. . . . SG3-15
s. 164. . . . SG2-4, SG24-7, SG24-22, SG26-37, SG28-6
s. 164(1) SG10-128
s. 164(2) SG3-14, SG10-128
s. 164(3) SG3-14
s. 164(4) SG10-128
s. 164(4A) SG10-148
s. 164(5) SG10-131
s. 165(2) SG10-131
s. 174. . . . SG2-11, SG10-18, SG10-19, SG10-34, SG10-40, SG10-41, SG10-48, SG10-54, SG10-67, SG10-75, SG10-77, SG10-79, SG10-82, SG10-99, SG10-101, SG10-106, SG10-110, SG10-111, SG10-112, SG10-113, SG10-114, SG10-115, SG10-116, SG10-117, SG10-118, SG10-119, SG11-9, SG11-19, SG11-29, SG11-39, SG11-48, SG12-3, SG12-11, SG14 11, SG14-21, SG15-23, SG19-11, SG20-13, SG20-25, SG21-9, SG23-10, SG24-16, SG24-30, SG25-11, SG25-31, SG25-43, SG26-11, SG26-43, SG28-12, SG27-15, SG27-28, SG27-46, SG30-11, SG31-11, SG31-37, SG31-48, SG32-13, SG32-25, SG32-35, SG32-45, SG32-75, SG32-87, SG33-9
s. 174(1) SG10-11

s. 174(2)(a) SG10-1, SG10-11, SG16-5, SG17-5, SG22-5
s. 174(2)(d) SG10-9
s. 177.......... SG14-30, SG15-51, SG20-37, SG27-49, SG32-101
s. 177(2A) SG9-3, SG9-4
s. 177(2B) SG9-3, SG9-4
s. 177(3) SG9-8
s. 177(3)(b) SG9-8
s. 189(1A) SG30-4
s. 202..... SG31-15, SG31-19, SG31-26, SG31-52, SG31-63, SG31-67, SG31-71, SG31-80, SG31-84, SG31-92, SG31-96, SG31-100, SG31-104, SG31-108, SG31-112, SG31-116, SG31-124, SG31-128, SG31-132, SG31-136, SG31-140, SG31-144
s. 207...... SG11-3, SG11-13, SG11-23, SG11-33, SG11-42, SG33-4, SG33-13
s. 209...... SG11-3, SG11-13, SG11-23, SG11-42, SG19-15, SG19-20, SG23-4, SG23-14, SG23-25, SG23-30
s. 212...... SG11-3, SG11-13, SG11-23, SG11-33, SG11-42, SG33-4, SG33-13
s. 215(2) SG9-8
s. 218(4) SG9-8
s. 224.......... SG2-7, SG5-6, SG11-1, SG11-31, SG12-13, SG12-22, SG12-28, SG13-7, SG18-4, SG19-3, SG19-13, SG19-18, SG22-7, SG22-9, SG25-3, SG25-13, SG25-23, SG25-33, SG30-3, SG30-13, SG30-17, SG31-13, SG31-24, SG31-28, SG31-39, SG31-57, SG31-103, SG31-106, SG31-118, SG31-135, SG31-150, SG32-3, SG32-15, SG32-77
ss. 224–281 .... SG22-6, SG22-8, SG22-10, SG22-12
s. 224–230.......... SG13-6
s. 224A SG2-7, SG25-3, SG25-8, SG25-13, SG25-18, SG25-23, SG25-28, SG25-33, SG25-36, SG30-8, SG31-3, SG31-8, SG31-13, SG31-24, SG31-28, SG31-33, SG31-44, SG31-55, SG31-57, SG31-61, SG31-65, SG31-69, SG31-73, SG31-74, SG31-86, SG31-98, SG31-106, SG31-110, SG31-118, SG31-150, SG32-3, SG32-9, SG32-15, SG32-21, SG32-77, SG32-83
s. 225.......... SG2-7, SG11-6, SG11-36, SG25-8, SG25-18, SG25-28, SG25-36, SG30-8, SG32-9
s. 225(2) SG3-15, SG25-3, SG25-13, SG25-23, SG25-33, SG31-3, SG31-8, SG31-13, SG31-24, SG31-28, SG31-33, SG31-39, SG31-44, SG31-57, SG31-106, SG31-110, SG31-118, SG31-150, SG32-3, SG32-15, SG32-21, SG32-77
s. 226(2) SG3-15
s. 226A.... SG2-7, SG11-6, SG11-36, SG20-3, SG20-16, SG25-3, SG25-8, SG25-13, SG25-16, SG25-18, SG25-23, SG25-28, SG25-33, SG25-36, SG27-6, SG27-12, SG27-38, SG30-8, SG31-3, SG31-8, SG31-13, SG31-17, SG31-24, SG31-28, SG31-30, SG31-33, SG31-39, SG31-44, SG31-50, SG31-55, SG31-57, SG31-61, SG31-65, SG31-69, SG31-73, SG31-74, SG31-78, SG31-82, SG31-86, SG31-90, SG31-98, SG31-102, SG31-106, SG31-110, SG31-114, SG31-118, SG31-122, SG31-126, SG31-130, SG31-134, SG31-138, SG31-142, SG31-146, SG31-150, SG31-151, SG31-155, SG32-3, SG32-9, SG32-15, SG32-21, SG32-77
s. 227(2B) SG3-12
s. 229.......... SG5-6
s. 236A SG31-28, SG31-34, SG31-39, SG31-45, SG31-157, SG32-5, SG32-10, SG32-17, SG32-15, SG32-22, SG32-31, SG32-77
s. 240.......... PD-85, SG9-12, SG12-12, SG19-12, SG23-11
s. 240A PD-85, SG2-12, SG10-19, SG10-34, SG10-110, SG11-10, SG11-20, SG11-30, SG11-40, SG11-49, SG12-3, SG12-12, SG14-12, SG14-21, SG14-22, SG15-24, SG19-12, SG20-14, SG20-26, SG20-36, SG21-4, SG21-10, SG23-11, SG24-31, SG25-12, SG25-22, SG25-32, SG25-44, SG26-9, SG26-12, SG27-16, SG27-29, SG27-47, SG30-12, SG31-12, SG31-38, SG31-49, SG32-14, SG32-36, SG32-46, SG32-56, SG32-66, SG32-76, SG32-88, SG33-10
s. 240ZA PD-85
s. 256AC SG15-14
s. 265.......... SG3-11
s. 269.......... PD-85
s. 270.......... PD-87
s. 271.......... PD-85
s. 272.......... PD-85
s. 274(3) R-437, R-438
s. 275.......... PD-85
s. 276.......... PD-85
s. 278.......... SG10-173
s. 282.......... SG22-10, SG22-12
s. 305.......... SG3-3
s. 321.......... PD-59
s. 332.......... SG3-11
sch. 3
para. 11 .... R-494
sch. 5, pt. 1 .... R-271
sch. 8.......... R-313, SG10-35, SG15-4
para. 9(1)(c).......... SG10-35
para. 9(8).......... R-387
para. 13(5).......... R-387
paras. 21–23 .... SG3-16
para. 22 .... SG1-1
sch. 12.......... R-313, SG15-9
para. 11(1).......... SG1-1
sch. 15.......... SG2-7, SG3-12, SG8-5
sch. 15A SG3-12
sch. 15B.......... SG2-7
pt. 1....... SG25-3, SG25-13, SG25-23, SG31-3, SG31-28, SG31-39, SG31-50, SG31-106, SG32-3, SG32-15, SG32-77
sch. 18.......... SG31-28
sch. 18A SG31-28, SG31-39, SG32-3, SG32-15, SG32-77
sch. 19A SG15-14
sch. 21.......... SG4-8, SG8-8, SG13-6, SG13-8
para. 4 .... SG13-3, SG13-6
para. 4(1).......... PD-85
para. 4(2).......... PD-85
para. 5 .... SG13-6
para. 5(1).......... PD-85
para. 5(2).......... PD-85
para. 5(2)(h) PD-85
para. 5A.......... PD-85
para. 5A(1) PD-85
para. 6 .... PD-85
para. 7 .... PD-85
para. 9 .... PD-85
para. 11 .... PD-85
para. 12 .... PD-85
sch. 22.......... PD-85
para. 14 .... R-437, R-438
sch. 23
para. 1 .... SG10-173
sch. 37, pt. 7 .... SG3-11
Criminal Justice and Court Services Act 2000 .... SG31-156
Criminal Justice and Courts Act 2015
s. 33.......... SG27-30
s. 35a.......... SG10-183
Criminal Justice and Immigration Act 2008... SG30-4
sch. 2.......... R-313
sch. 5.......... SG3-11
sch. 26, para. 4.......... SG3-11

Criminal Justice and Police Act 2001
s. 50 . . . R-548, R-548A
s. 51 . . . R-548, R-548A
s. 53(2) . . . R-548, R-548A
s. 54(2) . . . R-548, R-548A
s. 55 . . . R-548, R-548A
s. 56 . . . R-548, R-548A
s. 59 . . . R-548, R-548A, R-549, R-549A, R-551, R-551A
s. 59(4) . . . R-545, R-545A, R-548, R-548A
s. 59(5) . . . R-545, R-545A, R-548, R-548A
Criminal Justice and Public Order Act 1994
s. 35(2) . . . PD-71
s. 51 . . . SG10-105
s. 51(1) . . . R-269
s. 167 . . . SG10-82
Criminal Law Act 1977
s. 54 . . . SG31-158
Criminal Procedure and Investigations Act 1996 . . . PD-36, PD-45, PD-54, R-6, R-147, R-151, R-182
pt. I . . . R-143
pt. II . . . R-143
s. 3 . . . PD-52, R-144, R-212, R-220
s. 3(6) . . . R-5
s. 5 . . . PD-44, R-146, R-220
s. 6 . . . PD-44, R-146, R-220
s. 6C . . . R-146, R-220
s. 6E(4) . . . PD-56
s. 7A . . . PD-44, PD-52, R-220
s. 7A(8) . . . R-5
s. 8 . . . PD-45, PD-54, PD-122, R-220
s. 8(2) . . . R-220
s. 8(5) . . . R-5
s. 17 . . . R-150, R-590, R-597
s. 17(2)(a) . . . PD-52
s. 18 . . . PD-18, R-597
s. 20 . . . PD-47
s. 29 . . . R-20
s. 29(1B) . . . R-20
s. 29(1C) . . . R-20
s. 31 . . . R-202, R-207, R-208, R-212
s. 35(1) . . . R-418
s. 40 . . . R-202, R-207, R-208, R-212
s. 54 . . . R-268
s. 87 . . . PD-44
s. 87(4) . . . PD-44
s. 87(6) . . . PD-44
s. 87(7) . . . PD-44
s. 90(2) . . . PD-44
s. 91 . . . PD-44
Criminal Procedure (Attendance of Witnesses) Act 1965
s. 2 . . . R-156, R-354
s. 2C(8) . . . R-494
s. 3 . . . R-586
Criminal Procedure (Insanity) Act 1964 . . . PD-72
s. 4 . . . PD-16, R-34
s. 5(2) . . . R-449
Crown Proceedings Act 1947
s. 17(1) . . . R-414, R-643
Customs and Excise Management Act 1979
s. 50 . . . SG26-17
s. 50(1)(a) . . . SG26-19
s. 50(2) . . . SG26-19
s. 147(3) . . . R-387
s. 170 . . . SG26-17, SG26-33
s. 170(1)(a)(i) . . . SG26-19
s. 170(1)(a)(ii) . . . SG26-19
s. 170(1)(b) . . . SG26-19
s. 170(2) . . . SG23-2
s. 170(2)(a) . . . SG26-19
s. 170B . . . SG26-17, SG26-19
Dangerous Dogs Act 1991 . . . SG21-27
s. 1(7) . . . SG21-23
s. 3(1) . . . SG21-2, SG21-11, SG21-19
s. 4(7) . . . R-494
Data Protection Act 1998 . . . PD-18
s. 35 . . . PD-18
Domestic Violence, Crime and Victims Act 2004
s. 1 . . . SG18-2
s. 5 . . . PD-117, R-253, SG20-15, SG20-16
s. 12 . . . SG18-2
s. 17 . . . R-20
ss. 17–21 . . . PD-26
s. 32 . . . R-167, R-213
Drug Trafficking Act 1994 . . . PD-102
s. 3(4) . . . R-381
s. 3(5)(a) . . . R-381
s. 10 . . . R-384
s. 11 . . . R-380
s. 11(1) . . . R-380
s. 11(7) . . . R-380
s. 13 . . . R-382
s. 14 . . . R-382
s. 15 . . . R-382
s. 22(2) . . . R-385
s. 55 . . . R-383
Drugs Act 2005
s. 12 . . . SG10-40
Education Act 1996
s. 444 . . . SG10-168
s. 444(1) . . . SG10-77, SG10-192
s. 444(1A) . . . SG10-77
Education Act 2002
s. 141F . . . R-61
Environmental Protection Act 1990
s. 33 . . . SG24-2, SG24-18
s. 33C . . . SG24-14, SG24-28
s. 34 . . . SG24-17
s. 80 . . . SG24-17
Explosive Substances Act 1883
s. 2 . . . PD-126, SG32-15
s. 3 . . . PD-126, SG32-15
s. 5 . . . PD-126
Extradition Act 2003 . . . PD-102, PD-105, R-533, R-533A, R-590
pt. 1 . . . R-494, R-498, R-616, R-618, R-619, R-620, R-631, R-634, R-635, R-638, R-644, R-647
pt. 2 . . . R-494, R-498, R-616, R-618, R-625, R-631, R-634, R-635, R-638, R-619, R-623
s. 2(7A) . . . PD-104
s. 6 . . . R-631
s. 21A . . . PD-104
s. 21A(3)(a) . . . PD-104
s. 21A(4)(b) . . . PD-104
s. 21B . . . R-619
s. 27(4) . . . PD-106
s. 29(4) . . . PD-106
s. 28 . . . PD-105
s. 32 . . . R-616
s. 35 . . . R-631
s. 36 . . . PD-105, PD-107, R-631
s. 37 . . . R-631
s. 42 . . . PD-107
s. 46 . . . R-631
s. 47 . . . R-631
s. 54 . . . R-616
s. 55 . . . R-616
s. 56 . . . R-616
s. 57 . . . R-616
s. 74 . . . R-631
s. 105 . . . R-644
s. 110 . . . PD-105
s. 114 . . . R-616

s. 117 . . . R-631
s. 118 . . . R-631, PD-105
s. 124 . . . PD-107
s. 157 . . . R-514, R-514A, R-519, R-519A
s. 160 . . . R-534, R-534A, R-543, R-543A
s. 180 . . . R-631
s. 181 . . . R-631
s. 187 . . . R-631

Family Law Act 1994
s. 42 . . . SG18-2
s. 42A . . . SG10-69, SG18-2
s. 42A(1) . . . SG18-2
Family Law Act 1996
s. 42A . . . SG15-25, SG18-7
Female Genital Mutilation Act 2003
s. 3A . . . SG20-27
Firearms Act 1968
s. 51A . . . SG4-7
Football Offences Act 1991
s. 2 . . . SG10-54
s. 3 . . . SG10-54
s. 4 . . . SG10-54
Football Spectators Act 1989
s. 14A . . . SG10-163
s. 14A(5A) . . . R-387, R-437
s. 14H(5) . . . R-494, R-600
s. 14J . . . SG15-49
s. 22 . . . R-387
sch. 1 . . . SG10-163
Fraud Act 2006
s. 1 . . . SG26-4, SG26-6, SG26-17, SG26-19, SG26-21, SG26-23, SG26-33
s. 6 . . . SG26-13, SG26-15, SG26-33
s. 7 . . . SG26-13, SG26-15, SG26-33
Freedom of Information Act 2000 . . . PD-18

Geneva Conventions Act 1957
s. 1 . . . PD-117

Homicide Act 1957
s. 2 . . . SG25-33
Human Rights Act 1998 . . . R-610, R-611
s. 4 . . . R-414, R-643
s. 6 . . . PD-18

Identity Cards Act 2006
s. 25(1) . . . SG10-61
s. 25(5) . . . SG10-61
s. 26 . . . SG10-61
Immigration Act 1971
s. 28D . . . R-538, R-538A
Indecency with Children Act 1960
s. 1 . . . SG31-158
Indictments Act 1915
s. 5(3) . . . PD-26
Infant Life (Preservation) Act 1929
s. 1(1) . . . PD-117
Insolvency Act 1986
s. 306B . . . R-375
International Criminal Courts Act 2001
s. 51 . . . PD-117
s. 52 . . . PD-117

Judicial Proceedings (Regulation of Reports) Act 1926
s. 1 . . . PD-18
Juries Act 1974 . . . PD-69
s. 1 . . . PD-63
s. 6 . . . PD-63
s. 10 . . . PD-6, PD-60
s. 15A(1) . . . PD-69
s. 15A(5) . . . PD-69
s. 16(1) . . . PD-65, PD-69
s. 17 . . . PD-72
s. 17(1) . . . PD-72
s. 17(3) . . . PD-72
s. 17(4) . . . PD-72
s. 20 . . . R-586
ss. 20A-20D . . . PD-69
s. 20D . . . PD-69
s. 20D(1) . . . PD-69
s. 20E(2)(a) . . . PD-69
s. 20E(2)(b) . . . PD-69
s. 20E(5) . . . PD-69
s. 20F(1) . . . PD-69
s. 20F(2) . . . PD-69
s. 20F(4) . . . PD-69
s. 20F(10) . . . PD-69
s. 20G(1) . . . PD-69
Justices of the Peace Act 1361 . . . PD-82, SG10-153
Justice of the Peace Act 1968
s. 1(7) . . . PD-82

Legal Aid, Sentencing and Punishment of Offenders Act 2012
s. 16 . . . R-5
ss. 33–35 . . . PD-18
s. 65 . . . SG10-175
s. 85 . . . PD-125
s. 91 . . . R-117
s. 139 . . . SG8-8
Legal Services Act 2007
s. 13 . . . R-5
Licensing Act 2003
s. 128(1) . . . SG10-167
s. 129(2) . . . SG10-167
s. 129(3) . . . SG10-167
s. 141 . . . SG10-18, SG10-191
s. 146 . . . SG10-18, SG10-191
s. 147 . . . SG10-18
s. 147A . . . SG10-17
sch. 4 . . . SG10-167

Magistrates' Courts Act 1980
s. 1 . . . R-67, R-508
s. 8B . . . R-202, R-207, R-208, R-212
s. 10 . . . PD-55
s. 11 . . . PD-55
s. 11(3) . . . R-116
s. 11(4) . . . SG10-183
s. 11(7) . . . PD-55
s. 12(1)(a) . . . R-234
s. 14 . . . R-227, R-243
s. 16B(2) . . . R-235
s. 16E . . . R-227, R-243
ss. 17A–26 . . . R-75
s. 17E . . . PD-4
s. 18(5) . . . PD-4
ss. 19(1)–(4) . . . SG1-1
s. 22 . . . R-82, R-84
s. 22A . . . SG33-11
s. 24 . . . SG8-5
s. 24D . . . PD-4
s. 24(1) . . . PD-124
s. 51 . . . R-597
ss. 51–57 . . . PD-82
s. 54 . . . R-597
s. 55 . . . R-597
s. 76 . . . R-119
s. 77(6) . . . R-44
s. 80 . . . R-117
s. 82 . . . SG10-143
s. 82(1) . . . R-117
s. 82(4) . . . R-117
s. 83 . . . R-119
s. 86 . . . R-44, R-119
s. 97 . . . R-156

s. 97(1) R-597
s. 97(4) PD-103, R-586
s. 108. . . . . R-387, R-397, R-499
s. 109. . . . . R-494
s. 111. . . . . R-398
s. 115. . . . . PD-82, SG10-153
s. 115(3) PD-82
s. 121(1) R-597
s. 123. . . . . R-597
s. 125. . . . . R-118
s. 125A R-118
s. 125B R-118
s. 127. . . . . PD-30, R-597
s. 128(7) R-116
s. 135. . . . . SG10-25, SG16-6
s. 136. . . . . R-116, R-119
s. 142. . . . . R-227, R-244, SG16-4
s. 150(1) R-607

Magistrates' Courts (Appeals from Binding Over Orders) Act 1956
s. 1. . . . . R-387

Mental Health Act 1983. . . . . PD-45, SG8-4, SG25-37
s. 37. . . . . SG25-37
s. 37(1) R-449
s. 37(2)(a) SG25-37
s. 37(2)(b) SG25-37
s. 37(3) PD-16, R-34
s. 37(8) SG3-15
s. 41. . . . . SG25-37
s. 45. . . . . R-387, R-499
s. 45A SG25-37

Merchant Shipping and Maritime Security Act 1997 . . . . . PD-117

Misuse of Drugs Act 1971
s. 3. . . . . SG23-2
s. 4(2)(a) SG23-17
s. 4(2)(b) SG23-17
s. 4(3) SG23-12
s. 5(2) SG23-28
s. 5(3) SG23-12
s. 6(2) SG23-18
s. 8. . . . . SG23-23
s. 27(1) SG10-164

Modern Slavery Act 2015
s. 2. . . . . SG31-106
s. 14. . . . . SG31-156
sch. 5, para. 5. . . . . SG31-106

Oaths Act 1978
s. 5. . . . . R-603

Offences Against the Person Act 1861
s. 16. . . . . SG10-96, SG27-38
s. 18. . . . . PD-117, PD-126, R-253, SG12-3
s. 20. . . . . PD-117, R-253, SG12-13
s. 23. . . . . PD-126
s. 24. . . . . PD-126
s. 28. . . . . PD-126
s. 29. . . . . PD-126
s. 38. . . . . SG12-22
s. 47. . . . . SG12-19

Perjury Act 1911
s. 1. . . . . R-269

Police Act 1996
s. 89. . . . . SG12-25
s. 89(2) SG10-67

Police and Criminal Evidence Act 1984 . . . . . R-590
pt. V R-554, R-554A
s. 8. . . . . R-534, R-534A, R-538, R-538A
s. 10. . . . . R-515, R-515A
s. 11. . . . . R-515, R-515A, R-570, R-570A
s. 46. . . . . PD-126
s. 63B SG10-41
s. 63F(7) R-552, R-552A
s. 63F(10) R-552, R-552A
s. 63R(6) R-552, R-552A
s. 78. . . . . PD-74
s. 81. . . . . PD-47
sch. 1. . . . . PD-102
para. 2 . . . . . R-520, R-520A, R-540, R-540A
para. 3 . . . . . R-520, R-520A, R-540, R-540A
para. 4 . . . . . R-514, R-514A, R-519, R-519A, R-540, R-540A, R-548, R-548A
para. 12 . . . . . R-534, R-534A, R-540, R-540A

Police and Justice Act 2006
s. 34. . . . . SG16-2

Police (Property) Act 1897
s. 1. . . . . R-545, R-545A, R-547, R-547A

Powers of Criminal Courts (Sentencing) Act 2000 . . . . . SG4-7
s. 1. . . . . SG10-173
s. 1ZA SG10-173
s. 1ZA(3). SG10-173
s. 3. . . . . PD-125
s. 3(b) SG8-5, SG8-9
s. 3B SG1-1
s. 6. . . . . SG31-156
s. 8. . . . . SG8-5
s. 11. . . . . PD-16, PD-89
s. 12. . . . . PD-82
s. 12(6) PD-82
s. 14(1) SG8-8
s. 16(1) SG17-7
s. 17(1)(b) SG17-7
s. 17(1)(c) SG17-7
s. 83(3) R-246
s. 91. . . . . SG8-8, SG17-7, SG31-155
s. 91(1) SG8-5
s. 110 . . . . . SG4-7, SG23-2, SG23-4, SG23-7, SG23-12, SG23-14, SG23-17, SG23-23, SG23-25
s. 110(2) SG3-15
s. 111. . . . . SG4-7, SG19-13, SG19-15, SG19-17
s. 111(2) SG3-15
s. 116. . . . . SG3-11
s. 118(5) SG1-1, SG3-18
s. 130. . . . . SG10-145, SG24-3, SG24-19, SG26-34, SG31-156, SG32-4
s. 130(1) SG10-10
s. 130(3) SG10-10
s. 130(12) SG3-18
s. 131. . . . . SG10-145
s. 131(2) SG3-6
s. 133. . . . . R-41
s. 140(1) R-381, R-384
s. 143. . . . . SG10-156, SG24-28, SG31-156, SG32-4
s. 143(6) SG10-156
s. 143(7) SG10-156
s. 146. . . . . SG10-156
s. 147. . . . . SG24-28 , SG24-28
s. 148. . . . . SG3-6, SG31-2, SG10-169, SG31-2
s. 149. . . . . SG31-2
s. 150. . . . . PD-82, SG8-6
s. 161(1) SG3-3
sch. 3. . . . . R-313
sch. 3, para. 10. . . . . R-387
sch. 5. . . . . R-313
sch. 7. . . . . R-313
sch. 8. . . . . R-313

Prevention of Crime Act 1953 . . . . . SG4-7
s. 1A SG8-8, SG14-13
s. 1. . . . . SG4-7, SG8-8
s. 1(1) SG14-3
s. 1(2) SG10-165
s. 1A SG4-7

Prison Act 1952
s. 40CA. SG14-3

Prison Security Act 1992 . . . . . PD-117

Proceeds of Crime Act 2002 . . . . PD-122, R-527, R-527A, R-528, R-528A, R-529, R-529A, R-530, R-530A, R-531, R-531A, R-532, R-532A, SG10-154, SG31-51, SG32-4
pt. 2 . . . . . . R-3, R-317, R-318, R-319, R-324, R-328, R-467, R-468, R-470, R-471, R-474, R-475, R-476, R-590
pt. 7 . . . . . . R-530, R-530A
pt. 8 . . . . . . PD-102, R-514, R-514A
s. 6 . . . . . . SG24-4, SG24-20, SG26-35, SG31-156, SG32-99
s. 13 . . . . . . SG24-2, SG24-4, SG24-18, SG24-20, SG26-10, SG26-35, SG33-8
s. 13B R-480, R-481, R-482, R-483, R-484, R-485, R-486
s. 31 . . . . . . R-474, R-477, R-479
s. 31(2) R-476
s. 41(1) R-367
s. 41(4) R-368
s. 41(7) R-367, R-370, R-371
s. 42 . . . . . . R-317, R-367
s. 42(1) R-361
s. 42(3) R-371, R-369, R-370
s. 43 . . . . . . R-480, R-481, R-482, R-483, R-484, R-485, R-486
s. 47B R-344
s. 47C R-344
s. 47D R-344
s. 47E R-344
s. 47F R-344
s. 47G R-344
s. 47M R-345
s. 47N R-346
s. 47O(1) R-347
s. 47O(2) R-347
s. 48 . . . . . . R-317, R-376, R-377, R-378, R-379
s. 48(1) R-372
s. 49 . . . . . . R-317
s. 49(1) R-373
s. 49(2)(d) R-377
s. 50 . . . . . . R-317, R-376, R-377, R-378, R-379
s. 50(1) R-372
s. 51 . . . . . . R-317
s. 51(1) R-373
s. 54(4) R-317
s. 55(4)(b) R-377
s. 55(8) R-372, R-376, R-377
s. 58(2) R-317, R-348
s. 58(3) R-317, R-348
s. 59(2) R-348
s. 59(3) R-348
s. 62 . . . . . . R-317
s. 62(3) R-374
s. 63 . . . . . . R-317
s. 63(1) R-374
s. 63(2) R-374
s. 65 . . . . . . R-480, R-481, R-482, R-483, R-484, R-485, R-486
s. 67 . . . . . . R-340
s. 67A R-341
s. 67B R-341
s. 67C(1) R-342
s. 67C(2) R-342
s. 67C(4) R-342
s. 67D R-343
s. 68 . . . . . . R-367, R-370, R-372, R-373
s. 70 . . . . . . SG10-154, SG24-2, SG24-18, SG26-33
s. 75(2)(c) PD-26
s. 75(3)(a) PD-26
s. 85 . . . . . . R-479
s. 88(6) R-340
s. 327 . . . . . . SG26-25, SG26-27, SG26-33
s. 328 . . . . . . SG26-25, SG26-27, SG26-33
s. 329 . . . . . . SG26-25, SG26-27, SG26-33
s. 336A R-572
s. 336D R-572, R-574
s. 339ZH R-514, R-514A
s. 345 . . . . . . R-514, R-514A, R-519, R-519A, R-542, R-542A
s. 347 . . . . . . R-514, R-514A
s. 348 . . . . . . R-515, R-515A, R-570, R-570A
s. 351 . . . . . . R-514, R-514A, R-542, R-542A
s. 352 . . . . . . R-534, R-534A, R-542, R-542A
s. 357 . . . . . . R-514, R-514A
s. 361 . . . . . . R-515, R-515A, R-570, R-570A
s. 362 . . . . . . R-514, R-514A
s. 363 . . . . . . R-514, R-514A
s. 369 . . . . . . R-514, R-514A
s. 370 . . . . . . R-514, R-514A, R-519, R-519A
s. 373 . . . . . . R-514, R-514A
s. 375 . . . . . . R-514, R-514A
sch. 2 . . . . . . SG31-156, SG32-99
sch. 9, pt. 1 . . . . . . R-530, R-530A

Prosecution of Offences Act 1985 . . . . . . PD-96
s. 17 . . . . . . R-68
s. 18 . . . . . . SG10-147
s. 19(3) PD-52
s. 19(3ZA) PD-52
s. 20(1A)(d) PD-52
s. 21E R-296
s. 22 . . . . . . PD-121
s. 22(4) R-97
s. 22B R-91, R-97
s. 23 . . . . . . R-111, R-112, R-113
s. 23A R-111

Protection from Harassment Act 1997 . . . . . . SG18-2
s. 2 . . . . . . SG10-60, SG18-2, SG27-17, SG27-33, SG27-37
s. 2A SG27-18, SG27-33, SG27-37
s. 4 . . . . . . SG10-59, SG27-4, SG27-23
s. 4A SG27-5, SG27-23
s. 5 . . . . . . SG5-7, SG10-170, SG18-2, SG27-14, SG27-27, SG27-45, SG31-156
s. 5(5) SG10-69, SG15-25, SG18-2, SG18-7
s. 5A SG5-7, SG10-170, SG15-25, SG18-2, SG31-156
s. 19 . . . . . . SG31-156
sch. 1 . . . . . . SG31-156

Protection of Children Act 1978
s. 1 . . . . . . SG31-86, SG31-158

Public Order Act 1986
s. 2 . . . . . . SG10-70
s. 3 . . . . . . SG10-71
s. 4 . . . . . . SG10-72
s. 4A SG10-73
s. 5 . . . . . . SG10-74, SG10-191

Public Order Act 1994
s. 166 . . . . . . SG10-54

Regulation of Investigatory Powers Act 2000
s. 22(3) R-563, R-563A
s. 22(4) R-563, R-563A
s. 23A R-561, R-561A, R-563, R-563A
s. 23A(3) R-563, R-563A
s. 23A(4) R-563, R-563A
s. 23B R-563, R-563A
s. 23B(2) R-562, R-562A
s. 28 . . . . . . R-563, R-563A
s. 29 . . . . . . R-563, R-563A
s. 32A R-561, R-561A
s. 32A(3) R-563, R-563A
s. 32A(4) R-563, R-563A
s. 32A(5) R-563, R-563A
s. 32A(6) R-563, R-563A
s. 32B R-563, R-563A
s. 32B(2) R-562, R-562A
s. 43(6A) R-563, R-563A

Regulation of Railways Act 1889
s. 5(1) SG10-75
s. 5(3) SG10-75

Rehabilitation of Offenders Act 1974 . . . . PD-18
s. 4(1) PD-50
s. 7(2)(a) PD-50
s. 7(5) PD-82
Road Safety Act 2006
s. 61(5) SG22-10, SG22-12
Road Traffic Act 1988. . . . . . R-235, R-239, SG10-183
s. 1. . . . . SG22-7
s. 2. . . . . SG10-109
s. 3. . . . . SG10-106, SG10-192
s. 3A SG22-9
s. 3ZB SG10-108, SG22-13
s. 4(1) SG10-118
s. 4(2) SG10-119
s. 5(1)(a) SG10-111
s. 5(1)(b) SG10-112
s. 5A SG10-126
s. 7(6) SG10-114, SG10-115
s. 14. . . . . SG10-192
s. 15(2) SG10-192
s. 15(4) SG10-192
s. 35. . . . . SG10-192
s. 36. . . . . SG10-192
s. 40A SG10-122, SG10-123,
SG10-125, SG10-192
s. 41A SG10-192
s. 41B SG10-192
s. 41D SG10-192
s. 42. . . . . SG10-123, SG10-125, SG10-192
s. 47. . . . . SG10-192
s. 87(1) SG10-192
s. 103. . . . . SG10-110
s. 143. . . . . SG10-116, SG10-192, SG15-49
s. 170(4) SG10-113
s. 172. . . . . R-41, SG10-192
Road Traffic (Consequential Provisions)
Act 1988 . . . . R-234, R-235, R-239
Road Traffic (Driver Licensing and
Information Systems) Act 1989 . . . . R-234,
R-235, R-239
Road Traffic (New Drivers) Act 1995 . . . . . . SG10-183
Road Traffic Offenders Act 1988 . . . . R-234
s. 12. . . . . R-35, R-41
s. 25. . . . . R-44, R-242, R-262
s. 28. . . . . SG3-17
s. 34. . . . . SG10-183
s. 34(1) R-286, SG3-17, SG10-183
s. 34(3) SG3-17, SG10-183
s. 34(4) SG10-183
s. 34A SG10-183
s. 35. . . . . R-286, SG3-17, SG10-183
s. 35(1) SG3-17
s. 35(2) SG10-183
s. 36(1) SG22-4
s. 36(4) SG10-108, SG10-183, SG22-4,
SG22-10, SG22-12
s. 37(1A) SG10-183
s. 44. . . . . R-286
s. 71(6) R-44
Road Traffic Regulation Act 1984. . . . . R-234,
R-235, R-239
s. 25(5) SG10-192
s. 89(1) SG10-117, SG10-192
s. 112. . . . . R-41

Safeguarding Vulnerable Groups Act 2006
s. 2. . . . . SG31-156
sch. 3. . . . . SG31-156
sch. 10. . . . . SG31-156
Senior Courts Act 1981
s. 4. . . . . PD-105
s. 9(1) PD-111
s. 28. . . . . R-398
s. 48(2) R-397
s. 52. . . . . R-494
s. 81(1)(f) PD-35
s. 81(1B) PD-35
Serious Crime Act 2007
pt. 3. . . . . R-494
s. 19. . . . . SG2-10, SG30-10, SG31-156
s. 24. . . . . R-437
s. 74(8) R-437
sch. 1 . . . . SG31-156
Serious Crime Act 2015
s. 76. . . . . SG27-34
Serious Organised Crime and Police Act 2005
s. 73. . . . . SG2-5, SG10-18, SG10-19,
SG10-34, SG10-40, SG10-41, SG10-48,
SG10-54, SG10-67, SG10-77, SG10-79,
SG10-82, SG10-98, SG10-99, SG10-101,
SG10-106, SG10-110, SG10-111, SG10-112,
SG10-113, SG10-114, SG10-115, SG10-116,
SG10-117, SG10-118, SG10-119, SG11-4,
SG11-15, SG11-25, SG11-34, SG11-44,
SG12-3, SG12-6, SG12-16, SG14-7, SG14-17,
SG15-19, SG19-6, SG19-16, SG20-7, SG20-19,
SG20-30, SG21-5, SG23-6, SG24-12, SG24-26,
SG25-6, SG25-16, SG25-26, SG25-39, SG26-7,
SG26-39, SG27-10, SG27-24, SG27-41, SG28-8,
SG31-6, SG31-20, SG31-31, SG31-42, SG31-53,
SG32-7, SG32-19, SG32-31, SG32-41, SG32-51,
SG32-61, SG32-71, SG32-81, SG32-93, SG33-5
s. 74. . . . . SG2-5, SG10-18, SG10-19, SG10-34,
SG10-40, SG10-41, SG10-48, SG10-54,
SG10-67, SG10-75, SG10-77, SG10-79,
SG10-82, SG10-98, SG10-99, SG10-101,
SG10-106, SG10-110, SG10-111, SG10-112,
SG10-113, SG10-114, SG10-115, SG10-116,
SG10-117, SG10-118, SG10-119, SG11-4,
SG11-15, SG11-25, SG11-34, SG11-44, SG12-6,
SG12-16, SG14-7, SG14-17, SG15-19, SG19-6,
SG19-16, SG20-7, SG20-19, SG20-30, SG21-5,
SG21-6, SG23-6, SG24-12, SG24-26, SG25-6,
SG25-26, SG25-39, SG26-7, SG26-39, SG27-10,
SG27-24, SG27-41, SG28-8, SG31-6, SG31-20,
SG31-31, SG31-42, SG31-53, SG32-7, SG32-19,
SG32-41, SG32-51, SG32-61, SG32-71,
SG32-81, SG32-93, SG33-5
Sexual Offences Act 1956. . . . . SG31-157
s. 1. . . . . SG31-158
s. 2. . . . . SG31-158
s. 3. . . . . SG31-158
s. 4. . . . . SG31-158
s. 5. . . . . SG31-158
s. 7. . . . . SG31-158
s. 9. . . . . SG31-158
s. 10. . . . . SG31-158
s. 11. . . . . SG31-158
s. 12. . . . . SG31-158
s. 13. . . . . SG31-158
s. 14. . . . . SG31-158
s. 15. . . . . SG31-158
s. 22. . . . . SG31-158
s. 23. . . . . SG31-158
s. 24. . . . . SG31-158
s. 27. . . . . SG31-158
s. 28. . . . . SG31-158
s. 29. . . . . SG31-158
s. 30. . . . . SG31-158
s. 31. . . . . SG31-158
s. 33A SG31-94
Sexual Offences Act 2003. . . . . SG31-158
pt. 2. . . . . R-277
s. 1. . . . . SG31-3
s. 2. . . . . SG31-13
s. 3. . . . . PD-123, SG31-17
s. 4. . . . . SG31-24
s. 5. . . . . SG31-28, SG31-157
s. 6. . . . . SG31-39, SG31-157

s. 7 . . . . SG31-50
s. 8 . . . . SG31-57
s. 9 . . . . SG10-27, SG31-61
ss. 9–12 . . . . SG31-73, SG31-155
s. 10 . . . . SG10-27, SG31-61
s. 11 . . . . SG31-69
s. 12 . . . . SG31-69
s. 13 . . . . SG31-155
s. 14 . . . . SG31-61, SG31-69, SG31-73
s. 15 . . . . SG31-74
s. 16 . . . . SG31-78
s. 17 . . . . SG31-78
s. 18 . . . . SG31-82
s. 19 . . . . SG31-82
s. 25 . . . . SG31-65, SG31-155
s. 26 . . . . SG31-65, SG31-155
s. 30 . . . . SG31-110
s. 31 . . . . SG31-110
s. 32 . . . . SG31-114
s. 33 . . . . SG31-114
s. 34 . . . . SG31-118
s. 35 . . . . SG31-118
s. 36 . . . . SG31-122
s. 37 . . . . SG31-122
s. 38 . . . . SG31-126
s. 39 . . . . SG31-126
s. 40 . . . . SG31-130
s. 41 . . . . SG31-130
s. 47 . . . . SG31-102
s. 48 . . . . SG31-98
s. 49 . . . . SG31-98
s. 50 . . . . SG31-98
s. 52 . . . . SG31-90
s. 53 . . . . SG31-90
ss. 57–59 . . . . SG31-106, SG31-158
s. 59A SG31-106
s. 61 . . . . SG31-146
s. 62 . . . . SG31-150
s. 63 . . . . SG31-151
s. 64 . . . . SG31-142
s. 65 . . . . SG31-142
s. 66 . . . . SG31-134
s. 67 . . . . SG31-138
s. 71 . . . . SG10-79
ss. 80–88 . . . . SG31-156
s. 82 . . . . R-277
s. 91 . . . . SG15-37
s. 91(1)(a) SG10-78
s. 91(1)(b) SG10-78
s. 103I SG15-33
s. 104 . . . . SG31-156
sch. 3 . . . . R-277, SG31-156, SG10-171
sch. 5 . . . . SG31-141, SG10-171

Sexual Offences (Amendment) Act 1992
s. 1 . . . . PD-45

Sexual Offences (Amendment) Act 2000
s. 3 . . . . SG31-158

Social Security Administration Act 1992
s. 111A SG26-21, SG26-23
s. 112 . . . . SG26-21, SG26-23

Sporting Events (Control of Alcohol etc.) Act 1985
s. 2(1) SG10-54
s. 2(2) SG10-54

Street Offences Act 1959
sch. R-313

Tax Credits Act 2002
s. 35 . . . . SG26-21, SG26-23

Taxes Management Act 1970
s. 20BA R-548
s. 106(a) SG26-19
s. 106A SG26-17

Terrorism Act 2000 . . . . PD-102, PD-126, R-521, R-521A, R-522, R-522A, R-524, R-524A, R-525, R-525A, R-526, R-526A
pt. III R-523, R-523A
s. 1 . . . . PD-117, PD-126, SG32-6, SG32-18, SG32-30, SG32-40, SG32-50, SG32-60, SG32-70, SG32-80
s. 11 . . . . SG32-37
s. 12 . . . . SG32-47
s. 14 . . . . R-523, R-523A
s. 15 . . . . SG32-57
ss. 15–18 . . . . R-514, R-514A, R-523, R-523A
s. 16 . . . . SG32-57
s. 17 . . . . SG32-57
s. 18 . . . . SG32-57
s. 21A R-523, R-523A
s. 22B R-514, R-514A
ss. 23–23B SG32-99
s. 38B SG32-67
s. 41 . . . . R-554, R-554A
s. 56 . . . . PD-126
s. 57 . . . . SG32-77
s. 58 . . . . SG32-89
s. 59 . . . . PD-126
s. 62 . . . . PD-1269
sch. 3A
pt. 1 . . . . R-523, R-523A
sch. 5
para. 5 . . . . R-514, R-514A, R-519, R-519A, R-541, R-541A, R-548, R-548A
para. 10 . . . . R-514, R-514A
para. 11 . . . . R-534, R-534A, R-541, R-541A
para. 13 . . . . R-514, R-514A, R-519, R-519A
sch. 5A
para. 9 . . . . R-514, R-514A
para. 14 . . . . R-514, R-514A
sch. 6
para. 1 . . . . R-514, R-514A
para. 2 . . . . R-519, R-519A
para. 4 . . . . R-514, R-514A
sch. 6A
para. 2 . . . . R-514, R-514A
para. 4 . . . . R-514, R-514A
sch. 8 . . . . R-554, R-554A
para. 20B(5) R-552, R-552A
para. 20B(8) R-552, R-552A
para. 20G(6) R-552, R-552A

Terrorism Act 2006
s. 1 . . . . SG32-27
s. 2 . . . . SG32-27
s. 5 . . . . PD-126, SG32-3

Theft Act 1968
s. 1 . . . . SG10-191, SG33-2, SG33-11
s. 8(1) SG30-3, SG30-13, SG30-17, SG32-9
s. 9 . . . . SG19-13, SG19-18, SG31-156
s. 10 . . . . SG19-3
s. 12 . . . . SG10-101
s. 12A(2)(a) SG10-103
s. 12A(2)(b) SG10-103
s. 12A(2)(c) SG10-102
s. 12A(2)(d) SG10-102
s. 13 . . . . SG33-23
s. 17 . . . . SG26-4, SG26-6, SG26-17, SG26-19, SG26-21, SG26-23, SG26-33
s. 22 . . . . SG33-15
s. 25 . . . . SG33-19

Theft Act 1978
s. 3 . . . . SG33-27

Trade Marks Act 1994
s. 92 . . . . SG10-97, SG10-166
s. 97 . . . . SG10-166

Tribunals, Courts and Enforcement Act 2007
sch. 12 . . . . R-292, R-299, R-300

Value Added Tax Act 1994
s. 72 . . . . SG26-17, SG26-33, SG26-36
s. 72(1) SG26-19

s. 72(3) SG26-19
s. 72(8) SG26-19
Vehicle Excise and Registration Act 1994
s. 44. . . . . SG10-100

War Crimes Act 1991. . . . . PD-117
Water Industry Act 1991
s. 111. . . . . SG24-17
Welsh Language Act 1993 . . . . PD-12

Youth Justice and Criminal Evidence Act 1999 . . . . PD-8, R-178, R-180
s. 16. . . . . PD-6, PD-8, PD-45, PD-46, SG10-155
s. 17. . . . . PD-6, SG10-155
s. 19. . . . . R-62, R-164, R-182
s. 20. . . . . R-164
s. 21. . . . . PD-45, R-172
s. 22. . . . . PD-45, R-172
s. 23. . . . . PD-45, R-164
s. 24. . . . . R-164
s. 25. . . . . R-164
s. 26. . . . . R-164
s. 27. . . . . PD-38, R-164, SG8-5, SG1-1
s. 27(1) PD-38
s. 27(2) PD-38
s. 27(3) PD-38
s. 28. . . . . PD-45, PD-46, R-164, SG8-5
s. 28(2) PD-45
s. 28(4) PD-45
s. 28(5) PD-45
s. 28(6) PD-45
s. 29. . . . . PD-8, R-164
s. 30. . . . . R-164
s. 33A PD-9, PD-15, R-164
s. 33BA PD-8, R-164
s. 33BB PD-8, R-164
s. 34. . . . . R-219, R-220
s. 35. . . . . R-219, R-220
s. 36. . . . . R-219, R-220, R-221, R-222, R-223
s. 38(3) PD-52
s. 38(4) PD-52
s. 38(5) PD-52
s. 41. . . . . PD-45, PD-46, PD-51, R-211, R-214
s. 45. . . . . PD-45, PD-112, R-182
s. 45A PD-112, R-60, R-182
s. 46. . . . . PD-45, R-60, R-182

Table of Statutory Instruments

Civil Procedure Rules 1998 (SI 1998 No. 3132)
r. 3C R-387, R-437
r. 3H R-387, R-437
Costs in Criminal Cases (General) Regulations 1986 (SI 1986 No. 1335) PD-52
pt. II R-494
pt. IIA R-494
pt. IIB R-494
pt. III R-497
Criminal Justice Act 2003 (Commencement No. 8 and Transitional and Saving Provisions) Order 2005 (Supplementary Provisions) Order 2005 (SI 2005 No. 2122)
sch. 2, para. 29 . . . . SG3-11
Criminal Justice Act 2003 (Surcharge) Order 2012 (SI 2012 No. 1696)
art. 5(3) SG10-148
art. 7(2) SG10-148
Criminal Justice Act 2003 (Surcharge) (Amendment) Order 2014 (SI 2014 No. 2120) SG10-148
Criminal Justice and Data Protection (Protocol No. 36) Regulations 2014 (SI 2014 No. 3141)
reg. 10 . . . . R-610
reg. 15 . . . . R-611
Criminal Justice (European Investigation Order) Regulations 2017 (SI 2017 No. 730) R-569, R-569A
reg. 8 . . . . R-187, R-571
reg. 10 . . . . R-569, R-569A
reg. 14 . . . . R-187
reg. 35 . . . . R-612
reg. 36 . . . . R-613
reg. 37 . . . . R-613
reg. 38 . . . . R-614
reg. 39(1) R-614, R-615
reg. 39(2) R-614, R-615
reg. 39(8) R-614, R-615
reg. 41 . . . . R-615
reg. 44 . . . . R-614
reg. 43 . . . . R-614
reg. 44 . . . . R-615
reg. 45 . . . . R-614, R-615
reg. 48 . . . . R-615
sch. 5 . . . . R-612
para. 2 . . . . R-612
sch. 6 . . . . R-613
para. 2 . . . . R-613
Criminal Justice (International Co-operation) Act 1990 (Enforcement of Overseas Forfeiture Orders) Order 2005 (SI 2005 No. 3179)
art. 3 . . . . R-609
art. 5 . . . . R-609
art. 15 . . . . R-609
art. 19 . . . . R-609
Criminal Procedure and Investigations Act 1996 (Defence Disclosure Time Limits) Regulations 1997 (SI 1997 No. 2680) R-6
Criminal Procedure Rules 2012 (SI 2012 No. 1726)
pt. 17 . . . . R-4
Criminal Procedure Rules 2014 (SI 2014 No. 1610) R-4
Criminal Procedure Rules 2015 (SI 2015 No. 1490) PD-1, SG8-8
r. 1.1 . . . . R-1
r. 1.2 . . . . R-2
r. 1.3 . . . . R-3
r. 2.1 . . . . R-4
r. 2.2 . . . . R-5
r. 2.3 . . . . R-6
r. 3.1 . . . . R-7
r. 3.2 . . . . R-8
r. 3.3 . . . . R-9
r. 3.4 . . . . R-10
r. 3.5 . . . . R-11
r. 3.6 . . . . R-12
r. 3.7 . . . . R-13
r. 3.8 . . . . R-14
r. 3.9 . . . . R-15
r. 3.10 . . . . R-16
r. 3.11 . . . . R-17
r. 3.12 . . . . R-18
r. 3.13 . . . . R-19
r. 3.14 . . . . R-20
r. 3.15 . . . . R-21
r. 3.16 . . . . R-22
r. 3.17 . . . . R-23
r. 3.18 . . . . R-24
r. 3.19 . . . . R-25
r. 3.20 . . . . R-26
r. 3.21 . . . . R-27
r. 3.22 . . . . R-28
r. 3.23 . . . . R-29
r. 3.24 . . . . R-30
r. 3.25 . . . . R-31
r. 3.26 . . . . R-32
r. 3.27 . . . . R-33
r. 3.28 . . . . R-34
r. 4.1 . . . . R-35
r. 4.2 . . . . R-36
r. 4.3 . . . . R-37
r. 4.4 . . . . R-38
r. 4.5 . . . . R-39
r. 4.6 . . . . R-40
r. 4.7 . . . . R-41
r. 4.8 . . . . R-42
r. 4.9 . . . . R-43
r. 4.10 . . . . R-44
r. 4.11 . . . . R-45
r. 4.12 . . . . R-46
r. 4.13 . . . . R-47
r. 5.1 . . . . R-48
r. 5.2 . . . . R-49
r. 5.3 . . . . R-50
r. 5.4 . . . . R-51
r. 5.5 . . . . R-52
r. 5.6 . . . . R-53
r. 5.7 . . . . R-54
r. 5.8 . . . . R-55
r. 5.9 . . . . R-56
r. 6.1 . . . . R-57
r. 6.2 . . . . R-58
r. 6.3 . . . . R-59
r. 6.4 . . . . R-60
r. 6.5 . . . . R-61
r. 6.6 . . . . R-62
r. 6.7 . . . . R-63

r. 6.8 . . . . R-64
r. 6.9 . . . . R-65
r. 6.10 . . . . R-66
r. 7.1 . . . . R-67
r. 7.2 . . . . R-68
r. 7.3 . . . . R-69
r. 7.4 . . . . R-70
r. 8.1 . . . . R-71
r. 8.2 . . . . R-72
r. 8.3 . . . . R-73
r. 8.4 . . . . R-74
r. 9.1 . . . . R-75
r. 9.2 . . . . R-76
r. 9.3 . . . . R-77
r. 9.4 . . . . R-78
r. 9.5 . . . . R-79
r. 9.6 . . . . R-80
r. 9.7 . . . . R-81
r. 9.8 . . . . R-82
r. 9.9 . . . . R-83
r. 9.10 . . . . R-84
r. 9.11 . . . . R-85
r. 9.12 . . . . R-86
r. 9.13 . . . . R-87
r. 9.14 . . . . R-88
r. 9.15 . . . . R-89
r. 9.16 . . . . R-90
r. 10.1 . . . . R-91
r. 10.2 . . . . R-92
r. 10.3 . . . . R-93
r. 10.4 . . . . R-94
r. 10.5 . . . . R-95
r. 10.6 . . . . R-96
r. 10.7 . . . . R-97
r. 10.8 . . . . R-98
r. 10.9 . . . . R-99
r. 11.1 . . . . R-100
r. 11.2 . . . . R-101
r. 11.3 . . . . R-102
r. 11.4 . . . . R-103
r. 11.5 . . . . R-104
r. 11.6 . . . . R-105
r. 11.7 . . . . R-106
r. 11.8 . . . . R-107
r. 11.9 . . . . R-108
r. 11.10 . . . . R-109
r. 11.11 . . . . R-110
r. 12.1 . . . . R-111
r. 12.2 . . . . R-112
r. 12.3 . . . . R-113
r. 13.1 . . . . R-114
r. 13.2 . . . . R-115
r. 13.3 . . . . R-116
r. 13.4 . . . . R-117
r. 13.5 . . . . R-118
r. 13.6 . . . . R-119
r. 13.7 . . . . R-120
r. 14.1 . . . . R-121
r. 14.2 . . . . R-122
r. 14.3 . . . . R-123
r. 14.4 . . . . R-124
r. 14.5 . . . . R-125
r. 14.6 . . . . R-126
r. 14.7 . . . . R-127
r. 14.8 . . . . R-128
r. 14.9 . . . . R-129
r. 14.10 . . . . R-130
r. 14.11 . . . . R-131
r. 14.12 . . . . R-132
r. 14.13 . . . . R-133
r. 14.14 . . . . R-134
r. 14.15 . . . . R-135
r. 14.16 . . . . R-136
r. 14.17 . . . . R-137
r. 14.18 . . . . R-138
r. 14.19 . . . . R-139
r. 14.20 . . . . R-140
r. 14.21 . . . . R-141
r. 14.22 . . . . R-142
r. 15.1 . . . . R-143
r. 15.2 . . . . R-144
r. 15.3 . . . . R-145
r. 15.4 . . . . R-146
r. 15.5 . . . . R-147
r. 15.6 . . . . R-148
r. 15.7 . . . . R-149
r. 15.8 . . . . R-150
r. 15.9 . . . . R-151
r. 16.1 . . . . R-152
r. 16.2 . . . . R-153
r. 16.3 . . . . R-154
r. 16.4 . . . . R-155
r. 17.1 . . . . R-156
r. 17.2 . . . . R-157
r. 17.3 . . . . R-158
r. 17.4 . . . . R-159
r. 17.5 . . . . R-160
r. 17.6 . . . . R-161
r. 17.7 . . . . R-162
r. 17.8 . . . . R-163
r. 18.1 . . . . R-164
r. 18.2 . . . . R-165
r. 18.3 . . . . R-166
r. 18.4 . . . . R-167
r. 18.5 . . . . R-168
r. 18.6 . . . . R-169
r. 18.7 . . . . R-170
r. 18.8 . . . . R-171
r. 18.9 . . . . R-172
r. 18.10 . . . . R-173
r. 18.11 . . . . R-174
r. 18.12 . . . . R-175
r. 18.13 . . . . R-176
r. 18.14 . . . . R-177
r. 18.15 . . . . R-178
r. 18.16 . . . . R-179
r. 18.17 . . . . R-180
r. 18.18 . . . . R-181
r. 18.19 . . . . R-182
r. 18.20 . . . . R-183
r. 18.21 . . . . R-184
r. 18.22 . . . . R-185
r. 18.23 . . . . R-186
r. 18.24 . . . . R-187
r. 18.25 . . . . R-188
r. 18.26 . . . . R-189
r. 19.1 . . . . R-190
r. 19.2 . . . . R-191
r. 19.3 . . . . R-192
r. 19.4 . . . . R-193
r. 19.5 . . . . R-194
r. 19.6 . . . . R-195
r. 19.7 . . . . R-196
r. 19.8 . . . . R-197
r. 19.9 . . . . R-198
r. 19.10 . . . . R-199
r. 20.1 . . . . R-200
r. 20.2 . . . . R-201
r. 20.3 . . . . R-202
r. 20.4 . . . . R-203
r. 20.5 . . . . R-204
r. 21.1 . . . . R-205
r. 21.2 . . . . R-206
r. 21.3 . . . . R-207
r. 21.4 . . . . R-208
r. 21.5 . . . . R-209
r. 21.6 . . . . R-210
r. 22.1 . . . . R-211
r. 22.2 . . . . R-212
r. 22.3 . . . . R-213
r. 22.4 . . . . R-214
r. 22.5 . . . . R-215

r. 22.6 . . . . R-216
r. 22.7 . . . . R-217
r. 22.8 . . . . R-218
r. 23.1 . . . . R-219
r. 23.2 . . . . R-220
r. 23.3 . . . . R-221
r. 23.4 . . . . R-222
r. 23.5 . . . . R-223
r. 23.6 . . . . R-224
r. 23.7 . . . . R-225
r. 23.8 . . . . R-226
r. 24.1 . . . . R-227
r. 24.2 . . . . R-228
r. 24.3 . . . . R-229
r. 24.4 . . . . R-230
r. 24.5 . . . . R-231
r. 24.6 . . . . R-232
r. 24.7 . . . . R-233
r. 24.8 . . . . R-234
r. 24.9 . . . . R-235
r. 24.10 . . . . R-236
r. 24.11 . . . . R-237
r. 24.12 . . . . R-238
r. 24.13 . . . . R-239
r. 24.14 . . . . R-240
r. 24.15 . . . . R-241
r. 24.16 . . . . R-242
r. 24.17 . . . . R-243
r. 24.18 . . . . R-244
r. 25.1 . . . . R-245
r. 25.2 . . . . R-246
r. 25.3 . . . . R-247
r. 25.4 . . . . R-248
r. 25.5 . . . . R-249
r. 25.6 . . . . R-250
r. 25.7 . . . . R-251
r. 25.8 . . . . R-252
r. 25.9 . . . . R-253
r. 25.10 . . . . R-254
r. 25.11 . . . . R-255
r. 25.12 . . . . R-256
r. 25.13 . . . . R-257
r. 25.14 . . . . R-258
r. 25.15 . . . . R-259
r. 25.16 . . . . R-260
r. 25.17 . . . . R-261
r. 25.18 . . . . R-262
r. 26.1 . . . . R-263
r. 26.2 . . . . R-264
r. 26.3 . . . . R-265
r. 26.4 . . . . R-266
r. 26.5 . . . . R-267
r. 27.1 . . . . R-268
r. 27.2 . . . . R-269
r. 27.3 . . . . R-270
r. 27.4 . . . . R-271
r. 27.5 . . . . R-272
r. 27.6 . . . . R-273
r. 27.7 . . . . R-274
r. 28.1 . . . . R-275
r. 28.2 . . . . R-276
r. 28.3 . . . . R-277
r. 28.4 . . . . R-278
r. 28.5 . . . . R-279
r. 28.6 . . . . R-280
r. 28.7 . . . . R-281
r. 28.8 . . . . R-282
r. 28.9 . . . . R-283
r. 28.10 . . . . R-284
r. 28.11 . . . . R-285
r. 29.1 . . . . R-286
r. 29.2 . . . . R-287
r. 29.3 . . . . R-288
r. 29.4 . . . . R-289
r. 29.5 . . . . R-290
r. 29.6 . . . . R-291
r. 30.1 . . . . R-292
r. 30.2 . . . . R-293
r. 30.3 . . . . R-294
r. 30.4 . . . . R-295
r. 30.5 . . . . R-296
r. 30.6 . . . . R-297
r. 30.7 . . . . R-298
r. 30.8 . . . . R-299
r. 30.9 . . . . R-300
r. 30.10 . . . . R-301
r. 31.1 . . . . R-302
r. 31.2 . . . . R-303
r. 31.3 . . . . R-304
r. 31.4 . . . . R-305
r. 31.5 . . . . R-306
r. 31.6 . . . . R-307
r. 31.7 . . . . R-308
r. 31.8 . . . . R-309
r. 31.9 . . . . R-310
r. 31.10 . . . . R-311
r. 31.11 . . . . R-312
r. 32.1 . . . . R-313
r. 32.2 . . . . R-314
r. 32.3 . . . . R-315
r. 32.4 . . . . R-316
r. 33.1 . . . . R-317
r. 33.2 . . . . R-318
r. 33.3 . . . . R-319
r. 33.4 . . . . R-320
r. 33.5 . . . . R-321
r. 33.6 . . . . R-322
r. 33.7 . . . . R-323
r. 33.8 . . . . R-324
r. 33.9 . . . . R-325
r. 33.10 . . . . R-326
r. 33.11 . . . . R-327
r. 33.12 . . . . R-328
r. 33.13 . . . . R-329
r. 33.14 . . . . R-330
r. 33.15 . . . . R-331
r. 33.16 . . . . R-332
r. 33.17 . . . . R-333
r. 33.18 . . . . R-334
r. 33.19 . . . . R-335
r. 33.20 . . . . R-336
r. 33.21 . . . . R-337
r. 33.22 . . . . R-338
r. 33.23 . . . . R-339
r. 33.24 . . . . R-340
r. 33.25 . . . . R-341
r. 33.26 . . . . R-342
r. 33.27 . . . . R-343
r. 33.28 . . . . R-344
r. 33.29 . . . . R-345
r. 33.30 . . . . R-346
r. 33.31 . . . . R-347
r. 33.32 . . . . R-348
r. 33.33 . . . . R-349
r. 33.34 . . . . R-350
r. 33.35 . . . . R-351
r. 33.36 . . . . R-352
r. 33.37 . . . . R-353
r. 33.38 . . . . R-354
r. 33.39 . . . . R-355
r. 33.40 . . . . R-356
r. 33.41 . . . . R-357
r. 33.42 . . . . R-358
r. 33.43 . . . . R-359
r. 33.44 . . . . R-360
r. 33.45 . . . . R-361
r. 33.46 . . . . R-362
r. 33.47 . . . . R-363
r. 33.48 . . . . R-364
r. 33.49 . . . . R-365
r. 33.50 . . . . R-366
r. 33.51 . . . . R-367

r. 33.52 .... R-368
r. 33.53 .... R-369
r. 33.54 .... R-370
r. 33.55 .... R-371
r. 33.56 .... R-372
r. 33.57 .... R-373
r. 33.58 .... R-374
r. 33.59 .... R-375
r. 33.60 .... R-376
r. 33.61 .... R-377
r. 33.62 .... R-378
r. 33.63 .... R-379
r. 33.64 .... R-380
r. 33.65 .... R-381
r. 33.66 .... R-382
r. 33.67 .... R-383
r. 33.68 .... R-384
r. 33.69 .... R-385
r. 33.70 .... R-386
r. 34.1 .... R-387
r. 34.2 .... R-388
r. 34.3 .... R-389
r. 34.4 .... R-390
r. 34.5 .... R-391
r. 34.6 .... R-392
r. 34.7 .... R-393
r. 34.8 .... R-394
r. 34.9 .... R-395
r. 34.10 .... R-396
r. 34.11 .... R-397
r. 35.1 .... R-398
r. 35.2 .... R-399
r. 35.3 .... R-400
r. 35.4 .... R-401
r. 35.5 .... R-402
r. 36.1 .... R-403
r. 36.2 .... R-404
r. 36.3 .... R-405
r. 36.4 .... R-406
r. 36.5 .... R-407
r. 36.6 .... R-408
r. 36.7 .... R-409
r. 36.8 .... R-410
r. 36.9 .... R-411
r. 36.10 .... R-412
r. 36.11 .... R-413
r. 36.12 .... R-414
r. 36.13 .... R-415
r. 36.14 .... R-416
r. 36.15 .... R-417
r. 37.1 .... R-418
r. 37.2 .... R-419
r. 37.3 .... R-420
r. 37.4 .... R-421
r. 37.5 .... R-422
r. 37.6 .... R-423
r. 37.7 .... R-424
r. 37.8 .... R-425
r. 38.1 .... R-426
r. 38.2 .... R-427
r. 38.3 .... R-428
r. 38.4 .... R-429
r. 38.5 .... R-430
r. 38.6 .... R-431
r. 38.7 .... R-432
r. 38.8 .... R-433
r. 38.9 .... R-434
r. 38.10 .... R-435
r. 38.11 .... R-436
r. 39.1 .... R-437
r. 39.2 .... R-438
r. 39.3 .... R-439
r. 39.4 .... R-440
r. 39.5 .... R-441
r. 39.6 .... R-442
r. 39.7 .... R-443
r. 39.8 .... R-444
r. 39.9 .... R-445
r. 39.10 .... R-446
r. 39.11 .... R-447
r. 39.12 .... R-448
r. 39.13 .... R-449
r. 39.14 .... R-450
r. 40.1 .... R-451
r. 40.2 .... R-452
r. 40.3 .... R-453
r. 40.4 .... R-454
r. 40.5 .... R-455
r. 40.6 .... R-456
r. 40.7 .... R-457
r. 40.8 .... R-458
r. 40.9 .... R-459
r. 41.1 .... R-460
r. 41.2 .... R-461
r. 41.3 .... R-462
r. 41.4 .... R-463
r. 41.5 .... R-464
r. 41.6 .... R-465
r. 41.7 .... R-466
r. 42.1 .... R-467
r. 42.2 .... R-468
r. 42.3 .... R-469
r. 42.4 .... R-470
r. 42.5 .... R-471
r. 42.6 .... R-472
r. 42.7 .... R-473
r. 42.8 .... R-474
r. 42.9 .... R-475
r. 42.10 .... R-476
r. 42.11 .... R-477
r. 42.12 .... R-478
r. 42.13 .... R-479
r. 42.14 .... R-480
r. 42.15 .... R-481
r. 42.16 .... R-482
r. 42.17 .... R-483
r. 42.18 .... R-484
r. 42.19 .... R-485
r. 42.20 .... R-486
r. 43.1 .... R-487
r. 43.2 .... R-488
r. 43.3 .... R-489
r. 43.4 .... R-490
r. 44.1 .... R-491
r. 44.2 .... R-492
r. 44.3 .... R-493
r. 45.1 .... R-494
r. 45.2 .... R-495
r. 45.3 .... R-496
r. 45.4 .... R-497
r. 45.5 .... R-498
r. 45.6 .... R-499
r. 45.7 .... R-500
r. 45.8 .... R-501
r. 45.9 .... R-502
r. 45.10 .... R-503
r. 45.11 .... R-504
r. 45.12 .... R-505
r. 45.13 .... R-506
r. 45.14 .... R-507
r. 46.1 .... R-508
r. 46.2 .... R-509
r. 46.3 .... R-510
r. 47.1 .... R-511, R-511A
r. 47.2 .... R-512, R-512A
r. 47.3 .... R-513, R-513A
r. 47.4 .... R-514, R-514A
r. 47.5 .... R-515, R-515A
r. 47.6 .... R-516, R-516A
r. 47.7 .... R-517, R-517A
r. 47.8 .... R-518, R-518A
r. 47.9 .... R-519, R-519A

r. 47.10 .... R-520, R-520A
r. 47.11 .... R-521, R-521A
r. 47.12 .... R-522, R-522A
r. 47.13 .... R-523, R-523A
r. 47.14 .... R-524, R-524A
r. 47.15 .... R-525, R-525A
r. 47.16 .... R-526, R-526A
r. 47.17 .... R-527, R-527A
r. 47.18 .... R-528, R-528A
r. 47.19 .... R-529, R-529A
r. 47.20 .... R-530, R-530A
r. 47.21 .... R-531, R-531A
r. 47.22 .... R-532, R-532A
r. 47.23 .... R-533, R-533A
r. 47.24 .... R-534, R-534A
r. 47.25 .... R-535, R-535A
r. 47.26 .... R-536, R-536A
r. 47.27 .... R-537, R-537A
r. 47.28 .... R-538, R-538A
r. 47.29 .... R-539, R-539A
r. 47.30 .... R-540, R-540A
r. 47.31 .... R-541, R-541A
r. 47.32 .... R-542, R-542A
r. 47.33 .... R-543, R-543A
r. 47.34 .... R-544, R-544A
r. 47.35 .... R-545, R-545A
r. 47.36 .... R-546, R-546A
r. 47.37 .... R-547, R-547A
r. 47.38 .... R-548, R-548A
r. 47.39 .... R-549, R-549A
r. 47.40 .... R-550, R-550A
r. 47.41 .... R-551, R-551A
r. 47.42 .... R-552, R-552A
r. 47.43 .... R-553, R-553A
r. 47.44 .... R-554, R-554A
r. 47.45 .... R-555, R-555A
r. 47.46 .... R-556, R-556A
r. 47.47 .... R-557, R-557A
r. 47.48 .... R-558, R-558A
r. 47.49 .... R-559, R-559A
r. 47.50 .... R-560, R-560A
r. 47.51 .... R-561, R-561A
r. 47.52 .... R-562, R-562A
r. 47.53 .... R-563, R-563A
r. 47.54 .... R-564, R-564A
r. 47.55 .... R-565, R-565A
r. 47.56 .... R-566, R-566A
r. 47.57 .... R-567, R-567A
r. 47.58 .... R-568, R-568A
r. 47.59 .... R-569, R-569A
r. 47.60 .... R-570, R-570A
r. 47.61 .... R-571, R-571A
r. 47.62 .... R-572, R-572A
r. 47.63 .... R-573, R-573A
r. 47.64 .... R-574, R-574A
r. 47.65 .... R-575, R-575A
r. 47.66 .... R-576, R-576A
r. 47.67 .... R-577, R-577A
r. 47.68 .... R-578, R-578A
r. 47.69 .... R-579
r. 47.70 .... R-580
r. 47.71 .... R-581
r. 48.1 .... R-582
r. 48.2 .... R-583
r. 48.3 .... R-584
r. 48.4 .... R-585
r. 48.5 .... R-586
r. 48.6 .... R-587
r. 48.7 .... R-588
r. 48.8 .... R-589
r. 48.9 .... R-590
r. 48.10 .... R-591
r. 48.11 .... R-592
r. 48.12 .... R-593
r. 48.13 .... R-594
r. 48.14 .... R-595
r. 48.15 .... R-596
r. 48.16 .... R-597
r. 48.17 .... R-598
r. 49.1 .... R-599
r. 49.2 .... R-600
r. 49.3 .... R-601
r. 49.4 .... R-602
r. 49.5 .... R-603
r. 49.6 .... R-604
r. 49.7 .... R-605
r. 49.8 .... R-606
r. 49.9 .... R-607
r. 49.10 .... R-608
r. 49.11 .... R-609
r. 49.12 .... R-610
r. 49.13 .... R-611
r. 49.14 .... R-612
r. 49.15 .... R-613
r. 49.16 .... R-614
r. 49.17 .... R-615
r. 50.1 .... R-616
r. 50.2 .... R-617
r. 50.3 .... R-618
r. 50.4 .... R-619
r. 50.5 .... R-620
r. 50.6 .... R-621
r. 50.7 .... R-622
r. 50.8 .... R-623
r. 50.9 .... R-624
r. 50.10 .... R-625
r. 50.11 .... R-626
r. 50.12 .... R-627
r. 50.13 .... R-628
r. 50.14 .... R-629
r. 50.15 .... R-630
r. 50.16 .... R-631
r. 50.17 .... R-632
r. 50.18 .... R-633
r. 50.19 .... R-634
r. 50.20 .... R-635
r. 50.21 .... R-636
r. 50.22 .... R-637
r. 50.23 .... R-638
r. 50.24 .... R-639
r. 50.25 .... R-640
r. 50.26 .... R-641
r. 50.27 .... R-642
r. 50.28 .... R-643
r. 50.29 .... R-644
r. 50.30 .... R-645
r. 50.31 .... R-646
r. 50.32 .... R-647
pt. 76 .... SG10-147

Environmental Permitting (England and Wales) Regulations 2010 (SI 2010 No. 675)
reg. 12 .... SG24-2, SG24-18
reg. 38(1) SG24-2, SG24-14, SG24-18, SG24-28
reg. 38(2) SG24-2, SG24-14, SG24-18, SG24-28
reg. 38(3) SG24-2, SG24-14, SG24-18, SG24-28
reg. 44 .... SG24-14, SG24-28

Insolvency (Northern Ireland) Order 1989 (SI 1989 No. 2405) (N.I. 19)
art. 279B R-375

Magistrates' Courts (Anti-social Behaviour Orders) Rules 2002 (SI 2002 No. 2784) SG17-4

Proceeds of Crime Act 2002 (Appeals under Part 2) Order 2003 (SI 2003 No. 82) R-467, R-471
art. 6 .... R-468, R-477
art. 7 .... R-468, R-469
art. 8 .... R-472, R-473
art. 12 .... R-476
art. 15 .... R-476

Proceeds of Crime Act 2002 (Enforcement in different parts of the United Kingdom) Order 2002 (SI 2002 No. 3133)
art. 6 . . . . R-320, R-321, R-322
Proceeds of Crime Act 2002 (External Investigations) Order 2014 (SI 2014 No. 1893) . . . . R-514, , R-514A, R-590
art. 6 . . . . R-514, R-514A, R-519, R-519A, R-542, R-542A
art. 8 . . . . R-514, R-514A
art. 9 . . . . R-515, R-515A, R-570, R-570A
art. 12 . . . . R-514, R-514A, R-532, R-532A, R-542, R-542A
art. 13 . . . . R-534, R-534A, R-542, R-542A
art. 16 . . . . R-514, R-514A
art. 21 . . . . R-514, R-514A
art. 22 . . . . R-514, R-514A
art. 28 . . . . R-514, R-514A
art. 29 . . . . R-514, R-514A, R-519, R-519A
art. 32 . . . . R-514, R-514A
art. 34 . . . . R-514, R-514A
Proceeds of Crime Act 2002 (External Requests and Orders) Order 2005 (SI 2005 No. 3181) R-328
Prosecution of Offences (Custody Time-limits) Regulations 1987 (SI 1987 No. 299) PD-121
Protection of Freedoms Act 2012 (Commencement No. 6) Order 2013 (SI 2013 No. 1180) SG31-156
Railways (Penalty Fares) Regulations 1994 (SI 1994 No. 576) SG10-192
Safeguarding Vulnerable Groups Act 2006 (Commencement No. 8 and Saving) Order 2012 (SI 2012 No. 2231) SG31-156
Safeguarding Vulnerable Groups Act 2006 (Prescribed Criteria and Miscellaneous Provisions) Regulations 2009 (SI 2009 No. 37) SG31-156
Serious Crime Act 2007 (Appeals under Section 24) Order 2008 (SI 2008 No. 1863)
pt. 3. . . . . R-497
Transfrontier of Shipment of Waste Regulations 2007 (SI 2007 No. 1711) SG24-17

Table of Practice Directions

Consolidated Criminal Practice Directions [2002] 1 WLR 2870, [2002] 2 Cr App R 35 (533)
para. 1 5A PD-1
Annex D PD-1, PD-17
Annex E. PD-1, PD-17
Criminal Costs Practice Direction SG10-147
Criminal Practice Directions [2013] EWCA Crim 1631 .... PD-1
Criminal Practice Directions [2015] EWCA Crim 1567 .... SG8-8
CPD I
para. 3D PD-45
CPD II
para. 5B PD-45
para. 16B PD-45
CPD VI Trial
para. 26L.2 .... PD-45
CPD XIII Listing
E PD-45
Annex 3 .... SG10-141, SG10-144
Practice Direction (Citation of Authorities) [2012] 1 WLR 780 .... PD-113
Practice Direction (Committal for Contempt of Court - Open Court PD-69
Practice Direction (Costs in Criminal Proceedings) [2015] EWCA Crim 1568 .... SG10-147
Practice Direction (Magistrates' Courts: Anti-Social Behaviour Orders: Composition of Benches) [2006] 1 AER 886 .... SG17-4
Practice Direction (Supreme Court) (Devolution Issues) [1999] 1 WLR 1592, [1999] 3 All ER 466, [1999] 2 Cr App R 486 .... PD-10

Table of Codes of Conduct

Code of Practice for Victims of Crime (October 2013) PD-78, PD-79
para. 1.22 .... PD-45
Police and Criminal Evidence Act 1984 Codes of Practice
Code C PD-39
Code E PD-39
Note 5A. PD-39
Code F PD-39
Code H PD-39

Table of Guidelines

Attorney-General
Acceptance of Pleas and the Prosecutor's Role in the Sentencing Exercise PD-73
Plea Discussions in Cases of Serious or Complex Fraud PD-74
Crown Prosecution Service
HMCTS Guidance for summoning officers when considering deferral and excusal applications PD-59
Home Office Anti-social Behaviour, Crime and Policing Act 2014: Reform of anti-social behaviour
powers; Statutory guidance for frontline professionals (July 2014) SG10-155
Ministry of Justice
Achieving Best Evidence in Criminal Proceedings (2011) PD-6, PD-45
Sentencing Council
Allocation, offences taken into consideration and totality (December 2015) PD-77, SG31-46
Overraching Principles—Sentencing Youths (Nov 2009) PD-123
Reduction in Sentence for a Guilty Plea (June 2017) SG31-32, SG31-43, SG31-54, SG32-8, SG32-32, SG32-42, SG32-52, SG32-62, SG32-72, SG32-82, SG32-94

Table of Protocols and Circulars

Good Practice Model on Disclosure of Information in Cases of Alleged Child Abuse and Linked Criminal and Care Directions PD-45
Judicial Protocol on the Disclosure of Unused Material in Criminal Cases PD-44
Magistrates' Courts' Protocol for Listing Cases where the Welsh Language is used (January 2008) PD-12
Protocol between the Association of Chief Police Officers, the Crown Prosecution Service and Her Majesty's Courts and Tribunals Service to Expedite Cases Involving Witnesses under 10 years
sect. 8.6 .... PD-45
sect. 10.2 .... PD-45
Publicity and the Criminal Justice System PD-18
Sharing Court Registers and Court Lists with Local Newspapers (September 2011) PD-18

Table of International Treaties and Conventions and other Legal Instruments

European Convention on Human Rights
art. 6 .... PD-18, SG16-4
art. 8 .... PD-20, SG8-8
art. 10 .... PD-21

Table of European Legislation

Directive 2011/99/EU R-310
Directive 2014/41/EU R-187, R-571
Framework Decision 2002/584/JHA PD-104
Framework Decision 2009/829/JHA R-136
Recommendation 2012/C338/01 .... PD-99
Treaty on the Functioning of Europe, art. 267 .... R-491

CRIMINAL PROCEDURE RULES AND CRIMINAL PRACTICE DIRECTIONS

Criminal Procedure Rules (SI 2015 No. 1490) and Criminal Practice Directions

The following text reproduces the Criminal Procedure Rules 2015 and the Criminal Practice Directions. The Criminal Procedure Rules are shown as amended by the Criminal Procedure (Amendment) Rules 2016 (SI 2016 No. 120), the Criminal Procedure (Amendment No. 2) Rules 2016 (SI 2016 No. 705), the Criminal Procedure (Amendment) Rules 2017 (SI 2017 No. 144), the Criminal Procedure (Amendment No. 2) Rules 2017 (SI 2017 No. 282), the Criminal Procedure (Amendment No. 3) Rules 2017 (SI 2017 No. 755), the Criminal Procedure (Amendment No. 4) Rules 2017 (SI 2017 No. 915), the Criminal Procedure (Amendment) Rules 2018 (SI 2018 No. 132), the Criminal Procedure (Amendment No. 2) Rules 2018 (SI 2018 No. 847), the Criminal Procedure (Amendment) Rules 2019 (SI 2019 No. 143), and the Criminal Procedure (Amendment No. 2) Rules 2019, (SI 2019 No. 1119); the latter amendments will come into force on 7 October 2019.

Please note that the amendments to Part 47 will come into force on 7 October 2019 unless the Criminal Procedure (Amendment) (EU Exit) Regulations 2019 (SI 2019 No. 908) come into force before that date. In that event, Part 47A should be ignored.

If the above Regulations come into force before 7 October 2019, the amendments will come into force on 7 October 2019 as Part 47A and, in that event, Part 47 should be ignored.

The objective of the restructuring and revision of the Practice Direction in 2013 was to make it more accessible and useful to practitioners and a key part of that is arranging the Practice Direction so as to correspond so far as practicable with the related parts of the Criminal Procedure Rules. We have integrated the texts of the Rules and the Practice Direction so far as possible and have included amendments to the Practice Direction which have effect from 1 April 2019, using the most authoritative draft available at the time of going to press. The text of the Rules is displayed in black text and is accompanied by a number (e.g., **R-36**) in addition to the numbering in the rules themselves. The text of the Practice Direction is displayed in grey boxes and follows the relevant text of the Rules (save where this is impracticable) and is accompanied by a number (e.g., **PD-18**) in addition to the number used in the Practice Direction itself.

CRIMINAL PRACTICE DIRECTIONS GENERAL MATTERS

PD-1

CPD I General matters A

A.1 The Lord Chief Justice has power, including power under section 74 of the Courts Act 2003 and Part 1 of Schedule 2 to the Constitutional Reform Act 2005, to give directions as to the practice and procedure of the criminal courts. The following directions are given accordingly.

A.2 These Practice Directions replace the Criminal Practice Directions given on 7th October 2013 [2013] EWCA Crim 1631; [2013] 1 WLR 3164 as amended by the Directions given on (i) 10th December, 2013 [2013] EWCA Crim 2328; [2014] 1 WLR 35, (ii) 23rd July, 2014 [2014] EWCA Crim 1569; [2014] 1 WLR 3001, (iii) 18th March, 2015 [2015] EWCA Crim 430; [2015] 1 WLR 1643; (iv) 16th July, 2015 [2015] EWCA Crim 1253; [2015] 1 WLR 3582; (v) 4th April, 2016 [2016] EWCA Crim 97; (vi) 16th November, 2016 [2016] EWCA Crim 1714; (vii) 31st January, 2017 [2017] EWCA Crim 30; (viii) 3rd April, 2017 [2017] EWCA Crim 310; (ix) 2nd October, 2017 [2017] EWCA Crim 1076; and (x) 2nd April, [2018] EWCA Crim 516.

A.3 The Criminal Procedure Rules and the Criminal Practice Directions are the law. Together they provide a code of current practice that is binding on the courts to which they are directed, and which promotes the consistent administration of justice. Participants must comply with the Rules and Practice Direction, and directions made by the court, and so it is the responsibility of the courts and those who participate in cases to be familiar with, and to ensure that these provisions are complied with.

A.4 Annexes D and E to the Consolidated Criminal Practice Direction of 8th July, 2002, [2002] 1 W.L.R. 2870; [2002] 2 Cr. App. R. 35, as amended, which set out forms for use in connection with the Criminal Procedure Rules, remain in force. See also paragraph I 5A of these Practice Directions.

A.5 These Practice Directions supplement many, but not all, Parts of the Criminal Procedure Rules, and include other directions about practice and procedure in the courts to which they apply. They are to be known as the Criminal Practice Directions 2015. They come into force on 5th October, 2015. They apply to all cases in all the criminal courts of England and Wales from that date.

A.6 Consequent on the rearrangement of the Criminal Procedure Rules in the Criminal Procedure Rules 2015, S.I. 2015/1490:

(a) the content of these Practice Directions is arranged to correspond. Within each division of these Directions the paragraphs are numbered to correspond with the associated Part of the Criminal Procedure Rules 2015. Compared with the Criminal Practice Directions given in 2013, as amended, the numbering and content of some divisions is amended consequentially, as shown in this table:

Derivations	
Divisions of 2015 Directions	*Divisions of 2013 Directions*
I General matters	I General matters
II Preliminary proceedings	II Preliminary proceedings 16A–C II Preliminary proceedings 9A, 10A, 14A–B
III Custody and bail	III Custody and bail
IV Disclosure	IV Disclosure
V Evidence	V Evidence
VI Trial	VI Trial
VII Sentencing	VII Sentencing
VIII Confiscation and related proceedings [empty]	VIII Confiscation and related proceedings [empty]
IX Appeal	X Appeal
X Costs [Criminal Costs Practice Direction]	XI Costs [Criminal Costs Practice Direction]
XI Other proceedings	II Preliminary proceedings 6A, 17A–F IX Contempt of court
XII General application	XII General application
XIII Listing	XIII Listing

(b) the text of these Practice Directions is amended:
   (i) to bring up to date the cross-references to the Criminal Procedure Rules and to other paragraphs of these Directions which that text contains, and
   (ii) to adopt the abbreviation of references to the Criminal Procedure Rules ('CrimPR') for which rule 2.3(2) of the Criminal Procedure Rules 2015 provides.

A.7 In all other respects, the content of the Criminal Practice Directions 2015 reproduces that of the Criminal Practice Directions 2013, as amended.

Criminal Procedure Rules Part 1 The Overriding Objective

R-1 **The overriding objective**

1.1 (1) The overriding objective of this procedural code is that criminal cases be dealt with justly.
(2) Dealing with a criminal case justly includes—
   (a) acquitting the innocent and convicting the guilty;
   (b) dealing with the prosecution and the defence fairly;
   (c) recognising the rights of a defendant, particularly those under Article 6 of the European Convention on Human Rights;
   (d) respecting the interests of witnesses, victims and jurors and keeping them informed of the progress of the case;
   (e) dealing with the case efficiently and expeditiously;
   (f) ensuring that appropriate information is available to the court when bail and sentence are considered; and
   (g) dealing with the case in ways that take into account—
      (i) the gravity of the offence alleged,
      (ii) the complexity of what is in issue,
      (iii) the severity of the consequences for the defendant and others affected, and
      (iv) the needs of other cases.

R-2 **The duty of the participants in a criminal case**

1.2 (1) Each participant, in the conduct of each case, must—
   (a) prepare and conduct the case in accordance with the overriding objective;
   (b) comply with these Rules, practice directions and directions made by the court; and
   (c) at once inform the court and all parties of any significant failure (whether or not that participant is responsible for that failure) to take any procedural step required by these Rules, any practice direction or any direction of the court. A failure is significant if it might hinder the court in furthering the overriding objective.
(2) Anyone involved in any way with a criminal case is a participant in its conduct for the purposes of this rule.

R-3 **The application by the court of the overriding objective**

1.3 The court must further the overriding objective in particular when—
   (a) exercising any power given to it by legislation (including these Rules);
   (b) applying any practice direction; or
   (c) interpreting any rule or practice direction.

Criminal Practice Directions Part 1 The Overriding Objective

CPD I General matters 1A: The Overriding Objective PD-2

1A.1 The presumption of innocence and an adversarial process are essential features of English and Welsh legal tradition and of the defendant's right to a fair trial. But it is no part of a fair trial that questions of guilt and innocence should be determined by procedural manoeuvres. On the contrary, fairness is best served when the issues between the parties are identified as early and as clearly as possible. As Lord Justice Auld noted, a criminal trial is not a game under which a guilty defendant should be provided with a sporting chance. It is a search for truth in accordance with the twin principles that the prosecution must prove its case and that a defendant is not obliged to inculpate himself, the object being to convict the guilty and acquit the innocent.

1A.2 Further, it is not just for a party to obstruct or delay the preparation of a case for trial in order to secure some perceived procedural advantage, or to take unfair advantage of a mistake by someone else. If courts allow that to happen it damages public confidence in criminal justice. The Rules and the Practice Direction, taken together, make it clear that courts must not allow it to happen.

Criminal Procedure Rules Part 2 Understanding and Applying the Rules

When the Rules apply R-4

2.1 (1) In general, the Criminal Procedure Rules apply—
(a) in all criminal cases in magistrates' courts and in the Crown Court;
(b) in extradition cases in the High Court; and
(c) in all cases in the criminal division of the Court of Appeal.
(2) If a rule applies only in one or some of those courts, the rule makes that clear.
(3) These Rules apply on and after 5th October, 2015, but—
(a) unless the court otherwise directs, they do not affect a right or duty existing under the Criminal Procedure Rules 2014; and
(b) unless the High Court otherwise directs, Section 3 of Part 50 (Extradition—appeal to the High Court) does not apply to a case in which notice of an appeal was given before 6th October, 2014.
(4) In a case in which a request for extradition was received by a relevant authority in the United Kingdom on or before 31st December, 2003—
(a) the rules in Part 50 (Extradition) do not apply; and
(b) the rules in Part 17 of the Criminal Procedure Rules 2012 (Extradition) continue to apply as if those rules had not been revoked.

Definitions R-5

2.2 (1) In these Rules, unless the context makes it clear that something different is meant:
'advocate' means a person who is entitled to exercise a right of audience in the court under section 13 of the Legal Services Act 2007;
'business day' means any day except Saturday, Sunday, Christmas Day, Boxing Day, Good Friday, Easter Monday or a bank holiday;
'court' means a tribunal with jurisdiction over criminal cases. It includes a judge, recorder, District Judge (Magistrates' Court), lay justice and, when exercising their judicial powers, the Registrar of Criminal Appeals, a justices' clerk or assistant clerk;
'court officer' means the appropriate member of the staff of a court;
'justices' legal adviser' means a justices' clerk or an assistant to a justices' clerk;
'legal representative' means:
(i) the person for the time being named as a party's representative in any legal aid representation order made under section 16 of the Legal Aid, Sentencing and Punishment of Offenders Act 2012, or
(ii) subject to that, the person named as a party's representative in any notice for the time being given under **rule 46.2** (Notice of appointment, etc. of legal representative: general rules) provided that person is entitled to conduct litigation in the court under section 13 of the Legal Services Act 2007;
'live link' means an arrangement by which a person can see and hear, and be seen and heard by, the court when that person is not in the courtroom;
'Practice Direction' means the Lord Chief Justice's Criminal Practice Directions, as amended, and 'Criminal Costs Practice Direction' means the Lord Chief Justice's Practice Direction (Costs in Criminal Proceedings), as amended;
'public interest ruling' means a ruling about whether it is in the public interest to disclose prosecution material under sections 3(6), 7A(8) or 8(5) of the Criminal Procedure and Investigations Act 1996; and

'Registrar' means the Registrar of Criminal Appeals or a court officer acting with the Registrar's authority.

(2) Definitions of some other expressions are in the rules in which they apply.

R-6 References to legislation, including these Rules

2.3 (1) In these Rules, where a rule refers to an Act of Parliament or to subordinate legislation by title and year, subsequent references to that Act or to that legislation in the rule are shortened: so, for example, after a reference to the Criminal Procedure and Investigations Act 1996 that Act is called 'the 1996 Act'; and after a reference to the Criminal Procedure and Investigations Act 1996 (Defence Disclosure Time Limits) Regulations 2011 those Regulations are called 'the 2011 Regulations'.

(2) In the courts to which these Rules apply—

(a) unless the context makes it clear that something different is meant, a reference to the Criminal Procedure Rules, without reference to a year, is a reference to the Criminal Procedure Rules in force at the date on which the event concerned occurs or occurred;

(b) a reference to the Criminal Procedure Rules may be abbreviated to 'CrimPR'; and

(c) a reference to a Part or rule in the Criminal Procedure Rules may be abbreviated to, for example, 'CrimPR Part 3' or 'CrimPR 3.5'.

CRIMINAL PROCEDURE RULES PART 3 CASE MANAGEMENT

General rules

R-7 When this Part applies

3.1 (1) Rules 3.1 to 3.12 apply to the management of each case in a magistrates' court and in the Crown Court (including an appeal to the Crown Court) until the conclusion of that case.

(2) Rules 3.13 to 3.26 apply where—

(a) the defendant is sent to the Crown Court for trial;

(b) a High Court or Crown Court judge gives permission to serve a draft indictment; or

(c) the Court of Appeal orders a retrial.

(3) Rule 3.27 applies in a magistrates' court unless—

(a) the court sends the defendant for trial in the Crown Court; or

(b) the case is one to which rule 24.8 or rule 24.9 applies (Written guilty plea: special rules; Single justice procedure: special rules).

(4) Rule 3.28 applies in a magistrates' court and in the Crown Court (including on an appeal to the Crown Court).

R-8 The duty of the court

3.2 (1) The court must further the overriding objective by actively managing the case.

(2) Active case management includes—

(a) the early identification of the real issues;

(b) the early identification of the needs of witnesses;

(c) achieving certainty as to what must be done, by whom, and when, in particular by the early setting of a timetable for the progress of the case;

(d) monitoring the progress of the case and compliance with directions;

(e) ensuring that evidence, whether disputed or not, is presented in the shortest and clearest way;

(f) discouraging delay, dealing with as many aspects of the case as possible on the same occasion, and avoiding unnecessary hearings;

(g) encouraging the participants to co-operate in the progression of the case; and

(h) making use of technology.

(3) The court must actively manage the case by giving any direction appropriate to the needs of that case as early as possible.

(4) Where appropriate live links are available, making use of technology for the purposes of this rule includes directing the use of such facilities, whether an application for such a direction is made or not—

(a) for the conduct of a pre-trial hearing, including a pre-trial case management hearing;

(b) for the defendant's attendance at such a hearing—

(i) where the defendant is in custody, or where the defendant is not in custody and wants to attend by live link, but

(ii) only if the court is satisfied that the defendant can participate effectively by such means, having regard to all the circumstances including whether the defendant is represented or not; and

(c) for receiving evidence under one of the powers to which the rules in Part 18 apply (Measures to assist a witness or defendant to give evidence).

(5) Where appropriate telephone facilities are available, making use of technology for the purposes of this rule includes directing the use of such facilities, whether an applica-

tion for such a direction is made or not, for the conduct of a pre-trial case management hearing—
(a) if telephone facilities are more convenient for that purpose than live links;
(b) unless at that hearing the court expects to take the defendant's plea; and
(c) only if—
(i) the defendant is represented, or
(ii) exceptionally, the court is satisfied that the defendant can participate effectively by such means without a representative.

The duty of the parties R-9

3.3 (1) Each party must—
(a) actively assist the court in fulfilling its duty under rule 3.2, without or if necessary with a direction; and
(b) apply for a direction if needed to further the overriding objective. .
(2) Active assistance for the purposes of this rule includes—
(a) at the beginning of the case, communication between the prosecutor and the defendant at the first available opportunity and in any event no later than the beginning of the day of the first hearing;
(b) after that, communication between the parties and with the court officer until the conclusion of the case;
(c) by such communication establishing, among other things—
(i) whether the defendant is likely to plead guilty or not guilty,
(ii) what is agreed and what is likely to be disputed,
(iii) what information, or other material, is required by one party of another, and why, and
(iv) what is to be done, by whom, and when (without or if necessary with a direction);
(d) reporting on that communication to the court—
(i) at the first hearing, and
(ii) after that, as directed by the court; and
(e) alerting the court to any reason why—
(i) a direction should not be made in any of the circumstances listed in rule 3.2(4) or (5) (The duty of the court: use of live link or telephone facilities), or
(ii) such a direction should be varied or revoked.

Case progression officers and their duties R-10

3.4 (1) At the beginning of the case each party must, unless the court otherwise directs—
(a) nominate someone responsible for progressing that case; and
(b) tell other parties and the court who that is and how to contact that person.
(2) In fulfilling its duty under rule 3.2, the court must where appropriate—
(a) nominate a court officer responsible for progressing the case; and
(b) make sure the parties know who that is and how to contact that court officer.
(3) In this Part a person nominated under this rule is called a case progression officer.
(4) A case progression officer must—
(a) monitor compliance with directions;
(b) make sure that the court is kept informed of events that may affect the progress of that case;
(c) make sure that he or she can be contacted promptly about the case during ordinary business hours;
(d) act promptly and reasonably in response to communications about the case; and
(e) if he or she will be unavailable, appoint a substitute to fulfil his or her duties and inform the other case progression officers.

The court's case management powers R-11

3.5 (1) In fulfilling its duty under rule 3.2 the court may give any direction and take any step actively to manage a case unless that direction or step would be inconsistent with legislation, including these Rules.
(2) In particular, the court may—
(a) nominate a judge, magistrate or justices' legal adviser to manage the case;
(b) give a direction on its own initiative or on application by a party;
(c) ask or allow a party to propose a direction;
(d) receive applications, notices, representations and information by letter, by telephone, by live link, by email or by any other means of electronic communication, and conduct a hearing by live link, telephone or other such electronic means;
(e) give a direction—
(i) at a hearing, in public or in private, or
(ii) without a hearing;
(f) fix, postpone, bring forward, extend, cancel or adjourn a hearing;
(g) shorten or extend (even after it has expired) a time limit fixed by a direction;

(h) require that issues in the case should be—
(i) identified in writing,
(ii) determined separately, and decide in what order they will be determined; and
(i) specify the consequences of failing to comply with a direction.
(3) A magistrates' court may give a direction that will apply in the Crown Court if the case is to continue there.
(4) The Crown Court may give a direction that will apply in a magistrates' court if the case is to continue there.
(5) Any power to give a direction under this Part includes a power to vary or revoke that direction.
(6) If a party fails to comply with a rule or a direction, the court may—
(a) fix, postpone, bring forward, extend, cancel or adjourn a hearing;
(b) exercise its powers to make a costs order; and
(c) impose such other sanction as may be appropriate.

R-12 **Application to vary a direction**

3.6 (1) A party may apply to vary a direction if—
(a) the court gave it without a hearing;
(b) the court gave it at a hearing in that party's absence; or
(c) circumstances have changed.
(2) A party who applies to vary a direction must—
(a) apply as soon as practicable after becoming aware of the grounds for doing so; and
(b) give as much notice to the other parties as the nature and urgency of the application permits.

R-13 **Agreement to vary a time limit fixed by a direction**

3.7 (1) The parties may agree to vary a time limit fixed by a direction, but only if—
(a) the variation will not—
(i) affect the date of any hearing that has been fixed, or
(ii) significantly affect the progress of the case in any other way;
(b) the court has not prohibited variation by agreement; and
(c) the court's case progression officer is promptly informed.
(2) The court's case progression officer must refer the agreement to the court if in doubt that the condition in paragraph (1)(a) is satisfied.

R-14 **Court's power to vary requirements under this Part**

3.8 (1) The court may—
(a) shorten or extend (even after it has expired) a time limit set by this Part; and
(b) allow an application or representations to be made orally.
(2) A person who wants an extension of time must—
(a) apply when serving the application or representations for which it is needed; and
(b) explain the delay.

R-15 **Case preparation and progression**

3.9 (1) At every hearing, if a case cannot be concluded there and then the court must give directions so that it can be concluded at the next hearing or as soon as possible after that.
(2) At every hearing the court must, where relevant—
(a) if the defendant is absent, decide whether to proceed nonetheless;
(b) take the defendant's plea (unless already done) or if no plea can be taken then find out whether the defendant is likely to plead guilty or not guilty;
(c) set, follow or revise a timetable for the progress of the case, which may include a timetable for any hearing including the trial or (in the Crown Court) the appeal;
(d) in giving directions, ensure continuity in relation to the court and to the parties' representatives where that is appropriate and practicable; and
(e) where a direction has not been complied with, find out why, identify who was responsible, and take appropriate action.
(3) In order to prepare for the trial, the court must take every reasonable step—
(a) to encourage and to facilitate the attendance of witnesses when they are needed; and
(b) to facilitate the participation of any person, including the defendant.
(4) Facilitating the participation of the defendant includes finding out whether the defendant needs interpretation because—
(a) the defendant does not speak or understand English; or
(b) the defendant has a hearing or speech impediment.
(5) Where the defendant needs interpretation—
(a) the court officer must arrange for interpretation to be provided at every hearing which the defendant is due to attend;

(b) interpretation may be by an intermediary where the defendant has a speech impediment, without the need for a defendant's evidence direction;
(c) on application or on its own initiative, the court may require a written translation to be provided for the defendant of any document or part of a document, unless—
(i) translation of that document, or part, is not needed to explain the case against the defendant, or
(ii) the defendant agrees to do without and the court is satisfied that the agreement is clear and voluntary and that the defendant has had legal advice or otherwise understands the consequences;
(d) on application by the defendant, the court must give any direction which the court thinks appropriate, including a direction for interpretation by a different interpreter, where—
(i) no interpretation is provided,
(ii) no translation is ordered or provided in response to a previous application by the defendant, or
(iii) the defendant complains about the quality of interpretation or of any translation.

(6) Facilitating the participation of any person includes giving directions for the appropriate treatment and questioning of a witness or the defendant, especially where the court directs that such questioning is to be conducted through an intermediary.

(7) Where directions for appropriate treatment and questioning are required, the court must—
(a) invite representations by the parties and by any intermediary; and
(b) set ground rules for the conduct of the questioning, which rules may include—
(i) a direction relieving a party of any duty to put that party's case to a witness or a defendant in its entirety,
(ii) directions about the manner of questioning,
(iii) directions about the duration of questioning,
(iv) if necessary, directions about the questions that may or may not be asked,
(v) where there is more than one defendant, the allocation among them of the topics about which a witness may be asked, and
(vi) directions about the use of models, plans, body maps or similar aids to help communicate a question or an answer.

Readiness for trial or appeal R-16

3.10 (1) This rule applies to a party's preparation for trial or appeal, and in this rule and rule 3.11 'trial' includes any hearing at which evidence will be introduced.

(2) In fulfilling the duty under rule 3.3, each party must—
(a) comply with directions given by the court;
(b) take every reasonable step to make sure that party's witnesses will attend when they are needed;
(c) make appropriate arrangements to present any written or other material; and
(d) promptly inform the court and the other parties of anything that may—
(i) affect the date or duration of the trial or appeal, or
(ii) significantly affect the progress of the case in any other way.

(3) The court may require a party to give a certificate of readiness.

Conduct of a trial or an appeal R-17

3.11 In order to manage the trial or an appeal, the court—
(a) must establish, with the active assistance of the parties, what are the disputed issues;
(b) must consider setting a timetable that—
(i) takes account of those issues and any timetable proposed by a party, and
(ii) may limit the duration of any stage of the hearing;
(c) may require a party to identify—
(i) which witnesses that party wants to give evidence in person,
(ii) the order in which that party wants those witnesses to give their evidence,
(iii) whether that party requires an order compelling the attendance of a witness,
(iv) what arrangements are desirable to facilitate the giving of evidence by a witness,
(v) what arrangements are desirable to facilitate the participation of any other person, including the defendant,
(vi) what written evidence that party intends to introduce,
(vii) what other material, if any, that person intends to make available to the court in the presentation of the case, and
(viii) whether that party intends to raise any point of law that could affect the conduct of the trial or appeal; and
(d) may limit—
(i) the examination, cross-examination or re-examination of a witness, and
(ii) the duration of any stage of the hearing.

R-18 **Duty of court officer**

3.12 The court officer must—

(a) where a person is entitled or required to attend a hearing, give as much notice as reasonably practicable to—
(i) that person, and
(ii) that person's custodian (if any);

(b) where the court gives directions, promptly make a record available to the parties.

Preparation for trial in the Crown Court

R-19 **Pre-trial hearings in the Crown Court: general rules**

3.13 (1) The Crown Court—

(a) may, and in some cases must, conduct a preparatory hearing where rule 3.14 applies;
(b) must conduct a plea and trial preparation hearing;
(c) may conduct a further pre-trial case management hearing (and if necessary more than one such hearing) only where—
(i) the court anticipates a guilty plea,
(ii) it is necessary to conduct such a hearing in order to give directions for an effective trial, or
(iii) such a hearing is required to set ground rules for the conduct of the questioning of a witness or defendant.

(2) At the plea and trial preparation hearing the court must—

(a) satisfy itself that there has been explained to the defendant, in terms the defendant can understand (with help, if necessary), that the defendant will receive credit for a guilty plea;
(b) take the defendant's plea in accordance with rule 3.24 (Arraigning the defendant on the indictment) or if no plea can be taken then find out whether the defendant is likely to plead guilty or not guilty;
(c) unless the defendant pleads guilty, satisfy itself that there has been explained to the defendant, in terms the defendant can understand (with help, if necessary), that at the trial—
(i) the defendant will have the right to give evidence after the court has heard the prosecution case,
(ii) if the defendant does not attend, the trial may take place in the defendant's absence,
(iii) if the trial takes place in the defendant's absence, the judge may inform the jury of the reason for that absence, and
(iv) where the defendant is released on bail, failure to attend court when required is an offence for which the defendant may be arrested and punished and bail may be withdrawn; and
(d) give directions for an effective trial.

(3) A pre-trial case management hearing—

(a) must be in public, as a general rule, but all or part of the hearing may be in private if the court so directs; and
(b) must be recorded, in accordance with rule 5.5 (Recording and transcription of proceedings in the Crown Court).

(4) Where the court determines a pre-trial application in private, it must announce its decision in public.

(5) The court—

(a) at the first hearing in the Crown Court must require a defendant who is present
(i) to provide, in writing or orally, his or her name, date of birth and nationality, or
(ii) to confirm that information by those means, where the information was given to the magistrates' court which sent the defendant for trial; and
(b) at any subsequent hearing may require such a defendant to provide or confirm that information by those means.

R-20 **Preparatory hearing**

3.14 (1) This rule applies where the Crown Court—

(a) can order a preparatory hearing, under—
(i) section 7 of the Criminal Justice Act 1987 (cases of serious or complex fraud), or
(ii) section 29 of the Criminal Procedure and Investigations Act 1996 (other complex, serious or lengthy cases);
(b) must order such a hearing, to determine an application for a trial without a jury, under—
(i) section 44 of the Criminal Justice Act 2003 (danger of jury tampering), or
(ii) section 17 of the Domestic Violence, Crime and Victims Act 2004 (trial of sample counts by jury, and others by judge alone);
(c) must order such a hearing, under section 29 of the 1996 Act, where section 29(1B) or (1C) applies (cases in which a terrorism offence is charged, or other serious cases with a terrorist connection).

(2) The court may decide whether to order a preparatory hearing—

(a) on an application or on its own initiative;
(b) at a hearing (in public or in private), or without a hearing;

(c) in a party's absence, if that party—
(i) applied for the order, or
(ii) has had at least 14 days in which to make representations.

Application for preparatory hearing R-21

3.15 (1) A party who wants the court to order a preparatory hearing must—
(a) apply in writing—
(i) as soon as reasonably practicable, and in any event
(ii) not more than 14 days after the defendant pleads not guilty;
(b) serve the application on—
(i) the court officer, and
(ii) each other party.
(2) The applicant must—
(a) if relevant, explain what legislation requires the court to order a preparatory hearing;
(b) otherwise, explain—
(i) what makes the case complex or serious, or makes the trial likely to be long,
(ii) why a substantial benefit will accrue from a preparatory hearing, and
(iii) why the court's ordinary powers of case management are not adequate.
(3) A prosecutor who wants the court to order a trial without a jury must explain—
(a) where the prosecutor alleges a danger of jury tampering—
(i) what evidence there is of a real and present danger that jury tampering would take place,
(ii) what steps, if any, reasonably might be taken to prevent jury tampering, and
(iii) why, notwithstanding such steps, the likelihood of jury tampering is so substantial as to make it necessary in the interests of justice to order such a trial; or
(b) where the prosecutor proposes trial without a jury on some counts on the indictment—
(i) why a trial by jury involving all the counts would be impracticable,
(ii) how the counts proposed for jury trial can be regarded as samples of the others, and
(iii) why it would be in the interests of justice to order such a trial.

Application for non-jury trial containing information withheld from a defendant R-22

3.16 (1) This rule applies where—
(a) the prosecutor applies for an order for a trial without a jury because of a danger of jury tampering; and
(b) the application includes information that the prosecutor thinks ought not be revealed to a defendant.
(2) The prosecutor must—
(a) omit that information from the part of the application that is served on that defendant;
(b) mark the other part to show that, unless the court otherwise directs, it is only for the court; and
(c) in that other part, explain why the prosecutor has withheld that information from that defendant.
(3) The hearing of an application to which this rule applies—
(a) must be in private, unless the court otherwise directs; and
(b) if the court so directs, may be, wholly or in part, in the absence of a defendant from whom information has been withheld.
(4) At the hearing of an application to which this rule applies—
(a) the general rule is that the court will receive, in the following sequence—
(i) representations first by the prosecutor and then by each defendant, in all the parties' presence, and then
(ii) further representations by the prosecutor, in the absence of a defendant from whom information has been withheld; but
(b) the court may direct other arrangements for the hearing.
(5) Where, on an application to which this rule applies, the court orders a trial without a jury—
(a) the general rule is that the trial will be before a judge other than the judge who made the order; but
(b) the court may direct other arrangements.

Representations in response to application for preparatory hearing R-23

3.17 (1) This rule applies where a party wants to make representations about—
(a) an application for a preparatory hearing;
(b) an application for a trial without a jury.
(2) Such a party must—
(a) serve the representations on—
(i) the court officer, and
(ii) each other party;
(b) do so not more than 14 days after service of the application;
(c) ask for a hearing, if that party wants one, and explain why it is needed.

(3) Where representations include information that the person making them thinks ought not be revealed to another party, that person must—
(a) omit that information from the representations served on that other party;
(b) mark the information to show that, unless the court otherwise directs, it is only for the court; and
(c) with that information include an explanation of why it has been withheld from that other party.
(4) Representations against an application for an order must explain why the conditions for making it are not met.

R-24 **Commencement of preparatory hearing**

3.18 At the beginning of a preparatory hearing, the court must—
(a) announce that it is such a hearing; and
(b) take the defendant's plea under rule 3.24 (Arraigning the defendant on the indictment), unless already done.

R-25 **Defence trial advocate**

3.19 (1) The defendant must notify the court officer of the identity of the intended defence trial advocate—
(a) as soon as practicable, and in any event no later than the day of the plea and trial preparation hearing;
(b) in writing, or orally at that hearing.
(2) The defendant must notify the court officer in writing of any change in the identity of the intended defence trial advocate as soon as practicable, and in any event not more than 5 business days after that change.

R-26 **Application to stay case for abuse of process**

3.20 (1) This rule applies where a defendant wants the Crown Court to stay the case on the grounds that the proceedings are an abuse of the court, or otherwise unfair.
(2) Such a defendant must—
(a) apply in writing—
(i) as soon as practicable after becoming aware of the grounds for doing so,
(ii) at a pre-trial hearing, unless the grounds for the application do not arise until trial, and
(iii) in any event, before the defendant pleads guilty or the jury (if there is one) retires to consider its verdict at trial;
(b) serve the application on—
(i) the court officer, and
(ii) each other party; and
(c) in the application—
(i) explain the grounds on which it is made,
(ii) include, attach or identify all supporting material,
(iii) specify relevant events, dates and propositions of law, and
(iv) identify any witness the applicant wants to call to give evidence in person.
(3) A party who wants to make representations in response to the application must serve the representations on—
(a) the court officer; and
(b) each other party,
not more than 14 days after service of the application.

R-27 **Application for joint or separate trials, etc.**

3.21 (1) This rule applies where a party wants the Crown Court to order—
(a) the joint trial of—
(i) offences charged by separate indictments, or
(ii) defendants charged in separate indictments;
(b) separate trials of offences charged by the same indictment;
(c) separate trials of defendants charged in the same indictment; or
(d) the deletion of a count from an indictment.
(2) Such a party must—
(a) apply in writing—
(i) as soon as practicable after becoming aware of the grounds for doing so, and
(ii) before the trial begins, unless the grounds for the application do not arise until trial;
(b) serve the application on—
(i) the court officer, and
(ii) each other party; and
(c) in the application—
(i) specify the order proposed, and
(ii) explain why it should be made.

(3) A party who wants to make representations in response to the application must serve the representations on—
(a) the court officer; and
(b) each other party,
not more than 14 days after service of the application.
(4) Where the same indictment charges more than one offence, the court may exercise its power to order separate trials of those offences if of the opinion that—
(a) the defendant otherwise may be prejudiced or embarrassed in his or her defence (for example, where the offences to be tried together are neither founded on the same facts nor form or are part of a series of offences of the same or a similar character); or
(b) for any other reason it is desirable that the defendant should be tried separately for any one or more of those offences.

Order for joint or separate trials, or amendment of the indictment **R-28**

3.22 (1) This rule applies where the Crown Court makes an order—
(a) on an application under rule 3.21 applies (Application for joint or separate trials, etc.); or
(b) amending an indictment in any other respect.
(2) Unless the court otherwise directs, the court officer must endorse any paper copy of each affected indictment made for the court with—
(a) a note of the court's order; and
(b) the date of that order.

Application for indication of sentence **R-29**

3.23 (1) This rule applies where a defendant wants the Crown Court to give an indication of the maximum sentence that would be passed if a guilty plea were entered when the indication is sought.
(2) Such a defendant must—
(a) apply in writing as soon as practicable; and
(b) serve the application on—
(i) the court officer, and
(ii) the prosecutor.
(3) The application must—
(a) specify—
(i) the offence or offences to which it would be a guilty plea, and
(ii) the facts on the basis of which that plea would be entered; and
(b) include the prosecutor's agreement to, or representations on, that proposed basis of plea.
(4) The prosecutor must—
(a) provide information relevant to sentence, including—
(i) any previous conviction of the defendant, and the circumstances where relevant,
(ii) any statement of the effect of the offence on the victim, the victim's family or others; and
(b) identify any other matter relevant to sentence, including—
(i) the legislation applicable,
(ii) any sentencing guidelines, or guideline cases, and
(iii) aggravating and mitigating factors.
(5) The hearing of the application—
(a) may take place in the absence of any other defendant;
(b) must be attended by—
(i) the applicant defendant's legal representatives (if any), and
(ii) the prosecution advocate.

Arraigning the defendant on the indictment **R-30**

3.24 (1) In order to take the defendant's plea, the Crown Court must—
(a) obtain the prosecutor's confirmation, in writing or orally—
(i) that the indictment (or draft indictment, as the case may be) sets out a statement of each offence that the prosecutor wants the court to try and such particulars of the conduct constituting the commission of each such offence as the prosecutor relies upon to make clear what is alleged, and
(ii) of the order in which the prosecutor wants the defendants' names to be listed in the indictment, if the prosecutor proposes that more than one defendant should be tried at the same time;
(b) ensure that the defendant is correctly identified by the indictment or draft indictment;
(c) satisfy itself that there has been explained to the defendant, in terms the defendant can understand (with help, if necessary), each allegation against him or her; and
(d) in respect of each count—
(i) read the count aloud to the defendant, or arrange for it to be read aloud or placed before the defendant in writing,

(ii) ask whether the defendant pleads guilty or not guilty to the offence charged by that count, and
(iii) take the defendant's plea.

(2) Where a count is read which is substantially the same as one already read aloud, then only the materially different details need be read aloud.

(3) Where a count is placed before the defendant in writing, the court must summarise its gist aloud.

(4) In respect of each count in the indictment—
(a) if the defendant declines to enter a plea, the court must treat that as a not guilty plea unless rule 25.10 applies (Defendant unfit to plead);
(b) if the defendant pleads not guilty to the offence charged by that count but guilty to another offence of which the court could convict on that count—
(i) if the prosecutor and the court accept that plea, the court must treat the plea as one of guilty of that other offence, but
(ii) otherwise, the court must treat the plea as one of not guilty;
(c) if the defendant pleads a previous acquittal or conviction of the offence charged by that count—
(i) the defendant must identify that acquittal or conviction in writing, explaining the basis of that plea, and
(ii) the court must exercise its power to decide whether that plea disposes of that count.

(5) In a case in which a magistrates' court sends the defendant for trial, the Crown Court must take the defendant's plea—
(a) not less than 2 weeks after the date on which that sending takes place, unless the parties otherwise agree; and
(b) more than 16 weeks after that date, unless the court otherwise directs (either before or after that period expires).

R-31 Place of trial

3.25 (1) Unless the court otherwise directs, the court officer must arrange for the trial to take place in a courtroom provided by the Lord Chancellor.

(2) The court officer must arrange for the court and the jury (if there is one) to view any place required by the court.

R-32 Use of Welsh language at trial

3.26 Where the trial will take place in Wales and a participant wishes to use the Welsh language—
(a) that participant must serve notice on the court officer, or arrange for such a notice to be served on that participant's behalf—
(i) at or before the plea and trial preparation hearing, or
(ii) in accordance with any direction given by the court; and
(b) if such a notice is served, the court officer must arrange for an interpreter to attend.

Preparation for trial in a magistrates' court

R-33 Pre-trial hearings in a magistrates' court: general rules

3.27 (1) A magistrates' court—
(a) must conduct a preparation for trial hearing unless—
(i) the court sends the defendant for trial in the Crown Court, or
(ii) the case is one to which rule 24.8 or rule 24.9 applies (Written guilty plea: special rules; Single justice procedure: special rules);
(b) may conduct a further pre-trial case management hearing (and if necessary more than one such hearing) only where—
(i) the court anticipates a guilty plea,
(ii) it is necessary to conduct such a hearing in order to give directions for an effective trial, or
(iii) such a hearing is required to set ground rules for the conduct of the questioning of a witness or defendant.

(2) At a preparation for trial hearing the court must give directions for an effective trial.

(3) At a preparation for trial hearing, if the defendant is present the court must—
(a) satisfy itself that there has been explained to the defendant, in terms the defendant can understand (with help, if necessary), that the defendant will receive credit for a guilty plea;
(b) take the defendant's plea or if no plea can be taken then find out whether the defendant is likely to plead guilty or not guilty; and (c) unless the defendant pleads guilty, satisfy itself that there has been explained to the defendant, in terms the defendant can understand (with help, if necessary), that at the trial—
(i) the defendant will have the right to give evidence after the court has heard the prosecution case,
(ii) if the defendant does not attend, the trial is likely to take place in the defendant's absence, and
(iii) where the defendant is released on bail, failure to attend court when required is an offence for which the defendant may be arrested and punished and bail may be withdrawn.

(4) A pre-trial case management hearing must be in public, as a general rule, but all or part of the hearing may be in private if the court so directs.

(5) The court—

(a) at the first hearing in the case must require a defendant who is present to provide, in writing or orally, his or her name, date of birth and nationality; and

(b) at any subsequent hearing may require such a defendant to provide that information by those means.

Medical reports

Directions for commissioning medical reports, other than for sentencing purposes R-34

3.28 (1) This rule applies where, because of a defendant's suspected mental ill-health—

(a) a magistrates' court requires expert medical opinion about the potential suitability of a hospital order under section 37(3) of the Mental Health Act 1983(1) (hospital order without convicting the defendant);

(b) the Crown Court requires expert medical opinion about the defendant's fitness to participate at trial, under section 4 of the Criminal Procedure (Insanity) Act 1964(2); or

(c) a magistrates' court or the Crown Court requires expert medical opinion to help the court determine a question of intent or insanity,

other than such opinion introduced by a party.

(2) A court may exercise the power to which this rule applies on its own initiative having regard to—

(a) an assessment of the defendant's health by a mental health practitioner acting independently of the parties to assist the court;

(b) representations by a party; or

(c) observations by the court.

(3) A court that requires expert medical opinion to which this rule applies must—

(a) identify each issue in respect of which the court requires such opinion and any legislation applicable;

(b) specify the nature of the expertise likely to be required for giving such opinion;

(c) identify each party or participant by whom a commission for such opinion must be prepared, who may be—

(i) a party (or party's representative) acting on that party's own behalf,

(ii) a party (or party's representative) acting on behalf of the court, or

(iii) the court officer acting on behalf of the court;

(d) where there are available to the court arrangements with the National Health Service under which an assessment of a defendant's mental health may be prepared, give such directions as are needed under those arrangements for obtaining the expert report or reports required;

(e) where no such arrangements are available to the court, or they will not be used, give directions for the commissioning of an expert report or expert reports, including—

(i) such directions as can be made about supplying the expert or experts with the defendant's medical records,

(ii) directions about the other information, about the defendant and about the offence or offences alleged to have been committed by the defendant, which is to be supplied to each expert, and

(iii) directions about the arrangements that will apply for the payment of each expert;

(f) set a timetable providing for—

(i) the date by which a commission is to be delivered to each expert,

(ii) the date by which any failure to accept a commission is to be reported to the court,

(iii) the date or dates by which progress in the preparation of a report or reports is to be reviewed by the court officer, and

(iv) the date by which each report commissioned is to be received by the court; and

(g) identify the person (each person, if more than one) to whom a copy of a report is to be supplied, and by whom.

(4) A commission addressed to an expert must—

(a) identify each issue in respect of which the court requires expert medical opinion and any legislation applicable;

(b) include—

(i) the information required by the court to be supplied to the expert,

(ii) details of the timetable set by the court, and

(iii) details of the arrangements that will apply for the payment of the expert;

(c) identify the person (each person, if more than one) to whom a copy of the expert's report is to be supplied; and

(d) request confirmation that the expert from whom the opinion is sought—

(i) accepts the commission, and

(ii) will adhere to the timetable.

Criminal Practice Directions Part 3 Case Management

PD-3 **CPD I General matters 3A: Case Management**

3A.1 CrimPR 1.1(2)(e) requires that cases be dealt with efficiently and expeditiously. CrimPR 3.2 requires the court to further the overriding objective by actively managing the case, for example:

a) When dealing with an offence which is triable only on indictment the court must ask the defendant whether he or she intends to plead guilty at the Crown Court (CrimPR 9.7(5));

b) On a guilty plea, the court must pass sentence at the earliest opportunity, in accordance with CrimPR 24.11(9)(a) (magistrates' courts) and 25.16(7)(a) (the Crown Court).

3A.2 Given these duties, magistrates' courts and the Crown Court therefore will proceed as described in paragraphs 3A.3 to 3A.28 below. The parties will be expected to have prepared in accordance with CrimPR 3.3(1) to avoid unnecessary and wasted hearings. They will be expected to have communicated with each other by the time of the first hearing; to report to the court on that communication at the first hearing; and to continue thereafter to communicate with each other and with the court officer, in accordance with CrimPR 3.3(2).

3A.3 There is a Preparation for Effective Trial form for use in the magistrates' courts, and a Plea and Trial Preparation Hearing form for use in the Crown Court, each of which must be used as appropriate in connection with CrimPR Part 3: see paragraph 5A.2 of these Practice Directions. Versions of those forms in pdf and Word, together with guidance notes, are available on the Criminal Procedure Rules pages of the Ministry of Justice website.

Case progression and trial preparation in magistrates' courts

3A.4 CrimPR 8.3 applies in all cases and requires the prosecutor to serve:

i. a summary of the circumstances of the offence;
ii. any account given by the defendant in interview, whether contained in that summary or in another document;
iii. any written witness statement or exhibit that the prosecutor then has available and considers material to plea or to the allocation of the case for trial or sentence;
iv. a list of the defendant's criminal record, if any; and
v. any available statement of the effect of the offence on a victim, a victim's family or others.

The details must include sufficient information to allow the defendant and the court at the first hearing to take an informed view:

i. on plea;
ii. on venue for trial (if applicable);
iii. for the purposes of case management; or
iv. for the purposes of sentencing (including committal for sentence, if applicable).

Defendant in custody

3A.5 If the defendant has been detained in custody after being charged with an offence which is indictable only or triable either way, at the first hearing a magistrates' court will proceed at once with the allocation of the case for trial, where appropriate, and, if so required, with the sending of the defendant to the Crown Court for trial. The court will be expected to ask for and record any indication of plea and issues for trial to assist the Crown Court.

3A.6 If the offence charged is triable only summarily, or if at that hearing the case is allocated for summary trial, the court will forthwith give such directions as are necessary, either (on a guilty plea) to prepare for sentencing, or for a trial.

Defendant on bail

3A.7 If the defendant has been released on bail after being charged, the case must be listed for the first hearing 14 days after charge, or the next available court date thereafter when the prosecutor anticipates a guilty plea which is likely to be sentenced in the magistrates' court. In cases where there is an anticipated not guilty plea or the case is likely to be sent or committed to the Crown Court for either trial or sentence, then it must be listed for the first hearing 28 days after charge or the next available court date thereafter.

Guilty plea in the magistrates' courts

3A.8 Where a defendant pleads guilty or indicates a guilty plea in a magistrates' court the court should consider whether a pre-sentence report — a stand down report if possible — is necessary.

Guilty plea in the Crown Court

3A.9 Where a magistrates' court is considering committal for sentence or the defendant has indicated an intention to plead guilty in a matter which is to be sent to the Crown Court, the magistrates' court should request the preparation of a pre-sentence report for the Crown Court's use if the magistrates' court considers that:

(a) there is a realistic alternative to a custodial sentence; or
(b) the defendant may satisfy the criteria for classification as a dangerous offender; or
(c) there is some other appropriate reason for doing so.

3A.10 When a magistrates' court sends a case to the Crown Court for trial and the defendant indicates an intention to plead guilty at the Crown Court, then that magistrates' court must set a date for a Plea and Trial Preparation Hearing at the Crown Court, in accordance with CrimPR 9.7(5)(a)(i).

Case sent for Crown Court trial: no indication of guilty plea

3A.11 In any case sent to the Crown Court for trial, other than one in which the defendant indicates an intention to plead guilty, the magistrates' court must set a date for a Plea and Trial Preparation Hearing, in accordance with CrimPR 9.7(5)(a)(ii). The Plea and Trial Preparation Hearing must be held within 28 days of sending, unless the standard directions of the Presiding Judges of the circuit direct otherwise. Paragraph 3A.16 below additionally applies to the arrangements for such hearings. A magistrates' court may give other directions appropriate to the needs of the case, in accordance with CrimPR 3.5(3), and in accordance with any standard directions issued by the Presiding Judges of the circuit.

Defendant on bail: anticipated not guilty plea

3A.12 Where the defendant has been released on bail after being charged, and where the prosecutor does not anticipate a guilty plea at the first hearing in a magistrates' court, then it is essential that the initial details of the prosecution case that are provided for that first hearing are sufficient to assist the court, in order to identify the real issues and to give appropriate directions for an effective trial (regardless of whether the trial is to be heard in the magistrates' court or the Crown Court). In these circumstances, unless there is good reason not to do so, the prosecution should make available the following material in advance of the first hearing in the magistrates' court:

(a) A summary of the circumstances of the offence(s) including a summary of any account given by the defendant in interview;
(b) Statements and exhibits that the prosecution has identified as being of importance for the purpose of plea or initial case management, including any relevant CCTV that would be relied upon at trial and any Streamlined Forensic Report;
(c) Details of witness availability, as far as they are known at that hearing;
(d) Defendant's criminal record;
(e) Victim Personal Statements if provided;
(f) An indication of any medical or other expert evidence that the prosecution is likely to adduce in relation to a victim or the defendant;
(g) Any information as to special measures, bad character or hearsay, where applicable.

3A.13 In addition to the material required by CrimPR Part 8, the information required by the Preparation for Effective Trial form must be available to be submitted at the first hearing, and the parties must complete that form, in accordance with the guidance published with it. Where there is to be a contested trial in a magistrates' court, that form includes directions and a timetable that will apply in every case unless the court otherwise orders.

3A.14 Nothing in paragraph 3A.12-3A.13 shall preclude the court from taking a plea pursuant to CrimPR 3.9(2)(b) at the first hearing and for the court to case manage as far as practicable under Part 3 CrimPR.

Exercise of magistrates' court's powers

3A.15 In accordance with CrimPR 9.1, sections 49, 51(13) and 51A(11) of the Crime and Disorder Act 1998, and sections 17E, 18(5) and 24D of the Magistrates' Courts Act 1980 a single justice can:

a) allocate and send for trial;
b) take an indication of a guilty plea (but not pass sentence);
c) take a not guilty plea and give directions for the preparation of trial including:
    i. timetable for the proceedings;
    ii. the attendance of the parties;
    iii. the service of documents;
    iv. the manner in which evidence is to be given.

Case progression and trial preparation in the Crown Court

Plea and Trial Preparation Hearing

3A.16 In a case in which a magistrates' court has directed a Plea and Trial Preparation Hearing, the period which elapses between sending for trial and the date of that hearing must be consistent within each circuit. In every case, the time allowed for the conduct of the Plea and Trial Preparation Hearing must be sufficient for effective trial preparation. It is expected in every case that an indictment will be lodged at least 7 days in advance of the hearing. Please see the Note to the Practice Direction.

3A.17 In a case in which the defendant, not having done so before, indicates an intention to plead guilty to his representative after being sent for trial but before the Plea and Trial Preparation Hearing, the defence representative will notify the Crown Court and the prosecution forthwith. The court will ensure there is sufficient time at the Plea and Trial Preparation Hearing for sentence and a Judge should at once request the preparation of a pre-sentence report if it appears to the court that either:

(a) there is a realistic alternative to a custodial sentence; or
(b) the defendant may satisfy the criteria for classification as a dangerous offender; or
(c) there is some other appropriate reason for doing so.

3A.18 If at the Plea and Trial Preparation Hearing the defendant pleads guilty and no pre-sentence report has been prepared, if possible the court should obtain a stand down report.

3A.19 Where the defendant was remanded in custody after being charged and was sent for trial without initial details of the prosecution case having been served, then at least 7 days before the Plea and Trial Preparation Hearing the prosecutor should serve, as a minimum, the material identified in paragraph 3A.12 above. If at the Plea and Trial Preparation Hearing the defendant does not plead guilty, the court will be expected to identify the issues in the case and give appropriate directions for an effective trial. Please see the Note to the Practice Direction.

3A.20 At the Plea and Trial Preparation Hearing, in addition to the material required by paragraph 3A.12 above, the prosecutor must serve sufficient evidence to enable the court to case manage effectively without the need for a further case management hearing, unless the case falls within paragraph 3A.21. In addition, the information required by the Plea and Trial Preparation Hearing form must be available to the court at that hearing, and it must have been discussed between the parties in advance. The prosecutor must provide details of the availability of likely prosecution witnesses so that a trial date can immediately be arranged if the defendant does not plead guilty.

Further case management hearing

3A.21 In accordance with CrimPR 3.13(1)(c), after the Plea and Trial Preparation Hearing there will be no further case management hearing before the trial unless:

(i) a condition listed in that rule is met; and
(ii) the court so directs, in order to further the overriding objective.

The directions to be given at the Plea and Trial Preparation Hearing therefore may include a direction for a further case management hearing, but usually will do so only in one of the following cases:

(a) Class 1 cases;
(b) Class 2 cases which carry a maximum penalty of 10 years or more;
(c) cases involving death by driving (whether dangerous or careless), or death in the workplace;
(d) cases involving a vulnerable witness;
(e) cases in which the defendant is a child or otherwise under a disability, or requires special assistance;
(f) cases in which there is a corporate or unrepresented defendant;
(g) cases in which the expected trial length is such that a further case management hearing is desirable and any case in which the trial is likely to last longer than four weeks;
(h) cases in which expert evidence is to be introduced;
(i) cases in which a party requests a hearing to enter a plea;
(j) cases in which an application to dismiss or stay has been made;
(k) cases in which arraignment has not taken place, whether because of an issue relating to fitness to plead, or abuse of process or sufficiency of evidence, or for any other reason;
(l) cases in which there are likely to be linked criminal and care directions in accordance with the 2013 Protocol.

3A.22 If a further case management hearing is directed, a defendant in custody will not usually be expected to attend in person, unless the court otherwise directs.

Compliance hearing

3A.23 If a party fails to comply with a case management direction, that party may be required to attend the court to explain the failure. Unless the court otherwise directs a defendant in custody will not usually be expected to attend. See paragraph 3A.26-3A.28 below.

Conduct of case progression hearings

3A.24 As far as possible, case progression should be managed without a hearing in the courtroom, using electronic communication in accordance with CrimPR 3.5(2)(d). Court staff should be nominated to conduct case progression as part of their role, in accordance with CrimPR 3.4(2). To aid effective communication the prosecution and defence representative should notify the court and provide details of who shall be dealing with the case at the earliest opportunity.

Completion of Effective Trial Monitoring form

3A.25 It is imperative that the Effective Trial Monitoring form (as devised and issued by Her Majesty's Courts and Tribunals Service) is accurately completed by the parties for all cases that have been listed for trial. Advocates must engage with the process by providing the relevant details and completing the form.

Compliance courts

3A.26 To ensure effective compliance with directions of the courts made in accordance with the Criminal Procedure Rules and the overriding objective, courts should maintain a record whenever a party to the proceedings has failed to comply with a direction made by the court. The parties may have to attend a hearing to explain any lack of compliance.

3A.27 These hearings may be conducted by live link facilities or via other electronic means, as the court may direct.

3A.28 It will be for the Presiding Judges, Resident Judge and Justices' Clerks to decide locally how often compliance courts should be held, depending on the scale and nature of the problem at each court centre.

CPD I General matters 3B: Pagination and Indexing of Served Evidence PD-4

3B.1 The following directions apply to matters before the Crown Court, where
(a) there is an application to prefer a bill of indictment in relation to the case;
(b) a person is sent for trial under section 51 of the Crime and Disorder Act 1998 (sending cases to the Crown Court), to the service of copies of the documents containing the evidence on which the charge or charges are based under Paragraph 1 of Schedule 3 to that Act; or
(c) a defendant wishes to serve evidence.

3B.2 A party who serves documentary evidence in the Crown Court should:
(a) paginate each page in any bundle of statements and exhibits sequentially;
(b) provide an index to each bundle of statements produced including the following information:
i. the name of the case;
ii. the author of each statement;
iii. the start page number of the witness statement;
iv. the end page number of the witness statement.
(c) provide an index to each bundle of documentary and pictorial exhibits produced, including the following information:
i. the name of the case
ii. the exhibit reference;
iii. a short description of the exhibit;
iv. the start page number of the exhibit;
v. the end page number of the exhibit;
vi. where possible, the name of the person producing the exhibit should be added.

3B.3 Where additional documentary evidence is served, a party should paginate following on from the last page of the previous bundle or in a logical and sequential manner. A party should also provide notification of service of any amended index.

3B.4 The prosecution must ensure that the running total of the pages of prosecution evidence is easily identifiable on the most recent served bundle of prosecution evidence.

3B.5 For the purposes of these directions, the number of pages of prosecution evidence served on the court includes all
(a) witness statements;
(b) documentary and pictorial exhibits;
(c) records of interviews with the defendant; and
(d) records of interviews with other defendants which form part of the served prosecution documents or which are included in any notice of additional evidence,

but does not include any document provided on CD-ROM or by other means of electronic communication.

CPD I General matters 3C: Abuse of Process Stay Applications PD-5

3C.1 In all cases where a defendant in the Crown Court proposes to make an application to stay an indictment on the grounds of abuse of process, written notice of such application must be given to the prosecuting authority and to any co-defendant as soon as practicable after the defendant becomes aware of the grounds for doing so and not later than 14 days before the date fixed or warned for trial ('the relevant date'). Such notice must:
(a) give the name of the case and the indictment number;
(b) state the fixed date or the warned date as appropriate;
(c) specify the nature of the application;
(d) set out in numbered sub-paragraphs the grounds upon which the application is to be made;
(e) be copied to the chief listing officer at the court centre where the case is due to be heard.

3C.2 Any co-defendant who wishes to make a like application must give a like notice not later than seven days before the relevant date, setting out any additional grounds relied upon.

3C.3 In relation to such applications, the following automatic directions shall apply:
(a) the advocate for the applicant(s) must lodge with the court and serve on all other parties a skeleton argument in support of the application, at least five clear working days before the relevant

date. If reference is to be made to any document not in the existing trial documents, a paginated and indexed bundle of such documents is to be provided with the skeleton argument;

(b) the advocate for the prosecution must lodge with the court and serve on all other parties a responsive skeleton argument at least two clear working days before the relevant date, together with a supplementary bundle if appropriate.

3C.4 All skeleton arguments must specify any propositions of law to be advanced (together with the authorities relied upon in support, with paragraph references to passages relied upon) and, where appropriate, include a chronology of events and a list of dramatis personae. In all instances where reference is made to a document, the reference in the trial documents or supplementary bundle is to be given. Paragraphs XII D.17 to D.23 of these Practice Directions set out the general requirements for skeleton arguments.

3C.5 The above time limits are minimum time limits. In appropriate cases, the court will order longer lead times. To this end, in all cases where defence advocates are, at the time of the preliminary hearing or as soon as practicable after the case has been sent, considering the possibility of an abuse of process application, this must be raised with the judge dealing with the matter, who will order a different timetable if appropriate, and may wish, in any event, to give additional directions about the conduct of the application. If the trial judge has not been identified, the matter should be raised with the Resident Judge.

PD-6 **CPD I General matters 3D: Vulnerable People in the Courts**

3D.1 In respect of eligibility for special measures, 'vulnerable' and 'intimidated' witnesses are defined in sections 16 and 17 of the Youth Justice and Criminal Evidence Act 1999 (as amended by the Coroners and Justice Act 2009); 'vulnerable' includes those under 18 years of age and people with a mental disorder or learning disability; a physical disorder or disability; or who are likely to suffer fear or distress in giving evidence because of their own circumstances or those relating to the case.

3D.2 However, many other people giving evidence in a criminal case, whether as a witness or defendant, may require assistance: the court is required to take 'every reasonable step' to encourage and facilitate the attendance of witnesses and to facilitate the participation of any person, including the defendant (CrimPR 3.9(3)(a) and (b)). This includes enabling a witness or defendant to give their best evidence, and enabling a defendant to comprehend the proceedings and engage fully with his or her defence. The pre-trial and trial process should, so far as necessary, be adapted to meet those ends. Regard should be had to the welfare of a young defendant as required by section 44 of the Children and Young Persons Act 1933, and generally to Parts 1 and 3 of the Criminal Procedure Rules (the overriding objective and the court's powers of case management).

3D.3 Under Part 3 of the Rules, the court must identify the needs of witnesses at an early stage (CrimPR 3.2(2)(b)) and may require the parties to identify arrangements to facilitate the giving of evidence and participation in the trial (CrimPR 3.11(c)(iv) and (v)). There are various statutory special measures that the court may utilise to assist a witness in giving evidence. CrimPR Part 18 gives the procedures to be followed. Courts should note the 'primary rule' which requires the court to give a direction for a special measure to assist a child witness or qualifying witness and that in such cases an application to the court is not required (CrimPR 18.9).

3D.4 Court of Appeal decisions on this subject include a judgment from the Lord Chief Justice, Lord Judge in *R v Cox* [2012] EWCA Crim 549, [2012] 2 Cr App R 6; *R v Wills* [2011] EWCA Crim 1938, [2012] 1 Cr App R 2; and *R v E* [2011] EWCA Crim 3028, [2012] Crim LR 563.

3D.5 In *R v Wills*, the Court endorsed the approach taken by the report of the Advocacy Training Council (ATC) 'Raising the Bar: the Handling of Vulnerable Witnesses, Victims and Defendants in Court' (2011). The report includes and recommends the use of 'toolkits' to assist advocates as they prepare to question vulnerable people at court: http://www.advocacytrainingcouncil.org/vulnerable-witnesses/raising-the-bar

3D.6 Further toolkits are available through the Advocate's Gateway which is managed by the ATC's Management Committee: http://www.theadvocatesgateway.org/

3D.7 These toolkits represent best practice. Advocates should consult and follow the relevant guidance whenever they prepare to question a young or otherwise vulnerable witness or defendant. Judges may find it helpful to refer advocates to this material and to use the toolkits in case management.

3D.8 'Achieving Best Evidence in Criminal Proceedings' (Ministry of Justice 2011) describes best practice in preparation for the investigative interview and trial: http://www.cps.gov.uk/publications/docs/best_evidence_in_criminal_proceedings.pdf

PD-7 **CPD I General matters 3E: Ground Rules Hearings to Plan the Questioning of a Vulnerable Witness or Defendant**

3E.1 The judiciary is responsible for controlling questioning. Over-rigorous or repetitive cross-examination of a child or vulnerable witness should be stopped. Intervention by the judge, magistrates or intermediary (if any) is minimised if questioning, taking account of the individual's communication needs, is discussed in advance and ground rules are agreed and adhered to.

3E.2 Discussion of ground rules is required in all intermediary trials where they must be discussed between the judge or magistrates, advocates and intermediary before the witness gives evidence. The intermediary must be present but is not required to take the oath (the intermediary's declaration is made just before the witness gives evidence).

3E.3 Discussion of ground rules is good practice, even if no intermediary is used, in all young witness cases and in other cases where a witness or defendant has communication needs. Discussion before the day of trial is preferable to give advocates time to adapt their questions to the witness's needs. It may be helpful for a trial practice note of boundaries to be created at the end of the discussion. The judge may use such a document in ensuring that the agreed ground rules are complied with.

3E.4 All witnesses, including the defendant and defence witnesses, should be enabled to give the best evidence they can. In relation to young and/or vulnerable people, this may mean departing radically from traditional cross-examination. The form and extent of appropriate cross-examination will vary from case to case. For adult non vulnerable witnesses an advocate will usually put his case so that the witness will have the opportunity of commenting upon it and/or answering it. When the witness is young or otherwise vulnerable, the court may dispense with the normal practice and impose restrictions on the advocate 'putting his case' where there is a risk of a young or otherwise vulnerable witness failing to understand, becoming distressed or acquiescing to leading questions. Where limitations on questioning are necessary and appropriate, they must be clearly defined. The judge has a duty to ensure that they are complied with and should explain them to the jury and the reasons for them. If the advocate fails to comply with the limitations, the judge should give relevant directions to the jury when that occurs and prevent further questioning that does not comply with the ground rules settled upon in advance. Instead of commenting on inconsistencies during cross-examination, following discussion between the judge and the advocates, the advocate or judge may point out important inconsistencies after (instead of during) the witness's evidence. The judge should also remind the jury of these during summing up. The judge should be alert to alleged inconsistencies that are not in fact inconsistent, or are trivial.

3E.5 If there is more than one defendant, the judge should not permit each advocate to repeat the questioning of a vulnerable witness. In advance of the trial, the advocates should divide the topics between them, with the advocate for the first defendant leading the questioning, and the advocate(s) for the other defendant(s) asking only ancillary questions relevant to their client's case, without repeating the questioning that has already taken place on behalf of the other defendant(s).

3E.6 In particular in a trial of a sexual offence, 'body maps' should be provided for the witness' use. If the witness needs to indicate a part of the body, the advocate should ask the witness to point to the relevant part on the body map. In sex cases, judges should not permit advocates to ask the witness to point to a part of the witness' own body. Similarly, photographs of the witness' body should not be shown around the court while the witness is giving evidence.

CPD I General matters 3F: Intermediaries PD-8

Role and functions of intermediaries in criminal courts

3F.1 Intermediaries facilitate communication with witnesses and defendants who have communication needs. Their primary function is to improve the quality of evidence and aid understanding between the court, the advocates and the witness or defendant. For example, they commonly advise on the formulation of questions so as to avoid misunderstanding. On occasion, they actively assist and intervene during questioning. The extent to which they do so (if at all) depends on factors such as the communication needs of the witness or defendant, and the skills of the advocates in adapting their language and questioning style to meet those needs.

3F.2 Intermediaries are independent of parties and owe their duty to the court. The court and parties should be vigilant to ensure they act impartially and their assistance to witnesses and defendants is transparent. It is however permissible for an advocate to have a private consultation with an intermediary when formulating questions (although control of questioning remains the overall responsibility of the court).

3F.3 Further information is in *Intermediaries: Step by Step* (Toolkit 16; The Advocate's Gateway, 2015) and chapter 5 of the *Equal Treatment Bench Book* (Judicial College, 2013).

Links to publications

- http://www.theadvocatesgateway.org/images/toolkits/16intermediariesstepbystep060315.pdf
- https://www.judiciary.gov.uk/wp-content/uploads/2013/11/5-children-and-vulnerable-adults.pdf

Assessment

3F.4 The process of appointment should begin with assessment by an intermediary and a report. The report will make recommendations to address the communication needs of the witness or defendant during trial.

3F.5 In light of the scarcity of intermediaries, the appropriateness of assessment must be decided with care to ensure their availability for those witnesses and defendants who are most in need. The decision should be made on an individual basis, in the context of the circumstances of the particular case.

Intermediaries for prosecution and defence witnesses

3F.6 Intermediaries are one of the special measures available to witnesses under the Youth Justice and Criminal Evidence Act 1999 (YJCEA 1999). Witnesses deemed vulnerable in accordance with the criteria in s.16 YJCEA are eligible for the assistance of an intermediary when giving evidence pursuant to s. 29 YJCEA 1999. These provisions do not apply to defendants.

3F.7 An application for an intermediary to assist a witness when giving evidence must be made in accordance with Part 18 of the Criminal Procedure Rules. In addition, where an intermediary report is available (see 3F.4 above), it should be provided with the application.

3F.8 The Witness Intermediary Scheme (WIS) operated by the National Crime Agency identifies intermediaries for witnesses and may be used by the prosecution and defence. The WIS is contactable at wit@nca.x.gsi.gov.uk / 0845 000 5463. An intermediary appointed through the WIS is defined as a 'Registered Intermediary' and matched to the particular witness based on expertise, location and availability. Registered Intermediaries are accredited by the WIS and bound by Codes of Practice and Ethics issued by the Ministry of Justice (which oversees the WIS).

3F.9 Having identified a Registered Intermediary, the WIS does not provide funding. The party appointing the Registered Intermediary is responsible for payment at rates specified by the Ministry of Justice.

3F.10 Further information is in *The Registered Intermediaries Procedural Guidance Manual* (Ministry of Justice, 2015) and *Intermediaries: Step by Step* (see 3F.3 above).

Link to publication

- http://www.theadvocatesgateway.org/images/procedures/registered-intermediary-procedural-guidance-manual.pdf

Intermediaries for defendants

3F.11 Statutory provisions providing for defendants to be assisted by an intermediary when giving evidence (where necessary to ensure a fair trial) are not in force (because s.104 Coroners and Justice Act 2009, which would insert ss. 33BA and 33BB into the YJCEA 1999, has yet to be commenced).

3F.12 The court may direct the appointment of an intermediary to assist a defendant in reliance on its inherent powers (*C v Sevenoaks Youth Court* [2009] EWHC 3088 (Admin)). There is however no presumption that a defendant will be so assisted and, even where an intermediary would improve the trial process, appointment is not mandatory (*R v Cox* [2012] EWCA Crim 549). The court should adapt the trial process to address a defendant's communication needs (*R v Cox* [2012] EWCA Crim 549). It will rarely exercise its inherent powers to direct appointment of an intermediary but where a defendant is vulnerable or for some other reason experiences communication or hearing difficulties, such that he or she needs more help to follow the proceedings than her or his legal representatives readily can give having regard to their other functions on the defendant's behalf, then the court should consider sympathetically any application for the defendant to be accompanied throughout the trial by a support worker or other appropriate companion who can provide that assistance. This is consistent with CrimPR 3.9(3)(b) (see paragraph 3D.2 above); consistent with the observations in *R v Cox* (see paragraph 3D.4 above), *R (OP) v Ministry of Justice* [2014] EWHC 1944 (Admin) and *R v Rashid* [2017] EWCA Crim 2; and consistent with the arrangements contemplated at paragraph 3G.8 below.

3F.13 The court may exercise its inherent powers to direct appointment of an intermediary to assist a defendant giving evidence or for the entire trial. Terms of appointment are for the court and there is no illogicality in restricting the appointment to the defendant's evidence (*R v R* [2015] EWCA Crim 1870), when the 'most pressing need' arises (*OP v Secretary of State for Justice* [2014] EWHC 1944 (Admin)). Directions to appoint an intermediary for a defendant's evidence will thus be rare, but for the entire trial extremely rare, keeping in mind paragraph 3F.12 above.

3F.14 An application for an intermediary to assist a defendant must be made in accordance with Part 18 of the Criminal Procedure Rules. In addition, where an intermediary report is available (see 3F.4 above), it should be provided with the application.

3F.15 The WIS is not presently available to identify intermediaries for defendants (although in *OP v Secretary of State for Justice* [2014] EWHC 1944 (Admin), the Ministry of Justice was ordered to consider carefully whether it were justifiable to refuse equal provision to witnesses and defendants with respect to their evidence). 'Non-registered intermediaries' (intermediaries appointed other than through the WIS) must therefore be appointed for defendants. Although training is available, there is no accreditation process for non-registered intermediaries and rates of payment are unregulated.

3F.16 Arrangements for funding of intermediaries for defendants depend on the stage of the appointment process. Where the defendant is publicly funded, an application should be made to the Legal Aid Agency for prior authority to fund a pre-trial assessment. If the application is refused, an application may be made to the court to use its inherent powers to direct a pre-trial assessment and funding thereof. Where the court uses its inherent powers to direct assistance by an intermediary at trial (during evidence or for the entire trial), court staff are responsible for arranging payment from Central Funds. Internal guidance for court staff is in *Guidance for HMCTS Staff: Registered and Non-Registered Intermediaries for Vulnerable Defendants and Non-Vulnerable Defence and Prosecution Witnesses* (Her Majesty's Courts and Tribunals Service, 2014).

3F.17 The court should be satisfied that a non-registered intermediary has expertise suitable to meet the defendant's communication needs.

3F.18 Further information is in *Intermediaries: Step by Step* (see 3F.3 above).

Ineffective directions for intermediaries to assist defendants

3F.19 Directions for intermediaries to help defendants may be ineffective due to general unavailability, lack of suitable expertise, or non-availability for the purpose directed (for example, where the direction is for assistance during evidence, but an intermediary will only accept appointment for the entire trial).

3F.20 Intermediaries may contribute to the administration of justice by facilitating communication with appropriate defendants during the trial process. A trial will not be rendered unfair because a direction to appoint an intermediary for the defendant is ineffective. 'It would, in fact, be a most unusual case for a defendant who is fit to plead to be so disadvantaged by his condition that a properly brought prosecution would have to be stayed' because an intermediary with suitable expertise is not available for the purpose directed by the court (*R v Cox* [2012] EWCA Crim 549).

3F.21 Faced with an ineffective direction, it remains the court's responsibility to adapt the trial process to address the defendant's communication needs, as was the case prior to the existence of intermediaries (*R v Cox* [2012] EWCA Crim 549). In such a case, a ground rules hearing should be convened to ensure every reasonable step is taken to facilitate the defendant's participation in accordance with CrimPR 3.9. At the hearing, the court should make new, further and / or alternative directions. This includes setting ground rules to help the defendant follow proceedings and (where applicable) to give evidence.

3F.22 For example, to help the defendant follow proceedings the court may require evidence to be adduced by simple questions, with witnesses being asked to answer in short sentences. Regular breaks may assist the defendant's concentration and enable the defence advocate to summarise the evidence and take further instructions.

3F.23 Further guidance is available in publications such as *Ground Rules Hearings and the Fair Treatment of Vulnerable People in Court* (Toolkit 1; The Advocate's Gateway, 2015) and *General Principles from Research—Planning to Question a Vulnerable Person or Someone with Communication Needs* (Toolkit 2(a); The Advocate's Gateway, 2015). In the absence of an intermediary, these publications include information on planning how to manage the participation and questioning of the defendant, and the formulation of questions to avert misunderstanding (for example, by avoiding 'long and complicated questions... posed in a leading or 'tagged' manner' (*R v Wills* [2011] EWCA Crim 1938, [2012] 1 Cr App R 2)).

Links to publications

- http://www.theadvocatesgateway.org/images/toolkits/1groundruleshearingsandthefairtreatmentofvulnerablepeopleincourt060315.pdf
- http://www.theadvocatesgateway.org/images/toolkits/2generalprinciplesfromresearchpolicyandguidance-planningtoquestionavulnerablepersonorsomeonewithcommunicationneeds141215.pdf

Intermediaries for witnesses and defendants under 18

3F.24 Communication needs (such as short attention span, suggestibility and reticence in relation to authority figures) are common to many witnesses and defendants under 18. Consideration should therefore be given to the communication needs of all children and young people appearing in the criminal courts and to adapting the trial process to address any such needs. Guidance is available in publications such as *Planning to Question a Child or Young Person* (Toolkit 6; The Advocate's Gateway, 2015) and *Effective Participation of Young Defendants* (Toolkit 8; The Advocate's Gateway, 2013).

Links to publications

- http://www.theadvocatesgateway.org/images/toolkits/6planningtoquestionachildoryoungperson141215.pdf
- http://www.theadvocatesgateway.org/images/toolkits/8YoungDefendants211013.pdf

3F.25 For the reasons set out in 3F.5 above, the appropriateness of an intermediary assessment for witnesses and defendants under 18 must be decided with care. Whilst there is no presumption that they will be assessed by an intermediary (to evaluate their communication needs prior to trial) or assisted by an intermediary at court (for example, if / when giving evidence), the decision should be made on an individual basis in the context of the circumstances of the particular case.

3F.26 Assessment by an intermediary should be considered for witnesses and defendants under 18 who seem liable to misunderstand questions or to experience difficulty expressing answers, including those who seem unlikely to be able to recognise a problematic question (such as one that is misleading or not readily understood), and those who may be reluctant to tell a questioner in a position of authority if they do not understand.

Attendance at ground rules hearing

3F.27 Where the court directs questioning will be conducted through an intermediary, CrimPR 3.9 requires the court to set ground rules. The intermediary should be present at the ground rules hearing to make representations in accordance with CrimPR 3.9(7)(a).

Listing

3F.28 Where the court directs an intermediary will attend the trial, their dates of availability should be provided to the court. It is preferable that such trials are fixed rather than placed in warned lists.

Photographs of court facilities

3F.29 Resident Judges in the Crown Court or the Chief Clerk or other responsible person in the magistrates' courts should, in consultation with HMCTS managers responsible for court security matters, develop a policy to govern under what circumstances photographs or other visual recordings may be made of court facilities, such as a live link room, to assist vulnerable or child witnesses to familiarise themselves with the setting, so as to be enabled to give their best evidence. For example, a photograph may provide a helpful reminder to a witness whose court visit has taken place sometime earlier. Resident Judges should tend to permit photographs to be taken for this purpose by intermediaries or supporters, subject to whatever restrictions the Resident Judge or responsible person considers to be appropriate, having regard to the security requirements of the court.

PD-9 CPD I General matters 3G: Vulnerable Defendants

Before the trial, sentencing or appeal

3G.1 If a vulnerable defendant, especially one who is young, is to be tried jointly with one who is not, the court should consider at the plea and case management hearing, or at a case management hearing in a magistrates' court, whether the vulnerable defendant should be tried on his own, but should only so order if satisfied that a fair trial cannot be achieved by use of appropriate special measures or other support for the defendant. If a vulnerable defendant is tried jointly with one who is not, the court should consider whether any of the modifications set out in this direction should apply in the circumstances of the joint trial and, so far as practicable, make orders to give effect to any such modifications.

3G.2 It may be appropriate to arrange that a vulnerable defendant should visit, out of court hours and before the trial, sentencing or appeal hearing, the courtroom in which that hearing is to take place so that he or she can familiarise him or herself with it.

3G.3 Where an intermediary is being used to help the defendant to communicate at court, the intermediary should accompany the defendant on his or her pre-trial visit. The visit will enable the defendant to familiarise him or herself with the layout of the court, and may include matters such as: where the defendant will sit, either in the dock or otherwise; court officials (what their roles are and where they sit); who else might be in the court, for example those in the public gallery and press box; the location of the witness box; basic court procedure; and the facilities available in the court.

3G.4 If the defendant's use of the live link is being considered, he or she should have an opportunity to have a practice session.

3G.5 If any case against a vulnerable defendant has attracted or may attract widespread public or media interest, the assistance of the police should be enlisted to try and ensure that the defendant is not, when attending the court, exposed to intimidation, vilification or abuse. Section 41 of the Criminal Justice Act 1925 prohibits the taking of photographs of defendants and witnesses (among others) in the court building or in its precincts, or when entering or leaving those precincts. A direction reminding media representatives of the prohibition may be appropriate. The court should also be ready at this stage, if it has not already done so, where relevant to make a reporting restriction under section 39 of the Children and Young Persons Act 1933 or, on an appeal to the Crown Court from a youth court, to remind media representatives of the application of section 49 of that Act.

3G.6 The provisions of the Practice Direction accompanying Part 6 should be followed.

The trial, sentencing or appeal hearing

3G.7 Subject to the need for appropriate security arrangements, the proceedings should, if practicable, be held in a courtroom in which all the participants are on the same or almost the same level.

3G.8 Subject again to the need for appropriate security arrangements, a vulnerable defendant, especially if he is young, should normally, if he wishes, be free to sit with members of his family or others in a like relationship, and with some other suitable supporting adult such as a social worker, and in a place which permits easy, informal communication with his legal representatives. The court should ensure that a suitable supporting adult is available throughout the course of the proceedings.

3G.9 It is essential that at the beginning of the proceedings, the court should ensure that what is to take place has been explained to a vulnerable defendant in terms he or she can understand and, at trial in the Crown Court, it should ensure in particular that the role of the jury has been explained. It should remind those representing the vulnerable defendant and the supporting adult of their responsibility to explain each step as it takes place and, at trial, explain the possible consequences of a guilty verdict and credit for a guilty plea. The court should also remind any intermediary of the responsibility to ensure that the vulnerable defendant has understood the explanations given to him/her. Throughout the trial the court should continue to ensure, by any appropriate means, that the defendant understands what is happening and what has been said by those on the bench, the advocates and witnesses.

3G.10 A trial should be conducted according to a timetable which takes full account of a vulnerable defendant's ability to concentrate. Frequent and regular breaks will often be appropriate. The court should ensure, so far as practicable, that the whole trial is conducted in clear language that the defendant can understand and that evidence in chief and cross-examination are conducted using questions that are short and clear. The conclusions of the 'ground rules' hearing should be followed, and advocates should use and follow the 'toolkits' as discussed above.

3G.11 A vulnerable defendant who wishes to give evidence by live link, in accordance with section 33A of the Youth Justice and Criminal Evidence Act 1999, may apply for a direction to that effect; the procedure in CrimPR 18.14 to 18.17 should be followed. Before making such a direction, the court must be satisfied that it is in the interests of justice to do so and that the use of a live link would enable the defendant to participate more effectively as a witness in the proceedings. The direction will need to deal with the practical arrangements to be made, including the identity of the person or persons who will accompany him or her.

3G.12 In the Crown Court, the judge should consider whether robes and wigs should be worn, and should take account of the wishes of both a vulnerable defendant and any vulnerable witness. It is generally desirable that those responsible for the security of a vulnerable defendant who is in custody, especially if he or she is young, should not be in uniform, and that there should be no recognisable police presence in the courtroom save for good reason.

3G.13 The court should be prepared to restrict attendance by members of the public in the courtroom to a small number, perhaps limited to those with an immediate and direct interest in the outcome. The court should rule on any challenged claim to attend. However, facilities for reporting the proceedings (subject to any restrictions under section 39 or 49 of the Children and Young Persons Act 1933) must be provided. The court may restrict the number of reporters attending in the courtroom to such number as is judged practicable and desirable. In ruling on any challenged claim to attend in the courtroom for the purpose of reporting, the court should be mindful of the public's general right to be informed about the administration of justice.

3G.14 Where it has been decided to limit access to the courtroom, whether by reporters or generally, arrangements should be made for the proceedings to be relayed, audibly and if possible visually, to another room in the same court complex to which the media and the public have access if it appears that there will be a need for such additional facilities. Those making use of such a facility should be reminded that it is to be treated as an extension of the courtroom and that they are required to conduct themselves accordingly.

PD-10 **CPD I General matters 3H: Wales and the Welsh Language: Devolution Issues**

3H.1 These are the subject of Practice Direction: (Supreme Court) (Devolution Issues) [1999] 1 WLR 1592; [1999] 3 All ER 466; [1999] 2 Cr App R 486, to which reference should be made.

PD-11 **CPD I General matters 3J: Wales and the Welsh Language: Applications for Evidence to be Given in Welsh**

3J.1 If a defendant in a court in England asks to give or call evidence in the Welsh language, the case should not be transferred to Wales. In ordinary circumstances, interpreters can be provided on request.

PD-12 **CPD I General matters 3K: Wales and the Welsh Language: Use of the Welsh Language in Courts in Wales**

3K.1 The purpose of this direction is to reflect the principle of the Welsh Language Act 1993 that, in the administration of justice in Wales, the English and Welsh languages should be treated on a basis of equality.

General

3K.2 It is the responsibility of the legal representatives in every case in which the Welsh language may be used by any witness or party, or in any document which may be placed before the court, to inform the court of that fact, so that appropriate arrangements can be made for the listing of the case.

3K.3 Any party or witness is entitled to use Welsh in a magistrates' court in Wales without giving prior notice. Arrangements will be made for hearing such cases in accordance with the 'Magistrates' Courts' Protocol for Listing Cases where the Welsh Language is used' (January 2008) which is available on the Judiciary's website: https://www.judiciary.gov.uk/publications/mags-cts-protocol-for-listing-cases-in-welsh-language/. See also CrimPR 24.14.

3K.4 If the possible use of the Welsh language is known at the time of sending or appeal to the Crown Court, the court should be informed immediately after sending or when the notice of appeal is lodged. Otherwise, the court should be informed as soon as the possible use of the Welsh language becomes known.

3K.5 If costs are incurred as a result of failure to comply with these directions, a wasted costs order may be made against the defaulting party and / or his legal representatives.

3K.6 The law does not permit the selection of jurors in a manner which enables the court to discover whether a juror does or does not speak Welsh, or to secure a jury whose members are bilingual, to try a case in which the Welsh language may be used.

Preliminary and plea and case management hearings

3K.7 An advocate in a case in which the Welsh language may be used must raise that matter at the preliminary and/or the plea and case management hearing and endorse details of it on the advocates' questionnaire, so that appropriate directions may be given for the progress of the case.

Listing

3K.8 The listing officer, in consultation with the resident judge, should ensure that a case in which the Welsh language may be used is listed

(a) wherever practicable before a Welsh speaking judge, and
(b) in a court in Wales with simultaneous translation facilities.

Interpreters

3K.9 Whenever an interpreter is needed to translate evidence from English into Welsh or from Welsh into English, the court listing officer in whose court the case is to be heard shall contact the Welsh Language Unit who will ensure the attendance of an accredited interpreter.

Jurors

3K.10 The jury bailiff, when addressing the jurors at the start of their period of jury service, shall inform them that each juror may take an oath or affirm in Welsh or English as he wishes.

3K.11 After the jury has been selected to try a case, and before it is sworn, the court officer swearing in the jury shall inform the jurors in open court that each juror may take an oath or affirm in Welsh or English as he wishes. A juror who takes the oath or affirms in Welsh should not be asked to repeat it in English.

3K.12 Where Welsh is used by any party or witness in a trial, an accredited interpreter will provide simultaneous translation from Welsh to English for the jurors who do not speak Welsh. There is no provision for the translation of evidence from English to Welsh for a Welsh speaking juror.

3K.13 The jury's deliberations must be conducted in private with no other person present and therefore no interpreter may be provided to translate the discussion for the benefit of one or more of the jurors.

Witnesses

3K.14 When each witness is called, the court officer administering the oath or affirmation shall inform the witness that he may be sworn or affirm in Welsh or English, as he wishes. A witness who takes the oath or affirms in Welsh should not be asked to repeat it in English.

Opening / closing of Crown Courts

3K.15 Unless it is not reasonably practicable to do so, the opening and closing of the court should be performed in Welsh and English.

Role of Liaison Judge

3K.16 If any question or problem arises concerning the implementation of these directions, contact should in the first place be made with the Liaison Judge for the Welsh language through the Wales Circuit Office:

HMCTS WALES / GLITEM CYMRU
3rd Floor, Churchill House / 3ydd Llawr Tŷ Churchill
Churchill Way / Ffordd Churchill
Cardiff / Caerdydd
CF10 2HH
029 2067 8300

CPD I General Matters 3L: Security of Prisoners at Court PD-13

3L.1 High-risk prisoners identified to the court as presenting a significant risk of escape, violence in court or danger to those in the court and its environs, and to the public at large, will as far as possible, have administrative and remand appearances listed for disposal by way of live link. They will have priority for the use of video equipment.

3L.2 In all other proceedings that require the appearance in person of a high-risk prisoner, the proceedings will be listed at an appropriately secure court building and in a court with a secure (enclosed or ceiling-high) dock.

3L.3 Where a secure dock or live link is not available the court will be asked to consider an application for additional security measures, which may include:
(a) the use of approved restraints (but see below at 3L.6);
(b) the deployment of additional escort staff;
(c) securing the court room for all or part of the proceedings;
(d) in exceptional circumstances, moving the hearing to a prison.

3L.4 National Offender Management Service (NOMS) will be responsible for providing the assessment of the prisoner and it is accepted that this may change at short notice. NOMS must provide notification to the listing officer of all Category A prisoners, those on the Escape-list and Restricted Status prisoners or other prisoners who have otherwise been assessed as presenting a significant risk of violence or harm. There is a presumption that all prisoners notified as high-risk will be allocated a hearing by live link and/or secure dock facilities. Where the court cannot provide a secure listing, the reasons should be provided to the establishment so that alternative arrangements can be considered.

Applications for use of approved restraints

3L.5 It is the duty of the court to decide whether a prisoner who appears before them should appear in restraints or not. Their decision must comply with the requirements of the European Convention on Human Rights, particularly Article 3, which prohibits degrading treatment, see *Ranniman v Finland* (1997) 26 EHRR 56.

3L.6 No prisoner should be handcuffed in court unless there are reasonable grounds for apprehending that he will be violent or will attempt to escape. If an application is made, it must be entertained by the court and a ruling must be given. The defence should be given the opportunity to respond to the application: proceeding in the absence of the defendant or his representative may give rise to an issue under Article 6(1) of the European Convention on Human Rights: *R v Rollinson* (1996) 161 JP 107, CA. If an application is to be made ex parte then that application should be made inter partes and the defence should be given an opportunity to respond.

Additional security measures

3L.7 It may be in some cases that additional dock officers are deployed to mitigate the risk that a prisoner presents. When the nature of the risk is so serious that increased deployment will be insufficient or would in itself be so obtrusive as to prejudice a fair trial, then the court may be required to consider the following measures:
(a) reconsider the case for a live link hearing, including transferring the case to a court where the live link is available;

(b) transfer the case to an appropriately secure court;
(c) the use of approved restraints on the prisoner for all or part of the proceedings;
(d) securing the court room for all or part of the proceedings; and
(e) the use of (armed) police in the court building.

3L.8 The establishment seeking the additional security measures will submit a Court Management Directions Form setting out the evidence of the prisoners identified risk of escape or violence and requesting the courts approval of security measures to mitigate that risk. This must be sent to the listing officer along with current, specific and credible evidence that the security measures are both necessary and proportionate to the identified risk and that the risk cannot be managed in any other way.

3L.9 If the court is asked to consider transfer of the case, then this must be in accordance with the Listing and Allocation Practice Direction XIII F.11-F.13 post. The listing officer will liaise with the establishment, prosecution and the defence to ensure the needs of the witnesses are taken into account.

3L.10 The Judge who has conduct of the case must deal with any application for the use of restraints or any other security measure and will hear representations from the Crown Prosecution Service and the defence before proceeding. The application will only be granted if:
(a) there are good grounds for believing that the prisoner poses a significant risk of trying to escape from the court (beyond the assumed motivation of all prisoners to escape) and/or risk of serious harm towards those persons in court or the public generally should an escape attempt be successful; and
(b) where there is no other viable means of preventing escape or serious harm.

High-risk prisoners giving evidence from the witness box

3L.11 High-risk prisoners giving evidence from the witness box may pose a significant security risk. In circumstances where such prisoners are required to move from a secure dock to an insecure witness box, an application may be made for the court to consider the use of additional security measures including:
(a) the use of approved restraints;
(b) the deployment of additional escort staff or police in the courtroom or armed police in the building. The decision to deploy an armed escort is for the Chief Inspector of the relevant borough: the decision to allow the armed escort in or around the court room is for the Senior Presiding Judge (see below);
(c) securing the courtroom for all or part of the proceedings;
(d) giving evidence from the secure dock; and
(e) use of live link if the prisoner is not the defendant.

PD-14 CPD I General Matters 3M: Procedure for Application for Armed Police Presence in the Royal Courts of Justice, Crown Courts and Magistrates' Court Buildings

3M.1 This Practice Direction sets out the procedure for the making and handling of applications for authorisation for the presence of armed police officers within the precincts of any Crown Court and magistrates' court buildings at any time. It applies to an application to authorise the carriage of firearms or tasers in court. It does not apply to officers who are carrying CS spray or PAVA incapacitant spray, which is included in the standard equipment issued to officers in some forces and therefore no separate authorisation is required for its carriage in court.

3M.2 This Practice Direction applies to all cases in England and Wales in which a police unit intends to request authorisation for the presence of armed police officers in the Crown Court or in the magistrates' court buildings at any time and including during the delivery of prisoners to court.

3M.3 This Practice Direction allows applications to be made for armed police presence in the Royal Courts of Justice.

Emergency situations

3M.4 This Practice Direction does not apply in an emergency situation. In such circumstances, the police must be able to respond in a way in which their professional judgment deems most appropriate.

Designated court centres

3M.5 Applications may only be made for armed police presence in the designated Crown Court and magistrates' court centres (see below). This list may be revised from time to time in consultation with the Association of Chief Police Officers (ACPO) and HMCTS. It will be reviewed at least every five years in consultation with ACPO armed police secretariat and the Presiding Judges.

3M.6 The Crown Court centres designated for firearms deployment are:
(a) Northern Circuit: Carlisle, Chester, Liverpool, Preston, Manchester Crown Square & Manchester Minshull Street.
(b) North Eastern Circuit: Bradford, Leeds, Newcastle upon Tyne, Sheffield, Teesside and Kingston-upon-Hull.

(c) Western Circuit: Bristol, Winchester and Exeter.
(d) South Eastern Circuit (not including London): Canterbury, Chelmsford, Ipswich, Luton, Maidstone, Norwich, Reading and St Albans.
(e) South Eastern Circuit (London only): Central Criminal Court, Woolwich, Kingston and Snaresbrook.
(f) Midland Circuit: Birmingham, Northampton, Nottingham and Leicester.
(g) Wales Circuit: Cardiff, Swansea and Caernarfon.

3M.7 The magistrates' courts designated for firearms deployment are:
(a) South Eastern Circuit (London only): Westminster Magistrates' Court and Belmarsh Magistrates' Court.

Preparatory work prior to applications in all cases

3M.8 Prior to the making of any application for armed transport of prisoners or the presence of armed police officers in the court building, consideration must be given to making use of prison video link equipment to avoid the necessity of prisoners' attendance at court for the hearing in respect of which the application is to be made.

3M.9 Notwithstanding their designation, each requesting officer will attend the relevant court before an application is made to ensure that there have been no changes to the premises and that there are no circumstances that might affect security arrangements.

Applying in the Royal Courts of Justice

3M.10 All applications should be sent to the Listing Office of the Division in which the case is due to appear. The application should be sent by email if possible and must be on the standard form.

3M.11 The Listing Office will notify the Head of Division, providing a copy of the email and any supporting evidence. The Head of Division may ask to see the senior police officer concerned.

3M.12 The Head of Division will consider the application. If it is refused, the application fails and the police must be notified.

3M.13 In the absence of the Head of Division, the application should be considered by the Vice-President of the Division.

3M.14 The relevant Court Office will be notified of the decision and that office will immediately inform the police by telephone. The decision must then be confirmed in writing to the police.

Applying to the Crown Court

3M.15 All applications should be sent to the Cluster Manager and should be sent by email if possible and must be on the standard form.

3M.16 The Cluster Manager will notify the Presiding Judge on the circuit and the Resident Judge by email, providing a copy of the form and any supporting evidence. The Presiding Judge may ask to see the senior police officer concerned.

3M.17 The Presiding Judge will consider the application. If it is refused the application fails and the police must be informed.

3M.18 If the Presiding Judge approves the application it should be forwarded to the secretary in the Senior Presiding Judge's Office. The Senior Presiding Judge will make the final decision. The Presiding Judge will receive written confirmation of that decision.

3M.19 The Presiding Judge will notify the Cluster Manager and the Resident Judge of the decision. The Cluster Manager will immediately inform the police of the decision by telephone. The decision must then be confirmed in writing to the police.

Urgent applications to the Crown Court

3M.20 If the temporary deployment of armed police arises as an urgent issue and a case would otherwise have to be adjourned; or if the trial judge is satisfied that there is a serious risk to public safety, then the Resident Judge will have a discretion to agree such deployment without having obtained the consent of a Presiding Judge or the Senior Presiding Judge. In such a case:
(a) the Resident Judge should assess the facts and agree the proposed solution with a police officer of at least Superintendent level. That officer should agree the approach with the Firearms Division of the police.
(b) if the proposed solution involves the use of armed police officers, the Resident Judge must try to contact the Presiding Judge and/or the Senior Presiding Judge by email and telephone. The Cluster Manager should be informed of the situation.
(c) if the Resident Judge cannot obtain a response from the Presiding Judge or the Senior Presiding Judge, the Resident Judge may grant the application if satisfied:
(i) that the application is necessary;

(ii) that without such deployment there would be a significant risk to public safety; and
(iii) that the case would have to be adjourned at significant difficulty or inconvenience.

3M.21 The Resident Judge must keep the position under continual review, to ensure that it remains appropriate and necessary. The Resident Judge must make continued efforts to contact the Presiding Judge and the Senior Presiding Judge to notify them of the full circumstances of the authorisation.

Applying to the magistrates' courts

3M.22 All applications should be directed, by email if possible, to the Office of the Chief Magistrate, at Westminster Magistrates' Court and must be on the standard form.

3M.23 The Chief Magistrate should consider the application and, if approved, it should be forwarded to the Senior Presiding Judge's Office. The Senior Presiding Judge will make the final decision. The Chief Magistrate will receive written confirmation of that decision and will then notify the requesting police officer and, where authorisation is given, the affected magistrates' court of the decision.

Urgent applications in the magistrates' courts

3M.24 If the temporary deployment of armed police arises as an urgent issue and a case would otherwise have to be adjourned; or if the Chief Magistrate is satisfied that there is a serious risk to public safety, then the Chief Magistrate will have a discretion to agree such deployment without having obtained the consent of the Senior Presiding Judge. In such a case:

(a) the Chief Magistrate should assess the facts and agree the proposed solution with a police officer of at least Superintendent level. That officer should agree the approach with the Firearms Division of the police.
(b) if the proposed solution involves the use of armed police officers, the Chief Magistrate must try to contact the Senior Presiding Judge by email and telephone. The Cluster Manager should be informed of the situation.
(c) if the Chief Magistrate cannot obtain a response from the Senior Presiding Judge, the Chief Magistrate may grant the application if satisfied:
(i) that the application is necessary;
(ii) that without such deployment there would be a significant risk to public safety; and
(iii) that the case would have to be adjourned at significant difficulty or inconvenience.

3M.25 The Chief Magistrate must keep the position under continual review, to ensure that it remains appropriate and necessary. The Chief Magistrate must make continued efforts to contact the Senior Presiding Judge to notify him of the full circumstances of the authorisation.

PD-15 CPD I General Matters 3N: Use of Live Link and Telephone Facilities

3N.1 Where it is lawful and in the interests of justice to do so, courts should exercise their statutory and other powers to conduct hearings by live link or telephone. This is consistent with the Criminal Procedure Rules and with the recommendations of the President of the Queen's Bench Division's *Review of Efficiency in Criminal Proceedings* published in January 2015. Save where legislation circumscribes the court's jurisdiction, the breadth of that jurisdiction is acknowledged by CrimPR 3.5(1), (2)(d).

3N.2 It is the duty of the court to make use of technology actively to manage the case: CrimPR 3.2(1), (2)(h). That duty includes an obligation to give directions for the use of live links and telephone facilities in the circumstances listed in CrimPR 3.2(4) and (5) (pre-trial hearings, including pre-trial case management hearings). Where the court directs that evidence is to be given by live link, and especially where such a direction is given on the court's own initiative, it is essential that the decision is communicated promptly to the witness: CrimPR 18.4. Contrary to a practice adopted by some courts, none of those rules or other provisions require the renewal of a live link direction merely because a trial has had to be postponed or adjourned. Once made, such a direction applies until it is discharged by the court, having regard to the relevant statutory criteria.

3N.3 It is the duty of the parties to alert the court to any reason why live links or telephones should not be used where CrimPR 3.2 otherwise would oblige the court to do so; and, where a direction for the use of such facilities has been made, it is the duty of the parties as soon as practicable to alert the court to any reason why that direction should be varied CrimPR 3.3(2)(e) and 3.6.

3N.4 The word 'appropriate' in CrimPR 3.2(4) and (5) is not a term of art. It has the ordinary English meaning of 'fitting', or 'suitable'. Whether the facilities available to the court in any particular case can be considered appropriate is a matter for the court, but plainly to be appropriate such facilities must work, at the time at which they are required; all participants must be able to hear and, in the case of a live link, see each other clearly; and there must be no extraneous noise, movement or other distraction suffered by a participant, or transmitted by a participant to others. What degree of protection from accidental or deliberate interception should be considered appropriate will depend upon the purpose for which a live link or telephone is to be used. If it is to participate in a hearing which is open to the public anyway, then what is communicated by such means is by definition public and the use of links such as Skype or Facetime, which are not generally considered secure from interception, may not be objectionable. If it is to participate in a hearing in private, and especially one at which sensitive information will be discussed – for example, on an application for a search warrant – then a more secure service is likely to be required.

3N.5 There may be circumstances in which the court should not require the use of live link or telephone facilities despite their being otherwise appropriate at a pre-trial hearing. In every case, in deciding whether any such circumstances apply the court will keep in mind that, for the purposes of what may be an essentially administrative hearing, it may be compatible with the overriding objective to proceed in the defendant's absence altogether, especially if he or she is represented, unless, exceptionally, a rule otherwise requires. The principle that the court always must consider proceeding in a defendant's absence is articulated in CrimPR 3.9(2)(a). Where at a pre-trial hearing bail may be under consideration, the provisions of CrimPR 14.2 will be relevant.

3N.6 Such circumstances will include any case in which the defendant's effective participation cannot be achieved by his or her attendance by such means, and CrimPR 3.2(4) and (5) except such cases from the scope of the obligation which that rule otherwise imposes on the court. That exception may apply where (this list is not exhaustive) the defendant has a disorder or disability, including a hearing, speech or sight impediment, or has communication needs to which the use of a live link or telephone is inimical (whether or not those needs are such as to require the appointment of an intermediary); or where the defendant requires interpretation and effective interpretation cannot be provided by live link or telephone, as the case may be. In deciding whether to require a defendant to attend a first hearing in a magistrates' court by live link from a police station, the court should take into account any views expressed by the defendant, the terms of any mental health or other medical assessment of the defendant carried out at the police station, and all other relevant information and representations available. No single factor is determinative, but the court must keep in mind the terms of section 57C(6A) of the Crime and Disorder Act 1998 (Use of live link at preliminary hearings where accused is at police station) which provides that 'A live link direction under this section may not be given unless the court is satisfied that it is not contrary to the interests of justice to give the direction.'

3N.7 Finally, that exception sometimes may apply where the defendant's attendance in person at a pre-trial hearing will facilitate communication with his or her legal representatives. The court should not make such an exception merely to allow client and representatives to meet if that meeting can and should be held elsewhere. However, there will be cases in which defence representatives reasonably need to meet with a defendant, to take his or her instructions or to explain events to him or her, either shortly before or immediately after a pre-trial hearing and in circumstances in which that meeting cannot take place effectively by live link.

3N.8 Nothing prohibits the member or members of a court from conducting a pre-trial hearing by attending by live link or telephone from a location distant from all the other participants. Despite the conventional view that the venue for a court hearing is the court room in which that hearing has been arranged to take place, the Criminal Procedure Rules define 'court' as 'a tribunal with jurisdiction over criminal cases. It includes a judge, recorder, District Judge (Magistrates' Court), lay justice and, when exercising their judicial powers, the Registrar of Criminal Appeals, a justices' clerk or assistant clerk.' Neither CrimPR 3.25 (Place of trial), which applies in the Crown Court, nor CrimPR 24.14 (Place of trial), which applies in magistrates' courts, each of which requires proceedings to take place in a courtroom provided by the Lord Chancellor, applies for the purposes of a pre-trial hearing. Thus for the purposes of such a hearing there is no legal obstacle to the judge, magistrate or magistrates conducting it from elsewhere, with other participants assembled in a courtroom from which the member or members of the court are physically absent. In principle, nothing prohibits the conduct of a pre-trial hearing by live link or telephone with each participant, including the member or members of the court, in a different location (an arrangement sometimes described as a 'virtual hearing'). This is dependent upon there being means by which that hearing can be witnessed by the public – for example, by public attendance at a courtroom or other venue from which the participants all can be seen and heard (if by live link), or heard (if by telephone). The principle of open justice to which paragraph 3N.17 refers is relevant.

3N.9 Sections 57A to 57F of the Crime and Disorder Act 1998 allow a defendant who is in custody to enter a plea by live link, and allow for such a defendant who attends by live link to be sentenced. In appropriate circumstances, the court may allow a defendant who is not in custody to enter a plea by live link; but the same considerations as apply to sentencing in such a case will apply: see paragraph 3N.13 beneath.

3N.10 The Crime and Disorder Act 1998 does not allow for the attendance by live link at a contested trial of a defendant who is in custody. The court may allow a defendant who wishes to do so to observe all or part of his or her trial by live link, whether she or he is in custody or not, but (a) such a defendant cannot lawfully give evidence by such means unless he or she satisfies the criteria prescribed by section 33A of the Youth Justice and Criminal Evidence Act 1999 and the court so orders under that section (see also CrimPR 18.14–18.17); (b) a defendant who is in custody and who observes the trial by live link is not present, as a matter of law, and the trial must be treated as taking place in his or her absence, she or he having waived the right to attend; and (c) a defendant who has refused to attend his or her trial when required to do so, or who has absconded, must not be permitted to observe the proceedings by live link.

3N.11 Paragraphs I 3D to 3G inclusive of these Practice Directions (Vulnerable people in the courts; Ground rules hearings to plan the questioning of a vulnerable witness or defendant; Intermediaries; Vulnerable defendants) contain directions relevant to the use of a live link as a special measure for a young or otherwise vulnerable witness, or to facilitate the giving of evidence by a defendant who is likewise young or otherwise vulnerable, within the scope of the Youth Justice and Criminal Evidence Act 1999. Defence representatives and the court must keep in mind that special measures under the 1999 Act and CrimPR Part 18, including the use of a live link, are available to defence as well as to prosecution witnesses who meet the statutory criteria. Defence representatives should always consider whether their witnesses would benefit from giving evidence by live link and should apply for a direction if appropriate, either at the case management hearing or as soon as possible thereafter. A defence witness should be afforded the same facilities and treatment as a prosecution witness, including the same opportunity to make a pre-trial visit to the court building in order to familiarise himself or herself with it. Where a live link is sought as a special measure for a young or vulnerable witness or defendant, CrimPR 18.10 and 18.15 respectively require, among other things, that the applicant must identify someone to accompany that witness or defendant while they give evidence; must name the person, if possible; and must explain why that person would be an appropriate companion for that witness. The court must ensure that directions are given accordingly when ordering such a live link. Witness Service volunteers are available to support all witnesses, prosecution and defence, if required.

3N.12 Under sections 57A and 57D or 57E of the Crime and Disorder Act 1998 the court may pass sentence on a defendant in custody who attends by live link. The court may allow a defendant who is not in custody and who wishes to attend his or her sentencing by live link her or him by such means. Factors of which the court will wish to take account in exercising its discretion include, in particular, the penalty likely to be imposed; the importance of ensuring that the explanations of sentence required by CrimPR 24.11(9), in magistrates' courts, and in the Crown Court by CrimPR 25.16(7), can be given satisfactorily, for the defendant, for other participants and for the public, including reporters; and the preferences of the maker of any Victim Personal Statement which is to be read aloud or played pursuant to paragraph VII F.3(c) of these Practice Directions.

Youth defendants

3N.13 In the youth court or when a youth is appearing in the magistrates' court or the Crown Court, it will usually be appropriate for the youth to be produced in person at court. This is to ensure that the court can engage properly with the youth and that the necessary level of engagement can be facilitated with the Youth Offending Team worker, defence representative and/or appropriate adult. The court should deal with any application for use of a live-link on a case-by-case basis, after consultation with the parties and the Youth Offending Team. Such hearings that may be appropriate, include, onward remand hearings at which there is no bail application or case management hearings, particularly if the youth is already serving a custodial sentence.

3N.14 It rarely will be appropriate for a youth to be sentenced over a live link. However, notwithstanding the court's duties of engagement with a youth, the overriding welfare principle and the statutory responsibility of the youth offending worker to explain the sentence to the youth, after consultation with the parties and the Youth Offending Team, there may be circumstances in which it may be appropriate to sentence a youth over the live-link: a) If the youth is already serving a custodial sentence and the sentence to be imposed by the court is bound to be a further custodial sentence, whether concurrent or consecutive; b) If the youth is already serving a custodial sentence and the court is minded to impose a non-custodial sentence which will have no material impact on the sentence being served; c) The youth is being detained in a secure establishment at such a distance from the court that the travelling time from one to the other will be significant so as to materially affect the welfare of the youth; d) The youth's condition – whether mental or otherwise – is so disturbed that his or her production would be a significant detriment to his or her welfare.

3N.15 Arrangements must be made in advance of any live link hearing to enable the youth offending worker to be at the secure establishment where the youth is in custody. In the event that such arrangements are not practicable, the youth offending worker must have sufficient access to the youth via the live link booth before and after the hearing.

Conduct of participants

3N.16 Where a live link is used, the immediate vicinity of the device by which a person attends becomes, temporarily, part of the courtroom for the purposes of that person's participation. That person, and any advocate or legal representative, custodian, court officer, intermediary or other companion, whether immediately visible to the court or not, becomes a participant for the purposes of CrimPR 1.2(2) and is subject to the court's jurisdiction to regulate behaviour in the courtroom. The substance and effect of this direction must be drawn to the attention of all such participants.

Open justice and records of proceedings

3N.17 The principle of open justice to which CrimPR 6.2(1) gives effect applies as strongly where electronic means of communication are used to conduct a hearing as it applies in other circumstances. Open justice is the principal means by which courts are kept under scrutiny by the public. It follows that where a participant attends a hearing in public by live link or telephone then that person's participation must be, as nearly as may be, equally audible and, if applicable, equally visible to the public as it would be were he or she physically present. Where electronic means of communication are used to conduct a hearing, records of the event must be maintained in the usual way: CrimPR 5.4. In the Crown Court, this includes the recording of the proceedings: CrimPR 5.5.

CPD I General matters 3P: Commissioning Medical Reports PD-16

General observations

3P.1 CrimPR 24.3 and 25.10 concern procedures to be followed in magistrates' courts and in the Crown Court respectively where there is doubt about a defendant's mental health and, in the Crown Court, the defendant's capacity to participate in a trial. CrimPR 3.28 governs the procedure where, on the court's own initiative, a magistrates' court requires expert medical opinion about the potential suitability of a hospital order under section 37(3) of the Mental Health Act 1983 (hospital order without convicting the defendant), the Crown Court requires such opinion about the defendant's fitness to participate at trial, under section 4 of the Criminal Procedure (Insanity) Act 1964, or either a magistrates' court or the Crown Court requires such opinion to help the court determine a question of intent or insanity.

3P.2 Rule 3.28 governs the procedure to be followed where a report is commissioned at the instigation of the court. It is not a substitute for the prompt commissioning of a report or reports by a party or party's representatives where expert medical opinion is material to that party's case. In particular, those representing a defendant may wish to obtain a medical report or reports wholly independently of the court. Nothing in these directions, therefore, should be read as discouraging a party from commissioning a medical report before the case comes before the court, where that party believes such a report to be material to an issue in the case and where it is possible promptly to commission it. However, where a party has commissioned such a report then if that report has not been received by the time the court gives directions for preparation for trial, and if the court agrees that it seems likely that the report will be material to what is in issue, then when giving directions for trial the court should include a timetable for the reception of that report and should give directions for progress to be reviewed at intervals, adopting the timetable set out in these directions with such adaptations as are needed.

3P.3 In assessing the likely materiality of an expert medical report to help the court assess a defendant's health and capacity at the time of the alleged offence or the time of trial, or both, the court will be assisted by the parties' representations; by the views expressed in any assessment that may already have been prepared; and by the views of practitioners in local criminal justice mental health services, whose assistance is available to the court under local liaison arrangements.

3P.4 Where the court requires the assistance of such a report then it is essential that there should be (i) absolute clarity about who is expected to do what, by when, and at whose expense; and (ii) judicial directions for progress with that report to be monitored and reviewed at prescribed intervals, following a timetable set by the court which culminates in the consideration of the report at a hearing. This is especially important where the report in question is a psychiatric assessment of the defendant for the preparation of which specific expertise may be required which is not readily available and because in some circumstances a second such assessment, by another medical practitioner, may be required.

Timetable for the commissioning, preparation and consideration of a report or reports

3P.5 CrimPR 3.28 requires the court to set a timetable appropriate to the case for the preparation and reception of a report. That timetable must not be in substitution for the usual timetable for preparation for trial but must instead be incorporated within the trial preparation timetable. The fact that a medical report is to be obtained, whether that is commissioned at a party's instigation or on the court's own initiative, is never a reason to postpone a preparation for trial or a plea and trial preparation hearing, or to decline to give the directions needed for preparation for trial. It follows that a trial date must be set and other directions given in the usual way.

3P.6 In setting the timetable for obtaining a report or reports the court will take account of such representations and other information that it receives, including information about the anticipated availability and workload of medical practitioners with the appropriate expertise. However, the timetable ought not be a protracted one. It is essential to keep in mind the importance of maintaining progress: in recognition of the defendant's rights and with respect for the interests of victims and witnesses, as required by CrimPR Part 1 (the overriding objective). In a magistrates' court account must be taken, too, of section 11 of the Powers of Criminal Courts (Sentencing) Act 2000, which limits the duration of each remand pending the preparation of a report to 3 weeks, where the defendant is to be in custody, and to 4 weeks if the defendant is to be on bail.

3P.7 Subject, therefore, to contrary judicial direction the timetable set by the court should require:

(a) the convening of a further pre-trial case management hearing to consider the report and its implications for the conduct of the proceedings no more than 6 – 8 weeks after the court makes its request in a magistrates' court, and no more than 10 – 12 weeks after the request in the Crown Court (at the end of Stage 2 of the directions for pre-trial preparation in the Crown Court);

(b) the prompt identification of an appropriate medical practitioner or practitioners, if not already identified by the court, and the despatch of a commission or commissions accordingly, within 2 business days of the court's decision to request a report;

(c) acknowledgement of a commission by its recipient, and acceptance or rejection of that commission, within 5 business days of its receipt;

(d) enquiries by court staff to confirm that the commission has been received, and to ascertain the action being taken in response, in the event that no acknowledgement is received within 10 business days of its despatch;

(e) delivery of the report within 5 weeks of the despatch of the commission;

(f) enquiries into progress by court staff in the event that no report is received within 5 weeks of the despatch of the commission.

3P.8 The further pre-trial case management hearing that is convened for the court to consider the report should not be adjourned before it takes place save in exceptional circumstances and then only by explicit judicial direction the reasons for which must be recorded. If by the time of that hearing the report is available, as usually should be the case, then at that hearing the court can be expected to determine the issue in respect of which the report was commissioned and give further directions accordingly. If by that time, exceptionally, the report is not available then the court should take the opportunity provided by that hearing to enquire into the reasons, give such directions as are appropriate, and if necessary adjourn the hearing to a fixed date for further consideration then. Where it is known in advance of that hearing that the report will not be available in time, the hearing may be conducted by live link or telephone: subject, in the defendant's case, to the same considerations as are identified at paragraph 3N.6 of these Practice Directions. However, it rarely will be appropriate to dispense altogether with that hearing, or to make enquiries and give further directions without any hearing at all, in view of the arrangements for monitoring and review that the court already will have directed and which, by definition therefore, thus far will have failed to secure the report's timely delivery.

3P.9 Where a requirement of the timetable set by the court is not met, or where on enquiry by court staff it appears that the timetable is unlikely to be met, and in any instance in which a medical practitioner who accepts a commission asks for more time, then court staff should not themselves adjust the timetable or accede to such a request but instead should seek directions from an appropriate judicial authority. Subject to local judicial direction, that will be, in the Crown Court, the judge assigned to the case or the resident judge and, in a magistrates' court, a District Judge (Magistrates' Courts) or justice of the peace assigned to the case, or the Justices' Clerk, an assistant clerk or other senior legal adviser. Even if the timetable is adjusted in consequence:

(a) the further pre-trial case management hearing convened to consider the report rarely should be adjourned before it takes place: see paragraph 3O.13 [*sic*: 3P.8] above;
(b) directions should be given for court staff henceforth to make regular enquiries into progress, at prescribed intervals of not more than 2 weeks, and to report the outcome to an appropriate judicial authority who will decide what further directions, if any, to give.

3P.10 Any adjournment of a hearing convened to consider the report should be to a specific date: the hearing should not be adjourned generally, or to a date to be set in due course. The adjournment of such a hearing should not be for more than a further 6 – 8 weeks save in the most exceptional circumstances; and no more than one adjournment of the hearing should be allowed without obtaining written or oral representations from the commissioned medical practitioner explaining the reasons for the delay.

Commissioning a report

3P.11 Guidance entitled 'Good practice guidance: commissioning, administering and producing psychiatric reports for sentencing' prepared for and published by the Ministry of Justice and HM Courts and Tribunals Service in September 2010 contains material that will assist court staff and those who are asked to prepare such reports:
http://www.ohrn.nhs.uk/resource/policy/GoodPracticeGuidePsychReports.pdf
The guidance includes standard forms of letters of instruction and other documents.

3P.12 CrimPR 3.28 requires the commissioner of a report to explain why the court seeks the report and to include relevant information about the circumstances. The HMCTS Guidance contains forms for judicial use in the instruction of court staff, and guidance to court staff on the preparation of letters of instruction, where a report is required for sentencing purposes. Those forms and that guidance can be adapted for use where the court requires a report on the defendant's fitness to participate, in the Crown Court, or in a magistrates' court requires a report for the purposes of section 37(3) of the Mental Health Act 1983.

3P.13 The commission should invite a practitioner who is unable to accept it promptly to nominate a suitably qualified substitute, if possible, and to transfer the commission to that person, reporting the transfer when acknowledging the court officer's letter. It is entirely appropriate for the commission to draw the recipient's attention to CrimPR 1.2 (the duty of the participants in a criminal case) and to CrimPR 19.2(1)(b) (the obligation of an expert witness to comply with directions made by a court and at once to inform the court of any significant failure, by the expert or another, to take any step required by such a direction).

3P.14 Where the relevant legislation requires a second psychiatric assessment by a second medical practitioner, and where no commission already has been addressed to a second such practitioner, the commission may invite the person to whom it is addressed to nominate a suitably qualified second person and to pass a copy of the commission to that person forthwith.

Funding arrangements

3P.15 Where a medical report has been, or is to be, commissioned by a party then that party is responsible for arranging payment of the fees incurred, even though the report is intended for the court's use. That must be made clear in that party's commission.

3P.16 Where a medical report is requested by the court and commissioned by a party or by court staff at the court's direction then the commission must include (i) confirmation that the fees will be paid by HMCTS, (ii) details of how, and to whom, to submit an invoice or claim for fees, and (iii) notice of the prescribed rates of fees and of any legislative or other criteria applicable to the calculation of the fees that may be paid.

Remand in custody

3P.17 Where the defendant who is to be examined will be remanded in custody then notice that directions have been given for a medical report or reports to be prepared must be included in the information given to the defendant's custodian, to ensure that the preparation of the report or reports can be facilitated. This is especially important where bail is withheld on the ground that it would be otherwise impracticable to complete the required report, and in particular where that is the only ground for withholding bail.

Criminal Procedure Rules Part 4 Service of Documents

R-35 **When this Part applies**

4.1 (1) The rules in this Part apply—
(a) to the service of every document in a case to which these Rules apply; and
(b) for the purposes of section 12 of the Road Traffic Offenders Act 1988, to the service of a requirement to which that section applies.
(2) The rules apply subject to any special rules in other legislation (including other Parts of these Rules) or in the Practice Direction.

R-36 **Methods of service**

4.2 (1) A document may be served by any of the methods described in rules 4.3 to 4.6 (subject to rule 4.7 and 4.10), or in rule 4.8.
(2) Where a document may be served by electronic means under rule 4.6, the general rule is that the person serving it must use that method.

R-37 **Service by handing over a document**

4.3 (1) A document may be served on—
(a) an individual by handing it to him or her;
(b) a corporation by handing it to a person holding a senior position in that corporation;
(c) an individual or corporation who is legally represented in the case by handing it to that legal representative;
(d) the prosecution by handing it to the prosecutor or to the prosecution representative;
(e) the court officer by handing it to a court officer with authority to accept it at the relevant court office; and
(f) the Registrar of Criminal Appeals by handing it to a court officer with authority to accept it at the Criminal Appeal Office.
(2) If an individual is under 18, a copy of a document served under paragraph (1)(a) must be handed to his or her parent, or another appropriate adult, unless no such person is readily available.
(3) Unless the court otherwise directs, for the purposes of paragraph (1)(c) or (d) (service by handing a document to a party's representative) 'representative' includes an advocate appearing for that party at a hearing.
(4) In this rule, 'the relevant court office' means—
(a) in relation to a case in a magistrates' court or in the Crown Court, the office at the address advertised by the Lord Chancellor as the place at which that court's business is administered;
(b) in relation to an application to a High Court judge for permission to serve a draft indictment—
(i) in London, the Listing Office of the Queen's Bench Division of the High Court, and
(ii) elsewhere, the office at which court staff administer the business of any court then constituted of a High Court judge;
(c) in relation to an extradition appeal case in the High Court, the Administrative Court Office of the Queen's Bench Division of the High Court.

R-38 **Service by leaving or posting a document**

4.4 (1) A document may be served by addressing it to the person to be served and leaving it at the appropriate address for service under this rule, or by sending it to that address by first class post or by the equivalent of first class post.
(2) The address for service under this rule on—
(a) an individual is an address where it is reasonably believed that he or she will receive it;
(b) a corporation is its principal office, and if there is no readily identifiable principal office then any place where it carries on its activities or business;
(c) an individual or corporation who is legally represented in the case is that legal representative's office;
(d) the prosecution is the prosecutor's office;
(e) the court officer is the relevant court office; and
(f) the Registrar of Criminal Appeals is the Criminal Appeal Office, Royal Courts of Justice, Strand, London WC2A 2LL.
(3) In this rule, 'the relevant court office' means—
(a) in relation to a case in a magistrates' court or in the Crown Court, the office at the address advertised by the Lord Chancellor as the place at which that court's business is administered;

(b) in relation to an application to a High Court judge for permission to serve a draft indictment—
   (i) in London, the Listing Office of the Queen's Bench Division of the High Court, and
   (ii) elsewhere, the office at which court staff administer the business of any court then constituted of a High Court judge;
(c) in relation to an extradition appeal case in the High Court, the Administrative Court Office, Royal Courts of Justice, Strand, London WC2A 2LL.

Service by document exchange **R-39**

4.5 (1) This rule applies where—
(a) the person to be served—
   (i) has given a document exchange (DX) box number, and
   (ii) has not refused to accept service by DX; or
(b) the person to be served is legally represented in the case and the legal representative has given a DX box number.
(2) A document may be served by—
(a) addressing it to that person or legal representative, as appropriate, at that DX box number; and
(b) leaving it at—
   (i) the document exchange at which the addressee has that DX box number, or
   (ii) a document exchange at which the person serving it has a DX box number.

Service by electronic means **R-40**

4.6 (1) This rule applies where—
(a) the person to be served—
   (i) has given an electronic address and has not refused to accept service at that address, or
   (ii) is given access to an electronic address at which a document may be deposited and has not refused to accept service by the deposit of a document at that address; or
(b) the person to be served is legally represented in the case and the legal representative—
   (i) has given an electronic address, or
   (ii) is given access to an electronic address at which a document may be deposited.
(2) A document may be served—
(a) by sending it by electronic means to the address which the recipient has given; or
(b) by depositing it at an address to which the recipient has been given access and—
   (i) in every case, making it possible for the recipient to read the document, or view or listen to its content, as the case may be,
   (ii) unless the court otherwise directs, making it possible for the recipient to make and keep an electronic copy of the document, and
   (iii) notifying the recipient of the deposit of the document (which notice may be given by electronic means).
(3) Where a document is served under this rule the person serving it need not provide a paper copy as well.

Documents that must be served by specified methods **R-41**

4.7 (1) An application or written statement, and notice, under rule 48.9 alleging contempt of court may be served—
(a) on an individual, only under rule 4.3(1)(a) (by handing it to him or her);
(b) on a corporation, only under rule 4.3(1)(b) (by handing it to a person holding a senior position in that corporation).
(2) For the purposes of section 12 of the Road Traffic Offenders Act 1988, a notice of a requirement under section 172 of the Road Traffic Act 1988 or under section 112 of the Road Traffic Regulation Act 1984 to identify the driver of a vehicle may be served—
(a) on an individual, only by post under rule 4.4(1) and (2)(a);
(b) on a corporation, only by post under rule 4.4(1) and (2)(b).

Service by person in custody **R-42**

4.8 (1) A person in custody may serve a document by handing it to the custodian addressed to the person to be served.
(2) The custodian must—
(a) endorse it with the time and date of receipt;

(b) record its receipt; and
(c) forward it promptly to the addressee.

R-43 **Service by another method**

4.9 (1) The court may allow service of a document by a method—
(a) other than those described in rules 4.3 to 4.6 and in rule 4.8;
(b) other than one specified by rule 4.7, where that rule applies.
(2) An order allowing service by another method must specify—
(a) the method to be used; and
(b) the date on which the document will be served.

R-44 **Documents that may not be served on a legal representative**

4.10 Unless the court otherwise directs, service on a party's legal representative of any of the following documents is not service of that document on that party—
(a) a summons, requisition, single justice procedure notice or witness summons;
(b) notice of an order under section 25 of the Road Traffic Offenders Act 1988;
(c) a notice of registration under section 71(6) of that Act;
(d) notice of a hearing to review the postponement of the issue of a warrant of detention or imprisonment under section 77(6) of the Magistrates' Courts Act 1980;
(e) notice under section 86 of that Act of a revised date to attend a means inquiry;
(f) any notice or document served under Part 14 (Bail and custody time limits);
(g) notice under rule 24.16(a) of when and where an adjourned hearing will resume;
(h) notice under rule 28.5(3) of an application to vary or discharge a compensation order;
(i) notice under rule 28.10(2)(c) of the location of the sentencing or enforcing court;
(j) a collection order, or notice requiring payment, served under rule 30.2(a); or
(k) an application or written statement, and notice, under rule 48.9 alleging contempt of court.

R-45 **Date of service**

4.11 (1) A document served under rule 4.3 or rule 4.8 is served on the day it is handed over.
(2) Unless something different is shown, a document served on a person by any other method is served—
(a) in the case of a document left at an address, on the next business day after the day on which it was left;
(b) in the case of a document sent by first class post or by the equivalent of first class post, on the second business day after the day on which it was posted or despatched;
(c) in the case of a document served by document exchange, on the second business day after the day on which it was left at a document exchange allowed by rule 4.5;
(d) in the case of a document served by electronic means—
(i) on the day on which it is sent under rule 4.6(2)(a), if that day is a business day and if it is sent by no later than 2.30pm that day (4.30pm that day, in an extradition appeal case in the High Court),
(ii) on the day on which notice of its deposit is given under rule 4.6(2)(b), if that day is a business day and if that notice is given by no later than 2.30pm that day (4.30pm that day, in an extradition appeal case in the High Court), or
(iii) otherwise, on the next business day after it was sent or such notice was given; and
(e) in any case, on the day on which the addressee responds to it, if that is earlier.
(3) Unless something different is shown, a document produced by a computer system for dispatch by post is to be taken as having been sent by first class post, or by the equivalent of first class post, to the addressee on the business day after the day on which it was produced.
(4) Where a document is served on or by the court officer, 'business day' does not include a day on which the court office is closed.

R-46 **Proof of service**

4.12 The person who serves a document may prove that by signing a certificate explaining how and when it was served.

R-47 **Court's power to give directions about service**

4.13 (1) The court may specify the time as well as the date by which a document must be—
(a) served under rule 4.3 (Service by handing over a document) or rule 4.8 (Service by person in custody); or
(b) sent or deposited by electronic means, if it is served under rule 4.6.

(2) The court may treat a document as served if the addressee responds to it even if it was not served in accordance with the rules in this Part.

Criminal Procedure Rules Part 5 Forms and Court Records

Forms

Applications, etc. by forms or electronic means R-48

5.1 (1) This rule applies where a rule, a practice direction or the court requires a person to—
(a) make an application or give a notice;
(b) supply information for the purposes of case management by the court; or
(c) supply information needed for other purposes by the court.
(2) Unless the court otherwise directs, such a person must—
(a) use such electronic arrangements as the court officer may make for that purpose, in accordance with those arrangements; or
(b) if no such arrangements have been made, use the appropriate form set out in the Practice Direction or the Criminal Costs Practice Direction, in accordance with those Directions.

Forms in Welsh R-49

5.2 (1) Any Welsh language form set out in the Practice Direction, or in the Criminal Costs Practice Direction, is for use in connection with proceedings in courts in Wales.
(2) Both a Welsh form and an English form may be contained in the same document.
(3) Where only a Welsh form, or only the corresponding English form, is served—
(a) the following words in Welsh and English must be added:
'Darperir y ddogfen hon yn Gymraeg / Saesneg os bydd arnoch ei heisiau. Dylech wneud cais yn ddi-oed i (swyddog y llys) (rhodder yma'r cyfeiriad)
This document will be provided in Welsh / English if you require it. You should apply immediately to (the court officer) (address)'; and
(b) the court officer, or the person who served the form, must, on request, supply the corresponding form in the other language to the person served.

Signature of forms R-50

5.3 (1) This rule applies where a form provides for its signature.
(2) Unless other legislation otherwise requires, or the court otherwise directs, signature may be by any written or electronic authentication of the form by, or with the authority of, the signatory.

Court records

Duty to make records R-51

5.4 (1) For each case, as appropriate, the court officer must record, by such means as the Lord Chancellor directs—
(a) each charge or indictment against the defendant;
(b) the defendant's plea to each charge or count;
(c) each acquittal, conviction, sentence, determination, direction or order;
(d) each decision about bail;
(e) the power exercised where the court commits or adjourns the case to another court—
(i) for sentence, or
(ii) for the defendant to be dealt with for breach of a community order, a deferred sentence, a conditional discharge, or a suspended sentence of imprisonment, imposed by that other court;
(f) the court's reasons for a decision, where legislation requires those reasons to be recorded;
(g) any appeal;
(h) each party's presence or absence at each hearing;
(i) any consent that legislation requires before the court can proceed with the case, or proceed to a decision;
(j) in a magistrates' court—
(i) any indication of sentence given in connection with the allocation of a case for trial, and
(ii) the registration of a fixed penalty notice for enforcement as a fine, and any related endorsement on a driving record;
(k) in the Crown Court, any request for assistance or other communication about the case received from a juror;

(l) the identity of—
(i) the prosecutor,
(ii) the defendant,
(iii) any other applicant to whom these Rules apply,
(iv) any interpreter or intermediary,
(v) the parties' legal representatives, if any, and
(vi) the judge, magistrate or magistrates, justices' legal adviser or other person who made each recorded decision;
(m) where a defendant is entitled to attend a hearing, any agreement by the defendant to waive that right; and
(n) where interpretation is required for a defendant, any agreement by that defendant to do without the written translation of a document.

(2) Such records must include—
(a) each party's and representative's address, including any electronic address and telephone number available;
(b) the defendant's date of birth, if available; and
(c) the date of each event and decision recorded.

R-52 Recording and transcription of proceedings in the Crown Court

5.5 (1) Where someone may appeal to the Court of Appeal, the court officer must—
(a) arrange for the recording of the proceedings in the Crown Court, unless the court otherwise directs; and
(b) arrange for the transcription of such a recording if—
(i) the Registrar wants such a transcript, or
(ii) anyone else wants such a transcript (but that is subject to the restrictions in paragraph (2)).

(2) Unless the court otherwise directs, a person who transcribes a recording of proceedings under such arrangements—
(a) may only supply a transcript of a recording of a hearing in private to—
(i) the Registrar, or
(ii) an individual who was present at that hearing;
(b) if the recording of a hearing in public contains information to which reporting restrictions apply, may only supply a transcript containing that information to—
(i) the Registrar, or
(ii) a recipient to whom that supply will not contravene those reporting restrictions;
(c) subject to paragraph (2)(a) and (b), must supply any person with any transcript for which that person asks—
(i) in accordance with the transcription arrangements made by the court officer, and
(ii) on payment by that person of any fee prescribed.

(3) A party who wants to hear a recording of proceedings must—
(a) apply—
(i) in writing to the Registrar, if an appeal notice has been served where Part 36 applies (Appeal to the Court of Appeal: general rules), or
(ii) orally or in writing to the Crown Court officer;
(b) explain the reasons for the request; and
(c) pay any fee prescribed.

(4) If the Crown Court or the Registrar so directs, the Crown Court officer must allow that party to hear a recording of—
(a) a hearing in public;
(b) a hearing in private, if the applicant was present at that hearing.

R-53 Custody of case materials

5.6 Unless the court otherwise directs, in respect of each case the court officer may—
(a) keep any evidence, application, representation or other material served by the parties; or
(b) arrange for the whole or any part to be kept by some other appropriate person, subject to—
(i) any condition imposed by the court, and
(ii) the rules in Part 34 (Appeal to the Crown Court) and Part 36 (Appeal to the Court of Appeal: General Rules) about keeping exhibits pending any appeal.

R-54 Supply to a party of information or documents from records or case materials

5.7 (1) This rule applies where—
(a) applies where—
(i) a party wants information, or a copy of a document, from records or case materials kept by the court officer (for example, in case of loss, or to establish what is retained), or

(ii) a person affected by an order made, or warrant issued, by the court wants such information or such a copy; but

(b) does not apply to—

(i) a recording arranged under rule 5.5 (Recording and transcription of proceedings in the Crown Court),

(ii) a copy of such a recording, or

(iii) a transcript of such a recording.

(2) Such a party or person must—

(a) apply to the court officer;

(b) specify the information or document required; and

(c) pay any fee prescribed.

(3) The application—

(a) may be made orally, giving no reasons, if paragraph (4) requires the court officer to supply the information or document requested;

(b) must be in writing, unless the court otherwise permits, and must explain for what purpose the information is required, in any other case.

(4) The court officer must supply to the applicant party or person —

(a) a copy of any document served by, or on, that party or person (but not of any document not so served);

(b) by word of mouth, or in writing, as requested—

(i) information that was received from that party or person in the first place,

(ii) information about the terms of any direction or order directed to that party or person, or made on an application by that party or person, or at a hearing in public,

(iii) information about the outcome of the case.

(5) If the court so directs, the court officer must supply to the applicant party or person, by word of mouth or in writing, as requested, information that paragraph (4) does not require the court officer to supply.

(6) Where the information requested is about the grounds on which an order was made, or a warrant was issued, in the absence of the party or person applying for that information—

(a) that party or person must also serve the request on the person who applied for the order or warrant;

(b) if the person who applied for the order or warrant objects to the supply of the information requested, that objector must—

(i) give notice of the objection not more than 14 days after service of the request (or within any longer period allowed by the court),

(ii) serve that notice on the court officer and on the party or person requesting the information, and

(iii) if the objector wants a hearing, explain why one is needed;

(c) the court may determine the application for information at a hearing (which must be in private unless the court otherwise directs), or without a hearing;

(d) the court must not permit the information requested to be supplied unless the person who applied for the order or warrant has had at least 14 days (or any longer period allowed by the court) in which to make representations.

(7) A notice of objection under paragraph (6) must explain—

(a) whether the objection is to the supply of any part of the information requested, or only to the supply of a specified part, or parts, of it;

(b) whether the objection is to the supply of the information at any time, or only to its supply before a date or event specified by the objector; and

(c) the grounds of the objection.

(8) Where a notice of objection under paragraph (6) includes material that the objector thinks ought not be revealed to the party or person applying for information, the objector must—

(a) omit that material from the notice served on that party or person;

(b) mark the material to show that it is only for the court; and

(c) with that material include an explanation of why it has been withheld.

(9) Where paragraph (8) applies—

(a) a hearing of the application may take place, wholly or in part, in the absence of the party or person applying for information;

(b) at any such hearing, the general rule is that the court must consider, in the following sequence—

(i) representations first by the party or person applying for information and then by the objector, in the presence of both, and then

(ii) further representations by the objector, in the absence of that party or person

but the court may direct other arrangements for the hearing.

R-55 **Supply to the public, including reporters, of information about cases**

5.8 (1) This rule—
(a) applies where a member of the public, including a reporter, wants information about a case from the court officer;
(b) requires the court officer to publish information about cases due to be considered by the court.
(c) does not apply to—
(i) a recording arranged under rule 5.5 (Recording and transcription of proceedings in the Crown Court),
(ii) a copy of such a recording, or
(iii) a transcript of such a recording.

(2) A person who wants information about a case from the court officer must—
(a) apply to the court officer;
(b) specify the information requested; and
(c) pay any fee prescribed.

(3) The application—
(a) may be made orally, giving no reasons, if—
(i) paragraph (4) requires the court officer to supply the information requested, and
(ii) the information is to be supplied only by word of mouth;
(b) must be in writing, unless the court otherwise permits, and must explain for what purpose the information is required, in any other case.

(4) The court officer must supply to the applicant—
(a) any information listed in paragraph (6), if—
(i) the information is available to the court officer,
(ii) the supply of the information is not prohibited by a reporting restriction, and
(iii) the trial has not yet concluded, or the verdict was not more than 6 months ago; and
(b) details of any reporting or access restriction ordered by the court.

(5) The court officer must supply that information—
(a) by word of mouth; or
(b) in writing, including by—
(i) written certificate or extract, or
(ii) such arrangements as the Lord Chancellor directs.

(6) The information that paragraph (4) requires the court officer to supply is—
(a) the date of any hearing in public, unless any party has yet to be notified of that date;
(b) each alleged offence and any plea entered;
(c) the court's decision at any hearing in public, including any decision about—
(i) bail, or
(ii) the committal, sending or transfer of the case to another court;
(d) whether the case is under appeal;
(e) the outcome of the case; and
(f) the identity of—
(i) the prosecutor,
(ii) the defendant,
(iii) the parties' representatives, including their addresses, and
(iv) the judge, magistrate or magistrates, or justices' legal adviser by whom a decision at a hearing in public was made.

(7) If the court so directs, the court officer must—
(a) supply to the applicant, by word of mouth or in writing (including by written certificate or extract), other information about the case; or
(b) allow the applicant to inspect or copy a document, or part of a document, containing information about the case.

(8) The court may determine an application to which paragraph (7) applies—
(a) at a hearing, in public or in private; or
(b) without a hearing.

(9) Where a case is due to be heard in public, the court officer must—
(a) publish the information listed in paragraph (10) if—
(i) the information is available to the court officer, and
(ii) the publication of the information is not prohibited by a reporting restriction;
(b) publish that information—
(i) by notice displayed somewhere prominent in the vicinity of a court room in which the hearing is due to take place, or by such other arrangements as the Lord Chancellor directs (including arrangements for publication by electronic means), and
(ii) for no longer than 5 business days.

(10) The information that paragraph (9) requires the court officer to publish is—
(a) the date, time and place of the hearing;
(b) the identity of the defendant; and
(c) such other information as it may be practicable to publish concerning—
(i) the type of hearing,
(ii) the identity of the prosecutor,
(iii) the identity of the court,
(iv) the offence or offences alleged, and
(v) whether any reporting restriction applies.

(11) Where a case is ready to be tried without a hearing under rule 24.9 (Single justice procedure: special rules), the court officer must—
(a) publish the information listed in paragraph (12) if—
(i) the information is available to the court officer, and
(ii) the publication of the information is not prohibited by a reporting restriction;
(b) publish that information—
(i) by such arrangements as the Lord Chancellor directs, including arrangements for publication by electronic means, and
(ii) for no longer than 5 business days.

(12) The information that paragraph (11) requires the court officer to publish is—
(a) the identity of the defendant;
(b) the identity of the prosecutor;
(c) the offence or offences alleged; and
(d) whether any reporting restriction applies.

Supply of written certificate or extract from records for use in evidence, etc **R-56**

5.9 (1) This rule applies where legislation—
(a) allows a certificate of conviction or acquittal, or an extract from records kept by the court officer, to be introduced in evidence in criminal proceedings; or
(b) requires such a certificate or extract to be supplied by the court officer to a specified person for a specified purpose.

(2) A person who wants such a certificate or extract must—
(a) apply in writing to the court officer;
(b) specify the certificate or extract required;
(c) explain under what legislation and for what purpose it is required; and
(d) pay any fee prescribed.

(3) If the application satisfies the requirements of that legislation, the court officer must supply the certificate or extract requested—
(a) to a party;
(b) unless the court otherwise directs, to any other applicant.

Criminal Practice Directions Part 5 Forms and Court Records

CPD I General matters 5A: Forms **PD-17**

5A.1 The forms at Annex D to the Consolidated Criminal Practice Direction of 8th July 2002 [2002] 1 WLR 2870; [2002] 2 Cr App R 35, or forms to that effect, are to be used in the criminal courts, in accordance with CrimPR 5.1.

5A.2 The forms at Annex E to that Practice Direction, the case management forms, must be used in the criminal courts, in accordance with that rule.

5A.3 The table at the beginning of each section of each of those Annexes lists the forms and:
(a) shows the Rule in connection with which each applies;
(b) describes each form.

5A.4 The forms may be amended or withdrawn from time to time, or new forms added, under the authority of the Lord Chief Justice.

CPD I General matters 5B: Access to Information Held by the Court **PD-18**

5B.1 Open justice, as Lord Justice Toulson re-iterated in the case of *R (Guardian News and Media Ltd) v City of Westminster Magistrates' Court* [2012] EWCA Civ 420, [2013] QB 618, is a 'principle at the heart of our system of justice and vital to the rule of law'. There are exceptions but these 'have to be justified by some even more important principle'. However, the practical application of that undisputed principle, and the proper balancing of conflicting rights and principles, call for careful judgments to be made. The following is intended to provide some assistance to courts making decisions when asked to provide the public, including journalists, with access to or copies of information and documents held by the court, or when asked, exceptionally, to forbid the supply of transcripts that otherwise would have been supplied. It is not a prescriptive list, as the court will have to consider all the circumstances of each individual case.

5B.2 It remains the responsibility of the recipient of information or documents to ensure that they comply with any and all restrictions such as reporting restrictions (see Part 6 and the accompanying Practice Direction).

5B.3 For the purposes of this direction, the word document includes images in photographic, digital including DVD format, video, CCTV or any other form.

5B.4 Certain information can and should be provided to the public on request, subject to any restrictions, such as reporting restrictions, imposed in that particular case. CrimPR 5.5 governs the supply of transcript of a recording of proceedings in the Crown Court. CrimPR 5.8(4) and 5.8(6) read together specify the information that the court officer will supply to the public; an oral application is acceptable and no reason need be given for the request. There is no requirement for the court officer to consider the non-disclosure provisions of the Data Protection Act 1998 as the exemption under section 35 applies to all disclosure made under 'any enactment . . . or by the order of a court', which includes under the Criminal Procedure Rules.

5B.5 If the information sought is neither transcript nor listed at CrimPR 5.8(6), rule 5.8(7) will apply, and the provision of information is at the discretion of the court. The following guidance is intended to assist the court in exercising that discretion.

5B.6 A request for access to documents used in a criminal case should first be addressed to the party who presented them to the court or who, in the case of a written decision by the court, received that decision. Prosecuting authorities are subject to the Freedom of Information Act 2000 and the Data Protection Act 1998 and their decisions are susceptible to review.

5B.7 If the request is from a journalist or media organisation, note that there is a protocol between the NPCC, the CPS and the media entitled 'Publicity and the Criminal Justice System':

www.cps.gov.uk/publications/agencies/mediaprotocol.html
www.cps.gov.uk/publication/publicity-and-criminal-justice-system
There is additionally a protocol made under CrimPR 5.8(5)(b) between the media and HMCTS:
www.newsmediauk.org/write/MediaUploads/PDF%20Docs/Protocol_for_Sharing_Court_Documents.pdf
This Practice Direction does not affect the operation of those protocols. Material should generally be sought under the relevant protocol before an application is made to the court.

5B.8 An application to which CrimPR 5.8(7) applies must be made in accordance with rule 5.8; it must be in writing, unless the court permits otherwise, and 'must explain for what purpose the information is required.' A clear, detailed application, specifying the name and contact details of the applicant, whether or not he or she represents a media organisation, and setting out the reasons for the application and to what use the information will be put, will be of most assistance to the court. Applicants should state if they have requested the information under a protocol and include any reasons given for the refusal. Before considering such an application, the court will expect the applicant to have given notice of the request to the parties.

5B.9 The court will consider each application on its own merits. The burden of justifying a request for access rests on the applicant. Considerations to be taken into account will include:

i. whether or not the request is for the purpose of contemporaneous reporting; a request after the conclusion of the proceedings will require careful scrutiny by the court;
ii. the nature of the information or documents being sought;
iii. the purpose for which they are required;
iv. the stage of the proceedings at the time when the application is made;
v. the value of the documents in advancing the open justice principle, including enabling the media to discharge its role, which has been described as a 'public watchdog', by reporting the proceedings effectively;
vi. any risk of harm which access to them may cause to the legitimate interests of others; and
vii. any reasons given by the parties for refusing to provide the material requested and any other representations received from the parties.

Further, all of the principles below are subject to any specific restrictions in the case. Courts should be aware that the risk of providing a document may reduce after a particular point in the proceedings, and when the material requested may be made available.

Documents read aloud in their entirety

5B.10 If a document has been read aloud to the court in its entirety, it should usually be provided on request, unless to do so would be disruptive to the court proceedings or place an undue burden on the court, the advocates or others. It may be appropriate and convenient for material to be provided electronically, if this can be done securely.

5B.11 Documents likely to fall into this category are:

i. Opening notes;

ii. Statements agreed under section 9 of the Criminal Justice Act 1967, including experts' reports, if read in their entirety;
iii. Admissions made under section 10 of the Criminal Justice Act 1967.

Documents treated as read aloud in their entirety

5B.12 A document treated by the court as if it had been read aloud in public, though in fact it has been neither read nor summarised aloud, should generally be made available on request. The burden on the court, the advocates or others in providing the material should be considered, but the presumption in favour of providing the material is greater when the material has only been treated as having been read aloud. Again, subject to security considerations, it may be convenient for the material to be provided electronically.

5B.13 Documents likely to fall into this category include:
i. Skeleton arguments;
ii. Written submissions;
iii. Written decisions by the court.

Documents read aloud in part or summarised aloud

5B.14 Open justice requires only access to the part of the document that has been read aloud. If a member of the public requests a copy of such a document, the court should consider whether it is proportionate to order one of the parties to produce a suitably redacted version. If not, access to the document is unlikely to be granted; however open justice will generally have been satisfied by the document having been read out in court.

5B.15 If the request comes from an accredited member of the press (see *Access by reporters* below), there may be circumstances in which the court orders that a copy of the whole document be shown to the reporter, or provided, subject to the condition that those matters that had not been read out to the court may not be used or reported. A breach of such an order would be treated as a contempt of court.

5B.16 Documents in this category are likely to include:
i. Section 9 statements that are edited.

Jury bundles and exhibits (including video footage shown to the jury)

5B.17 The court should consider:
i. whether access to the specific document is necessary to understand or effectively to report the case;
ii. the privacy of third parties, such as the victim (in some cases, the reporting restriction imposed by section 1 of the Judicial Proceedings (Regulation of Reports) Act 1926 will apply (indecent or medical matter));
iii. whether the reporting of anything in the document may be prejudicial to a fair trial in this or another case, in which case whether it may be necessary to make an order under section 4(2) of the Contempt of Court Act 1981.

The court may order one of the parties to provide a copy of certain pages (or parts of the footage), but these should not be provided electronically.

Statements of witnesses who give oral evidence

5B.18 A witness statement does not become evidence unless it is agreed under section 9 of the Criminal Justice Act 1967 and presented to the court. Therefore the statements of witnesses who give oral evidence, including ABE interview and transcripts and experts' reports, should not usually be provided. Open justice is generally satisfied by public access to the court.

Confidential documents

5B.19 A document the content of which, though relied upon by the court, has not been communicated to the public or reporters, nor treated as if it had been, is likely to have been supplied in confidence and should be treated accordingly. This will apply even if the court has made reference to the document or quoted from the document. There is most unlikely to be a sufficient reason to displace the expectation of confidentiality ordinarily attaching to a document in this category, and it would be exceptional to permit the inspection or copying by a member of the public or of the media of such a document. The rights and legitimate interests of others are likely to outweigh the interests of open justice with respect these documents.

5B.20 Documents in this category are likely to include:
i. Pre-sentence reports;
ii. Medical reports;
iii. Victim Personal Statements;
iv. Reports and summaries for confiscation.

Prohibitions against the provision of information

5B.21 Statutory provisions may impose specific prohibitions against the provision of information. Those most likely to be encountered are listed in the note to CrimPR 5.8 and include the Rehabilitation of Offenders Act 1974, section 18 of the Criminal Procedure and Investigations Act 1996 ('unused material' disclosed by the prosecution), sections 33, 34 and 35 of the Legal Aid, Sentencing and Punishment of Offenders Act 2012 ('LASPO Act 2012') (privileged information furnished to the Legal Aid Agency) and reporting restrictions generally.

5B.22 Reports of allocation or sending proceedings are restricted by section 52A of the Crime and Disorder Act 1998, so that only limited information, as specified in the statute, may be reported, whether it is referred to in the court room or not. The magistrates' court has power to order that the restriction shall not apply; if any defendant objects the court must apply the interests of justice test as specified in section 52A. The restriction ceases to apply either after all defendants indicate a plea of guilty, or after the conclusion of the trial of the last defendant to be tried. If the case does not result in a guilty plea, a finding of guilt or an acquittal, the restriction does not lift automatically and an application must be made to the court.

5B.23 Extradition proceedings have some features in common with committal proceedings, but no automatic reporting restrictions apply.

5B.24 Public Interest Immunity and the rights of a defendant, witnesses and victims under Article 6 and 8 of the European Convention on Human Rights may also restrict the power to release material to third parties.

Other documents

5B.25 The following table indicates the considerations likely to arise on an application to inspect or copy other documents.

Document	Considerations
Charge sheet Indictment	The alleged offence(s) will have been read aloud in court, and their terms must be supplied under CrimPR 5.8(4)
Material disclosed under CPIA 1996	To the extent that the content is deployed at trial, it becomes public at that hearing. Otherwise, it is a criminal offence for it to be disclosed: section 18 of the 1996 Act.
Written notices, applications, replies (including any application for representation)	To the extent that evidence is introduced, or measures taken, at trial, the content becomes public at that hearing. A statutory prohibition against disclosure applies to an application for representation: sections 33, 34 and 35 of the LASPO Act 2012.
Written decisions by the court, other than those read aloud in public or treated as if so read	Such decisions should usually be provided, subject to the criteria listed in CrimPR 5.8(4)(a) (and see also paragraph 5B.31 below).
Sentencing remarks	Sentencing remarks should usually be provided to the accredited Press, if the judge was reading from a prepared script which was handed out immediately afterwards; if not, then permission for a member of the accredited Press to obtain a transcript should usually be given (see also paragraphs 5B.26 and 29 below).
Official recordings	See CrimPR 5.5.
Transcript	See CrimPR 5.5 (and see also paragraphs 5B.32 to 36 below).

Access by reporters

5B.26 Under CrimPR Part 5, the same procedure applies to applications for access to information by reporters as to other members of the public. However, if the application is made by legal representatives instructed by the media, or by an accredited member of the media, who is able to produce in support of the application a valid Press Card (http://www.ukpresscardauthority.co.uk/) then there is a greater presumption in favour of providing the requested material, in recognition of the press' role as 'public watch dog' in a democratic society (*Observer and Guardian v United Kingdom* (1992) 14 EHRR 153, Times November 27, 1991). The general principle in those circumstances is that the court should supply documents and information unless there is a good reason not to in order to protect the rights or legitimate interests of others and the request will not place an undue burden on the court *R* (*Guardian News and Media Ltd*) at [87]. Subject to that, the paragraphs above relating to types of documents should be followed.

5B.27 Court staff should usually verify the authenticity of cards, checking the expiry date on the card and where necessary may consider telephoning the number on the reverse of the card to verify the card holder. Court staff may additionally request sight of other identification if necessary to ensure that the card holder has been correctly identified. The supply of information under CrimPR 5.8(7) is at the discretion of the court, and court staff must ensure that they have received a clear direction from the court before providing any information or material under rule 5.8(7) to a member of the public, including to the accredited media or their legal representatives.

5B.28 Opening notes and skeleton arguments or written submissions, once they have been placed before the court, should usually be provided to the media. If there is no opening note, permission for the media to obtain a transcript of the prosecution opening should usually be given (see below). It may be convenient for copies to be provided electronically by counsel, provided that the documents are kept suitably secure. The media are expected to be aware of the limitations on the use to which such material can be put, for example that legal argument held in the absence of the jury must not be reported before the conclusion of the trial.

5B.29 The media should also be able to obtain transcripts of hearings held in open court directly from the transcription service provider, on payment of any required fee. The service providers commonly require the judge's authorisation before they will provide a transcript, as an additional verification to ensure that the correct material is released and reporting restrictions are noted. However, responsibility for compliance with any restriction always rests with the person receiving the information or material: see CPD I General Matters 6B beneath.

5B.30 It is not for the judge to exercise an editorial judgment about 'the adequacy of the material already available to the paper for its journalistic purpose' (*Guardian* at 82) but the responsibility for complying with the Contempt of Court Act 1981 and any and all restrictions on the use of the material rests with the recipient.

Written decisions

5B.31 Where the Criminal Procedure Rules allow for a determination without a hearing there may be occasions on which it furthers the overriding objective to deliver the court's decision to the parties in writing, without convening a public hearing at which that decision will be pronounced: on an application for costs made at the conclusion of a trial, for example. If the only reason for delivering a decision in that way is to promote efficiency and expedition and if no other consideration arises then usually a copy of the decision should be provided in response to any request once the decision is final. However, had the decision been announced in public then the criteria in CrimPR 5.8(4)(a) would have applied to the supply of information by the court officer; and ordinarily those same criteria should be applied by the court, therefore. Moreover, where considerations other than efficiency and expedition have influenced the court's decision to reach a determination without convening a hearing then those same considerations may be inimical to the supply of the written decision to any applicant other than a party. Reporting restrictions may be relevant, for example; as may the considerations listed in paragraph 5B.9 above. In such a case the court should consider supplying a redacted version of the decision in response to a request by anyone who is not a party; or it may be appropriate to give the decision in terms that can be supplied to the public, supplemented by additional reasons provided only to the parties.

Transcript

5B.32 CrimPR 5.5 does not require an application to the court for transcript, nor does the rule anticipate recourse to the court for a judicial decision about the supply of transcript in any but unusual circumstances. Ordinarily it is the rule itself that determines the circumstances in which the transcriber of a recording may or may not supply transcript to an applicant.

5B.33 Where reporting restrictions apply to information contained in the recording from which the transcript is prepared then unless the court otherwise directs it is for the transcriber to redact that transcript where redaction is necessary to permit its supply to that applicant. Having regard to the

Criminal Procedure Rules and Criminal Practice Directions

terms of the statutes that impose reporting restrictions, however, it is unlikely that redaction will be required frequently. Statutory restrictions prohibit publication 'to the public at large or any section of the public', or some comparable formulation. They do not ordinarily prohibit a publication constituted only of the supply of transcript to an individual applicant. However, any reporting restrictions will continue to apply to a recipient of transcript, and where they apply the recipient must be alerted to them by the endorsement on the transcript of a suitable warning notice, to this or the like effect:

> 'WARNING: reporting restrictions may apply to the contents transcribed in this document, particularly if the case concerned a sexual offence or involved a child. Reporting restrictions prohibit the publication of the applicable information to the public or any section of the public, in writing, in a broadcast or by means of the internet, including social media. Anyone who receives a copy of this transcript is responsible in law for making sure that applicable restrictions are not breached. A person who breaches a reporting restriction is liable to a fine and/or imprisonment. For guidance on whether reporting restrictions apply, and to what information, ask at the court office or take legal advice.'

5B.34 Exceptionally, court staff may invite the court to direct that transcript must be redacted before it is supplied to an applicant, or that transcript must not be supplied to an applicant pending the supply of further information or assurances by that applicant, or at all, in exercise of the judicial discretion to which CrimPR 5.5(2) refers. Circumstances giving rise to concern may include, for example, the occurrence of events causing staff reasonably to suspect that an applicant intends or is likely to disregard a reporting restriction that applies, despite the warning notice endorsed on the transcript, or reasonably to suspect that an applicant has malicious intentions towards another person. Given that the proceedings will have taken place in public, despite any such suspicions, cogent and compelling reasons will be required to deny a request for transcript of such proceedings and the onus rests always on the court to justify such a denial, not on the applicant to justify the request. Even where there are reasons to suspect a criminal intent, the appropriate course may be to direct that the police be informed of those reasons rather than to direct that the transcript be withheld. Nevertheless, it may be appropriate in such a case to direct that an application for the transcript should be made which complies with paragraph 5B.8 above (even though that paragraph does not apply); and then for the court to review that application with regard to the considerations listed in paragraph 5B.9 above (but the usual burden of justifying a request under that paragraph does not apply).

5B.35 Some applicants for transcript may be taken to be aware of the significance of reporting restrictions, where they apply, and, by reason of such an applicant's statutory or other public or quasi-public functions, in any event unlikely to contravene any such restriction. Such applicants include public authorities within the meaning of section 6 of the Human Rights Act 1998 (a definition which extends to government departments and their agencies, local authorities, prosecuting authorities, and institutions such as the Parole Board and the Sentencing Council) and include public or private bodies exercising disciplinary functions in relation to practitioners of a regulated profession such as doctors, lawyers, accountants, etc. It would be only in the most exceptional circumstances that a court might conclude that any such body should not receive unredacted transcript of proceedings in public, irrespective of whether reporting restrictions do or do not apply.

5B.36 The rule imposes no time limit on a request for the supply of transcript. The assumption is that transcript of proceedings in public in the Crown Court will continue to be available for as long as relevant records are maintained by the Lord Chancellor under the legislation to which CrimPR 5.4 refers.

PD-19 **CPD I General matters 5C: Issue of Medical Certificates**

5C.1 Doctors will be aware that medical notes are normally submitted by defendants in criminal proceedings as justification for not answering bail. Medical notes may also be submitted by witnesses who are due to give evidence and jurors.

5C.2 If a medical certificate is accepted by the court, this will result in cases (including contested hearings and trials) being adjourned rather than the court issuing a warrant for the defendant's arrest without bail. Medical certificates will also provide the defendant with sufficient evidence to defend a charge of failure to surrender to bail.

5C.3 However, a court is not absolutely bound by a medical certificate. The medical practitioner providing the certificate may be required by the court to give evidence. Alternatively the court may exercise its discretion to disregard a certificate which it finds unsatisfactory: *R v Ealing Magistrates' Court ex parte Burgess* [2001] 165 JP 82.

5C.4 Circumstances where the court may find a medical certificate unsatisfactory include:
(a) where the certificate indicates that the defendant is unfit to attend work (rather than to attend court);
(b) where the nature of the defendant's ailment (e.g. a broken arm) does not appear to be capable of preventing his attendance at court;
(c) where the defendant is certified as suffering from stress/anxiety/depression and there is no indication of the defendant recovering within a realistic timescale.

5C.5 It therefore follows that the minimum standards a medical certificate should set out are:
(a) the date on which the medical practitioner examined the defendant;
(b) the exact nature of the defendant's ailments;
(c) if it is not self-evident, why the ailment prevents the defendant attending court;
(d) an indication as to when the defendant is likely to be able to attend court, or a date when the current certificate expires.

5C.6 Medical practitioners should be aware that when issuing a certificate to a defendant in criminal proceedings they make themselves liable to being summonsed to court to give evidence about the content of the certificate, and they may be asked to justify their statements.

Criminal Procedure Rules Part 6 Reporting, etc. Restrictions

General rules

When this Part applies **R-57**

6.1 (1) This Part applies where the court can—
(a) impose a restriction on—
(i) reporting what takes place at a public hearing, or
(ii) public access to what otherwise would be a public hearing;
(b) vary or remove a reporting or access restriction that is imposed by legislation;
(c) withhold information from the public during a public hearing;
(d) order a trial in private;
(e) allow there to take place during a hearing—
(i) sound recording, or
(ii) communication by electronic means.

(2) This Part does not apply to arrangements required by legislation, or directed by the court, in connection with—
(a) sound recording during a hearing, or the transcription of such a recording; or
(b) measures to assist a witness or defendant to give evidence.

Exercise of court's powers to which this Part applies **R-58**

6.2 (1) When exercising a power to which this Part applies, as well as furthering the overriding objective, in accordance with rule 1.3, the court must have regard to the importance of—
(a) dealing with criminal cases in public; and
(b) allowing a public hearing to be reported to the public.

(2) The court may determine an application or appeal under this Part—
(a) at a hearing, in public or in private; or
(b) without a hearing.

(3) But the court must not exercise a power to which this Part applies unless each party and any other person directly affected—
(a) is present; or
(b) has had an opportunity—
(i) to attend, or
(ii) to make representations.

Court's power to vary requirements under this Part **R-59**

6.3 (1) The court may—
(a) shorten or extend (even after it has expired) a time limit under this Part;
(b) require an application to be made in writing instead of orally;
(c) consider an application or representations made orally instead of in writing;
(d) dispense with a requirement to—
(i) give notice, or
(ii) serve an application.

(2) Someone who wants an extension of time must—
(a) apply when making the application or representations for which it is needed; and
(b) explain the delay.

Reporting and access restrictions

R-60 Reporting and access restrictions

6.4 (1) This rule applies where the court can—
(a) impose a restriction on—
(i) reporting what takes place at a public hearing, or
(ii) public access to what otherwise would be a public hearing;
(b) withhold information from the public during a public hearing.
(2) Unless other legislation otherwise provides, the court may do so—
(a) on application by a party; or
(b) on its own initiative.
(3) A party who wants the court to do so must—
(a) apply as soon as reasonably practicable;
(b) notify—
(i) each other party, and
(ii) such other person (if any) as the court directs;
(c) specify the proposed terms of the order, and for how long it should last;
(d) explain—
(i) what power the court has to make the order, and
(ii) why an order in the terms proposed is necessary;
(e) where the application is for a reporting direction under section 45A of the Youth Justice and Criminal Evidence Act 1999 (Power to restrict reporting of criminal proceedings for lifetime of witnesses and victims under 18), explain—
(i) how the circumstances of the person whose identity is concerned meet the conditions prescribed by that section, having regard to the factors which that section lists; and
(ii) why such a reporting direction would be likely to improve the quality of any evidence given by that person, or the level of co-operation given by that person to any party in connection with the preparation of that party's case, taking into account the factors listed in that section;
(f) where the application is for a reporting direction under section 46 of the Youth Justice and Criminal Evidence Act 1999 (Power to restrict reports about certain adult witnesses in criminal proceedings), explain—
(i) how the witness is eligible for assistance, having regard to the factors listed in that section, and
(ii) why such a reporting direction would be likely to improve the quality of the witness' evidence, or the level of co-operation given by the witness to the applicant in connection with the preparation of the applicant's case, taking into account the factors which that section lists.

R-61 Varying or removing restrictions

6.5 (1) This rule applies where the court can vary or remove a reporting or access restriction.
(2) Unless other legislation otherwise provides, the court may do so—
(a) on application by a party or person directly affected; or
(b) on its own initiative.
(3) A party or person who wants the court to do so must—
(a) apply as soon as reasonably practicable;
(b) notify—
(i) each other party, and
(ii) such other person (if any) as the court directs;
(c) specify the restriction;
(d) explain, as appropriate, why it should be varied or removed.
(4) A person who wants to appeal to the Crown Court under section 141F of the Education Act 2002 must—
(a) serve an appeal notice on—
(i) the Crown Court officer, and
(ii) each other party;
(b) serve on the Crown Court officer, with the appeal notice, a copy of the application to the magistrates' court;

(c) serve the appeal notice not more than 21 days after the magistrates' court's decision against which the appellant wants to appeal; and
(d) in the appeal notice, explain, as appropriate, why the restriction should be maintained, varied or removed.
(5) Rule 34.11 (Constitution of the Crown Court) applies on such an appeal.

Trial in private **R-62**

6.6 (1) This rule applies where the court can order a trial in private.
(2) A party who wants the court to do so must—
(a) apply in writing not less than 5 business days before the trial is due to begin; and
(b) serve the application on—
(i) the court officer, and
(ii) each other party.
(3) The applicant must explain—
(a) the reasons for the application;
(b) how much of the trial the applicant proposes should be in private; and
(c) why no measures other than trial in private will suffice, such as—
(i) reporting restrictions,
(ii) an admission of facts,
(iii) the introduction of hearsay evidence,
(iv) a direction for a special measure under section 19 of the Youth Justice and Criminal Evidence Act 1999,
(v) a witness anonymity order under section 86 of the Coroners and Justice Act 2009, or
(vi) arrangements for the protection of a witness.
(4) Where the application includes information that the applicant thinks ought not be revealed to another party, the applicant must—
(a) omit that information from the part of the application that is served on that other party;
(b) mark the other part to show that, unless the court otherwise directs, it is only for the court; and
(c) in that other part, explain why the applicant has withheld that information from that other party.
(5) The court officer must at once—
(a) display notice of the application somewhere prominent in the vicinity of the courtroom; and
(b) give notice of the application to reporters by such other arrangements as the Lord Chancellor directs.
(6) The application must be determined at a hearing which—
(a) must be in private, unless the court otherwise directs;
(b) if the court so directs, may be, wholly or in part, in the absence of a party from whom information has been withheld; and
(c) in the Crown Court, must be after the defendant is arraigned but before the jury is sworn.
(7) At the hearing of the application—
(a) the general rule is that the court must consider, in the following sequence—
(i) representations first by the applicant and then by each other party, in all the parties' presence, and then
(ii) further representations by the applicant, in the absence of a party from whom information has been withheld; but
(b) the court may direct other arrangements for the hearing.
(8) The court must not hear a trial in private until—
(a) the business day after the day on which it orders such a trial, or
(b) the disposal of any appeal against, or review of, any such order, if later.

Representations in response **R-63**

6.7 (1) This rule applies where a party, or person directly affected, wants to make representations about an application or appeal.
(2) Such a party or person must—
(a) serve the representations on—
(i) the court officer,
(ii) the applicant,
(iii) each other party, and
(iv) such other person (if any) as the court directs;

(b) do so as soon as reasonably practicable after notice of the application; and
(c) ask for a hearing, if that party or person wants one, and explain why it is needed.

(3) Representations must—
(a) explain the reasons for any objection;
(b) specify any alternative terms proposed.

R-64 **Order about restriction or trial in private**

6.8 (1) This rule applies where the court—
(a) orders, varies or removes a reporting or access restriction; or
(b) orders a trial in private.

(2) The court officer must—
(a) record the court's reasons for the decision; and
(b) as soon as reasonably practicable, arrange for notice of the decision to be—
(i) displayed somewhere prominent in the vicinity of the courtroom, and
(ii) communicated to reporters by such other arrangements as the Lord Chancellor directs.

Sound recording and electronic communication

R-65 **Sound recording and electronic communication**

6.9 (1) This rule applies where the court can give permission to—
(a) bring into a hearing for use, or use during a hearing, a device for—
(i) recording sound, or
(ii) communicating by electronic means; or
(b) publish a sound recording made during a hearing.

(2) The court may give such permission—
(a) on application; or
(b) on its own initiative.

(3) A person who wants the court to give such permission must—
(a) apply as soon as reasonably practicable;
(b) notify—
(i) each party, and
(ii) such other person (if any) as the court directs; and
(c) explain why the court should permit the use or publication proposed.

(4) As a condition of the applicant using such a device, the court may direct arrangements to minimise the risk of its use—
(a) contravening a reporting restriction;
(b) disrupting the hearing; or
(c) compromising the fairness of the hearing, for example by affecting—
(i) the evidence to be given by a witness, or
(ii) the verdict of a jury.

(5) Such a direction may require that the device is used only—
(a) in a specified part of the courtroom;
(b) for a specified purpose;
(c) for a purpose connected with the applicant's activity as a member of a specified group, for example representatives of news-gathering or reporting organisations;
(d) at a specified time, or in a specified way.

R-66 **Forfeiture of unauthorised sound recording**

6.10 (1) This rule applies where someone without the court's permission—
(a) uses a device for recording sound during a hearing; or
(b) publishes a sound recording made during a hearing.

(2) The court may exercise its power to forfeit the device or recording—
(a) on application by a party, or on its own initiative;
(b) provisionally, despite rule 6.2(3), to allow time for representations.

(3) A party who wants the court to forfeit a device or recording must—
(a) apply as soon as reasonably practicable;
(b) notify—
(i) as appropriate, the person who used the device, or who published the recording, and
(ii) each other party; and
(c) explain why the court should exercise that power.

Criminal Practice Directions Part 6 Reporting, etc. Restrictions

CPD II Preliminary proceedings 6A: Unofficial Sound Recording of Proceedings PD-20

6A.1 Section 9 of the Contempt of Court Act 1981 contains provisions governing the unofficial use of equipment for recording sound in court.

Section 9(1) provides that it is a contempt of court:

(a) to use in court, or bring into court for use, any tape recorder or other instrument for recording sound, except with the permission of the court;

(b) to publish a recording of legal proceedings made by means of any such instrument, or any recording derived directly or indirectly from it, by playing it in the hearing of the public or any section of the public, or to dispose of it or any recording so derived, with a view to such publication;

(c) to use any such recording in contravention of any conditions of leave granted under paragraph (a).

These provisions do not apply to the making or use of sound recordings for purposes of official transcripts of the proceedings, upon which the Act imposes no restriction whatever.

6A.2 The discretion given to the court to grant, withhold or withdraw leave to use equipment for recording sound or to impose conditions as to the use of the recording is unlimited, but the following factors may be relevant to its exercise:

(a) the existence of any reasonable need on the part of the applicant for leave, whether a litigant or a person connected with the press or broadcasting, for the recording to be made;

(b) the risk that the recording could be used for the purpose of briefing witnesses out of court;

(c) any possibility that the use of the recorder would disturb the proceedings or distract or worry any witnesses or other participants.

6A.3 Consideration should always be given whether conditions as to the use of a recording made pursuant to leave should be imposed. The identity and role of the applicant for leave and the nature of the subject matter of the proceedings may be relevant to this.

6A.4 The particular restriction imposed by section 9(1) (b) applies in every case, but may not be present in the mind of every applicant to whom leave is given. It may therefore be desirable on occasion for this provision to be drawn to the attention of those to whom leave is given.

6A.5 The transcript of a permitted recording is intended for the use of the person given leave to make it and is not intended to be used as, or to compete with, the official transcript mentioned in section 9(4).

6A.6 Where a contravention of section 9(1) is alleged, the procedure in section 2 of Part 48 of the Rules should be followed. Section 9(3) of the 1981 Act permits the court to 'order the instrument, or any recording made with it, or both, to be forfeited'. The procedure at CrimPR 6.10 should be followed.

CPD II Preliminary proceedings 6B: Restrictions on Reporting Proceedings PD-21

6B.1 Open justice is an essential principle in the criminal courts but the principle is subject to some statutory restrictions. These restrictions are either automatic or discretionary. Guidance is provided in the joint publication, *Reporting Restrictions in the Criminal Courts* issued by the Judicial College, the Newspaper Society, the Society of Editors and the Media Lawyers Association. The current version is the fourth edition and has been updated to be effective from May 2015.

6B.2 Where a restriction is automatic no order can or should be made in relation to matters falling within the relevant provisions. However, the court may, if it considers it appropriate to do so, give a reminder of the existence of the automatic restriction. The court may also discuss the scope of the restriction and any particular risks in the specific case in open court with representatives of the press present. Such judicial observations cannot constitute an order binding on the editor or the reporter although it is anticipated that a responsible editor would consider them carefully before deciding what should be published. It remains the responsibility of those reporting a case to ensure that restrictions are not breached.

6B.3 Before exercising its discretion to impose a restriction the court must follow precisely the statutory provisions under which the order is to be made, paying particular regard to what has to be established, by whom and to what standard.

6B.4 Without prejudice to the above paragraph, certain general principles apply to the exercise of the court's discretion:

(a) The court must have regard to CrimPR Parts 6 and 18.

(b) The court must keep in mind the fact that every order is a departure from the general principle that proceedings shall be open and freely reported.

(c) Before making any order the court must be satisfied that the purpose of the proposed order cannot be achieved by some lesser measure e.g., the grant of special measures, screens or the clearing of the public gallery (usually subject to a representative(s) of the media remaining).

(d) The terms of the order must be proportionate so as to comply with Article 10 ECHR (freedom of expression).

(e) No order should be made without giving other parties to the proceedings and any other interested party, including any representative of the media, an opportunity to make representations.
(f) Any order should provide for any interested party who has not been present or represented at the time of the making of the order to have permission to apply within a limited period e.g., 24 hours.
(g) The wording of the order is the responsibility of the judge or Bench making the order: it must be in precise terms and, if practicable, agreed with the advocates.
(h) The order must be in writing and must state:
  (i) the power under which it is made;
  (ii) its precise scope and purpose; and
  (iii) the time at which it shall cease to have effect, if appropriate.
(i) The order must specify, in every case, whether or not the making or terms of the order may be reported or whether this itself is prohibited. Such a report could cause the very mischief which the order was intended to prevent.

6B.5 A series of template orders have been prepared by the Judicial College and are available as an appendix to the Crown Court Bench Book Companion; these template orders should generally be used.

6B.6 A copy of the order should be provided to any person known to have an interest in reporting the proceedings and to any local or national media who regularly report proceedings in the court.

6B.7 Court staff should be prepared to answer any enquiry about a specific case; but it is and will remain the responsibility of anyone reporting a case to ensure that no breach of any order occurs and the onus rests on such person to make enquiry in case of doubt.

PD-22 CPD I General Matters 6C: Use of live text-based forms of communication (including *Twitter*) from court for the purposes of fair and accurate reporting

6C.1 This part clarifies the use which may be made of live text-based communications, such as mobile email, social media (including *Twitter*) and internet-enabled laptops in and from courts throughout England and Wales. For the purpose of this part these means of communication are referred to, compendiously, as 'live text-based communications'. It is consistent with the legislative structure which:
(a) prohibits:
  (i) the taking of photographs in court (section 41 of the Criminal Justice Act 1925);
  (ii) the use of sound recording equipment in court unless the leave of the judge has first been obtained (section 9 of the Contempt of Court Act 1981); and
(b) requires compliance with the strict prohibition rules created by sections 1, 2 and 4 of the Contempt of Court Act 1981 in relation to the reporting of court proceedings.

General Principles

6C.2 The judge has an overriding responsibility to ensure that proceedings are conducted consistently, with the proper administration of justice, and to avoid any improper interference with its processes.

6C.3 A fundamental aspect of the proper administration of justice is the principle of open justice. Fair and accurate reporting of court proceedings forms part of that principle. The principle is, however, subject to well-known statutory and discretionary exceptions. Two such exceptions are the prohibitions, set out in paragraph 6C.1(a), on photography in court and on making sound recordings of court proceedings.

6C.4 The statutory prohibition on photography in court, by any means, is absolute. There is no judicial discretion to suspend or dispense with it. Any equipment which has photographic capability must not have that function activated.

6C.5 Sound recordings are also prohibited unless, in the exercise of its discretion, the court permits such equipment to be used. In criminal proceedings, some of the factors relevant to the exercise of that discretion are contained in paragraph 6A.2. The same factors are likely to be relevant when consideration is being given to the exercise of this discretion in civil or family proceedings.

Use of Live Text-based Communications: General Considerations

6C.6 The normal, indeed almost invariable, rule has been that mobile phones must be turned off in court. There is however no statutory prohibition on the use of live text-based communications in open court.

6C.7 Where a member of the public, who is in court, wishes to use live text-based communications during court proceedings an application for permission to activate and use, in silent mode, a mobile phone, small laptop or similar piece of equipment, solely in order to make live text-based communications of the proceedings will need to be made. The application may be made formally or informally (for instance by communicating a request to the judge through court staff).

6C.8 It is presumed that a representative of the media or a legal commentator using live text-based communications from court does not pose a danger of interference to the proper administration of justice in the individual case. This is because the most obvious purpose of permitting the use of live text-based communications would be to enable the media to produce fair and accurate reports of the proceedings. As such, a representative of the media or a legal commentator who wishes to use live text-based communications from court may do so without making an application to the court.

6C.9 When considering, either generally on its own motion, or following a formal application or informal request by a member of the public, whether to permit live text-based communications, and if so by whom, the paramount question for the judge will be whether the application may interfere with the proper administration of justice.

6C.10 In considering the question of permission, the factors listed in paragraph 6A.2 are likely to be relevant.

6C.11 Without being exhaustive, the danger to the administration of justice is likely to be at its most acute in the context of criminal trials e.g., where witnesses who are out of court may be informed of what has already happened in court and so coached or briefed before they then give evidence, or where information posted on, for instance, *Twitter* about inadmissible evidence may influence members of the jury. However, the danger is not confined to criminal proceedings; in civil and sometimes family proceedings, simultaneous reporting from the courtroom may create pressure on witnesses, by distracting or worrying them.

6C.12 It may be necessary for the judge to limit live text-based communications to representatives of the media for journalistic purposes but to disallow its use by the wider public in court. That may arise if it is necessary, for example, to limit the number of mobile electronic devices in use at any given time because of the potential for electronic interference with the court's own sound recording equipment, or because the widespread use of such devices in court may cause a distraction in the proceedings.

6C.13 Subject to these considerations, the use of an unobtrusive, hand-held, silent piece of modern equipment, for the purposes of simultaneous reporting of proceedings to the outside world as they unfold in court, is generally unlikely to interfere with the proper administration of justice.

6C.14 Permission to use live text-based communications from court may be withdrawn by the court at any time.

CPD I General matters 6D: Taking Notes in Court PD-23

6D.1 As long as it does not interfere with the proper administration of justice, anyone who attends a court hearing may quietly take notes, on paper or by silent electronic means. If that person is a participant, including an expert witness who is in the courtroom under CrimPR 24.4(2)(a)(ii) or 25.11(2)(a)(ii), note taking may be an essential aid to that person's own or (if they are a representative) to their client's effective participation. If that person is a reporter or a member of the public, attending a hearing to which, by definition, they have been admitted, note taking is a feature of the principle of open justice. The permission of the court is not required, and the distinctions between members of the public and others which are drawn at paragraphs 6C.7 and 6C.8 of these Practice Directions do not apply.

6D.2 However, where there is reason to suspect that the taking of notes may be for an unlawful purpose, or that it may disrupt the proceedings, then it is entirely proper for court staff to make appropriate enquiries, and ultimately it is within the power of the court to prohibit note taking by a specified individual or individuals in the court room if that is necessary and proportionate to prevent unlawful conduct. If, for example, there is reason to believe that notes are being taken in order to influence the testimony of a witness who is due to give evidence, perhaps by briefing that witness on what another witness has said, then because such conduct is unlawful (it is likely to be in contempt of court, and it may constitute a perversion of the course of justice) it is within the court's power to prohibit such note taking. If there is reason to believe that what purports to be taking notes with an electronic device is in fact the transmission of live text-based communications from court without the permission required by paragraph 6C.7 of these Practice Directions, or where permission to transmit such communications has been withdrawn under paragraph 6C.14, then that, too, would constitute grounds for prohibiting the taking of such notes.

6D.3 The existence of a reporting restriction, without more, is not a sufficient reason to prohibit note taking (though it may need to be made clear to those who take notes that the reporting restriction affects how much, if any, of what they have noted may be communicated to anyone else). However, if there is reason to believe that notes are being taken in order to facilitate the contravention of a reporting restriction then that, too, would constitute grounds for prohibiting such note taking.

Criminal Procedure Rules Part 7 Starting a Prosecution in a Magistrates' Court

R-67 When this Part applies

7.1 (1) This Part applies in a magistrates' court where—

(a) a prosecutor wants the court to issue a summons or warrant under section 1 of the Magistrates' Courts Act 1980;

(b) a prosecutor with the power to do so issues—

(i) a written charge and requisition, or

(ii) a written charge and single justice procedure notice under section 29 of the Criminal Justice Act 2003; or

(c) a person who is in custody is charged with an offence.

(2) In this Part, 'authorised prosecutor' means a prosecutor authorised under section 29 of the Criminal Justice Act 2003 to issue a written charge and requisition or single justice procedure notice.

R-68 Application for summons, etc.

7.2 (1) A prosecutor who wants the court to issue a summons must—

(a) serve on the court officer a written application; or

(b) unless other legislation prohibits this, present an application orally to the court, with a written statement of the allegation or allegations made by the prosecutor.

(2) A prosecutor who wants the court to issue a warrant must—

(a) serve on the court officer—

(i) a written application, or

(ii) a copy of a written charge that has been issued; or

(b) present to the court either of those documents.

(3) An application for the issue of a summons or warrant must—

(a) set out the allegation or allegations made by the applicant in terms that comply with rule 7.3 (Allegation of offence in application or charge); and

(b) demonstrate—

(i) that the application is made in time, if legislation imposes a time limit, and

(ii) that the applicant has the necessary consent, if legislation requires it.

(4) As well as complying with paragraph (3), an application for the issue of a warrant must—

(a) demonstrate that the offence or offences alleged can be tried in the Crown Court;

(b) demonstrate that the offence or offences alleged can be punished with imprisonment; or

(c) concisely outline the applicant's grounds for asserting that the defendant's address is not sufficiently established for a summons to be served.

(5) Paragraph (6) applies unless the prosecutor is—

(a) a public authority within the meaning of section 17 of the Prosecution of Offences Act 1985; or

(b) a person acting—

(i) on behalf of such an authority, or

(ii) in that person's capacity as an official appointed by such an authority.

(6) Where this paragraph applies, as well as complying with paragraph (3), and with paragraph (4) if applicable, an application for the issue of a summons or warrant must—

(a) concisely outline the grounds for asserting that the defendant has committed the alleged offence or offences;

(b) disclose—

(i) details of any previous such application by the same applicant in respect of any allegation now made, and

(ii) details of any current or previous proceedings brought by another prosecutor in respect of any allegation now made; and

(c) include a statement that to the best of the applicant's knowledge, information and belief—

(i) the allegations contained in the application are substantially true,

(ii) the evidence on which the applicant relies will be available at the trial,

(iii) the details given by the applicant under paragraph (6)(b) are true, and

(iv) the application discloses all the information that is material to what the court must decide

(7) Where the statement required by paragraph (6)(c) is made orally—

(a) the statement must be on oath or affirmation, unless the court otherwise directs; and

(b) the court must arrange for a record of the making of the statement.

(8) An authorised prosecutor who issues a written charge must notify the court officer immediately.

(9) A single document may contain—

(a) more than one application; or

(b) more than one written charge.

(10) Where an offence can be tried only in a magistrates' court, then unless other legislation otherwise provides—

(a) a prosecutor must serve an application for the issue of a summons or warrant on the court officer or present it to the court; or

(b) an authorised prosecutor must issue a written charge, not more than 6 months after the offence alleged.

(11) Where an offence can be tried in the Crown Court then—

(a) a prosecutor must serve an application for the issue of a summons or warrant on the court officer or present it to the court; or

(b) an authorised prosecutor must issue a written charge, within any time limit that applies to that offence.

(12) The court may determine an application to issue or withdraw a summons or warrant—

(a) without a hearing, as a general rule, or at a hearing (which must be in private unless the court otherwise directs);

(b) in the absence of—

(i) the prosecutor,

(ii) the defendant;

(c) with or without representations by the defendant.

(13) If the court so directs, a party to an application to issue or withdraw a summons or warrant may attend a hearing by live link or telephone.

Allegation of offence in application for summons, etc. or charge **R-69**

7.3 (1) An allegation of an offences in an application for the issue of a summons or warrant or in a charge must contain—

(a) a statement of the offence that—

(i) describes the offence in ordinary language, and

(ii) identifies any legislation that creates it; and

(b) such particulars of the conduct constituting the commission of the offence as to make clear what the prosecutor alleges against the defendant.

(2) More than one incident of the commission of the offence may be included in the allegation if those incidents taken together amount to a course of conduct having regard to the time, place or purpose of commission.

Summons, warrant and requisition **R-70**

7.4 (1) A summons, warrant or requisition may be issued in respect of more than one offence.

(2) A summons or requisition must—

(a) contain notice of when and where the defendant is required to attend the court;

(b) specify each offence in respect of which it is issued;

(c) in the case of a summons, identify—

(i) the court that issued it, unless that is otherwise recorded by the court officer, and

(ii) the court office for the court that issued it; and

(d) in the case of a requisition, identify the person under whose authority it is issued.

(3) A summons may be contained in the same document as an application for the issue of that summons.

(4) A requisition may be contained in the same document as a written charge.

(5) Where the court issues a summons—

(a) the prosecutor must—

(i) serve it on the defendant, and

(ii) notify the court officer; or

(b) the court officer must—

(i) serve it on the defendant, and

(ii) notify the prosecutor.

(6) Where an authorised prosecutor issues a requisition that prosecutor must—

(a) serve on the defendant—

(i) the requisition, and

(ii) the written charge; and

(b) serve a copy of each on the court officer.

(7) Unless it would be inconsistent with other legislation, a replacement summons or requisition may be issued without a fresh information or written charge where the one replaced—

(a) Was served under rule 4.4 (Service by leaving or posting a document) ; but

(b) is shown not to have been received by the addressee.

(8) A summons or requisition issued to a defendant under 18 may require that defendant's parent or guardian to attend the court with the defendant, or a separate summons or requisition may be issued for that purpose.

Criminal Procedure Rules Part 8 Initial Details of the Prosecution Case

R-71 **When this Part applies**

8.1 This Part applies in a magistrates' court.

R-72 **Providing initial details of the prosecution case**

8.2 (1) The prosecutor must serve initial details of the prosecution case on the court officer—

(a) as soon as practicable; and

(b) in any event, no later than the beginning of the day of the first hearing.

(2) Where a defendant requests those details, the prosecutor must serve them on the defendant—

(a) as soon as practicable; and

(b) in any event, no later than the beginning of the day of the first hearing.

(3) Where a defendant does not request those details, the prosecutor must make them available to the defendant at, or before, the beginning of the day of the first hearing.

R-73 **Content of initial details**

8.3 Initial details of the prosecution case must include—

(a) where, immediately before the first hearing in the magistrates' court, the defendant was in police custody for the offence charged—

(i) a summary of the circumstances of the offence, and

(ii) the defendant's criminal record, if any;

(b) where paragraph (a) does not apply—

(i) a summary of the circumstances of the offence,

(ii) any account given by the defendant in interview, whether contained in that summary or in another document,

(iii) any written witness statement or exhibit that the prosecutor then has available and considers material to plea, or to the allocation of the case for trial, or to sentence,

(iv) the defendant's criminal record, if any, and

(v) any available statement of the effect of the offence on a victim, a victim's family or others.

R-74 **Use of initial details**

8.4 (1) This rule applies where—

(a) the prosecutor wants to introduce information contained in a document listed in rule 8.3; and

(b) the prosecutor has not—

(i) served that document on the defendant, or

(ii) made that information available to the defendant.

(2) The court must not allow the prosecutor to introduce that information unless the court first allows the defendant sufficient time to consider it.

Criminal Practice Directions Part 8 Initial Details of the Prosecution Case

CPD II Preliminary proceedings 8A: Defendant's Record PD-24

Copies of record

8A.1 The defendant's record (previous convictions, cautions, reprimands, etc) may be taken into account when the court decides not only on sentence but also, for example, about bail, or when allocating a case for trial. It is therefore important that up to date and accurate information is available. Previous convictions must be provided as part of the initial details of the prosecution case under CrimPR Part 8.

8A.2 The record should usually be provided in the following format:

Personal details and summary of convictions and cautions—Police National Computer ['PNC'] Court/Defence/Probation Summary Sheet;

Previous convictions — PNC Court/Defence/Probation printout, supplemented by Form MG16 if the police force holds convictions not shown on PNC;

Recorded cautions—PNC Court/Defence/Probation printout, supplemented by Form MG17 if the police force holds cautions not shown on PNC.

8A.3 The defence representative should take instructions on the defendant's record and if the defence wish to raise any objection to the record, this should be made known to the prosecutor immediately.

8A.4 It is the responsibility of the prosecutor to ensure that a copy of the defendant's record has been provided to the Probation Service.

8A.5 Where following conviction a custodial order is made, the court must ensure that a copy is attached to the order sent to the prison.

Additional information

8A.6 In the Crown Court, the police should also provide brief details of the circumstances of the last three similar convictions and/or of convictions likely to be of interest to the court, the latter being judged on a case-by-case basis.

8A.7 Where the current alleged offence could constitute a breach of an existing sentence such as a suspended sentence, community order or conditional discharge, and it is known that that sentence is still in force then details of the circumstances of the offence leading to the sentence should be included in the antecedents. The detail should be brief and include the date of the offence.

8A.8 On occasions the PNC printout provided may not be fully up to date. It is the responsibility of the prosecutor to ensure that all of the necessary information is available to the court and the Probation Service and provided to the defence. Oral updates at the hearing will sometimes be necessary, but it is preferable if this information is available in advance.

Criminal Procedure Rules Part 9 Allocation and Sending for Trial

General rules

When this Part applies R-75

9.1 (1) This Part applies to the allocation and sending of cases for trial under—

(a) sections 17A to 26 of the Magistrates' Courts Act 1980; and

(b) sections 50A to 52 of the Crime and Disorder Act 1998.

(2) Rules 9.6 and 9.7 apply in a magistrates' court where the court must, or can, send a defendant to the Crown Court for trial, without allocating the case for trial there.

(3) Rules 9.8 to 9.14 apply in a magistrates' court where the court must allocate the case to a magistrates' court or to the Crown Court for trial.

(4) Rules 9.15 and 9.16 apply in the Crown Court, where a defendant is sent for trial there.

Exercise of magistrates' court's powers R-76

9.2 (1) This rule applies to the exercise of the powers to which rules 9.6 to 9.14 apply.

(2) The general rule is that the court must exercise its powers at a hearing in public, but it may exercise any power it has to—

(a) withhold information from the public; or

(b) order a hearing in private.

(3) The general rule is that the court must exercise its powers in the defendant's presence, but it may exercise the powers to which the following rules apply in the defendant's absence on the conditions specified—
 (a) where rule 9.8 (Adult defendant: request for plea), rule 9.9 (Adult defendant: guilty plea) or rule 9.13 (Young defendant) applies, if—
  (i) the defendant is represented, and
  (ii) the defendant's disorderly conduct makes his or her presence in the courtroom impracticable;
 (b) where rule 9.10 (Adult defendant: not guilty plea) or rule 9.11 (Adult defendant: allocation for magistrates' court trial) applies, if—
  (i) the defendant is represented and waives the right to be present, or
  (ii) the defendant's disorderly conduct makes his or her presence in the courtroom impracticable.

(4) The court may exercise its power to adjourn—
 (a) if either party asks; or
 (b) on its own initiative.

(5) Where the court on the same occasion deals with two or more offences alleged against the same defendant, the court must deal with those offences in the following sequence—
 (a) any to which rule 9.6 applies (Prosecutor's notice requiring Crown Court trial);
 (b) any to which rule 9.7 applies (sending for Crown Court trial, without allocation there), in this sequence—
  (i) any the court must send for trial, then
  (ii) any the court can send for trial; and
 (c) any to which rule 9.14 applies (Allocation and sending for Crown Court trial).

(6) Where the court on the same occasion deals with two or more defendants charged jointly with an offence that can be tried in the Crown Court then in the following sequence—
 (a) the court must explain, in terms each defendant can understand (with help, if necessary), that if the court sends one of them to the Crown Court for trial then the court must send for trial in the Crown Court, too, any other of them—
  (i) who is charged with the same offence as the defendant sent for trial, or with an offence which the court decides is related to that offence,
  (ii) who does not wish to plead guilty to each offence with which he or she is charged, and
  (iii) (if that other defendant is under 18, and the court would not otherwise have sent him or her for Crown Court trial) where the court decides that sending is necessary in the interests of justice
 even if the court by then has decided to allocate that other defendant for magistrates' court trial; and
 (b) the court may ask the defendants questions to help it decide in what order to deal with them.

(7) After following paragraph (5), if it applies, where the court on the same occasion—
 (a) deals with two or more defendants charged jointly with an offence that can be tried in the Crown Court;
 (b) allocates any of them to a magistrates' court for trial; and
 (c) then sends another one of them to the Crown Court for trial,
the court must deal again with each one whom, on that occasion, it has allocated for magistrates' court trial.

R-77 Matters to be specified on sending for trial

9.3 (1) Where the court sends a defendant to the Crown Court for trial, it must specify—
 (a) each offence to be tried;
 (b) in respect of each, the power exercised to send the defendant for trial for that offence; and
 (c) the Crown Court centre at which the trial will take place.

(2) In a case in which the prosecutor serves a notice to which rule 9.6(1)(a) applies (notice requiring Crown Court trial in a case of serious or complex fraud), the court must specify the Crown Court centre identified by that notice.

(3) In any other case, in deciding the Crown Court centre at which the trial will take place, the court must take into account—
 (a) the convenience of the parties and witnesses;

(b) how soon a suitable courtroom will be available; and
(c) the directions on the allocation of Crown Court business contained in the Practice Direction.

Duty of justices' legal adviser R-78

9.4 (1) This rule applies—
(a) only in a magistrates' court; and
(b) unless the court—
(i) includes a District Judge (Magistrates' Courts), and
(ii) otherwise directs.
(2) On the court's behalf, a justices' legal adviser may—
(a) read the allegation of the offence to the defendant;
(b) give any explanation and ask any question required by the rules in this Part;
(c) make any announcement required by the rules in this Part, other than an announcement of—
(i) the court's decisions about allocation and sending,
(ii) any indication by the court of likely sentence, or
(iii) sentence.
(3) A justices' legal adviser must—
(a) assist an unrepresented defendant;
(b) give the court such advice as is required to enable it to exercise its powers;
(c) if required, attend the members of the court outside the courtroom to give such advice, but inform the parties of any advice so given.

Duty of magistrates' court officer R-79

9.5 (1) The magistrates' court officer must—
(a) serve notice of a sending for Crown Court trial on—
(i) the Crown Court officer, and
(ii) the parties;
(b) in that notice record—
(i) the matters specified by the court under rule 9.3 (Matters to be specified on sending for trial),
(ii) any indication of intended guilty plea given by the defendant under rule 9.7 (Sending for Crown Court trial),
(iii) any decision by the defendant to decline magistrates' court trial under rule 9.11 (Adult defendant: allocation to magistrates' court for trial), and
(iv) the date on which any custody time limit will expire;
(c) record any indication of likely sentence to which rule 9.11 applies; and
(d) give the court such other assistance as it requires.
(2) The magistrates' court officer must include with the notice served on the Crown Court officer—
(a) the initial details of the prosecution case served by the prosecutor under rule 8.2;
(b) a record of any—
(i) listing or case management direction affecting the Crown Court,
(ii) direction about reporting restrictions,
(iii) decision about bail, for the purposes of section 5 of the Bail Act 1976,
(iv) recognizance given by a surety, or
(v) representation order; and
(c) if relevant, any available details of any—
(i) interpreter,
(ii) intermediary, or
(iii) other supporting adult, where the defendant is assisted by such a person.

Sending without allocation for Crown Court trial

Prosecutor's notice requiring Crown Court trial R-80

9.6 (1) This rule applies where a prosecutor with power to do so requires a magistrates' court to send for trial in the Crown Court—
(a) a case of serious or complex fraud; or
(b) a case which will involve a child witness.
(2) The prosecutor must serve notice of that requirement—
(a) on the magistrates' court officer and on the defendant; and

(b) before trial in a magistrates' court begins under Part 24 (Trial and sentence in a magistrates' court).

(3) The notice must identify—

(a) the power on which the prosecutor relies; and

(b) the Crown Court centre at which the prosecutor wants the trial to take place.

(4) The prosecutor—

(a) must, when choosing a Crown Court centre, take into account the matters listed in rule 9.3(3) (court deciding to which Crown Court centre to send a case); and

(b) may change the centre identified before the case is sent for trial.

R-81 **Sending for Crown Court trial**

9.7 (1) This rule applies where a magistrates' court must, or can, send a defendant to the Crown Court for trial without first allocating the case for trial there.

(2) The court must read the allegation of the offence to the defendant.

(3) The court must explain, in terms the defendant can understand (with help, if necessary)—

(a) the allegation, unless it is self-explanatory;

(b) that the offence is one for which the court, as appropriate—

(i) must send the defendant to the Crown Court for trial because the offence is one which can only be tried there or because the court for some other reason is required to send that offence for trial,

(ii) may send the defendant to the Crown Court for trial if the magistrates' court decides that the offence is related to one already sent for trial there; or

(iii) (where the offence is low-value shoplifting and the defendant is 18 or over) must send the defendant to the Crown Court for trial if the defendant wants to be tried there;

(c) that reporting restrictions apply, which the defendant may ask the court to vary or remove.

(4) In the following sequence, the court must then—

(a) invite the prosecutor to—

(i) identify the court's power to send the defendant to the Crown Court for trial for the offence, and

(ii) make representations about any ancillary matters, including bail and directions for the management of the case in the Crown Court;

(b) invite the defendant to make representations about—

(i) the court's power to send the defendant to the Crown Court, and

(ii) any ancillary matters;

(c) (where the offence is low-value shoplifting and the defendant is 18 or over) offer the defendant the opportunity to require trial in the Crown Court; and

(d) decide whether or not to send the defendant to the Crown Court for trial.

(5) If the court sends the defendant to the Crown Court for trial, it must—

(a) ask whether the defendant intends to plead guilty in the Crown Court and—

(i) if the answer is 'yes', make arrangements for the Crown Court to take the defendant's plea as soon as possible, or

(ii) if the defendant does not answer, or the answer is 'no', make arrangements for a case management hearing in the Crown Court; and

(b) give any other ancillary directions.

Allocation for magistrates' court or Crown Court trial

R-82 **Adult defendant: request for plea**

9.8 (1) This rule applies where—

(a) the defendant is 18 or over; and

(b) the court must decide whether a case is more suitable for trial in a magistrates' court or in the Crown Court.

(2) The court must read the allegation of the offence to the defendant.

(3) The court must explain, in terms the defendant can understand (with help, if necessary)—

(a) the allegation, unless it is self-explanatory;

(b) that the offence is one which can be tried in a magistrates' court or in the Crown Court;

(c) that the court is about to ask whether the defendant intends to plead guilty;

(d) that if the answer is 'yes', then the court must treat that as a guilty plea and must sentence the defendant, or commit the defendant to the Crown Court for sentence;

(e) that if the defendant does not answer, or the answer is 'no', then—
(i) the court must decide whether to allocate the case to a magistrates' court or to the Crown Court for trial,
(ii) the value involved may require the court to order trial in a magistrates' court (where the offence is one to which section 22 of the Magistrates' Courts Act 1980 applies), and
(iii) if the court allocates the case to a magistrates' court for trial, the defendant can nonetheless require trial in the Crown Court (unless the offence is one to which section 22 of the Magistrates' Courts Act 1980 applies and the value involved requires magistrates' court trial); and
(f) that reporting restrictions apply, which the defendant may ask the court to vary or remove.
(4) The court must then ask whether the defendant intends to plead guilty.

Adult defendant: guilty plea R-83

9.9 (1) This rule applies where—
(a) rule 9.8 applies; and
(b) the defendant indicates an intention to plead guilty.
(2) The court must exercise its power to deal with the case—
(a) as if the defendant had just pleaded guilty at a trial in a magistrates' court; and
(b) in accordance with rule 24.11 (Procedure if the court convicts).

Adult defendant: not guilty plea R-84

9.10 (1) This rule applies where—
(a) rule 9.8 applies; and
(b) the defendant—
(i) indicates an intention to plead not guilty, or
(ii) gives no indication of intended plea.
(2) In the following sequence, the court must then—
(a) where the offence is one to which section 22 of the Magistrates' Courts Act 1980 applies, explain in terms the defendant can understand (with help, if necessary) that—
(i) if the court decides that the value involved clearly is less than £5,000, the court must order trial in a magistrates' court,
(ii) if the court decides that it is not clear whether that value is more or less than £5,000, then the court will ask whether the defendant agrees to be tried in a magistrates' court, and
(iii) if the answer to that question is 'yes', then the court must order such a trial and if the defendant is convicted then the maximum sentence is limited;
(b) invite the prosecutor to—
(i) identify any previous convictions of which it can take account, and
(ii) make representations about how the court should allocate the case for trial, including representations about the value involved, if relevant;
(c) invite the defendant to make such representations;
(d) where the offence is one to which section 22 of the Magistrates' Courts Act 1980 applies—
(i) if it is not clear whether the value involved is more or less than £5,000, ask whether the defendant agrees to be tried in a magistrates' court,
(ii) if the defendant's answer to that question is 'yes', or if that value clearly is less than £5,000, order a trial in a magistrates' court,
(iii) if the defendant does not answer that question, or the answer is 'no', or if that value clearly is more than £5,000, apply paragraph (2)(e);
(e) exercise its power to allocate the case for trial, taking into account—
(i) the adequacy of a magistrates' court's sentencing powers,
(ii) any representations by the parties, and
(iii) any allocation guidelines issued by the Sentencing Council.

Adult defendant: allocation for magistrates' court trial R-85

9.11 (1) This rule applies where—
(a) rule 9.10 applies; and
(b) the court allocates the case to a magistrates' court for trial.
(2) The court must explain, in terms the defendant can understand (with help, if necessary) that—
(a) the court considers the case more suitable for trial in a magistrates' court than in the Crown Court;

(b) if the defendant is convicted at a magistrates' court trial, then in some circumstances the court may commit the defendant to the Crown Court for sentence;
(c) if the defendant does not agree to a magistrates' court trial, then the court must send the defendant to the Crown Court for trial; and
(d) before deciding whether to accept magistrates' court trial, the defendant may ask the court for an indication of whether a custodial or non-custodial sentence is more likely in the event of a guilty plea at such a trial, but the court need not give such an indication.

(3) If the defendant asks for such an indication of sentence and the court gives such an indication—
(a) the court must then ask again whether the defendant intends to plead guilty;
(b) if, in answer to that question, the defendant indicates an intention to plead guilty, then the court must exercise its power to deal with the case—
(i) as if the defendant had just pleaded guilty to an offence that can be tried only in a magistrates' court, and
(ii) in accordance with rule 24.11 (Procedure if the court convicts);
(c) if, in answer to that question, the defendant indicates an intention to plead not guilty, or gives no indication of intended plea, in the following sequence the court must then—
(i) ask whether the defendant agrees to trial in a magistrates' court,
(ii) if the defendant's answer to that question is 'yes', order such a trial,
(iii) if the defendant does not answer that question, or the answer is 'no', apply rule 9.14.

(4) If the defendant asks for an indication of sentence but the court gives none, or if the defendant does not ask for such an indication, in the following sequence the court must then—
(a) ask whether the defendant agrees to trial in a magistrates' court;
(b) if the defendant's answer to that question is 'yes', order such a trial;
(c) if the defendant does not answer that question, or the answer is 'no', apply rule 9.14.

R-86 Adult defendant: prosecutor's application for Crown Court trial

9.12 (1) This rule applies where—
(a) rule 9.11 applies;
(b) the defendant agrees to trial in a magistrates' court; but
(c) the prosecutor wants the court to exercise its power to send the defendant to the Crown Court for trial instead.

(2) The prosecutor must—
(a) apply before trial in a magistrates' court begins under Part 24 (Trial and sentence in a magistrates' court); and
(b) notify—
(i) the defendant, and
(ii) the magistrates' court officer.

(3) The court must determine an application to which this rule applies before it deals with any other pre-trial application.

R-87 Young defendant

9.13 (1) This rule applies where—
(a) the defendant is under 18; and
(b) the court must decide whether to send the defendant for Crown Court trial instead of ordering trial in a youth court.

(2) The court must read the allegation of the offence to the defendant.

(3) The court must explain, in terms the defendant can understand (with help, if necessary)—
(a) the allegation, unless it is self-explanatory;
(b) that the offence is one which can be tried in the Crown Court instead of in a youth court;
(c) that the court is about to ask whether the defendant intends to plead guilty;
(d) that if the answer is 'yes', then the court must treat that as a guilty plea and must sentence the defendant, or commit the defendant to the Crown Court for sentence;
(e) that if the defendant does not answer, or the answer is 'no', then the court must decide whether to send the defendant for Crown Court trial instead of ordering trial in a youth court; and
(f) that reporting restrictions apply, which the defendant may ask the court to vary or remove.

(4) The court must then ask whether the defendant intends to plead guilty.

(5) If the defendant's answer to that question is 'yes', the court must exercise its power to deal with the case—
(a) as if the defendant had just pleaded guilty at a trial in a youth court; and
(b) in accordance with rule 24.11 (Procedure if the court convicts).
(6) If the defendant does not answer that question, or the answer is 'no', in the following sequence the court must then—
(a) invite the prosecutor to make representations about whether Crown Court or youth court trial is more appropriate;
(b) invite the defendant to make such representations;
(c) exercise its power to allocate the case for trial, taking into account—
(i) the offence and the circumstances of the offence,
(ii) the suitability of a youth court's sentencing powers,
(iii) where the defendant is jointly charged with an adult, whether it is necessary in the interests of justice for them to be tried together in the Crown Court, and
(iv) any representations by the parties.

Allocation and sending for Crown Court trial R-88

9.14 (1) This rule applies where—
(a) under rule 9.10 or rule 9.13, the court allocates the case to the Crown Court for trial;
(b) under rule 9.11, the defendant does not agree to trial in a magistrates' court; or
(c) under rule 9.12, the court grants the prosecutor's application for Crown Court trial.
(2) In the following sequence, the court must—
(a) invite the prosecutor to make representations about any ancillary matters, including bail and directions for the management of the case in the Crown Court;
(b) invite the defendant to make any such representations; and
(c) exercise its powers to—
(i) send the defendant to the Crown Court for trial, and
(ii) give any ancillary directions.

Crown Court initial procedure after sending for trial

Service of prosecution evidence R-89

9.15 (1) This rule applies where—
(a) a magistrates' court sends the defendant to the Crown Court for trial; and
(b) the prosecutor serves on the defendant copies of the documents containing the evidence on which the prosecution case relies.
(2) The prosecutor must at the same time serve copies of those documents on the Crown Court officer.

Application to dismiss offence sent for Crown Court trial R-90

9.16 (1) This rule applies where a defendant wants the Crown Court to dismiss an offence sent for trial there.
(2) The defendant must—
(a) apply in writing—
(i) not more than 28 days after service of the prosecution evidence, and
(ii) before the defendant's arraignment;
(b) serve the application on—
(i) the Crown Court officer, and
(ii) each other party;
(c) in the application—
(i) explain why the prosecution evidence would not be sufficient for the defendant to be properly convicted,
(ii) ask for a hearing, if the defendant wants one, and explain why it is needed,
(iii) identify any witness whom the defendant wants to call to give evidence in person, with an indication of what evidence the witness can give,
(iv) identify any material already served that the defendant thinks the court will need to determine the application, and
(v) include any material not already served on which the defendant relies.
(3) A prosecutor who opposes the application must—
(a) serve notice of opposition, not more than 14 days after service of the defendant's notice, on—
(i) the Crown Court officer, and
(ii) each other party;

(b) in the notice of opposition—
(i) explain the grounds of opposition,
(ii) ask for a hearing, if the prosecutor wants one, and explain why it is needed,
(iii) identify any witness whom the prosecutor wants to call to give evidence in person, with an indication of what evidence the witness can give,
(iv) identify any material already served that the prosecutor thinks the court will need to determine the application, and
(v) include any material not already served on which the prosecutor relies.

(4) The court may determine an application under this rule—
(a) at a hearing, in public or in private, or without a hearing;
(b) in the absence of—
(i) the defendant who made the application,
(ii) the prosecutor, if the prosecutor has had at least 14 days in which to serve notice opposing the application.

(5) The court may—
(a) shorten or extend (even after it has expired) a time limit under this rule;
(b) allow a witness to give evidence in person even if that witness was not identified in the defendant's application or in the prosecutor's notice.

Criminal Practice Directions Part 9 Allocation and Sending for Trial

PD-25 **CPD II Preliminary proceedings 9A: Allocation (Mode of Trial)**

9A.1 Courts must follow the Sentencing Council's guideline on Allocation (mode of trial) when deciding whether or not to send defendants charged with 'either way' offences for trial in the Crown Court under section 51(1) of the Crime and Disorder Act 1998.

Criminal Procedure Rules Part 10 The Indictment

R-91 **When this Part applies**

10.1 This Part applies where—
(a) a magistrates' court sends a defendant to the Crown Court for trial under section 51 or section 51A of the Crime and Disorder Act 1998;
(b) a prosecutor wants a High Court judge's permission to serve a draft indictment;
(c) the Crown Court approves a proposed indictment under paragraph 2 of Schedule 17 to the Crime and Courts Act 2013 and rule 11.4 (Deferred prosecution agreements: Application to approve the terms of an agreement);
(d) a prosecutor wants to re-institute proceedings in the Crown Court under section 22B of the Prosecution of Offences Act 1985;
(e) the Court of Appeal orders a retrial, under section 8 of the Criminal Appeal Act 1968 or under section 77 of the Criminal Justice Act 2003.

R-92 **The indictment: general rules**

10.2 (1) The indictment on which the defendant is arraigned under rule 3.24 (Arraigning the defendant on the indictment) must be in writing and must contain, in a paragraph called a 'count'—
(a) a statement of the offence charged that—
(i) describes the offence in ordinary language, and
(ii) identifies any legislation that creates it; and
(b) such particulars of the conduct constituting the commission of the offence as to make clear what the prosecutor alleges against the defendant.

(2) More than one incident of the commission of the offence may be included in a count if those incidents taken together amount to a course of conduct having regard to the time, place or purpose of commission.

(3) The counts must be numbered consecutively.

(4) An indictment may contain—
(a) any count charging substantially the same offence as one for which the defendant was sent for trial;
(b) any count contained in a draft indictment served with the permission of a High Court judge or at the direction of the Court of Appeal; and
(c) any other count charging an offence that the Crown Court can try and which is based on the prosecution evidence that has been served.

(5) For the purposes of section 2 of the Administration of Justice (Miscellaneous Provisions) Act 1933—
(a) a draft indictment constitutes a bill of indictment;
(b) the draft, or bill, is preferred before the Crown Court and becomes the indictment—

(i) where rule 10.3 applies (Draft indictment generated electronically on sending for trial), immediately before the first count (or the only count, if there is only one) is read to or placed before the defendant to take the defendant's plea under rule 3.24(1)(d),
(ii) when the prosecutor serves the draft indictment on the Crown Court officer, where rule 10.4 (Draft indictment served by the prosecutor after sending for trial), rule 10.5 (Draft indictment served by the prosecutor with a High Court judge's permission), rule 10.7 (Draft indictment served by the prosecutor on re-instituting proceedings) or rule 10.8 (Draft indictment served by the prosecutor at the direction of the Court of Appeal) applies,
(iii) when the Crown Court approves the proposed indictment, where rule 10.6 applies (Draft indictment approved by the Crown Court with deferred prosecution agreement).

(6) An indictment must be in one of the forms set out in the Practice Direction unless—
(a) rule 10.3 applies; or
(b) the Crown Court otherwise directs.

(7) Unless the Crown Court otherwise directs, the court officer must—
(a) endorse any paper copy of the indictment made for the court with—
(i) a note to identify it as a copy of the indictment, and
(ii) the date on which the draft indictment became the indictment under paragraph (5); and
(b) where rule 10.4, 10.5, 10.7 or 10.8 applies, serve a copy of the indictment on all parties.

(8) The Crown Court may extend the time limit under rule 10.4, 10.5, 10.7 or 10.8, even after it has expired.

Draft indictment generated electronically on sending for trial **R-93**

10.3 (1) Unless the Crown Court otherwise directs before the defendant is arraigned, this rule applies where—
(a) a magistrates' court sends a defendant to the Crown Court for trial;
(b) the magistrates' court officer serves on the Crown Court officer the notice required by rule 9.5 (Duty of magistrates' court officer); and
(c) by means of such electronic arrangements as the court officer may make for the purpose, there is presented to the Crown Court as a count—
(i) each allegation of an indictable offence specified in the notice, and
(ii) each allegation specified in the notice to which section 40 of the Criminal Justice Act 1988 applies (specified summary offences founded on the prosecution evidence).

(2) Where this rule applies—
(a) each such allegation constitutes a count;
(b) the allegation or allegations so specified together constitute a draft indictment;
(c) before the draft indictment so constituted is preferred before the Crown Court under rule 10.2(5)(b)(i) the prosecutor may substitute for any count an amended count to the same effect and charging the same offence;
(d) if under rule 9.15 (Service of prosecution evidence) the prosecutor has served copies of the documents containing the evidence on which the prosecution case relies then, before the draft indictment is preferred before the Crown Court under rule 10.2(5)(b)(i), the prosecutor may substitute or add—
(i) any count charging substantially the same offence as one specified in the notice, and
(ii) any other count charging an offence which the Crown Court can try and which is based on the prosecution evidence so served; and
(e) a prosecutor who substitutes or adds a count under paragraph (2)(c) or (d) must serve that count on the Crown Court officer and the defendant.

Draft indictment served by the prosecutor after sending for trial **R-94**

10.4 (1) This rule applies where—
(a) a magistrates' court sends a defendant to the Crown Court for trial; and
(b) rule 10.3 (Draft indictment generated electronically on sending for trial) does not apply.

(2) The prosecutor must serve a draft indictment on the Crown Court officer not more than 28 days after serving under rule 9.15 (Service of prosecution evidence) copies of the documents containing the evidence on which the prosecution case relies.

Draft indictment served by the prosecutor with a High Court judge's permission **R-95**

10.5 (1) This rule applies where—
(a) the prosecutor applies to a High Court judge under rule 10.9 (Application to a High Court judge for permission to serve a draft indictment); and
(b) the judge gives permission to serve a proposed indictment.

(2) Where this rule applies—
(a) that proposed indictment constitutes the draft indictment; and

(b) the prosecutor must serve the draft indictment on the Crown Court officer not more than 28 days after the High Court judge's decision.

R-96 **Draft indictment approved with deferred prosecution agreement**

10.6 (1) This rule applies where—

(a) the prosecutor applies to the Crown Court under rule 11.4 (Deferred prosecution agreements: Application to approve the terms of an agreement); and

(b) the Crown Court approves the proposed indictment served with that application.

(2) Where this rule applies, that proposed indictment constitutes the draft indictment.

R-97 **Draft indictment served by the prosecutor on re-instituting proceedings**

10.7 (1) This rule applies where the prosecutor wants to re-institute proceedings in the Crown Court under section 22B of the Prosecution of Offences Act 1985.

(2) The prosecutor must serve a draft indictment on the Crown Court officer not more than 3 months after the proceedings were stayed under section 22(4) of that Act.

R-98 **Draft indictment served by the prosecutor at the direction of the Court of Appeal**

10.8 (1) This rule applies where the Court of Appeal orders a retrial.

(2) The prosecutor must serve a draft indictment on the Crown Court officer not more than 28 days after that order.

R-99 **Application to a High Court judge for permission to serve a draft indictment**

10.9 (1) This rule applies where a prosecutor wants a High Court judge's permission to serve a draft indictment.

(2) Such a prosecutor must—

(a) apply in writing;

(b) serve the application on—

(i) the court officer, and

(ii) the proposed defendant, unless the judge otherwise directs; and

(c) ask for a hearing, if the prosecutor wants one, and explain why it is needed.

(3) The application must—

(a) attach—

(i) the proposed indictment,

(ii) copies of the documents containing the evidence on which the prosecutor relies, including any written witness statement or statements complying with rule 16.2 (Content of written witness statement) and any documentary exhibit to any such statement,

(iii) a copy of any indictment on which the defendant already has been arraigned, and

(iv) if not contained in such an indictment, a list of any offence or offences for which the defendant already has been sent for trial;

(b) include—

(i) a concise statement of the circumstances in which, and the reasons why, the application is made, and

(ii) a concise summary of the evidence contained in the documents accompanying the application, identifying each passage in those documents said to evidence each offence alleged by the prosecutor and relating that evidence to each count in the proposed indictment; and

(c) contain a statement that, to the best of the prosecutor's knowledge, information and belief—

(i) the evidence on which the prosecutor relies will be available at the trial, and

(ii) the allegations contained in the application are substantially true

unless the application is made by or on behalf of the Director of Public Prosecutions or the Director of the Serious Fraud Office.

(4) A proposed defendant served with an application who wants to make representations to the judge must—

(a) serve the representations on the court officer and on the prosecutor;

(b) do so as soon as practicable, and in any event within such period as the judge directs; and

(c) ask for a hearing, if the proposed defendant wants one, and explain why it is needed.

(5) The judge may determine the application—

(a) without a hearing, or at a hearing in public or in private;

(b) with or without receiving the oral evidence of any proposed witness.

(6) At any hearing, if the judge so directs a statement required by paragraph (3)(c) must be repeated on oath or affirmation.
(7) If the judge gives permission to serve a draft indictment, the decision must be recorded in writing and endorsed on, or annexed to, the proposed indictment.

Criminal Practice Directions Part 10 The Indictment

CPD II Preliminary proceedings 10A: Preparation and Content of the Indictment PD-26

Preferring the indictment

10A.1 Section 2 of the Administration of Justice (Miscellaneous Provisions) Act 1933 allows Criminal Procedure Rules to 'make provision... as to the manner in which and the time at which bills of indictment are to be preferred'. CrimPR 10.2(5) lists the events which constitute preferment for the purposes of that Act. Where a defendant is contemplating an application to the Crown Court to dismiss an offence sent for trial, under the provisions to which CrimPR 9.16 applies, or where the prosecutor is contemplating discontinuance, under the provisions to which CrimPR Part 12 applies, the parties and the court must be astute to the effect of the occurrence of those events: the right to apply for dismissal is lost if the defendant is arraigned, and the right to discontinue is lost if the indictment is preferred.

Printing and signature of indictment

10A.2 Neither Section 2 of the Administration of Justice (Miscellaneous Provisions) Act 1933 nor the Criminal Procedure Rules require an indictment to be printed or signed. Section 2(1) of the Act was amended by section 116 of the Coroners and Justice Act 2009 to remove the requirement for signature. For the potential benefit of the Criminal Appeal Office, CrimPR 10.2(7) requires only that any paper copy of the indictment which for any reason in fact is made for the court must be endorsed with a note to identify it as a copy of the indictment, and with the date on which the indictment came into being. For the same reason, CrimPR 3.22 requires only that any paper copy of an indictment which in fact has been made must be endorsed with a note of the order and of its date where the court makes an order for joint or separate trials affecting that indictment or makes an order for the amendment of that indictment in any respect.

Content of indictment; joint and separate trials

10A.3 The rule has been abolished which formerly required an indictment containing more than one count to include only offences founded on the same facts, or offences which constitute all or part of a series of the same or a similar character. However, if an indictment charges more than one offence, and if at least one of those offences does not meet those criteria, then CrimPR 3.21(4) cites that circumstance as an example of one in which the court may decide to exercise its power to order separate trials under section 5(3) of the Indictments Act 1915. It is for the court to decide which allegations, against whom, should be tried at the same time, having regard to the prosecutor's proposals, the parties' representations, the court's powers under the 1915 Act (see also CrimPR 3.21(4)) and the overriding objective. Where necessary the court should be invited to exercise those powers. It is generally undesirable for a large number of counts to be tried at the same time and the prosecutor may be required to identify a selection of counts on which the trial should proceed, leaving a decision to be taken later whether to try any of the remainder.

10A.4 Where an indictment contains substantive counts and one or more related conspiracy counts, the court will expect the prosecutor to justify their joint trial. Failing justification, the prosecutor should be required to choose whether to proceed on the substantive counts or on the conspiracy counts. In any event, if there is a conviction on any counts that are tried, then those that have not been proceeded with can remain on the file marked 'not to be proceeded with without the leave of the court or the Court of Appeal'. In the event that a conviction is later quashed on appeal, the remaining counts can be tried.

10A.5 There is no rule of law or practice which prohibits two indictments being in existence at the same time for the same offence against the same person and on the same facts. However, the court will not allow the prosecutor to proceed on both indictments. They cannot be tried together and the court will require the prosecutor to elect the one on which the trial will proceed. Where different defendants have been separately sent for trial for offences which properly may be tried together then it is permissible to join in one indictment counts based on the separate sendings for trial even if an indictment based on one of them already exists.

Draft indictment generated electronically on sending for trial

10A.6 CrimPR 10.3 applies where court staff have introduced arrangements for the charges sent for trial to be presented in the Crown Court as the counts of a draft indictment without the need for those charges to be rewritten and served a second time on the defendant and on the court office. Where such arrangements are introduced, court users will be informed (and the fact will become apparent on the sending for trial).

10A.7 Now that there is no restriction on the counts that an indictment may contain (see paragraph 10A.3 above), and given the Crown Court's power, and in some cases obligation, to order separate trials, few circumstances will arise in which the court will wish to exercise the discretion conferred by rule 10.3(1) to direct that the rule will not apply, thus discarding such an electronically generated draft indictment. The most likely such circumstance to arise would be in a case in which prosecution evidence emerging soon after sending requires such a comprehensive amendment of the counts as to make it more convenient to all participants for the prosecutor to prepare and serve under CrimPR 10.4 a complete new draft indictment than to amend the electronically generated draft.

Draft indictment served by the prosecutor

10A.8 CrimPR 10.4 applies after sending for trial wherever CrimPR 10.3 does not. It requires the prosecutor to prepare a draft indictment and serve it on the Crown Court officer, who by CrimPR 10.2(7)(b) then must serve it on the defendant. In most instances service will be by electronic means, usually by making use of the Crown Court digital case system to which the prosecutor will upload the draft (which at once then becomes the indictment, under section 2 of the Administration of Justice (Miscellaneous Provisions) Act 1933 and CrimPR 10.2(5)(b)(ii)).

10A.9 The prosecutor's time limit for service of the draft indictment under CrimPR 10.4 is 28 days after serving under CrimPR 9.15 the evidence on which the prosecution case relies. The Crown Court may extend that time limit, under CrimPR 10.2(8). However, under paragraph CrimPD I 3A.16 of these Practice Directions the court will expect that in every case a draft indictment will be served at least 7 days before the plea and trial preparation hearing, whether the time prescribed by the rule will have expired or not.

Amending the content of the indictment

10A.10 Where the prosecutor wishes to substitute or add counts to a draft indictment, or to invite the court to allow an indictment to be amended, so that the draft indictment, or indictment, will charge offences which differ from those with which the defendant first was charged, the defendant should be given as much notice as possible of what is proposed. It is likely that the defendant will need time to consider his or her position and advance notice will help to avoid delaying the proceedings.

Multiple offending: count charging more than one incident

10A.11 CrimPR 10.2(2) allows a single count to allege more than one incident of the commission of an offence in certain circumstances. Each incident must be of the same offence. The circumstances in which such a count may be appropriate include, but are not limited to, the following:

(a) the victim on each occasion was the same, or there was no identifiable individual victim as, for example, in a case of the unlawful importation of controlled drugs or of money laundering;

(b) the alleged incidents involved a marked degree of repetition in the method employed or in their location, or both;

(c) the alleged incidents took place over a clearly defined period, typically (but not necessarily) no more than about a year;

(d) in any event, the defence is such as to apply to every alleged incident. Where what is in issue differs in relation to different incidents, a single 'multiple incidents' count will not be appropriate (though it may be appropriate to use two or more such counts according to the circumstances and to the issues raised by the defence).

10A.12 Even in circumstances such as those set out above, there may be occasions on which a prosecutor chooses not to use such a count, in order to bring the case within section 75(3)(a) of the Proceeds of Crime Act 2002 (criminal lifestyle established by conviction of three or more offences in the same proceedings): for example, because section 75(2)(c) of that Act does not apply (criminal lifestyle established by an offence committed over a period of at least six months). Where the prosecutor proposes such a course, it is unlikely that CrimPR Part 1 (the overriding objective) will require an indictment to contain a single 'multiple incidents' count in place of a larger number of counts, subject to the general principles set out at paragraph 10A.3.

10A.13 For some offences, particularly sexual offences, the penalty for the offence may have changed during the period over which the alleged incidents took place. In such a case, additional 'multiple incidents' counts should be used so that each count only alleges incidents to which the same maximum penalty applies.

10A.14 In other cases, such as sexual or physical abuse, a complainant may be in a position only to give evidence of a series of similar incidents without being able to specify when or the precise circumstances in which they occurred. In these cases, a 'multiple incidents' count may be desirable. If on the other hand the complainant is able to identify particular incidents of the offence by reference to a date or other specific event, but alleges that in addition there were other incidents which the complainant is unable to specify, then it may be desirable to include separate counts for the identified incidents and a 'multiple incidents' count or counts alleging that incidents of the same offence occurred 'many' times. Using a 'multiple incidents' count may be an appropriate alternative to using 'specimen' counts in some cases where repeated sexual or physical abuse is alleged. The choice of count will depend on the particular circumstances of the case and should be determined bearing in mind the implications for sentencing set out in *R v Canavan*; *R v Kidd*; *R v Shaw* [1998] 1 WLR 604, [1998] 1 Cr App R 79, [1998] 1 Cr App R (S) 243. In *R v A* [2015] EWCA Crim 177, [2015] 2 Cr App R (S) 115(12) the Court of Appeal reviewed the circumstances in which a mixture of multiple incident and single incident counts might be appropriate where the prosecutor alleged sustained sexual abuse.

Multiple offending: trial by jury and then by judge alone

10A.15 Under sections 17 to 21 of the Domestic Violence, Crime and Victims Act 2004, the court may order that the trial of certain counts will be by jury in the usual way and, if the jury convicts, that other associated counts will be tried by judge alone. The use of this power is likely to be appropriate where justice cannot be done without charging a large number of separate offences and the allegations against the defendant appear to fall into distinct groups by reference to the identity of the victim, by reference to the dates of the offences, or by some other distinction in the nature of the offending conduct alleged.

10A.16 In such a case, it is essential to make clear from the outset the association asserted by the prosecutor between those counts to be tried by a jury and those counts which it is proposed should be tried by judge alone, if the jury convict on the former. A special form of indictment is prescribed for this purpose.

10A.17 An order for such a trial may be made only at a preparatory hearing. It follows that where the prosecutor intends to invite the court to order such a trial it will normally be appropriate to proceed as follows. A draft indictment in the form appropriate to such a trial should be served with an application under CrimPR 3.15 for a preparatory hearing. This will ensure that the defendant is aware at the earliest possible opportunity of what the prosecutor proposes and of the proposed association of counts in the indictment.

10A.18 At the start of the preparatory hearing, the defendant should be arraigned on all counts in Part One of the indictment. Arraignment on Part Two need not take place until after there has been either a guilty plea to, or finding of guilt on, an associated count in Part One of the indictment.

10A.19 If the prosecutor's application is successful, the prosecutor should prepare an abstract of the indictment, containing the counts from Part One only, for use in the jury trial. Preparation of such an abstract does not involve 'amendment' of the indictment. It is akin to where a defendant pleads guilty to certain counts in an indictment and is put in the charge of the jury on the remaining counts only.

10A.20 If the prosecutor's application for a two stage trial is unsuccessful, the prosecutor may apply to amend the indictment to remove from it any counts in Part Two which would make jury trial on the whole indictment impracticable and to revert to a standard form of indictment. It will be a matter for the court whether arraignment on outstanding counts takes place at the preparatory hearing, or at a future date.

CPD II Preliminary proceedings 10B: Voluntary Bills of Indictment PD-27

10B.1 Section 2(2)(b) of the Administration of Justice (Miscellaneous Provisions) Act 1933 and paragraph 2(6) of Schedule 3 to the Crime and Disorder Act 1998 allow the preferment of a bill of indictment by the direction or with the consent of a judge of the High Court. Bills so preferred are known as 'voluntary bills'.

10B.2 Applications for such consent must comply with CrimPR 10.3.

10B.3 Those requirements should be complied with in relation to each defendant named in the indictment for which consent is sought, whether or not it is proposed to prefer any new count against him or her.

10B.4 The preferment of a voluntary bill is an exceptional procedure. Consent should only be granted where good reason to depart from the normal procedure is clearly shown and only where the interests of justice, rather than considerations of administrative convenience, require it.

10B.5 Prosecutors must follow the procedures prescribed by the rule unless there are good reasons for not doing so, in which case prosecutors must inform the judge that the procedures have not been followed and seek leave to dispense with all or any of them. Judges should not give leave to dispense unless good reasons are shown.

10B.6 A judge to whom application for consent to the preferment of a documents submitted by the prosecutor and any written submissions made by the prospective defendant, and may properly seek any necessary amplification. CrimPR 10.3(4)(b) allows the judge to set a timetable for representations. The judge may invite oral submissions from either party, or accede to a request for an opportunity to make oral submissions, if the judge considers it necessary or desirable to receive oral submissions in order to make a sound and fair decision on the application. Any such oral submissions should be made on notice to the other party and in open court unless the judge otherwise directs.

Criminal Procedure Rules Part 11 Deferred Prosecution Agreements

R-100 **When this Part applies**

11.1 (1) This Part applies to proceedings in the Crown Court under Schedule 17 to the Crime and Courts Act 2013.

(2) In this Part—

(a) 'agreement' means a deferred prosecution agreement under paragraph 1 of that Schedule;

(b) 'prosecutor' means a prosecutor designated by or under paragraph 3 of that Schedule; and

(c) 'defendant' means the corporation, partnership or association with whom the prosecutor proposes to enter, or enters, an agreement.

R-101 **Exercise of court's powers**

11.2 (1) The court must determine an application to which this Part applies at a hearing, which—

(a) must be in private, under rule 11.3 (Application to approve a proposal to enter an agreement);

(b) may be in public or private, under rule 11.4 (Application to approve the terms of an agreement), rule 11.6 (Application to approve a variation of the terms of an agreement) or rule 11.9 (Application to postpone the publication of information by the prosecutor);

(c) must be in public, under rule 11.5 (Application on breach of agreement) or rule 11.7 (Application to lift suspension of prosecution), unless the court otherwise directs.

(2) If at a hearing in private to which rule 11.4 or rule 11.6 applies the court approves the agreement or the variation proposed, the court must announce its decision and reasons at a hearing in public.

(3) The court must not determine an application under rule 11.3, rule 11.4 or rule 11.6 unless—

(a) both parties are present;

(b) the prosecutor provides the court with a written declaration that, for the purposes of the application—

(i) the investigator enquiring into the alleged offence or offences has certified that no information has been supplied which the investigator knows to be inaccurate, misleading or incomplete, and

(ii) the prosecutor has complied with the prosecution obligation to disclose material to the defendant; and

(c) the defendant provides the court with a written declaration that, for the purposes of the application—

(i) the defendant has not supplied any information which the defendant knows to be inaccurate, misleading or incomplete, and

(ii) the individual through whom the defendant makes the declaration has made reasonable enquiries and believes the defendant's declaration to be true.

(4) The court must not determine an application under rule 11.5 or rule 11.7—

(a) in the prosecutor's absence; or

(b) in the absence of the defendant, unless the defendant has had at least 28 days in which to make representations.

(5) If the court approves a proposal to enter an agreement—

(a) the general rule is that any further application to which this Part applies must be made to the same judge; but

(b) the court may direct other arrangements.

(6) The court may adjourn a hearing—
(a) if either party asks, or on its own initiative;
(b) in particular, if the court requires more information about—
(i) the facts of an alleged offence,
(ii) the terms of a proposal to enter an agreement, or of a proposed agreement or variation of an agreement, or
(iii) the circumstances in which the prosecutor wants the court to decide whether the defendant has failed to comply with the terms of an agreement.
(7) The court may—
(a) hear an application under rule 11.4 immediately after an application under rule 11.3, if the court approves a proposal to enter an agreement;
(b) hear an application under rule 11.7 immediately after an application under rule 11.5, if the court terminates an agreement.

Application to approve a proposal to enter an agreement **R-102**

11.3 (1) This rule applies where a prosecutor wants the court to approve a proposal to enter an agreement.
(2) The prosecutor must—
(a) apply in writing after the commencement of negotiations between the parties but before the terms of agreement have been settled; and
(b) serve the application on—
(i) the court officer, and
(ii) the defendant.
(3) The application must—
(a) identify the parties to the proposed agreement;
(b) attach a proposed indictment setting out such of the offences listed in Part 2 of Schedule 17 to the Crime and Courts Act 2013 as the prosecutor is considering;
(c) include or attach a statement of facts proposed for inclusion in the agreement, which must give full particulars of each alleged offence, including details of any alleged financial gain or loss;
(d) include any information about the defendant that would be relevant to sentence in the event of conviction for the offence or offences;
(e) specify the proposed expiry date of the agreement;
(f) describe the proposed terms of the agreement, including details of any—
(i) monetary penalty to be paid by the defendant, and the time within which any such penalty is to be paid,
(ii) compensation, reparation or donation to be made by the defendant, the identity of the recipient of any such payment and the time within which any such payment is to be made,
(iii) surrender of profits or other financial benefit by the defendant, and the time within which any such sum is to be surrendered,
(iv) arrangement to be made in relation to the management or conduct of the defendant's business,
(v) co-operation required of the defendant in any investigation related to the offence or offences,
(vi) other action required of the defendant,
(vii) arrangement to monitor the defendant's compliance with a term,
(viii) consequence of the defendant's failure to comply with a term, and
(ix) prosecution costs to be paid by the defendant, and the time within which any such costs are to be paid;
(g) in relation to those terms, explain how they comply with—
(i) the requirements of the code issued under paragraph 6 of Schedule 17 to the Crime and Courts Act 2013, and
(ii) any sentencing guidelines or guideline cases which apply;
(h) contain or attach the defendant's written consent to the proposal; and
(i) explain why—
(i) entering into an agreement is likely to be in the interests of justice, and
(ii) the proposed terms of the agreement are fair, reasonable and proportionate.
(4) If the proposed statement of facts includes assertions that the defendant does not admit, the application must—
(a) specify the facts that are not admitted; and
(b) explain why that is immaterial for the purposes of the proposal to enter an agreement.

R-103 **Application to approve the terms of an agreement**

11.4 (1) This rule applies where—
(a) the court has approved a proposal to enter an agreement on an application under rule 11.3; and
(b) the prosecutor wants the court to approve the terms of the agreement.
(2) The prosecutor must—
(a) apply in writing as soon as practicable after the parties have settled the terms; and
(b) serve the application on—
(i) the court officer, and
(ii) the defendant.
(3) The application must—
(a) attach the agreement;
(b) indicate in what respect, if any, the terms of the agreement differ from those proposed in the application under rule 11.3;
(c) contain or attach the defendant's written consent to the agreement;
(d) explain why—
(i) the agreement is in the interests of justice, and
(ii) the terms of the agreement are fair, reasonable and proportionate;
(e) attach a draft indictment, charging the defendant with the offence or offences the subject of the agreement; and
(f) include any application for the hearing to be in private.
(4) If the court approves the agreement and the draft indictment, the court officer must—
(a) endorse any paper copy of the indictment made for the court with—
(i) a note to identify it as the indictment approved by the court, and
(ii) the date of the court's approval; and
(b) treat the case as if it had been suspended by order of the court.

R-104 **Application on breach of agreement**

11.5 (1) This rule applies where—
(a) the prosecutor believes that the defendant has failed to comply with the terms of an agreement; and
(b) the prosecutor wants the court to decide—
(i) whether the defendant has failed to comply, and
(ii) if so, whether to terminate the agreement, or to invite the parties to agree proposals to remedy that failure.
(2) The prosecutor must—
(a) apply in writing, as soon as practicable after becoming aware of the grounds for doing so; and
(b) serve the application on—
(i) the court officer, and
(ii) the defendant.
(3) The application must—
(a) specify each respect in which the prosecutor believes the defendant has failed to comply with the terms of the agreement, and explain the reasons for the prosecutor's belief; and
(b) attach a copy of any document containing evidence on which the prosecutor relies.
(4) A defendant who wants to make representations in response to the application must serve the representations on—
(a) the court officer; and
(b) the prosecutor,
not more than 28 days after service of the application.

R-105 **Application to approve a variation of the terms of an agreement**

11.6 (1) This rule applies where the parties have agreed to vary the terms of an agreement because—
(a) on an application under rule 11.5 (Application on breach of agreement), the court has invited them to do so; or
(b) variation of the agreement is necessary to avoid a failure by the defendant to comply with its terms in circumstances that were not, and could not have been, foreseen by either party at the time the agreement was made.

(2) The prosecutor must—
(a) apply in writing, as soon as practicable after the parties have settled the terms of the variation; and
(b) serve the application on—
(i) the court officer, and
(ii) the defendant.
(3) The application must—
(a) specify each variation proposed;
(b) contain or attach the defendant's written consent to the variation;
(c) explain why—
(i) the variation is in the interests of justice, and
(ii) the terms of the agreement as varied are fair, reasonable and proportionate; and
(d) include any application for the hearing to be in private.

Application to lift suspension of prosecution R-106

11.7 (1) This rule applies where—
(a) the court terminates an agreement before its expiry date; and
(b) the prosecutor wants the court to lift the suspension of the prosecution that applied when the court approved the terms of the agreement.
(2) The prosecutor must—
(a) apply in writing, as soon as practicable after the termination of the agreement; and
(b) serve the application on—
(i) the court officer, and
(ii) the defendant.
(3) A defendant who wants to make representations in response to the application must serve the representations on—
(a) the court officer; and
(b) the prosecutor,
not more than 28 days after service of the application.

Notice to discontinue prosecution R-107

11.8 (1) This rule applies where an agreement expires—
(a) on its expiry date, or on a date treated as its expiry date; and
(b) without having been terminated by the court.
(2) The prosecutor must—
(a) as soon as practicable give notice in writing discontinuing the prosecution on the indictment approved by the court under rule 11.4 (Application to approve the terms of an agreement); and
(b) serve the notice on—
(i) the court officer, and
(ii) the defendant.

Application to postpone the publication of information by the prosecutor R-108

11.9 (1) This rule applies where the prosecutor—
(a) makes an application under rule 11.4 (Application to approve the terms of an agreement), rule 11.5 (Application on breach of agreement) or rule 11.6 (Application to approve a variation of the terms of an agreement);
(b) decides not to make an application under rule 11.5, despite believing that the defendant has failed to comply with the terms of the agreement; or
(c) gives a notice under rule 11.8 (Notice to discontinue prosecution).
(2) A party who wants the court to order that the publication of information by the prosecutor about the court's or the prosecutor's decision should be postponed must—
(a) apply in writing, as soon as practicable and in any event before such publication occurs;
(b) serve the application on—
(i) the court officer, and
(ii) the other party; and
(c) in the application—
(i) specify the proposed terms of the order, and for how long it should last, and
(ii) explain why an order in the terms proposed is necessary.

Duty of court officer, etc. R-109

11.10 (1) Unless the court otherwise directs, the court officer must—
(a) arrange for the recording of proceedings on an application to which this Part applies;

(b) arrange for the transcription of such a recording if—
(i) a party wants such a transcript, or
(ii) anyone else wants such a transcript (but that is subject to the restrictions in paragraph (2)).

(2) Unless the court otherwise directs, a person who transcribes a recording of proceedings under such arrangements—
(a) must not supply anyone other than a party with a transcript of a recording of—
(i) a hearing in private, or
(ii) a hearing in public to which reporting restrictions apply;
(b) subject to that, must supply any person with any transcript for which that person asks—
(i) in accordance with the transcription arrangements made by the court officer, and
(ii) on payment by that person of any fee prescribed.

(3) The court officer must not identify either party to a hearing in private under rule 11.3 (Application to approve a proposal to enter an agreement) or rule 11.4 (Application to approve the terms of an agreement)—
(a) in any notice displayed in the vicinity of the courtroom; or
(b) in any other information published by the court officer.

R-110 Court's power to vary requirements under this Part

11.11 (1) The court may—
(a) shorten or extend (even after it has expired) a time limit under this Part;
(b) allow there to be made orally—
(i) an application under rule 11.4 (Application to approve the terms of an agreement), or
(ii) an application under rule 11.7 (Application to lift suspension of prosecution)
where the court exercises its power under rule 11.2(7) to hear one application immediately after another.

(2) A party who wants an extension of time must—
(a) apply when serving the application or notice for which it is needed; and
(b) explain the delay.

Criminal Procedure Rules Part 12 Discontinuing a Prosecution

R-111 When this Part applies

12.1 (1) This Part applies where—
(a) the Director of Public Prosecutions can discontinue a case in a magistrates' court, under section 23 of the Prosecution of Offences Act 1985;
(b) the Director of Public Prosecutions, or another public prosecutor, can discontinue a case sent for trial in the Crown Court, under section 23A of the Prosecution of Offences Act 1985.

(2) In this Part, 'prosecutor' means one of those authorities.

R-112 Discontinuing a case

12.2 (1) A prosecutor exercising a power to which this Part applies must serve notice on—
(a) the court officer;
(b) the defendant; and
(c) any custodian of the defendant.

(2) Such a notice must—
(a) identify—
(i) the defendant and each offence to which the notice relates,
(ii) the person serving the notice, and
(iii) the power that that person is exercising;
(b) explain—
(i) in the copy of the notice served on the court officer, the reasons for discontinuing the case,
(ii) that the notice brings the case to an end,
(iii) if the defendant is in custody for any offence to which the notice relates, that the defendant must be released from that custody, and
(iv) if the notice is under section 23 of the 1985 Act, that the defendant has a right to require the case to continue.

(3) Where the defendant is on bail, the court officer must notify—
(a) any surety; and
(b) any person responsible for monitoring or securing the defendant's compliance with a condition of bail.

Defendant's notice to continue R-113

12.3 (1) This rule applies where a prosecutor serves a notice to discontinue under section 23 of the 1985 Act.
(2) A defendant who wants the case to continue must serve notice—
(a) on the court officer; and
(b) not more than 35 days after service of the notice to discontinue.
(3) If the defendant serves such a notice, the court officer must—
(a) notify the prosecutor; and
(b) refer the case to the court.

Criminal Procedure Rules Part 13 Warrants for Arrest, Detention or Imprisonment

When this Part applies R-114

13.1 (1) This Part applies where the court can issue a warrant for arrest, detention or imprisonment.
(2) In this Part, 'defendant' means anyone against whom such a warrant is issued.

Terms of a warrant for arrest R-115

13.2 A warrant for arrest must require each person to whom it is directed to arrest the defendant and—
(a) bring the defendant to a court—
(i) specified in the warrant, or
(ii) required or allowed by law; or
(b) release the defendant on bail (with conditions or without) to attend court at a date, time and place—
(i) specified in the warrant, or
(ii) to be notified by the court.

Terms of a warrant for detention or imprisonment R-116

13.3 (1) A warrant for detention or imprisonment must—
(a) require each person to whom it is directed to detain the defendant and—
(i) take the defendant to any place specified in the warrant or required or allowed by law, and
(ii) deliver the defendant to the custodian of that place; and
(b) require that custodian to detain the defendant, as ordered by the court, until in accordance with the law—
(i) the defendant is delivered to the appropriate court or place, or
(ii) the defendant is released.
(2) Where a magistrates' court remands a defendant to police detention under section 128(7) or section 136 of the Magistrates' Courts Act 1980, or to customs detention under section 152 of the Criminal Justice Act 1988, the warrant it issues must—
(a) be directed, as appropriate, to—
(i) a constable, or
(ii) an officer of Her Majesty's Revenue and Customs; and
(b) require that constable or officer to detain the defendant—
(i) for a period (not exceeding the maximum permissible) specified in the warrant, or
(ii) until in accordance with the law the defendant is delivered to the appropriate court or place.
(3) Where a magistrates' court sentences a defendant to imprisonment or detention and section 11(3) of the Magistrates' Courts Act 1980(a) applies (custodial sentence imposed in the defendant's absence), the warrant it issues must—
(a) require each person to whom the warrant is directed—
(i) to arrest the defendant and bring him or her to a court specified in the warrant, and
(ii) unless the court then otherwise directs, after that to act as required by paragraph (1)(a) of this rule; and

(b) require the custodian to whom the defendant is delivered in accordance with that paragraph to act as required by paragraph (1)(b) of this rule.

R-117 **Information to be included in a warrant**

13.4 (1) A warrant must identify—
(a) each person to whom it is directed;
(b) the defendant against whom it was issued;
(c) the reason for its issue;
(d) the court that issued it, unless that is otherwise recorded by the court officer; and
(e) the court office for the court that issued it.

(2) A warrant for detention or imprisonment must contain a record of any decision by the court under—
(a) section 91 of the Legal Aid, Sentencing and Punishment of Offenders Act 2012 (remands of children otherwise than on bail), including in particular—
(i) whether the defendant must be detained in local authority accommodation or youth detention accommodation,
(ii) the local authority designated by the court,
(iii) any requirement imposed by the court on that authority,
(iv) any condition imposed by the court on the defendant, and
(v) the reason for any such requirement or condition;
(b) section 80 of the Magistrates' Courts Act 1980 (application of money found on defaulter to satisfy sum adjudged); or
(c) section 82(1) or (4) of the 1980 Act (conditions for issue of a warrant).

(3) A warrant that contains an error is not invalid, as long as—
(a) it was issued in respect of a lawful decision by the court; and
(b) it contains enough information to identify that decision.

R-118 **Execution of a warrant**

13.5 (1) A warrant may be executed—
(a) by any person to whom it is directed; or
(b) if the warrant was issued by a magistrates' court, by anyone authorised to do so by section 125 (warrants), 125A (civilian enforcement officers) or 125B (execution by approved enforcement agency) of the Magistrates' Courts Act 1980.

(2) The person who executes a warrant must—
(a) explain, in terms the defendant can understand, what the warrant requires, and why;
(b) show the defendant the warrant, if that person has it; and
(c) if the defendant asks—
(i) arrange for the defendant to see the warrant, if that person does not have it, and
(ii) show the defendant any written statement of that person's authority required by section 125A or 125B of the 1980 Act.

(3) The person who executes a warrant of arrest that requires the defendant to be released on bail must—
(a) make a record of—
(i) the defendant's name,
(ii) the reason for the arrest,
(iii) the defendant's release on bail, and
(iv) when and where the warrant requires the defendant to attend court; and
(b) serve the record on—
(i) the defendant, and
(ii) the court officer.

(4) The person who executes a warrant of detention or imprisonment must—
(a) take the defendant—
(i) to any place specified in the warrant, or
(ii) if that is not immediately practicable, to any other place at which the defendant may be lawfully detained (and the warrant then has effect as if it specified that place);
(b) obtain a receipt from the custodian; and
(c) notify the court officer that the defendant has been taken to that place.

R-119 **Warrants that cease to have effect on payment**

13.6 (1) This rule applies to a warrant issued by a magistrates' court under any of the following provisions of the Magistrates' Courts Act 1980—
(a) section 76 (enforcement of sums adjudged to be paid);

(b) section 83 (process for securing attendance of offender);
(c) section 86 (power of magistrates' court to fix day for appearance of offender at means inquiry, etc.);
(d) section 136 (committal to custody overnight at police station for non-payment of sum adjudged by conviction).

(2) The warrant no longer has effect if—
(a) the sum in respect of which the warrant was issued is paid to the person executing it;
(b) that sum is offered to, but refused by, that person; or
(c) that person is shown a receipt for that sum given by—
(i) the court officer, or
(ii) the authority to which that sum is due.

Warrant issued when the court office is closed R-120

13.7 (1) This rule applies where the court issues a warrant when the court office is closed.
(2) The applicant for the warrant must, not more than 72 hours later, serve on the court officer—
(a) a copy of the warrant; and
(b) any written material that was submitted to the court.

Criminal Procedure Rules Part 14 Bail and Custody Time Limits

Section 1: general rules

When this Part applies R-121

14.1 (1) This Part applies where—
(a) a magistrates' court or the Crown Court can—
(i) grant or withhold bail, or impose or vary a condition of bail, and
(ii) where bail has been withheld, extend a custody time limit;
(b) a magistrates' court can monitor and enforce compliance with a supervision measure imposed in another European Union member State.
(2) Rules 14.20, 14.21 and 14.22 apply where a magistrates' court can authorise an extension of the period for which a defendant is released on bail before being charged with an offence.
(3) In this Part, 'defendant' includes a person who has been granted bail by a police officer.

Exercise of court's powers: General R-122

14.2 (1) The court must not make a decision to which this Part applies unless—
(a) each party to the decision and any surety directly affected by the decision—
(i) is present, in person or by live link, or
(ii) has had an opportunity to make representations;
(b) on an application for bail by a defendant who is absent and in custody, the court is satisfied that the defendant—
(i) has waived the right to attend, or
(ii) was present when a court withheld bail in the case on a previous occasion and has been in custody continuously since then;
(c) on a prosecutor's appeal against a grant of bail, application to extend a custody time limit or appeal against a refusal to extend such a time limit—
(i) the court is satisfied that a defendant who is absent has waived the right to attend, or
(ii) the court is satisfied that it would be just to proceed even though the defendant is absent;
(d) the court is satisfied that sufficient time has been allowed—
(i) for the defendant to consider the information provided by the prosecutor under rule 14.5(2), and
(ii) for the court to consider the parties' representations and make the decision required.
(2) The court may make a decision to which this Part applies at a hearing, in public or in private.
(3) The court may determine without a hearing an application to vary a condition of bail if—
(a) the parties to the application have agreed the terms of the variation proposed; or
(b) on an application by a defendant, the court determines the application no sooner than the fifth business day after the application was served.
(4) The court may adjourn a determination to which this Part applies, if that is necessary to obtain information sufficient to allow the court to make the decision required.

(5) At any hearing at which the court makes one of the following decisions, the court must announce in terms the defendant can understand (with help, if necessary, and by reference to the circumstances of the defendant and the case) its reasons for—
(a) withholding bail, or imposing or varying a bail condition;
(b) granting bail, where the prosecutor opposed the grant; or
(c) where the defendant is under 18—
(i) imposing or varying a bail condition when ordering the defendant to be detained in local authority accommodation, or
(ii) ordering the defendant to be detained in youth detention accommodation.
(6) At any hearing at which the court grants bail, the court must—
(a) tell the defendant where and when to surrender to custody; or
(b) arrange for the court officer to give the defendant, as soon as practicable, notice of where and when to surrender to custody.
(7) This rule does not apply on an application to a magistrates' court to authorise an extension of pre-charge bail.

R-123 Duty of justices' legal adviser

14.3 (1) This rule applies—
(a) only in a magistrates' court; and
(b) unless the court—
(i) includes a District Judge (Magistrates' Courts), and
(ii) otherwise directs.
(2) A justices' legal adviser must—
(a) assist an unrepresented defendant;
(b) give the court such advice as is required to enable it to exercise its powers;
(c) if required, attend the members of the court outside the courtroom to give such advice, but inform the parties of any advice so given.

R-124 General duties of court officer

14.4 (1) The court officer must arrange for a note or other record to be made of—
(a) the parties' representations about bail; and
(b) the court's reasons for a decision—
(i) to withhold bail, or to impose or vary a bail condition,
(ii) to grant bail, where the prosecutor opposed the grant or,
(iii) on an application to which rule 14.21 applies (Application to authorise extension of pre-charge bail).
(2) The court officer must serve notice of a decision about bail on—
(a) the defendant (but, in the Crown Court, only where the defendant's legal representative asks for such a notice, or where the defendant has no legal representative);
(b) the prosecutor (but only where the court granted bail, the prosecutor opposed the grant, and the prosecutor asks for such a notice);
(c) a party to the decision who was absent when it was made;
(d) a surety who is directly affected by the decision;
(e) the defendant's custodian, where the defendant is in custody and the decision requires the custodian—
(i) to release the defendant (or will do so, if a requirement ordered by the court is met), or
(ii) to transfer the defendant to the custody of another custodian;
(f) the court officer for any other court at which the defendant is required by that decision to surrender to custody.
(3) Where the court postpones the date on which a defendant who is on bail must surrender to custody, the court officer must serve notice of the postponed date on—
(a) the defendant; and
(b) any surety.
(4) Where a magistrates' court withholds bail in a case to which section 5(6A) of the Bail Act 1976 applies (remand in custody after hearing full argument on an application for bail), the court officer must serve on the defendant a certificate that the court heard full argument.
(5) Where the court determines without a hearing an application to which rule 14.21 applies (Application to authorise extension of pre-charge bail), the court officer must—
(a) if the court allows the application, notify the applicant;
(b) if the court refuses the application, notify the applicant and the defendant.

Section 2: bail

Prosecutor's representations about bail R-125

14.5 (1) This rule applies whenever the court can grant or withhold bail.
(2) The prosecutor must as soon as practicable—
(a) provide the defendant with all the information in the prosecutor's possession which is material to what the court must decide; and
(b) provide the court with the same information.
(3) A prosecutor who opposes the grant of bail must specify—
(a) each exception to the general right to bail on which the prosecutor relies; and
(b) each consideration that the prosecutor thinks relevant.
(4) A prosecutor who wants the court to impose a condition on any grant of bail must—
(a) specify each condition proposed; and
(b) explain what purpose would be served by such a condition.

Reconsideration of police bail by magistrates' court R-126

14.6 (1) This rule applies where—
(a) a party wants a magistrates' court to reconsider a bail decision by a police officer after the defendant is charged with an offence;
(b) a defendant wants a magistrates' court to reconsider a bail condition imposed by a police officer before the defendant is charged with an offence.
(2) An application under this rule must be made to—
(a) the magistrates' court to whose custody the defendant is under a duty to surrender, if any; or
(b) any magistrates' court acting for the police officer's local justice area, in any other case.
(3) The applicant party must—
(a) apply in writing; and
(b) serve the application on—
(i) the court officer,
(ii) the other party, and
(iii) any surety affected or proposed.
(4) The application must—
(a) specify—
(i) the decision that the applicant wants the court to make,
(ii) each offence charged, or for which the defendant was arrested, and
(iii) the police bail decision to be reconsidered and the reasons given for it;
(b) explain, as appropriate—
(i) why the court should grant bail itself, or withdraw it, or impose or vary a condition, and
(ii) if the applicant is the prosecutor, what material information has become available since the police bail decision was made;
(c) propose the terms of any suggested condition of bail; and
(d) if the applicant wants an earlier hearing than paragraph (7) requires, ask for that, and explain why it is needed.
(5) A prosecutor who applies under this rule must serve on the defendant, with the application, notice that the court has power to withdraw bail and, if the defendant is absent when the court makes its decision, order the defendant's arrest.
(6) A party who opposes an application must—
(a) so notify the court officer and the applicant at once; and
(b) serve on each notice of the reasons for opposition.
(7) Unless the court otherwise directs, the court officer must arrange for the court to hear the application as soon as practicable and in any event—
(a) if it is an application to withdraw bail, no later than the second business day after it was served;
(b) in any other case, no later than the fifth business day after it was served.
(8) The court may—
(a) vary or waive a time limit under this rule;
(b) allow an application to be in a different form to one set out in the Practice Direction;
(c) if rule 14.2 allows, determine without a hearing an application to vary a condition.

Notice of application to consider bail R-127

14.7 (1) This rule applies where—
(a) in a magistrates' court—
(i) a prosecutor wants the court to withdraw bail granted by the court, or to impose or vary a condition of such bail, or

(ii) a defendant wants the court to reconsider such bail before the next hearing in the case;

(b) in the Crown Court,

(i) a party wants the court to grant bail that has been withheld, or to withdraw bail that has been granted, or to impose a new bail condition or to vary a present one, or

(ii) a prosecutor wants the court to consider whether to grant or withhold bail, or impose or vary a condition of bail, under section 88 or section 89 of the Criminal Justice Act 2003 (bail and custody in connection with an intended application to the Court of Appeal to which Part 27 (Retrial after acquittal) applies).

(2) Such a party must—

(a) apply in writing;

(b) serve the application on—

(i) the court officer,

(ii) the other party, and

(iii) any surety affected or proposed; and

(c) serve the application not less than 2 business days before any hearing in the case at which the applicant wants the court to consider it, if such a hearing is already due.

(3) The application must—

(a) specify—

(i) the decision that the applicant wants the court to make,

(ii) each offence charged, and

(iii) each relevant previous bail decision and the reasons given for each;

(b) if the applicant is a defendant, explain—

(i) as appropriate, why the court should not withhold bail, or why it should vary a condition, and

(ii) what further information or legal argument, if any, has become available since the most recent previous bail decision was made;

(c) if the applicant is the prosecutor, explain—

(i) as appropriate, why the court should withdraw bail, or impose or vary a condition, and

(ii) what material information has become available since the most recent previous bail decision was made;

(d) propose the terms of any suggested condition of bail; and

(e) if the applicant wants an earlier hearing than paragraph (6) requires, ask for that, and explain why it is needed.

(4) A prosecutor who applies under this rule must serve on the defendant, with the application, notice that the court has power to withdraw bail and, if the defendant is absent when the court makes its decision, order the defendant's arrest.

(5) A party who opposes an application must—

(a) so notify the court officer and the applicant at once; and

(b) serve on each notice of the reasons for opposition.

(6) Unless the court otherwise directs, the court officer must arrange for the court to hear the application as soon as practicable and in any event—

(a) if it is an application to grant or withdraw bail, no later than the second business day after it was served;

(b) if it is an application to impose or vary a condition, no later than the fifth business day after it was served.

(7) The court may—

(a) vary or waive a time limit under this rule;

(b) allow an application to be in a different form to one set out in the Practice Direction, or to be made orally;

(c) if rule 14.2 allows, determine without a hearing an application to vary a condition.

R-128 Defendant's application or appeal to the Crown Court after magistrates' court bail decision

14.8 (1) This rule applies where a defendant wants to—

(a) apply to the Crown Court for bail after a magistrates' court has withheld bail; or

(b) appeal to the Crown Court after a magistrates' court has refused to vary a bail condition as the defendant wants.

(2) The defendant must—
(a) apply to the Crown Court in writing as soon as practicable after the magistrates' court's decision; and
(b) serve the application on—
(i) the Crown Court officer,
(ii) the magistrates' court officer,
(iii) the prosecutor, and
(iv) any surety affected or proposed.
(3) The application must—
(a) specify—
(i) the decision that the applicant wants the Crown Court to make, and
(ii) each offence charged;
(b) explain—
(i) as appropriate, why the Crown Court should not withhold bail, or why it should vary the condition under appeal, and
(ii) what further information or legal argument, if any, has become available since the magistrates' court's decision;
(c) propose the terms of any suggested condition of bail;
(d) if the applicant wants an earlier hearing than paragraph (6) requires, ask for that, and explain why it is needed; and
(e) on an application for bail, attach a copy of the certificate of full argument served on the defendant under rule 14.4(4).
(4) The magistrates' court officer must as soon as practicable serve on the Crown Court officer—
(a) a copy of the note or record made under rule 14.4(1) in connection with the magistrates' court's decision; and
(b) the date of the next hearing, if any, in the magistrates' court.
(5) A prosecutor who opposes the application must—
(a) so notify the Crown Court officer and the defendant at once; and
(b) serve on each notice of the reasons for opposition.
(6) Unless the Crown Court otherwise directs, the court officer must arrange for the court to hear the application or appeal as soon as practicable and in any event no later than the business day after it was served.
(7) The Crown Court may vary a time limit under this rule.

Prosecutor's appeal against grant of bail **R-129**

14.9 (1) This rule applies where a prosecutor wants to appeal—
(a) to the Crown Court against a grant of bail by a magistrates' court, in a case in which the defendant has been charged with, or convicted of, an offence punishable with imprisonment; or
(b) to the High Court against a grant of bail—
(i) by a magistrates' court, in an extradition case, or
(ii) by the Crown Court, in a case in which the defendant has been charged with, or convicted of, an offence punishable with imprisonment (but not in a case in which the Crown Court granted bail on an appeal to which paragraph (1)(a) applies).
(2) The prosecutor must tell the court which has granted bail of the decision to appeal—
(a) at the end of the hearing during which the court granted bail; and
(b) before the defendant is released on bail.
(3) The court which has granted bail must exercise its power to remand the defendant in custody pending determination of the appeal.
(4) The prosecutor must serve an appeal notice—
(a) on the court officer for the court which has granted bail and on the defendant;
(b) not more than 2 hours after telling that court of the decision to appeal.
(5) The appeal notice must specify—
(a) each offence with which the defendant is charged;
(b) the decision under appeal;
(c) the reasons given for the grant of bail; and
(d) the grounds of appeal.
(6) On an appeal to the Crown Court, the magistrates' court officer must, as soon as practicable, serve on the Crown Court officer—
(a) the appeal notice;

(b) a copy of the note or record made under rule 14.4(1) (record of bail decision); and
(c) notice of the date of the next hearing in the court which has granted bail.

(7) If the Crown Court so directs, the Crown Court officer must arrange for the defendant to be assisted by the Official Solicitor in a case in which the defendant—
(a) has no legal representative; and
(b) asks for such assistance.

(8) On an appeal to the Crown Court, the Crown Court officer must arrange for the court to hear the appeal as soon as practicable and in any event no later than the second business day after the appeal notice was served.

(9) The prosecutor—
(a) may abandon an appeal to the Crown Court without the court's permission, by serving a notice of abandonment, signed by or on behalf of the prosecutor, on—
(i) the defendant,
(ii) the Crown Court officer, and
(iii) the magistrates' court officer
before the hearing of the appeal begins; but
(b) after the hearing of the appeal begins, may only abandon the appeal with the Crown Court's permission.

(10) The court officer for the court which has granted bail must instruct the defendant's custodian to release the defendant on the bail granted by that court, subject to any condition or conditions of bail imposed, if—
(a) the prosecutor fails to serve an appeal notice within the time to which paragraph (4) refers; or
(b) the prosecutor serves a notice of abandonment under paragraph (9).

R-130 **Consideration of bail in a murder case**

14.10 (1) This rule applies in a case in which—
(a) the defendant is charged with murder; and
(b) the Crown Court has not yet considered bail.

(2) The magistrates' court officer must arrange with the Crown Court officer for the Crown Court to consider bail as soon as practicable and in any event no later than the second business day after—
(a) a magistrates' court sends the defendant to the Crown Court for trial; or
(b) the first hearing in the magistrates' court, if the defendant is not at once sent for trial.

R-131 **Condition of residence**

14.11 (1) The defendant must notify the prosecutor of the address at which the defendant will live and sleep if released on bail with a condition of residence—
(a) as soon as practicable after the institution of proceedings, unless already done; and
(b) as soon as practicable after any change of that address.

(2) The prosecutor must help the court to assess the suitability of an address proposed as a condition of residence.

R-132 **Electronic monitoring requirements**

14.12 (1) This rule applies where the court imposes electronic monitoring requirements, where available, as a condition of bail.

(2) The court officer must—
(a) inform the person responsible for the monitoring ('the monitor') of—
(i) the defendant's name, and telephone number if available,
(ii) each offence with which the defendant is charged,
(iii) details of the place at which the defendant's presence must be monitored,
(iv) the period or periods during which the defendant's presence at that place must be monitored, and
(v) if fixed, the date on which the defendant must surrender to custody;
(b) inform the defendant and, where the defendant is under 16, an appropriate adult, of the monitor's identity and the means by which the monitor may be contacted; and
(c) notify the monitor of any subsequent—
(i) variation or termination of the electronic monitoring requirements, or
(ii) fixing or variation of the date on which the defendant must surrender to custody.

R-133 **Accommodation or support requirements**

14.13 (1) This rule applies where the court imposes as a condition of bail a requirement, where available, that the defendant must—
(a) reside in accommodation provided for that purpose by, or on behalf of, a public authority;
(b) receive bail support provided by, or on behalf of, a public authority.

(2) The court officer must—
(a) inform the person responsible for the provision of any such accommodation or support ('the service provider') of—
(i) the defendant's name, and telephone number if available,
(ii) each offence with which the defendant is charged,
(iii) details of the requirement,
(iv) any other bail condition, and
(v) if fixed, the date on which the defendant must surrender to custody;
(b) inform the defendant and, where the defendant is under 16, an appropriate adult, of—
(i) the service provider's identity and the means by which the service provider may be contacted, and
(ii) the address of any accommodation in which the defendant must live and sleep; and
(c) notify the service provider of any subsequent—
(i) variation or termination of the requirement,
(ii) variation or termination of any other bail condition, and
(iii) fixing or variation of the date on which the defendant must surrender to custody.

Requirement for a surety or payment, etc. R-134

14.14 (1) This rule applies where the court imposes as a condition of bail a requirement for—
(a) a surety;
(b) a payment;
(c) the surrender of a document or thing.
(2) The court may direct how such a condition must be met.
(3) Unless the court otherwise directs, if any such condition or direction requires a surety to enter into a recognizance—
(a) the recognizance must specify—
(i) the amount that the surety will be required to pay if the purpose for which the recognizance is entered is not fulfilled, and
(ii) the date, or the event, upon which the recognizance will expire;
(b) the surety must enter into the recognizance in the presence of—
(i) the court officer,
(ii) the defendant's custodian, where the defendant is in custody, or
(iii) someone acting with the authority of either; and
(c) the person before whom the surety enters into the recognizance must at once serve a copy on—
(i) the surety, and
(ii) as appropriate, the court officer and the defendant's custodian.
(4) Unless the court otherwise directs, if any such condition or direction requires someone to make a payment, or surrender a document or thing—
(a) that payment, document or thing must be made or surrendered to—
(i) the court officer,
(ii) the defendant's custodian, where the defendant is in custody, or
(iii) someone acting with the authority of either; and
(b) the court officer or the custodian, as appropriate, must serve immediately on the other a statement that the payment, document or thing has been made or surrendered.
(5) The custodian must release the defendant when each requirement ordered by the court has been met.

Forfeiture of a recognizance given by a surety R-135

14.15 (1) This rule applies where the court imposes as a condition of bail a requirement that a surety enter into a recognizance and, after the defendant is released on bail,—
(a) the defendant fails to surrender to custody as required, or
(b) it appears to the court that the surety has failed to comply with a condition or direction.
(2) The court officer must serve notice on—
(a) the surety; and
(b) each party to the decision to grant bail,
of the hearing at which the court will consider the forfeiture of the recognizance.
(3) The court must not forfeit the recognizance less than 5 business days after service of notice under paragraph (2).

Bail condition to be enforced in another European Union member State R-136

14.16 (1) This rule applies where the court can impose as a condition of bail pending trial a requirement—
(a) with which the defendant must comply while in another European Union member State; and
(b) which that other member State can monitor and enforce.

(2) The court—

(a) must not exercise its power to impose such a requirement until the court has decided what, if any, condition or conditions of bail to impose while the defendant is in England and Wales;

(b) subject to that, may exercise its power to make a request for the other member State to monitor and enforce that requirement.

(3) Where the court makes such a request, the court officer must—

(a) issue a certificate requesting the monitoring and enforcement of the defendant's compliance with that requirement, in the form required by EU Council Framework Decision 2009/829/JHA;

(b) serve on the relevant authority of the other member State—

(i) the court's decision or a certified copy of that decision,

(ii) the certificate, and

(iii) a copy of the certificate translated into an official language of the other member State, unless English is such a language or the other member State has declared that it will accept a certificate in English; and

(c) report to the court—

(i) any request for further information returned by the competent authority in the other member State, and

(ii) that authority's decision.

(4) Where the competent authority in the other member State agrees to monitor and enforce the requirement—

(a) the court—

(i) may exercise its power to withdraw the request (where it can), but

(ii) whether or not it does so, must continue to exercise the powers to which this Part applies in accordance with the rules in this Part;

(b) the court officer must immediately serve notice on that authority if—

(i) legal proceedings are brought in relation to the requirement being monitored and enforced, or

(ii) the court decides to vary or revoke that requirement, or to issue a warrant for the defendant's arrest; and

(c) the court officer must promptly report to the court any information and any request received from that authority.

(5) A party who wants the court to exercise the power to which this rule applies must serve with an application under rule 14.7 (Notice of application to consider bail)—

(a) a draft order; and

(b) a draft certificate in the form required by EU Council Framework Decision 2009/829/JHA.

R-137 Enforcement of measure imposed in another European Union member State

14.17 (1) This rule applies where the Lord Chancellor serves on the court officer a certificate requesting the monitoring and enforcement of a defendant's compliance with a supervision measure imposed by an authority in another European Union member State.

(2) The court officer must arrange for the court to consider the request—

(a) as a general rule—

(i) within 20 business days of the date on which the Lord Chancellor received it from the requesting authority, or

(ii) within 40 business days of that date, if legal proceedings in relation to the supervision measure are brought within the first 20 business days;

(b) exceptionally, later than that, but in such a case the court officer must immediately serve on the requesting authority—

(i) an explanation for the delay, and

(ii) an indication of when the court's decision is expected.

(3) On consideration of the request by the court, the court officer must—

(a) without delay serve on the requesting authority—

(i) notice of any further information required by the court, and

(ii) subject to any such requirement and any response, notice of the court's decision; and

(b) where the court agrees to monitor the supervision measure, serve notice of the court's decision on any supervisor specified by the court.

(4) Where the court agrees to monitor the supervision measure—

(a) the court officer must immediately serve notice on the requesting authority if there is reported to the court—

(i) a breach of the measure, or

(ii) any other event that might cause the requesting authority to review its decision;

(b) the court officer must without delay serve notice on the requesting authority if—
(i) legal proceedings are brought in relation to the decision to monitor compliance with the bail condition,
(ii) there is reported to the court a change of the defendant's residence, or
(iii) the court decides (where it can) to stop monitoring the defendant's compliance with the measure.

Section 3: custody time limits

Application to extend a custody time limit R-138

14.18 (1) This rule applies where the prosecutor gives notice of application to extend a custody time limit.
(2) The court officer must arrange for the court to hear that application as soon as practicable after the expiry of—
(a) 5 days from the giving of notice, in the Crown Court; or
(b) 2 days from the giving of notice, in a magistrates' court.
(3) The court may shorten a time limit under this rule.

Appeal against custody time limit decision R-139

14.19 (1) This rule applies where—
(a) a defendant wants to appeal to the Crown Court against a decision by a magistrates' court to extend a custody time limit;
(b) a prosecutor wants to appeal to the Crown Court against a decision by a magistrates' court to refuse to extend a custody time limit.
(2) The appellant must serve an appeal notice—
(a) on—
(i) the other party to the decision,
(ii) the Crown Court officer, and
(iii) the magistrates' court officer;
(b) in a defendant's appeal, as soon as practicable after the decision under appeal;
(c) in a prosecutor's appeal—
(i) as soon as practicable after the decision under appeal, and
(ii) before the relevant custody time limit expires.
(3) The appeal notice must specify—
(a) each offence with which the defendant is charged;
(b) the decision under appeal;
(c) the date on which the relevant custody time limit will expire;
(d) on a defendant's appeal, the date on which the relevant custody time limit would have expired but for the decision under appeal; and
(e) the grounds of appeal.
(4) The Crown Court officer must arrange for the Crown Court to hear the appeal as soon as practicable and in any event no later than the second business day after the appeal notice was served.
(5) The appellant—
(a) may abandon an appeal without the Crown Court's permission, by serving a notice of abandonment, signed by or on behalf of the appellant, on—
(i) the other party,
(ii) the Crown Court officer, and
(iii) the magistrates' court officer
before the hearing of the appeal begins; but
(b) after the hearing of the appeal begins, may only abandon the appeal with the Crown Court's permission.

Extension of bail before charge

Exercise of court's powers: extension of pre-charge bail R-140

14.20 (1) The court must determine an application to which rule 14.21 (Application to authorise extension of pre-charge bail) applies—
(a) without a hearing, subject to paragraph (2); and
(b) as soon as practicable, but as a general rule no sooner than the fifth business day after the application was served.

(2) The court must determine an application at a hearing where—
(a) if the application succeeds, its effect will be to extend the period for which the defendant is on bail to less than 12 months from the day after the defendant's arrest for the offence and the court considers that the interests of justice require a hearing;
(b) if the application succeeds, its effect will be to extend that period to more than 12 months from that day and the applicant or the defendant asks for a hearing;
(c) it is an application to withhold information from the defendant and the court considers that the interests of justice require a hearing.
(3) Any hearing must be in private.
(4) Subject to rule 14.22 (Application to withhold information from the defendant), at a hearing the court may determine an application in the absence of—
(a) the applicant;
(b) the defendant, if the defendant has had at least 5 business days in which to make representations.
(5) If the court so directs, a party to an application may attend a hearing by live link or telephone.
(6) The court must not authorise an extension of the period for which a defendant is on bail before being charged unless—
(a) the applicant states, in writing or orally, that to the best of the applicant's knowledge and belief—
(i) the application discloses all the information that is material to what the court must decide, and
(ii) the content of the application is true; or
(b) the application includes a statement by an investigator of the suspected offence that to the best of that investigator's knowledge and belief those requirements are met.
(7) Where the statement required by paragraph (6) is made orally—
(a) the statement must be on oath or affirmation, unless the court otherwise directs; and
(b) the court must arrange for a record of the making of the statement.
(8) The court may shorten or extend (even after it has expired) a time limit imposed by this rule or by rule 14.21 (Application to authorise extension of pre-charge bail).

R-141 Application to authorise extension of pre-charge bail

14.21 (1) This rule applies where an applicant wants the court to authorise an extension of the period for which a defendant is released on bail before being charged with an offence.
(2) The applicant must—
(a) apply in writing before the date on which the defendant's pre-charge bail is due to end;
(b) demonstrate that the applicant is entitled to apply as a constable, a member of staff of the Financial Conduct Authority, a member of the Serious Fraud Office or a Crown Prosecutor;
(c) serve the application on—
(i) the court officer, and
(ii) the defendant; and
(d) serve on the defendant, with the application, a form of response notice for the defendant's use.
(3) The application must specify—
(a) the offence or offences for which the defendant was arrested;
(b) the date on which the defendant's pre-charge bail began;
(c) the date and period of any previous extension of that bail;
(d) the date on which that bail is due to end;
(e) the conditions of that bail; and
(f) if different, the bail conditions which are to be imposed if the court authorises an extension, or further extension, of the period for which the defendant is released on pre-charge bail.
(4) The application must explain—
(a) the grounds for believing that, as applicable—
(i) further investigation is needed of any matter in connection with the offence or offences for which the defendant was released on bail, or
(ii) further time is needed for making a decision as to whether to charge the defendant with that offence or those offences;

(b) the grounds for believing that, as applicable—
(i) the investigation into the offence or offences for which the defendant was released on bail is being conducted diligently and expeditiously, or
(ii) the decision as to whether to charge the defendant with that offence or those offences is being made diligently and expeditiously; and
(c) the grounds for believing that the defendant's further release on bail is necessary and proportionate in all the circumstances having regard, in particular, to any conditions of bail imposed.
(5) The application must—
(a) indicate whether the applicant wants the court to authorise an extension of the defendant's bail for 3 months or for 6 months; and
(b) if for 6 months, explain why the investigation is unlikely to be completed or the charging decision made, as the case may be, within 3 months.
(6) The application must explain why it was not made earlier where—
(a) the application is made before the date on which the defendant's bail is due to end; but
(b) it is not likely to be practicable for the court to determine the application before that date.
(7) A defendant who objects to the application must—
(a) serve notice on—
(i) the court officer, and
(ii) the applicant, not more than 5 business days after service of the application; and
(b) in the notice explain the grounds of the objection.

Application to withhold information from the defendant **R-142**

14.22 (1) This rule applies where an application to authorise an extension of pre-charge bail includes an application to withhold information from the defendant.
(2) The applicant must—
(a) omit that information from the part of the application that is served on the defendant;
(b) mark the other part to show that, unless the court otherwise directs, it is only for the court; and
(c) in that other part, explain the grounds for believing that the disclosure of that information would have one or more of the following results—
(i) evidence connected with an indictable offence would be interfered with or harmed,
(ii) a person would be interfered with or physically injured,
(iii) a person suspected of having committed an indictable offence but not yet arrested for the offence would be alerted, or
(iv) the recovery of property obtained as a result of an indictable offence would be hindered.
(3) At any hearing of an application to which this rule applies—
(a) the court must first determine the application to withhold information, in the defendant's absence and that of any legal representative of the defendant;
(b) if the court allows the application to withhold information, then in the following sequence—
(i) the court must consider representations first by the applicant and then by the defendant, in the presence of both, and
(ii) the court may consider further representations by the applicant in the defendant's absence and that of any legal representative of the defendant, if satisfied that there are reasonable grounds for believing that information withheld from the defendant would be disclosed during those further representations.
(4) If the court refuses an application to withhold information from the defendant, the applicant may withdraw the application to authorise an extension of pre-charge bail.

Criminal Practice Directions Part 14 Bail and Custody Time Limits

CPD III Custody and bail 14A: Bail Before Sending for Trial **PD-28**

14A.1 Before the Crown Court can deal with an application under CrimPR 14.8 by a defendant after a magistrates' court has withheld bail, it must be satisfied that the magistrates' court has issued a certificate, under section 5(6A) of the Bail Act 1976, that it heard full argument on the application for bail before it refused the application. The certificate of full argument is produced by the magistrates' court's computer system, Libra, as part of the GENORD (General Form of Order). Two hard copies are produced, one for the defence and one for the prosecution. (Some magistrates' courts may also produce a manual certificate which will usually be available from the justices' legal adviser at the conclusion of the hearing; the GENORD may not be produced until the following day.) Under CrimPR 14.4(4), the magistrates' court officer will provide the defendant with a certificate that the court heard full argument. However, it is the responsibility of the defence, as the applicant in the Crown Court, to ensure that a copy of the certificate of full argument is provided to the Crown Court as part of the application (CrimPR 14.8(3)(e)). The applicant's solicitors should attach a copy of the certificate to the bail application form. If the certificate is not enclosed with the application form, it will be difficult to avoid some delay in listing.

Venue

14A.2 Applications should be made to the court to which the defendant will be, or would have been, sent for trial. In the event of an application in a purely summary case, it should be made to the Crown Court centre which normally receives Class 3 work. The hearing will be listed as a chambers matter, unless a judge has directed otherwise.

PD-29 **CPD III Custody and bail 14B: Bail: Failure to Surrender and Trials in Absence**

14B.1 The failure of defendants to comply with the terms of their bail by not surrendering, or not doing so at the appointed time, undermines the administration of justice and disrupts proceedings. The resulting delays impact on victims, witnesses and other court users and also waste costs. A defendant's failure to surrender affects not only the case with which he or she is concerned, but also the court's ability to administer justice more generally, by damaging the confidence of victims, witnesses and the public in the effectiveness of the court system and the judiciary. It is, therefore, most important that defendants who are granted bail appreciate the significance of the obligation to surrender to custody in accordance with the terms of their bail and that courts take appropriate action, if they fail to do so.

14B.2 A defendant who will be unable for medical reasons to attend court in accordance with his or her bail must obtain a certificate from his or her general practitioner or another appropriate medical practitioner such as the doctor with care of the defendant at a hospital. This should be obtained in advance of the hearing and conveyed to the court through the defendant's legal representative. In order to minimise the disruption to the court and to others, particularly witnesses if the case is listed for trial, the defendant should notify the court through his legal representative as soon as his inability to attend court becomes known.

14B.3 Guidance has been produced by the British Medical Association and the Crown Prosecution Service on the roles and responsibilities of medical practitioners when issuing medical certificates in criminal proceedings. Judges and magistrates should seek to ensure that this guidance is followed. However, it is a matter for each individual court to decide whether, in any particular case, the issued certificate should be accepted. Without a medical certificate or if an unsatisfactory certificate is provided, the court is likely to consider that the defendant has failed to surrender to bail.

14B.4 If a defendant fails to surrender to his or her bail there are at least four courses of action for the courts to consider taking:

(a) imposing penalties for the failure to surrender;
(b) revoking bail or imposing more stringent conditions;
(c) conducting trials in the absence of the defendant; and
(d) ordering that some or all of any sums of money lodged with the court as a security or pledged by a surety as a condition on the grant of bail be forfeit.

The relevant sentencing guideline is the Definitive Guideline Fail to Surrender to Bail. Under section 125(1) of the Coroners and Justice Act 2009, for offences committed on or after 6 April 2010, the court must follow the relevant guideline unless it would be contrary to the interests of justice to do so. The guideline can be obtained from the Sentencing Council's website: http://sentencingcouncil.judiciary.gov.uk/guidelines/guidelines-to-download.htm/

PD-30 **CPD III Custody and bail 14C: Penalties for Failure to Surrender**

Initiating Proceedings — Bail granted by a police officer

14C.1 When a person has been granted bail by a police officer to attend court and subsequently fails to surrender to custody, the decision whether to initiate proceedings for a section 6(1) or section 6(2) offence will be for the police/prosecutor and proceedings are commenced in the usual way.

14C.2 The offence in this form is a summary offence although section 6(10) to (14) of the Bail Act 1976, inserted by section 15(3) of the Criminal Justice Act 2003, disapplies section 127 of the Magistrates' Courts Act 1980 and provides for alternative time limits for the commencement of proceedings. The offence should be dealt with on the first appearance after arrest, unless an adjournment is necessary, as it will be relevant in considering whether to grant bail again.

Initiating Proceedings — Bail granted by a court

14C.3 Where a person has been granted bail by a court and subsequently fails to surrender to custody, on arrest that person should normally be brought as soon as appropriate before the court at which the proceedings in respect of which bail was granted are to be heard. (There is no requirement to lay an information within the time limit for a Bail Act offence where bail was granted by the court).

14C.4 Given that bail was granted by a court, it is more appropriate that the court itself should initiate the proceedings by its own motion although the prosecutor may invite the court to take proceedings, if the prosecutor considers proceedings are appropriate.

Timing of disposal

14C.5 Courts should not, without good reason, adjourn the disposal of a section 6(1) or section 6(2) Bail Act 1976 offence (failure to surrender) until the conclusion of the proceedings in respect of which bail was granted but should deal with defendants as soon as is practicable. In deciding what is practicable, the court must take into account when the proceedings in respect of which bail was granted are expected to conclude, the seriousness of the offence for which the defendant is already being prosecuted, the type of penalty that might be imposed for the Bail Act offence and the original offence, as well as any other relevant circumstances.

14C.6 If the Bail Act offence is adjourned alongside the substantive proceedings, then it is still necessary to consider imposing a separate penalty at the trial. In addition, bail should usually be revoked in the meantime. Trial in the absence of the defendant is not a penalty for the Bail Act offence and a separate penalty may be imposed for the Bail Act offence.

Conduct of Proceedings

14C.7 Proceedings under section 6 of the Bail Act 1976 may be conducted either as a summary offence or as a criminal contempt of court. Where proceedings are commenced by the police or prosecutor, the prosecutor will conduct the proceedings and, if the matter is contested, call the evidence. Where the court initiates proceedings, with or without an invitation from the prosecutor, the court may expect the assistance of the prosecutor, such as in cross-examining the defendant, if required.

14C.8 The burden of proof is on the defendant to prove that he had reasonable cause for his failure to surrender to custody (section 6(3) of the Bail Act 1976).

Sentencing for a Bail Act offence

14C.9 A defendant who commits an offence under section 6(1) or section 6(2) of the Bail Act 1976 commits an offence that stands apart from the proceedings in respect of which bail was granted. The seriousness of the offence can be reflected by an appropriate and generally separate penalty being imposed for the Bail Act offence.

14C.10 As noted above, there is a sentencing guideline on sentencing offenders for Bail Act offences and this must be followed unless it would be contrary to the interests of justice to do so. Where the appropriate penalty is a custodial sentence, consecutive sentences should be imposed unless there are circumstances that make this inappropriate.

CPD III Custody and bail 14D: Relationship between the Bail Act Offence and Further Remands on Bail or in Custody **PD-31**

14D.1 The court at which the defendant is produced should, where practicable and legally permissible, arrange to have all outstanding cases brought before it (including those from different courts) for the purpose of progressing matters and dealing with the question of bail. This is likely to be practicable in the magistrates' court where cases can easily be transferred from one magistrates' court to another. Practice is likely to vary in the Crown Court. If the defendant appears before a different court, for example because he is charged with offences committed in another area, and it is not practicable for all matters to be concluded by that court then the defendant may be remanded on bail or in custody, if appropriate, to appear before the first court for the outstanding offences to be dealt with.

14D.2 When a defendant has been convicted of a Bail Act offence, the court should review the remand status of the defendant, including the conditions of that bail, in respect of all outstanding proceedings against the defendant.

14D.3 Failure by the defendant to surrender or a conviction for failing to surrender to bail in connection with the main proceedings will be significant factors weighing against the re-granting of bail.

14D.4 Whether or not an immediate custodial sentence has been imposed for the Bail Act offence, the court may, having reviewed the defendant's remand status, also remand the defendant in custody in the main proceedings.

PD-32 **CPD III Custody and bail 14E: Trials in Absence**

14E.1 Paragraphs VI 24C and 25B of these Practice Directions (Trial adjournment in magistrates' courts; Trial adjournment in the Crown Court) include guidance on the circumstances in which the court should proceed with or adjourn a trial from which the defendant absents himself or herself voluntarily.

PD-33 **CPD III Custody and bail 14F: Forfeiture of Monies Lodged as Security or Pledged by a Surety/ Estreatment of Recognisances**

14F.1 A surety undertakes to forfeit a sum of money if the defendant fails to surrender as required. Considerable care must be taken to explain that obligation and the consequences before a surety is taken. This system, in one form or another, has great antiquity. It is immensely valuable. A court concerned that a defendant will fail to surrender will not normally know that defendant personally, nor indeed much about him. When members of the community who do know the defendant say they trust him to surrender and are prepared to stake their own money on that trust, that can have a powerful influence on the decision of the court as to whether or not to grant bail. There are two important side-effects. The first is that the surety will keep an eye on the defendant, and report to the authorities if there is a concern that he will abscond. In those circumstances, the surety can withdraw. The second is that a defendant will be deterred from absconding by the knowledge that if he does so then his family or friends who provided the surety will lose their money. In the experience of the courts, it is comparatively rare for a defendant to fail to surrender when meaningful sureties are in place.

14F.2 Any surety should have the opportunity to make representations to the defendant to surrender himself, in accordance with their obligations.

14F.3 The court should not wait or adjourn a decision on estreatment of sureties or securities until such time, if any, that the bailed defendant appears before the court. It is possible that any defendant who apparently absconds may have a defence of reasonable cause to the allegation of failure to surrender. If that happens, then any surety or security estreated would be returned. The reason for proceeding is that the defendant may never surrender, or may not surrender for many years. The court should still consider the sureties' obligations if that happens. Moreover, the longer the matter is delayed the more probable it is that the personal circumstances of the sureties will change.

14F.4 The court should follow the procedure at CrimPR 14.15. Before the court makes a decision, it should give the sureties the opportunity to make representations, either in person, through counsel or by statement.

14F.5 The court has discretion to forfeit the whole sum, part only of the sum, or to remit the sum. The starting point is that the surety is forfeited in full. It would be unfortunate if this valuable method of allowing a defendant to remain at liberty were undermined. Courts would have less confidence in the efficacy of sureties. It is also important to note that a defendant who absconds without in any way forewarning his sureties does not thereby release them from any or all of their responsibilities. Even if a surety does his best, he remains liable for the full amount, except at the discretion of the court. However, all factors should be taken into account and the following are noted for guidance only:

i) The presence or absence of culpability is a factor, but is not in itself a reason to reduce or set aside the obligations entered into by the surety.

ii) The means of a surety, and in particular changed means, are relevant.
iii) The court should forfeit no more than is necessary, in public policy, to maintain the integrity and confidence of the system of taking sureties.

CPD III Custody and bail 14G: Bail During Trial PD-34

14G.1 The following should be read subject to the Bail Act 1976.

14G.2 Once a trial has begun the further grant of bail, whether during the short adjournment or overnight, is in the discretion of the trial judge or trial Bench. It may be a proper exercise of this discretion to refuse bail during the short adjournment if the accused cannot otherwise be segregated from witnesses and jurors.

14G.3 An accused who was on bail while on remand should not be refused bail during the trial unless, in the opinion of the court, there are positive reasons to justify this refusal. Such reasons might include:

(a) that a point has been reached where there is a real danger that the accused will abscond, either because the case is going badly for him, or for any other reason;

(b) that there is a real danger that he may interfere with witnesses, jurors or co-defendants.

14G.4 Once the jury has returned a guilty verdict or a finding of guilt has been made, a further renewal of bail should be decided in the light of the gravity of the offence, any friction between co-defendants and the likely sentence to be passed in all the circumstances of the case.

CPD III Custody and bail 14H: Crown Court Judge's Certification of Fitness to Appeal and Applications to the Crown Court for Bail Pending Appeal PD-35

14H.1 The trial or sentencing judge may grant a certificate of fitness for appeal (see, for example, sections 1(2) (b) and 11(1A) of the Criminal Appeal Act 1968); the judge in the Crown Court should only certify cases in exceptional circumstances. The Crown Court judge should use the Criminal Appeal Office Form C (Crown Court Judge's Certificate of fitness for appeal) which is available to court staff on the HMCTS intranet.

14H.2 The judge may well think it right to encourage the defendant's advocate to submit to the court, and serve on the prosecutor, before the hearing of the application, a draft of the grounds of appeal which he will ask the judge to certify on Form C.

14H.3 The first question for the judge is then whether there exists a particular and cogent ground of appeal. If there is no such ground, there can be no certificate; and if there is no certificate there can be no bail. A judge should not grant a certificate with regard to sentence merely in the light of mitigation to which he has, in his opinion, given due weight, nor in regard to conviction on a ground where he considers the chance of a successful appeal is not substantial. The judge should bear in mind that, where a certificate is refused, application may be made to the Court of Appeal for leave to appeal and for bail; it is expected that certificates will only be granted in exceptional circumstances.

14H.4 Defence advocates should note that the effect of a grant of a certificate is to remove the need for leave to appeal to be granted by the Court of Appeal. It does not in itself commence the appeal. The completed Form C will be sent by the Crown Court to the Criminal Appeal Office; it is not copied to the parties. The procedures in CrimPR Part 39 should be followed.

14H.5 Bail pending appeal to the Court of Appeal (Criminal Division) may be granted by the trial or sentencing judge if they have certified the case as fit for appeal (see sections 81(1)(f) and 81(1B) of the Senior Courts Act 1981). Bail can only be granted in the Crown Court within 28 days of the conviction or sentence which is to be the subject of the appeal and may not be granted if an application for bail has already been made to the Court of Appeal. The procedure for bail to be granted by a judge of the Crown Court pending an appeal is governed by CrimPR Part 14. The Crown Court judge should use the Criminal Appeal Office Form BC (Crown Court Judge's Order granting bail) which is available to court staff on the HMCTS intranet.

14H.6 The length of the period which might elapse before the hearing of any appeal is not relevant to the grant of a certificate; but, if the judge does decide to grant a certificate, it may be one factor in the decision whether or not to grant bail. If bail is granted, the judge should consider imposing a condition of residence in line with the practice in the Court of Appeal (Criminal Division).

CRIMINAL PROCEDURE RULES PART 15 DISCLOSURE

R-143 **When this Part applies**

15.1 This Part applies—
(a) in a magistrates' court and in the Crown Court;
(b) where Parts I and II of the Criminal Procedure and Investigations Act 1996 apply.

R-144 **Prosecution disclosure**

15.2 (1) This rule applies in the Crown Court where, under section 3 of the Criminal Procedure and Investigations Act 1996, the prosecutor—
(a) discloses prosecution material to the defendant; or
(b) serves on the defendant a written statement that there is no such material to disclose.
(2) The prosecutor must at the same time so inform the court officer.

R-145 **Prosecutor's application for public interest ruling**

15.3 (1) This rule applies where—
(a) without a court order, the prosecutor would have to disclose material; and
(b) the prosecutor wants the court to decide whether it would be in the public interest to disclose it.
(2) The prosecutor must—
(a) apply in writing for such a decision; and
(b) serve the application on—
(i) the court officer,
(ii) any person who the prosecutor thinks would be directly affected by disclosure of the material, and
(iii) the defendant, but only to the extent that serving it on the defendant would not disclose what the prosecutor thinks ought not be disclosed.
(3) The application must—
(a) describe the material, and explain why the prosecutor thinks that—
(i) it is material that the prosecutor would have to disclose,
(ii) it would not be in the public interest to disclose that material, and
(iii) no measure such as the prosecutor's admission of any fact, or disclosure by summary, extract or edited copy, adequately would protect both the public interest and the defendant's right to a fair trial;
(b) omit from any part of the application that is served on the defendant anything that would disclose what the prosecutor thinks ought not be disclosed (in which case, paragraph (4) of this rule applies); and
(c) explain why, if no part of the application is served on the defendant.
(4) Where the prosecutor serves only part of the application on the defendant, the prosecutor must—
(a) mark the other part, to show that it is only for the court; and
(b) in that other part, explain why the prosecutor has withheld it from the defendant.
(5) Unless already done, the court may direct the prosecutor to serve an application on—
(a) the defendant;
(b) any other person who the court considers would be directly affected by the disclosure of the material.
(6) The court must determine the application at a hearing which—
(a) must be in private, unless the court otherwise directs; and
(b) if the court so directs, may take place, wholly or in part, in the defendant's absence.
(7) At a hearing at which the defendant is present—
(a) the general rule is that the court must consider, in the following sequence—
(i) representations first by the prosecutor and any other person served with the application, and then by the defendant, in the presence of them all, and then
(ii) further representations by the prosecutor and any such other person in the defendant's absence; but
(b) the court may direct other arrangements for the hearing.
(8) The court may only determine the application if satisfied that it has been able to take adequate account of—
(a) such rights of confidentiality as apply to the material; and
(b) the defendant's right to a fair trial.

(9) Unless the court otherwise directs, the court officer—
(a) must not give notice to anyone other than the prosecutor—
(i) of the hearing of an application under this rule, unless the prosecutor served the application on that person, or
(ii) of the court's decision on the application;
(b) may—
(i) keep a written application or representations, or
(ii) arrange for the whole or any part to be kept by some other appropriate person, subject to any conditions that the court may impose.

Defence disclosure R-146

15.4 (1) This rule applies where—
(a) under section 5 or 6 of the Criminal Procedure and Investigations Act 1996, the defendant gives a defence statement;
(b) under section 6C of the 1996 Act, the defendant gives a defence witness notice.
(2) The defendant must serve such a statement or notice on—
(a) the court officer; and
(b) the prosecutor.

Defendant's application for prosecution disclosure R-147

15.5 (1) This rule applies where the defendant—
(a) has served a defence statement given under the Criminal Procedure and Investigations Act 1996; and
(b) wants the court to require the prosecutor to disclose material.
(2) The defendant must serve an application on—
(a) the court officer; and
(b) the prosecutor.
(3) The application must—
(a) describe the material that the defendant wants the prosecutor to disclose;
(b) explain why the defendant thinks there is reasonable cause to believe that—
(i) the prosecutor has that material, and
(ii) it is material that the Criminal Procedure and Investigations Act 1996 requires the prosecutor to disclose; and
(c) ask for a hearing, if the defendant wants one, and explain why it is needed.
(4) The court may determine an application under this rule—
(a) at a hearing, in public or in private; or
(b) without a hearing.
(5) The court must not require the prosecutor to disclose material unless the prosecutor—
(a) is present; or
(b) has had at least 14 days in which to make representations.

Review of public interest ruling R-148

15.6 (1) This rule applies where the court has ordered that it is not in the public interest to disclose material that the prosecutor otherwise would have to disclose, and—
(a) the defendant wants the court to review that decision; or
(b) the Crown Court reviews that decision on its own initiative.
(2) Where the defendant wants the court to review that decision, the defendant must—
(a) serve an application on—
(i) the court officer, and
(ii) the prosecutor; and
(b) in the application—
(i) describe the material that the defendant wants the prosecutor to disclose, and
(ii) explain why the defendant thinks it is no longer in the public interest for the prosecutor not to disclose it.
(3) The prosecutor must serve any such application on any person who the prosecutor thinks would be directly affected if that material were disclosed.
(4) The prosecutor, and any such person, must serve any representations on—
(a) the court officer; and
(b) the defendant, unless to do so would in effect reveal something that either thinks ought not be disclosed.

(5) The court may direct—
(a) the prosecutor to serve any such application on any person who the court considers would be directly affected if that material were disclosed;
(b) the prosecutor and any such person to serve any representations on the defendant.
(6) The court must review a decision to which this rule applies at a hearing which—
(a) must be in private, unless the court otherwise directs; and
(b) if the court so directs, may take place, wholly or in part, in the defendant's absence.
(7) At a hearing at which the defendant is present—
(a) the general rule is that the court must consider, in the following sequence—
(i) representations first by the defendant, and then by the prosecutor and any other person served with the application, in the presence of them all, and then
(ii) further representations by the prosecutor and any such other person in the defendant's absence; but
(b) the court may direct other arrangements for the hearing.
(8) The court may only conclude a review if satisfied that it has been able to take adequate account of—
(a) such rights of confidentiality as apply to the material; and
(b) the defendant's right to a fair trial.

R-149 Defendant's application to use disclosed material

15.7 (1) This rule applies where a defendant wants the court's permission to use disclosed prosecution material—
(a) otherwise than in connection with the case in which it was disclosed; or
(b) beyond the extent to which it was displayed or communicated publicly at a hearing.
(2) The defendant must serve an application on—
(a) the court officer; and
(b) the prosecutor.
(3) The application must—
(a) specify what the defendant wants to use or disclose; and
(b) explain why.
(4) The court may determine an application under this rule—
(a) at a hearing, in public or in private; or
(b) without a hearing.
(5) The court must not permit the use of such material unless—
(a) the prosecutor has had at least 28 days in which to make representations; and
(b) the court is satisfied that it has been able to take adequate account of any rights of confidentiality that may apply to the material.

R-150 Unauthorised use of disclosed material

15.8 (1) This rule applies where a person is accused of using disclosed prosecution material in contravention of section 17 of the Criminal Procedure and Investigations Act 1996.
(2) A party who wants the court to exercise its power to punish that person for contempt of court must comply with the rules in Part 48 (Contempt of court).
(3) The court must not exercise its power to forfeit material used in contempt of court unless—
(a) the prosecutor; and
(b) any other person directly affected by the disclosure of the material.
is present, or has had at least 14 days in which to make representations.

R-151 Court's power to vary requirements under this Part

15.9 The court may—
(a) shorten or extend (even after it has expired) a time limit under this Part;
(b) allow a defence statement, or a defence witness notice, to be in a different written form to one set out in the Practice Direction, as long as it contains what the Criminal Procedure and Investigations Act 1996 requires;
(c) allow an application under this Part to be in a different form to one set out in the Practice Direction, or to be presented orally; and
(d) specify the period within which—
(i) any application under this Part must be made, or
(ii) any material must be disclosed, on an application to which rule 15.5 applies (Defendant's application for prosecution disclosure).

Criminal Practice Directions Part 15 Disclosure

CPD IV Disclosure 15A: Disclosure of Unused Material PD-36

15A.1 Disclosure is a vital part of the preparation for trial, both in the magistrates' courts and in the Crown Court. All parties must be familiar with their obligations, in particular under the Criminal Procedure and Investigations Act 1996 as amended and the Code issued under that Act, and must comply with the relevant judicial protocol and guidelines from the Attorney-General. These documents have recently been revised and the new guidance will be issued shortly as *Judicial Protocol on the Disclosure of Unused Material in Criminal Cases* and the *Attorney-General's Guidelines on Disclosure*. The new documents should be read together as complementary, comprehensive guidance. They will be available electronically on the respective websites.

15A.2 In addition, certain procedures are prescribed under CrimPR Part 15 and these should be followed. The notes to Part 15 contain a useful summary of the requirements of the CPIA 1996 as amended.

Criminal Procedure Rules Part 16 Written Witness Statements

When this Part applies R-152

16.1 This Part applies where a party wants to introduce a written witness statement in evidence under section 9 of the Criminal Justice Act 1967.

Content of written witness statement R-153

16.2 The statement must contain—
(a) at the beginning—
(i) the witness' name, and
(ii) the witness' age, if under 18;
(b) a declaration by the witness that—
(i) it is true to the best of the witness' knowledge and belief, and
(ii) the witness knows that if it is introduced in evidence, then it would be an offence wilfully to have stated in it anything that the witness knew to be false or did not believe to be true;
(c) if the witness cannot read the statement, a signed declaration by someone else that that person read it to the witness; and
(d) the witness' signature.

Reference to exhibit R-154

16.3 Where the statement refers to a document or object as an exhibit, it must identify that document or object clearly.

Written witness statement in evidence R-155

16.4 (1) A party who wants to introduce in evidence a written witness statement must—
(a) before the hearing at which that party wants to introduce it, serve a copy of the statement on—
(i) the court officer, and
(ii) each other party; and
(b) at or before that hearing, serve on the court officer the statement or an authenticated copy.
(2) If that party relies on only part of the statement, that party must mark the copy in such a way as to make that clear.
(3) A prosecutor must serve on a defendant, with the copy of the statement, a notice—
(a) of the right to object to the introduction of the statement in evidence instead of the witness giving evidence in person;
(b) of the time limit for objecting under this rule; and
(c) that if the defendant does not object in time, the court—
(i) can nonetheless require the witness to give evidence in person, but
(ii) may decide not to do so.
(4) A party served with a written witness statement who objects to its introduction in evidence must—
(a) serve notice of the objection on—
(i) the party who served it, and
(ii) the court officer; and

(b) serve the notice of objection not more than 7 days after service of the statement unless—
 (i) the court extends that time limit, before or after the statement was served,
 (ii) rule 24.8 (Written guilty plea: special rules) applies, in which case the time limit is the later of 7 days after service of the statement or 7 days before the hearing date, or
 (iii) rule 24.9 (Single justice procedure: special rules) applies, in which case the time limit is 21 days after service of the statement.

(5) The court may exercise its power to require the witness to give evidence in person—
 (a) on application by any party; or
 (b) on its own initiative.

(6) A party entitled to receive a copy of a statement may waive that entitlement by so informing—
 (a) the party who would have served it; and
 (b) the court.

Criminal Practice Directions Part 16 Written Witness Statements

PD-37 **CPD V Evidence 16A: Evidence by Written Statement**

16A.1 Where the prosecution proposes to tender written statements in evidence under section 9 of the Criminal Justice Act 1967, it will frequently be necessary for certain statements to be edited. This will occur either because a witness has made more than one statement whose contents should conveniently be reduced into a single, comprehensive statement, or where a statement contains inadmissible, prejudicial or irrelevant material. Editing of statements must be done by a Crown Prosecutor (or by a legal representative, if any, of the prosecutor if the case is not being conducted by the Crown Prosecution Service) and not by a police officer.

Composite statements

16A.2 A composite statement giving the combined effect of two or more earlier statements must be prepared in compliance with the requirements of section 9 of the 1967 Act; and must then be signed by the witness.

Editing single statements

16A.3 There are two acceptable methods of editing single statements. They are:

(a) By marking copies of the statement in a way which indicates the passages on which the prosecution will not rely. This merely indicates that the prosecution will not seek to adduce the evidence so marked. The original signed statement to be tendered to the court is not marked in any way.
 The marking on the copy statement is done by lightly striking out the passages to be edited, so that what appears beneath can still be read, or by bracketing, or by a combination of both. It is not permissible to produce a photocopy with the deleted material obliterated, since this would be contrary to the requirement that the defence and the court should be served with copies of the signed original statement.
 Whenever the striking out/bracketing method is used, it will assist if the following words appear at the foot of the frontispiece or index to any bundle of copy statements to be tendered: '*The prosecution does not propose to adduce evidence of those passages of the attached copy statements which have been struck out and/or bracketed (nor will it seek to do so at the trial unless a notice of further evidence is served)*'.

(b) By obtaining a fresh statement, signed by the witness, which omits the offending material, applying the procedure for composite statements above.

16A.4 In most cases where a single statement is to be edited, the striking out/bracketing method will be the more appropriate, but the taking of a fresh statement is preferable in the following circumstances:

(a) When a police (or other investigating) officer's statement contains details of interviews with more suspects than are eventually charged, a fresh statement should be prepared and signed, omitting all details of interview with those not charged except, insofar as it is relevant, for the bald fact that a certain named person was interviewed at a particular time, date and place.

(b) When a suspect is interviewed about more offences than are eventually made the subject of charges, a fresh statement should be prepared and signed, omitting all questions and answers about the uncharged offences unless either they might appropriately be taken into consideration, or evidence about those offences is admissible on the charges preferred. It may, however, be desirable to replace the omitted questions and answers with a phrase such as: '*After referring to some other matters, I then said, ". . . . ."*', so as to make it clear that part of the interview has been omitted.

(c) A fresh statement should normally be prepared and signed if the only part of the original on which the prosecution is relying is only a small proportion of the whole, although it remains desirable to use the alternative method if there is reason to believe that the defence might itself wish to rely, in mitigation or for any other purpose, on at least some of those parts which the prosecution does not propose to adduce.

(d) When the passages contain material which the prosecution is entitled to withhold from disclosure to the defence.

16A.5 Prosecutors should also be aware that, where statements are to be tendered under section 9 of the 1967 Act in the course of summary proceedings, there will be a need to prepare fresh statements excluding inadmissible or prejudicial material, rather than using the striking out or bracketing method.

16A.6 Whenever a fresh statement is taken from a witness and served in evidence, the earlier, unedited statement(s) becomes unused material and should be scheduled and reviewed for disclosure to the defence in the usual way.

CPD V Evidence 16B: Video Recorded Evidence in Chief PD-38

16B.1 The procedure for making an application for leave to admit into evidence video recorded evidence in chief under section 27 of the Youth Justice and Criminal Evidence Act 1999 is given in CrimPR Part 18.

16B.2 Where a court, on application by a party to the proceedings or of its own motion, grants leave to admit a video recording in evidence under section 27(1) of the 1999 Act, it may direct that any part of the recording be excluded (section 27(2) and (3)). When such direction is given, the party who made the application to admit the video recording must edit the recording in accordance with the judge's directions and send a copy of the edited recording to the appropriate officer of the Crown Court and to every other party to the proceedings.

16B.3 Where a video recording is to be adduced during proceedings before the Crown Court, it should be produced and proved by the interviewer, or any other person who was present at the interview with the witness at which the recording was made. The applicant should ensure that such a person will be available for this purpose, unless the parties have agreed to accept a written statement in lieu of attendance by that person.

16B.4 Once a trial has begun, if, by reason of faulty or inadequate preparation or for some other cause, the procedures set out above have not been properly complied with and an application is made to edit the video recording, thereby necessitating an adjournment for the work to be carried out, the court may, at its discretion, make an appropriate award of costs.

CPD V Evidence 16C: Evidence of Audio and Video Recorded Interviews PD-39

16C.1 The interrogation of suspects is primarily governed by Code C, one of the Codes of Practice under the Police and Criminal Evidence Act 1984 ('PACE'). Under that Code, interviews must normally be contemporaneously recorded. Under PACE Code E, interviews conducted at a police station concerning an indictable offence must normally be audio-recorded. In practice, most interviews are audio-recorded under Code E, or video-recorded under Code F, and it is best practice to do so. The questioning of terrorism suspects is governed separately by Code H. The Codes are available electronically on the Home Office website.

16C.2 Where a record of the interview is to be prepared, this should be in accordance with the current national guidelines, as envisaged by Note 5A of Code E.

16C.3 If the prosecution wishes to rely on the defendant's interview in evidence, the prosecution should seek to agree the record with the defence. Both parties should have received a copy of the audio or video recording, and can check the record against the recording. The record should be edited (see below) if inadmissible matters are included within it and, in particular if the interview is lengthy, the prosecution should seek to shorten it by editing or summary.

16C.4 If the record is agreed there is usually no need for the audio or video recording to be played in court. It is a matter for the discretion of the trial judge, but usual practice is for edited copies of the record to be provided to the court, and to the jury if there is one, and for the prosecution advocate to read the interview with the interviewing officer or the officer in the case, as part of the officer's evidence in chief, the officer reading the interviewer and the advocate reading the defendant and defence representative. In the magistrates' court, the Bench sometimes retire to read the interview themselves, and the document is treated as if it had been read aloud in court. This is permissible, but CrimPR 24.5 should be followed.

16C.5 Where the prosecution intends to adduce the interview in evidence, and agreement between the parties has not been reached about the record, sufficient notice must be given to allow consideration of any amendment to the record, or the preparation of any transcript of the interview, or any editing of a recording for the purpose of playing it in court. To that end, the following practice should be followed:

(a) Where the defence is unable to agree a record of interview or transcript (where one is already available) the prosecution should be notified at latest at the Plea and Case Management

Hearing ('PCMH'), with a view to securing agreement to amend. The notice should specify the part to which objection is taken, or the part omitted which the defence consider should be included. A copy of the notice should be supplied to the court within the period specified above. The PCMH form inquires about the admissibility of the defendant's interview and shortening by editing or summarising for trial.

(b) If agreement is not reached and it is proposed that the audio or video recording or part of it be played in court, notice should be given to the prosecution by the defence as ordered at the PCMH, in order that the advocates for the parties may agree those parts of the audio or video recording that should not be adduced and that arrangements may be made, by editing or in some other way, to exclude that material. A copy of the notice should be supplied to the court.

(c) Notice of any agreement reached should be supplied to the court by the prosecution, as soon as is practicable.

16C.6 Alternatively, if, the prosecution advocate proposes to play the audio or video recording or part of it, the prosecution should at latest at the PCMH, notify the defence and the court. The defence should notify the prosecution and the court within 14 days of receiving the notice, if they object to the production of the audio or video recording on the basis that a part of it should be excluded. If the objections raised by the defence are accepted, the prosecution should prepare an edited recording, or make other arrangements to exclude the material part; and should notify the court of the arrangements made.

16C.7 If the defendant wishes to have the audio or video recording or any part of it played to the court, the defence should provide notice to the prosecution and the court at latest at the PCMH. The defence should also, at that time, notify the prosecution of any proposals to edit the recording and seek the prosecution's agreement to those amendments.

16C.8 Whenever editing or amendment of a record of interview or of an audio or video recording or of a transcript takes place, the following general principles should be followed:

(i) Where a defendant has made a statement which includes an admission of one or more other offences, the portion relating to other offences should be omitted unless it is or becomes admissible in evidence;

(ii) Where the statement of one defendant contains a portion which exculpates him or her and partly implicates a co-defendant in the trial, the defendant making the statement has the right to insist that everything relevant which is exculpatory goes before the jury. In such a case the judge must be consulted about how best to protect the position of the co-defendant.

16C.9 If it becomes necessary for either party to access the master copy of the audio or video recording, they should give notice to the other party and follow the procedure in PACE Code E at section 6.

16C.10 If there is a challenge to the integrity of the master recording, notice and particulars should be given to the court and to the prosecution by the defence as soon as is practicable. The court may then, at its discretion, order a case management hearing or give such other directions as may be appropriate.

16C.11 If an audio or video recording is to be adduced during proceedings before the Crown Court, it should be produced and proved in a witness statement by the interviewing officer or any other officer who was present at the interview at which the recording was made. The prosecution should ensure that the witness is available to attend court if required by the defence in the usual way.

16C.12 It is the responsibility of the prosecution to ensure that there is a person available to operate any audio or video equipment needed during the course of the proceedings. Subject to their other responsibilities, the court staff may be able to assist.

16C.13 If either party wishes to present audio or video evidence, that party must ensure, in advance of the hearing, that the evidence is in a format that is compatible with the court's equipment, and that the material to be used does in fact function properly in the relevant court room.

16C.14 In order to avoid the necessity for the court to listen to or watch lengthy or irrelevant material before the relevant part of a recording is reached, counsel shall indicate to the equipment operator those parts of a recording which it may be necessary to play. Such an indication should, so far as possible, be expressed in terms of the time track or other identifying process used by the interviewing police force and should be given in time for the operator to have located those parts by the appropriate point in the trial.

16C.15 Once a trial has begun, if, by reason of faulty preparation or for some other cause, the procedures above have not been properly complied with, and an application is made to amend the record of interview or transcript or to edit the recording, as the case may be, thereby making necessary an adjournment for the work to be carried out, the court may make at its discretion an appropriate award of costs.

16C.16 Where a case is listed for hearing on a date which falls within the time limits set out above, it is the responsibility of the parties to ensure that all the necessary steps are taken to comply with this Practice Direction within such shorter period as is available.

Criminal Procedure Rules Part 17 Witness Summonses, Warrants and Orders

When this Part applies R-156

17.1 (1) This Part applies in magistrates' courts and in the Crown Court where—
(a) a party wants the court to issue a witness summons, warrant or order under—
(i) section 97 of the Magistrates' Courts Act 1980,
(ii) paragraph 4 of Schedule 3 to the Crime and Disorder Act 1998,
(iii) section 2 of the Criminal Procedure (Attendance of Witnesses) Act 1965, or
(iv) section 7 of the Bankers' Books Evidence Act 1879;
(b) the court considers the issue of such a summons, warrant or order on its own initiative as if a party had applied; or
(c) one of those listed in rule 17.7 wants the court to withdraw such a summons, warrant or order.
(2) A reference to a 'witness' in this Part is a reference to a person to whom such a summons, warrant or order is directed.

Issue etc. of summons, warrant or order with or without a hearing R-157

17.2 (1) The court may issue or withdraw a witness summons, warrant or order with or without a hearing.
(2) A hearing under this Part must be in private unless the court otherwise directs.

Application for summons, warrant or order: general rules R-158

17.3 (1) A party who wants the court to issue a witness summons, warrant or order must apply as soon as practicable after becoming aware of the grounds for doing so.
(2) A party applying for a witness summons must—
(a) identify the proposed witness;
(b) explain—
(i) what evidence the proposed witness can give or produce,
(ii) why it is likely to be material evidence, and
(iii) why it would be in the interests of justice to issue a summons, order or warrant as appropriate.
(3) A party applying for an order to be allowed to inspect and copy an entry in bank records must—
(a) identify the entry;
(b) explain the purpose for which the entry is required; and
(c) propose—
(i) the terms of the order, and
(ii) the period within which the order should take effect, if 3 days from the date of service of the order would not be appropriate.
(4) The application may be made orally unless—
(a) rule 17.5 applies; or
(b) the court otherwise directs.
(5) The applicant must serve any order made on the witness to whom, or the bank to which, it is directed.

Written application: form and service R-159

17.4 (1) An application in writing under rule 17.3 must be in the form set out in the Practice Direction, containing the same declaration of truth as a witness statement.
(2) The party applying must serve the application—
(a) in every case, on the court officer and as directed by the court; and
(b) as required by rule 17.5, if that rule applies.

Application for summons to produce a document, etc.: special rules R-160

17.5 (1) This rule applies to an application under rule 17.3 for a witness summons requiring the proposed witness—
(a) to produce in evidence a document or thing; or
(b) to give evidence about information apparently held in confidence, that relates to another person.
(2) The application must be in writing in the form required by rule 17.4.
(3) The party applying must serve the application—
(a) on the proposed witness, unless the court otherwise directs; and
(b) on one or more of the following, if the court so directs—
(i) a person to whom the proposed evidence relates,
(ii) another party.

(4) The court must not issue a witness summons where this rule applies unless—
(a) everyone served with the application has had at least 14 days in which to make representations, including representations about whether there should be a hearing of the application before the summons is issued; and
(b) the court is satisfied that it has been able to take adequate account of the duties and rights, including rights of confidentiality, of the proposed witness and of any person to whom the proposed evidence relates.

(5) This rule does not apply to an application for an order to produce in evidence a copy of an entry in a banker's book.

R-161 Application for summons to produce a document, etc.: court's assessment of relevance and confidentiality

17.6 (1) This rule applies where a person served with an application for a witness summons requiring the proposed witness to produce in evidence a document or thing objects to its production on the ground that—
(a) it is not likely to be material evidence; or
(b) even if it is likely to be material evidence, the duties or rights, including rights of confidentiality, of the proposed witness or of any person to whom the document or thing relates, outweigh the reasons for issuing a summons.

(2) The court may require the proposed witness to make the document or thing available for the objection to be assessed.

(3) The court may invite—
(a) the proposed witness or any representative of the proposed witness; or
(b) a person to whom the document or thing relates or any representative of such a person, to help the court assess the objection.

R-162 Application to withdraw a summons, warrant or order

17.7 (1) The court may withdraw a witness summons, warrant or order if one of the following applies for it to be withdrawn—
(a) the party who applied for it, on the ground that it no longer is needed;
(b) the witness, on the grounds that—
(i) he was not aware of any application for it, and
(ii) he cannot give or produce evidence likely to be material evidence, or
(iii) even if he can, his duties or rights, including rights of confidentiality, or those of any person to whom the evidence relates, outweigh the reasons for the issue of the summons, warrant or order; or
(c) any person to whom the proposed evidence relates, on the grounds that—
(i) he was not aware of any application for it, and
(ii) that evidence is not likely to be material evidence, or
(iii) even if it is, his duties or rights, including rights of confidentiality, or those of the witness, outweigh the reasons for the issue of the summons, warrant or order.

(2) A person applying under the rule must—
(a) apply in writing as soon as practicable after becoming aware of the grounds for doing so, explaining why he wants the summons, warrant or order to be withdrawn; and
(b) serve the application on the court officer and as appropriate on—
(i) the witness,
(ii) the party who applied for the summons, warrant or order, and
(iii) any other person who he knows was served with the application for the summons, warrant or order.

(3) Rule 17.6 applies to an application under this rule that concerns a document or thing to be produced in evidence.

R-163 Court's power to vary requirements under this Part

17.8 (1) The court may—
(a) shorten or extend (even after it has expired) a time limit under this Part; and
(b) where a rule or direction requires an application under this Part to be in writing, allow that application to be made orally instead.

(2) Someone who wants the court to allow an application to be made orally under paragraph (1)(b) of this rule must—
(a) give as much notice as the urgency of his application permits to those on whom he would otherwise have served an application in writing; and
(b) in doing so explain the reasons for the application and for wanting the court to consider it orally.

Criminal Practice Directions Part 17 Witness Summonses, Warrants and Orders

CPD V Evidence 17A: Wards of Court and Children Subject to Current Family Proceedings **PD-40**

17A.1 Where police wish to interview a child who is subject to current family proceedings, leave of the Family Court is only required where such an interview may lead to a child disclosing information confidential to those proceedings and not otherwise available to the police under Working Together to Safeguard Children (March 2013), a guide to inter-agency working to safeguard and promote the welfare of children: www.workingtogetheronline.co.uk/chapters/contents.html

17A.2 Where exceptionally the child to be interviewed or called as a witness in criminal proceedings is a Ward of Court then the leave of the court which made the wardship order will be required.

17A.3 Any application for leave in respect of any such child must be made to the court in which the relevant family proceedings are continuing and must be made on notice to the parents, any actual carer (e.g., relative or foster parent) and, in care proceedings, to the local authority and the guardian. In private proceedings the Family Court Reporter (if appointed) should be notified.

17A.4 If the police need to interview the child without the knowledge of another party (usually a parent or carer), they may make the application for leave without giving notice to that party.

17A.5 Where leave is given the order should ordinarily give leave for any number of interviews that may be required. However, anything beyond that actually authorised will require a further application.

17A.6 Exceptionally the police may have to deal with complaints by or allegations against such a child immediately without obtaining the leave of the court as, for example:
(a) a serious offence against a child (like rape) where immediate medical examination and collection of evidence is required; or
(b) where the child is to be interviewed as a suspect.

When any such action is necessary, the police should, in respect of each and every interview, notify the parents and other carer (if any) and the Family Court Reporter (if appointed). In care proceedings the local authority and guardian should be notified. The police must comply with all relevant Codes of Practice when conducting any such interview.

17A.7 The Family Court should be appraised of the position at the earliest reasonable opportunity by one of the notified parties and should thereafter be kept informed of any criminal proceedings.

17A.8 No evidence or document in the family proceedings or information about the proceedings should be disclosed into criminal proceedings without the leave of the Family Court.

Criminal Procedure Rules Part 18 Measures to Assist a Witness or Defendant to Give Evidence

General rules

When this Part applies **R-164**

18.1 This Part applies—
(a) where the court can give a direction (a 'special measures direction'), under section 19 of the Youth Justice and Criminal Evidence Act 1999, on an application or on its own initiative, for any of the following measures—
(i) preventing a witness from seeing the defendant (section 23 of the 1999 Act),
(ii) allowing a witness to give evidence by live link (section 24 of the 1999 Act),
(iii) hearing a witness' evidence in private (section 25 of the 1999 Act),
(iv) dispensing with the wearing of wigs and gowns (section 26 of the 1999 Act),
(v) admitting video recorded evidence (sections 27 and 28 of the 1999 Act),
(vi) questioning a witness through an intermediary (section 29 of the 1999 Act),
(vii) using a device to help a witness communicate (section 30 of the 1999 Act);
(b) where the court can vary or discharge such a direction, under section 20 of the 1999 Act;
(c) where the court can give, vary or discharge a direction (a 'defendant's evidence direction') for a defendant to give evidence—
(i) by live link, under section 33A of the 1999 Act, or
(ii) through an intermediary, under sections 33BA and 33BB of the 1999 Act;
(d) where the court can—
(i) make a witness anonymity order, under section 86 of the Coroners and Justice Act 2009, or
(ii) vary or discharge such an order, under section 91, 92 or 93 of the 2009 Act;
(e) where the court can give or discharge a direction (a 'live link direction'), on an application or on its own initiative, for a witness to give evidence by live link under—
(i) section 32 of the Criminal Justice Act 1988, or
(ii) sections 51 and 52 of the Criminal Justice Act 2003;

(f) where the court can exercise any other power it has to give, vary or discharge a direction for a measure to help a witness give evidence.

R-165 Meaning of 'witness'

18.2 In this Part, 'witness' means anyone (other than a defendant) for whose benefit an application, direction or order is made.

R-166 Making an application for a direction or order

18.3 A party who wants the court to exercise its power to give or make a direction or order must—
(a) apply in writing as soon as reasonably practicable, and in any event not more than—
(i) 28 days after the defendant pleads not guilty, in a magistrates' court, or
(ii) 14 days after the defendant pleads not guilty, in the Crown Court; and
(b) serve the application on—
(i) the court officer, and
(ii) each other party.

R-167 Decisions and reasons

18.4 (1) A party who wants to introduce the evidence of a witness who is the subject of an application, direction or order must—
(a) inform the witness of the court's decision as soon as reasonably practicable; and
(b) explain to the witness the arrangements that as a result will be made for him or her to give evidence.
(2) The court must—
(a) promptly determine an application; and
(b) allow a party sufficient time to comply with the requirements of—
(i) paragraph (1), and
(ii) the code of practice issued under section 32 of the Domestic Violence, Crime and Victims Act 2004.
(3) The court must announce, at a hearing in public before the witness gives evidence, the reasons for a decision—
(a) to give, make, vary or discharge a direction or order; or
(b) to refuse to do so.

R-168 Court's power to vary requirements under this Part

18.5 (1) The court may—
(a) shorten or extend (even after it has expired) a time limit under this Part; and
(b) allow an application or representations to be made in a different form to one set out in the Practice Direction, or to be made orally.
(2) A person who wants an extension of time must—
(a) apply when serving the application or representations for which it is needed; and
(b) explain the delay.

R-169 Custody of documents

18.6 Unless the court otherwise directs, the court officer may—
(a) keep a written application or representations; or
(b) arrange for the whole or any part to be kept by some other appropriate person, subject to any conditions that the court may impose.

R-170 Declaration by intermediary

18.7 (1) This rule applies where—
(a) a video recorded interview with a witness is conducted through an intermediary;
(b) the court directs the examination of a witness or defendant through an intermediary.
(2) An intermediary must make a declaration—
(a) before such an interview begins;
(b) before the examination begins (even if such an interview with the witness was conducted through the same intermediary).
(3) The declaration must be in these terms—
'I solemnly, sincerely and truly declare [*or* I swear by Almighty God] that I will well and faithfully communicate questions and answers and make true explanation of all matters and things as shall be required of me according to the best of my skill and understanding.'

Special measures directions

Exercise of court's powers R-171

18.8 The court may decide whether to give, vary or discharge a special measures direction—
(a) at a hearing, in public or in private, or without a hearing;
(b) in a party's absence, if that party—
(i) applied for the direction, variation or discharge, or
(ii) has had at least 14 days in which to make representations.

Special measures direction for a young witness R-172

18.9 (1) This rule applies where, under section 21 or section 22 of the Youth Justice and Criminal Evidence Act 1999, the primary rule requires the court to give a direction for a special measure to assist a child witness or a qualifying witness—
(a) on an application, if one is made; or
(b) on the court's own initiative, in any other case.
(2) A party who wants to introduce the evidence of such a witness must as soon as reasonably practicable—
(a) notify the court that the witness is eligible for assistance;
(b) provide the court with any information that the court may need to assess the witness' views, if the witness does not want the primary rule to apply; and
(c) serve any video recorded evidence on—
(i) the court officer, and
(ii) each other party.

Content of application for a special measures direction R-173

18.10 An applicant for a special measures direction must—
(a) explain how the witness is eligible for assistance;
(b) explain why special measures would be likely to improve the quality of the witness' evidence;
(c) propose the measure or measures that in the applicant's opinion would be likely to maximise, so far as practicable, the quality of that evidence;
(d) report any views that the witness has expressed about—
(i) his or her eligibility for assistance,
(ii) the likelihood that special measures would improve the quality of his or her evidence, and
(iii) the measure or measures proposed by the applicant;
(e) in a case in which a child witness or a qualifying witness does not want the primary rule to apply, provide any information that the court may need to assess the witness' views;
(f) in a case in which the applicant proposes that the witness should give evidence by live link—
(i) identify someone to accompany the witness while the witness gives evidence,
(ii) name that person, if possible, and
(iii) explain why that person would be an appropriate companion for the witness, including the witness' own views;
(g) in a case in which the applicant proposes the admission of video recorded evidence, identify—
(i) the date and duration of the recording,
(ii) which part the applicant wants the court to admit as evidence, if the applicant does not want the court to admit all of it;
(h) attach any other material on which the applicant relies; and
(i) if the applicant wants a hearing, ask for one, and explain why it is needed.

Application to vary or discharge a special measures direction R-174

18.11 (1) A party who wants the court to vary or discharge a special measures direction must—
(a) apply in writing, as soon as reasonably practicable after becoming aware of the grounds for doing so; and
(b) serve the application on—
(i) the court officer, and
(ii) each other party.
(2) The applicant must—
(a) explain what material circumstances have changed since the direction was given (or last varied, if applicable);

(b) explain why the direction should be varied or discharged; and
(c) ask for a hearing, if the applicant wants one, and explain why it is needed.

R-175 Application containing information withheld from another party

18.12 (1) This rule applies where—
(a) an applicant serves an application for a special measures direction, or for its variation or discharge; and
(b) the application includes information that the applicant thinks ought not be revealed to another party.
(2) The applicant must—
(a) omit that information from the part of the application that is served on that other party;
(b) mark the other part to show that, unless the court otherwise directs, it is only for the court; and
(c) in that other part, explain why the applicant has withheld that information from that other party.
(3) Any hearing of an application to which this rule applies—
(a) must be in private, unless the court otherwise directs; and
(b) if the court so directs, may be, wholly or in part, in the absence of a party from whom information has been withheld.
(4) At any hearing of an application to which this rule applies—
(a) the general rule is that the court must consider, in the following sequence—
(i) representations first by the applicant and then by each other party, in all the parties' presence, and then
(ii) further representations by the applicant, in the absence of a party from whom information has been withheld; but
(b) the court may direct other arrangements for the hearing.

R-176 Representations in response

18.13 (1) This rule applies where a party wants to make representations about—
(a) an application for a special measures direction;
(b) an application for the variation or discharge of such a direction; or
(c) a direction, variation or discharge that the court proposes on its own initiative.
(2) Such a party must—
(a) serve the representations on—
(i) the court officer, and
(ii) each other party;
(b) do so not more than 14 days after, as applicable—
(i) service of the application, or
(ii) notice of the direction, variation or discharge that the court proposes; and
(c) ask for a hearing, if that party wants one, and explain why it is needed.
(3) Where representations include information that the person making them thinks ought not be revealed to another party, that person must—
(a) omit that information from the representations served on that other party;
(b) mark the information to show that, unless the court otherwise directs, it is only for the court; and
(c) with that information include an explanation of why it has been withheld from that other party.
(4) Representations against a special measures direction must explain, as appropriate—
(a) why the witness is not eligible for assistance; or
(b) if the witness is eligible for assistance, why—
(i) no special measure would be likely to improve the quality of the witness' evidence,
(ii) the proposed measure or measures would not be likely to maximise, so far as practicable, the quality of the witness' evidence, or
(iii) the proposed measure or measures might tend to inhibit the effective testing of that evidence;
(c) in a case in which the admission of video recorded evidence is proposed, why it would not be in the interests of justice for the recording, or part of it, to be admitted as evidence.
(5) Representations against the variation or discharge of a special measures direction must explain why it should not be varied or discharged.

Defendant's evidence directions

R-177 Exercise of court's powers

18.14 The court may decide whether to give, vary or discharge a defendant's evidence direction—
(a) at a hearing, in public or in private, or without a hearing;

(b) in a party's absence, if that party—
(i) applied for the direction, variation or discharge, or
(ii) has had at least 14 days in which to make representations.

Content of application for a defendant's evidence direction R-178

18.15 An applicant for a defendant's evidence direction must—
(a) explain how the proposed direction meets the conditions prescribed by the Youth Justice and Criminal Evidence Act 1999;
(b) in a case in which the applicant proposes that the defendant give evidence by live link—
(i) identify a person to accompany the defendant while the defendant gives evidence, and
(ii) explain why that person is appropriate;
(c) ask for a hearing, if the applicant wants one, and explain why it is needed.

Application to vary or discharge a defendant's evidence direction R-179

18.16 (1) A party who wants the court to vary or discharge a defendant's evidence direction must—
(a) apply in writing, as soon as reasonably practicable after becoming aware of the grounds for doing so; and
(b) serve the application on—
(i) the court officer, and
(ii) each other party.
(2) The applicant must—
(a) on an application to discharge a live link direction, explain why it is in the interests of justice to do so;
(b) on an application to discharge a direction for an intermediary, explain why it is no longer necessary in order to ensure that the defendant receives a fair trial;
(c) on an application to vary a direction for an intermediary, explain why it is necessary for the direction to be varied in order to ensure that the defendant receives a fair trial; and
(d) ask for a hearing, if the applicant wants one, and explain why it is needed.

Representations in response R-180

18.17 (1) This rule applies where a party wants to make representations about—
(a) an application for a defendant's evidence direction;
(b) an application for the variation or discharge of such a direction; or
(c) a direction, variation or discharge that the court proposes on its own initiative.
(2) Such a party must—
(a) serve the representations on—
(i) the court officer, and
(ii) each other party;
(b) do so not more than 14 days after, as applicable—
(i) service of the application, or
(ii) notice of the direction, variation or discharge that the court proposes; and
(c) ask for a hearing, if that party wants one, and explain why it is needed.
(3) Representations against a direction, variation or discharge must explain why the conditions prescribed by the Youth Justice and Criminal Evidence Act 1999 are not met.

Witness anonymity orders

Exercise of court's powers R-181

18.18 (1) The court may decide whether to make, vary or discharge a witness anonymity order—
(a) at a hearing (which must be in private, unless the court otherwise directs), or without a hearing (unless any party asks for one);
(b) in the absence of a defendant.
(2) The court must not exercise its power to make, vary or discharge a witness anonymity order, or to refuse to do so—
(a) before or during the trial, unless each party has had an opportunity to make representations;
(b) on an appeal by the defendant to which applies Part 34 (Appeal to the Crown Court) or Part 39 (Appeal to the Court of Appeal about conviction or sentence), unless in each party's case—
(i) that party has had an opportunity to make representations, or
(ii) the appeal court is satisfied that it is not reasonably practicable to communicate with that party;
(c) after the trial and any such appeal are over, unless in the case of each party and the witness—
(i) each has had an opportunity to make representations, or
(ii) the court is satisfied that it is not reasonably practicable to communicate with that party or witness.

R-182 Content and conduct of application for a witness anonymity order

18.19 (1) An applicant for a witness anonymity order must—
(a) include in the application nothing that might reveal the witness' identity;
(b) describe the measures proposed by the applicant;
(c) explain how the proposed order meets the conditions prescribed by section 88 of the Coroners and Justice Act 2009;
(d) explain why no measures other than those proposed will suffice, such as—
(i) an admission of the facts that would be proved by the witness,
(ii) an order restricting public access to the trial,
(iii) reporting restrictions, in particular under sections 45, 45A or 46 of the Youth Justice and Criminal Evidence Act 1999,
(iv) a direction for a special measure under section 19 of the Youth Justice and Criminal Evidence Act 1999,
(v) introduction of the witness' written statement as hearsay evidence, under section 116 of the Criminal Justice Act 2003, or
(vi) arrangements for the protection of the witness;
(e) attach to the application—
(i) a witness statement setting out the proposed evidence, edited in such a way as not to reveal the witness' identity,
(ii) where the prosecutor is the applicant, any further prosecution evidence to be served, and any further prosecution material to be disclosed under the Criminal Procedure and Investigations Act 1996, similarly edited, and
(iii) any defence statement that has been served, or as much information as may be available to the applicant that gives particulars of the defence; and
(f) ask for a hearing, if the applicant wants one.

(2) At any hearing of the application, the applicant must—
(a) identify the witness to the court, unless at the prosecutor's request the court otherwise directs; and
(b) present to the court, unless it otherwise directs—
(i) the unedited witness statement from which the edited version has been prepared,
(ii) where the prosecutor is the applicant, the unedited version of any further prosecution evidence or material from which an edited version has been prepared, and
(iii) such further material as the applicant relies on to establish that the proposed order meets the conditions prescribed by section 88 of the 2009 Act.

(3) At any such hearing—
(a) the general rule is that the court must consider, in the following sequence—
(i) representations first by the applicant and then by each other party, in all the parties' presence, and then
(ii) information withheld from a defendant, and further representations by the applicant, in the absence of any (or any other) defendant; but
(b) the court may direct other arrangements for the hearing.

(4) Before the witness gives evidence, the applicant must identify the witness to the court—
(a) if not already done;
(b) without revealing the witness' identity to any other party or person; and
(c) unless at the prosecutor's request the court otherwise directs.

R-183 Duty of court officer to notify the Director of Public Prosecutions

18.20 The court officer must notify the Director of Public Prosecutions of an application, unless the prosecutor is, or acts on behalf of, a public authority.

R-184 Application to vary or discharge a witness anonymity order

18.21 (1) A party who wants the court to vary or discharge a witness anonymity order, or a witness who wants the court to do so when the case is over, must—
(a) apply in writing, as soon as reasonably practicable after becoming aware of the grounds for doing so; and
(b) serve the application on—
(i) the court officer, and
(ii) each other party.

(2) The applicant must—
(a) explain what material circumstances have changed since the order was made (or last varied, if applicable);

(b) explain why the order should be varied or discharged, taking account of the conditions for making an order; and
(c) ask for a hearing, if the applicant wants one.

(3) Where an application includes information that the applicant thinks might reveal the witness' identity, the applicant must—
(a) omit that information from the application that is served on a defendant;
(b) mark the information to show that it is only for the court and the prosecutor (if the prosecutor is not the applicant); and
(c) with that information include an explanation of why it has been withheld.

(4) Where a party applies to vary or discharge a witness anonymity order after the trial and any appeal are over, the party who introduced the witness' evidence must serve the application on the witness.

Representations in response R-185

18.22 (1) This rule applies where a party or, where the case is over, a witness, wants to make representations about—
(a) an application for a witness anonymity order;
(b) an application for the variation or discharge of such an order; or
(c) a variation or discharge that the court proposes on its own initiative.

(2) Such a party or witness must—
(a) serve the representations on—
(i) the court officer, and
(ii) each other party;
(b) do so not more than 14 days after, as applicable—
(i) service of the application, or
(ii) notice of the variation or discharge that the court proposes; and
(c) ask for a hearing, if that party or witness wants one.

(3) Where representations include information that the person making them thinks might reveal the witness' identity, that person must—
(a) omit that information from the representations served on a defendant;
(b) mark the information to show that it is only for the court (and for the prosecutor, if relevant); and
(c) with that information include an explanation of why it has been withheld.

(4) Representations against a witness anonymity order must explain why the conditions for making the order are not met.

(5) Representations against the variation or discharge of such an order must explain why it would not be appropriate to vary or discharge it, taking account of the conditions for making an order.

(6) A prosecutor's representations in response to an application by a defendant must include all information available to the prosecutor that is relevant to the conditions and considerations specified by sections 88 and 89 of the Coroners and Justice Act 2009.

Live link directions

Exercise of court's powers R-186

18.23 The court may decide whether to give or discharge a live link direction—
(a) at a hearing, in public or in private, or without a hearing;
(b) in a party's absence, if that party—
(i) applied for the direction or discharge, or
(ii) has had at least 14 days in which to make representations in response to an application by another party.

Content of application for a live link direction R-187

18.24 (1) An applicant for a live link direction must—
(a) unless the court otherwise directs, identify the place from which the witness will give evidence;
(b) if that place is in the United Kingdom, explain why it would be in the interests of the efficient or effective administration of justice for the witness to give evidence by live link;
(c) if the applicant wants the witness to be accompanied by another person while giving evidence—
(i) name that person, if possible, and
(ii) explain why it is appropriate for the witness to be accompanied;
(d) ask for a hearing, if the applicant wants one, and explain why it is needed.

(2) An applicant for a live link direction under section 32 of the Criminal Justice Act 1988 who wants the court also to make a European investigation order must—
(a) identify the participating State in which, and the place in that State from which, the witness will give evidence;
(b) explain why it is necessary and proportionate to make a European investigation order;
(c) if applicable, explain how the requirements of regulation 14 of the Criminal Justice (European Investigation Order) Regulations 2017 are met (Hearing a person by videoconference or telephone); and
(d) attach a draft order in the form required by regulation 8 of the 2017 Regulations (Form and content of a European investigation order) and Directive 2014/41/EU.

(3) Where the court makes a European investigation order, the court officer must promptly—
(a) issue an order in the form required by regulation 8 of the 2017 Regulations (Form and content of a European investigation order) and Directive 2014/41/EU;
(b) where the applicant is a constable or a prosecuting authority, serve that order on the applicant;
(c) in any other case, serve that order on the appropriate authority in the participating State in which the measure or measures are to be carried out.

R-188 Application to discharge a live link direction, etc

18.25 (1) A party who wants the court to discharge a live link direction must—
(a) apply in writing, as soon as reasonably practicable after becoming aware of the grounds for doing so; and
(b) serve the application on—
(i) the court officer, and
(ii) each other party.

(2) The applicant must—
(a) explain what material circumstances have changed since the direction was given;
(b) explain why it is in the interests of justice to discharge the direction; and
(c) ask for a hearing, if the applicant wants one, and explain why it is needed.

(3) An applicant for the variation or revocation of a European investigation order made on an application under rule 18.24 must demonstrate that the applicant is, as the case may be—
(a) the person who applied for the order;
(b) a prosecuting authority; or
(c) any other person affected by the order.

(4) Where the court varies or revokes such an order, the court officer must promptly notify the appropriate authority in the participating State in which the measure or measures are to be carried out.

R-189 Representations in response

18.26 (1) This rule applies where a party wants to make representations about an application for a live link direction or for the discharge of such a direction.

(2) Such a party must—
(a) serve the representations on—
(i) the court officer, and
(ii) each other party;
(b) do so not more than 14 days after service of the application; and—
(c) ask for a hearing, if that party wants one, and explain why it is needed.

(3) Representations against a direction or discharge must explain, as applicable, why the conditions prescribed by the Criminal Justice Act 1988 or the Criminal Justice Act 2003 are not met.

Criminal Practice Directions Part 18 Measures to Assist a Witness or Defendant to Give Evidence

PD-41 CPD V Evidence 18A: Measures to Assist a Witness or Defendant to give Evidence

18A.1 For special measures applications, the procedures at CrimPR Part 18 should be followed. However, assisting a vulnerable witness to give evidence is not merely a matter of ordering the appropriate measure. Further directions about vulnerable people in the courts, ground rules hearings and intermediaries are given in paragraphs I 3D to 3G.

18A.2 Special measures need not be considered or ordered in isolation. The needs of the individual witness should be ascertained, and a combination of special measures may be appropriate. For example, if a witness who is to give evidence by live link wishes, screens can be used to shield the live link screen from the defendant and the public, as would occur if screens were being used for a witness giving evidence in the court room.

CPD V Evidence 18B: Witnesses giving Evidence by Live Link PD-42

18B.1 A special measures direction for the witness to give evidence by live link may also provide for a specified person to accompany the witness (CrimPR 18.10(f)). In determining who this should be, the court must have regard to the wishes of the witness. The presence of a supporter is designed to provide emotional support to the witness, helping reduce the witness's anxiety and stress and contributing to the ability to give best evidence. It is preferable for the direction to be made well before the trial begins and to ensure that the designated person is available on the day of the witness's testimony so as to provide certainty for the witness.

18B.2 An increased degree of flexibility is appropriate as to who can act as supporter. This can be anyone known to and trusted by the witness who is not a party to the proceedings and has no detailed knowledge of the evidence in the case. The supporter may be a member of the Witness Service but need not be an usher or court official. Someone else may be appropriate.

18B.3 The usher should continue to be available both to assist the witness and the witness supporter, and to ensure that the court's requirements are properly complied with in the live link room.

18B.4 In order to be able to express an informed view about special measures, the witness is entitled to practise speaking using the live link (and to see screens in place). Simply being shown the room and equipment is inadequate for this purpose.

18B.5 If, with the agreement of the court, the witness has chosen not to give evidence by live link but to do so in the court room, it may still be appropriate for a witness supporter to be selected in the same way, and for the supporter to sit alongside the witness while the witness is giving evidence.

CPD V Evidence 18C: Visually Recorded Interviews: Memory Refreshing and Watching at a Different Time from the Trial Court PD-43

18C.1 Witnesses are entitled to refresh their memory from their statement or visually recorded interview. The court should enquire at the PTPH or other case management hearing about arrangements for memory refreshing. The witness's first viewing of the visually recorded interview can be distressing or distracting. It should not be seen for the first time immediately before giving evidence. Depending upon the age and vulnerability of the witness several competing issues have to be considered and it may be that the assistance of the intermediary is needed to establish exactly how memory refreshing should be managed.

18C.2 If the interview is ruled inadmissible, the court must decide what constitutes an acceptable alternative method of memory refreshing.

18C.3 Decisions about how, when and where refreshing should take place should be court-led and made on a case-by-case basis in respect of each witness. General principles to be addressed include:

i. the venue for viewing. The delicate balance between combining the court familiarisation visit and watching the DVD, and having them on two separate occasions, needs to be considered in respect of each witness as combining the two may lead to 'information overload'. Refreshing need not necessarily take place within the court building but may be done, for example, at the police ABE suite;
ii. requiring that any viewing is monitored by a person (usually the officer in the case) who will report to the court about anything said by the witness;
iii. whether it is necessary for the witness to see the DVD more than once for the purpose of refreshing. The court will need to ask the advice of the intermediary, if any, with respect to this;
iv. arrangements, if the witness will not watch the DVD at the same time as the trial bench or judge and jury, for the witness to watch it before attending to be cross examined, (depending upon their ability to retain information this may be the day before).

18C.4 There is no legal requirement that the witness should watch the interview at the same time as the trial bench or jury. Increasingly, this is arranged to occur at a different time, with the advantages that breaks can be taken as needed without disrupting the trial, and cross-examination starts while the witness is fresh. An intermediary may be present to facilitate communication but should not act as the independent person designated to take a note and report to the court if anything is said.

18C.5 Where the viewing takes place at a different time from that of the trial bench or jury, the witness is sworn (or promises) just before cross-examination and, unless the judge otherwise directs:

(a) it is good practice for the witness to be asked by the prosecutor, (or the judge/magistrate if they so direct), in appropriate language if, and when, he or she has watched the recording of the interview;
(b) if, in watching the recording of the interview or otherwise the witness has indicated that there is something he or she wishes to correct or to add then it is good practice for the prosecutor (or the judge/magistrate if they so direct) to deal with that before cross-examination provided that proper notice has been given to the defence.

PD-44 **CPD V Evidence 18D: Witness Anonymity Orders**

18D.1 This direction supplements CrimPR 18.18 to 18.22, which governs the procedure to be followed on an application for a witness anonymity order. The court's power to make such an order is conferred by the Coroners and Justice Act 2009 (in this section, 'the Act'); section 87 of the Act provides specific relevant powers and obligations.

18D.2 As the Court of Appeal stated in *R v Mayers and Others* [2008] EWCA Crim 2989, [2009] 1 WLR 1915, [2009] 1 Cr App R 30 and emphasised again in *R v Donovan and Kafunda* [2012] EWCA Crim 2749, unreported, 'a witness anonymity order is to be regarded as a special measure of the last practicable resort': Lord Chief Justice, Lord Judge. In making such an application, the prosecution's obligations of disclosure 'go much further than the ordinary duties of disclosure' (*R v Mayers*); reference should be made to the Judicial Protocol on Disclosure, see paragraph IV 15A.1.

Case management

18D.3 Where such an application is proposed, with the parties' active assistance the court should set a realistic timetable, in accordance with the duties imposed by CrimPR 3.2 and 3.3. Where possible, the trial judge should determine the application, and any hearing should be attended by the parties' trial advocates.

Service of evidence and disclosure of prosecution material pending an application

18D.4 Where the prosecutor proposes an application for a witness anonymity order, it is not necessary for that application to have been determined before the proposed evidence is served. In most cases, an early indication of what that evidence will be if an order is made will be consistent with a party's duties under CrimPR 1.2 and 3.3. The prosecutor should serve with the other prosecution evidence a witness statement setting out the proposed evidence, redacted in such a way as to prevent disclosure of the witness' identity, as permitted by section 87(4) of the Act. Likewise the prosecutor should serve with other prosecution material disclosed under the Criminal Procedure and Investigations Act 1996 any such material appertaining to the witness, similarly redacted.

The application

18D.5 An application for a witness anonymity order should be made as early as possible and within the period for which CrimPR 18.3 provides. The application, and any hearing of it, must comply with the requirements of that rule and with those of rule 18.19. In accordance with CrimPR 1.2 and 3.3, the applicant must provide the court with all available information relevant to the considerations to which the Act requires a court to have regard.

Response to the application

18D.6 A party upon whom an application for a witness anonymity order is served must serve a response in accordance with CrimPR 18.22. That period may be extended or shortened in the court's discretion: CrimPR 18.5.

18D.7 To avoid the risk of injustice, a respondent, whether the Prosecution or a defendant, must actively assist the court. If not already done, a respondent defendant should serve a defence statement under section 5 or 6 of the Criminal Procedure and Investigations Act 1996, so that the court is fully informed of what is in issue. When a defendant makes an application for a witness anonymity order the prosecutor should consider the continuing duty to disclose material under section 7A of the Criminal Procedure and Investigations Act 1996; therefore a prosecutor's response should include confirmation that that duty has been considered. Great care should be taken to ensure that nothing disclosed contains anything that might reveal the witness' identity. A respondent prosecutor should provide the court with all available information relevant to the considerations to which the Act requires a court to have regard, whether or not that information falls to be disclosed under the 1996 Act.

Determination of the application

18D.8 All parties must have an opportunity to make oral representations to the court on an application for a witness anonymity order: section 87(6) of the Act. However, a hearing may not be needed if none is sought: CrimPR 18.18(1) (a). Where, for example, the witness is an investigator who is recognisable by the defendant but known only by an assumed name, and there is no likelihood that the witness' credibility will be in issue, then the court may indicate a provisional decision and invite representations within a defined period, usually 14 days, including representations about whether there should be a hearing. In such a case, where the parties do not object the court may make an order without a hearing. Or where the court provisionally considers an application to be misconceived, an applicant may choose to withdraw it without requiring a hearing. Where the court directs a hearing of the application then it should allow adequate time for service of the representations in response.

18D.9 The hearing of an application for a witness anonymity order usually should be in private: CrimPR 18.18(1)(a), and before the trial judge wherever possible. The court has power to hear a party in the absence of a defendant and that defendant's representatives: section 87(7) of the Act and rule 18.18(1)(b). In the Crown Court, a recording of the proceedings will be made, in accordance with CrimPR 5.5. The Crown Court officer must treat such a recording in the same way as the recording of an application for a public interest ruling. It must be kept in secure conditions, and the arrangements made by the Crown Court officer for any transcription must impose restrictions that correspond with those under CrimPR 5.5(2).

18D.10 The hearing of an application for a witness anonymity order usually should be in private: CrimPR 18.18(1)(a). The court has power to hear a party in the absence of a defendant and that defendant's representatives: section 87(7) of the Act and rule 18.18(1)(b). In the Crown Court, a recording of the proceedings will be made, in accordance with CrimPR 5.5. The Crown Court officer must treat such a recording in the same way as the recording of an application for a public interest ruling. It must be kept in secure conditions, and the arrangements made by the Crown Court officer for any transcription must impose restrictions that correspond with those under CrimPR 5.5(2).

18D.11 Where confidential supporting information is presented to the court before the last stage of the hearing, the court may prefer not to read that information until that last stage.

18D.12 The court may adjourn the hearing at any stage, and should do so if its duty under CrimPR 3.2 so requires.

18D.13 On a prosecutor's application, the court is likely to be assisted by the attendance of a senior investigator or other person of comparable authority who is familiar with the case.

18D.14 During the last stage of the hearing it is essential that the court test thoroughly the information supplied in confidence in order to satisfy itself that the conditions prescribed by the Act are met. At that stage, if the court concludes that this is the only way in which it can satisfy itself as to a relevant condition or consideration, exceptionally it may invite the applicant to present the proposed witness to be questioned by the court. Any such questioning should be carried out at such a time, and the witness brought to the court in such a way, as to prevent disclosure of his or her identity.

18D.15 The court may ask the Attorney General to appoint special counsel to assist. However, it must be kept in mind that, 'Such an appointment will always be exceptional, never automatic; a course of last and never first resort. It should not be ordered unless and until the trial judge is satisfied that no other course will adequately meet the overriding requirement of fairness to the defendant': *R v H* [2004] UKHL 3, [2004] 2 AC 134 (at paragraph 22), [2004] 2 Cr App R 10. Whether to accede to such a request is a matter for the Attorney General, and adequate time should be allowed for the consideration of such a request.

18D.16 The Court of Appeal in *R v Mayers* 'emphasise[d] that all three conditions, A, B and C, must be met before the jurisdiction to make a witness anonymity order arises. Each is mandatory. Each is distinct.' The Court also noted that if there is more than one anonymous witness in a case any link, and the nature of any link, between the witnesses should be investigated: 'questions of possible improper collusion between them, or cross-contamination of one another, should be addressed.'

18D.17 Following a hearing the court should announce its decision on an application for a witness anonymity order in the parties' presence and in public: CrimPR 18.4(2). The court should give such reasons as it is possible to give without revealing the witness' identity. In the Crown Court, the court will be conscious that reasons given in public may be reported and reach the jury. Consequently, the court should ensure that nothing in its decision or its reasons could undermine any warning it may give jurors under section 90(2) of the Act. A record of the reasons must be kept. In the Crown Court, the announcement of those reasons will be recorded.

18D.18 Should the judge grant the anonymity then the following should be considered by the judge with the assistance of the court staff, so that the practical arrangements (confidentially recorded) are in place to ensure that the witness's anonymity is not compromised:

i. Any pre-trial visit by the anonymous witness;
ii. How the witness will enter and leave the court building;
iii. Where the witness will wait until they give evidence;
iv. Provision for prosecution counsel to speak to the anonymous witness at court before they give evidence;
v. Provision for the anonymous witness to see their statement or view their ABEs;
vi. How the witness will enter and leave the court room;
vii. Provisions to disguise the identity of the anonymous witness whilst they give evidence (voice modulation and screens);
viii. Provisions for the anonymous witness to have any breaks required;
ix. Provisions to protect the anonymity of the witness in the event of an emergency such as a security alert.

Order

18D.19 Where the court makes a witness anonymity order, it is essential that the measures to be taken are clearly specified in a written record of that order approved by the court and issued on its behalf. An order made in a magistrates' court must be recorded in the court register, in accordance with CrimPR 5.4.

18D.20 Should the application for anonymity be refused, consideration will be given as to whether the witness to whom the application related can be compelled to give evidence despite any risk to their safety and what special measures could support them to give their evidence.

18D.21 Self-evidently, the written record of the order must not disclose the identity of the witness to whom it applies. However, it is essential that there be maintained some means of establishing a clear correlation between witness and order, and especially where in the same proceedings witness anonymity orders are made in respect of more than one witness, specifying different measures in respect of each. Careful preservation of the application for the order, including the confidential part, ordinarily will suffice for this purpose.

Discharge or variation of the order

18D.22 Section 91 of the Act allows the court to discharge or vary a witness anonymity order: on application, if there has been a material change of circumstances since the order was made or since any previous variation of it; or on its own initiative. CrimPR 18.21 allows the parties to apply for the variation of a pre-trial direction where circumstances have changed.

18D.23 The court should keep under review the question of whether the conditions for making an order are met. In addition, consistently with the parties' duties under CrimPR 1.2 and 3.3, it is incumbent on each, and in particular on the applicant for the order, to keep the need for it under review.

18D.24 Where the court considers the discharge or variation of an order, the procedure that it adopts should be appropriate to the circumstances. As a general rule, that procedure should approximate to the procedure for determining an application for an order. The court may need to hear further representations by the applicant for the order in the absence of a respondent defendant and that defendant's representatives.

Arrangements at trial

18D.25 At trial the greatest possible care must be taken to ensure that nothing will compromise the witness' anonymity. Detailed arrangements may have been proposed by the applicant under CrimPR 18.19(1)(b) and directed by the court on determining the application for the order. Such arrangements must take account of the layout of the courtroom and of the means of access for the witness, for the defendant or defendants, and for members of the public. The risk of a chance encounter between the witness and someone who may recognise him or her, either then or subsequently, must be rigorously excluded. Subject to contrary direction by the trial judge, the court staff and those accompanying the witness must adopt necessary measures to ensure that the witness is neither seen nor heard by anyone whose observation would, or might, render nugatory the court's order. Further HMCTS guidance for court staff can be found in Guidance for Criminal Courts for England and Wales for Anonymous/Protected Witnesses.

Retention of confidential material

18D.26 If retained by the court, confidential material must be stored in secure conditions by the court officer. Alternatively, subject to such directions as the court may give, such material may be committed to the safe keeping of the applicant or any other appropriate person in exercise of the powers conferred by CrimPR 18.6. If the material is released to any such person, the court should ensure that it will be available to the court at trial.

PD-45 **CPD V Evidence 18E: Use of s. 28 Youth Justice and Criminal Evidence Act 1999; Pre-recording of Cross-examination and Re-examination for Witnesses Captured by s. 16 YJCEA 1999**

18E.1 When Section 28 of the Youth Justice and Criminal Evidence Act 1999 (s.28 YJCEA 1999) is bought into force by Statutory Instrument for a particular Crown Court, under that S.I., a witness will be eligible for special measures under s.28 if

i. he or she is under the age of 18 at the time of the special measures hearing; or
ii. he or she suffers from a mental disorder within the meaning of the Mental Health Act 1983, or has a significant impairment of intelligence and social functioning, or has a physical disability or a physical disorder, and the quality of his or her evidence is likely to be diminished as a consequence.

18E.2 This process is governed by the Criminal Procedure Rules and careful attention should be paid to the court's case management powers and the obligations on the parties. Advocates should also refer to the annex of this practice direction which contains further detailed guidance on ground rules hearings.

18E.3 The Resident Judge may appoint a judicial lead from full time judges at the court centre who will be responsible for monitoring and supervision of the scheme. The Plea and Trial Preparation Hearing (PTPH) must be conducted by a full time judge authorised by the Resident Judge to sit on that class of case and who has been authorised to deal with s.28 YJCEA 1999 cases by the Resident Judge.

18E.4 Reference should be made to the joint protocol agreed between the police and the Crown Prosecution Service.

18E.5 Witnesses eligible for special measures under s.28 YJCEA 1999 should be identified by the police. The police and Crown Prosecution Service should discuss, with the witness or with the witness' parent or carer, special measures available and the witness' needs, such that the most appropriate package of special measures can be identified. This may include use of a Registered Intermediary. See Criminal Practice Directions of 2015 (CPD) General matters 3D: Vulnerable people in the courts and 3F: Intermediaries.

18E.6 For access to special measures under s.28 YJCEA 1999, the witness' interview must be recorded in accordance with the Achieving Best Evidence ('ABE') guidance which is available on the Ministry of Justice website.

18E.7 For timetabling of the case, it is imperative that the investigators and prosecutor commence the disclosure process at the start of the investigation. The *Judicial Protocol on Disclosure of Unused Material in Criminal Proceedings* (November 2013) must be followed, and if applicable, the *2013 Protocol and Good Practice Model on Disclosure of information in cases of alleged child abuse and linked criminal and care directions.* Local Implementation Teams (LITs) should encourage all appropriate agencies to endorse and follow both the Protocol and the Good Practice Model. LITs should monitor compliance and issues should initially be raised at the LITs.

The first hearing in the magistrates' court

18E.8 Initial details of the prosecution case must be served in accordance with Part 8 of the Rules.

18E.9 The prosecutor must formally notify the court at the first hearing that the case is eligible for special measures under s.28 YJCEA 1999.

18E.10 At the hearing the court must follow part 9 of the Rules (Allocation) and refer to the Sentencing Council's guideline on Allocation. This practice direction applies only where the defendant indicates a not guilty plea or does not indicate a plea, and the case is sent for trial in the Crown Court, either with or without allocation.

18E.11 If the case is to be sent to the Crown Court, the prosecutor should inform the court and the defence if not already notified that the prosecution will seek special measures including under s.28 YJCEA 1999.

18E.12 In any case that is sent to the Crown Court for trial in which the prosecution has notified the court of its intention to make an application for special measures under s.28 of the YJCEA 1999 the timetable is that as established by the Better Case Management initiative. The Court must be mindful of its duties under Parts 1 and 3 of the Rules to manage the case effectively. Wherever the Crown Prosecution Service will seek a s.28 YJCEA 1999 special measures direction this should, where possible, be listed for PTPH within 28 days of the date of sending from the magistrates' court. Section 10.2 of *A protocol between the Association of Chief Police Officers, the Crown Prosecution Service and Her Majesty's Courts and Tribunals Service to expedite cases involving witnesses under 10 years* does not apply.

18E.13 From the point of grant of the s.28 YJCEA 1999 special measures application, timescales provided by section 8.6 of *A protocol between the Association of Chief Police Officers, the Crown Prosecution Service and Her Majesty's Courts and Tribunals Service to expedite cases involving witnesses under 10 years* will cease to apply and the case should be managed in accordance with the timescales established in this practice direction.

Before the PTPH hearing in the Crown Court

18E.14 On being notified of the sending of the case by the magistrates' court, the case should be flagged as a s.28 case and referred to the Resident Judge or the judicial lead at that Crown Court, according to instructions issued by the Resident Judge.

18E.15 A transcript of the ABE interview and the application for special measures, including under s.28 YJCEA 1999, must be served on the Court and defence at least 7 days prior to the PTPH. The report of any Registered Intermediary must be served with the application for special measures.

18E.16 Any defence representations about the application for special measures must be served before the PTPH, within 28 days from the first hearing at the magistrates' court, when notice was first given of the application.

Plea and Trial Preparation Hearing

18E.17 The s.28 YJCEA 1999 part of the PTPH form should, on enquiry of the parties, be completed by the judge during the hearing. Orders should be recorded on the form, and uploaded onto the Digital Case System (DCS) as the record of orders made by the court. Any unrepresented defendant should be served with a paper copy of the orders.

18E.18 A plea should be taken and recorded and the defence required to identify the issues. The detail of a defence statement is not required at this stage, but the defence should identify the core issues in dispute.

The application

18E.19 The judge may hear submissions from the advocates and will rule on the application. If it is refused (see the assumptions to be applied by the courts in s.21 and s.22 of the YJCEA 1999), this practice direction ceases to apply.

18E.20 If the application is granted, the judge should make orders and give directions for preparation for the recorded cross-examination and re-examination hearing and advance preparation for the trial, including for disclosure of unused material. The correct and timely application of the Criminal Procedure and Investigations Act 1996 ('CPIA 1996') will be vital and close attention should be paid to the *2013 Protocol and Good Practice Model on Disclosure* (November 2013), above.

18E.21 The orders made are likely to include:

i. Service of the prosecution evidence within 50 days of sending;
ii. Directions for service of defence witness requirements;
iii. Service of initial disclosure; under the CPIA 1996, as soon as reasonably practical; in this context, this should be interpreted as being simultaneous with the service of the prosecution evidence, i.e. within 50 days of sending for both bail and custody cases. This will be within 3 weeks of the PTPH;
iv. Orders on disclosure material held by a third party;
v. Service of the defence statement; under the CPIA 1996, this must be served within 28 days of the prosecutor serving or purporting to serve initial disclosure;
vi. Any editing of the ABE interview;
vii. Fixing a date for a ground rules hearing, about one week prior to the recorded cross-examination and re-examination hearing, see CPD General matters 3E: Ground rules hearings to plan questioning of a vulnerable witness or defendant;
viii. Service of the Ground Rules Hearing Form by the defence advocate;
ix. Making arrangements for the witness to refresh his or her memory by viewing the recorded examination-in-chief ('ABE interview'), see CPD Evidence 18C: Visually recorded interviews: memory refreshing and watching at a different time from the jury;
x. Making arrangements for the recorded cross-examination and re-examination hearing under s.28, including fixing a date, time and location;
xi. Other special measures;
xii. Directions for any further directions hearing whether at the conclusion of the recorded cross-examination and re-examination hearing or subsequently;
xiii. Fixing a date for trial.

18E.22 The timetable should ensure the prosecution evidence and initial disclosure are served swiftly. The ground rules hearing will usually be soon after the deadline for service of the defence statement, the recorded cross-examination and re-examination hearing about one week later. However, there must be time afforded for any further disclosure of unused material following service of the defence statement and for determination of any application under s.8 of the CPIA 1996. Subject to judicial discretion applications for extensions of time for service of disclosure by either party should generally be refused.

18E.23 Where the defendant may be unfit to plead, a timetable for s.28 should usually still be set, taking into account extra time needed for the obtaining of medical reports, save in cases where it is indicated that it is unlikely that there would be a trial if the defendant is found fit.

18E.24 As far as possible, without diminishing the defendant's right to a fair trial, the timing and duration of the recorded cross-examination should take into account the needs of the witness. For a young child, the hearing should usually be in the morning and conclude before lunch time.

18E.25 An application for a witness summons to obtain material held by a third party, should be served in advance of the PTPH and determined at that hearing, or as soon as reasonably practicable thereafter. The timetable should accommodate any consequent hearings or applications, but it is imperative parties are prompt to obtain third party disclosure material. The prosecution must make the court and the defence aware of any difficulty as soon as it arises. As noted above, the *2013 Protocol and Good Practice Model on Disclosure of information in cases of alleged child abuse and linked criminal and care directions hearings* should be followed, if applicable. Engagement with the Protocol is to be overseen by LITs. A single point of contact in each relevant agency can facilitate speedy disclosure.

18E.26 The needs of other witnesses should not be neglected. Witness and intermediary availability dates should be available for the PTPH.

Prior to ground rules hearing and hearing under section 28

18E.27 It is imperative parties abide by orders made at the PTPH, including the completion and service of the Ground Rules Hearing Form by the defence advocate. Delays or failures must be reported to the judge as soon as they arise; this is the responsibility of each legal representative. If ordered, the lead lawyer for the prosecution and defence must provide a weekly update to the court Case Progression Officer, copied to the judge and parties, detailing the progress and any difficulties or delays in complying with orders. The court may order a further case management hearing if necessary.

18E.28 Any applications under s.100 of the Criminal Justice Act 2003 ('CJA 2003') (non-defendant's bad character) or under s.41 of the YJCEA 1999 (evidence or cross-examination about complainants sexual behaviour) or any other application which may affect the cross-examination must be made promptly, and responses submitted in time for the judge to rule on the application at the ground rules hearing. Parts 21 and 22 of the Rules apply to applications under s.100 and s.41 respectively.

18E.29 The witness' court familiarisation visit must take place, including an opportunity to practice on the live link/recording facilities, see the Code of Practice for Victims of Crime, October 2013, Chapter 3, paragraph 1.22. The witness must have the opportunity to view his or her ABE interview to refresh his or her memory. It may or may not be appropriate for this to take place on the day of the court visit: CPD Evidence 18C must be followed.

18E.30 When the court has deemed that the case is suitable for the witness to give evidence from a remote site then a familiarisation visit should take place at that site. At the ground rules hearing the judge and advocates should consider appropriate arrangements for them to talk to the witness before the cross examination hearing.

18E.31 Applications to vary or discharge a special measures declaration must comply with Rule 18.11. Although the need for prompt action will make case preparation tight.

Ground rules hearing

18E.32 Advocates should master the toolkits available through The Advocate's Gateway. These provide guidance on questioning a vulnerable witness, see CPD General matters 3D and the annex to this practice direction.

18E.33 Any appointed Registered Intermediary must attend the ground rules hearing, see CPD General matters 3E.2.

18E.34 The defence advocate at the ground rules hearing must be she or he who will conduct the recorded cross-examination. See listing and allocation below on continuity of counsel and release from other cases.

18E.35 Topics for discussion and agreement at the ground rules hearing will depend on the individual needs of the witness, and an intermediary may provide advance indications. CPD General matters 3E must be followed. Topics that will need discussion in every case will include:

i. the overall length of cross-examination;
ii. cross-examination by a single advocate in a multi-handed case;
iii. any restrictions on the advocate's usual duty to 'put the defence case'.

18E.36 It may be helpful to discuss at this stage how any limitations on questioning will be explained to the jury.

18E.37 At the ground rules hearing, the judge should:

i. rule on any application under s.100 of the CJA 2003 or s.41 of the YJCEA 1999, or other applications that may affect the cross-examination;
ii. decide how the witness may view exhibits or documents;
iii. review progress in complying with orders made at the preliminary hearing and make any necessary orders.

Recording of cross-examination and re-examination: hearing under s.28

18E.38 At the hearing, the witness will be cross-examined and re-examined, if required, via the live link from the court room to the witness suite (unless provision has been made for the use of a remote link) and the examination will be recorded. It is the responsibility of the designated court clerk to ensure in advance that all of the equipment is working and to contact the provider's Service Desk if support is required. Any other special measures must be in place and any intermediary or supporter should sit in the live link room with the witness. The intermediary's role is transparent and therefore must be visible and audible to the judge and advocates at the cross-examination and in the subsequent replaying.

18E.39 The judge, advocates and parties, including the defendant will usually assemble in the court room for the hearing. In some cases the judge and advocates may be in the witness suite with the witness, for example when questioning a very young child or where the witness has a particular communication need. The court will decide this on a case-by-case basis. The defendant should be able to communicate with his or her representatives and should be able to hear the witness via the live link and see the proceedings: s.28 (2). Whether the witness is screened or not will depend on the other special measures ordered, for example screens may have been ordered under s.23 YJCEA 1999.

18E.40 On the admission of the public or media to the hearing, please see below.

18E.41 At the conclusion of the hearing, the judge will issue further orders, such as for the editing of the recorded cross-examination and may set a timetable for progress.

18E.42 Under s.28(4) YJCEA 1999, the judge, on application of any parties or on the court's own motion may direct that the recorded examination is not admitted into evidence, despite any previous direction. Such direction must be given promptly, preferably immediately after the conclusion of the examination.

18E.43 Without exception, editing of the ABE interview/examination-in-chief or recorded cross-examination is precluded without an order of the court.

18E.44 The ability to record simultaneously from a court and a witness room and to play back the recording at trial will be provided in all Crown Courts as an additional facility within the existing Justice Video Service (JVS). Courts will book recording slots with the Service Desk who will launch the recording at the scheduled time when the court is ready. Recordings will be stored in a secure data centre with backup and resiliency, for authorised access.

After the recording

18E.45 Following the recording the judge should review compliance with orders and progress towards preparation for trial, make any further orders necessary and confirm the date of the trial. Any further orders made by the judge should be recorded and uploaded onto the relevant section of the DCS.

18E.46 If the defendant enters a guilty plea, the judge should proceed towards sentence, making any appropriate orders, such as for a Pre-Sentence Report and setting a date for sentencing. Any reduction for a guilty plea shall reflect the day of the recorded cross-examination as the first day of trial; the Sentencing Council guideline on guilty plea reductions should be applied.

Preparation for trial

18E.47 Parties must notify the court promptly if any difficulties arise or any orders are not complied with. The court may order a further case management hearing (FCMH).

18E.48 In accordance with orders, either after recorded cross-examination or at the FCMH, necessary editing of the ABE interview/examination-in-chief and/or the recorded cross-examination must be done only on the order of the court. Any editing must be done promptly.

18E.49 Recorded cross-examinations and re-examinations will be stored securely by the service provider so as to be accessible to the advocates and the court. It will not usually be necessary to obtain a transcript of the recorded cross-examination, but if it is difficult to comprehend, a transcript should be obtained and served. The ground rules hearing form outlines questions to the witness that might be completed electronically by the judge during cross-examination forming a contemporaneous note of the hearing, served on the parties as an agreed record.

18E.50 Editing, authorised by the judge, is to be submitted by the court to the Service Desk, who produce an edited copy. The master and all edited copy versions are retained in the secure data centre from where they can be accessed. Courts book playback timeslots with the Service Desk for the trial date. The court may authorise parties to view playback at JVS endpoints, by submitting a request form to the Service Desk. Access for those so authorised is via the Quickcode (recording ID) and a security PIN (password) on the courtroom touch panel or remote control.

18E.51 No further cross-examination or re-examination of the witness may take place unless the criteria in section 28(6) are satisfied and the judge makes a further special measures direction under section 28(5). Any such further examination must be recorded via live link as described above.

18E.52 Section 28(6) of the YJCEA 1999 provides as follows:

(6) *The court may only give such a further direction if it appears to the court—*

(a) *that the proposed cross-examination is sought by a party to the proceedings as a result of that party having become aware, since the time when the original recording was made in pursu-*

ance of subsection (1), of a matter which that party could not with reasonable diligence have ascertained by then, or

(b) *that for any other reason it is in the interests of justice to give the further direction.*

18E.53 Any application under section 28(5) must be in writing and be served on the court and the prosecution at least 28 days before the date of trial. The application must specify:

i. the topics on which further cross-examination is sought;
ii. the material or matter of which the defence has become aware since the original recording;
iii. why it was not possible for the defence to have obtained the material or ascertained the matter earlier; and
iv. the expected impact on the issues before the court at trial.

18E.54 The prosecution should respond in writing within 7 days of the application. The judge may determine the application on the papers or order a hearing. Any further cross-examination ordered must be recorded via live link in advance of the trial and served on the court and the parties.

Trial

18E.55 In accordance with the judge's directions, the ABE interview/examination-in-chief and the recorded cross-examination and re-examination, edited as directed, should be played to the jury at the appropriate point within the trial.

18E.56 The jury should not usually receive transcripts of the recordings, and if they do these should be removed from the jury as soon as the recording has been played, see CPD Trial 26L.2.

18E.57 If the matter was not addressed at the ground rules hearing, the judge should discuss with the advocates how any limitations on questioning should be explained to the jury before summing-up.

After conclusion of trial

18E.58 Immediately after the trial, the ABE interview/examination-in-chief and the recorded cross-examination and re-examination should be stored securely on the cloud.

Listing and allocation

18E.59 **Advocates:** It is the responsibility of the defence advocate, on accepting the brief, to ensure that he or she is available for both the ground rules hearing and the hearing under section 28; continuity at trial is obligatory except in exceptional circumstances. The judge and list office will make whatever reasonable arrangements are possible to achieve this, assisted by the Resident Judge where necessary.

18E.60 When the timetable for the case is being set, advocates must have their up to date availability with them (in so far as is possible). When an advocate who is part-heard in another trial at a different Crown Court centre finds themselves in difficulties in attending either the ground rules hearing, s.28 hearing itself or the trial where s.28 has been utilised, they must inform the Resident Judges of both courts as soon as practicable. The Resident Judges must resolve any conflict with the advocate's availability. The starting point should be that the case involving s.28 hearing takes priority. However, due consideration should also be given to custody time limits, other issues which make either case particularly complex or sensitive, high profile cases and anything else that the judges should take into consideration in the interests of justice.

18E.61 **Judicial:** All PTPHs must be listed before judges who have been authorised to deal with s.28 cases by the Resident Judge at the relevant court centre. The nominated lead judge (if there is one) or Resident Judge may allocate individual cases to one of the judges in the court centre identified to deal with the case if necessary. The Resident Judge, lead judge or allocated judge may make directions in the case if required.

18E.62 It is essential that the ground rules hearing and the s. 28 YJCEA 1999 hearing are before the same judge. Once the s.28 hearing has taken place, any judge, in accordance with CPD XIII Listing E, including recorders, can deal with the trial.

18E.63 LITs should be established with all relevant agencies represented by someone of sufficient seniority. Their task will be to monitor the operation of the scheme and compliance with this practice direction and other relevant protocols.

18E.64 **Listing:** Due to the limited availability of recording facilities, the hearing held under section 28 must take precedence over other hearings. Section 28 hearings should be listed as the first matter in the morning and will usually conclude before lunch time. Ground rules hearings may be held at any time, including towards the end of the court day, to accommodate the advocates and intermediary (if there is one) and to minimise disruption to other trials.

Public, including media access, and reporting restrictions

18E.65 Open justice is an essential principle of the common law. However, certain automatic statutory restrictions may apply, and the judge may consider it appropriate in the specific circumstances of a case to make an order applying discretionary restrictions. CPD Preliminary proceedings 16B must be followed and the templates published by the Judicial College (available on LMS) should be used. The parties to the proceedings, and interested parties such as the media, should have the opportunity to make representations before an order is made.

18E.66 The statutory powers most likely to be available to the judge are listed below. The judge should consider the specific statutory requirements necessary for the making of the particular order carefully, and the order made must be in writing.

a) Provisions to exclude the public from hearings:
   i. Section 37 of the Children and Young Persons Act 1933, applicable to witnesses under 18;
   ii. Section 25 of the YJCEA 1999, applicable to the evidence of a child or vulnerable adult in sexual offences cases.
b) Automatic reporting restrictions:
   i. Section 1 of the Sexual Offences (Amendment) Act 1992, applicable to the complainant in any sex offence case.
c) Discretionary reporting restrictions:
   i. Section 45 of the YJCEA 1999, applicable to under 18s concerned in criminal proceedings;
   ii. Section 46 of the YJCEA 1999, applicable to an adult witness whose evidence would be diminished by fear or distress.
d) Postponement of fair and accurate reports under section 4(2) of the Contempt of Court Act 1981.

18E.67 Note that public access to information held by the court is now the subject of Rule 5.8 and CPD General matters 5B that must be followed.

PD-46 **Annex for section 28 ground rules hearings at the Crown Court when dealing with witnesses under s.16 YJCEA 1999**

Introduction

1. This annex is designed to assist all advocates in their preparation for cross-examination of vulnerable witnesses.
2. Adherence to the principles below will avoid interruption during the pre-recorded cross-examination and reduce any ordered editing.
3. Issues concerning the vulnerable witness and the nature of the cross-examination will be addressed by the judge at the Ground Rules Hearing (GRH).
4. In appropriate cases and in particular where the witness is of very young years or suffers from a disability or disorder it is expected that the advocate will have prepared his or her cross-examination in writing for consideration by the court.
5. It is thus incumbent on the Defence to ensure that full instructions have been taken prior to the GRH.

Required preparation prior to the GRH

6. All advocates should be familiar with the relevant toolkits, available through **The Advocates Gateway** www.theadvocatesgateway.org/toolkits which provide guidance on questioning a vulnerable witness. A synopsis of this guidance, which advocates should have read prior to any GRH, is included in this annex.

Attendance at, and procedure during, the GRH

7. In preparation for trial, courts must take every reasonable step to facilitate the participation of witnesses and defendants CPR 3.8(4) (d). The court should order that the defendant attends the GRH.
8. The defence advocate must complete and submit the Ground Rules Hearing form by the time and date ordered at the PTPH.
9. The hearing facilitates the judge's duty to control questioning if and when necessary.
10. The hearing enables the court to ensure its process is adapted to enable the witness to give his or her best evidence whilst ensuring the defendant's right to a fair trial is not diminished. Accordingly the ground rules and the nature of the questioning of the witness by the advocate (and limitations imposed if necessary in accordance with principles above) will be discussed.
11. Prior to the hearing it is necessary for both advocates and the judge to have viewed the ABE evidence.
12. The judge will state what ground rules will apply. The advocates must comply with them.
13. Any intermediary must attend the GRH. It is the responsibility of those instructing the intermediary to ensure this.
14. The defendant's advocate attending the hearing must be the same advocate who will be conducting the recorded cross-examination (and the subsequent trial, if any).
15. Any intermediary for the witness should only be warned for the GRH and the section 28 hearing they are assisting with. An Intermediary should not be instructed unless available to attend the GRH and the section 28 hearings ordered by the court.

16. Topics for discussion and agreement at the GRH will depend on the individual needs of the witness. CPD I General Matters 3E must be followed.
17. Topics of discussion at the hearing will include the length of cross-examination and any restrictions on the advocate's usual duty to 'put the defence case'. As was made plain by the Vice President of the Court of Appeal Criminal Division in *Regina v Lubemba and Pooley* 2014 EWCA Crim 2064, advocates cannot insist upon any supposed right 'to put one's case' or previous inconsistent statements to a vulnerable witness. If there is a right to 'put one's case' it must be modified for young or vulnerable witnesses. It is perfectly possible to ensure the jury are made aware of the defence case and of significant inconsistencies without intimidation or distressing a witness. It is expected that all advocates will be familiar with and have read this case.
18. At the GRH counsel need to agree with the judge how and when the matters referred to in paragraph 11 will be explained to the jury. This explanation will normally be done by the judge, but may exceptionally, and only with the permission of the judge, be explained by counsel. If there is no agreement the judge will rule on it.
19. A Section 28 Defence GRH form should be completed as far as possible prior to attendance at the GRH before the judge.
20. Rulings will be made on any application under section 100 of the CJA 2003 or section 41 of the YCEA 1999, and on any other application that may affect the conduct of the cross examination. Any ruling will be included in the trial practice note.
21. A review will take place of the progress made by the parties in complying with the orders made at the PTPH and the court will make any other necessary orders.
22. Additional information can be found in the Inns of Court College of Advocacy training document 'Advocacy and the vulnerable: 20 principles of questioning' at the following link: www.icca.ac.uk/images/download/advocacy-and-the-vulnerable/20-principles-of-questioning.pdf. This document is part of a suite of training materials available to assist advocates in dealing with questioning vulnerable victims in the criminal justice system.

Court of Appeal guidance

In a series of decisions the Court of Appeal has made it clear that there has to be a different and fresh approach to the cross-examination of, in particular, children of tender years, and witnesses who are vulnerable as a result of mental incapacity. The following propositions have support in decisions on appeal: (*R v B 2010 EWCA Crim 4; R v F 2013 EWCA Crim 424; Wills v R 2011 EWCA Crim 1938; R v Edwards 2011 EWCA Crim 3028; R v Watts 2010 EWCA Crim 1824; R v W and M 2010 EWCA Crim 1926)*

'The reality of questioning children of tender years is that direct challenge that he or she is wrong or lying could lead to confusion and, worse, to capitulation which the child does not, in reality, accept.

Capitulation is not a consequence of unreliability but a function of the youngster's age. Experience has shown that young children are scared of disagreeing with a mature adult whom they do not wish to confront.

It is common, in the trial of an adult, to hear, once the nursery slopes of cross-examination have been skied, the assertion "you were never punched or kicked, as you have suggested, were you?"

It was precisely that approach which the Court is anxious to avoid. Such an approach risks confusion in the minds of the witness whose evidence was bound to take centre stage, and it is difficult to see how it can be helpful. We struggle to understand how the defendant's right to a fair trial was in any way compromised simply because Mr X was not allowed to ask the question "Simon did not punch you in the way you suggest?"

The overriding objective. The Criminal Procedure Rules objective is that criminal cases be dealt with justly. Dealing with a criminal case justly includes dealing with the case efficiently and expeditiously in ways that take account of the gravity of the offence alleged and the complexity of what is in issue.

In our collective experience the age of a witness is not determinative of his or her ability to give truthful and accurate evidence. Like adults some children will provide truthful and accurate testimony, and some will not. However children are not miniature adults, but children, and to be treated for what they are, not what they will, in the years ahead, grow to be.

There is undoubtedly a danger of a child witness wishing simply to please.

There is undoubtedly a danger of a child witness assenting to what is put rather than disagreeing during the questioning process in an endeavour to bring that process to a speedier conclusion.

It is particularly important in the case of a child witness to keep a question short and simple, and even more important than it is with an adult witness to avoid questions which are rolled up and contain, inadvertently two or three questions at once. It is generally recognised that, particularly with child witnesses, short and untagged questions are best at eliciting the evidence. By untagged we mean questions that do not contain a statement of the answer which is sought. That said, when it comes to directly contradicting a particular statement and inviting the witness to face a directly contradictory suggestion, it may often be difficult to examine otherwise.

No doubt if a way can be found of engaging the witness to tell the story, and the content then differs from what had been said before, that will be a yet better indication that the original account is wrong. But that is difficult to achieve and indeed may itself have the disadvantage of prolonging the child's time giving evidence. Even then there may be no guarantee as to which account is the more reliable.

Most of the questions which produced the answers which were chiefly relied upon, unlike many others, constituted the putting of direct suggestions with an indication of the answer "this happened didn't it?" Or "this didn't happen, did it?" The consequence of that is that it can be very difficult to tell whether the child is truly changing her account or simply taking the line of least resistance.

At the same time the right of the defendant to a fair trial must be undiminished. When the issue is whether the child is lying or mistaken, when claiming that the defendant behaved indecently towards him or her, it should not be over problematic for the advocate to formulate short, simple questions, which put the essential elements of the defendant's case to the witness, and fully ventilate before the jury the areas of evidence which bear on the child's credibility.

Aspects of evidence which undermine or are believed to undermine the child's credibility must, of course, be revealed to the jury. However it is not necessarily appropriate for them to form the subject matter of detailed cross-examination of the child, and the advocate may have to forego much of the kind of contemporary cross-examination which consists of no more than comment on matters which will be before the jury, in any event, from different sources.

Notwithstanding some of the difficulties; when all is said and done, the witness whose cross-examination is in contemplation is a child, sometimes very young, and it should not take very lengthy cross examination to demonstrate, when it is the case, that the child may indeed be fabricating, or fantasising, or imagining, or reciting a well-rehearsed untruthful script, learned by rote; or simply just suggestible, or contaminated by or in collusion with others to make false allegations, or making assertions in language which is beyond his or her level of comprehension; and are therefore likely to be derived from another source. Comment on the evidence, including comment on evidence which may bear adversely on the credibility of the child, should be addressed after the child has finished giving evidence. Clear limitations have to be imposed on the cross-examination of vulnerable young complainants.'

Criminal Procedure Rules Part 19 Expert Evidence

R-190 When this Part applies

19.1 (1) This Part applies where a party wants to introduce expert opinion evidence.

(2) A reference to an 'expert' in this Part is a reference to a person who is required to give or prepare expert evidence for the purpose of criminal proceedings, including evidence required to determine fitness to plead or for the purpose of sentencing.

R-191 Expert's duty to the court

19.2 (1) An expert must help the court to achieve the overriding objective—

(a) by giving opinion which is—

(i) objective and unbiased, and

(ii) within the expert's area or areas of expertise; and

(b) by actively assisting the court in fulfilling its duty of case management under rule 3.2, in particular by—

(i) complying with directions made by the court, and

(iii) at once informing the court of any significant failure (by the expert or another) to take any step required by such a direction.

(2) This duty overrides any obligation to the person from whom the expert receives instructions or by whom the expert is paid.

(3) This duty includes obligations—

(a) to define the expert's area or areas of expertise—

(i) in the expert's report, and

(ii) when giving evidence in person;

(b) when giving evidence in person, to draw the court's attention to any question to which the answer would be outside the expert's area or areas of expertise;

(c) inform all parties and the court if the expert's opinion changes from that contained in a report served as evidence or given in a statement; and

(d) to disclose to the party for whom the expert's evidence is commissioned anything—

(i) of which the expert is aware, and

(ii) of which that party, if aware of it, would be required to give notice under rule 19.3(3)(c).

[Note. The Practice Direction lists examples of matters that should be disclosed under this rule and rule 19.3(3)(c).]

Introduction of expert evidence **R-192**

19.3 (1) A party who wants another party to admit as fact a summary of an expert's conclusions must serve that summary—

(a) on the court officer and on each party from whom that admission is sought;

(b) as soon as practicable after the defendant whom it affects pleads not guilty.

(2) A party on whom such a summary is served must—

(a) serve a response stating—

(i) which, if any, of the expert's conclusions are admitted as fact, and

(ii) where a conclusion is not admitted, what are the disputed issues concerning that conclusion; and

(b) serve the response—

(i) on the court officer and on the party who served the summary,

(ii) as soon as practicable, and in any event not more than 14 days after service of the summary.

(3) A party who wants to introduce expert evidence otherwise than as admitted fact must—

(a) serve a report by the expert which complies with rule 19.4 (Content of expert's report) on—

(i) the court officer, and

(ii) each other party;

(b) serve the report as soon as practicable, and in any event with any application in support of which that party relies on that evidence;

(c) serve with the report notice of anything of which the party serving it is aware which might reasonably be thought capable of—

(i) undermining the reliability of the expert's opinion, or

(ii) detracting from the credibility or impartiality of the expert;

(d) if another party so requires, give that party a copy of, or a reasonable opportunity to inspect—

(i) a record of any examination, measurement, test or experiment on which the expert's findings and opinion are based, or that were carried out in the course of reaching those findings and opinion, and

(ii) anything on which any such examination, measurement, test or experiment was carried out.

(4) Unless the parties otherwise agree or the court directs, a party may not—

(a) introduce expert evidence if that party has not complied with paragraph (3);

(b) introduce in evidence an expert report if the expert does not give evidence in person.

Content of expert's report **R-193**

19.4 (1) Where rule 19.3(3) applies, an expert's report must—

(a) give details of the expert's qualifications, relevant experience and accreditation;

(b) give details of any literature or other information which the expert has relied on in making the report;

(c) contain a statement setting out the substance of all facts given to the expert which are material to the opinions expressed in the report, or upon which those opinions are based;

(d) make clear which of the facts stated in the report are within the expert's own knowledge;

(e) where the expert has based an opinion or inference on a representation of fact or opinion made by another person for the purposes of criminal proceedings (for example, as to the outcome of an examination, measurement, test or experiment)—

(i) identify the person who made that representation to the expert,

(ii) give the qualifications, relevant experience and any accreditation of that person, and

(iii) certify that that person had personal knowledge of the matters stated in that representation;

(f) where there is a range of opinion on the matters dealt with in the report—

(i) summarise the range of opinion, and

(ii) give reasons for the expert's own opinion;

(g) if the expert is not able to give an opinion without qualification, state the qualification;

(h) include such information as the court may need to decide whether the expert's opinion is sufficiently reliable to be admissible as evidence;

(i) contain a summary of the conclusions reached;
(j) contain a statement that the expert understands an expert's duty to the court, and has complied and will continue to comply with that duty; and
(k) contain the same declaration of truth as a witness statement.

R-194 **Expert to be informed of service of report**

19.5 A party who serves on another party or on the court a report by an expert must, at once, inform that expert of that fact.

R-195 **Pre-hearing discussion of expert evidence**

19.6 (1) This rule applies where more than one party wants to introduce expert evidence.
(2) The court may direct the experts to—
(a) discuss the expert issues in the proceedings; and
(b) prepare a statement for the court of the matters on which they agree and disagree, giving their reasons.
(3) Except for that statement, the content of that discussion must not be referred to without the court's permission.
(4) A party may not introduce expert evidence without the court's permission if the expert has not complied with a direction under this rule.

R-196 **Court's power to direct that evidence is to be given by a single joint expert**

19.7 (1) Where more than one defendant wants to introduce expert evidence on an issue at trial, the court may direct that the evidence on that issue is to be given by one expert only.
(2) Where the co-defendants cannot agree who should be the expert, the court may—
(a) select the expert from a list prepared or identified by them; or
(b) direct that the expert be selected in another way.

R-197 **Instructions to a single joint expert**

19.8 (1) Where the court gives a direction under rule 19.7 for a single joint expert to be used, each of the co-defendants may give instructions to the expert.
(2) A co-defendant who gives instructions to the expert must, at the same time, send a copy of the instructions to each other co-defendant.
(3) The court may give directions about—
(a) the payment of the expert's fees and expenses; and
(b) any examination, measurement, test or experiment which the expert wishes to carry out.
(4) The court may, before an expert is instructed, limit the amount that can be paid by way of fees and expenses to the expert.
(5) Unless the court otherwise directs, the instructing co-defendants are jointly and severally liable for the payment of the expert's fees and expenses.

R-198 **Application to withhold information from another party**

19.9 (1) This rule applies where—
(a) a party introduces expert evidence under rule 19.3(3);
(b) the evidence omits information which it otherwise might include because the party introducing it thinks that that information ought not be revealed to another party; and
(c) the party introducing the evidence wants the court to decide whether it would be in the public interest to withhold that information.
(2) The party who wants to introduce the evidence must—
(a) apply for such a decision; and
(b) serve the application on—
(i) the court officer, and
(ii) the other party, but only to the extent that serving it would not reveal what the applicant thinks ought to be withheld.
(3) The application must—
(a) identify the information;
(b) explain why the applicant thinks that it would be in the public interest to withhold it; and
(c) omit from the part of the application that is served on the other party anything that would reveal what the applicant thinks ought to be withheld.
(4) Where the applicant serves only part of the application on the other party, the applicant must—
(a) mark the other part, to show that it is only for the court; and
(b) in that other part, explain why the applicant has withheld it from the other party.
(5) The court may—
(a) direct the applicant to serve on the other party any part of the application which has been withheld;
(b) determine the application at a hearing or without a hearing.

(6) Any hearing of an application to which this rule applies—
(a) must be in private, unless the court otherwise directs; and
(b) if the court so directs, may be, wholly or in part, in the absence of the party from whom information has been withheld.

(7) At any hearing of an application to which this rule applies—
(a) the general rule is that the court must consider, in the following sequence—
(i) representations first by the applicant and then by the other party, in both parties' presence, and then
(ii) further representations by the applicant, in the absence of the party from whom information has been withheld; but
(b) the court may direct other arrangements for the hearing.

Court's power to vary requirements under this Part R-199

19.10 (1) The court may extend (even after it has expired) a time limit under this Part.
(2) A party who wants an extension of time must—
(a) apply when serving the report, summary or notice for which it is required; and
(b) explain the delay.

Criminal Practice Directions Part 19 Expert Evidence

CPD V Evidence 19A: Expert Evidence PD-47

19A.1 Expert opinion evidence is admissible in criminal proceedings at common law if, in summary, (i) it is relevant to a matter in issue in the proceedings; (ii) it is needed to provide the court with information likely to be outside the court's own knowledge and experience; and (iii) the witness is competent to give that opinion.

19A.2 Legislation relevant to the introduction and admissibility of such evidence includes section 30 of the Criminal Justice Act 1988, which provides that an expert report shall be admissible as evidence in criminal proceedings whether or not the person making it gives oral evidence, but that if he or she does not give oral evidence then the report is admissible only with the leave of the court; and CrimPR Part 19, which in exercise of the powers conferred by section 81 of the Police and Criminal Evidence Act 1984 and section 20 of the Criminal Procedure and Investigations Act 1996 requires the service of expert evidence in advance of trial in the terms required by those rules.

19A.3 In the Law Commission report entitled 'Expert Evidence in Criminal Proceedings in England and Wales', report number 325, published in March, 2011, the Commission recommended a statutory test for the admissibility of expert evidence. However, in its response the government declined to legislate. The common law, therefore, remains the source of the criteria by reference to which the court must assess the admissibility and weight of such evidence; and CrimPR 19.4 lists those matters with which an expert's report must deal, so that the court can conduct an adequate such assessment.

19A.4 In its judgment in *R v Dlugosz and Others* [2013] EWCA Crim 2, the Court of Appeal observed (at paragraph 11): 'It is essential to recall the principle which is applicable, namely in determining the issue of admissibility, the court must be satisfied that there is a sufficiently reliable scientific basis for the evidence to be admitted. If there is then the court leaves the opposing views to be tested before the jury.' Nothing at common law precludes assessment by the court of the reliability of an expert opinion by reference to substantially similar factors to those the Law Commission recommended as conditions of admissibility, and courts are encouraged actively to enquire into such factors.

19A.5 Therefore factors which the court may take into account in determining the reliability of expert opinion, and especially of expert scientific opinion, include:
(a) the extent and quality of the data on which the expert's opinion is based, and the validity of the methods by which they were obtained;
(b) if the expert's opinion relies on an inference from any findings, whether the opinion properly explains how safe or unsafe the inference is (whether by reference to statistical significance or in other appropriate terms);
(c) if the expert's opinion relies on the results of the use of any method (for instance, a test, measurement or survey), whether the opinion takes proper account of matters, such as the degree of precision or margin of uncertainty, affecting the accuracy or reliability of those results;
(d) the extent to which any material upon which the expert's opinion is based has been reviewed by others with relevant expertise (for instance, in peer-reviewed publications), and the views of those others on that material;
(e) the extent to which the expert's opinion is based on material falling outside the expert's own field of expertise;
(f) the completeness of the information which was available to the expert, and whether the expert took account of all relevant information in arriving at the opinion (including information as to the context of any facts to which the opinion relates);

(g) if there is a range of expert opinion on the matter in question, where in the range the expert's own opinion lies and whether the expert's preference has been properly explained; and
(h) whether the expert's methods followed established practice in the field and, if they did not, whether the reason for the divergence has been properly explained.

19A.6 In addition, in considering reliability, and especially the reliability of expert scientific opinion, the court should be astute to identify potential flaws in such opinion which detract from its reliability, such as:
(a) being based on a hypothesis which has not been subjected to sufficient scrutiny (including, where appropriate, experimental or other testing), or which has failed to stand up to scrutiny;
(b) being based on an unjustifiable assumption;
(c) being based on flawed data;
(d) relying on an examination, technique, method or process which was not properly carried out or applied, or was not appropriate for use in the particular case; or
(e) relying on an inference or conclusion which has not been properly reached.

19A.7 To assist in the assessment described above, CrimPR 19.3(3)(c) requires a party who introduces expert evidence to give notice of anything of which that party is aware which might reasonably be thought capable of undermining the reliability of the expert's opinion, or detracting from the credibility or impartiality of the expert; and CrimPR 19.2(3)(d) requires the expert to disclose to that party any such matter of which the expert is aware. Examples of matters that should be disclosed pursuant to those rules include (this is not a comprehensive list), both in relation to the expert and in relation to any corporation or other body with which the expert works, as an employee or in any other capacity:
(a) any fee arrangement under which the amount or payment of the expert's fees is in any way dependent on the outcome of the case (see also the declaration required by paragraph 19B.1 of these directions);
(b) any conflict of interest of any kind, other than a potential conflict disclosed in the expert's report (see also the declaration required by paragraph 19B.1 of these directions);
(c) adverse judicial comment;
(d) any case in which an appeal has been allowed by reason of a deficiency in the expert's evidence;
(e) any adverse finding, disciplinary proceedings or other criticism by a professional, regulatory or registration body or authority, including the Forensic Science Regulator;
(f) any such adverse finding or disciplinary proceedings against, or other such criticism of, others associated with the corporation or other body with which the expert works which calls into question the quality of that corporation's or body's work generally;
(g) conviction of a criminal offence in circumstances that suggest:
(i) a lack of respect for, or understanding of, the interests of the criminal justice system (for example, perjury; acts perverting or tending to pervert the course of public justice),
(ii) dishonesty (for example, theft or fraud), or
(iii) a lack of personal integrity (for example, corruption or a sexual offence);
(h) lack of an accreditation or other commitment to prescribed standards where that might be expected;
(i) a history of failure or poor performance in quality or proficiency assessments;
(j) a history of lax or inadequate scientific methods;
(k) a history of failure to observe recognised standards in the expert's area of expertise;
(l) a history of failure to adhere to the standards expected of an expert witness in the criminal justice system.

19A.8 In a case in which an expert, or a corporation or body with which the expert works, has been criticised without a full investigation, for example by adverse comment in the course of a judgment, it would be reasonable to expect those criticised to supply information about the conduct and conclusions of any independent investigation into the incident, and to explain what steps, if any, have been taken to address the criticism.

19A.9 The rules require disclosure of that of which the expert, or the party who introduces the expert evidence, is aware. The rules do not require persistent or disproportionate enquiry, and courts will recognise that there may be occasions on which neither the expert nor the party has been made aware of criticism. Nevertheless, where matters ostensibly within the scope of the disclosure obligations come to the attention of the court without their disclosure by the party who introduces the evidence then that party, and the expert, should expect a searching examination of the circumstances by the court; and, subject to what emerges, the court may exercise its power under section 81 of the Police and Criminal Evidence Act 1984 or section 20 of the Criminal Procedure and Investigations Act 1996 to exclude the expert evidence.

CPD V Evidence 19B: Statements of Understanding and Declarations of Truth in Expert Reports PD-48

19B.1 The statement and declaration required by CrimPR 19.4(j), (k) should be in the following terms, or in terms substantially the same as these:

'I (name) DECLARE THAT:

1. I understand that my duty is to help the court to achieve the overriding objective by giving independent assistance by way of objective, unbiased opinion on matters within my expertise, both in preparing reports and giving oral evidence. I understand that this duty overrides any obligation to the party by whom I am engaged or the person who has paid or is liable to pay me. I confirm that I have complied with and will continue to comply with that duty.
2. I confirm that I have not entered into any arrangement where the amount or payment of my fees is in any way dependent on the outcome of the case.
3. I know of no conflict of interest of any kind, other than any which I have disclosed in my report.
4. I do not consider that any interest which I have disclosed affects my suitability as an expert witness on any issues on which I have given evidence.
5. I will advise the party by whom I am instructed if, between the date of my report and the trial, there is any change in circumstances which affect my answers to points 3 and 4 above.
6. I have shown the sources of all information I have used.
7. I have exercised reasonable care and skill in order to be accurate and complete in preparing this report.
8. I have endeavoured to include in my report those matters, of which I have knowledge or of which I have been made aware, that might adversely affect the validity of my opinion. I have clearly stated any qualifications to my opinion.
9. I have not, without forming an independent view, included or excluded anything which has been suggested to me by others including my instructing lawyers.
10. I will notify those instructing me immediately and confirm in writing if for any reason my existing report requires any correction or qualification.
11. I understand that:
    (a) my report will form the evidence to be given under oath or affirmation;
    (b) the court may at any stage direct a discussion to take place between experts;
    (c) the court may direct that, following a discussion between the experts, a statement should be prepared showing those issues which are agreed and those issues which are not agreed, together with the reasons;
    (d) I may be required to attend court to be cross-examined on my report by a cross-examiner assisted by an expert.
    (e) I am likely to be the subject of public adverse criticism by the judge if the Court concludes that I have not taken reasonable care in trying to meet the standards set out above.
12. I have read Part 19 of the Criminal Procedure Rules and I have complied with its requirements.
13. I confirm that I have acted in accordance with the code of practice or conduct for experts of my discipline, namely [*identify the code*].
14. [For Experts instructed by the Prosecution only] I confirm that I have read guidance contained in a booklet known as *Disclosure: Experts' Evidence and Unused Material* which details my role and documents my responsibilities, in relation to revelation as an expert witness. I have followed the guidance and recognise the continuing nature of my responsibilities of disclosure. In accordance with my duties of disclosure, as documented in the guidance booklet, I confirm that:
    (a) I have complied with my duties to record, retain and reveal material in accordance with the Criminal Procedure and Investigations Act 1996, as amended;
    (b) I have compiled an Index of all material. I will ensure that the Index is updated in the event I am provided with or generate additional material;
    (c) in the event my opinion changes on any material issue, I will inform the investigating officer, as soon as reasonably practicable and give reasons.

I confirm that the contents of this report are true to the best of my knowledge and belief and that I make this report knowing that, if it is tendered in evidence, I would be liable to prosecution if I have wilfully stated anything which I know to be false or that I do not believe to be true.'

CPD V Evidence 19C: Pre-Hearing Discussion of Expert Evidence PD-49

19C.1. To assist the court in the preparation of the case for trial, parties must consider, with their experts, at an early stage, whether there is likely to be any useful purpose in holding an experts' discussion and, if so, when. Under CrimPR 19.6 such pre-trial discussions are not compulsory unless directed by the court. However, such a direction is listed in the magistrates' courts Preparation for

Effective Trial form and in the Crown Court Plea and Trial Preparation Hearing form as one to be given by default, and therefore the court can be expected to give such a direction in every case unless persuaded otherwise. Those standard directions include a timetable to which the parties must adhere unless it is varied.

19C.2. The purpose of discussions between experts is to agree and narrow issues and in particular to identify:
(a) the extent of the agreement between them;
(b) the points of and short reasons for any disagreement;
(c) action, if any, which may be taken to resolve any outstanding points of disagreement; and
(d) any further material issues not raised and the extent to which these issues are agreed.

19C.3. Where the experts are to meet, that meeting conveniently may be conducted by telephone conference or live link; and experts' meetings always should be conducted by those means where that will avoid unnecessary delay and expense.

19C.4. Where the experts are to meet, the parties must discuss and if possible agree whether an agenda is necessary, and if so attempt to agree one that helps the experts to focus on the issues which need to be discussed. The agenda must not be in the form of leading questions or hostile in tone. The experts may not be required to avoid reaching agreement, or to defer reaching agreement, on any matter within the experts' competence.

19C.5. If the legal representatives do attend:
(a) they should not normally intervene in the discussion, except to answer questions put to them by the experts or to advise on the law; and
(b) the experts may if they so wish hold part of their discussions in the absence of the legal representatives.

19C.6. A statement must be prepared by the experts dealing with paragraphs 19C.2(a)–(d) above. Individual copies of the statements must be signed or otherwise authenticated by the experts, in manuscript or by electronic means, at the conclusion of the discussion, or as soon thereafter as practicable, and in any event within 5 business days. Copies of the statements must be provided to the parties no later than 10 business days after signing.

19C.7. Experts must give their own opinions to assist the court and do not require the authority of the parties to sign a joint statement. The joint statement should include a brief re-statement that the experts recognise their duties, which should be in the following terms, or in terms substantially the same as these:

'We each DECLARE THAT:
1. We individually here re-state the Expert's Declaration contained in our respective reports that we understand our overriding duties to the court, have complied with them and will continue to do so.
2. We have neither jointly nor individually been instructed to, nor has it been suggested that we should, avoid reaching agreement, or defer reaching agreement, on any matter within our competence.'

19C.8. If an expert significantly alters an opinion, the joint statement must include a note or addendum by that expert explaining the change of opinion.

CRIMINAL PROCEDURE RULES PART 20 HEARSAY EVIDENCE

R-200 When this Part applies

20.1 This Part applies—
(a) in a magistrates' court and in the Crown Court;
(b) where a party wants to introduce hearsay evidence, within the meaning of section 114 of the Criminal Justice Act 2003.

R-201 Notice to introduce hearsay evidence

20.2 (1) This rule applies where a party wants to introduce hearsay evidence for admission under any of the following sections of the Criminal Justice Act 2003—
(a) section 114(1)(d) (evidence admissible in the interests of justice);
(b) section 116 (evidence where a witness is unavailable);
(c) section 117(1)(c) (evidence in a statement prepared for the purposes of criminal proceedings);
(d) section 121 (multiple hearsay).
(2) That party must—
(a) serve notice on—
(i) the court officer, and
(ii) each other party;

(b) in the notice—
(i) identify the evidence that is hearsay,
(ii) set out any facts on which that party relies to make the evidence admissible,
(iii) explain how that party will prove those facts if another party disputes them, and
(iv) explain why the evidence is admissible; and
(c) attach to the notice any statement or other document containing the evidence that has not already been served.
(3) A prosecutor who wants to introduce such evidence must serve the notice not more than—
(a) 28 days after the defendant pleads not guilty, in a magistrates' court; or
(b) 14 days after the defendant pleads not guilty, in the Crown Court.
(4) A defendant who wants to introduce such evidence must serve the notice as soon as reasonably practicable.
(5) A party entitled to receive a notice under this rule may waive that entitlement by so informing—
(a) the party who would have served it; and
(b) the court.

Opposing the introduction of hearsay evidence R-202

20.3 (1) This rule applies where a party objects to the introduction of hearsay evidence.
(2) That party must—
(a) apply to the court to determine the objection;
(b) serve the application on—
(i) the court officer, and
(ii) each other party;
(c) serve the application as soon as reasonably practicable, and in any event not more than 14 days after—
(i) service of notice to introduce the evidence under rule 20.2,
(ii) service of the evidence to which that party objects, if no notice is required by that rule, or
(iii) the defendant pleads not guilty
whichever of those events happens last; and
(d) in the application, explain—
(i) which, if any, facts set out in a notice under rule 20.2 that party disputes,
(ii) why the evidence is not admissible, and
(iii) any other objection to the evidence.
(3) The court—
(a) may determine an application—
(i) at a hearing, in public or in private, or
(ii) without a hearing;
(b) must not determine the application unless the party who served the notice—
(i) is present, or
(ii) has had a reasonable opportunity to respond;
(c) may adjourn the application; and
(d) may discharge or vary a determination where it can do so under—
(i) section 8B of the Magistrates' Courts Act 1980 (ruling at pre-trial hearing in a magistrates' court), or
(ii) section 9 of the Criminal Justice Act 1987, or section 31 or 40 of the Criminal Procedure and Investigations Act 1996 (ruling at preparatory or other pre-trial hearing in the Crown Court).

Unopposed hearsay evidence R-203

20.4 (1) This rule applies where—
(a) a party has served notice to introduce hearsay evidence under rule 20.2; and
(b) no other party has applied to the court to determine an objection to the introduction of the evidence.
(2) The court must treat the evidence as if it were admissible by agreement.

Court's power to vary requirements under this Part R-204

20.5 (1) The court may—
(a) shorten or extend (even after it has expired) a time limit under this Part;

(b) allow an application or notice to be given in a different form to one set out in the Practice Direction, or to be made or given orally;
(c) dispense with the requirement for notice to introduce hearsay evidence.

(2) A party who wants an extension of time must—
(a) apply when serving the application or notice for which it is needed; and
(b) explain the delay.

Criminal Procedure Rules Part 21 Evidence of Bad Character

R-205 **When this Part applies**

21.1 This Part applies—
(a) in a magistrates' court and in the Crown Court;
(b) where a party wants to introduce evidence of bad character, within the meaning of section 98 of the Criminal Justice Act 2003.

R-206 **Content of application or notice**

21.2 (1) A party who wants to introduce evidence of bad character must—
(a) make an application under rule 21.3, where it is evidence of a non-defendant's bad character;
(b) give notice under rule 21.4, where it is evidence of a defendant's bad character.

(2) An application or notice must—
(a) set out the facts of the misconduct on which that party relies,
(b) explain how that party will prove those facts (whether by certificate of conviction, other official record, or other evidence), if another party disputes them, and
(c) explain why the evidence is admissible.

R-207 **Application to introduce evidence of a non-defendant's bad character**

21.3 (1) This rule applies where a party wants to introduce evidence of the bad character of a person other than the defendant.

(2) That party must serve an application to do so on—
(a) the court officer; and
(b) each other party.

(3) The applicant must serve the application—
(a) as soon as reasonably practicable; and in any event
(b) not more than 14 days after the prosecutor discloses material on which the application is based (if the prosecutor is not the applicant).

(4) A party who objects to the introduction of the evidence must—
(a) serve notice on—
(i) the court officer, and
(ii) each other party
not more than 14 days after service of the application; and
(b) in the notice explain, as applicable—
(i) which, if any, facts of the misconduct set out in the application that party disputes,
(ii) what, if any, facts of the misconduct that party admits instead,
(iii) why the evidence is not admissible, and
(iv) any other objection to the application.

(5) The court—
(a) may determine an application—
(i) at a hearing, in public or in private, or
(ii) without a hearing;
(b) must not determine the application unless each party other than the applicant—
(i) is present, or
(ii) has had at least 14 days in which to serve a notice of objection;
(c) may adjourn the application; and
(d) may discharge or vary a determination where it can do so under—
(i) section 8B of the Magistrates' Courts Act 1980 (ruling at pre-trial hearing in a magistrates' court), or
(ii) section 9 of the Criminal Justice Act 1987, or section 31 or 40 of the Criminal Procedure and Investigations Act 1996 (ruling at preparatory or other pre-trial hearing in the Crown Court).

Notice to introduce evidence of a defendant's bad character R-208

21.4 (1) This rule applies where a party wants to introduce evidence of a defendant's bad character.
(2) A prosecutor or co-defendant who wants to introduce such evidence must serve notice on—
(a) the court officer; and
(b) each other party.
(3) A prosecutor must serve any such notice not more than—
(a) 28 days after the defendant pleads not guilty, in a magistrates' court; or
(b) 14 days after the defendant pleads not guilty, in the Crown Court.
(4) A co-defendant must serve any such notice—
(a) as soon as reasonably practicable; and in any event
(b) not more than 14 days after the prosecutor discloses material on which the notice is based.
(5) A party who objects to the introduction of the evidence identified by such a notice must—
(a) apply to the court to determine the objection;
(b) serve the application on—
(i) the court officer, and
(ii) each other party
not more than 14 days after service of the notice; and
(c) in the application explain, as applicable—
(i) which, if any, facts of the misconduct set out in the notice that party disputes,
(ii) what, if any, facts of the misconduct that party admits instead,
(iii) why the evidence is not admissible,
(iv) why it would be unfair to admit the evidence, and
(v) any other objection to the notice.
(6) The court—
(a) may determine such an application—
(i) at a hearing, in public or in private, or
(ii) without a hearing;
(b) must not determine the application unless the party who served the notice—
(i) is present, or
(ii) has had a reasonable opportunity to respond;
(c) may adjourn the application; and
(d) may discharge or vary a determination where it can do so under—
(i) section 8B of the Magistrates' Courts Act 1980 (ruling at pre-trial hearing in a magistrates' court), or
(ii) section 9 of the Criminal Justice Act 1987, or section 31 or 40 of the Criminal Procedure and Investigations Act 1996 (ruling at preparatory or other pre-trial hearing in the Crown Court).
(7) A party entitled to receive such a notice may waive that entitlement by so informing—
(a) the party who would have served it; and
(b) the court.
(8) A defendant who wants to introduce evidence of his or her own bad character must—
(a) give notice, in writing or orally—
(i) as soon as reasonably practicable, and in any event
(ii) before the evidence is introduced, either by the defendant or in reply to a question asked by the defendant of another party's witness in order to obtain that evidence; and
(b) in the Crown Court, at the same time give notice (in writing, or orally) of any direction about the defendant's character that the defendant wants the court to give the jury under rule 25.14 (Directions to the jury and taking the verdict).

Reasons for decisions R-209

21.5 The court must announce at a hearing in public (but in the absence of the jury, if there is one) the reasons for a decision—
(a) to admit evidence as evidence of bad character, or to refuse to do so; or
(b) to direct an acquittal or a retrial under section 107 of the Criminal Justice Act 2003.

Court's power to vary requirements under this Part R-210

21.6 (1) The court may—
(a) shorten or extend (even after it has expired) a time limit under this Part;
(b) allow an application or notice to be in a different form to one set out in the Practice Direction, or to be made or given orally;

(c) dispense with a requirement for notice to introduce evidence of a defendant's bad character.

(2) A party who wants an extension of time must—

(a) apply when serving the application or notice for which it is needed; and

(b) explain the delay.

Criminal Practice Directions Part 21 Evidence of Bad Character

PD-50 **CPD V Evidence 21A: Spent Convictions**

21A.1 The effect of section 4(1) of the Rehabilitation of Offenders Act 1974 is that a person who has become a rehabilitated person for the purpose of the Act in respect of a conviction (known as a 'spent' conviction) shall be treated for all purposes in law as a person who has not committed, or been charged with or prosecuted for, or convicted of or sentenced for, the offence or offences which were the subject of that conviction.

21A.2 Section 4(1) of the 1974 Act does not apply, however, to evidence given in criminal proceedings: section 7(2)(a). During the trial of a criminal charge, reference to previous convictions (and therefore to spent convictions) can arise in a number of ways. The most common is when a bad character application is made under the Criminal Justice Act 2003. When considering bad character applications under the 2003 Act, regard should always be had to the general principles of the Rehabilitation of Offenders Act 1974.

21A.3 On conviction, the court must be provided with a statement of the defendant's record for the purposes of sentence. The record supplied should contain all previous convictions, but those which are spent should, so far as practicable, be marked as such. No one should refer in open court to a spent conviction without the authority of the judge, which authority should not be given unless the interests of justice so require. When passing sentence the judge should make no reference to a spent conviction unless it is necessary to do so for the purpose of explaining the sentence to be passed.

Criminal Procedure Rules Part 22 Evidence of a Complainant's Previous Sexual Behaviour

R-211 **When this Part applies**

22.1 This Part applies—

(a) in a magistrates' court and in the Crown Court;

(b) where—

(i) section 41 of the Youth Justice and Criminal Evidence Act 1999(a) prohibits the introduction of evidence or cross-examination about any sexual behaviour of the complainant of a sexual offence, and

(ii) despite that prohibition, a defendant wants to introduce such evidence or to cross-examine a witness about such behaviour.

R-212 **Exercise of court's powers**

22.2 The court—

(a) must determine an application under rule 22.4 (Application for permission to introduce evidence or cross-examine)—

(i) at a hearing in private, and

(ii) in the absence of the complainant;

(b) must not determine the application unless—

(i) each party other than the applicant is present, or has had at least 14 days in which to make representations, and

(ii) the court is satisfied that it has been able to take adequate account of the complainant's rights;

(c) may adjourn the application; and

(d) may discharge or vary a determination where it can do so under—

(i) section 8B of the Magistrates' Courts Act 1980(a) (ruling at pre-trial hearing in a magistrates' court), or

(ii) section 9 of the Criminal Justice Act 1987(b), or section 31 or 40 of the Criminal Procedure and Investigations Act 1996(c) (ruling at preparatory or other pre-trial hearing in the Crown Court).

Decisions and reasons R-213

22.3 (1) A prosecutor who wants to introduce the evidence of a complainant in respect of whom the court allows the introduction of evidence or cross-examination about any sexual behaviour must—

(a) inform the complainant of the court's decision as soon as reasonably practicable; and

(b) explain to the complainant any arrangements that as a result will be made for him or her to give evidence.

(2) The court must—

(a) promptly determine an application; and

(b) allow the prosecutor sufficient time to comply with the requirements of—

(i) paragraph (1), and

(ii) the code of practice issued under section 32 of the Domestic Violence, Crime and Victims Act 2004(g).

(3) The court must announce at a hearing in public—

(a) the reasons for a decision to allow or refuse an application under rule 22.4; and

(b) if it allows such an application, the extent to which evidence may be introduced or questions asked.

Application for permission to introduce evidence or cross-examine R-214

22.4. (1) A defendant who wants to introduce evidence or cross-examine a witness about any sexual behaviour of the complainant must—

(a) serve an application for permission to do so on—

(i) the court officer, and

(ii) each other party;

(b) serve the application—

(i) as soon as reasonably practicable after becoming aware of the grounds for doing so, and in any event

(ii) not more than 14 days after the prosecutor discloses material on which the application is based.

(2) The application must—

(a) identify the issue to which the defendant says the complainant's sexual behaviour is relevant;

(b) give particulars of—

(i) any evidence that the defendant wants to introduce, and

(ii) any questions that the defendant wants to ask;

(c) identify the exception to the prohibition in section 41 of the Youth Justice and Criminal Evidence Act 1999 on which the defendant relies; and

(d) give the name and date of birth of any witness whose evidence about the complainant's sexual behaviour the defendant wants to introduce.

Reply to application R-215

22.5. (1) This rule applies where—

(a) an applicant serves an application under rule 22.4 (Application for permission to introduce evidence or cross-examine); and

(b) the application includes information that the applicant thinks ought not be revealed to another party.

(2) The applicant must—

(a) omit that information from the part of the application that is served on that other party;

(b) mark the other part to show that, unless the court otherwise directs, it is only for the court; and

(c) in that other part, explain why the applicant has withheld that information from that other party.

(3) If the court so directs, the hearing of an application to which this rule applies may be, wholly or in part, in the absence of a party from whom information has been withheld.

(4) At the hearing of an application to which this rule applies—

(a) the general rule is that the court must consider, in the following sequence—

(i) representations first by the applicant and then by each other party, in all the parties' presence, and then

(ii) further representations by the applicant, in the absence of a party from whom information has been withheld; but

(b) the court may direct other arrangements for the hearing.

R-216 **Application for special measures**

22.6. (1) This rule applies where a party wants to make representations about—
(a) an application under rule 22.4 (Application for permission to introduce evidence or cross-examine); or
(b) a proposed variation or discharge of a decision allowing such an application.
(2) Such a party must—
(a) serve the representations on—
(i) the court officer, and
(ii) each other party; and
(b) do so not more than 14 days after, as applicable—
(i) service of the application, or
(ii) notice of the proposal to vary or discharge.
(3) Where representations include information that the person making them thinks ought not be revealed to another party, that person must—
(a) omit that information from the representations served on that other party;
(b) mark the information to show that, unless the court otherwise directs, it is only for the court; and
(c) with that information include an explanation of why it has been withheld from that other party.
(4) Representations against an application under rule 22.4 must explain the grounds of objection.
(5) Representations against the variation or discharge of a decision must explain why it should not be varied or discharged.

R-217 **Special measures, etc. for a witness**

22.7 (1) This rule applies where the court allows an application under rule 22.4 (Application for permission to introduce evidence or cross-examine).
(2) Despite the time limits in rule 18.3 (Making an application for a direction or order)—
(a) a party may apply not more than 14 days after the court's decision for a special measures direction or for the variation of an existing special measures direction; and
(b) the court may shorten the time for opposing that application.
(3) Where the court allows the cross-examination of a witness, the court must give directions for the appropriate treatment and questioning of that witness in accordance with rule 3.9(6) and (7) (setting ground rules for the conduct of questioning).

R-218 **Court's power to vary requirements under this Part**

22.8. The court may shorten or extend (even after it has expired) a time limit under this Part."

Criminal Practice Directions Part 22 Evidence of a Complainant's Previous Sexual Behaviour

PD-51 **CPD V Evidence 22A: Use of Ground Rules Hearing when Dealing with S.41 Youth Justice and Criminal Evidence Act 1999 (YJCEA 1999) Evidence of Complainant's Previous Sexual Behaviour**

The Application

22A.1 When a defendant wishes to introduce evidence, or cross-examine about the previous sexual behaviour of the complainant, then it is imperative that the timetable and procedure as laid down in the Criminal Procedure Rules Part 22 is followed. The application must be submitted in writing as soon as reasonably practicable and not more than 14 days after the prosecutor has disclosed material on which the application is based. Should the prosecution wish to make any representations then these should be served on the court and other parties not more than 14 days after receiving the application.

22A.2 The application must clearly state the issue to which the defendant says the complainant's sexual behaviour is relevant and the reasons why it should be admitted. It must outline the evidence which the defendant wants to introduce and articulate the questions which it is proposed should be asked. The application must identify the statutory exception to the prohibition in section 41 YJCEA 1999 on which the defendant relies and give the name and date of birth of any witness whose evidence about the complainant's sexual behaviour the defendant wants to introduce.

The Hearing

22A.3 When determining the application, the judge should examine the questions with the usual level of scrutiny expected at a ground rules hearing. For each question that it is sought to put to a witness, or evidence it is sought to adduce, the defence should identify clearly for the judge the suggested relevance it has to an issue in the case. In order for the judge to rule on which evidence can be adduced or questions put, the defence must set out individual questions for the judge; merely identifying a topic is not sufficient for this type of application. The judge should make it clear that if the application is granted then no other questions on this topic will be allowed to be asked, unless with the express permission of the court.

22A.4 The application should be dealt with in private and in the absence of the complainant, but the judge must state in open court, without the jury or complainant present, the reasons for the decision, and if leave is granted, the extent of the questions or evidence that is allowed.

Late applications

22A.5 Late applications should be considered with particular scrutiny especially if there is a suggestion of tactical thinking behind the timing of the application and/or when the application is based on material that has been available for some time. If consideration of a late application has the potential to disrupt the timetabling of witnesses, then the judge will need to take account of the potential impact of delay upon a witness who is due to give evidence. If necessary, the judge may defer consideration of any such application until later in the trial.

22A.6 By analogy, following the approach adopted by the Court of Appeal in *R v Musone* [2007] 1 WLR 2467, the trial judge is entitled to refuse the application where (s)he is satisfied that the applicant is seeking to manipulate the court process so as to prevent the respondent from being able to prepare an adequate response. This may be the only remedy available to the court to ensure that the fairness of the trial is upheld and will be particularly relevant when the application is made on the day of trial.

22A.7 Where the application has been granted in good time before the trial, the complainant is entitled to be made aware that such evidence is part of the defence case.

At the trial

22A.8 Advocates should be reminded that the questioning must be conducted in an appropriate manner. Any aggressive, repetitive and oppressive questioning will be stopped by the judge. Judges should intervene and stop any attempts to refer to evidence that might have been adduced under section 41, but for which no leave has been given and/or should have formed the basis of a section 41 application, but did not do so. When evidence about the complainant's previous sexual behaviour is referred to without an application, the judge may be required to consider whether the impact of that happening is so prejudicial to the overall fairness of the trial that the trial should be stopped and a re-trial should be ordered, should the impact not be capable of being ameliorated by way of jury direction.

Criminal Procedure Rules Part 23 Restriction on Cross-Examination by a Defendant

General rules

When this Part applies R-219

23.1 This Part applies where—

(a) a defendant may not cross-examine in person a witness because of section 34 or section 35 of the Youth Justice and Criminal Evidence Act 1999 (Complainants in proceedings for sexual offences; Child complainants and other child witnesses);

(b) the court can prohibit a defendant from cross-examining in person a witness under section 36 of that Act (Direction prohibiting accused from cross-examining particular witness).

Appointment of advocate to cross-examine witness R-220

23.2 (1) This rule applies where a defendant may not cross-examine in person a witness in consequence of—

(a) the prohibition imposed by section 34 or section 35 of the Youth Justice and Criminal Evidence Act 1999; or

(b) a prohibition imposed by the court under section 36 of the 1999 Act.

(2) The court must, as soon as practicable, explain in terms the defendant can understand (with help, if necessary)—

(a) the prohibition and its effect;

(b) that if the defendant will not be represented by a lawyer with a right of audience in the court for the purposes of the case then the defendant is entitled to arrange for such a lawyer to cross-examine the witness on his or her behalf;
(c) that the defendant must notify the court officer of the identity of any such lawyer, with details of how to contact that person, by no later than a date set by the court;
(d) that if the defendant does not want to make such arrangements, or if the defendant gives no such notice by that date, then—
(i) the court must decide whether it is necessary in the interests of justice to appoint such a lawyer to cross-examine the witness in the defendant's interests, and
(ii) if the court decides that that is necessary, the court will appoint a lawyer chosen by the court who will not be responsible to the defendant.

(3) Having given those explanations, the court must—
(a) ask whether the defendant wants to arrange for a lawyer to cross-examine the witness, and set a date by when the defendant must notify the court officer of the identity of that lawyer if the answer to that question is 'yes';
(b) if the answer to that question is 'no', or if by the date set the defendant has given no such notice—
(i) decide whether it is necessary in the interests of justice for the witness to be cross-examined by an advocate appointed to represent the defendant's interests, and
(ii) if the court decides that that is necessary, give directions for the appointment of such an advocate.

(4) The court may give the explanations and ask the questions required by this rule—
(a) at a hearing, in public or in private; or
(b) without a hearing, by written notice to the defendant.

(5) The court may extend (even after it has expired) the time limit that it sets under paragraph (3)(a)—
(a) on application by the defendant; or
(b) on its own initiative.

(6) Paragraphs (7), (8), (9) and (10) apply where the court appoints an advocate.

(7) The directions that the court gives under paragraph (3)(b)(ii) must provide for the supply to the advocate of a copy of—
(a) all material served by one party on the other, whether before or after the advocate's appointment, to which applies—
(i) Part 8 (Initial details of the prosecution case),
(ii) in the Crown Court, rule 9.15 (service of prosecution evidence in a case sent for trial),
(iii) Part 16 (Written witness statements),
(iv) Part 19 (Expert evidence),
(v) Part 20 (Hearsay evidence),
(vi) Part 21 (Evidence of bad character),
(vii) Part 22 (Evidence of a complainant's previous sexual behaviour);
(b) any material disclosed, given or served, whether before or after the advocate's appointment, which is—
(i) prosecution material disclosed to the defendant under section 3 (Initial duty of prosecutor to disclose) or section 7A (Continuing duty of prosecutor to disclose) of the Criminal Procedure and Investigations Act 1996(a),
(ii) a defence statement given by the defendant under section 5 (Compulsory disclosure by accused) or section 6 (Voluntary disclosure by accused) of the 1996 Act (b),
(iii) a defence witness notice given by the defendant under section 6C of that Act (c) (Notification of intention to call defence witnesses), or
(iv) an application by the defendant under section 8 of that Act (d) (Application by accused for disclosure);
(c) any case management questionnaire prepared for the purposes of the trial or, as the case may be, the appeal; and
(d) all case management directions given by the court for the purposes of the trial or the appeal.

(8) Where the defendant has given a defence statement—
(a) section 8(2) of the Criminal Procedure and Investigations Act 1996 is modified to allow the advocate, as well as the defendant, to apply for an order for prosecution disclosure under that subsection if the advocate has reasonable cause to believe that there is prosecu-

tion material concerning the witness which is required by section 7A of the Act to be disclosed to the defendant and has not been; and

(b) rule 15.5 (Defendant's application for prosecution disclosure) applies to an application by the advocate as it does to an application by the defendant.

(9) Before receiving evidence the court must establish, with the active assistance of the parties and of the advocate, and in the absence of any jury in the Crown Court—

(a) what issues will be the subject of the advocate's cross-examination; and

(b) whether the court's permission is required for any proposed question, for example where Part 21 or Part 22 applies.

(10) The appointment terminates at the conclusion of the cross-examination of the witness.

Application to prohibit cross-examination

Exercise of court's powers R-221

23.3 (1) The court may decide whether to impose or discharge a prohibition against cross-examination under section 36 of the Youth Justice and Criminal Evidence Act 1999—

(a) at a hearing, in public or in private, or without a hearing;

(b) in a party's absence, if that party—

(i) applied for the prohibition or discharge, or

(ii) has had at least 14 days in which to make representations.

(2) The court must announce, at a hearing in public before the witness gives evidence, the reasons for a decision—

(a) to impose or discharge such a prohibition; or

(b) to refuse to do so.

Application to prohibit cross-examination R-222

23.4 (1) This rule applies where under section 36 of the Youth Justice and Criminal Evidence Act 1999 the prosecutor wants the court to prohibit the cross-examination of a witness by a defendant in person.

(2) The prosecutor must—

(a) apply in writing, as soon as reasonably practicable after becoming aware of the grounds for doing so; and

(b) serve the application on—

(i) the court officer,

(ii) the defendant who is the subject of the application, and

(iii) any other defendant, unless the court otherwise directs.

(3) The application must—

(a) report any views that the witness has expressed about whether he or she is content to be cross-examined by the defendant in person;

(b) identify—

(i) the nature of the questions likely to be asked, having regard to the issues in the case,

(ii) any relevant behaviour of the defendant at any stage of the case, generally and in relation to the witness,

(iii) any relationship, of any nature, between the witness and the defendant,

(iv) any other defendant in the case who is subject to such a prohibition in respect of the witness, and

(v) any special measures direction made in respect of the witness, or for which an application has been made;

(c) explain why the quality of evidence given by the witness on cross-examination—

(i) is likely to be diminished if no such prohibition is imposed, and

(ii) would be likely to be improved if it were imposed; and

(d) explain why it would not be contrary to the interests of justice to impose the prohibition.

Application to discharge prohibition imposed by the court R-223

23.5 (1) A party who wants the court to discharge a prohibition against cross-examination which the court imposed under section 36 of the Youth Justice and Criminal Evidence Act 1999 must—

(a) apply in writing, as soon as reasonably practicable after becoming aware of the grounds for doing so; and

(b) serve the application on—

(i) the court officer, and

(ii) each other party.

(2) The applicant must—
(a) explain what material circumstances have changed since the prohibition was imposed; and
(b) ask for a hearing, if the applicant wants one, and explain why it is needed.

R-224 Application containing information withheld from another party

23.6 (1) This rule applies where—
(a) an applicant serves an application for the court to impose a prohibition against cross-examination, or for the discharge of such a prohibition; and
(b) the application includes information that the applicant thinks ought not be revealed to another party.
(2) The applicant must—
(a) omit that information from the part of the application that is served on that other party;
(b) mark the other part to show that, unless the court otherwise directs, it is only for the court; and
(c) in that other part, explain why the applicant has withheld that information from that other party.
(3) Any hearing of an application to which this rule applies—
(a) must be in private, unless the court otherwise directs; and
(b) if the court so directs, may be, wholly or in part, in the absence of a party from whom information has been withheld.
(4) At any hearing of an application to which this rule applies—
(a) the general rule is that the court must consider, in the following sequence—
(i) representations first by the applicant and then by each other party, in all the parties' presence, and then
(ii) further representations by the applicant, in the absence of a party from whom information has been withheld; but
(b) the court may direct other arrangements for the hearing.

R-225 Representations in response

23.7 (1) This rule applies where a party wants to make representations about—
(a) an application under rule 23.4 for a prohibition against cross-examination;
(b) an application under rule 23.5 for the discharge of such a prohibition; or
(c) a prohibition or discharge that the court proposes on its own initiative.
(2) Such a party must—
(a) serve the representations on—
(i) the court officer, and
(ii) each other party;
(b) do so not more than 14 days after, as applicable—
(i) service of the application, or
(ii) notice of the prohibition or discharge that the court proposes; and
(c) ask for a hearing, if that party wants one, and explain why it is needed.
(3) Representations against a prohibition must explain in what respect the conditions for imposing it are not met.
(4) Representations against the discharge of a prohibition must explain why it should not be discharged.
(5) Where representations include information that the person making them thinks ought not be revealed to another party, that person must—
(a) omit that information from the representations served on that other party;
(b) mark the information to show that, unless the court otherwise directs, it is only for the court; and
(c) with that information include an explanation of why it has been withheld from that other party.

R-226 Court's power to vary requirements

23.8 (1) The court may—
(a) shorten or extend (even after it has expired) a time limit under rule 23.4 (Application to prohibit cross-examination), rule 23.5 (Application to discharge prohibition imposed by the court) or rule 23.7 (Representations in response); and
(b) allow an application or representations required by any of those rules to be made in a different form to one set out in the Practice Direction, or to be made orally.
(2) A person who wants an extension of time must—
(a) apply when serving the application or representations for which it is needed; and
(b) explain the delay.

Criminal Practice Directions Part 23 Cross-Examination Advocates

CPD V Evidence 23A: Cross-Examination Advocates PD-52

Provisional appointment of advocate

23A.1 At the first hearing in the court in the case, and in a magistrates' court in particular, there may be occasions on which a defendant has engaged no legal representative, within the meaning of the Criminal Procedure Rules, for the purposes of the case generally, but still intends to do so – for example, where he or she has made an application for legal aid which has yet to be determined. Where the defendant nonetheless has identified a prospective legal representative who has a right of audience in the court; where the court is satisfied that that representative will be willing to cross-examine the relevant witness or witnesses in the interests of the defendant should it transpire that the defendant will not be represented for the purposes of the case generally; and if the court is in a position there and then to make, contingently, the decision required by section 38(3) of the Youth Justice and Criminal Evidence Act 1999 ('the court must consider whether it is necessary in the interests of justice for the witness to be cross-examined by a legal representative appointed to represent the interests of the accused'); then the court may appoint that representative under section 38(4) of the 1999 Act contingently, the appointment to come into effect only if, and when, it is established that the defendant will not be represented for the purposes of the case generally.

23A.2 Where such a provisional appointment is made it is essential that the role and status of the representative is clearly established at the earliest possible opportunity. The court's directions under CrimPR 23.2(3) should require the defendant to notify the court officer, by the date set by the court, whether:

(i) the defendant will be represented by a legal representative for the purposes of the case generally, and if so by whom (in which event the court's provisional appointment has no effect);

(ii) the defendant will not be represented for the purposes of the case generally, but the defendant and the legal representative provisionally appointed by the court remain content with that provisional appointment (in which event the court's provisional appointment takes effect); or

(iii) the defendant will not be represented for the purposes of the case generally, but will arrange for a lawyer to cross-examine the relevant witness or witnesses on his or her behalf, giving that lawyer's name and contact details.

If in the event the defendant fails to give notice by the due date then, unless it is apparent that she or he will, in fact, be represented for the purposes of the case generally, the court may decide to confirm the provisional appointment and proceed accordingly.

Supply of case papers

23A.3 For the advocate to fulfil the duty imposed by the appointment, and to achieve a responsible, professional and appropriate treatment both of the defendant and of the witness, it is essential for the advocate to establish what is in issue. To that end, it is likewise essential for the advocate to have been supplied with the material listed in CrimPR 23.2(7).

23A.4 In the Crown Court, much of this this can be achieved most conveniently by giving the advocate access to the Crown Court Digital Case System. However, material disclosed by the prosecutor to the defendant under section 3 or section 7A of the Criminal Procedure and Investigations Act 1996 is not stored in that system and therefore must be supplied to the advocate either by the defendant or by the prosecutor. In the latter case, the prosecutor reasonably may omit from the copies supplied to the advocate any material that can have no bearing on the cross-examination for which the advocate has been appointed – the medical or social services records of another witness, for example.

23A.5 In a magistrates' court, pending the introduction of comparable electronic arrangements:

i. in some instances the advocate may have received the relevant material at a point at which he or she was acting as the defendant's legal representative subject to a restriction on the purpose or duration of that appointment notified under CrimPR 46.2(5) – for example, pending the outcome of an application for legal aid.

ii. in some instances the defendant may be able to provide spare copies of relevant material. Where that material has been disclosed by the prosecutor under section 3 or section 7A of the Criminal Procedure and Investigations Act 1996 then its supply to the advocate by the defendant is permitted by section 17(2)(a) of the 1996 Act (exception to the prohibition against further disclosure where that further disclosure is 'in connection with the proceedings for whose purposes [the defendant] was given the object or allowed to inspect it').

iii. in some instances the prosecutor may be able to supply the relevant material, or some of it, at no, or minimal, expense by electronic means.

iv. in the event that, unusually, none of those sources of supply is available, then the court's directions under CrimPR 23.2(3) should require the court officer to provide copies from the court's own records, as if the advocate were a party and had applied under CrimPR 5.7.

Obtaining information and observations from the defendant

23A.6 Advocates and courts should keep in mind section 38(5) of the 1999 Act, which provides 'A person so appointed shall not be responsible to the accused.' The advocate therefore cannot and should not take instructions from the defendant, in the usual sense; and to avoid any misapprehension in that respect, either by the defendant or by others, some advocates may prefer to avoid direct oral communication with the defendant before, and even perhaps during, the trial.

23A.7 However, as remarked above at paragraph 23A.3, for the advocate to fulfil the duty imposed by the appointment it is essential for him or her to establish what is in issue; which may require communication with the defendant both before and at the trial as well as a thorough examination of the case papers. CrimPR 23.2(7)(a) in effect requires the advocate to have identified the issues on which the cross-examination of the witness is expected to proceed before the court begins to receive prosecution evidence, and to have taken part in their discussion with the court. To that end, communication with the defendant may be necessary.

Extent of cross-examination advocate's appointment

23A.8 In *Abbas v Crown Prosecution Service* [2015] EWHC 579 (Admin); [2015] 2 Cr.App.R. 11 the Divisional Court observed:

> 'The role of a section 38 advocate is, undoubtedly, limited to the proper performance of their duty as a cross examiner of a particular witness. Sections 36 and 38 are all about protecting vulnerable witnesses from cross examination by the accused. Therefore, it should not be thought that an advocate appointed under section 38 has a free ranging remit to conduct the trial on the accused's behalf. Their professional duty and their statutory duty would be to ensure that they are in a position properly to conduct the cross examination. Their duties might include therefore applications to admit bad character of the witness and or applications for disclosure of material relevant to the cross examination. That is as far as one can go. All these matters must be entirely fact specific. The important thing to note is that the section 38 advocate must ensure that s/he performs his/her duties in accordance with the words of the statute. It means also that their appointment comes to an end, under section 38, at the conclusion of the cross examination, save to the extent that the court otherwise determines. Technically the lawyer no longer has a role in the proceedings thereafter. However, if the lawyer is prepared to stay and assist the defendant on a pro bono basis, I see nothing in the Act and no logical reason why the court should oblige them to leave. The advocate may well prove beneficial to the efficient and fair resolution of the proceedings. The aim of the legislation as I have said is simply to stop the accused cross examining the witness. It is not to prevent the person appointed to cross examine from playing any other part in the trial.'

23A.9 Advocates will be alert to, and courts should keep in mind, the extent of the remuneration available to a cross-examination advocate, in assessing the amount of which the court has only a limited role: see section 19(3) of the Prosecution of Offences Act 1985, which empowers the Lord Chancellor to make regulations authorising payments out of central funds 'to cover the proper fee or costs of a legal representative appointed under section 38(4) of the Youth Justice and Criminal Evidence Act 1999 and any expenses properly incurred in providing such a person with evidence or other material in connection with his appointment', and also sections 19(3ZA) and 20(1A)(d) of the 1985 Act and the Costs in Criminal Cases (General) Regulations 1986, as amended.

23A.10 Advocates and courts must be alert, too, to the possibility that were an advocate to agree to represent a defendant generally at trial, for no payment save that to which such regulations entitled him or her, then the statutory condition precedent for the appointment might be removed and the appointment in consequence withdrawn.

Criminal Procedure Rules Part 24 Trial and Sentence in a Magistrates' Court

When this Part applies R-227

24.1 (1) This Part applies in a magistrates' court where—
(a) the court tries a case;
(b) the defendant pleads guilty;
(c) under section 14 or 16E of the Magistrates' Courts Act 1980, the defendant makes a statutory declaration of not having found out about the case until after the trial began;
(d) under section 142 of the 1980 Act, the court can—
(i) set aside a conviction, or
(ii) vary or rescind a costs order, or an order to which Part 31 applies (Behaviour orders).
(2) Where the defendant is under 18, in this Part—
(a) a reference to convicting the defendant includes a reference to finding the defendant guilty of an offence; and
(b) a reference to sentence includes a reference to an order made on a finding of guilt.

General rules R-228

24.2 (1) Where this Part applies—
(a) the general rule is that the hearing must be in public; but
(b) the court may exercise any power it has to—
(i) impose reporting restrictions,
(ii) withhold information from the public, or
(iii) order a hearing in private; and
(c) unless the court otherwise directs, only the following may attend a hearing in a youth court—
(i) the parties and their legal representatives,
(ii) a defendant's parents, guardian or other supporting adult,
(iii) a witness,
(iv) anyone else directly concerned in the case, and
(v) a representative of a news-gathering or reporting organisation.
(2) Unless already done, the justices' legal adviser or the court must—
(a) read the allegation of the offence to the defendant;
(b) explain, in terms the defendant can understand (with help, if necessary)—
(i) the allegation, and
(ii) what the procedure at the hearing will be;
(c) ask whether the defendant has been advised about the potential effect on sentence of a guilty plea;
(d) ask whether the defendant pleads guilty or not guilty; and
(e) take the defendant's plea.
(3) The court may adjourn the hearing—
(a) at any stage, to the same or to another magistrates' court; or
(b) to a youth court, where the court is not itself a youth court and the defendant is under 18.
(4) Paragraphs (1) and (2) of this rule do not apply where the court tries a case under rule 24.9 (Single justice procedure: special rules).

Procedure on plea of not guilty R-229

24.3 (1) This rule applies—
(a) if the defendant has—
(i) entered a plea of not guilty, or
(ii) not entered a plea; or
(b) if, in either case, it appears to the court that there may be grounds for making a hospital order without convicting the defendant.
(2) If a not guilty plea was taken on a previous occasion, the justices' legal adviser or the court must ask the defendant to confirm that plea.
(3) In the following sequence—
(a) the prosecutor may summarise the prosecution case, concisely identifying the relevant law, outlining the facts and indicating the matters likely to be in dispute;
(b) to help the members of the court to understand the case and resolve any issue in it, the court may invite the defendant concisely to identify what is in issue;
(c) the prosecutor must introduce the evidence on which the prosecution case relies;
(d) at the conclusion of the prosecution case, on the defendant's application or on its own initiative, the court—

(i) may acquit on the ground that the prosecution evidence is insufficient for any reasonable court properly to convict, but
(ii) must not do so unless the prosecutor has had an opportunity to make representations;
(e) the justices' legal adviser or the court must explain, in terms the defendant can understand (with help, if necessary)—
(i) the right to give evidence, and
(ii) the potential effect of not doing so at all, or of refusing to answer a question while doing so;
(f) the defendant may introduce evidence;
(g) a party may introduce further evidence if it is then admissible (for example, because it is in rebuttal of evidence already introduced);
(h) the prosecutor may make final representations in support of the prosecution case, where—
(i) the defendant is represented by a legal representative, or
(ii) whether represented or not, the defendant has introduced evidence other than his or her own; and
(i) the defendant may make final representations in support of the defence case.
(4) Where a party wants to introduce evidence or make representations after that party's opportunity to do so under paragraph (3), the court—
(a) may refuse to receive any such evidence or representations; and
(b) must not receive any such evidence or representations after it has announced its verdict.
(5) If the court—
(a) convicts the defendant; or
(b) makes a hospital order instead of doing so,
it must give sufficient reasons to explain its decision.
(6) If the court acquits the defendant, it may—
(a) give an explanation of its decision; and
(b) exercise any power it has to make—
(i) a behaviour order,
(ii) a costs order.

R-230 Evidence of a witness in person

24.4 (1) This rule applies where a party wants to introduce evidence by calling a witness to give that evidence in person.
(2) Unless the court otherwise directs—
(a) a witness waiting to give evidence must not wait inside the courtroom, unless that witness is—
(i) a party, or
(ii) an expert witness;
(b) a witness who gives evidence in the courtroom must do so from the place provided for that purpose; and
(c) a witness' address must not be announced unless it is relevant to an issue in the case.
(3) Unless other legislation otherwise provides, before giving evidence a witness must take an oath or affirm.
(4) In the following sequence—
(a) the party who calls a witness must ask questions in examination-in-chief;
(b) every other party may ask questions in cross-examination;
(c) the party who called the witness may ask questions in re-examination.
(5) If other legislation so permits, at any time while giving evidence a witness may refer to a record of that witness' recollection of events.
(6) The justices' legal adviser or the court may—
(a) ask a witness questions; and in particular
(b) where the defendant is not represented, ask any question necessary in the defendant's interests.

R-231 Evidence of a witness in writing

24.5 (1) This rule applies where a party wants to introduce in evidence the written statement of a witness to which applies—
(a) Part 16 (Written witness statements);
(b) Part 19 (Expert evidence); or
(c) Part 20 (Hearsay evidence).

(2) If the court admits such evidence—
(a) the court must read the statement; and
(b) unless the court otherwise directs, if any member of the public, including any reporter, is present, each relevant part of the statement must be read or summarised aloud.

Evidence by admission R-232

24.6 (1) This rule applies where—
(a) a party introduces in evidence a fact admitted by another party; or
(b) parties jointly admit a fact.
(2) Unless the court otherwise directs, a written record must be made of the admission.

Procedure on plea of guilty R-233

24.7 (1) This rule applies if—
(a) the defendant pleads guilty; and
(b) the court is satisfied that the plea represents a clear acknowledgement of guilt.
(2) The court may convict the defendant without receiving evidence.

Written guilty plea: special rules R-234

24.8 (1) This rule applies where—
(a) the offence alleged—
(i) can be tried only in a magistrates' court, and
(ii) is not one specified under section 12(1)(a) of the Magistrates' Courts Act 1980;
(b) the defendant is at least 16 years old;
(c) the prosecutor has served on the defendant—
(i) the summons or requisition,
(ii) the material listed in paragraph (2) on which the prosecutor relies to set out the facts of the offence,
(iii) the material listed in paragraph (3) on which the prosecutor relies to provide the court with information relevant to sentence,
(iv) a notice that the procedure set out in this rule applies, and
(v) a notice for the defendant's use if the defendant wants to plead guilty without attending court; and
(d) the prosecutor has served on the court officer—
(i) copies of those documents, and
(ii) a certificate of service of those documents on the defendant.
(2) The material that the prosecutor must serve to set out the facts of the offence is—
(a) a summary of the evidence on which the prosecution case is based;
(b) any—
(i) written witness statement to which Part 16 (Written witness statements) applies, or
(ii) document or extract setting out facts; or
(c) any combination of such a summary, statement, document or extract.
(3) The material that the prosecutor must serve to provide information relevant to sentence is—
(a) details of any previous conviction of the defendant which the prosecutor considers relevant, other than any conviction listed in the defendant's driving record;
(b) if applicable, a notice that the defendant's driving record will be made available to the court;
(c) a notice containing or describing any other information about the defendant, relevant to sentence, which will be made available to the court.
(4) A defendant who wants to plead guilty without attending court must, before the hearing date specified in the summons or requisition—
(a) serve a notice of guilty plea on the court officer; and
(b) include with that notice—
(i) any representations that the defendant wants the court to consider, and
(ii) a statement of the defendant's assets and other financial circumstances.
(5) A defendant who wants to withdraw such a notice must notify the court officer in writing before the hearing date.
(6) If the defendant does not withdraw the notice before the hearing date, then on or after that date—
(a) to establish the facts of the offence and other information about the defendant relevant to sentence, the court may take account only of—
(i) information contained in a document served by the prosecutor under paragraph (1),

(ii) any previous conviction listed in the defendant's driving record, where the offence is under the Road Traffic Regulation Act 1984, the Road Traffic Act 1988, the Road Traffic (Consequential Provisions) Act 1988 or the Road Traffic (Driver Licensing and Information Systems) Act 1989,
(iii) any other information about the defendant, relevant to sentence, of which the prosecutor served notice under paragraph (1), and
(iv) any representations and any other information served by the defendant under paragraph (4)

and rule 24.11(3) to (9) inclusive must be read accordingly;
(b) unless the court otherwise directs, the prosecutor need not attend; and
(c) the court may accept such a guilty plea and pass sentence in the defendant's absence.

(7) With the defendant's agreement, the court may deal with the case in the same way as under paragraph (6) where the defendant is present and—
(a) has served a notice of guilty plea under paragraph (4); or
(b) pleads guilty there and then.

R-235 Single justice procedure: special rules

24.9 (1) This rule applies where—
(a) the offence alleged—
(i) can be tried only in a magistrates' court, and
(ii) is not one punishable with imprisonment;
(b) the defendant is at least 18 years old;
(c) the prosecutor has served on the defendant—
(i) a written charge,
(ii) the material listed in paragraph (2) on which the prosecutor relies to set out the facts of the offence,
(iii) the material listed in paragraph (3) on which the prosecutor relies to provide the court with information relevant to sentence,
(iv) a notice that the procedure set out in this rule applies,
(v) a notice for the defendant's use if the defendant wants to plead guilty,
(vi) a notice for the defendant's use if the defendant wants to plead guilty but wants the case dealt with at a hearing by a court comprising more than one justice, and
(vii) a notice for the defendant's use if the defendant wants to plead not guilty; and
(d) the prosecutor has served on the court officer—
(i) copies of those documents, and
(ii) a certificate of service of those documents on the defendant.

(2) The material that the prosecutor must serve to set out the facts of the offence is—
(a) a summary of the evidence on which the prosecution case is based;
(b) any—
(i) written witness statement to which Part 16 (Written witness statements) applies, or
(ii) document or extract setting out facts; or
(c) any combination of such a summary, statement, document or extract.

(3) The material that the prosecutor must serve to provide information relevant to sentence is—
(a) details of any previous conviction of the defendant which the prosecutor considers relevant, other than any conviction listed in the defendant's driving record;
(b) if applicable, a notice that the defendant's driving record will be made available to the court;
(c) a notice containing or describing any other information about the defendant, relevant to sentence, which will be made available to the court.

(4) Not more than 21 days after service on the defendant of the documents listed in paragraph (1)(c)—
(a) a defendant who wants to plead guilty must serve a notice to that effect on the court officer and include with that notice—
(i) any representations that the defendant wants the court to consider, and
(ii) a statement of the defendant's assets and other financial circumstances;
(b) a defendant who wants to plead guilty but wants the case dealt with at a hearing by a court comprising more than one justice must serve a notice to that effect on the court officer;
(c) a defendant who wants to plead not guilty must serve a notice to that effect on the court officer.

(5) If within 21 days of service on the defendant of the documents listed in paragraph (1)(c) the defendant serves a notice to plead guilty under paragraph (4)(a)—
(a) the court officer must arrange for the court to deal with the case in accordance with that notice; and
(b) the time for service of any other notice under paragraph (4) expires at once.
(6) If within 21 days of service on the defendant of the documents listed in paragraph (1)(c) the defendant wants to withdraw a notice which he or she has served under paragraph (4)(b) (notice to plead guilty at a hearing) or under paragraph (4)(c) (notice to plead not guilty), the defendant must—
(a) serve notice of that withdrawal on the court officer; and
(b) serve any substitute notice under paragraph (4).
(7) Paragraph (8) applies where by the date of trial the defendant has not—
(a) served notice under paragraph (4)(b) or (c) of wanting to plead guilty at a hearing, or wanting to plead not guilty; or
(b) given notice to that effect under section 16B(2) of the Magistrates' Courts Act 1980.
(8) Where this paragraph applies—
(a) the court may try the case in the parties' absence and without a hearing;
(b) the court may accept any guilty plea of which the defendant has given notice under paragraph (4)(a);
(c) to establish the facts of the offence and other information about the defendant relevant to sentence, the court may take account only of—
(i) information contained in a document served by the prosecutor under paragraph (1),
(ii) any previous conviction listed in the defendant's driving record, where the offence is under the Road Traffic Regulation Act 1984, the Road Traffic Act 1988, the Road Traffic (Consequential Provisions) Act 1988 or the Road Traffic (Driver Licensing and Information Systems) Act 1989,
(iii) any other information about the defendant, relevant to sentence, of which the prosecutor served notice under paragraph (1), and
(iv) any representations and any other information served by the defendant under paragraph (4)(a)
and rule 24.11(3) to (9) inclusive must be read accordingly.
(9) Paragraph (10) applies where—
(a) the defendant serves on the court officer a notice under paragraph (4)(b) or (c); or
(b) the court which tries the defendant under paragraph (8) adjourns the trial for the defendant to attend a hearing by a court comprising more than one justice.
(10) Where this paragraph applies, the court must exercise its power to issue a summons and—
(a) the rules in Part 7 apply (Starting a prosecution in a magistrates' court) as if the prosecutor had just served an application for a summons to be issued in the same terms as the written charge;
(b) the rules in Part 8 (Initial details of the prosecution case) apply as if the documents served by the prosecutor under paragraph (1) had been served under that Part;
(c) except for rule 24.8 (Written guilty plea: special rules) and this rule, the rules in this Part apply.

Application to withdraw a guilty plea R-236

24.10 (1) This rule applies where the defendant wants to withdraw a guilty plea.
(2) The defendant must apply to do so—
(a) as soon as practicable after becoming aware of the reasons for doing so; and
(b) before sentence.
(3) Unless the court otherwise directs, the application must be in writing and the defendant must serve it on—
(a) the court officer; and
(b) the prosecutor.
(4) The application must—
(a) explain why it would be unjust not to allow the defendant to withdraw the guilty plea;
(b) identify—
(i) any witness that the defendant wants to call, and
(ii) any other proposed evidence; and
(c) say whether the defendant waives legal professional privilege, giving any relevant name and date.

R-237 **Procedure if the court convicts**

24.11 (1) This rule applies if the court convicts the defendant.

(2) The court—

(a) may exercise its power to require—

(i) a statement of the defendant's financial circumstances,

(ii) a pre-sentence report; and

(b) may (and in some circumstances must) remit the defendant to a youth court for sentence where—

(i) the defendant is under 18, and

(ii) the convicting court is not itself a youth court.

(3) The prosecutor must—

(a) summarise the prosecution case, if the sentencing court has not heard evidence;

(b) identify any offence to be taken into consideration in sentencing;

(c) provide information relevant to sentence, including any statement of the effect of the offence on the victim, the victim's family and others; and

(d) where it is likely to assist the court, identify any other matter relevant to sentence, including—

(i) the legislation applicable,

(ii) any sentencing guidelines, or guideline cases,

(iii) aggravating and mitigating features affecting the defendant's culpability and the harm which the offence caused, was intended to cause or might forseeably have caused, and

(iv) the effect of such of the information listed in paragraph (2)(a) as the court may need to take into account.

(4) The defendant must provide details of financial circumstances—

(a) in any form required by the court officer;

(b) by any date directed by the court or by the court officer.

(5) Where the defendant pleads guilty but wants to be sentenced on a different basis to that disclosed by the prosecution case—

(a) the defendant must set out that basis in writing, identifying what is in dispute;

(b) the court may invite the parties to make representations about whether the dispute is material to sentence; and

(c) if the court decides that it is a material dispute, the court must—

(i) invite such further representations or evidence as it may require, and

(ii) decide the dispute.

(6) Where the court has power to order the endorsement of the defendant's driving record, or power to order the defendant to be disqualified from driving—

(a) if other legislation so permits, a defendant who wants the court not to exercise that power must introduce the evidence or information on which the defendant relies;

(b) the prosecutor may introduce evidence; and

(c) the parties may make representations about that evidence or information.

(7) Before the court passes sentence—

(a) the court must—

(i) give the defendant an opportunity to make representations and introduce evidence relevant to sentence, and

(ii) where the defendant is under 18, give the defendant's parents, guardian or other supporting adult, if present, such an opportunity as well; and

(b) the justices' legal adviser or the court must elicit any further information relevant to sentence that the court may require.

(8) If the court requires more information, it may exercise its power to adjourn the hearing for not more than—

(a) 3 weeks at a time, if the defendant will be in custody; or

(b) 4 weeks at a time.

(9) When the court has taken into account all the evidence, information and any report available, the court must—

(a) as a general rule, pass sentence there and then;

(b) when passing sentence, explain the reasons for deciding on that sentence, unless neither the defendant nor any member of the public, including any reporter, is present;

(c) when passing sentence, explain to the defendant its effect, the consequences of failing to comply with any order or pay any fine, and any power that the court has to vary or review the sentence, unless—

(i) the defendant is absent, or

(ii) the defendant's ill-health or disorderly conduct makes such an explanation impracticable;

(d) give any such explanation in terms the defendant, if present, can understand (with help, if necessary); and
(e) consider exercising any power it has to make a costs or other order.

(10) Despite the general rule—
(a) the court must adjourn the hearing if the defendant is absent, the case started with a summons, requisition or single justice procedure notice, and either—
(i) the court considers passing a custodial sentence (where it can do so), or
(ii) the court considers imposing a disqualification (unless it has already adjourned the hearing to give the defendant an opportunity to attend);
(b) the court may exercise any power it has to—
(i) commit the defendant to the Crown Court for sentence (and in some cases it must do so), or
(ii) defer sentence for up to 6 months.

Procedure where a party is absent R-238

24.12 (1) This rule—
(a) applies where a party is absent; but
(b) does not apply where—
(i) the defendant has served a notice of guilty plea under rule 24.8 (Written guilty plea: special rules), or
(ii) the court tries a case under rule 24.9 (Single justice procedure: special rules).

(2) Where the prosecutor is absent, the court may—
(a) if it has received evidence, deal with the case as if the prosecutor were present; and
(b) in any other case—
(i) enquire into the reasons for the prosecutor's absence, and
(ii) if satisfied there is no good reason, exercise its power to dismiss the allegation.

(3) Where the defendant is absent—
(a) the general rule is that the court must proceed as if the defendant—
(i) were present, and
(ii) had pleaded not guilty (unless a plea already has been taken)
and the court must give reasons if it does not do so; but
(b) the general rule does not apply if the defendant is under 18;
(c) the general rule is subject to the court being satisfied that—
(i) any summons or requisition was served on the defendant a reasonable time before the hearing, or
(ii) in a case in which the hearing has been adjourned, the defendant had reasonable notice of where and when it would resume;
(d) the general rule is subject also to rule 24.11(10)(a) (restrictions on passing sentence in the defendant's absence).

(4) Where the defendant is absent, the court—
(a) must exercise its power to issue a warrant for the defendant's arrest and detention in the terms required by rule 13.3(3) (Terms of a warrant for detention or imprisonment), if it passes a custodial sentence; and
(b) may exercise its power to issue a warrant for the defendant's arrest in any other case, if it does not apply the general rule in paragraph (3)(a) of this rule about proceeding in the defendant's absence.

Provision of documents for the court R-239

24.13 (1) A party who introduces a document in evidence, or who otherwise uses a document in presenting that party's case, must provide a copy for—
(a) each other party;
(b) any witness that party wants to refer to that document;
(c) the court; and
(d) the justices' legal adviser.

(2) Unless the court otherwise directs, on application or on its own initiative, the court officer must provide for the court—
(a) any copy received under paragraph (1) before the hearing begins; and
(b) a copy of the court officer's record of—
(i) information supplied by each party for the purposes of case management, including any revision of information previously supplied,
(ii) each pre-trial direction for the management of the case,

(iii) any pre-trial decision to admit evidence,
(iv) any pre-trial direction about the giving of evidence, and
(v) any admission to which rule 24.6 applies.

(3) Where rule 24.8 (Written guilty plea: special rules) applies, the court officer must provide for the court—
(a) each document served by the prosecutor under rule 24.8(1)(d);
(b) the defendant's driving record, where the offence is under the Road Traffic Regulation Act 1984, the Road Traffic Act 1988, the Road Traffic (Consequential Provisions) Act 1988 or the Road Traffic (Driver Licensing and Information Systems) Act 1989);
(c) any other information about the defendant, relevant to sentence, of which the prosecutor served notice under rule 24.8(1); and
(d) the notice of guilty plea and any representations and other information served by the defendant under rule 24.8(4).

(4) Where the court tries a case under rule 24.9 (Single justice procedure: special rules), the court officer must provide for the court—
(a) each document served by the prosecutor under rule 24.9(1)(d);
(b) the defendant's driving record, where the offence is under the Road Traffic Regulation Act 1984, the Road Traffic Act 1988, the Road Traffic (Consequential Provisions) Act 1988 or the Road Traffic (Driver Licensing and Information Systems) Act 1989;
(c) any other information about the defendant, relevant to sentence, of which the prosecutor served notice under rule 24.9(1); and
(d) any notice, representations and other information served by the defendant under rule 29.9(4)(a).

R-240 **Place of trial**

24.14 (1) The hearing must take place in a courtroom provided by the Lord Chancellor, unless—
(a) the court otherwise directs; or
(b) the court tries a case under rule 24.9 (Single justice procedure: special rules).

(2) Where the hearing takes place in Wales—
(a) any party or witness may use the Welsh language; and
(b) if practicable, at least one member of the court must be Welsh-speaking.

R-241 **Duty of justices' legal adviser**

24.15 (1) A justices' legal adviser must attend the court and carry out the duties listed in this rule, as applicable, unless the court—
(a) includes a District Judge (Magistrates' Courts); and
(b) otherwise directs.

(2) A justices' legal adviser must—
(a) before the hearing begins, by reference to what is provided for the court under rule 24.13 (Provision of documents for the court) draw the court's attention to—
(i) what the prosecutor alleges,
(ii) what the parties say is agreed,
(iii) what the parties say is in dispute, and
(iv) what the parties say about how each expects to present the case, especially where that may affect its duration and timetabling;
(b) whenever necessary, give the court legal advice and—
(i) if necessary, attend the members of the court outside the courtroom to give such advice, but
(ii) inform the parties (if present) of any such advice given outside the courtroom; and
(c) assist the court, where appropriate, in the formulation of its reasons and the recording of those reasons.

(3) A justices' legal adviser must—
(a) assist an unrepresented defendant;
(b) assist the court by—
(i) making a note of the substance of any oral evidence or representations, to help the court recall that information,
(ii) if the court rules inadmissible part of a written statement introduced in evidence, marking that statement in such a way as to make that clear,
(iii) ensuring that an adequate record is kept of the court's decisions and the reasons for them, and
(iv) making any announcement, other than of the verdict or sentence.

(4) Where the defendant has served a notice of guilty plea to which rule 24.8 (Written guilty plea: special rules) applies, a justices' legal adviser must—
(a) unless the court otherwise directs, if any member of the public, including any reporter, is present, read aloud to the court—
(i) the material on which the prosecutor relies to set out the facts of the offence and to provide information relevant to sentence (or summarise any written statement included in that material, if the court so directs), and
(ii) any written representations by the defendant;
(b) otherwise, draw the court's attention to—
(i) what the prosecutor alleges, and any significant features of the material listed in paragraph (4)(a)(i), and
(ii) any written representations by the defendant.
(5) Where the court tries a case under rule 24.9 (Single justice procedure: special rules), a justices' legal adviser must draw the court's attention to—
(a) what the prosecutor alleges, and any significant features of the material on which the prosecutor relies to prove the alleged offence and to provide information relevant to sentence; and
(b) any representations served by the defendant.

Duty of court officer **R-242**

24.16 The court officer must—
(a) serve on each party notice of where and when an adjourned hearing will resume, unless—
(i) the party was present when that was arranged,
(ii) the defendant has served a notice of guilty plea to which rule 24.8 (Written guilty plea: special rules) applies, and the adjournment is for not more than 4 weeks, or
(iii) the court tries a case under rule 24.9 (Single justice procedure: special rules), and the adjourned trial will resume under that rule;
(b) if the reason for the adjournment was to postpone sentence, include that reason in any such notice to the defendant;
(c) unless the court otherwise directs, make available to the parties any written report to which rule 24.11 (Procedure if the court convicts) applies;
(d) where the court has ordered a defendant to provide information under section 25 of the Road Traffic Offenders Act 1988, serve on the defendant notice of that order unless the defendant was present when it was made;
(e) serve on the prosecutor—
(i) any notice of guilty plea to which rule 24.8 (Written guilty plea: special rules) applies, and
(ii) any declaration served under rule 24.17 (Statutory declaration of ignorance of proceedings) that the defendant did not know about the case;
(f) serve on the prosecutor notice of any hearing date arranged in consequence of such a declaration, unless—
(i) the prosecutor was present when that was arranged, or
(ii) the court otherwise directs;
(g) serve on the prosecutor—
(i) notice of any hearing date arranged in consequence of the issue of a summons under rule 24.9 (Single justice procedure: special rules), and in that event
(ii) any notice served by the defendant under rule 24.9(2)(b) or (c);
(h) record the court's reasons for not proceeding in the defendant's absence where rule 24.12(3)(a) applies; and
(i) give the court such other assistance as it requires.

Statutory declaration of ignorance of proceedings **R-243**

24.17 (1) This rule applies where—
(a) the case started with—
(i) an application for a summons,
(ii) a written charge and requisition, or
(iii) a written charge and single justice procedure notice; and
(b) under section 14 or 16E of the Magistrates' Courts Act 1980, the defendant makes a statutory declaration of not having found out about the case until after the trial began.
(2) The defendant must—
(a) serve such a declaration on the court officer—
(i) not more than 21 days after the date of finding out about the case; or
(ii) with an explanation for the delay, if serving it more than 21 days after that date;

(b) serve with the declaration one of the following, as appropriate, if the case began with a written charge and single justice procedure notice—
(i) a notice under rule 24.9(4)(a) (notice of guilty plea), with any representations that the defendant wants the court to consider and a statement of the defendant's assets and other financial circumstances, as required by that rule,
(ii) a notice under rule 24.9(4)(b) (notice of intention to plead guilty at a hearing before a court comprising more than one justice), or
(iii) a notice under rule 24.9(4)(c) (notice of intention to plead not guilty).

(3) The court may extend that time limit, even after it has expired—
(a) at a hearing, in public or in private; or
(b) without a hearing.

(4) Where the defendant serves such a declaration, in time or with an extension of time in which to do so, and the case began with a summons or requisition—
(a) the court must treat the summons or requisition and all subsequent proceedings as void (but not the application for the summons or the written charge with which the case began);
(b) if the defendant is present when the declaration is served, the rules in this Part apply as if the defendant had been required to attend the court on that occasion;
(c) if the defendant is absent when the declaration is served—
(i) the rules in Part 7 apply (Starting a prosecution in a magistrates' court) as if the prosecutor had just served an application for a summons in the same terms as the original application or written charge;
(ii) the court may exercise its power to issue a summons in accordance with those rules; and
(iii) except for rule 24.8 (Written guilty plea: special rules), the rules in this Part then apply.

(5) Where the defendant serves such a declaration, in time or with an extension of time in which to do so, and the case began with a single justice procedure notice—
(a) the court must treat the single justice procedure notice and all subsequent proceedings as void (but not the written charge with which the case began);
(b) rule 24.9 (Single justice procedure: special rules) applies as if the defendant had served the notice required by paragraph (2)(b) of this rule within the time allowed by rule 24.9(4); and
(c) where that notice is under rule 24.9(4)(b) (notice of intention to plead guilty at a hearing before a court comprising more than one justice) or under rule 24.9(4)(c) (notice of intention to plead not guilty), then—
(i) if the defendant is present when the declaration is served, the rules in this Part apply as if the defendant had been required to attend the court on that occasion,
(ii) if the defendant is absent when the declaration is served, paragraph (6) of this rule applies.

(6) Where this paragraph applies, the court must exercise its power to issue a summons and—
(a) the rules in Part 7 apply (Starting a prosecution in a magistrates' court) as if the prosecutor had just served an application for a summons in the same terms as the written charge;
(b) except for rule 24.8 (Written guilty plea: special rules) and rule 24.9 (Single justice procedure: special rules), the rules in this Part apply.

(7) A court officer may take the statutory declaration to which this rule refers if that officer—
(a) is a justices' legal adviser; or
(b) is nominated for the purpose by such a legal adviser.

R-244 Setting aside a conviction or varying a costs etc. order

24.18 (1) This rule applies where under section 142 of the Magistrates' Courts Act 1980, the court can—
(a) set aside a conviction, or
(b) vary or rescind—
(i) a costs order, or
(ii) an order to which Part 31 applies (Behaviour orders).

(2) The court may exercise its power—
(a) on application by a party, or on its own initiative;
(b) at a hearing, in public or in private, or without a hearing.

(3) The court must not exercise its power in a party's absence unless—
(a) the court makes a decision proposed by that party;
(b) the court makes a decision to which that party has agreed in writing; or
(c) that party has had an opportunity to make representations at a hearing (whether or not that party in fact attends).

(4) A party who wants the court to exercise its power must—
(a) apply in writing as soon as reasonably practicable after the conviction or order that that party wants the court to set aside, vary or rescind;

(b) serve the application on—
   (i) the court officer, and
   (ii) each other party; and
(c) in the application—
   (i) explain why, as appropriate, the conviction should be set aside, or the order varied or rescinded,
   (ii) specify any variation of the order that the applicant proposes,
   (iii) identify any witness that the defendant wants to call, and any other proposed evidence,
   (iv) say whether the defendant waives legal professional privilege, giving any relevant name and date, and
   (v) if the application is late, explain why.

(5) The court may—
   (a) extend (even after it has expired) the time limit under paragraph (4), unless the court's power to set aside the conviction, or vary the order, can no longer be exercised;
   (b) allow an application to be made orally.

Criminal Practice Directions Part 24 Trial and Sentence in a Magistrates' Court

CPD VI Trial 24A: Role of the Justices' Clerk/Legal Adviser PD-53

24A.1 The role of the justices' clerk/legal adviser is a unique one, which carries with it independence from direction when undertaking a judicial function and when advising magistrates. These functions must be carried out in accordance with the Bangalore Principles of Judicial Conduct (judicial independence, impartiality, integrity, propriety, ensuring fair treatment and competence and diligence). More specifically, duties must be discharged in accordance with the relevant professional Code of Conduct and the Legal Adviser Competence Framework.

24A.2 A justices' clerk is responsible for:
(a) the legal advice tendered to the justices within the area;
(b) the performance of any of the functions set out below by any member of his staff acting as justices' legal adviser;
(c) ensuring that competent advice is available to justices when the justices' clerk is not personally present in court; and
(d) ensuring that advice given at all stages of proceedings and powers exercised (including those delegated to justices' legal advisers) take into account the court's duty to deal with cases justly and actively to manage the case.

24A.3 Where a person other than the justices' clerk (a justices' legal adviser), who is authorised to do so, performs any of the functions referred to in this direction, he or she will have the same duties, powers and responsibilities as the justices' clerk. The justices' legal adviser may consult the justices' clerk, or other person authorised by the justices' clerk for that purpose, before tendering advice to the bench. If the justices' clerk or that person gives any advice directly to the bench, he or she should give the parties or their advocates an opportunity of repeating any relevant submissions, prior to the advice being given.

24A.4 When exercising judicial powers, a justices' clerk or legal adviser is acting in exactly the same capacity as a magistrate. The justices' clerk may delegate powers to a justices' legal adviser in accordance with the relevant statutory authority. The scheme of delegation must be clear and in writing, so that all justices' legal advisers are certain of the extent of their powers. Once a power is delegated, judicial discretion in an individual case lies with the justices' legal adviser exercising the power. When exercise of a power does not require the consent of the parties, a justices' clerk or legal adviser may deal with and decide a contested issue or may refer that issue to the court.

24A.5 It shall be the responsibility of the justices' clerk or legal adviser to provide the justices with any advice they require to perform their functions justly, whether or not the advice has been requested, on:
(a) questions of law;
(b) questions of mixed law and fact;
(c) matters of practice and procedure;
(d) the process to be followed at sentence and the matters to be taken into account, together with the range of penalties and ancillary orders available, in accordance with the relevant sentencing guidelines;
(e) any relevant decisions of the superior courts or other guidelines;
(f) the appropriate decision-making structure to be applied in any given case; and
(g) other issues relevant to the matter before the court.

24A.6 In addition to advising the justices, it shall be the justices' legal adviser's responsibility to assist the court, where appropriate, as to the formulation of reasons and the recording of those reasons.

24A.7 The justices' legal adviser has a duty to assist an unrepresented defendant, see CrimPR 9.4(3)(a), 14.3(2)(a) and 24.15(3)(a), in particular when the court is making a decision on allocation, bail, at trial and on sentence.

24A.8 Where the court must determine allocation, the legal adviser may deal with any aspect of the allocation hearing save for the decision on allocation, indication of sentence and sentence.

24A.9 When a defendant acting in person indicates a guilty plea, the legal adviser must explain the procedure and inform the defendant of their right to address the court on the facts and to provide details of their personal circumstances in order that the court can decide the appropriate sentence.

24A.10 When a defendant indicates a not guilty plea but has not completed the relevant sections of the Magistrates' Courts Trial Preparation Form, the legal adviser must either ensure that the Form is completed or, in appropriate cases, assist the court to obtain and record the essential information on the form.

24A.11 Immediately prior to the commencement of a trial, the legal adviser must summarise for the court the agreed and disputed issues, together with the way in which the parties propose to present their cases. If this is done by way of pre-court briefing, it should be confirmed in court or agreed with the parties.

24A.12 A justices' clerk or legal adviser must not play any part in making findings of fact, but may assist the bench by reminding them of the evidence, using any notes of the proceedings for this purpose, and clarifying the issues which are agreed and those which are to be determined.

24A.13 A justices' clerk or legal adviser may ask questions of witnesses and the parties in order to clarify the evidence and any issues in the case. A legal adviser has a duty to ensure that every case is conducted justly.

24A.14 When advising the justices, the justices' clerk or legal adviser, whether or not previously in court, should:

(a) ensure that he is aware of the relevant facts; and

(b) provide the parties with an opportunity to respond to any advice given.

24A.15 At any time, justices are entitled to receive advice to assist them in discharging their responsibilities. If they are in any doubt as to the evidence which has been given, they should seek the aid of their legal adviser, referring to his notes as appropriate. This should ordinarily be done in open court. Where the justices request their adviser to join them in the retiring room, this request should be made in the presence of the parties in court. Any legal advice given to the justices other than in open court should be clearly stated to be provisional; and the adviser should subsequently repeat the substance of the advice in open court and give the parties the opportunity to make any representations they wish on that provisional advice. The legal adviser should then state in open court whether the provisional advice is confirmed or, if it is varied, the nature of the variation.

24A.16 The legal adviser is under a duty to assist unrepresented parties, whether defendants or not, to present their case, but must do so without appearing to become an advocate for the party concerned. The legal adviser should also ensure that members of the court are aware of obligations under the Victims' Code.

24A.17 The role of legal advisers in fine default proceedings, or any other proceedings for the enforcement of financial orders, obligations or penalties, is to assist the court. They must not act in an adversarial or partisan manner, such as by attempting to establish wilful refusal or neglect or any other type of culpable behaviour, to offer an opinion on the facts, or to urge a particular course of action upon the justices. The expectation is that a legal adviser will ask questions of the defaulter to elicit information which the justices will require to make an adjudication, such as the explanation for the default. A legal adviser may also advise the justices as to the options open to them in dealing with the case.

24A.18 The performance of a legal adviser is subject to regular appraisal. For that purpose the appraiser may be present in the justices' retiring room. The content of the appraisal is confidential, but the fact that an appraisal has taken place, and the presence of the appraiser in the retiring room, should be briefly explained in open court.

PD-54 **CPD VI Trial 24B: Identification for the Court of the Issues in the Case**

24B.1 CrimPR 3.11(a) requires the court, with the active assistance of the parties, to establish what are the disputed issues in order to manage the trial. To that end, the purpose of the prosecutor's summary of the prosecution case is to explain briefly, in the prosecutor's own terms, what the case is about, including any relevant legislation or case law relevant to the particular case. It will not usually be necessary, or helpful, to present a detailed account of all the prosecution evidence due to be introduced.

24B.2 CrimPR 24.3(3)(b) provides for a defendant, or his or her advocate, immediately after the prosecution opening to set out the issues in the defendant's own terms, if invited to do so by the court. The purpose of any such identification of issues is to provide the court with focus as to what it is likely to be called upon to decide, so that the members of the court will be alert to those issues from the outset and can evaluate the prosecution evidence that they hear accordingly.

24B.3 The parties should keep in mind that, in most cases, the members of the court already will be aware of what has been declared to be in issue. The court will have access to any written admissions and to information supplied for the purposes of case management: CrimPR 24.13(2). The court's legal adviser will have drawn the court's attention to what is alleged and to what is understood to be in dispute: CrimPR 24.15(2). If a party has nothing of substance to add to that, then he or she should say so. The requirement to be concise will be enforced and the exchange with the court properly may be confined to enquiry and confirmation that the court's understanding of those allegations and issues is correct. Nevertheless, for the defendant to be offered an opportunity to identify issues at this stage may assist even if all he or she wishes to announce, or confirm, is that the prosecution is being put to proof.

24B.4 The identification of issues at the case management stage will have been made without the risk that they would be used at trial as statements of the defendant admissible in evidence against the defendant, provided the advocate follows the letter and the spirit of the Criminal Procedure Rules. The court may take the view that a party is not acting in the spirit of the Criminal Procedure Rules in seeking to ambush the other party or raising late and technical legal arguments that were not previously raised as issues. No party that seeks to ambush the other at trial should derive an advantage from such a course of action. The court may also take the view that a defendant is not acting in the spirit of the Criminal Procedure Rules if he or she refuses to identify the issues and puts the prosecutor to proof at the case management stage. In both such circumstances the court may limit the proceedings on the day of trial in accordance with CrimPR 3.11(d). In addition any significant divergence from the issues identified at case management at this late stage may well result in the exercise of the court's powers under CrimPR 3.5(6), the powers to impose sanctions.

CPD VI Trial 24C: Trial Adjournment in Magistrates' Courts PD-55

24C.1 Courts are entitled to expect the parties and other participants to adhere to CrimPR 1.2 (The duty of the participants in a criminal case) and to prepare accordingly for the trial to proceed on the date arranged. The court will expect communication between the parties and with the court regarding any issues which are likely to affect the effectiveness of any trial: CrimPR 3.2(2)(b)-(e). In particular, any revision of the information provided in the preparation for effective trial form must be reported to the court and each other party well in advance of the trial, not at trial or shortly before; and in considering any application to adjourn a trial the court will regard as especially significant any failure in this respect. Any communication should clearly identify the issue and any direction sought. and should require reference to a legal adviser or case progression officer. The parties and other participants are entitled to expect the court and its staff to adhere to CrimPR 1.3 (The application by the court of the overriding objective) and to conduct its business accordingly. If relevant Criminal Procedure Rules, Criminal Practice Directions and judicial directions for trial preparation are followed, an effective trial on the date arranged will be the result.

24C.2 In some circumstances during preparation for trial it will become apparent to a party that a trial will not be required. It is in the interests of victims, witnesses, defendants, the court and legal representatives that these decisions are made at the earliest opportunity and that the other party, or parties, and the court are notified immediately. The requirements for an application to vacate a trial fixture are set out at paragraphs 24C.30 to 24C.32 beneath.

24C.3 Where a defendant who previously has pleaded not guilty decides to enter a guilty plea, notice of that decision, and the basis of plea, should be given to the prosecution and court as soon as possible so that a decision can be taken about the need for witnesses to attend (but caution should be exercised before the witnesses' attendance is dispensed with, and usually it will be advisable to set a date for the plea to be taken in advance of the date already set for trial). The sooner that notice of such a plea is given, the greater the reduction in sentence the defendant can expect. The court will expect an explanation for the change of plea to assess the level of credit to be applied.

24C.4 Where a party is unable to comply with a direction within the time set by the court, and that failure will have implications for preparation by another party or for the likelihood of the trial proceeding within the time allocated, the party concerned should advise each other party and the court immediately of the failure and of the anticipated date for compliance: CrimPR 1.2(1)(c) and 3.10(2)(d). Parties are encouraged to communicate with each other to agree alternative dates consistent with maintaining the trial fixture: CrimPR 3.7.

Application to adjourn on day of trial

General principles

24C.5 The court is entitled to expect that trials will start on time with all case management issues dealt with in advance of the trial date. Early engagement between the parties and communication with the court should mean that it is rare for applications to adjourn trials to be made on the day of trial, except in circumstances that could not have been foreseen. However, there will be occasions on which, on the day set for trial, the court is invited without prior warning to adjourn to another day in consequence of an event or events said to make it unjust to proceed as planned; and in some circumstances it may have been necessary to arrange to hear a contested application to adjourn a trial on the very date on which that trial is due to begin (though before making such arrangements the court should have kept in mind the need to make time available for other cases, too, where the time available for the trial will be abbreviated by the time required to hear the application to adjourn it).

24C.6 Section 10 of the Magistrates' Courts Act 1980 confers a discretionary power to adjourn, and see also CrimPR 24.2(3). The following directions codify and restate procedural principles established in a long line of judgments of the senior courts, to some of which they refer. Therefore these directions supersede those judgments and it is to these directions that magistrates' courts must refer in the first instance.

24C.7 The starting point is that the trial should proceed. The basic approach was explained by Gross LJ in *Director of Public Prosecutions v Petrie* [2015] EWHC 48 (Admin):

> *'...successive initiatives... have repeatedly exhorted the magistracy and District Bench to case manage robustly and to resist the granting of adjournments. Although there are of course instances where the interests of justice require the grant of an adjournment, this should be a course of last rather than first resort – and after other alternatives have been considered.... It is essential that parties to proceedings in a magistrates' court should proceed on the basis of a need to get matters right first time; any suggestion of a culture readily permitting an opportunity to correct failures of preparation should be firmly dispelled.'*

24C.8 A magistrates' court may keep in mind that, if appropriate, the court's decision may be re-opened (see CrimPR 24.18), and that avenues of appeal by way of rehearing or of review are open to the parties, including in a case in which it is later discovered that the court has acted on a material mistake of fact (see *R (Director of Public Prosecutions) v Sunderland Magistrates' Court, R (Kharaghan) v City of London Magistrates' Court* [2018] EWHC 229 (Admin)). The court should not be deterred from a prompt and robust determination therefore. Only if there are compelling reasons for doing so will the High Court interfere with the court's exercise of its discretion.

24C.9 In general, the relevant principles relating to trial adjournment are these:

- the court's duty is to deal justly with the case, which includes doing justice between the parties.
- the court must have regard to the need for expedition. Delay is generally inimical to the interests of justice and brings the criminal justice system into disrepute. Proceedings in a magistrates' court should be simple and speedy.
- applications for adjournments should be rigorously scrutinised and the court must have a clear reason for adjourning. To do this, the court must review the history of the case.
- where the prosecutor asks for an adjournment the court must consider not only the interest of the defendant in getting the matter dealt with without delay but also the public interest in ensuring that criminal charges are adjudicated upon thoroughly, with the guilty convicted as well as the innocent acquitted.
- with a more serious charge the public interest that there be a trial will carry greater weight. It is, however, reasonable for the court to expect that parties should have given especially careful attention to the preparation of trials involving serious offences or where the trial has significant implications for victims or witnesses.
- where the defendant asks for an adjournment the court must consider whether he or she will be able to present the defence fully without and, if not, the extent to which his or her ability to do so is compromised.
- the court must consider the consequences of an adjournment and its impact on the ability of witnesses and defendants accurately to recall events.
- the impact of adjournment on other cases. The relisting of one case almost inevitably delays or displaces the hearing of others. The length of the hearing and the extent of delay in other cases will need to be considered.

The relevance of fault

24C.10 As the starting point is that the trial should proceed, a consequence of doing so without adjournment may be that the prosecutor is unable to prove the prosecution case, or that the defendant is unable to explore an issue. That may be a just consequence of inadequate preparation. Even in the absence of fault on the part of either party it may not be in the interests of justice to adjourn, notwithstanding that an imperfect trial may be the result.

24C.11 The reason why the adjournment is required should be examined and if it arises through the fault of the applicant for that adjournment then that weighs against its grant, carrying weight in accordance with the gravity of the fault. For the purposes of this paragraph, the prosecutor and those who investigated the case usually should be treated as one.

24C.12 If the applicant was at fault, was it serious? A fault will be serious if the relevant act or omission has been repeated, especially where it has caused a previous adjournment, or where there is no reasonable explanation for that act or omission. The more serious the default, the less willing the court will be to adjourn.

24C.13 Where a party has been at fault, did the other party, if aware of it, draw attention to that fault promptly and explicitly? CrimPR 1.2(1)(c) imposes a collective responsibility on participants promptly to draw attention to a significant failure to take a required procedural step. CrimPR 3.10(2)(d) requires each party promptly to inform the court and the other parties of anything that may affect the date or duration of the trial or significantly affect the progress of the case in any other way. If no such action has been taken by a party who could have done so then the court may look less favourably on any application by that same party to adjourn, and especially if that application reasonably might have been made before the trial date.

Length of adjournment

24C.14 Were an adjournment granted, for how long would it need to be? The shorter the necessary adjournment, the less objectionable it will be – although much will depend on the ability of the court to accommodate it without undue impact on other cases. Courts must make every effort to make the adjournment as short as possible, for example by using time vacated by another trial or by conducting the hearing at another court house. In some cases it may be possible to achieve a just outcome by a short adjournment to later on the same day.

24C.15 If the reason for the application to adjourn is that the applicant party seeks more time in which to raise or explore an issue, has that party reasonable grounds for its late identification despite the requirements of CrimPR 3.3(1) read with 3.2(2) (early identification of issues)? In the absence of such grounds, that failure will constitute a fault for the purposes of these directions.

Particular grounds of applications to adjourn trials

24C.16 The following paragraphs identify some particular factors which may need to be taken into account in addition to those identified in paragraphs 24C.5 – 24C15.

Absence of defendant

24C.17 If a defendant has attained the age of 18 years, the court shall proceed in his absence unless it appears to the court to be contrary to the interests of justice to do so: section 11 of the Magistrates' Courts Act 1980. In marked contrast to the position in the Crown Court, in magistrates' courts proceeding in the absence of a defendant is the default position where the defendant is aware of the date of trial and no acceptable reason is offered for that absence. The court is not obliged to investigate if no reason is offered. In assessing where the interests of justice lie the court will take into account all factors, including such reasons for absence as may be offered; the reliability of the information supplied in support of those reasons; the date on which the reasons for absence became known to the defendant; and what action the defendant thereafter took in response. Where the defendant provides a medical note to excuse his or her non-attendance the court must consider 5C of these Practice Directions (issue of medical certificates) and give reasons if deciding to proceed notwithstanding.

24C.18 If the court does not proceed to trial in the absence of the defendant it is required by the 1980 Act to give its reasons, which must be specific to the case: section 11(7), and see also CrimPR 24.16(h).

24C.19 Where a defendant is under 18, there is no presumption that the court should proceed in absence. In deciding whether it is in the interests of justice to proceed the court should take into account:

- that trial in absence can and sometimes does result in acquittal and that it is in nobody's interests to delay an acquittal;
- that if convicted the defendant can ask that the conviction be re-opened in the interests of justice, for example if absence was involuntary;

- that if convicted the defendant has a right to a rehearing on appeal to the Crown Court;
- the age, vulnerability, or experience of the defendant;
- whether a parent or guardian is present, whether a parent or guardian ordinarily would be required to attend and whether such a person has attended a previous hearing;
- the interests of any co-defendant in the case proceeding;
- the interests of witnesses who have attended, including the age of any such witness;
- the nature of the evidence and whether memories of relevant evidence are liable to fade;
- how soon an adjourned trial can be accommodated in the court list.

When proceeding in absence or adjourning the court must give its reasons.

Absence of witness

24C.20 Where the court is asked to adjourn because a witness has failed to attend, the court must:

- rigorously investigate the steps taken to secure that witness' attendance, the reasons given for absence and the likelihood of the witness attending should the case be adjourned;
- consider the relevance of the witness to the case, and whether the witness' statement can be agreed or admitted, in whole or part, as hearsay, including under section 114(1)(d) of the Criminal Justice Act 2003;
- in the case of a defence witness, consider whether proper notice has been given of the intention to call that witness;
- consider whether an absent witness can be heard later in the trial;
- where other witnesses have attended and the court has determined that the absent witness is required, consider hearing those witnesses who are present and adjourning the case part-heard, provided the next hearing can be held conveniently in a matter of days or weeks, not months, to avoid having to recall all the witnesses.

Failure to serve evidence in time

24C.21 It should rarely be the case that an application to adjourn based on a failure to serve evidence is made on the day of trial. The court is entitled to expect that evidence will have been served in good time and in accordance with the directions of the court. The court should consider whether the party who complains of the failure had drawn attention to it: CrimPR 1.2(1)(c) and 3.10(2)(d), and see paragraphs 24C.10 – 24C.13 above.

24C.22 The court must conduct a rigorous inquiry into the nature of the evidence and must consider whether any of what is sought has been served, and if so when; the volume and the significance of what is sought; and the time likely to be needed for its consideration. In particular, the court must satisfy itself that any material still sought is relevant and that the party seeking it has a right to it. In some circumstances a failure to serve evidence can be addressed by refusing to admit it instead of by adjourning the trial to allow it to be served: see *R v Boardman* [2015] EWCA Crim 175; [2015] 1 Cr. App. R. 33; [2015] Crim. L.R. 451.

Failure to comply with disclosure obligations

24C.23 The parties' disclosure obligations arise from the Criminal Procedure and Investigations Act 1996. The procedure to comply with those duties is set out at CrimPR Part 15. Disclosure is not a trial issue. It should have been resolved by the parties complying with their statutory obligations and with the Rules in advance of the trial.

24C.24 Where a defendant complains of a prosecution failure to disclose material that ought to have been disclosed the court must first establish whether either party is applying for an adjournment as a result. If an adjournment is sought, the court should consider whether the matter can be resolved by the giving of disclosure immediately. If it cannot, the court should consider whether the parties have complied with their obligations under CrimPR 3.3 and under the provisions listed in paragraph 24C.1 above, and should consider the relevance of fault.

24C.25 If the prosecutor has complied or purported to comply with his or her initial disclosure obligations, no further material is disclosable and consequently no application to adjourn should be entertained unless the defendant has served a defence statement in accordance with section 6 of the Criminal Procedure and Investigations Act 1996 and CrimPR 15.4.

24C.26 If the defendant has served a defence statement and asks for further disclosure, in consequence of the prosecutor's allegedly inadequate response or in consequence of a failure to respond at all, the court has no power to entertain an application for that further disclosure unless it is made pursuant to section 8 of the Criminal Procedure and Investigations Act 1996 and CrimPR 15.5. The court should consider hearing such an application immediately, provided that there is sufficient time available for the application itself and then for the defence to consider any material disclosed in consequence of it.

Managing trials within available court time

24C.27 Where there is a risk of a trials being adjourned for lack of court time the court or legal adviser must assess the priority to be assigned to each trial listed for hearing that day based on the needs of the parties, whether the case has been adjourned before and the seriousness of the offence; giving priority to any cases in which the defendant is in custody by reason only of a trial due to be heard that day. Where more than one court is sitting to deal with trials, liaison between courtrooms should occur to determine the potential for all listed trials to be heard through movement of cases. Where a case is moved from one courtroom to another and as a result is assigned to a different advocate, the court must allow the fresh advocate adequate time in which to prepare. Courts should always begin a trial by reviewing the need for witnesses and the timetable set during pre-trial case management. The court will be slow to adjourn a trial until it is clear that all other trials assessed as having an equal or higher priority for hearing that day will be effective.

24C.28 The court is entitled to expect that parties will present their case within the time set during pre-trial case management. In entertaining additional applications for which no time has been allowed the court must keep in mind the expectation that the trial will be completed within the allocated time with minimal impact on other cases.

24C.29 While it is preferable to complete a trial on the date allocated, there will be occasions on which it is appropriate to adjourn part-heard, particularly where it is possible to hear the majority of witnesses. If necessary future listings will be moved to accommodate the hearing.

Applications to vacate trials

24C.30 To make the best use of the court's and the parties' time it is expected that applications to vacate trials will be made promptly and in writing, in advance of the date of trial. Any application should be served on each other party at the same time as it is served on the court. As a general rule, such an application will be dealt with outside the courtroom under CrimPR 3.5. An application to vacate a trial will be considered in accordance with the same principles as those identified in paragraphs 24C.5 – 24C.26 of these Directions.

24C.31 Given the binding nature of any decision on an application to vacate and refix a trial, absent a change of circumstances, it is incumbent on the parties to provide full and accurate information to the court to enable it to assess where the interests of justice lie: see *R (on the application of F and another) v Knowsley Magistrates Court* [2006] EWHC 695 (Admin); *R (Jones) v South East Surrey Local Justice Area* [2010] EWHC 916 (Admin), (2010) 174 JP 342; *DPP v Woods* [2017] EWHC 1070 (Admin). Any application should, as a minimum, include (as should, as appropriate, any response):

- the reason for the application;
- a chronology of the case, recording the dates of compliance with any directions and of communication between the parties;
- an assessment of the interests of justice, addressing the factors identified in these Practice Directions and indicating the likely effect should the court conclude that the trial should proceed on the date fixed;
- any restrictions on the future availability of witnesses;
- any likely changes to the number of witnesses or the way in which the evidence will be presented and any impact on the trial time estimate.

24C.32 On receipt of an application each other party should serve that party's response on the court and on the applicant within 2 business days unless the court otherwise directs. Any request for the matter to be determined at a hearing should be served with the application to vacate the trial or with the response to that application, as the case may be, together with the reasons for that request, to enable the court to decide whether a hearing is needed.

CRIMINAL PROCEDURE RULES PART 25 TRIAL AND SENTENCE IN THE CROWN COURT

When this Part applies R-245

25.1 This Part applies in the Crown Court where—
(a) the court tries a case; or
(b) the defendant pleads guilty.

General powers and requirements R-246

25.2 (1) Where this Part applies, the general rule is that—
(a) the trial must be in public, but that is subject to the court's power to—
(i) impose a restriction on reporting what takes place at a public hearing, or public access to what otherwise would be a public hearing,

(ii) withhold information from the public during a public hearing, or
(iii) order a trial in private;
(b) the court must not proceed if the defendant is absent, unless the court is satisfied that—
(i) the defendant has waived the right to attend, and
(ii) the trial will be fair despite the defendant's absence;
(c) the court must not sentence the defendant to imprisonment or detention unless—
(i) the defendant has a legal representative,
(ii) the defendant has been sentenced to imprisonment or detention on a previous occasion in the United Kingdom, or
(iii) the defendant could have been represented under legal aid but is not because section 83(3) of the Powers of Criminal Courts (Sentencing) Act 2000 applies to him or her.
(2) Before proceeding to trial the court must—
(a) obtain the prosecutor's confirmation, in writing or orally, that the indictment on which the defendant is about to be tried sets out—
(i) a statement of each offence that the prosecutor wants the court to try, and
(ii) such particulars of the conduct constituting the commission of each such offence as the prosecutor relies upon to make clear what is alleged;
(b) ensure that the defendant is correctly identified by that indictment;
(c) satisfy itself that there has been explained to the defendant, in terms the defendant can understand (with help, if necessary), each allegation in that indictment against him or her; and
(d) invite any objection to the terms or validity of that indictment.
(3) The court may adjourn the trial at any stage.

R-247 Application for ruling on procedure, evidence or other question of law

25.3 (1) This rule applies to an application—
(a) about—
(i) case management, or any other question of procedure, or
(ii) the introduction or admissibility of evidence, or any other question of law;
(b) that has not been determined before the trial begins.
(2) The application is subject to any other rule that applies to it (for example, as to the time and form in which the application must be made).
(3) Unless the court otherwise directs, the application must be made, and the court's decision announced, in the absence of the jury (if there is one).

R-248 Procedure on plea of guilty

25.4 (1) This rule applies if—
(a) the defendant pleads guilty to an offence; and
(b) the court is satisfied that the plea represents a clear acknowledgement of guilt.
(2) The court need not receive evidence unless rule 25.16(4) applies (determination of facts for sentencing).

R-249 Application to vacate a guilty plea

25.5 (1) This rule applies where a party wants the court to vacate a guilty plea.
(2) Such a party must—
(a) apply in writing—
(i) as soon as practicable after becoming aware of the grounds for doing so, and
(ii) in any event, before the final disposal of the case, by sentence or otherwise; and
(b) serve the application on—
(i) the court officer, and
(ii) the prosecutor.
(3) Unless the court otherwise directs, the application must—
(a) explain why it would be unjust for the guilty plea to remain unchanged;
(b) indicate what, if any, evidence the applicant wishes to call;
(c) identify any proposed witness; and
(d) indicate whether legal professional privilege is waived, specifying any material name and date.

R-250 Selecting the jury

25.6 (1) This rule—
(a) applies where—
(i) the defendant pleads not guilty,
(ii) the defendant declines to enter a plea and the court treats that as a not guilty plea, or
(iii) the court determines that the defendant is not fit to be tried;
(b) does not apply where—
(i) the court orders a trial without a jury because of a danger of jury tampering or where jury tampering appears to have taken place, or

(ii) the court tries without a jury counts on an indictment after a trial of sample counts with a jury.

(2) The court must select a jury to try the case from the panel, or part of the panel, of jurors summoned by the Lord Chancellor to attend at that time and place.

(3) Where it appears that too few jurors to constitute a jury will be available from among those so summoned, the court—
(a) may exercise its own power to summon others in the court room, or in the vicinity, up to the number likely to be required, and add their names to the panel summoned by the Lord Chancellor; but
(b) must inform the parties, if they are absent when the court exercises that power.

(4) The court must select the jury by drawing at random each juror's name from among those so summoned and—
(a) announcing each name so drawn; or
(b) announcing an identifying number assigned by the court officer to that person, where the court is satisfied that that is necessary.

(5) If too few jurors to constitute a jury are available from the panel after all their names have been drawn, the court may—
(a) exercise its own power to summon others in the court room, or in the vicinity, up to the number required; and
(b) announce—
(i) the name of each person so summoned, or
(ii) an identifying number assigned by the court officer to that person, where the court is satisfied that that is necessary.

(6) The jury the court selects—
(a) must comprise no fewer than 12 jurors;
(b) may comprise as many as 14 jurors to begin with, where the court expects the trial to last for more than 4 weeks.

(7) Where the court selects a jury comprising more than 12 jurors, the court must explain to them that—
(a) the purpose of selecting more than 12 jurors to begin with is to fill any vacancy or vacancies caused by the discharge of any of the first 12 before the prosecution evidence begins;
(b) any such vacancy or vacancies will be filled by the extra jurors in order of their selection from the panel;
(c) the court will discharge any extra juror or jurors remaining by no later than the beginning of the prosecution evidence; and
(d) any juror who is discharged for that reason then will be available to be selected for service on another jury, during the period for which that juror has been summoned.

(8) Each of the 12 or more jurors the court selects—
(a) must take an oath or affirm; and
(b) becomes a full jury member until discharged.

(9) The oath or affirmation must be in these terms, or in any corresponding terms that the juror declares to be binding on him or her—
'I swear by Almighty God [*or* I do solemnly, sincerely and truly declare and affirm] that I will faithfully try the defendant and give a true verdict according to the evidence.'

Discharging jurors **R-251**

25.7 (1) The court may exercise its power to discharge a juror at any time—
(a) after the juror completes the oath or affirmation; and
(b) before the court discharges the jury.

(2) No later than the beginning of the prosecution evidence, if the jury then comprises more than 12 jurors the court must discharge any in excess of 12 in reverse order of their selection from the panel.

(3) The court may exercise its power to discharge the jury at any time—
(a) after each juror has completed the oath or affirmation; and
(b) before the jury has delivered its verdict on each offence charged in the indictment.

(4) The court must exercise its power to discharge the jury when, in respect of each offence charged in the indictment, either—
(a) the jury has delivered its verdict on that offence; or
(b) the court has discharged the jury from reaching a verdict.

Objecting to jurors **R-252**

25.8 (1) A party who objects to the panel of jurors must serve notice explaining the objection on the court officer and on the other party before the first juror's name or number is drawn.

(2) A party who objects to the selection of an individual juror must—
(a) tell the court of the objection—
(i) after the juror's name or number is announced, and
(ii) before the juror completes the oath or affirmation; and
(b) explain the objection.
(3) A prosecutor who exercises the prosecution right without giving reasons to prevent the court selecting an individual juror must announce the exercise of that right before the juror completes the oath or affirmation.
(4) The court must determine an objection under paragraph (1) or (2)—
(a) at a hearing, in public or in private; and
(b) in the absence of the jurors, unless the court otherwise directs.

R-253 **Procedure on plea of not guilty**

25.9 (1) This rule applies where—
(a) the defendant pleads not guilty; or
(b) the defendant declines to enter a plea and the court treats that as a not guilty plea.
(2) In the following sequence—
(a) where there is a jury, the court must—
(i) inform the jurors of each offence charged in the indictment to which the defendant pleads not guilty, and
(ii) explain to the jurors that it is their duty, after hearing the evidence, to decide whether the defendant is guilty or not guilty of each offence;
(b) the prosecutor may summarise the prosecution case, concisely outlining the facts and the matters likely to be in dispute;
(c) where there is a jury, to help the jurors to understand the case and resolve any issue in it the court may—
(i) invite the defendant concisely to identify what is in issue, if necessary in terms approved by the court,
(ii) if the defendant declines to do so, direct that the jurors be given a copy of any defence statement served under rule 15.4 (Defence disclosure), edited if necessary to exclude any reference to inappropriate matters or to matters evidence of which would not be admissible;
(d) the prosecutor must introduce the evidence on which the prosecution case relies;
(e) subject to paragraph (3), at the end of the prosecution evidence, on the defendant's application or on its own initiative, the court—
(i) may direct the jury (if there is one) to acquit on the ground that the prosecution evidence is insufficient for any reasonable court properly to convict, but
(ii) must not do so unless the prosecutor has had an opportunity to make representations;
(f) subject to paragraph (4), at the end of the prosecution evidence, the court must ask whether the defendant intends to give evidence in person and, if the answer is 'no', then the court must satisfy itself that there has been explained to the defendant, in terms the defendant can understand (with help, if necessary)—
(i) the right to give evidence in person, and
(ii) that if the defendant does not give evidence in person, or refuses to answer a question while giving evidence, the court may draw such inferences as seem proper;
(g) the defendant may summarise the defence case, if he or she intends to call at least one witness other than him or herself to give evidence in person about the facts of the case;
(h) in this order (or in a different order, if the court so directs) the defendant may—
(i) give evidence in person,
(ii) call another witness, or witnesses, to give evidence in person, and
(iii) introduce any other evidence;
(i) a party may introduce further evidence if it is then admissible (for example, because it is in rebuttal of evidence already introduced);
(j) the prosecutor may make final representations, where—
(i) the defendant has a legal representative,
(ii) the defendant has called at least one witness, other than the defendant him or herself, to give evidence in person about the facts of the case, or
(iii) the court so permits; and
(k) the defendant may make final representations.
(3) Paragraph (2)(e) does not apply in relation to a charge of murder, manslaughter, attempted murder, or causing harm contrary to section 18 or 20 of the Offences against the Person Act 1861 until the court has heard all the evidence (including any defence evidence), where the defendant is charged with—
(a) any of those offences; and

(b) an offence of causing or allowing a child or vulnerable adult to die or to suffer serious physical harm, contrary to section 5 of the Domestic Violence, Crime and Victims Act 2004.

(4) Paragraph (2)(f) does not apply where it appears to the court that, taking account of all the circumstances, the defendant's physical or mental condition makes it undesirable for the defendant to give evidence in person.

(5) Where there is more than one defendant, this rule applies to each in the order their names appear in the indictment, or in an order directed by the court.

(6) Unless the jury (if there is one) has retired to consider its verdict, the court may allow a party to introduce evidence, or make representations, after that party's opportunity to do so under paragraph (2).

(7) Unless the jury has already reached a verdict on a count, the court may exercise its power to—
(a) discharge the jury from reaching a verdict on that count;
(b) direct the jury to acquit the defendant on that count; or
(c) invite the jury to convict the defendant, if the defendant pleads guilty to the offence charged by that count.

Defendant unfit to plead **R-254**

25.10 (1) This rule applies where—
(a) it appears to the court, on application or on its own initiative, that the defendant may not be fit to be tried; and
(b) the defendant has not by then been acquitted of each offence charged by the indictment.

(2) The court—
(a) must exercise its power to decide, without a jury, whether the defendant is fit to be tried;
(b) may postpone the exercise of that power until immediately before the opening of the defence case.

(3) Where the court determines that the defendant is not fit to be tried—
(a) the court must exercise its power to appoint a person to put the case for the defence, taking account of all the circumstances and in particular—
(i) the willingness and suitability (including the qualifications and experience) of that person,
(ii) the nature and complexity of the case,
(iii) any advantage of continuity of representation, and
(iv) the defendant's wishes and needs;
(b) the court must select a jury, if none has been selected yet; and
(c) rule 25.9 (Procedure on plea of not guilty) applies, if the steps it lists have not already been taken, except that—
(i) everything which that rule requires to be done by the defendant may be done instead by the person appointed to put the case for the defence,
(ii) under rule 25.9(2)(a), the court must explain to the jurors that their duty is to decide whether or not the defendant did the act or made the omission charged as an offence, not whether the defendant is guilty of that offence, and
(iii) rule 25.9(2)(e) does not apply (warning of consequences of defendant not giving evidence).

Evidence of a witness in person **R-255**

25.11 (1) This rule applies where a party wants to introduce evidence by calling a witness to give that evidence in person.

(2) Unless the court otherwise directs—
(a) a witness waiting to give evidence must not wait inside the courtroom, unless that witness is—
(i) a party, or
(ii) an expert witness;
(b) a witness who gives evidence in the courtroom must do so from the place provided for that purpose; and
(c) a witness' address—
(i) must not be given in public unless the address is relevant to an issue in the case,
(ii) may be given in writing to the court, parties and jury.

(3) Unless other legislation otherwise provides, before giving evidence a witness must take an oath or affirm.

(4) In the following sequence—
(a) the party who calls a witness may ask questions in examination-in-chief;
(b) if the witness gives evidence for the prosecution—
(i) the defendant, if there is only one, may ask questions in cross-examination, or
(ii) subject to the court's directions, each defendant, if there is more than one, may ask such questions, in the order their names appear in the indictment or as directed by the court;

(c) if the witness gives evidence for a defendant—
   (i) subject to the court's directions, each other defendant, if there is more than one, may ask questions in cross-examination, in the order their names appear in the indictment or as directed by the court, and
   (ii) the prosecutor may ask such questions;
(d) the party who called the witness may ask questions in re-examination arising out of any cross-examination.

(5) If other legislation so permits, at any time while giving evidence a witness may refer to a record of that witness' recollection of events.

(6) The court may—
(a) ask a witness questions; and in particular
(b) where the defendant is not represented, ask a witness any question necessary in the defendant's interests.

R-256 Evidence of a witness in writing

25.12 (1) This rule applies where a party wants to introduce in evidence the written statement of a witness to which applies—
(a) Part 16 (Written witness statements);
(b) Part 19 (Expert evidence); or
(c) Part 20 (Hearsay evidence).

(2) If the court admits such evidence each relevant part of the statement must be read or summarised aloud, unless the court otherwise directs.

R-257 Evidence by admission

25.13 (1) This rule applies where—
(a) a party introduces in evidence a fact admitted by another party; or
(b) parties jointly admit a fact.

(2) Unless the court otherwise directs, a written record must be made of the admission.

R-258 Directions to the jury and taking the verdict

25.14 (1) This rule applies where there is a jury.

(2) The court must give the jury directions about the relevant law at any time at which to do so will assist jurors to evaluate the evidence.

(3) After following the sequence in rule 25.9 (Procedure on plea of not guilty), the court must—
(a) summarise for the jury, to such extent as is necessary, the evidence relevant to the issues they must decide;
(b) give the jury such questions, if any, as the court invites jurors to answer in coming to a verdict;
(c) direct the jury to retire to consider its verdict;
(d) if necessary, recall the jury
   (i) to answer jurors' questions, or
   (ii) to give directions, or further directions, about considering and delivering its verdict or verdicts, including, if appropriate, directions about reaching a verdict by a majority;
(e) in a case in which the jury is required to return a single verdict—
   (i) recall the jury (unless already recalled) when it informs the court that it has reached its verdict, and
   (ii) direct the delivery of that verdict there and then;
(f) in a case in which the jury is required to return two or more verdicts—
   (i) recall the jury (unless already recalled) when it informs the court that it has reached a verdict or verdicts, and
   (ii) ask the jury whether its members all agree on every verdict required;
(g) if the answer to that question is 'yes', direct the delivery of each of those verdicts there and then; and
(h) if the answer to that question is 'no'—
   (i) direct the delivery there and then of any unanimous verdict that has been reached, or
   (ii) postpone the taking of any such verdict while the jury considers each other verdict required.

(4) The court may give the jury directions, questions or other assistance in writing.
(5) When the court directs the jury to deliver its verdict or verdicts, the court must ask the foreman chosen by the jury, in respect of each count—
(a) whether the jury has reached a verdict on which all the jurors agree;
(b) if so, whether that verdict is guilty or not guilty;
(c) if not, where the jury has deliberated for at least 2 hours and if the court decides to invite a majority verdict, then—
(i) whether at least 10 (of 11 or 12 jurors), or 9 (of 10 jurors), agreed on a verdict,
(ii) if so, is that verdict guilty or not guilty, and
(iii) if (and only if) such a verdict is guilty, how many jurors agreed to that verdict and how many disagreed.
(6) Where evidence has been given that the defendant was insane, so as not to be responsible for the act or omission charged as the offence, then under paragraph (5)(b) the court must ask whether the jury's verdict is guilty, not guilty, or not guilty by reason of insanity.

Conviction or acquittal without a jury **R-259**

25.15 (1) This rule applies where—
(a) the court tries the case without a jury; and
(b) after following the sequence in rule 25.9 (Procedure on plea of not guilty).
(2) In respect of each count, the court must give reasons for its decision to convict or acquit.

Procedure if the court convicts **R-260**

25.16 (1) This rule applies where, in respect of any count in the indictment—
(a) the defendant pleads guilty; or
(b) the court convicts the defendant.
(2) The court may exercise its power—
(a) if the defendant is an individual—
(i) to require a pre-sentence report,
(ii) to commission a medical report,
(iii) to require a statement of the defendant's assets and other financial circumstances;
(b) if the defendant is a corporation, to require such information as the court directs about the defendant's corporate structure and financial resources;
(c) to adjourn sentence pending—
(i) receipt of any such report, statement or information,
(ii) the verdict in a related case.
(3) The prosecutor must—
(a) summarise the prosecution case, if the sentencing court has not heard evidence;
(b) identify in writing any offence that the prosecutor proposes should be taken into consideration in sentencing;
(c) provide information relevant to sentence, including—
(i) any previous conviction of the defendant, and the circumstances where relevant,
(ii) any statement of the effect of the offence on the victim, the victim's family or others; and
(d) identify any other matter relevant to sentence, including—
(i) the legislation applicable,
(ii) any sentencing guidelines, or guideline cases,
(iii) aggravating and mitigating features affecting the defendant's culpability and the harm which the offence caused, was intended to cause or might forseeably have caused, and
(iv) the effect of such of the information listed in paragraph (2) as the court may need to take into account.
(4) Where the defendant pleads guilty, the court may give directions for determining the facts on the basis of which sentence must be passed if—
(a) the defendant wants to be sentenced on a basis agreed with the prosecutor; or
(b) in the absence of such agreement, the defendant wants to be sentenced on the basis of different facts to those disclosed by the prosecution case.
(5) Where the court has power to order the endorsement of the defendant's driving record, or power to order the defendant to be disqualified from driving—
(a) if other legislation so permits, a defendant who wants the court not to exercise that power must introduce the evidence or information on which the defendant relies;

(b) the prosecutor may introduce evidence; and
(c) the parties may make representations about that evidence or information.

(6) Before passing sentence—
(a) the court must give the defendant an opportunity to make representations and introduce evidence relevant to sentence;
(b) where the defendant is under 18, the court may give the defendant's parents, guardian or other supporting adult, if present, such an opportunity as well; and
(c) if the court requires more information, it may exercise its power to adjourn the hearing.

(7) When the court has taken into account all the evidence, information and any report available, the court must—
(a) as a general rule, pass sentence at the earliest opportunity;
(b) when passing sentence—
(i) explain the reasons,
(ii) explain to the defendant its effect, the consequences of failing to comply with any order or pay any fine, and any power that the court has to vary or review the sentence, unless the defendant is absent or the defendant's ill-health or disorderly conduct makes such an explanation impracticable, and
(iii) give any such explanation in terms the defendant, if present, can understand (with help, if necessary); and
(c) deal with confiscation, costs and any behaviour order.

(8) The general rule is subject to the court's power to defer sentence for up to 6 months.

R-261 Provision of documents for the court

25.17 (1) Unless the court otherwise directs, a party who introduces a document in evidence, or who otherwise uses a document in presenting that party's case, must provide a copy for—
(a) each other party;
(b) any witness that party wants to refer to the document; and
(c) the court.

(2) If the court so directs, a party who introduces or uses a document for such a purpose must provide a copy for the jury.

(3) Unless the court otherwise directs, on application or on its own initiative, the court officer must provide for the court—
(a) any copy received under paragraph (1) before the trial begins; and
(b) a copy of the court officer's record of—
(i) information supplied by each party for the purposes of case management, including any revision of information previously supplied,
(ii) each pre-trial direction for the management of the case,
(iii) any pre-trial decision to admit evidence,
(iv) any pre-trial direction about the giving of evidence, and
(v) any admission to which rule 25.13 (Evidence by admission) applies; and
(c) any other document served on the court officer for the use of the court.

R-262 Duty of court officer

25.18 The court officer must—
(a) serve on each party notice of where and when an adjourned hearing will resume, unless that party was present when that was arranged;
(b) if the reason for the adjournment was to postpone sentence, include that reason in any such notice to the defendant;
(c) unless the court otherwise directs, make available to the parties any written report to which rule 25.16(2) applies (pre-sentence and medical reports);
(d) where the court has ordered a defendant to provide information under section 25 of the Road Traffic Offenders Act 1988, serve on the defendant notice of that order unless the defendant was present when it was made;
(e) give the court such other assistance as it requires, including—
(i) selecting jurors from the panel summoned by the Lord Chancellor, under rule 25.6 (Selecting the jury),
(ii) taking the oaths or affirmations of jurors and witnesses, under rules 25.6 and 25.11 (Evidence of a witness in person),
(iii) informing the jurors of the offence or offences charged in the indictment, and of their duty, under rule 25.9 (Procedure on plea of not guilty),

(iv) recording the date and time at which the court gives the jury oral directions under rule 25.14(2) (directions about the law),
(v) recording the date and time at which the court gives the jury any written directions, questions or other assistance under rule 25.14(4), and
(vi) asking the jury foreman to deliver the verdict, under rule 25.14(5).

Criminal Practice Directions Part 25 Trial and Sentence in the Crown Court

CPD VI Trial 25A: Identification for the Jury of the Issues in the Case PD-56

25A.1 CrimPR 3.11(a) requires the court, with the active assistance of the parties, to establish what are the disputed issues in order to manage the trial. To that end, prosecution opening speeches are invaluable. They set out for the jury the principal issues in the trial, and the evidence which is to be introduced in support of the prosecution case. They should clarify, not obfuscate. The purpose of the prosecution opening is to help the jury understand what the case concerns, not necessarily to present a detailed account of all the prosecution evidence due to be introduced.

25A.2 CrimPR 25.9(2)(c) provides for a defendant, or his or her advocate, to set out the issues in the defendant's own terms (subject to superintendence by the court), immediately after the prosecution opening. Any such identification of issues at this stage is not to be treated as a substitute for or extension of the summary of the defence case which can be given later, under CrimPR 25.9(2)(g). Its purpose is to provide the jury with focus as to the issues that they are likely to be called upon to decide, so that jurors will be alert to those issues from the outset and can evaluate the prosecution evidence that they hear accordingly. For that purpose, the defendant is not confined to what is included in the defence statement (though any divergence from the defence statement will expose the defendant to adverse comment or inference), and for the defendant to take the opportunity at this stage to identify the issues may assist even if all he or she wishes to announce is that the prosecution is being put to proof.

25A.3 To identify the issues for the jury at this stage also provides an opportunity for the judge to give appropriate directions about the law; for example, as to what features of the prosecution evidence they should look out for in a case in which what is in issue is the identification of the defendant by an eye-witness. Giving such directions at the outset is another means by which the jury can be helped to focus on the significant features of the evidence, in the interests of a fair and effective trial.

25A.4 A defendant is not entitled to identify issues at this stage by addressing the jury unless the court invites him or her to do so. Given the advantages described above, usually the court should extend such an invitation but there may be circumstances in which, in the court's judgment, it furthers the overriding objective not to do so. Potential reasons for denying the defendant the opportunity at this stage to address the jury about the issues include (i) that the case is such that the issues are apparent; (ii) that the prosecutor has given a fair, accurate and comprehensive account of the issues in opening, rendering repetition superfluous; and (iii) where the defendant is not represented, that there is a risk of the defendant, at this early stage, inflicting injustice on him or herself by making assertions to the jury to such an extent, or in such a manner, as is unfairly detrimental to his or her subsequent standing.

25A.5 Whether or not there is to be a defence identification of issues, and, if there is, in what manner and in what terms it is to be presented to the jury, are questions that must be resolved in the absence of the jury and that should be addressed at the opening of the trial.

25A.6 Even if invited to identify the issues by addressing the jury, the defendant is not obliged to accept the invitation. However, where the court decides that it is important for the jury to be made aware of what the defendant has declared to be in issue in the defence statement then the court may require the jury to be supplied with copies of the defence statement, edited at the court's direction if necessary, in accordance with section 6E(4) of the Criminal Procedure and Investigations Act 1996.

CPD VI Trial 25B: Trial Adjournment in the Crown Court PD-57

25B.1 A defendant has a right, in general, to be present and to be represented at his trial. However, a defendant may choose not to exercise those rights, such as by voluntarily absenting himself and failing to instruct his lawyers adequately so that they can represent him.

25B.2 The court has a discretion as to whether a trial should take place or continue in the defendant's absence and must exercise its discretion with due regard for the interests of justice. The overriding concern must be to ensure that such a trial is as fair as circumstances permit and leads to a just outcome. If the defendant's absence is due to involuntary illness or incapacity it would very rarely be right to exercise the discretion in favour of commencing or continuing the trial.

25B.3 Proceeding in the absence of a defendant is a step which ought normally to be taken only if it is unavoidable. The court must exercise its discretion as to whether a trial should take place or continue in the defendant's absence with the utmost care and caution. Due regard should be had to the judgment of Lord Bingham in *R v Jones (Anthony William)* [2002] UKHL 5, [2003] 1 A.C. 1, [2002] 2 Cr. App. R. 9. Circumstances to be taken into account before proceeding include:

i) the conduct of the defendant,
ii) the disadvantage to the defendant,
iii) the public interest, taking account of the inconvenience and hardship to witnesses, and especially to any complainant, of a delay; if the witnesses have attended court and are ready to give evidence, that will weigh in favour of continuing with the trial,
iv) the effect of any delay,
v) whether the attendance of the defendant could be secured at a later hearing, and
vii) the likely outcome if the defendant is found guilty.

Even if the defendant is voluntarily absent, it is still generally desirable that he or she is represented.

Criminal Procedure Rules Part 26 Jurors

R-263 Appeal against officer's refusal to excuse or postpone jury service

26.1 (1) This rule applies where a person summoned for jury service in the Crown Court, the High Court or the county court wants to appeal against a refusal by an officer on the Lord Chancellor's behalf—
(a) to excuse that person from such service; or
(b) to postpone the date on which that person is required to attend for such service.
(2) The appellant must appeal to the court to which the appellant has been summoned.
(3) The appellant must—
(a) apply in writing, as soon as reasonably practicable; and
(b) serve the application on the court officer.
(4) The application must—
(a) attach a copy of—
(i) the jury summons, and
(ii) the refusal to excuse or postpone which is under appeal; and
(b) explain why the court should excuse the appellant from jury service, or postpone its date, as appropriate.
(5) The court to which the appeal is made—
(a) may extend the time for appealing, and may allow the appeal to be made orally;
(b) may determine the appeal at a hearing in public or in private, or without a hearing;
(c) may adjourn any hearing of the appeal;
(d) must not determine an appeal unless the appellant has had a reasonable opportunity to make representations in person.

R-264 Excusal from jury service by court

26.2 At any time before a juror completes the oath or affirmation, the court may exercise its power to excuse him or her from jury service for lack of capacity to act effectively as a juror because of an insufficient understanding of English—
(a) on the court's own initiative, or where the court officer refers the juror to the court; and
(b) after enquiry of the juror.

R-265 Provision of information for jurors

26.3 The court officer must arrange for each juror to receive—
(a) by such means as the Lord Chancellor directs, general information about jury service and about a juror's responsibilities;
(b) written notice of the prohibitions against—
(i) research by a juror into the case,
(ii) disclosure by a juror of any such research to another juror during the trial,
(iii) conduct by a juror which suggests that that juror intends to try the case otherwise than on the evidence,

(iv) disclosure by a juror of the deliberations of the jury;

(c) written warning that breach of those prohibitions is an offence, for which the penalty is imprisonment or a fine or both, and may be a contempt of court.

Assessment of juror's availability for long trial, etc. **R-266**

26.4 (1) The court may invite each member of a panel of jurors to provide such information, by such means and at such a time as the court directs, about—

(a) that juror's availability to try a case expected to last for longer than the juror had expected to serve;

(b) any association of that juror with, or any knowledge by that juror of—

(i) a party or witness, or

(ii) any other person, or any place, of significance to the case.

(2) Where jurors provide information under this rule, the court may postpone the selection of the jury to try a case to allow each juror an opportunity to review and amend that information before that selection.

(3) Using that information, the court may exercise its power to excuse a juror from selection as a member of the jury to try a case, but the court must not—

(a) excuse a juror without allowing the parties an opportunity to make representations; or

(b) refuse to excuse a juror without allowing that juror such an opportunity.

Surrender of electronic communication devices by jurors **R-267**

26.5 (1) This rule applies where the court can order the members of a jury to surrender for a specified period any electronic communication devices that they possess.

(2) The court may make such an order—

(a) on application; or

(b) on its own initiative.

(3) A party who wants the court to make such an order must—

(a) apply as soon as reasonably practicable;

(b) notify each other party;

(c) specify for what period any device should be surrendered; and

(d) explain why—

(i) the proposed order is necessary or expedient in the interest of justice, and

(ii) the terms of the proposed order are a proportionate means of safeguarding those interests.

Criminal Practice Directions Part 26 Jurors

CPD VI Trial 26A: Juries: introduction **PD-58**

26A.1 Jury service is an important public duty which individual members of the public are chosen at random to undertake. As the Court has acknowledged: 'Jury service is not easy; it never has been. It involves a major civic responsibility' (*R v Thompson* [2010] EWCA Crim 1623, [9] per Lord Judge CJ, [2011] 1 WLR 200, [2010] 2 Cr App R 27).

Provision of information to prospective jurors

26A.2 HMCTS provide every person summoned as a juror with information about the role and responsibilities of a juror. Prospective jurors are provided with a pamphlet, 'Your Guide to Jury Service', and may also view the film 'Your Role as a Juror' online at any time on the Ministry of Justice YouTube site www.youtube.com/watch?v=JP7slp-X9Pc There is also information at https://www.gov.uk/jury-service/overview

CPD VI Trial 26B: Juries: Preliminary Matters Arising before Jury Service Commences **PD-59**

26B.1 The effect of section 321 of the Criminal Justice Act 2003 was to remove certain categories of persons from those previously ineligible for jury service (the judiciary and others concerned with the administration of justice) and certain other categories ceased to be eligible for excusal as of right, (such as members of Parliament and medical professionals). The normal presumption is that everyone, unless ineligible or disqualified, will be required to serve when summoned to do so.

Excusal and deferral

26B.2 The jury summoning officer is empowered to defer or excuse individuals in appropriate circumstances and in accordance with the HMCTS *Guidance for summoning officers when considering deferral and excusal applications* (2009): http://www.official-documents.gov.uk/document/other/9780108508400/9780108508400.pdf

Appeals from officer's refusal to excuse or postpone jury service

26B.3 CrimPR 26.1 governs the procedure for a person's appeal against a summoning officer's decision in relation to excusal or deferral of jury service.

Provision of information at court

26B.4 The court officer is expected to provide relevant further information to jurors on their arrival in the court centre.

PD-60 **CPD VI Trial 26C: Juries: Eligibility**

English language ability

26C.1 Under the Juries Act 1974 section 10, a person summoned for jury service who applies for excusal on the grounds of insufficient understanding of English may, where necessary, be brought before the judge.

26C.2 The court may exercise its power to excuse any person from jury service for lack of capacity to act effectively as a juror because of an insufficient understanding of English.

26C.3 The judge has the discretion to stand down jurors who are not competent to serve by reason of a personal disability: *R v Mason* [1981] QB 881, (1980) 71 Cr App R 157; *R v Jalil* [2008] EWCA Crim 2910, [2009] 2 Cr App R (S.) 40.

Jurors with professional and public service commitments

26C.4 The legislative change in the Criminal Justice Act 2003 means that more individuals are eligible to serve as jurors, including those previously excused as of right or ineligible. Judges need to be vigilant to the need to exercise their discretion to adjourn a trial, excuse or discharge a juror should the need arise.

26C.5 Whether or not an application has already been made to the jury summoning officer for deferral or excusal, it is also open to the person summoned to apply to the court to be excused. Such applications must be considered with common sense and according to the interests of justice. An explanation should be required for an application being much later than necessary.

Serving police officers, prison officers or employees of prosecuting agencies

26C.6 A judge should always be made aware at the stage of jury selection if any juror in waiting is in these categories. The juror summons warns jurors in these categories that they will need to alert court staff.

26C.7 In the case of police officers an inquiry by the judge will have to be made to assess whether a police officer may serve as a juror. Regard should be had to: whether evidence from the police is in dispute in the case and the extent to which that dispute involves allegations made against the police; whether the potential juror knows or has worked with the officers involved in the case; whether the potential juror has served or continues to serve in the same police units within the force as those dealing with the investigation of the case or is likely to have a shared local service background with police witnesses in a trial.

26C.8 In the case of a serving prison officer summoned to a court, the judge will need to inquire whether the individual is employed at a prison linked to that court or is likely to have special knowledge of any person involved in a trial.

26C.9 The judge will need to ensure that employees of prosecuting authorities do not serve on a trial prosecuted by the prosecuting authority by which they are employed. They can serve on a trial prosecuted by another prosecuting authority: *R v Abdroikov* [2007] UKHL 37, [2007] 1 WLR 2679, [2008] 1 Cr App R 21; *Hanif v UK* [2011] ECHR 2247, (2012) 55 EHRR 16; *R v L* [2011] EWCA Crim 65, [2011] 1 Cr App R 27. Similarly, a serving police officer can serve where there is no particular link between the court and the station where the police officer serves.

26C.10 Potential jurors falling into these categories should be excused from jury service unless there is a suitable alternative court/trial to which they can be transferred.

PD-61 **CPD VI Trial 26D: Juries: Precautionary Measures before Swearing**

26D.1 There should be a consultation with the advocates as to the questions, if any, it may be appropriate to ask potential jurors. Topics to be considered include:

a. the availability of jurors for the duration of a trial that is likely to run beyond the usual period for which jurors are summoned;
b. whether any juror knows the defendant or parties to the case;

c. whether potential jurors are so familiar with any locations that feature in the case that they may have, or come to have, access to information not in evidence;
d. in cases where there has been any significant local or national publicity, whether any questions should be asked of potential jurors.

26D.2 Judges should however exercise caution. At common law a judge has a residual discretion to discharge a particular juror who ought not to be serving, but this discretion can only be exercised to prevent an individual juror who is not competent from serving. It does not include a discretion to discharge a jury drawn from particular sections of the community or otherwise to influence the overall composition of the jury. However, if there is a risk that there is widespread local knowledge of the defendant or a witness in a particular case, the judge may, after hearing submissions from the advocates, decide to exclude jurors from particular areas to avoid the risk of jurors having or acquiring personal knowledge of the defendant or a witness.

Length of trial

26D.3 Where the length of the trial is estimated to be significantly longer than the normal period of jury service, it is good practice for the trial judge to enquire whether the potential jurors on the jury panel foresee any difficulties with the length and if the judge is satisfied that the jurors' concerns are justified, he may say that they are not required for that particular jury. This does not mean that the judge must excuse the juror from sitting at that court altogether, as it may well be possible for the juror to sit on a shorter trial at the same court.

Juror with potential connection to the case or parties

26D.4 Where a juror appears on a jury panel, it will be appropriate for a judge to excuse the juror from that particular case where the potential juror is personally concerned with the facts of the particular case, or is closely connected with a prospective witness. Judges need to exercise due caution as noted above.

CPD VI Trial 26E: Juries: Swearing in Jurors PD-62

Swearing Jury for trial

26E.1 All jurors shall be sworn or affirm. All jurors shall take the oath or affirmation in open court in the presence of one another. If, as a result of the juror's delivery of the oath or affirmation, a judge has concerns that a juror has such difficulties with language comprehension or reading ability that might affect that juror's capacity to undertake his or her duties, bearing in mind the likely evidence in the trial, the judge should make appropriate inquiry of that juror.

Form of oath or affirmation

26E.2 Each juror should have the opportunity to indicate to the court the Holy Book on which he or she wishes to swear. The precise wording will depend on his or her faith as indicated to the court.

26E.3 Any person who prefers to affirm shall be permitted to make a solemn affirmation instead. The wording of the affirmation is: 'I do solemnly, sincerely and truly declare and affirm that I will faithfully try the defendant and give a true verdict according to the evidence'.

CPD VI Trial 26F: Juries: Ensuring an effective jury panel PD-63

Adequacy of numbers

26F.1 By section 6 of the Juries Act 1974, if it appears to the court that a jury to try any issue before the court will be, or probably will be, incomplete, the court may, if the court thinks fit, require any persons who are in, or in the vicinity of, the court, to be summoned (without any written notice) for jury service up to the number needed (after allowing for any who may not be qualified under section 1 of the Act, and for excusals and challenges) to make up a full jury.

CPD VI Trial 26G: Juries: Preliminary Instructions to Jurors PD-64

26G.1 After the jury has been sworn and the defendant has been put in charge the judge will want to give directions to the jury on a number of matters.

26G.2 Jurors can be expected to follow the instructions diligently. As the Privy Council stated in *Taylor* [2013] UKPC 8, [2013] 1 WLR 1144:

> The assumption must be that the jury understood and followed the direction that they were given: ... the experience of trial judges is that juries perform their duty according to law. ... [T]he law proceeds on the footing that the jury, acting in accordance with the instructions given to them by the trial judge, will render a true verdict in accordance with

the evidence. To conclude otherwise would be to underrate the integrity of the system of trial by jury and the effect on the jury of the instructions by the trial judge.

At the start of the trial

26G.3 Trial judges should instruct the jury on general matters which will include the time estimate for the trial and normal sitting hours. The jury will always need clear guidance on the following:

i. The need to try the case only on the evidence and remain faithful to their oath or affirmation;
ii. The prohibition on internet searches for matters related to the trial, issues arising or the parties;
iii. The importance of not discussing any aspect of the case with anyone outside their own number or allowing anyone to talk to them about it, whether directly, by telephone, through internet facilities such as Facebook or Twitter or in any other way;
iv. The importance of taking no account of any media reports about the case;
v. The collective responsibility of the jury. As the Lord Chief Justice made clear in *R v Thompson and Others* [2010] EWCA Crim 1623, [2011] 1 WLR 200, [2010] 2 Cr App R 27:
   [T]here is a collective responsibility for ensuring that the conduct of each member is consistent with the jury oath and that the directions of the trial judge about the discharge of their responsibilities are followed.... The collective responsibility of the jury for its own conduct must be regarded as an integral part of the trial itself.
vi. The need to bring any concerns, including concerns about the conduct of other jurors, to the attention of the judge at the time, and not to wait until the case is concluded. The point should be made that, unless that is done while the case is continuing, it may not be possible to deal with the problem at all.

Subsequent reminder of the jury instructions

26G.4 Judges should consider reminding jurors of these instructions as appropriate at the end of each day and in particular when they separate after retirement.

26G.5 Following the judge's direction to the jury, each member of the jury must be provided with a copy of the notice 'Your Legal Responsibilities as a Juror'. This notice outlines what is required of the juror during and after their time on the jury. It is not a substitute for the judge's direction, but is designed to reinforce what the judge has outlined in the direction. The court clerk should ensure a record is made of service of the notice. Jurors are advised to keep their copy of the notice with their summons and at the end of the trial, they are allowed to retain it for future information.

PD-65 **CPD VI Trial 26H: Juries: Discharge of a juror for personal reasons**

26H.1 Where a juror unexpectedly finds him or herself in difficult professional or personal circumstances during the course of the trial, the juror should be encouraged to raise such problems with the trial judge. This might apply, for example, to a parent whose childcare arrangements unexpectedly fail, or a worker who is engaged in the provision of services the need for which can be critical, or a Member of Parliament who has deferred their jury service to an apparently more convenient time, but is unexpectedly called back to work for a very important reason. Such difficulties would normally be raised through a jury note in the normal manner.

26H.2 In such circumstances, the judge must exercise his or her discretion according to the interests of justice and the requirements of each individual case. The judge must decide for him or herself whether the juror has presented a sufficient reason to interfere with the course of the trial. If the juror has presented a sufficient reason, in longer trials it may well be possible to adjourn for a short period in order to allow the juror to overcome the difficulty.

26H.3 In shorter cases, it may be more appropriate to discharge the juror and to continue the trial with a reduced number of jurors. The power to do this is implicit in section 16(1) of the Juries Act 1974. In unusual cases (such as an unexpected emergency arising overnight) a juror need not be discharged in open court. The good administration of justice depends on the co-operation of jurors, who perform an essential public service. All such applications should be dealt with sensitively and sympathetically and the trial judge should always seek to meet the interests of justice without unduly inconveniencing any juror.

PD-66 **CPD VI Trial 26J: Juries: Views**

26J.1 In each case in which it is necessary for the jury to view a location, the judge should produce ground rules for the view, after discussion with the advocates. The rules should contain details of what the jury will be shown and in what order and who, if anyone, will be permitted to speak and what will be said. The rules should also make provision for the jury to ask questions and receive a response from the judge, following submissions from the advocates, while the view is taking place.

CPD VI Trial 26K: Juries: Directions, Written Materials and Summing Up **PD-67**

Overview

26K.1 Sir Brian Leveson's *Review of Efficiency in Criminal Proceedings 2015* contained recommendations to improve the efficiency of jury trials including:

- Early provision of appropriate directions;
- Provision of a written route to verdict;
- Provision of a split summing up (a summing up delivered in two parts – the first part prior to the closing speeches and the second part afterwards); and
- Streamlining the summing up to help the jury focus on the issues.

The purpose of this practice direction, and the associated criminal procedure rules, is to give effect to these recommendations.

Record-keeping

26K.2 Full and accurate record-keeping is essential to enable the Registrar of Criminal Appeals to obtain transcripts in the event of an application or appeal to the Court of Appeal (Criminal Division).

26K.3 A court officer is required to record the date and time at which the court provides directions and written materials (CrimPR 25.18(e)(iv)–(v)).

26K.4 The judge should ensure that a court officer (such as a court clerk or usher) is present in court to record the information listed in paragraph 26K.5.

26K.5 A court officer should clearly record the:

- Date, time and subject of submissions and rulings relating to directions and written materials;
- Date, time and subject of directions and written materials provided prior to the summing up; and
- Date and time of the summing up, including both parts of a split summing up.

26K.6 A court officer should retain a copy of written materials on the court file or database.

26K.7 The parties should also record the information listed in paragraph 26K.5 and retain a copy of written materials. Where relevant to a subsequent application or appeal to the Court of Appeal (Criminal Division), the information listed in paragraph 26K.5 should be provided in the notice of appeal, and any written materials should be identified.

Early provision of appropriate directions

26K.8 The court is required to provide directions about the relevant law at any time that will assist the jury to evaluate the evidence (CrimPR 25.14(2)). The judge may provide an early direction prior to any evidence being called, prior to the evidence to which it relates or shortly thereafter.

26K.9 Where the judge decides it will assist the jury in:

- their approach to the evidence; and / or
- evaluating the evidence as they hear it

an early direction should be provided.

26K.10 For example:

- Where identification is in issue, an early *Turnbull* direction is likely to assist the jury in approaching the evidence with the requisite caution; and by having the relevant considerations in mind when listening to the evidence.
- Where special measures are to be used and / or ground rules will restrict the manner and scope of questioning, an early explanation may assist the jury in their approach to the evidence.
- An early direction may also assist the jury, by having the relevant approach, considerations and / or test in mind, when listening to:
  - Expert witnesses; and
  - Evidence of bad character;
  - Hearsay;
  - Interviews of co-defendants; and
  - Evidence involving legal concepts such as knowledge, dishonesty, consent, recklessness, conspiracy, joint enterprise, attempt, self-defence, excessive force, voluntary intoxication and duress.

Written route to verdict

26K.11 A route to verdict, which poses a series of questions that lead the jury to the appropriate verdict, may be provided by the court (CrimPR 25.14(3)(b)). Each question should tailor the law to the issues and evidence in the case.

26K.12 Save where the case is so straightforward that it would be superfluous to do so, the judge should provide a written route to verdict. It may be presented (on paper or digitally) in the form of text, bullet points, a flowchart or other graphic.

Other written materials

26K.13 Where the judge decides it will assist the jury, written materials should be provided. They may be presented (on paper or digitally) in the form of text, bullet points, a table, a flowchart or other graphic.

26K.14 For example, written materials may assist the jury in relation to a complex direction or where the case involves:

- A complex chronology;
- Competing expert evidence; or
- Differing descriptions of a suspect.

26K.15 Such written materials may be prepared by the judge or the parties at the direction of the judge. Where prepared by the parties at the direction of the judge, they will be subject to the judge's approval.

Split summing up and provision of appropriate directions prior to closing speeches

26K.16 Where the judge decides it will assist the jury when listening to the closing speeches, a split summing up should be provided. For example, the provision of appropriate directions prior to the closing speeches may avoid repetitious explanations of the law by the advocates.

26K.17 By way of illustration, such directions may include:

- Functions of the judge and jury;
- Burden and standard of proof;
- Separate consideration of counts;
- Separate consideration of defendants;
- Elements of offence(s);
- Defence(s);
- Route to verdict;
- Circumstantial evidence; and
- Inferences from silence.

Closing speeches

26K.18 The advocates closing speeches should be consistent with any directions and route to verdict already provided by the judge.

Summing up

26K.19 Prior to beginning or resuming the summing up at the conclusion of the closing speeches, the judge should briefly list (without repeating) any directions provided earlier in the trial. The purpose of this requirement is to provide a definitive account of all directions for the benefit of the Registrar of Criminal Appeals and the Court of Appeal (Criminal Division), in the event of an application or appeal.

26K.20 The court is required to summarise the evidence relevant to the issues to such extent as is necessary (CrimPR 25.14(3)(a)).

26K.21 To assist the jury to focus on the issues during retirement, save where the case is so straightforward that it would be superfluous to do so, the judge should provide:

- A reminder of the issues;
- A summary of the nature of the evidence relating to each issue;
- A balanced account of the points raised by the parties; and
- Any outstanding directions.

It is not necessary for the judge to recount all relevant evidence or to rehearse all of the significant points raised by the parties.

26K.22 At the conclusion of the summing up, the judge should provide final directions to the jury on the need:

- For unanimity (in respect of each count and defendant, where relevant);

- To dismiss any thoughts of majority verdicts until further direction; and
- To select a juror to chair their discussions and speak on their behalf to the court.

CPD VI Trial 26L: Juries: Jury access to exhibits and evidence in retirement PD-68

26L.1 At the end of the summing up it is also important that the judge informs the jury that any exhibits they wish to have will be made available to them.

26L.2 Judges should invite submissions from the advocates as to what material the jury should retire with and what material before them should be removed, such as the transcript of an ABE interview (which should usually be removed from the jury as soon as the recording has been played.)

26L.3 Judges will also need to inform the jury of the opportunity to view certain audio, DVD or CCTV evidence that has been played (excluding, for example ABE interviews). If possible, it may be appropriate for the jury to be able to view any such material in the jury room alone, such as on a sterile laptop, so that they can discuss it freely; this will be a matter for the judge's discretion, following discussion with counsel.

CPD VI Trial 26M: Juries: Jury Irregularities PD-69

26M.1 This practice direction replaces the protocol regarding jury irregularities issued by the President of the Queen's Bench Division in November 2012, and the subsequent practice direction, in light of sections 20A to 20D of the Juries Act 1974 and the associated repeal of section 8 of the Contempt of Court Act 1981 (confidentiality of jury's deliberations).
It applies to juries sworn on or after 13 April 2015.

26M.2 A jury irregularity is anything that may prevent one or more jurors from remaining faithful to their oath or affirmation to 'faithfully try the defendant and give a true verdict according to the evidence.' Jury irregularities take many forms. Some are clear-cut such as a juror conducting research about the case or an attempt to suborn or intimidate a juror. Others are less clear-cut — for example, when there is potential bias or friction between jurors.

26M.3 A jury irregularity may involve contempt of court and / or the commission of an offence by or in relation to a juror.

26M.4 Under the previous version of this practice direction, the Crown Court required approval from the Vice-President of the Court of Appeal (Criminal Division) (CACD) prior to providing a juror's details to the police for the purposes of an investigation into a jury irregularity. Such approval is no longer required. Provision of a juror's details to the police is now a matter for the Crown Court.

Jury Irregularity During Trial

26M.5 A jury irregularity that comes to light during a trial may impact on the conduct of the trial. It may also involve contempt of court and / or the commission of an offence by or in relation to a juror. **The primary concern of the judge should be the impact on the trial.**

26M.6 A jury irregularity should be drawn to the attention of the judge in the absence of the jury as soon as it becomes known.

26M.7 **When the judge becomes aware of a jury irregularity, the judge should follow the procedure set out below:**

STEP 1: **Consider isolating juror(s)**
STEP 2: **Consult with advocates**
STEP 3: **Consider appropriate provisional measures (which may include surrender / seizure of electronic communications devices and taking defendant into custody)**
STEP 4: **Seek to establish basic facts of jury irregularity**
STEP 5: **Further consult with advocates**
STEP 6: **Decide what to do in relation to conduct of trial**
STEP 7: **Consider ancillary matters (contempt in face of court and / or commission of criminal offence)**

STEP 1: Consider isolating juror(*s*)

26M.8 The judge should consider whether the juror(s) concerned should be isolated from the rest of the jury, particularly if the juror(s) may have conducted research about the case.

26M.9 If two or more jurors are concerned, the judge should consider whether they should also be isolated from each other, particularly if one juror has made an accusation against another.

STEP 2: Consult with advocates

26M.10 The judge should consult with the advocates and invite submissions about appropriate provisional measures (Step 3) and how to go about establishing the basic facts of the jury irregularity (Step 4).

26M.11 The consultation should be conducted
— in open court;
— in the presence of the defendant; and
— with all parties represented
unless there is good reason not to do so.

26M.12 If the jury irregularity involves a suspicion about the conduct of the defendant or another party, there may be good reason for the consultation to take place in the absence of the defendant or the other party. There may also be good reason for it to take place in private. If so, the proper location is in the court room, with DARTS recording, rather than in the judge's room.

26M.13 If the jury irregularity relates to the jury's deliberations, the judge should warn all those present that it is an offence to disclose, solicit or obtain information about a jury's deliberations (section 20D(1) of the Juries Act 1974—see 26M.35 to 26M.38 regarding the offence and exceptions). This would include disclosing information about the jury's deliberations divulged in court during consultation with the advocates (Step 2 and Step 5) or when seeking to establish the basic facts of the jury irregularity (Step 4). The judge should emphasise that the advocates, court staff and those in the public gallery would commit the offence by explaining to another what is said in court about the jury's deliberations.

STEP 3: Consider appropriate provisional measures

26M.14 **The judge should consider appropriate provisional measures which may include surrender / seizure of electronic communications devices and taking the defendant into custody.**

Surrender / seizure of electronic communications devices

26M.15 The judge should consider whether to make an order under section 15A(1) of the Juries Act 1974 requiring the juror(s) concerned to surrender electronic communications devices, such as mobile telephones or smart phones.

26M.16 Having made an order for surrender, the judge may require a court security officer to search a juror to determine whether the juror has complied with the order. Section 54A of the Courts Act 2003 contains the court security officer's powers of search and seizure.

26M.17 Section 15A(5) of the Juries Act 1974 provides that it is contempt of court for a juror to fail to surrender an electronic communications device in accordance with an order for surrender (see paragraphs 26M.29 to 26M.30 regarding the procedure for dealing with such a contempt).

26M.18 Any electronic communications device surrendered or seized under these provisions should be kept safe by the court until returned to the juror or handed to the police as evidence.

Taking defendant into custody

26M.19 If the defendant is on bail, and the jury irregularity involves a suspicion about the defendant's conduct, the judge should consider taking the defendant into custody. If that suspicion involves an attempt to suborn or intimidate a juror, the defendant should be taken into custody.

STEP 4: Seek to establish basic facts of jury irregularity

26M.20 The judge should seek to establish the basic facts of the jury irregularity for the purpose of determining how to proceed in relation to the conduct of the trial. The judge's enquiries may involve having the juror(s) concerned write a note of explanation and / or questioning the juror(s). The judge may enquire whether the juror(s) feel able to continue and remain faithful to their oath or affirmation. If there is questioning, each juror should be questioned separately, in the absence of the rest of the jury, unless there is good reason not to do so.

26M.21 In accordance with paragraphs 26M.10 to 26M.13, the enquiries should be conducted in open court; in the presence of the defendant; and with all parties represented unless there is good reason not to do so.

STEP 5: Further consult with advocates

26M.22 The judge should further consult with the advocates and invite submissions about how to proceed in relation to the conduct of the trial and what should be said to the jury (Step 6).

26M.23 In accordance with paragraphs 26M.10 to 26M.13, the consultation should be conducted in open court; in the presence of the defendant; and with all parties represented unless there is good reason not to do so.

STEP 6: Decide what to do in relation to conduct of trial

26M.24 When deciding how to proceed, the judge may take time to reflect.

26M.25 Considerations may include the stage the trial has reached. The judge should be alert to attempts by the defendant or others to thwart the trial. In cases of potential bias, the judge should consider whether a fair minded and informed observer would conclude that there was a real possibility that the juror(s) or jury would be biased (*Porter v Magill* [2001] UKHL 67, [2002] 2 AC 357).

26M.26 **In relation to the conduct of the trial, there are three possibilities:**

1. ***Take no action and continue with the trial***
   If so, the judge should consider what, if anything, to say to the jury. For example, the judge may reassure the jury nothing untoward has happened or remind them their verdict is a decision of the whole jury and that they should try to work together. Anything said should be tailored to the circumstances of the case.
2. ***Discharge the juror(s) concerned and continue with the trial***
   If so, the judge should consider what to say to the discharged juror(s) and the jurors who remain. All jurors should be warned not to discuss what has happened.
3. ***Discharge the whole jury***
   If so, the judge should consider what to say to the jury and they should be warned not to discuss what has happened.
   If the judge is satisfied that jury tampering has taken place, depending on the circumstances, the judge may continue the trial without a jury (section 46(3) of the Criminal Justice Act 2003) or order a new trial without a jury (section 46(5) of the Criminal Justice Act 2003). Alternatively, the judge may re-list the trial. If there is a real and present danger of jury tampering in the new trial, the prosecution may apply for a trial without a jury (section 44 of the Criminal Justice Act 2003).

STEP 7: Consider ancillary matters

26M.27 **A jury irregularity may also involve contempt in the face of the court and / or the commission of a criminal offence. The possibilities include the following:**

— **Contempt in the face of the court by a juror**

— **An offence by a juror or a non-juror under the Juries Act 1974**

Offences that may be committed by jurors are researching the case, sharing research, engaging in prohibited conduct or disclosing information about the jury's deliberations (sections 20A to 20D of the Juries Act 1974). Non-jurors may commit the offence of disclosing, soliciting or obtaining information about the jury's deliberations (section 20D of the Juries Act 1974).

— **An offence by juror or a non-juror other than under the Juries Act 1974** A juror may commit an offence such as assault or theft. A non-juror may commit an offence in relation to a juror such as attempting to pervert the course of justice — for example, if the defendant or another attempts to suborn or intimidate a juror.

Contempt in the face of the court by a juror

26M.28 If a juror commits contempt in the face of the court, the juror's conduct may also constitute an offence. If so, the judge should decide whether to deal with the juror summarily under the procedure for contempt in the face of the court or refer the matter to the Attorney General's Office or the police (see paragraphs 26M.31 and 26M.33).

26M.29 In the case of a *minor and clear* contempt in the face of the court, the judge may deal with the juror summarily. The judge should follow the procedure in CrimPR 48.5 to 48.8. The judge should also have regard to the practice direction regarding contempt of court issued in March 2015 (Practice Direction: Committal for Contempt of Court — Open Court), which emphasises the principle of open justice in relation to proceedings for contempt before all courts.

26M.30 If a juror fails to comply with an order for surrender of an electronic communications device (see paragraphs 26M.15 to 26M.18), the judge should deal with the juror summarily following the procedure for contempt in the face of the court.

Offence by a juror or non-juror under the Juries Act 1974

26M.31 If it appears that an offence under the Juries Act 1974 may have been committed by a juror or non-juror (and the matter has not been dealt with summarily under the procedure for contempt in the face of the court), **the judge** should contact the Attorney General's Office to consider a police investigation, setting out the position neutrally. The officer in the case should not be asked to investigate.

Contact details for the Attorney General's Office are set out at the end of this practice direction.

26M.32 If relevant to an investigation, any electronic communications device surrendered or seized pursuant to an order for surrender should be passed to the police as soon as practicable.

Offence by a juror or non-juror other than under the Juries Act 1974

26M.33 If it appears that an offence, other than an offence under the Juries Act 1974, may have been committed by a juror or non-juror (and the matter has not been dealt with summarily under the procedure for contempt in the face of the court), **the judge or a member of court staff** should contact the police setting out the position neutrally. The officer in the case should not be asked to investigate.

26M.34 If relevant to an investigation, any electronic communications device surrendered or seized pursuant to an order for surrender should be passed to the police as soon as practicable.

Other matters to consider

Jury deliberations

26M.35 **In light of the offence of disclosing, soliciting or obtaining information about a jury's deliberations (section 20D(1) of the Juries Act 1974), great care is required if a jury irregularity relates to the jury's deliberations.**

26M.36 *During the trial*, there are exceptions to this offence that enable the judge (and only the judge) to:

— Seek to establish the basic facts of a jury irregularity involving the jury's deliberations (Step 4); and

— Disclose information about the jury's deliberations to the Attorney General's Office if it appears that an offence may have been committed (Step 7).

26M.37 With regard to seeking to establish the basic facts of a jury irregularity involving the jury's deliberations (Step 4), it is to be noted that during the trial it is not an offence for the judge to disclose, solicit or obtain information about the jury's deliberations for the purposes of dealing with the case (sections 20E(2)(a) and 20G(1) of the Juries Act 1974).

26M.38 With regard to disclosing information about the jury's deliberations to the Attorney General's Office if it appears that an offence may have been committed (Step 7), it is to be noted that during the trial:

— It is not an offence for the judge to disclose information about the jury's deliberations for the purposes of an investigation by a relevant investigator into whether an offence or contempt of court has been committed by or in relation to a juror (section 20E(2)(b) of the Juries Act 1974); and

— A relevant investigator means a police force or the Attorney General (section 20E(5) of the Juries Act 1974).

Minimum number of jurors

26M.39 If it is decided to discharge one or more jurors (Step 6), a minimum of nine jurors must remain if the trial is to continue (section 16(1) of the Juries Act 1974).

Preparation of statement by judge

26M.40 If a jury irregularity occurs, and the trial continues, the judge should have regard to the remarks of Lord Hope in *R v Connors and Mirza* [2004] UKHL 2 at [127] and [128], [2004] 1 AC 1118, [2004] 2 Cr App R 8 and consider whether to prepare a statement that could be used in an application for leave to appeal or an appeal relating to the jury irregularity.

Jury Irregularity After Jury Discharged

26M.41 A jury irregularity that comes to light after the jury has been discharged may involve the commission of an offence by or in relation to a juror. It may also provide a ground of appeal.

26M.42 A jury irregularity after the jury has been discharged may come to the attention of the:
- **Trial judge or court**
- **Registrar of Criminal Appeals (the Registrar)**
- **Prosecution**
- **Defence**

Role of the trial judge or court

26M.43 The judge has no jurisdiction in relation to a jury irregularity that comes to light after the jury has been discharged (*R v Thompson and others* [2010] EWCA Crim 1623, [2011] 1 WLR 200, [2010] 2 Cr App R 27A). The jury will be deemed to have been discharged when all verdicts on all defendants have been delivered or when the jury has been discharged from giving all verdicts on all defendants.

26M.44 The judge will be *functus officio* in relation to a jury irregularity that comes to light during an adjournment between verdict and sentence. The judge should proceed to sentence unless there is good reason not to do so.

26M.45 In practice, a jury irregularity often comes to light when the judge or court receives a communication from a former juror.

26M.46 If a jury irregularity comes to the attention of a judge or court after the jury has been discharged, and regardless of the result of the trial, the judge or a member of court staff should contact the Registrar setting out the position neutrally. Any communication from a former juror should be forwarded to the Registrar.
Contact details for the Registrar are set out at the end of this practice direction.

Role of the Registrar

26M.47 If a jury irregularity comes to the attention of the Registrar after the jury has been discharged, and regardless of the result of the trial, the Registrar should consider if it appears that an offence may have been committed by or in relation to a juror. The Registrar should also consider if there may be a ground of appeal.

26M.48 When deciding how to proceed, particularly in relation to a communication from a former juror, the Registrar may seek the direction of the Vice-President of the Court of Appeal (Criminal Division) (CACD) or another judge of the CACD in accordance with instructions from the Vice-President.

26M.49 If it appears that an offence may have been committed by or in relation to a juror, the Registrar should contact the Private Office of the Director of Public Prosecutions to consider a police investigation.

26M.50 If there may be a ground of appeal, the Registrar should inform the defence.

26M.51 If a communication from a former juror is not of legal significance, the Registrar should respond explaining that no action is required. An example of such a communication is if it is restricted to a general complaint about the verdict from a dissenting juror or an expression of doubt or second thoughts.

Role of the prosecution

26M.52 If a jury irregularity comes to the attention of the prosecution after the jury has been discharged, which may provide a ground of appeal, they should notify the defence in accordance with their duties to act fairly and assist in the administration of justice (*R v Makin* [2004] EWCA Crim 1607, 148 SJLB 821).

Role of the defence

26M.53 If a jury irregularity comes to the attention of the defence after the jury has been discharged, which provides an arguable ground of appeal, an application for leave to appeal may be made.

Other matters to consider

Jury deliberations

26M.54 **In light of the offence of disclosing, soliciting or obtaining information about a jury's deliberations (section 20D(1) of the Juries Act 1974), great care is required if a jury irregularity relates to the jury's deliberations.**

26M.55 *After the jury has been discharged*, there are exceptions to this offence that enable a judge, a member of court staff, the Registrar, the prosecution and the defence to disclose information about the jury's deliberations if it appears that an offence may have been committed by or in relation to a juror or if there may be a ground of appeal.

26M.56 For example, it is to be noted that:

— After the jury has been discharged, it is not an offence for a person to disclose information about the jury's deliberations to defined persons if the person reasonably believes that an offence or contempt of court may have been committed by or in relation to a juror or the conduct of a juror may provide grounds of appeal (section 20F(1) (2) of the Juries Act 1974).

— The defined persons to whom such information may be disclosed are a member of a police force, a judge of the CACD, the Registrar of Criminal Appeals (the Registrar), a judge where the trial took place or a member of court staff where the trial took place who would reasonably be expected to disclose the information only to one of the aforementioned defined persons (section 20F(2) of the Juries Act 1974).

— After the jury has been discharged, it is not an offence for a judge of the CACD or the Registrar to disclose information about the jury's deliberations for the purposes of an investigation by a relevant investigator into whether an offence or contempt of court has been committed by or in relation to a juror or the conduct of a juror may provide grounds of appeal (section 20F(4) of the Juries Act 1974).

— A relevant investigator means a police force, the Attorney General, the Criminal Cases Review Commission (CCRC) or the Crown Prosecution Service (section 20F(10) of the Juries Act 1974).

Investigation by the Criminal Cases Review Commission (CCRC)

26M.57 If an application for leave to appeal, or an appeal, includes a ground of appeal relating to a jury irregularity, the Registrar may refer the case to the Full Court to decide whether to direct the CCRC to conduct an investigation under section 23A of the Criminal Appeal Act 1968.

26M.58 If the Court directs the CCRC to conduct an investigation, directions should be given as to the scope of the investigation.

Contact Details

Attorney General's Office
Contempt.SharedMailbox@attorneygeneral.gsi.gov.uk
Telephone: 020 7271 2492

The Registrar
penny.donnelly@hmcts.x.gsi.gov.uk (Secretary) or
criminalappealoffice.generaloffice@hmcts.gsi.gov.uk
Telephone: 020 7947 6103 (Secretary) or 020 7947 6011

PD-70 CPD VI Trial 26N: Open Justice

26N.1 There must be freedom of access between advocate and judge. Any discussion must, however, be between the judge and the advocates on both sides. If an advocate is instructed by a solicitor who is in court, he or she, too, should be allowed to attend the discussion. This freedom of access is important because there may be matters calling for communication or discussion of such a nature that the advocate cannot, in the client's interest, mention them in open court, e.g. the advocate, by way of mitigation, may wish to tell the judge that reliable medical evidence shows that the defendant is suffering from a terminal illness and may not have long to live. It is imperative that, so far as possible, justice must be administered in open court. Advocates should, therefore, only ask to see the judge when it is felt to be really necessary. The judge must be careful only to treat such communications as private where, in the interests of justice, this is necessary. Where any such discussion takes place it should be recorded, preferably by audio recording.

PD-71 CPD VI Trial 26P: Defendant's Right to Give or Not to Give Evidence

26P.1 At the conclusion of the evidence for the prosecution, section 35(2) of the Criminal Justice and Public Order Act 1994 requires the court to satisfy itself that the defendant is aware that the stage has been reached at which evidence can be given for the defence and that the defendant's failure to give evidence, or if he does so his failure to answer questions, without a good reason, may lead to inferences being drawn against him.

If the defendant is legally represented

26P.2 After the close of the prosecution case, if the defendant's representative requests a brief adjournment to advise his client on this issue the request should, ordinarily, be granted. When appropriate the judge should, in the presence of the jury, inquire of the representative in these terms:

'Have you advised your client that the stage has now been reached at which he may give evidence and, if he chooses not to do so or, having been sworn, without good cause refuses to answer any question, the jury may draw such inferences as appear proper from his failure to do so?

26P.3 If the representative replies to the judge that the defendant has been so advised, then the case shall proceed. If counsel replies that the defendant has not been so advised, then the judge shall direct the representative to advise his client of the consequences and should adjourn briefly for this purpose, before proceeding further.

If the defendant is not legally represented

26P.4 If the defendant is not represented, the judge shall, at the conclusion of the evidence for the prosecution, in the absence of the jury, indicate what he will say to him in the presence of the jury and ask if he understands and whether he would like a brief adjournment to consider his position.

26P.5 When appropriate, and in the presence of the jury, the judge should say to the defendant:

'You have heard the evidence against you. Now is the time for you to make your defence. You may give evidence on oath, and be cross-examined like any other witness. If you do not give evidence or, having been sworn, without good cause refuse to answer any question, the jury may draw such inferences as appear proper. That means they may hold it against you. You may also call any witness or witnesses whom you have arranged to attend court or lead any agreed evidence. Afterwards you may also, if you wish, address the jury. But you cannot at that stage give evidence. Do you now intend to give evidence?

CPD VI Trial 26Q: Majority Verdicts PD-72

26Q.1 It is very important that all those trying indictable offences should, so far as possible, adopt a uniform practice when complying with section 17 of the Juries Act 1974, both in directing the jury in summing-up and also in receiving the verdict or giving further directions after retirement. So far as the summing-up is concerned, it is inadvisable for the judge, and indeed for advocates, to attempt an explanation of the section for fear that the jury will be confused. Before the jury retires, however, the judge should direct the jury in some such words as the following:

'As you may know, the law permits me, in certain circumstances, to accept a verdict which is not the verdict of you all. Those circumstances have not as yet arisen, so that when you retire I must ask you to reach a verdict upon which each one of you is agreed. Should, however, the time come when it is possible for me to accept a majority verdict, I will give you a further direction.'

26Q.2 Thereafter, the practice should be as follows:

Should the jury return before two hours and ten minutes has elapsed since the last member of the jury left the jury box to go to the jury room (or such longer time as the judge thinks reasonable) (see section 17(4)), they should be asked:

(a) 'Have you reached a verdict upon which you are all agreed? Please answer "Yes" or "No".';

(b) (i) If unanimous, 'What is your verdict?';

(ii) If not unanimous, the jury should be sent out again for further deliberation, with a further direction to arrive if possible at a unanimous verdict.

26Q.3 Should the jury return (whether for the first time or subsequently) or be sent for after the two hours and ten minutes (or the longer period) has elapsed, questions (a) and (b)(i) in the paragraph above should be put to them and, if it appears that they are not unanimous, they should be asked to retire once more and told they should continue to endeavour to reach a unanimous verdict but that, if they cannot, the judge will accept a majority verdict as in section 17(1).

26Q.4 When the jury finally return, they should be asked:

(a) 'Have at least ten (or nine as the case may be) of you agreed on your verdict?';

(b) If 'Yes', 'What is your verdict? Please only answer "Guilty" or "Not Guilty".';

(c) (i) If 'Not Guilty', accept the verdict without more ado;
(ii) If 'Guilty', 'Is that the verdict of you all, or by a majority?';
(d) If 'Guilty' by a majority, 'How many of you agreed to the verdict and how many dissented?'

26Q.5 At whatever stage the jury return, before question (a) is asked, the senior officer of the court present shall state in open court, for each period when the jury was out of court for the purpose of considering their verdict(s), the time at which the last member of the jury left the jury box to go to the jury room and the time of their return to the jury box; and will additionally state in open court the total of such periods.

26Q.6 The reason why section 17(3) is confined to a majority verdict of 'Guilty', and for the somewhat complicated procedure set out above, is to prevent it being known that a verdict of 'Not Guilty' is a majority verdict. If the final direction continues to require the jury to arrive, if possible, at a unanimous verdict and the verdict is received as specified, it will not be known for certain that the acquittal is not unanimous.

26Q.7 Where there are several counts (or alternative verdicts) left to the jury the above practice will, of course, need to be adapted to the circumstances. The procedure will have to be repeated in respect of each count (or alternative verdict), the verdict being accepted in those cases where the jury are unanimous and the further direction being given in cases in which they are not unanimous. The judge may exercise discretion in deciding when to record the unanimous verdict; the circumstances of the case may dictate that it is more desirable to give the majority direction before the recording of any unanimous verdicts. If so, then instead of being asked about each count in turn, the jury should be asked 'Have you reached verdicts upon which you are all agreed in respect of all defendants and/or all counts?'.

26Q.8 Should the jury in the end be unable to agree on a verdict by the required majority, the judge in his discretion will either ask them to deliberate further, or discharge them.

26Q.9 Section 17 will, of course, apply also to verdicts other than 'Guilty' or 'Not Guilty', e.g. to special verdicts under the Criminal Procedure (Insanity) Act 1964, following a finding by the judge that the defendant is unfit to be tried, and special verdicts on findings of fact. Accordingly, in such cases the questions to jurors will have to be suitably adjusted.

Criminal Procedure Rules Part 27 Retrial After Acquittal

General

R-268 When this Part applies

27.1 (1) Rule 27.2 applies where, under section 54 of the Criminal Procedure and Investigations Act 1996, the Crown Court or a magistrates' court can certify for the High Court that interference or intimidation has been involved in proceedings leading to an acquittal.

(2) Rules 27.3 to 27.7 apply where, under section 77 of the Criminal Justice Act 2003, the Court of Appeal can—
(a) quash an acquittal for a serious offence and order a defendant to be retried; or
(b) order that an acquittal outside the United Kingdom is no bar to the defendant being tried in England and Wales,

if there is new and compelling evidence and it is in the interests of justice to make the order.

Application for certificate to allow order for retrial

R-269 Application for certificate

27.2 (1) This rule applies where—
(a) a defendant has been acquitted of an offence;
(b) a person has been convicted of one of the following offences involving interference with or intimidation of a juror or a witness (or potential witness) in any proceedings which led to the defendant's acquittal—
(i) perverting the course of justice,
(ii) intimidation etc. of witnesses, jurors and others under section 51(1) of the Criminal Justice and Public Order Act 1994, or
(iii) aiding, abetting, counselling, procuring, suborning or inciting another person to commit an offence under section 1 of the Perjury Act 1911; and

(c) the prosecutor wants the court by which that person was convicted to certify for the High Court that there is a real possibility that, but for the interference or intimidation, the defendant would not have been acquitted.

(2) The prosecutor must—
(a) apply in writing as soon as practicable after that person's conviction; and
(b) serve the application on—
(i) the court officer, and
(ii) the defendant who was acquitted, if the court so directs.

(3) The application must—
(a) give details, with relevant facts and dates, of—
(i) the conviction for interference or intimidation, and
(ii) the defendant's acquittal; and
(b) explain—
(i) why there is a real possibility that, but for the interference or intimidation, the defendant would not have been acquitted, and
(ii) why it would not be contrary to the interests of justice to prosecute the defendant again for the offence of which he or she was acquitted, despite any lapse of time or other reason.

(4) The court may—
(a) extend the time limit under paragraph (2);
(b) allow an application to be in a different form to one set out in the Practice Direction, or to be made orally;
(c) determine an application under this rule—
(i) at a hearing, in private or in public; or
(ii) without a hearing.

(5) If the court gives a certificate, the court officer must serve it on—
(a) the prosecutor; and
(b) the defendant who was acquitted.

Application to Court of Appeal to quash acquittal and order retrial

Application for reporting restriction pending application for order for retrial R-270

27.3 (1) This rule applies where—
(a) no application has been made under rule 27.4 (Application for order for retrial);
(b) an investigation by officers has begun into an offence with a view to an application under that rule; and
(c) the Director of Public Prosecutions wants the Court of Appeal to make, vary or remove an order for a reporting restriction under section 82 of the Criminal Justice Act 2003 (Restrictions on publication in the interests of justice).

(2) The Director must—
(a) apply in writing;
(b) serve the application on—
(i) the Registrar, and
(ii) the defendant, unless the court otherwise directs.

(3) The application must, as appropriate—
(a) explain why the Director wants the court to direct that it need not be served on the defendant until the application under rule 27.4 is served;
(b) specify the proposed terms of the order, and for how long it should last;
(c) explain why an order in the terms proposed is necessary;
(d) explain why an order should be varied or removed.

Application for order for retrial R-271

27.4 (1) This rule applies where—
(a) a defendant has been acquitted—
(i) in the Crown Court, or on appeal from the Crown Court, of an offence listed in Part 1 of Schedule 5 to the Criminal Justice Act 2003 (qualifying offences),
(ii) in proceedings elsewhere than in the United Kingdom of an offence under the law of that place, if what was alleged would have amounted to or included one of those listed offences;

(b) with the Director of Public Prosecutions' written consent, a prosecutor wants the Court of Appeal to make an order, as the case may be—
   (i) quashing the acquittal in the Crown Court and ordering the defendant to be retried for the offence, or
   (ii) declaring whether the acquittal outside the United Kingdom is a bar to the defendant's trial in England and Wales and, if it is, whether that acquittal shall not be such a bar.

(2) Such a prosecutor must—
(a) apply in writing;
(b) serve the application on the Registrar;
(c) not more than 2 business days later serve on the defendant who was acquitted—
   (i) the application, and
   (ii) a notice charging the defendant with the offence, unless the defendant has already been arrested and charged under section 87 of the Criminal Justice Act 2003 (arrest, under warrant or otherwise, and charge).

(3) The application must—
(a) give details, with relevant facts and dates, of the defendant's acquittal;
(b) explain—
   (i) what new and compelling evidence there is against the defendant, and
   (ii) why in all the circumstances it would be in the interests of justice for the court to make the order sought;
(c) include or attach any application for the following, with reasons—
   (i) an order under section 80(6) of the Criminal Justice Act 2003 (Procedure and evidence) for the production of any document, exhibit or other thing which in the prosecutor's opinion is necessary for the determination of the application,
   (ii) an order under that section for the attendance before the court of any witness who would be a compellable witness at the trial the prosecutor wants the court to order,
   (iii) an order for a reporting restriction under section 82 of the Criminal Justice Act 2003 (Restrictions on publication in the interests of justice); and
(d) attach—
   (i) written witness statements of the evidence on which the prosecutor relies as new and compelling evidence against the defendant,
   (ii) relevant documents from the trial at which the defendant was acquitted, including a record of the offence or offences charged and of the evidence given, and
   (iii) any other document or thing that the prosecutor thinks the court will need to decide the application.

R-272 Respondent's notice

27.5 (1) A defendant on whom a prosecutor serves an application may serve a respondent's notice, and must do so if the defendant wants to make representations to the court.

(2) Such a defendant must serve the respondent's notice on—
(a) the Registrar; and
(b) the prosecutor,

not more than 28 days after service of the application.

(3) The respondent's notice must—
(a) give the date on which the respondent was served with the prosecutor's application;
(b) summarise any relevant facts not contained in that application;
(c) explain the defendant's grounds for opposing that application;
(d) include or attach any application for the following, with reasons—
   (i) an extension of time within which to serve the respondent's notice,
   (ii) bail pending the hearing of the prosecutor's application, if the defendant is in custody,
   (iii) a direction to attend in person any hearing that the defendant could attend by live link, if the defendant is in custody,
   (iv) an order under section 80(6) of the Criminal Justice Act 2003 (Procedure and evidence) for the production of any document, exhibit or other thing which in

the defendant's opinion is necessary for the determination of the prosecutor's application,

(v) an order under that section for the attendance before the court of any witness who would be a compellable witness at the trial the prosecutor wants the court to order; and

(e) attach or identify any other document or thing that the defendant thinks the court will need to decide the application.

Application to Crown Court for summons or warrant R-273

27.6 (1) This rule applies where—

(a) the prosecutor has served on the Registrar an application under rule 27.4 (Application for order for retrial);

(b) the defendant is not in custody as a result of arrest under section 88 of the Criminal Justice Act 2003 (Bail and custody before application); and

(c) the prosecutor wants the Crown Court to issue—

(i) a summons requiring the defendant to appear before the Court of Appeal at the hearing of the prosecutor's application, or

(ii) a warrant for the defendant's arrest

under section 89 of the 2003 Act (Bail and custody before hearing).

(2) The prosecutor must—

(a) apply in writing; and

(b) serve the application on the Crown Court officer.

(3) The application must—

(a) explain what the case is about, including a brief description of the defendant's acquittal, the new evidence and the stage that the application to the Court of Appeal has reached;

(b) specify—

(i) the decision that the prosecutor wants the Crown Court to make,

(ii) each offence charged, and

(iii) any relevant previous bail decision and the reasons given for it;

(c) propose the terms of any suggested condition of bail.

Application of other rules about procedure in the Court of Appeal R-274

27.7 On an application under rule 27.4 (Application for order for retrial)—

(a) the rules in Part 36 (Appeal to the Court of Appeal: general rules) apply with the necessary modifications;

(b) rules 39.8, 39.9 and 39.10 (bail and bail conditions in the Court of Appeal) apply as if the references in those rules to appeal included references to an application under rule 27.4; and

(c) rule 39.14 (Renewal or setting aside of order for retrial) applies as if the reference to section 7 of the Criminal Appeal Act 1968 were a reference to section 84 of the Criminal Justice Act 2003 (Retrial).

Criminal Practice Directions: Sentencing

CPD VII Sentencing A: Pleas of Guilty in the Crown Court PD-73

A.1 Prosecutors and Prosecution Advocates should be familiar with and follow the Attorney-General's Guidelines on the Acceptance of Pleas and the Prosecutor's Role in the Sentencing Exercise.

CPD VII Sentencing B: Determining the Factual Basis of Sentence PD-74

'Where a guilty plea is offered to less than the whole indictment and the prosecution is minded to accept pleas tendered to some counts or to lesser alternative counts.'

B.1 In some cases, defendants wishing to plead guilty will simply plead guilty to all charges on the basis of the facts as alleged and opened by the prosecution, with no dispute as to the factual basis or the extent of offending. Alternatively a defendant may plead guilty to some of the charges brought; in such a case, the judge will consider whether that plea represents a proper plea on the basis of the facts set out by the papers.

B.2 Where the prosecution advocate is considering whether to accept a plea to a lesser charge, the advocate may invite the judge to approve the proposed course of action. In such circumstances, the advocate must abide by the decision of the judge.

B.3 If the prosecution advocate does not invite the judge to approve the acceptance by the prosecution of a lesser charge, it is open to the judge to express his or her dissent with the course proposed and invite the advocate to reconsider the matter with those instructing him or her.

B.4 In any proceedings where the judge is of the opinion that the course proposed by the advocate may lead to serious injustice, the proceedings may be adjourned to allow the following procedure to be followed:

(a) as a preliminary step, the prosecution advocate must discuss the judge's observations with the Chief Crown Prosecutor or the senior prosecutor of the relevant prosecuting authority as appropriate, in an attempt to resolve the issue;
(b) where the issue remains unresolved, the Director of Public Prosecutions or the Director of the relevant prosecuting authority should be consulted;
(c) in extreme circumstances the judge may decline to proceed with the case until the prosecuting authority has consulted with the Attorney General, as may be appropriate.

B.5 Prior to entering a plea of guilty, a defendant may seek an indication of sentence under the procedure set out in *R v Goodyear* [2005] EWCA Crim 888, [2005] 1 WLR 2532, [2005] 2 Cr App R 20; see below.

Where a guilty plea is offered on a limited basis

B.6 A defendant may put forward a plea of guilty without accepting all of the facts as alleged by the prosecution. The basis of plea offered may seek to limit the facts or the extent of the offending for which the defendant is to be sentenced. Depending on the view taken by the prosecution, and the content of the offered basis, the case will fall into one of the following categories:

(a) a plea of guilty upon a basis of plea agreed by the prosecution and defence;
(b) a plea of guilty on a basis signed by the defendant but in respect of which there is no or only partial agreement by the prosecution;
(c) a plea of guilty on a basis that contains within it matters that are purely mitigation and which do not amount to a contradiction of the prosecution case; or
(d) in cases involving serious or complex fraud, a plea of guilty upon a basis of plea agreed by the prosecution and defence accompanied by joint submissions as to sentence.

(a) A plea of guilty upon a basis of plea agreed by the prosecution and defence

B.7 The prosecution may reach an agreement with the defendant as to the factual basis on which the defendant will plead guilty, often known as an 'agreed basis of plea'. It is always subject to the approval of the court, which will consider whether it adequately and appropriately reflects the evidence as disclosed on the papers, whether it is fair and whether it is in the interests of justice.

B.8 *R v Underwood* [2004] EWCA Crim 2256, [2005] 1 Cr App R 13, [2005] 1 Cr App R (S) 90 outlines the principles to be applied where the defendant admits that he or she is guilty, but disputes the basis of offending alleged by the prosecution:

(a) The prosecution may accept and agree the defendant's account of the disputed facts or reject it in its entirety, or in part. If the prosecution accepts the defendant's basis of plea, it must ensure that the basis of plea is factually accurate and enables the sentencing judge to impose a sentence appropriate to reflect the justice of the case;
(b) In resolving any disputed factual matters, the prosecution must consider its primary duty to the court and must not agree with or acquiesce in an agreement which contains material factual disputes;
(c) If the prosecution does accept the defendant's basis of plea, it must be reduced to writing, be signed by advocates for both sides, and made available to the judge prior to the prosecution's opening;
(d) An agreed basis of plea that has been reached between the parties should not contain matters which are in dispute and any aspects upon which there is not agreement should be clearly identified;
(e) On occasion, the prosecution may lack the evidence positively to dispute the defendant's account, for example, where the defendant asserts a matter outside the knowledge of the

prosecution. Simply because the prosecution does not have evidence to contradict the defendant's assertions does not mean those assertions should be agreed. In such a case, the prosecution should test the defendant's evidence and submissions by requesting a *Newton* hearing (*R v Newton* (1982) 77 Cr App R 13, (1982) 4 Cr App R (S) 388), following the procedure set out below;

(f) If it is not possible for the parties to resolve a factual dispute when attempting to reach a plea agreement under this part, it is the responsibility of the prosecution to consider whether the matter should proceed to trial, or to invite the court to hold a *Newton* hearing as necessary.

B.9 *R v Underwood* emphasises that, whether or not pleas have been 'agreed', the judge is not bound by any such agreement and is entitled of his or her own motion to insist that any evidence relevant to the facts in dispute (or upon which the judge requires further evidence for whatever reason) should be called. Any view formed by the prosecution on a proposed basis of plea is deemed to be conditional on the judge's acceptance of the basis of plea.

B.10 A judge is not entitled to reject a defendant's basis of plea absent a *Newton* hearing unless it is determined by the court that the basis is manifestly false and as such does not merit examination by way of the calling of evidence or alternatively the defendant declines the opportunity to engage in the process of the *Newton* hearing whether by giving evidence on his own behalf or otherwise.

(b) A plea of guilty on a basis signed by the defendant but in respect of which there is no or only partial agreement by the prosecution

B.11 Where the defendant pleads guilty, but disputes the basis of offending alleged by the prosecution and agreement as to that has not been reached, the following procedure should be followed:

(a) The defendant's basis of plea must be set out in writing, identifying what is in dispute and must be signed by the defendant;

(b) The prosecution must respond in writing setting out their alternative contentions and indicating whether or not they submit that a *Newton* hearing is necessary;

(c) The court may invite the parties to make representations about whether the dispute is material to sentence; and

(d) If the court decides that it is a material dispute, the court will invite such further representations or evidence as it may require and resolve the dispute in accordance with the principles set out in *R v Newton*.

B.12 Where the disputed issue arises from facts which are within the exclusive knowledge of the defendant and the defendant is willing to give evidence in support of his case, the defence advocate should be prepared to call the defendant. If the defendant is not willing to testify, and subject to any explanation which may be given, the judge may draw such inferences as appear appropriate.

B.13 The decision whether or not a *Newton* hearing is required is one for the judge. Once the decision has been taken that there will be a *Newton* hearing, evidence is called by the parties in the usual way and the criminal burden and standard of proof applies. Whatever view has been taken by the prosecution, the prosecutor should not leave the questioning to the judge, but should assist the court by exploring the issues which the court wishes to have explored. The rules of evidence should be followed as during a trial, and the judge should direct himself appropriately as the tribunal of fact. Paragraphs 6 to 10 of *Underwood* provide additional guidance regarding the *Newton* hearing procedure.

(c) A plea of guilty on a basis that contains within it matters that are purely mitigation and which do not amount to a contradiction of the prosecution case

B.14 A basis of plea should not normally set out matters of mitigation but there may be circumstances where it is convenient and sensible for the document outlining a basis to deal with facts closely aligned to the circumstances of the offending which amount to mitigation and which may need to be resolved prior to sentence. The resolution of these matters does not amount to a *Newton* hearing properly so defined and in so far as facts fall to be established the defence will have to discharge the civil burden in order to do so. The scope of the evidence required to resolve issues that are purely matters of mitigation is for the court to determine.

(d) Cases involving serious fraud — a plea of guilty upon a basis of plea agreed by the prosecution and defence accompanied by joint submissions as to sentence

B.15 This section applies when the prosecution and the defendant(s) to a matter before the Crown Court involving allegations of serious or complex fraud have agreed a basis of plea and seek to make submissions to the court regarding sentence.

B.16 Guidance for prosecutors regarding the operation of this procedure is set out in the 'Attorney General's Guidelines on Plea Discussions in Cases of Serious or Complex Fraud', which came into force on 5 May 2009 and is referred to in this direction as the 'Attorney General's Plea Discussion Guidelines'.

B.17 In this part—

(a) 'a plea agreement' means a written basis of plea agreed between the prosecution and defendant(s) in accordance with the principles set out in *R v Underwood*, supported by admissible documentary evidence or admissions under section 10 of the Criminal Justice Act 1967;

(b) 'a sentencing submission' means sentencing submissions made jointly by the prosecution and defence as to the appropriate sentencing authorities and applicable sentencing range in the relevant sentencing guideline relating to the plea agreement;

(c) 'serious or complex fraud' includes, but is not limited to, allegations of fraud where two or more of the following are present:

(i) the amount obtained or intended to be obtained exceeded £500,000;
(ii) there is a significant international dimension;
(iii) the case requires specialised knowledge of financial, commercial, fiscal or regulatory matters such as the operation of markets, banking systems, trusts or tax regimes;
(iv) the case involves allegations of fraudulent activity against numerous victims;
(v) the case involves an allegation of substantial and significant fraud on a public body;
(vi) the case is likely to be of widespread public concern;
(vii) the alleged misconduct endangered the economic well-being of the United Kingdom, for example by undermining confidence in financial markets.

Procedure

B.18 The procedure regarding agreed bases of plea outlined above, applies with equal rigour to the acceptance of pleas under this procedure. However, because under this procedure the parties will have been discussing the plea agreement and the charges from a much earlier stage, it is vital that the judge is fully informed of all relevant background to the discussions, charges and the eventual basis of plea.

B.19 Where the defendant has not yet appeared before the Crown Court, the prosecutor must send full details of the plea agreement and sentencing submission(s) to the court, at least 7 days in advance of the defendant's first appearance. Where the defendant has already appeared before the Crown Court, the prosecutor must notify the court as soon as is reasonably practicable that a plea agreement and sentencing submissions under the Attorney General's Plea Discussion Guidelines are to be submitted. The court should set a date for the matter to be heard, and the prosecutor must send full details of the plea agreement and sentencing submission(s) to the court as soon as practicable, or in accordance with the directions of the court.

B.20 The provision to the judge of full details of the plea agreement requires sufficient information to be provided to allow the judge to understand the facts of the case and the history of the plea discussions, to assess whether the plea agreement is fair and in the interests of justice, and to decide the appropriate sentence. This will include, but is not limited to:

(i) the plea agreement;
(ii) the sentencing submission(s);
(iii) all of the material provided by the prosecution to the defendant in the course of the plea discussions;
(iv) relevant material provided by the defendant, for example documents relating to personal mitigation; and
(v) the minutes of any meetings between the parties and any correspondence generated in the plea discussions.

The parties should be prepared to provide additional material at the request of the court.

B.21 The court should at all times have regard to the length of time that has elapsed since the date of the occurrence of the events giving rise to the plea discussions, the time taken to interview the defendant, the date of charge and the prospective trial date (if the matter were to proceed to trial) so as to ensure that its consideration of the plea agreement and sentencing submissions does not cause any unnecessary further delay.

Status of plea agreement and joint sentencing submissions

B.22 Where a plea agreement and joint sentencing submissions are submitted, it remains entirely a matter for the court to decide how to deal with the case. The judge retains the absolute discretion to refuse to accept the plea agreement and to sentence otherwise than in accordance with the sentencing submissions made under the Attorney General's Plea Discussion Guidelines.

B.23 Sentencing submissions should draw the court's attention to any applicable range in any relevant guideline, and to any ancillary orders that may be applicable. Sentencing submissions should not include a specific sentence or agreed range other than the ranges set out in sentencing guidelines or authorities.

B.24 Prior to pleading guilty in accordance with the plea agreement, the defendant(s) may apply to the court for an indication of the likely maximum sentence under the procedure set out below (a '*Goodyear* indication').

B.25 In the event that the judge indicates a sentence or passes a sentence which is not within the submissions made on sentencing, the plea agreement remains binding.

B.26 If the defendant does not plead guilty in accordance with the plea agreement, or if a defendant who has pleaded guilty in accordance with a plea agreement, successfully applies to withdraw his plea under CrimPR 25.5, the signed plea agreement may be treated as confession evidence, and may be used against the defendant at a later stage in these or any other proceedings. Any credit for a timely guilty plea may be lost. The court may exercise its discretion under section 78 of the Police and Criminal Evidence Act 1984 to exclude any such evidence if it appears to the court that, having regard to all the circumstances, including the circumstances in which the evidence was obtained, the admission of the evidence would have such an adverse effect on the fairness of the proceedings that the court ought not to admit it.

B.27 Where a defendant has failed to plead guilty in accordance with a plea agreement, the case is unlikely to be ready for trial immediately. The prosecution may have been commenced earlier than it otherwise would have been, in reliance upon the defendant's agreement to plead guilty. This is likely to be a relevant consideration for the court in deciding whether or not to grant an application to adjourn or stay the proceedings to allow the matter to be prepared for trial in accordance with the protocol on the 'Control and Management of Heavy Fraud and other Complex Criminal Cases', or as required.

CPD VII Sentencing C: Indications of Sentence: *R v Goodyear* PD-75

C.1 Prior to pleading guilty, it is open to a defendant in the Crown Court to request from the judge an indication of the maximum sentence that would be imposed if a guilty plea were to be tendered at that stage in the proceedings, in accordance with the guidance in *R v Goodyear* [2005] EWCA Crim 888, [2005] 1 WLR 2532, [2005] 2 Cr App R 20. The defence should notify the court and the prosecution of the intention to seek an indication in advance of any hearing.

C.2 Attention is drawn to the guidance set out in paragraphs 53 and following of *R v Goodyear*. The objective of the *Goodyear* guidelines is to safeguard against the creation or appearance of judicial pressure on a defendant. Any advance indication given should be the maximum sentence if a guilty plea were to be tendered at that stage of the proceedings only; the judge should not indicate the maximum possible sentence following conviction by a jury after trial. The judge should only give a *Goodyear* indication if one is requested by the defendant, although the judge can, in an appropriate case, remind the defence advocate of the defendant's entitlement to seek an advance indication of sentence.

C.3 Whether to give a *Goodyear* indication, and whether to give reasons for a refusal, is a matter for the discretion of the judge, to be exercised in accordance with the principles outlined by the Court of Appeal in that case. Such indications should normally not be given if there is a dispute as to the basis of plea unless the judge concludes that he or she can properly deal with the case without the need for a *Newton* hearing. If there is a basis of plea agreed by the prosecution and defence, it must be reduced into writing and a copy provided to the judge. As always, any basis of plea will be subject to the approval of the court. In cases where a dispute arises, the procedure in *R v Underwood* should be followed prior to the court considering a sentence indication further, as set out above. The judge should not become involved in negotiations about the acceptance of pleas or any agreed basis of plea, nor should a request be made for an indication of the different sentences that might be imposed if various different pleas were to be offered.

C.4 There should be no prosecution opening nor should the judge hear mitigation. However, during the sentence indication process the prosecution advocate is expected to assist the court by ensuring that the court has received all of the prosecution evidence, any statement from the victim about the impact of the offence, and any relevant previous convictions. Further, where appropriate, the prosecution should provide references to the relevant statutory powers of the court, relevant sentencing guidelines and authorities, and such other assistance as the court requires.

C.5 Attention is drawn to paragraph 70(d) of *Goodyear* which emphasises that the prosecution 'should not say anything which may create the impression that the sentence indication has the support or approval of the Crown.' This prohibition against the Crown indicating its approval of a particular sentence applies in all circumstances when a defendant is being sentenced, including when joint sentencing submissions are made.

C.6 An indication, once given, is, save in exceptional circumstances (such as arose in *R v Newman* [2010] EWCA Crim 1566, [2011] 1 Cr App R (S) 68), binding on the judge who gave it, and any other judge, subject to overriding statutory obligations such as those following a finding of 'dangerousness'. In circumstances where a judge proposes to depart from a *Goodyear* indication this must only be done in a way that does not give rise to unfairness (see *Newman*). However, if the defendant does not plead guilty, the indication will not thereafter bind the court.

C.7 If the offence is a specified offence such that the defendant might be liable to an assessment of 'dangerousness' in accordance with the Criminal Justice Act 2003 it is unlikely that the necessary material for such an assessment will be available. The court can still proceed to give an indication of sentence, but should state clearly the limitations of the indication that can be given.

C.8 A *Goodyear* indication should be given in open court in the presence of the defendant but any reference to the hearing is not admissible in any subsequent trial; and reporting restrictions should normally be imposed.

PD-76 **CPD VII Sentencing D: Facts to be Stated on Pleas of Guilty**

D.1 To enable the press and the public to know the circumstances of an offence of which an accused has been convicted and for which he is to be sentenced, in relation to each offence to which an accused has pleaded guilty the prosecution shall state those facts in open court, before sentence is imposed.

PD-77 **CPD VII Sentencing E: Concurrent and Consecutive Sentences**

E.1 Where a court passes on a defendant more than one term of imprisonment, the court should state in the presence of the defendant whether the terms are to be concurrent or consecutive. Should this not be done, the court clerk should ask the court, before the defendant leaves court, to do so.

E.2 If a defendant is, at the time of sentence, already serving two or more consecutive terms of imprisonment and the court intends to increase the total period of imprisonment, it should use the expression 'consecutive to the total period of imprisonment to which you are already subject' rather than 'at the expiration of the term of imprisonment you are now serving', as the defendant may not then be serving the last of the terms to which he is already subject.

E.3 The Sentencing Council has issued a definitive guideline on Totality which should be consulted. Under section 125(1) of the Coroners and Justice Act 2009, for offences committed after 6 April 2010, the guideline must be followed unless it would be contrary to the interests of justice to do so.

PD-78 **CPD VII Sentencing F: Victim Personal Statements**

F.1 Victims of crime are invited to make a statement, known as a Victim Personal Statement ('VPS'). The statement gives victims a formal opportunity to say how a crime has affected them. It may help to identify whether they have a particular need for information, support and protection. The court will take the statement into account when determining sentence. In some circumstances, it may be appropriate for relatives of a victim to make a VPS, for example where the victim has died as a result of the relevant criminal conduct. The revised Code of Practice for Victims of Crime, published on 29 October 2013 gives further information about victims' entitlements within the criminal justice system, and the duties placed on criminal justice agencies when dealing with victims of crime.

F.2 When a police officer takes a statement from a victim, the victim should be told about the scheme and given the chance to make a VPS. The decision about whether or not to make a VPS is entirely a matter for the victim; no pressure should be brought to bear on their decision, and no conclusion should be drawn if they choose not to make such a statement. A VPS or a further VPS may be made (in proper s.9 form, see below) at any time prior to the disposal of the case. It will not normally be appropriate for a VPS to be made after the disposal of the case; there may be rare occasions between sentence and appeal when a further VPS may be necessary, for example, when the victim was injured and the final prognosis was not available at the date of sentence. However, VPS after disposal should be confined to presenting up to date factual material, such as medical information, and should be used sparingly.

F.3 If the court is presented with a VPS the following approach, subject to the further guidance given by the Court of Appeal in *R v Perkins; Bennett; Hall* [2013] EWCA Crim 323, [2013] Crim LR 533, should be adopted:

a) The VPS and any evidence in support should be considered and taken into account by the court, prior to passing sentence.
b) Evidence of the effects of an offence on the victim contained in the VPS or other statement, must be in proper form, that is a witness statement made under section 9 of the Criminal Justice Act 1967 or an expert's report; and served in good time upon the defendant's solicitor or the defendant, if he or she is not represented. Except where inferences can properly be drawn from the nature of or circumstances surrounding the offence, a sentencing court must not make assumptions unsupported by evidence about the effects of an offence on the victim. The maker of a VPS may be cross-examined on its content.
c) At the discretion of the court, the VPS may also be read aloud or played in open court, in whole or in part, or it may be summarised. If the VPS is to be read aloud, the court should also determine who should do so. In making these decisions, the court should take account of the victim's preferences, and follow them unless there is good reason not to do so; examples of this include the inadmissibility of the content or the potentially harmful consequences for the victim or others. Court hearings should not be adjourned solely to allow the victim to attend court to read the VPS. For the purposes of CPD I General matters 5B: Access to information held by the court, a VPS that is read aloud or played in open court in whole or in part should be considered as such, and no longer treated as a confidential document.
d) In all cases it will be appropriate for a VPS to be referred to in the course of the sentencing hearing and/or in the sentencing remarks.
e) The court must pass what it judges to be the appropriate sentence having regard to the circumstances of the offence and of the offender, taking into account, so far as the court considers it appropriate, the impact on the victim. The opinions of the victim or the victim's close relatives as to what the sentence should be are therefore not relevant, unlike the consequences of the offence on them. Victims should be advised of this. If, despite the advice, opinions as to sentence are included in the statement, the court should pay no attention to them.

CPD VII Sentencing G: Families Bereaved by Homicide and other Criminal Conduct PD-79

G.1 In cases in which the victim has died as a result of the relevant criminal conduct, the victim's family is not a party to the proceedings, but does have an interest in the case. Bereaved families have particular entitlements under the Code of Practice for Victims of Crime. All parties should have regard to the needs of the victim's family and ensure that the trial process does not expose bereaved families to avoidable intimidation, humiliation or distress.

G.2 In so far as it is compatible with family members' roles as witnesses, the court should consider the following measures:

a) Practical arrangements being discussed with the family and made in good time before the trial, such as seating for family members in the courtroom; if appropriate, in an alternative area, away from the public gallery;
b) Warning being given to families if the evidence on a certain day is expected to be particularly distressing;
c) Ensuring that appropriate use is made of the scheme for Victim Personal Statements, in accordance with the paragraphs above.

G.3 The sentencer should consider providing a written copy of the sentencing remarks to the family after sentence has been passed. Sentencers should tend in favour of providing such a copy, unless there is good reason not to do so, and the copy should be provided as soon as is reasonably practicable after the sentencing hearing.

PD-80 **CPD VII Sentencing H: Community Impact Statements**

H.1 A community impact statement may be prepared by the police to make the court aware of particular crime trends in the local area and the impact of these on the local community.

H.2 Such statements must be in proper form, that is a witness statement made under section 9 of the Criminal Justice Act 1967 or an expert's report; and served in good time upon the defendant's solicitor or the defendant, if he is not represented.

H.3 The community impact statement and any evidence in support should be considered and taken into account by the court, prior to passing sentence. The statement should be referred to in the course of the sentencing hearing and/or in the sentencing remarks. Subject to the court's discretion, the contents of the statement may be summarised or read out in open court.

H.4 The court must pass what it judges to be the appropriate sentence having regard to the circumstances of the offence and of the offender, taking into account, so far as the court considers it appropriate, the impact on the local community. Opinions as to what the sentence should be are therefore not relevant. If, despite the advice, opinions as to sentence are included in the statement, the court should pay no attention to them.

H.5 Except where inferences can properly be drawn from the nature of or circumstances surrounding the offence, a sentencing court must not make assumptions unsupported by evidence about the effects of an offence on the local community.

H.6 It will not be appropriate for a Community Impact Statement to be made after disposal of the case but before an appeal.

PD-81 **CPD VII Sentencing I: Impact Statements for Businesses**

I.1 Individual victims of crime are invited to make a statement, known as a Victim Personal Statement ('VPS'), see CPD VII Sentencing F. If a victim, or one of those others affected by a crime, is a business, enterprise or other body (including a charity or public body, for example a school or hospital), of any size, a nominated representative may make an Impact Statement for Business ('ISB'). The ISB gives a formal opportunity for the court to be informed how a crime has affected a business or other body. The court will take the statement into account when determining sentence. This does not prevent individual employees from making a VPS about the impact of the same crime on them as individuals. Indeed, the ISB should be about the impact on the business or other body exclusively, and the impact on any individual included within a VPS.

I.2 When a police officer takes statements about the alleged offence, he or she should also inform the business or other body about the scheme. An ISB may be made to the police at that time, or the ISB template may be downloaded from www.police.uk, completed and emailed or posted to the relevant police contact. Guidance on how to complete the form is available on www.police.uk and on the CPS website. There is no obligation to make an ISB.

I.3 An ISB or an updated ISB may be made (in proper s.9 form, see below) at any time prior to the disposal of the case. It will not be appropriate for an ISB to be made after disposal of the case but before an appeal.

I.4 A business or other body wishing to make an ISB should consider carefully who to nominate as the representative to make the statement on its behalf. A person making an ISB on behalf of such a business or body, the nominated representative, must be authorised to do so on its behalf, either by nature of their position, such as a director or owner or a senior official, or by having been suitably authorised, such as by the owner or Board of Directors or governing body. The nominated representative must also be in a position to give admissible evidence about the impact of the crime on the business or body. This will usually be through first hand personal knowledge, or using business documents (as defined in section 117 of the Criminal Justice Act 2003). The most appropriate person will vary depending on the nature of the crime, and the size and structure of the business or other body and may for example include a manager, director, chief executive or shop owner.

I.5 If the nominated representative leaves the business before the case comes to court, he or she will usually remain the representative, as the ISB made by him or her will still provide the best evidence of the impact of the crime, and he or she could still be asked to attend court. Nominated representatives should be made aware of the on-going nature of the role at the time of making the ISB.

I.6 If necessary a further ISB may be provided to the police if there is a change in circumstances. This could be made by an alternative nominated representative. However, the new ISB will usually supplement, not replace, the original ISB and again must contain admissible evidence. The prosecutor will decide which ISB to serve on the defence as evidence, and any ISB that is not served in evidence will be included in the unused material and considered for disclosure to the defence.

I.7 The ISB must be made in proper form, that is as a witness statement made under section 9 of the Criminal Justice Act 1967 or an expert's report; and served in good time upon the defendant's solicitor or the defendant, if he or she is not represented. The maker of an ISB can be cross-examined on its content.

I.8 The ISB and any evidence in support should be considered and taken into account by the court, prior to passing sentence. The statement should be referred to in the course of the sentencing hearing and/or in the sentencing remarks. Subject to the court's discretion, the contents of the statement may be summarised or read out in open court; the views of the business or body should be taken into account in reaching a decision.

I.9 The court must pass what it judges to be the appropriate sentence having regard to the circumstances of the offence and of the offender, taking into account, so far as the court considers it appropriate, the impact on the victims and others affected, including any business or other corporate victim. Opinions as to what the sentence should be are therefore not relevant. If, despite the advice, opinions as to sentence are included in the statement, the court should pay no attention to them.

I.10 Except where inferences can properly be drawn from the nature of or circumstances surrounding the offence, a sentencing court must not make assumptions unsupported by evidence about the effects of an offence on a business or other body.

CPD VII Sentencing J: Binding Over Orders and Conditional Discharges PD-82

J.1 This direction takes into account the judgments of the European Court of Human Rights in *Steel v United Kingdom* (1999) 28 EHRR 603, [1998] Crim LR 893 and in *Hashman and Harrup v United Kingdom* (2000) 30 EHRR 241, [2000] Crim LR 185. Its purpose is to give practical guidance, in the light of those two judgments, on the practice of imposing binding over orders. The direction applies to orders made under the court's common law powers, under the Justices of the Peace Act 1361, under section 1(7) of the Justices of the Peace Act 1968 and under section 115 of the Magistrates' Courts Act 1980. This direction also gives guidance concerning the court's power to bind over parents or guardians under section 150 of the Powers of Criminal Courts (Sentencing) Act 2000 and the Crown Court's power to bind over to come up for judgment. The court's power to impose a conditional discharge under section 12 of the Powers of Criminal Courts (Sentencing) Act 2000 is also covered by this direction.

Binding over to keep the peace

J.2 Before imposing a binding over order, the court must be satisfied so that it is sure that a breach of the peace involving violence, or an imminent threat of violence, has occurred or that there is a real risk of violence in the future. Such violence may be perpetrated by the individual who will be subject to the order or by a third party as a natural consequence of the individual's conduct.

J.3 In light of the judgment in *Hashman*, courts should no longer bind an individual over 'to be of good behaviour'. Rather than binding an individual over to 'keep the peace' in general terms, the court should identify the specific conduct or activity from which the individual must refrain.

Written order

J.4 When making an order binding an individual over to refrain from specified types of conduct or activities, the details of that conduct or those activities should be specified by the court in a written order, served on all relevant parties. The court should state its reasons for the making of the order, its length and the amount of the recognisance. The length of the order should be proportionate to the harm sought to be avoided and should not generally exceed 12 months.

Evidence

J.5 Sections 51 to 57 of the Magistrates' Courts Act 1980 set out the jurisdiction of the magistrates' court to hear an application made on complaint and the procedure which is to be followed. This includes a requirement under section 53 to hear evidence and the parties, before making any order. This practice should be applied to all cases in the magistrates' court and the Crown Court where the court is considering imposing a binding over order. The court should give the individual who would be subject to the order and the prosecutor the opportunity to make representations, both as to the making of the order and as to its terms. The court should also hear any admissible evidence the parties wish to call and which has not already been heard in the proceedings. Particularly careful consideration may be required where the individual who would be subject to the order is a witness in the proceedings.

J.6 Where there is an admission which is sufficient to found the making of a binding over order and/or the individual consents to the making of the order, the court should nevertheless hear sufficient representations and, if appropriate, evidence, to satisfy itself that an order is appropriate in all the circumstances and to be clear about the terms of the order.

J.7 Where there is an allegation of breach of a binding over order and this is contested, the court should hear representations and evidence, including oral evidence, from the parties before making a finding. If unrepresented and no opportunity has been given previously the court should give a reasonable period for the person said to have breached the binding over order to find representation.

Burden and standard of proof

J.8 The court should be satisfied so that it is sure of the matters complained of before a binding over order may be imposed. Where the procedure has been commenced on complaint, the burden of proof rests on the complainant. In all other circumstances, the burden of proof rests upon the prosecution.

J.9 Where there is an allegation of breach of a binding over order, the court should be satisfied on the balance of probabilities that the defendant is in breach before making any order for forfeiture of a recognisance. The burden of proof shall rest on the prosecution.

Recognisance

J.10 The court must be satisfied on the merits of the case that an order for binding over is appropriate and should announce that decision before considering the amount of the recognisance. If unrepresented, the individual who is made subject to the binding over order should be told he has a right of appeal from the decision.

J.11 When fixing the amount of recognisance, courts should have regard to the individual's financial resources and should hear representations from the individual or his legal representatives regarding finances.

J.12 A recognisance is made in the form of a bond giving rise to a civil debt on breach of the order.

Refusal to enter into a recognisance

J.13 If there is any possibility that an individual will refuse to enter a recognisance, the court should consider whether there are any appropriate alternatives to a binding over order (for example, continuing with a prosecution). Where there are no appropriate alternatives and the individual continues to refuse to enter into the recognisance, the court may commit the individual to custody. In the magistrates' court, the power to do so will derive from section 1(7) of the Justices of the Peace Act 1968 or, more rarely, from section 115(3) of the Magistrates' Courts Act 1980, and the court should state which power it is acting under; in the Crown Court, this is a common law power.

J.14 Before the court exercises a power to commit the individual to custody, the individual should be given the opportunity to see a duty solicitor or another legal representative and be represented in proceedings if the individual so wishes. Public funding should generally be granted to cover representation. In the Crown Court this rests with the Judge who may grant a Representation Order.

J.15 In the event that the individual does not take the opportunity to seek legal advice, the court shall give the individual a final opportunity to comply with the request and shall explain the consequences of a failure to do so.

Antecedents

J.16 Courts are reminded of the provisions of section 7(5) of the Rehabilitation of Offenders Act 1974 which excludes from a person's antecedents any order of the court 'with respect to any person otherwise than on a conviction'.

Binding over to come up for judgment

J.17 If the Crown Court is considering binding over an individual to come up for judgment, the court should specify any conditions with which the individual is to comply in the meantime and not specify that the individual is to be of good behaviour.

J.18 The Crown Court should, if the individual is unrepresented, explain the consequences of a breach of the binding over order in these circumstances.

Binding over of parent or guardian

J.19 Where a court is considering binding over a parent or guardian under section 150 of the Powers of Criminal Courts (Sentencing) Act 2000 to enter into a recognisance to take proper care of and exercise proper control over a child or young person, the court should specify the actions which the parent or guardian is to take.

Security for good behaviour

J.20 Where a court is imposing a conditional discharge under section 12 of the Powers of Criminal Courts (Sentencing) Act 2000, it has the power, under section 12(6) to make an order that a person who consents to do so give security for the good behaviour of the offender. When making such an order, the court should specify the type of conduct from which the offender is to refrain.

CPD VII Sentencing K: Committal for Sentence PD-83

K.1 CrimPR 28.10 applies when a case is committed to the Crown Court for sentence and specifies the information and documentation that must be provided by the magistrates' court. On a committal for sentence any reasons given by the magistrates for their decision should be included with the documents. All of these documents should be made available to the judge in the Crown Court if the judge requires them, in order to decide before the hearing questions of listing or representation or the like. They will also be available to the court during the hearing if it becomes necessary or desirable for the court to see what happened in the lower court.

CPD VII Sentencing L: Imposition of Life Sentences PD-84

L.1 Section 82A of the Powers of Criminal Courts (Sentencing) Act 2000 empowers a judge when passing a sentence of life imprisonment, where such a sentence is not fixed by law, to specify by order such part of the sentence ('the relevant part') as shall be served before the prisoner may require the Secretary of State to refer his case to the Parole Board. This is applicable to defendants under the age of 18 years as well as to adult defendants.

L.2 Thus the life sentence falls into two parts:

(a) the relevant part, which consists of the period of detention imposed for punishment and deterrence, taking into account the seriousness of the offence; and

(b) the remaining part of the sentence, during which the prisoner's detention will be governed by consideration of risk to the public.

L.3 The judge is not obliged by statute to make use of the provisions of section 82A when passing a life sentence. However, the judge should do so, save in the very exceptional case where the judge considers that the offence is so serious that detention for life is justified by the seriousness of the offence alone, irrespective of the risk to the public. In such a case, the judge should state this in open court when passing sentence.

L.4 In cases where the judge is to specify the relevant part of the sentence under section 82A, the judge should permit the advocate for the defendant to address the court as to the appropriate length of the relevant part. Where no relevant part is to be specified, the advocate for the defendant should be permitted to address the court as to the appropriateness of this course of action.

L.5 In specifying the relevant part of the sentence, the judge should have regard to the specific terms of section 82A and should indicate the reasons for reaching his decision as to the length of the relevant part.

CPD VII Sentencing M: Mandatory Life Sentences PD-85

M.1 The purpose of this section is to give practical guidance as to the procedure for passing a mandatory life sentence under section 269 and schedule 21 of the Criminal Justice Act 2003 ('the Act'). This direction also gives guidance as to the transitional arrangements under section 276 and schedule 22 of the Act. It clarifies the correct approach to looking at the practice of the Secretary of State prior to December 2002 for the purposes of schedule 22 of the Act, in the light of the judgment in *R v Sullivan, Gibbs, Elener and Elener* [2004] EWCA Crim 1762, [2005] 1 Cr App R 3, [2005] 1 Cr App R (S) 67.

M.2 Section 269 came into force on 18 December 2003. Under section 269, all courts passing a mandatory life sentence must either announce in open court the minimum term the prisoner must serve before the Parole Board can consider release on licence under the provisions of section 28 of the Crime (Sentences) Act 1997 (as amended by section 275 of the Act), or announce that the seriousness of the offence is so exceptionally high that the early release provisions should not apply at all (a 'whole life order').

M.3 In setting the minimum term, the court must set the term it considers appropriate taking into account the seriousness of the offence. In considering the seriousness of the offence, the court must have regard to the general principles set out in Schedule 21 of the Act as amended and any guidelines relating to offences in general which are relevant to the case and not incompatible with the provisions of Schedule 21. Although it is necessary to have regard to such guidance, it is always permissible not to apply the guidance if a judge considers there are reasons for not following it. It is always necessary to have regard to the need to do justice in the particular case. However, if a court departs from any of the starting points given in Schedule 21, the court is under a duty to state its reasons for doing so (section 270(2)(b) of the Act).

M.4 Schedule 21 states that the first step is to choose one of five starting points: 'whole life', 30 years, 25 years, 15 years or 12 years. Where the 15 year starting point has been chosen, judges should have in mind that this starting point encompasses a very broad range of murders. At paragraph 35 of *Sullivan*, the court found it should not be assumed that Parliament intended to raise all minimum terms that would previously have had a lower starting point, to 15 years.

M.5 Where the offender was 21 or over at the time of the offence, and the court takes the view that the murder is so grave that the offender ought to spend the rest of his life in prison, the appropriate starting point is a 'whole life order' (paragraph 4(1) of Schedule 21). The effect of such an order is that the early release provisions in section 28 of the Crime (Sentences) Act 1997 will not apply. Such an order should only be specified where the court considers that the seriousness of the offence (or the combination of the offence and one or more other offences associated with it) is exceptionally high. Paragraph 4(2) sets out examples of cases where it would normally be appropriate to take the 'whole life order' as the appropriate starting point.

M.6 Where the offender is aged 18 to 20 and commits a murder that is so serious that it would require a whole life order if committed by an offender aged 21 or over, the appropriate starting point will be 30 years. (Paragraph 5(2)(h) of Schedule 21).

M.7 Where a case is not so serious as to require a 'whole life order' but where the seriousness of the offence is particularly high and the offender was aged 18 or over when he committed the offence, the appropriate starting point is 30 years (paragraph 5(1) of Schedule 21). Paragraph 5(2) sets out examples of cases where a 30 year starting point would normally be appropriate (if they do not require a 'whole life order').

M.8 Where the offender was aged 18 or over when he committed the offence, took a knife or other weapon to the scene intending to commit any offence or have it available to use as a weapon, and used it in committing the murder, the offence is normally to be regarded as sufficiently serious for an appropriate starting point of 25 years (paragraph 5A of Schedule 21).

M.9 Where the offender was aged 18 or over when he committed the offence and the case does not fall within paragraph 4(1), 5(1) or 5A(1) of Schedule 21, the appropriate starting point is 15 years (see paragraph 6).

M.10 18 to 20 year olds are only the subject of the 30-year, 25-year and 15-year starting points.

M.11 The appropriate starting point when setting a sentence of detention during Her Majesty's pleasure for offenders aged under 18 when they committed the offence is always 12 years (paragraph 7 of Schedule 21).

M.12 The second step after choosing a starting point is to take account of any aggravating or mitigating factors which would justify a departure from the starting point. Additional aggravating factors (other than those specified in paragraphs 4(2), 5(2) and 5A) are listed at paragraph 10 of Schedule 21. Examples of mitigating factors are listed at paragraph 11 of Schedule 21. Taking into account the aggravating and mitigating features, the court may add to or subtract from the starting point to arrive at the appropriate punitive period.

M.13 The third step is that the court should consider the effect of section 143(2) of the Act in relation to previous convictions; section 143(3) of the Act where the offence was committed whilst the offender was on bail; and section 144 of the Act where the offender has pleaded guilty (paragraph 12 of Schedule 21). The court should then take into account what credit the offender would have received for a remand in custody under section 240 or 240ZA of the Act and/or for a remand on bail subject to a qualifying curfew condition under section 240A, but for the fact that the mandatory sentence is one of life imprisonment. Where the offender has been thus remanded in connection with the offence or a related offence, the court should have in mind that no credit will otherwise be given for this time when the prisoner is considered for early release. The appropriate time to take it into account is when setting the minimum term. The court should make any appropriate subtraction from the punitive period it would otherwise impose, in order to reach the minimum term.

M.14 Following these calculations, the court should have arrived at the appropriate minimum term to be announced in open court. As paragraph 9 of Schedule 21 makes clear, the judge retains ultimate discretion and the court may arrive at any minimum term from any starting point. The minimum term is subject to appeal by the offender under section 271 of the Act and subject to review on a reference by the Attorney-General under section 272 of the Act.

PD-86 **CPD VII Sentencing N: Transitional Arrangements for Sentences where the Offence was Committed before 18 December 2003**

N.1 Where the court is passing a sentence of mandatory life imprisonment for an offence committed before 18 December 2003, the court should take a fourth step in determining the minimum term in accordance with section 276 and Schedule 22 of the Act.

N.2 The purpose of those provisions is to ensure that the sentence does not breach the principle of non-retroactivity, by ensuring that a lower minimum term would not have been imposed for the offence when it was committed. Before setting the minimum term, the court must check whether the proposed term is greater than that which the Secretary of State would probably have notified under the practice followed by the Secretary of State before December 2002.

N.3 The decision in *Sullivan, Gibbs, Elener and Elener* [2004] EWCA Crim 1762, [2005] 1 Cr App R 3, [2005] 1 Cr App R (S) 67 gives detailed guidance as to the correct approach to this practice and judges passing mandatory life sentences where the murder was committed prior to 18 December 2003 are well advised to read that judgment before proceeding.

N.4 The practical result of that judgment is that in sentences where the murder was committed before 31 May 2002, the best guide to what would have been the practice of the Secretary of State is the letter sent to judges by Lord Bingham CJ on 10th February 1997, the relevant parts of which are set out below.

N.5 The practice of Lord Bingham, as set out in his letter of 10 February 1997, was to take 14 years as the period actually to be served for the 'average', 'normal' or 'unexceptional' murder. Examples of factors he outlined as capable, in appropriate cases, of mitigating the normal penalty were:

(1) Youth;
(2) Age (where relevant to physical capacity on release or the likelihood of the defendant dying in prison);
(3) [Intellectual disability or mental disorder];
(4) Provocation (in a non-technical sense), or an excessive response to a personal threat;
(5) The absence of an intention to kill;
(6) Spontaneity and lack of premeditation (beyond that necessary to constitute the offence: e.g., a sudden response to family pressure or to prolonged and eventually insupportable stress);
(7) Mercy killing;
(8) A plea of guilty, or hard evidence of remorse or contrition.

N.6 Lord Bingham then listed the following factors as likely to call for a sentence more severe than the norm:

(1) Evidence of planned, professional, revenge or contract killing;
(2) The killing of a child or a very old or otherwise vulnerable victim;
(3) Evidence of sadism, gratuitous violence, or sexual maltreatment, humiliation or degradation before the killing;
(4) Killing for gain (in the course of burglary, robbery, blackmail, insurance fraud, etc.);
(5) Multiple killings;
(6) The killing of a witness, or potential witness, to defeat the ends of justice;
(7) The killing of those doing their public duty (policemen, prison officers, postmasters, firemen, judges, etc.);
(8) Terrorist or politically motivated killings;
(9) The use of firearms or other dangerous weapons, whether carried for defensive or offensive reasons;
(10) A substantial record of serious violence;
(11) Macabre attempts to dismember or conceal the body.

N.7 Lord Bingham further stated that the fact that a defendant was under the influence of drink or drugs at the time of the killing is so common he would be inclined to treat it as neutral. But in the not unfamiliar case in which a couple, inflamed by drink, indulge in a violent quarrel in which one dies, often against a background of longstanding drunken violence, then he would tend to recommend a term somewhat below the norm.

N.8 Lord Bingham went on to say that given the intent necessary for proof of murder, the consequences of taking life and the understandable reaction of relatives to the deceased, a substantial term will almost always be called for, save perhaps in a truly venial case of mercy killing. While a recommendation of a punitive term longer than, say, 30 years will be very rare indeed, there should not be any upper limit. Some crimes will certainly call for terms very well in excess of the norm.

N.9 For the purposes of sentences where the murder was committed after 31 May 2002 and before 18 December 2003, the judge should apply the Practice Statement handed down on 31 May 2002 reproduced at paragraphs N.10 to N.20 below.

N.10 This Statement replaces the previous single normal tariff of 14 years by substituting a higher and a normal starting point of respectively 16 (comparable to 32 years) and 12 years (comparable to 24 years). These starting points have then to be increased or reduced because of aggravating or mitigating factors such as those referred to below. It is emphasised that they are no more than starting points.

The normal starting point of 12 years

N.11 Cases falling within this starting point will normally involve the killing of an adult victim, arising from a quarrel or loss of temper between two people known to each other. It will not have the characteristics referred to in paragraph N.13. Exceptionally, the starting point may be reduced because of the sort of circumstances described in the next paragraph.

N.12 The normal starting point can be reduced because the murder is one where the offender's culpability is significantly reduced, for example, because:

(a) the case came close to the borderline between murder and manslaughter; or

(b) the offender suffered from mental disorder, or from a mental disability which lowered the degree of his criminal responsibility for the killing, although not affording a defence of diminished responsibility; or

(c) the offender was provoked (in a non-technical sense) such as by prolonged and eventually unsupportable stress; or

(d) the case involved an over-reaction in self-defence; or

(e) the offence was a mercy killing.

These factors could justify a reduction to 8/9 years (equivalent to 16/18 years).

The higher starting point of 15/16 years

N.13 The higher starting point will apply to cases where the offender's culpability was exceptionally high, or the victim was in a particularly vulnerable position. Such cases will be characterised by a feature which makes the crime especially serious, such as:

(a) the killing was 'professional' or a contract killing;

(b) the killing was politically motivated;

(c) the killing was done for gain (in the course of a burglary, robbery etc.);

(d) the killing was intended to defeat the ends of justice (as in the killing of a witness or potential witness);

(e) the victim was providing a public service;

(f) the victim was a child or was otherwise vulnerable;

(g) the killing was racially aggravated;

(h) the victim was deliberately targeted because of his or her religion or sexual orientation;

(i) there was evidence of sadism, gratuitous violence or sexual maltreatment, humiliation or degradation of the victim before the killing;

(j) extensive and/or multiple injuries were inflicted on the victim before death;

(k) the offender committed multiple murders.

Variation of the starting point

N.14 Whichever starting point is selected in a particular case, it may be appropriate for the trial judge to vary the starting point upwards or downwards, to take account of aggravating or mitigating factors, which relate to either the offence or the offender, in the particular case.

N.15 Aggravating factors relating to the offence can include:

(a) the fact that the killing was planned;

(b) the use of a firearm;

(c) arming with a weapon in advance;

(d) concealment of the body, destruction of the crime scene and/or dismemberment of the body;

(e) particularly in domestic violence cases, the fact that the murder was the culmination of cruel and violent behaviour by the offender over a period of time.

N.16 Aggravating factors relating to the offender will include the offender's previous record and failures to respond to previous sentences, to the extent that this is relevant to culpability rather than to risk.

N.17 Mitigating factors relating to the offence will include:

(a) an intention to cause grievous bodily harm, rather than to kill;

(b) spontaneity and lack of pre-meditation.

N.18 Mitigating factors relating to the offender may include:

(a) the offender's age;

(b) clear evidence of remorse or contrition;

(c) a timely plea of guilty.

Very serious cases

N.19 A substantial upward adjustment may be appropriate in the most serious cases, for example, those involving a substantial number of murders, or if there are several factors identified as attracting the higher starting point present. In suitable cases, the result might even be a minimum term of 30 years (equivalent to 60 years) which would offer little or no hope of the offender's eventual release. In cases of exceptional gravity, the judge, rather than setting a whole life minimum term, can state that there is no minimum period which could properly be set in that particular case.

N.20 Among the categories of case referred to in paragraph N.13, some offences may be especially grave. These include cases in which the victim was performing his duties as a prison officer at the time of the crime, or the offence was a terrorist or sexual or sadistic murder, or involved a young child. In such a case, a term of 20 years and upwards could be appropriate.

N.21 In following this guidance, judges should bear in mind the conclusion of the Court in *Sullivan* that the general effect of both these statements is the same. While Lord Bingham does not identify as many starting points, it is open to the judge to come to exactly the same decision irrespective of which was followed. Both pieces of guidance give the judge a considerable degree of discretion.

CPD VII Sentencing P: Procedure for Announcing the Minimum Term in Open Court PD-87

P.1 Having gone through the three or four steps outlined above, the court is then under a duty, under section 270 of the Act, to state in open court, in ordinary language, its reasons for deciding on the minimum term or for passing a whole life order.

P.2 In order to comply with this duty, the court should state clearly the minimum term it has determined. In doing so, it should state which of the starting points it has chosen and its reasons for doing so. Where the court has departed from that starting point due to mitigating or aggravating features, it must state the reasons for that departure and any aggravating or mitigating features which have led to that departure. At that point, the court should also declare how much, if any, time is being deducted for time spent in custody and/or on bail subject to a qualifying curfew condition. The court must then explain that the minimum term is the minimum amount of time the prisoner will spend in prison, from the date of sentence, before the Parole Board can order early release. If it remains necessary for the protection of the public, the prisoner will continue to be detained after that date. The court should also state that where the prisoner has served the minimum term and the Parole Board has decided to direct release, the prisoner will remain on licence for the rest of his life and may be recalled to prison at any time.

P.3 Where the offender was 21 or over when he committed the offence and the court considers that the seriousness of the offence is so exceptionally high that a 'whole life order' is appropriate, the court should state clearly its reasons for reaching this conclusion. It should also explain that the early release provisions will not apply.

CPD VII Sentencing Q: Financial, Etc. Information Required for Sentencing PD-88

Q.1 These directions supplement CrimPR 24.11 and 25.16, which set out the procedure to be followed where a defendant pleads guilty, or is convicted, and is to be sentenced. They are not concerned exclusively with corporate defendants, or with offences of an environmental, public health, health and safety or other regulatory character, but the guidance which they contain is likely to be of particular significance in such cases.

Q.2 The rules set out the prosecutor's responsibilities in all cases. Where the offence is of a character, or is against a prohibition, with which the sentencing court is unlikely to be familiar, those responsibilities are commensurately more onerous. The court is entitled to the greatest possible assistance in identifying information relevant to sentencing.

Q.3 In such a case, save where the circumstances are very straightforward, it is likely that justice will best be served by the submission of the required information in writing: see *R v Friskies Petcare (UK) Ltd* [2000] 2 Cr App R (S) 401. Though it is the prosecutor's responsibility to the court to prepare any such document, if the defendant pleads guilty, or indicates a guilty plea, then it is very highly desirable that such sentencing information should be agreed between the parties and jointly submitted. If agreement cannot be reached in all particulars, then the nature and extent of the disagreement should be indicated. If the court concludes that what is in issue is material to sentence, then it will give directions for resolution of the dispute, whether by hearing oral evidence or by other means. In every case, when passing sentence the sentencing court must make clear on what basis sentence is passed: in fairness to the defendant, and for the information of any other person, or court, who needs or wishes to understand the reasons for sentence.

Q.4 If so directed by or on behalf of the court, a defendant must supply accurate information about financial circumstances. In fixing the amount of any fine the court must take into account, amongst other considerations, the financial circumstances of the offender (whether an individual or other person) as they are known or as they appear to be. Before fixing the amount of fine when the defendant is an individual, the court must inquire into his financial circumstances. Where the defendant is an individual the court may make a financial circumstances order in respect of him. This means an order in which the court requires an individual to provide a statement as to his financial means, within a specified time. It is an offence, punishable with imprisonment, to fail to comply with such an order or for knowingly/recklessly furnishing a false statement or knowingly failing to disclose a material fact. The provisions of section 20A Criminal Justice Act 1991 apply to any person (thereby including a corporate organisation) and place the offender under a statutory duty to provide the court with a statement as to his financial means in response to an official request. There are offences for non-compliance, false statements or non-disclosure. It is for the court to decide how much information is required, having regard to relevant sentencing guidelines or guideline cases. However, by reference to those same guidelines and cases the parties should anticipate what the court will require, and prepare accordingly. In complex cases, and in cases involving a corporate defendant, the information required will be more extensive than in others. In the case of a corporate defendant, that information usually will include details of the defendant's corporate structure; annual profit and loss accounts, or extracts; annual balance sheets, or extracts; details of shareholders' receipts; and details of the remuneration of directors or other officers.

Q.5 In *R v F Howe and Son (Engineers) Ltd* [1999] 2 Cr App R (S) 37 the Court of Appeal observed:

> 'If a defendant company wishes to make any submission to the court about its ability to pay a fine it should supply copies of its accounts and any other financial information on which it intends to rely in good time before the hearing both to the court and to the prosecution. This will give the prosecution the opportunity to assist the court should the court wish it. Usually accounts need to be considered with some care to avoid reaching a superficial and perhaps erroneous conclusion. Where accounts or other financial information are deliberately not supplied the court will be entitled to conclude that the company is in a position to pay any financial penalty it is minded to impose. Where the relevant information is provided late it may be desirable for sentence to be adjourned, if necessary at the defendant's expense, so as to avoid the risk of the court taking what it is told at face value and imposing an inadequate penalty.'

Q.6 In the case of an individual, the court is likewise entitled to conclude that the defendant is able to pay any fine imposed unless the defendant has supplied financial information to the contrary. It is the defendant's responsibility to disclose to the court such information relevant to his or her financial position as will enable it to assess what he or she reasonably can afford to pay. If necessary, the court may compel the disclosure of an individual defendant's financial circumstances. In the absence of such disclosure, or where the court is not satisfied that it has been given sufficient reliable information, the court will be entitled to draw reasonable inferences as to the offender's means from evidence it has heard and from all the circumstances of the case.

PD-89 CPD VII Sentencing R: Medical Reports for Sentencing Puposes

General observations

R.1 CrimPR 24.11 and 25.16 concern standard sentencing procedures in magistrates' courts and in the Crown Court respectively. CrimPR 28.8 deals with the obtaining of medical reports for sentencing purposes.

R.2 Rule 28.8 governs the procedure to be followed where a report is commissioned at the instigation of the court. It is not a substitute for the prompt commissioning of a report or reports by a defendant or defendant's representatives where expert medical opinion is material to the defence case. In particular, the defendant's representatives may wish to obtain a medical report or reports wholly independently of the court. Nothing in these directions, therefore, should be read as discouraging the commissioning of a medical report before the case comes before the court, where such a report is expected to be material and where it is possible promptly to commission it. However, where such a report has been commissioned then if that report has not been received in time for sentencing and if the court agrees that it seems likely to be material, then the court should set a timetable for the reception of that report and should give directions for progress to be reviewed at intervals, adopting the timetable set out in these directions with such adaptations as are needed.

R.3 In assessing the likely materiality of an expert medical report for sentencing purposes the court will be assisted by the parties' representations; by the views expressed in any pre-sentence report that may have been prepared; and by the views of practitioners in local criminal justice mental health services, whose assistance is available to the court under local liaison arrangements.

R.4 Where the court requires the assistance of such a report then it is essential that there should be (i) absolute clarity about who is expected to do what, by when, and at whose expense; and (ii) judicial directions for progress with that report to be monitored and reviewed at prescribed intervals, following a timetable set by the court which culminates in the consideration of the report at a hearing. This is especially important where the report in question is a psychiatric assessment of the defendant for the preparation of which specific expertise may be required which is not readily available and because in some circumstances a second such assessment, by another medical practitioner, may be required.

Timetable for the commissioning, preparation and consideration of a report or reports

R.5 CrimPR 28.8 requires the court to set a timetable appropriate to the case for the preparation and reception of a report. In doing so the court will take account of such representations and other information that it receives, including information about the anticipated availability and workload of practitioners with the appropriate expertise. However, the timetable ought not be a protracted one. It is essential to keep in mind the importance of maintaining progress: in recognition of the defendant's rights and with respect for the interests of victims and witnesses, as required by CrimPR Part 1 (the overriding objective). In a magistrates' court account must be taken, too, of section 11 of the Powers of Criminal Courts (Sentencing) Act 2000, which limits the duration of each remand pending the preparation of a report to 3 weeks, where the defendant is to be in custody, and to 4 weeks if the defendant is to be on bail.

R.6 Subject, therefore, to contrary judicial direction the timetable set by the court should require:

(a) the convening of a hearing to consider the report no more than 6 – 8 weeks after the court makes its request;
(b) the prompt identification of an appropriate medical practitioner or practitioners, if not already identified by the court, and the despatch of a commission or commissions accordingly, within 2 business days of the court's decision to request a report;
(c) acknowledgement of a commission by its recipient, and acceptance or rejection of that commission, within 5 business days of its receipt;
(d) enquiries by court staff to confirm that the commission has been received, and to ascertain the action being taken in response, in the event that no acknowledgement is received within 10 business days of its despatch;
(e) delivery of the report within 5 weeks of the despatch of the commission;
(f) enquiries into progress by court staff in the event that no report is received within 5 weeks of the despatch of the commission.

R.7 The hearing that is convened for the court to consider the report, at 6 – 8 weeks after the court requests that report, should not be adjourned before it takes place save in exceptional circumstances and then only by explicit judicial direction the reasons for which must be recorded. If by the time of that hearing the report is available, as usually should be the case, then at that hearing the court can be expected to determine the issue in respect of which the report was commissioned and pass sentence. If by that time, exceptionally, the report is not available then the court should take the opportunity provided by that hearing to enquire into the reasons, give such directions as are appropriate, and if necessary adjourn the hearing to a fixed date for further consideration then. Where it is known in advance of that hearing that the report will not be available in time, the hearing may be conducted by live link or telephone: subject, in the defendant's case, to the same considerations as are identified at paragraph I.3N.6 of these Practice Directions. However, it rarely will be appropriate to dispense altogether with that hearing, or to make enquiries and give further directions without any hearing at all, in view of the arrangements for monitoring and review that the court already will have directed and which, by definition therefore, thus far will have failed to secure the report's timely delivery.

R.8 Where a requirement of the timetable set by the court is not met, or where on enquiry by court staff it appears that the timetable is unlikely to be met, and in any instance in which a medical practitioner who accepts a commission asks for more time, then court staff should not themselves adjust the timetable or accede to such a request but instead should seek directions from an appropriate judicial authority. Subject to local judicial direction, that will be, in the Crown Court, the judge assigned to the case or the resident judge and, in a magistrates' court, a District Judge (Magistrates' Courts) or justice of the peace assigned to the case, or the Justices' Clerk, an assistant clerk or other senior legal adviser. Even if the timetable is adjusted in consequence:

(a) the hearing convened to consider the report (that is, the hearing set for no more than 6 – 8 weeks after the court made its request) rarely should be adjourned before it takes place: see paragraph R.13 above;

(b) directions should be given for court staff henceforth to make regular enquiries into progress, at intervals of not more than 2 weeks, and to report the outcome to an appropriate judicial authority who will decide what further directions, if any, to give.

R.9 Any adjournment of a hearing convened to consider the report should be to a specific date: the hearing should not be adjourned generally, or to a date to be set in due course. The adjournment of such a hearing should not be for more than a further 6 – 8 weeks save in the most exceptional circumstances; and no more than one adjournment of the hearing should be allowed without obtaining written or oral representations from the commissioned medical practitioner explaining the reasons for the delay.

Commissioning a report

R.10 Guidance entitled 'Good practice guidance: commissioning, administering and producing psychiatric reports for sentencing' prepared for and published by the Ministry of Justice and HM Courts and Tribunals Service in September 2010 contains material that will assist court staff and those who are asked to prepare such reports:
http://www.ohrn.nhs.uk/resource/policy/GoodPracticeGuidePsychReports.pdf
That guidance includes standard forms of letters of instruction and other documents.

R.11 CrimPR 28.8 requires the commissioner of a report to explain why the court seeks the report and to include relevant information about the circumstances. The HMCTS Guidance contains forms for judicial use in the instruction of court staff, and guidance to court staff on the preparation of letters of instruction, where a report is required for sentencing purposes. Where a report is requested in a case involving manslaughter by reason of diminished responsibility, the report writer should have regard to the Sentencing Council's guideline on Manslaughter by reason of Diminished Responsibility. This should assist the report writer in providing the most helpful assessment to enable the court to determine the level of diminution involved in the case.

R.12 The commission should invite a practitioner who is unable to accept it promptly to nominate a suitably qualified substitute, if possible, and to transfer the commission to that person, reporting the transfer when acknowledging the court officer's letter. It is entirely appropriate for the commission to draw the recipient's attention to CrimPR 1.2 (the duty of the participants in a criminal case) and to CrimPR 19.2(1)(b) (the obligation of an expert witness to comply with directions made by a court and at once to inform the court of any significant failure, by the expert or another, to take any step required by such a direction).

R.13 Where the relevant legislation requires a second psychiatric assessment by a second medical practitioner, and where no commission already has been addressed to a second such practitioner, the commission may invite the person to whom it is addressed to nominate a suitably qualified second person and to pass a copy of the commission to that person forthwith.

Funding arrangements

R.14 Where a medical report has been, or is to be, commissioned by a party then that party is responsible for arranging payment of the fees incurred, even though the report is intended for the court's use. That must be made clear in that party's commission.

R.15 Where a medical report is requested by the court and commissioned by a party or by court staff at the court's direction then the commission must include (i) confirmation that the fees will be paid by HMCTS, (ii) details of how, and to whom, to submit an invoice or claim for fees, and (iii) notice of the prescribed rates of fees and of any legislative or other criteria applicable to the calculation of the fees that may be paid.

Remand in custody

R.16 Where the defendant who is to be examined will be remanded in custody then notice that directions have been given for a medical report or reports to be prepared must be included in the information given to the defendant's custodian, to ensure that the preparation of the report or reports can be facilitated. This is especially important where bail is withheld on the ground that it would be otherwise impracticable to complete the required report, and in particular where that is the only ground for withholding bail.

Criminal Procedure Rules Part 28 Sentencing Procedures in Special Cases

R-275 **Reasons for not following usual sentencing requirements**

28.1 (1) This rule applies where the court decides—

(a) not to follow a relevant sentencing guideline;

(b) not to make, where it could—
  (i) a reparation order (unless it passes a custodial or community sentence),
  (ii) a compensation order,
  (iii) a slavery and trafficking reparation order, or
  (iv) a travel restriction order;
(c) not to order, where it could—
  (i) that a suspended sentence of imprisonment is to take effect,
  (ii) the endorsement of the defendant's driving record, or
  (iii) the defendant's disqualification from driving, for the usual minimum period or at all;
(d) to pass a lesser sentence than it otherwise would have passed because the defendant has assisted, or has agreed to assist, an investigator or prosecutor in relation to an offence.

(2) The court must explain why it has so decided, when it explains the sentence that it has passed.
(3) Where paragraph (1)(d) applies, the court must arrange for such an explanation to be given to the defendant and to the prosecutor in writing, if the court thinks that it would not be in the public interest to explain in public.

Notice of requirements of suspended sentence and community, etc. orders **R-276**

28.2 (1) This rule applies where the court—
(a) makes a suspended sentence order;
(b) imposes a requirement under—
  (i) a community order,
  (ii) a youth rehabilitation order, or
  (iii) a suspended sentence order; or
(c) orders the defendant to attend meetings with a supervisor.

(2) The court officer must notify—
(a) the defendant of—
  (i) the length of the sentence suspended by a suspended sentence order, and
  (ii) the period of the suspension;
(b) the defendant and, where the defendant is under 14, an appropriate adult, of—
  (i) any requirement or requirements imposed, and
  (ii) the identity of any responsible officer or supervisor, and the means by which that person may be contacted;
(c) any responsible officer or supervisor, and, where the defendant is under 14, the appropriate qualifying officer (if that is not the responsible officer), of—
  (i) the defendant's name, address and telephone number (if available),
  (ii) the offence or offences of which the defendant was convicted, and
  (iii) the requirement or requirements imposed; and
(d) the person affected, where the court imposes a requirement—
  (i) for the protection of that person from the defendant, or
  (ii) requiring the defendant to reside with that person.

(3) If the court imposes an electronic monitoring requirement, the monitor of which is not the responsible officer, the court officer must—
(a) notify the defendant and, where the defendant is under 16, an appropriate adult, of the monitor's name, and the means by which the monitor may be contacted; and
(b) notify the monitor of—
  (i) the defendant's name, address and telephone number (if available),
  (ii) the offence or offences of which the defendant was convicted,
  (iii) the place or places at which the defendant's presence must be monitored,
  (iv) the period or periods during which the defendant's presence there must be monitored, and
  (v) the identity of the responsible officer, and the means by which that officer may be contacted.

Notification requirements **R-277**

28.3 (1) This rule applies where, on a conviction, sentence or order, legislation requires the defendant—
(a) Part 2 of, and Schedule 3 to, the Sexual Offences Act 2003 (notification for the period specified by section 82 of the Act after conviction, etc. of an offence listed in Schedule 3 and committed in the circumstances specified in that Schedule);
(b) to be included in a barred list.

(2) The court must tell the defendant that such requirements apply, and under what legislation.

R-278 Variation of sentence

28.4 (1) This rule—

(a) applies where a magistrates' court or the Crown Court can vary or rescind a sentence or order, other than an order to which rule 24.18 applies (Setting aside a conviction or varying a costs etc. order); and

(b) authorises the Crown Court, in addition to its other powers, to do so within the period of 56 days beginning with another defendant's acquittal or sentencing where—

(i) defendants are tried separately in the Crown Court on the same or related facts alleged in one or more indictments, and

(ii) one is sentenced before another is acquitted or sentenced.

(2) The court—

(a) may exercise its power—

(i) on application by a party, or on its own initiative,

(ii) at a hearing, in public or in private, or without a hearing;

(b) must announce, at a hearing in public—

(i) a decision to vary or rescind a sentence or order, or to refuse to do so, and

(ii) the reasons for that decision.

(3) A party who wants the court to exercise that power must—

(a) apply in writing as soon as reasonably practicable after—

(i) the sentence or order that that party wants the court to vary or rescind, or

(ii) where paragraph (1)(b) applies, the other defendant's acquittal or sentencing;

(b) serve the application on—

(i) the court officer, and

(ii) each other party; and

(c) in the application—

(i) explain why the sentence should be varied or rescinded,

(ii) specify the variation that the applicant proposes, and

(iii) if the application is late, explain why.

(4) The court must not exercise its power in the defendant's absence unless—

(a) the court makes a variation—

(i) which is proposed by the defendant, or

(ii) the effect of which is that the defendant is no more severely dealt with under the sentence as varied than before; or

(b) the defendant has had an opportunity to make representations at a hearing (whether or not the defendant in fact attends).

(5) The court may—

(a) extend (even after it has expired) the time limit under paragraph (3), unless the court's power to vary or rescind the sentence cannot be exercised;

(b) allow an application to be made orally.

(6) For the purposes of the announcement required by paragraph (2)(b), the court need not comprise the same member or members as the court by which the decision to be announced was made.

R-279 Application to vary or discharge a compensation, etc. order

28.5 (1) This rule applies where on application by the defendant a magistrates' court can vary or discharge—

(a) a compensation order; or

(b) a slavery and trafficking reparation order.

(2) A defendant who wants the court to exercise that power must—

(a) apply in writing as soon as practicable after becoming aware of the grounds for doing so;

(b) serve the application on the magistrates' court officer;

(c) where the order was made in the Crown Court, serve a copy of the application on the Crown Court officer; and

(d) in the application, specify the order that the defendant wants the court to vary or discharge and explain (as applicable)—

(i) what civil court finding shows that the injury, loss or damage was less than it had appeared to be when the order was made,

(ii) in what circumstances the person for whose benefit the order was made has recovered the property for the loss of which it was made,

(iii) why a confiscation order, unlawful profit order or slavery and trafficking reparation order makes the defendant now unable to pay compensation or reparation in full, or

(iv) in what circumstances the defendant's means have been reduced substantially and unexpectedly, and why they seem unlikely to increase for a considerable period.

(3) The court officer must serve a copy of the application on the person for whose benefit the order was made.

(4) The court must not vary or discharge the order unless—

(a) the defendant, and the person for whose benefit it was made, each has had an opportunity to make representations at a hearing (whether or not either in fact attends); and

(b) where the order was made in the Crown Court, the Crown Court has notified its consent.

Application to remove, revoke or suspend a disqualification or restriction **R-280**

28.6 (1) This rule applies where, on application by the defendant, the court can remove, revoke or suspend a disqualification or restriction included in a sentence (except a disqualification from driving).

(2) A defendant who wants the court to exercise such a power must—

(a) apply in writing, no earlier than the date on which the court can exercise the power;

(b) serve the application on the court officer; and

(c) in the application—

(i) specify the disqualification or restriction, and

(ii) explain why the defendant wants the court to remove, revoke or suspend it.

(3) The court officer must serve a copy of the application on the chief officer of police for the local justice area.

Application for a restitution order by the victim of a theft **R-281**

28.7 (1) This rule applies where, on application by the victim of a theft, the court can order a defendant to give that person goods obtained with the proceeds of goods stolen in that theft.

(2) A person who wants the court to exercise that power if the defendant is convicted must—

(a) apply in writing as soon as practicable (without waiting for the verdict);

(b) serve the application on the court officer; and

(c) in the application—

(i) identify the goods, and

(ii) explain why the applicant is entitled to them.

(3) The court officer must serve a copy of the application on each party.

(4) The court must not determine the application unless the applicant and each party has had an opportunity to make representations at a hearing (whether or not each in fact attends).

(5) The court may—

(a) extend (even after it has expired) the time limit under paragraph (2); and

(b) allow an application to be made orally.

Directions for commissioning medical reports for sentencing purposes **R-282**

28.8 (1) This rule applies where for sentencing purposes the court requires—

(a) a medical examination of the defendant and a report; or

(b) information about the arrangements that could be made for the defendant where the court is considering—

(i) a hospital order, or

(ii) a guardianship order.

(2) The court must—

(a) identify each issue in respect of which the court requires expert medical opinion and the legislation applicable;

(b) specify the nature of the expertise likely to be required for giving such opinion;

(c) identify each party or participant by whom a commission for such opinion must be prepared, who may be—

(i) a party (or party's representative) acting on that party's own behalf,

(ii) a party (or party's representative) acting on behalf of the court, or

(iii) the court officer acting on behalf of the court;

(d) where there are available to the court arrangements with the National Health Service under which an assessment of a defendant's mental health may be prepared, give such directions as are needed under those arrangements for obtaining the expert report or reports required;

(e) where no such arrangements are available to the court, or they will not be used, give directions for the commissioning of an expert report or expert reports, including—

(i) such directions as can be made about supplying the expert or experts with the defendant's medical records,

(ii) directions about the other information, about the defendant and about the offence or offences alleged to have been committed by the defendant, which is to be supplied to each expert, and
(iii) directions about the arrangements that will apply for the payment of each expert;
(f) set a timetable providing for—
(i) the date by which a commission is to be delivered to each expert,
(ii) the date by which any failure to accept a commission is to be reported to the court,
(iii) the date or dates by which progress in the preparation of a report or reports is to be reviewed by the court officer, and
(iv) the date by which each report commissioned is to be received by the court; and
(g) identify the person (each person, if more than one) to whom a copy of a report is to be supplied, and by whom.

(3) A commission addressed to an expert must—
(a) identify each issue in respect of which the court requires expert medical opinion and the legislation applicable;
(b) include—
(i) the information required by the court to be supplied to the expert,
(ii) details of the timetable set by the court, and
(iii) details of the arrangements that will apply for the payment of the expert;
(c) identify the person (each person, if more than one) to whom a copy of the expert's report is to be supplied; and
(d) request confirmation that the expert from whom the opinion is sought—
(i) accepts the commission, and
(ii) will adhere to the timetable.

R-283 **Information to be supplied on admission to hospital or guardianship**

28.9 (1) This rule applies where the court—
(a) orders the defendant's detention and treatment in hospital; or
(b) makes a guardianship order.

(2) Unless the court otherwise directs, the court officer must, as soon as practicable, serve on (as applicable) the hospital or the guardian—
(a) a record of the court's order;
(b) such information as the court has received that appears likely to assist in treating or otherwise dealing with the defendant, including information about—
(i) the defendant's mental condition,
(ii) the defendant's other circumstances, and
(iii) the circumstances of the offence.

R-284 **Information to be supplied on committal for sentence, etc.**

28.10 (1) This rule applies where a magistrates' court or the Crown Court convicts the defendant and—
(a) commits or adjourns the case to another court—
(i) for sentence, or
(ii) for the defendant to be dealt with for breach of a deferred sentence, a conditional discharge, or a suspended sentence of imprisonment, imposed by that other court;
(b) deals with a deferred sentence, a conditional discharge, or a suspended sentence of imprisonment, imposed by another court; or
(c) makes an order that another court is, or may be, required to enforce.

(2) Unless the convicting court otherwise directs, the court officer must, as soon as practicable—
(a) where paragraph (1)(a) applies, arrange the transmission from the convicting to the other court of a record of any relevant—
(i) certificate of conviction,
(ii) magistrates' court register entry,
(iii) decision about bail, for the purposes of section 5 of the Bail Act 1976,
(iv) note of evidence,
(v) statement or other document introduced in evidence,
(vi) medical or other report,
(vii) representation order or application for such order, and
(viii) interim driving disqualification;

(b) where paragraph (1)(b) or (c) applies, arrange—
(i) the transmission from the convicting to the other court of notice of the convicting court's order, and
(ii) the recording of that order at the other court;
(c) in every case, notify the defendant and, where the defendant is under 14, an appropriate adult, of the location of the other court.

Application to review sentence because of assistance given or withheld **R-285**

28.11 (1) This rule applies where the Crown Court can reduce or increase a sentence on application by a prosecutor in a case in which—
(a) since being sentenced, the defendant has assisted, or has agreed to assist, an investigator or prosecutor in relation to an offence; or
(b) since receiving a reduced sentence for agreeing to give such assistance, the defendant has failed to do so.
(2) A prosecutor who wants the court to exercise that power must—
(a) apply in writing as soon as practicable after becoming aware of the grounds for doing so;
(b) serve the application on—
(i) the court officer, and
(ii) the defendant; and
(c) in the application—
(i) explain why the sentence should be reduced, or increased, as appropriate, and
(ii) identify any other matter relevant to the court's decision, including any sentencing guideline or guideline case.
(3) The general rule is that the application must be determined by the judge who passed the sentence, unless that judge is unavailable.
(4) The court must not determine the application in the defendant's absence unless the defendant has had an opportunity to make representations at a hearing (whether or not the defendant in fact attends).

Criminal Procedure Rules Part 29 Road Traffic Penalties

Representations about obligatory disqualification or endorsement **R-286**

29.1 (1) This rule applies—
(a) where the court—
(i) convicts the defendant of an offence involving obligatory disqualification from driving and section 34(1) of the Road Traffic Offenders Act 1988 (Disqualification for certain offences) applies,
(ii) convicts the defendant of an offence where section 35 of the 1988 Act (Disqualification for repeated offences) applies, or
(iii) convicts the defendant of an offence involving obligatory endorsement of the defendant's driving record and section 44 of the 1988 Act (Orders for endorsement) applies;
(b) unless the defendant is absent.
(2) The court must explain, in terms the defendant can understand (with help, if necessary)—
(a) where paragraph (1)(a)(i) applies (obligatory disqualification under section 34)—
(i) that the court must order the defendant to be disqualified from driving for a minimum of 12 months (or 2 or 3 years, as the case may be, according to the offence and the defendant's driving record), unless the court decides that there are special reasons to order disqualification for a shorter period, or not to order disqualification at all, and
(ii) if applicable, that the period of disqualification will be reduced by at least 3 months if, by no later than 2 months before the end of the reduced period, the defendant completes an approved driving course;
(b) where paragraph (1)(a)(ii) applies (disqualification under section 35)—
(i) that the court must order the defendant to be disqualified from driving for a minimum of 6 months (or 1 or 2 years, as the case may be, according to the defendant's driving record), unless, having regard to all the circumstances, the court decides to order disqualification for a shorter period, or not to order disqualification at all, and
(ii) that circumstances of which the court cannot take account in making its decision are any that make the offence not a serious one; hardship (other than exceptional hard-

ship); and any that during the last 3 years already have been taken into account by a court when ordering disqualification for less than the usual minimum period, or not at all, for repeated driving offences;

(c) where paragraph (1)(a)(iii) applies (obligatory endorsement), that the court must order the endorsement of the defendant's driving record unless the court decides that there are special reasons not to do so;

(d) in every case, as applicable—

(i) that the court already has received representations from the defendant about whether any such special reasons or mitigating circumstances apply and will take account of them, or

(ii) that the defendant may make such representations now, on oath or affirmation.

(3) Unless the court already has received such representations from the defendant, before it applies rule 24.11 (magistrates' court procedure if the court convicts) or rule 25.16 (Crown Court procedure if the court convicts), as the case may be, the court must—

(a) ask whether the defendant wants to make any such representations; and

(b) if the answer to that question is 'yes', require the defendant to take an oath or affirm and make them.

R-287 Application to remove a disqualification from driving

29.2 (1) This rule applies where, on application by the defendant, the court can remove a disqualification from driving.

(2) A defendant who wants the court to exercise that power must—

(a) apply in writing, no earlier than the date on which the court can exercise the power;

(b) serve the application on the court officer; and

(c) in the application—

(i) specify the disqualification, and

(ii) explain why the defendant wants the court to remove it.

(3) The court officer must serve a copy of the application on the chief officer of police for the local justice area.

R-288 Information to be supplied on order for endorsement of driving record, etc.

29.3 (1) This rule applies where the court—

(a) convicts the defendant of an offence involving obligatory endorsement, and orders there to be endorsed on the defendant's driving record (and on any counterpart licence, if other legislation requires)—

(i) particulars of the conviction,

(ii) particulars of any disqualification from driving that the court imposes, and

(iii) the penalty points to be attributed to the offence;

(b) disqualifies the defendant from driving for any other offence; or

(c) suspends or removes a disqualification from driving.

(2) The court officer must, as soon as practicable, serve on the Secretary of State notice that includes details of—

(a) where paragraph (1)(a) applies—

(i) the local justice area in which the court is acting,

(ii) the dates of conviction and sentence,

(iii) the offence, and the date on which it was committed,

(iv) the sentence, and

(v) the date of birth, and sex, of the defendant, where those details are available;

(b) where paragraph (1)(b) applies—

(i) the date and period of the disqualification,

(ii) the power exercised by the court;

(c) where paragraph (1)(c) applies—

(i) the date and period of the disqualification,

(ii) the date and terms of the order for its suspension or removal,

(iii) the power exercised by the court, and

(iv) where the court suspends the disqualification pending appeal, the court to which the defendant has appealed.

R-289 Statutory declaration to avoid fine after fixed penalty notice

29.4 (1) This rule applies where—

(a) a chief officer of police, or the Secretary of State, serves on the magistrates' court officer a certificate registering, for enforcement as a fine, a sum payable by a defendant after failure to comply with a fixed penalty notice;

(b) the court officer notifies the defendant of the registration; and

(c) the defendant makes a statutory declaration with the effect that there become void—
(i) the fixed penalty notice, or any associated notice sent to the defendant as owner of the vehicle concerned, and
(ii) the registration and any enforcement proceedings.

(2) The defendant must serve that statutory declaration not more than 21 days after service of notice of the registration, unless the court extends that time limit.

(3) The court officer must—
(a) serve a copy of the statutory declaration on the person by whom the certificate was registered;
(b) cancel any endorsement on the defendant's driving record (and on any counterpart licence, if other legislation requires); and
(c) notify the Secretary of State of any such cancellation.

(4) A court officer may take the statutory declaration to which this rule refers if that officer—
(a) is a justices' legal adviser; or
(b) is nominated for the purpose by such a legal adviser.

Application for declaration about a course or programme certificate decision **R-290**

29.5 (1) This rule applies where the court can declare unjustified—
(a) a course provider's failure or refusal to give a certificate of the defendant's satisfactory completion of an approved course; or
(b) a programme provider's giving of a certificate of the defendant's failure fully to participate in an approved programme.

(2) A defendant who wants the court to exercise that power must—
(a) apply in writing, not more than 28 days after—
(i) the date by which the defendant was required to complete the course, or
(ii) the giving of the certificate of failure fully to participate in the programme;
(b) serve the application on the court officer; and
(c) in the application, specify the course or programme and explain (as applicable)—
(i) that the course provider has failed to give a certificate,
(ii) where the course provider has refused to give a certificate, why the defendant disagrees with the reasons for that decision, or
(iii) where the programme provider has given a certificate, why the defendant disagrees with the reasons for that decision.

(3) The court officer must serve a copy of the application on the course or programme provider.

(4) The court must not determine the application unless the defendant, and the course or programme provider, each has had an opportunity to make representations at a hearing (whether or not either in fact attends).

Appeal against recognition of foreign driving disqualification **R-291**

29.6 (1) This rule applies where—
(a) a Minister gives a disqualification notice under section 57 of the Crime (International Co-operation) Act 2003; and
(b) the person to whom it is given wants to appeal under section 59 of the Act to a magistrates' court.

(2) That person ('the appellant') must serve an appeal notice on—
(a) the court officer, at a magistrates' court in the local justice area in which the appellant lives; and
(b) the Minister, at the address given in the disqualification notice.

(3) The appellant must serve the appeal notice within the period for which section 59 of the 2003 Act provides.

(4) The appeal notice must—
(a) attach a copy of the disqualification notice;
(b) explain which of the conditions in section 56 of the 2003 Act is not met, and why section 57 of the Act therefore does not apply; and
(c) include any application to suspend the disqualification, under section 60 of the Act.

(5) The Minister may serve a respondent's notice, and must do so if—
(a) the Minister wants to make representations to the court; or
(b) the court so directs.

(6) The Minister must—
(a) unless the court otherwise directs, serve any such respondent's notice not more than 14 days after—
(i) the appellant serves the appeal notice, or
(ii) a direction to do so;
(b) in any such respondent's notice—
(i) identify the grounds of opposition on which the Minister relies,

(ii) summarise any relevant facts not already included in the disqualification and appeal notices, and
(iii) identify any other document that the Minister thinks the court will need to decide the appeal (and serve any such document with the notice).

(7) Where the court determines an appeal, the general rule is that it must do so at a hearing (which must be in public, unless the court otherwise directs).

(8) The court officer must serve on the Minister—
(a) notice of the outcome of the appeal;
(b) notice of any suspension of the disqualification; and
(c) the appellant's driving licence, if surrendered to the court officer.

Criminal Procedure Rules Part 30 Enforcement of Fines and Other Orders for Payment

R-292 When this Part applies

30.1 (1) This Part applies where a magistrates' court can enforce payment of—
(a) a fine, or a sum that legislation requires the court to treat as a fine; or
(b) any other sum that a court has ordered to be paid—
(i) on a conviction, or
(ii) on the forfeiture of a surety.

(2) Rules 30.7 to 30.9 apply where the court, or a fines officer, issues a warrant for an enforcement agent to take control of a defendant's goods and sell them, using the procedure in Schedule 12 to the Tribunals, Courts and Enforcement Act 2007.

(3) In this Part—
(a) 'defendant' means anyone liable to pay a sum to which this Part applies;
(b) 'payment terms' means by when, and by what (if any) instalments, such a sum must be paid.

R-293 Exercise of court's powers

30.2 The court must not exercise its enforcement powers unless—
(a) the court officer has served on the defendant any collection order or other notice of—
(i) the obligation to pay,
(ii) the payment terms, and
(iii) how and where the defendant must pay; and
(b) the defendant has failed to comply with the payment terms.

R-294 Duty to give receipt

30.3 (1) This rule applies where the defendant makes a payment to—
(a) the court officer specified in an order or notice served under rule 30.2;
(b) another court officer;
(c) any—
(i) custodian of the defendant,
(ii) supervisor appointed to encourage the defendant to pay, or
(iii) responsible officer appointed under a community sentence or a suspended sentence of imprisonment; or
(d) a person executing a warrant to which rule 13.6 (warrants for arrest, detention or imprisonment that cease to have effect on payment) or this Part applies.

(2) The person receiving the payment must—
(a) give the defendant a receipt unless the method of payment generates an independent record (for example, a bank record)
(b) as soon as practicable transmit the payment to the court officer specified in an order or notice served under rule 30.2, if the recipient is not that court officer.

R-295 Appeal against decision of fines officer

30.4 (1) This rule applies where—
(a) a collection order is in force;
(b) a fines officer makes a decision under one of these paragraphs of Schedule 5 to the Courts Act 2003—
(i) paragraph 22 (Application to fines officer for variation of order or attachment of earnings order, etc.),

(ii) paragraph 31 (Application to fines officer for variation of reserve terms), or
(iii) paragraph 37 (Functions of fines officer in relation to defaulters: referral or further steps notice); and
(c) the defendant wants to appeal against that decision.
(2) Unless the court otherwise directs, the defendant must—
(a) appeal in writing not more than 10 business days after the decision;
(b) serve the appeal on the court officer; and
(c) in the appeal—
(i) explain why a different decision should be made, and
(ii) specify the decision that the defendant proposes.
(3) Where the court determines an appeal the general rule is that it must do so at a hearing.

Application to reduce a fine, vary payment terms or remit a courts charge **R-296**

30.5 (1) This rule applies where—
(a) no collection order is in force; and the defendant wants the court to—
(i) reduce the amount of a fine, or
(ii) vary payment terms;
(b) the defendant, a fines officer or an enforcement agent wants the court to remit a criminal courts charge.
(2) Unless the court otherwise directs, such a defendant, fines officer or enforcement agent must—
(a) apply in writing;
(b) serve the application on the court officer;
(c) if the application is to reduce a fine or vary payment terms, explain—
(i) what relevant circumstances have not yet been considered by the court, and
(ii) why the fine should be reduced, or the payment terms varied;
(d) if the application is to remit a criminal courts charge, explain—
(i) how the circumstances meet the time limits and other conditions in section 21E of the Prosecution of Offences Act 1985, and
(ii) why the charge should be remitted.
(3) The court may determine an application—
(a) at a hearing, which may be in public or in private; or
(b) without a hearing.

Claim to avoid fine after penalty notice **R-297**

30.6 (1) This rule applies where—
(a) a chief officer of police serves on the magistrates' court officer a certificate registering, for enforcement as a fine, a sum payable by a defendant after failure to comply with a penalty notice; and
(b) the court or a fines officer enforces the fine.
(2) A defendant who claims not to be the person to whom the penalty notice was issued must, unless the court otherwise directs—
(a) make that claim in writing; and
(b) serve it on the court officer.
(3) The court officer must—
(a) notify the chief officer of police by whom the certificate was registered; and
(b) refer the case to the court.
(4) Where such a claim is made—
(a) the general rule is that the court must adjourn the enforcement for 28 days and fix a hearing; but
(b) the court may make a different order.
(5) At any such hearing, the chief officer of police must introduce any evidence to contradict the defendant's claim.

Information to be included in a warrant of control **R-298**

30.7 (1) A warrant must identify—
(a) each person to whom it is directed;
(b) the defendant against whom it was issued;
(c) the sum for which it was issued and the reason that sum is owed;
(d) the court or fines officer who issued it, unless that is otherwise recorded by the court officer; and
(e) the court office for the court or fines officer who issued it.

(2) A person to whom a warrant is directed must record on it the date and time at which it is received.
(3) A warrant that contains an error is not invalid, as long as—
(a) it was issued in respect of a lawful decision by the court or fines officer; and
(b) it contains enough information to identify that decision.

R-299 Warrant of control: application by enforcement agent for extension of time, etc.

30.8 (1) This rule applies where an enforcement agent wants the court to exercise a power under Schedule 12 to the Tribunals, Courts and Enforcement Act 2007, or under regulations made under that Schedule, to—
(a) shorten or extend a time limit;
(b) give the agent authority to—
(i) enter premises which the agent would not otherwise have authority to enter,
(ii) enter or remain on premises at a time at which the agent would not otherwise have authority to be there,
(iii) use reasonable force, in circumstances in which the agent would not otherwise have authority to use such force,
(iv) sell goods by a method which the agent would not otherwise have authority to use, or
(v) recover disbursements which the agent would not otherwise have authority to recover;
(c) specify the manner in which goods which have not been sold must be disposed of.
(2) Such an enforcement agent must—
(a) apply in writing;
(b) serve the application on the court officer; and
(c) pay any fee prescribed.
(3) The application must—
(a) identify the power that the agent wants the court to exercise;
(b) explain how the conditions for the exercise of that power are satisfied, including any condition that requires the agent to give another person notice of the application;
(c) specify those persons, if any, to whom the agent has given notice in accordance with such a condition; and
(d) propose the terms of the order that the agent wants the court to make.
(4) A person to whom the enforcement agent has given notice of an application and who wants to make representations to the court must—
(a) serve the representations on—
(i) the court officer,
(ii) the enforcement agent, and
(iii) any other person to whom the enforcement agent gave notice;
(b) do so as soon as reasonably practicable and in any event within such period as the court directs; and
(c) in the representations, propose the terms of the order that that person wants the court to make, and explain why.
(5) The court—
(a) must not determine an application unless any person to whom the enforcement agent gave notice—
(i) is present, or
(ii) has had a reasonable opportunity to respond;
(b) subject to that, may determine an application—
(i) at a hearing, which must be in private unless the court otherwise directs, or
(ii) without a hearing.

R-300 Warrant of control: application to resolve dispute

30.9 (1) This rule applies where a defendant's goods are sold using the procedure in Schedule 12 to the Tribunals, Courts and Enforcement Act 2007 and there is a dispute about—
(a) what share of the proceeds of those goods should be paid by the enforcement agent to a co-owner; or
(b) the fees or disbursements sought or recovered by the enforcement agent out of the proceeds.
(2) An enforcement agent, a defendant or a co-owner who wants the court to resolve the dispute must—
(a) apply in writing as soon as practicable after becoming aware of the grounds for doing so;

(b) serve the application on—
(i) the court officer,
(ii) each other party to the dispute, and
(iii) any other co-owner; and
(c) pay any fee prescribed.
(3) The application must—
(a) identify the warrant of control;
(b) specify the goods sold, the proceeds, and the fees and disbursements sought or recovered by the enforcement agent;
(c) identify the power that the applicant wants the court to exercise;
(d) specify the persons served with the application;
(e) explain the circumstances of the dispute; and
(f) propose the terms of the order that the applicant wants the court to make.
(4) A person served with an application who wants to make representations to the court must—
(a) serve the representations on—
(i) the court officer,
(ii) the applicant, and
(iii) any other person on whom the application was served;
(b) do so as soon as reasonably practicable and in any event within such period as the court directs; and
(c) in the representations, propose the terms of the order that that person wants the court to make, and explain why.
(5) The court—
(a) must determine an application at a hearing, which must be in private unless the court otherwise directs;
(b) must not determine an application unless each party—
(i) is present, or
(ii) has had a reasonable opportunity to attend.

Financial penalties imposed in other European Union member States R-301

30.10 (1) This rule applies where the Lord Chancellor gives the court officer a request to enforce a financial penalty imposed in another European Union member State.
(2) The court officer must serve on the defendant—
(a) notice of the request for enforcement, and of its effect;
(b) a copy of—
(i) the certificate requesting enforcement, and
(ii) the decision requiring payment to which that certificate relates; and
(c) notice that the procedure set out in this rule applies.
(3) A defendant who wants the court to refuse enforcement must—
(a) serve notice of objection on the court officer;
(b) unless the court otherwise directs, serve that notice not more than 14 days after service of notice of the request; and
(c) in the notice of objection—
(i) identify each ground for refusal on which the defendant relies,
(ii) summarise any relevant facts not already included in the certificate and decision served with the notice of the request, and
(iii) identify any other document that the defendant thinks the court will need to determine the request (and serve any such document with the notice).
(4) The court—
(a) may determine a request for enforcement—
(i) at a hearing, which must be in public unless the court otherwise directs, or
(ii) without a hearing; but
(b) must not allow enforcement unless the defendant has had at least 14 days in which to serve notice of objection.
(5) Paragraphs (2) and (3) do not apply if, on receipt of the request, the court decides that a ground for refusal applies.
(6) The court officer must serve on the Lord Chancellor notice of the court's decision.

R-302 When this Part applies

31.1 (1) This Part applies where—
(a) a magistrates' court or the Crown Court can make, vary or revoke a civil order—
(i) as well as, or instead of, passing a sentence, or in any other circumstances in which other legislation allows the court to make such an order, and
(ii) that requires someone to do, or not do, something;
(b) a magistrates' court or the Crown Court can make a European protection order;
(c) a magistrates' court can give effect to a European protection order made in another European Union member State.
(2) A reference to a 'behaviour order' in this Part is a reference to any such order.
(3) A reference to 'hearsay evidence' in this Part is a reference to evidence consisting of hearsay within the meaning of section 1(2) of the Civil Evidence Act 1995.

R-303 Behaviour orders: general rules

31.2 (1) The court must not make a behaviour order unless the person to whom it is directed has had an opportunity—
(a) to consider—
(i) what order is proposed and why, and
(ii) the evidence in support; and
(b) to make representations at a hearing (whether or not that person in fact attends).
(2) That restriction does not apply to making —
(a) an interim behaviour order, but unless other legislation otherwise provides such an order has no effect unless the person to whom it is directed—
(i) is present when it is made, or
(ii) is handed a document recording the order not more than 7 days after it is made;
(b) a restraining order that gives effect to a European protection order, where rule 31.10 applies (Giving effect to a European protection order made in another EU member State).
(3) Where the court decides not to make, where it could—
(a) a football banning order; or
(b) a parenting order, after a person under 16 is convicted of an offence,
the court must announce, at a hearing in public, the reasons for its decision.
(4) Where the court makes an order which imposes one or more of the prohibitions or restrictions listed in rule 31.9(1), the court must arrange for someone to explain to the person who benefits from that protection—
(a) that person may apply for a European protection order, if he or she decides to reside or stay in another European Union member State;
(b) the basic conditions for making such an application; and
(c) that it is advisable to make any such application before leaving the United Kingdom.

R-304 Application for behaviour order and notice of terms of proposed order: special rules

31.3 (1) This rule applies where—
(a) a prosecutor wants the court to make one of the following orders if the defendant is convicted—
(i) an anti-social behaviour order (but this rule does not apply to an application for an interim anti-social behaviour order),
(ii) a serious crime prevention order,
(iii) a criminal behaviour order, or
(iv) a prohibition order;
(b) a prosecutor proposes, on the prosecutor's initiative or at the court's request, a sexual harm prevention order if the defendant is convicted;
(c) a prosecutor proposes a restraining order whether the defendant is convicted or acquitted.
(2) Where paragraph (1)(a) applies (order on application), the prosecutor must serve a notice of intention to apply for such an order on—
(a) the court officer;
(b) the defendant against whom the prosecutor wants the court to make the order; and
(c) any person on whom the order would be likely to have a significant adverse effect, as soon as practicable (without waiting for the verdict).
(3) A notice under paragraph (2) must—
(a) summarise the relevant facts;
(b) identify the evidence on which the prosecutor relies in support;
(c) attach any written statement that the prosecutor has not already served; and
(d) specify the order that the prosecutor wants the court to make.

(4) A defendant served with a notice under paragraph (2) must—
   (a) serve notice of any evidence on which the defendant relies on—
      (i) the court officer, and
      (ii) the prosecutor,
   as soon as practicable (without waiting for the verdict); and
   (b) in the notice, identify that evidence and attach any written statement that has not already been served.

(5) Where paragraph (1)(b) applies (sexual harm prevention order proposed), the prosecutor must—
   (a) serve a draft order on the court officer and on the defendant not less than 2 business days before the hearing at which the order may be made;
   (b) in the draft order specify those prohibitions which the prosecutor proposes as necessary for the purpose of—
      (i) protecting the public or any particular members of the public from sexual harm from the defendant, or
      (ii) protecting children or vulnerable adults generally, or any particular children or vulnerable adults, from sexual harm from the defendant outside the United Kingdom.

(6) Where paragraph (1)(c) applies (restraining order proposed), the prosecutor must—
   (a) serve a draft order on the court officer and on the defendant as soon as practicable (without waiting for the verdict);
   (b) in the draft order specify—
      (i) those prohibitions which, if the defendant is convicted, the prosecutor proposes for the purpose of protecting a person from conduct which amounts to harassment or will cause fear of violence, or
      (ii) those prohibitions which, if the defendant is acquitted, the prosecutor proposes as necessary to protect a person from harassment by the defendant.

(7) Where the prosecutor wants the court to make an anti-social behaviour order, a criminal behaviour order or a prohibition order, the rules about special measures directions in Part 18 (Measures to assist a witness or defendant to give evidence) apply, but—
   (a) the prosecutor must apply when serving a notice under paragraph (2); and
   (b) the time limits in rule 18.3(a) do not apply.

Evidence to assist the court: special rules **R-305**

31.4 (1) This rule applies where the court can make on its own initiative—
   (a) a football banning order;
   (b) a restraining order; or
   (c) an anti-social behaviour order.

(2) A party who wants the court to take account of evidence not already introduced must—
   (a) serve notice on—
      (i) the court officer, and
      (ii) every other party,
   as soon as practicable (without waiting for the verdict); and
   (b) in the notice, identify that evidence; and
   (c) attach any written statement containing such evidence.

Application to vary or revoke behaviour order **R-306**

31.5 (1) The court may vary or revoke a behaviour order if—
   (a) the legislation under which it is made allows the court to do so; and
   (b) one of the following applies—
      (i) the prosecutor,
      (ii) the person to whom the order is directed,
      (iii) any other person protected or affected by the order,
      (iv) the relevant authority or responsible officer,
      (v) the relevant Chief Officer of Police,
      (vi) the Director of Public Prosecutions, or
      (vii) the Director of the Serious Fraud Office.

(2) A person applying under this rule must—
   (a) apply in writing as soon as practicable after becoming aware of the grounds for doing so, explaining—
      (i) what material circumstances have changed since the order was made, and
      (ii) why the order should be varied or revoked as a result; and
   (b) serve the application on—
      (i) the court officer,
      (ii) as appropriate, the prosecutor or defendant, and
      (iii) any other person listed in paragraph (1)(b), if the court so directs.

(3) A party who wants the court to take account of any particular evidence before making its decision must, as soon as practicable—
(a) serve notice on—
(i) the court officer,
(ii) as appropriate, the prosecutor or defendant, and
(iii) any other person listed in paragraph (1)(b) on whom the court directed the application to be served; and
(b) in that notice identify the evidence and attach any written statement that has not already been served.
(4) The court may decide an application under this rule with or without a hearing.
(5) But the court must not—
(a) dismiss an application under this rule unless the applicant has had an opportunity to make representations at a hearing (whether or not the applicant in fact attends); or
(b) allow an application under this rule unless everyone required to be served, by this rule or by the court, has had at least 14 days in which to make representations, including representations about whether there should be a hearing.
(6) The court officer must—
(a) serve the application on any person, if the court so directs; and
(b) give notice of any hearing to—
(i) the applicant, and
(ii) any person required to be served, by this rule or by the court.

R-307 Notice of hearsay evidence

31.6 (1) A party who wants to introduce hearsay evidence must—
(a) serve notice on—
(i) the court officer, and
(ii) every other party directly affected; and
(b) in that notice—
(i) explain that it is a notice of hearsay evidence,
(ii) identify that evidence,
(iii) identify the person who made the statement which is hearsay, or explain why if that person is not identified, and
(iv) explain why that person will not be called to give oral evidence.
(2) A party may serve one notice under this rule in respect of more than one notice and more than one witness.

R-308 Cross-examination of maker of hearsay statement

31.7 (1) This rule applies where a party wants the court's permission to cross-examine a person who made a statement which another party wants to introduce as hearsay.
(2) The party who wants to cross-examine that person must—
(a) apply in writing, with reasons, not more than 7 days after service of the notice of hearsay evidence; and
(b) serve the application on—
(i) the court officer,
(ii) the party who served the hearsay evidence notice, and
(iii) every party on whom the hearsay evidence notice was served.
(3) The court may decide an application under this rule with or without a hearing.
(4) But the court must not—
(a) dismiss an application under this rule unless the applicant has had an opportunity to make representations at a hearing (whether or not the applicant in fact attends); or
(b) allow an application under this rule unless everyone served with the application has had at least 7 days in which to make representations, including representations about whether there should be a hearing.

R-309 Credibility and consistency of maker of hearsay statement

31.8 (1) This rule applies where a party wants to challenge the credibility or consistency of a person who made a statement which another party wants to introduce as hearsay.
(2) The party who wants to challenge the credibility or consistency of that person must—
(a) serve notice of intention to do so on—
(i) the court officer, and
(ii) the party who served the notice of hearsay evidence
not more than 7 days after service of that hearsay evidence notice; and
(b) in the notice, identify any statement or other material on which that party relies.

(3) The party who served the hearsay notice—
(a) may call that person to give oral evidence instead; and
(b) if so, must serve notice of intention to do so on—
(i) the court officer, and
(ii) every party on whom the hearsay notice was served
not more than 7 days after service of the notice under paragraph (2).

European protection order to be given effect in another EU member State R-310

31.9 (1) This rule applies where—
(a) a person benefits from the protection of one or more of the following prohibitions or restrictions imposed on another person by an order of a court in England and Wales when dealing with a criminal cause or matter—
(i) a prohibition from entering certain localities, places or defined areas where the protected person resides or visits,
(ii) a prohibition or restriction of contact with the protected person by any means (including by telephone, post, facsimile transmission or electronic mail),
(iii) a prohibition or restriction preventing the other person from approaching the protected person whether at all or to within a particular distance; and either
(b) that protected person wants the Crown Court or a magistrates' court to make a European protection order to supplement such an order; or
(c) the court varies or revokes such a prohibition or restriction in such an order and correspondingly amends or revokes a European protection order already made.
(2) Such a protected person—
(a) may apply orally or in writing to the Crown Court at the hearing at which the order imposing the prohibition or restriction is made by that court; or
(b) in any other case, must apply in writing to a magistrates' court and serve the application on the court officer.
(3) The application must—
(a) identify the prohibition or restriction that the European protection order would supplement;
(b) identify the date, if any, on which that prohibition or restriction will expire;
(c) specify the European Union member State in which the applicant has decided to reside or stay, or in which he or she already is residing or staying;
(d) indicate the length of the period for which the applicant intends to reside or stay in that member State;
(e) explain why the applicant needs the protection of that measure while residing or staying in that member State; and
(f) include any other information of which the applicant wants the court to take account.
(4) Where the court makes or amends a European protection order, the court officer must—
(a) issue an order in the form required by Directive 2011/99/EU;
(b) serve on the competent authority of the European Union member State in which the protected person has decided to reside or stay—
(i) a copy of that form, and
(ii) a copy of the form translated into an official language of that member State, or into an official language of the European Union if that member State has declared that it will accept a translation in that language.
(5) Where the court revokes a European protection order, the court officer must without delay so inform that authority.
(6) Where the court refuses to make a European protection order, the court officer must arrange for the protected person to be informed of any available avenue of appeal or review against the court's decision.

Giving effect to a European protection order made in another EU member State R-311

31.10 (1) This rule applies where the Lord Chancellor serves on the court officer—
(a) a request by an authority in another European Union member State to give effect to a European protection order;
(b) a request by such an authority to give effect to a variation of such an order; or
(c) notice by such an authority of the revocation or withdrawal of such an order.
(2) In the case of a request to which paragraph (1) refers, the court officer must, without undue delay—
(a) arrange for the court to consider the request;
(b) serve on the requesting authority—
(i) notice of any further information required by the court, and
(ii) subject to any such requirement and any response, notice of the court's decision;

(c) where the court gives effect to the European protection order—
   (i) include in the notice served on the requesting authority the terms of the restraining order made by the court,
   (ii) serve notice of those terms, and of the potential legal consequences of breaching them, on the person restrained by the order made by the court and on the person protected by that order, and
   (iii) serve notice on the Lord Chancellor of any breach of the restraining order which is reported to the court;

(d) where the court refuses to give effect to the European protection order—
   (i) include in the notice served on the requesting authority the grounds for the refusal,
   (ii) where appropriate, inform the protected person, or any representative or guardian of that person, of the possibility of applying for a comparable order under the law of England and Wales, and
   (iii) arrange for that person, representative or guardian to be informed of any available avenue of appeal or review against the court's decision.

(3) In the case of a notice to which paragraph (1) refers, the court officer must, as soon as possible, arrange for the court to act on that notice.

(4) Unless the court otherwise directs, the court officer must omit from any notice served on a person against whom a restraining order may be, or has been, made the address or contact details of the person who is the object of the European protection order.

R-312 Court's power to vary requirements under this Part

31.11 Unless other legislation otherwise provides, the court may—
(a) shorten a time limit or extend it (even after it has expired);
(b) allow a notice or application to be given in a different form, or presented orally.

Criminal Procedure Rules Part 32 Breach, Revocation and Amendment of Community and Other Orders

R-313 When this Part applies

32.1 This Part applies where—
(a) the person responsible for a defendant's compliance with an order to which applies—
   (i) Schedule 3, 5, 7 or 8 to the Powers of Criminal Courts (Sentencing) Act 2000,
   (ii) Schedule 8 or 12 to the Criminal Justice Act 2003,
   (iii) Schedule 2 to the Criminal Justice and Immigration Act 2008, or
   (iv) the Schedule to the Street Offences Act 1959

   wants the court to deal with that defendant for failure to comply;
(b) one of the following wants the court to exercise any power it has to revoke or amend such an order—
   (i) the responsible officer or supervisor,
   (ii) the defendant, or
   (iii) where the legislation allows, a person affected by the order; or
(c) the court considers exercising on its own initiative any power it has to revoke or amend such an order.

R-314 Application by responsible officer or supervisor

32.2 (1) This rule applies where—
(a) the responsible officer wants the court to—
   (i) deal with a defendant for failure to comply with an order to which this Part applies, or
   (ii) revoke or amend such an order; or
(b) the court considers exercising on its own initiative any power it has to—
   (i) revoke or amend such an order, and
   (ii) summon the defendant to attend for that purpose.

(2) Rules 7.2 to 7.4, which deal, among other things, with starting a prosecution in a magistrates' court, apply—
(a) as if—
   (i) a reference in those rules to an allegation of an offence included a reference to an allegation of failure to comply with an order to which this Part applies, and
   (ii) a reference to the prosecutor included a reference to the responsible officer or supervisor; and
(b) with the necessary consequential modifications.

Application by defendant or person affected R-315

32.3 (1) This rule applies where—
(a) the defendant wants the court to exercise any power it has to revoke or amend an order to which this Part applies; or
(b) where the legislation allows, a person affected by such an order wants the court to exercise any such power.
(2) That defendant, or person affected, must—
(a) apply in writing, explaining why the order should be revoked or amended; and
(b) serve the application on—
(i) the court officer,
(ii) the responsible officer or supervisor, and
(iii) as appropriate, the defendant or the person affected.

Procedure on application by responsible officer or supervisor R-316

32.4 (1) Except for rules 24.8 (Written guilty plea; special rules) and 24.9 (Single justice procedure: special rules), the rules in Part 24, which deal with the procedure at a trial in a magistrates' court, apply—
(a) as if—
(i) a reference in those rules to an allegation of an offence included a reference to an allegation of failure to comply with an order to which this Part applies,
(ii) a reference to the court's verdict included a reference to the court's decision to revoke or amend such an order, or to exercise any other power it has to deal with the defendant, and
(iii) a reference to the court's sentence included a reference to the exercise of any such power; and
(b) with the necessary consequential modifications.
(2) The court officer must serve on each party any order revoking or amending an order to which this Part applies.

Criminal Procedure Rules Part 33 Confiscation and Related Proceedings

General rules

Interpretation R-317

33.1 In this Part:
'document' means anything in which information of any description is recorded;
'hearsay evidence' means evidence consisting of hearsay within the meaning of section 1(2) of the Civil Evidence Act 1995;
'restraint proceedings' means proceedings under sections 42 and 58(2) and (3) of the Proceeds of Crime Act 2002;
'receivership proceedings' means proceedings under sections 48, 49, 50, 51, 54(4), 59(2) and (3), 62 and 63 of the 2002 Act;
'witness statement' means a written statement signed by a person which contains the evidence, and only that evidence, which that person would be allowed to give orally; and
words and expressions used have the same meaning as in Part 2 of the 2002 Act.

Calculation of time R-318

33.2 (1) This rule shows how to calculate any period of time for doing any act which is specified by this Part for the purposes of any proceedings under Part 2 of the Proceeds of Crime Act 2002 or by an order of the Crown Court in restraint proceedings or receivership proceedings.
(2) A period of time expressed as a number of days shall be computed as clear days.
(3) In this rule 'clear days' means that in computing the number of days—
(a) the day on which the period begins; and
(b) if the end of the period is defined by reference to an event, the day on which that event occurs,
are not included.
(4) Where the specified period is 5 days or less and includes a day which is not a business day that day does not count.

Court office closed R-319

33.3 When the period specified by this Part, or by an order of the Crown Court under Part 2 of the Proceeds of Crime Act 2002, for doing any act at the court office falls on a day on which the office is closed, that act shall be in time if done on the next day on which the court office is open.

R-320 **Application for registration of Scottish or Northern Ireland Order**

33.4 (1) This rule applies to an application for registration of an order under article 6 of the Proceeds of Crime Act 2002 (Enforcement in different parts of the United Kingdom) Order 2002.

(2) The application may be made without notice.

(3) The application must be in writing and may be supported by a witness statement which must—

(a) exhibit the order or a certified copy of the order; and

(b) to the best of the witness's ability, give full details of the realisable property located in England and Wales in respect of which the order was made and specify the person holding that realisable property.

(4) If the court registers the order, the applicant must serve notice of the registration on—

(a) any person who holds realisable property to which the order applies; and

(b) any other person whom the applicant knows to be affected by the order.

(5) The permission of the Crown Court under rule 33.10 is not required to serve the notice outside England and Wales.

R-321 **Application to vary or set aside registration**

33.5 (1) An application to vary or set aside registration of an order under article 6 of the Proceeds of Crime Act 2002 (Enforcement in different parts of the United Kingdom) Order 2002 may be made to the Crown Court by—

(a) any person who holds realisable property to which the order applies; and

(b) any other person affected by the order.

(2) The application must be in writing and may be supported by a witness statement.

(3) The application and any witness statement must be lodged with the Crown Court.

(4) The application must be served on the person who applied for registration at least 7 days before the date fixed by the court for hearing the application, unless the Crown Court specifies a shorter period.

(5) No property in England and Wales may be realised in pursuance of the order before the Crown Court has decided the application.

R-322 **Register of orders**

33.6 (1) The Crown Court must keep, under the direction of the Lord Chancellor, a register of the orders registered under article 6 of the Proceeds of Crime Act 2002 (Enforcement in different parts of the United Kingdom) Order 2002.

(2) The register must include details of any variation or setting aside of a registration under rule 33.5 and of any execution issued on a registered order.

(3) If the person who applied for registration of an order which is subsequently registered notifies the Crown Court that the court which made the order has varied or discharged the order, details of the variation or discharge, as the case may be, must be entered in the register.

R-323 **Statements of truth**

33.7 (1) Any witness statement required to be served by this Part must be verified by a statement of truth contained in the witness statement.

(2) A statement of truth is a declaration by the person making the witness statement to the effect that the witness statement is true to the best of his knowledge and belief and that he made the statement knowing that, if it were tendered in evidence, he would be liable to prosecution if he wilfully stated in it anything which he knew to be false or did not believe to be true.

(3) The statement of truth must be signed by the person making the witness statement.

(4) If the person making the witness statement fails to verify the witness statement by a statement of truth, the Crown Court may direct that it shall not be admissible as evidence.

R-324 **Use of witness statements for other purposes**

33.8 (1) Except as provided by this rule, a witness statement served in proceedings under Part 2 of the Proceeds of Crime Act 2002 may be used only for the purpose of the proceedings in which it is served.

(2) Paragraph (1) does not apply if and to the extent that—

(a) the witness gives consent in writing to some other use of it;

(b) the Crown Court gives permission for some other use; or

(c) the witness statement has been put in evidence at a hearing held in public.

R-325 **Service of documents**

33.9 (1) Rule 49.1 (Notice required to accompany process served outside the United Kingdom and translations) shall not apply in restraint proceedings and receivership proceedings.

(2) An order made in restraint proceedings or receivership proceedings may be enforced against the defendant or any other person affected by it notwithstanding that service of a copy of the order has not been effected in accordance with Part 4 if the Crown Court is satisfied that the person had notice of the order by being present when the order was made.

Service outside the jurisdiction **R-326**

33.10 (1) Where this Part requires a document to be served on someone who is outside England and Wales, it may be served outside England and Wales with the permission of the Crown Court.

(2) Where a document is to be served outside England and Wales it may be served by any method permitted by the law of the country in which it is to be served.

(3) Nothing in this rule or in any court order shall authorise or require any person to do anything in the country where the document is to be served which is against the law of that country.

(4) Where this Part requires a document to be served a certain period of time before the date of a hearing and the recipient does not appear at the hearing, the hearing must not take place unless the Crown Court is satisfied that the document has been duly served.

Certificates of service **R-327**

33.11 (1) Where this Part requires that the applicant for an order in restraint proceedings or receivership proceedings serve a document on another person, the applicant must lodge a certificate of service with the Crown Court within 7 days of service of the document.

(2) The certificate must state—

(a) the method of service;

(b) the date of service; and

(c) if the document is served under rule 4.9 (Service by another method), such other information as the court may require when making the order permitting service by that method.

(3) Where a document is to be served by the Crown Court in restraint proceedings and receivership proceedings and the court is unable to serve it, the court must send a notice of non-service stating the method attempted to the party who requested service.

External requests and orders **R-328**

33.12 (1) The rules in this Part and in Part 42 (Appeal to the Court of Appeal in confiscation and related proceedings) apply with the necessary modifications to proceedings under the Proceeds of Crime Act 2002 (External Requests and Orders) Order 2005 in the same way that they apply to corresponding proceedings under Part 2 of the Proceeds of Crime Act 2002.

(2) This table shows how provisions of the 2005 Order correspond with provisions of the 2002 Act.

Article of the Proceeds of Crime Act 2002 (External Requests and Orders) Order 2005	*Section of the Proceeds of Crime Act 2002*
8	41
9	42
10	43
11	44
15	48
16	49
17	58
23	31
27	50
28	51
41	62
42	63
44	65
45	66

Confiscation proceedings

R-329 Statements in connection with confiscation orders

33.13 (1) This rule applies where—
(a) the court can make a confiscation order; and
(b) the prosecutor asks the court to make such an order, or the court decides to make such an order on its own initiative.

(2) Within such periods as the court directs—
(a) if the court so orders, the defendant must give such information, in such manner, as the court directs;
(b) the prosecutor must serve a statement of information relevant to confiscation on the court officer and the defendant;
(c) if the court so directs—
(i) the defendant must serve a response notice on the court officer and the prosecutor, and
(ii) the parties must identify what is in dispute.

(3) Where it appears to the court that a person other than the defendant holds, or may hold, an interest in property held by the defendant which property is likely to be realised or otherwise used to satisfy a confiscation order—
(a) the court must not determine the extent of the defendant's interest in that property unless that other person has had a reasonable opportunity to make representations; and
(b) the court may order that other person to give such information, in such manner and within such a period, as the court directs.

(4) The court may—
(a) shorten or extend a time limit which it has set;
(b) vary, discharge or supplement an order which it has made;
(c) postpone confiscation proceedings without a hearing.

(5) A prosecutor's statement of information must—
(a) identify the maker of the statement and show its date;
(b) identify the defendant in respect of whom it is served;
(c) specify the conviction which gives the court power to make the confiscation order, or each conviction if more than one;
(d) if the prosecutor believes the defendant to have a criminal lifestyle, include such matters as the prosecutor believes to be relevant in connection with deciding—
(i) whether the defendant has such a lifestyle,
(ii) whether the defendant has benefited from his or her general criminal conduct,
(iii) the defendant's benefit from that conduct, and
(iv) whether the court should or should not make such assumptions about the defendant's property as legislation permits;
(e) if the prosecutor does not believe the defendant to have a criminal lifestyle, include such matters as the prosecutor believes to be relevant in connection with deciding—
(i) whether the defendant has benefited from his or her particular criminal conduct, and
(ii) the defendant's benefit from that conduct;
(f) in any case, include such matters as the prosecutor believes to be relevant in connection with deciding—
(i) whether to make a determination about the extent of the defendant's interest in property in which another person holds, or may hold, an interest, and
(ii) what determination to make, if the court decides to make one.

(6) A defendant's response notice must—
(a) indicate the extent to which the defendant accepts the allegations made in the prosecutor's statement of information; and
(b) so far as the defendant does not accept an allegation, give particulars of any matters on which the defendant relies,

in any manner directed by the court.

(7) The court must satisfy itself that there has been explained to the defendant, in terms the defendant can understand (with help, if necessary)—
(a) that if the defendant accepts to any extent an allegation in a prosecutor's statement of information, then the court may treat that as conclusive for the purposes of deciding whether the defendant has benefited from general or particular criminal conduct, and if so by how much;
(b) that if the defendant fails in any respect to comply with a direction to serve a response notice, then the court may treat that as acceptance of each allegation to which the defendant has not replied, except the allegation that the defendant has benefited from general or particular criminal conduct; and

(c) that if the defendant fails without reasonable excuse to comply with an order to give information, then the court may draw such inference as it believes is appropriate.

Application for compliance order R-330

33.14 (1) This rule applies where—

(a) the prosecutor wants the court to make a compliance order after a confiscation order has been made;

(b) the prosecutor or a person affected by a compliance order wants the court to vary or discharge the order.

(2) Such a prosecutor or person must—

(a) apply in writing; and

(b) serve the application on—

(i) the court officer, and

(ii) as appropriate, the prosecutor and any person who is affected by the compliance order (or who would be affected if it were made), unless the court otherwise directs.

(3) The application must—

(a) specify—

(i) the confiscation order,

(ii) the compliance order, if it is an application to vary or discharge that order;

(b) if it is an application for a compliance order—

(i) specify each measure that the prosecutor proposes to ensure that the confiscation order is effective, including in particular any restriction or prohibition on the defendant's travel outside the United Kingdom, and

(ii) explain why each such measure is appropriate;

(c) if it is an application to vary or discharge a compliance order, as appropriate—

(i) specify any proposed variation, and

(ii) explain why it is appropriate for the order to be varied or discharged;

(d) attach any material on which the applicant relies;

(e) propose the terms of the order; and

(f) ask for a hearing, if the applicant wants one, and explain why it is needed.

(4) A person who wants to make representations about the application must—

(a) serve the representations on—

(i) the court officer, and

(ii) the applicant;

(b) do so as soon as reasonably practicable after service of the application;

(c) attach any material on which that person relies; and

(d) ask for a hearing, if that person wants one, and explain why it is needed.

(5) The court—

(a) may determine the application at a hearing (which must be in private unless the court otherwise directs), or without a hearing;

(b) may dispense with service on any person of a prosecutor's application for a compliance order if, in particular—

(i) the application is urgent, or

(ii) there are reasonable grounds for believing that to give notice of the application would cause the dissipation of property that otherwise would be available to satisfy the confiscation order.

Application for reconsideration R-331

33.15 (1) This rule applies where the prosecutor wants the court, in view of fresh evidence—

(a) to consider making a confiscation order where the defendant was convicted but no such order was considered;

(b) to reconsider a decision that the defendant had not benefited from criminal conduct;

(c) to reconsider a decision about the amount of the defendant's benefit.

(2) The application must—

(a) be in writing and give—

(i) the name of the defendant,

(ii) the date on which and the place where any relevant conviction occurred,

(iii) the date on which and the place where any relevant confiscation order was made or varied,

(iv) details of any slavery and trafficking reparation order made by virtue of any relevant confiscation order,

(v) the grounds for the application, and

(vi) an indication of the evidence available to support the application; and

(b) where the parties are agreed on the terms of the proposed order include, in one or more documents—
(i) a draft order in the terms proposed, and
(ii) evidence of the parties' agreement.
(3) The application must be served on—
(a) the court officer; and
(b) the defendant.
(4) The court—
(a) may determine the application without a hearing where the parties are agreed on the terms of the proposed order;
(b) must determine the application at a hearing in any other case.
(5) Where this rule or the court requires the application to be heard, the court officer must arrange for the court to hear it no sooner than the eighth day after it was served unless the court otherwise directs.

R-332 Application for new calculation of available amount

33.16 (1) This rule applies where the prosecutor or a receiver wants the court to make a new calculation of the amount available for confiscation.
(2) The application—
(a) must be in writing and may be supported by a witness statement;
(b) must identify any slavery and trafficking reparation order made by virtue of the confiscation order; and
(c) where the parties are agreed on the terms of the proposed order, must include in one or more documents—
(i) a draft order in the terms proposed, and
(ii) evidence of the parties' agreement.
(3) The application and any witness statement must be served on the court officer.
(4) The application and any witness statement must be served on—
(a) the defendant;
(b) the receiver, if the prosecutor is making the application and a receiver has been appointed; and
(c) the prosecutor, if the receiver is making the application,
(5) The court—
(a) may determine the application without a hearing where the parties are agreed on the terms of the proposed order;
(b) must determine the application at a hearing in any other case.
(6) Where this rule or the court requires the application to be heard, the court officer must arrange for the court to hear it no sooner than the eighth day after it was served unless the court otherwise directs.

R-333 Variation of confiscation order due to inadequacy of available amount

33.17 (1) This rule applies where the defendant, the prosecutor or a receiver wants the court to vary a confiscation order because the amount available is inadequate.
(2) The application—
(a) must be in writing and may be supported by a witness statement;
(b) must identify any slavery and trafficking reparation order made by virtue of the confiscation order; and
(c) where the parties are agreed on the terms of the proposed order, must include in one or more documents—
(i) a draft order in the terms proposed, and
(ii) evidence of the parties' agreement.
(3) The application and any witness statement must be served on the court officer.
(4) The application and any witness statement must be served on—
(a) the prosecutor;
(b) the defendant, if the receiver is making the application; and
(c) the receiver, if the defendant is making the application and a receiver has been appointed.
(5) The court—
(a) may determine the application without a hearing where the parties are agreed on the terms of the proposed order;
(a) must determine the application at a hearing in any other case.
(6) Where this rule or the court requires the application to be heard, the court officer must arrange for the court to hear it no sooner than the eighth day after it was served unless the court otherwise directs.

R-334 Application by magistrates' court officer to discharge confiscation order

33.18 (1) This rule applies where a magistrates' court officer wants the court to discharge a confiscation order because the amount available is inadequate or the sum outstanding is very small.

(2) The application must be in writing and give details of—
(a) the confiscation order;
(b) any slavery and trafficking reparation order made by virtue of the confiscation order;
(c) the amount outstanding under the order; and
(d) the grounds for the application.
(3) The application must be served on—
(a) the defendant;
(b) the prosecutor; and
(c) any receiver.
(4) The court may determine the application without a hearing unless a person listed in paragraph (3) indicates, within 7 days after the application was served, that he or she would like to make representations.
(5) If the court makes an order discharging the confiscation order, the court officer must, at once, send a copy of the order to—
(a) the magistrates' court officer who applied for the order;
(b) the defendant;
(c) the prosecutor; and
(d) any receiver.

Application for variation of confiscation order made against an absconder **R-335**

33.19 (1) This rule applies where the defendant wants the court to vary a confiscation order made while the defendant was an absconder.
(2) The application must be in writing and supported by a witness statement which must give details of—
(a) the confiscation order;
(b) any slavery and trafficking reparation order made by virtue of the confiscation order;
(c) the circumstances in which the defendant ceased to be an absconder;
(d) the defendant's conviction of the offence or offences concerned; and
(e) the reason why the defendant believes the amount required to be paid under the confiscation order was too large.
(3) The application and witness statement must be served on the court officer.
(4) The application and witness statement must be served on the prosecutor at least 7 days before the date fixed by the court for hearing the application, unless the court specifies a shorter period.

Application for discharge of confiscation order made against an absconder **R-336**

33.20 (1) This rule applies where the defendant wants the court to discharge a confiscation order made while the defendant was an absconder and—
(a) the defendant since has been tried and acquitted of each offence concerned; or
(b) the prosecution has not concluded or is not to proceed.
(2) The application must be in writing and supported by a witness statement which must give details of—
(a) the confiscation order;
(b) the date on which the defendant ceased to be an absconder;
(c) the acquittal of the defendant if he or she has been acquitted of the offence concerned; and
(d) if the defendant has not been acquitted of the offence concerned—
(i) the date on which the defendant ceased to be an absconder,
(ii) the date on which the proceedings taken against the defendant were instituted and a summary of steps taken in the proceedings since then, and
(iii) any indication that the prosecutor does not intend to proceed against the defendant.
(3) The application and witness statement must be served on the court officer.
(4) The application and witness statement must be served on the prosecutor at least 7 days before the date fixed by the court for hearing the application, unless the court specifies a shorter period.
(5) If the court orders the discharge of the confiscation order, the court officer must serve notice on any other court responsible for enforcing the order.

Application for increase in term of imprisonment in default **R-337**

33.21 (1) This rule applies where —
(a) a court varies a confiscation order; and
(b) the prosecutor wants the court in consequence to increase the term of imprisonment to be served in default of payment.
(2) The application must be made in writing and give details of—
(a) the name and address of the defendant;
(b) the confiscation order;

(c) the grounds for the application; and
(d) the enforcement measures taken, if any.

(3) On receipt of the application, the court officer must—
(a) at once, send to the defendant and any other court responsible for enforcing the order, a copy of the application; and
(b) fix a time, date and place for the hearing and notify the applicant and the defendant of that time, date and place.

(4) If the court makes an order increasing the term of imprisonment in default, the court officer must, at once, send a copy of the order to—
(a) the applicant;
(b) the defendant;
(c) where the defendant is in custody at the time of the making of the order, the person having custody of the defendant; and
(d) any other court responsible for enforcing the order.

R-338 **Compensation—general**

33.22 (1) This rule applies where a person who held realisable property wants the court to award compensation for loss suffered in consequence of anything done in relation to that property in connection with confiscation proceedings.
(2) The application must be in writing and may be supported by a witness statement.
(3) The application and any witness statement must be served on the court officer.
(4) The application and any witness statement must be served on—
(a) the person alleged to be in default; and
(b) the person or authority by whom the compensation would be payable,
at least 7 days before the date fixed by the court for hearing the application, unless the court directs otherwise.

R-339 **Compensation—confiscation order made against absconder**

33.23 (1) This rule applies where—
(a) the court varies or discharges a confiscation order made against an absconder;
(b) a person who held realisable property suffered loss as a result of the making of that confiscation order; and
(c) that person wants the court to award compensation for that loss.
(2) The application must be in writing and supported by a witness statement which must give details of—
(a) the confiscation order;
(b) the variation or discharge of the confiscation order;
(c) the realisable property to which the application relates; and
(d) the loss suffered by the applicant as a result of the confiscation order.
(3) The application and witness statement must be served on the court officer.
(4) The application and witness statement must be served on the prosecutor at least 7 days before the date fixed by the court for hearing the application, unless the court specifies a shorter period.

R-340 **Payment of money held or detained in satisfaction of confiscation order**

33.24 (1) An order under section 67 of the Proceeds of Crime Act 2002 requiring the payment of money to a magistrates' court officer ('a payment order') shall—
(a) be directed to—
(i) the bank or building society concerned, where the money is held in an account maintained with that bank or building society, or
(ii) the person on whose authority the money is detained, in any other case;
(b) name the person against whom the confiscation order has been made;
(c) state the amount which remains to be paid under the confiscation order;
(d) state the name and address of the branch at which the account in which the money ordered to be paid is held and the sort code of that branch, if the sort code is known;
(e) state the name in which the account in which the money ordered to be paid is held and the account number of that account, if the account number is known;
(f) state the amount which the bank or building society is required to pay to the court officer under the payment order;
(g) give the name and address of the court officer to whom payment is to be made; and
(h) require the bank or building society to make payment within a period of 7 days beginning on the day on which the payment order is made, unless it appears to the court that a longer or shorter period would be appropriate in the particular circumstances.
(2) In this rule 'confiscation order' has the meaning given to it by section 88(6) of the Proceeds of Crime Act 2002.

Application to realise seized property R-341

33.25 (1) This rule applies where—
(a) property is held by a defendant against whom a confiscation order has been made;
(b) the property has been seized by or produced to an officer; and
(c) an officer who is entitled to apply wants a magistrates' court—
(i) to make an order under section 67A of the Proceeds of Crime Act 2002 authorising the realisation of the property towards satisfaction of the confiscation order, or
(ii) to determine any storage, insurance or realisation costs in respect of the property which may be recovered under section 67B of the 2002 Act.
(2) Such an officer must—
(a) apply in writing; and
(b) serve the application on—
(i) the court officer, and
(ii) any person whom the applicant believes would be affected by an order.
(3) The application must—
(a) specify the property;
(b) explain—
(i) the applicant's entitlement to apply,
(ii) how the proposed realisation meets the conditions prescribed by section 67A of the 2002 Act, and
(iii) how any storage, etc. costs have been calculated;
(c) attach any material on which the applicant relies; and
(d) propose the terms of the order.
(4) The court may—
(a) determine the application at a hearing, or without a hearing;
(b) consider an application made orally instead of in writing;
(c) consider an application which has not been served on a person likely to be affected by an order.
(5) If the court authorises the realisation of the property, the applicant must—
(a) notify any person affected by the order who was absent when it was made; and
(b) serve on the court officer a list of those so notified.

Appeal about decision on application to realise seized property R-342

33.26 (1) This rule applies where on an application under rule 33.25 for an order authorising the realisation of property—
(a) a magistrates' court decides not to make such an order and an officer who is entitled to apply wants to appeal against that decision to the Crown Court, under section 67C(1) of the Proceeds of Crime Act 2002;
(b) a magistrates' court makes such an order and a person who is affected by that decision, other than the defendant against whom the confiscation order was made, wants to appeal against it to the Crown Court, under section 67C(2) of the 2002 Act;
(c) a magistrates' court makes a decision about storage, etc. costs and an officer who is entitled to apply wants to appeal against that decision to the Crown Court, under section 67C(4) of the 2002 Act.
(2) The appellant must serve an appeal notice—
(a) on the Crown Court officer and on any other party;
(b) not more than 21 days after the magistrates' court's decision, or, if applicable, service of notice under rule 33.25(5).
(3) The appeal notice must—
(a) specify the decision under appeal;
(b) where paragraph (1)(a) applies, explain why the property should be realised;
(c) in any other case, propose the order that the appellant wants the court to make, and explain why.
(4) Rule 34.11 (Constitution of the Crown Court) applies on such an appeal.

Application for direction about surplus proceeds R-343

33.27 (1) This rule applies where—
(a) on an application under rule 33.25, a magistrates' court has made an order authorising an officer to realise property;
(b) an officer so authorised holds proceeds of that realisation;
(c) the confiscation order has been fully paid; and
(d) the officer, or a person who had or has an interest in the property represented by the proceeds, wants a magistrates' court or the Crown Court to determine under section 67D of the Proceeds of Crime Act 2002—
(i) to whom the remaining proceeds should be paid, and
(ii) in what amount or amounts.

(2) Such a person must—
(a) apply in writing; and
(b) serve the application on—
(i) the court officer, and
(ii) as appropriate, the officer holding the proceeds, or any person to whom such proceeds might be paid.

(3) The application must—
(a) specify the property which was realised;
(b) explain the applicant's entitlement to apply;
(c) describe the distribution proposed by the applicant and explain why that is proposed;
(d) attach any material on which the applicant relies; and
(e) ask for a hearing, if the applicant wants one, and explain why it is needed.

(4) A person who wants to make representations about the application must—
(a) serve the representations on—
(i) the court officer,
(ii) the applicant, and
(iii) any other person to whom proceeds might be paid;
(b) do so as soon as reasonably practicable after service of the application;
(c) attach any material on which that person relies; and
(d) ask for a hearing, if that person wants one, and explain why it is needed.

(5) The court—
(a) must not determine the application unless the applicant and each person on whom it was served—
(i) is present, or
(ii) has had an opportunity to attend or to make representations;
(b) subject to that, may determine the application—
(i) at a hearing (which must be in private unless the court otherwise directs), or without a hearing,
(ii) in the absence of any party to the application.

Seizure and detention proceedings

R-344 Application for approval to seize property or to search

33.28 (1) This rule applies where an officer who is entitled to apply wants the approval of a magistrates' court, under section 47G of the Proceeds of Crime Act 2002—
(a) to seize property, under section 47C of that Act;
(b) to search premises or a person or vehicle for property to be seized, under section 47D, 47E or 47F of that Act.

(2) Such an officer must—
(a) apply in writing; and
(b) serve the application on the court officer.

(3) The application must—
(a) explain—
(i) the applicant's entitlement to apply, and
(ii) how the proposed seizure meets the conditions prescribed by sections 47B, 47C and, if applicable, 47D, 47E or 47F of the 2002 Act;
(b) if applicable, specify any premises, person or vehicle to be searched;
(c) attach any material on which the applicant relies; and
(d) propose the terms in which the applicant wants the court to give its approval.

(4) The court—
(a) must determine the application—
(i) at a hearing, which must be in private unless the court otherwise directs, and
(ii) in the applicant's presence;
(b) may consider an application made orally instead of in writing.

R-345 Application to extend detention period

33.29 (1) This rule applies where an officer who is entitled to apply, or the prosecutor, wants a magistrates' court to make an order, under section 47M of the Proceeds of Crime Act 2002, extending the period for which seized property may be detained.

(2) Such an officer or prosecutor must—
(a) apply in writing; and
(b) serve the application on—
(i) the court officer, and
(ii) any person whom the applicant believes would be affected by an order.

(3) The application must—
(a) specify—
(i) the property to be detained, and
(ii) whether the applicant wants it to be detained for a specified period or indefinitely;
(b) explain—
(i) the applicant's entitlement to apply, and
(ii) how the proposed detention meets the conditions prescribed by section 47M of the 2002 Act;
(c) attach any material on which the applicant relies; and
(d) propose the terms of the order.
(4) The court—
(a) must determine the application—
(i) at a hearing, which must be in private unless the court otherwise directs, and
(ii) in the applicant's presence;
(b) may—
(i) consider an application made orally instead of in writing,
(ii) require service of the application on the court officer after it has been heard, instead of before.
(5) If the court extends the period for which the property may be detained, the applicant must—
(a) notify any person affected by the order who was absent when it was made; and
(b) serve on the court officer a list of those so notified.

Application to vary or discharge order for extended detention R-346

33.30 (1) This rule applies where an officer who is entitled to apply, the prosecutor, or a person affected by an order to which rule 33.29 applies, wants a magistrates' court to vary or discharge that order, under section 47N of the Proceeds of Crime Act 2002.
(2) Such a person must—
(a) apply in writing; and
(b) serve the application on—
(i) the court officer, and
(ii) as appropriate, the applicant for the order, or any person affected by the order.
(3) The application must—
(a) specify the order and the property detained;
(b) explain—
(i) the applicant's entitlement to apply,
(ii) why it is appropriate for the order to be varied or discharged,
(iii) if applicable, on what grounds the court must discharge the order;
(c) attach any material on which the applicant relies;
(d) if applicable, propose the terms of any variation; and
(e) ask for a hearing, if the applicant wants one, and explain why it is needed.
(4) A person who wants to make representations about the application must—
(a) serve the representations on—
(i) the court officer, and
(ii) the applicant;
(b) do so as soon as reasonably practicable after service of the application;
(c) attach any material on which that person relies;
(d) ask for a hearing, if that person wants one, and explain why it is needed.
(5) The court—
(a) must not determine the application unless the applicant and each person on whom it was served—
(i) is present, or
(ii) has had an opportunity to attend or to make representations;
(b) subject to that, may determine the application—
(i) at a hearing (which must be in private unless the court otherwise directs), or without a hearing,
(ii) in the absence of any party to the application.

Appeal about property detention decision R-347

33.31 (1) This rule applies where—
(a) on an application under rule 33.29 for an order extending the period for which property may be detained—
(i) a magistrates' court decides not to make such an order, and
(ii) an officer who is entitled to apply for such an order, or the prosecutor, wants to appeal against that decision to the Crown Court under section 47O(1) of the Proceeds of Crime Act 2002;

(b) on an application under rule 33.30 to vary or discharge an order under rule 33.29—
(i) a magistrates' court determines the application, and
(ii) a person who is entitled to apply under that rule wants to appeal against that decision to the Crown Court under section 47O(2) of the 2002 Act.
(2) The appellant must serve an appeal notice—
(a) on the Crown Court officer and on any other party;
(b) not more than 21 days after the magistrates' court's decision, or, if applicable, service of notice under rule 33.29(5).
(3) The appeal notice must—
(a) specify the decision under appeal;
(b) where paragraph (1)(a) applies, explain why the detention period should be extended;
(c) where paragraph (1)(b) applies, propose the order that the appellant wants the court to make, and explain why.
(4) Rule 34.11 (Constitution of the Crown Court) applies on such an appeal.

Restraint and receivership proceedings: rules that apply generally

R-348 Taking control of goods and forfeiture

33.32 (1) This rule applies to applications under sections 58(2) and (3) and 59(2) and (3) of the Proceeds of Crime Act 2002 for leave of the Crown Court to take control of goods or levy distress against property, or to exercise a right of forfeiture by peaceable re-entry in relation to a tenancy, in circumstances where the property or tenancy is the subject of a restraint order or a receiver has been appointed in respect of the property or tenancy.
(2) The application must be made in writing to the Crown Court.
(3) The application must be served on—
(a) the person who applied for the restraint order or the order appointing the receiver; and
(b) any receiver appointed in respect of the property or tenancy,
at least 7 days before the date fixed by the court for hearing the application, unless the Crown Court specifies a shorter period.

R-349 Joining of applications

33.33 An application for the appointment of a management receiver or enforcement receiver under rule 33.56 may be joined with—
(a) an application for a restraint order under rule 33.51; and
(b) an application for the conferral of powers on the receiver under rule 33.57.

R-350 Applications to be dealt with in writing

33.34 Applications in restraint proceedings and receivership proceedings are to be dealt with without a hearing, unless the Crown Court orders otherwise.

R-351 Business in chambers

33.35 Restraint proceedings and receivership proceedings may be heard in chambers.

R-352 Power of court to control evidence

33.36 (1) When hearing restraint proceedings and receivership proceedings, the Crown Court may control the evidence by giving directions as to—
(a) the issues on which it requires evidence;
(b) the nature of the evidence which it requires to decide those issues; and
(c) the way in which the evidence is to be placed before the court.
(2) The court may use its power under this rule to exclude evidence that would otherwise be admissible.
(3) The court may limit cross-examination in restraint proceedings and receivership proceedings.

R-353 Evidence of witnesses

33.37 (1) The general rule is that, unless the Crown Court orders otherwise, any fact which needs to be proved in restraint proceedings or receivership proceedings by the evidence of a witness is to be proved by their evidence in writing.
(2) Where evidence is to be given in writing under this rule, any party may apply to the Crown Court for permission to cross-examine the person giving the evidence.
(3) If the Crown Court gives permission under paragraph (2) but the person in question does not attend as required by the order, his evidence may not be used unless the court gives permission.

R-354 Witness summons

33.38 (1) Any party to restraint proceedings or receivership proceedings may apply to the Crown Court to issue a witness summons requiring a witness to—
(a) attend court to give evidence; or
(b) produce documents to the court.

(2) Rule 17.3 (Application for summons, warrant or order: general rules) applies to an application under this rule as it applies to an application under section 2 of the Criminal Procedure (Attendance of Witnesses) Act 1965.

Hearsay evidence R-355

33.39 Section 2(1) of the Civil Evidence Act 1995 (duty to give notice of intention to rely on hearsay evidence) does not apply to evidence in restraint proceedings and receivership proceedings.

Disclosure and inspection of documents R-356

33.40 (1) This rule applies where, in the course of restraint proceedings or receivership proceedings, an issue arises as to whether property is realisable property.

(2) The Crown Court may make an order for disclosure of documents.

(3) Part 31 of the Civil Procedure Rules 1998 as amended from time to time shall have effect as if the proceedings were proceedings in the High Court.

Court documents R-357

33.41 (1) Any order which the Crown Court issues in restraint proceedings or receivership proceedings must—

(a) state the name and judicial title of the person who made it;

(b) bear the date on which it is made; and

(c) be sealed by the Crown Court.

(2) The Crown Court may place the seal on the order—

(a) by hand; or

(b) by printing a facsimile of the seal on the order whether electronically or otherwise.

(3) A document purporting to bear the court's seal shall be admissible in evidence without further proof.

Consent orders R-358

33.42 (1) This rule applies where all the parties to restraint proceedings or receivership proceedings agree the terms in which an order should be made.

(2) Any party may apply for a judgment or order in the terms agreed.

(3) The Crown Court may deal with an application under paragraph (2) without a hearing.

(4) Where this rule applies—

(a) the order which is agreed by the parties must be drawn up in the terms agreed;

(b) it must be expressed as being 'By Consent'; and

(c) it must be signed by the legal representative acting for each of the parties to whom the order relates or by the party if he is a litigant in person.

(5) Where an application is made under this rule, then the requirements of any other rule as to the procedure for making an application do not apply.

Slips and omissions R-359

33.43 (1) The Crown Court may at any time correct an accidental slip or omission in an order made in restraint proceedings or receivership proceedings.

(2) A party may apply for a correction without notice.

Supply of documents from court records R-360

33.44 (1) No document relating to restraint proceedings or receivership proceedings may be supplied from the records of the Crown Court for any person to inspect or copy unless the Crown Court grants permission.

(2) An application for permission under paragraph (1) must be made on notice to the parties to the proceedings.

Disclosure of documents in criminal proceedings R-361

33.45 (1) This rule applies where—

(a) proceedings for an offence have been started in the Crown Court and the defendant has not been either convicted or acquitted on all counts; and

(b) an application for a restraint order under section 42(1) of the Proceeds of Crime Act 2002 has been made.

(2) The judge presiding at the proceedings for the offence may be supplied from the records of the Crown Court with documents relating to restraint proceedings and any receivership proceedings.

(3) Such documents must not otherwise be disclosed in the proceedings for the offence.

R-362 Preparation of documents

33.46 (1) Every order in restraint proceedings or receivership proceedings must be drawn up by the Crown Court unless—
(a) the Crown Court orders a party to draw it up;
(b) a party, with the permission of the Crown Court, agrees to draw it up; or
(c) the order is made by consent under rule 33.42.
(2) The Crown Court may direct that—
(a) an order drawn up by a party must be checked by the Crown Court before it is sealed; or
(b) before an order is drawn up by the Crown Court, the parties must lodge an agreed statement of its terms.
(3) Where an order is to be drawn up by a party—
(a) he must lodge it with the Crown Court no later than 7 days after the date on which the court ordered or permitted him to draw it up so that it can be sealed by the Crown Court; and
(b) if he fails to lodge it within that period, any other party may draw it up and lodge it.
(4) Nothing in this rule shall require the Crown Court to accept a document which is illegible, has not been duly authorised, or is unsatisfactory for some other similar reason.

R-363 Order for costs

33.47 (1) This rule applies where the Crown Court is deciding whether to make an order for costs in restraint proceedings or receivership proceedings.
(2) The court has discretion as to—
(a) whether costs are payable by one party to another;
(b) the amount of those costs; and
(c) when they are to be paid.
(3) If the court decides to make an order about costs—
(a) the general rule is that the unsuccessful party must be ordered to pay the costs of the successful party; but
(b) the court may make a different order.
(4) In deciding what order (if any) to make about costs, the court must have regard to all of the circumstances, including—
(a) the conduct of all the parties; and
(b) whether a party has succeeded on part of an application, even if he has not been wholly successful.
(5) The orders which the court may make include an order that a party must pay—
(a) a proportion of another party's costs;
(b) a stated amount in respect of another party's costs;
(c) costs from or until a certain date only;
(d) costs incurred before proceedings have begun;
(e) costs relating to particular steps taken in the proceedings;
(f) costs relating only to a distinct part of the proceedings; and
(g) interest on costs from or until a certain date, including a date before the making of an order.
(6) Where the court would otherwise consider making an order under paragraph (5)(f), it must instead, if practicable, make an order under paragraph (5)(a) or (c).
(7) Where the court has ordered a party to pay costs, it may order an amount to be paid on account before the costs are assessed.

R-364 Assessment of costs

33.48 (1) Where the Crown Court has made an order for costs in restraint proceedings or receivership proceedings it may either—
(a) make an assessment of the costs itself; or
(b) order assessment of the costs under rule 45.11.
(2) In either case, the Crown Court or the assessing authority, as the case may be, must—
(a) only allow costs which are proportionate to the matters in issue; and
(b) resolve any doubt which it may have as to whether the costs were reasonably incurred or reasonable and proportionate in favour of the paying party.
(3) The Crown Court or the assessing authority, as the case may be, is to have regard to all the circumstances in deciding whether costs were proportionately or reasonably incurred or proportionate and reasonable in amount.
(4) In particular, the Crown Court or the assessing authority must give effect to any orders which have already been made.

(5) The Crown Court or the assessing authority must also have regard to—
(a) the conduct of all the parties, including in particular, conduct before, as well as during, the proceedings;
(b) the amount or value of the property involved;
(c) the importance of the matter to all the parties;
(d) the particular complexity of the matter or the difficulty or novelty of the questions raised;
(e) the skill, effort, specialised knowledge and responsibility involved;
(f) the time spent on the application; and
(g) the place where and the circumstances in which work or any part of it was done.

Time for complying with an order for costs **R-365**

33.49 A party to restraint proceedings or receivership proceedings must comply with an order for the payment of costs within 14 days of—
(a) the date of the order if it states the amount of those costs;
(b) if the amount of those costs is decided later under rule 45.11, the date of the assessing authority's decision; or
(c) in either case, such later date as the Crown Court may specify.

Application of costs rules **R-366**

33.50 Rules 33.47, 33.48 and 33.49 do not apply to the assessment of costs in proceedings to the extent that section 11 of the Access to Justice Act 1999 applies and provisions made under that Act make different provision.

Restraint proceedings

Application for restraint order or ancillary order **R-367**

33.51 (1) This rule applies where the prosecutor, or an accredited financial investigator, makes an application under section 42 of the Proceeds of Crime Act 2002 for—
(a) a restraint order, under section 41(1) of the 2002 Act; or
(b) an ancillary order, under section 41(7) of that Act, for the purpose of ensuring that a restraint order is effective.
(2) The application may be made without notice if the application is urgent or if there are reasonable grounds for believing that giving notice would cause the dissipation of realisable property which is the subject of the application.
(3) An application for a restraint order must be in writing and supported by a witness statement which must—
(a) give the grounds for the application;
(b) to the best of the witness's ability, give full details of the realisable property in respect of which the applicant is seeking the order and specify the person holding that realisable property;
(c) include the proposed terms of the order.
(4) An application for an ancillary order must be in writing and supported by a witness statement which must—
(a) give the grounds for, and full details of, the application;
(b) include, if appropriate—
(i) any request for an order for disclosure of documents to which rule 33.40 applies (Disclosure and inspection of documents),
(ii) the identity of any person whom the applicant wants the court to examine about the extent or whereabouts of realisable property,
(iii) a list of the main questions that the applicant wants to ask any such person, and
(iv) a list of any documents to which the applicant wants to refer such a person; and
(c) include the proposed terms of the order.
(5) An application for a restraint order and an application for an ancillary order may (but need not) be made at the same time and contained in the same documents.
(6) An application by an accredited financial investigator must include a statement that, under section 68 of the 2002 Act, the applicant has authority to apply.

Restraint and ancillary orders **R-368**

33.52 (1) The Crown Court may make a restraint order subject to exceptions, including, but not limited to, exceptions for reasonable living expenses and reasonable legal expenses, and for the purpose of enabling any person to carry on any trade, business or occupation.

(2) But the Crown Court must not make an exception for legal expenses where this is prohibited by section 41(4) of the Proceeds of Crime Act 2002.
(3) An exception to a restraint order may be made subject to conditions.
(4) The Crown Court must not require the applicant for a restraint order to give any undertaking relating to damages sustained as a result of the restraint order by a person who is prohibited from dealing with realisable property by the restraint order.
(5) The Crown Court may require the applicant for a restraint order to give an undertaking to pay the reasonable expenses of any person, other than a person who is prohibited from dealing with realisable property by the restraint order, which are incurred in complying with the restraint order.
(6) An order must include a statement that disobedience of the order, either by a person to whom the order is addressed, or by another person, may be contempt of court and the order must include details of the possible consequences of being held in contempt of court.
(7) Unless the Crown Court otherwise directs, an order made without notice has effect until the court makes an order varying or discharging it.
(8) The applicant for an order must—
(a) serve copies of the order and of the witness statement made in support of the application on the defendant and any person who is prohibited by the order from dealing with realisable property; and
(b) notify any person whom the applicant knows to be affected by the order of its terms.

R-369 Application for discharge or variation of restraint or ancillary order by a person affected by the order

33.53 (1) This rule applies where a person affected by a restraint order makes an application to the Crown Court under section 42(3) of the Proceeds of Crime Act 2002 to discharge or vary the restraint order or any ancillary order made under section 41(7) of the Act.
(2) The application must be in writing and may be supported by a witness statement.
(3) The application and any witness statement must be lodged with the Crown Court.
(4) The application and any witness statement must be served on the person who applied for the restraint order and any person who is prohibited from dealing with realisable property by the restraint order (if he is not the person making the application) at least 2 days before the date fixed by the court for hearing the application, unless the Crown Court specifies a shorter period.

R-370 Application for variation of restraint or ancillary order by the person who applied for the order

33.54 (1) This rule applies where the applicant for a restraint order makes an application under section 42(3) of the Proceeds of Crime Act 2002 to the Crown Court to vary the restraint order or any ancillary order made under section 41(7) of the 2002 Act (including where the court has already made a restraint order and the applicant is seeking to vary the order in order to restrain further realisable property).
(2) The application may be made without notice if the application is urgent or if there are reasonable grounds for believing that giving notice would cause the dissipation of realisable property which is the subject of the application.
(3) The application must be in writing and must be supported by a witness statement which must—
(a) give the grounds for the application;
(b) where the application is for the inclusion of further realisable property in a restraint order give full details, to the best of the witness's ability, of the realisable property in respect of which the applicant is seeking the order and specify the person holding that realisable property;
(c) where the application is to vary an ancillary order, include, if appropriate—
(i) any request for an order for disclosure of documents to which rule 33.40 applies (Disclosure and inspection of documents),
(ii) the identity of any person whom the applicant wants the court to examine about the extent or whereabouts of realisable property,
(iii) a list of the main questions that the applicant wants to ask any such person, and
(iv) a list of any documents to which the applicant wants to refer such a person; and
(d) include the proposed terms of the variation.
(4) An application by an accredited financial investigator must include a statement that, under section 68 of the 2002 Act, the applicant has authority to apply.
(5) The application and witness statement must be lodged with the Crown Court.
(6) Except where, under paragraph (2), notice of the application is not required to be served, the application and witness statement must be served on any person who is prohibited from

dealing with realisable property by the restraint order at least 2 days before the date fixed by the court for hearing the application, unless the Crown Court specifies a shorter period.

(7) If the court makes an order for the variation of a restraint or ancillary order, the applicant must serve copies of the order and of the witness statement made in support of the application on—
(a) the defendant;
(b) any person who is prohibited from dealing with realisable property by the restraint order (whether before or after the variation); and
(c) any other person whom the applicant knows to be affected by the order.

Application for discharge of restraint or ancillary order by the person who applied for the order **R-371**

33.55 (1) This rule applies where the applicant for a restraint order makes an application under section 42(3) of the Proceeds of Crime Act 2002 to discharge the order or any ancillary order made under section 41(7) of the 2002 Act.
(2) The application may be made without notice.
(3) The application must be in writing and must state the grounds for the application.
(4) If the court makes an order for the discharge of a restraint or ancillary order, the applicant must serve copies of the order on—
(a) the defendant;
(b) any person who is prohibited from dealing with realisable property by the restraint order (whether before or after the discharge); and
(c) any other person whom the applicant knows to be affected by the order.

Receivership proceedings

Application for appointment of a management or an enforcement receiver **R-372**

33.56 (1) This rule applies to an application for the appointment of a management receiver under section 48(1) of the Proceeds of Crime Act 2002 and an application for the appointment of an enforcement receiver under section 50(1) of the 2002 Act.
(2) The application may be made without notice if—
(a) the application is joined with an application for a restraint order under rule 35.51 (Application for restraint order or ancillary order);
(b) the application is urgent; or
(c) there are reasonable grounds for believing that giving notice would cause the dissipation of realisable property which is the subject of the application.
(3) The application must be in writing and must be supported by a witness statement which must—
(a) give the grounds for the application;
(b) give full details of the proposed receiver;
(c) to the best of the witness's ability, give full details of the realisable property in respect of which the applicant is seeking the order and specify the person holding that realisable property;
(d) where the application is made by an accredited financial investigator, include a statement that, under section 68 of the 2002 Act, the applicant has authority to apply; and
(e) if the proposed receiver is not a person falling within section 55(8) of the 2002 Act and the applicant is asking the court to allow the receiver to act—
(i) without giving security, or
(ii) before he has given security or satisfied the court that he has security in place,
explain the reasons why that is necessary.
(4) Where the application is for the appointment of an enforcement receiver, the applicant must provide the Crown Court with a copy of the confiscation order made against the defendant.
(5) The application and witness statement must be lodged with the Crown Court.
(6) Except where, under paragraph (2), notice of the application is not required to be served, the application and witness statement must be lodged with the Crown Court and served on—
(a) the defendant;
(b) any person who holds realisable property to which the application relates; and
(c) any other person whom the applicant knows to be affected by the application,
at least 7 days before the date fixed by the court for hearing the application, unless the Crown Court specifies a shorter period.
(7) If the court makes an order for the appointment of a receiver, the applicant must serve copies of the order and of the witness statement made in support of the application on—
(a) the defendant;
(b) any person who holds realisable property to which the order applies; and
(c) any other person whom the applicant knows to be affected by the order.

R-373 Application for conferral of powers on a management receiver or an enforcement receiver

33.57 (1) This rule applies to an application for the conferral of powers on a management receiver under section 49(1) of the Proceeds of Crime Act 2002 or an enforcement receiver under section 51(1) of the 2002 Act.

(2) The application may be made without notice if the application is to give the receiver power to take possession of property and—
(a) the application is joined with an application for a restraint order under rule 33.51 (Application for restraint order or ancillary order);
(b) the application is urgent; or
(c) there are reasonable grounds for believing that giving notice would cause the dissipation of the property which is the subject of the application.

(3) The application must be made in writing and supported by a witness statement which must—
(a) give the grounds for the application;
(b) give full details of the realisable property in respect of which the applicant is seeking the order and specify the person holding that realisable property;
(c) where the application is made by an accredited financial investigator, include a statement that, under section 68 of the 2002 Act, the applicant has authority to apply; and
(d) where the application is for power to start, carry on or defend legal proceedings in respect of the property, explain—
(i) what proceedings are concerned, in what court, and
(ii) what powers the receiver will ask that court to exercise.

(4) Where the application is for the conferral of powers on an enforcement receiver, the applicant must provide the Crown Court with a copy of the confiscation order made against the defendant.

(5) The application and witness statement must be lodged with the Crown Court.

(6) Except where, under paragraph (2), notice of the application is not required to be served, the application and witness statement must be served on—
(a) the defendant;
(b) any person who holds realisable property in respect of which a receiver has been appointed or in respect of which an application for a receiver has been made;
(c) any other person whom the applicant knows to be affected by the application; and
(d) the receiver (if one has already been appointed),
at least 7 days before the date fixed by the court for hearing the application, unless the Crown Court specifies a shorter period.

(7) If the court makes an order for the conferral of powers on a receiver, the applicant must serve copies of the order on—
(a) the defendant;
(b) any person who holds realisable property in respect of which the receiver has been appointed; and
(c) any other person whom the applicant knows to be affected by the order.

R-374 Applications for discharge or variation of receivership orders, and applications for other orders

33.58 (1) This rule applies to applications under section 62(3) of the Proceeds of Crime Act 2002 for orders (by persons affected by the action of receivers) and applications under section 63(1) of the 2002 Act for the discharge or variation of orders relating to receivers.

(2) The application must be made in writing and lodged with the Crown Court.

(3) The application must be served on the following persons (except where they are the person making the application)—
(a) the person who applied for appointment of the receiver;
(b) the defendant;
(c) any person who holds realisable property in respect of which the receiver has been appointed;
(d) the receiver; and
(e) any other person whom the applicant knows to be affected by the application,
at least 7 days before the date fixed by the court for hearing the application, unless the Crown Court specifies a shorter period.

(4) If the court makes an order for the discharge or variation of an order relating to a receiver under section 63(2) of the 2002 Act, the applicant must serve copies of the order on any persons whom he knows to be affected by the order.

Sums in the hands of receivers R-375

33.59 (1) This rule applies where the amount payable under a confiscation order has been fully paid and any sums remain in the hands of an enforcement receiver.

(2) The receiver must make an application to the Crown Court for directions as to the distribution of the sums in his hands.

(3) The application and any evidence which the receiver intends to rely on in support of the application must be served on—

(a) the defendant; and

(b) any other person who held (or holds) interests in any property realised by the receiver,

at least 7 days before the date fixed by the court for hearing the application, unless the Crown Court specifies a shorter period.

(4) If any of the provisions listed in paragraph (5) (provisions as to the vesting of funds in a trustee in bankruptcy) apply, then the Crown Court must make a declaration to that effect.

(5) These are the provisions—

(a) section 31B of the Bankruptcy (Scotland) Act 1985;

(b) section 306B of the Insolvency Act 1986; and

(c) article 279B of the Insolvency (Northern Ireland) Order 1989.

Security R-376

33.60 (1) This rule applies where the Crown Court appoints a receiver under section 48 or 50 of the Proceeds of Crime Act 2002 and the receiver is not a person falling within section 55(8) of the 2002 Act (and it is immaterial whether the receiver is a permanent or temporary member of staff or on secondment from elsewhere).

(2) The Crown Court may direct that before the receiver begins to act, or within a specified time, he must either—

(a) give such security as the Crown Court may determine; or

(b) file with the Crown Court and serve on all parties to any receivership proceedings evidence that he already has in force sufficient security,

to cover his liability for his acts and omissions as a receiver.

(3) The Crown Court may terminate the appointment of a receiver if he fails to—

(a) give the security; or

(b) satisfy the court as to the security he has in force,

by the date specified.

Remuneration R-377

33.61 (1) This rule applies where the Crown Court appoints a receiver under section 48 or 50 of the Proceeds of Crime Act 2002 and the receiver is not a person falling within section 55(8) of the 2002 Act (and it is immaterial whether the receiver is a permanent or temporary member of staff or on secondment from elsewhere).

(2) The receiver may only charge for his services if the Crown Court—

(a) so directs; and

(b) specifies the basis on which the receiver is to be remunerated.

(3) Unless the Crown Court orders otherwise, in determining the remuneration of the receiver, the Crown Court shall award such sum as is reasonable and proportionate in all the circumstances and which takes into account—

(a) the time properly given by him and his staff to the receivership;

(b) the complexity of the receivership;

(c) any responsibility of an exceptional kind or degree which falls on the receiver in consequence of the receivership;

(d) the effectiveness with which the receiver appears to be carrying out, or to have carried out, his duties; and

(e) the value and nature of the subject matter of the receivership.

(4) The Crown Court may refer the determination of a receiver's remuneration to be ascertained by the taxing authority of the Crown Court and rules 45.11 (Assessment and re-assessment) to 45.14 (Application for an extension of time) shall have effect as if the taxing authority was ascertaining costs.

(5) A receiver appointed under section 48 of the 2002 Act is to receive his remuneration by realising property in respect of which he is appointed, in accordance with section 49(2)(d) of the 2002 Act.

(6) A receiver appointed under section 50 of the 2002 Act is to receive his remuneration by applying to the magistrates' court officer for payment under section 55(4)(b) of the 2002 Act.

R-378 **Accounts**

33.62 (1) The Crown Court may order a receiver appointed under section 48 or 50 of the Proceeds of Crime Act 2002 to prepare and serve accounts.

(2) A party to receivership proceedings served with such accounts may apply for an order permitting him to inspect any document in the possession of the receiver relevant to those accounts.

(3) Any party to receivership proceedings may, within 14 days of being served with the accounts, serve notice on the receiver—

(a) specifying any item in the accounts to which he objects;

(b) giving the reason for such objection; and

(c) requiring the receiver within 14 days of receipt of the notice, either—

(i) to notify all the parties who were served with the accounts that he accepts the objection, or

(ii) if he does not accept the objection, to apply for an examination of the accounts in relation to the contested item.

(4) When the receiver applies for the examination of the accounts he must at the same time lodge with the Crown Court—

(a) the accounts; and

(b) a copy of the notice served on him under this section of the rule.

(5) If the receiver fails to comply with paragraph (3)(c) of this rule, any party to receivership proceedings may apply to the Crown Court for an examination of the accounts in relation to the contested item.

(6) At the conclusion of its examination of the accounts the court must certify the result.

R-379 **Non-compliance by receiver**

33.63 (1) If a receiver appointed under section 48 or 50 of the Proceeds of Crime Act 2002 fails to comply with any rule, practice direction or direction of the Crown Court, the Crown Court may order him to attend a hearing to explain his non-compliance.

(2) At the hearing, the Crown Court may make any order it considers appropriate, including—

(a) terminating the appointment of the receiver;

(b) reducing the receiver's remuneration or disallowing it altogether; and

(c) ordering the receiver to pay the costs of any party.

Proceedings under the Criminal Justice Act 1988 and the Drug Trafficking Act 1994

R-380 **Statements, etc. relevant to making confiscation orders**

33.64 (1) Where a prosecutor or defendant—

(a) serves on the magistrates' court officer any statement or other document under section 73 of the Criminal Justice Act 1988 in any proceedings in respect of an offence listed in Schedule 4 to that Act; or

(b) serves on the Crown Court officer any statement or other document under section 11 of the Drug Trafficking Act 1994 or section 73 of the 1988 Act in any proceedings in respect of a drug trafficking offence or in respect of an offence to which Part VI of the 1988 Act applies,

that party must serve a copy as soon as practicable on the defendant or the prosecutor, as the case may be.

(2) Any statement tendered by the prosecutor to the magistrates' court under section 73 of the 1988 Act or to the Crown Court under section 11(1) of the 1994 Act or section 73(1A) of the 1988 Act must include the following particulars—

(a) the name of the defendant;

(b) the name of the person by whom the statement is made and the date on which it was made;

(c) where the statement is not tendered immediately after the defendant has been convicted, the date on which and the place where the relevant conviction occurred; and

(d) such information known to the prosecutor as is relevant to the determination as to whether or not the defendant has benefited from drug trafficking or relevant criminal conduct and to the assessment of the value of any proceeds of drug trafficking or, as the case may be, benefit from relevant criminal conduct.

(3) Where, in accordance with section 11(7) of the 1994 Act or section 73(1C) of the 1988 Act, the defendant indicates in writing the extent to which he or she accepts any allegation contained within the prosecutor's statement, the defendant must serve a copy of that reply on the court officer.

(4) Expressions used in this rule shall have the same meanings as in the 1994 Act or, where appropriate, the 1988 Act.

Postponed determinations R-381

33.65 (1) Where an application is made by the defendant or the prosecutor—
(a) to a magistrates' court under section 72A(5)(a) of the Criminal Justice Act 1988 asking the court to exercise its powers under section 72A(4) of that Act; or
(b) to the Crown Court under section 3(5)(a) of the Drug Trafficking Act 1994 asking the Court to exercise its powers under section 3(4) of that Act, or under section 72A(5)(a) of the 1988 Act asking the court to exercise its powers under section 72A(4) of the 1988 Act,
the application must be made in writing and the applicant must serve a copy on the prosecutor or the defendant, as the case may be.
(2) A party served with a copy of an application under paragraph (1) must, within 28 days of the date of service, notify the applicant and the court officer, in writing, whether or not that party opposes the application, giving his reasons for any opposition.
(3) After the expiry of the period referred to in paragraph (2), the court may determine an application under paragraph (1) —
(a) without a hearing; or
(b) at a hearing at which the parties may be represented.

Confiscation orders—revised assessments R-382

33.66 (1) Where the prosecutor makes an application under section 13, 14 or 15 of the Drug Trafficking Act 1994 or section 74A, 74B or 74C of the Criminal Justice Act 1988, the application must be in writing and a copy must be served on the defendant.
(2) The application must include the following particulars—
(a) the name of the defendant;
(b) the date on which and the place where any relevant conviction occurred;
(c) the date on which and the place where any relevant confiscation order was made or, as the case may be, varied;
(d) the grounds on which the application is made; and
(e) an indication of the evidence available to support the application.

Application to the Crown Court to discharge or vary order to make material available R-383

33.67 (1) Where an order under section 93H of the Criminal Justice Act 1988 (order to make material available) or section 55 of the Drug Trafficking Act 1994 (order to make material available) has been made by the Crown Court, any person affected by it may apply in writing to the court officer for the order to be discharged or varied, and on hearing such an application the court may discharge the order or make such variations to it as the court thinks fit.
(2) Subject to paragraph (3), where a person proposes to make an application under paragraph (1) for the discharge or variation of an order, that person shall give a copy of the application, not later than 48 hours before the making of the application—
(a) to a constable at the police station specified in the order; or
(b) to the office of the appropriate officer who made the application, as specified in the order,
in either case together with a notice indicating the time and place at which the application for discharge or variation is to be made.
(3) The court may direct that paragraph (2) need not be complied with if satisfied that the person making the application has good reason to seek a discharge or variation of the order as soon as possible and it is not practicable to comply with that paragraph.
(4) In this rule:
'constable' includes a person commissioned by the Commissioners for Her Majesty's Revenue and Customs;
'police station' includes a place for the time being occupied by Her Majesty's Revenue and Customs.

Application to the Crown Court for increase in term of imprisonment in default of payment R-384

33.68 (1) This rule applies to applications made, or that have effect as made, to the Crown Court under section 10 of the Drug Trafficking Act 1994 and section 75A of the Criminal Justice Act 1988 (interest on sums unpaid under confiscation orders).
(2) Notice of an application to which this rule applies to increase the term of imprisonment or detention fixed in default of payment of a confiscation order by a person ('the defendant') shall be made by the prosecutor in writing to the court officer.
(3) A notice under paragraph (2) shall—
(a) state the name and address of the defendant;
(b) specify the grounds for the application;

(c) give details of the enforcement measures taken, if any; and
(d) include a copy of the confiscation order.

(4) On receiving a notice under paragraph (2), the court officer must—
(a) forthwith send to the defendant and the magistrates' court required to enforce payment of the confiscation order under section 140(1) of the Powers of Criminal Courts (Sentencing) Act 2000, a copy of the said notice; and
(b) notify in writing the applicant and the defendant of the date, time and place appointed for the hearing of the application.

(5) Where the Crown Court makes an order pursuant to an application mentioned in paragraph (1) above, the court officer shall send forthwith a copy of the order—
(a) to the applicant;
(b) to the defendant;
(c) where the defendant is at the time of the making of the order in custody, to the person having custody of him or her; and
(d) to the magistrates' court mentioned in paragraph (4)(a).

R-385 Drug trafficking—compensation on acquittal in the Crown Court

33.69 Where the Crown Court cancels a confiscation order under section 22(2) of the Drug Trafficking Act 1994, the Crown Court officer must serve notice to that effect on the High Court officer and on the court officer of the magistrates' court which has responsibility for enforcing the order.

Contempt proceedings

R-386 Application to punish for contempt of court

33.70 (1) This rule applies where a person is accused of disobeying—
(a) a compliance order made for the purpose of ensuring that a confiscation order is effective;
(b) a restraint order; or
(c) an ancillary order made for the purpose of ensuring that a restraint order is effective.

(2) An applicant who wants the Crown Court to exercise its power to punish that person for contempt of court must comply with the rules in Part 48 (Contempt of court).

Criminal Procedure Rules Part 34 Appeal to the Crown Court

R-387 When this Part applies

34.1 (1) This part applies where—
(a) a defendant wants to appeal under—
(i) section 108 of the Magistrates' Courts Act 1980,
(ii) section 45 of the Mental Health Act 1983,
(iii) paragraph 10 of Schedule 3 to the Powers of Criminal Courts (Sentencing) Act 2000, or paragraphs 9(8) or 13(5) of Schedule 8 to the Criminal Justice Act 2003,
(iv) section 42 of the Counter Terrorism Act 2008;
(b) the Criminal Cases Review Commission refers a defendant's case to the Crown Court under section 11 of the Criminal Appeal Act 1995;
(c) a prosecutor wants to appeal under—
(i) section 14A(5A) of the Football Spectators Act 1989, or
(ii) section 147(3) of the Customs and Excise Management Act 1979; or
(d) a person wants to appeal under—
(i) section 1 of the Magistrates' Courts (Appeals from Binding Over Orders) Act 1956,
(ii) section 12(5) of the Contempt of Court Act 1981,
(iii) regulation 3C or 3H of the Costs in Criminal Cases (General) Regulations 1986,
(iv) section 22 of the Football Spectators Act 1989,
(v) section 10(4) or (5) of the Crime and Disorder Act 1998.

(2) A reference to an 'appellant' in this part is a reference to such a party or person.

R-388 Service of appeal and respondent's notices

34.2 (1) An appellant must serve an appeal notice on—
(a) the magistrates' court officer; and
(b) every other party.

(2) The appellant must serve the appeal notice—
(a) as soon after the decision appealed against as the appellant wants; but
(b) not more than 21 days after—
(i) sentence or the date sentence is deferred, whichever is earlier, if the appeal is against conviction or against a finding of guilt,

(ii) sentence, if the appeal is against sentence, or
(iii) the order or failure to make an order about which the appellant wants to appeal, in any other case.

(3) The appellant must serve with the appeal notice any application for the following, with reasons—
(a) an extension of the time limit under this rule, if the appeal notice is late;
(b) bail pending appeal, if the appellant is in custody;
(c) the suspension of any disqualification imposed or order made in the case, where the magistrates' court or the Crown Court can order such a suspension pending appeal.

(4) Where both the magistrates' court and the Crown Court can grant bail or suspend a disqualification or order pending appeal, an application must indicate by which court the appellant wants the application determined.

(5) Where the appeal is against conviction or against a finding of guilt, unless the respondent agrees that the court should allow the appeal—
(a) the respondent must serve a respondent's notice on—
(i) the Crown Court officer; and
(ii) the appellant; and
(b) the respondent must serve that notice not more than 21 days after service of the appeal notice.

Form of appeal and respondent's notices **R-389**

34.3 (1) The appeal notice must—
(a) specify—
(i) the conviction or finding of guilt,
(ii) the sentence, or
(iii) the order, or the failure to make an order,
about which the appellant wants to appeal;
(b) summarise the issues;
(c) in an appeal against conviction or against a finding of guilt, to the best of the appellant's ability and to assist the court in fulfilling its duty under rule 3.2 (the court's duty of case management)—
(i) identify the witnesses who gave oral evidence in the magistrates' court,
(ii) identify the witnesses who gave written evidence in the magistrates' court,
(iii) identify the prosecution witnesses whom the appellant will want to question if they are called to give oral evidence in the Crown Court,
(iv) identify the likely defence witnesses,
(v) give notice of any special arrangements or other measures that the appellant thinks are needed for witnesses,
(vi) explain whether the issues in the Crown Court differ from the issues in the magistrates' court, and if so how, and
(vii) say how long the trial lasted in the magistrates' court and how long the appeal is likely to last in the Crown Court;
(d) in an appeal against a sentence, order or failure to make an order—
(i) identify any circumstances, report or other information of which the appellant wants the court to take account, and
(ii) explain the significance of those circumstances or that information to what is in issue;
(e) in an appeal against a finding that the appellant insulted someone or interrupted proceedings in the magistrates' court, attach—
(i) the magistrates' court's written findings of fact, and
(ii) the appellant's response to those findings;
(f) say whether the appellant has asked the magistrates' court to reconsider the case; and
(g) include a list of those on whom the appellant has served the appeal notice.

(2) A respondent's notice must—
(a) give the date on which the respondent was served with the appeal notice; and
(b) to assist the court in fulfilling its duty under rule 3.2—
(i) identify the witnesses who gave oral evidence in the magistrates' court,
(ii) identify the witnesses who gave written evidence in the magistrates' court,
(iii) identify the prosecution witnesses whom the respondent intends to call to give oral evidence in the Crown Court,
(iv) give notice of any special arrangements or other measures that the respondent thinks are needed for witnesses,
(v) explain whether the issues in the Crown Court differ from the issues in the magistrates' court, and if so how, and

(vi) say how long the trial lasted in the magistrates' court and how long the appeal is likely to last in the Crown Court.

(3) Paragraph (4) applies in an appeal against conviction or against a finding of guilt where in the magistrates' court a party to the appeal—
(a) introduced in evidence material to which applies—
(i) Part 16 (Written witness statements),
(ii) Part 19 (Expert evidence),
(iii) Part 20 (Hearsay evidence),
(iv) Part 21 (Evidence of bad character), or
(v) Part 22 (Evidence of a complainant's previous sexual behaviour); or
(b) made an application to which applies—
(i) Part 17 (Witness summonses, warrants and orders),
(ii) Part 18 (Measures to assist a witness or defendant to give evidence), or
(iii) Part 23 (Restriction on cross-examination by a defendant).

(4) If such a party wants to reintroduce that material or to renew that application in the Crown Court that party must include a notice to that effect in the appeal or respondent's notice, as the case may be.

R-390 **Duty of magistrates' court officer**

34.4 (1) The magistrates' court officer must—
(a) arrange for the magistrates' court to hear as soon as practicable any application to that court under rule 34.2(3)(c) (suspension of disqualification or order pending appeal); and
(b) as soon as practicable notify the Crown Court officer of the service of the appeal notice and make available to that officer—
(i) the appeal notice and any accompanying application served by the appellant,
(ii) details of the parties including their addresses, and
(iii) a copy of each magistrates' court register entry relating to the decision under appeal and to any application for bail or for the suspension of a disqualification or order pending appeal.

(2) Where the appeal is against conviction or against a finding of guilt, the magistrates' court officer must make available to the Crown Court officer as soon as practicable—
(a) all material served on the magistrate's court officer to which applies—
(i) Part 8 (Initial details of the prosecution case),
(ii) Part 16 (Written witness statements),
(iii) Part 17 (Witness summonses, warrants and orders),
(iv) Part 18 (Measures to assist a witness or defendant to give evidence),
(v) Part 19 (Expert evidence),
(vi) Part 20 (Hearsay evidence),
(vii) Part 21 (Evidence of bad character),
(viii) Part 22 (Evidence of a complainant's previous sexual behaviour),
(ix) Part 23 (Restriction on cross-examination by a defendant);
(b) any case management questionnaire prepared for the purposes of the trial;
(c) all case management directions given by the magistrates' court for the purposes of the trial; and
(d) any other document, object or information for which the Crown Court officer asks.

(3) Where the appeal is against sentence, the magistrates' court officer must make available to the Crown Court officer as soon as practicable any report received for the purposes of sentencing.

(4) Unless the magistrates' court otherwise directs, the magistrates' court officer—
(a) must keep any document or object exhibited in the proceedings in the magistrates' court, or arrange for it to be kept by some other appropriate person, until at least—
(i) 6 weeks after the conclusion of those proceedings, or
(ii) the conclusion of any proceedings in the Crown Court that begin within that 6 weeks; but
(b) need not keep such a document if—
(i) the document that was exhibited is a copy of a document retained by the party who produced it, and
(ii) what was in evidence in the magistrates' court was the content of that document.

R-391 **Duty of person keeping exhibit**

34.5 A person who, under arrangements made by the magistrates' court officer, keeps a document or object exhibited in the proceedings in the magistrates' court must—
(a) keep that exhibit until—
(i) 6 weeks after the conclusion of those proceedings, or

(ii) the conclusion of any proceedings in the Crown Court that begin within that 6 weeks, unless the magistrates' court or the Crown Court otherwise directs; and

(b) provide the Crown Court with any such document or object for which the Crown Court officer asks, within such period as the Crown Court officer may require.

Reference by the Criminal Cases Review Commission R-392

34.6 (1) The Crown Court officer must, as soon as practicable, serve a reference by the Criminal Cases Review Commission on—

(a) the appellant;

(b) every other party; and

(c) the magistrates' court officer.

(2) The appellant may serve an appeal notice on—

(a) the Crown Court officer; and

(b) every other party,

not more than 21 days later.

(3) The Crown Court must treat the reference as the appeal notice if the appellant does not serve an appeal notice.

Preparation for appeal R-393

34.7 (1) The Crown Court may conduct a preparation for appeal hearing (and if necessary more than one such hearing) where—

(a) it is necessary to conduct such a hearing in order to give directions for the effective determination of the appeal; or

(b) such a hearing is required to set ground rules for the conduct of the questioning of a witness or appellant.

(2) Where under rule 34.3(4) a party gives notice to reintroduce material or to renew an application first introduced or made in the magistrates' court—

(a) no other notice or application to the same effect otherwise required by these Rules need be served; and

(b) any objection served by the other party in the magistrates' court is treated as renewed unless within 21 days that party serves notice withdrawing it.

(3) Paragraphs (4) and (5) apply where—

(a) the appeal is against conviction or against a finding of guilt;

(b) a party wants to introduce material or make an application under a Part of these Rules listed in rule 34.3(3); and

(c) that party gives no notice of reintroduction or renewal under rule 34.3(4) (whether because the conditions for giving such a notice are not met or for any other reason).

(4) Such a party must serve the material, notice or application required by that Part not more than 21 days after service of the appeal notice.

(5) Subject to paragraph (4), the requirements of that Part apply (for example, as to the form in which a notice must be given or an application made and as to the time and form in which such a notice or application may be opposed).

Hearings and decisions R-394

34.8 (1) The Crown Court as a general rule must hear in public an appeal or reference to which this part applies, but—

(a) may order any hearing to be in private; and

(b) where a hearing is about a public interest ruling, must hold that hearing in private.

(2) The Crown Court officer must give as much notice as reasonably practicable of every hearing to—

(a) the parties;

(b) any party's custodian; and

(c) any other person whom the Crown Court requires to be notified.

(3) The Crown Court officer must serve every decision on—

(a) the parties;

(b) any other person whom the Crown Court requires to be served; and

(c) the magistrates' court officer and any party's custodian, where the decision determines an appeal.

(4) But where a hearing or decision is about a public interest ruling, the Crown Court officer must not—

(a) give notice of that hearing to; or

(b) serve that decision on,

anyone other than the prosecutor who applied for that ruling, unless the court otherwise directs.

R-395 **Abandoning an appeal**

34.9 (1) The appellant—

(a) may abandon an appeal without the Crown Court's permission, by serving a notice of abandonment on—
   (i) the magistrates' court officer,
   (ii) the Crown Court officer, and
   (iii) every other party
   before the hearing of the appeal begins; but
(b) after the hearing of the appeal begins, may only abandon the appeal with the Crown Court's permission.

(2) A notice of abandonment must be signed by or on behalf of the appellant.

(3) Where an appellant who is on bail pending appeal abandons an appeal—
(a) the appellant must surrender to custody as directed by the magistrates' court officer; and
(b) any conditions of bail apply until then.

R-396 **Court's power to vary requirements under this Part**

34.10 The Crown Court may—
(a) shorten or extend (even after it has expired) a time limit under this Part;
(b) allow an appellant to vary an appeal notice that that appellant has served;
(c) direct that an appeal notice be served on any person;
(d) allow an appeal notice or a notice of abandonment to be in a different form to one set out in the Practice Direction, or to be presented orally.

R-397 **Constitution of the Crown Court**

34.11 (1) On the hearing of an appeal the general rule is that—
(a) the Crown Court must comprise—
   (i) a judge of the High Court, a Circuit judge, a Recorder or a qualifying judge advocate, and
   (ii) no less than two and no more than four justices of the peace, none of whom took part in the decision under appeal; and
(b) if the appeal is from a youth court, each justice of the peace must be qualified to sit as a member of a youth court.

(2) Despite the general rule—
(a) the Crown Court may include only one justice of the peace if—
   (i) the presiding judge decides that otherwise the start of the appeal hearing will be delayed unreasonably, or
   (ii) one or more of the justices of the peace who started hearing the appeal is absent; and
(b) the Crown Court may comprise only a judge of the High Court, a Circuit judge, a Recorder or a qualifying judge advocate if—
   (i) the appeal is against conviction, under section 108 of the Magistrates' Courts Act 1980, and
   (ii) the respondent agrees that the court should allow the appeal, under section 48(2) of the Senior Courts Act 1981.

(3) Before the hearing of an appeal begins and after that hearing ends—
(a) the Crown Court may comprise only a judge of the High Court, a Circuit judge, a Recorder or a qualifying judge advocate; and
(b) so constituted, the court may, among other things, exercise the powers to which apply—
   (i) the rules in this Part and in Part 3 (Case management), and
   (ii) rule 35.2 (stating a case for the opinion of the High Court, or refusing to do so).

Criminal Practice Directions Part 34 Appeal to the Crown Court

PD-90 **CPD IX Appeal 34A: Appeals to the Crown Court**

34A.1 On an appeal against conviction CrimPR 34.3 requires the appellant and respondent to supply information needed for the effective case management of the appeal, but allows the Crown Court to relieve the appellant – not the respondent – of that obligation, in whole or part.

34A.2 The court is most likely to exercise that discretion in an appellant's favour where he or she is not represented and is unable, without assistance, to provide reliable such information. The notes to the standard form of appeal notice invite the appellant to answer the relevant questions in that form to the extent that he or she is able, explaining that while the appellant may not be able to answer all those questions nevertheless any answers that can be given will assist in making arrangements for the hearing of the appeal. Where an appellant uses the prescribed form of easy read appeal notice the court usually should assume that the appellant will not be able to supply case management information, and that form contains no questions corresponding with those in the standard appeal notice. In such a case relevant information will be supplied by the respondent in the respondent's notice and may be gleaned from material obtained from magistrates' court records by Crown Court staff.

CPD IX Appeal 34B: Appeal to the Crown Court: Information from the Magistrates' Court PD-91

34B.1 CrimPR 34.4 applies when a defendant appeals to the Crown Court against conviction or sentence and specifies the information and documentation that must be made available by the magistrates' court.

34B.2 In all cases magistrates' court staff must ensure that Crown Court staff are notified of the appeal as soon as practicable: CrimPR 34.4(2)(b). In most cases Crown Court staff will be able to obtain the other information required by CrimPR 34.4(3) or (4) by direct access to the electronic records created by magistrates' court staff. However, if such access is not available then alternative arrangements must be made for the transfer of such information to Crown Court staff by electronic means. Paper copies of documents should be created and sent only as a last resort.

34B.3 On an appeal against conviction, the reasons given by the magistrates for their decision should not be included with the documents; the appeal hearing is not a review of the magistrates' court's decision but a re-hearing. There is no requirement for the Notice of Appeal form to be redacted in any way; the judge and magistrates presiding over the rehearing will base their decision on the evidence presented during the re-hearing itself.

34B.4 On an appeal solely against sentence, the magistrates' court's reasons and factual finding leading to the finding of guilt should be included, but any reasons for the sentence imposed should be omitted as the Crown Court will be conducting a fresh sentencing exercise. Whilst reasons for the sentence imposed are not necessary for the re-hearing, the Notice of Appeal form may include references to the sentence that is being appealed. There is no requirement to redact this before the form is given to the judge and magistrates hearing the appeal.

Criminal Procedure Rules Part 35 Appeal to the High Court by Case Stated

When this Part applies R-398

35.1 This Part applies where a person wants to appeal to the High Court by case stated—
(a) under section 111 of the Magistrates' Courts Act 1980, against a decision of a magistrates' court; or
(b) under section 28 of the Senior Courts Act 1981, against a decision of the Crown Court.

Application to state a case R-399

35.2 (1) A party who wants the court to state a case for the opinion of the High Court must—
(a) apply in writing, not more than 21 days after the decision against which the applicant wants to appeal; and
(b) serve the application on—
(i) the court officer, and
(ii) each other party.

(2) The application must—
(a) specify the decision in issue;
(b) specify the proposed question or questions of law or jurisdiction on which the opinion of the High Court will be asked;
(c) indicate the proposed grounds of appeal; and
(d) include or attach any application for the following, with reasons—
(i) if the application is to the Crown Court, an extension of time within which to apply to state a case,
(ii) bail pending appeal,
(iii) the suspension of any disqualification imposed in the case, where the court can order such a suspension pending appeal.

(3) A party who wants to make representations about the application must—
(a) serve the representations on—
(i) the court officer, and
(ii) each other party; and
(b) do so not more than 14 days after service of the application.
(4) The court may determine the application without a hearing.
(5) If the court decides not to state a case, the court officer must serve on each party—
(a) notice of that decision; and
(b) the court's written reasons for that decision, if not more than 21 days later the applicant asks for those reasons.

R-400 Preparation of case stated

35.3 (1) This rule applies where the court decides to state a case for the opinion of the High Court.
(2) The court officer must serve on each party notice of—
(a) the decision to state a case, and
(b) any recognizance ordered by the court.
(3) Unless the court otherwise directs, not more than 21 days after the court's decision to state a case—
(a) in a magistrates' court, the court officer must serve a draft case on each party;
(b) in the Crown Court, the applicant must serve a draft case on the court officer and each other party.
(4) The draft case must—
(a) specify the decision in issue;
(b) specify the question(s) of law or jurisdiction on which the opinion of the High Court will be asked;
(c) include a succinct summary of—
(i) the nature and history of the proceedings,
(ii) the court's relevant findings of fact, and
(iii) the relevant contentions of the parties;
(d) if a question is whether there was sufficient evidence on which the court reasonably could reach a finding of fact—
(i) specify that finding, and
(ii) include a summary of the evidence on which the court reached that finding.
(5) Except to the extent that paragraph (4)(d) requires, the draft case must not include an account of the evidence received by the court.
(6) A party who wants to make representations about the content of the draft case, or to propose a revised draft, must—
(a) serve the representations, or revised draft, on—
(i) the court officer, and
(ii) each other party; and
(b) do so not more than 21 days after service of the draft case.
(7) The court must state the case not more than 21 days after the time for service of representations under paragraph (6) has expired.
(8) A case stated for the opinion of the High Court must—
(a) comply with paragraphs (4) and (5); and
(b) identify—
(i) the court that stated it, and
(ii) the court office for that court.
(9) The court officer must serve the case stated on each party.

R-401 Duty of justices' legal adviser

35.4 (1) This rule applies—
(a) only in a magistrates' court; and
(b) unless the court—
(i) includes a District Judge (Magistrates' Courts), and
(ii) otherwise directs.
(2) A justices' legal adviser must—
(a) give the court legal advice; and
(b) if the court so requires, assist it by—
(i) preparing and amending the draft case, and
(ii) completing the case stated.

Court's power to vary requirements under this Part R-402

35.5 (1) The court may shorten or extend (even after it has expired) a time limit under this Part.

(2) A person who wants an extension of time must—

(a) apply when serving the application, representations or draft case for which it is needed; and

(b) explain the delay.

Criminal Procedure Rules Part 36 Appeal to the Court of Appeal: General Rules

When this Part applies R-403

36.1 (1) This Part applies to all applications, appeals and references to the Court of Appeal to which Parts 37, 38, 39, 40, 41 and 43 apply.

(2) In this Part and in those, unless the context makes it clear that something different is meant, 'court' means the Court of Appeal or any judge of that court.

Case management in the Court of Appeal R-404

36.2 (1) The court and the parties have the same duties and powers as under Part 3 (Case management).

(2) The Registrar—

(a) must fulfil the duty of active case management under rule 3.2; and

(b) in fulfilling that duty may exercise any of the powers of case management under—

(i) rule 3.5 (the court's general powers of case management),

(ii) rule 3.10(3) (requiring a certificate of readiness), and

(iii) rule 3.11 (requiring a party to identify intentions and anticipated requirements) subject to the directions of the court.

(3) The Registrar must nominate a case progression officer under rule 3.4.

Power to vary requirements R-405

36.3 The court or the Registrar may—

(a) shorten a time limit or extend it (even after it has expired) unless that is inconsistent with other legislation;

(b) allow a party to vary any notice that that party has served;

(c) direct that a notice or application be served on any person;

(d) allow a notice or application to be in a different form, or presented orally.

Application for extension of time R-406

36.4 A person who wants an extension of time within which to serve a notice or make an application must—

(a) apply for that extension of time when serving that notice or making that application; and

(b) give the reasons for the application for an extension of time.

Renewing an application refused by a judge or the Registrar R-407

36.5 (1) This rule applies where a party with the right to do so wants to renew—

(a) to a judge of the Court of Appeal an application refused by the Registrar; or

(b) to the Court of Appeal an application refused by a judge of that court.

(2) That party must—

(a) renew the application in the form set out in the Practice Direction, signed by or on behalf of the applicant;

(b) serve the renewed application on the Registrar not more than 14 days after—

(i) the refusal of the application that the applicant wants to renew; or

(ii) the Registrar serves that refusal on the applicant, if the applicant was not present in person or by live link when the original application was refused.

Hearings R-408

36.6 (1) The general rule is that the Court of Appeal must hear in public—

(a) an application, including an application for permission to appeal; and

(b) an appeal or reference,

but it may order any hearing to be in private.

(2) Where a hearing is about a public interest ruling, that hearing must be in private unless the court otherwise directs.

(3) Where the appellant wants to appeal against an order restricting public access to a trial, the court—

(a) may decide without a hearing—

(i) an application, including an application for permission to appeal, and

(ii) an appeal; but

(b) must announce its decision on such an appeal at a hearing in public.

(4) Where the appellant wants to appeal or to refer a case to the Supreme Court, the court—
(a) may decide without a hearing an application—
(i) for permission to appeal or to refer a sentencing case, or
(ii) to refer a point of law; but
(b) must announce its decision on such an application at a hearing in public.
(5) Where a party wants the court to reopen the determination of an appeal—
(a) the court—
(i) must decide the application without a hearing, as a general rule, but
(ii) may decide the application at a hearing; and
(b) need not announce its decision on such an application at a hearing in public.
(6) A judge of the Court of Appeal and the Registrar may exercise any of their powers—
(a) at a hearing in public or in private; or
(b) without a hearing.

R-409 Notice of hearings and decisions

36.7 (1) The Registrar must give as much notice as reasonably practicable of every hearing to—
(a) the parties;
(b) any party's custodian;
(c) any other person whom the court requires to be notified; and
(d) the Crown Court officer, where Parts 37, 38 or 40 apply.
(2) The Registrar must serve every decision on—
(a) the parties;
(b) any other person whom the court requires to be served; and
(c) the Crown Court officer and any party's custodian, where the decision determines an appeal or application for permission to appeal.
(3) But where a hearing or decision is about a public interest ruling, the Registrar must not—
(a) give notice of that hearing to; or
(b) serve that decision on,
anyone other than the prosecutor who applied for that ruling, unless the court otherwise directs.

R-410 Duty of Crown Court officer

36.8 (1) The Crown Court officer must provide the Registrar with any document, object or information for which the Registrar asks, within such period as the Registrar may require.
(2) Where someone may appeal to the Court of Appeal, the Crown Court officer must keep any document or object exhibited in the proceedings in the Crown Court, or arrange for it to be kept by some other appropriate person, until—
(a) 6 weeks after the conclusion of those proceedings; or
(b) the conclusion of any appeal proceedings that begin within that 6 weeks,
unless the court, the Registrar or the Crown Court otherwise directs.
(3) Where Part 37 applies (Appeal to the Court of Appeal against ruling at preparatory hearing), the Crown Court officer must as soon as practicable serve on the appellant a transcript or note of—
(a) each order or ruling against which the appellant wants to appeal; and
(b) the decision by the Crown Court judge on any application for permission to appeal.
(4) Where Part 38 applies (Appeal to the Court of Appeal against ruling adverse to prosecution), the Crown Court officer must as soon as practicable serve on the appellant a transcript or note of—
(a) each ruling against which the appellant wants to appeal;
(b) the decision by the Crown Court judge on any application for permission to appeal; and
(c) the decision by the Crown Court judge on any request to expedite the appeal.
(5) Where Part 39 applies (Appeal to the Court of Appeal about conviction or sentence), the Crown Court officer must as soon as practicable serve on or make available to the Registrar—
(a) any Crown Court judge's certificate that the case is fit for appeal;
(b) the decision on any application at the Crown Court centre for bail pending appeal;
(c) such of the Crown Court case papers as the Registrar requires; and
(d) such transcript of the Crown Court proceedings as the Registrar requires.
(6) Where Part 40 applies (Appeal to the Court of Appeal about reporting or public access) and an order is made restricting public access to a trial, the Crown Court officer must—
(a) immediately notify the Registrar of that order, if the appellant has given advance notice of intention to appeal; and

(b) as soon as practicable provide the applicant for that order with a transcript or note of the application.

Duty of person transcribing proceedings in the Crown Court **R-411**

36.9 A person who transcribes a recording of proceedings in the Crown Court under arrangements made by the Crown Court officer must provide the Registrar with any transcript for which the Registrar asks, within such period as the Registrar may require.

Duty of person keeping exhibit **R-412**

36.10 A person who under arrangements made by the Crown Court officer keeps a document or object exhibited in the proceedings in the Crown Court must—

(a) keep that exhibit until—
  (i) 6 weeks after the conclusion of the Crown Court proceedings, or
  (ii) the conclusion of any appeal proceedings that begin within that 6 weeks,
  unless the court, the Registrar or the Crown Court otherwise directs; and
(b) provide the Registrar with any such document or object for which the Registrar asks, within such period as the Registrar may require.

Registrar's duty to provide copy documents for appeal or reference **R-413**

36.11 Unless the court otherwise directs, for the purposes of an appeal or reference—

(a) the Registrar must—
  (i) provide a party with a copy of any document or transcript held by the Registrar for such purposes, or
  (ii) allow a party to inspect such a document or transcript,
  on payment by that party of any charge fixed by the Treasury; but
(b) the Registrar must not provide a copy or allow the inspection of—
  (i) a document provided only for the court and the Registrar, or
  (ii) a transcript of a public interest ruling or of an application for such a ruling.

Declaration of incompatibility with a Convention right **R-414**

36.12 (1) This rule applies where a party—

(a) wants the court to make a declaration of incompatibility with a Convention right under section 4 of the Human Rights Act 1998; or
(b) raises an issue that the Registrar thinks may lead the court to make such a declaration.

(2) The Registrar must serve notice on—

(a) the relevant person named in the list published under section 17(1) of the Crown Proceedings Act 1947; or
(b) the Treasury Solicitor, if it is not clear who is the relevant person.

(3) That notice must include or attach details of—

(a) the legislation affected and the Convention right concerned;
(b) the parties to the appeal; and
(c) any other information or document that the Registrar thinks relevant.

(4) A person who has a right under the 1998 Act to become a party to the appeal must—

(a) serve notice on—
  (i) the Registrar, and
  (ii) the other parties,
  if that person wants to exercise that right; and
(b) in that notice—
  (i) indicate the conclusion that that person invites the court to reach on the question of incompatibility, and
  (ii) identify each ground for that invitation, concisely outlining the arguments in support.

(5) The court must not make a declaration of incompatibility—

(a) less than 21 days after the Registrar serves notice under paragraph (2); and
(b) without giving any person who serves a notice under paragraph (4) an opportunity to make representations at a hearing.

Abandoning an appeal **R-415**

36.13 (1) This rule applies where an appellant wants to—

(a) abandon—
  (i) an application to the court for permission to appeal, or
  (ii) an appeal; or
(b) reinstate such an application or appeal after abandoning it.

(2) The appellant—
(a) may abandon such an application or appeal without the court's permission by serving a notice of abandonment on—
(i) the Registrar, and
(ii) any respondent
before any hearing of the application or appeal; but
(b) at any such hearing, may only abandon that application or appeal with the court's permission.
(3) A notice of abandonment must be in the form set out in the Practice Direction, signed by or on behalf of the appellant.
(4) On receiving a notice of abandonment the Registrar must—
(a) date it;
(b) serve a dated copy on—
(i) the appellant,
(ii) the appellant's custodian, if any,
(iii) the Crown Court officer, and
(iv) any other person on whom the appellant or the Registrar served the appeal notice; and
(c) treat the application or appeal as if it had been refused or dismissed by the Court of Appeal.
(5) An appellant who wants to reinstate an application or appeal after abandoning it must—
(a) apply in writing, with reasons; and
(b) serve the application on the Registrar.

R-416 Abandoning a ground of appeal or opposition

36.14 (1) If the court gives permission to appeal then unless the court otherwise directs the decision indicates that—
(a) the appellant has permission to appeal on every ground identified by the appeal notice; and
(b) the court finds reasonably arguable each ground on which the appellant has permission to appeal.
(2) If the court gives permission to appeal but not on every ground identified by the appeal notice the decision indicates that—
(a) at the hearing of the appeal the court will not consider representations that address any ground thus excluded from argument; and
(b) an appellant who wants to rely on such an excluded ground needs the court's permission to do so.
(3) An appellant who wants to rely at the hearing of an appeal on a ground of appeal excluded from argument by a judge of the Court of Appeal when giving permission to appeal must—
(a) apply for permission to do so, with reasons, and identify each such ground;
(b) serve the application on—
(i) the Registrar, and
(ii) any respondent;
(c) serve the application not more than 14 days after—
(i) the giving of permission to appeal, or
(ii) the Registrar serves notice of that decision on the applicant, if the applicant was not present in person or by live link when permission to appeal was given.
(4) Paragraph (5) applies where one of the following Parts applies—
(a) Part 37 (Appeal to the Court of Appeal against ruling at preparatory hearing);
(b) Part 38 (Appeal to the Court of Appeal against ruling adverse to prosecution);
(c) Part 39 (Appeal to the Court of Appeal about conviction or sentence); or
(d) Part 40 (Appeal to the Court of Appeal about reporting or public access restriction).
(5) An appellant who wants to rely on a ground of appeal not identified by the appeal notice must—
(a) apply for permission to do so and identify each such ground;
(b) in respect of each such ground—
(i) explain why it was not included in the appeal notice, and
(ii) where Part 39 applies, comply with rule 39.3(2);
(c) serve the application on—
(i) the Registrar, and
(ii) any respondent;
(d) serve the application—
(i) as soon as reasonably practicable, and in any event
(ii) at the same time as serving any renewed application for permission to appeal which relies on that ground.

(6) Paragraph (5) applies where a party wants to abandon—
(a) a ground of appeal on which that party has permission to appeal; or
(b) a ground of opposition identified in a respondent's notice.
(7) Such a party must serve notice on—
(a) the Registrar; and
(b) each other party,
before any hearing at which that ground will be considered by the court.

Reopening the determination of an appeal R-417

36.15 (1) This rule applies where—
(a) a party wants the court to reopen a decision which determines an appeal or reference to which this Part applies (including a decision on an application for permission to appeal or refer);
(b) the Registrar refers such a decision to the court for the court to consider reopening it.
(2) Such a party must—
(a) apply in writing for permission to reopen that decision, as soon as practicable after becoming aware of the grounds for doing so; and
(b) serve the application on the Registrar.
(3) The application must—
(a) specify the decision which the applicant wants the court to reopen; and
(b) explain—
(i) why it is necessary for the court to reopen that decision in order to avoid real injustice
(ii) how the circumstances are exceptional and make it appropriate to reopen the decision notwithstanding the rights and interests of other participants and the importance of finality,
(iii) why there is no alternative effective remedy among any potentially available, and
(iv) any delay in making the application.
(4) The Registrar—
(a) may invite a party's representations on—
(i) an application to reopen a decision, or
(ii) a decision that the Registrar has referred, or intends to refer, to the court; and
(b) must do so if the court so directs.
(5) A party invited to make representations must serve them on the Registrar within such period as the Registrar directs.
(6) The court must not reopen a decision to which this rule applies unless each other party has had an opportunity to make representations.,

Criminal Procedure Rules Part 37 Appeal to the Court of Appeal against Ruling at Preparatory Hearing

When this Part applies R-418

37.1 (1) This Part applies where a party wants to appeal under—
(a) section 9(11) of the Criminal Justice Act 1987 or section 35(1) of the Criminal Procedure and Investigations Act 1996; or
(b) section 47(1) of the Criminal Justice Act 2003.
(2) A reference to an 'appellant' in this Part is a reference to such a party.

Service of appeal notice R-419

37.2 (1) An appellant must serve an appeal notice on—
(a) the Crown Court officer;
(b) the Registrar; and
(c) every party directly affected by the order or ruling against which the appellant wants to appeal.
(2) The appellant must serve the appeal notice not more than 5 business days after—
(a) the order or ruling against which the appellant wants to appeal; or
(b) the Crown Court judge gives or refuses permission to appeal.

Form of appeal notice R-420

37.3 (1) An appeal notice must be in the form set out in the Practice Direction.
(2) The appeal notice must—
(a) specify each order or ruling against which the appellant wants to appeal;
(b) identify each ground of appeal on which the appellant relies, numbering them consecutively (if there is more than one) and concisely outlining each argument in support;
(c) summarise the relevant facts;

(d) identify any relevant authorities;
(e) include or attach any application for the following, with reasons—
(i) permission to appeal, if the appellant needs the court's permission,
(ii) an extension of time within which to serve the appeal notice,
(iii) a direction to attend in person a hearing that the appellant could attend by live link, if the appellant is in custody;
(f) include a list of those on whom the appellant has served the appeal notice; and
(g) attach—
(i) a transcript or note of each order or ruling against which the appellant wants to appeal,
(ii) all relevant skeleton arguments considered by the Crown Court judge,
(iii) any written application for permission to appeal that the appellant made to the Crown Court judge,
(iv) a transcript or note of the decision by the Crown Court judge on any application for permission to appeal, and
(v) any other document or thing that the appellant thinks the court will need to decide the appeal.

R-421 **Crown Court judge's permission to appeal**

37.4 (1) An appellant who wants the Crown Court judge to give permission to appeal must—
(a) apply orally, with reasons, immediately after the order or ruling against which the appellant wants to appeal; or
(b) apply in writing and serve the application on—
(i) the Crown Court officer, and
(ii) every party directly affected by the order or ruling
not more than 2 business days after that order or ruling.
(2) A written application must include the same information (with the necessary adaptations) as an appeal notice.

R-422 **Respondent's notice**

37.5 (1) A party on whom an appellant serves an appeal notice may serve a respondent's notice, and must do so if—
(a) that party wants to make representations to the court; or
(b) the court so directs.
(2) Such a party must serve the respondent's notice on—
(a) the appellant;
(b) the Crown Court officer;
(c) the Registrar; and
(d) any other party on whom the appellant served the appeal notice.
(3) Such a party must serve the respondent's notice not more than 5 business days after—
(a) the appellant serves the appeal notice; or
(b) a direction to do so.
(4) The respondent's notice must be in the form set out in the Practice Direction.
(5) The respondent's notice must—
(a) give the date on which the respondent was served with the appeal notice;
(b) identify each ground of opposition on which the respondent relies, numbering them consecutively (if there is more than one), concisely outlining each argument in support and identifying the ground of appeal to which each relates;
(c) summarise any relevant facts not already summarised in the appeal notice;
(d) identify any relevant authorities;
(e) include or attach any application for the following, with reasons—
(i) an extension of time within which to serve the respondent's notice,
(ii) a direction to attend in person any hearing that the respondent could attend by live link, if the respondent is in custody;
(f) identify any other document or thing that the respondent thinks the court will need to decide the appeal.

R-423 **Powers of Court of Appeal judge**

37.6 A judge of the Court of Appeal may give permission to appeal as well as exercising the powers given by other legislation (including these Rules).

R-424 **Renewing applications**

37.7 Rule 36.5 (Renewing an application refused by a judge or the Registrar) applies with a time limit of 5 business days.

Right to attend hearing R-425

37.8 (1) A party who is in custody has a right to attend a hearing in public.
(2) The court or the Registrar may direct that such a party is to attend a hearing by live link.

Criminal Procedure Rules Part 38 Appeal to the Court of Appeal against Ruling Adverse to Prosecution

When this Part applies R-426

38.1 (1) This Part applies where a prosecutor wants to appeal under section 58(2) of the Criminal Justice Act 2003.
(2) A reference to an 'appellant' in this Part is a reference to such a prosecutor.

Decision to appeal R-427

38.2 (1) An appellant must tell the Crown Court judge of any decision to appeal—
(a) immediately after the ruling against which the appellant wants to appeal; or
(b) on the expiry of the time to decide whether to appeal allowed under paragraph (2).
(2) If an appellant wants time to decide whether to appeal—
(a) the appellant must ask the Crown Court judge immediately after the ruling; and
(b) the general rule is that the judge must not require the appellant to decide there and then but instead must allow until the next business day.

Service of appeal notice R-428

38.3 (1) An appellant must serve an appeal notice on—
(a) the Crown Court officer;
(b) the Registrar; and
(c) every defendant directly affected by the ruling against which the appellant wants to appeal.
(2) The appellant must serve the appeal notice not later than—
(a) the next business day after telling the Crown Court judge of the decision to appeal, if the judge expedites the appeal; or
(b) 5 business days after telling the Crown Court judge of that decision, if the judge does not expedite the appeal.

Form of appeal notice R-429

38.4 (1) An appeal notice must be in the form set out in the Practice Direction.
(2) The appeal notice must—
(a) specify each ruling against which the appellant wants to appeal;
(b) identify each ground of appeal on which the appellant relies, numbering them consecutively (if there is more than one) and concisely outlining each argument in support;
(c) summarise the relevant facts;
(d) identify any relevant authorities;
(e) include or attach any application for the following, with reasons—
(i) permission to appeal, if the appellant needs the court's permission,
(ii) an extension of time within which to serve the appeal notice,
(iii) expedition of the appeal, or revocation of a direction expediting the appeal;
(f) include a list of those on whom the appellant has served the appeal notice;
(g) attach—
(i) a transcript or note of each ruling against which the appellant wants to appeal,
(ii) all relevant skeleton arguments considered by the Crown Court judge,
(iii) any written application for permission to appeal that the appellant made to the Crown Court judge,
(iv) a transcript or note of the decision by the Crown Court judge on any application for permission to appeal,
(v) a transcript or note of the decision by the Crown Court judge on any request to expedite the appeal, and
(vi) any other document or thing that the appellant thinks the court will need to decide the appeal; and
(h) attach a form of respondent's notice for any defendant served with the appeal notice to complete if that defendant wants to do so.

Crown Court judge's permission to appeal R-430

38.5 (1) An appellant who wants the Crown Court judge to give permission to appeal must—
(a) apply orally, with reasons, immediately after the ruling against which the appellant wants to appeal; or

(b) apply in writing and serve the application on—
(i) the Crown Court officer, and
(ii) every defendant directly affected by the ruling
on the expiry of the time allowed under rule 38.2 to decide whether to appeal.

(2) A written application must include the same information (with the necessary adaptations) as an appeal notice.

(3) The Crown Court judge must allow every defendant directly affected by the ruling an opportunity to make representations.

(4) The general rule is that the Crown Court judge must decide whether or not to give permission to appeal on the day that the application for permission is made.

R-431 **Expediting an appeal**

38.6 (1) An appellant who wants the Crown Court judge to expedite an appeal must ask, giving reasons, on telling the judge of the decision to appeal.

(2) The Crown Court judge must allow every defendant directly affected by the ruling an opportunity to make representations.

(3) The Crown Court judge may revoke a direction expediting the appeal unless the appellant has served the appeal notice.

R-432 **Respondent's notice**

38.7 (1) A defendant on whom an appellant serves an appeal notice may serve a respondent's notice, and must do so if—
(a) the defendant wants to make representations to the court; or
(b) the court so directs.

(2) Such a defendant must serve the respondent's notice on—
(a) the appellant;
(b) the Crown Court officer;
(c) the Registrar; and
(d) any other defendant on whom the appellant served the appeal notice.

(3) Such a defendant must serve the respondent's notice—
(a) not later than the next business day after—
(i) the appellant serves the appeal notice, or
(ii) a direction to do so
if the Crown Court judge expedites the appeal; or
(b) not more than 5 business days after—
(i) the appellant serves the appeal notice, or
(ii) a direction to do so
if the Crown Court judge does not expedite the appeal.

(4) The respondent's notice must be in the form set out in the Practice Direction.

(5) The respondent's notice must—
(a) give the date on which the respondent was served with the appeal notice;
(b) identify each ground of opposition on which the respondent relies, numbering them consecutively (if there is more than one), concisely outlining each argument in support and identifying the ground of appeal to which each relates;
(c) summarise any relevant facts not already summarised in the appeal notice;
(d) identify any relevant authorities;
(e) include or attach any application for the following, with reasons—
(i) an extension of time within which to serve the respondent's notice,
(ii) a direction to attend in person any hearing that the respondent could attend by live link, if the respondent is in custody;
(f) identify any other document or thing that the respondent thinks the court will need to decide the appeal.

R-433 **Public interest ruling**

38.8 (1) This rule applies where the appellant wants to appeal against a public interest ruling.

(2) The appellant must not serve on any defendant directly affected by the ruling—
(a) any written application to the Crown Court judge for permission to appeal; or
(b) an appeal notice,
if the appellant thinks that to do so in effect would reveal something that the appellant thinks ought not be disclosed.

(3) The appellant must not include in an appeal notice—
 (a) the material that was the subject of the ruling; or
 (b) any indication of what sort of material it is,
 if the appellant thinks that to do so in effect would reveal something that the appellant thinks ought not be disclosed.
(4) The appellant must serve on the Registrar with the appeal notice an annex—
 (a) marked to show that its contents are only for the court and the Registrar;
 (b) containing whatever the appellant has omitted from the appeal notice, with reasons; and
 (c) if relevant, explaining why the appellant has not served the appeal notice.
(5) Rules 38.5(3) and 38.6(2) do not apply.

Powers of Court of Appeal judge R-434

38.9 A judge of the Court of Appeal may—
 (a) give permission to appeal;
 (b) revoke a Crown Court judge's direction expediting an appeal; and
 (c) where an appellant abandons an appeal, order a defendant's acquittal, his release from custody and the payment of his costs,
as well as exercising the powers given by other legislation (including these Rules).

Renewing applications R-435

38.10 Rule 36.5 (Renewing an application refused by a judge or the Registrar) applies with a time limit of 5 business days.

Right to attend hearing R-436

38.11 (1) A respondent who is in custody has a right to attend a hearing in public.
(2) The court or the Registrar may direct that such a respondent is to attend a hearing by live link.

Criminal Procedure Rules Part 39 Appeal to the Court of Appeal about Conviction or Sentence

When this Part applies R-437

39.1 (1) This Part applies where—
 (a) a defendant wants to appeal under—
  (i) Part 1 of the Criminal Appeal Act 1968,
  (ii) section 274(3) of the Criminal Justice Act 2003,
  (iii) paragraph 14 of Schedule 22 to the Criminal Justice Act 2003, or
  (iv) section 42 of the Counter-Terrorism Act 2008;
 (b) the Criminal Cases Review Commission refers a case to the Court of Appeal under section 9 of the Criminal Appeal Act 1995;
 (c) a prosecutor wants to appeal to the Court of Appeal under section 14A(5A) of the Football Spectators Act 1989;
 (d) a party wants to appeal under section 74(8) of the Serious Organised Crime and Police Act 2005;
 (e) a person found to be in contempt of court wants to appeal under section 13 of the Administration of Justice Act 1960 and section 18A of the Criminal Appeal Act 1968; or
 (f) a person wants to appeal to the Court of Appeal under—
  (i) section 24 of the Serious Crime Act 2007, or
  (ii) regulation 3C or 3H of the Costs in Criminal Cases (General) Regulations 1986.
(2) A reference to an 'appellant' in this Part is a reference to such a party or person.

Service of appeal notice R-438

39.2 (1) The appellant must serve an appeal notice on the Registrar—
 (a) not more than 28 days after—
  (i) the conviction, verdict, or finding,
  (ii) the sentence,
  (iii) the order (subject to paragraph (b)), or the failure to make an order, or
  (iv) the minimum term review decision under section 274(3) of, or paragraph 14 of Schedule 22 to, the Criminal Justice Act 2003
  about which the appellant wants to appeal;
 (b) not more than 21 days after the order in a case in which the appellant appeals against a wasted or third party costs order;

(c) not more than 28 days after the Registrar serves notice that the Criminal Cases Review Commission has referred a conviction to the court.

R-439 Form of appeal notice

39.3 (1) An appeal notice must—
(a) specify—
(i) the conviction, verdict, or finding,
(ii) the sentence, or
(iii) the order, or the failure to make an orderabout which the appellant wants to appeal;
(b) identify each ground of appeal on which the appellant relies (and see paragraph (2));
(c) identify the transcript that the appellant thinks the court will need, if the appellant wants to appeal against a conviction;
(d) identify the relevant sentencing powers of the Crown Court, if sentence is in issue;
(e) include or attach any application for the following, with reasons—
(i) permission to appeal, if the appellant needs the court's permission,
(ii) an extension of time within which to serve the appeal notice,
(iii) bail pending appeal,
(iv) a direction to attend in person a hearing that the appellant could attend by live link, if the appellant is in custody,
(v) the introduction of evidence, including hearsay evidence and evidence of bad character,
(vi) an order requiring a witness to attend court,
(vii) a direction for special measures for a witness,
(viii) a direction for special measures for the giving of evidence by the appellant;
(ix) the suspension of any disqualification imposed, or order made, in the case, where the Court of Appeal can order such a suspension pending appeal.
(f) identify any other document or thing that the appellant thinks the court will need to decide the appeal.

(2) The grounds of appeal must—
(a) include in no more than the first two pages a summary of the grounds that makes what then follows easy to understand;
(b) in each ground of appeal identify the event or decision to which that ground relates;
(c) in each ground of appeal summarise the facts relevant to that ground, but only to the extent necessary to make clear what is in issue;
(d) concisely outline each argument in support of each ground;
(e) number each ground consecutively, if there is more than one;
(f) identify any relevant authority and—
(i) state the proposition of law that the authority demonstrates, and
(ii) identify the parts of the authority that support that proposition; and
(g) where the Criminal Cases Review Commission refers a case to the court, explain how each ground of appeal relates (if it does) to the reasons for the reference.

R-440 Crown Court judge's certificate that case is fit for appeal

39.4 (1) An appellant who wants the Crown Court judge to certify that a case is fit for appeal must—
(a) apply orally, with reasons, immediately after there occurs—
(i) the conviction, verdict, or finding,
(ii) the sentence, or
(iii) the order, or the failure to make an order
about which the appellant wants to appeal; or
(b) apply in writing and serve the application on the Crown Court officer not more than 14 days after that occurred.

(2) A written application must include the same information (with the necessary adaptations) as an appeal notice.

R-441 Reference by Criminal Cases Review Commission

39.5 (1) The Registrar must serve on the appellant a reference by the Criminal Cases Review Commission.
(2) The court must treat that reference as the appeal notice if the appellant does not serve such a notice under rule 39.2.

R-442 Respondent's notice

39.6 (1) The Registrar—
(a) may serve an appeal notice on any party directly affected by the appeal; and
(b) must do so if the Criminal Cases Review Commission refers a conviction, verdict, finding or sentence to the court.

(2) Such a party may serve a respondent's notice, and must do so if—
(a) that party wants to make representations to the court; or
(b) the court or the Registrar so directs.
(3) Such a party must serve the respondent's notice on—
(a) the appellant;
(b) the Registrar; and
(c) any other party on whom the Registrar served the appeal notice.
(4) Such a party must serve the respondent's notice—
(a) not more than 14 days after the Registrar serves—
(i) the appeal notice, or
(ii) a direction to do so; or
(b) not more than 28 days after the Registrar serves notice that the Commission has referred a conviction.
(5) The respondent's notice must be in the form set out in the Practice Direction.
(6) The respondent's notice must—
(a) give the date on which the respondent was served with the appeal notice;
(b) identify each ground of opposition on which the respondent relies, numbering them consecutively (if there is more than one), concisely outlining each argument in support and identifying the ground of appeal to which each relates;
(c) identify the relevant sentencing powers of the Crown Court, if sentence is in issue;
(d) summarise any relevant facts not already summarised in the appeal notice;
(e) identify any relevant authorities;
(f) include or attach any application for the following, with reasons—
(i) an extension of time within which to serve the respondent's notice,
(ii) bail pending appeal,
(iii) a direction to attend in person a hearing that the respondent could attend by live link, if the respondent is in custody,
(iv) the introduction of evidence, including hearsay evidence and evidence of bad character,
(v) an order requiring a witness to attend court,
(vi) a direction for special measures for a witness; and
(g) identify any other document or thing that the respondent thinks the court will need to decide the appeal.

Adaptation of rules about introducing evidence **R-443**

39.7 (1) (1) The following Parts apply with such adaptations as the court or the Registrar may direct—
(a) Part 16 (Written witness statements);
(b) Part 18 (Measures to assist a witness or defendant to give evidence);
(c) Part 19 (Expert evidence);
(d) Part 20 (Hearsay evidence);
(e) Part 21 (Evidence of bad character); and
(f) Part 22 (Evidence of a complainant's previous sexual behaviour).
(2) But the general rule is that—
(a) a respondent who opposes an appellant's application or notice to which one of those Parts applies must do so in the respondent's notice, with reasons;
(b) an appellant who opposes a respondent's application or notice to which one of those Parts applies must serve notice, with reasons, on—
(i) the Registrar, and
(ii) the respondent
not more than 14 days after service of the respondent's notice; and
(c) the court or the Registrar may give directions with or without a hearing.
(3) A party who wants the court to order the production of a document, exhibit or other thing connected with the proceedings must—
(a) identify that item; and
(b) explain—
(i) how it is connected with the proceedings,
(ii) why its production is necessary for the determination of the case, and
(iii) to whom it should be produced (the court, appellant or respondent, or any two or more of them).
(4) A party who wants the court to order a witness to attend to be questioned must—
(a) identify the proposed witness; and

(b) explain—
   (i) what evidence the proposed witness can give,
   (ii) why that evidence is capable of belief,
   (iii) if applicable, why that evidence may provide a ground for allowing the appeal,
   (iv) on what basis that evidence would have been admissible in the case which is the subject of the application for permission to appeal or appeal, and
   (v) why that evidence was not introduced in that case.

(5) Where the court orders a witness to attend to be questioned, the witness must attend the hearing of the application for permission to appeal or of the appeal, as applicable, unless the court otherwise directs.

(6) Where the court orders a witness to attend to be questioned before an examiner on the court's behalf, the court must identify the examiner and may give directions about—
(a) the time and place, or times and places, at which that questioning must be carried out;
(b) the manner in which that questioning must be carried out, in particular as to—
   (i) the service of any report, statement or questionnaire in preparation for the questioning,
   (ii) the sequence in which the parties may ask questions, and
   (iii) if more than one witness is to be questioned, the sequence in which those witnesses may be questioned; and
(c) the manner in which, and when, a record of the questioning must be submitted to the court.

(7) Where the court orders the questioning of a witness before an examiner, the court may delegate to that examiner the giving of directions under paragraph (6)(a), (b) and (c).

R-444 Application for bail, or to suspend a disqualification or order, pending appeal or retrial

39.8 (1) This rule applies where—
(a) a party wants to make an application to the court about bail pending appeal or retrial;
(b) an appellant wants to apply to the court to suspend a disqualification or order pending appeal.

(2) That party must serve an application in the form set out in the Practice Direction on—
(a) the Registrar, unless the application is with the appeal notice; and
(b) the other party.

(3) The court must not decide such an application without giving the other party an opportunity to make representations, including, in the case of a bail application, representations about any condition or surety proposed by the applicant.

(4) This rule and rule 14.16 (Bail condition to be enforced in another European Union member State) apply where the court can impose as a condition of bail pending retrial a requirement—
(a) with which a defendant must comply while in another European Union member State; and
(b) which that other member State can monitor and enforce.

R-445 Conditions of bail pending appeal or retrial

39.9 (1) This rule applies where the court grants a party bail pending appeal or retrial subject to any condition that must be met before that party is released.

(2) The court may direct how such a condition must be met.

(3) The Registrar must serve a certificate in the form set out in the Practice Direction recording any such condition and direction on—
(a) that party;
(b) that party's custodian; and
(c) any other person directly affected by any such direction.

(4) A person directly affected by any such direction need not comply with it until the Registrar serves that person with that certificate.

(5) Unless the court otherwise directs, if any such condition or direction requires someone to enter into a recognizance it must be—
(a) in the form set out in the Practice Direction and signed before—
   (i) the Registrar,
   (ii) the custodian, or
   (iii) someone acting with the authority of the Registrar or custodian;
(b) copied immediately to the person who enters into it; and
(c) served immediately by the Registrar on the appellant's custodian or vice versa, as appropriate.

(6) Unless the court otherwise directs, if any such condition or direction requires someone to make a payment, surrender a document or take some other step—
(a) that payment, document or step must be made, surrendered or taken to or before—
   (i) the Registrar,
   (ii) the custodian, or
   (iii) someone acting with the authority of the Registrar or custodian;

(b) the Registrar or the custodian, as appropriate, must serve immediately on the other a statement that the payment, document or step has been made, surrendered or taken, as appropriate.

(7) The custodian must release the appellant where it appears that any condition ordered by the court has been met.

(8) For the purposes of section 5 of the Bail Act 1976 (record of decision about bail), the Registrar must keep a copy of—

(a) any certificate served under paragraph (3);

(b) a notice of hearing given under rule 36.7(1); and

(c) a notice of the court's decision served under rule 36.7(2).

(9) Where the court grants bail pending retrial the Registrar must serve on the Crown Court officer copies of the documents kept under paragraph (8).

Forfeiture of a recognizance given as a condition of bail **R-446**

39.10 (1) This rule applies where—

(a) the court grants a party bail pending appeal or retrial; and

(b) the bail is subject to a condition that that party provides a surety to guarantee that he will surrender to custody as required; but

(c) that party does not surrender to custody as required.

(2) The Registrar must serve notice on—

(a) the surety; and

(b) the prosecutor,

of the hearing at which the court may order the forfeiture of the recognizance given by that surety.

(3) The court must not forfeit a surety's recognizance—

(a) less than 7 days after the Registrar serves notice under paragraph (2); and

(b) without giving the surety an opportunity to make representations at a hearing.

Right to attend hearing **R-447**

39.11 A party who is in custody has a right to attend a hearing in public unless—

(a) it is a hearing preliminary or incidental to an appeal, including the hearing of an application for permission to appeal;

(b) it is the hearing of an appeal and the court directs that—

(i) the appeal involves a question of law alone, and

(ii) for that reason the appellant has no permission to attend; or

(c) that party is in custody in consequence of—

(i) a verdict of not guilty by reason of insanity, or

(ii) a finding of disability.

Power to vary determination of appeal against sentence **R-448**

39.12 (1) This rule applies where the court decides an appeal affecting sentence in a party's absence.

(2) The court may vary such a decision if it did not take account of something relevant because that party was absent.

(3) A party who wants the court to vary such a decision must—

(a) apply in writing, with reasons;

(b) serve the application on the Registrar not more than 7 days after—

(i) the decision, if that party was represented at the appeal hearing, or

(ii) the Registrar serves the decision, if that party was not represented at that hearing.

Directions about re-admission to hospital on dismissal of appeal **R-449**

39.13 (1) This rule applies where—

(a) an appellant subject to—

(i) an order under section 37(1) of the Mental Health Act 1983 (detention in hospital on conviction), or

(ii) an order under section 5(2) of the Criminal Procedure (Insanity) Act 1964 (detention in hospital on finding of insanity or disability)

has been released on bail pending appeal; and

(b) the court—

(i) refuses permission to appeal,

(ii) dismisses the appeal, or

(iii) affirms the order under appeal.

(2) The court must give appropriate directions for the appellant's—
(a) re-admission to hospital; and
(b) if necessary, temporary detention pending re-admission.

R-450 **Renewal or setting aside of order for retrial**

39.14 (1) This rule applies where—
(a) a prosecutor wants a defendant to be arraigned more than 2 months after the court ordered a retrial under section 7 of the Criminal Appeal Act 1968; or
(b) a defendant wants such an order set aside after 2 months have passed since it was made.
(2) That party must apply in writing, with reasons, and serve the application on—
(a) the Registrar;
(b) the other party.

Criminal Practice Directions Part 39 Appeal to the Court of Appeal about Conviction or Sentence

PD-92 **CPD IX Appeal 39A: Appeals Against Conviction and Sentence — The Provision of Notice to the Prosecution**

39A.1 When an appeal notice served under CrimPR 39.2 is received by the Registrar of Criminal Appeals, the Registrar will notify the relevant prosecution authority, giving the case name, reference number and the trial or sentencing court.

39A.2 If the court or the Registrar directs, or invites, the prosecution authority to serve a respondent's notice under CrimPR 39.6, prior to the consideration of leave, the Registrar will also at that time serve on the prosecution authority the appeal notice containing the grounds of appeal and the transcripts, if available. If the prosecution authority is not directed or invited to serve a respondent's notice but wishes to do so, the authority should request the grounds of appeal and any existing transcript from the Criminal Appeal Office. Any respondent's notice received prior to the consideration of leave will be made available to the single judge.

39A.3 The Registrar of Criminal Appeals will notify the relevant prosecution authority in the event that:
(a) leave to appeal against conviction or sentence is granted by the single Judge; or
(b) the single Judge or the Registrar refers an application for leave to appeal against conviction or sentence to the Full Court for determination; or
(c) there is to be a renewed application for leave to appeal against sentence only.
If the prosecution authority has not yet been served with the appeal notice and transcript, the Registrar will serve these with the notification, and if leave is granted, the Registrar will also serve the authority with the comments of the single judge.

39A.4 The prosecution should notify the Registrar without delay if they wish to be represented at the hearing. The prosecution should note that the Registrar will not delay listing to await a response from the Prosecution as to whether they wish to attend. Prosecutors should note that occasionally, for example, where the single Judge fixes a hearing date at short notice, the case may be listed very quickly.

39A.5 If the prosecution wishes to be represented at any hearing, the notification should include details of Counsel instructed and a time estimate. An application by the prosecution to remove a case from the list for Counsel's convenience, or to allow further preparation time, will rarely be granted.

39A.6 There may be occasions when the Court of Appeal Criminal Division will grant leave to appeal to an unrepresented applicant and proceed forthwith with the appeal in the absence of the appellant and Counsel. The prosecution should not attend any hearing at which the appellant is unrepresented. *Nasteska v The former Yugoslav Republic of Macedonia (Application No.23152/05)* As a Court of Review, the Court of Appeal Criminal Division would expect the prosecution to have raised any specific matters of relevance with the sentencing Judge in the first instance.

39A.7 Where there is a renewed application for leave to appeal against a sentence imposed for an offence involving a fatality, the Crown Prosecution Service has indicated that it wishes to be represented at all sentence appeals in order to ensure that they are in a position, if appropriate, to make representations as to the impact of the offence upon the victim and their family. In those circumstances, if the court is minded to grant the application for leave to appeal the court should consider adjourning the hearing of the appeal to allow prosecution counsel to attend and for the victim's family to be notified and attend if they so wish.

CPD IX Appeal 39B: Listing of Appeals against Conviction and Sentence in the Court of Appeal Criminal Division (CACD) PD-93

39B.1 Arrangements for the fixing of dates for the hearing of appeals will be made by the Criminal Appeal Office Listing Officer, under the superintendence of the Registrar of Criminal Appeals who may give such directions as he deems necessary.

39B.2 Where possible, regard will be had to an advocate's existing commitments. However, in relation to the listing of appeals, the Court of Appeal takes precedence over all lower courts, including the Crown Court. Wherever practicable, a lower court will have regard to this principle when making arrangements to release an advocate to appear in the Court of Appeal. In case of difficulty the lower court should communicate with the Registrar. In general an advocate's commitment in a lower court will not be regarded as a good reason for failing to accept a date proposed for a hearing in the Court of Appeal.

39B.3 Similarly when the Registrar directs that an appellant should appear by video link, the prison must give precedence to video-links to the Court of Appeal over video-links to the lower courts, including the Crown Court.

39B.4 The copy of the Criminal Appeal Office summary provided to advocates will contain the summary writer's time estimate for the whole hearing including delivery of judgment. It will also contain a time estimate for the judges' reading time of the core material. The Listing Officer will rely on those estimates, unless the advocate for the appellant or the Crown provides different time estimates to the Listing Officer, in writing, within 7 days of the receipt of the summary by the advocate. Where the time estimates are considered by an advocate to be inadequate, or where the estimates have been altered because, for example, a ground of appeal has been abandoned, it is the duty of the advocate to inform the Court promptly, in which event the Registrar will reconsider the time estimates and inform the parties accordingly.

39B.5 The following target times are set for the hearing of appeals. Target times will run from the receipt of the appeal by the Listing Officer, as being ready for hearing.

39B.6

Nature of Appeal:	*From Receipt by Listing Officer to Fixing of Hearing Date:*	*From Fixing of Hearing Date to Hearing:*	*Total Time From Receipt by Listing Officer to Hearing:*
Sentence Appeal	14 days	14 days	28 days
Conviction Appeal	21 days	42 days	63 days
Conviction Appeal where witness to attend	28 days	52 days	80 days

39B.7 Where legal vacations impinge, these periods may be extended. Where expedition is required, the Registrar may direct that these periods be abridged.

39B.8 'Appeal' includes an application for leave to appeal which requires an oral hearing.

CPD IX Appeal 39C: Appeal Notices Containing Grounds of Appeal PD-94

39C.1 The requirements for the service of notices of appeal and the time limits for doing so are as set out in CrimPR Part 39. The Court must be provided with an appeal notice as a single document which sets out the grounds of appeal. Advocates should not provide the Court with an advice addressed to lay or professional clients. Any appeal notice or grounds of appeal served on the Court will usually be provided to the respondent.

39C.2 Advocates should not settle grounds unless they consider that they are properly arguable. Grounds should be carefully drafted; the court is not assisted by grounds of appeal which are not properly set out and particularised in accordance with CrimPR 39.3. The grounds must:

i. be concise; and
ii. be presented in A4 page size and portrait orientation, in not less than 12 point font and in 1.5 line spacing.

Appellants and advocates should keep in mind the powers of the court and the Registrar to return for revision, within a directed period, grounds that do not comply with the rule or with these directions, including grounds that are so prolix or diffuse as to render them incomprehensible. They should keep in mind also the court's powers to refuse permission to appeal on any ground that is so poorly presented as to render it unarguable and thus to exclude it from consideration by the court: see CrimPR 36.14. Should leave to amend the grounds be granted, it is most unlikely that further grounds will be entertained.

39C.3 Where the appellant wants to appeal against conviction, transcripts must be identified in accordance with CrimPR 39.3(1)(c). This includes specifying the date and time of transcripts in the notice of appeal. Accordingly, the date and time of the summing up should be provided, including both parts of a split summing-up. Where relevant, the date and time of additional transcripts (such as rulings or early directions) should be provided. Similarly, any relevant written materials (such as route to verdict) should be identified.

39C.4 Where the appellant wants to rely on a ground of appeal that is not identified by the appeal notice, an application under CrimPR 36.14(5) is required. In *R v James and Others* [2018] EWCA Crim 285 the Court of Appeal identified as follows the considerations that obtain and the criteria that the court will apply on any such application:

(a) as a general rule all the grounds of appeal that an appellant wishes to advance should be lodged with the appeal notice, subject to their being perfected on receipt of transcripts from the Registrar.

(b) the application for permission to appeal under section 31 of the Criminal Appeal Act 1968 is an important stage in the process. It may not be treated lightly or its determination in effect ignored merely because fresh representatives would have done or argued things differently to their predecessors. Fresh grounds advanced by fresh representatives must be particularly cogent.

(c) as well as addressing the factors material to the determination of an application for an extension of time within which to renew an application for permission to appeal, if that is required, on an application under CrimPR 36.14(5) the appellant or his or her representatives must address directly the factors which the court is likely to consider relevant when deciding whether to allow the substitution or addition of grounds of appeal. Those factors include (but this list is not exhaustive):
   (i) the extent of the delay in advancing the fresh ground or grounds;
   (ii) the reasons for that delay;
   (iii) whether the facts or issues the subject of the fresh ground were known to the appellant's representatives when they advised on appeal;
   (iv) the interests of justice and the overriding objective in Part 1 of the Criminal Procedure Rules.

(d) on the assumption that an appellant will have received advice on appeal from his or her trial advocate, who will have settled the grounds of appeal in the original appeal notice or who will have advised that there are no reasonably arguable grounds to challenge the safety of the conviction:
   (i) fresh representatives should comply with the duty of due diligence explained in *McCook* [2014] EWCA Crim 734. Waiver of privilege by the appellant is very likely to be required.
   (ii) once the trial lawyers have responded, the fresh representatives should again consider with great care their duty to the court and whether the proposed fresh grounds should be advanced as reasonably arguable and particularly cogent.
   (iii) the Registrar will obtain, before the determination of the application under CrimPR 36.14(5), transcripts relevant to the fresh grounds and, where required, a respondents' notice relating to the fresh grounds.

(e) while an application under CrimPR 36.14(5) will not require "exceptional leave", and hence the demonstration of substantial injustice should it not be granted, the hurdle for the applicant is a high one nonetheless. Representatives should remind themselves of the provisions of paragraph 39C.2 above.

(f) permission to renew out of time an application for permission to appeal is not given unless the applicant can persuade the court that very good reasons exist. If that application to renew out of time is accompanied by an application to vary the grounds of appeal, the hurdle will be higher still.

(g) any application to substitute or add grounds will be considered by a fully constituted court and at a hearing, not on the papers.

(h) on any renewal of an application for permission to appeal accompanied by an application under CrimPR 36.14(5), if the court refuses those applications it has the power to make a loss of time order or an order for costs in line with *R v Gray and Others* [2014] EWCA Crim 2372. By analogy with *R v Kirk* [2015] EWCA Crim 1764 (where the court refused an extension of time) the court has the power to order payment of the costs of obtaining the respondent's notice and any additional transcripts.

Direct Lodgement

39C.5 With effect from 1st October 2018, Forms NG and Grounds of Appeal which are covered by Part 39 of the Criminal Procedure Rules (appeal to the Court of Appeal about conviction or sentence) are to be lodged directly with the Criminal Appeal Office and not with the Crown Court where the appellant was convicted or sentenced. This Practice Direction must be read alongside the detailed guidance notes that have been produced to accompany the new forms. They are available: https://www.justice.gov.uk/courts/procedure-rules/criminal/forms

From this date the Crown Court will no longer accept Forms NG and will return them to the sender. Forms NG and Grounds of Appeal should only be lodged once. They should, where possible, be lodged by email. Applications should not be lodged directly onto the Digital Case System. Applications must be lodged at the following address: criminalappealoffice.applications@hmcts.x.gsi.gov.uk

If you do not have access to an email account, you should post Form NG and the Grounds of Appeal to:

The Registrar, Criminal Appeal Office, Royal Courts of Justice, Strand, London WC2A 2LL.

Once an application has been effectively lodged, the Registrar will confirm receipt within 7 days.

Service

39C.6 Legal representatives should make sure they provide their secure email address for the purposes of correspondence and service of document. The date of service for new applications lodged by email will be the day on which it is sent, if that day is a business day and if sent no later than 2:30pm on that day, otherwise the date of service will be on the next business day after it was sent.

Completing the Form NG

39C.7 All applications must be compliant with the relevant Criminal Procedure Rules, particularly those in Part 39. A separate Form NG should be completed for each substantive application which is being made. Each application (conviction, sentence and confiscation order) has its own Form NG and must be drafted and lodged as a stand-alone application.

CPD IX Appeal 39D: Respondents' Notices **PD-95**

39D.1 The requirements for the service of respondents' notices and the time limits for doing so are as set out in Part 39 of the Criminal Procedure Rules. Any respondent's notice served should be in accordance with Rule 39.6. The Court does not require a response to the respondent's notice.

CPD IX Appeal 39E: Loss of Time **PD-96**

39E.1 Both the Court and the single judge have power, in their discretion, under the Criminal Appeal Act 1968 sections 29 and 31, to direct that part of the time during which an applicant is in custody after lodging his notice of application for leave to appeal should not count towards sentence. When leave to appeal has been refused by the single judge, it is necessary to consider the reasons given by the single judge before making a decision whether to renew the application. Where an application devoid of merit has been refused by the single judge he may indicate that the Full Court should consider making a direction for loss of time on renewal of the application. However, the Full Court may make such a direction whether or not such an indication has been given by the single judge.

39E.2 The case of *R v Gray and Others* [2014] EWCA Crim 2372 makes clear 'that unmeritorious renewal applications took up a wholly disproportionate amount of staff and judicial resources in preparation and hearing time. They also wasted significant sums of public money.... The more time the Court of Appeal Office and the judges spent on unmeritorious applications, the longer the waiting times were likely to be.... The only means the court has of discouraging unmeritorious applications which waste precious time and resources is by using the powers given to us by Parliament in the Criminal Appeal Act 1968 and the Prosecution of Offenders Act 1985.'

39E.3 Further, applicants and counsel are reminded of the warning given by the Court of Appeal in *R v Hart and Others* [2006] EWCA Crim 3239, [2007] 1 Cr. App. R. 31, [2007] 2 Cr. App. R. (S.) 34 and should 'heed the fact that this court is prepared to exercise its power.... The mere fact that counsel has advised that there are grounds of appeal will not always be a sufficient answer to the question as to whether or not an application has indeed been brought which was totally without merit.'

39E.4 Where the Single Judge has not indicated that the Full Court should consider making a Loss of Time Order because the defendant has already been released, the case of *R v Terence Nolan* [2017] EWCA Crim 2449 indicates that the Single Judge should consider what, if any, costs have been incurred by the Registrar and the Prosecution and should make directions accordingly. Reference should be made to the relevant Costs Division of the Criminal Practice Direction.

PD-97 **CPD IX Appeal 39F: Skeleton Arguments**

39F.1 Advocates should always ensure that the court, and any other party as appropriate, has a single document containing all of the points that are to be argued. The appeal notice must comply with the requirements of CrimPR 39.3. In cases of an appeal against conviction, advocates must serve a skeleton argument when the appeal notice does not sufficiently outline the grounds of the appeal, particularly in cases where a complex or novel point of law has been raised. In an appeal against sentence it may be helpful for an advocate to serve a skeleton argument when a complex issue is raised.

39F.2 The appellant's skeleton argument, if any, must be served no later than 21 days before the hearing date, and the respondent's skeleton argument, if any, no later than 14 days before the hearing date, unless otherwise directed by the Court.

39F.3 Paragraphs XII D.17 to D.23 of these Practice Directions set out the general requirements for skeleton arguments. A skeleton argument, if provided, should contain a numbered list of the points the advocate intends to argue, grouped under each ground of appeal, and stated in no more than one or two sentences. It should be as succinct as possible. Advocates should ensure that the correct Criminal Appeal Office number and the date on which the document was served appear at the beginning of any document and that their names are at the end.

PD-98 **CPD IX Appeal 39G: Criminal Appeal Office Summaries**

39G.1 To assist the Court, the Criminal Appeal Office prepares summaries of the cases coming before it. These are entirely objective and do not contain any advice about how the Court should deal with the case or any view about its merits. They consist of two Parts.

39G.2 Part I, which is provided to all of the advocates in the case, generally contains:
(a) particulars of the proceedings in the Crown Court, including representation and details of any co-accused;
(b) particulars of the proceedings in the Court of Appeal (Criminal Division);
(c) the facts of the case, as drawn from the transcripts, appeal notice, respondent's notice, witness statements and/or the exhibits;
(d) the submissions and rulings, summing up and sentencing remarks.

39G.3 The contents of the summary are a matter for the professional judgment of the writer, but an advocate wishing to suggest any significant alteration to Part I should write to the Registrar of Criminal Appeals. If the Registrar does not agree, the summary and the letter will be put to the Court for decision. The Court will not generally be willing to hear oral argument about the content of the summary.

39G.4 Advocates may show Part I of the summary to their professional or lay clients (but to no one else) if they believe it would help to check facts or formulate arguments, but summaries are not to be copied or reproduced without the permission of the Criminal Appeal Office; permission for this will not normally be given in cases involving children, or sexual offences, or where the Crown Court has made an order restricting reporting.

39G.5 Unless a judge of the High Court or the Registrar of Criminal Appeals gives a direction to the contrary, in any particular case involving material of an explicitly salacious or sadistic nature, Part I will also be supplied to appellants who seek to represent themselves before the Full Court, or who renew to the full court their applications for leave to appeal against conviction or sentence.

39G.6 Part II, which is supplied to the Court alone, contains:
(a) a summary of the grounds of appeal; and
(b) in appeals against sentence (and applications for such leave), summaries of the antecedent histories of the parties and of any relevant pre-sentence, medical or other reports.

39G.7 All of the source material is provided to the Court and advocates are able to draw attention to anything in it which may be of particular relevance.

Criminal Procedure Rules Part 40 Appeal to the Court of Appeal about Reporting or Public Access Restriction

R-451 **When this Part applies**

40.1 (1) This Part applies where a person directly affected by an order to which section 159(1) of the Criminal Justice Act 1988 applies wants to appeal against that order.
(2) A reference to an 'appellant' in this Part is a reference to such a party.

Service of appeal notice R-452

40.2 (1) An appellant must serve an appeal notice on—
(a) the Crown Court officer;
(b) the Registrar;
(c) the parties; and
(d) any other person directly affected by the order against which the appellant wants to appeal.
(2) The appellant must serve the appeal notice not later than—
(a) the next business day after an order restricting public access to the trial;
(b) 10 business days after an order restricting reporting of the trial.

Form of appeal notice R-453

40.3 (1) An appeal notice must be in the form set out in the Practice Direction.
(2) The appeal notice must—
(a) specify the order against which the appellant wants to appeal;
(b) identify each ground of appeal on which the appellant relies, numbering them consecutively (if there is more than one) and concisely outlining each argument in support;
(c) summarise the relevant facts;
(d) identify any relevant authorities;
(e) include or attach, with reasons—
(i) an application for permission to appeal,
(ii) any application for an extension of time within which to serve the appeal notice,
(iii) any application for a direction to attend in person a hearing that the appellant could attend by live link, if the appellant is in custody,
(iv) any application for permission to introduce evidence, and
(v) a list of those on whom the appellant has served the appeal notice; and
(f) attach any document or thing that the appellant thinks the court will need to decide the appeal.

Advance notice of appeal against order restricting public access R-454

40.4 (1) This rule applies where the appellant wants to appeal against an order restricting public access to a trial.
(2) The appellant may serve advance written notice of intention to appeal against any such order that may be made.
(3) The appellant must serve any such advance notice—
(a) on—
(i) the Crown Court officer,
(ii) the Registrar,
(iii) the parties, and
(iv) any other person who will be directly affected by the order against which the appellant intends to appeal, if it is made; and
(b) not more than 5 business days after the Crown Court officer displays notice of the application for the order.
(4) The advance notice must include the same information (with the necessary adaptations) as an appeal notice.
(5) The court must treat that advance notice as the appeal notice if the order is made.

Duty of applicant for order restricting public access R-455

40.5 (1) This rule applies where the appellant wants to appeal against an order restricting public access to a trial.
(2) The party who applied for the order must serve on the Registrar—
(a) a transcript or note of the application for the order; and
(b) any other document or thing that that party thinks the court will need to decide the appeal.
(3) That party must serve that transcript or note and any such other document or thing as soon as practicable after—
(a) the appellant serves the appeal notice; or
(b) the order, where the appellant served advance notice of intention to appeal.

Respondent's notice on appeal against reporting restriction R-456

40.6 (1) This rule applies where the appellant wants to appeal against an order restricting the reporting of a trial.

(2) A person on whom an appellant serves an appeal notice may serve a respondent's notice, and must do so if—
(a) that person wants to make representations to the court; or
(b) the court so directs.
(3) Such a person must serve the respondent's notice on—
(a) the appellant;
(b) the Crown Court officer;
(c) the Registrar;
(d) the parties; and
(e) any other person on whom the appellant served the appeal notice.
(4) Such a person must serve the respondent's notice not more than 3 business days after—
(a) the appellant serves the appeal notice; or
(b) a direction to do so.
(5) The respondent's notice must be in the form set out in the Practice Direction.
(6) The respondent's notice must—
(a) give the date on which the respondent was served with the appeal notice;
(b) identify each ground of opposition on which the respondent relies, numbering them consecutively (if there is more than one), concisely outlining each argument in support and identifying the ground of appeal to which each relates;
(c) summarise any relevant facts not already summarised in the appeal notice;
(d) identify any relevant authorities;
(e) include or attach any application for the following, with reasons—
(i) an extension of time within which to serve the respondent's notice,
(ii) a direction to attend in person any hearing that the respondent could attend by live link, if the respondent is in custody,
(iii) permission to introduce evidence; and
(f) identify any other document or thing that the respondent thinks the court will need to decide the appeal.

R-457 Renewing applications

40.7 Rule 36.5 (Renewing an application refused by a judge or the Registrar) applies with a time limit of 5 business days.

R-458 Right to introduce evidence

40.8 No person may introduce evidence without the court's permission.

R-459 Right to attend hearing

40.9 (1) A party who is in custody has a right to attend a hearing in public of an appeal against an order restricting the reporting of a trial.
(2) The court or the Registrar may direct that such a party is to attend a hearing by live link.

Criminal Procedure Rules Part 41 Reference to the Court of Appeal of Point of Law or Unduly Lenient Sentencing

R-460 When this Part applies

41.1 This Part applies where the Attorney General wants to—
(a) refer a point of law to the Court of Appeal under section 36 of the Criminal Justice Act 1972; or
(b) refer a sentencing case to the Court of Appeal under section 36 of the Criminal Justice Act 1988.

R-461 Service of notice of reference and application for permission

41.2 (1) The Attorney General must serve any notice of reference and any application for permission to refer a sentencing case on—
(a) the Registrar; and
(b) the defendant.
(2) Where the Attorney General refers a point of law—
(a) the Attorney must give the Registrar details of—
(i) the defendant affected,
(ii) the date and place of the relevant Crown Court decision, and
(iii) the relevant verdict and sentencing; and
(b) the Attorney must give the defendant notice that—
(i) the outcome of the reference will not make any difference to the outcome of the trial, and
(ii) the defendant may serve a respondent's notice.

(3) Where the Attorney General applies for permission to refer a sentencing case, the Attorney must give the defendant notice that—
(a) the outcome of the reference may make a difference to that sentencing, and in particular may result in a more severe sentence; and
(b) the defendant may serve a respondent's notice.

(4) The Attorney General must serve an application for permission to refer a sentencing case on the Registrar not more than 28 days after the last of the sentences in that case.

Form of notice of reference and application for permission **R-462**

41.3 (1) A notice of reference and an application for permission to refer a sentencing case must give the year and number of that reference or that case.

(2) A notice of reference of a point of law must—
(a) specify the point of law in issue and indicate the opinion that the Attorney General invites the court to give;
(b) identify each ground for that invitation, numbering them consecutively (if there is more than one) and concisely outlining each argument in support;
(c) exclude any reference to the defendant's name and any other reference that may identify the defendant;
(d) summarise the relevant facts; and
(e) identify any relevant authorities.

(3) An application for permission to refer a sentencing case must—
(a) give details of—
(i) the defendant affected,
(ii) the date and place of the relevant Crown Court decision, and
(iii) the relevant verdict and sentencing;
(b) explain why that sentencing appears to the Attorney General unduly lenient, concisely outlining each argument in support; and
(c) include the application for permission to refer the case to the court.

(4) A notice of reference of a sentencing case must—
(a) include the same details and explanation as the application for permission to refer the case;
(b) summarise the relevant facts; and
(c) identify any relevant authorities.

(5) Where the court gives the Attorney General permission to refer a sentencing case, it may treat the application for permission as the notice of reference.

Respondent's notice **R-463**

41.4 (1) A defendant on whom the Attorney General serves a notice of reference or an application for permission to refer a sentencing case may serve a respondent's notice, and must do so if—
(a) the defendant wants to make representations to the court; or
(b) the court so directs.

(2) Such a defendant must serve the respondent's notice on—
(a) the Attorney General; and
(b) the Registrar.

(3) Such a defendant must serve the respondent's notice—
(a) where the Attorney General refers a point of law, not more than 28 days after—
(i) the Attorney serves the reference, or
(ii) a direction to do so;
(b) where the Attorney General applies for permission to refer a sentencing case, not more than 14 days after—
(i) the Attorney serves the application, or
(ii) a direction to do so.

(4) Where the Attorney General refers a point of law, the respondent's notice must—
(a) give the date on which the respondent was served with the notice of reference;
(b) identify each ground of opposition on which the respondent relies, numbering them consecutively (if there is more than one), concisely outlining each argument in support and identifying the Attorney General's groud or reason to which each relates;

(c) summarise any relevant facts not already summarised in the reference;
(d) identify any relevant authorities; and
(e) include or attach any application for the following, with reasons—
(i) an extension of time within which to serve the respondent's notice,
(ii) permission to attend a hearing that the respondent does not have a right to attend,
(iii) a direction to attend in person a hearing that the respondent could attend by live link, if the respondent is in custody.

(5) Where the Attorney General applies for permission to refer a sentencing case, the respondent's notice must—
(a) give the date on which the respondent was served with the application;
(b) say if the respondent wants to make representations at the hearing of the application or reference; and
(c) include or attach any application for the following, with reasons—
(i) an extension of time within which to serve the respondent's notice,
(ii) permission to attend a hearing that the respondent does not have a right to attend,
(iii) a direction to attend in person a hearing that the respondent could attend by live link, if the respondent is in custody.

R-464 **Variation or withdrawal of notice of reference or application for permission**

41.5 (1) This rule applies where the Attorney General wants to vary or withdraw—
(a) a notice of reference; or
(b) an application for permission to refer a sentencing case.
(2) The Attorney General—
(a) may vary or withdraw the notice or application without the court's permission by serving notice on—
(i) the Registrar, and
(ii) the defendant
before any hearing of the reference or application; but
(b) at any such hearing, may only vary or withdraw that notice or application with the court's permission.

R-465 **Right to attend hearing**

41.6 (1) A respondent who is in custody has a right to attend a hearing in public unless it is a hearing preliminary or incidental to a reference, including the hearing of an application for permission to refer a sentencing case.
(2) The court or the Registrar may direct that such a respondent is to attend a hearing by live link.

R-466 **Anonymity of defendant on reference of point of law**

41.7 Where the Attorney General refers a point of law, the court must not allow anyone to identify the defendant during the proceedings unless the defendant gives permission.

Criminal Procedure Rules Part 42 Appeal to the Court of Appeal in Confiscation and Related Proceedings

General rules

R-467 **Extension of time**

42.1 (1) An application to extend the time limit for giving notice of application for permission to appeal under Part 2 of the Proceeds of Crime Act 2002 must—
(a) be included in the notice of appeal; and
(b) state the grounds for the application.
(2) The parties may not agree to extend any date or time limit set by this Part or by the Proceeds of Crime Act 2002 (Appeals under Part 2) Order 2003.

R-468 **Other applications**

42.2 Rules 39.3(2)(h) (Form of appeal notice) applies in relation to an application—
(a) by a party to an appeal under Part 2 of the Proceeds of Crime Act 2002 that, under article 7 of the Proceeds of Crime Act 2002 (Appeals under Part 2) Order 2003, a witness be ordered to attend or that the evidence of a witness be received by the Court of Appeal; or
(b) by the defendant to be given permission by the court to be present at proceedings for which permission is required under article 6 of the 2003 Order,

as it applies in relation to applications under Part I of the Criminal Appeal Act 1968 and the form in which rules 39.3 requires notice to be given may be modified as necessary.

Examination of witness by court **R-469**

42.3 Rule 36.7 (Notice of hearings and decisions) shall apply in relation to an order of the court under article 7 of the Proceeds of Crime Act 2002 (Appeals under Part 2) Order 2003 to require a person to attend for examination as it applies in relation to such an order of the court under Part I of the Criminal Appeal Act 1968.

Supply of documentary and other exhibits **R-470**

42.4 Rule 36.11 (Registrar's duty to provide copy documents for appeal or reference) applies in relation to an appellant or respondent under Part 2 of the Proceeds of Crime Act 2002 as it applies in relation to an appellant and respondent under Part I of the Criminal Appeal Act 1968.

Registrar's power to require information from court of trial **R-471**

42.5 The Registrar may require the Crown Court to provide the Court of Appeal with any assistance or information which it requires for the purposes of exercising its jurisdiction under Part 2 of the Proceeds of Crime Act 2002, the Proceeds of Crime Act 2002 (Appeals under Part 2) Order 2003 or this Part.

Hearing by single judge **R-472**

42.6 Rule 36.6(6) (Hearings) applies in relation to a judge exercising any of the powers referred to in article 8 of the Proceeds of Crime Act 2002 (Appeals under Part 2) Order 2003 or the powers in rules 42.12(3) and (4) (Respondent's notice), 42.15(2) (Notice of appeal) and 42.16(6) (Respondent's notice), as it applies in relation to a judge exercising the powers referred to in section 31(2) of the Criminal Appeal Act 1968.

Determination by full court **R-473**

42.7 Rule 36.5 (Renewing an application refused by a single judge or the Registrar) applies where a single judge has refused an application by a party to exercise in that party's favour any of the powers listed in article 8 of the Proceeds of Crime Act 2002 (Appeals under Part 2) Order 2003, or the power in rule 42.12(3) or (4) as it applies where the judge has refused to exercise the powers referred to in section 31(2) of the Criminal Appeal Act 1968.

Notice of determination **R-474**

42.8 (1) This rule applies where a single judge or the Court of Appeal has determined an application or appeal under the Proceeds of Crime Act 2002 (Appeals under Part 2) Order 2003 or under Part 2 of the Proceeds of Crime Act 2002.

(2) The Registrar must, as soon as practicable, serve notice of the determination on all of the parties to the proceedings.

(3) Where a single judge or the Court of Appeal has disposed of an application for permission to appeal or an appeal under section 31 of the 2002 Act, the Registrar must also, as soon as practicable, serve the order on a court officer of the court of trial and any magistrates' court responsible for enforcing any confiscation order which the Crown Court has made.

Record of proceedings and transcripts **R-475**

42.9 Rule 5.5 (Recording and transcription of proceedings in the Crown Court) and rule 36.9 (Duty of person transcribing proceedings in the Crown Court) apply in relation to proceedings in respect of which an appeal lies to the Court of Appeal under Part 2 of the Proceeds of Crime Act 2002 as they apply in relation to proceedings in respect of which an appeal lies to the Court of Appeal under Part I of the Criminal Appeal Act 1968.

Appeal to the Supreme Court **R-476**

42.10 (1) An application to the Court of Appeal for permission to appeal to the Supreme Court under Part 2 of the Proceeds of Crime Act 2002 must be made—

(a) orally after the decision of the Court of Appeal from which an appeal lies to the Supreme Court; or

(b) in the form set out in the Practice Direction, in accordance with article 12 of the Proceeds of Crime Act 2002 (Appeals under Part 2) Order 2003 and served on the Registrar.

(2) The application may be abandoned at any time before it is heard by the Court of Appeal by serving notice in writing on the Registrar.

(3) Rule 36.6(6) (Hearings) applies in relation to a single judge exercising any of the powers referred to in article 15 of the 2003 Order, as it applies in relation to a single judge exercising the powers referred to in section 31(2) of the Criminal Appeal Act 1968.

(4) Rules 36.5 (Renewing an application refused by a judge or the Registrar) applies where a single judge has refused an application by a party to exercise in that party's favour any of the powers listed in article 15 of the 2003 Order as they apply where the judge has refused to exercise the powers referred to in section 31(2) of the 1968 Act.

(5) The form in which rule 36.5(2) requires an application to be made may be modified as necessary.

Confiscation: appeal by prosecutor or by person with interest in property

R-477 Notice of appeal

42.11 (1) Where an appellant wishes to apply to the Court of Appeal for permission to appeal under section 31 of the Proceeds of Crime Act 2002, the appellant must serve a notice of appeal in the form set out in the Practice Direction on—

(a) the Crown Court officer; and

(b) the defendant.

(2) When the notice of a prosecutor's appeal about a confiscation order is served on the defendant, it must be accompanied by a respondent's notice in the form set out in the Practice Direction for the defendant to complete and a notice which—

(a) informs the defendant that the result of an appeal could be that the Court of Appeal would increase a confiscation order already imposed, make a confiscation order itself or direct the Crown Court to hold another confiscation hearing;

(b) informs the defendant of any right under article 6 of the Proceeds of Crime Act 2002 (Appeals under Part 2) Order 2003 to be present at the hearing of the appeal, although in custody;

(c) invites the defendant to serve any notice on the Registrar —

(i) to apply to the Court of Appeal for permission to be present at proceedings for which such permission is required under article 6 of the 2003 Order, or

(ii) to present any argument to the Court of Appeal on the hearing of the application or, if permission is given, the appeal, and whether the defendant wishes to present it in person or by means of a legal representative;

(d) draws to the defendant's attention the effect of rule 42.4 (Supply of documentary and other exhibits); and

(e) advises the defendant to consult a solicitor as soon as possible.

(3) The appellant must provide a Crown Court officer with a certificate of service stating that the appellant has served the notice of appeal on the defendant in accordance with paragraph (1) or explaining why it has not been possible to do so.

R-478 Respondent's notice

42.12 (1) This rule applies where a defendant is served with a notice of appeal under rule 42.11.

(2) If the defendant wishes to oppose the application for permission to appeal, the defendant must, not later than 14 days after service of the notice of appeal, serve on the Registrar and on the appellant a notice in the form set out in the Practice Direction—

(a) stating the date on which the notice of appeal was served;

(b) summarising the defendant's response to the arguments of the appellant; and

(c) specifying the authorities which the defendant intends to cite.

(3) The time for giving notice under this rule may be extended by the Registrar, a single judge or by the Court of Appeal.

(4) Where the Registrar refuses an application under paragraph (3) for the extension of time, the defendant is entitled to have the application determined by a single judge.

(5) Where a single judge refuses an application under paragraph (3) or (4) for the extension of time, the defendant is entitled to have the application determined by the Court of Appeal.

R-479 Amendment and abandonment of appeal

42.13 (1) The appellant may amend a notice of appeal served under rule 42.11 or abandon an appeal under section 31 of the Proceeds of Crime Act 2002—

(a) without the permission of the court at any time before the Court of Appeal has begun hearing the appeal; and

(b) with the permission of the court after the Court of Appeal has begun hearing the appeal,

by serving notice in writing on the Registrar.

(2) Where the appellant serves a notice abandoning an appeal under paragraph (1), the appellant must send a copy of it to—

(a) the defendant;

(b) a court officer of the court of trial; and

(c) the magistrates' court responsible for enforcing any confiscation order which the Crown Court has made.

(3) Where the appellant serves a notice amending a notice of appeal under paragraph (1), the appellant must send a copy of it to the defendant.

(4) Where an appeal is abandoned under paragraph (1), the application for permission to appeal or appeal must be treated, for the purposes of section 85 of the 2002 Act (Conclusion of proceedings), as having been refused or dismissed by the Court of Appeal.

Appeal about compliance, restraint or receivership order

Permission to appeal R-480

42.14 (1) Permission to appeal to the Court of Appeal under section 13B, section 43 or section 65 of the Proceeds of Crime Act 2002 may only be given where—

(a) the Court of Appeal considers that the appeal would have a real prospect of success; or

(b) there is some other compelling reason why the appeal should be heard.

(2) An order giving permission to appeal may limit the issues to be heard and be made subject to conditions.

Notice of appeal R-481

42.15 (1) Where an appellant wishes to apply to the Court of Appeal for permission to appeal under section 13B, 43 or 65 of the Proceeds of Crime Act 2002 Act, the appellant must serve a notice of appeal in the form set out in the Practice Direction on the Crown Court officer.

(2) Unless the Registrar, a single judge or the Court of Appeal directs otherwise, the appellant must serve the notice of appeal, accompanied by a respondent's notice in the form set out in the Practice Direction for the respondent to complete, on—

(a) each respondent;

(b) any person who holds realisable property to which the appeal relates; and

(c) any other person affected by the appeal

as soon as practicable and in any event not later than 5 business days after.the notice of appeal is served on the Crown Court officer.

(3) The appellant must serve the following documents with the notice of appeal—

(a) four additional copies of the notice of appeal for the Court of Appeal;

(b) four copies of any skeleton argument;

(c) one sealed copy and four unsealed copies of any order being appealed;

(d) four copies of any witness statement or affidavit in support of the application for permission to appeal;

(e) four copies of a suitable record of the reasons for judgment of the Crown Court; and

(f) four copies of the bundle of documents used in the Crown Court proceedings from which the appeal lies.

(4) Where it is not possible to serve all of the documents referred to in paragraph (3), the appellant must indicate which documents have not yet been served and the reasons why they are not currently available.

(5) The appellant must provide a Crown Court officer with a certificate of service stating that the notice of appeal has been served on each respondent in accordance with paragraph (2) and including full details of each respondent or explaining why it has not been possible to effect service.

Respondent's notice R-482

42.16 (1) This rule applies to an appeal under section 13B, 43 or 65 of the Proceeds of Crime Act 2002.

(2) A respondent may serve a respondent's notice on the Registrar.

(3) A respondent who—

(a) is seeking permission to appeal from the Court of Appeal; or

(b) wishes to ask the Court of Appeal to uphold the decision of the Crown Court for reasons different from or additional to those given by the Crown Court,

must serve a respondent's notice on the Registrar.

(4) A respondent's notice must be in the form set out in the Practice Direction and where the respondent seeks permission to appeal to the Court of Appeal it must be requested in the respondent's notice.

(5) A respondent's notice must be served on the Registrar not later than 14 days after—

(a) the date the respondent is served with notification that the Court of Appeal has given the appellant permission to appeal; or

(b) the date the respondent is served with notification that the application for permission to appeal and the appeal itself are to be heard together.

(6) Unless the Registrar, a single judge or the Court of Appeal directs otherwise, the respondent serving a respondent's notice must serve the notice on the appellant and any other respondent—
(a) as soon as practicable; and
(b) in any event not later than 5 business days,
after it is served on the Registrar.

R-483 Amendment and abandonment of appeal

42.17 (1) The appellant may amend a notice of appeal served under rule 42.15 or abandon an appeal under section 13B, 43 or 65 of the Proceeds of Crime Act 2002—
(a) without the permission of the court at any time before the Court of Appeal has begun hearing the appeal; and
(b) with the permission of the court after the Court of Appeal has begun hearing the appeal,
by serving notice in writing on the Registrar.

(2) Where the appellant serves a notice under paragraph (1), the appellant must send a copy of it to each respondent.

R-484 Stay

42.18 Unless the Court of Appeal or the Crown Court orders otherwise, an appeal under section 13B, 43 or 65 of the Proceeds of Crime Act 2002 does not operate as a stay of any order or decision of the Crown Court.

R-485 Striking out appeal notices and setting aside or imposing conditions on permission to appeal

42.19 (1) The Court of Appeal may—
(a) strike out the whole or part of a notice of appeal served under rule 42.15; or
(b) impose or vary conditions upon which an appeal under section 13B, 43 or 65 of the Proceeds of Crime Act 2002 may be brought.

(2) The Court of Appeal will only exercise its powers under paragraph (1) where there is a compelling reason for doing so.

(3) Where a party is present at the hearing at which permission to appeal was given, that party may not subsequently apply for an order that the Court of Appeal exercise its powers under paragraph (1)(b).

R-486 Hearing of appeals

42.20 (1) This rule applies to appeals under section 13B, 43 or 65 of the Proceeds of Crime Act 2002.

(2) Every appeal must be limited to a review of the decision of the Crown Court unless the Court of Appeal considers that in the circumstances of an individual appeal it would be in the interests of justice to hold a re-hearing.

(3) The Court of Appeal may allow an appeal where the decision of the Crown Court was—
(a) wrong; or
(b) unjust because of a serious procedural or other irregularity in the proceedings in the Crown Court.

(4) The Court of Appeal may draw any inference of fact which it considers justified on the evidence.

(5) At the hearing of the appeal a party may not rely on a matter not contained in that party's notice of appeal unless the Court of Appeal gives permission.

Criminal Procedure Rules Part 43 Appeal or Reference to the Supreme Court

R-487 When this Part applies

43.1 (1) This Part applies where—
(a) a party wants to appeal to the Supreme Court after—
(i) an application to the Court of Appeal to which Part 27 applies (Retrial following acquittal), or
(ii) an appeal to the Court of Appeal to which applies Part 37 (Appeal to the Court of Appeal against ruling at preparatory hearing), Part 38 (Appeal to the Court of Appeal against ruling adverse to prosecution), or Part 39 (Appeal to the Court of Appeal about conviction or sentence); or

(b) a party wants to refer a case to the Supreme Court after a reference to the Court of Appeal to which Part 41 applies (Reference to the Court of Appeal of point of law or unduly lenient sentencing).

(2) A reference to an 'appellant' in this Part is a reference to such a party.

Application for permission or reference R-488

43.2 (1) An appellant must—

(a) apply orally to the Court of Appeal—

(i) for permission to appeal or to refer a sentencing case, or

(ii) to refer a point of law

immediately after the court gives the reasons for its decision; or

(b) apply in writing and serve the application on the Registrar and every other party not more than—

(i) 14 days after the court gives the reasons for its decision if that decision was on a sentencing reference to which Part 41 applies (Attorney General's reference of sentencing case), or

(ii) 28 days after the court gives those reasons in any other case.

(2) An application for permission to appeal or to refer a sentencing case must—

(a) identify the point of law of general public importance that the appellant wants the court to certify is involved in the decision; and

(b) give reasons why—

(i) that point of law ought to be considered by the Supreme Court, and

(ii) the court ought to give permission to appeal.

(3) An application to refer a point of law must give reasons why that point ought to be considered by the Supreme Court.

(4) An application must include or attach any application for the following, with reasons—

(a) an extension of time within which to make the application for permission or for a reference;

(b) bail pending appeal;

(c) permission to attend any hearing in the Supreme Court, if the appellant is in custody.

(5) A written application must be in the form set out in the Practice Direction.

Determination of detention pending appeal, etc. R-489

43.3 On an application for permission to appeal, the Court of Appeal must—

(a) decide whether to order the detention of a defendant who would have been liable to be detained but for the decision of the court; and

(b) determine any application for—

(i) bail pending appeal,

(ii) permission to attend any hearing in the Supreme Court, or

(iii) a representation order.

Bail pending appeal R-490

43.4 Rules 39.8 (Application for bail pending appeal or retrial), 39.9 (Conditions of bail pending appeal or re-trial) and 39.10 (Forfeiture of a recognizance given as a condition of bail) apply.

Criminal Procedure Rules Part 44 Request to the European Court for a Preliminary Ruling

When this Part applies R-491

44.1 This Part applies where the court can request the Court of Justice of the European Union ('the European Court') to give a preliminary ruling, under Article 267 of the Treaty on the Functioning of the European Union.

Preparation of request R-492

44.2 (1) The court may—

(a) make an order for the submission of a request—

(i) on application by a party, or

(ii) on its own initiative;

(b) give directions for the preparation of the terms of such a request.

(2) The court must—

(a) include in such a request—

(i) the identity of the court making the request,

(ii) the parties' identities,

(iii) a statement of whether a party is in custody,
(iv) a succinct statement of the question on which the court seeks the ruling of the European Court,
(v) a succinct statement of any opinion on the answer that the court may have expressed in any judgment that it has delivered,
(vi) a summary of the nature and history of the proceedings, including the salient facts and an indication of whether those facts are proved, admitted or assumed,
(vii) the relevant rules of national law,
(viii) a summary of the relevant contentions of the parties,
(ix) an indication of the provisions of European Union law that the European Court is asked to interpret, and
(x) an explanation of why a ruling of the European Court is requested;

(b) express the request in terms that can be translated readily into other languages; and
(c) set out the request in a schedule to the order.

R-493 **Submission of request**

44.3 (1) The court officer must serve the order for the submission of the request on the Senior Master of the Queen's Bench Division of the High Court.

(2) The Senior Master must—
(a) submit the request to the European Court; but
(b) unless the court otherwise directs, postpone the submission of the request until—
(i) the time for any appeal against the order has expired, and
(ii) any appeal against the order has been determined.

Criminal Practice Directions Part 44 Request to the European Court for a Preliminary Ruling

PD-99 **CPD IX Appeal 44A: References to the European Court of Justice**

44A.1 Further to rule 44.3 of the Criminal Procedure Rules, the order containing the reference shall be filed with the Senior Master of the Queen's Bench Division of the High Court for onward transmission to the Court of Justice of the European Union. The order should be marked for the attention of Mrs Isaac and sent to the Senior Master:

c/o Queen's Bench Division Associates Dept
Room WG03
Royal Courts of Justice
Strand
London
WC2A 2LL

44A.2 There is no longer a requirement that the relevant court file be sent to the Senior Master. The parties should ensure that all appropriate documentation is sent directly to the European Court at the following address:

The Registrar
Court of Justice of the European Union
Kirchberg
L-2925 Luxemburg

44A.3 There is no prescribed form for use but the following details must be included in the back sheet to the order:

i. Solicitor's full address;
ii. Solicitor's and Court references;
iii. Solicitor's e-mail address.

44A.4 The European Court of Justice regularly updates its Recommendation to national courts and tribunals in relation to the initiation of preliminary ruling proceedings. The current Recommendation is 2012/C 338/01: http://eur-lex.europa.eu/legal-content/EN/TXT/PDF/?uri=CELEX:32012H1106(01)&qid=1440325685329&from=EN

44A.5 The referring court may request the Court of Justice of the European Union to apply its urgent preliminary ruling procedure where the referring court's proceedings relate to a person in custody. For further information see Council Decision 2008/79/EC [2008] OJ L24/42: http://eur-lex.europa.eu/legal-content/EN/TXT/?qid=1440325784497&uri=CELEX:32008L0079

44A.6 Any such request must be made in a document separate from the order or in a covering letter and must set out:
iv. The matters of fact and law which establish the urgency;
v. The reasons why the urgent preliminary ruling procedure applies; and
vi. In so far as possible, the court's view on the answer to the question referred to the Court of Justice of the European Union for a preliminary ruling.

44A.7 Any request to apply the urgent preliminary ruling procedure should be filed with the Senior Master as described above.

CRIMINAL PROCEDURE RULES PART 45 COSTS

General rules

When this Part applies R-494

45.1 (1) This Part applies where the court can make an order about costs under—
(a) Part II of the Prosecution of Offences Act 1985 and Part II, IIA or IIB of The Costs in Criminal Cases (General) Regulations 1986;
(b) section 109 of the Magistrates' Courts Act 1980;
(c) section 52 of the Senior Courts Act 1981 and rule 45.6 or rule 45.7;
(d) section 8 of the Bankers Books Evidence Act 1879;
(e) section 2C(8) of the Criminal Procedure (Attendance of Witnesses) Act 1965;
(f) section 36(5) of the Criminal Justice Act 1972;
(g) section 159(5) and Schedule 3, paragraph 11, of the Criminal Justice Act 1988;
(h) section 14H(5) of the Football Spectators Act 1989;
(i) section 4(7) of the Dangerous Dogs Act 1991;
(j) Part 3 of The Serious Crime Act 2007 (Appeals under Section 24) Order 2008; or
(k) Part 1 or 2 of the Extradition Act 2003.
(2) In this Part, 'costs' means—
(a) the fees payable to a legal representative;
(b) the disbursements paid by a legal representative; and
(c) any other expenses incurred in connection with the case.

Costs orders: general rules R-495

45.2 (1) The court must not make an order about costs unless each party and any other person directly affected—
(a) is present; or
(b) has had an opportunity—
(i) to attend, or
(ii) to make representations.
(2) The court may make an order about costs—
(a) at a hearing in public or in private; or
(b) without a hearing.
(3) In deciding what order, if any, to make about costs, the court must have regard to all the circumstances, including—
(a) the conduct of all the parties; and
(b) any costs order already made.
(4) If the court makes an order about costs, it must—
(a) specify who must, or must not, pay what, to whom; and
(b) identify the legislation under which the order is made, where there is a choice of powers.
(5) The court must give reasons if it—
(a) refuses an application for a costs order; or
(b) rejects representations opposing a costs order.
(6) If the court makes an order for the payment of costs—
(a) the general rule is that it must be for an amount that is sufficient reasonably to compensate the recipient for costs—
(i) actually, reasonably and properly incurred, and
(ii) reasonable in amount; but
(b) the court may order the payment of—
(i) a proportion of that amount,
(ii) a stated amount less than that amount,
(iii) costs from or until a certain date only,

(iv) costs relating only to particular steps taken, or
(v) costs relating only to a distinct part of the case.

(7) On an assessment of the amount of costs, relevant factors include—
(a) the conduct of all the parties;
(b) the particular complexity of the matter or the difficulty or novelty of the questions raised;
(c) the skill, effort, specialised knowledge and responsibility involved;
(d) the time spent on the case;
(e) the place where and the circumstances in which work or any part of it was done; and
(f) any direction or observations by the court that made the costs order.

(8) If the court orders a party to pay costs to be assessed under rule 45.11, it may order that party to pay an amount on account.

(9) An order for the payment of costs takes effect when the amount is assessed, unless the court exercises any power it has to order otherwise.

R-496 **Court's power to vary requirements**

45.3 (1) Unless other legislation otherwise provides, the court may—
(a) extend a time limit for serving an application or representations under rules 45.4 to 45.10, even after it has expired; and
(b) consider an application or representations—
(i) made in a different form to one set out in the Practice Direction, or
(ii) made orally instead of in writing.

(2) A person who wants an extension of time must—
(a) apply when serving the application or representations for which it is needed; and
(b) explain the delay.

Costs out of central funds

R-497 **Costs out of central funds**

45.4 (1) This rule applies where the court can order the payment of costs out of central funds.

(2) In this rule, costs—
(a) include—
(i) on an appeal, costs incurred in the court that made the decision under appeal, and
(ii) at a retrial, costs incurred at the initial trial and on any appeal; but
(b) do not include costs met by legal aid.

(3) The court may make an order—
(a) on application by the person who incurred the costs; or
(b) on its own initiative.

(4) Where a person wants the court to make an order that person must—
(a) apply as soon as practicable; and
(b) outline the type of costs and the amount claimed, if that person wants the court to direct an assessment; or
(c) specify the amount claimed, if that person wants the court to assess the amount itself.

(5) The general rule is that the court must make an order, but—
(a) the court may decline to make a defendant's costs order if, for example—
(i) the defendant is convicted of at least one offence, or
(ii) the defendant's conduct led the prosecutor reasonably to think the prosecution case stronger than it was; and
(b) the court may decline to make a prosecutor's costs order if, for example, the prosecution was started or continued unreasonably.

(6) If the court makes an order—
(a) the court may direct an assessment under, as applicable—
(i) Part III of the Costs in Criminal Cases (General) Regulations 1986, or
(ii) Part 3 of The Serious Crime Act 2007 (Appeals under Section 24) Order 2008;
(b) the court may assess the amount itself in a case in which either—
(i) the recipient agrees the amount, or
(ii) the court decides to allow a lesser sum than that which is reasonably sufficient to compensate the recipient for expenses properly incurred in the proceedings;
(c) an order for the payment of a defendant's costs which includes an amount in respect of fees payable to a legal representative, or disbursements paid by a legal representative, must include a statement to that effect.

(7) If the court directs an assessment, the order must specify any restriction on the amount to be paid that the court considers appropriate.

(8) If the court assesses the amount itself, it must do so subject to any restriction on the amount to be paid that is imposed by regulations made by the Lord Chancellor.

Payment of costs by one party to another

Costs on conviction and sentence, etc. **R-498**

45.5 (1) This rule applies where the court can order a defendant to pay the prosecutor's costs if the defendant is—

(a) convicted or found guilty;
(b) dealt with in the Crown Court after committal for sentence there;
(c) dealt with for breach of a sentence; or
(d) in an extradition case—
   (i) ordered to be extradited, under Part 1 of the Extradition Act 2003,
   (ii) sent for extradition to the Secretary of State, under Part 2 of that Act, or
   (iii) unsuccessful on an appeal by the defendant to the High Court, or on an application by the defendant for permission to appeal from the High Court to the Supreme Court.

(2) The court may make an order—
(a) on application by the prosecutor; or
(b) on its own initiative.

(3) Where the prosecutor wants the court to make an order—
(a) the prosecutor must—
   (i) apply as soon as practicable, and
   (ii) specify the amount claimed; and
(b) the general rule is that the court must make an order if it is satisfied that the defendant can pay;

(4) A defendant who wants to oppose an order must make representations as soon as practicable.

(5) If the court makes an order, it must assess the amount itself.

Costs on appeal **R-499**

45.6 (1) This rule—
(a) applies where a magistrates' court, the Crown Court or the Court of Appeal can order a party to pay another person's costs on an appeal, or an application for permission to appeal;
(b) authorises the Crown Court, in addition to its other powers, to order a party to pay another party's costs on an appeal to that court, except on an appeal under—
   (i) section 108 of the Magistrates' Courts Act 1980, or
   (ii) section 45 of the Mental Health Act 1983.

(2) In this rule, costs include—
(a) costs incurred in the court that made the decision under appeal; and
(b) costs met by legal aid.

(3) The court may make an order—
(a) on application by the person who incurred the costs; or
(b) on its own initiative.

(4) A person who wants the court to make an order must—
(a) apply as soon as practicable;
(b) notify each other party;
(c) specify—
   (i) the amount claimed, and
   (ii) against whom; and
(d) where an appellant abandons an appeal to the Crown Court by serving a notice of abandonment—
   (i) apply in writing not more than 14 days later, and
   (ii) serve the application on the appellant and on the Crown Court officer.

(5) A party who wants to oppose an order must—
(a) make representations as soon as practicable; and
(b) where the application was under paragraph (4)(d), serve representations on the applicant, and on the Crown Court officer, not more than 7 days after it was served.

(6) Where the application was under paragraph (4)(d), the Crown Court officer may—
(a) submit it to the Crown Court; or
(b) serve it on the magistrates' court officer, for submission to the magistrates' court.

(7) If the court makes an order, it may direct an assessment under rule 45.11, or assess the amount itself where—
(a) the appellant abandons an appeal to the Crown Court;
(b) the Crown Court decides an appeal, except an appeal under—
(i) section 108 of the Magistrates' Courts Act 1980, or
(ii) section 45 of the Mental Health Act 1983; or
(c) the Court of Appeal decides an appeal to which Part 40 applies (Appeal to the Court of Appeal about reporting or public access restriction).
(8) If the court makes an order in any other case, it must assess the amount itself.

R-500 **Costs on an application**

45.7 (1) This rule—
(a) applies where the court can order a party to pay another person's costs in a case in which—
(i) the court decides an application for the production in evidence of a copy of a bank record,
(ii) a magistrates' court or the Crown Court decides an application to terminate a football banning order,
(iii) a magistrates' court or the Crown Court decides an application to terminate a disqualification for having custody of a dog,
(iv) the Crown Court allows an application to withdraw a witness summons, or
(v) the Crown Court decides an application relating to a deferred prosecution agreement under rule 11.5 (breach), rule 11.6 (variation) or rule 11.7 (lifting suspension of prosecution);
(b) authorises the Crown Court, in addition to its other powers, to order a party to pay another party's costs on an application to that court under rule 11.5, 11.6 or 11.7.
(2) The court may make an order—
(a) on application by the person who incurred the costs; or
(b) on its own initiative.
(3) A person who wants the court to make an order must—
(a) apply as soon as practicable;
(b) notify each other party; and
(c) specify—
(i) the amount claimed, and
(ii) against whom.
(4) A party who wants to oppose an order must make representations as soon as practicable.
(5) If the court makes an order, it may direct an assessment under rule 45.11, or assess the amount itself.

R-501 **Costs resulting from unnecessary or improper act, etc.**

45.8 (1) This rule applies where the court can order a party to pay another party's costs incurred as a result of an unnecessary or improper act or omission by or on behalf of the first party.
(2) In this rule, costs include costs met by legal aid.
(3) The court may make an order—
(a) on application by the party who incurred such costs; or
(b) on its own initiative.
(4) A party who wants the court to make an order must—
(a) apply in writing as soon as practicable after becoming aware of the grounds for doing so and in any event no later than the end of the case;
(b) serve the application on—
(i) the court officer (or, in the Court of Appeal, the Registrar), and
(ii) each other party;
(c) in that application specify—
(i) the party by whom costs should be paid,
(ii) the relevant act or omission,
(iii) the reasons why that act or omission meets the criteria for making an order,
(iv) the amount claimed, and
(v) those on whom the application has been served.
(5) Where the court considers making an order on its own initiative, it must—
(a) identify the party against whom it proposes making the order; and
(b) specify—
(i) the relevant act or omission,

(ii) the reasons why that act or omission meets the criteria for making an order, and
(iii) with the assistance of the party who incurred the costs, the amount involved.

(6) A party who wants to oppose an order must—
(a) make representations as soon as practicable; and
(b) in reply to an application, serve representations on the applicant and on the court officer (or Registrar) not more than 7 days after it was served.

(7) If the court makes an order, it must assess the amount itself.

(8) To help assess the amount, the court may direct an enquiry by—
(a) the Lord Chancellor, where the assessment is by a magistrates' court or by the Crown Court; or
(b) the Registrar, where the assessment is by the Court of Appeal.

(9) In deciding whether to direct such an enquiry, the court must have regard to all the circumstances including—
(a) any agreement between the parties about the amount to be paid;
(b) the amount likely to be allowed;
(c) the delay and expense that may be incurred in the conduct of the enquiry; and
(d) the particular complexity of the assessment, or the difficulty or novelty of any aspect of the assessment.

(10) If the court directs such an enquiry—
(a) paragraphs (3) to (8) inclusive of rule 45.11 (Assessment and re-assessment) apply as if that enquiry were an assessment under that rule (but rules 45.12 (Appeal to a costs judge) and 45.13 (Appeal to a High Court judge) do not apply);
(b) the authority that carries out the enquiry must serve its conclusions on the court officer as soon as reasonably practicable after following that procedure; and
(c) the court must then assess the amount to be paid.

Other costs orders

Costs against a legal representative **R-502**

45.9 (1) This rule applies where—
(a) a party has incurred costs—
(i) as a result of an improper, unreasonable or negligent act or omission by a legal or other representative or representative's employee, or
(ii) which it has become unreasonable for that party to have to pay because of such an act or omission occurring after those costs were incurred; and
(b) the court can—
(i) order the representative responsible to pay such costs, or
(ii) prohibit the payment of costs to that representative.

(2) In this rule, costs include costs met by legal aid.

(3) The court may make an order—
(a) on application by the party who incurred such costs; or
(b) on its own initiative.

(4) A party who wants the court to make an order must—
(a) apply in writing as soon as practicable after becoming aware of the grounds for doing so and in any event no later than the end of the case;
(b) serve the application on—
(i) the court officer (or, in the Court of Appeal, the Registrar),
(ii) the representative responsible,
(iii) each other party, and
(iv) any other person directly affected;
(c) in that application specify—
(i) the representative responsible,
(ii) the relevant act or omission,
(iii) the reasons why that act or omission meets the criteria for making an order,
(iv) the amount claimed, and
(v) those on whom the application has been served.

(5) Where the court considers making an order on its own initiative, it must—
(a) identify the representative against whom it proposes making that order; and
(b) specify—
(i) the relevant act or omission,
(ii) the reasons why that act or omission meets the criteria for making an order, and
(iii) with the assistance of the party who incurred the costs, the amount involved.

(6) A representative who wants to oppose an order must—
(a) make representations as soon as practicable; and
(b) in reply to an application, serve representations on the applicant and on the court officer (or Registrar) not more than 7 days after it was served.

(7) If the court makes an order—
(a) the general rule is that it must do so without waiting until the end of the case, but it may postpone making the order; and
(b) it must assess the amount itself.

(8) To help assess the amount, the court may direct an enquiry by—
(a) the Lord Chancellor, where the assessment is by a magistrates' court or by the Crown Court; or
(b) the Registrar, where the assessment is by the Court of Appeal.

(9) In deciding whether to direct such an enquiry, the court must have regard to all the circumstances including—
(a) any agreement between the parties about the amount to be paid;
(b) the amount likely to be allowed;
(c) the delay and expense that may be incurred in the conduct of the enquiry; and
(d) the particular complexity of the assessment, or the difficulty or novelty of any aspect of the assessment.

(10) If the court directs such an enquiry—
(a) paragraphs (3) to (8) inclusive of rule 45.11 (Assessment and re-assessment) apply as if that enquiry were an assessment under that rule (but rules 45.12 (Appeal to a costs judge) and 45.13 (Appeal to a High Court judge) do not apply);
(b) the authority that carries out the enquiry must serve its conclusions on the court officer as soon as reasonably practicable after following that procedure; and
(c) the court must then assess the amount to be paid.

(11) Instead of making an order, the court may make adverse observations about the representative's conduct for use in an assessment where—
(a) a party's costs are—
(i) to be met by legal aid, or
(ii) to be paid out of central funds; or
(b) there is to be an assessment under rule 45.11.

R-503 Costs against a third party

45.10 (1) This rule applies where—
(a) there has been serious misconduct by a person who is not a party; and
(b) the court can order that person to pay a party's costs.

(2) In this rule, costs include costs met by legal aid.

(3) The court may make an order—
(a) on application by the party who incurred the costs; or
(b) on its own initiative.

(4) A party who wants the court to make an order must—
(a) apply in writing as soon as practicable after becoming aware of the grounds for doing so;
(b) serve the application on—
(i) the court officer (or, in the Court of Appeal, the Registrar),
(ii) the person responsible,
(iii) each other party, and
(iv) any other person directly affected;
(c) in that application specify—
(i) the person responsible,
(ii) the relevant misconduct,
(iii) the reasons why the criteria for making an order are met,
(iv) the amount claimed, and
(v) those on whom the application has been served.

(5) Where the court considers making an order on its own initiative, it must—
(a) identify the person against whom it proposes making that order; and
(b) specify—
(i) the relevant misconduct,
(ii) the reasons why the criteria for making an order are met, and
(iii) with the assistance of the party who incurred the costs, the amount involved.

(6) A person who wants to oppose an order must—
(a) make representations as soon as practicable; and

(b) in reply to an application, serve representations on the applicant and on the court officer (or Registrar) not more than 7 days after it was served.

(7) If the court makes an order—

(a) the general rule is that it must do so at the end of the case, but it may do so earlier; and

(b) it must assess the amount itself.

(8) To help assess the amount, the court may direct an enquiry by—

(a) the Lord Chancellor, where the assessment is by a magistrates' court or by the Crown Court; or

(b) the Registrar, where the assessment is by the Court of Appeal.

(9) In deciding whether to direct such an enquiry, the court must have regard to all the circumstances including—

(a) any agreement between the parties about the amount to be paid;

(b) the amount likely to be allowed;

(c) the delay and expense that may be incurred in the conduct of the enquiry; and

(d) the particular complexity of the assessment, or the difficulty or novelty of any aspect of the assessment.

(10) If the court directs such an enquiry—

(a) paragraphs (3) to (8) inclusive of rule 45.11 (Assessment and re-assessment) apply as if that enquiry were an assessment under that rule (but rules 45.12 (Appeal to a costs judge) and 45.13 (Appeal to a High Court judge) do not apply);

(b) the authority that carries out the enquiry must serve its conclusions on the court officer as soon as reasonably practicable after following that procedure; and

(c) the court must then assess the amount to be paid.

Assessment of costs

Assessment and re-assessment **R-504**

45.11 (1) This rule applies where the court directs an assessment under—

(a) rule 33.48 (Confiscation and related proceedings—restraint and receivership proceedings; rules that apply generally — assessment of costs);

(b) rule 45.6 (Costs on appeal); or

(c) rule 45.7 (Costs on an application).

(2) The assessment must be carried out by the relevant assessing authority, namely—

(a) the Lord Chancellor, where the direction was given by a magistrates' court or by the Crown Court; or

(b) the Registrar, where the direction was given by the Court of Appeal.

(3) The party in whose favour the court made the costs order ('the applicant') must—

(a) apply for an assessment—

(i) in writing, in any form required by the assessing authority, and

(ii) not more than 3 months after the costs order; and

(b) serve the application on—

(i) the assessing authority, and

(ii) the party against whom the court made the costs order ('the respondent').

(4) The applicant must—

(a) summarise the work done;

(b) specify—

(i) each item of work done, giving the date, time taken and amount claimed,

(ii) any disbursements or expenses, including the fees of any advocate, and

(iii) any circumstances of which the applicant wants the assessing authority to take particular account; and

(c) supply—

(i) receipts or other evidence of the amount claimed, and

(ii) any other information or document for which the assessing authority asks, within such period as that authority may require.

(5) A respondent who wants to make representations about the amount claimed must—

(a) do so in writing; and

(b) serve the representations on the assessing authority, and on the applicant, not more than 21 days after service of the application.

(6) The assessing authority must—

(a) if it seems likely to help with the assessment, obtain any other information or document;

(b) resolve in favour of the respondent any doubt about what should be allowed; and

(c) serve the assessment on the parties.

(7) Where either party wants the amount allowed re-assessed—
(a) that party must—
(i) apply to the assessing authority, in writing and in any form required by that authority,
(ii) serve the application on the assessing authority, and on the other party, not more than 21 days after service of the assessment,
(iii) explain the objections to the assessment,
(iv) supply any additional supporting information or document, and
(v) ask for a hearing, if that party wants one; and
(b) a party who wants to make representations about an application for re-assessment must—
(i) do so in writing,
(ii) serve the representations on the assessing authority, and on the other party, not more than 21 days after service of the application, and
(iii) ask for a hearing, if that party wants one;
(c) the assessing authority—
(i) must arrange a hearing, in public or in private, if either party asks for one,
(ii) subject to that, may re-assess the amount allowed with or without a hearing,
(iii) must re-assess the amount allowed on the initial assessment, taking into account the reasons for disagreement with that amount and any other representations,
(iv) may maintain, increase or decrease the amount allowed on the assessment,
(v) must serve the re-assessment on the parties, and
(vi) must serve reasons on the parties, if not more than 21 days later either party asks for such reasons.
(8) A time limit under this rule may be extended even after it has expired—
(a) by the assessing authority, or
(b) by the Senior Costs Judge, if the assessing authority declines to do so.

R-505 **Appeal to a costs judge**

45.12 (1) This rule applies where—
(a) the assessing authority has re-assessed the amount allowed under rule 45.11; and
(b) either party wants to appeal against that amount.
(2) That party must—
(a) serve an appeal notice on—
(i) the Senior Costs Judge,
(ii) the other party, and
(iii) the assessing authority
not more than 21 days after service of the written reasons for the re-assessment;
(b) explain the objections to the re-assessment;
(c) serve on the Senior Costs Judge with the appeal notice—
(i) the applications for assessment and re-assessment,
(ii) any other information or document considered by the assessing authority,
(iii) the assessing authority's written reasons for the re-assessment, and
(iv) any other information or document for which a costs judge asks, within such period as the judge may require; and
(d) ask for a hearing, if that party wants one.
(3) A party who wants to make representations about an appeal must—
(a) serve representations in writing on—
(i) the Senior Costs Judge, and
(ii) the applicant
not more than 21 days after service of the appeal notice; and
(b) ask for a hearing, if that party wants one.
(4) Unless a costs judge otherwise directs, the parties may rely only on—
(a) the objections to the amount allowed on the initial assessment; and
(b) any other representations and material considered by the assessing authority.
(5) A costs judge—
(a) must arrange a hearing, in public or in private, if either party asks for one;
(b) subject to that, may determine an appeal with or without a hearing;
(c) may—
(i) consult the assessing authority,

(ii) consult the court which made the costs order, and
(iii) obtain any other information or document;
(d) must reconsider the amount allowed by the assessing authority, taking into account the objections to the re-assessment and any other representations;
(e) may maintain, increase or decrease the amount allowed on the re-assessment;
(f) may provide for the costs incurred by either party to the appeal; and
(g) must serve reasons for the decision on—
(i) the parties, and
(ii) the assessing authority.
(6) A costs judge may extend a time limit under this rule, even after it has expired.

Appeal to a High Court judge R-506

45.13 (1) This rule applies where—
(a) a costs judge has determined an appeal under rule 45.12; and
(b) either party wants to appeal against the amount allowed.
(2) A party who wants to appeal—
(a) may do so only if a costs judge certifies that a point of principle of general importance was involved in the decision on the review; and
(b) must apply in writing for such a certificate and serve the application on—
(i) the costs judge,
(ii) the other party
not more than 21 days after service of the decision on the review.
(3) That party must—
(a) appeal to a judge of the High Court attached to the Queen's Bench Division as if it were an appeal from the decision of a master under Part 52 of the Civil Procedure Rules 1998; and
(b) serve the appeal not more than 21 days after service of the costs judge's certificate under paragraph (2).
(4) A High Court judge—
(a) may extend a time limit under this rule even after it has expired;
(b) has the same powers and duties as a costs judge under rule 45.12; and
(c) may hear the appeal with one or more assessors.

Application for an extension of time R-507

45.14 A party who wants an extension of time under rule 45.11, 45.12 or 45.13 must—
(a) apply in writing;
(b) explain the delay; and
(c) attach the application, representations or appeal for which the extension of time is needed.

Criminal Practice Directions Part 45 Costs

CPD X CrimPR Part 45 Costs PD-100

Reference should be made to the Practice Direction (Costs in Criminal Proceedings) 2015.

Criminal Procedure Rules Part 46 Representatives

Functions of representatives and supporters R-508

46.1 (1) Under these Rules, anything that a party may or must do may be done—
(a) by a legal representative on that party's behalf;
(b) by a person with the corporation's written authority, where that corporation is a defendant;
(c) with the help of a parent, guardian or other suitable supporting adult where that party is a defendant—
(i) who is under 18, or
(ii) whose understanding of what the case involves is limited
unless other legislation (including a rule) otherwise requires.
(2) A member, officer or employee of a prosecutor may, on the prosecutor's behalf—
(a) serve on the magistrates' court officer, or present to a magistrates' court, an application for a summons or warrant under section 1 of the Magistrates' Courts Act 1980; or
(b) issue a written charge and requisition, or single justice procedure notice, under section 29 of the Criminal Justice Act 2003.

R-509 Notice of appointment, etc. of legal representative: general rules

46.2 (1) This rule applies—
(a) in relation to—
(i) a party who does not have legal aid for the purposes of a case, and
(ii) a party to an extradition case in the High Court, whether that party has legal
(b) where such a party—
(i) appoints a legal representative for the purposes of the case, or
(ii) dismisses such a representative, with or without appointing another;
(c) where a legal representative for such a party withdraws from the case.
(2) Where paragraph (1)(b) applies, that party must give notice of the appointment or dismissal to—
(a) the court officer;
(b) each other party; and
(c) where applicable, the legal representative who has been dismissed,
as soon as practicable and in any event within 5 business days.
(3) Where paragraph (1)(c) applies, that legal representative must—
(a) as soon as practicable give notice to—
(i) the court officer,
(ii) the party whom he or she has represented, and
(iii) each other party; and
(b) where that legal representative has represented the defendant in an extradition case in the High Court, include with the notice—
(i) confirmation that the defendant has notice of when and where the appeal hearing will take place and of the need to attend, if the defendant is on bail,
(ii) details sufficient to locate the defendant, including details of the custodian and of the defendant's date of birth and custody reference, if the defendant is in custody, and
(iii) details of any arrangements likely to be required by the defendant to facilitate his or her participation in consequence of the representative's withdrawal, including arrangements for interpretation.
(4) Any such notice—
(a) may be given orally, but only if—
(i) it is given at a hearing, and
(ii) it specifies no restriction under paragraph (5)(b) (restricted scope of appointment);
(b) otherwise, must be in writing.
(5) A notice of the appointment of a legal representative—
(a) must identify—
(i) the legal representative who has been appointed, with details of how to contact that representative, and
(ii) all those to whom the notice is given;
(b) may specify a restriction, or restrictions, on the purpose or duration of the appointment; and
(c) if it specifies any such restriction, may nonetheless provide that documents may continue to be served on the represented party at the representative's address until—
(i) further notice is given under this rule, or
(ii) that party obtains legal aid for the purposes of the case.
(6) A legal representative who is dismissed by a party or who withdraws from representing a party must, as soon as practicable, make available to that party such documents in the representative's possession as have been served on that party.

R-510 Application to change legal representative: legal aid

46.3 (1) This rule applies in a magistrates' court, the Crown Court and the Court of Appeal—
(a) in relation to a party who has legal aid for the purposes of a case;
(b) where such a party wants to select a legal representative in place of the representative named in the legal aid representation order.
(2) Such a party must—
(a) apply in writing as soon as practicable after becoming aware of the grounds for doing so; and
(b) serve the application on—
(i) the court officer, and
(ii) the legal representative named in the legal aid representation order.
(3) The application must—
(a) explain what the case is about, including what offences are alleged, what stage it has reached and what is likely to be in issue at trial;

(b) explain how and why the applicant chose the legal representative named in the legal aid representation order;
(c) if an advocate other than that representative has been instructed for the applicant, explain whether the applicant wishes to replace that advocate;
(d) explain, giving relevant facts and dates—
(i) in what way, in the applicant's opinion, there has been a breakdown in the relationship between the applicant and the current representative such that neither the individual representing the applicant nor any colleague of his or hers any longer can provide effective representation, or
(ii) what other compelling reason, in the applicant's opinion, means that neither the individual representing the applicant nor any colleague of his or hers any longer can provide effective representation;
(e) give details of any previous application by the applicant to replace the legal representative named in the legal aid representation order;
(f) state whether the applicant—
(i) waives the legal professional privilege attaching to the applicant's communications with the current representative, to the extent required to allow that representative to respond to the matters set out in the application, or
(ii) declines to waive that privilege and acknowledges that the court may draw such inferences as it thinks fit in consequence;
(g) explain how and why the applicant has chosen the proposed new representative;
(h) include or attach a statement by the proposed new representative which—
(i) confirms that that representative is eligible and willing to conduct the case for the applicant,
(ii) confirms that that representative can and will meet the current timetable for the case, including any hearing date or dates that have been set, if the application succeeds,
(iii) explains what, if any, dealings that representative has had with the applicant before the present case; and
(i) ask for a hearing, if the applicant wants one, and explain why it is needed.

(4) The legal representative named in the legal aid representation order must—
(a) respond in writing no more than 5 business days after service of the application; and
(b) serve the response on—
(i) the court officer,
(ii) the applicant, and
(iii) the proposed new representative.

(5) The response must—
(a) explain which, if any, of the matters set out in the application the current representative disputes;
(b) explain, as appropriate, giving relevant facts and dates—
(i) whether, and if so in what way, in the current representative's opinion, there has been a breakdown in the relationship with the applicant such that neither the individual representing the applicant nor any colleague of his or hers any longer can provide effective representation,
(ii) whether, in the current representative's opinion, there is some other compelling reason why neither the individual representing the applicant nor any colleague of his or hers any longer can provide effective representation, and if so what reason,
(iii) whether the current representative considers there to be a duty to withdraw from the case in accordance with professional rules of conduct, and if so the nature of that duty, and
(iv) whether the current representative no longer is able to represent the applicant through circumstances outside the representative's control, and if so the particular circumstances that render the representative unable to do so;
(c) explain what, if any, dealings the current representative had had with the applicant before the present case; and
(d) ask for a hearing, if the current representative wants one, and explain why it is needed.

(6) The court may determine the application—
(a) without a hearing, as a general rule; or
(b) at a hearing, which must be in private unless the court otherwise directs.

(7) Unless the court otherwise directs, any hearing must be in the absence of each other party and each other party's representative and advocate (if any).

(8) If the court allows the application, as soon as practicable—
(a) the current representative must make available to the new representative such documents in the current representative's possession as have been served on the applicant party; and
(b) the new representative must serve notice of appointment on each other party.

(9) Paragraph (10) applies where—
(a) the court refuses the application;
(b) in response to that decision—
(i) the applicant declines further representation by the current representative or asks for legal aid to be withdrawn, or
(ii) the current representative declines further to represent the applicant; and
(c) the court in consequence withdraws the applicant's legal aid.
(10) The court officer must serve notice of the withdrawal of legal aid on—
(a) the applicant; and
(b) the current representative.

Criminal Procedure Rules Part 47 Investigation Orders and Warrants*

* [Editorial note: This Part only applies in the event that the Criminal Procedure (Amendment) (EU Exit) Regulations 2019 (SI 2019 No. 908) come into force on or after 7 October 2019. Otherwise, Part 47A applies and Part 47 should be ignored.]

Section 1: General Rules

R-511 **When this Part applies**

47.1 This Part applies to the exercise of the powers listed in each of rules 47.4, 47.24, 47.35, 47.42, 47.46, 47.51, 47.54, 47.59, and 47,63.

R-512 **Meaning of 'court', 'applicant' and 'respondent'**

47.2 In this Part—
(a) a reference to the 'court' includes a reference to any justice of the peace or judge who can exercise a power to which this Part applies;
(b) 'applicant' means a person who, or an authority which, can apply for an order or warrant to which this Part applies; and
(c) 'respondent' means any person—
(i) against whom such an order is sought or made, or
(ii) on whom an application for such an order is served.

R-513 **Documents served on the court officer**

47.3 (1) Unless the court otherwise directs, the court officer may—
(a) keep a written application; or
(b) arrange for the whole or any part to be kept by some other appropriate person, subject to any conditions that the court may impose.
(2) Where the court makes an order when the court office is closed, the applicant must, not more than 72 hours later, serve on the court officer—
(a) a copy of the order; and
(b) any written material that was submitted to the court.
(3) Where the court issues a warrant—
(a) the applicant must return it to the court officer as soon as practicable after it has been executed, and in any event not more than 3 months after it was issued (unless other legislation otherwise provides); and
(b) the court officer must—
(i) keep the warrant for 12 months after its return, and
(ii) during that period, make it available for inspection by the occupier of the premises to which it relates, if that occupier asks to inspect it.

Section 2: Investigation Orders

R-514 **When this Section applies**

47.4 This Section applies where—
(a) a Circuit judge can make, vary or discharge an order for the production of, or for giving access to, material under paragraph 4 of Schedule 1 to the Police and Criminal Evidence Act 1984, other than material that consists of or includes journalistic material;
(b) for the purposes of a terrorist investigation, a Circuit judge can make, vary or discharge—
(i) an order for the production of, or for giving access to, material, or for a statement of its location, under paragraphs 5 and 10 of Schedule 5 to the Terrorism Act 2000,
(ii) an explanation order, under paragraphs 10 and 13 of Schedule 5 to the 2000 Act,
(iii) a customer information order, under paragraphs 1 and 4 of Schedule 6 to the 2000 Act;

(c) for the purposes of—
  (i) a terrorist investigation, a Circuit judge can make, and the Crown Court can vary or discharge, an account monitoring order, under paragraphs 2 and 4 of Schedule 6A to the 2000 Act,
  (ii) a terrorist financing investigation, a judge entitled to exercise the jurisdiction of the Crown Court can make, and the Crown Court can vary or discharge, a disclosure order, under paragraphs 9 and 14 of Schedule 5A to the 2000 Act;
(d) for the purposes of an investigation to which Part 8 of the Proceeds of Crime Act 2002 or the Proceeds of Crime Act 2002 (External Investigations) Order 2014 applies, a Crown Court judge can make, and the Crown Court can vary or discharge—
  (i) a production order, under sections 345 and 351 of the 2002 Act or under articles 6 and 12 of the 2014 Order,
  (ii) an order to grant entry, under sections 347 and 351 of the 2002 Act or under articles 8 and 12 of the 2014 Order,
  (iii) a disclosure order, under sections 357 and 362 of the 2002 Act or under articles 16 and 21 of the 2014 Order,
  (iv) a customer information order, under sections 363 and 369 of the 2002 Act or under articles 22 and 28 of the 2014 Order,
  (v) an account monitoring order, under sections 370, 373 and 375 of the 2002 Act or under articles 29, 32 and 34 of the 2014 Order;
(e) in connection with an extradition request, a Circuit judge can make an order for the production of, or for giving access to, material under section 157 of the Extradition Act 2003.
(f) a magistrates' court can make a further information order under section 22B of the Terrorism Act 2000(a) in connection with—
  (i) an investigation into whether a person is involved in the commission of an offence under any of sections 15 to 18 of the 2000 Act
  (ii) determining whether such an investigation should be started, or
  (iii) identifying terrorist property or its movement or use;
(g) a magistrates' court can make a further information order under section 339ZH of the Proceeds of Crime Act 2002(c) in connection with—
  (i) an investigation into whether a person is engaged in money laundering,
  (ii) determining whether such an investigation should be started, or
  (iii) an investigation into money laundering by an authority in a country outside the United Kingdom.

Exercise of court's powers **R-515**

47.5 (1) Subject to paragraphs (2), (3) and (4), the court may determine an application for an order, or to vary or discharge an order—
  (a) at a hearing (which must be in private unless the court otherwise directs), or without a hearing; and
  (b) in the absence of—
    (i) the applicant,
    (ii) the respondent (if any),
    (iii) any other person affected by the order.
(2) The court must not determine such an application in the applicant's absence if—
  (a) the applicant asks for a hearing; or
  (b) it appears to the court that—
    (i) the proposed order may infringe legal privilege, within the meaning of section 10 of the Police and Criminal Evidence Act 1984, section 348 or 361 of the Proceeds of Crime Act 2002 or article 9 of the Proceeds of Crime Act 2002 (External Investigations) Order 2014,
    (ii) the proposed order may require the production of excluded material, within the meaning of section 11 of the 1984 Act, or
    (iii) for any other reason the application is so complex or serious as to require the court to hear the applicant.
(3) The court must not determine such an application in the absence of any respondent or other person affected, unless—
  (a) the absentee has had at least 2 business days in which to make representations; or
  (b) the court is satisfied that—
    (i) the applicant cannot identify or contact the absentee,
    (ii) it would prejudice the investigation if the absentee were present,

(iii) it would prejudice the investigation to adjourn or postpone the application so as to allow the absentee to attend, or
(iv) the absentee has waived the opportunity to attend.

(4) The court must not determine such an application in the absence of any respondent who, if the order sought by the applicant were made, would be required to produce or give access to journalistic material, unless that respondent has waived the opportunity to attend.

(5) The court officer must arrange for the court to hear such an application no sooner than 2 business days after it was served, unless—
(a) the court directs that no hearing need be arranged; or
(b) the court gives other directions for the hearing.

(6) The court must not determine an application unless satisfied that sufficient time has been allowed for it.

(7) If the court so directs, the parties to an application may attend a hearing by live link or telephone.

(8) The court must not make, vary or discharge an order unless the applicant states, in writing or orally, that to the best of the applicant's knowledge and belief—
(a) the application discloses all the information that is material to what the court must decide; and
(b) the content of the application is true.

(9) Where the statement required by paragraph (8) is made orally—
(a) the statement must be on oath or affirmation, unless the court otherwise directs; and
(b) the court must arrange for a record of the making of the statement.

(10) The court may—
(a) shorten or extend (even after it has expired) a time limit under this Section;
(b) dispense with a requirement for service under this Section (even after service was required); and
(c) consider an application made orally instead of in writing.

(11) A person who wants an extension of time must—
(a) apply when serving the application for which it is needed; and
(b) explain the delay.

R-516 Application for order: general rules

47.6 (1) This rule applies to each application for an order to which this Section applies.

(2) The applicant must—
(a) apply in writing and serve the application on the court officer;
(b) demonstrate that the applicant is entitled to apply, for example as a constable or under legislation that applies to other officers;
(c) give the court an estimate of how long the court should allow—
(i) to read the application and prepare for any hearing, and
(ii) for any hearing of the application;
(d) attach a draft order in the terms proposed by the applicant;
(e) serve notice of the application on the respondent, unless the court otherwise directs;
(f) serve the application on the respondent to such extent, if any, as the court directs.

(3) A notice served on the respondent must—
(a) specify the material or information in respect of which the application is made; and
(b) identify—
(i) the power that the applicant invites the court to exercise, and
(ii) the conditions for the exercise of that power which the applicant asks the court to find are met.

(4) The applicant must serve any order made on the respondent.

R-517 Application containing information withheld from a respondent or other person

47.7 (1) This rule applies where an application includes information that the applicant thinks ought to be revealed only to the court.

(2) The application must—
(a) identify that information; and
(b) explain why that information ought not to be served on the respondent or another person.

(3) At a hearing of an application to which this rule applies—
(a) the general rule is that the court must consider, in the following sequence—
(i) representations first by the applicant and then by the respondent and any other person, in the presence of them all, and then
(ii) further representations by the applicant, in the others' absence; but
(b) the court may direct other arrangements for the hearing.

Application to vary or discharge an order R-518

47.8 (1) This rule applies where one of the following wants the court to vary or discharge an order to which a rule in this Section refers—
(a) an applicant;
(b) the respondent; or
(c) a person affected by the order.
(2) That applicant, respondent or person affected must—
(a) apply in writing as soon as practicable after becoming aware of the grounds for doing so;
(b) serve the application on—
(i) the court officer, and
(ii) the respondent, applicant, or any person known to be affected, as applicable;
(c) explain why it is appropriate for the order to be varied or discharged;
(d) propose the terms of any variation; and
(e) ask for a hearing, if one is wanted, and explain why it is needed.

Application to punish for contempt of court R-519

47.9 (1) This rule applies where a person is accused of disobeying—
(a) a production order made under paragraph 4 of Schedule 1 to the Police and Criminal Evidence Act 1984;
(b) a production etc. order made under paragraph 5 of Schedule 5 to the Terrorism Act 2000;
(c) an explanation order made under paragraph 13 of that Schedule;
(d) an account monitoring order made under paragraph 2 of Schedule 6A to that Act;
(e) a production order made under section 345 of the Proceeds of Crime Act 2002 or article 6 of the Proceeds of Crime Act 2002 (External Investigations) Order 2014;
(f) an account monitoring order made under section 370 of the 2002 Act or article 29 of the 2014 Order; or
(g) a production order made under section 157 of the Extradition Act 2003.
(2) An applicant who wants the court to exercise its power to punish that person for contempt of court must comply with the rules in Part 48 (Contempt of court).

Orders under the Police and Criminal Evidence Act 1984

Application for a production order under the Police and Criminal Evidence Act 1984 R-520

47.10 (1) This rule applies where an applicant wants the court to make an order to which rule 47.4(a) refers.
(2) As well as complying with rule 47.6 (Application for order: general rules), the application must, in every case—
(a) specify the offence under investigation (and see paragraph (3)(a));
(b) describe the material sought;
(c) identify the respondent;
(d) specify the premises on which the material is believed to be, or explain why it is not reasonably practicable to do so;
(e) explain the grounds for believing that the material is on the premises specified, or (if applicable) on unspecified premises of the respondent;
(f) specify the set of access conditions on which the applicant relies (and see paragraphs (3) and (4)); and
(g) propose—
(i) the terms of the order, and
(ii) the period within which it should take effect.
(3) Where the applicant relies on paragraph 2 of Schedule 1 to the Police and Criminal Evidence Act 1984 ('the first set of access conditions': general power to gain access to special procedure material), the application must—
(a) specify the indictable offence under investigation;
(b) explain the grounds for believing that the offence has been committed;
(c) explain the grounds for believing that the material sought—
(i) is likely to be of substantial value to the investigation (whether by itself, or together with other material),
(ii) is likely to be admissible evidence at trial for the offence under investigation, and
(iii) does not consist of or include items subject to legal privilege or excluded material;

(d) explain what other methods of obtaining the material—
(i) have been tried without success, or
(ii) have not been tried because they appeared bound to fail; and
(e) explain why it is in the public interest for the respondent to produce the material, having regard to—
(i) the benefit likely to accrue to the investigation if the material is obtained, and
(ii) the circumstances under which the respondent holds the material.

(4) Where the applicant relies on paragraph 3 of Schedule 1 to the Police and Criminal Evidence Act 1984 ('the second set of access conditions': use of search warrant power to gain access to excluded or special procedure material), the application must—
(a) state the legislation under which a search warrant could have been issued, had the material sought not been excluded or special procedure material (in this paragraph, described as 'the main search power');
(b) include or attach the terms of the main search power;
(c) explain how the circumstances would have satisfied any criteria prescribed by the main search power for the issue of a search warrant; and
(d) explain why the issue of such a search warrant would have been appropriate.

Orders under the Terrorism Act 2000

R-521 Application for an order under the Terrorism Act 2000

47.11 (1) This rule applies where an applicant wants the court to make one of the orders to which rule 47.4(b) and (c) refers.
(2) As well as complying with rule 47.6 (Application for order: general rules), the application must—
(a) specify the offence under investigation;
(b) explain how the investigation constitutes a terrorist investigation or terrorist financing investigation, as appropriate, within the meaning of the Terrorism Act 2000;
(c) identify the respondent; and
(d) give the information required by whichever of rules 47.12 to 47.16 applies.

R-522 Content of application for a production etc. order under the Terrorism Act 2000

47.12 (1) As well as complying with rules 47.6 and 47.11, an applicant who wants the court to make an order for the production of, or for giving access to, material, or for a statement of its location, must—
(a) describe that material;
(b) explain why the applicant thinks the material is—
(i) in the respondent's possession, custody or power, or
(ii) expected to come into existence and then to be in the respondent's possession, custody or power within 28 days of the order;
(c) explain how the material constitutes or contains excluded material or special procedure material;
(d) confirm that none of the material is expected to be subject to legal privilege;
(e) explain why the material is likely to be of substantial value to the investigation;
(f) explain why it is in the public interest for the material to be produced, or for the applicant to be given access to it, having regard to—
(i) the benefit likely to accrue to the investigation if it is obtained, and
(ii) the circumstances in which the respondent has the material, or is expected to have it; and
(g) propose—
(i) the terms of the order, and
(ii) the period within which it should take effect.
(2) An applicant who wants the court to make an order to grant entry in aid of a production order must—
(a) specify the premises to which entry is sought;
(b) explain why the order is needed; and
(c) propose the terms of the order.

R-523 Content of application for a disclosure order or further information order under the Terrorism Act 2000

47.13 (1) As well as complying with rules 47.6 and 47.11, an applicant who wants the court to make a disclosure order must—
(a) explain why the applicant thinks that—
(i) a person has committed an offence under any of sections 15 to 18 of the Terrorism Act 2000, or

(ii) property described in the application is terrorist property within the meaning of section 14 of the 2000 Act;
(b) describe in general terms the information that the applicant wants the respondent to provide;
(c) confirm that none of the information is—
(i) expected to be subject to legal privilege, or
(ii) excluded material;
(d) explain why the information is likely to be of substantial value to the investigation;
(e) explain why it is in the public interest for the information to be provided, having regard to the benefit likely to accrue to the investigation if it is obtained; and
(f) propose the terms of the order.

(2) As well as complying with rule 47.6, an applicant who wants the court to make a further information order must—
(a) identify the respondent from whom the information is sought and explain—
(i) whether the respondent is the person who made the disclosure to which the information relates or is otherwise carrying on a business in the regulated sector within the meaning of Part 1 of Schedule 3A to the 2000 Act, and
(ii) why the applicant thinks that the information is in the possession, or under the control, of the respondent;
(b) specify or describe the information that the applicant wants the respondent to provide;
(c) where the information sought relates to a disclosure of information by someone under section 21A of the 2000 Act (Failure to disclose: regulated sector), explain—
(i) how the information sought relates to a matter arising from that disclosure,
(ii) how the information would assist in investigating whether a person is involved in the commission of an offence under any of sections 15 to 18 of that Act, or in determining whether an investigation of that kind should be started, or in identifying terrorist property or its movement or use, and
(iii) why it is reasonable in all the circumstances for the information to be provided;
(d) where the information sought relates to a disclosure made under a requirement of the law of a country outside the United Kingdom which corresponds with Part III of the 2000 Act (Terrorist property), and an authority in that country which investigates offences corresponding with sections 15 to 18 of that Act has asked the National Crime Agency for information in connection with that disclosure, explain—
(i) how the information sought relates to a matter arising from that disclosure,
(ii) why the information is likely to be of substantial value to the authority that made the request in determining any matter in connection with the disclosure, and
(iii) why it is reasonable in all the circumstances for the information to be provided;
(e) confirm that none of the information is expected to be subject to legal privilege; and
(f) propose the terms of the order, including—
(i) how the respondent must provide the information required, and
(ii) the date by which the information must be provided.

(3) Rule 47.8 (Application to vary or discharge an order) does not apply to a further information order.

(4) Paragraph (5) applies where a party to an application for a further information order wants to appeal to the Crown Court from the decision of the magistrates' court.

(5) The appellant must—
(a) serve an appeal notice—
(i) on the Crown Court officer and on the other party,
(ii) not more than 21 days after the magistrates' court's decision; and
(b) in the appeal notice, explain, as appropriate, why the Crown Court should (as the case may be) make, discharge or vary a further information order.

(6) Rule 34.11 (Constitution of the Crown Court) applies on such an appeal.

Content of application for an explanation order under the Terrorism Act 2000 **R-524**

47.14 As well as complying with rules 47.6 and 47.11, an applicant who wants the court to make an explanation order must—
(a) identify the material that the applicant wants the respondent to explain;
(b) confirm that the explanation is not expected to infringe legal privilege; and
(c) propose the terms of the order.

Content of application for a customer information order under the Terrorism Act 2000 **R-525**

47.15 As well as complying with rules 47.6 and 47.11, an applicant who wants the court to make a customer information order must—
(a) explain why it is desirable for the purposes of the investigation to trace property said to be terrorist property within the meaning of the Terrorism Act 2000;

(b) explain why the order will enhance the effectiveness of the investigation; and
(c) propose the terms of the order.

R-526 **Content of application for an account monitoring order under the Terrorism Act 2000**

47.16 As well as complying with rules 47.6 and 47.11, an applicant who wants the court to make an account monitoring order must—
(a) specify—
(i) the information sought,
(ii) the period during which the applicant wants the respondent to provide that information (to a maximum of 90 days), and
(iii) where, when and in what manner the applicant wants the respondent to provide that information;
(b) explain why it is desirable for the purposes of the investigation to trace property said to be terrorist property within the meaning of the Terrorism Act 2000;
(c) explain why the order will enhance the effectiveness of the investigation; and
(d) propose the terms of the order.

Orders under the Proceeds of Crime Act 2002

R-527 **Application for an order under the Proceeds of Crime Act 2002**

47.17 (1) This rule applies where an applicant wants the court to make one of the orders to which rule 47.4(d) refers.
(2) As well as complying with rule 47.6 (Application for order: general rules), the application must—
(a) identify—
(i) the respondent, and
(ii) the person or property the subject of the investigation;
(b) in the case of an investigation in the United Kingdom, explain why the applicant thinks that—
(i) the person under investigation has benefited from criminal conduct, in the case of a confiscation investigation, or committed a money laundering offence, in the case of a money laundering investigation, or
(ii) in the case of a detained cash investigation, a detained property investigation or a frozen funds investigation, the cash or property involved, or the money held in the frozen account, was obtained through unlawful conduct or is intended to be used in unlawful conduct;
(c) in the case of an investigation outside the United Kingdom, explain why the applicant thinks that—
(i) there is an investigation by an overseas authority which relates to a criminal investigation or to criminal proceedings (including proceedings to remove the benefit of a person's criminal conduct following that person's conviction), and
(ii) the investigation is into whether property has been obtained as a result of or in connection with criminal conduct, or into the extent or whereabouts of such property;
(d) give the additional information required by whichever of rules 47.18 to 47.22 applies.

R-528 **Content of application for a production order under the Proceeds of Crime Act 2002**

47.18 As well as complying with rules 47.6 and 47.17, an applicant who wants the court to make an order for the production of, or for giving access to, material, must—
(a) describe that material;
(b) explain why the applicant thinks the material is in the respondent's possession or control;
(c) confirm that none of the material is—
(i) expected to be subject to legal privilege, or
(ii) excluded material;
(d) explain why the material is likely to be of substantial value to the investigation;
(e) explain why it is in the public interest for the material to be produced, or for the applicant to be given access to it, having regard to—
(i) the benefit likely to accrue to the investigation if it is obtained, and
(ii) the circumstances in which the respondent has the material; and
(f) propose—
(i) the terms of the order, and
(ii) the period within which it should take effect, if 7 days from the date of the order would not be appropriate.

Content of application for an order to grant entry under the Proceeds of Crime Act 2002 R-529

47.19 An applicant who wants the court to make an order to grant entry in aid of a production order must—
(a) specify the premises to which entry is sought;
(b) explain why the order is needed; and
(c) propose the terms of the order.

Content of application for a disclosure order or further information order under the Proceeds of Crime Act 2002 R-530

47.20 (1) As well as complying with rules 47.6 and 47.17, an applicant who wants the court to make a disclosure order must—
(a) describe in general terms the information that the applicant wants the respondent to provide;
(b) confirm that none of the information is—
(i) expected to be subject to legal privilege, or
(ii) excluded material;
(c) explain why the information is likely to be of substantial value to the investigation;
(d) explain why it is in the public interest for the information to be provided, having regard to the benefit likely to accrue to the investigation if it is obtained; and
(e) propose the terms of the order.
(2) As well as complying with rule 47.6, an applicant who wants the court to make a further information order must—
(a) identify the respondent from whom the information is sought and explain—
(i) whether the respondent is the person who made the disclosure to which the information relates or is otherwise carrying on a business in the regulated sector within the meaning of Part 1 of Schedule 9 to the Proceeds of Crime Act 2002, and
(ii) why the applicant thinks that the information is in the possession, or under the control, of the respondent;
(b) specify or describe the information that the applicant wants the respondent to provide;
(c) where the information sought relates to a disclosure of information under Part 7 of the Proceeds of Crime Act 2002 (Money laundering), explain—
(i) how the information sought relates to a matter arising from that disclosure,
(ii) how the information would assist in investigating whether a person is engaged in money laundering or in determining whether an investigation of that kind should be started, and
(iii) why it is reasonable in all the circumstances for the information to be provided;
(d) where the information sought relates to a disclosure made under a requirement of the law of a country outside the United Kingdom which corresponds with Part 7 of the 2002 Act, and an authority in that country which investigates money laundering has asked the National Crime Agency for information in connection with that disclosure, explain—
(i) how the information sought relates to a matter arising from that disclosure,
(ii) why the information is likely to be of substantial value to the authority that made the request in determining any matter in connection with the disclosure, and
(iii) why it is reasonable in all the circumstances for the information to be provided;
(e) confirm that none of the information is expected to be subject to legal privilege; and
(f) propose the terms of the order, including—
(i) how the respondent must provide the information required, and
(ii) the date by which the information must be provided.
(3) Rule 47.8 (Application to vary or discharge an order) does not apply to a further information order.
(4) Paragraph (5) applies where a party to an application for a further information order wants to appeal to the Crown Court from the decision of the magistrates' court.
(5) The appellant must—
(a) serve an appeal notice—
(i) on the Crown Court officer and on the other party,
(ii) not more than 21 days after the magistrates' court's decision; and
(b) in the appeal notice, explain, as appropriate, why the Crown Court should (as the case may be) make, discharge or vary a further information order.
(6) Rule 34.11 (Constitution of the Crown Court) applies on such an appeal.

R-531 **Content of application for a customer information order under the Proceeds of Crime Act 2002**

47.21 As well as complying with rules 47.6 and 47.17, an applicant who wants the court to make a customer information order must—

(a) explain why customer information about the person under investigation is likely to be of substantial value to that investigation;
(b) explain why it is in the public interest for the information to be provided, having regard to the benefit likely to accrue to the investigation if it is obtained; and
(c) propose the terms of the order.

R-532 **Content of application for an account monitoring order under the Proceeds of Crime Act 2002**

47.22 As well as complying with rules 47.6 and 47.17, an applicant who wants the court to make an account monitoring order for the provision of account information must—

(a) specify—
  (i) the information sought,
  (ii) the period during which the applicant wants the respondent to provide that information (to a maximum of 90 days), and
  (iii) when and in what manner the applicant wants the respondent to provide that information;
(b) explain why the information is likely to be of substantial value to the investigation;
(c) explain why it is in the public interest for the information to be provided, having regard to the benefit likely to accrue to the investigation if it is obtained; and
(d) propose the terms of the order.

Orders under the Extradition Act 2003

R-533 **Application for a production order under the Extradition Act 2003**

47.23 (1) This rule applies where an applicant wants the court to make an order to which rule 47.4(e) refers.

(2) As well as complying with rule 47.6 (Application for order: general rules), the application must—
  (a) identify the person whose extradition is sought;
  (b) specify the extradition offence of which that person is accused;
  (c) identify the respondent; and
  (d) describe the special procedure or excluded material sought.

(3) In relation to the person whose extradition is sought, the application must explain the grounds for believing that—
  (a) that person has committed the offence for which extradition is sought;
  (b) that offence is an extradition offence; and
  (c) that person is in the United Kingdom or is on the way to the United Kingdom.

(4) In relation to the material sought, the application must—
  (a) specify the premises on which the material is believed to be;
  (b) explain the grounds for believing that—
    (i) the material is on those premises,
    (ii) the material consists of or includes special procedure or excluded material, and
    (iii) the material would be likely to be admissible evidence at a trial in England and Wales for the offence for which extradition is sought;
  (c) explain what other methods of obtaining the material—
    (i) have been tried without success, or
    (ii) have not been tried because they appeared bound to fail; and
  (d) explain why it is in the public interest for the respondent to produce or give access to the material.

(5) The application must propose—
  (a) the terms of the order, and
  (b) the period within which it should take effect.

Section 3: Investigation Warrants

R-534 **When this Section applies**

47.24 This Section applies where—

(a) a justice of the peace can issue a warrant under—
  (i) section 8 of the Police and Criminal Evidence Act 1984,
  (ii) section 2 of the Criminal Justice Act 1987;

(b) a Circuit judge can issue a warrant under—
(i) paragraph 12 of Schedule 1 to the Police and Criminal Evidence Act 1984,
(ii) paragraph 11 of Schedule 5 to the Terrorism Act 2000,
(iii) section 160 of the Extradition Act 2003;
(c) a Crown Court judge can issue a warrant under—
(i) section 352 of the Proceeds of Crime Act 2002, or
(ii) article 13 of the Proceeds of Crime Act 2002 (External Investigations) Order 2014;
(d) a court to which these Rules apply can issue a warrant to search for and seize articles or persons under a power not listed in paragraphs (a), (b) or (c).

Exercise of court's powers R-535

47.25 (1) The court must determine an application for a warrant—
(a) at a hearing, which must be in private unless the court otherwise directs;
(b) in the presence of the applicant; and
(c) in the absence of any person affected by the warrant, including any person in occupation or control of premises which the applicant wants to search.
(2) If the court so directs, the applicant may attend the hearing by live link or telephone.
(3) The court must not determine an application unless satisfied that sufficient time has been allowed for it.
(4) The court must not determine an application unless the applicant confirms, on oath or affirmation, that to the best of the applicant's knowledge and belief—
(a) the application discloses all the information that is material to what the court must decide, including any circumstances that might reasonably be considered capable of undermining any of the grounds of the application; and
(b) the content of the application is true.
(5) If the court requires the applicant to answer a question about an application—
(a) the applicant's answer must be on oath or affirmation;
(b) the court must arrange for a record of the gist of the question and reply; and
(c) if the applicant cannot answer to the court's satisfaction, the court may—
(i) specify the information the court requires, and
(ii) give directions for the presentation of any renewed application.
(6) Unless to do so would be inconsistent with other legislation, on an application the court may issue—
(a) a warrant in respect of specified premises;
(b) a warrant in respect of all premises occupied or controlled by a specified person;
(c) a warrant in respect of all premises occupied or controlled by a specified person which specifies some of those premises; or
(d) more than one warrant—
(i) each one in respect of premises specified in the warrant,
(ii) each one in respect of all premises occupied or controlled by a person specified in the warrant (whether or not such a warrant also specifies any of those premises), or
(iii) at least one in respect of specified premises and at least one in respect of all premises occupied or controlled by a specified person (whether or not such a warrant also specifies any of those premises).

Application for warrant: general rules R-536

47.26 (1) This rule applies to each application to which this Section applies.
(2) The applicant must—
(a) apply in writing;
(b) serve the application on—
(i) the court officer, or
(ii) if the court office is closed, the court;
(c) demonstrate that the applicant is entitled to apply, for example as a constable or under legislation that applies to other officers;
(d) give the court an estimate of how long the court should allow—
(i) to read and prepare for the application, and
(ii) for the hearing of the application; and
(e) tell the court when the applicant expects any warrant issued to be executed.
(3) The application must disclose anything known or reported to the applicant that might reasonably be considered capable of undermining any of the grounds of the application.

(4) Where the application includes information that the applicant thinks should not be supplied under rule 5.7 (Supply to a party of information or documents from records or case materials) to a person affected by a warrant, the applicant may—
(a) set out that information in a separate document, marked accordingly; and
(b) in that document, explain why the applicant thinks that that information ought not to be supplied to anyone other than the court.

(5) The application must include—
(a) a declaration by the applicant that to the best of the applicant's knowledge and belief—
(i) the application discloses all the information that is material to what the court must decide, including anything that might reasonably be considered capable of undermining any of the grounds of the application, and
(ii) the content of the application is true; and
(b) a declaration by an officer senior to the applicant that the senior officer has reviewed and authorised the application.

(6) The application must attach a draft warrant or warrants in the terms proposed by the applicant.

R-537 Information to be included in a warrant

47.27 (1) A warrant must identify—
(a) the person or description of persons by whom it may be executed;
(b) any person who may accompany a person executing the warrant;
(c) so far as practicable, the material, documents, articles or persons to be sought;
(d) the legislation under which it was issued;
(e) the name of the applicant;
(f) the court that issued it, unless that is otherwise recorded by the court officer;
(g) the court office for the court that issued it; and
(h) the date on which it was issued.

(2) A warrant must specify—
(a) either—
(i) the premises to be searched, where the application was for authority to search specified premises, or
(ii) the person in occupation or control of premises to be searched, where the application was for authority to search any premises occupied or controlled by that person; and
(b) the number of occasions on which specified premises may be searched, if more than one.

(3) A warrant must include, by signature, initial, or otherwise, an indication that it has been approved by the court that issued it.

(4) Where a warrant comprises more than a single page, each page must include such an indication.

(5) A copy of a warrant must include a prominent certificate that it is such a copy.

R-538 Application for warrant under section 8 of the Police and Criminal Evidence Act 1984

47.28 (1) This rule applies where an applicant wants a magistrates' court to issue a warrant or warrants under section 8 of the Police and Criminal Evidence Act 1984.

(2) As well as complying with rule 47.26, the application must—
(a) specify the offence under investigation (and see paragraph (3));
(b) so far as practicable, identify the material sought (and see paragraph (4));
(c) specify the premises to be searched (and see paragraphs (5) and (6));
(d) state whether the applicant wants the premises to be searched on more than one occasion (and see paragraph (7)); and
(e) state whether the applicant wants other persons to accompany the officers executing the warrant or warrants (and see paragraph (8)).

(3) In relation to the offence under investigation, the application must—
(a) state whether that offence is—
(i) an indictable offence, or
(ii) a relevant offence as defined in section 28D of the Immigration Act 1971; and
(b) explain the grounds for believing that the offence has been committed.

(4) In relation to the material sought, the application must explain the grounds for believing that that material—
(a) is likely to be of substantial value to the investigation (whether by itself, or together with other material);

(b) is likely to be admissible evidence at trial for the offence under investigation; and
(c) does not consist of or include items subject to legal privilege, excluded material or special procedure material.

(5) In relation to premises which the applicant wants to be searched and can specify, the application must—
(a) specify each set of premises;
(b) in respect of each set of premises, explain the grounds for believing that material sought is on those premises; and
(c) in respect of each set of premises, explain the grounds for believing that—
(i) it is not practicable to communicate with any person entitled to grant entry to the premises,
(ii) it is practicable to communicate with such a person but it is not practicable to communicate with any person entitled to grant access to the material sought,
(iii) entry to the premises will not be granted unless a warrant is produced, or
(iv) the purpose of a search may be frustrated or seriously prejudiced unless a constable arriving at the premises can secure immediate entry to them.

(6) In relation to premises which the applicant wants to be searched but at least some of which the applicant cannot specify, the application must—
(a) explain the grounds for believing that—
(i) because of the particulars of the offence under investigation it is necessary to search any premises occupied or controlled by a specified person, and
(ii) it is not reasonably practicable to specify all the premises which that person occupies or controls which might need to be searched;
(b) specify as many sets of premises as is reasonably practicable;
(c) in respect of each set of premises, whether specified or not, explain the grounds for believing that material sought is on those premises; and
(d) in respect of each specified set of premises, explain the grounds for believing that—
(i) it is not practicable to communicate with any person entitled to grant entry to the premises,
(ii) it is practicable to communicate with such a person but it is not practicable to communicate with any person entitled to grant access to the material sought,
(iii) entry to the premises will not be granted unless a warrant is produced, or
(iv) the purpose of a search may be frustrated or seriously prejudiced unless a constable arriving at the premises can secure immediate entry to them.

(7) In relation to any set of premises which the applicant wants to be searched on more than one occasion, the application must—
(a) explain why it is necessary to search on more than one occasion in order to achieve the purpose for which the applicant wants the court to issue the warrant; and
(b) specify any proposed maximum number of occasions.

(8) In relation to any set of premises which the applicant wants to be searched by the officers executing the warrant with other persons authorised by the court, the application must—
(a) identify those other persons, by function or description; and
(b) explain why those persons are required.

Application for warrant under section 2 of the Criminal Justice Act 1987 **R-539**

47.29 (1) This rule applies where an applicant wants a magistrates' court to issue a warrant or warrants under section 2 of the Criminal Justice Act 1987.

(2) As well as complying with rule 47.26, the application must—
(a) describe the investigation being conducted by the Director of the Serious Fraud Office and include—
(i) an explanation of what is alleged and why, and
(ii) a chronology of relevant events;
(b) specify the document, documents or description of documents sought by the applicant (and see paragraphs (3) and (4)); and
(c) specify the premises which the applicant wants to be searched (and see paragraph (5)).

(3) In relation to each document or description of documents sought, the application must—
(a) explain the grounds for believing that each such document—
(i) relates to a matter relevant to the investigation, and
(ii) could not be withheld from disclosure or production on grounds of legal professional privilege; and
(b) explain the grounds for believing that—
(i) a person has failed to comply with a notice by the Director to produce the document or documents,

(ii) it is not practicable to serve such a notice, or
(iii) the service of such a notice might seriously impede the investigation.

(4) In relation to any document or description of documents which the applicant wants to be preserved but not seized under a warrant, the application must—
(a) specify the steps for which the applicant wants the court's authority in order to preserve and prevent interference with the document or documents; and
(b) explain why such steps are necessary.

(5) In respect of each set of premises which the applicant wants to be searched, the application must explain the grounds for believing that a document or description of documents sought by the applicant is on those premises.

(6) If the court so directs, the applicant must make available to the court material on which is based the information given under paragraph (2).

R-540 Application for warrant under paragraph 12 of Schedule 1 to the Police and Criminal Evidence Act 1984

47.30 (1) This rule applies where an applicant wants a Circuit judge to issue a warrant or warrants under paragraph 12 of Schedule 1 to the Police and Criminal Evidence Act 1984.

(2) As well as complying with rule 47.26, the application must—
(a) specify the offence under investigation (and see paragraph (3)(a));
(b) specify the set of access conditions on which the applicant relies (and see paragraphs (3) and (4));
(c) so far as practicable, identify the material sought;
(d) specify the premises to be searched (and see paragraphs (6) and (7)); and
(e) state whether the applicant wants other persons to accompany the officers executing the warrant or warrants (and see paragraph (8)).

(3) Where the applicant relies on paragraph 2 of Schedule 1 to the Police and Criminal Evidence Act 1984 ('the first set of access conditions': general power to gain access to special procedure material), the application must—
(a) specify the indictable offence under investigation;
(b) explain the grounds for believing that the offence has been committed;
(c) explain the grounds for believing that the material sought—
(i) is likely to be of substantial value to the investigation (whether by itself, or together with other material),
(ii) is likely to be admissible evidence at trial for the offence under investigation, and
(iii) does not consist of or include items subject to legal privilege or excluded material;
(d) explain what other methods of obtaining the material—
(i) have been tried without success, or
(ii) have not been tried because they appeared bound to fail; and
(e) explain why it is in the public interest to obtain the material, having regard to—
(i) the benefit likely to accrue to the investigation if the material is obtained, and
(ii) the circumstances under which the material is held.

(4) Where the applicant relies on paragraph 3 of Schedule 1 to the Police and Criminal Evidence Act 1984 ('the second set of access conditions': use of search warrant power to gain access to excluded or special procedure material), the application must—
(a) state the legislation under which a search warrant could have been issued, had the material sought not been excluded or special procedure material (in this paragraph, described as 'the main search power');
(b) include or attach the terms of the main search power;
(c) explain how the circumstances would have satisfied any criteria prescribed by the main search power for the issue of a search warrant;
(d) explain why the issue of such a search warrant would have been appropriate.

(5) Where the applicant relies on the second set of access conditions and on an assertion that a production order made under paragraph 4 of Schedule 1 to the 1984 Act in respect of the material sought has not been complied with—
(a) the application must—
(i) identify that order and describe its terms, and
(ii) specify the date on which it was served; but
(b) the application need not comply with paragraphs (6) or (7).

(6) In relation to premises which the applicant wants to be searched and can specify, the application must (unless paragraph (5) applies)—
(a) specify each set of premises;

(b) in respect of each set of premises, explain the grounds for believing that material sought is on those premises; and
(c) in respect of each set of premises, explain the grounds for believing that—
(i) it is not practicable to communicate with any person entitled to grant entry to the premises,
(ii) it is practicable to communicate with such a person but it is not practicable to communicate with any person entitled to grant access to the material sought,
(iii) the material sought contains information which is subject to a restriction on disclosure or an obligation of secrecy contained in an enactment and is likely to be disclosed in breach of the restriction or obligation if a warrant is not issued, or
(iv) service of notice of an application for a production order under paragraph 4 of Schedule 1 to the 1984 Act may seriously prejudice the investigation.

(7) In relation to premises which the applicant wants to be searched but at least some of which the applicant cannot specify, the application must (unless paragraph (5) applies)—
(a) explain the grounds for believing that—
(i) because of the particulars of the offence under investigation it is necessary to search any premises occupied or controlled by a specified person, and
(ii) it is not reasonably practicable to specify all the premises which that person occupies or controls which might need to be searched;
(b) specify as many sets of premises as is reasonably practicable;
(c) in respect of each set of premises, whether specified or not, explain the grounds for believing that material sought is on those premises; and
(d) in respect of each specified set of premises, explain the grounds for believing that—
(i) it is not practicable to communicate with any person entitled to grant entry to the premises,
(ii) it is practicable to communicate with such a person but it is not practicable to communicate with any person entitled to grant access to the material sought,
(iii) the material sought contains information which is subject to a restriction on disclosure or an obligation of secrecy contained in an enactment and is likely to be disclosed in breach of the restriction or obligation if a warrant is not issued, or
(iv) service of notice of an application for a production order under paragraph 4 of Schedule 1 to the 1984 Act may seriously prejudice the investigation.

(8) In relation to any set of premises which the applicant wants to be searched by the officers executing the warrant with other persons authorised by the court, the application must—
(a) identify those other persons, by function or description; and
(b) explain why those persons are required.

Application for warrant under paragraph 11 of Schedule 5 to the Terrorism Act 2000 **R-541**

47.31 (1) This rule applies where an applicant wants a Circuit judge to issue a warrant or warrants under paragraph 11 of Schedule 5 to the Terrorism Act 2000.

(2) As well as complying with rule 47.26, the application must—
(a) specify the offence under investigation;
(b) explain how the investigation constitutes a terrorist investigation within the meaning of the Terrorism Act 2000;
(c) so far as practicable, identify the material sought (and see paragraph (4));
(d) specify the premises to be searched (and see paragraph (5)); and
(e) state whether the applicant wants other persons to accompany the officers executing the warrant or warrants (and see paragraph (6)).

(3) Where the applicant relies on an assertion that a production order made under paragraph 5 of Schedule 5 to the 2000 Act in respect of material on the premises has not been complied with—
(a) the application must—
(i) identify that order and describe its terms, and
(ii) specify the date on which it was served; but
(b) the application need not comply with paragraphs (4) or (5)(b).

(4) In relation to the material sought, unless paragraph (3) applies the application must explain the grounds for believing that—
(a) the material consists of or includes excluded material or special procedure material but does not include items subject to legal privilege;
(b) the material is likely to be of substantial value to a terrorist investigation (whether by itself, or together with other material); and

(c) it is not appropriate to make an order under paragraph 5 of Schedule 11 to the 2000 Act in relation to the material because—
(i) it is not practicable to communicate with any person entitled to produce the material,
(ii) it is not practicable to communicate with any person entitled to grant access to the material or entitled to grant entry to premises to which the application for the warrant relates, or
(iii) a terrorist investigation may be seriously prejudiced unless a constable can secure immediate access to the material.

(5) In relation to the premises which the applicant wants to be searched, the application must—
(a) specify—
(i) where paragraph (3) applies, the respondent and any premises to which the production order referred, or
(ii) in any other case, one or more sets of premises, or any premises occupied or controlled by a specified person (which may include one or more specified sets of premises); and
(b) unless paragraph (3) applies, in relation to premises which the applicant wants to be searched but cannot specify, explain why—
(i) it is necessary to search any premises occupied or controlled by the specified person, and
(ii) it is not reasonably practicable to specify all the premises which that person occupies or controls which might need to be searched;
(c) explain the grounds for believing that material sought is on those premises.

(6) In relation to any set of premises which the applicant wants to be searched by the officers executing the warrant with other persons authorised by the court, the application must—
(a) identify those other persons, by function or description; and
(b) explain why those persons are required.

R-542 Application for warrant under section 352 of the Proceeds of Crime Act 2002

47.32 (1) This rule applies where an applicant wants a Crown Court judge to issue a warrant or warrants under—
(a) section 352 of the Proceeds of Crime Act 2002; or
(b) article 13 of the Proceeds of Crime Act 2002 (External Investigations) Order 2014.

(2) As well as complying with rule 47.26, the application must—
(a) explain whether the investigation is a confiscation investigation, a money laundering investigation, a detained cash investigation, a detained property investigation, a frozen funds investigation or an external investigation;
(b) in the case of an investigation in the United Kingdom, explain why the applicant suspects that—
(i) the person under investigation has benefited from criminal conduct, in the case of a confiscation investigation, or committed a money laundering offence, in the case of a money laundering investigation, or
(ii) in the case of a detained cash investigation, a detained property investigation or a frozen funds investigation, the cash or property involved, or the money held in the frozen account, was obtained through unlawful conduct or is intended to be used in unlawful conduct;
(c) in the case of an investigation outside the United Kingdom, explain why the applicant believes that—
(i) there is an investigation by an overseas authority which relates to a criminal investigation or to criminal proceedings (including proceedings to remove the benefit of a person's criminal conduct following that person's conviction), and
(ii) the investigation is into whether property has been obtained as a result of or in connection with criminal conduct, or into the extent or whereabouts of such property;
(d) indicate what material is sought (and see paragraphs (4) and (5));
(e) specify the premises to be searched (and see paragraph (6)); and
(f) state whether the applicant wants other persons to accompany the officers executing the warrant or warrants (and see paragraph (7)).

(3) Where the applicant relies on an assertion that a production order made under sections 345 and 351 of the 2002 Act or under articles 6 and 12 of the 2014 Order has not been complied with—
(a) the application must—
(i) identify that order and describe its terms,

(ii) specify the date on which it was served, and
(iii) explain the grounds for believing that the material in respect of which the order was made is on the premises specified in the application for the warrant; but
(b) the application need not comply with paragraphs (4) or (5).
(4) Unless paragraph (3) applies, in relation to the material sought the application must—
(a) specify the material; or
(b) give a general description of the material and explain the grounds for believing that it relates to the person, cash, property or money under investigation and—
(i) in the case of a confiscation investigation, relates to the question whether that person has benefited from criminal conduct, or to any question about the extent or whereabouts of that benefit,
(ii) in the case of a money laundering investigation, relates to the question whether that person has committed a money laundering offence,
(iii) in the case of a detained cash investigation, a detained property investigation or a frozen funds investigation into the derivation of cash, property or money, relates to the question whether that cash, property or money is recoverable property,
(iv) in the case of a detained cash investigation, a detained property investigation or a frozen funds investigation into the intended use of cash, property or money, relates to the question whether that cash, property or money is intended by any person to be used in unlawful conduct,
(v) in the case of an investigation outside the United Kingdom, relates to that investigation.
(5) Unless paragraph (3) applies, in relation to the material sought the application must explain also the grounds for believing that—
(a) the material consists of or includes special procedure material but does not include excluded material or privileged material;
(b) the material is likely to be of substantial value to the investigation (whether by itself, or together with other material); and
(c) it is in the public interest for the material to be obtained, having regard to—
(i) other potential sources of information,
(ii) the benefit likely to accrue to the investigation if the material is obtained.
(6) In relation to the premises which the applicant wants to be searched, unless paragraph (3) applies the application must—
(a) explain the grounds for believing that material sought is on those premises;
(b) if the application specifies the material sought, explain the grounds for believing that it is not appropriate to make a production order under sections 345 and 351 of the 2002 Act or under articles 6 and 12 of the 2014 Order because—
(i) it is not practicable to communicate with any person against whom the production order could be made,
(ii) it is not practicable to communicate with any person who would be required to comply with an order to grant entry to the premises, or
(iii) the investigation might be seriously prejudiced unless an appropriate person is able to secure immediate access to the material;
(c) if the application gives a general description of the material sought, explain the grounds for believing that—
(i) it is not practicable to communicate with any person entitled to grant entry to the premises,
(ii) entry to the premises will not be granted unless a warrant is produced, or
(iii) the investigation might be seriously prejudiced unless an appropriate person arriving at the premises is able to secure immediate access to them;
(7) In relation to any set of premises which the applicant wants to be searched by those executing the warrant with other persons authorised by the court, the application must—
(a) identify those other persons, by function or description; and
(b) explain why those persons are required.

Application for warrant under section 160 of the Extradition Act 2003 **R-543**

47.33 (1) This rule applies where an applicant wants a Circuit judge to issue a warrant or warrants under section 160 of the Extradition Act 2003.
(2) As well as complying with rule 47.26, the application must—
(a) identify the person whose extradition is sought (and see paragraph (3));
(b) specify the extradition offence of which that person is accused;

Criminal Procedure Rules and Criminal Practice Directions

(c) specify the material, or description of material, sought (and see paragraph (4)); and
(d) specify the premises to be searched (and see paragraph (5)).

(3) In relation to the person whose extradition is sought, the application must explain the grounds for believing that—
(a) that person has committed the offence for which extradition is sought;
(b) that offence is an extradition offence; and
(c) that person is in the United Kingdom or is on the way to the United Kingdom.

(4) In relation to the material sought, the application must explain the grounds for believing that—
(a) the material consists of or includes special procedure or excluded material; and
(b) the material would be likely to be admissible evidence at a trial in England and Wales for the offence for which extradition is sought.

(5) In relation to the premises which the applicant wants to search, the application must explain the grounds for believing that—
(a) material sought is on those premises;
(b) one or more of the following conditions is satisfied, namely—
(i) it is not practicable to communicate with any person entitled to grant entry to the premises,
(ii) it is practicable to communicate with such a person but it is not practicable to communicate with any person entitled to grant access to the material sought, or
(iii) the material contains information which is subject to a restriction on disclosure or an obligation of secrecy contained in an enactment and is likely to be disclosed in breach of the restriction or obligation if a warrant is not issued.

(6) In relation to any set of premises which the applicant wants to be searched by the officers executing the warrant with other persons authorised by the court, the application must—
(a) identify those other persons, by function or description; and
(b) explain why those persons are required.

R-544 Application for warrant under any other power

47.34 (1) This rule applies—
(a) where an applicant wants a court to issue a warrant or warrants under a power (in this rule, 'the relevant search power') to which rule 47.24(d) (other powers) refers; but
(b) subject to any inconsistent provision in legislation that applies to the relevant search power.

(2) As well as complying with rule 47.26, the application must—
(a) demonstrate the applicant's entitlement to apply;
(b) identify the relevant search power (and see paragraph (3));
(c) so far as practicable, identify the articles or persons sought (and see paragraph (4));
(d) specify the premises to be searched (and see paragraphs (5) and (6));
(e) state whether the applicant wants the premises to be searched on more than one occasion, if the relevant search power allows (and see paragraph (7)); and
(f) state whether the applicant wants other persons to accompany the officers executing the warrant or warrants, if the relevant search power allows (and see paragraph (8)).

(3) The application must—
(a) include or attach the terms of the relevant search power; and
(b) explain how the circumstances satisfy the criteria prescribed by that power for making the application.

(4) In relation to the articles or persons sought, the application must explain how they satisfy the criteria prescribed by the relevant search power about such articles or persons.

(5) In relation to premises which the applicant wants to be searched and can specify, the application must—
(a) specify each set of premises; and
(b) in respect of each, explain how the circumstances satisfy any criteria prescribed by the relevant search power—
(i) for asserting that the articles or persons sought are on those premises, and
(ii) for asserting that the court can exercise its power to authorise the search of those particular premises.

(6) In relation to premises which the applicant wants to be searched but at least some of which the applicant cannot specify, the application must—
(a) explain how the relevant search power allows the court to authorise such searching;

(b) specify the person who occupies or controls such premises;
(c) specify as many sets of such premises as is reasonably practicable;
(d) explain why—
(i) it is necessary to search more premises than those specified, and
(ii) it is not reasonably practicable to specify all the premises which the applicant wants to be searched;
(e) in respect of each set of premises, whether specified or not, explain how the circumstances satisfy any criteria prescribed by the relevant search power for asserting that the articles or persons sought are on those premises; and
(f) in respect of each specified set of premises, explain how the circumstances satisfy any criteria prescribed by the relevant search power for asserting that the court can exercise its power to authorise the search of those premises.

(7) In relation to any set of premises which the applicant wants to be searched on more than one occasion, the application must—
(a) explain how the relevant search power allows the court to authorise such searching;
(b) explain why the applicant wants the premises to be searched more than once; and
(c) specify any proposed maximum number of occasions.

(8) In relation to any set of premises which the applicant wants to be searched by the officers executing the warrant with other persons authorised by the court, the application must—
(a) identify those other persons, by function or description; and
(b) explain why those persons are required.

Section 4: Orders for the Retention or Return of Property

When this Section applies R-545

47.35 (1) This Section applies where—
(a) under section 1 of the Police (Property) Act 1897, a magistrates' court can—
(i) order the return to the owner of property which has come into the possession of the police or the National Crime Agency in connection with an investigation of a suspected offence, or
(ii) make such order with respect to such property as the court thinks just, where the owner cannot be ascertained;
(b) a Crown Court judge can—
(i) order the return of seized property under section 59(4) of the Criminal Justice and Police Act 2001, or
(ii) order the examination, retention, separation or return of seized property under section 59(5) of the Act.

(2) In this Section, a reference to a person with 'a relevant interest' in seized property means someone from whom the property was seized, or someone with a proprietary interest in the property, or someone who had custody or control of it immediately before it was seized.

Exercise of court's powers R-546

47.36 (1) The court may determine an application for an order—
(a) at a hearing (which must be in private unless the court otherwise directs), or without a hearing;
(b) in a party's absence, if that party—
(i) applied for the order, or
(ii) has had at least 14 days in which to make representations.

(2) The court officer must arrange for the court to hear such an application no sooner than 14 days after it was served, unless—
(a) the court directs that no hearing need be arranged; or
(b) the court gives other directions for the hearing.

(3) If the court so directs, the parties to an application may attend a hearing by live link or telephone.

(4) The court may—
(a) shorten or extend (even after it has expired) a time limit under this Section;
(b) dispense with a requirement for service under this Section (even after service was required); and
(c) consider an application made orally instead of in writing.

(5) A person who wants an extension of time must—
(a) apply when serving the application or representations for which it is needed; and
(b) explain the delay.

R-547 Application for an order under section 1 of the Police (Property) Act 1897

47.37 (1) This rule applies where an applicant wants the court to make an order to which rule 47.35(1)(a) refers.

(2) The applicant must apply in writing and serve the application on—

(a) the court officer; and

(b) as appropriate—

(i) the officer who has the property,

(ii) any person who appears to be its owner.

(3) The application must—

(a) explain the applicant's interest in the property (either as a person who claims to be its owner or as an officer into whose possession the property has come);

(b) specify the direction that the applicant wants the court to make, and explain why; and

(c) include or attach a list of those on whom the applicant has served the application.

R-548 Application for an order under section 59 of the Criminal Justice and Police Act 2001

47.38 (1) This rule applies where an applicant wants the court to make an order to which rule 47.35(1)(b) refers.

(2) The applicant must apply in writing and serve the application on—

(a) the court officer; and

(b) as appropriate—

(i) the person who for the time being has the seized property,

(ii) each person whom the applicant knows or believes to have a relevant interest in the property.

(3) In each case, the application must—

(a) explain the applicant's interest in the property (either as a person with a relevant interest, or as possessor of the property in consequence of its seizure, as appropriate);

(b) explain the circumstances of the seizure of the property and identify the power that was exercised to seize it (or which the person seizing it purported to exercise, as appropriate); and

(c) include or attach a list of those on whom the applicant has served the application.

(4) On an application for an order for the return of property under section 59(4) of the Criminal Justice and Police Act 2001, the application must explain why any one or more of these applies—

(a) there was no power to make the seizure;

(b) the property seized is, or contains, an item subject to legal privilege which is not an item that can be retained lawfully in the circumstances listed in section 54(2) of the Act;

(c) the property seized is, or contains, excluded or special procedure material which is not material that can be retained lawfully in the circumstances listed in sections 55 and 56 of the Act;

(d) the property seized is, or contains, something taken from premises under section 50 of the Act, or from a person under section 51 of the Act, in the circumstances listed in those sections and which cannot lawfully be retained on the conditions listed in the Act.

(5) On an application for an order for the examination, retention, separation or return of property under section 59(5) of the 2001 Act, the application must—

(a) specify the direction that the applicant wants the court to make, and explain why;

(b) if applicable, specify each requirement of section 53(2) of the Act (examination and return of property) which is not being complied with;

(c) if applicable, explain why the retention of the property by the person who now has it would be justified on the grounds that, even if it were returned, it would immediately become appropriate for that person to get it back under—

(i) a warrant for its seizure, or

(ii) a production order made under paragraph 4 of Schedule 1 to the Police and Criminal Evidence Act 1984, section 20BA of the Taxes Management Act 1970 or paragraph 5 of Schedule 5 to the Terrorism Act 2000.

R-549 Application containing information withheld from another party

47.39 (1) This rule applies where—

(a) an applicant serves an application to which rule 47.37 (Application for an order under section 59 of the Criminal Justice and Police Act 2001) applies; and

(b) the application includes information that the applicant thinks ought not be revealed to another party.

(2) The applicant must—

(a) omit that information from the part of the application that is served on that other party;

(b) mark the other part to show that, unless the court otherwise directs, it is only for the court; and

(c) in that other part, explain why the applicant has withheld that information from that other party.

(3) If the court so directs, any hearing of an application to which this rule applies may be, wholly or in part, in the absence of a party from whom information has been withheld.

(4) At any hearing of an application to which this rule applies—
(a) the general rule is that the court must consider, in the following sequence—
(i) representations first by the applicant and then by each other party, in all the parties' presence, and then
(ii) further representations by the applicant, in the absence of a party from whom information has been withheld; but
(b) the court may direct other arrangements for the hearing.

Representations in response **R-550**

47.40 (1) This rule applies where a person wants to make representations about an application under rule 47.37 or rule 47.38.
(2) Such a person must—
(a) serve the representations on—
(i) the court officer, and
(ii) the applicant and any other party to the application;
(b) do so not more than 14 days after service of the application; and
(c) ask for a hearing, if that person wants one.
(3) Representations in opposition to an application must explain why the grounds on which the applicant relies are not met.
(4) Where representations include information that the person making them thinks ought not be revealed to another party, that person must—
(a) omit that information from the representations served on that other party;
(b) mark the information to show that, unless the court otherwise directs, it is only for the court; and
(c) with that information include an explanation of why it has been withheld from that other party.

Application to punish for contempt of court **R-551**

47.41 (1) This rule applies where a person is accused of disobeying an order under section 59 of the Criminal Justice and Police Act 2001.
(2) A person who wants the court to exercise its power to punish that person for contempt of court must comply with the rules in Part 48 (Contempt of court).

Section 5: Orders for the Retention of Fingerprints, etc.

When this Section applies **R-552**

47.42 This Section applies where—
(a) a District Judge (Magistrates' Court) can make an order under—
(i) section 63F(7) or 63R(6) of the Police and Criminal Evidence Act 1984, or
(ii) paragraph 20B(5) or 20G(6) of Schedule 8 to the Terrorism Act 2000;
(b) the Crown Court can determine an appeal under—
(i) section 63F(10) of the Police and Criminal Evidence Act 1984, or
(ii) paragraph 20B(8) of Schedule 8 to the Terrorism Act 2000.

Exercise of court's powers **R-553**

47.43 (1) The court must determine an application under rule 47.44, and an appeal under rule 47.45—
(a) at a hearing, which must be in private unless the court otherwise directs; and
(b) in the presence of the applicant or appellant.
(2) The court must not determine such an application or appeal unless any person served under those rules—
(a) is present; or
(b) has had an opportunity—
(i) to attend, or
(ii) to make representations.

Application to extend retention period **R-554**

47.44 (1) This rule applies where a magistrates' court can make an order extending the period for which there may be retained material consisting of—
(a) fingerprints taken from a person—
(i) under a power conferred by Part V of the Police and Criminal Evidence Act 1984,
(ii) with that person's consent, in connection with the investigation of an offence by the police, or

(iii) under a power conferred by Schedule 8 to the Terrorism Act 2000 in relation to a person detained under section 41 of that Act;
(b) a DNA profile derived from a DNA sample so taken; or
(c) a sample so taken.
(2) A chief officer of police who wants the court to make such an order must—
(a) apply in writing—
(i) within the period of 3 months ending on the last day of the retention period, where the application relates to fingerprints or a DNA profile, or
(ii) before the expiry of the retention period, where the application relates to a sample;
(b) in the application—
(i) identify the material,
(ii) state when the retention period expires,
(iii) give details of any previous such application relating to the material, and
(iv) outline the circumstances in which the material was acquired;
(c) serve the application on the court officer, in every case; and
(d) serve the application on the person from whom the material was taken, where—
(i) the application relates to fingerprints or a DNA profile, or
(ii) the application is for the renewal of an order extending the retention period for a sample.
(3) An application to extend the retention period for fingerprints or a DNA profile must explain why that period should be extended.
(4) An application to extend the retention period for a sample must explain why, having regard to the nature and complexity of other material that is evidence in relation to the offence, the sample is likely to be needed in any proceedings for the offence for the purposes of—
(a) disclosure to, or use by, a defendant; or
(b) responding to any challenge by a defendant in respect of the admissibility of material that is evidence on which the prosecution proposes to rely.
(5) On an application to extend the retention period for fingerprints or a DNA profile, the applicant must serve notice of the court's decision on any respondent where—
(a) the court makes the order sought; and
(b) the respondent was absent when it was made.

R-555 Appeal

47.45 (1) This rule applies where, under rule 47.44, a magistrates' court determines an application relating to fingerprints or a DNA profile and—
(a) the person from whom the material was taken wants to appeal to the Crown Court against an order extending the retention period; or
(b) a chief officer of police wants to appeal to the Crown Court against a refusal to make such an order.
(2) The appellant must—
(a) serve an appeal notice—
(i) on the Crown Court officer and on the other party, and
(ii) not more than 21 days after the magistrates' court's decision, or, if applicable, service of notice under rule 47.44(5); and
(b) in the appeal notice, explain, as appropriate, why the retention period should, or should not, be extended.
(3) Rule 34.11 (Constitution of the Crown Court) applies on such an appeal.

Section 6: Investigation Anonymity Orders under the Coroners and Justice Act 2009

R-556 When this Section applies

47.46 This Section applies where—
(a) a justice of the peace can make or discharge an investigation anonymity order, under sections 76 and 80(1) of the Coroners and Justice Act 2009;
(b) a Crown Court judge can determine an appeal against—
(i) a refusal of such an order, under section 79 of the 2009 Act,
(ii) a decision on an application to discharge such an order, under section 80(6) of the 2009 Act.

R-557 Exercise of court's powers

47.47 (1) The court may determine an application for an investigation anonymity order, and any appeal against the refusal of such an order—
(a) at a hearing (which must be in private unless the court otherwise directs); or
(b) without a hearing.

(2) The court must determine an application to discharge an investigation anonymity order, and any appeal against the decision on such an application—
(a) at a hearing (which must be in private unless the court otherwise directs); and
(b) in the presence of the person specified in the order, unless—
(i) that person applied for the discharge of the order,
(ii) that person has had an opportunity to make representations, or
(iii) the court is satisfied that it is not reasonably practicable to communicate with that person.
(3) The court may consider an application or an appeal made orally instead of in writing.

Application for an investigation anonymity order R-558

47.48 (1) This rule applies where an applicant wants a magistrates' court to make an investigation anonymity order.
(2) The applicant must—
(a) apply in writing;
(b) serve the application on the court officer;
(c) identify the person to be specified in the order, unless—
(i) the applicant wants the court to determine the application at a hearing, or
(ii) the court otherwise directs;
(d) explain how the proposed order meets the conditions prescribed by section 78 of the Coroners and Justice Act 2009;
(e) say if the applicant intends to appeal should the court refuse the order;
(f) attach any material on which the applicant relies; and
(g) propose the terms of the order.
(3) At any hearing of the application, the applicant must—
(a) identify to the court the person to be specified in the order, unless—
(i) the applicant has done so already, or
(ii) the court otherwise directs; and
(b) unless the applicant has done so already, inform the court if the applicant intends to appeal should the court refuse the order.

Application to discharge an investigation anonymity order R-559

47.49 (1) This rule applies where one of the following wants a magistrates' court to discharge an investigation anonymity order—
(a) an applicant; or
(b) the person specified in the order.
(2) That applicant or the specified person must—
(a) apply in writing as soon as practicable after becoming aware of the grounds for doing so;
(b) serve the application on—
(i) the court officer, and as applicable
(ii) the applicant for the order, and
(iii) the specified person;
(c) explain—
(i) what material circumstances have changed since the order was made, or since any previous application was made to discharge it, and
(ii) why it is appropriate for the order to be discharged; and
(d) attach—
(i) a copy of the order, and
(ii) any material on which the applicant relies.
(3) A party must inform the court if that party intends to appeal should the court discharge the order.

Appeal R-560

47.50 (1) This rule applies where one of the following ('the appellant') wants to appeal to the Crown Court—
(a) the applicant for an investigation anonymity order, where a magistrates' court has refused to make the order;
(b) a party to an application to discharge such an order, where a magistrates' court has decided that application.
(2) The appellant must—
(a) serve on the Crown Court officer a copy of the application to the magistrates' court; and

(b) where the appeal concerns a discharge decision, notify each other party, not more than 21 days after the decision against which the appellant wants to appeal.

(3) The Crown Court must hear the appeal without justices of the peace.

Section 7: Investigation Approval Orders under the Regulation of Investigatory Powers Act 2000

R-561 **When this Section applies**

47.51 This Section applies where a justice of the peace can make an order approving—

(a) the grant or renewal of an authorisation, or the giving or renewal of a notice, under section 23A of the Regulation of Investigatory Powers Act 2000;

(b) the grant or renewal of an authorisation under section 32A of the 2000 Act.

R-562 **Exercise of court's powers**

47.52 (1) Rule 47.5 (Investigation orders; Exercise of court's powers) applies, subject to sections 23B(2) and 32B(2) of the Regulation of Investigatory Powers Act 2000.

(2) Where a magistrates' court refuses to approve the grant, giving or renewal of an authorisation or notice, the court must not exercise its power to quash that authorisation or notice unless the applicant has had at least 2 business days from the date of the refusal in which to make representations.

R-563 **Application for approval for authorisation or notice**

47.53 (1) This rule applies where an applicant wants a magistrates' court to make an order approving—

(a) under sections 23A and 23B of the Regulation of Investigatory Powers Act 2000—

(i) an authorisation to obtain or disclose communications data, under section 22(3) of the 2000 Act, or

(ii) a notice that requires a postal or telecommunications operator if need be to obtain, and in any case to disclose, communications data, under section 22(4) of the 2000 Act;

(b) under sections 32A and 32B of the Regulation of Investigatory Powers Act 2000, an authorisation for—

(i) the carrying out of directed surveillance, under section 28 of the 2000 Act, or

(ii) the conduct or use of a covert human intelligence source, under section 29 of the 2000 Act.

(2) The applicant must—

(a) apply in writing and serve the application on the court officer;

(b) attach the authorisation or notice which the applicant wants the court to approve;

(c) attach such other material (if any) on which the applicant relies to satisfy the court—

(i) as required by section 23A(3) and (4) of the 2000 Act, in relation to communications data,

(ii) as required by section 32A(3) and (4) of the 2000 Act, in relation to directed surveillance, or

(iii) as required by section 32A(5) and (6), and, if relevant, section 43(6A), of the 2000 Act, in relation to a covert human intelligence source; and

(d) propose the terms of the order.

Section 8: Orders for Access to Documents, etc. under the Criminal Appeal Act 1995

R-564 **When this Section applies**

47.54 This Section applies where the Crown Court can order a person to give the Criminal Cases Review Commission access to a document or other material under section 18A of the Criminal Appeal Act 1995.

R-565 **Exercise of court's powers**

47.55 (1) Subject to paragraphs (2), (3) and (4), the court may determine an application by the Criminal Cases Review Commission for an order—

(a) at a hearing (which must be in private unless the court otherwise directs), or without a hearing; and

(b) in the absence of—

(i) the Commission,

(ii) the respondent,

(iii) any other person affected by the order.

(2) The court must not determine such an application in the Commission's absence if—

(a) the Commission asks for a hearing; or

(b) it appears to the court that the application is so complex or serious as to require the court to hear the Commission.

(3) The court must not determine such an application in the absence of any respondent or other person affected, unless—

(a) the absentee has had at least 2 business days in which to make representations; or

(b) the court is satisfied that—

(i) the Commission cannot identify or contact the absentee,

(ii) it would prejudice the exercise of the Commission's functions to adjourn or postpone the application so as to allow the absentee to attend, or

(iii) the absentee has waived the opportunity to attend.

(4) The court must not determine such an application in the absence of any respondent who, if the order sought by the Commission were made, would be required to produce or give access to journalistic material, unless that respondent has waived the opportunity to attend.

(5) The court officer must arrange for the court to hear such an application no sooner than 2 business days after it was served, unless—

(a) the court directs that no hearing need be arranged; or

(b) the court gives other directions for the hearing.

(6) The court must not determine an application unless satisfied that sufficient time has been allowed for it.

(7) If the court so directs, the parties to an application may attend a hearing by live link or telephone.

(8) The court must not make an order unless an officer of the Commission states, in writing or orally, that to the best of that officer's knowledge and belief—

(a) the application discloses all the information that is material to what the court must decide; and

(b) the content of the application is true.

(9) Where the statement required by paragraph (8) is made orally—

(a) the statement must be on oath or affirmation, unless the court otherwise directs; and

(b) the court must arrange for a record of the making of the statement.

(10) The court may shorten or extend (even after it has expired) a time limit under this Section.

Application for an order for access **R-566**

47.56 (1) Where the Criminal Cases Review Commission wants the court to make an order for access to a document or other material, the Commission must—

(a) apply in writing and serve the application on the court officer;

(b) give the court an estimate of how long the court should allow—

(i) to read the application and prepare for any hearing, and

(ii) for any hearing of the application;

(c) attach a draft order in the terms proposed by the Commission; and

(d) serve the application and draft order on the respondent.

(2) The application must—

(a) identify the respondent;

(b) describe the document, or documents, or other material sought;

(c) explain the reasons for thinking that—

(i) what is sought is in the respondent's possession or control, and

(ii) access to what is sought may assist the Commission in the exercise of any of its functions; and

(d) explain the Commission's proposals for—

(i) the manner in which the respondent should give access, and

(ii) the period within which the order should take effect.

(3) The Commission must serve any order made on the respondent.

Application containing information withheld from a respondent or other person **R-567**

47.57 (1) This rule applies where—

(a) the Criminal Cases Review Commission serves an application under rule 47.56 (Application for an order for access); and

(b) the application includes information that the Commission thinks ought not be revealed to a recipient.

(2) The Commission must—

(a) omit that information from the part of the application that is served on that recipient;

(b) mark the other part, to show that it is only for the court; and
(c) in that other part, explain why the Commission has withheld it from that recipient.

(3) A hearing of an application to which this rule applies may take place, wholly or in part, in the absence of that recipient and any other person.

(4) At a hearing of an application to which this rule applies—
(a) the general rule is that the court must consider, in the following sequence—
(i) representations first by the Commission and then by the other parties, in the presence of them all, and then
(ii) further representations by the Commission, in the others' absence; but
(b) the court may direct other arrangements for the hearing.

R-568 Application to punish for contempt of court

47.58 (1) This rule applies where a person is accused of disobeying an order for access made under section 18A of the Criminal Appeal Act 1995.

(2) An applicant who wants the court to exercise its power to punish that person for contempt of court must comply with the rules in Part 48 (Contempt of court).

Section 9: European Investigation Orders

R-569 When this Section applies

47.59 This Section—
(a) applies where the court can—
(i) make a European investigation order under regulation 6 of the Criminal Justice (European Investigation Order) Regulations 2017,
(ii) vary or revoke such an order under regulation 10 of the 2017 Regulations;
(b) does not apply where rule 18.24 or rule 18.25 applies (application to make or discharge, etc. a live link direction supplemented by a European investigation order).

R-570 Exercise of court's powers

47.60 (1) Subject to paragraphs (2) and (3), the court may determine an application under rule 47.61 to make, vary or revoke a European investigation order—
(a) at a hearing (which must be in private unless the court otherwise directs), or without a hearing; and
(b) in the absence of—
(i) the applicant,
(ii) the respondent (if any),
(iii) any other person affected by the order.

(2) The court must not determine such an application in the applicant's absence if—
(a) under the same conditions in a similar domestic case the investigative measure to be specified in the order would be a search warrant;
(b) the applicant asks for a hearing;
(c) it appears to the court that the investigative measure which the applicant wants the court to specify in the European investigation order—
(i) may infringe legal privilege, within the meaning of section 10 of the Police and Criminal Evidence Act 1984, section 348 or 361 of the Proceeds of Crime Act 2002 or article 9 of the Proceeds of Crime Act 2002 (External Investigations) Order 2014, or
(ii) may require the production of excluded material, within the meaning of section 11 of the 1984 Act; or
(d) it appears to the court that for any other reason the application is so complex or serious as to require the court to hear the applicant.

(3) The court—
(a) must determine such an application in the absence of any respondent or other person affected if under the same conditions in a similar domestic case—
(i) an investigative measure to be specified in the European investigation order would be a search warrant, or
(ii) each investigative measure to be specified in the European investigation order would be one to an application for which no Criminal Procedure Rule would apply other than the rules in Section 1 and this Section of this Part;
(b) may determine such an application in the absence of any respondent or other person affected where the court considers that—
(i) no requirement for the absentee's participation could be applied effectively because the application is for a European investigation order and not for a warrant, order, notice or summons to be given effect in England and Wales,

(ii) the applicant cannot identify or contact the absentee,
(iii) it would prejudice the investigation if the absentee were present,
(iv) it would prejudice the investigation to adjourn or postpone the application so as to allow the absentee to attend, or
(v) the absentee has waived the opportunity to attend.

(4) The court must not determine an application unless satisfied that sufficient time has been allowed for it.

(5) If the court so directs, a party to an application may attend a hearing by live link or telephone.

(6) The court must not make, vary or discharge an order unless the applicant states, in writing or orally, that to the best of the applicant's knowledge and belief—
(a) the application discloses all the information that is material to what the court must decide; and
(b) the content of the application is true.

(7) Where the statement required by paragraph (6) is made orally—
(a) the statement must be on oath or affirmation, unless the court otherwise directs; and
(b) the court must arrange for a record of the making of the statement.

(8) The court may—
(a) dispense with a requirement for service under this Section (even after service was required); and
(b) consider an application made orally instead of in writing.

Application to make, vary or revoke a European investigation order **R-571**

47.61 (1) This rule applies where—
(a) one of the following wants the court to make a European investigation order—
(i) a constable, acting with the consent of a prosecuting authority,
(ii) a prosecuting authority, or
(iii) a party to a prosecution;
(b) one of the following wants the court to vary or revoke a European investigation order made by the court—
(i) the person who applied for the order,
(ii) a prosecuting authority, or
(iii) any other person affected by the order.

(2) The applicant must—
(a) apply in writing and serve the application on the court officer;
(b) demonstrate that the applicant is entitled to apply;
(c) if, and only if, the court cannot determine an application for a European investigation order in the absence of a respondent or other person affected (see rule 47.60(3)), serve on that respondent or other person such notice of the application as the court may direct;
(d) serve notice of an application to vary or revoke a European investigation order on, as appropriate, the person who applied for the order and any other person affected by the order.

(3) An application for the court to make a European investigation order must—
(a) specify the offence under prosecution or investigation;
(b) explain why it is suspected that the offence has been committed;
(c) describe, as appropriate—
(i) the proceedings for the offence, or
(ii) the investigation;
(d) specify the investigative measure or measures sought for the purpose of obtaining evidence for use in the proceedings or investigation, as the case may be;
(e) specify the participating State in which the measure or measures are to be carried out;
(f) explain why it is necessary and proportionate to make a European investigation order for the purposes of the proceedings or investigation;
(g) where a measure is one which would require the issue of a warrant, order, notice or witness summons before it could be lawfully carried out in England and Wales, explain how such an instrument could have been issued taking into account—
(i) the nature of the evidence to be obtained,
(ii) the purpose for which that evidence is sought (including its relevance to the investigation or proceedings in respect of which the European investigation order is sought),
(iii) the circumstances in which the evidence is held,

(iv) the nature and seriousness of the offence to which the investigation or proceedings relates, and
(v) any provision or rule of domestic law applicable to the issuing of such an instrument;
(h) where a measure is one which would require authorisation under any enactment relating to the acquisition and disclosure of data relating to communications, or the carrying out of surveillance, before it could be lawfully carried out in England and Wales, explain whether such authorisation has in fact been granted, or could have been granted, taking into account—
(i) the factors listed in paragraph (3)(g)(i) to (iv), and
(ii) the provisions of the legislation applicable to the granting of such authorisation;
(i) where a measure is in connection with, or in the form of, the interception of communications, explain whether any additional requirements imposed by legislation relating to the making of such a request have been complied with;
(j) where the application is for an order specifying one of the measures listed in any of regulations 15 to 19 of the Criminal Justice (European Investigation Order) Regulations 2017 (banking and other financial information; gathering of evidence in real time; covert investigations; provisional measures; interception of telecommunications where technical assistance is needed), explain how the requirements of that regulation are met;
(k) attach a draft order in the form required by regulation 8 of the 2017 Regulations (Form and content of a European investigation order) and Directive 2014/41/EU.

(4) An application for the court to vary or revoke a European investigation order must—
(a) explain why it is appropriate for the order to be varied or revoked;
(b) propose the terms of any variation; and
(c) ask for a hearing, if one is wanted, and explain why it is needed.

(5) Where the court—
(a) makes a European investigation order the court officer must promptly—
(i) issue an order in the form required by regulation 8 of the 2017 Regulations (Form and content of a European investigation order) and Directive 2014/41/EU,
(ii) where the applicant is a constable or a prosecuting authority, serve that order on the applicant,
(iii) in any other case, serve that order on the appropriate authority in the participating State in which the measure or measures are to be carried out;
(b) varies or revokes a European investigation order the court officer must promptly notify the appropriate authority in the participating State in which the measure or measures are to be carried out.

Section 10: Order for the Extension of a Moratorium Period under the Proceeds of Crime Act 2002

R-572 When this Section applies

47.62 (1) This Section applies where the Crown Court can extend a moratorium period under section 336A of the Proceeds of Crime Act 2002.

(2) In this Section, 'respondent' means, as well as a person within the meaning of rule 47.2(c), an 'interested person' within the meaning of section 336D of the 2002 Act.

R-573 Exercise of court's powers

47.63 (1) The court may determine an application to which rule 47.64 (Application for extension of moratorium period) applies—
(a) at a hearing (which must be in private unless the court otherwise directs), or without a hearing; and
(b) in the absence of—
(i) the applicant,
(ii) a respondent.

(2) The court must not determine such an application in the applicant's absence if the applicant asks for a hearing.

(3) The court must not determine such an application in the absence of a respondent unless—
(a) the absentee has had at least 2 business days in which to make representations; or
(b) the court is satisfied that—
(i) the applicant cannot identify or contact the absentee,
(ii) it would prejudice the investigation if the absentee were present,
(iii) it would prejudice the investigation to adjourn or postpone the application so as to allow the absentee to attend, or
(iv) the absentee has waived the opportunity to attend.

(4) The court officer must arrange for the court to hear such an application no sooner than 2 business days after notice of the application was served, unless—
(a) the court directs that no hearing need be arranged; or
(b) the court gives other directions for the hearing.
(5) If the court so directs, the parties to an application may attend a hearing by live link or telephone.
(6) The court must not extend a moratorium period unless the applicant states, in writing or orally, that to the best of the applicant's knowledge and belief—
(a) the application discloses all the information that is material to what the court must decide; and
(b) the content of the application is true.
(7) Where the statement required by paragraph (6) is made orally—
(a) the statement must be on oath or affirmation, unless the court otherwise directs; and
(b) the court must arrange for a record of the making of the statement.
(8) The court may—
(a) shorten or extend (even after it has expired) a time limit imposed by this rule;
(b) dispense with a requirement for service under this Section (even after service was required); and
(c) consider an application made orally instead of in writing.

Application for extension of moratorium period **R-574**

47.64 (1) This rule applies where an applicant wants the court to extend a moratorium period.
(2) The applicant must—
(a) apply in writing before the date on which the moratorium period otherwise would end;
(b) demonstrate that the applicant is entitled to apply as a senior officer within the meaning of section 336D of the Proceeds of Crime Act 2002;
(c) serve the application on the court officer;
(d) serve notice on each respondent that an application has been made; and
(e) serve the application on each respondent to such extent, if any, as the court directs.
(3) The application must specify—
(a) the disclosure in respect of which the application is made;
(b) the date on which the moratorium period began;
(c) the date and period of any previous extension of that period; and
(d) the date on which that period is due to end.
(4) The application must—
(a) describe the investigation being carried out in relation to that disclosure; and
(b) explain the grounds for believing that—
(i) the investigation is being conducted diligently and expeditiously,
(ii) further time is needed for conducting the investigation, and
(iii) it would be reasonable in all the circumstances for the moratorium period to be extended.
(5) A respondent who objects to the application must—
(a) serve notice of the objection on—
(i) the court officer, and
(ii) the applicant,
not more than 2 business days after service of notice of the application; and
(b) in that notice explain the grounds of the objection.
(6) The applicant must serve any order made on each respondent.

Application containing information withheld from a respondent **R-575**

47.65 (1) This rule applies where an application to extend a moratorium period includes an application to withhold information from a respondent.
(2) The applicant must—
(a) omit that information from any part of the application that is served on the respondent;
(b) mark the other part to show that, unless the court otherwise directs, it is only for the court; and
(c) in that other part, explain the grounds for believing that the disclosure of that information would have one or more of the following results—
(i) evidence of an offence would be interfered with or harmed,
(ii) the gathering of information about the possible commission of an offence would be interfered with,

(iii) a person would be interfered with or physically injured,
(iv) the recovery of property under this Act would be hindered, or
(v) national security would be put at risk.

(3) At any hearing of an application to which this rule applies—
(a) the court must first determine the application to withhold information, in the respondent's absence and that of any legal representative of the respondent;
(b) if the court allows the application to withhold information, then in the following sequence—
(i) the court must consider representations first by the applicant and then by the respondent, in the presence of both, and
(ii) the court may consider further representations by the applicant in the respondent's absence and that of any legal representative of the respondent.

(4) If the court refuses an application to withhold information from the respondent, the applicant may withdraw the application to extend the moratorium period.

Section 11: Orders for Access to Electronic Data under the Crime (Overseas Production Orders) Act 2019

R-576 When this Section applies

47.66 (1) This Section applies where the Crown Court can make an overseas production order under section 1 of the Crime (Overseas Production Orders) Act 2019.

(2) In this Section, a reference to a person affected by such an order includes a person by whom or on whose behalf there is stored any journalistic data specified or described in the application for that order.

R-577 Exercise of court's powers

47.67 (1) Subject to paragraphs (2), (3) and (4), the court may determine an application under rule 47.68 for an overseas production order, or an application under rule 47.69 to vary or revoke an order—
(a) at a hearing (which must be in private unless the court otherwise directs), or without a hearing; and
(b) in the absence of—
(i) the applicant,
(ii) the respondent,
(iii) any other person affected by the order.

(2) The court must not determine such an application in the applicant's absence if—
(a) the applicant asks for a hearing; or
(b) it appears to the court that—
(i) the proposed order may require the production of excepted electronic data, within the meaning of section 3 of the Crime (Overseas Production Orders) Act 2019, or
(ii) for any other reason the application is so complex or serious as to require the court to hear the applicant.

(3) The court must not determine such an application in the absence of any respondent or other person affected unless—
(a) the absentee has had at least 2 business days in which to make representations; or
(b) the court is satisfied that—
(i) the applicant cannot identify or contact the absentee,
(ii) it would prejudice the investigation if the absentee were present,
(iii) where journalistic data is sought, it would prejudice the investigation of another indictable offence or another terrorist investigation if the absentee were present,
(iv) it would prejudice the investigation to adjourn or postpone the application so as to allow the absentee to attend, or
(v) the absentee has waived the opportunity to attend.

(4) The court must not determine such an application in the absence of any respondent who, if the order sought by the applicant were made, would be required to produce or give access to journalistic data, unless that respondent has waived the opportunity to attend.

(5) The court officer must arrange for the court to hear such an application no sooner than 2 business days after notice of the application was served, unless—
(a) the court directs that no hearing need be arranged; or
(b) the court gives other directions for the hearing.

(6) The court must not determine an application unless satisfied that sufficient time has been allowed for it.

(7) If the court so directs, the parties to an application may attend a hearing by live link or telephone.

(8) The court must not make, vary or revoke an order unless the applicant states, in writing or orally, that to the best of the applicant's knowledge and belief—
(a) the application discloses all the information that is material to what the court must decide; and
(b) the content of the application is true.

(9) Where the statement required by paragraph (8) is made orally—
(a) the statement must be on oath or affirmation, unless the court otherwise directs; and
(b) the court must arrange for a record of the making of the statement.

(10) The court may—
(a) shorten or extend (even after it has expired) a time limit under this Section;
(b) dispense with a requirement for service under this Section (even after service was required); and
(c) consider an application made orally instead of in writing.

(11) A person who wants an extension of time must—
(a) apply when serving the application for which it is needed; and
(b) explain the delay.

Application for order R-578

47.68 (1) An applicant who wants the court to make an overseas production order must—
(a) apply in writing and serve the application on the court officer;
(b) demonstrate that the applicant is entitled to apply;
(c) give the court an estimate of how long the court should allow—
(i) to read the application and prepare for any hearing, and
(ii) for any hearing of the application;
(d) attach a draft order in the terms proposed by the applicant;
(e) serve notice of the application on the respondent and on any other person affected by the order, unless the court otherwise directs;
(f) serve the application on the respondent and on any such other person to such extent, if any, as the court directs.

(2) A notice served on the respondent and on any other person affected by the order must—
(a) specify or describe the electronic data in respect of which the application is made; and
(b) identify—
(i) the power that the applicant invites the court to exercise, and
(ii) the conditions for the exercise of that power which the applicant asks the court to find are met.

(3) The application must—
(a) specify the designated international co-operation arrangement by reference to which the application is made;
(b) identify the respondent;
(c) explain the grounds for believing that the respondent operates in, or is based in, a country or territory outside the United Kingdom which is a party to, or participates in, that designated international co-operation arrangement;
(d) specify or describe the electronic data in respect of which the order is sought;
(e) explain the grounds for believing that the electronic data sought does not consist of or include excepted electronic data;
(f) briefly describe the investigation for the purposes of which the electronic data is sought and explain—
(i) the grounds for believing that an indictable offence has been committed which is under investigation or in respect of which proceedings have begun, or
(ii) how the investigation constitutes a terrorist investigation within the meaning of the Terrorism Act 2000;
(g) explain the grounds for believing that the respondent has possession or control of all or part of the electronic data sought;
(h) explain the grounds for believing that the electronic data sought is likely to be of substantial value to the investigation, or to the proceedings (as the case may be), whether by itself or together with other material;
(i) where paragraph (3)(f)(i) applies, explain the grounds for believing that all or part of the electronic data sought is likely to be relevant evidence in respect of the offence concerned;

(j) explain the grounds for believing that it is in the public interest for the respondent to produce or give access to the electronic data sought, having regard to—
  (i) the benefit likely to accrue to the investigation, or to the proceedings (as the case may be), if that data is obtained, and
  (ii) the circumstances under which the respondent has possession or control of any of that data;
(k) specify—
  (i) the person, or the description of person, to whom the applicant wants the court to order that electronic data must be produced or made accessible, and
  (ii) the period by the end of which the applicant wants the court to order that that electronic data must be produced or made accessible (which must be a period of 7 days beginning with the day on which the order is served on the respondent, unless the court otherwise directs); and
(l) where the applicant wants the court to include a non-disclosure requirement in the order—
  (i) explain why such a requirement would be appropriate, and
  (ii) specify or describe when the applicant wants that requirement, if ordered, to expire.

(4) In the event that an overseas production order is made, the applicant must serve the order on the Secretary of State for service on the respondent.

(5) Where notice of the application was served on a respondent, in the event that the application is dismissed or abandoned the applicant must—
(a) promptly so notify that respondent; and
(b) where the application is dismissed, promptly inform that respondent if the court nonetheless orders that for a period that respondent must not—
  (i) conceal, destroy, alter or dispose of any of the electronic data specified or described in the application, or
  (ii) disclose the making of the application or its contents to any person.

R-579 **Application to vary or revoke an order**

47.69 (1) The orders to which this rule applies are—
(a) an overseas production order;
(b) an order under section 8(4) of the Crime (Overseas Production Orders) Act 2019 maintaining an unexpired non-disclosure requirement;
(c) an order under section 13(3) of the 2019 Act maintaining a duty not to conceal, destroy, alter or dispose of electronic data, and not to disclose the making or content of an application for an overseas production order;
(d) an order under section 13(4)(b) of the Act maintaining a duty not to conceal, destroy, alter or dispose of electronic data.

(2) This rule applies where one of the following wants the court to vary, to further vary or to revoke an order listed in paragraph (1)—
(a) the applicant for that order, or an equivalent appropriate officer;
(b) the respondent;
(c) another person affected by the order; or
(d) the Secretary of State.

(3) The applicant for the variation or revocation must—
(a) apply in writing as soon as practicable after becoming aware of the grounds for doing so;
(b) serve the application on—
  (i) the court officer, and
  (ii) as applicable, the applicant for the order, the respondent, any other person known to be affected and the Secretary of State; and
(c) ask for a hearing, if one is wanted, and explain why it is needed.

(4) Where the applicant wants the court to vary, or further vary, an overseas production order, the application must—
(a) specify or describe the electronic data in respect of which the varied order is sought (which may include electronic data not specified or described in the original order);
(b) satisfy or, as the case may be, continue to satisfy, the requirements of rule 47.68(3)(a) and (c) to (i) (which may be done by reference to the original application); and
(c) meet the requirements of rule 47.68(3)(j).

(5) Where the applicant wants the court to revoke an overseas production order, the application must—
(a) explain why revocation is appropriate;
(b) if the applicant wants the court, despite revocation, to maintain the requirement that for a period the respondent must not conceal, destroy, alter or dispose of any of the electronic data specified or described in the order—
(i) explain why it would be appropriate to maintain that requirement, and
(ii) specify or describe when the applicant wants that requirement, if maintained, to expire; and
(c) if the order includes an unexpired non-disclosure requirement that the applicant wants the court, despite revocation, to maintain—
(i) explain why it would be appropriate to maintain that requirement, and
(ii) specify or describe when the applicant wants that requirement, if maintained, to expire.
(6) Where the applicant wants the court to vary, to further vary or to revoke an order under section 8(4), section 13(3) or section 13(4)(b) of the 2019 Act the application must—
(a) explain—
(i) what material circumstances have changed since the order was made, and
(ii) why the order should be varied or revoked, as the case may be, as a result; and
(b) if applicable, specify the variation proposed.

Application containing information withheld from a respondent or other person **R-580**

47.70 (1) This rule applies where an application under rule 47.68 or 47.69 includes information that the applicant thinks ought to be revealed only to the court.
(2) The application must—
(a) identify that information; and
(b) explain why that information ought not to be served on the respondent or another person.
(3) At a hearing of an application to which this rule applies—
(a) the general rule is that the court must consider, in the following sequence—
(i) representations first by the applicant and then by the respondent and any other person, in the presence of them all, and then
(ii) further representations by the applicant, in the others' absence; but
(b) the court may direct other arrangements for the hearing.

Application to punish for contempt of court **R-581**

47.71 (1) This rule applies where a person is accused of disobeying an order made by the court under the Crime (Overseas Production Orders) Act 2019.
(2) An applicant who wants the court to exercise its power to punish that person for contempt of court must comply with the rules in Part 48 (Contempt of court).

Criminal Practice Directions Part 47 Investigation Orders and Warrants

CPD XI Other Proceedings 47A: Investigation Orders and Warrants **PD-101**

47A.1 Powers of entry, search and seizure, and powers to obtain banking and other confidential information, are among the most intrusive that investigators can exercise. Every application must be carefully scrutinised with close attention paid to what the relevant statutory provision requires of the applicant and to what it permits. CrimPR Part 47 must be followed, and the prescribed forms (retaining the Notes for Guidance section) must be used. These are designed to prompt applicants, and the courts, to deal with all of the relevant criteria.

47A.2 The issuing of a warrant or the making of such an order is never to be treated as a formality and it is therefore essential that the judge or magistrate considering the application is given, and must take, sufficient time for the purpose. The prescribed forms require the applicant to provide a time estimate, and listing officers and justices' legal advisers should take account of these.

47A.3 Applicants for orders and warrants owe the court duties of candour and truthfulness. On any application made without notice to the respondent, and so on all applications for search warrants, the duty of frank and complete disclosure is especially onerous. The applicant must draw the court's attention to any information that is unfavourable to the application. The existence of unfavourable information will not necessarily lead to the application being refused; it will be a matter for the court what weight to place on each piece of information. As Hughes LJ made clear in *Re Stanford International Limited*[2] 'In effect a prosecutor seeking an *ex parte* order must put on his defence hat and ask himself what, if he was representing the defendant or a third party with a relevant interest, he would be saying to the judge, and, having answered that question, that is what he must tell the judge'. This is, as Aitkins LJ recognised, 'a heavy burden but a vital safeguard. Full details must be given[3].'

47A.4 Where an applicant supplements an application with additional oral or written information, on questioning by the court or otherwise, it is essential that the court keeps an adequate record. What is needed will depend upon the circumstances. The Rules require that a record of the 'gist' be retained. The purpose of such a record is to allow the sufficiency of the court's reasons for its decision subsequently to be assessed. The gravity of such decisions requires that their exercise should be susceptible to scrutiny and to explanation by reference to all of the information that was taken into account.

47A.5 The forms that accompany CrimPR Part 47 provide for the most frequently encountered applications. The included Notes for Guidance summarise for the applicant and the court the relevant criteria for making and considering an application. However, there are some hundreds of powers of entry, search and seizure, supplied by a corresponding number of legislative provisions. In any criminal matter, if there is no form designed for the particular warrant or order sought, the forms should still be used, as far as is practicable, and adapted as necessary. The applicant should pay particular attention to the specific legislative requirements for the granting of such an application to ensure that the court has all of the necessary information, and, if the court might be unfamiliar with the legislation, should provide a copy of the relevant provisions. Applicants must comply with the duties of candour and truthfulness, and include in their application the declarations required by the Rules and must make disclosure of any unfavourable information to the court.

PD-102 CPD XI Other Proceedings 47B: Investigation Orders and Warrants in the Crown Court

47B.1 This section covers applications made under:
(i) Schedule 1 Police and Criminal Evidence Act 1984 (PACE);
(ii) Section 2 Criminal Justice Act 1987;
(iii) Drug Trafficking Act 1994;
(iv) Part 8 of the Proceeds of Crime Act 2002;
(v) Section 5 Coroners and Justice Act 2009;
(vi) Terrorism Act 2000.
It does NOT cover applications under the Extradition Act 2003.

Crown Court Centres

47B.2 Investigators must give careful consideration to which Crown Court centre is most appropriate to hear the application. In all cases, the application must explain the rationale for choosing the particular court centre. Relevant considerations will usually be:
(i) where any subsequent proceedings are likely to be commenced;
(ii) where a main suspect has some geographical connection; and/or
(iii) where, in broad terms, the offending has taken place.
A court centre should not be chosen simply because it is most convenient or proximate to the investigator's location. Any dispute over the proper venue for an application should be determined by the relevant Presiding Judges.

47B.3 Where the investigation is complex, lengthy and/or involves multiple suspects all applications should be made to one court centre. To ensure consistency, all subsequent applications arising out of the same or any connected investigation should be made to the same court centre and, where practicable, the same judge.

47B.4 Judges can refuse to determine applications and request they be resubmitted (if necessary to another court) where:
(i) the application is not in the proper form;
(ii) there is an inaccurate reading time estimate; and/or
(iii) there is insufficient justification for the application to be made at that court centre.

[2] [2010] EWCA Civ 137 at para 159.
[3] *R (On the Application of S, F and L) v Chief Constable of the British Transport Police and Southwark Crown Court* [2013] EWHC 2189 (Admin) at [45 (d)].

Dealing with applications without a hearing

47B.5 The court must not determine an application in the applicant's absence in the circumstances set out in CrimPR 47.5(2); or in the absence of any respondent in the circumstances set out in CrimPR 47.5(3) and (4).

47B.6 When permitted by the rules, and where the application has been sufficiently completed and submitted on the correct form, there is a presumption that the application will be dealt with without a hearing. The judge is always entitled to require a hearing to clarify omissions or ambiguity on the application, or for any other reason.

47B.7 It will often not be appropriate for a court to deal with an application without a hearing in the following situations:

(i) where the investigation involved covert activity or the application is based on material gathered covertly;

(ii) where the application is based on material which is especially sensitive and/or where it will be necessary to ensure the security at court of the material produced in support of the application;

(iii) where the case may result in substantial local and/or national public interest;

(iv) where the application is particularly lengthy, serious or complex.

47B.8 Applications should be sent electronically to the designated secure email address at the relevant court centre.

47B.9 A judge considering an application without a hearing will subject the application to the usual intense level of scrutiny ensuring that the relevant statutory requirements have been met. If the judge is not so satisfied then the judge will refuse the application, require further information to be served or adjourn it for a hearing in court, which can be carried out via live link or telephone, where permitted by the Rules. The Court will inform the applicant of the outcome and make the necessary arrangements for any additional hearings that may be required. There is no requirement for any order to be signed by the judge with a 'wet ink' signature. The applicant will be notified electronically of any orders that are made.

47B.10 Applications considered without a hearing will be determined by a judge as soon as practicable. Approved orders will be returned electronically to the applicant and an electronic copy must be securely saved by the court. If there is a particular urgency with any application, that fact should be made clear to the court when it is served and the judge should expedite it where possible.

Listing

47B.11 To assist the listing process, the applicant must supply a realistic estimate of the reading time required when the application is served. This estimate should be provided in the application and in the covering email to which it is attached. The covering email should also stipulate whether there have been any previous applications in the same or any connected investigation and provide the name of the judge who granted any previous Orders.

47B.12 Where the judge has decided that a hearing is required to determine or further consider the application, the expectation is that this hearing should usually take place by live link or telephone.[4] Where the judge directs a hearing at court, any additional material relied on by the applicant must be brought to court on the day of the hearing. Any additional material should not be retained by the court once the application has been determined, but must be taken away by the applicant at the end of the hearing.[5]

47B.13 When listing such hearings consideration should be given to Division XIII Listing of these practice directions which states at A.1 that listing is a judicial responsibility and function. G.3(1) of that division envisages that such applications will be completed by 10.30am or start after 4.30pm so as not to interfere with trials. This general direction does not prevent a judge from considering applications outside of these times where other court business allows.

47B.14 However, as paragraph G.8 of Division XIII Listing makes clear, along with the relevant case law, that the search powers in PACE constitute 'a serious inroad upon the liberty of the subject. The responsibility for ensuring that the procedure is not abused lies with circuit judges. It is of cardinal importance that circuit judges should be scrupulous in discharging that responsibility.'[6] Accordingly, there must be adequate time allowed for the judge to read care-

[4] Although the court cannot receive evidence by telephone, information in support of the application can be given on oath by this means.

[5] Generally, there are no secure storage at facilities at court centres where sensitive material can be safely left.

[6] *per* Lloyd LJ *R v Maidstone Crown Court, ex p Waitt* [1988] Crim LR 384.

fully the application and all the supporting evidence supplied with it. The judge will require sufficient time to enable a short judgment to be given, where necessary so that in the event of challenge in the Administrative Court there is an explanation of the reasons for the decision for that court to consider.

DARTS Recording

47B.15 Hearings in court are required to be recorded whether on DARTS or some other secure method such as on a hand-held machine. Determination of the method of recording is a matter for the judge.

Criminal Procedure Rules Part 47A Investigation Orders and Warrants*

* [Editorial note: This Part only applies in the event that the Criminal Procedure (Amendment) (EU Exit) Regulations 2019 come into force before 7 October 2019. Otherwise, Part 47 applies and Part 47A should be ignored.]

Section 1: General Rules

R-511A **When this Part applies**

47.1 This Part applies to the exercise of the powers listed in each of rules 47.4, 47.24, 47.35, 47.42, 47.46, 47.51, 47.54, 47.59, and 47,63.

R-512A **Meaning of 'court', 'applicant' and 'respondent'**

47.2 In this Part—

(a) a reference to the 'court' includes a reference to any justice of the peace or judge who can exercise a power to which this Part applies;
(b) 'applicant' means a person who, or an authority which, can apply for an order or warrant to which this Part applies; and
(c) 'respondent' means any person—
(i) against whom such an order is sought or made, or
(ii) on whom an application for such an order is served.

R-513A **Documents served on the court officer**

47.3 (1) Unless the court otherwise directs, the court officer may—
(a) keep a written application; or
(b) arrange for the whole or any part to be kept by some other appropriate person, subject to any conditions that the court may impose.
(2) Where the court makes an order when the court office is closed, the applicant must, not more than 72 hours later, serve on the court officer—
(a) a copy of the order; and
(b) any written material that was submitted to the court.
(3) Where the court issues a warrant—
(a) the applicant must return it to the court officer as soon as practicable after it has been executed, and in any event not more than 3 months after it was issued (unless other legislation otherwise provides); and
(b) the court officer must—
(i) keep the warrant for 12 months after its return, and
(ii) during that period, make it available for inspection by the occupier of the premises to which it relates, if that occupier asks to inspect it.

Section 2: Investigation Orders

R-514A **When this Section applies**

47.4 This Section applies where—

(a) a Circuit judge can make, vary or discharge an order for the production of, or for giving access to, material under paragraph 4 of Schedule 1 to the Police and Criminal Evidence Act 1984, other than material that consists of or includes journalistic material;
(b) for the purposes of a terrorist investigation, a Circuit judge can make, vary or discharge—
(i) an order for the production of, or for giving access to, material, or for a statement of its location, under paragraphs 5 and 10 of Schedule 5 to the Terrorism Act 2000,
(ii) an explanation order, under paragraphs 10 and 13 of Schedule 5 to the 2000 Act,
(iii) a customer information order, under paragraphs 1 and 4 of Schedule 6 to the 2000 Act;

(c) for the purposes of—
   (i) a terrorist investigation, a Circuit judge can make, and the Crown Court can vary or discharge, an account monitoring order, under paragraphs 2 and 4 of Schedule 6A to the 2000 Act,
   (ii) a terrorist financing investigation, a judge entitled to exercise the jurisdiction of the Crown Court can make, and the Crown Court can vary or discharge, a disclosure order, under paragraphs 9 and 14 of Schedule 5A to the 2000 Act;
(d) for the purposes of an investigation to which Part 8 of the Proceeds of Crime Act 2002 or the Proceeds of Crime Act 2002 (External Investigations) Order 2014 applies, a Crown Court judge can make, and the Crown Court can vary or discharge—
   (i) a production order, under sections 345 and 351 of the 2002 Act or under articles 6 and 12 of the 2014 Order,
   (ii) an order to grant entry, under sections 347 and 351 of the 2002 Act or under articles 8 and 12 of the 2014 Order,
   (iii) a disclosure order, under sections 357 and 362 of the 2002 Act or under articles 16 and 21 of the 2014 Order,
   (iv) a customer information order, under sections 363 and 369 of the 2002 Act or under articles 22 and 28 of the 2014 Order,
   (v) an account monitoring order, under sections 370, 373 and 375 of the 2002 Act or under articles 29, 32 and 34 of the 2014 Order;
(e) in connection with an extradition request, a Circuit judge can make an order for the production of, or for giving access to, material under section 157 of the Extradition Act 2003.
(f) a magistrates' court can make a further information order under section 22B of the Terrorism Act 2000(a) in connection with—
   (i) an investigation into whether a person is involved in the commission of an offence under any of sections 15 to 18 of the 2000 Act
   (ii) determining whether such an investigation should be started, or
   (iii) identifying terrorist property or its movement or use;
(g) a magistrates' court can make a further information order under section 339ZH of the Proceeds of Crime Act 2002(c) in connection with—
   (i) an investigation into whether a person is engaged in money laundering,
   (ii) determining whether such an investigation should be started, or
   (iii) an investigation into money laundering by an authority in a country outside the United Kingdom.

Exercise of court's powers **R-515A**

47.5 (1) Subject to paragraphs (2), (3) and (4), the court may determine an application for an order, or to vary or discharge an order—
   (a) at a hearing (which must be in private unless the court otherwise directs), or without a hearing; and
   (b) in the absence of—
      (i) the applicant,
      (ii) the respondent (if any),
      (iii) any other person affected by the order.
(2) The court must not determine such an application in the applicant's absence if—
   (a) the applicant asks for a hearing; or
   (b) it appears to the court that—
      (i) the proposed order may infringe legal privilege, within the meaning of section 10 of the Police and Criminal Evidence Act 1984, section 348 or 361 of the Proceeds of Crime Act 2002 or article 9 of the Proceeds of Crime Act 2002 (External Investigations) Order 2014,
      (ii) the proposed order may require the production of excluded material, within the meaning of section 11 of the 1984 Act, or
      (iii) for any other reason the application is so complex or serious as to require the court to hear the applicant.
(3) The court must not determine such an application in the absence of any respondent or other person affected, unless—
   (a) the absentee has had at least 2 business days in which to make representations; or
   (b) the court is satisfied that—
      (i) the applicant cannot identify or contact the absentee,
      (ii) it would prejudice the investigation if the absentee were present,

(iii) it would prejudice the investigation to adjourn or postpone the application so as to allow the absentee to attend, or

(iv) the absentee has waived the opportunity to attend.

(4) The court must not determine such an application in the absence of any respondent who, if the order sought by the applicant were made, would be required to produce or give access to journalistic material, unless that respondent has waived the opportunity to attend.

(5) The court officer must arrange for the court to hear such an application no sooner than 2 business days after it was served, unless—

(a) the court directs that no hearing need be arranged; or

(b) the court gives other directions for the hearing.

(6) The court must not determine an application unless satisfied that sufficient time has been allowed for it.

(7) If the court so directs, the parties to an application may attend a hearing by live link or telephone.

(8) The court must not make, vary or discharge an order unless the applicant states, in writing or orally, that to the best of the applicant's knowledge and belief—

(a) the application discloses all the information that is material to what the court must decide; and

(b) the content of the application is true.

(9) Where the statement required by paragraph (8) is made orally—

(a) the statement must be on oath or affirmation, unless the court otherwise directs; and

(b) the court must arrange for a record of the making of the statement.

(10) The court may—

(a) shorten or extend (even after it has expired) a time limit under this Section;

(b) dispense with a requirement for service under this Section (even after service was required); and

(c) consider an application made orally instead of in writing.

(11) A person who wants an extension of time must—

(a) apply when serving the application for which it is needed; and

(b) explain the delay.

R-516A Application for order: general rules

47.6 (1) This rule applies to each application for an order to which this Section applies.

(2) The applicant must—

(a) apply in writing and serve the application on the court officer;

(b) demonstrate that the applicant is entitled to apply, for example as a constable or under legislation that applies to other officers;

(c) give the court an estimate of how long the court should allow—

(i) to read the application and prepare for any hearing, and

(ii) for any hearing of the application;

(d) attach a draft order in the terms proposed by the applicant;

(e) serve notice of the application on the respondent, unless the court otherwise directs;

(f) serve the application on the respondent to such extent, if any, as the court directs.

(3) A notice served on the respondent must—

(a) specify the material or information in respect of which the application is made; and

(b) identify—

(i) the power that the applicant invites the court to exercise, and

(ii) the conditions for the exercise of that power which the applicant asks the court to find are met.

(4) The applicant must serve any order made on the respondent.

R-517A Application containing information withheld from a respondent or other person

47.7 (1) This rule applies where an application includes information that the applicant thinks ought to be revealed only to the court.

(2) The application must—

(a) identify that information; and

(b) explain why that information ought not to be served on the respondent or another person.

(3) At a hearing of an application to which this rule applies—

(a) the general rule is that the court must consider, in the following sequence—

(i) representations first by the applicant and then by the respondent and any other person, in the presence of them all, and then

(ii) further representations by the applicant, in the others' absence; but

(b) the court may direct other arrangements for the hearing.

Application to vary or discharge an order R-518A

47.8 (1) This rule applies where one of the following wants the court to vary or discharge an order to which a rule in this Section refers—
(a) an applicant;
(b) the respondent; or
(c) a person affected by the order.
(2) That applicant, respondent or person affected must—
(a) apply in writing as soon as practicable after becoming aware of the grounds for doing so;
(b) serve the application on—
(i) the court officer, and
(ii) the respondent, applicant, or any person known to be affected, as applicable;
(c) explain why it is appropriate for the order to be varied or discharged;
(d) propose the terms of any variation; and
(e) ask for a hearing, if one is wanted, and explain why it is needed.

Application to punish for contempt of court R-519A

47.9 (1) This rule applies where a person is accused of disobeying—
(a) a production order made under paragraph 4 of Schedule 1 to the Police and Criminal Evidence Act 1984;
(b) a production etc. order made under paragraph 5 of Schedule 5 to the Terrorism Act 2000;
(c) an explanation order made under paragraph 13 of that Schedule;
(d) an account monitoring order made under paragraph 2 of Schedule 6A to that Act;
(e) a production order made under section 345 of the Proceeds of Crime Act 2002 or article 6 of the Proceeds of Crime Act 2002 (External Investigations) Order 2014;
(f) an account monitoring order made under section 370 of the 2002 Act or article 29 of the 2014 Order; or
(g) a production order made under section 157 of the Extradition Act 2003.
(2) An applicant who wants the court to exercise its power to punish that person for contempt of court must comply with the rules in Part 48 (Contempt of court).

Orders under the Police and Criminal Evidence Act 1984

Application for a production order under the Police and Criminal Evidence Act 1984 R-520A

47.10 (1) This rule applies where an applicant wants the court to make an order to which rule 47.4(a) refers.
(2) As well as complying with rule 47.6 (Application for order: general rules), the application must, in every case—
(a) specify the offence under investigation (and see paragraph (3)(a));
(b) describe the material sought;
(c) identify the respondent;
(d) specify the premises on which the material is believed to be, or explain why it is not reasonably practicable to do so;
(e) explain the grounds for believing that the material is on the premises specified, or (if applicable) on unspecified premises of the respondent;
(f) specify the set of access conditions on which the applicant relies (and see paragraphs (3) and (4)); and
(g) propose—
(i) the terms of the order, and
(ii) the period within which it should take effect.
(3) Where the applicant relies on paragraph 2 of Schedule 1 to the Police and Criminal Evidence Act 1984 ('the first set of access conditions': general power to gain access to special procedure material), the application must—
(a) specify the indictable offence under investigation;
(b) explain the grounds for believing that the offence has been committed;
(c) explain the grounds for believing that the material sought—
(i) is likely to be of substantial value to the investigation (whether by itself, or together with other material),
(ii) is likely to be admissible evidence at trial for the offence under investigation, and
(iii) does not consist of or include items subject to legal privilege or excluded material;
(d) explain what other methods of obtaining the material—
(i) have been tried without success, or
(ii) have not been tried because they appeared bound to fail; and

(e) explain why it is in the public interest for the respondent to produce the material, having regard to—
(i) the benefit likely to accrue to the investigation if the material is obtained, and
(ii) the circumstances under which the respondent holds the material.

(4) Where the applicant relies on paragraph 3 of Schedule 1 to the Police and Criminal Evidence Act 1984 ('the second set of access conditions': use of search warrant power to gain access to excluded or special procedure material), the application must—
(a) state the legislation under which a search warrant could have been issued, had the material sought not been excluded or special procedure material (in this paragraph, described as 'the main search power');
(b) include or attach the terms of the main search power;
(c) explain how the circumstances would have satisfied any criteria prescribed by the main search power for the issue of a search warrant; and
(d) explain why the issue of such a search warrant would have been appropriate.

Orders under the Terrorism Act 2000

R-521A **Application for an order under the Terrorism Act 2000**

47.11 (1) This rule applies where an applicant wants the court to make one of the orders to which rule 47.4(b) and (c) refers.

(2) As well as complying with rule 47.6 (Application for order: general rules), the application must—
(a) specify the offence under investigation;
(b) explain how the investigation constitutes a terrorist investigation or terrorist financing investigation, as appropriate, within the meaning of the Terrorism Act 2000;
(c) identify the respondent; and
(d) give the information required by whichever of rules 47.12 to 47.16 applies.

R-522A **Content of application for a production etc. order under the Terrorism Act 2000**

47.12 (1) As well as complying with rules 47.6 and 47.11, an applicant who wants the court to make an order for the production of, or for giving access to, material, or for a statement of its location, must—
(a) describe that material;
(b) explain why the applicant thinks the material is—
(i) in the respondent's possession, custody or power, or
(ii) expected to come into existence and then to be in the respondent's possession, custody or power within 28 days of the order;
(c) explain how the material constitutes or contains excluded material or special procedure material;
(d) confirm that none of the material is expected to be subject to legal privilege;
(e) explain why the material is likely to be of substantial value to the investigation;
(f) explain why it is in the public interest for the material to be produced, or for the applicant to be given access to it, having regard to—
(i) the benefit likely to accrue to the investigation if it is obtained, and
(ii) the circumstances in which the respondent has the material, or is expected to have it; and
(g) propose—
(i) the terms of the order, and
(ii) the period within which it should take effect.

(2) An applicant who wants the court to make an order to grant entry in aid of a production order must—
(a) specify the premises to which entry is sought;
(b) explain why the order is needed; and
(c) propose the terms of the order.

R-523A **Content of application for a disclosure order or further information order under the Terrorism Act 2000**

47.13 (1) As well as complying with rules 47.6 and 47.11, an applicant who wants the court to make a disclosure order must—
(a) explain why the applicant thinks that—
(i) a person has committed an offence under any of sections 15 to 18 of the Terrorism Act 2000, or
(ii) property described in the application is terrorist property within the meaning of section 14 of the 2000 Act;

(b) describe in general terms the information that the applicant wants the respondent to provide;
(c) confirm that none of the information is—
(i) expected to be subject to legal privilege, or
(ii) excluded material;
(d) explain why the information is likely to be of substantial value to the investigation;
(e) explain why it is in the public interest for the information to be provided, having regard to the benefit likely to accrue to the investigation if it is obtained; and
(f) propose the terms of the order.

(2) As well as complying with rule 47.6, an applicant who wants the court to make a further information order must—
(a) identify the respondent from whom the information is sought and explain—
(i) whether the respondent is the person who made the disclosure to which the information relates or is otherwise carrying on a business in the regulated sector within the meaning of Part 1 of Schedule 3A to the 2000 Act, and
(ii) why the applicant thinks that the information is in the possession, or under the control, of the respondent;
(b) specify or describe the information that the applicant wants the respondent to provide;
(c) where the information sought relates to a disclosure of information by someone under section 21A of the 2000 Act (Failure to disclose: regulated sector), explain—
(i) how the information sought relates to a matter arising from that disclosure,
(ii) how the information would assist in investigating whether a person is involved in the commission of an offence under any of sections 15 to 18 of that Act, or in determining whether an investigation of that kind should be started, or in identifying terrorist property or its movement or use, and
(iii) why it is reasonable in all the circumstances for the information to be provided;
(d) where the information sought relates to a disclosure made under a requirement of the law of a country outside the United Kingdom which corresponds with Part III of the 2000 Act (Terrorist property), and an authority in that country which investigates offences corresponding with sections 15 to 18 of that Act has asked the National Crime Agency for information in connection with that disclosure, explain—
(i) how the information sought relates to a matter arising from that disclosure,
(ii) why the information is likely to be of substantial value to the authority that made the request in determining any matter in connection with the disclosure, and
(iii) why it is reasonable in all the circumstances for the information to be provided;
(e) confirm that none of the information is expected to be subject to legal privilege; and
(f) propose the terms of the order, including—
(i) how the respondent must provide the information required, and
(ii) the date by which the information must be provided.

(3) Rule 47.8 (Application to vary or discharge an order) does not apply to a further information order.
(4) Paragraph (5) applies where a party to an application for a further information order wants to appeal to the Crown Court from the decision of the magistrates' court.
(5) The appellant must—
(a) serve an appeal notice—
(i) on the Crown Court officer and on the other party,
(ii) not more than 21 days after the magistrates' court's decision; and
(b) in the appeal notice, explain, as appropriate, why the Crown Court should (as the case may be) make, discharge or vary a further information order.
(6) Rule 34.11 (Constitution of the Crown Court) applies on such an appeal.

Content of application for an explanation order under the Terrorism Act 2000 **R-524A**

47.14 As well as complying with rules 47.6 and 47.11, an applicant who wants the court to make an explanation order must—
(a) identify the material that the applicant wants the respondent to explain;
(b) confirm that the explanation is not expected to infringe legal privilege; and
(c) propose the terms of the order.

Content of application for a customer information order under the Terrorism Act 2000 **R-525A**

47.15 As well as complying with rules 47.6 and 47.11, an applicant who wants the court to make a customer information order must—
(a) explain why it is desirable for the purposes of the investigation to trace property said to be terrorist property within the meaning of the Terrorism Act 2000;

(b) explain why the order will enhance the effectiveness of the investigation; and
(c) propose the terms of the order.

R-526A **Content of application for an account monitoring order under the Terrorism Act 2000**

47.16 As well as complying with rules 47.6 and 47.11, an applicant who wants the court to make an account monitoring order must—
(a) specify—
(i) the information sought,
(ii) the period during which the applicant wants the respondent to provide that information (to a maximum of 90 days), and
(iii) where, when and in what manner the applicant wants the respondent to provide that information;
(b) explain why it is desirable for the purposes of the investigation to trace property said to be terrorist property within the meaning of the Terrorism Act 2000;
(c) explain why the order will enhance the effectiveness of the investigation; and
(d) propose the terms of the order.

Orders under the Proceeds of Crime Act 2002

R-527A **Application for an order under the Proceeds of Crime Act 2002**

47.17 (1) This rule applies where an applicant wants the court to make one of the orders to which rule 47.4(d) refers.
(2) As well as complying with rule 47.6 (Application for order: general rules), the application must—
(a) identify—
(i) the respondent, and
(ii) the person or property the subject of the investigation;
(b) in the case of an investigation in the United Kingdom, explain why the applicant thinks that—
(i) the person under investigation has benefited from criminal conduct, in the case of a confiscation investigation, or committed a money laundering offence, in the case of a money laundering investigation, or
(ii) in the case of a detained cash investigation, a detained property investigation or a frozen funds investigation, the cash or property involved, or the money held in the frozen account, was obtained through unlawful conduct or is intended to be used in unlawful conduct;
(c) in the case of an investigation outside the United Kingdom, explain why the applicant thinks that—
(i) there is an investigation by an overseas authority which relates to a criminal investigation or to criminal proceedings (including proceedings to remove the benefit of a person's criminal conduct following that person's conviction), and
(ii) the investigation is into whether property has been obtained as a result of or in connection with criminal conduct, or into the extent or whereabouts of such property;
(d) give the additional information required by whichever of rules 47.18 to 47.22 applies.

R-528A **Content of application for a production order under the Proceeds of Crime Act 2002**

47.18 As well as complying with rules 47.6 and 47.17, an applicant who wants the court to make an order for the production of, or for giving access to, material, must—
(a) describe that material;
(b) explain why the applicant thinks the material is in the respondent's possession or control;
(c) confirm that none of the material is—
(i) expected to be subject to legal privilege, or
(ii) excluded material;
(d) explain why the material is likely to be of substantial value to the investigation;
(e) explain why it is in the public interest for the material to be produced, or for the applicant to be given access to it, having regard to—
(i) the benefit likely to accrue to the investigation if it is obtained, and
(ii) the circumstances in which the respondent has the material; and
(f) propose—
(i) the terms of the order, and
(ii) the period within which it should take effect, if 7 days from the date of the order would not be appropriate.

Content of application for an order to grant entry under the Proceeds of Crime Act 2002 R-529A

47.19 An applicant who wants the court to make an order to grant entry in aid of a production order must—
(a) specify the premises to which entry is sought;
(b) explain why the order is needed; and
(c) propose the terms of the order.

Content of application for a disclosure order or further information order under the Proceeds of Crime Act 2002 R-530A

47.20 (1) As well as complying with rules 47.6 and 47.17, an applicant who wants the court to make a disclosure order must—
(a) describe in general terms the information that the applicant wants the respondent to provide;
(b) confirm that none of the information is—
(i) expected to be subject to legal privilege, or
(ii) excluded material;
(c) explain why the information is likely to be of substantial value to the investigation;
(d) explain why it is in the public interest for the information to be provided, having regard to the benefit likely to accrue to the investigation if it is obtained; and
(e) propose the terms of the order.
(2) As well as complying with rule 47.6, an applicant who wants the court to make a further information order must—
(a) identify the respondent from whom the information is sought and explain—
(i) whether the respondent is the person who made the disclosure to which the information relates or is otherwise carrying on a business in the regulated sector within the meaning of Part 1 of Schedule 9 to the Proceeds of Crime Act 2002, and
(ii) why the applicant thinks that the information is in the possession, or under the control, of the respondent;
(b) specify or describe the information that the applicant wants the respondent to provide;
(c) where the information sought relates to a disclosure of information under Part 7 of the Proceeds of Crime Act 2002 (Money laundering), explain—
(i) how the information sought relates to a matter arising from that disclosure,
(ii) how the information would assist in investigating whether a person is engaged in money laundering or in determining whether an investigation of that kind should be started, and
(iii) why it is reasonable in all the circumstances for the information to be provided;
(d) where the information sought relates to a disclosure made under a requirement of the law of a country outside the United Kingdom which corresponds with Part 7 of the 2002 Act, and an authority in that country which investigates money laundering has asked the National Crime Agency for information in connection with that disclosure, explain—
(i) how the information sought relates to a matter arising from that disclosure,
(ii) why the information is likely to be of substantial value to the authority that made the request in determining any matter in connection with the disclosure, and
(iii) why it is reasonable in all the circumstances for the information to be provided;
(e) confirm that none of the information is expected to be subject to legal privilege; and
(f) propose the terms of the order, including—
(i) how the respondent must provide the information required, and
(ii) the date by which the information must be provided.
(3) Rule 47.8 (Application to vary or discharge an order) does not apply to a further information order.
(4) Paragraph (5) applies where a party to an application for a further information order wants to appeal to the Crown Court from the decision of the magistrates' court.
(5) The appellant must—
(a) serve an appeal notice—
(i) on the Crown Court officer and on the other party,
(ii) not more than 21 days after the magistrates' court's decision; and
(b) in the appeal notice, explain, as appropriate, why the Crown Court should (as the case may be) make, discharge or vary a further information order.
(6) Rule 34.11 (Constitution of the Crown Court) applies on such an appeal.

R-531A **Content of application for a customer information order under the Proceeds of Crime Act 2002**

47.21 As well as complying with rules 47.6 and 47.17, an applicant who wants the court to make a customer information order must—
(a) explain why customer information about the person under investigation is likely to be of substantial value to that investigation;
(b) explain why it is in the public interest for the information to be provided, having regard to the benefit likely to accrue to the investigation if it is obtained; and
(c) propose the terms of the order.

R-532A **Content of application for an account monitoring order under the Proceeds of Crime Act 2002**

47.22 As well as complying with rules 47.6 and 47.17, an applicant who wants the court to make an account monitoring order for the provision of account information must—
(a) specify—
(i) the information sought,
(ii) the period during which the applicant wants the respondent to provide that information (to a maximum of 90 days), and
(iii) when and in what manner the applicant wants the respondent to provide that information;
(b) explain why the information is likely to be of substantial value to the investigation;
(c) explain why it is in the public interest for the information to be provided, having regard to the benefit likely to accrue to the investigation if it is obtained; and
(d) propose the terms of the order.

Orders under the Extradition Act 2003

R-533A **Application for a production order under the Extradition Act 2003**

47.23 (1) This rule applies where an applicant wants the court to make an order to which rule 47.4(e) refers.
(2) As well as complying with rule 47.6 (Application for order: general rules), the application must—
(a) identify the person whose extradition is sought;
(b) specify the extradition offence of which that person is accused;
(c) identify the respondent; and
(d) describe the special procedure or excluded material sought.
(3) In relation to the person whose extradition is sought, the application must explain the grounds for believing that—
(a) that person has committed the offence for which extradition is sought;
(b) that offence is an extradition offence; and
(c) that person is in the United Kingdom or is on the way to the United Kingdom.
(4) In relation to the material sought, the application must—
(a) specify the premises on which the material is believed to be;
(b) explain the grounds for believing that—
(i) the material is on those premises,
(ii) the material consists of or includes special procedure or excluded material, and
(iii) the material would be likely to be admissible evidence at a trial in England and Wales for the offence for which extradition is sought;
(c) explain what other methods of obtaining the material—
(i) have been tried without success, or
(ii) have not been tried because they appeared bound to fail; and
(d) explain why it is in the public interest for the respondent to produce or give access to the material.
(5) The application must propose—
(a) the terms of the order, and
(b) the period within which it should take effect.

Section 3: Investigation Warrants

R-534A **When this Section applies**

47.24 This Section applies where—
(a) a justice of the peace can issue a warrant under—
(i) section 8 of the Police and Criminal Evidence Act 1984,
(ii) section 2 of the Criminal Justice Act 1987;

(b) a Circuit judge can issue a warrant under—
(i) paragraph 12 of Schedule 1 to the Police and Criminal Evidence Act 1984,
(ii) paragraph 11 of Schedule 5 to the Terrorism Act 2000,
(iii) section 160 of the Extradition Act 2003;
(c) a Crown Court judge can issue a warrant under—
(i) section 352 of the Proceeds of Crime Act 2002, or
(ii) article 13 of the Proceeds of Crime Act 2002 (External Investigations) Order 2014;
(d) a court to which these Rules apply can issue a warrant to search for and seize articles or persons under a power not listed in paragraphs (a), (b) or (c).

Exercise of court's powers **R-535A**

47.25 (1) The court must determine an application for a warrant—
(a) at a hearing, which must be in private unless the court otherwise directs;
(b) in the presence of the applicant; and
(c) in the absence of any person affected by the warrant, including any person in occupation or control of premises which the applicant wants to search.
(2) If the court so directs, the applicant may attend the hearing by live link or telephone.
(3) The court must not determine an application unless satisfied that sufficient time has been allowed for it.
(4) The court must not determine an application unless the applicant confirms, on oath or affirmation, that to the best of the applicant's knowledge and belief—
(a) the application discloses all the information that is material to what the court must decide, including any circumstances that might reasonably be considered capable of undermining any of the grounds of the application; and
(b) the content of the application is true.
(5) If the court requires the applicant to answer a question about an application—
(a) the applicant's answer must be on oath or affirmation;
(b) the court must arrange for a record of the gist of the question and reply; and
(c) if the applicant cannot answer to the court's satisfaction, the court may—
(i) specify the information the court requires, and
(ii) give directions for the presentation of any renewed application.
(6) Unless to do so would be inconsistent with other legislation, on an application the court may issue—
(a) a warrant in respect of specified premises;
(b) a warrant in respect of all premises occupied or controlled by a specified person;
(c) a warrant in respect of all premises occupied or controlled by a specified person which specifies some of those premises; or
(d) more than one warrant—
(i) each one in respect of premises specified in the warrant,
(ii) each one in respect of all premises occupied or controlled by a person specified in the warrant (whether or not such a warrant also specifies any of those premises), or
(iii) at least one in respect of specified premises and at least one in respect of all premises occupied or controlled by a specified person (whether or not such a warrant also specifies any of those premises).

Application for warrant: general rules **R-536A**

47.26 (1) This rule applies to each application to which this Section applies.
(2) The applicant must—
(a) apply in writing;
(b) serve the application on—
(i) the court officer, or
(ii) if the court office is closed, the court;
(c) demonstrate that the applicant is entitled to apply, for example as a constable or under legislation that applies to other officers;
(d) give the court an estimate of how long the court should allow—
(i) to read and prepare for the application, and
(ii) for the hearing of the application; and
(e) tell the court when the applicant expects any warrant issued to be executed.
(3) The application must disclose anything known or reported to the applicant that might reasonably be considered capable of undermining any of the grounds of the application.

(4) Where the application includes information that the applicant thinks should not be supplied under rule 5.7 (Supply to a party of information or documents from records or case materials) to a person affected by a warrant, the applicant may—
(a) set out that information in a separate document, marked accordingly; and
(b) in that document, explain why the applicant thinks that that information ought not to be supplied to anyone other than the court.
(5) The application must include—
(a) a declaration by the applicant that to the best of the applicant's knowledge and belief—
(i) the application discloses all the information that is material to what the court must decide, including anything that might reasonably be considered capable of undermining any of the grounds of the application, and
(ii) the content of the application is true; and
(b) a declaration by an officer senior to the applicant that the senior officer has reviewed and authorised the application.
(6) The application must attach a draft warrant or warrants in the terms proposed by the applicant.

R-537A **Information to be included in a warrant**

47.27 (1) A warrant must identify—
(a) the person or description of persons by whom it may be executed;
(b) any person who may accompany a person executing the warrant;
(c) so far as practicable, the material, documents, articles or persons to be sought;
(d) the legislation under which it was issued;
(e) the name of the applicant;
(f) the court that issued it, unless that is otherwise recorded by the court officer;
(g) the court office for the court that issued it; and
(h) the date on which it was issued.
(2) A warrant must specify—
(a) either—
(i) the premises to be searched, where the application was for authority to search specified premises, or
(ii) the person in occupation or control of premises to be searched, where the application was for authority to search any premises occupied or controlled by that person; and
(b) the number of occasions on which specified premises may be searched, if more than one.
(3) A warrant must include, by signature, initial, or otherwise, an indication that it has been approved by the court that issued it.
(4) Where a warrant comprises more than a single page, each page must include such an indication.
(5) A copy of a warrant must include a prominent certificate that it is such a copy.

R-538A **Application for warrant under section 8 of the Police and Criminal Evidence Act 1984**

47.28 (1) This rule applies where an applicant wants a magistrates' court to issue a warrant or warrants under section 8 of the Police and Criminal Evidence Act 1984.
(2) As well as complying with rule 47.26, the application must—
(a) specify the offence under investigation (and see paragraph (3));
(b) so far as practicable, identify the material sought (and see paragraph (4));
(c) specify the premises to be searched (and see paragraphs (5) and (6));
(d) state whether the applicant wants the premises to be searched on more than one occasion (and see paragraph (7)); and
(e) state whether the applicant wants other persons to accompany the officers executing the warrant or warrants (and see paragraph (8)).
(3) In relation to the offence under investigation, the application must—
(a) state whether that offence is—
(i) an indictable offence, or
(ii) a relevant offence as defined in section 28D of the Immigration Act 1971; and
(b) explain the grounds for believing that the offence has been committed.
(4) In relation to the material sought, the application must explain the grounds for believing that that material—
(a) is likely to be of substantial value to the investigation (whether by itself, or together with other material);

(b) is likely to be admissible evidence at trial for the offence under investigation; and
(c) does not consist of or include items subject to legal privilege, excluded material or special procedure material.

(5) In relation to premises which the applicant wants to be searched and can specify, the application must—
(a) specify each set of premises;
(b) in respect of each set of premises, explain the grounds for believing that material sought is on those premises; and
(c) in respect of each set of premises, explain the grounds for believing that—
(i) it is not practicable to communicate with any person entitled to grant entry to the premises,
(ii) it is practicable to communicate with such a person but it is not practicable to communicate with any person entitled to grant access to the material sought,
(iii) entry to the premises will not be granted unless a warrant is produced, or
(iv) the purpose of a search may be frustrated or seriously prejudiced unless a constable arriving at the premises can secure immediate entry to them.

(6) In relation to premises which the applicant wants to be searched but at least some of which the applicant cannot specify, the application must—
(a) explain the grounds for believing that—
(i) because of the particulars of the offence under investigation it is necessary to search any premises occupied or controlled by a specified person, and
(ii) it is not reasonably practicable to specify all the premises which that person occupies or controls which might need to be searched;
(b) specify as many sets of premises as is reasonably practicable;
(c) in respect of each set of premises, whether specified or not, explain the grounds for believing that material sought is on those premises; and
(d) in respect of each specified set of premises, explain the grounds for believing that—
(i) it is not practicable to communicate with any person entitled to grant entry to the premises,
(ii) it is practicable to communicate with such a person but it is not practicable to communicate with any person entitled to grant access to the material sought,
(iii) entry to the premises will not be granted unless a warrant is produced, or
(iv) the purpose of a search may be frustrated or seriously prejudiced unless a constable arriving at the premises can secure immediate entry to them.

(7) In relation to any set of premises which the applicant wants to be searched on more than one occasion, the application must—
(a) explain why it is necessary to search on more than one occasion in order to achieve the purpose for which the applicant wants the court to issue the warrant; and
(b) specify any proposed maximum number of occasions.

(8) In relation to any set of premises which the applicant wants to be searched by the officers executing the warrant with other persons authorised by the court, the application must—
(a) identify those other persons, by function or description; and
(b) explain why those persons are required.

Application for warrant under section 2 of the Criminal Justice Act 1987 **R-539A**

47.29 (1) This rule applies where an applicant wants a magistrates' court to issue a warrant or warrants under section 2 of the Criminal Justice Act 1987.

(2) As well as complying with rule 47.26, the application must—
(a) describe the investigation being conducted by the Director of the Serious Fraud Office and include—
(i) an explanation of what is alleged and why, and
(ii) a chronology of relevant events;
(b) specify the document, documents or description of documents sought by the applicant (and see paragraphs (3) and (4)); and
(c) specify the premises which the applicant wants to be searched (and see paragraph (5)).

(3) In relation to each document or description of documents sought, the application must—
(a) explain the grounds for believing that each such document—
(i) relates to a matter relevant to the investigation, and
(ii) could not be withheld from disclosure or production on grounds of legal professional privilege; and
(b) explain the grounds for believing that—
(i) a person has failed to comply with a notice by the Director to produce the document or documents,

(ii) it is not practicable to serve such a notice, or
(iii) the service of such a notice might seriously impede the investigation.

(4) In relation to any document or description of documents which the applicant wants to be preserved but not seized under a warrant, the application must—
(a) specify the steps for which the applicant wants the court's authority in order to preserve and prevent interference with the document or documents; and
(b) explain why such steps are necessary.

(5) In respect of each set of premises which the applicant wants to be searched, the application must explain the grounds for believing that a document or description of documents sought by the applicant is on those premises.

(6) If the court so directs, the applicant must make available to the court material on which is based the information given under paragraph (2).

R-540A **Application for warrant under paragraph 12 of Schedule 1 to the Police and Criminal Evidence Act 1984**

47.30 (1) This rule applies where an applicant wants a Circuit judge to issue a warrant or warrants under paragraph 12 of Schedule 1 to the Police and Criminal Evidence Act 1984.

(2) As well as complying with rule 47.26, the application must—
(a) specify the offence under investigation (and see paragraph (3)(a));
(b) specify the set of access conditions on which the applicant relies (and see paragraphs (3) and (4));
(c) so far as practicable, identify the material sought;
(d) specify the premises to be searched (and see paragraphs (6) and (7)); and
(e) state whether the applicant wants other persons to accompany the officers executing the warrant or warrants (and see paragraph (8)).

(3) Where the applicant relies on paragraph 2 of Schedule 1 to the Police and Criminal Evidence Act 1984 ('the first set of access conditions': general power to gain access to special procedure material), the application must—
(a) specify the indictable offence under investigation;
(b) explain the grounds for believing that the offence has been committed;
(c) explain the grounds for believing that the material sought—
(i) is likely to be of substantial value to the investigation (whether by itself, or together with other material),
(ii) is likely to be admissible evidence at trial for the offence under investigation, and
(iii) does not consist of or include items subject to legal privilege or excluded material;
(d) explain what other methods of obtaining the material—
(i) have been tried without success, or
(ii) have not been tried because they appeared bound to fail; and
(e) explain why it is in the public interest to obtain the material, having regard to—
(i) the benefit likely to accrue to the investigation if the material is obtained, and
(ii) the circumstances under which the material is held.

(4) Where the applicant relies on paragraph 3 of Schedule 1 to the Police and Criminal Evidence Act 1984 ('the second set of access conditions': use of search warrant power to gain access to excluded or special procedure material), the application must—
(a) state the legislation under which a search warrant could have been issued, had the material sought not been excluded or special procedure material (in this paragraph, described as 'the main search power');
(b) include or attach the terms of the main search power;
(c) explain how the circumstances would have satisfied any criteria prescribed by the main search power for the issue of a search warrant;
(d) explain why the issue of such a search warrant would have been appropriate.

(5) Where the applicant relies on the second set of access conditions and on an assertion that a production order made under paragraph 4 of Schedule 1 to the 1984 Act in respect of the material sought has not been complied with—
(a) the application must—
(i) identify that order and describe its terms, and
(ii) specify the date on which it was served; but
(b) the application need not comply with paragraphs (6) or (7).

(6) In relation to premises which the applicant wants to be searched and can specify, the application must (unless paragraph (5) applies)—
(a) specify each set of premises;

(b) in respect of each set of premises, explain the grounds for believing that material sought is on those premises; and
(c) in respect of each set of premises, explain the grounds for believing that—
(i) it is not practicable to communicate with any person entitled to grant entry to the premises,
(ii) it is practicable to communicate with such a person but it is not practicable to communicate with any person entitled to grant access to the material sought,
(iii) the material sought contains information which is subject to a restriction on disclosure or an obligation of secrecy contained in an enactment and is likely to be disclosed in breach of the restriction or obligation if a warrant is not issued, or
(iv) service of notice of an application for a production order under paragraph 4 of Schedule 1 to the 1984 Act may seriously prejudice the investigation.

(7) In relation to premises which the applicant wants to be searched but at least some of which the applicant cannot specify, the application must (unless paragraph (5) applies)—
(a) explain the grounds for believing that—
(i) because of the particulars of the offence under investigation it is necessary to search any premises occupied or controlled by a specified person, and
(ii) it is not reasonably practicable to specify all the premises which that person occupies or controls which might need to be searched;
(b) specify as many sets of premises as is reasonably practicable;
(c) in respect of each set of premises, whether specified or not, explain the grounds for believing that material sought is on those premises; and
(d) in respect of each specified set of premises, explain the grounds for believing that—
(i) it is not practicable to communicate with any person entitled to grant entry to the premises,
(ii) it is practicable to communicate with such a person but it is not practicable to communicate with any person entitled to grant access to the material sought,
(iii) the material sought contains information which is subject to a restriction on disclosure or an obligation of secrecy contained in an enactment and is likely to be disclosed in breach of the restriction or obligation if a warrant is not issued, or
(iv) service of notice of an application for a production order under paragraph 4 of Schedule 1 to the 1984 Act may seriously prejudice the investigation.

(8) In relation to any set of premises which the applicant wants to be searched by the officers executing the warrant with other persons authorised by the court, the application must—
(a) identify those other persons, by function or description; and
(b) explain why those persons are required.

Application for warrant under paragraph 11 of Schedule 5 to the Terrorism Act 2000 **R-541A**

47.31 (1) This rule applies where an applicant wants a Circuit judge to issue a warrant or warrants under paragraph 11 of Schedule 5 to the Terrorism Act 2000.

(2) As well as complying with rule 47.26, the application must—
(a) specify the offence under investigation;
(b) explain how the investigation constitutes a terrorist investigation within the meaning of the Terrorism Act 2000;
(c) so far as practicable, identify the material sought (and see paragraph (4));
(d) specify the premises to be searched (and see paragraph (5)); and
(e) state whether the applicant wants other persons to accompany the officers executing the warrant or warrants (and see paragraph (6)).

(3) Where the applicant relies on an assertion that a production order made under paragraph 5 of Schedule 5 to the 2000 Act in respect of material on the premises has not been complied with—
(a) the application must—
(i) identify that order and describe its terms, and
(ii) specify the date on which it was served; but
(b) the application need not comply with paragraphs (4) or (5)(b).

(4) In relation to the material sought, unless paragraph (3) applies the application must explain the grounds for believing that—
(a) the material consists of or includes excluded material or special procedure material but does not include items subject to legal privilege;
(b) the material is likely to be of substantial value to a terrorist investigation (whether by itself, or together with other material); and

(c) it is not appropriate to make an order under paragraph 5 of Schedule 11 to the 2000 Act in relation to the material because—
(i) it is not practicable to communicate with any person entitled to produce the material,
(ii) it is not practicable to communicate with any person entitled to grant access to the material or entitled to grant entry to premises to which the application for the warrant relates, or
(iii) a terrorist investigation may be seriously prejudiced unless a constable can secure immediate access to the material.

(5) In relation to the premises which the applicant wants to be searched, the application must—
(a) specify—
(i) where paragraph (3) applies, the respondent and any premises to which the production order referred, or
(ii) in any other case, one or more sets of premises, or any premises occupied or controlled by a specified person (which may include one or more specified sets of premises); and
(b) unless paragraph (3) applies, in relation to premises which the applicant wants to be searched but cannot specify, explain why—
(i) it is necessary to search any premises occupied or controlled by the specified person, and
(ii) it is not reasonably practicable to specify all the premises which that person occupies or controls which might need to be searched;
(c) explain the grounds for believing that material sought is on those premises.

(6) In relation to any set of premises which the applicant wants to be searched by the officers executing the warrant with other persons authorised by the court, the application must—
(a) identify those other persons, by function or description; and
(b) explain why those persons are required.

R-542A **Application for warrant under section 352 of the Proceeds of Crime Act 2002**

47.32 (1) This rule applies where an applicant wants a Crown Court judge to issue a warrant or warrants under—
(a) section 352 of the Proceeds of Crime Act 2002; or
(b) article 13 of the Proceeds of Crime Act 2002 (External Investigations) Order 2014.

(2) As well as complying with rule 47.26, the application must—
(a) explain whether the investigation is a confiscation investigation, a money laundering investigation, a detained cash investigation, a detained property investigation, a frozen funds investigation or an external investigation;
(b) in the case of an investigation in the United Kingdom, explain why the applicant suspects that—
(i) the person under investigation has benefited from criminal conduct, in the case of a confiscation investigation, or committed a money laundering offence, in the case of a money laundering investigation, or
(ii) in the case of a detained cash investigation, a detained property investigation or a frozen funds investigation, the cash or property involved, or the money held in the frozen account, was obtained through unlawful conduct or is intended to be used in unlawful conduct;
(c) in the case of an investigation outside the United Kingdom, explain why the applicant believes that—
(i) there is an investigation by an overseas authority which relates to a criminal investigation or to criminal proceedings (including proceedings to remove the benefit of a person's criminal conduct following that person's conviction), and
(ii) the investigation is into whether property has been obtained as a result of or in connection with criminal conduct, or into the extent or whereabouts of such property;
(d) indicate what material is sought (and see paragraphs (4) and (5));
(e) specify the premises to be searched (and see paragraph (6)); and
(f) state whether the applicant wants other persons to accompany the officers executing the warrant or warrants (and see paragraph (7)).

(3) Where the applicant relies on an assertion that a production order made under sections 345 and 351 of the 2002 Act or under articles 6 and 12 of the 2014 Order has not been complied with—
(a) the application must—
(i) identify that order and describe its terms,

(ii) specify the date on which it was served, and
(iii) explain the grounds for believing that the material in respect of which the order was made is on the premises specified in the application for the warrant; but
(b) the application need not comply with paragraphs (4) or (5).

(4) Unless paragraph (3) applies, in relation to the material sought the application must—
(a) specify the material; or
(b) give a general description of the material and explain the grounds for believing that it relates to the person, cash, property or money under investigation and—
(i) in the case of a confiscation investigation, relates to the question whether that person has benefited from criminal conduct, or to any question about the extent or whereabouts of that benefit,
(ii) in the case of a money laundering investigation, relates to the question whether that person has committed a money laundering offence,
(iii) in the case of a detained cash investigation, a detained property investigation or a frozen funds investigation into the derivation of cash, property or money, relates to the question whether that cash, property or money is recoverable property,
(iv) in the case of a detained cash investigation, a detained property investigation or a frozen funds investigation into the intended use of cash, property or money, relates to the question whether that cash, property or money is intended by any person to be used in unlawful conduct,
(v) in the case of an investigation outside the United Kingdom, relates to that investigation.

(5) Unless paragraph (3) applies, in relation to the material sought the application must explain also the grounds for believing that—
(a) the material consists of or includes special procedure material but does not include excluded material or privileged material;
(b) the material is likely to be of substantial value to the investigation (whether by itself, or together with other material); and
(c) it is in the public interest for the material to be obtained, having regard to—
(i) other potential sources of information,
(ii) the benefit likely to accrue to the investigation if the material is obtained.

(6) In relation to the premises which the applicant wants to be searched, unless paragraph (3) applies the application must—
(a) explain the grounds for believing that material sought is on those premises;
(b) if the application specifies the material sought, explain the grounds for believing that it is not appropriate to make a production order under sections 345 and 351 of the 2002 Act or under articles 6 and 12 of the 2014 Order because—
(i) it is not practicable to communicate with any person against whom the production order could be made,
(ii) it is not practicable to communicate with any person who would be required to comply with an order to grant entry to the premises, or
(iii) the investigation might be seriously prejudiced unless an appropriate person is able to secure immediate access to the material;
(c) if the application gives a general description of the material sought, explain the grounds for believing that—
(i) it is not practicable to communicate with any person entitled to grant entry to the premises,
(ii) entry to the premises will not be granted unless a warrant is produced, or
(iii) the investigation might be seriously prejudiced unless an appropriate person arriving at the premises is able to secure immediate access to them;

(7) In relation to any set of premises which the applicant wants to be searched by those executing the warrant with other persons authorised by the court, the application must—
(a) identify those other persons, by function or description; and
(b) explain why those persons are required.

Application for warrant under section 160 of the Extradition Act 2003 **R-543A**

47.33 (1) This rule applies where an applicant wants a Circuit judge to issue a warrant or warrants under section 160 of the Extradition Act 2003.

(2) As well as complying with rule 47.26, the application must—
(a) identify the person whose extradition is sought (and see paragraph (3));
(b) specify the extradition offence of which that person is accused;

(c) specify the material, or description of material, sought (and see paragraph (4)); and
(d) specify the premises to be searched (and see paragraph (5)).

(3) In relation to the person whose extradition is sought, the application must explain the grounds for believing that—
(a) that person has committed the offence for which extradition is sought;
(b) that offence is an extradition offence; and
(c) that person is in the United Kingdom or is on the way to the United Kingdom.

(4) In relation to the material sought, the application must explain the grounds for believing that—
(a) the material consists of or includes special procedure or excluded material; and
(b) the material would be likely to be admissible evidence at a trial in England and Wales for the offence for which extradition is sought.

(5) In relation to the premises which the applicant wants to search, the application must explain the grounds for believing that—
(a) material sought is on those premises;
(b) one or more of the following conditions is satisfied, namely—
(i) it is not practicable to communicate with any person entitled to grant entry to the premises,
(ii) it is practicable to communicate with such a person but it is not practicable to communicate with any person entitled to grant access to the material sought, or
(iii) the material contains information which is subject to a restriction on disclosure or an obligation of secrecy contained in an enactment and is likely to be disclosed in breach of the restriction or obligation if a warrant is not issued.

(6) In relation to any set of premises which the applicant wants to be searched by the officers executing the warrant with other persons authorised by the court, the application must—
(a) identify those other persons, by function or description; and
(b) explain why those persons are required.

R-544A Application for warrant under any other power

47.34 (1) This rule applies—
(a) where an applicant wants a court to issue a warrant or warrants under a power (in this rule, 'the relevant search power') to which rule 47.24(d) (other powers) refers; but
(b) subject to any inconsistent provision in legislation that applies to the relevant search power.

(2) As well as complying with rule 47.26, the application must—
(a) demonstrate the applicant's entitlement to apply;
(b) identify the relevant search power (and see paragraph (3));
(c) so far as practicable, identify the articles or persons sought (and see paragraph (4));
(d) specify the premises to be searched (and see paragraphs (5) and (6));
(e) state whether the applicant wants the premises to be searched on more than one occasion, if the relevant search power allows (and see paragraph (7)); and
(f) state whether the applicant wants other persons to accompany the officers executing the warrant or warrants, if the relevant search power allows (and see paragraph (8)).

(3) The application must—
(a) include or attach the terms of the relevant search power; and
(b) explain how the circumstances satisfy the criteria prescribed by that power for making the application.

(4) In relation to the articles or persons sought, the application must explain how they satisfy the criteria prescribed by the relevant search power about such articles or persons.

(5) In relation to premises which the applicant wants to be searched and can specify, the application must—
(a) specify each set of premises; and
(b) in respect of each, explain how the circumstances satisfy any criteria prescribed by the relevant search power—
(i) for asserting that the articles or persons sought are on those premises, and
(ii) for asserting that the court can exercise its power to authorise the search of those particular premises.

(6) In relation to premises which the applicant wants to be searched but at least some of which the applicant cannot specify, the application must—
(a) explain how the relevant search power allows the court to authorise such searching;

(b) specify the person who occupies or controls such premises;
(c) specify as many sets of such premises as is reasonably practicable;
(d) explain why—
(i) it is necessary to search more premises than those specified, and
(ii) it is not reasonably practicable to specify all the premises which the applicant wants to be searched;
(e) in respect of each set of premises, whether specified or not, explain how the circumstances satisfy any criteria prescribed by the relevant search power for asserting that the articles or persons sought are on those premises; and
(f) in respect of each specified set of premises, explain how the circumstances satisfy any criteria prescribed by the relevant search power for asserting that the court can exercise its power to authorise the search of those premises.

(7) In relation to any set of premises which the applicant wants to be searched on more than one occasion, the application must—
(a) explain how the relevant search power allows the court to authorise such searching;
(b) explain why the applicant wants the premises to be searched more than once; and
(c) specify any proposed maximum number of occasions.

(8) In relation to any set of premises which the applicant wants to be searched by the officers executing the warrant with other persons authorised by the court, the application must—
(a) identify those other persons, by function or description; and
(b) explain why those persons are required.

Section 4: Orders for the Retention or Return of Property

When this Section applies R-545A

47.35 (1) This Section applies where—
(a) under section 1 of the Police (Property) Act 1897, a magistrates' court can—
(i) order the return to the owner of property which has come into the possession of the police or the National Crime Agency in connection with an investigation of a suspected offence, or
(ii) make such order with respect to such property as the court thinks just, where the owner cannot be ascertained;
(b) a Crown Court judge can—
(i) order the return of seized property under section 59(4) of the Criminal Justice and Police Act 2001, or
(ii) order the examination, retention, separation or return of seized property under section 59(5) of the Act.

(2) In this Section, a reference to a person with 'a relevant interest' in seized property means someone from whom the property was seized, or someone with a proprietary interest in the property, or someone who had custody or control of it immediately before it was seized.

Exercise of court's powers R-546A

47.36 (1) The court may determine an application for an order—
(a) at a hearing (which must be in private unless the court otherwise directs), or without a hearing;
(b) in a party's absence, if that party—
(i) applied for the order, or
(ii) has had at least 14 days in which to make representations.

(2) The court officer must arrange for the court to hear such an application no sooner than 14 days after it was served, unless—
(a) the court directs that no hearing need be arranged; or
(b) the court gives other directions for the hearing.

(3) If the court so directs, the parties to an application may attend a hearing by live link or telephone.

(4) The court may—
(a) shorten or extend (even after it has expired) a time limit under this Section;
(b) dispense with a requirement for service under this Section (even after service was required); and
(c) consider an application made orally instead of in writing.

(5) A person who wants an extension of time must—
(a) apply when serving the application or representations for which it is needed; and
(b) explain the delay.

R-547A **Application for an order under section 1 of the Police (Property) Act 1897**

47.37 (1) This rule applies where an applicant wants the court to make an order to which rule 47.35(1)(a) refers.

(2) The applicant must apply in writing and serve the application on—

(a) the court officer; and

(b) as appropriate—

(i) the officer who has the property,

(ii) any person who appears to be its owner.

(3) The application must—

(a) explain the applicant's interest in the property (either as a person who claims to be its owner or as an officer into whose possession the property has come);

(b) specify the direction that the applicant wants the court to make, and explain why; and

(c) include or attach a list of those on whom the applicant has served the application.

R-548A **Application for an order under section 59 of the Criminal Justice and Police Act 2001**

47.38 (1) This rule applies where an applicant wants the court to make an order to which rule 47.35(1)(b) refers.

(2) The applicant must apply in writing and serve the application on—

(a) the court officer; and

(b) as appropriate—

(i) the person who for the time being has the seized property,

(ii) each person whom the applicant knows or believes to have a relevant interest in the property.

(3) In each case, the application must—

(a) explain the applicant's interest in the property (either as a person with a relevant interest, or as possessor of the property in consequence of its seizure, as appropriate);

(b) explain the circumstances of the seizure of the property and identify the power that was exercised to seize it (or which the person seizing it purported to exercise, as appropriate); and

(c) include or attach a list of those on whom the applicant has served the application.

(4) On an application for an order for the return of property under section 59(4) of the Criminal Justice and Police Act 2001, the application must explain why any one or more of these applies—

(a) there was no power to make the seizure;

(b) the property seized is, or contains, an item subject to legal privilege which is not an item that can be retained lawfully in the circumstances listed in section 54(2) of the Act;

(c) the property seized is, or contains, excluded or special procedure material which is not material that can be retained lawfully in the circumstances listed in sections 55 and 56 of the Act;

(d) the property seized is, or contains, something taken from premises under section 50 of the Act, or from a person under section 51 of the Act, in the circumstances listed in those sections and which cannot lawfully be retained on the conditions listed in the Act.

(5) On an application for an order for the examination, retention, separation or return of property under section 59(5) of the 2001 Act, the application must—

(a) specify the direction that the applicant wants the court to make, and explain why;

(b) if applicable, specify each requirement of section 53(2) of the Act (examination and return of property) which is not being complied with;

(c) if applicable, explain why the retention of the property by the person who now has it would be justified on the grounds that, even if it were returned, it would immediately become appropriate for that person to get it back under—

(i) a warrant for its seizure, or

(ii) a production order made under paragraph 4 of Schedule 1 to the Police and Criminal Evidence Act 1984, section 20BA of the Taxes Management Act 1970 or paragraph 5 of Schedule 5 to the Terrorism Act 2000.

R-549A **Application containing information withheld from another party**

47.39 (1) This rule applies where—

(a) an applicant serves an application to which rule 47.37 (Application for an order under section 59 of the Criminal Justice and Police Act 2001) applies; and

(b) the application includes information that the applicant thinks ought not be revealed to another party.

(2) The applicant must—

(a) omit that information from the part of the application that is served on that other party;

(b) mark the other part to show that, unless the court otherwise directs, it is only for the court; and

(c) in that other part, explain why the applicant has withheld that information from that other party.

(3) If the court so directs, any hearing of an application to which this rule applies may be, wholly or in part, in the absence of a party from whom information has been withheld.
(4) At any hearing of an application to which this rule applies—
(a) the general rule is that the court must consider, in the following sequence—
(i) representations first by the applicant and then by each other party, in all the parties' presence, and then
(ii) further representations by the applicant, in the absence of a party from whom information has been withheld; but
(b) the court may direct other arrangements for the hearing.

Representations in response R-550A

47.40 (1) This rule applies where a person wants to make representations about an application under rule 47.37 or rule 47.38.
(2) Such a person must—
(a) serve the representations on—
(i) the court officer, and
(ii) the applicant and any other party to the application;
(b) do so not more than 14 days after service of the application; and
(c) ask for a hearing, if that person wants one.
(3) Representations in opposition to an application must explain why the grounds on which the applicant relies are not met.
(4) Where representations include information that the person making them thinks ought not be revealed to another party, that person must—
(a) omit that information from the representations served on that other party;
(b) mark the information to show that, unless the court otherwise directs, it is only for the court; and
(c) with that information include an explanation of why it has been withheld from that other party.

Application to punish for contempt of court R-551A

47.41 (1) This rule applies where a person is accused of disobeying an order under section 59 of the Criminal Justice and Police Act 2001.
(2) A person who wants the court to exercise its power to punish that person for contempt of court must comply with the rules in Part 48 (Contempt of court).

Section 5: Orders for the Retention of Fingerprints, etc.

When this Section applies R-552A

47.42 This Section applies where—
(a) a District Judge (Magistrates' Court) can make an order under—
(i) section 63F(7) or 63R(6) of the Police and Criminal Evidence Act 1984, or
(ii) paragraph 20B(5) or 20G(6) of Schedule 8 to the Terrorism Act 2000;
(b) the Crown Court can determine an appeal under—
(i) section 63F(10) of the Police and Criminal Evidence Act 1984, or
(ii) paragraph 20B(8) of Schedule 8 to the Terrorism Act 2000.

Exercise of court's powers R-553A

47.43 (1) The court must determine an application under rule 47.44, and an appeal under rule 47.45—
(a) at a hearing, which must be in private unless the court otherwise directs; and
(b) in the presence of the applicant or appellant.
(2) The court must not determine such an application or appeal unless any person served under those rules—
(a) is present; or
(b) has had an opportunity—
(i) to attend, or
(ii) to make representations.

Application to extend retention period R-554A

47.44 (1) This rule applies where a magistrates' court can make an order extending the period for which there may be retained material consisting of—
(a) fingerprints taken from a person—
(i) under a power conferred by Part V of the Police and Criminal Evidence Act 1984,
(ii) with that person's consent, in connection with the investigation of an offence by the police, or
(iii) under a power conferred by Schedule 8 to the Terrorism Act 2000 in relation to a person detained under section 41 of that Act;

(b) a DNA profile derived from a DNA sample so taken; or
(c) a sample so taken.

(2) A chief officer of police who wants the court to make such an order must—
(a) apply in writing—
(i) within the period of 3 months ending on the last day of the retention period, where the application relates to fingerprints or a DNA profile, or
(ii) before the expiry of the retention period, where the application relates to a sample;
(b) in the application—
(i) identify the material,
(ii) state when the retention period expires,
(iii) give details of any previous such application relating to the material, and
(iv) outline the circumstances in which the material was acquired;
(c) serve the application on the court officer, in every case; and
(d) serve the application on the person from whom the material was taken, where—
(i) the application relates to fingerprints or a DNA profile, or
(ii) the application is for the renewal of an order extending the retention period for a sample.

(3) An application to extend the retention period for fingerprints or a DNA profile must explain why that period should be extended.

(4) An application to extend the retention period for a sample must explain why, having regard to the nature and complexity of other material that is evidence in relation to the offence, the sample is likely to be needed in any proceedings for the offence for the purposes of—
(a) disclosure to, or use by, a defendant; or
(b) responding to any challenge by a defendant in respect of the admissibility of material that is evidence on which the prosecution proposes to rely.

(5) On an application to extend the retention period for fingerprints or a DNA profile, the applicant must serve notice of the court's decision on any respondent where—
(a) the court makes the order sought; and
(b) the respondent was absent when it was made.

R-555A **Appeal**

47.45 (1) This rule applies where, under rule 47.44, a magistrates' court determines an application relating to fingerprints or a DNA profile and—
(a) the person from whom the material was taken wants to appeal to the Crown Court against an order extending the retention period; or
(b) a chief officer of police wants to appeal to the Crown Court against a refusal to make such an order.

(2) The appellant must—
(a) serve an appeal notice—
(i) on the Crown Court officer and on the other party, and
(ii) not more than 21 days after the magistrates' court's decision, or, if applicable, service of notice under rule 47.44(5); and
(b) in the appeal notice, explain, as appropriate, why the retention period should, or should not, be extended.

(3) Rule 34.11 (Constitution of the Crown Court) applies on such an appeal.

Section 6: Investigation Anonymity Orders under the Coroners and Justice Act 2009

R-556A **When this Section applies**

47.46 This Section applies where—
(a) a justice of the peace can make or discharge an investigation anonymity order, under sections 76 and 80(1) of the Coroners and Justice Act 2009;
(b) a Crown Court judge can determine an appeal against—
(i) a refusal of such an order, under section 79 of the 2009 Act,
(ii) a decision on an application to discharge such an order, under section 80(6) of the 2009 Act.

R-557A **Exercise of court's powers**

47.47 (1) The court may determine an application for an investigation anonymity order, and any appeal against the refusal of such an order—
(a) at a hearing (which must be in private unless the court otherwise directs); or
(b) without a hearing.

(2) The court must determine an application to discharge an investigation anonymity order, and any appeal against the decision on such an application—
(a) at a hearing (which must be in private unless the court otherwise directs); and

(b) in the presence of the person specified in the order, unless—
(i) that person applied for the discharge of the order,
(ii) that person has had an opportunity to make representations, or
(iii) the court is satisfied that it is not reasonably practicable to communicate with that person.

(3) The court may consider an application or an appeal made orally instead of in writing.

Application for an investigation anonymity order R-558A

47.48 (1) This rule applies where an applicant wants a magistrates' court to make an investigation anonymity order.

(2) The applicant must—
(a) apply in writing;
(b) serve the application on the court officer;
(c) identify the person to be specified in the order, unless—
(i) the applicant wants the court to determine the application at a hearing, or
(ii) the court otherwise directs;
(d) explain how the proposed order meets the conditions prescribed by section 78 of the Coroners and Justice Act 2009;
(e) say if the applicant intends to appeal should the court refuse the order;
(f) attach any material on which the applicant relies; and
(g) propose the terms of the order.

(3) At any hearing of the application, the applicant must—
(a) identify to the court the person to be specified in the order, unless—
(i) the applicant has done so already, or
(ii) the court otherwise directs; and
(b) unless the applicant has done so already, inform the court if the applicant intends to appeal should the court refuse the order.

Application to discharge an investigation anonymity order R-559A

47.49 (1) This rule applies where one of the following wants a magistrates' court to discharge an investigation anonymity order—
(a) an applicant; or
(b) the person specified in the order.

(2) That applicant or the specified person must—
(a) apply in writing as soon as practicable after becoming aware of the grounds for doing so;
(b) serve the application on—
(i) the court officer, and as applicable
(ii) the applicant for the order, and
(iii) the specified person;
(c) explain—
(i) what material circumstances have changed since the order was made, or since any previous application was made to discharge it, and
(ii) why it is appropriate for the order to be discharged; and
(d) attach—
(i) a copy of the order, and
(ii) any material on which the applicant relies.

(3) A party must inform the court if that party intends to appeal should the court discharge the order.

Appeal R-560A

47.50 (1) This rule applies where one of the following ('the appellant') wants to appeal to the Crown Court—
(a) the applicant for an investigation anonymity order, where a magistrates' court has refused to make the order;
(b) a party to an application to discharge such an order, where a magistrates' court has decided that application.

(2) The appellant must—
(a) serve on the Crown Court officer a copy of the application to the magistrates' court; and
(b) where the appeal concerns a discharge decision, notify each other party,

not more than 21 days after the decision against which the appellant wants to appeal.

(3) The Crown Court must hear the appeal without justices of the peace.

Section 7: Investigation Approval Orders under the Regulation of Investigatory Powers Act 2000

R-561A **When this Section applies**

47.51 This Section applies where a justice of the peace can make an order approving—
(a) the grant or renewal of an authorisation, or the giving or renewal of a notice, under section 23A of the Regulation of Investigatory Powers Act 2000;
(b) the grant or renewal of an authorisation under section 32A of the 2000 Act.

R-562A **Exercise of court's powers**

47.52 (1) Rule 47.5 (Investigation orders; Exercise of court's powers) applies, subject to sections 23B(2) and 32B(2) of the Regulation of Investigatory Powers Act 2000.
(2) Where a magistrates' court refuses to approve the grant, giving or renewal of an authorisation or notice, the court must not exercise its power to quash that authorisation or notice unless the applicant has had at least 2 business days from the date of the refusal in which to make representations.

R-563A **Application for approval for authorisation or notice**

47.53 (1) This rule applies where an applicant wants a magistrates' court to make an order approving—
(a) under sections 23A and 23B of the Regulation of Investigatory Powers Act 2000—
(i) an authorisation to obtain or disclose communications data, under section 22(3) of the 2000 Act, or
(ii) a notice that requires a postal or telecommunications operator if need be to obtain, and in any case to disclose, communications data, under section 22(4) of the 2000 Act;
(b) under sections 32A and 32B of the Regulation of Investigatory Powers Act 2000, an authorisation for—
(i) the carrying out of directed surveillance, under section 28 of the 2000 Act, or
(ii) the conduct or use of a covert human intelligence source, under section 29 of the 2000 Act.
(2) The applicant must—
(a) apply in writing and serve the application on the court officer;
(b) attach the authorisation or notice which the applicant wants the court to approve;
(c) attach such other material (if any) on which the applicant relies to satisfy the court—
(i) as required by section 23A(3) and (4) of the 2000 Act, in relation to communications data,
(ii) as required by section 32A(3) and (4) of the 2000 Act, in relation to directed surveillance, or
(iii) as required by section 32A(5) and (6), and, if relevant, section 43(6A), of the 2000 Act, in relation to a covert human intelligence source; and
(d) propose the terms of the order.

Section 8: Orders for Access to Documents, etc. under the Criminal Appeal Act 1995

R-564A **When this Section applies**

47.54 This Section applies where the Crown Court can order a person to give the Criminal Cases Review Commission access to a document or other material under section 18A of the Criminal Appeal Act 1995.

R-565A **Exercise of court's powers**

47.55 (1) Subject to paragraphs (2), (3) and (4), the court may determine an application by the Criminal Cases Review Commission for an order—
(a) at a hearing (which must be in private unless the court otherwise directs), or without a hearing; and
(b) in the absence of—
(i) the Commission,
(ii) the respondent,
(iii) any other person affected by the order.
(2) The court must not determine such an application in the Commission's absence if—
(a) the Commission asks for a hearing; or
(b) it appears to the court that the application is so complex or serious as to require the court to hear the Commission.
(3) The court must not determine such an application in the absence of any respondent or other person affected, unless—
(a) the absentee has had at least 2 business days in which to make representations; or
(b) the court is satisfied that—
(i) the Commission cannot identify or contact the absentee,

(ii) it would prejudice the exercise of the Commission's functions to adjourn or postpone the application so as to allow the absentee to attend, or
(iii) the absentee has waived the opportunity to attend.

(4) The court must not determine such an application in the absence of any respondent who, if the order sought by the Commission were made, would be required to produce or give access to journalistic material, unless that respondent has waived the opportunity to attend.

(5) The court officer must arrange for the court to hear such an application no sooner than 2 business days after it was served, unless—
(a) the court directs that no hearing need be arranged; or
(b) the court gives other directions for the hearing.

(6) The court must not determine an application unless satisfied that sufficient time has been allowed for it.

(7) If the court so directs, the parties to an application may attend a hearing by live link or telephone.

(8) The court must not make an order unless an officer of the Commission states, in writing or orally, that to the best of that officer's knowledge and belief—
(a) the application discloses all the information that is material to what the court must decide; and
(b) the content of the application is true.

(9) Where the statement required by paragraph (8) is made orally—
(a) the statement must be on oath or affirmation, unless the court otherwise directs; and
(b) the court must arrange for a record of the making of the statement.

(10) The court may shorten or extend (even after it has expired) a time limit under this Section.

Application for an order for access **R-566A**

47.56 (1) Where the Criminal Cases Review Commission wants the court to make an order for access to a document or other material, the Commission must—
(a) apply in writing and serve the application on the court officer;
(b) give the court an estimate of how long the court should allow—
(i) to read the application and prepare for any hearing, and
(ii) for any hearing of the application;
(c) attach a draft order in the terms proposed by the Commission; and
(d) serve the application and draft order on the respondent.

(2) The application must—
(a) identify the respondent;
(b) describe the document, or documents, or other material sought;
(c) explain the reasons for thinking that—
(i) what is sought is in the respondent's possession or control, and
(ii) access to what is sought may assist the Commission in the exercise of any of its functions; and
(d) explain the Commission's proposals for—
(i) the manner in which the respondent should give access, and
(ii) the period within which the order should take effect.

(3) The Commission must serve any order made on the respondent.

Application containing information withheld from a respondent or other person **R-567A**

47.57 (1) This rule applies where—
(a) the Criminal Cases Review Commission serves an application under rule 47.56 (Application for an order for access); and
(b) the application includes information that the Commission thinks ought not be revealed to a recipient.

(2) The Commission must—
(a) omit that information from the part of the application that is served on that recipient;
(b) mark the other part, to show that it is only for the court; and
(c) in that other part, explain why the Commission has withheld it from that recipient.

(3) A hearing of an application to which this rule applies may take place, wholly or in part, in the absence of that recipient and any other person.

(4) At a hearing of an application to which this rule applies—
(a) the general rule is that the court must consider, in the following sequence—
(i) representations first by the Commission and then by the other parties, in the presence of them all, and then
(ii) further representations by the Commission, in the others' absence; but
(b) the court may direct other arrangements for the hearing.

R-568A **Application to punish for contempt of court**

47.58 (1) This rule applies where a person is accused of disobeying an order for access made under section 18A of the Criminal Appeal Act 1995.

(2) An applicant who wants the court to exercise its power to punish that person for contempt of court must comply with the rules in Part 48 (Contempt of court).

Section 9: Order for the Extension of a Moratorium Period under the Proceeds of Crime Act 2002

R-569A **When this Section applies**

47.59 (1) This Section applies where the Crown Court can extend a moratorium period under section 336A of the Proceeds of Crime Act 2002.

(2) In this Section, 'respondent' means, as well as a person within the meaning of rule 47.2(c), an 'interested person' within the meaning of section 336D of the 2002 Act.

R-570A **Exercise of court's powers**

47.60 (1) The court may determine an application to which rule 47.64 (Application for extension of moratorium period) applies—

(a) at a hearing (which must be in private unless the court otherwise directs), or without a hearing; and

(b) in the absence of—

(i) the applicant,

(ii) a respondent.

(2) The court must not determine such an application in the applicant's absence if the applicant asks for a hearing.

(3) The court must not determine such an application in the absence of a respondent unless—

(a) the absentee has had at least 2 business days in which to make representations; or

(b) the court is satisfied that—

(i) the applicant cannot identify or contact the absentee,

(ii) it would prejudice the investigation if the absentee were present,

(iii) it would prejudice the investigation to adjourn or postpone the application so as to allow the absentee to attend, or

(iv) the absentee has waived the opportunity to attend.

(4) The court officer must arrange for the court to hear such an application no sooner than 2 business days after notice of the application was served, unless—

(a) the court directs that no hearing need be arranged; or

(b) the court gives other directions for the hearing.

(5) If the court so directs, the parties to an application may attend a hearing by live link or telephone.

(6) The court must not extend a moratorium period unless the applicant states, in writing or orally, that to the best of the applicant's knowledge and belief—

(a) the application discloses all the information that is material to what the court must decide; and

(b) the content of the application is true.

(7) Where the statement required by paragraph (6) is made orally—

(a) the statement must be on oath or affirmation, unless the court otherwise directs; and

(b) the court must arrange for a record of the making of the statement.

(8) The court may—

(a) shorten or extend (even after it has expired) a time limit imposed by this rule;

(b) dispense with a requirement for service under this Section (even after service was required); and

(c) consider an application made orally instead of in writing.

R-571A **Application for extension of moratorium period**

47.61 (1) This rule applies where an applicant wants the court to extend a moratorium period.

(2) The applicant must—

(a) apply in writing before the date on which the moratorium period otherwise would end;

(b) demonstrate that the applicant is entitled to apply as a senior officer within the meaning of section 336D of the Proceeds of Crime Act 2002;

(c) serve the application on the court officer;

(d) serve notice on each respondent that an application has been made; and

(e) serve the application on each respondent to such extent, if any, as the court directs.

(3) The application must specify—

(a) the disclosure in respect of which the application is made;

(b) the date on which the moratorium period began;

(c) the date and period of any previous extension of that period; and
(d) the date on which that period is due to end.

(4) The application must—
(a) describe the investigation being carried out in relation to that disclosure; and
(b) explain the grounds for believing that—
(i) the investigation is being conducted diligently and expeditiously,
(ii) further time is needed for conducting the investigation, and
(iii) it would be reasonable in all the circumstances for the moratorium period to be extended.

(5) A respondent who objects to the application must—
(a) serve notice of the objection on—
(i) the court officer, and
(ii) the applicant,
not more than 2 business days after service of notice of the application; and
(b) in that notice explain the grounds of the objection.

(6) The applicant must serve any order made on each respondent.

Application containing information withheld from a respondent R-572A

47.62 (1) This rule applies where an application to extend a moratorium period includes an application to withhold information from a respondent.

(2) The applicant must—
(a) omit that information from any part of the application that is served on the respondent;
(b) mark the other part to show that, unless the court otherwise directs, it is only for the court; and
(c) in that other part, explain the grounds for believing that the disclosure of that information would have one or more of the following results—
(i) evidence of an offence would be interfered with or harmed,
(ii) the gathering of information about the possible commission of an offence would be interfered with,
(iii) a person would be interfered with or physically injured,
(iv) the recovery of property under this Act would be hindered, or
(v) national security would be put at risk.

(3) At any hearing of an application to which this rule applies—
(a) the court must first determine the application to withhold information, in the respondent's absence and that of any legal representative of the respondent;
(b) if the court allows the application to withhold information, then in the following sequence—
(i) the court must consider representations first by the applicant and then by the respondent, in the presence of both, and
(ii) the court may consider further representations by the applicant in the respondent's absence and that of any legal representative of the respondent.

(4) If the court refuses an application to withhold information from the respondent, the applicant may withdraw the application to extend the moratorium period.

Section 10: Orders for Access to Electronic Data under the Crime (Overseas Production Orders) Act 2019

When this Section applies R-573A

47.63 (1) This Section applies where the Crown Court can make an overseas production order under section 1 of the Crime (Overseas Production Orders) Act 2019 [the Act comes into force on a date to be appointed]

(2) In this Section, a reference to a person affected by such an order includes a person by whom or on whose behalf there is stored any journalistic data specified or described in the application for that order.

Exercise of court's powers R-574A

47.64 (1) Subject to paragraphs (2), (3) and (4), the court may determine an application under rule 47.65 for an overseas production order, or an application under rule 47.66 to vary or revoke an order—
(a) at a hearing (which must be in private unless the court otherwise directs), or without a hearing; and
(b) in the absence of—
(i) the applicant,
(ii) the respondent,
(iii) any other person affected by the order.

(2) The court must not determine such an application in the applicant's absence if—
(a) the applicant asks for a hearing; or
(b) it appears to the court that—
(i) the proposed order may require the production of excepted electronic data, within the meaning of section 3 of the Crime (Overseas Production Orders) Act 2019, or
(ii) for any other reason the application is so complex or serious as to require the court to hear the applicant.
(3) The court must not determine such an application in the absence of any respondent or other person affected unless—
(a) the absentee has had at least 2 business days in which to make representations; or
(b) the court is satisfied that—
(i) the applicant cannot identify or contact the absentee,
(ii) it would prejudice the investigation if the absentee were present,
(iii) where journalistic data is sought, it would prejudice the investigation of another indictable offence or another terrorist investigation if the absentee were present,
(iv) it would prejudice the investigation to adjourn or postpone the application so as to allow the absentee to attend, or
(v) the absentee has waived the opportunity to attend.
(4) The court must not determine such an application in the absence of any respondent who, if the order sought by the applicant were made, would be required to produce or give access to journalistic data, unless that respondent has waived the opportunity to attend.
(5) The court officer must arrange for the court to hear such an application no sooner than 2 business days after notice of the application was served, unless—
(a) the court directs that no hearing need be arranged; or
(b) the court gives other directions for the hearing.
(6) The court must not determine an application unless satisfied that sufficient time has been allowed for it.
(7) If the court so directs, the parties to an application may attend a hearing by live link or telephone.
(8) The court must not make, vary or revoke an order unless the applicant states, in writing or orally, that to the best of the applicant's knowledge and belief—
(a) the application discloses all the information that is material to what the court must decide; and
(b) the content of the application is true.
(9) Where the statement required by paragraph (8) is made orally—
(a) the statement must be on oath or affirmation, unless the court otherwise directs; and
(b) the court must arrange for a record of the making of the statement.
(10) The court may—
(a) shorten or extend (even after it has expired) a time limit under this Section;
(b) dispense with a requirement for service under this Section (even after service was required); and
(c) consider an application made orally instead of in writing.
(11) A person who wants an extension of time must—
(a) apply when serving the application for which it is needed; and
(b) explain the delay.

R-575A **Application for order**

47.65 (1) An applicant who wants the court to make an overseas production order must—
(a) apply in writing and serve the application on the court officer;
(b) demonstrate that the applicant is entitled to apply;
(c) give the court an estimate of how long the court should allow—
(i) to read the application and prepare for any hearing, and
(ii) for any hearing of the application;
(d) attach a draft order in the terms proposed by the applicant;
(e) serve notice of the application on the respondent and on any other person affected by the order, unless the court otherwise directs;
(f) serve the application on the respondent and on any such other person to such extent, if any, as the court directs.
(2) A notice served on the respondent and on any other person affected by the order must—
(a) specify or describe the electronic data in respect of which the application is made; and
(b) identify—
(i) the power that the applicant invites the court to exercise, and
(ii) the conditions for the exercise of that power which the applicant asks the court to find are met.

(3) The application must—
(a) specify the designated international co-operation arrangement by reference to which the application is made;
(b) identify the respondent;
(c) explain the grounds for believing that the respondent operates in, or is based in, a country or territory outside the United Kingdom which is a party to, or participates in, that designated international co-operation arrangement;
(d) specify or describe the electronic data in respect of which the order is sought;
(e) explain the grounds for believing that the electronic data sought does not consist of or include excepted electronic data;
(f) briefly describe the investigation for the purposes of which the electronic data is sought and explain—
(i) the grounds for believing that an indictable offence has been committed which is under investigation or in respect of which proceedings have begun, or
(ii) how the investigation constitutes a terrorist investigation within the meaning of the Terrorism Act 2000;
(g) explain the grounds for believing that the respondent has possession or control of all or part of the electronic data sought;
(h) explain the grounds for believing that the electronic data sought is likely to be of substantial value to the investigation, or to the proceedings (as the case may be), whether by itself or together with other material;
(i) where paragraph (3)(f)(i) applies, explain the grounds for believing that all or part of the electronic data sought is likely to be relevant evidence in respect of the offence concerned;
(j) explain the grounds for believing that it is in the public interest for the respondent to produce or give access to the electronic data sought, having regard to—
(i) the benefit likely to accrue to the investigation, or to the proceedings (as the case may be), if that data is obtained, and
(ii) the circumstances under which the respondent has possession or control of any of that data;
(k) specify—
(i) the person, or the description of person, to whom the applicant wants the court to order that electronic data must be produced or made accessible, and
(ii) the period by the end of which the applicant wants the court to order that that electronic data must be produced or made accessible (which must be a period of 7 days beginning with the day on which the order is served on the respondent, unless the court otherwise directs); and
(l) where the applicant wants the court to include a non-disclosure requirement in the order—
(i) explain why such a requirement would be appropriate, and
(ii) specify or describe when the applicant wants that requirement, if ordered, to expire.

(4) In the event that an overseas production order is made, the applicant must serve the order on the Secretary of State for service on the respondent.

(5) Where notice of the application was served on a respondent, in the event that the application is dismissed or abandoned the applicant must—
(a) promptly so notify that respondent; and
(b) where the application is dismissed, promptly inform that respondent if the court nonetheless orders that for a period that respondent must not—
(i) conceal, destroy, alter or dispose of any of the electronic data specified or described in the application, or
(ii) disclose the making of the application or its contents to any person.

Application to vary or revoke an order R-576A

47.66 (1) The orders to which this rule applies are—
(a) an overseas production order;
(b) an order under section 8(4) of the Crime (Overseas Production Orders) Act 2019 maintaining an unexpired non-disclosure requirement;
(c) an order under section 13(3) of the 2019 Act maintaining a duty not to conceal, destroy, alter or dispose of electronic data, and not to disclose the making or content of an application for an overseas production order;
(d) an order under section 13(4)(b) of the Act maintaining a duty not to conceal, destroy, alter or dispose of electronic data.

(2) This rule applies where one of the following wants the court to vary, to further vary or to revoke an order listed in paragraph (1)—
(a) the applicant for that order, or an equivalent appropriate officer;
(b) the respondent;
(c) another person affected by the order; or
(d) the Secretary of State.
(3) The applicant for the variation or revocation must—
(a) apply in writing as soon as practicable after becoming aware of the grounds for doing so;
(b) serve the application on—
(i) the court officer, and
(ii) as applicable, the applicant for the order, the respondent, any other person known to be affected and the Secretary of State; and
(c) ask for a hearing, if one is wanted, and explain why it is needed.
(4) Where the applicant wants the court to vary, or further vary, an overseas production order, the application must—
(a) specify or describe the electronic data in respect of which the varied order is sought (which may include electronic data not specified or described in the original order);
(b) satisfy or, as the case may be, continue to satisfy, the requirements of rule 47.68(3)(a) and (c) to (i) (which may be done by reference to the original application); and
(c) meet the requirements of rule 47.68(3)(j).
(5) Where the applicant wants the court to revoke an overseas production order, the application must—
(a) explain why revocation is appropriate;
(b) if the applicant wants the court, despite revocation, to maintain the requirement that for a period the respondent must not conceal, destroy, alter or dispose of any of the electronic data specified or described in the order—
(i) explain why it would be appropriate to maintain that requirement, and
(ii) specify or describe when the applicant wants that requirement, if maintained, to expire; and
(c) if the order includes an unexpired non-disclosure requirement that the applicant wants the court, despite revocation, to maintain—
(i) explain why it would be appropriate to maintain that requirement, and
(ii) specify or describe when the applicant wants that requirement, if maintained, to expire.
(6) Where the applicant wants the court to vary, to further vary or to revoke an order under section 8(4), section 13(3) or section 13(4)(b) of the 2019 Act the application must—
(a) explain—
(i) what material circumstances have changed since the order was made, and
(ii) why the order should be varied or revoked, as the case may be, as a result; and
(b) if applicable, specify the variation proposed.

R-577A Application containing information withheld from a respondent or other person

47.67 (1) This rule applies where an application under rule 47.65 or 47.66 includes information that the applicant thinks ought to be revealed only to the court.
(2) The application must—
(a) identify that information; and
(b) explain why that information ought not to be served on the respondent or another person.
(3) At a hearing of an application to which this rule applies—
(a) the general rule is that the court must consider, in the following sequence—
(i) representations first by the applicant and then by the respondent and any other person, in the presence of them all, and then
(ii) further representations by the applicant, in the others' absence; but
(b) the court may direct other arrangements for the hearing.

R-578A Application to punish for contempt of court

47.68 (1) This rule applies where a person is accused of disobeying an order made by the court under the Crime (Overseas Production Orders) Act 2019.
(2) An applicant who wants the court to exercise its power to punish that person for contempt of court must comply with the rules in Part 48 (Contempt of court).

Criminal Procedure Rules Part 48 Contempt of Court

General rules

When this Part applies R-582

48.1 (1) This Part applies where the court can deal with a person for conduct—
(a) in contempt of court; or
(b) in contravention of the legislation to which rules 48.5 and 48.9 refer.
(2) In this Part, 'respondent' means any such person.

Exercise of court's power to deal with contempt of court R-583

48.2 (1) The court must determine at a hearing—
(a) an enquiry under rule 48.8;
(b) an allegation under rule 48.9.
(2) The court must not proceed in the respondent's absence unless—
(a) the respondent's behaviour makes it impracticable to proceed otherwise; or
(b) the respondent has had at least 14 days' notice of the hearing, or was present when it was arranged.
(3) If the court hears part of an enquiry or allegation in private, it must announce at a hearing in public—
(a) the respondent's name;
(b) in general terms, the nature of any conduct that the respondent admits, or the court finds proved; and
(c) any punishment imposed.

Notice of suspension of imprisonment by Court of Appeal or Crown Court R-584

48.3 (1) This rule applies where—
(a) the Court of Appeal or the Crown Court suspends an order of imprisonment for contempt of court; and
(b) the respondent is absent when the court does so.
(2) The respondent must be served with notice of the terms of the court's order—
(a) by any applicant under rule 48.9; or
(b) by the court officer, in any other case.

Application to discharge an order for imprisonment R-585

48.4 (1) This rule applies where the court can discharge an order for a respondent's imprisonment for contempt of court.
(2) A respondent who wants the court to discharge such an order must—
(a) apply in writing, unless the court otherwise directs, and serve any written application on—
(i) the court officer, and
(ii) any applicant under rule 48.9 on whose application the respondent was imprisoned;
(b) in the application—
(i) explain why it is appropriate for the order for imprisonment to be discharged, and
(ii) give details of any appeal, and its outcome; and
(c) ask for a hearing, if the respondent wants one.

Contempt of court by obstruction, disruption, etc.

Initial procedure on obstruction, disruption etc. R-586

48.5 (1) This rule applies where the court observes, or someone reports to the court—
(a) in the Court of Appeal or the Crown Court, obstructive, disruptive, insulting or intimidating conduct, in the courtroom or in its vicinity, or otherwise immediately affecting the proceedings;
(b) in the Crown Court, a contravention of—
(i) section 3 of the Criminal Procedure (Attendance of Witnesses) Act 1965 (disobeying a witness summons);
(ii) section 20 of the Juries Act 1974 (disobeying a jury summons);
(c) in a magistrates' court, a contravention of—
(i) section 97(4) of the Magistrates' Courts Act 1980 (refusing to give evidence), or
(ii) section 12 of the Contempt of Court Act 1981 (insulting or interrupting the court, etc.);
(d) a contravention of section 9 of the Contempt of Court Act 1981 (without the court's permission, recording the proceedings, etc.);

(e) any other conduct with which the court can deal as, or as if it were, a criminal contempt of court, except failure to surrender to bail under section 6 of the Bail Act 1976.

(2) Unless the respondent's behaviour makes it impracticable to do so, the court must—

(a) explain, in terms the respondent can understand (with help, if necessary)—

(i) the conduct that is in question,

(ii) that the court can impose imprisonment, or a fine, or both, for such conduct,

(iii) (where relevant) that the court has power to order the respondent's immediate temporary detention, if in the court's opinion that is required,

(iv) that the respondent may explain the conduct,

(v) that the respondent may apologise, if he or she so wishes, and that this may persuade the court to take no further action, and

(vi) that the respondent may take legal advice; and

(b) allow the respondent a reasonable opportunity to reflect, take advice, explain and, if he or she so wishes, apologise.

(3) The court may then—

(a) take no further action in respect of that conduct;

(b) enquire into the conduct there and then; or

(c) postpone that enquiry (if a magistrates' court, only until later the same day).

R-587 Review after temporary detention

48.6 (1) This rule applies in a case in which the court has ordered the respondent's immediate temporary detention for conduct to which rule 48.5 applies.

(2) The court must review the case—

(a) if a magistrates' court, later the same day;

(b) in the Court of Appeal or the Crown Court, no later than the next business day.

(3) On the review, the court must—

(a) unless the respondent is absent, repeat the explanations required by rule 48.5(2)(a); and

(b) allow the respondent a reasonable opportunity to reflect, take advice, explain and, if he or she so wishes, apologise.

(4) The court may then—

(a) take no further action in respect of the conduct;

(b) if a magistrates' court, enquire into the conduct there and then; or

(c) if the Court of Appeal or the Crown Court—

(i) enquire into the conduct there and then, or

(ii) postpone the enquiry, and order the respondent's release from such detention in the meantime.

R-588 Postponement of enquiry

48.7 (1) This rule applies where the Court of Appeal or the Crown Court postpones the enquiry.

(2) The court must arrange for the preparation of a written statement containing such particulars of the conduct in question as to make clear what the respondent appears to have done.

(3) The court officer must serve on the respondent—

(a) that written statement;

(b) notice of where and when the postponed enquiry will take place; and

(c) a notice that—

(i) reminds the respondent that the court can impose imprisonment, or a fine, or both, for contempt of court, and

(ii) warns the respondent that the court may pursue the postponed enquiry in the respondent's absence, if the respondent does not attend.

R-589 Procedure on enquiry

48.8 (1) At an enquiry, the court must—

(a) ensure that the respondent understands (with help, if necessary) what is alleged, if the enquiry has been postponed from a previous occasion;

(b) explain what the procedure at the enquiry will be; and

(c) ask whether the respondent admits the conduct in question.

(2) If the respondent admits the conduct, the court need not receive evidence.

(3) If the respondent does not admit the conduct, the court must consider—

(a) any statement served under rule 48.7;

(b) any other evidence of the conduct;

(c) any evidence introduced by the respondent; and

(d) any representations by the respondent about the conduct.

(4) If the respondent admits the conduct, or the court finds it proved, the court must—
(a) before imposing any punishment for contempt of court, give the respondent an opportunity to make representations relevant to punishment;
(b) explain, in terms the respondent can understand (with help, if necessary)—
(i) the reasons for its decision, including its findings of fact, and
(ii) the punishment it imposes, and its effect; and
(c) if a magistrates' court, arrange for the preparation of a written record of those findings.
(5) The court that conducts an enquiry—
(a) need not include the same member or members as the court that observed the conduct; but
(b) may do so, unless that would be unfair to the respondent.

Contempt of court by failure to comply with court order, etc.

Initial procedure on failure to comply with court order, etc. **R-590**

48.9 (1) This rule applies where—
(a) a party, or other person directly affected, alleges—
(i) in the Crown Court, a failure to comply with an order to which applies rule 33.70 (compliance order, restraint order or ancillary order), rule 47.9 (certain investigation orders under the Police and Criminal Evidence Act 1984, the Terrorism Act 2000, the Proceeds of Crime Act 2002, the Proceeds of Crime Act 2002 (External Investigations) Order 2014 and the Extradition Act 2003), rule 47.41 (order for retention or return of property under section 59 of the Criminal Justice and Police Act 2001) or rule 47.58 (order for access under section 18A of the Criminal Appeal Act 1995),
(ii) in the Court of Appeal or the Crown Court, any other conduct with which that court can deal as a civil contempt of court, or
(iii) in the Crown Court or a magistrates' court, unauthorised use of disclosed prosecution material under section 17 of the Criminal Procedure and Investigations Act 1996;
(b) the court deals on its own initiative with conduct to which paragraph (1)(a) applies.
(2) Such a party or person must—
(a) apply in writing and serve the application on the court officer; and
(b) serve on the respondent—
(i) the application, and
(ii) notice of where and when the court will consider the allegation (not less than 14 days after service).
(3) The application must—
(a) identify the respondent;
(b) explain that it is an application for the respondent to be dealt with for contempt of court;
(c) contain such particulars of the conduct in question as to make clear what is alleged against the respondent; and
(d) include a notice warning the respondent that the court—
(i) can impose imprisonment, or a fine, or both, for contempt of court, and
(ii) may deal with the application in the respondent's absence, if the respondent does not attend the hearing.
(4) A court which acts on its own initiative under paragraph (1)(b) must—
(a) arrange for the preparation of a written statement containing the same information as an application; and
(b) arrange for the service on the respondent of—
(i) that written statement, and
(ii) notice of where and when the court will consider the allegation (not less than 14 days after service).

Procedure on hearing **R-591**

48.10 (1) At the hearing of an allegation under rule 48.9, the court must—
(a) ensure that the respondent understands (with help, if necessary) what is alleged;
(b) explain what the procedure at the hearing will be; and
(c) ask whether the respondent admits the conduct in question.
(2) If the respondent admits the conduct, the court need not receive evidence.
(3) If the respondent does not admit the conduct, the court must consider—
(a) the application or written statement served under rule 48.9;
(b) any other evidence of the conduct;
(c) any evidence introduced by the respondent; and
(d) any representations by the respondent about the conduct.

(4) If the respondent admits the conduct, or the court finds it proved, the court must—
(a) before imposing any punishment for contempt of court, give the respondent an opportunity to make representations relevant to punishment;
(b) explain, in terms the respondent can understand (with help, if necessary)—
(i) the reasons for its decision, including its findings of fact, and
(ii) the punishment it imposes, and its effect; and
(c) in a magistrates' court, arrange for the preparation of a written record of those findings.

R-592 Introduction of written witness statement or other hearsay

48.11 (1) Where rule 48.9 applies, an applicant or respondent who wants to introduce in evidence the written statement of a witness, or other hearsay, must—
(a) serve a copy of the statement, or notice of other hearsay, on—
(i) the court officer, and
(ii) the other party; and
(b) serve the copy or notice—
(i) when serving the application under rule 48.9, in the case of an applicant, or
(ii) not more than 7 days after service of that application or of the court's written statement, in the case of the respondent.
(2) Such service is notice of that party's intention to introduce in evidence that written witness statement, or other hearsay, unless that party otherwise indicates when serving it.
(3) A party entitled to receive such notice may waive that entitlement.

R-593 Content of written witness statement

48.12 (1) This rule applies to a written witness statement served under rule 48.11.
(2) Such a written witness statement must contain a declaration by the person making it that it is true to the best of that person's knowledge and belief.

R-594 Content of notice of other hearsay

48.13 (1) This rule applies to a notice of hearsay, other than a written witness statement, served under rule 48.11.
(2) Such a notice must—
(a) set out the evidence, or attach the document that contains it; and
(b) identify the person who made the statement that is hearsay.

R-595 Cross-examination of maker of written witness statement or other hearsay

48.14 (1) This rule applies where a party wants the court's permission to cross-examine a person who made a statement which another person wants to introduce as hearsay.
(2) The party who wants to cross-examine that person must—
(a) apply in writing, with reasons; and
(b) serve the application on—
(i) the court officer, and
(ii) the party who served the hearsay.
(3) A respondent who wants to cross-examine such a person must apply to do so not more than 7 days after service of the hearsay by the applicant.
(4) An applicant who wants to cross-examine such a person must apply to do so not more than 3 days after service of the hearsay by the respondent.
(5) The court—
(a) may decide an application under this rule without a hearing; but
(b) must not dismiss such an application unless the person making it has had an opportunity to make representations at a hearing.

R-596 Credibility and consistency of maker of written witness statement or other hearsay

48.15 (1) This rule applies where a party wants to challenge the credibility or consistency of a person who made a statement which another party wants to introduce as hearsay.
(2) The party who wants to challenge the credibility or consistency of that person must—
(a) serve notice of intention to do so on—
(i) the court officer, and
(ii) the party who served the hearsay; and
(b) in it, identify any statement or other material on which that party relies.
(3) A respondent who wants to challenge such a person's credibility or consistency must serve such a notice not more than 7 days after service of the hearsay by the applicant.
(4) An applicant who wants to challenge such a person's credibility or consistency must serve such a notice not more than 3 days after service of the hearsay by the respondent.

(5) The party who served the hearsay—
(a) may call that person to give oral evidence instead; and
(b) if so, must serve notice of intention to do so on—
(i) the court officer, and
(ii) the other party
as soon as practicable after service of the notice under paragraph (2).

Magistrates' courts' powers to adjourn, etc. R-597

48.16 (1) This rule applies where a magistrates' court deals with unauthorised disclosure of prosecution material under sections 17 and 18 of the Criminal Procedure and Investigations Act 1996.
(2) The sections of the Magistrates' Courts Act 1980 listed in paragraph (3) apply as if in those sections—
(a) 'complaint' and 'summons' each referred to an application or written statement under rule 48.9;
(b) 'complainant' meant an applicant; and
(c) 'defendant' meant the respondent.
(3) Those sections are—
(a) section 51 (issue of summons on complaint);
(b) section 54 (adjournment);
(c) section 55 (non-appearance of defendant);
(d) section 97(1) (summons to witness);
(e) section 121(1) (constitution and place of sitting of court);
(f) section 123 (defect in process).
(4) Section 127 of the 1980 Act (limitation of time) does not apply.

Court's power to vary requirements R-598

48.17 (1) The court may shorten or extend (even after it has expired) a time limit under rule 48.11, 48.14 or 48.15.
(2) A person who wants an extension of time must—
(a) apply when serving the statement, notice or application for which it is needed; and
(b) explain the delay.

Criminal Practice Directions Part 48 Contempt of Court

CPD XI Other proceedings 48A: Contempt in the Face of the Magistrates' Court PD-103

General

48A.1 The procedure to be followed in cases of contempt of court is given in CrimPR Part 48. The magistrates' courts' power to deal with contempt in the face of the court is contained within section 12 of the Contempt of Court Act 1981. Magistrates' courts also have the power to punish a witness who refuses to be sworn or give evidence under section 97(4) of the Magistrates' Courts Act 1980.

Contempt consisting of wilfully insulting anyone specified in section 12 or interrupting proceedings

48A.2 In the majority of cases, an apology and a promise as to future conduct should be sufficient for the court to order a person's release. However, there are likely to be certain cases where the nature and seriousness of the misconduct requires the court to consider using its powers, under section 12(2) of the Contempt of Court Act 1981, either to fine or to order the person's committal to custody.

Imposing a penalty for contempt

48A.3 The court should allow the person a further opportunity to apologise for his or her contempt, and should follow the procedure at CrimPR 48.8(4). The court should consider whether it is appropriate to release the person or whether it must exercise its powers to fine the person or to commit the person to custody under section 12(2) of the 1981 Act. In deciding how to deal with the person, the court should have regard to the period for which he or she has been detained, whether the conduct was admitted and the seriousness of the contempt. Any period of committal to custody should be for the shortest period of time commensurate with the interests of preserving good order in the administration of justice.

Criminal Procedure Rules Part 49 International Co-operation

Notice required to accompany process served outside the United Kingdom and translations R-599

49.1 (1) The notice which by virtue of section 3(4)(b) of the Crime (International Co-operation) Act 2003 (general requirements for service of process) must accompany any process served outside the United Kingdom must give the information specified in paragraphs (2) and (4) below.

(2) The notice must—
(a) state that the person required by the process to appear as a party or attend as a witness can obtain information about his rights in connection therewith from the relevant authority; and
(b) give the particulars specified in paragraph (4) about that authority.
(3) The relevant authority where the process is served—
(a) at the request of the prosecuting authority, is that authority; or
(b) at the request of the defendant or the prosecutor in the case of a private prosecution, is the court by which the process is served.
(4) The particulars referred to in paragraph (2) are—
(a) the name and address of the relevant authority, together with its telephone and fax numbers and e-mail address; and
(b) the name of a person at the relevant authority who can provide the information referred to in paragraph (2)(a), together with his telephone and fax numbers and e-mail address.
(5) The justices' clerk or Crown Court officer must send, together with any process served outside the United Kingdom—
(a) any translation which is provided under section 3(3)(b) of the 2003 Act; and
(b) any translation of the information required to be given by this rule which is provided to him.
(6) In this rule 'process' has the same meaning as in section 51(3) of the 2003 Act.

R-600 Proof of service outside the United Kingdom

49.2 (1) A statement in a certificate given by or on behalf of the Secretary of State—
(a) that process has been served on any person under section 4(1) of the Crime (International Co-operation) Act 2003 (service of process otherwise than by post);
(b) of the manner in which service was effected; and
(c) of the date on which process was served;
shall be admissible as evidence of any facts so stated.
(2) In this rule 'process' has the same meaning as in section 51(3) of the 2003 Act.

R-601 Supply of copy of notice of request for assistance abroad

49.3 Where a request for assistance under section 7 of the Crime (International Co-operation) Act 2003 is made by a justice of the peace or a judge exercising the jurisdiction of the Crown Court and is sent in accordance with section 8(1) of the 2003 Act, the justices' clerk or the Crown Court officer shall send a copy of the letter of request to the Secretary of State as soon as practicable after the request has been made.

R-602 Persons entitled to appear and take part in proceedings before a nominated court, and exclusion of the public

49.4 A court nominated under section 15(1) of the Crime (International Co-operation) Act 2003 (nominating a court to receive evidence) may—
(a) determine who may appear or take part in the proceedings under Schedule 1 to the 2003 Act before the court and whether a party to the proceedings is entitled to be legally represented; and
(b) direct that the public be excluded from those proceedings if it thinks it necessary to do so in the interests of justice.

R-603 Record of proceedings to receive evidence before a nominated court

49.5 (1) Where a court is nominated under section 15(1) of the Crime (International Co-operation) Act 2003 the justices' clerk or Crown Court officer shall enter in an overseas record—
(a) details of the request in respect of which the notice under section 15(1) of the 2003 Act was given;
(b) the date on which, and place at which, the proceedings under Schedule 1 to the 2003 Act in respect of that request took place;
(c) the name of any witness who gave evidence at the proceedings in question;
(d) the name of any person who took part in the proceedings as a legal representative or an interpreter;
(e) whether a witness was required to give evidence on oath or (by virtue of section 5 of the Oaths Act 1978) after making a solemn affirmation; and
(f) whether the opportunity to cross-examine any witness was refused.
(2) When the court gives the evidence received by it under paragraph 6(1) of Schedule 1 to the 2003 Act to the court or authority that made the request or to the territorial authority for forwarding to the court or authority that made the request, the justices' clerk or Crown Court officer shall send to the court, authority or territorial authority (as the case may be) a copy of an extract of so much of the overseas record as relates to the proceedings in respect of that request.

Interpreter for the purposes of proceedings involving a television or telephone link R-604

49.6 (1) This rule applies where a court is nominated under section 30(3) (hearing witnesses in the UK through television links) or section 31(4) (hearing witnesses in the UK by telephone) of the Crime (International Co-operation) Act 2003.

(2) Where it appears to the justices' clerk or the Crown Court officer that the witness to be heard in the proceedings under Part 1 or 2 of Schedule 2 to the 2003 Act ('the relevant proceedings') is likely to give evidence in a language other than English, he shall make arrangements for an interpreter to be present at the proceedings to translate what is said into English.

(3) Where it appears to the justices' clerk or the Crown Court officer that the witness to be heard in the relevant proceedings is likely to give evidence in a language other than that in which the proceedings of the court referred to in section 30(1) or, as the case may be, 31(1) of the 2003 Act ('the external court') will be conducted, he shall make arrangements for an interpreter to be present at the relevant proceedings to translate what is said into the language in which the proceedings of the external court will be conducted.

(4) Where the evidence in the relevant proceedings is either given in a language other than English or is not translated into English by an interpreter, the court shall adjourn the proceedings until such time as an interpreter can be present to provide a translation into English.

(5) Where a court in Wales understands Welsh—

(a) paragraph (2) does not apply where it appears to the justices' clerk or Crown Court officer that the witness in question is likely to give evidence in Welsh;

(b) paragraph (4) does not apply where the evidence is given in Welsh; and

(c) any translation which is provided pursuant to paragraph (2) or (4) may be into Welsh instead of English.

Record of television link hearing before a nominated court R-605

49.7 (1) This rule applies where a court is nominated under section 30(3) of the Crime (International Co-operation) Act 2003.

(2) The justices' clerk or Crown Court officer shall enter in an overseas record—

(a) details of the request in respect of which the notice under section 30(3) of the 2003 Act was given;

(b) the date on which, and place at which, the proceedings under Part 1 of Schedule 2 to that Act in respect of that request took place;

(c) the technical conditions, such as the type of equipment used, under which the proceedings took place;

(d) the name of the witness who gave evidence;

(e) the name of any person who took part in the proceedings as a legal representative or an interpreter; and

(f) the language in which the evidence was given.

(3) As soon as practicable after the proceedings under Part 1 of Schedule 2 to the 2003 Act took place, the justices' clerk or Crown Court officer shall send to the external authority that made the request a copy of an extract of so much of the overseas record as relates to the proceedings in respect of that request.

Record of telephone link hearing before a nominated court R-606

49.8 (1) This rule applies where a court is nominated under section 31(4) of the Crime (International Co-operation) Act 2003.

(2) The justices' clerk or Crown Court officer shall enter in an overseas record—

(a) details of the request in respect of which the notice under section 31(4) of the 2003 Act was given;

(b) the date, time and place at which the proceedings under Part 2 of Schedule 2 to the 2003 Act took place;

(c) the name of the witness who gave evidence;

(d) the name of any interpreter who acted at the proceedings; and

(e) the language in which the evidence was given.

Overseas record R-607

49.9 (1) The overseas records of a magistrates' court shall be part of the register (within the meaning of section 150(1) of the Magistrates' Courts Act 1980).

(2) The overseas records of any court shall not be open to inspection by any person except—

(a) as authorised by the Secretary of State; or

(b) with the leave of the court.

R-608 **Overseas freezing orders**

49.10 (1) This rule applies where a court is nominated under section 21(1) of the Crime (International Co-operation) Act 2003 to give effect to an overseas freezing order.

(2) Where the Secretary of State serves a copy of such an order on the court officer—

(a) the general rule is that the court must consider the order no later than the next business day;

(b) exceptionally, the court may consider the order later than that, but not more than 5 business days after service.

(3) The court must not consider the order unless—

(a) it is satisfied that the chief officer of police for the area in which the evidence is situated has had notice of the order; and

(b) that chief officer of police has had an opportunity to make representations, at a hearing if that officer wants.

(4) The court may consider the order—

(a) without a hearing; or

(b) at a hearing, in public or in private.

R-609 **Overseas forfeiture orders**

49.11 (1) This rule applies where—

(a) the Crown Court can—

(i) make a restraint order under article 5 of the Criminal Justice (International Cooperation) Act 1990 (Enforcement of Overseas Forfeiture Orders) Order 2005, or

(ii) give effect to an external forfeiture order under article 19 of that Order;

(b) the Director of Public Prosecutions or the Director of the Serious Fraud Office receives—

(i) a request for the restraint of property to which article 3 of the 2005 Order applies, or

(ii) a request to give effect to an external forfeiture order to which article 15 of the Order applies; and

(c) the Director wants the Crown Court to—

(i) make such a restraint order, or

(ii) give effect to such a forfeiture order.

(2) The Director must—

(a) apply in writing;

(b) serve the application on the court officer; and

(c) serve the application on the defendant and on any other person affected by the order, unless the court is satisfied that—

(i) the application is urgent, or

(ii) there are reasonable grounds for believing that to give notice of the application would cause the dissipation of the property which is the subject of the application.

(3) The application must—

(a) identify the property the subject of the application;

(b) identify the person who is or who may become the subject of such a forfeiture order;

(c) explain how the requirements of the 2005 Order are satisfied, as the case may be—

(i) for making a restraint order, or

(ii) for giving effect to a forfeiture order;

(d) where the application is to give effect to a forfeiture order, include an application to appoint the Director as the enforcement authority; and

(e) propose the terms of the Crown Court order.

(4) If the court allows the application, it must—

(a) where it decides to make a restraint order—

(i) specify the property the subject of the order,

(ii) specify the person or persons who are prohibited from dealing with that property,

(iii) specify any exception to that prohibition, and

(iv) include any ancillary order that the court believes is appropriate to ensure that the restraint order is effective;

(b) where it decides to give effect to a forfeiture order, exercise its power to—

(i) direct the registration of the order as an order of the Crown Court,

(ii) give directions for notice of the order to be given to any person affected by it, and

(iii) appoint the applicant Director as the enforcement authority.

(5) Paragraph (6) applies where a person affected by an order, or the Director, wants the court to vary or discharge a restraint order or cancel the registration of a forfeiture order.

(6) Such a person must—
(a) apply in writing as soon as practicable after becoming aware of the grounds for doing so;
(b) serve the application on the court officer and, as applicable—
(i) the other party, and
(ii) any other person who will or may be affected;
(c) explain why it is appropriate, as the case may be—
(i) for the restraint order to be varied or discharged, or
(ii) for the registration of the forfeiture order to be cancelled;
(d) propose the terms of any variation; and
(e) ask for a hearing, if one is wanted, and explain why it is needed.
(7) The court may—
(a) consider an application
(i) at a hearing, which must be in private unless the court otherwise directs, or
(ii) without a hearing;
(b) allow an application to be made orally.

Overseas restraint orders **R-610**

49.12 (1) This rule applies where—
(a) the Crown Court can give effect to an overseas restraint order under regulation 10 of the Criminal Justice and Data Protection (Protocol No. 36) Regulations 2014;
(b) the Director of Public Prosecutions or the Director of the Serious Fraud Office receives a request from a court or authority in another European Union member State to give effect to such an order; and
(c) the Director serves on the Crown Court officer—
(i) the certificate which accompanied the request for enforcement of the order,
(ii) a copy of the order restraining the property to which that certificate relates, and
(iii) a copy of an order confiscating the property in respect of which the restraint order was made, or an indication of when such a confiscation order is expected.
(2) On service of those documents on the court officer—
(a) the general rule is that the Crown Court must consider the order, with a view to its registration, no later than the next business day;
(b) exceptionally, the court may consider the order later than that, but not more than 5 business days after service.
(3) The court—
(a) must not consider the order unless the Director—
(i) is present, or
(ii) has had a reasonable opportunity to make representations;
(b) subject to that, may consider the order—
(i) at a hearing, which must be in private unless the court otherwise directs, or
(ii) without a hearing.
(4) If the court decides to give effect to the order, the court must—
(a) direct its registration as an order of the Crown Court; and
(b) give directions for notice of the order to be given to any person affected by it.
(5) Paragraph (6) applies where a person affected by the order, or the Director, wants the court to cancel the registration or vary the property to which the order applies.
(6) Such a person must—
(a) apply in writing as soon as practicable after becoming aware of the grounds for doing so;
(b) serve the application on the court officer and, as applicable—
(i) the other party, and
(ii) any other person who will or may be affected;
(c) explain, as applicable—
(i) when the overseas restraint order ceased to have effect in the European Union member State in which it was made,
(ii) why continuing to give effect to that order would be impossible as a consequence of an immunity under the law of England and Wales,
(iii) why continuing to give effect to that order would be incompatible with a Convention right within the meaning of the Human Rights Act 1998,
(iv) why therefore it is appropriate for the registration to be cancelled or varied;
(d) include with the application any evidence in support;
(e) propose the terms of any variation; and
(f) ask for a hearing, if one is wanted, and explain why it is needed.

R-611 **Overseas confiscation orders**

49.13 (1) This rule applies where—
(a) the Crown Court can give effect to an overseas confiscation order under regulation 15 of the Criminal Justice and Data Protection (Protocol No. 36) Regulations 2014;
(b) the Director of Public Prosecutions or the Director of the Serious Fraud Office receives a request from a court or authority in another European Union member State to give effect to such an order; and
(c) the Director serves on the Crown Court officer—
(i) the certificate which accompanied the request for enforcement of the order, and
(ii) a copy of the confiscation order to which that certificate relates.

(2) The court—
(a) must not consider the order unless the Director—
(i) is present, or
(ii) has had a reasonable opportunity to make representations;
(b) subject to that, may consider the order—
(i) at a hearing, which must be in private unless the court otherwise directs, or
(ii) without a hearing.

(3) If the court decides to give effect to the order, the court must—
(a) direct its registration as an order of the Crown Court; and
(b) give directions for notice of the order to be given to any person affected by it.

(4) Paragraph (5) applies where a person affected by the order, or the Director, wants the court to cancel the registration or vary the property to which the order applies.

(5) Such a person must—
(a) apply in writing as soon as practicable after becoming aware of the grounds for doing so;
(b) serve the application on the court officer and, as applicable—
(i) the other party, and
(ii) any other person who will or may be affected;
(c) explain, as applicable—
(i) when the overseas confiscation order ceased to have effect in the European Union member State in which it was made,
(ii) why continuing to give effect to that order would be statute-barred, provided that the criminal conduct that gave rise to the order falls within the jurisdiction of England and Wales,
(iii) why continuing to give effect to that order would be impossible as a consequence of an immunity under the law of England and Wales,
(iv) why continuing to give effect to that order would be incompatible with a Convention right within the meaning of the Human Rights Act 1998,
(v) why therefore it is appropriate for the registration to be cancelled or varied;
(d) include with the application any evidence in support;
(e) propose the terms of any variation; and
(f) ask for a hearing, if one is wanted, and explain why it is needed.

R-612 **Giving effect to a European investigation order for the receipt of oral evidence**

49.14 (1) This rule applies where a court is nominated under regulation 35 of the Criminal Justice (European Investigation Order) Regulations 2017 to give effect to a European investigation order by—
(a) examining a witness; and
(b) transmitting the product to the participating State in which the order was made.

(2) The court—
(a) must give effect to the order within 90 days beginning with the day after the day on which the court is nominated, unless a different period is agreed between the court, the Secretary of State and the issuing authority in the participating State in which the order was made;
(b) must conduct the examination in accordance with Schedule 5 to the 2017 Regulations;
(c) subject to that, may conduct the examination—
(i) in public or in private,
(ii) in the presence of such other persons as the court allows.

(3) Subject to paragraph (2) and to such adaptations as the court directs, the court must receive the witness' evidence as if it were given at trial and to that extent—
(a) Part 17 (Witness summonses, warrants and orders) applies to the exercise of the power to secure a witness' attendance under paragraph 2 of Schedule 5 to the 2017 Regulations as if that power were one of those listed in rule 17.1(a) (When this Part applies);
(b) rule 24.4 (Evidence of a witness in person) applies where the evidence is received in a magistrates' court;

(c) rule 25.11 (Evidence of a witness in person) applies where the evidence is received in the Crown Court.

Giving effect to a European investigation order for hearing a person by live link R-613

49.15 (1) This rule applies where a court is nominated under regulation 36 or 37 of the Criminal Justice (European Investigation Order) Regulations 2017 to give effect to a European investigation order by—

(a) facilitating the giving of oral evidence by live video or audio link by a person who is in England and Wales in proceedings in the participating State in which the order was made; and

(b) superintending the giving of evidence by that person by those means.

(2) The court—

(a) must give effect to the order within 90 days beginning with the day after the day on which the court is nominated, unless a different period is agreed between the court, the Secretary of State and the issuing authority in the participating State in which the order was made;

(b) must conduct the proceedings—

(i) in accordance with Schedule 6 to the 2017 Regulations,

(ii) subject to that, under the supervision of the court which receives the evidence in the participating State in which the order was made;

(c) subject to paragraph (2)(b), may conduct the proceedings—

(i) in public or in private,

(ii) in the presence of such other persons as the court allows.

(3) Subject to paragraph (2) and to such adaptations as the court directs, the court must conduct the proceedings as if the witness were giving evidence at a trial in England and Wales and to that extent—

(a) Part 17 (Witness summonses, warrants and orders) applies to the exercise of the power to secure a witness' attendance under paragraph 2 of Schedule 6 to the 2017 Regulations as if that power were one of those listed in rule 17.1(a) (When this Part applies);

(b) rule 24.4 (Evidence of a witness in person) applies where the proceedings take place in a magistrates' court;

(c) rule 25.11 (Evidence of a witness in person) applies where the proceedings take place in the Crown Court.

Giving effect to a European investigation order by issuing a search warrant or production, etc. order R-614

49.16 (1) This rule applies where—

(a) a court is nominated under regulation 38 of the Criminal Justice (European Investigation Order) Regulations 2017 (Search warrants and production orders: nominating a court) to give effect to a European investigation order by issuing—

(i) a search warrant under regulation 39(1) (Search warrants and production orders: giving effect to the European investigation order),

(ii) a production order in respect of excluded material or special procedure material under regulation 39(2), or

(iii) a search warrant in respect of excluded material or special procedure material under regulation 39(8);

(b) a court is nominated under regulation 43 of the 2017 Regulations (Nominating a court to make a customer information order or an account monitoring order) to give effect to a European investigation order by making—

(i) a customer information order under regulation 44 (Court's power to make a customer information order), or

(ii) an account monitoring order under regulation 45 (Court's power to make an account monitoring order).

(2) The Secretary of State must serve on the court officer a draft warrant or order in terms that give effect to the European investigation order.

(3) The court must consider the European investigation order—

(a) without a hearing, as a general rule; and

(b) within 5 business days beginning with the day after the day on which the court is nominated, unless a different period is agreed between the court and the Secretary of State.

(4) The court must not give effect to the European investigation order unless it is satisfied that each of the following authorities has had notice of that order and has had an opportunity to make representations, at a hearing if that authority wants—

(a) the relevant chief officer of police; and

(b) any other authority that will be responsible for the execution of the warrant or order.

R-615 Application to vary or revoke a search warrant or production etc. order issued to give effect to a European investigation order

49.17 (1) This rule applies where—
(a) under regulation 41 of the Criminal Justice (European Investigation Order) Regulations 2017 (Power to revoke or vary a search warrant or production order or to authorise the release of evidence seized or produced) the court can vary or revoke—
(i) a search warrant issued under regulation 39(1) of the 2017 Regulations,
(ii) a production order issued in respect of excluded material or special procedure material under regulation 39(2),
(iii) a search warrant issued in respect of excluded material or special procedure material under regulation 39(8);
(b) under regulation 41 of the 2017 Regulations the court can authorise the release of evidence seized by or produced to a constable on the execution of a search warrant or production order issued on an application under rule 49.16;
(c) under regulation 48 of the 2017 Regulations (Power to vary or revoke customer information and account monitoring orders) the court can vary or revoke—
(i) a customer information order issued under regulation 44,
(ii) an account monitoring order issued under regulation 45.
(2) The applicant must—
(a) apply in writing and serve the application on—
(i) the court officer, and as appropriate
(ii) the chief officer of police to whom the European investigation order was sent by the Secretary of State,
(iii) any other person affected by the warrant or order;
(b) demonstrate that the applicant is, as the case may be—
(i) the chief officer of police to whom the European investigation order was sent by the Secretary of State, or
(ii) any other person affected by the warrant or order.
(3) An application to vary a warrant or order must propose the terms of the variation.
(4) An application to revoke a warrant or order or to authorise the release of evidence seized or produced must indicate, as the case may be, that—
(a) the European investigation order has been withdrawn or no longer has effect in the participating State in which it was issued; or
(b) one of the grounds for refusing to give effect to the order obtains.
(5) Where the court—
(a) varies a warrant or order to which this rule applies the court officer must promptly serve a copy of that warrant or order, as varied, on the Secretary of State;
(b) revokes such a warrant or order the court officer must promptly notify the Secretary of State.

Criminal Procedure Rules Part 50 Extradition

Section 1: general rules

R-616 When this Part applies

50.1 (1) This Part applies to extradition under Part 1 or Part 2 of the Extradition Act 2003.
(2) Section 2 of this Part applies to proceedings in a magistrates' court, and in that Section—
(a) rules 50.3 to 50.7, 50.15 and 50.16 apply to extradition under Part 1 of the Act;
(b) rules 50.3, 50.4 and 50.8 to 50.16 apply to extradition under Part 2 of the Act.
(3) Section 3 of this Part applies where—
(a) a party wants to appeal to the High Court against an order by the magistrates' court or by the Secretary of State;
(b) a party to an appeal to the High Court wants to appeal further to the Supreme Court under—
(i) section 32 of the Act (appeal under Part 1 of the Act), or
(ii) section 114 of the Act (appeal under Part 2 of the Act).
(4) Section 4 of this Part applies to proceedings in a magistrates' court under—
(a) sections 54 and 55 of the Act (Request for consent to other offence being dealt with; Questions for decision at consent hearing);
(b) sections 56 and 57 of the Act (Request for consent to further extradition to category 1 territory; Questions for decision at consent hearing).
(5) In this Part, and for the purposes of this Part in other rules—
(a) 'magistrates' court' means a District Judge (Magistrates' Courts) exercising the powers to which Section 2 of this Part applies;

(b) 'presenting officer' means an officer of the National Crime Agency, a police officer, a prosecutor or other person representing an authority or territory seeking the extradition of a defendant;
(c) 'defendant' means a person arrested under Part 1 or Part 2 of the Extradition Act 2003.

Further objective in extradition proceedings **R-617**

50.2 When exercising a power to which this Part applies, in furthering the overriding objective, in accordance with rule 1.3, the court must have regard to the importance of—
(a) mutual confidence and recognition between judicial authorities in the United Kingdom and in requesting territories; and
(b) the conduct of extradition proceedings in accordance with international obligations, including obligations to deal swiftly with extradition requests.

Section 2: extradition proceedings in a magistrates' court

Exercise of magistrates' court's powers **R-618**

50.3 (1) The general rule is that the magistrates' court must exercise its powers at a hearing in public, but—
(a) that is subject to any power the court has to—
(i) impose reporting restrictions,
(ii) withhold information from the public, or
(iii) order a hearing in private; and
(b) despite the general rule the court may, without a hearing—
(i) give any directions to which rule 50.4 applies (Case management in the magistrates' court and duty of court officer), or
(ii) determine an application which these Rules allow to be determined by a magistrates' court without a hearing in a case to which this Part does not apply.
(2) If the court so directs, a party may attend by live link any hearing except an extradition hearing under rule 50.6 or 50.13.
(3) Where the defendant is absent from a hearing—
(a) the general rule is that the court must proceed as if the defendant—
(i) were present, and
(ii) opposed extradition on any ground of which the court has been made aware;
(b) the general rule does not apply if the defendant is under 18;
(c) the general rule is subject to the court being satisfied that—
(i) the defendant had reasonable notice of where and when the hearing would take place,
(ii) the defendant has been made aware that the hearing might proceed in his or her absence, and
(iii) there is no good reason for the defendant's absence; and
(d) the general rule does not apply but the court may exercise its powers in the defendant's absence where—
(i) the court discharges the defendant,
(ii) the defendant is represented and the defendant's presence is impracticable by reason of his or her ill health or disorderly conduct, or
(iii) on an application under rule 50.32 (Application for consent to deal with another offence or for consent to further extradition), the defendant is represented or the defendant's presence is impracticable by reason of his or her detention in the territory to which he or she has been extradited.
(4) The court may exercise its power to adjourn—
(a) if either party asks, or on its own initiative; and
(b) in particular—
(i) to allow there to be obtained information that the court requires,
(ii) following a provisional arrest under Part 1 of the Extradition Act 2003, pending receipt of the warrant,
(iii) following a provisional arrest under Part 2 of the Act, pending receipt of the extradition request,
(iv) if the court is informed that the defendant is serving a custodial sentence in the United Kingdom,
(v) if it appears to the court that the defendant is not fit to be extradited, unless the court discharges the defendant for that reason,
(vi) where a court dealing with a warrant to which Part 1 of the Act applies is informed that another such warrant has been received in the United Kingdom,
(vii) where a court dealing with a warrant to which Part 1 of the Act applies is informed of a request for the temporary transfer of the defendant to the territory to which the

defendant's extradition is sought, or a request for the defendant to speak to the authorities of that territory, or

(viii) during a hearing to which rule 50.32 applies (Application for consent to deal with another offence or for consent to further extradition).

(5) The court must exercise its power to adjourn if informed that the defendant has been charged with an offence in the United Kingdom.

(6) The general rule is that, before exercising a power to which this Part applies, the court must give each party an opportunity to make representations, unless that party is absent without good reason.

(7) The court may—

(a) shorten a time limit or extend it (even after it has expired), unless that is inconsistent with other legislation;

(b) direct that a notice or application be served on any person;

(c) allow a notice or application to be in a different form to one set out in the Practice Direction, or to be presented orally.

(8) A party who wants an extension of time within which to serve a notice or make an application must—

(a) apply for that extension of time when serving that notice or making that application; and

(b) give the reasons for the application for an extension of time.

R-619 Case management in the magistrates' court and duty of court officer

50.4 (1) The magistrates' court and the parties have the same duties and powers as under Part 3 (Case management), subject to—

(a) rule 50.2 (Further objective in extradition proceedings); and

(b) paragraph (2) of this rule.

(2) Rule 3.6 (Application to vary a direction) does not apply to a decision to extradite or discharge.

(3) Where this rule applies, active case management by the court includes—

(a) if the court requires information from the authorities in the requesting territory—

(i) nominating a court officer, the designated authority which certified the arrest warrant where Part 1 of the Extradition Act 2003 Act applies, a party or other person to convey that request to those authorities, and

(ii) in a case in which the terms of that request need to be prepared in accordance with directions by the court, giving such directions accordingly;

(b) giving such directions as are required where, under section 21B of the Extradition Act 2003, the parties agree—

(i) to the temporary transfer of the defendant to the requesting territory, or

(ii) that the defendant should speak with representatives of an authority in that territory.

(4) Where this rule applies, active assistance by the parties includes—

(a) applying for any direction needed as soon as reasonably practicable;

(b) concisely explaining the reasons for any application for the court to direct—

(i) the preparation of a request to which paragraph (3)(a) applies,

(ii) the making of arrangements to which paragraph (3)(b) applies.

(5) Where this rule applies, active assistance by the presenting officer includes—

(a) taking reasonable steps to ensure that the defendant will be able to understand (with help, if necessary)—

(i) what is alleged by the warrant, if Part 1 of the 2003 Act applies, or

(ii) the content of the extradition request, if Part 2 of the Act applies; and

(b) providing in writing identification of the equivalent offence or offences under the law of England and Wales for the conduct being relied on if—

(i) this is raised for the defence as an issue and the court considers it necessary to identify the equivalent offence or offences in writing, or

(ii) the defendant is not represented.

(6) The court officer must—

(a) as soon as practicable, serve notice of the court's decision to extradite or discharge—

(i) on the defendant,

(ii) on the designated authority which certified the arrest warrant, where Part 1 of the 2003 Act applies,

(iii) on the Secretary of State, where Part 2 of the Act applies; and

(b) give the court such assistance as it requires.

Extradition under Part 1 of the Extradition Act 2003

R-620 Preliminary hearing after arrest

50.5 (1) This rule applies where the defendant is first brought before the court after—

(a) arrest under a warrant to which Part 1 of the Extradition Act 2003 applies; or

(b) provisional arrest under Part 1 of the Act.

(2) The presenting officer must—
(a) serve on the court officer—
(i) the arrest warrant, and
(ii) a certificate, given by the authority designated by the Secretary of State, that the warrant was issued by an authority having the function of issuing such warrants in the territory to which the defendant's extradition is sought; or
(b) apply at once for an extension of time within which to serve that warrant and that certificate.
(3) An application under paragraph (2)(b) must—
(a) explain why the requirement to serve the warrant and certificate at once could not reasonably be complied with; and
(b) include—
(i) any written material in support of that explanation, and
(ii) representations about bail pending service of those documents.
(4) When the presenting officer serves the warrant and certificate, in the following sequence the court must—
(a) decide whether the defendant is the person in respect of whom the warrant was issued;
(b) explain, in terms the defendant can understand (with help, if necessary)—
(i) the allegation made in the warrant, and
(ii) that the defendant may consent to extradition, and how that may be done and with what effect;
(c) give directions for an extradition hearing to begin—
(i) no more than 21 days after the defendant's arrest, or
(ii) if either party so applies, at such a later date as the court decides is in the interests of justice;
(d) consider any ancillary application, including an application about bail pending the extradition hearing; and
(e) give such directions as are required for the preparation and conduct of the extradition hearing.

Extradition hearing **R-621**

50.6 (1) This rule applies at the extradition hearing directed under rule 50.5.
(2) In the following sequence, the court must decide—
(a) whether the offence specified in the warrant is an extradition offence;
(b) whether a bar to extradition applies, namely—
(i) the rule against double jeopardy,
(ii) absence of prosecution decision,
(iii) extraneous considerations,
(iv) the passage of time,
(v) the defendant's age,
(vi) speciality,
(vii) earlier extradition or transfer to the United Kingdom, or
(viii) forum;
(c) where the warrant alleges that the defendant is unlawfully at large after conviction, whether conviction was in the defendant's presence and if not—
(i) whether the defendant was absent deliberately,
(ii) if the defendant was not absent deliberately, whether the defendant would be entitled to a retrial (or to a review of the conviction, amounting to a retrial);
(d) whether extradition would be—
(i) compatible with the defendant's human rights, and
(ii) proportionate;
(e) whether it would be unjust or oppressive to extradite the defendant because of his or her physical or mental condition;
(f) after deciding each of (a) to (e) above, before progressing to the next, whether to order the defendant's discharge,
(g) whether to order the temporary transfer of the defendant to the territory to which the defendant's extradition is sought.
(3) If the court discharges the defendant, the court must consider any ancillary application, including an application about—
(a) reporting restrictions; or
(b) costs.
(4) If the court does not discharge the defendant, the court must—
(a) exercise its power to order the defendant's extradition;
(b) explain, in terms the defendant can understand (with help, if necessary), that the defendant may appeal to the High Court within the next 7 days; and

(c) consider any ancillary application, including an application about—
(i) bail pending extradition,
(ii) reporting restrictions, or
(iii) costs.

(5) If the court orders the defendant's extradition, the court must order its postponement where—
(a) the defendant has been charged with an offence in the United Kingdom; or
(b) the defendant has been sentenced to imprisonment or detention in the United Kingdom.

R-622 **Discharge where warrant withdrawn**

50.7 (1) This rule applies where the authority that certified the warrant gives the court officer notice that the warrant has been withdrawn—
(a) after the start of the hearing under rule 50.5; and
(b) before the court orders the defendant's extradition or discharge.

(2) The court must exercise its power to discharge the defendant.

Extradition under Part 2 of the Extradition Act 2003

R-623 **Issue of arrest warrant**

50.8 (1) This rule applies where the Secretary of State serves on the court officer—
(a) an extradition request to which Part 2 of the Extradition Act 2003 applies;
(b) a certificate given by the Secretary of State that the request was received in the way approved for the request; and
(c) a copy of any Order in Council which applies to the request.

(2) In the following sequence, the court must decide—
(a) whether the offence in respect of which extradition is requested is an extradition offence; and
(b) whether there is sufficient evidence, or (where the Secretary of State has so ordered, for this purpose) information, to justify the issue of a warrant of arrest.

(3) The court may issue an arrest warrant—
(a) without giving the parties an opportunity to make representations; and
(b) without a hearing, or at a hearing in public or in private.

R-624 **Preliminary hearing after arrest**

50.9 (1) This rule applies where a defendant is first brought before the court after arrest under a warrant to which rule 50.8 applies.

(2) In the following sequence, the court must—
(a) explain, in terms the defendant can understand (with help, if necessary)—
(i) the content of the extradition request, and
(ii) that the defendant may consent to extradition, and how that may be done and with what effect;
(b) give directions for an extradition hearing to begin—
(i) no more than 2 months later, or
(ii) if either party so applies, at such a later date as the court decides is in the interests of justice;
(c) consider any ancillary application, including an application about bail pending the extradition hearing; and
(d) give such directions as are required for the preparation and conduct of the extradition hearing.

R-625 **Issue of provisional arrest warrant**

50.10 (1) This rule applies where a presenting officer wants a justice of the peace to issue a provisional arrest warrant under Part 2 of the Extradition Act 2003, pending receipt of an extradition request.

(2) The presenting officer must—
(a) serve an application for a warrant on the court officer; and
(b) verify that application on oath or affirmation.

(3) In the following sequence, the justice must decide—
(a) whether the alleged offence is an extradition offence; and
(b) whether there is sufficient evidence, or (where the Secretary of State has so ordered, for this purpose) information, to justify the issue of a warrant of arrest.

R-626 **Preliminary hearing after provisional arrest**

50.11 (1) This rule applies where a defendant is first brought before the court after arrest under a provisional arrest warrant to which rule 50.10 applies.

(2) The court must—
(a) explain, in terms the defendant can understand (with help, if necessary)—
(i) the allegation in respect of which the warrant was issued, and
(ii) that the defendant may consent to extradition, and how that may be done and with what effect; and
(b) consider any ancillary application, including an application about bail pending receipt of the extradition request.

Arrangement of extradition hearing after provisional arrest R-627

50.12 (1) This rule applies when the Secretary of State serves on the court officer—
(a) a request for extradition in respect of which a defendant has been arrested under a provisional arrest warrant to which rule 50.10 applies;
(b) a certificate given by the Secretary of State that the request was received in the way approved for the request; and
(c) a copy of any Order in Council which applies to the request.
(2) Unless a time limit for service of the request has expired, the court must—
(a) give directions for an extradition hearing to begin—
(i) no more than 2 months after service of the request, or
(ii) if either party so applies, at such a later date as the court decides is in the interests of justice;
(b) consider any ancillary application, including an application about bail pending the extradition hearing; and
(c) give such directions as are required for the preparation and conduct of the extradition hearing.

Extradition hearing R-628

50.13 (1) This rule applies at the extradition hearing directed under rule 50.9 or rule 50.12.
(2) In the following sequence, the court must decide—
(a) whether the documents served on the court officer by the Secretary of State include—
(i) those listed in rule 50.8(1) or rule 50.12(1), as the case may be,
(ii) particulars of the person whose extradition is requested,
(iii) particulars of the offence specified in the request, and
(iv) as the case may be, a warrant for the defendant's arrest, or a certificate of the defendant's conviction and (if applicable) sentence, issued in the requesting territory;
(b) whether the defendant is the person whose extradition is requested;
(c) whether the offence specified in the request is an extradition offence;
(d) whether the documents served on the court officer by the Secretary of State have been served also on the defendant;
(e) whether a bar to extradition applies, namely—
(i) the rule against double jeopardy,
(ii) extraneous considerations,
(iii) the passage of time,
(iv) hostage-taking considerations, or
(v) forum;
(f) where the request accuses the defendant of an offence, whether there is evidence which would be sufficient to make a case requiring an answer by the defendant if the extradition proceedings were a trial (unless the Secretary of State has otherwise ordered, for this purpose);
(g) where the request accuses the defendant of being unlawfully at large after conviction, whether the defendant was—
(i) convicted in his or her presence, or
(ii) absent deliberately;
(h) where the request accuses the defendant of being unlawfully at large after conviction, and the defendant was absent but not deliberately—
(i) whether the defendant would be entitled to a retrial (or to a review of the conviction amounting to a retrial), and
(ii) if so, whether there is evidence which would be sufficient to make a case requiring an answer by the defendant if the extradition proceedings were a trial (unless the Secretary of State has otherwise ordered, for this purpose);
(i) whether extradition would be compatible with the defendant's human rights;
(j) whether it would be unjust or oppressive to extradite the defendant because of his or her physical or mental condition;

(k) after deciding each of (a) to (j) above, before progressing to the next, whether to order the defendant's discharge.

(3) If the court discharges the defendant, the court must consider any ancillary application, including an application about—

(a) reporting restrictions; or

(b) costs.

(4) If the court does not discharge the defendant, the court must—

(a) exercise its power to send the case to the Secretary of State to decide whether to extradite the defendant;

(b) explain, in terms the defendant can understand (with help, if necessary), that—

(i) the defendant may appeal to the High Court not more than 14 days after being informed of the Secretary of State's decision, and

(ii) any such appeal brought before the Secretary of State's decision has been made will not be heard until after that decision; and

(c) consider any ancillary application, including an application about—

(i) bail pending extradition,

(ii) reporting restrictions, or

(iii) costs.

(5) If the Secretary of State orders the defendant's extradition, the court must order its postponement where—

(a) the defendant has been charged with an offence in the United Kingdom; or

(b) the defendant has been sentenced to imprisonment or detention in the United Kingdom.

R-629 Discharge where extradition request withdrawn

50.14 (1) This rule applies where the Secretary of State gives the court officer notice that the extradition request has been withdrawn—

(a) after the start of the hearing under rule 50.9 or 50.11; and

(b) before the court—

(i) sends the case to the Secretary of State to decide whether to extradite the defendant, or

(ii) discharges the defendant.

(2) The court must exercise its power to discharge the defendant.

Evidence at extradition hearing

R-630 Introduction of additional evidence

50.15 (1) Where a party wants to introduce evidence at an extradition hearing under the law that would apply if that hearing were a trial, the relevant Part of these Rules applies with such adaptations as the court directs.

(2) If the court admits as evidence the written statement of a witness—

(a) each relevant part of the statement must be read or summarised aloud; or

(b) the court must read the statement and its gist must be summarised aloud.

(3) If a party introduces in evidence a fact admitted by another party, or the parties jointly admit a fact, a written record must be made of the admission.

Discharge after failure to comply with a time limit

R-631 Defendant's application to be discharged

50.16 (1) This rule applies where a defendant wants to be discharged—

(a) because of a failure—

(i) to give the defendant a copy of any warrant under which the defendant is arrested as soon as practicable after arrest,

(ii) to bring the defendant before the court as soon as practicable after arrest under a warrant,

(iii) to bring the defendant before the court no more than 48 hours after provisional arrest under Part 1 of the Extradition Act 2003;

(b) following the expiry of a time limit for—

(i) service of a warrant to which Part 1 of the 2003 Act applies, after provisional arrest under that Part of the Act (48 hours, under section 6 of the Act, unless the court otherwise directs),

(ii) service of an extradition request to which Part 2 of the Act applies, after provisional arrest under that Part of the Act (45 days, under section 74 of the Act, unless the Secretary of State has otherwise ordered for this purpose),

(iii) receipt of an undertaking that the defendant will be returned to complete a sentence in the United Kingdom, where the court required such an undertaking (21 days, under section 37 of the Act),
(iv) making an extradition order, after the defendant has consented to extradition under Part 1 of the Act (10 days, under section 46 of the Act),
(v) extradition, where an extradition order has been made under Part 1 of the Act and any appeal by the defendant has failed (10 days, under sections 35, 36 and 47 of the Act, unless the court otherwise directs),
(vi) extradition, where an extradition order has been made under Part 2 of the Act and any appeal by the defendant has failed (28 days, under sections 117 and 118 of the Act),
(vii) the resumption of extradition proceedings, where those proceedings were adjourned pending disposal of another extradition claim which has concluded (21 days, under section 180 of the Act),
(viii) extradition, where extradition has been deferred pending the disposal of another extradition claim which has concluded (21 days, under section 181 of the Act), or
(ix) re-extradition, where the defendant has been returned to the United Kingdom to serve a sentence before serving a sentence overseas (as soon as practicable, under section 187 of the Act); or

(c) because an extradition hearing does not begin on the date arranged by the court.

(2) Unless the court otherwise directs—
(a) such a defendant must apply in writing and serve the application on—
(i) the magistrates' court officer,
(ii) the High Court officer, where paragraph (1)(b)(v) applies, and
(iii) the prosecutor;
(b) the application must explain the grounds on which it is made; and
(c) the court officer must arrange a hearing as soon as practicable, and in any event no later than the second business day after an application is served.

Section 3: appeal to the High Court

Exercise of the High Court's powers R-632

50.17 (1) The general rule is that the High Court must exercise its powers at a hearing in public, but—
(a) that is subject to any power the court has to—
(i) impose reporting restrictions,
(ii) withhold information from the public, or
(iii) order a hearing in private;
(b) despite the general rule, the court may determine without a hearing—
(i) an application for the court to consider out of time an application for permission to appeal to the High Court,
(ii) an application for permission to appeal to the High Court (but a renewed such application must be determined at a hearing),
(iii) an application for permission to appeal from the High Court to the Supreme Court,
(iv) an application for permission to reopen a decision under rule 50.27 (Reopening the determination of an appeal), or
(v) an application concerning bail; and
(c) despite the general rule the court may, without a hearing—
(i) give case management directions,
(ii) reject a notice or application and, if applicable, dismiss an application for permission to appeal, where rule 50.31 (Payment of High Court fees) applies and the party who served the notice or application fails to comply with that rule, or
(iii) make a determination to which the parties have agreed in writing.

(2) If the High Court so directs, a party may attend a hearing by live link.

(3) The general rule is that where the High Court exercises its powers at a hearing it may do so only if the defendant attends, in person or by live link, but, despite the general rule, the court may exercise its powers in the defendant's absence if—
(a) the defendant waives the right to attend;
(b) subject to any appeal to the Supreme Court, the result of the court's order would be the discharge of the defendant; or
(c) the defendant is represented and—
(i) the defendant is in custody, or

(ii) the defendant's presence is impracticable by reason of his or her ill health or disorderly conduct.

(4) If the High Court gives permission to appeal to the High Court—

(a) unless the court otherwise directs, the decision indicates that the appellant has permission to appeal on every ground identified by the appeal notice;

(b) unless the court otherwise directs, the decision indicates that the court finds reasonably arguable each ground on which the appellant has permission to appeal; and

(c) the court must give such directions as are required for the preparation and conduct of the appeal, including a direction as to whether the appeal must be heard by a single judge of the High Court or by a divisional court.

(5) If the High Court decides without a hearing an application for permission to appeal from the High Court to the Supreme Court, the High Court must announce its decision at a hearing in public.

(6) The High Court may—

(a) shorten a time limit or extend it (even after it has expired), unless that is inconsistent with other legislation;

(b) allow or require a party to vary or supplement a notice that that party has served;

(c) direct that a notice or application be served on any person;

(d) allow a notice or application to be in a different form to one set out in the Practice Direction, or to be presented orally.

(7) A party who wants an extension of time within which to serve a notice or make an application must—

(a) apply for that extension of time when serving that notice or making that application; and

(b) give the reasons for the application for an extension of time.

R-633 **Case management in the High Court**

50.18 (1) The High Court and the parties have the same duties and powers as under Part 3 (Case management), subject to—

(a) rule 50.2 (Further objective in extradition proceedings); and

(b) paragraph (3) of this rule.

(2) A master of the High Court, a deputy master, or a court officer nominated for the purpose by the Lord Chief Justice—

(a) must fulfil the duty of active case management under rule 3.2, and in fulfilling that duty may exercise any of the powers of case management under—

(i) rule 3.5 (the court's general powers of case management),

(ii) rule 3.10(3) (requiring a certificate of readiness), and

(iii) rule 3.11 (requiring a party to identify intentions and anticipated requirements)

subject to the directions of a judge of the High Court; and

(b) must nominate a case progression officer under rule 3.4.

(3) Rule 3.6 (Application to vary a direction) does not apply to a decision to give or to refuse—

(a) permission to appeal; or

(b) permission to reopen a decision under rule 50.27 (Reopening the determination of an appeal).

R-634 **Service of appeal notice**

50.19 (1) A party who wants to appeal to the High Court must serve an appeal notice on—

(a) in every case—

(i) the High Court officer,

(ii) the other party, and

(iii) the Director of Public Prosecutions, unless the Director already has the conduct of the proceedings;

(b) the designated authority which certified the arrest warrant, where Part 1 of the Extradition Act 2003 applies; and

(c) the Secretary of State, where the appeal is against—

(i) an order by the Secretary of State, or

(ii) an order by the magistrates' court sending a case to the Secretary of State.

(2) A defendant who wants to appeal must serve the appeal notice—

(a) not more than 7 days after the day on which the magistrates' court makes an order for the defendant's extradition, starting with that day, where that order is under Part 1 of the Extradition Act 2003;

(b) not more than 14 days after the day on which the Secretary of State informs the defendant of the Secretary of State's decision, starting with that day, where under Part 2 of the Act—

(i) the magistrates' court sends the case to the Secretary of State for a decision whether to extradite the defendant, or
(ii) the Secretary of State orders the defendant's extradition.

(3) An authority or territory seeking the defendant's extradition which wants to appeal against an order for the defendant's discharge must serve the appeal notice—
(a) not more than 7 days after the day on which the magistrates' court makes that order, starting with that day, if the order is under Part 1 of the Extradition Act 2003;
(b) not more than 14 days after the day on which the magistrates' court makes that order, starting with that day, if the order is under Part 2 of the Act;
(c) not more than 14 days after the day on which the Secretary of State informs the territory's representative of the Secretary of State's order, starting with that day, where the order is under Part 2 of the Act.

Form of appeal notice R-635

50.20 (1) An appeal notice constitutes—
(a) an application to the High Court for permission to appeal to that court; and
(b) an appeal to that court, if the court gives permission.

(2) An appeal notice must be in writing.

(3) In every case, the appeal notice must—
(a) specify—
(i) the date of the defendant's arrest under Part 1 or Part 2 of the Extradition Act 2003, and
(ii) the decision about which the appellant wants to appeal, including the date of that decision;
(b) identify each ground of appeal on which the appellant relies;
(c) summarise the relevant facts;
(d) identify any document or other material that the appellant thinks the court will need to decide the appeal; and
(e) include or attach a list of those on whom the appellant has served the appeal notice.

(4) If a defendant serves an appeal notice after the expiry of the time limit specified in rule 50.19 (Service of appeal notice)—
(a) the notice must—
(i) explain what the defendant did to ensure that it was served as soon as it could be, and
(ii) include or attach such evidence as the defendant relies upon to support that explanation; and
(b) where the appeal is on human rights grounds against an order for extradition made by the Secretary of State, the notice must explain why—
(i) the appeal is necessary to avoid real injustice, and
(ii) the circumstances are exceptional and make it appropriate to consider the appeal.

(5) Unless the High Court otherwise directs, the appellant may amend the appeal notice—
(a) by serving on those listed in rule 50.19(1) the appeal notice as so amended;
(b) not more than 10 business days after service of the appeal notice.

(6) Where the appeal is against an order by the magistrates' court—
(a) if the grounds of appeal are that the magistrates' court ought to have decided differently a question of fact or law at the extradition hearing, the appeal notice must—
(i) identify that question,
(ii) explain what decision the magistrates' court should have made, and why, and
(iii) explain why the magistrates' court would have been required not to make the order under appeal, if that question had been decided differently;
(b) if the grounds of appeal are that there is an issue which was not raised at the extradition hearing, or that evidence is available which was not available at the extradition hearing, the appeal notice must—
(i) identify that issue or evidence,
(ii) explain why it was not then raised or available,
(iii) explain why that issue or evidence would have resulted in the magistrates' court deciding a question differently at the extradition hearing, and
(iv) explain why, if the court had decided that question differently, the court would have been required not to make the order it made.

(7) Where the appeal is against an order by the Secretary of State—
(a) if the grounds of appeal are that the Secretary of State ought to have decided differently a question of fact or law, the appeal notice must—
(i) identify that question,
(ii) explain what decision the Secretary of State should have made, and why, and

(iii) explain why the Secretary of State would have been required not to make the order under appeal, if that question had been decided differently;

(b) if the grounds of appeal are that there is an issue which was not raised when the case was being considered by the Secretary of State, or that information is available which was not then available, the appeal notice must—

(i) identify that issue or information,

(ii) explain why it was not then raised or available,

(iii) explain why that issue or information would have resulted in the Secretary of State deciding a question differently, and

(iv) explain why, if the Secretary of State had decided that question differently, the order under appeal would not have been made.

R-636 Respondent's notice

50.21 (1) A party on whom an appellant serves an appeal notice under rule 50.19 may serve a respondent's notice, and must do so if—

(a) that party wants to make representations to the High Court; or

(b) the court so directs.

(2) Such a party must serve any such notice on—

(a) the High Court officer;

(b) the appellant;

(c) the Director of Public Prosecutions, unless the Director already has the conduct of the proceedings; and

(d) any other person on whom the appellant served the appeal notice.

(3) Such a party must serve any such notice, as appropriate—

(a) not more than 10 business days after—

(i) service on that party of an amended appeal notice under rule 50.20(5) (Form of appeal notice), or

(ii) the expiry of the time for service of any such amended appeal notice

whichever of those events happens first;

(b) not more than 5 business days after service on that party of—

(i) an appellant's notice renewing an application for permission to appeal,

(ii) a direction to serve a respondent's notice.

(4) A respondent's notice must—

(a) give the date or dates on which the respondent was served with, as appropriate—

(i) the appeal notice,

(ii) the appellant's notice renewing the application for permission to appeal,

(iii) the direction to serve a respondent's notice;

(b) identify each ground of opposition on which the respondent relies and the ground of appeal to which each such ground of opposition relates;

(c) summarise any relevant facts not already summarised in the appeal notice; and

(d) identify any document or other material that the respondent thinks the court will need to decide the appeal.

R-637 Renewing an application for permission to appeal, restoring excluded grounds, etc.

50.22 (1) This rule—

(a) applies where the High Court—

(i) refuses permission to appeal to the High Court, or

(ii) gives permission to appeal to the High Court but not on every ground identified by the appeal notice;

(b) does not apply where—

(i) a defendant applies out of time for permission to appeal to the High Court, and

(ii) the court for that reason refuses to consider that application.

(2) Unless the court refuses permission to appeal at a hearing, the appellant may renew the application for permission by serving notice on—

(a) the High Court officer;

(b) the respondent; and

(c) any other person on whom the appellant served the appeal notice, not more than 5 business days after service of notice of the court's decision on the appellant.

(3) If the court refuses permission to appeal, the renewal notice must explain the grounds for the renewal.

(4) If the court gives permission to appeal but not on every ground identified by the appeal notice the decision indicates that—

(a) at the hearing of the appeal the court will not consider representations that address any ground thus excluded from argument; and

(b) an appellant who wants to rely on such an excluded ground needs the court's permission to do so.

(5) An appellant who wants to rely at the hearing of an appeal on a ground of appeal excluded from argument must—
- (a) apply in writing, with reasons, and identify each such ground;
- (b) serve the application on—
  - (i) the High Court officer, and
  - (ii) the respondent;
- (c) serve the application not more than 5 business days after—
  - (i) the giving of permission to appeal, or
  - (ii) the High Court officer serves notice of that decision on the applicant, if the applicant was not present in person or by live link when permission to appeal was given.

(6) Paragraph (7) applies where a party wants to abandon—
- (a) a ground of appeal on which that party has permission to appeal; or
- (b) a ground of opposition identified in a respondent's notice.

(7) Such a party must serve notice on—
- (a) the High Court officer; and
- (b) each other party,

before any hearing at which that ground will be considered by the court.

Appeal hearing **R-638**

50.23 (1) Unless the High Court otherwise directs, where the appeal to the High Court is under Part 1 of the Extradition Act 2003 the hearing of the appeal must begin no more than 40 days after the defendant's arrest.

(2) Unless the High Court otherwise directs, where the appeal to the High Court is under Part 2 of the 2003 Act the hearing of the appeal must begin no more than 76 days after the later of—
- (a) service of the appeal notice; or
- (b) the day on which the Secretary of State informs the defendant of the Secretary of State's order, in a case in which—
  - (i) the appeal is by the defendant against an order by the magistrates' court sending the case to the Secretary of State, and
  - (ii) the appeal notice is served before the Secretary of State decides whether the defendant should be extradited.

(3) If the effect of the decision of the High Court on the appeal is that the defendant is to be extradited—
- (a) the High Court must consider any ancillary application, including an application about—
  - (i) bail pending extradition,
  - (ii) reporting restrictions,
  - (iii) costs;
- (b) the High Court is the appropriate court to order a postponement of the defendant's extradition where—
  - (i) the defendant has been charged with an offence in the United Kingdom, or
  - (ii) the defendant has been sentenced to imprisonment or detention in the United Kingdom.

(4) If the effect of the decision of the High Court on the appeal is that the defendant is discharged, the High Court must consider any ancillary application, including an application about—
- (a) reporting restrictions;
- (b) costs.

Early termination of appeal: order by consent, etc. **R-639**

50.24 (1) This rule applies where—
- (a) an appellant has served an appeal notice under rule 50.19; and
- (b) the High Court—
  - (i) has not determined the application for permission to appeal, or
  - (ii) where the court has given permission to appeal, has not determined the appeal.

(2) Where the warrant or extradition request with which the appeal is concerned is withdrawn—
- (a) the party or person so informing the court must serve on the High Court officer—
  - (i) notice to that effect by the authority or territory requesting the defendant's extradition,
  - (ii) details of how much of the warrant or extradition request remains outstanding, if any, and of any other warrant or extradition request outstanding in respect of the defendant,

(iii) details of any bail condition to which the defendant is subject, if the defendant is on bail, and

(iv) details sufficient to locate the defendant, including details of the custodian and of the defendant's date of birth and custody reference, if the defendant is in custody; and

(b) paragraph (5) applies but only to the extent that the parties want the court to deal with an ancillary matter.

(3) Where a defendant with whose discharge the appeal is concerned consents to extradition, paragraph (5) applies but only to the extent that the parties want the court to—

(a) give directions for that consent to be given to the magistrates' court or to the Secretary of State, as the case may be;

(b) deal with an ancillary matter.

(4) Paragraph (5) applies where the parties want the court to make a decision on which they are agreed—

(a) determining the application for permission to appeal or the appeal, as the case may be;

(b) specifying the date on which that application or appeal is to be treated as discontinued; and

(c) determining an ancillary matter, including costs, if applicable.

(5) The parties must serve on the High Court officer, in one or more documents—

(a) a draft order in the terms proposed;

(b) evidence of each party's agreement to those terms; and

(c) concise reasons for the request that the court make the proposed order.

R-640 Application for permission to appeal to the Supreme Court

50.25 (1) This rule applies where a party to an appeal to the High Court wants to appeal to the Supreme Court.

(2) Such a party must—

(a) apply orally to the High Court for permission to appeal immediately after the court's decision; or

(b) apply in writing and serve the application on the High Court officer and every other party not more than 14 days after that decision.

(3) Such a party must—

(a) identify the point of law of general public importance that the appellant wants the High Court to certify is involved in the decision;

(b) serve on the High Court officer a statement of that point of law; and

(c) give reasons why—

(i) that point of law ought to be considered by the Supreme Court, and

(ii) the High Court ought to give permission to appeal.

(4) As well as complying with paragraph (3), a defendant's application for permission to appeal to the Supreme Court must include or attach any application for the following, with reasons—

(a) bail pending appeal;

(b) permission to attend any hearing in the Supreme Court, if the appellant is in custody.

R-641 Determination of detention pending appeal to the Supreme Court against discharge

50.26 On an application for permission to appeal to the Supreme Court against a decision of the High Court which, but for that appeal, would have resulted in the defendant's discharge, the High Court must—

(a) decide whether to order the detention of the defendant; and

(b) determine any application for—

(i) bail pending appeal,

(ii) permission to attend any hearing in the Supreme Court,

(iii) a representation order.

R-642 Reopening the determination of an appeal

50.27 (1) This rule applies where a party wants the High Court to reopen a decision of that court which determines an appeal or an application for permission to appeal.

(2) Such a party must—

(a) apply in writing for permission to reopen that decision, as soon as practicable after becoming aware of the grounds for doing so; and

(b) serve the application on the High Court officer and every other party.

(3) The application must—

(a) specify the decision which the applicant wants the court to reopen; and

(b) give reasons why—
(i) it is necessary for the court to reopen that decision in order to avoid real injustice,
(ii) the circumstances are exceptional and make it appropriate to reopen the decision, and
(iii) there is no alternative effective remedy.

(4) The court must not give permission to reopen a decision unless each other party has had an opportunity to make representations.

Declaration of incompatibility with a Convention right R-643

50.28 (1) This rule applies where a party—
(a) wants the High Court to make a declaration of incompatibility with a Convention right under section 4 of the Human Rights Act 1998; or
(b) raises an issue that appears to the High Court may lead to the court making such a declaration.

(2) If the High Court so directs, the High Court officer must serve notice on—
(a) the relevant person named in the list published under section 17(1) of the Crown Proceedings Act 1947; or
(b) the Treasury Solicitor, if it is not clear who is the relevant person.

(3) That notice must include or attach details of—
(a) the legislation affected and the Convention right concerned;
(b) the parties to the appeal; and
(c) any other information or document that the High Court thinks relevant.

(4) A person who has a right under the 1998 Act to become a party to the appeal must—
(a) serve notice on—
(i) the High Court officer, and
(ii) the other parties,

if that person wants to exercise that right; and
(b) in that notice—
(i) indicate the conclusion that that person invites the High Court to reach on the question of incompatibility, and
(ii) identify each ground for that invitation, concisely outlining the arguments in support.

(5) The High Court must not make a declaration of incompatibility—
(a) less than 21 days after the High Court officer serves notice under paragraph (2); and
(b) without giving any person who serves a notice under paragraph (4) an opportunity to make representations at a hearing.

Duties of court officers R-644

50.29 (1) The magistrates' court officer must—
(a) keep any document or object exhibited in the proceedings in the magistrates' court, or arrange for it to be kept by some other appropriate person, until—
(i) 6 weeks after the conclusion of those proceedings, or
(ii) the conclusion of any proceedings in the High Court that begin within that 6 weeks;
(b) provide the High Court with any document, object or information for which the High Court officer asks, within such period as the High Court officer may require; and
(c) arrange for the magistrates' court to hear as soon as practicable any application to that court for bail pending appeal.

(2) A person who, under arrangements made by the magistrates' court officer, keeps a document or object exhibited in the proceedings in the magistrates' court must—
(a) keep that exhibit until—
(i) 6 weeks after the conclusion of those proceedings, or
(ii) the conclusion of any proceedings in the High Court that begin within that 6 weeks,

unless the magistrates' court or the High Court otherwise directs; and
(b) provide the High Court with any such document or object for which the High Court officer asks, within such period as the High Court officer may require.

(3) The High Court officer must—
(a) give as much notice as reasonably practicable of each hearing to—
(i) the parties,
(ii) the defendant's custodian, if any, and
(iii) any other person whom the High Court requires to be notified;
(b) serve a record of each order or direction of the High Court on—
(i) the parties,
(ii) any other person whom the High Court requires to be notified;

(c) if the High Court's decision determines an appeal or application for permission to appeal, serve a record of that decision on—
(i) the defendant's custodian, if any,
(ii) the magistrates' court officer, and
(iii) the designated authority which certified the arrest warrant, where Part 1 of the Extradition Act 2003 applies;
(d) where rule 50.24 applies (Early termination of appeal: order by consent, etc.), arrange for the High Court to consider the document or documents served under that rule;
(e) treat the appeal as if it had been dismissed by the High Court where—
(i) the hearing of the appeal does not begin within the period required by rule 50.23 (Appeal hearing) or ordered by the High Court, or
(ii) on an appeal by a requesting territory under section 105 of the Extradition Act 2003, the High Court directs the magistrates' court to decide a question again and the magistrates' court comes to the same conclusion as it had done before.

R-645 Constitution of the High Court

50.30 (1) A master of the High Court, a deputy master, or a court officer nominated for the purpose by the Lord Chief Justice, may exercise any power of the High Court to which the rules in this Section apply, except the power to—
(a) give or refuse permission to appeal;
(b) determine an appeal;
(c) reopen a decision which determines an appeal or an application for permission to appeal;
(d) grant or withhold bail; or
(e) impose or vary a condition of bail.
(2) Despite paragraph (1), such a master, deputy master or court officer may exercise one of the powers listed in paragraph (1)(a), (b), (d) or (e) if making a decision to which the parties have agreed in writing.
(3) A renewed application for permission to appeal to the High Court may be determined by—
(a) a single judge of the High Court other than the judge who first refused permission, or
(b) a divisional court.
(4) An appeal may be determined by—
(a) a single judge of the High Court; or
(b) a divisional court.

R-646 Payment of High Court fees

50.31 (1) This rule applies where a party serves on the High Court officer a notice or application in respect of which a court fee is payable under legislation that requires the payment of such a fee.
(2) Such a party must pay the fee, or satisfy the conditions for any remission of the fee, when so serving the notice or application.
(3) If such a party fails to comply with paragraph (2), then unless the High Court otherwise directs—
(a) the High Court officer must serve on that party a notice requiring payment of the fee due, or satisfaction of the conditions for any remission of that fee, within a period specified in the notice;
(b) that party must comply with such a requirement; and
(c) until the expiry of the period specified in the notice, the High Court must not exercise its power—
(i) to reject the notice or application in respect of which the fee is payable, or
(ii) to dismiss an application for permission to appeal, in consequence of rejecting an appeal notice.

Section 4: post-extradition proceedings

R-647 Application for consent to deal with another offence or for consent to further extradition

50.32 (1) This rule applies where—
(a) a defendant has been extradited to a territory under Part 1 of the Extradition Act 2003; and
(b) the court officer receives from the authority designated by the Secretary of State a request for the court's consent to—
(i) the defendant being dealt with in that territory for an offence other than one in respect of which the extradition there took place, or
(ii) the defendant's further extradition from there to another such territory for an offence.

(2) The presenting officer must serve on the court officer—
   (a) the request; and
   (b) a certificate given by the designated authority that the request was made by a judicial authority with the function of making such requests in the territory to which the defendant was extradited.
(3) The court must—
   (a) give directions for service by a party or other person on the defendant of notice that the request for consent has been received, unless satisfied that it would not be practicable for such notice to be served;
   (b) give directions for a hearing to consider the request to begin—
      (i) no more than 21 days after the request was received by the designated authority, or
      (ii) at such a later date as the court decides is in the interests of justice; and
   (c) give such directions as are required for the preparation and conduct of that hearing.
(4) At the hearing directed under paragraph (3), in the following sequence the court must decide—
   (a) whether the consent requested is required, having regard to—
      (i) any opportunity given for the defendant to leave the requesting territory after extradition which the defendant did not take within 45 days of arrival there,
      (ii) if the defendant did not take such an opportunity, any requirements for consent imposed by the law of the requesting territory or by arrangements between that territory and the United Kingdom where the request is for consent to deal with the defendant in that territory for another offence,
      (iii) if the defendant did not take such an opportunity, any requirements for consent imposed by arrangements between the requesting territory and the United Kingdom where the request is for consent to extradite the defendant to another territory for an offence;
   (b) if such consent is required, then—
      (i) whether the offence in respect of which consent is requested is an extradition offence, and
      (ii) if it is, whether the court would order the defendant's extradition under sections 11 to 25 of the Extradition Act 2003 (bars to extradition and other considerations) were the defendant in the United Kingdom and the court was considering extradition for that offence.
(5) The court must give directions for notice of its decision to be conveyed to the authority which made the request.
(6) Rules 50.3 (Exercise of magistrates' court's powers) and 50.4 (Case management in the magistrates' court and duty of court officer) apply on an application under this rule.

Criminal Practice Directions Part 50 Extradition

CPD XI Other Proceedings 50A: Extradition: General Matters and Management of the Appeal PD-104

General matters: expedition at all times

50A.1 Compliance with these directions is essential to ensure that extradition proceedings are dealt with expeditiously, both in accordance with the spirit of the Council Framework Decision of 13 June 2002 on the European Arrest Warrant and surrender procedures between Member States and the United Kingdom's other treaty obligations. It is of the utmost importance that orders which provide directions for the proper management and progress of cases are obeyed so that the parties can fulfil their duty to assist the court in furthering the overriding objective and in making efficient use of judicial resources. To that end:
(i) the court may, and usually should, give case management directions, which may be based on a model, but adapted to the needs of the individual case, requiring the parties to supply case management information, consistently with the overriding objective of the Criminal Procedure Rules and compatibly with the parties' entitlement to legal professional and litigation privilege;
(ii) a defendant whose extradition is requested must expect to be required to identify what he or she intends to put in issue so that directions can be given to achieve a single, comprehensive and effective extradition hearing at the earliest possible date;
(iii) where the issues are such that further information from the requesting authority or state is needed then it is essential that the request is formulated clearly and in good time, in terms to which the parties can expect to contribute but which terms must be approved by the court, in order that those to whom the request is addressed will be able to understand what is sought, and why, and so can respond promptly;

(iv) where such a request or other document, including a formal notice to the defendant of a post-extradition consent request, requires transmission to an authority or other person in a requesting state or other place outside the UK, it is essential that clear and realistic directions for the transmission are given, identifying who is to be responsible and to what timetable, having regard to the capacity of the proposed courier. Once given, such directions must be promptly complied with and the court at once informed if difficulties are encountered.

General guidance under s. 2(7A) Extradition Act 2003 (as amended by the Anti-Social Behaviour, Crime and Policing Act 2014)

50A.2 When proceeding under section 21A of the Act and considering under subsection (3)(a) of the Act the seriousness of the conduct alleged to constitute the extradition offence, the judge will determine the issue on the facts of each case as set out in the warrant, subject to the guidance in paragraph 50A.3 below.

50A.3 In any case where the conduct alleged to constitute the offence falls into one of the categories in the table at paragraph 50A.5 below, unless there are exceptional circumstances, the judge should generally determine that extradition would be disproportionate. It would follow under the terms of s. 21A(4)(b) of the Act that the judge must order the person's discharge.

50A.4 The exceptional circumstances referred to above in paragraph 50A.3 will include:

i. Vulnerable victim
ii. Crime committed against someone because of their disability, gender-identity, race, religion or belief, or sexual orientation
iii. Significant premeditation
iv. Multiple counts
v. Extradition also sought for another offence
vi. Previous offending history

50A.5 The table is as follows:

Category of offence	Examples
Minor **theft** — (not robbery/ burglary or theft from the person)	Where the theft is of a low monetary value and there is a low impact on the victim or indirect harm to others, for example: (a) Theft of an item of food from a supermarket (b) Theft of a small amount of scrap metal from company premises (c) Theft of a very small sum of money
Minor financial offences (**forgery, fraud** and **tax** offences)	Where the sums involved are small and there is a low impact on the victim and / or low indirect harm to others, for example: (a) Failure to file a tax return or invoices on time (b) Making a false statement in a tax return (c) Dishonestly applying for a tax refund (d) Obtaining a bank loan using a forged or falsified document (e) Non-payment of child maintenance
Minor **road traffic, driving** and related offences	Where no injury, loss or damage was incurred to any person or property, for example: (a) Driving whilst using a mobile phone (b) Use of a bicycle whilst intoxicated
Minor **public order** offences	Where there is no suggestion the person started the trouble, and the offending behaviour was for example: (a) Non-threatening verbal abuse of a law enforcement officer or government official (b) Shouting or causing a disturbance, without threats (c) Quarrelling in the street, without threats
Minor **criminal damage**, (other than by fire)	For example, breaking a window
Possession of controlled substance (other than one with a high capacity for harm such as heroin, cocaine, LSD or crystal meth)	Where it was possession of a very small quantity and intended for personal use

CPD XI Other Proceedings 50B Management of the Appeal to the High Court PD-105

50B.1 Applications for permission to appeal to the High Court under the Extradition Act 2003 must be started in the Administrative Court of the Queen's Bench Division at the Royal Courts of Justice in London.

50.B.2 A Lord Justice of Appeal appointed by the Lord Chief Justice will have responsibility to assist the President of the Queen's Bench Division with overall supervision of extradition appeals.

Definitions

50B.3 Where appropriate 'appeal' includes 'application for permission to appeal'.

50B.4 'EAW' means European Arrest Warrant.

50B.5 A 'nominated legal officer of the court' is a court officer assigned to the Administrative Court Office who is a barrister or solicitor and who has been nominated for the purpose by the Lord Chief Justice under CrimPR 50.18 and 50.30.

Forms

50B.6 The forms are to be used in the High Court, in accordance with the CrimPR 50.19, 50.20, 50.21 and 50.22.

50B.7 The forms may be amended or withdrawn from time to time, or new forms added, under the authority of the Lord Chief Justice: see CrimPD I 5A.

Management of the Appeal

50B.8 Where it is not possible for the High Court to begin to hear the appeal in accordance with time limits contained in Crim PR 50.23(1) and (2), the Court may extend the time limit if it believes it to be in the interests of justice to do so and may do so even after the time limit has expired.

50B.9 The power to extend those time limits may be exercised by a Lord Justice of Appeal, a Single Judge of the High Court, a Master of the Administrative Court or a nominated legal officer of the court.

50B.10 Case Management directions setting down a timetable may be imposed upon the parties by a Lord Justice of Appeal, a Single Judge of the High Court, a Master of the Administrative Court or a nominated legal officer of the court. For the court's constitution and relevant powers and duties see section 4 of the Senior Courts Act 1981 and CrimPR 50.18 and 50.30.

Listing of Oral, Renewal Hearings and Substantive Hearings

50B.11 Arrangements for the fixing of dates for hearings will be made by a Listing Officer of the Administrative Court under the direction of the Judge with overall responsibility for supervision of extradition appeals.

50B.12 A Lord Justice of Appeal, a Single Judge of the High Court, a Master of the Administrative Court or a nominated legal officer of the court may give such directions to the Listing Officer as they deem necessary with regard to the fixing of dates, including as to whether cases in the same/related proceedings or raising the same or similar issues should be heard together or consecutively under the duty imposed by Crim PR 1.1(2)(e). Parties must alert the nominated legal officer of the court for the need for such directions.

50B.13 Save in exceptional circumstances, regard will not be given to an advocate's existing commitments. This is in accordance with the spirit of the legislation that extradition matters should be dealt with expeditiously. Extradition matters are generally not so complex that an alternative advocate cannot be instructed.

50B.14 If a party disagrees with the time estimate given by the Court, they must inform the Listing Office within 5 business days of the notification of the listing and they must provide a time estimate of their own.

Expedited appeals

50B.15 The Court may direct that the hearing of an appeal be expedited.

50B.16 The Court will deal with requests for an expedited appeal without a hearing. Requests for expedition must be made in writing, either within the appeal notice, or by application notice, clearly marked with the Administrative Court reference number, which must be lodged with the Administrative Court Office or emailed to the appropriate email address: administrativecourtoffice.crimex@hmcts.x.gsi.gov.uk and notice must be given to the other parties.

50B.17 Any requests for an expedited appeal made to an out of hours Judge must be accompanied by:

i) A detailed chronology;
ii) Reasons why the application could not be made within Court hours;
iii) Any Orders or Judgments made in the proceedings.

Amendment to Notices

50B.18 Amendment to Notice of Appeal requiring permission

(i) Subject to Crim PR 50.20(5), an appeal notice may not be amended without the permission of the Court: CrimPR 50.17(6)(b);

(ii) An application for permission to amend made before permission to appeal has been considered will be determined without a hearing;

(iii) An application for permission to amend after permission to appeal has been granted and any submissions in opposition will normally be dealt with at the hearing unless there is any risk that the hearing may have to be adjourned. If there is any risk that the application to amend may lead the other party to seek time to answer the proposed amendment, the application must be made as soon as practicable and well in advance of the hearing. A failure to make immediate applications for such an amendment is likely to result in refusal.

(iv) Legal representatives or the appellant, if acting in person, must

a. Inform the Court at the time they make the application if the existing time estimate is affected by the proposed amendment; and

b. Attempt to agree any revised time estimate no later than 5 business days after service of the application.

(v) where the appellant wishes to restore grounds of appeal excluded on the grant of permission to appeal, the procedure is governed by CrimPR 50.22.

50B.19 Amendment to Respondent's Notice

(i) A respondent's notice may not be amended without the permission of the Court: CrimPR 50.17(6)(b);

(ii) An application for permission to amend made before permission to appeal has been considered will be determined without a hearing.

(iii) An application for permission to amend after permission to appeal has been granted and any submissions in opposition will normally be dealt with at the hearing unless there is any risk that the hearing may have to be adjourned. If there is any risk that the application to amend may require the other party to seek time to answer the proposed amendment, the application must be made as soon as practicable and well in advance of the hearing. A failure to make immediate applications for such an amendment is likely to result in refusal.

(iv) Legal representatives or the appellant, if acting in person, must

a. Inform the Court at the time they make the application if the existing time estimate is affected by the proposed amendment; and

b. Attempt to agree any revised time estimate no later than 5 business days after service of the application.

Use of Live-Links

50B.20 When a party acting in person is in custody, the Court office will request the institution to use live-link for attendance at any oral or renewal hearing or substantive appeal. The institution must give precedence to all such applications in the High Court over live-links to the lower courts, including the Crown Court.

Interpreters

50B.21 It is the responsibility of the Court Listing Officer to ensure the attendance of an accredited interpreter when an unrepresented party in extradition proceedings is acting in person and does not understand or speak English.

50B.22 Where a party who does not understand or speak English is legally represented it is the responsibility of his/her solicitors to instruct an interpreter if required for any hearing in extradition proceedings.

Disposing of applications and appeals by way of consent

50B.23 CrimPR 50.24 governs the submission of Consent Orders and lists the essential requirements for such orders. Any Consent Order, the effect of which will be to allow extradition to proceed, must specify the date on which the appeal proceedings are to be treated as discontinued, for the purposes of section 36 or 118, as the case may be, of the Extradition Act 2003: whether that is to be the date on which the order is made or some later date. A Consent Order may be approved by a Lord Justice of Appeal, a Single Judge of the High Court or, under CrimPR 50.30(2), a nominated legal officer of the court. The order may, but need not, be pronounced in open court: CrimPR 50.17(1)(c)(iii). Once approved, the order will be sent to the parties and to any other person as required by CrimPR 50.29(3)(b), (c).

50B.24 A consent order to allow an appeal brought under s.28 of the Extradition Act 2003 must provide—

(i) for the quashing of the decision of the District Judge in Westminster Magistrates' Court discharging the Requested Person;

(ii) for the matter to be remitted to the District Judge to hold fresh extradition proceedings;

(iii) for any ancillary matter, such as bail or costs.

50B.25 A consent order to allow an appeal brought under s.110 of the Extradition Act 2003 must provide—

(i) for the quashing of the decision of the Secretary of State for the Home Department not to order extradition;

(ii) for the matter to be remitted to the Secretary of State to make a fresh decision on whether or not to order extradition;

(iii) for any ancillary matter, such as bail or costs.

50B.26 (a) a Consent Order is intended to dispose of an application for permission to appeal which has not yet been considered by the court, the order must make clear by what means that will be achieved, bearing in mind that an application for permission which is refused without a hearing can be renewed under CrimPR 50.22(2). If the parties intend to exclude the possibility of renewal the order should declare either (i) that the time limit under rule 50.22(2) is reduced to nil, or (ii) permission to appeal is given and the appeal determined on the other terms of the order.

(b) one of the parties is a child or protected party, the documents served under CrimPR 50.24(5) must include an opinion from the advocate acting on behalf of the child or protected party and, in the case of a protected party, any relevant documents prepared for the Court of Protection.

Fees

50B.27 Applications to extend representation orders do not attract any fee.

50B.28 Fees are payable for all other applications in accordance with the current Fees Order.

CPD XI Other Proceedings 50C: Extradition: Representation Orders **PD-106**

50C.1 Representation orders may be granted by a Lord Justice of Appeal, a Single Judge of the High Court, a Master of the Administrative Court or a nominated legal officer of the court upon a properly completed CRM14 being lodged with the Court. A representation order will cover junior advocate and solicitors for the preparation of the Notice of Appeal to determination of the appeal.

50C.2 Applications to extend representation orders may be granted by a Lord Justice of Appeal, a Single Judge of the High Court, a Master of the Administrative Court or a nominated Court Officer who may direct a case management hearing before a Lord Justice of Appeal, a Single Judge, or a Master of the Administrative Court. Since these applications do not attract a fee, parties may lodge them with the Court by attaching them to an email addressed to the nominated legal officer of the court.

50C.3 Applications to extend representation orders to cover the instruction of Queen's Counsel to appear either alone or with junior advocate must be made in writing, either by letter or application notice, clearly marked with the Administrative Court reference number, which must be lodged with the Administrative Court Office or emailed to the appropriate email address: administrativecourtoffice.crimex@hmcts.x.gsi.gov.uk.

The request must:

(i) identify the substantial novel or complex issues of law or fact in the case;

(ii) explain why these may only be adequately presented by a Queen's Counsel;

(iii) state whether a Queen's Counsel has been instructed on behalf of the respondent;

(iv) explain any delay in making the request;

(v) be supported by advice from junior advocate or Queen's Counsel.

50C.4 Applications for prior authority to cover the cost of obtaining expert evidence must be made in writing, either by letter, clearly marked with the Administrative Court reference number, which must be sent or emailed to the Administrative Court Office.

The request must:

(i) confirm that the evidence sought has not been considered in any previous appeals determined by the appellate courts;

(ii) explain why the evidence was not called at the extradition hearing in Westminster Magistrates' Court and what evidence can be produced to support that;

(iii) explain why the new evidence would have resulted in the District Judge deciding a question at the extradition hearing differently and whether, if so, the District Judge would have been required to make a different order as to discharge of the requested person;

(iv) explain why the evidence was not raised when the case was being considered by the Secretary of State for the Home Department or information was available that was not available at that time;

(v) explain why the new evidence would have resulted in the Secretary of State deciding a question differently, and if the question had been decided differently, the Secretary of State would not have ordered the person's extradition;
(vi) state when the need for the new evidence first became known;
(vii) explain any delay in making the request;
(viii) explain what relevant factual, as opposed to expert evidence, is being given by whom to create the factual basis for the expert's opinion;
(ix) explain why this particular area of expertise is relevant: for example why a child psychologist should be appointed as opposed to a social worker;
(x) state whether the requested person has capacity;
(xi) set out a full breakdown of all costs involved including any VAT or other tax payable, including alternative quotes or explaining why none are available;
(xii) provide a list of all previous extensions of the representation order and the approval of expenditure to date;
(xiii) provide a timetable for the production of the evidence and its anticipated effect on the time estimate and hearing date;
(xiv) set out the level of compliance to date with any directions order.

50C.5 Experts must have direct personal experience of and proven expertise in the issue on which a report is sought; it is only if they do have such experience and it is relevant, that they can give evidence of what they have observed.

50C.6 Where an order is granted to extend a representation order to obtain further evidence it will still be necessary for the party seeking to rely on the new evidence to satisfy the Court hearing the application for permission or the substantive appeal that the evidence obtained should be admitted having regard to sections 27(4) and 29(4) of the Extradition Act 2003 and the judgment in *Szombathely City Court v Fenyvesi* [2009] EWHC 231 (Admin).

50C.7 Applications to extend representation for the translation of documents must be made in writing, either by letter, clearly marked with the Administrative Court reference number, which must be sent to Administrative Court Office, The Royal Courts of Justice, Strand, London, WC2A 2LL or emailed to the appropriate email address: administrativecourtoffice.crimex@hmcts.x.gsi.gov.uk

The request should:
(i) explain the importance of the document for which a translation is being sought and the justification for obtaining it;
(ii) explain what it is believed the contents of the document is and the issues it will assist the court to address in hearing the appeal;
(iii) confirm that the evidence sought has not been considered in any previous appeals determined by the appellate courts;
(iv) confirm that the evidence sought was not called at the extradition hearing in the Westminster Magistrates' Court;
(v) explain why the evidence sought would have resulted in the District Judge deciding a question at the extradition hearing differently and whether, if so, the District Judge would have been required to make a different order as to discharge of the requested person;
(vi) confirm that the new evidence was not raised when the case was being considered by the Secretary of State for the Home Department;
(vii) explain why the new evidence sought would have resulted in the Secretary of State deciding a question differently, and if the question had been decided differently, the Secretary of State would not have ordered the person's extradition;
(viii) confirm when the need for the new evidence first became known;
(ix) explain any delay in making the request;
(x) explain fully the evidential basis for incurring the expenditure;
(xi) explain why the appellant cannot produce the evidence himself or herself in the form of a statement of truth;
(xii) set out a full breakdown of all costs involved including any VAT or other tax payable and the Legal Aid Agency contractual rates;
(xiii) provide a list of all previous extensions of the representation order and the expenditure to date.

50C.8 Where an order is made to extend representation to cover the cost of the translation of documents it will still be necessary for the party seeking to rely on the documents as evidence to satisfy the Court that it should be admitted at the hearing of the appeal having regard to sections 27(4) and

29(4) of the Extradition Act 2003 and the judgment in *Szombathely City Court v Fenyvesi* [2009] EWHC 231 (Admin).

CPD XI Other Proceedings 50D: Extradition: Applications, etc **PD-107**

Extension or abridgement of time

50D.1

(i) Any party who seeks extension or abridgment of time for the service of documents, evidence or skeleton arguments must apply to the High Court on the appropriate form and pay the appropriate fee.
(ii) Applications for extension or abridgment of time may be determined by a Lord Justice of Appeal, a Single Judge of the High Court, a Master of the Administrative Court or a nominated legal officer of the court.
(iii) Applications for extension of time must include a witness statement setting out the reasons for non-compliance with any previous order and the proposed timetable for compliance.
(iv) Any application made to an out of hours Judge must be accompanied with:
  a. A detailed chronology;
  b. Reasons why the application could not be made within Court hours;
  c. Any Orders or Judgments made in the proceedings

Representatives

50D.2 CrimPR Part 46 applies.

50D.3 Where under CrimPR 46.2(1)(c) a legal representative withdraws from the case then that representative should satisfy him or herself that the defendant is aware of the time and date of the appeal hearing and of the need to attend, by live link if the court has so directed. If the legal representative has any reason to doubt that the defendant is so aware then he or she should promptly notify the Administrative Court Office.

Application to adjourn

50D.4 Where a hearing date has been fixed, any application to vacate the hearing must be made on the appropriate form. A fee is required for the application if it is made within 14 days of the hearing date. The application must:

(i) explain the reasons why an application is being made to vacate the hearing;
(ii) detail the views of the other parties to the appeal;
(iii) include a draft order with the application notice.

50D.5 If the parties both seek an adjournment then the application must be submitted for consideration by a Lord Justice of Appeal, a Single Judge of the High Court or a Master of the Administrative Court. Exceptional circumstances must be shown if a date for the hearing has been fixed or the adjournment will result in material delay to the determination of the appeal.

50D.6 An application to adjourn following a compromise agreement must be supported by evidence justifying exceptional circumstances and why it is in compliance with the overriding objective.

Variation of directions

50D.7 Where parties are unable to comply with any order of the court they must apply promptly to vary directions before deadlines for compliance have expired and seek further directions. An application to vary directions attracts a fee and the application notice, to be submitted on the appropriate form, must:

(i) provide full and proper explanations for why the current and existing directions have not been complied with;
(ii) detail the views of the other parties to the appeal;
(iii) include a draft order setting out in full the timetable and directions as varied i.e. a superseding order which stands alone.

50D.8 A failure to make the application prior to the expiry of the date specified in the order will generally result in the refusal of the application unless good reasons are shown.

Application to certify a point of law of general public importance

50D.9 Where an application is made under CrimPR 50.25(2)(b) the application must be made on the appropriate form accompanied by the relevant fee.

50D.10 Any response to the application must be made within 10 business days.

50D.11 Where an application to certify is granted but permission to appeal to the Supreme Court is refused, it shall be for those representing the Requested Person to apply for an extension of the Representation Order to cover proceedings in the Supreme Court, if so advised.

50D.12 The representation order may be extended by a Lord Justice of Appeal, a Single Judge of the High Court, a Master of the Administrative Court or a nominated legal officer of the court.

50D.13 The result of the application to certify a point of law of general public importance and permission to appeal to the Supreme Court may be notified in advance to the legal representatives but legal representatives must not communicate it to the Requested Person until 1 hour before the pronouncement is made in open court.

50D.14 There shall be no public announcement of the result until after it has been formally pronounced.

Application to reopen the determination of an appeal

50D.15 An application under CrimPR 50.27 to reopen an appeal must be referred to the court that determined the appeal, but may if circumstances require be considered by a judge or judges other than those who determined the original appeal.

Application to extend required period for removal pursuant to section 36 of the Extradition Act 2003

50D.16 Where an application is made for an extension of the required period within which to extradite a Requested Person it must be accompanied by:

(i) a witness statement explaining why it is not possible to remove the Requested Person within the required period and the proposed timetable for removal;

(ii) a draft order.

50D.17 The application to extend time may be made before or after the expiry of the required period for extradition, but the court will scrutinise with particular care an application made after its expiry.

50D.18 Where extensions of time are sought for the same reason in respect of a number of Requested Persons who are due to be extradited at the same time, a single application may be made to the court listing each of the Requested Persons for whom an extension is sought.

50D.19 The application may be determined by a Lord Justice of Appeal, a Single Judge of the High Court, a Master of the Administrative listing those persons may be granted.

Application for directions ancillary to a discharge pursuant to section 42 or 124 of the Extradition Act 2003

50D.20 Where the High Court is informed that the warrant or extradition request has been withdrawn then unless ancillary matters are dealt with by Consent Order an application notice must be issued seeking any such directions. The notice of discharge of a Requested Person must be accompanied by:

(i) the notification by the requesting state that the EAW has been withdrawn together with a translation of the same;

(ii) a witness statement containing:

a. details of whether the withdrawn EAW is the only EAW outstanding in respect of the Requested Person;

b. details of other EAWs outstanding in respect of the Requested Person and the stage which the proceedings have reached;

c. whether only part of the EAW has been withdrawn;

d. details of any bail conditions;

e. details of any institution in which the Requested Person is being detained, the Requested Person's prison number and date of birth.

50D.21 The order for discharge may be made by a Lord Justice of Appeal, a Single Judge of the High Court, a Master of the Administrative Court or a nominated legal officer of the court.

50D.22 It is the responsibility of the High Court to serve the approved order on the appropriate institution and Westminster Magistrates' Court.

PD-108 **CPD XI Other Proceedings 50E: Extradition: Court Papers**

Skeleton arguments

50E.1 The Court on granting permission to appeal or directing an oral hearing for permission to appeal will give directions as to the filing of skeleton arguments. Strict compliance is required with all time limits.

50E.2 A skeleton argument must:

(a) not normally exceed 25 pages (excluding front sheets and back sheets) and be concise;

(b) be printed on A4 paper in not less than 12 point font and 1.5 line spacing;

(c) define the issues in the appeal;

(d) be set out in numbered paragraphs;
(e) be cross-referenced to any relevant document in the bundle;
(f) be self-contained and not incorporate by reference material from previous skeleton arguments;
(g) not include extensive quotations from documents or authorities.

50E.3 Where it is necessary to refer to an authority, the skeleton argument must
(a) state the proposition of law the authority demonstrates; and
(b) identify but not quote the parts of the authority that support the proposition.

50E.4 If more than one authority is cited in support of a given proposition, the skeleton argument must briefly state why.

50E.5 A chronology of relevant events will be necessary in most appeals.

50E.6 Where a skeleton argument has been prepared in respect of an application for permission to appeal, the same skeleton argument may be relied upon in the appeal upon notice being given to the Court or a replacement skeleton may be lodged not less than 10 business days before the hearing of the appeal.

50E.7 At the hearing the Court may refuse to hear argument on a point not included in a skeleton argument filed within the prescribed time.

Bundles

50E.8 The bundle for the hearing should be agreed by the parties save where the Requested Person is acting in person. In those circumstances the Court expects the Requesting State to prepare the bundle.

50E.9 The bundle must be paginated and indexed.

50E.10 Subject to any order made by the Court, the following documents must be included in the appeal bundle:
(i) a copy of the appellant's notice;
(ii) a copy of any respondent's notice;
(iii) a copy of any appellant's or respondent's skeleton argument;
(iv) a copy of the order under appeal;
(v) a copy of any order made by the Court in the exercise of its case management powers;
(vi) any judgment of the Court made in a previous appeal involving the party or parties which is relevant to the present proceedings.
(vii) where the bundle of papers reaches more than 200 pages, the parties should agree a core appeal bundle which must contain (i)–(vi) above.

50E.11 The Bundle should only contain relevant documents and must not include duplicate documents.

50E.12 Bundles lodged with the Court will not be returned to the parties but will be destroyed in the confidential waste system at the conclusion of the proceedings and without further notification.

CPD XI Other Proceedings 50F: Extradition: Consequences of Non Compliance with Directions **PD-109**

50F.1 Failure to comply with these directions will lead to applications for permission and appeals being dealt with on the material available to the Court at the time when the decision is made.

50F.2 Judges dealing with extradition appeals will seek full and proper explanations for any breaches of the rules and the provisions of this Practice Direction.

50F.3 If no good explanation can be given immediately by counsel or solicitors, the senior partner or the departmental head responsible is likely to be called to court to explain any failure to comply with a court order. Where counsel or solicitors fail to obey orders of the Court and are unable to provide proper and sufficient reasons for their disobedience they may anticipate the matter being formally referred to the President of the Queen's Bench Division with a recommendation that the counsel or solicitors involved be reported to their professional bodies.

50F.4 The court may also refuse to admit any material or any evidence not filed in compliance with the order for Directions or outside a time limit specified by the court.

50F.5 A failure to comply with the time limits or other requirements for skeleton arguments will have the consequences specified in 50E.7.

Criminal Practice Directions: General Application

CPD XII General Application A: Court Dress **PD-110**

A.1 In magistrates' courts, advocates appear without robes or wigs. In all other courts, Queen's Counsel wear a short wig and a silk (or stuff) gown over a court coat with bands, junior counsel wear a short wig and stuff gown with bands. Solicitors and other advocates authorised under the Courts and Legal

Services Act 1990 wear a black solicitor's gown with bands; they may wear short wigs in circumstances where they would be worn by Queen's Counsel or junior counsel.

A.2 High Court Judges hearing criminal cases may wear the winter criminal robe year-round. However, scarlet summer robes may be worn.

PD-111 **CPD XII General Application B: Modes of Address and Titles of Judges and Magistrates**

Modes of Address

B.1 The following judges, when sitting in court, should be addressed as 'My Lord' or 'My Lady', as the case may be, whatever their personal status:
(a) Judges of the Court of Appeal and of the High Court;
(b) any Circuit Judge sitting as a judge of the Court of Appeal (Criminal Division) or the High Court under section 9(1) of the Senior Courts Act 1981;
(c) any judge sitting at the Central Criminal Court;
(d) any Senior Circuit Judge who is an Honorary Recorder.

B.2 Subject to the paragraph above, Circuit Judges, qualifying judge advocates, Recorders and Deputy Circuit Judges should be addressed as 'Your Honour' when sitting in court.

District Judges (Magistrates' Courts) should be addressed as 'Sir [or Madam]' or 'Judge' when sitting in Court.

Magistrates in court should be addressed through the Chairperson as 'Sir [or Madam]' or collectively as 'Your Worships'.

Description

B.3 In cause lists, forms and orders members of the judiciary should be described as follows:
(a) Circuit Judges, as 'His [or Her] Honour Judge A'.
When the judge is sitting as a judge of the High Court under section 9(1) of the Senior Courts Act 1981, the words 'sitting as a judge of the High Court' should be added;
(b) Recorders, as 'Mr [or Mrs, Ms or Miss] Recorder B'.
This style is appropriate irrespective of any honour or title which the recorder might possess, but if in any case it is desired to include an honour or title, the alternative description, 'Sir CD, Recorder' or 'The Lord D, Recorder' may be used;
(c) Deputy Circuit Judges, as 'His [or Her] Honour EF, sitting as a Deputy Circuit Judge';
(d) qualifying judge advocates, as 'His [or Her] Honour GH, sitting as a qualifying judge advocate.';
(e) District Judges (Magistrates' Courts), as 'District Judge (Magistrates' Courts) J'.

PD-112 **CPD XII General Application D: Citation of Authority, and Provision of Copies of Judgments to the Court and Skeleton Arguments**

C.1 For cases in the High Court, reference should be made to Practice Direction 40E, the supplementary Practice Direction to the Civil Procedure Rules Part 40.

C.2 For cases in the Court of Appeal (Criminal Division), the following provisions apply.

Availability of reserved judgments before handing down, corrections and applications consequential on judgment

C.3 Where judgment is to be reserved the Presiding Judge may, at the conclusion of the hearing, invite the views of the parties' legal representatives as to the arrangements to be made for the handing down of the judgment.

C.4 Unless the court directs otherwise, the following provisions apply where the Presiding Judge is satisfied that the judgment will attract no special degree of confidentiality or sensitivity.

C.5 The court will provide a copy of the draft judgment to the parties' legal representatives about three working days before handing down, or at such other time as the court may direct. Every page of every judgment which is made available in this way will be marked 'Unapproved judgment: No permission is granted to copy or use in court.' The draft is supplied in confidence and on the conditions that:
(a) neither the draft judgment nor its substance will be disclosed to any other person or used in the public domain; and
(b) no action will be taken (other than internally) in response to the draft judgment, before the judgment is handed down.

C.6 Unless the parties' legal representatives are told otherwise when the draft judgment is circulated, any proposed corrections to the draft judgment should be sent to the clerk of the judge who prepared the draft (or to the associate, if the judge has no clerk) with a copy to any other party's legal representatives, by 12 noon on the day before judgment is handed down.

C.7 If, having considered the draft judgment, the prosecution will be applying to the Court for a retrial or either party wishes to make any other application consequent on the judgment, the judge's clerk should be informed with a time estimate for the application by 12 noon on the day before judgment is handed down. This will enable the court to make appropriate listing arrangements and notify advocates to attend if the court so requires. There is no fee payable to advocates who attend the hand down hearing if not required to do so by the court. If either party is considering applying to the Court to certify a point for appeal to the Supreme Court, it would assist if the judge's clerk could be informed at the same time, although this is not obligatory as under section 34 of the Criminal Appeal Act 1968, the time limit for such applications is 28 days.

Communication to the parties including the defendant or the victim

C.8 The contents are not to be communicated to the parties, including to the defendant, respondent or the victim (defined as a person entitled to receive services under the Code of Practice for Victims of Crime) until two hours before the listed time for pronouncement of judgment.

C.9 Judges may permit more information about the result of a case to be communicated on a confidential basis to the parties including to the defendant, respondent or the victim at an earlier stage if good reason is shown for making such a direction.

C.10 If, for any reason, the parties' legal representatives have special grounds for seeking a relaxation of the usual condition restricting disclosure to the parties, a request for relaxation of the condition may be made informally through the judge's clerk (or through the associate, if the judge has no clerk).

C.11 If the parties or their legal representatives are in any doubt about the persons to whom copies of the draft judgment may be distributed they should enquire of the judge or Presiding Judge.

C.12 Any breach of the obligations or restrictions in this section or failure to take reasonable steps to ensure compliance may be treated as contempt of court.

Restrictions on disclosure or reporting

C.13 Anyone who is supplied with a copy of the handed-down judgment, or who reads it in court, will be bound by any direction which the court may have given in a child case under section 39 of the Children and Young Persons Act 1933 or section 45 or 45A of the Youth Justice and Criminal Evidence Act 1999, or any other form of restriction on disclosure, or reporting, of information in the judgment.

C.14 Copies of the approved judgment can be ordered from the official shorthand writers, on payment of the appropriate fee. Judgments identified as of legal or public interest will generally be made available on the website managed by BAILLI: http://www.bailii.org/

CPD XII General Application D: Citation of Authority and Provision of Copies of Judgments to the Court **PD-113**

D.1 This Practice Direction applies to all criminal matters before the Court of Appeal (Criminal Division), the Crown Court and the magistrates' courts. In relation to those matters only, Practice Direction (Citation of Authorities) [2012] 1 WLR 780 is hereby revoked.

Citation of authority

D.2 In *R v Erskine; R v Williams* [2009] EWCA Crim 1425, [2010] 1 WLR 183, (2009) 2 Cr App R 29 the Lord Chief Justice stated:

75. The essential starting point, relevant to any appeal against conviction or sentence, is that, adapting the well known aphorism of Viscount Falkland in 1641: if it is not necessary to refer to a previous decision of the court, it is necessary not to refer to it. Similarly, if it is not necessary to include a previous decision in the bundle of authorities, it is necessary to exclude it. That approach will be rigidly enforced.

76. It follows that when the advocate is considering what authority, if any, to cite for a proposition, only an authority which establishes the principle should be cited. Reference should not be made to authorities which do no more than either (a) illustrate the principle or (b) restate it.

78. Advocates must expect to be required to justify the citation of each authority relied on or included in the bundle. The court is most unlikely to be prepared to look at an authority which does no more than illustrate or restate an established proposition.

80. . . .In particular, in sentencing appeals, where a definitive Sentencing Guidelines Council guideline is available there will rarely be any advantage in citing an authority reached before the issue of the guideline, and authorities after its issue which do not refer to it will rarely be of assistance. In any event, where the authority does no more than uphold a sentence imposed at

the Crown Court, the advocate must be ready to explain how it can assist the court to decide that a sentence is manifestly excessive or wrong in principle.

D.3 Advocates should only cite cases when it is necessary to do so; when the case identifies or represents a principle or the development of a principle. In sentencing appeals, other cases are rarely helpful, providing only an illustration, and this is especially true if there is a sentencing guideline. Unreported cases should only be cited in exceptional circumstances, and the advocate must expect to explain why such a case has been cited.

D.4 Advocates should not assume that because a case cited to the court is not referred to in the judgment the court has not considered it; it is more likely that the court was not assisted by it.

D.5 When an authority is to be cited, whether in written or oral submissions, the advocate should always provide the neutral citation followed by the law report reference.

D.6 The following practice should be followed:

i) Where a judgment is reported in the Official Law Reports (A.C., Q.B., Ch., Fam.) published by the Incorporated Council of Law Reporting for England and Wales or the Criminal Appeal Reports or the Criminal Appeal Reports (Sentencing) one of those two series of reports must be cited; either is equally acceptable. However, where a judgment is reported in the Criminal Appeal Reports or the Criminal Appeal Reports (Sentencing) that reference must be given in addition to any other reference. Other series of reports and official transcripts of judgment may only be used when a case is not reported, or not yet reported, in the Official Law Reports or the Criminal Appeal Reports or the Criminal Appeal Reports (Sentencing).

ii) If a judgment is not reported in the Official Law Reports, the Criminal Appeal Reports or the Criminal Appeal Reports (Sentencing), but it is reported in an authoritative series of reports which contains a headnote and is made by individuals holding a Senior Courts qualification (for the purposes of section 115 of the Courts and Legal Services Act 1990), that report should be cited.

iii) Where a judgment is not reported in any of the reports referred to above, but is reported in other reports, they may be cited.

iv) Where a judgment has not been reported, reference may be made to the official transcript if that is available, not the handed-down text of the judgment, as this may have been subject to late revision after the text was handed down. Official transcripts may be obtained from, for instance, BAILLI (http://www.bailii.org/).

D.7 In the majority of cases, it is expected that all references will be to the Official Law Reports and the Criminal Appeal Reports or the Criminal Appeal Reports (Sentencing); it will be rare for there to be a need to refer to any other reports. An unreported case should not be cited unless it contains a relevant statement of legal principle not found in reported authority, and it is expected that this will only occur in exceptional circumstances.

Provision of copies of judgments to the Court

D.8 The paragraphs below specify whether or not copies should be provided to the court. Authorities should not be included for propositions not in dispute. If more than one authority is to be provided, the copies should be presented in paginated and tagged bundles.

D.9 If required, copies of judgments should be provided either by way of a photocopy of the published report or by way of a copy of a reproduction of the judgment in electronic form that has been authorised by the publisher of the relevant series, but in any event:

i) the report must be presented to the court in an easily legible form (a 12-point font is preferred but a 10 or 11-point font is acceptable); and

ii) the advocate presenting the report must be satisfied that it has not been reproduced in a garbled form from the data source.

In any case of doubt the court will rely on the printed text of the report (unless the editor of the report has certified that an electronic version is more accurate because it corrects an error contained in an earlier printed text of the report).

D.10 If such a copy is unavailable, a printed transcript such as from BAILLI may be included.

Provision of copies to the Court of Appeal (Criminal Division)

D.11 Advocates must provide to the Registrar of Criminal Appeals, with their appeal notice, respondent's notice or skeleton argument, a list of authorities upon which they wish to rely in their written or oral submissions. The list of authorities should contain the name of the applicant, appellant or respondent and the Criminal Appeal Office number where known. The list should include reference to the relevant paragraph numbers in each authority. An updated list can be provided if a new authority is issued, or in response to a respondent's notice or skeleton argument. From time to time, the Registrar may issue guidance as to the style or content of lists of authorities, including a suggested format; this guidance should be followed by all parties. The latest guidance is available from the Criminal Appeal Office.

D.12 If the case cited is reported in the Official Law Reports, the Criminal Appeal Reports or the Criminal Appeal Reports (Sentencing), the law report reference must be given after the neutral citation, and the relevant paragraphs listed, but copies should not be provided to the court.

D.13 If, exceptionally, reference is made to a case that is not reported in the Official Law Reports, the Criminal Appeal Reports or the Criminal Appeal Reports (Sentencing), three copies must be provided to the Registrar with the list of authorities and the relevant appeal notice or respondent's notice (or skeleton argument, if provided). The relevant passages of the authorities should be marked or sidelined.

Provision of copies to the Crown Court and the magistrates' courts

D.14 When the court is considering routine applications, it may be sufficient for the court to be referred to the applicable legislation or to one of the practitioner texts. However, it is the responsibility of the advocate to ensure that the court is provided with the material that it needs properly to consider any matter.

D.15 If it would assist the court to consider any authority, the directions at paragraphs D.2 to D.7 above relating to citation will apply and a list of authorities should be provided.

D.16 Copies should be provided by the party seeking to rely upon the authority in accordance with CrimPR 24.13. This Rule is applicable in the magistrates' courts, and in relation to the provision of authorities, should also be followed in the Crown Court since courts often do not hold library stock (see CrimPR 25.17). Advocates should comply with paragraphs D.8 to D.10 relating to the provision of copies to the court.

D.17 The court may give directions for the preparation of skeleton arguments. Such directions will provide for the time within which skeleton arguments must be served and for the issues which they must address. Such directions may provide for the number of pages, or the number of words, to which a skeleton argument is to be confined. Any such directions displace the following to the extent of any inconsistency. Subject to that, however, a skeleton argument must:

i. not normally exceed 15 pages (excluding front sheets and back sheets) and be concise;
ii. be presented in A4 page size and portrait orientation, in not less than 12 point font and in 1.5 line spacing;
iii. define the issues;
iv. be set out in numbered paragraphs;
v. be cross-referenced to any relevant document in any bundle prepared for the court;
vi. be self-contained and not incorporate by reference material from previous skeleton arguments;
vii. not include extensive quotations from documents or authorities.

D.18 Where it is necessary to refer to an authority, the skeleton argument must:

i. state the proposition of law the authority demonstrates; and
ii. identify but not quote the parts of the authority that support the proposition.

D.19 If more than one authority is cited in support of a given proposition, the skeleton argument must briefly state why.

D.20 A chronology of relevant events will be necessary in most cases.

D.21 There are directions at paragraphs I 3C.3 and 3C.4 of these Practice Directions that apply to the service of skeleton arguments in support of, and in opposition to, an application to stay an indictment on the grounds of abuse of process; and directions at paragraphs IX 39F.1 to 39F.3 that apply to the service of skeleton arguments in the Court of Appeal. Where a skeleton argument has been prepared in respect of an application for permission to appeal, the same skeleton argument may be relied upon in the appeal upon notice being given to the court, or a replacement skeleton may be served to the timetable set out in those paragraphs.

D.22 At the hearing the court may refuse to hear argument on a point not included in a skeleton argument served within the prescribed time.

D.23 In *R v James, R v Selby* [2016] EWCA Crim 1639; [2017] Crim.L.R. 228 the Court of Appeal observed (at paragraphs 52 to 54):

'Legal documents of unnecessary and too often of excessive length offer very little assistance to the court. In *Tombstone Ltd v Raja* [2008] EWCA Civ 1441, [2009] 1 WLR 1143 Mummery LJ said:

"Practitioners . . . are well advised to note the risk of the court's negative reaction to unnecessarily long written submissions. The skeleton argument procedure was introduced to assist the court, as well as the parties, by improving preparations for, and the efficiency of, adversarial oral hearings, which remain central to this court's public role. . . . An unintended and unfortunate side effect of the growth in written advocacy. . . has been that too many practitioners, at increased cost to their clients and diminishing assistance to the court, burden their opponents and the court with written briefs."

He might have penned those remarks had he been sitting in these two cases, and many more, in this Division.

In *Standard Bank PLC v Via Mat International* [2013] EWCA Civ 490, [2013] 2 All ER (Comm) 1222 the excessive length of court documents prompted:

"It is important that both practitioners and their clients understand that skeleton arguments are not intended to serve as vehicles for extended advocacy and that in general a short, concise skeleton is both more helpful to the court and more likely to be persuasive than a longer document which seeks to develop every point which the advocate would wish to make in oral argument."

No area of law is exempt from the requirement to produce careful and concise documents: *Tchenquiz v Director of the Serious Fraud Office* [2014] EWCA Civ 1333, [2015] 1 WLR 838, paragraph 10.'

PD-114 **CPD XII General application E: Preparation of Judgments: Neutral Citation**

E.1 Since 11 January 2001 every judgment of the Court of Appeal, and of the Administrative Court, and since 14 January 2002 every judgment of the High Court, has been prepared and issued as approved with single spacing, paragraph numbering (in the margins) and no page numbers. In courts with more than one judge, the paragraph numbering continues sequentially through each judgment and does not start again at the beginning of each judgment. Indented paragraphs are not numbered. A unique reference number is given to each judgment. For judgments of the Court of Appeal, this number is given by the official shorthand writers, Merrill Legal Solutions (Tel: 020 7421 4000 ext.4036). For judgments of the High Court, it is provided by the Courts Recording and Transcription Unit at the Royal Courts of Justice. Such a number will also be furnished, on request to the Courts Recording and Transcription Unit, Royal Courts of Justice, Strand, London WC2A 2LL (Tel: 020 7947 7820), (e-mail: rcj.cratu@hmcts.gsi.gov.uk) for High Court judgments delivered outside London.

E.2 Each Court of Appeal judgment starts with the year, followed by EW (for England and Wales), then CA (for Court of Appeal), followed by Civ or Crim and finally the sequential number. For example, '*Smith v Jones* [2001] EWCA Civ 10'.

E.3 In the High Court, represented by HC, the number comes before the divisional abbreviation and, unlike Court of Appeal judgments, the latter is bracketed: (Ch), (Pat), (QB), (Admin), (Comm), (Admlty), (TCC) or (Fam), as appropriate. For example, '[2002] EWHC 123 (Fam)', or '[2002] EWHC 124 (QB)', or '[2002] EWHC 125 (Ch)'.

E.4 This 'neutral citation', as it is called, is the official number attributed to the judgment and must always be used at least once when the judgment is cited in a later judgment. Once the judgment is reported, this neutral citation appears in front of the familiar citation from the law reports series. Thus: '*Smith v Jones* [2001] EWCA Civ 10; [2001] QB 124; [2001] 2 All ER 364', etc.

E.5 Paragraph numbers are referred to in square brackets. When citing a paragraph from a High Court judgment, it is unnecessary to include the descriptive word in brackets: (Admin), (QB), or whatever. When citing a paragraph from a Court of Appeal judgment, however, 'Civ' or 'Crim' is included. If it is desired to cite more than one paragraph of a judgment, each numbered paragraph should be enclosed with a square bracket. Thus paragraph 59 in *Green v White* [2002] EWHC 124 (QB) would be cited: '*Green v White* [2002] EWHC 124 at [59]'; paragraphs 30–35 in *Smith v Jones* would be '*Smith v Jones* [2001] EWCA Civ 10 at [30]–[35]'; similarly, where a number of paragraphs are cited: '*Smith v Jones* [2001] EWCA Civ 10 at [30], [35] and [40–43]'.

E.6 If a judgment is cited more than once in a later judgment, it is helpful if only one abbreviation is used, e.g., '*Smith v Jones*' or 'Smith's case', but preferably not both (in the same judgment).

PD-115 **CPD XII General application F: Citation of Hansard**

F.1 Where any party intends to refer to the reports of Parliamentary proceedings as reported in the Official Reports of either House of Parliament ('Hansard') in support of any such argument as is permitted by the decisions in *Pepper v Hart* [1993] AC 593 and *Pickstone v Freemans PLC* [1989] AC 66, or otherwise, he must, unless the court otherwise directs, serve upon all other parties and the court copies of any such extract, together with a brief summary of the argument intended to be based upon such extract. No other report of Parliamentary proceedings may be cited.

F.2 Unless the court otherwise directs, service of the extract and summary of the argument shall be effected not less than 5 clear working days before the first day of the hearing, whether or not it has a fixed date. Advocates must keep themselves informed as to the state of the lists where no fixed date has been given. Service on the court shall be effected by sending three copies to the Registrar of Criminal Appeals, Royal Courts of Justice, Strand, London, WC2A 2LL or to the court manager of the relevant Crown Court centre, as appropriate. If any party fails to do so, the court may make such order (relating to costs or otherwise) as is, in all the circumstances, appropriate.

Criminal Practice Directions Listing

CPD XIII Listing A: Judicial Responsibility for Listing and Key Principles PD-116

Listing as a judicial responsibility and function

A.1 Listing is a judicial responsibility and function. The purpose is to ensure that all cases are brought to a hearing or trial in accordance with the interests of justice, that the resources available for criminal justice are deployed as effectively as possible, and that cases are heard by an appropriate judge or bench with the minimum of delay.

A.2 The agreement reached between the Lord Chief Justice and the Secretary of State for Constitutional Affairs and Lord Chancellor set out in a statement to the House of Lords on 26 January 2004 ('the Concordat'), states that judges, working with HMCTS, are responsible for deciding on the assignment of cases to particular courts and the listing of those cases before particular judges. Therefore:

(a) The Presiding Judges of each circuit have the overall responsibility for listing at all courts, Crown and magistrates', on their circuit;

(b) Subject to the supervision of the Presiding Judges, the Resident Judge at each Crown Court has the general responsibility within his or her court centre for the allocation of criminal judicial work, to ensure the just and efficient despatch of the business of the court or group of courts. This includes overseeing the deployment of allocated judges at the court or group, including the distribution of work between all the judges allocated to that court. A Resident Judge must appoint a deputy or deputies to exercise his or her functions when he or she is absent from his or her court centre. See also paragraph A.5: Discharge of judicial responsibilities;

(c) The listing officer in the Crown Court is responsible for carrying out the day-to-day operation of listing practice under the direction of the Resident Judge. The listing officer at each Crown Court centre has one of the most important functions at that Crown Court and makes a vital contribution to the efficient running of that Crown Court and to the efficient operation of the administration of criminal justice;

(d) In the magistrates' courts, the Judicial Business Group, subject to the supervision of the Presiding Judges of the circuit, is responsible for determining the listing practice in that area. The day-to-day operation of that listing practice is the responsibility of the justices' clerk with the assistance of the listing officer.

Key principles of listing

A.3 When setting the listing practice, the Resident Judge or the Judicial Business Group should take into account principles a-j:

(a) Ensure the timely trial of cases and resolution of other issues (such as confiscation) so that justice is not delayed. The following factors are relevant:

i. In general, each case should be tried within as short a time of its arrival in the court as is consistent with the interests of justice, the needs of victims and witnesses, and with the proper and timely preparation by the prosecution and defence of their cases in accordance with the directions and timetable set;

ii. Priority should be accorded to the trial of young defendants, and cases where there are vulnerable or young witnesses. In *R v Barker* [2010] EWCA Crim 4, the Lord Chief Justice highlighted 'the importance to the trial and investigative process of keeping any delay in a case involving a child complainant to an irreducible minimum';

iii. Custody time limits (CTLs) should be observed, see CPD XIII Listing F;

iv. Every effort must be made to avoid delay in cases in which the defendant is on bail;

(b) Ensure that in the magistrates' court unless impracticable, non-custody anticipated guilty plea cases are listed 14 days after charge, and non-custody anticipated not guilty pleas are listed 28 days after charge;
(c) Provide, when possible, for certainty and/or as much advance notice as possible, of the trial date; and take all reasonable steps to ensure that the trial date remains fixed;
(d) Ensure that a judge or bench with any necessary authorisation and of appropriate experience is available to try each case and, wherever desirable and practicable, there is judicial continuity, including in relation to post-trial hearings;
(e) Strike an appropriate balance in the use of resources, by taking account of:
  i. The efficient deployment of the judiciary in the Crown Court and the magistrates' courts taking into account relevant sitting requirements for magistrates. See CPD XIII Annex 1 for information to support judicial deployment in the magistrates' courts;
  ii. The proper use of the courtrooms available at the court;
  iii. The provision in long and/or complex cases for adequate reading time for the judiciary;
  iv. The facilities in the available courtrooms, including the security needs (such as a secure dock), size and equipment, such as video and live link facilities;
  v. The proper use of those who attend the Crown Court as jurors;
  vi. The availability of legal advisers in the magistrates' courts;
  vii. The need to return those sentenced to custody as soon as possible after the sentence is passed, and to facilitate the efficient operation of the prison escort contract;
(f) Provide where practicable:
  i. the defendant and the prosecution with the advocate of their choice where this does not result in any delay to the trial of the case; and,
  ii. for the efficient deployment of advocates, lawyers and associate prosecutors of the Crown Prosecution Service, and other prosecuting authorities, and of the resources available to the independent legal profession, for example by trying to group certain cases together;
(g) Meet the need for special security measures for category A and other high-risk defendants;
(h) Ensure that proper time (including judicial reading time) is afforded to hearings in which the court is exercising powers that impact on the rights of individuals, such as applications for investigative orders or warrants;
(i) Consider the significance of ancillary proceedings, such as confiscation hearings, and the need to deal with such hearings promptly and, where possible, for such hearings to be conducted by the trial judge;
(j) Provide for government initiatives or projects approved by the Lord Chief Justice.

A.4 Although the listing practice at each Crown Court centre and magistrates' court will take these principles into account, the listing practice adopted will vary from court to court depending particularly on the number of courtrooms and the facilities available, the location and the workload, its volume and type.

Discharge of judicial responsibilities

A.5 The Resident Judge of each court is responsible for:
  i. ensuring that good practice is implemented throughout the court, such that all hearings commence on time;
  ii. ensuring that the causes of trials that do not proceed on the date originally fixed are examined to see if there is any systemic issue;
  iii. monitoring the general performance of the court and the listing practices;
  iv. monitoring the timeliness of cases and reporting any cases of serious concern to the Presiding Judge;
  v. maintaining and reviewing annually a list of Recorders, qualifying judge advocates and Deputy Circuit Judges authorised to hear appeals from the magistrates' courts unless such a list is maintained by the Presiding Judge.

A.6 The Judicial Business Group for each clerkship subject to the overall jurisdiction of the Presiding Judge is responsible for:
  i. monitoring the workload and anticipated changes which may impact on listing policies;
  ii. ensuring that any listing practice meets the needs of the system as a whole.

PD-117 **CPD XIII Listing B: Classification**

B.1 The classification structure outlined below is solely for the purposes of trial in the Crown Court. The structure has been devised to accommodate practical administrative functions and is not intended to reflect a hierarchy of the offences therein.

Offences are classified as follows:

Class 1: A:

i. Murder;
ii. Attempted Murder;
iii. Manslaughter;
iv. Infanticide;
v. Child destruction (section 1(1) of the Infant Life (Preservation) Act 1929);
vi. Abortion (section 58 of the Offences against the Person Act 1861);
vii. Assisting a suicide;
viii. Cases including section 5 of the Domestic Violence, Crime and Victims Act 2004, as amended (if a fatality has resulted);
ix. Soliciting, inciting, encouraging or assisting, attempting or conspiring to commit any of the above offences or assisting an offender having committed such an offence.

Class 1: B:

i. Genocide;
ii. Torture, hostage-taking and offences under the War Crimes Act 1991;
iii. Offences under ss. 51 and 52 International Criminal Courts Act 2001;
iv. An offence under section 1 of the Geneva Conventions Act 1957;
v. Terrorism offences (where offence charged is indictable only and took place during an act of terrorism or for the purposes of terrorism as defined in s.1 of the Terrorism Act 2000);
vi. Piracy, under the Merchant Shipping and Maritime Security Act 1997;
vii. Treason;
viii. An offence under the Official Secrets Acts;
ix. Incitement to disaffection;
x. Soliciting, inciting, encouraging or assisting, attempting or conspiring to commit any of the above offences or assisting an offender having committed such an offence.

Class 1: C:

i. Prison mutiny, under the Prison Security Act 1992;
ii. Riot in the course of serious civil disturbance;
iii. Serious gang related crime resulting in the possession or discharge of firearms, particularly including a campaign of firebombing or extortion, especially when accompanied by allegations of drug trafficking on a commercial scale;
iv. Complex sexual offence cases in which there are many complainants (often under age, in care or otherwise particularly vulnerable) and/or many defendants who are alleged to have systematically groomed and abused them, often over a long period of time;
v. Cases involving people trafficking for sexual, labour or other exploitation and cases of human servitude;
vi. Soliciting, inciting, encouraging or assisting, attempting or conspiring to commit any of the above offences or assisting an offender having committed such an offence.

Class 1: D:

i. Causing death by dangerous driving;
ii. Causing death by careless driving;
iii. Causing death by unlicensed, disqualified or uninsured driving;
iv. Any Health and Safety case resulting in a fatality or permanent serious disability;
v. Any other case resulting in a fatality or permanent serious disability;
vi. Soliciting, inciting, encouraging or assisting, attempting or conspiring to commit any of the above offences or assisting an offender having committed such an offence.

Class 2: A

i. Arson with intent to endanger life or reckless as to whether life was endangered;
ii. Cases in which explosives, firearms or imitation firearms are used or carried or possessed;
iii. Kidnapping or false imprisonment (without intention to commit a sexual offence but charged on the same indictment as a serious offence of violence such as under section 18 or section 20 of the Offences Against the Person Act 1861);
iv. Cases in which the defendant is a police officer, member of the legal profession or a high profile or public figure;
v. Cases in which the complainant or an important witness is a high profile or public figure;
vi. Riot otherwise than in the course of serious civil disturbance;
vii. Child cruelty;

viii. Cases including section 5 of the Domestic Violence, Crime and Victims Act 2004, as amended (if no fatality has resulted);
ix. Soliciting, inciting, encouraging or assisting, attempting or conspiring to commit any of the above offences or assisting an offender having committed such an offence.

Class 2: B

i. Any sexual offence, with the exception of those included in Class 1C;
ii. Kidnapping or false imprisonment (with intention to commit a sexual offence or charged on the same indictment as a sexual offence);
iii. Soliciting, inciting, encouraging or assisting, attempting or conspiring to commit any of the above offences or assisting an offender having committed such an offence.

Class 2: C:

i. Serious, complex fraud;
ii. Serious and/or complex money laundering;
iii. Serious and/or complex bribery;
iv. Corruption;
v. Complex cases in which the defendant is a corporation (including cases for sentence as well as for trial);
vi. Any case in which the defendant is a corporation with a turnover in excess of £1bn (including cases for sentence as well as for trial);
vii. Soliciting, inciting, encouraging or assisting, attempting or conspiring to commit any of the above offences or assisting an offender having committed such an offence.

Class 3: All other offences not listed in the classes above.

Deferred Prosecution Agreements

B.2 Cases coming before the court under section 45 [of] and Schedule 17 [to] the Crime and Courts Act 2013 must be referred to the President of the Queen's Bench Division who will allocate the matter to a judge from a list of judges approved by the Lord Chief Justice. Only the allocated judge may thereafter hear any matter or make any decision in relation to that case.

Criminal Cases Review Commission

B.3 Where the CCRC refers a case upon conviction from the magistrates' courts to the Crown Court, this shall be dealt with at a Crown Court centre designated by the Senior Presiding Judge.

PD-118 **CPD XIII Listing C: Referral of Cases in the Crown Court to the Resident Judge and to the Presiding Judges**

C.1 This Practice Direction specifies:

(a) cases which must be referred to a Presiding Judge for release; and
(b) cases which must be referred to the Resident Judge before being assigned to a judge, Recorder or qualifying judge advocate to hear.

It is applicable to all Crown Courts, but its application may be modified by the Senior Presiding Judge or the Presiding Judges, with the approval of the Senior Presiding Judge, through the provision of further specific guidance to Resident Judges in relation to the allocation and management of the work at their court.

C.2 This Practice Direction does not prescribe the way in which the Resident Judge gives directions as to listing policy to the listing officer; its purpose is to ensure that there is appropriate judicial control over the listing of cases. However, the Resident Judge must arrange with the listing officers a satisfactory means of ensuring that all cases listed at their court are listed before judges, Recorders or qualifying judge advocates of suitable seniority and experience, subject to the requirements of this Practice Direction. The Resident Judge should ensure that listing officers are made aware of the contents and importance of this Practice Direction, and that listing officers develop satisfactory procedures for referral of cases to him or her.

C.3 In order to assist the Resident Judge and the listing officer, all cases sent to the Crown Court should where possible include a brief case summary prepared by the prosecution. The prosecutor should ensure that any factors that make the case complex, or would lead it to be referred to the Resident Judge or a Presiding Judge are highlighted. The defence may also send submissions to the court, again highlighting any areas of complexity or any other factors that might assist in the case being allocated to an appropriate judge.

Cases in the Crown Court to be referred to the Resident Judge

C.4 All cases in Class 1A, 1B, 1C, 1D, 2A and 2C must be referred to the Resident Judge as must any case which appears to raise particularly complex, sensitive or serious issues.

C.5 Resident Judges should give guidance to the judges and staff of their respective courts as to which Class 2B cases should be referred to them following consultation with the Senior Presiding Judge. This will include any cases that may be referred to the Presiding Judge, see below. Class 2B cases to be referred to the Resident Judge are likely to be identified by the list officer, or by the judge at the first hearing in the Crown Court. Any appeal against conviction and/or sentence from a Youth Court involving a Class 2B case must be brought to the attention of the Resident Judge as soon as practicable. Where not provided with the appeal papers, the list officer must obtain a full summary of the prosecution case so as to allow an informed allocation decision to be made.

C.6 Once a case has been referred to the Resident Judge, the Resident Judge should refer the case to the Presiding Judge, following the guidance below, or allocate the case to an appropriate category of judge, and if possible to a named judge.

Cases in the Crown Court to be referred to a Presiding Judge

C.7 All cases in Class 1A, 1B and 1C must be referred by the Resident Judge to a Presiding Judge, as must a case in any class which is:

i. An usually grave or complex case or one in which a novel and important point of law is to be raised;
ii. A case where it is alleged that the defendant caused more than 1 fatality;
iii. A non-fatal case of baby shaking where serious injury resulted;
iv. A case where the defendant is a police officer, or a member of the legal profession or a high profile figure;
v. A case which for any reason is likely to attract exceptional media attention;
vi. A case where a large organisation or corporation may, if convicted, be ordered to pay a very large fine;
vii. Any case likely to last more than three months.

C.8 Resident Judges are encouraged to refer any other case if they think it is appropriate to do so.

C.9 Presiding Judges and Resident Judges should agree a system for the referral of cases to the Presiding Judge, ideally by electronic means. The system agreed should include provision for the Resident Judge to provide the Presiding Judge with a brief summary of the case, a clear recommendation by the Resident Judge about the judges available to try the case and any other comments. A written record of the decision and brief reasons for it must be made and retained.

C.10 Once a case has been referred to the Presiding Judge, the Presiding Judge may retain the case for trial by a High Court Judge, or release the case back to the Resident Judge, either for trial by a named judge, or for trial by an identified category of judges, to be allocated by the Resident Judge.

CPD XIII Listing D: Authorisation of Judges **PD-119**

D.1 Judges must be authorised by the Lord Chief Justice before they may hear certain types of case.

D.2 Judges (other than High Court Judges) to hear Class 1A cases must be authorised to hear such cases. Any judge previously granted a 'Class 1' or 'murder' authorisation is authorised to hear Class 1A cases. Judges previously granted an 'attempted murder' (including soliciting, incitement or conspiracy thereof) authorisation can only deal with these cases within Class 1A.

D.3 Judges (other than High Court Judges) to hear sexual offences cases in Class 1C or any case within Class 2B must be authorised to hear such cases. Any judge previously granted a 'Class 2' or 'serious sex offences' authorisation is authorised to hear sexual offences cases in Class 1C or 2B. It is a condition of the authorisation that it does not take effect until the judge has attended the relevant Judicial College course; the Resident Judge should check in the case of newly authorised judges that they have attended the course. Judges who have been previously authorised to try such cases should make every effort to ensure their training is up-to-date and maintained by attending the Serious Sexual Offences Seminar at least once every three years. See CPD XIII Annex 2 for guidance in dealing with sexual offences in the youth court.

D.4 Cases in the magistrates' courts involving the imposition of very large fines

i. Where a defendant appears before a magistrates' court for an either way offence, to which CPD XIII Annex 3 applies the case must be dealt with by a DJ (MC) who has been authorised to deal with such cases by the Chief Magistrate.
ii. The authorised DJ (MC) must first consider whether such cases should be allocated to the Crown Court or, where the defendant pleads guilty, committed for sentence under s. 3 Powers of [Criminal] Courts (Sentenc[ing]) Act 2000, and must do so when the DJ (MC) considers the offence or combination of offences so serious that the Crown Court should deal with the defendant had they been convicted on indictment.
iii. If an authorised DJ (MC) decides not to commit such a case the reasons must be recorded in writing to be entered onto the court register.

PD-120 **CPD XIII Listing E: Allocation of Business within the Crown Court**

E.1 Cases in Class 1A may only be tried by:

i. a High Court Judge, or
ii. a Circuit Judge, or Deputy High Court Judge, authorised to try such cases and provided that the Presiding Judge has released the case for trial by such a judge; or
iii. a Deputy Circuit Judge to whom the case has been specifically released by the Presiding Judge.

E.2 Cases in Class 1B may only be tried by:

i. a High Court Judge, or
ii. a Circuit Judge, or a Deputy High Court Judge, provided that the Presiding Judge has released the case for trial by such a judge; or
iii. a Deputy Circuit Judge to whom the case has been specifically released by the Presiding Judge.

E.3 Cases in Class 1C may only be tried by:

i. a High Court Judge, or
ii. a Circuit Judge, or a Deputy High Court Judge, or Deputy Circuit Judge, authorised to try such cases (if the case requires the judge to be authorised to hear sexual offences cases), provided that the Presiding Judge has released the case for trial by such a judge, or, if the case is a sexual offence, the Presiding Judge has assigned the case to that named judge.

See also CPD XIII Listing C.10.

E.4 Cases in Class 1D and 2A may be tried by:

i. a High Court Judge, or
ii. a Circuit Judge, or Deputy High Court Judge, or Deputy Circuit Judge, or a Recorder or a qualifying judge advocate, provided that either the Presiding Judge has released the case or the Resident Judge has allocated the case for trial by such a judge; with the exception that Class 2A i) cases may not be tried by a Recorder or qualifying judge advocate.

E.5 Cases in Class 2B may be tried by:

i. a High Court Judge, or
ii. a Circuit Judge, or Deputy High Court Judge, or Deputy Circuit Judge, or a Recorder or a qualifying judge advocate, authorised to try such cases and provided that either the Presiding Judge has released the case or the Resident Judge has allocated the case for trial by such a judge.

E.6 Cases in Class 2C may be tried by:

i. a High Court Judge, or
ii. a Circuit Judge, or Deputy High Court Judge, or Deputy Circuit Judge, or a Recorder or a qualifying judge advocate, with suitable experience (for example, with company accounts or other financial information) and provided that either the Presiding Judge has released the case or the Resident Judge has allocated the case for trial by such a judge.

E.7 Cases in Classes 1D, 2A and 2C will usually be tried by a Circuit Judge.

E.8 Cases in Class 3 may be tried by a High Court Judge, or a Circuit Judge, a Deputy Circuit Judge, a Recorder or a qualifying judge advocate. A case in Class 3 shall not be listed for trial by a High Court Judge except with the consent of a Presiding Judge.

E.9 If a case has been allocated to a judge, Recorder or qualifying judge advocate, the preliminary hearing should be conducted by the allocated judge if practicable, and if not, if possible by a judge of at least equivalent standing. PCMHs should only be heard by Recorders or qualifying judge advocates with the approval of the Resident Judge.

E.10 For cases in Class 1A, 1B or 1C, or any case that has been referred to the Presiding Judge, the preliminary hearing and PCMH must be conducted by a High Court Judge; by a Circuit Judge; or by a judge authorised by the Presiding Judges to conduct such hearings. In the event of a guilty plea before such an authorised judge, the case will be adjourned for sentencing and will immediately be referred to the Presiding Judge who may retain the case for sentence by a High Court Judge, or release the case back to the Resident Judge, either for sentence by a named judge, or for sentence by an identified category of judges, to be allocated by the Resident Judge.

E.11 Appeals from decisions of magistrates' courts shall be heard by:

i. a Resident Judge, or
ii. a Circuit Judge, nominated by the Resident Judge, or
iii. a Recorder or qualifying judge advocate or a Deputy Circuit Judge listed by the Presiding Judge to hear such appeals; or, if there is no such list nominated by the Resident Judge to hear such appeals;
iv. and, no less than two and no more than four justices of the peace, none of whom took part in the decision under appeal;
v. where no Circuit Judge or Recorder or qualifying judge advocate satisfying the requirements above is available, by a Circuit Judge, Recorder, qualifying judge advocate or Deputy Circuit Judge selected by the Resident Judge to hear a specific case or cases listed on a specific day.

E.12 Appeals from the youth court in relation to sexual offences shall be heard by:
i. A Resident Judge or;
ii. a Circuit Judge nominated by the Resident Judge who is authorised under D.3 to hear sexual offences in Class 1C or Class 2B;
iii. and no less than two and no more than four justices of the peace, none of whom took part in the decision under appeal. The justices of the peace must have undertaken specific training to deal with youth matters.
iv. No appeal against conviction and/or sentence from a Youth Court involving a Class 1C or Class 2B offence shall be heard by a Recorder save with the express permission of the Presiding Judge of the Circuit.

E.13 Allocation or committal for sentence following breach (such as a matter in which a community order has been made, or a suspended sentence passed), should, where possible, be listed before the judge who originally dealt with the matter or, if not, before a judge of the same or higher level.

E.14 Applications for removal of a driving disqualification should be made to the location of the Crown Court where the order of disqualification was made. Where possible, the matter should be listed before the judge who originally dealt with the matter or, if not, before a judge of the same or higher level.

CPD XIII Listing F: Listing of Trials, Custody Time Limits and Transfer of Cases PD-121

Estimates of trial length

F.1 Under the regime set out in the Criminal Procedure Rules, the parties will be expected to provide an accurate estimate of the length of trial at the hearing where the case is to be managed based on a detailed estimate of the time to be taken with each witness to be called, and accurate information about the availability of witnesses.

F.2 At the hearing the judge will ask the prosecution to clarify any custody time limit ('CTL') dates. The court clerk must ensure the CTL date is marked clearly on the court file or electronic file. When a case is subject to a CTL all efforts must be made at the first hearing to list the case within the CTL and the judge should seek to ensure this. Further guidance on listing CTL cases can be found below.

Cases that should usually have fixed trial dates

F.3 The cases where fixtures should be given will be set out in the listing practice applicable at the court, but should usually include the following:
i. Cases in classes 1A, 1B, 1C, 2B and 2C;
ii. Cases involving vulnerable and intimidated witnesses (including domestic violence cases), whether or not special measures have been ordered by the court;
iii. Cases where the witnesses are under 18 or have to come from overseas;
iv. Cases estimated to last more than a certain time — the period chosen will depend on the size of the centre and the available judges;
v. Cases where a previous fixed hearing has not been effective;
vi. Re-trials; and,
vii. Cases involving expert witnesses.

Custody Time Limits

F.4 Every effort must be made to list cases for trial within the CTL limits set by Parliament. The guiding principles are:
i. At the first hearing in the Crown Court, prosecution will inform the court when the CTL lapses.
ii. All efforts must be made to list the case within the CTL. The CTL may only be extended in accordance with s. 22 Prosecution of Offences Act 1985 and the Prosecution of Offences (Custody Time Limits) Regulations 1987.
iii. If suitable, given priority and listed on a date not less than 2 weeks before the CTL expires, the case may be placed in a warned list.
iv. The CTL must be kept under continual review by the parties, HMCTS and the Resident Judge.
v. If the CTL is at risk of being exceeded, an additional hearing should take place and should be listed before the Resident Judge or trial judge or other judge nominated by the Resident Judge.
vi. An application to extend the CTL in any case listed outside the CTL must be considered by the court whether or not it was listed with the express consent of the defence.
vii. Any application to extend CTLs must be considered as a matter of urgency. The reasons for needing the extension must be ascertained and fully explained to the court.
viii. Where courtroom or judge availability is an issue, the court must itself list the case to consider the extension of any CTL. The Delivery Director of the circuit must provide a statement setting out in detail what has been done to try to accommodate the case within the CTL.
ix. Where courtroom or judge availability is not in issue, but all parties and the court agree that the case will not be ready for trial before the expiration of the CTL, a date may be fixed outside

the CTL. This may be done without prejudice to any application to extend the CTLs or with the express consent of the defence; this must be noted on the papers.

F.5 As legal argument may delay the swearing in of a jury, it is desirable to extend the CTL to a date later than the first day of the trial.

Re-trials ordered by the Court of Appeal

F.6 The Crown Court must comply with the directions of the Court of Appeal and cannot vary those directions without reference to the Court of Appeal.

F.7 In cases where a retrial is ordered by the Court of Appeal the CTL is 112 days starting from the date that the new indictment is preferred i.e. from the date that the indictment is delivered to the Crown Court. Court centres should check that CREST has calculated the dates correctly and that it has not used 182 days on cases that have previously been 'sent'.

Changes to the date of fixed cases

F.8 Once a trial date or window is fixed, it should not be vacated or moved without good reason. Under the Criminal Procedure Rules, parties are expected to be ready by the trial date.

F.9 The listing officer may, in circumstances determined by the Resident Judge, agree to the movement of the trial to a date to which the defence and prosecution both consent, provided the timely hearing of the case is not delayed. The prosecution will be expected to have consulted the witnesses before agreeing to any change.

F.10 In all other circumstances, requests to adjourn or vacate fixtures or trial windows must be referred to the Resident Judge for his or her personal attention; the Resident Judge may delegate the decision to a named deputy.

Transferring cases to another court

F.11 Transfer between courts on the same circuit must be agreed by the Resident Judges of each court, subject to guidance from the Presiding Judges of the circuit.

F.12 Transfer of trials between circuits must be agreed between the Presiding Judges and Delivery Directors of the respective circuits.

F.13 Transfers may be agreed either in specific cases or in accordance with general principles agreed between those cited above.

PD-122 CPD XIII Listing G: Listing of Hearings other than Trials

G.1 In addition to trials, the court's listing practice will have to provide court time for shorter matters, such as those listed below. These hearings are important, often either for setting the necessary case management framework for the proper and efficient preparation of cases for trial, or for determining matters that affect the rights of individuals. They must be afforded the appropriate level of resource that they require to be considered properly, and this may include judicial reading time as well as an appropriate length of hearing.

G.2 The applicant is responsible for notifying the court, and the other party if appropriate, and ensuring that the papers are served in good time, including a time estimate for judicial reading time and for the hearing. The applicant must endeavour to complete the application within the time estimate provided unless there are exceptional circumstances.

G.3 Hearings other than trials include the following:

i. Applications for search warrants and Production Orders, sufficient reading time must be provided, see G.8 below;
ii. Bail applications;
iii. Applications to vacate or adjourn hearings;
iv. Applications for dismissal of charges;
v. Pre-Trial and Preparation Hearing;
vi. Applications for disclosure of further unused material under section 8 of CPIA 1996;
vii. Case progression or case management hearings;
viii. Applications in respect of sentence indications not sought at the PTPH;
ix. Sentences;
x. Civil applications under the Anti-Social Behaviour, Crime and Policing Act 2014;
xi. Appeals from the magistrates' court: it is essential in all cases where witnesses are likely to be needed on the appeal to check availability before a date is fixed
xii. Appeals from the youth court: where the case involves a Class 2B offence then a directions hearing will be required before the re-hearing to consider special measures, ground rules and appropriate adjustments for the hearing of the trial.

G.4 Short hearings should not generally be listed before a judge such that they may delay the start or continuation of a trial at the Crown Court. It is envisaged that any such short hearing will be completed by 10.30am or start after 4.30pm.

G.5 Each Crown Court equipped with a video link with a prison must have in place arrangements for the conduct of PCMHs, other pre-trial hearings and sentencing hearings by video link.

Notifying sureties of hearing dates

G.6 Where a surety has entered into a recognizance in the magistrates' court in respect of a case allocated or sent to the Crown Court and where the bail order or recognizance refers to attendance at the first hearing in the Crown Court, the defendant should be reminded by the listing officer that the surety should attend the first hearing in the Crown Court in order to provide further recognizance. If attendance is not arranged, the defendant may be remanded in custody pending the recognisance being provided.

G.7 The Court should also notify sureties of the dates of the hearing at the Crown Court at which the defendant is ordered to appear in as far in advance as possible: see the observations of Parker LJ in *R v Crown Court at Reading ex p. Bello* [1992] 3 All ER 353.

Applications for Production Orders and Search Warrants

G.8 The use of production orders and search warrants involve the use of intrusive state powers that affect the rights and liberties of individuals. It is the responsibility of the court to ensure that those powers are not abused. To do so, the court must be presented with a properly completed application, on the appropriate form, which includes a summary of the investigation to provide the context for the order, a clear explanation of how the statutory requirements are fulfilled, and full and frank disclosure of anything that might undermine the basis for the application. Further directions on the proper making and consideration of such applications will be provided by Practice Direction. However, the complexity of the application must be taken into account in listing it such that the judge is afforded appropriate reading time and the hearing is given sufficient time for the issues to be considered thoroughly, and a short judgment given.

Confiscation and Related Hearings

G.9 Applications for restraint orders should be determined by the Resident Judge, or a judge nominated by the Resident Judge, at the Crown Court location at which they are lodged.

G.10 In order to prevent possible dissipation of assets of significant value, applications under the Proceeds of Crime Act 2002 should be considered urgent when lists are being fixed. In order to prevent potential prejudice, applications for the variation and discharge of orders, for the appointment of receivers, and applications to punish alleged breaches of orders as a contempt of court should similarly be treated as urgent and listed expeditiously.

Confiscation Hearings

G.11 It is important that confiscation hearings take place in good time after the defendant is convicted or sentenced.

CPD XIII Annex 1: General Principles for the Deployment of the Judiciary in the Magistrates' Court **PD-123**

This distils the full deployment guidance issued in November 2012. The relevant sections dealing specifically with the allocation of work within the magistrates' court have been incorporated into this Practice Direction. It does not seek to replace the guidance in its entirety.

Presumptions

1. The presumptions which follow are intended to provide an acceptable and flexible framework establishing the deployment of the DJ (MC)s and magistrates. The system must be capable of adaptation to meet particular needs, whether of locality or caseload. In any event, the presumptions which follow are illustrative not exhaustive.
2. DJ(MC)s should generally (not invariably) be deployed in accordance with the following presumptions ('the Presumptions'):
   (a) Cases involving complex points of law and evidence.
   (b) Cases involving complex procedural issues.
   (c) Long cases (included on grounds of practicality).
   (d) Interlinked cases (given the need for consistency, together with their likely complexity and novelty).
   (e) Cases for which armed police officers are required in court, such as high end firearms cases.
   (f) A share of the more routine business of the Court, including case management and pre-trial reviews, (for a variety of reasons, including the need for DJ(MC)s to have competence in all areas of work and the desirability of an equitable division of work between magistrates and DJ(MC)s, subject always to the interests of the administration of justice).

(g) Where appropriate, in supporting the training of magistrates.
(h) Occasionally, in mixed benches of DJ(MC)s and magistrates (with a particular view both to improving the case management skills of magistrates and to improving the culture of collegiality).
(i) In the short term tackling of particular local backlogs ('backlog busting'), sometimes in combination with magistrates from the local or (with the SPJ's approval) adjoining benches.

3. In accordance with current arrangements certain classes of cases necessarily require DJ(MC)s and have therefore been excluded from the above presumptions; these are as follows:
(a) Extradition;
(b) Terrorism;
(c) Prison Adjudications;
(d) Sex cases in the Youth Court as per Annex 2;
(e) Cases where the defendant is likely to be sentenced to a very large fine, see Annex 3;
(f) The Special Jurisdiction of the Chief Magistrate.

4. In formulating the Presumptions, the following considerations have been taken into account:
(a) The listing of cases is here, as elsewhere, a judicial function, see CPD XIII A.1. In the magistrates' courts the Judicial Business Group, subject to the supervision of the Presiding Judges of the circuit, is responsible for determining the day to day listing practice in that area. The day-to-day operation of that listing practice is the responsibility of the justices' clerk with the assistance of the listing officer.
(b) Equally, providing the training of magistrates is a responsibility of justices' clerks.
(c) It is best not to treat 'high profile' cases as a separate category but to consider their listing in the light of the principles and presumptions. The circumstances surrounding high profile cases do not permit ready generalisation, save that they are likely to require especially sensitive handling. Listing decisions involving such cases will often benefit from good communication at a local level between the justices' clerk, the DJ (MC) and the Bench Chairman.
Account must be taken of the need to maintain the competences of all members of the judiciary sitting in the magistrates' court.

5. The Special Jurisdiction of the Senior District Judge (Chief Magistrate) concerns cases which fall into the following categories:
i. cases with a terrorism connection;
ii. cases involving war crimes and crimes against humanity;
iii. matters affecting state security;
iv. cases brought under the Official Secrets Act;
v. offences involving royalty or parliament;
vi. offences involving diplomats;
vii. corruption of public officials;
viii. police officers charged with serious offences;
ix. cases of unusual sensitivity.

6. Where cases fall within the category of the Special Jurisdiction they must be heard by:-
i. the Senior District Judge (or if not available);
ii. the Deputy Senior District Judge (or if not available);
iii. a District Judge approved by the Senior District Judge or his/her deputy for the particular case.

7. Where a doubt may exist as to whether or not a case falls within the Special Jurisdiction, reference should always be made to the Senior District Judge or to the Deputy Senior District Judge for clarification.

PD-124 **CPD XIII Annex 2: Sexual Offences in the Youth Court**

Introduction

1. This annex sets out the procedure to be applied in the Youth Court in all cases involving allegations of sexual offences which are capable of being sent for trial at the Crown Court under the grave crime provisions.
2. This applies to all cases involving such charges, irrespective of the gravity of the allegation, the age of the defendant and / or the antecedent history of the defendant[7].
3. This does not alter the test[8] that the Youth Court must apply when determining whether a case is a 'grave crime'.

[7] So, for example, every allegation of sexual touching, under s3 of the Sexual Offences Act 2003, is covered by this protocol.
[8] Set out in the Sentencing Guidelines Council's definitive guideline, entitled 'Overarching Principles — Sentencing Youths' Published by the Sentencing Guidelines Council in November 2009.

4. In the Crown Court, cases involving allegations of sexual offences frequently involve complex and sensitive issues and only those Circuit Judges and Recorders who have been specifically authorised and who have attended the appropriate Judicial College course may try this type of work.
5. A number of District Judges (Magistrates' Courts) have now undertaken training in dealing with these difficult cases and have been specifically authorised to hear cases involving serious sexual offences which fall short of requiring to be sent to the Crown Court ('an authorised DJ(MC)'). As such, a procedure similar to that of the Crown Court will now apply to allegations of sexual offences in the Youth Court.

Procedure

6. The determination of venue in the Youth Court is governed by section 51 Crime and Disorder Act 1998, which provides that the youth must be tried summarily unless charged with such a grave crime that long term detention is a realistic possibility[9], or that one of the other exceptions to this presumption arises.
7. Wherever possible such cases should be listed before an authorised DJ(MC), to decide whether the case falls within the grave crime provisions and should therefore be sent for trial. If jurisdiction is retained and the allegation involves actual, or attempted, penetrative activity, the case must be tried by an authorised DJ(MC). In all other cases, the authorised DJ(MC) must consider whether the case is so serious and / or complex that it must be tried by an authorised DJ(MC), or whether the case can be heard by any DJ(MC) or any Youth Court Bench.
8. If it is not practicable for an authorised DJ(MC) to determine venue, any DJ(MC) or any Youth Court Bench may consider that issue. If jurisdiction is retained, appropriate directions may be given but the case papers, including a detailed case summary and a note of any representations made by the parties, must be sent to an authorised DJ(MC) to consider. As soon as possible the authorised DJ(MC) must decide whether the case must be tried by an authorised DJ(MC) or whether the case is suitable to be heard by any DJ(MC) or any Youth Court Bench; however, if the case involves actual, or alleged, penetrative activity, the trial must be heard by an authorised DJ(MC).
9. Once an authorised DJ(MC) has decided that the case is one which must be tried by an authorised DJ(MC), and in all cases involving actual or alleged penetrative activity, all further procedural hearings should, so far as practicable, be heard by an authorised DJ(MC).

Cases remitted for sentence

10. All cases which are remitted for sentence from the Crown Court to the Youth Court should be listed for sentence before an authorised DJ(MC).

Arrangements for an authorised DJ(MC) to be appointed

11. Where a case is to be tried by an authorised DJ(MC) but no such Judge is available, the Bench Legal Adviser should contact the Chief Magistrates Office for an authorised DJ(MC) to be assigned.

CPD XIII Annex 3: Cases Involving Very Large Fines in the Magistrates' Court **PD-125**

1. This Annex applies when s. 85 Legal Aid, Sentencing and Punishment of Offenders Act 2012 comes into force and the magistrates' court has the power to impose a maximum fine of any amount.
2. An authorised DJ(MC) must deal with any allocation decision, trial and sentencing hearing in the following types of cases which are triable either way:
   a) Cases involving death or significant, life changing injury or a high risk of death or significant, life-changing injury;
   b) Cases involving substantial environmental damage or polluting material of a dangerous nature;
   c) Cases where major adverse effect on human health or quality of life, animal health or flora has resulted;
   d) Cases where major costs through clean up, site restoration or animal rehabilitation have been incurred;
   e) Cases where the defendant corporation has a turnover in excess of £10 million but does not exceed £250 million, and has acted in a deliberate, reckless or negligent manner;
   f) Cases where the defendant corporation has a turnover in excess of £250 million;
   g) Cases where the court will be expected to analyse complex company accounts;
   h) High profile cases or ones of an exceptionally sensitive nature.

[9] Section 24(1) of the Magistrates Court Act 1980.

3. The prosecution agency must notify the justices' clerk where practicable of any case of the type mentioned in paragraph 2 of this Annex, no less than 7 days before the first hearing to ensure that an authorised DJ(MC) is available at the first hearing.
4. The justices' clerk shall contact the Office of the Chief Magistrate to ensure that an authorised DJ(MC) can be assigned to deal with such a case if there is not such a person available in the courthouse. The justices' clerk shall also notify a Presiding Judge of the Circuit that such a case has been listed.
5. Where an authorised DJ(MC) is not appointed at the first hearing the court shall adjourn the case. The court shall ask the accused for an indication of his plea, but shall not allocate the case nor, if the accused indicates a guilty plea, sentence him, commit him for sentence, ask for a pre-sentence report or give any indication as to likely sentence that will be imposed. The justices' clerk shall ensure an authorised DJ(MC) is appointed for the following hearing and notify the Presiding Judge of the Circuit that the case has been listed.
6. When dealing with sentence, section 3 of the Powers of Criminal Courts (Sentenc[ing]) Act 2000 can be invoked where, despite the magistrates' court having maximum fine powers available to it, the offence or combination of offences make it so serious that the Crown Court should deal with it as though the person had been convicted on indictment.
7. An authorised DJ(MC) should consider allocating the case to the Crown Court or committing the accused for sentence.

PD-126 **CPD XIII Annex 4: Application This annex replaces the Protocol on the case management of Terrorism Cases issued in December 2006 by the President of the Queen's Bench Division**

1. This annex applies to 'terrorism cases'. For the purposes of this annex a case is a 'terrorism case' where:
   (a) one of the offences charged against any of the defendants is indictable only and it is alleged by the prosecution that there is evidence that it took place during an act of terrorism or for the purposes of terrorism as defined in s1 of the Terrorist Act 2000. This may include, but is not limited to:
      (i) murder;
      (ii) manslaughter;
      (iii) an offence under section 18 of the Offences against the Person Act 1861 (wounding with intent);
      (iv) an offence under section 23 or 24 of that Act (administering poison etc);
      (v) an offence under section 28 or 29 of that Act (explosives);
      (vi) an offence under section 2, 3 or 5 of the Explosive Substances Act 1883 (causing explosions);
      (vii) an offence under section 1(2) of the Criminal Damage Act 1971 (endangering life by damaging property);
      (viii) an offence under section 1 of the Biological Weapons Act 1974 (biological weapons);
      (ix) an offence under section 2 of the Chemical Weapons Act 1996 (chemical weapons);
      (x) an offence under section 56 of the Terrorism Act 2000 (directing a terrorist organisation);
      (xi) an offence under section 59 of that Act (inciting terrorism overseas);
      (xii) offences under (v), (vii) and (viii) above given jurisdiction by virtue of section 62 of that Act (terrorist bombing overseas); and
      (xiii) an offence under section 5 of the Terrorism Act 2006 (preparation of terrorism acts).
   (b) one of the offences charged is indictable only and includes an allegation by the prosecution of serious fraud that took place during an act of terrorism or for the purposes of terrorism as defined in s1 of the Terrorist Act 2000 and the prosecutor gives a notice under section 51B of the Crime and Disorder Act 1998 (Notices in serious or complex fraud cases);
   (c) one of the offences charged is indictable only, which includes an allegation that a defendant conspired, incited or attempted to commit an offence under sub paragraphs (1)(a) or (b) above; or
   (d) it is a case (which can be indictable only or triable either way) that a judge of the terrorism cases list (see paragraph 2(a) below) considers should be a terrorism case. In deciding whether a case not covered by subparagraphs (1)(a), (b) or (c) above should be a terrorism case, the judge may hear representations from the Crown Prosecution Service.

The terrorism cases list

2. (a) All terrorism cases, wherever they originate in England and Wales, will be managed in a list known as the 'terrorism cases list' by such judges of the High Court as are nominated by the President of the Queen's Bench Division.

(b) Such cases will be tried, unless otherwise directed by the President of the Queen's Bench Division, by a judge of the High Court as nominated by the President of the Queen's Bench Division.

3. The judges managing the terrorism cases referred to in paragraph 2(a) will be supported by the London and South Eastern Regional Co-ordinator's Office (the 'Regional Co-ordinator's Office'). An official of that office or an individual nominated by that office will act as the case progression officer for cases in that list for the purposes of CrimPR 3.4.

Procedure after charge

4. Immediately after a person has been charged in a terrorism case, anywhere in England and Wales, a representative of the Crown Prosecution Service will notify the person on the 24 hour rota for special jurisdiction matters at Westminster Magistrates' Court of the following information:
   (a) the full name of each defendant and the name of his solicitor of other legal representative, if known;
   (b) the charges laid;
   (c) the name and contact details of the Crown Prosecutor with responsibility for the case, if known; and
   (d) confirmation that the case is a terrorism case.
5. The person on the 24-hour rota will then ensure that all terrorism cases wherever they are charged in England and Wales are listed before the Chief Magistrate or other District Judge designated under the Terrorism Act 2000. Unless the Chief Magistrate or other District Judge designated under the Terrorism Act 2000 directs otherwise, the first appearance of all defendants accused of terrorism offences will be listed at Westminster Magistrates' Court.
6. In order to comply with section 46 of the Police and Criminal Evidence Act 1984, if a defendant in a terrorism case is charged at a police station within the local justice area in which Westminster Magistrates' Court is situated, the defendant must be brought before Westminster Magistrates' Court as soon as is practicable and in any event not later than the first sitting after he is charged with the offence. If a defendant in a terrorism case is charged in a police station outside the local justice area in which Westminster Magistrates' Court is situated, unless the Chief Magistrate or other designated judge directs otherwise, the defendant must be removed to that area as soon as is practicable. He must then be brought before Westminster Magistrates' Court as soon as is practicable after his arrival in the area and in any event not later than the first sitting of Westminster Magistrates' Court after his arrival in that area.
7. As soon as is practicable after charge a representative of the Crown Prosecution Service will also provide the Regional Listing Co-ordinator's Office with the information listed in paragraph 4 above.
8. The Regional Co-ordinator's Office will then ensure that the Chief Magistrate and the Legal Aid Agency have the same information.

Cases to be sent to the Crown Court under section 51 of the Crime and Disorder Act 1998

9. The court should ordinarily direct that the plea and trial preparation hearing should take place about 14 days after charge.
10. The sending magistrates' court should contact the Regional Listing Co-ordinator's Office who will be responsible for notifying the magistrates' court as to the relevant Crown Court to which to send the case.
11. In all terrorism cases, the magistrates' court case progression form for cases sent to the Crown Court under section 51 of the Crime and Disorder Act 1998 should not be used. Instead of the automatic directions set out in that form, the magistrates' court shall make the following directions to facilitate the preliminary hearing at the Crown Court:
    (a) three days prior to the preliminary hearing in the terrorism cases list, the prosecution must serve upon each defendant and the Regional Listing co-ordinator:
        (i) a preliminary summary of the case;
        (ii) the names of those who are to represent the prosecution, if known;
        (iii) an estimate of the length of the trial;
        (iv) a suggested provisional timetable which should generally include:
            - the general nature of further enquiries being made by the prosecution,
            - the time needed for the completion of such enquiries,
            - the time required by the prosecution to review the case,
            - a timetable for the phased service of the evidence,
            - the time for the provision by the Attorney General for his consent if necessary,
            - the time for service of the detailed defence case statement,

- the date for the case management hearing, and
- the estimated trial date;

(v) a preliminary statement of the possible disclosure issues setting out the nature and scale of the problem, including the amount of unused material, the manner in which the prosecution seeks to deal with these matters and a suggested timetable for discharging their statutory duty; and

(vi) any information relating to bail and custody time limits.

(b) one day prior to the preliminary hearing in the terrorist cases list, each defendant must serve in writing on the Regional Listing Co-ordinator and the prosecution:

(i) the proposed representation;

(ii) observations on the timetable; and

(iii) an indication of plea and the general nature of the defence.

Cases to be sent to the Crown Court after the prosecutor gives notice under section 51B of the Crime and Disorder Act 1998

12. If a terrorism case is to be sent to the Crown Court after the prosecutor gives a notice under section 51B of the Crime and Disorder Act 1998 the magistrates' court should proceed as in paragraphs 9-11 above.

13. When a terrorism case is so sent or transferred the case will go into the terrorism list and be managed by a judge as described in paragraph 2(a) above.

The plea and trial preparation hearing at the Crown Court

14. At the plea and trial preparation hearing, the judge will determine whether the case is one to remain in the terrorism list and if so, give directions setting the provisional timetable.

15. The Legal Aid Agency must attend the hearing by an authorised officer to assist the court.

Use of video links

16. Unless a judge otherwise directs, all Crown Court hearings prior to the trial will be conducted by video link for all defendants in custody.

Security

17. The police service and the prison service will provide the Regional Listing Co-ordinator's Office with an initial joint assessment of the security risks associated with any court appearance by the defendants within 14 days of charge. Any subsequent changes in circumstances or the assessment of risk which have the potential to impact upon the choice of trial venue will be notified to the Regional Listing Co-ordinator's Office immediately.

PD-127 **CPD XIII Annex 5: Management of cases from the organised crime division of the Crown Prosecution Service This annex replaces the guidance issued by the Senior Presiding Judge in January 2014**

1. The Organised Crime Division (OCD) of the CPS is responsible for prosecution of cases from the National Crime Agency (NCA). Typically, these cases involve more than one defendant, are voluminous and raise complex and specialised issues of law. It is recognised that if not closely managed, such cases have the potential to cost vast amounts of public money and take longer than necessary.
2. This annex applies to all cases handled by the OCD.

Designated court centres

3. Subject to the overriding discretion of the Presiding Judges of the circuit, OCD cases should normally be heard at Designated Court Centres (DCC). The process of designating court centres for this purpose has taken into account geographical factors and the size, security and facilities of those court centres. The designated court centres are:

(a) Northern Circuit: Manchester, Liverpool and Preston.

(b) North Eastern Circuit: Leeds, Newcastle and Sheffield.

(c) Western Circuit: Bristol and Winchester.

(d) South Eastern Circuit (not including London): Reading, Luton, Chelmsford, Ipswich, Maidstone, Lewes and Hove.

(e) South Eastern Circuit (London only): Southwark, Blackfriars, Kingston, Woolwich, Croydon and the Central Criminal Court.

(f) Midland Circuit: Birmingham, Leicester and Nottingham.

(g) Wales Circuit: Cardiff, Swansea and Mold.

Selection of designated court centres

4. If arrests are made in different parts of the country and the OCD seeks to have all defendants tried by one Crown Court, the OCD will, at the earliest opportunity, write to the relevant court cluster manager with a recommendation as to the appropriate designated court centre, requesting that the decision be made by the relevant Presiding Judges. In the event that the designated court centre within one region is unable to accommodate a case, for example, as a result of a custody time limit expiry date, consideration may be given to transferring the case to a DCC in another region with the consent of the relevant Presiding Judges.
5. There will be a single point of contact person at the OCD for each HMCTS region, to assist listing co-ordinators.
6. The single contact person for each HMCTS region will be the relevant Cluster Manager, with the exception of the South Eastern Circuit, where the appropriate person will be the Regional Listing Co-ordinator.

Designation of the trial judge

7. The trial judge will be assigned by the Presiding Judge at the earliest opportunity, and in accordance with CPD XIII Listing E: Allocation of Business within the Crown Court. Where the trial judge is unable to continue with the case, all further pre-trial hearings should be by a single judge until a replacement has been assigned.

Procedure after charge

8. Within 24 hours of the laying of a charge, a representative of the OCD will notify the relevant Cluster Manager of the following information to enable an agreement to be reached between that Cluster Manager and the reviewing CPS lawyer before the first appearance as to the DCC to which the case should be sent:
   (a) the full name of each defendant and the name of his legal representatives, if known;
   (b) the charges laid; and
   (c) the name and contact details of the Crown Prosecutor with responsibility for the case.

Exceptions

9. Where it is not possible to have a case dealt with at a DCC, the OCD should liaise closely with the relevant Cluster Manager and the Presiding Judges to ensure that the cases are sent to the most appropriate court centre. This will, among other things, take into account the location of the likely source of the case, convenience of the witnesses, travelling distance for OCD staff and facilities at the court centres.
10. In the event that it is allocated to a non-designated court centre, the OCD should be permitted to make representations in writing to the Presiding Judges within 14 days as to why the venue is not suitable. The Presiding Judges will consider the reasons and, if necessary, hold a hearing. The CPS may renew their request at any stage where further reasons come to light that may affect the original decision on venue.
11. Nothing in this annex should be taken to remove the right of the defence to make representations as to the venue.

SENTENCING GUIDELINES

Sentencing Guidelines

This is an edited version of the various definitive sentencing guidelines, both those originally issued by the Sentencing Guidelines Council and those issued by the Sentencing Council for England and Wales. It contains all of the essential guideline material relevant to offences in *Blackstone's Criminal Practice*. Fuller versions are available on the Sentencing Council website at www.sentencingcouncil.org.uk. By virtue of the Coroners and Justice Act 2009 (Commencement No. 4, Transitional and Saving Provisions) Order 2010 (SI 2010 No. 816), art. 7, guidelines issued by the SGC 'are to be treated as guidelines issued by the Sentencing Council'. For more on the status of guidelines and the duty of courts to follow them, see **E1.3** in the main work.

The Sentencing Guidelines Council now make changes to these guidelines directly on their website. Whilst we update the guidelines contained in this supplement as frequently as possible, readers are advised that only the online version of a guideline is guaranteed to be up to date.

Up to date versions of the Sentencing Guidelines for use in Magistrates' Court can be found here: https://www.sentencingcouncil.org.uk/the-magistrates-court-sentencing-guidelines/

Up to date versions of the Sentencing Guidelines for use in Crown Court can be found here: https://www.sentencingcouncil.org.uk/crown-court/

Paragraph numbering and marginal notation

'SG1-1', 'SG1-2' (etc.) paragraph numbers are used as a cross-referencing aid for readers.

The marginal numbers in square brackets denote the page of the original guideline, where these were issued in PDF format, from which the corresponding material in the Sentencing Guidelines has been reproduced. The dotted lines denote the precise location of the page break.

For example, the content between ------------------------ [10] and ------------------------ [11] can be found on Page 10 of the original guideline as published either by the Sentencing Guidelines Council or the Sentencing Council of England and Wales (as appropriate).

Expanded Explanations in Guidelines

On 24 July 2019 the Sentencing Council published the following on their website:

Judges and magistrates across England and Wales will have access to expanded explanations embedded in offence specific guidelines. The expanded explanations add extra information to aggravating and mitigating factors to make it easier for courts to maintain consistency and transparency in sentencing.

They are designed to reflect and encourage current best practice rather than to alter sentencing practice. They will provide court users with useful information relating to fines, community and custodial sentences and commonly used factors. They will also improve transparency for victims, defendants and the wider public.

The expanded explanations, which supplement the General guideline are effective from 1 October 2019 but are now available online, with an accompanying video.

For more information please visit: https://www.sentencingcouncil.org.uk/blog/post/expanded-explanations-in-guidelines/

Where an aggravating or mitigating factor appears in the Sentencing Guidelines as reproduced this supplement, please consult the Table of Expanded Explanations for Aggravating Factors and the Table of Expanded Explanations for Factors Reducing Seriousness or Reflecting Personal Mitigation at SA1-A23 and M1-M17 respectively.

TABLE OF EXPANDED EXPLANATIONS FOR AGGRAVATING FACTORS

Previous convictions, having regard to a) the **nature** of the offence to which the conviction relates and its **relevance** to the current offence; and b) the **time** that has elapsed since the conviction	SA1
Offence committed whilst on bail	SA2
Offence motivated by, or demonstrating hostility based on any of the following characteristics or presumed characteristics of the victim: religion, race, disability, sexual orientation or transgender identity.	SA3
Offence was committed against an emergency worker acting in the exercise of functions as such a worker	SA4
Other aggravating factors:	
Commission of offence whilst under the influence of alcohol or drugs	A1
Offence was committed as part of a group	A2
Offence involved use or threat of use of a weapon	A3
Planning of an offence	A4
Commission of the offence for financial gain	A5
High level of profit from the offence	A6
Abuse of trust or dominant position	A7
Gratuitous degradation of victim/maximising distress to victim	A8
Vulnerable victim	A9
Victim was providing a public service or performing a public duty at the time of the offence	A10
Other(s) put at risk of harm by the offending	A11
Offence committed in the presence of other(s) (especially children)	A12
Actions after the event including but not limited to attempts to cover up/conceal evidence	A13
Blame wrongly placed on other(s)	A14
Failure to respond to warnings or concerns expressed by others about the offender's behaviour	A15
Offence committed on licence or post sentence supervision or while subject to court order(s)	A16
Offence committed on licence or post sentence supervision	A16L
Offence committed while subject to court order(s)	A16CO
Offence committed in custody	A17
Offences taken into consideration	A18
Offence committed in a domestic context	A19
Offence committed in a terrorist context	A20
Location and/or timing of offence	A21
Location	A21L
Timing	A21T
Established evidence of community/ wider impact	A22
Prevalence	A23

Care should be taken to avoid double counting factors including those already taken into account in assessing culpability or harm or those inherent in the offence

SA1: Previous convictions, having regard to a) the nature of the offence to which the conviction relates and its relevance to the current offence; and b) the time that has elapsed since the conviction

Effective from: 01 October 2019

Guidance on the use of previous convictions

The following guidance should be considered when seeking to determine the degree to which previous convictions should aggravate sentence:

Section 143 of the Criminal Justice Act states that:

> In considering the seriousness of an offence ("the current offence") committed by an offender who has one or more previous convictions, the court must treat each previous conviction as an aggravating factor if (in the case of that conviction) the court considers that it can reasonably be so treated having regard, in particular, to—
> (a) the nature of the offence to which the conviction relates and its relevance to the current offence, and
> (b) the time that has elapsed since the conviction.

1. Previous convictions are considered at step two in the Council's offence-specific guidelines.
2. The primary significance of previous convictions (including convictions in other jurisdictions) is the extent to which they indicate trends in offending behaviour and possibly the offender's response to earlier sentences.
3. Previous convictions are normally **relevant** to the current offence when they are of a similar type.
4. Previous convictions of a type different from the current offence **may** be relevant where they are an indication of persistent offending or escalation and/or a failure to comply with previous court orders.
5. Numerous and frequent previous convictions might indicate an underlying problem (for example, an addiction) that could be addressed more effectively in the community and will not necessarily indicate that a custodial sentence is necessary.
6. If the offender received a non-custodial disposal for the previous offence, a court should not necessarily move to a custodial sentence for the fresh offence.
7. In cases involving significant persistent offending, the community and custody thresholds may be crossed even though the current offence normally warrants a lesser sentence. If a custodial sentence is imposed it should be proportionate and kept to the necessary minimum.
8. The aggravating effect of relevant previous convictions reduces with the passage of time; **older convictions are less relevant** to the offender's culpability for the current offence and less likely to be predictive of future offending.
9. Where the previous offence is particularly old it will normally have little relevance for the current sentencing exercise.
10. The court should consider the time gap since the previous conviction and the reason for it. Where there has been a significant gap between previous and current convictions or a reduction in the frequency of offending this may indicate that the offender has made attempts to desist from offending in which case the aggravating effect of the previous offending will diminish.
11. Where the current offence is significantly less serious than the previous conviction (suggesting a decline in the gravity of offending), the previous conviction may carry less weight.
12. When considering the totality of previous offending a court should take a rounded view of the previous crimes and not simply aggregate the individual offences.
13. Where information is available on the context of previous offending this may assist the court in assessing the relevance of that prior offending to the current offence

SA2: Offence committed whilst on bail

Effective from: 01 October 2019

S143 (3) Criminal Justice Act 2003 states:

In considering the seriousness of any offence committed while the offender was on bail, the court must treat the fact that it was committed in those circumstances as an aggravating factor.

SA3: Offence motivated by, or demonstrating hostility based on any of the following characteristics or presumed characteristics of the victim: religion, race, disability, sexual orientation or transgender identity.

Effective from: 01 October 2019

See below for the statutory provisions.

- **Note the requirement for the court to state that the offence has been aggravated by the relevant hostility.**

- **Where the element of hostility is core to the offending, the aggravation will be higher than where it plays a lesser role.**

Increase in sentences for racial or religious aggravation

s145(2) of the Criminal Justice Act 2003 states:

If the offence was racially or religiously aggravated, the court—

(a) must treat that fact as an aggravating factor, and
(b) must state in open court that the offence was so aggravated.

An offence is racially or religiously aggravated for these purposes if—

- at the time of committing the offence, or immediately before or after doing so, the offender demonstrates towards the victim of the offence, hostility based on the victim's membership (or presumed membership) of a racial or religious group; **or**
- the offence is motivated (wholly or partly) by hostility towards members of a racial or religious group based on their membership of that group.

"membership", in relation to a racial or religious group, includes association with members of that group;

"presumed" means presumed by the offender.

It is immaterial whether or not the offender's hostility is also based, to any extent, on any other factor not mentioned above.

"racial group" means a group of persons defined by reference to race, colour, nationality (including citizenship) or ethnic or national origins.

"religious group" means a group of persons defined by reference to religious belief or lack of religious belief.

Increase in sentences for aggravation related to disability, sexual orientation or transgender identity

s146 of the Criminal Justice Act 2003 states:

(1) This section applies where the court is considering the seriousness of an offence committed in any of the circumstances mentioned in subsection (2).
(2) Those circumstances are—
    (a) that, at the time of committing the offence, or immediately before or after doing so, the offender demonstrated towards the victim of the offence hostility based on—
        (i) the sexual orientation (or presumed sexual orientation) of the victim,
        (ii) a disability (or presumed disability) of the victim, or
        (iii) the victim being (or being presumed to be) transgender, or
    (b) that the offence is motivated (wholly or partly)—
        (i) by hostility towards persons who are of a particular sexual orientation,
        (ii) by hostility towards persons who have a disability or a particular disability or
        (iii) by hostility towards persons who are transgender.
(3) The court—
    (a) must treat the fact that the offence was committed in any of those circumstances as an aggravating factor, and
    (b) must state in open court that the offence was committed in such circumstances.
(4) It is immaterial for the purposes of paragraph (a) or (b) of subsection (2) whether or not the offender's hostility is also based, to any extent, on any other factor not mentioned in that paragraph.
(5) In this section "disability" means any physical or mental impairment.
(6) In this section references to being transgender include references to being transsexual, or undergoing, proposing to undergo or having undergone a process or part of a process of gender reassignment.

SA4: Offence was committed against an emergency worker acting in the exercise of functions as such a worker

Effective from: 01 October 2019

See below for the statutory provisions.

- **Note the requirement for the court to state that the offence has been so aggravated.**
- **Note this statutory factor only applies to certain violent or sexual offences as listed below which were committed on or after 13 November 2018.**
- **For other offences the factor 'Victim was providing a public service or performing a public duty at the time of the offence' can be applied where relevant.**

The Assaults on Emergency Worker (Offences) Act 2018 states:

2 Aggravating factor

(1) This section applies where—
 (a) the court is considering for the purposes of sentencing the seriousness of an offence listed in subsection (3), and
 (b) the offence was committed against an emergency worker acting in the exercise of functions as such a worker.

(2) The court—
 (a) must treat the fact mentioned in subsection (1)(b) as an aggravating factor (that is to say, a factor that increases the seriousness of the offence), and
 (b) must state in open court that the offence is so aggravated.

(3) The offences referred to in subsection (1)(a) are—
 (a) an offence under any of the following provisions of the Offences against the Person Act 1861—
  (i) section 16 (threats to kill);
  (ii) section 18 (wounding with intent to cause grievous bodily harm);
  (iii) section 20 (malicious wounding);
  (iv) section 23 (administering poison etc);
  (v) section 28 (causing bodily injury by gunpowder etc);
  (vi) section 29 (using explosive substances etc with intent to cause grievous bodily harm);
  (vii) section 47 (assault occasioning actual bodily harm);
 (b) an offence under section 3 of the Sexual Offences Act 2003 (sexual assault);
 (c) manslaughter;
 (d) kidnapping;
 (e) an ancillary offence in relation to any of the preceding offences.

(4) For the purposes of subsection (1)(b), the circumstances in which an offence is to be taken as committed against a person acting in the exercise of functions as an emergency worker include circumstances where the offence takes place at a time when the person is not at work but is carrying out functions which, if done in work time, would have been in the exercise of functions as an emergency worker.

(5) In this section—
 "ancillary offence", in relation to an offence, means any of the following—
 (a) aiding, abetting, counselling or procuring the commission of the offence;
 (b) an offence under Part 2 of the Serious Crime Act 2007 (encouraging or assisting crime) in relation to the offence;
 (c) attempting or conspiring to commit the offence;
 "emergency worker" has the meaning given by section 3.

(6) Nothing in this section prevents a court from treating the fact mentioned in subsection (1)(b) as an aggravating factor in relation to offences not listed in subsection (3).

(7) This section applies only in relation to offences committed on or after the day it comes into force.

3 Meaning of "emergency worker"

(1) In sections 1 and 2, "emergency worker" means—
 (a) a constable;
 (b) a person (other than a constable) who has the powers of a constable or is otherwise employed for police purposes or is engaged to provide services for police purposes;
 (c) a National Crime Agency officer;
 (d) a prison officer;
 (e) a person (other than a prison officer) employed or engaged to carry out functions in a custodial institution of a corresponding kind to those carried out by a prison officer;
 (f) a prisoner custody officer, so far as relating to the exercise of escort functions;
 (g) a custody officer, so far as relating to the exercise of escort functions;
 (h) a person employed for the purposes of providing, or engaged to provide, fire services or fire and rescue services;
 (i) a person employed for the purposes of providing, or engaged to provide, search services or rescue services (or both);
 (j) a person employed for the purposes of providing, or engaged to provide—
  (i) NHS health services, or
  (ii) services in the support of the provision of NHS health services, and whose general activities in doing so involve face to face interaction with individuals receiving the services or with other members of the public.

(2) It is immaterial for the purposes of subsection (1) whether the employment or engagement is paid or unpaid.

(3) In this section—

"custodial institution" means any of the following—

(a) a prison;

(b) a young offender institution, secure training centre, secure college or remand centre;

(c) a removal centre, a short-term holding facility or pre-departure accommodation, as defined by section 147 of the Immigration and Asylum Act 1999;

(d) services custody premises, as defined by section 300(7) of the Armed Forces Act 2006;

"custody officer" has the meaning given by section 12(3) of the Criminal Justice and Public Order Act 1994;

"escort functions"—

(a) in the case of a prisoner custody officer, means the functions specified in section 80(1) of the Criminal Justice Act 1991;

(b) in the case of a custody officer, means the functions specified in paragraph 1 of Schedule 1 to the Criminal Justice and Public Order Act 1994;

"NHS health services" means any kind of health services provided as part of the health service continued under section 1(1) of the National Health Service Act 2006 and under section 1(1) of the National Health Service (Wales) Act 2006;

"prisoner custody officer" has the meaning given by section 89(1) of the Criminal Justice Act 1991.

Other aggravating factors:

A1: Commission of offence whilst under the influence of alcohol or drugs

Effective from: 01 October 2019

The fact that an offender is **voluntarily** intoxicated at the time of the offence will tend to increase the seriousness of the offence provided that the intoxication has **contributed to the offending.**

This applies regardless of whether the offender is under the influence of legal or illegal substance(s).

In the case of a person addicted to drugs or alcohol the intoxication may be considered not to be voluntary, but the court should have regard to the extent to which the offender has sought help or engaged with any assistance which has been offered or made available in dealing with the addiction.

An offender who has voluntarily consumed drugs and/or alcohol must accept the consequences of the behaviour that results, even if it is out of character.

A2: Offence was committed as part of a group

Effective from: 01 October 2019

The mere membership of a group (two or more persons) should not be used to increase the sentence, but where the **offence was committed as part** of a group this will normally make it more serious because:

- the **harm** caused (both physical or psychological) or the potential for harm may be greater and/or
- the **culpability** of the offender may be higher (the role of the offender within the group will be a relevant consideration).

Culpability based on role in group offending could range from:

- Higher culpability indicated by a leading role in the group and/or the involvement by the offender of others through coercion, intimidation or exploitation, to
- Lower culpability indicated by a lesser or subordinate role under direction and/or involvement of the offender through coercion, intimidation or exploitation.

Courts should be alert to factors that suggest that an offender may have been the subject of coercion, intimidation or exploitation (including as a result of domestic abuse, trafficking or modern slavery) which the offender may find difficult to articulate, and where appropriate ask for this to be addressed in a PSR.

Where the offending is part of an organised criminal network, this will make it more serious, and the role of the offender in the organisation will also be relevant.

When sentencing young adult offenders (typically aged 18-25), consideration should also be given to the guidance on the mitigating factor relating to age and/or lack of maturity when considering the significance of group offending.

A3: Offence involved use or threat of use of a weapon

Effective from: 01 October 2019

- A 'weapon' can take many forms
- The use or production of a weapon has relevance
  - o to the **culpability** of the offender where it indicates planning or intention to cause harm; and
  - o to the **harm** caused (both physical or psychological) or the potential for harm.
- Relevant considerations will include:
  - o the dangerousness of the weapon;
  - o whether the offender brought the weapon to the scene, or just used what was available on impulse;
  - o whether the offender made or adapted something for use as a weapon;
  - o the context in which the weapon was threatened, used or produced.

When sentencing young adult offenders (typically aged 18-25), consideration should also be given to the guidance on the mitigating factor relating to age and/or lack of maturity when assessing the relevance of this factor to culpability.

A4: Planning of an offence

Effective from: 01 October 2019

- Evidence of planning normally indicates a higher level of intention and pre-meditation which increases the level of culpability.
- Planning may be inferred from the scale and sophistication of the offending and/or the role of the offender.
- The greater the degree of planning the greater the culpability.

A5: Commission of the offence for financial gain

Effective from: 01 October 2019

- Where an offence (which is not one which by its nature is an acquisitive offence) has been committed wholly or in part for financial gain or the avoidance of cost, this will increase the seriousness.
- Where the offending is committed in a commercial context for financial gain or the avoidance of costs, this will normally indicate a higher level of culpability:
  - o examples would include, but are not limited to, dealing in unlawful goods, failing to disclose relevant matters to an authority or regulator, failing to comply with a regulation or failing to obtain the necessary licence or permission in order to avoid costs.
  - o offending of this type can undermine legitimate businesses.
- See the guidance on fines if considering a financial penalty.

A6: High level of profit from the offence

Not yet applicable

A7: Abuse of trust or dominant position

Effective from: 01 October 2019

- A close examination of the facts is necessary and a clear justification should be given if abuse of trust is to be found.
- In order for an abuse of trust to make an offence more serious the relationship between the offender and victim(s) must be one that would give rise to the offender having a significant level of responsibility towards the victim(s) on which the victim(s) would be entitled to rely.
- Abuse of trust may occur in many factual situations. Examples may include relationships such as teacher and pupil, parent and child, employer and employee, professional adviser and client, or carer (whether paid or unpaid) and dependant. It may also include ad hoc situations such as a late-night taxi driver and a lone passenger. These examples are not exhaustive and do not necessarily indicate that abuse of trust is present.
- Additionally an offence may be made more serious where an offender has abused their position to facilitate and/or conceal offending.
- Where an offender has been given an inappropriate level of responsibility, abuse of trust is unlikely to apply.

A8: Gratuitous degradation of victim / maximising distress to victim

Effective from: 01 October 2019

Where an offender deliberately causes **additional** harm to a victim over and above that which is an essential element of the offence - this will increase seriousness. Examples may include, but are not limited to, posts of images on social media designed to cause additional distress to the victim.

Where any such actions are the subject of separate charges, this should be taken into account when assessing totality.

When sentencing young adult offenders (typically aged 18-25), consideration should also be given to the guidance on the mitigating factor relating to age and/or lack of maturity when considering the significance of this factor.

A9: Vulnerable victim

Effective from: 01 October 2019

- An offence is more serious if the victim is vulnerable because of personal circumstances such as (but not limited to) age, illness or disability (unless the vulnerability of the victim is an element of the offence).
- Other factors such as the victim being isolated, incapacitated through drink or being in an unfamiliar situation **may** lead to a court considering that the offence is more serious.
- The extent to which any vulnerability may impact on the sentence is a matter for the court to weigh up in each case.
- Culpability will be increased if the offender **targeted** a victim because of an actual or perceived vulnerability.
- Culpability will be increased if the victim is made vulnerable by the actions of the offender (such as a victim who has been intimidated or isolated by the offender).
- Culpability is increased if an offender persisted in the offending once it was obvious that the victim was vulnerable (for example continuing to attack an injured victim).
- The level of harm (physical, psychological or financial) is likely to be increased if the victim is vulnerable.

A10: Victim was providing a public service or performing a public duty at the time of the offence

Effective from: 01 October 2019

This reflects:

- the fact that people in public facing roles are more exposed to the possibility of harm and consequently more vulnerable and/or
- the fact that someone is working in the public interest merits the additional protection of the courts.

This applies whether the victim is a public or private employee or acting in a voluntary capacity.

Care should be taken to avoid double counting where the statutory aggravating factor relating to emergency workers applies.

A11: Other(s) put at risk of harm by the offending

Effective from: 01 October 2019

- Where there is risk of harm to other(s) not taken in account at step one and not subject to a separate charge, this makes the offence more serious.
- Dealing with a risk of harm involves consideration of both the likelihood of harm occurring and the extent of it if it does.

Where any such risk of harm is the subject of separate charges, this should be taken into account when assessing totality.

When sentencing young adult offenders (typically aged 18-25), consideration should also be given to the guidance on the mitigating factor relating to age and/or lack of maturity when considering the significance of this factor.

A12: Offence committed in the presence of other(s) (especially children)

Effective from: 01 October 2019

- This reflects the psychological harm that may be caused to those who witnessed the offence.
- The presence of one or more children may in some situations make the primary victim more vulnerable – for example an adult may be less able to resist the offender if concerned about the safety or welfare of children present.
- When sentencing young adult offenders (typically aged 18-25), consideration should also be given to the guidance on the mitigating factor relating to age and/or lack of maturity when considering the significance of this factor.

A13: Actions after the event including but not limited to attempts to cover up/conceal evidence

Effective from: 01 October 2019

The more sophisticated, extensive or persistent the actions after the event, the more likely it is to increase the seriousness of the offence.

When sentencing young adult offenders (typically aged 18-25), consideration should also be given to the guidance on the mitigating factor relating to age and lack of maturity when considering the significance of such conduct.

Where any such actions are the subject of separate charges, this should be taken into account when assessing totality.

A14: Blame wrongly placed on other(s)

Effective from: 01 October 2019

- Where the investigation has been hindered and/or other(s) have suffered as a result of being wrongly blamed by the offender, this will make the offence more serious.
- This factor will **not** be engaged where an offender has simply exercised his or her right not to assist the investigation or accept responsibility for the offending.

When sentencing young adult offenders (typically aged 18-25), consideration should also be given to the guidance on the mitigating factor relating to age and lack of maturity when considering the significance of such conduct.

A15: Failure to respond to warnings or concerns expressed by others about the offender's behaviour

Effective from: 01 October 2019

Where an offender has had the benefit of warnings or advice about their conduct but has failed to heed it, this would make the offender more blameworthy.

This may particularly be the case when:

- such warning(s) or advice were of an official nature or from a professional source, and/or
- the warning(s) were made at the time of or shortly before the commission of the offence.

When sentencing young adult offenders (typically aged 18-25), consideration should also be given to the guidance on the mitigating factor relating to age and/or lack of maturity when considering the significance of this factor.

A16: Offence committed on licence or post sentence supervision or while subject to court order(s)

Effective from: 01 October 2019

- An offender who is subject to licence or post sentence supervision is under a particular obligation to desist from further offending.
- Commission of an offence while subject to a **relevant** court order makes the offence more serious.
- The extent to which the offender has complied with the conditions of a licence or order (including the time that has elapsed since its commencement) will be a relevant consideration.
- Where the offender is dealt with separately for a breach of a licence or order regard should be had to totality.
- Care should be taken to avoid double counting matters taken into account when considering previous convictions.

When sentencing young adult offenders (typically aged 18-25), consideration should also be given to the guidance on the mitigating factor relating to age and/or lack of maturity when considering the significance of this factor.

A16L: Offence committed on licence or post sentence supervision

Effective from: 01 October 2019

- An offender who is subject to licence or post sentence supervision is under a particular obligation to desist from further offending.
- The extent to which the offender has complied with the conditions of a licence or order (including the time that has elapsed since its commencement) will be a relevant consideration.

- Where the offender is dealt with separately for a breach of a licence or order regard should be had to totality.
- Care should be taken to avoid double counting matters taken into account when considering previous convictions.

When sentencing young adult offenders (typically aged 18-25), consideration should also be given to the guidance on the mitigating factor relating to age and/or lack of maturity when considering the significance of this factor.

A16CO: Offence committed while subject to court order(s)

Effective from: 01 October 2019

- Commission of an offence while subject to a **relevant** court order makes the offence more serious.
- The extent to which the offender has complied with the conditions of an order (including the time that has elapsed since its commencement) will be a relevant consideration.
- Where the offender is dealt with separately for a breach of an order regard should be had to totality.
- Care should be taken to avoid double counting matters taken into account when considering previous convictions.

When sentencing young adult offenders (typically aged 18-25), consideration should also be given to the guidance on the mitigating factor relating to age and/or lack of maturity when considering the significance of this factor.

A17: Offence committed in custody

Effective from: 01 October 2019

- Offences committed in custody are more serious because they undermine the fundamental need for control and order which is necessary for the running of prisons and maintaining safety.
- Generally the sentence for the new offence will be consecutive to the sentence being served as it will have arisen out of an unrelated incident. The court must have regard to the totality of the offender's criminality when passing the second sentence, to ensure that the total sentence to be served is just and proportionate. Refer to the Totality guideline (SG3-7-SG3-18) for detailed guidance [see **SG3-7 *et seq.***].
- Care should be taken to avoid double counting matters taken into account when considering previous convictions.

A18: Offences taken into consideration

Effective from: 01 October 2019

Taken from the **Offences Taken into Consideration Definitive Guideline**: (SG3-1-SG3-6)

General principles

When sentencing an offender who requests offences to be taken into consideration (TICs), courts should pass a total sentence which reflects all the offending behaviour. The sentence must be just and proportionate and must not exceed the statutory maximum for the conviction offence.

Offences to be Taken into Consideration

The court has discretion as to whether or not to take TICs into account. In exercising its discretion the court should take into account that TICs are capable of reflecting the offender's overall criminality. The court is likely to consider that the fact that the offender has assisted the police (particularly if the offences would not otherwise have been detected) and avoided the need for further proceedings demonstrates a genuine determination by the offender to 'wipe the slate clean'.

It is generally **undesirable** for TICs to be accepted in the following circumstances:

- where the TIC is likely to attract a greater sentence than the conviction offence;
- where it is in the public interest that the TIC should be the subject of a separate charge;
- where the offender would avoid a prohibition, ancillary order or similar consequence which it would have been desirable to impose on conviction. For example:
  - o where the TIC attracts mandatory disqualification or endorsement and the offence(s) for which the defendant is to be sentenced do not;
  - o where the TIC constitutes a breach of an earlier sentence;
  - o where the TIC is a specified offence for the purposes of section 224 of the Criminal Justice Act 2003, but the conviction offence is non-specified; or
  - o where the TIC is not founded on the same facts or evidence or part of a series of offences of the same or similar character (unless the court is satisfied that it is in the interests of justice to do so).

Jurisdiction

The magistrates' court cannot take into consideration an indictable only offence.

The Crown Court can take into account summary only offences provided the TICs are founded on the same facts or evidence as the indictable charge, or are part of a series of offences of the same or similar character as the indictable conviction offence.

Procedural safeguards

A court should generally only take offences into consideration if the following procedural provisions have been satisfied:

- the police or prosecuting authorities have prepared a schedule of offences (TIC schedule) that they consider suitable to be taken into consideration. The TIC schedule should set out the nature of each offence, the date of the offence(s), relevant detail about the offence(s) (including, for example, monetary values of items) and any other brief details that the court should be aware of;
- a copy of the TIC schedule must be provided to the defendant and his representative (if he has one) before the sentence hearing. The defendant should sign the TIC schedule to provisionally admit the offences;
- at the sentence hearing, the court should ask the defendant in open court whether he admits each of the offences on the TIC schedule and whether he wishes to have them taken into consideration;
- if there is any doubt about the admission of a particular offence, it should not be accepted as a TIC. Special care should be taken with vulnerable and/or unrepresented defendants;
- if the defendant is committed to the Crown Court for sentence, this procedure must take place again at the Crown Court even if the defendant has agreed to the schedule in the magistrates' court.

Application

The sentence imposed on an offender should, in most circumstances, be increased to reflect the fact that other offences have been taken into consideration. The court should:

1. Determine the sentencing starting point for the conviction offence, referring to the relevant definitive sentencing guidelines. No regard should be had to the presence of TICs at this stage.
2. Consider whether there are any aggravating or mitigating factors that justify an upward or downward adjustment from the starting point.

The presence of TICs should generally be treated as an aggravating feature that justifies an adjustment from the starting point. Where there is a large number of TICs, it may be appropriate to move outside the category range, although this must be considered in the context of the case and subject to the principle of totality. The court is limited to the statutory maximum for the conviction offence.

3. Continue through the sentencing process including:
   - consider whether the frank admission of a number of offences is an indication of a defendant's remorse or determination and/ or demonstration of steps taken to address addiction or offending behaviour;
   - any reduction for a guilty plea should be applied to the overall sentence;
   - the principle of totality;
   - when considering ancillary orders these can be considered in relation to any or all of the TICs, specifically:
     - o compensation orders;
     - o restitution orders

A19: Offence committed in a domestic context

Refer to the <u>**Overarching Principles: Domestic Abuse Definitive Guideline**</u> (SG5-1-SG5-8)

A20: Offence committed in a terrorist context

Not yet applicable

A21: Location and/or timing of offence

Not yet applicable

A21L: Location

Effective from: 01 October 2019

- In general, an offence is not made more serious by the location of the offence except in ways taken into account by other factors in this guideline (such as planning, vulnerable victim, offence committed in a domestic context, maximising distress to victim, others put at risk of harm by the offending, offence committed in the presence of others). Care should be taken to avoid double counting.

Sentencing Guidelines

- Courts should be cautious about aggravating an offence by reason of it being committed for example in a crowded place or in an isolated place unless it also indicates increased harm or culpability not already accounted for.
- An offence may be more serious when it is committed in places in which there is a particular need for discipline or safety such as prisons, courts, schools or hospitals.

A21T: Timing

Effective from: 01 October 2019

- In general, an offence is not made more serious by the timing of the offence except in ways taken into account by other factors in this guideline (such as planning, vulnerable victim, offence committed in a domestic context, maximising distress to victim, others put at risk of harm by the offending, offence committed in the presence of others). Care should be taken to avoid double counting.
- Courts should be cautious about aggravating an offence by reason of it being committed for example at night, or in broad daylight unless it also indicates increased harm or culpability not already accounted for.

A22: Established evidence of community/ wider impact

Effective from: 01 October 2019

- This factor should increase the sentence only where there is clear evidence of wider harm not already taken into account elsewhere. A community impact statement will assist the court in assessing the level of impact.
- For issues of prevalence see the separate guidance below.

Prevalence

- Sentencing levels in offence specific guidelines take account of collective social harm. Accordingly offenders should normally be sentenced by straightforward application of the guidelines without aggravation for the fact that their activity contributed to a harmful social effect upon a neighbourhood or community.
- It is not open to a sentencer to increase a sentence for prevalence in ordinary circumstances or in response to a personal view that there is 'too much of this sort of thing going on in this area'.
- First, there must be evidence provided to the court by a responsible body or by a senior police officer.
- Secondly, that evidence must be before the court in the specific case being considered with the relevant statements or reports having been made available to the Crown and defence in good time so that meaningful representations about that material can be made.
- Even if such material is provided, a sentencer will only be entitled to treat prevalence as an aggravating factor if satisfied:
  - o that the level of harm caused in a particular locality is significantly higher than that caused elsewhere (and thus already inherent in the guideline levels);
  - o that the circumstances can properly be described as exceptional; **and**
  - o that it is just and proportionate to increase the sentence for such a factor in the particular case being sentenced.

A23: Prevalence

Effective from: 01 October 2019

- Sentencing levels in offence specific guidelines take account of collective social harm. Accordingly offenders should normally be sentenced by straightforward application of the guidelines without aggravation for the fact that their activity contributed to a harmful social effect upon a neighbourhood or community.
- It is not open to a sentencer to increase a sentence for prevalence in ordinary circumstances or in response to a personal view that there is 'too much of this sort of thing going on in this area'.
- First, there must be evidence provided to the court by a responsible body or by a senior police officer.
- Secondly, that evidence must be before the court in the specific case being considered with the relevant statements or reports having been made available to the Crown and defence in good time so that meaningful representations about that material can be made.
- Even if such material is provided, a sentencer will only be entitled to treat prevalence as an aggravating factor if satisfied
  - o that the level of harm caused in a particular locality is significantly higher than that caused elsewhere (and thus already inherent in the guideline levels);
  - o that the circumstances can properly be described as exceptional; **and**
  - o that it is just and proportionate to increase the sentence for such a factor in the particular case being sentenced.

TABLE OF EXPANDED EXPLANATIONS FOR FACTORS REDUCING SERIOUSNESS OR REFLECTING PERSONAL MITIGATION

No previous convictions or no relevant/recent convictions:	M1
Good character and/or exemplary conduct:	M2
Remorse:	M3
Self-reporting:	M4
Cooperation with the investigation/ early admissions:	M5
Little or no planning:	M6
The offender was in a lesser or subordinate role if acting with others/performed limited role under direction:	M7
Involved through coercion, intimidation or exploitation:	M8
Limited awareness or understanding of the offence:	M9
Little or no financial gain:	M10
Delay since apprehension:	M11
Activity originally legitimate:	M12
Age and/or lack of maturity:	M13
Sole or primary carer for dependent relatives:	M14
Physical disability or serious medical conditions requiring urgent, intensive or long-term treatment:	M15
Mental disorder or learning disability:	M16
Determination and/or demonstration of steps having been taken to address addiction or offending behaviour:	M17

> Care should be taken to avoid double counting factors including those already taken into account in assessing culpability or harm

M1: No previous convictions or no relevant/recent convictions

Effective from: 01 October 2019

- First time offenders usually represent a lower risk of reoffending. Reoffending rates for first offenders are significantly lower than rates for repeat offenders. In addition, first offenders are normally regarded as less blameworthy than offenders who have committed the same crime several times already. For these reasons first offenders receive a mitigated sentence.
- Where there are previous offences but these are old and/or are for offending of a different nature, the sentence will normally be reduced to reflect that the new offence is not part of a pattern of offending and there is therefore a lower likelihood of reoffending.
- When assessing whether a previous conviction is 'recent' the court should consider the time gap since the previous conviction and the reason for it.
- Previous convictions are likely to be 'relevant' when they share characteristics with the current offence (examples of such characteristics include, but are not limited to: dishonesty, violence, abuse of position or trust, use or possession of weapons, disobedience of court orders). In general the more serious the previous offending the longer it will retain relevance.

M2: Good character and/or exemplary conduct

Effective from: 01 October 2019

This factor may apply whether or not the offender has previous convictions. Evidence that an offender has demonstrated positive good character through, for example, charitable works may reduce the sentence.

However, this factor is less likely to be relevant where the offending is very serious. Where an offender has used their good character or status to facilitate or conceal the offending it could be treated as an aggravating factor.

M3: Remorse

Effective from: 01 October 2019

The court will need to be satisfied that the offender is genuinely remorseful for the offending behaviour in order to reduce the sentence (separate from any guilty plea reduction).

Lack of remorse should never be treated as an aggravating factor.

M4: Self-reporting

Effective from: 01 October 2019

Where an offender has self-reported to the authorities, particularly in circumstances where the offence may otherwise have gone undetected, this should reduce the sentence (separate from any guilty plea reduction).

M5: Cooperation with the investigation/early admissions

Effective from: 01 October 2019

Assisting or cooperating with the investigation and/or making pre-court admissions may ease the effect on victims and witnesses and save valuable police time justifying a reduction in sentence (separate from any guilty plea reduction).

M6: Little or no planning

Effective from: 01 October 2019

Where an offender has committed the offence with little or no prior thought, this is likely to indicate a lower level of culpability and therefore justify a reduction in sentence.

However, impulsive acts of unprovoked violence or other types of offending may indicate a propensity to behave in a manner that would not normally justify a reduction in sentence.

M7: The offender was in a lesser or subordinate role if acting with others/performed limited role under direction

Effective from: 01 October 2019

Whereas acting as part of a group may make an offence more serious, if the offender's role was minor this may indicate lower culpability and justify a reduction in sentence.

M8: Involved through coercion, intimidation or exploitation

Effective from: 01 October 2019

- Where this applies it will reduce the culpability of the offender.
- This factor may be of particular relevance where the offender has been the victim of domestic abuse, trafficking or modern slavery, but may also apply in other contexts.
- Courts should be alert to factors that suggest that an offender may have been the subject of coercion, intimidation or exploitation which the offender may find difficult to articulate, and where appropriate ask for this to be addressed in a PSR.
- This factor may indicate that the offender is vulnerable and would find it more difficult to cope with custody or to complete a community order.

M9: Limited awareness or understanding of the offence

Effective from: 01 October 2019

The factor may apply to reduce the culpability

- of an offender acting alone who has not appreciated the seriousness of the offence **or**
- of an offender who is acting with others and does not appreciate the extent of the overall offending.

If the offender had genuinely failed to understand or appreciate the seriousness of the offence, the sentence may be reduced from that which would have applied if the offender had understood the full extent of the offence and the likely harm that would be caused.

Where an offender lacks capacity to understand the full extent of the offending see the guidance under 'Mental disorder or learning disability'.

M10: Little or no financial gain

Effective from: 01 October 2019

Where an offence (which is not one which by its nature is an acquisitive offence) is committed in a context where financial gain could arise, the culpability of the offender may be reduced where it can be shown that the offender **did not seek to gain financially** from the conduct and did not in fact do so.

M11: Delay since apprehension

Effective from: 01 October 2019

Where there has been an unreasonable delay in proceedings since apprehension which is not the fault of the offender, the court may take this into account by reducing the sentence **if this has had a detrimental effect on the offender.**

Note: No fault should attach to an offender for not admitting an offence and/or putting the prosecution to proof of its case.

M12: Activity originally legitimate

Effective from: 01 October 2019

Where the offending arose from an activity which was originally legitimate, but became unlawful (for example because of a change in the offender's circumstances or a change in regulations), this **may** indicate lower culpability and thereby a reduction in sentence.

This factor will not apply where the offender has used a legitimate activity to mask a criminal activity.

M13: Age and/or lack of maturity

Effective from: 01 October 2019

Age and/or lack of maturity can affect:

- the offender's responsibility for the offence and
- the effect of the sentence on the offender.

Either or both of these considerations may justify a reduction in the sentence.

The emotional and developmental age of an offender is of at least equal importance to their chronological age (if not greater).

In particular young adults (typically aged 18-25) are still developing neurologically and consequently may be less able to:

- evaluate the consequences of their actions
- limit impulsivity
- limit risk taking

Young adults are likely to be susceptible to peer pressure and are more likely to take risks or behave impulsively when in company with their peers.

Immaturity can also result from atypical brain development. Environment plays a role in neurological development and factors such as adverse childhood experiences including deprivation and/or abuse may affect development.

An immature offender may find it particularly difficult to cope with custody and therefore may be more susceptible to self-harm in custody.

An immature offender may find it particularly difficult to cope with the requirements of a community order without appropriate support.

There is a greater capacity for change in immature offenders and they may be receptive to opportunities to address their offending behaviour and change their conduct.

Many young people who offend either stop committing crime, or begin a process of stopping, in their late teens and early twenties. Therefore a young adult's previous convictions may not be indicative of a tendency for further offending.

Where the offender is a care leaver the court should enquire as to any effect a sentence may have on the offender's ability to make use of support from the local authority. (Young adult care leavers are entitled to time limited support. Leaving care services may change at the age of 21 and cease at the age of 25, unless the young adult is in education at that point). See also the Sentencing Children and Young People Guideline (paragraphs 1.16 and 1.17).

Where an offender has turned 18 between the commission of the offence and conviction the court should take as its starting point the sentence likely to have been imposed on the date at which the offence was committed, but applying the purposes of sentencing adult offenders. See also the **Sentencing Children and Young People Guideline** (paragraphs 6.1 to 6.3) [see **SG8-1** ***et seq.***].

When considering a custodial or community sentence for a young adult the National Probation Service should address these issues in a PSR.

M14: Sole or primary carer for dependent relatives

Effective from: 01 October 2019

This factor is particularly relevant where an offender is on the cusp of custody or where the suitability of a community order is being considered. See also the **Imposition of community and custodial sentences guideline**. (SG9-1-SG9-12)

For offenders on the cusp of custody, imprisonment should not be imposed where there would be an impact on dependants which would make a custodial sentence disproportionate to achieving the aims of sentencing.

Where custody is unavoidable consideration of the impact on dependants may be relevant to the length of the sentence imposed and whether the sentence can be suspended.

For more serious offences where a substantial period of custody is appropriate, this factor will carry less weight.

When imposing a community sentence on an offender with primary caring responsibilities the effect on dependants must be considered in determining suitable requirements.

In addition when sentencing an offender who is pregnant relevant considerations may include:

- any effect of the sentence on the health of the offender, and
- any effect of the sentence on the unborn child.

The court should ensure that it has all relevant information about dependent children before deciding on sentence.

When an immediate custodial sentence is necessary, the court must consider whether proper arrangements have been made for the care of any dependent children and if necessary consider adjourning sentence for this to be done.

When considering a community or custodial sentence for an offender who has, or may have, caring responsibilities the court should ask the National Probation Service to address these issues in a PSR.

Useful information can be found in the **Equal Treatment Bench Book** (see in particular Chapter 6 paragraphs 94-100)

M15: Physical disability or serious medical conditions requiring urgent, intensive or long-term treatment

Effective from: 01 October 2019

- The court can take account of physical disability or a serious medical condition by way of mitigation as a reason for reducing the length of the sentence, either on the ground of the greater impact which imprisonment will have on the offender, or as a matter of generally expressed mercy in the individual circumstances of the case.
- However, such a condition, even when it is difficult to treat in prison, will not automatically entitle the offender to a lesser sentence than would otherwise be appropriate.
- There will always be a need to balance issues personal to an offender against the gravity of the offending (including the harm done to victims), and the public interest in imposing appropriate punishment for serious offending.
- A terminal prognosis is not in itself a reason to reduce the sentence even further. The court must impose a sentence that properly meets the aims of sentencing even if it will carry the clear prospect that the offender will die in custody. The prospect of death in the near future will be a matter considered by the prison authorities and the Secretary of State under the early release on compassionate grounds procedure (ERCG).

- But, an offender's knowledge that he will likely face the prospect of death in prison, subject only to the ERCG provisions, is a factor that can be considered by the sentencing judge when determining the sentence that it would be just to impose.

M16: Mental disorder or learning disability

Effective from: 01 October 2019

Mental disorders and learning disabilities are different things, although an individual may suffer from both. A **learning disability** is a permanent condition developing in childhood, whereas **mental illness** (or a mental health problem) can develop at any time, and is not necessarily permanent; people can get better and resolve mental health problems with help and treatment.

In the context of sentencing a broad interpretation of the terms 'mental disorder' and learning disabilities' should be adopted to include:

- Offenders with an intellectual impairment (low IQ);
- Offenders with a cognitive impairment such as (but not limited to) dyslexia, attention deficit hyperactivity disorder (ADHD);
- Offenders with an autistic spectrum disorder (ASD) including Asperger's syndrome;
- Offenders with a personality disorder;
- Offenders with a mental illness.

Offenders may have a combination of the above conditions.

Sentencers should be alert to the fact that not all mental disorders or learning disabilities are visible or obvious.

A mental disorder or learning disability can affect both:

1. the offender's responsibility for the offence, and
2. the impact of the sentence on the offender.

The court will be assisted by a PSR and, where appropriate, medical reports (including from court mental health teams) in assessing:

1. the degree to which a mental disorder or learning disability has reduced the offender's responsibility for the offence. This may be because the condition had an impact on the offender's ability to understand the consequences of their actions, to limit impulsivity and/or to exercise self-control.
   - a relevant factor will be the degree to which a mental disorder or learning disability has been exacerbated by the actions of the offender (for example by the **voluntary** abuse of drugs or alcohol or by **voluntarily** failing to follow medical advice);
   - in considering the extent to which the offender's actions were voluntary, the extent to which a mental disorder or learning disability has an impact on the offender's ability to exercise self-control or to engage with medical services will be a relevant consideration.
2. any effect of the mental disorder or learning disability on the impact of the sentence on the offender; a mental disorder or learning disability may make it more difficult for the offender to cope with custody or comply with a community order.

M17: Determination and/or demonstration of steps having been taken to address addiction or offending behaviour

Effective from: 01 October 2019

Where offending is driven by or closely associated with drug or alcohol abuse (for example stealing to feed a habit, or committing acts of disorder or violence whilst drunk) a commitment to address the underlying issue may justify a reduction in sentence. This will be particularly relevant where the court is considering whether to impose a sentence that focuses on rehabilitation.

Similarly, a commitment to address other underlying issues that may influence the offender's behaviour may justify the imposition of a sentence that focusses on rehabilitation.

The court will be assisted by a PSR in making this assessment.

PART 1 ALLOCATION

SG1-1

Definitive Guideline

Applicability of guideline [1]

In accordance with section 122(2) of the Coroners and Justice Act 2009, the Sentencing Council issues this definitive guideline. It applies to all defendants in the magistrates' court (including youths jointly charged with adults) whose cases are dealt with on or after 1 March 2016.

It also applies to allocation decisions made in the Crown Court pursuant to Schedule 3 of the Crime and Disorder Act 1998. It will not be applicable in the youth court where a separate statutory procedure applies.

Venue for trial

It is important to ensure that all cases are tried at the appropriate level.

1. In general, either way offences should be tried summarily unless:
   - the outcome would clearly be a sentence in excess of the court's powers for the offence(s) concerned after taking into account personal mitigation and any potential reduction for a guilty plea; or
   - for reasons of unusual legal, procedural or factual complexity, the case should be tried in the Crown Court. This exception may apply in cases where a very substantial fine is the likely sentence. Other circumstances where this exception will apply are likely to be rare and case specific; the court will rely on the submissions of the parties to identify relevant cases.
2. In cases with no factual or legal complications the court should bear in mind its **power to commit for sentence after a trial** and **may retain jurisdiction** notwithstanding that the likely sentence might exceed its powers.
3. Cases may be tried summarily even where the defendant is subject to a Crown Court Suspended Sentence Order or Community Order.[1]
4. All parties should be asked by the court to make representations as to whether the case is suitable for summary trial. The court should refer to definitive guidelines (if any) to assess the likely sentence for the offence in the light of the facts alleged by the prosecution case, taking into account all aspects of the case including those advanced by the defence, including any personal mitigation to which the defence wish to refer.

Where the court decides that the case is suitable to be dealt with in the magistrates' court, it must warn the defendant that all sentencing options remain open and, if the defendant consents to summary trial and is convicted by the court or pleads guilty, the defendant may be committed to the Crown Court for sentence.

Committal for sentence [2]

There is ordinarily no statutory restriction on committing an either way case for sentence following conviction. The general power of the magistrates' court to commit to the Crown Court for sentence after a finding that a case is suitable for summary trial and/or conviction continues to be available where the court is of the opinion 'that the offence or the combination of the offence and one or more offences associated with it was so serious that the Crown Court should, in the court's opinion, have the power to deal with the offender in any way it could deal with him if he had been convicted on indictment'.[2]

However, where the court proceeds to the summary trial of certain offences relating to criminal damage, upon conviction there is no power to commit to the Crown Court for sentence.[3]

The court should refer to any definitive guideline to arrive at the appropriate sentence taking into account all of the circumstances of the case including personal mitigation and the appropriate guilty plea reduction.

In borderline cases the court should consider obtaining a pre-sentence report before deciding whether to commit to the Crown Court for sentence.

---

1 The power to commit the case to the Crown Court to be dealt with under para. 11(1) of Schedule 12 or para. 22 of Schedule 8 to the Criminal Justice Act 2003 can be exercised if the defendant is convicted.

2 Powers of Criminal Courts (Sentencing) Act 2000, s. 3

3 Magistrates' Courts Act 1980, s. 3(4) and s. 22

[2] Where the offending is so serious that the court is of the opinion that the Crown Court should have the power to deal with the offender, the case should be committed to the Crown Court for sentence even if a community order may be the appropriate sentence (this will allow the Crown Court to deal with any breach of a community order, if that is the sentence passed).

Youths jointly charged with adults — interests of justice test

The proper venue for the trial of any youth is normally the youth court. Subject to statutory restrictions, that remains the case where a youth is charged jointly with an adult.

This guideline does not provide information on the complex statutory framework for dealing with a youth jointly charged with an adult . . .

The following guidance must be applied in those cases where the interests of justice test falls to be considered:

1. If the adult is sent for trial to the Crown Court, the court should conclude that the youth must be tried separately in the youth court unless it is in the interests of justice for the youth and the adult to be tried jointly.
2. Examples of factors that should be considered when deciding whether it is in the interests of justice to send the youth to the Crown Court (rather than having a trial in the youth court) include:
   - whether separate trials will cause injustice to witnesses or to the case as a whole (consideration should be given to the provisions of sections 27 and 28 of the Youth Justice and Criminal Evidence Act 1999);
   - the age of the youth: the younger the youth, the greater the desirability that the youth be tried in the youth court;
   - the age gap between the youth and the adult: a substantial gap in age militates in favour of the youth being tried in the youth court;
   - the lack of maturity of the youth;
   - the relative culpability of the youth compared with the adult and whether the alleged role played by the youth was minor;
   - the lack of previous convictions on the part of the youth.

[3] The court should bear in mind that the youth court now has a general power to commit for sentence following conviction pursuant to Section 3B of the Powers of Criminal Courts (Sentencing) Act 2000 (as amended). In appropriate cases this will permit the same court to sentence adults and youths who have been tried separately.

[Sets out the MCA 1980, s. 19(1) to (4) (see **D6.21**) and the CAJA 2009, s. 125(1) (see **SG19-1**).]

PART 2 GENERAL GUIDELINE: OVERARCHING PRINCIPLES

SG2-1 [The new guideline and expanded explanations replace and update the 2004 Seriousness guideline. Once they come into force on 1 October 2019, all old pdfs and paper versions will be obsolete and the Seriousness guideline will be withdrawn.]

Effective from: 1 October 2019

- For sentencing offences for which there is no offence specific sentencing guideline, and
- For use in conjunction with offence specific sentencing guidelines

Guideline users should be aware that the **Equal Treatment Bench Book** covers important aspects of fair treatment and disparity of outcomes for different groups in the criminal justice system. It provides guidance which sentencers are encouraged to take into account wherever applicable, to ensure that there is fairness for all involved in court proceedings.

SG2-2 **Applicability**

In accordance with section 120 of the Coroners and Justice Act 2009, the Sentencing Council issues this definitive guideline. It applies to all individual offenders aged 18 and older and organisations that are sentenced on or after the effective date of this guideline, regardless of the date of the offence.

Section 125(1) of the Coroners and Justice Act 2009 provides that when sentencing offences committed after 6 April 2010:

'Every court –

1. must, in sentencing an offender, follow any sentencing guideline which is relevant to the offender's case, and
2. must, in exercising any other function relating to the sentencing of offenders, follow any sentencing guidelines which are relevant to the exercise of the function,

unless the court is satisfied that it would be contrary to the interests of justice to do so.'

This guideline applies only to individual offenders aged 18 and older or organisations. General principles to be considered in the sentencing of youths are in Sentencing Council's definitive guideline, the **Overarching Principles - Sentencing Children and Young People** (SG8-1–SG8-12)

SG2-3 STEP ONE **Reaching a provisional sentence**

a) Where there is no definitive sentencing guideline for the offence, to arrive at a provisional sentence the court should take account of all of the following (if they apply):
   - the statutory maximum sentence (and if appropriate minimum sentence) for the offence;
   - sentencing judgments of the Court of Appeal (Criminal Division) for the offence; and
   - definitive sentencing guidelines for analogous offences.

The court will be assisted by the parties in identifying the above.

For the avoidance of doubt the court should **not** take account of any draft sentencing guidelines.

When considering definitive guidelines for analogous offences the court must apply these carefully, making adjustments for any differences in the statutory maximum sentence and in the elements of the offence. This will not be a merely arithmetical exercise.

b) Where possible the court should follow the stepped approach of sentencing guidelines to arrive at the sentence.

The seriousness of the offence is assessed by considering:

- the **culpability** of the offender

and

- the **harm** caused by the offending.

c) The initial assessment of harm and culpability should take no account of plea or previous convictions.

The court should consider which of the five purposes of sentencing (below) it is seeking to achieve through the sentence that is imposed. More than one purpose might be relevant and the importance of each must be weighed against the particular offence and offender characteristics when determining sentence.

- The punishment of offenders
- The reduction of crime (including its reduction by deterrence)
- The reform and rehabilitation of offenders
- The protection of the public
- The making of reparation by offenders to persons affected by their offences

STEP TWO **Aggravating and mitigating factors** SG2-4

Once a provisional sentence is arrived at the court should take into account factors that may make the offence more serious and factors which may reduce seriousness or reflect personal mitigation.

- Identify whether a combination of these or other relevant factors should result in any upward or downward adjustment from the sentence arrived at so far.
- It is for the sentencing court to determine how much weight should be assigned to the aggravating and mitigating factors taking into account all of the circumstances of the offence and the offender.
- Not all factors that apply will necessarily influence the sentence.
- When sentencing an offence for which a **fixed penalty notice** was available the reason why the offender did not take advantage of the fixed penalty will be a relevant consideration.
- **If considering a fine – see information on fine band ranges below.**
- **If considering a community or custodial sentence refer also to the Imposition of community and custodial sentences definitive guideline (SG9-2–SG9-12) – see information on community orders and custodial sentences below.**

Fines	Starting point	Range
Fine Band A	50% of relevant weekly income	25 – 75% of relevant weekly income
Fine Band B	100% of relevant weekly income	75 – 125% of relevant weekly income
Fine Band C	150% of relevant weekly income	125 – 175% of relevant weekly income
Fine Band D	250% of relevant weekly income	200 – 300% of relevant weekly income
Fine Band E	400% of relevant weekly income	300 – 500% of relevant weekly income
Fine Band F	600% of relevant weekly income	500 – 700% of relevant weekly income

- The court should determine the appropriate level of fine in accordance with this guideline and section 164 of the Criminal Justice Act 2003, which requires that the fine must reflect the seriousness of the offence and that the court must take into account the financial circumstances of the offender.
- Where possible, if a financial penalty is imposed, it should remove any economic benefit the offender has derived through the commission of the offence including:
  o avoided costs;
  o operating savings;
  o any gain made as a direct result of the offence.
- The fine should meet, in a fair and proportionate way, the objectives of punishment, deterrence and the removal of gain derived through the commission of the offence; **it should not be cheaper to offend than to comply with the law.**
- In considering economic benefit, the court should avoid double recovery.
- Where the means of the offender are limited, priority should be given to compensation (where applicable) over payment of any other financial penalty.
- Where it is not possible to calculate or estimate the economic benefit, the court may wish to draw on information from the enforcing authorities about the general costs of operating within the law.
- When sentencing **organisations** the fine must be sufficiently substantial to have a real economic impact which will bring home to both management and shareholders the need to comply with the law. The court should ensure that the effect of the fine (particularly if it will result in closure of the business) is proportionate to the gravity of the offence.

- Obtaining financial information: It is for the offender to disclose to the court such data relevant to their financial position as will enable it to assess what they can reasonably afford to pay. If necessary, the court may compel the disclosure of an individual offender's financial circumstances pursuant to section 162 of the Criminal Justice Act 2003. In the absence of such disclosure, or where the court is not satisfied that it has been given sufficient reliable information, the court will be entitled to draw reasonable inferences as to the offender's means from evidence it has heard and from all the circumstances of the case. In setting a fine, the court may conclude that the offender is able to pay any fine imposed unless the offender has supplied financial information to the contrary.

Community Orders and Custodial Sentences

For the imposition of community orders, including the community orders table, see Imposition of Community and Custodial Sentences **SG9-2–SG9-8**.

For the imposition of custodial sentences see Imposition of Community and Custodial Sentences **SG9-9–SG9-12**.

Factors increasing seriousness

(Factors are not listed in any particular order and are not exhaustive)

Statutory aggravating factors

- Previous convictions, having regard to a) the **nature** of the offence to which the conviction relates and its **relevance** to the current offence; and b) the **time** that has elapsed since the conviction
- Offence committed whilst on bail
- Offence motivated by, or demonstrating hostility based on any of the following characteristics or presumed characteristics of the victim: religion, race, disability, sexual orientation, or transgender identity
- Offence was committed against an emergency worker acting in the exercise of functions as such a worker

Other aggravating factors

- Commission of offence whilst under the influence of alcohol or drugs
- Offence was committed as part of a group
- Offence involved use or threat of a weapon
- Planning of an offence
- Commission of the offence for financial gain
- High level of profit from the offence
- Abuse of trust or dominant position
- Restraint, detention or additional degradation of the victim
- Vulnerable victim
- Victim was providing a public service or performing a public duty at the time of the offence
- Other(s) put at risk of harm by the offending
- Offence committed in the presence of other(s) (especially children)
- Actions after the event including but not limited to attempts to cover up/conceal evidence
- Blame wrongly placed on other(s)
- Failure to respond to warnings or concerns expressed by others about the offender's behaviour
- Offence committed on licence or while subject to court order(s)
- Offence committed in custody
- Offences taken into consideration
- Offence committed in a domestic context
- Offence committed in a terrorist context
- Location and/or timing of offence
- Established evidence of community/wider impact
- Prevalence

Factors reducing seriousness or reflecting personal mitigation
(Factors are not listed in any particular order and are not exhaustive)

- No previous convictions or no relevant/recent convictions
- Good character and/or exemplary conduct
- Remorse
- Self-reporting
- Cooperation with the investigation/early admissions
- Little or no planning
- The offender was in a lesser or subordinate role if acting with others/performed limited role under direction
- Involved through coercion, intimidation or exploitation
- Limited awareness or understanding of the offence
- Little or no financial gain
- Delay since apprehension
- Activity originally legitimate
- Age and/or lack of maturity
- Sole or primary carer for dependent relatives
- Physical disability or serious medical condition requiring urgent, intensive or long-term treatment
- Mental disorder or learning disability
- Determination and/or demonstration of steps having been taken to address addiction or offending behaviour

STEP THREE Consider any factors which indicate a reduction for assistance to the prosecution **SG2-5**

The court should take into account sections 73 and 74 of the Serious Organised Crime and Police Act 2005 (assistance by defendants: reduction or review of sentence) and any other rule of law by virtue of which an offender may receive a discounted sentence in consequence of assistance given (or offered) to the prosecutor or investigator.

STEP FOUR Reduction for guilty pleas **SG2-6**

The court should take account of any potential reduction for a guilty plea in accordance with section 144 of the Criminal Justice Act 2003 and the guideline for Reduction in Sentence for a Guilty Plea (where <u>first hearing is on or after 1 June 2017</u>, or <u>first hearing before 1 June 2017</u>).

STEP FIVE Dangerousness **SG2-7**

Where the offence is listed in Schedule 15 and/or Schedule 15B of the Criminal Justice Act 2003

The court should consider whether having regard to the criteria contained in Chapter 5 of Part 12 of the Criminal Justice Act 2003 it would be appropriate to impose a life sentence (section 224A or section 225) or an extended sentence (section 226A). When sentencing offenders to a life sentence under these provisions, the notional determinate sentence should be used as the basis for the setting of a minimum term.

STEP SIX Special custodial sentence for certain offenders of particular concern **SG2-8**

Where the offence is listed in Schedule 18A of the Criminal Justice Act 2003 and the court does not impose a sentence of imprisonment for life or an extended sentence, but does impose a period of imprisonment, the term of the sentence must be equal to the aggregate of the appropriate custodial term and a further period of 1 year for which the offender is to be subject to a licence.

See the <u>**Crown Court Compendium**</u>, Part II Sentencing S4-3 for further details.

STEP SEVEN Totality principle **SG2-9**

If sentencing an offender for more than one offence, or where the offender is already serving a sentence, consider whether the total sentence is just and proportionate to the overall offending behaviour in accordance with the <u>**Offences Taken into Consideration**</u> and <u>**Totality**</u> (SG3-1–SG3-18) guidelines.

SG2-10 **STEP EIGHT Compensation and ancillary orders**

In all cases the court should consider whether to make compensation and/or other ancillary orders.

Where the offence involves a firearm, an imitation firearm or an offensive weapon the court may consider the criteria in section 19 of the Serious Crime Act 2007 for the imposition of a Serious Crime Prevention Order.

- **Ancillary orders – Magistrates' Court** (SG10–SG151)
- **Ancillary orders – Crown Court Compendium, Part II Sentencing, s 7**

SG2-11 **STEP NINE Reasons**

Section 174 of the Criminal Justice Act 2003 imposes a duty to give reasons for, and explain the effect of, the sentence.

SG2-12 **STEP TEN Consideration for time spent on bail (tagged curfew)**

The court must consider whether to give credit for time spent on bail in accordance with section 240A of the Criminal Justice Act 2003.

[2] PART 3 OFFENCES TAKEN INTO CONSIDERATION AND TOTALITY

OFFENCES TAKEN INTO CONSIDERATION

Definitive Guideline SG3-1

Applicability of guideline

In accordance with section 120 of the Coroners and Justice Act 2009, the Sentencing Council issues this definitive guideline. It applies to all offenders whose cases are dealt with on or after 11 June 2012.

[Sets out the CAJA 2009, s. 125(1): see **SG19-1**.]

This guideline applies where an offender admits the commission of other offences in the course of sentencing proceedings and requests those other offences to be taken into consideration.[4]

General principles SG3-2

When sentencing an offender who requests offences to be taken into consideration (TICs), courts should pass a total sentence which reflects *all* the offending behaviour. The sentence must be just and proportionate and must not exceed the statutory maximum for the conviction offence.

Offences to be Taken Into Consideration SG3-3

The court has discretion as to whether or not to take TICs into account. In exercising its discretion the court should take into account that TICs are capable of reflecting the offender's overall criminality. The court is likely to consider that the fact that the offender has assisted the police (particularly if the offences would not otherwise have been detected) and avoided the need for further proceedings demonstrates a genuine determination by the offender to 'wipe the slate clean'.[5]

It is generally **undesirable** for TICs to be accepted in the following circumstances:

- where the TIC is likely to attract a greater sentence than the conviction offence;
- where it is in the public interest that the TIC should be the subject of a separate charge;
- [3] where the offender would avoid a prohibition, ancillary order or similar consequence which it would have been desirable to impose on conviction. For example:
- where the TIC attracts mandatory disqualification or endorsement and the offence(s) for which the defendant is to be sentenced do not;
- where the TIC constitutes a breach of an earlier sentence;[6]
- where the TIC is a specified offence for the purposes of section 224 of the Criminal Justice Act 2003, but the conviction offence is non-specified; or
- where the TIC is not founded on the same facts or evidence or part of a series of offences of the same or similar character (unless the court is satisfied that it is in the interests of justice to do so).

Jurisdiction SG3-4

The magistrates' court cannot take into consideration an indictable only offence.

The Crown Court can take into account summary only offences provided the TICs are founded on the same facts or evidence as the indictable charge, or are part of a series of offences of the same or similar character as the indictable conviction offence.[7]

4 Criminal Justice Act 2003, s. 305 and Powers of Criminal Courts (Sentencing) Act 2000, s. 161(1)
5 Per Lord Chief Justice, *R v Miles* [2006] EWCA Crim 256
6 *R v Webb* (1953) 37 Cr App 82
7 Criminal Justice Act 1988, s. 40

SG3-5 **Procedural safeguards** [3]

A court should generally only take offences into consideration if the following procedural provisions have been satisfied:

- the police or prosecuting authorities have prepared a schedule of offences (TIC schedule) that they consider suitable to be taken into consideration. The TIC schedule should set out the nature of each offence, the date of the offence(s), relevant detail about the offence(s) (including, for example, monetary values of items) and any other brief details that the court should be aware of;
- a copy of the TIC schedule must be provided to the defendant and his representative (if he has one) before the sentence hearing. The defendant should sign the TIC schedule to provisionally admit the offences;
- at the sentence hearing, the court should ask the defendant in open court whether he admits each of the offences on the TIC schedule and whether he wishes to have them taken into consideration;[8]
- if there is any doubt about the admission of a particular offence, it should not be accepted as a TIC. Special care should be taken with vulnerable and/or unrepresented defendants;
- if the defendant is committed to the Crown Court for sentence, this procedure must take place again at the Crown Court even if the defendant has agreed to the schedule in the magistrates' court.

SG3-6 **Application**

The sentence imposed on an offender should, in most circumstances, be increased to reflect the fact that other offences have been taken into consideration. The court should:

1. Determine the sentencing starting point for the conviction offence, referring to the relevant definitive sentencing guidelines. No regard should be had to the presence of TICs at this stage.
2. Consider whether there are any aggravating or mitigating factors that justify an upward or downward adjustment from the starting point.

The presence of TICs should generally be treated as an aggravating feature that justifies an upward adjustment from the starting point. Where there is a large number of TICs, it may be appropriate to move outside the category range, although this must be considered in the context of the case and subject to the principle of totality. The court is limited to the statutory maximum for the conviction offence. [4]

3. Continue through the sentencing process including:
   - consider whether the frank admission of a number of offences is an indication of a defendant's remorse or determination and/or demonstration of steps taken to address addiction or offending behaviour;
   - any reduction for a guilty plea should be applied to the overall sentence;
   - the principle of totality;
   - when considering ancillary orders these can be considered in relation to any or all of the TICs, specifically:
   - compensation orders[9]—in the magistrate[s'] court the total compensation cannot exceed the limit for the conviction offence;
   - restitution orders.[10]

TOTALITY

SG3-7 ## Definitive Guideline

Applicability of guideline [5]

In accordance with section 120 of the Coroners and Justice Act 2009, the Sentencing Council issues this definitive guideline. It applies to all offenders whose cases are dealt with on or after 11 June 2012.

[8] *Anderson v DPP* [1978] AC 964
[9] Powers of Criminal Courts (Sentencing) Act 2000, s. 131(2)
[10] ibid, s. 148

[5] [Sets out the CAJA 2009, s. 125(1): see **SG19-1**.]

This guideline applies when sentencing an offender for multiple offences or when sentencing an offender who is already serving an existing sentence. In these situations, the courts should apply the principle of totality.

General principles **SG3-8**

The principle of totality comprises two elements:

1. All courts, when sentencing for more than a single offence, should pass a total sentence which reflects *all* the offending behaviour before it and is just and proportionate. This is so whether the sentences are structured as concurrent or consecutive. Therefore, concurrent sentences will ordinarily be longer than a single sentence for a single offence.
2. It is usually impossible to arrive at a just and proportionate sentence for multiple offending simply by adding together notional single sentences. It is necessary to address the offending behaviour, together with the factors personal to the offender as a whole.

Concurrent/consecutive sentences **SG3-9**

There is no inflexible rule governing whether sentences should be structured as concurrent or consecutive components. The overriding principle is that the overall sentence must be just and proportionate.

[6] **General approach (as applied to Determinate Custodial Sentences)** **SG3-10**

1. **Consider the sentence for each individual offence, referring to the relevant sentencing guidelines.**
2. **Determine whether the case calls for concurrent or consecutive sentences.**

Concurrent Sentences will ordinarily be appropriate where:

a) **offences arise out of the same incident or facts.**

Examples include:

- a single incident of dangerous driving resulting in injuries to multiple victims;[11]
- robbery with a weapon where the weapon offence is ancillary to the robbery and is not distinct and independent of it;[12]
- fraud and associated forgery;
- separate counts of supplying different types of drugs of the same class as part of the same transaction.

b) **there is a series of offences of the same or similar kind, especially when committed against the same person.**

Examples include:

- repetitive small thefts from the *same* person, such as by an employee;
- repetitive benefit frauds of the same kind, committed in each payment period.

Where concurrent sentences are to be passed the sentence should reflect the overall criminality involved. The sentence should be appropriately aggravated by the presence of the associated offences.

Examples include:

- a single incident of dangerous driving resulting in injuries to multiple victims where there are separate charges relating to each victim. The sentences should generally be passed concurrently, but each sentence should be aggravated to take into account the harm caused;
- repetitive fraud or theft, where charged as a series of small frauds/thefts, would be properly considered in relation to the total amount of money obtained and the period of time over which the

[11] *R v Lawrence* (1989) 11 Cr App R (S) 580

[12] *R v Poulton and Celaire* [2002] EWCA Crim 2487; *Attorney General's Reference No 21 & 22 of 2003* [2003] EWCA Crim 3089

offending took place. The sentences should generally be passed concurrently, each one reflecting the overall seriousness; [6]

- robbery with a weapon where the weapon offence is ancillary to the robbery and is not distinct and independent of it. The principal sentence for the robbery should properly reflect the presence of the weapon. The court must avoid double-counting and may deem it preferable for the possession of the weapon's offence to run concurrently to avoid the appearance of under-sentencing in respect of the robbery.[13]

Consecutive sentences will ordinarily be appropriate where: [7]

a) offences arise out of unrelated facts or incidents.

Examples include:

- where the offender commits a theft on one occasion and a common assault against a different victim on a separate occasion;
- an attempt to pervert the course of justice in respect of another offence also charged;[14]
- a Bail Act offence;[15]
- any offence committed within the prison context;
- offences that are unrelated because whilst they were committed simultaneously they are distinct and there is an aggravating element that requires separate recognition, for example:
  - an assault on a constable committed to try to evade arrest for another offence also charged;[16]
  - where the defendant is convicted of drug dealing and possession of a firearm offence. The firearm offence is not the essence or the intrinsic part of the drugs offence and requires separate recognition;[17]
  - where the defendant is convicted of threats to kill in the context of an indecent assault on the same occasion, the threats to kill could be distinguished as a separate element.[18]

b) offences that are of the same or similar kind but where the overall criminality will not sufficiently be reflected by concurrent sentences.

Examples include:

- where offences committed against *different* people, such as repeated thefts involving attacks on several different shop assistants;[19]
- where offences of domestic violence or sexual offences are committed against the *same* individual.

c) one of more offence(s) qualifies for a statutory minimum sentence and concurrent sentences would improperly undermine that minimum[20]

However it is not permissible to impose consecutive sentences for offences committed at the same time in order to evade the statutory maximum penalty.[21]

Where consecutive sentences are to be passed add up the sentences for each offence and consider if the aggregate length is just and appropriate.

If the aggregate length is not just and proportionate the court should consider how to reach a just and proportionate sentence. There are a number of ways in which this could be achieved.

Examples include:

- when sentencing for similar offence types or offences of a similar level of severity the court can consider:
  - whether all of the offences can be proportionately reduced (with particular reference to the category ranges within the sentencing guidelines) and passed consecutively;

---

13 *Attorney General's Reference Nos 21 & 22 of 2003*

14 *Attorney General's Reference No 1 of 1990* (1990) 12 Cr App R (S) 245

15 *R v Millen* (1980) 2 Cr App R (S) 357

16 *R v Kastercum* (1972) 56 Cr App R 298

17 *R v Poulton and Celaire* [2002] EWCA Crim 2487; *Attorney General's Reference Nos 21 & 22 of 2003* [2003] EWCA Crim 3089

18 *R v Fletcher* [2002] 2 CAR (S) 127

19 *R v Jamieson & Jamieson* [2008] EWCA Crim 2761

20 *R v Raza* (2010) 1 Cr App R (S) 56

21 *R v Ralphs* [2009] EWCA Crim 2555

[7] • whether, despite their similarity, a most serious principal offence can be identified and the other sentences can all be proportionately reduced (with particular reference to the category ranges within sentencing guidelines) and passed consecutively in order that the sentence for the lead offence can be clearly identified.

[8] • when sentencing for two or more offences of differing levels of seriousness the court can consider:

- whether some offences are of such low seriousness in the context of the most serious offence(s) that they can be recorded as 'no separate penalty' (for example technical breaches or minor driving offences not involving mandatory disqualification);
- whether some of the offences are of lesser seriousness and are unrelated to the most serious offence(s), that they can be ordered to run concurrently so that the sentence for the most serious offence(s) can be clearly identified.

3. **Test the overall sentence(s) against the requirement that they be just and proportionate.**
4. **Consider whether the sentence is structured in a way that will be best understood by all concerned with it.**

[9] **Specific applications — Custodial sentences**

SG3-11

Sentencing Guidelines

Existing Determinate Sentence, where Determinate Sentence to be Passed

Circumstance	Approach
Offender serving a determinate sentence (offence(s) committed before original sentence imposed)	Consider what the sentence length would have been if the court had dealt with the offences at the same time and ensure that the totality of the sentence is just and proportionate in all the circumstances. If it is not, an adjustment should be made to the sentence imposed for the latest offence.
Offender serving a determinate sentence (offence(s) committed after original sentence imposed)	Generally the sentence will be consecutive as it will have arisen out of an unrelated incident. The court must have regard to the totality of the offender's criminality when passing the second sentence, to ensure that the total sentence to be served is just and proportionate. Where a prisoner commits acts of violence in prison, any reduction for totality is likely to be minimal.[22]
Offender serving a determinate sentence but released from custody	The new sentence should start on the day it is imposed: s.265 Criminal Justice Act 2003 prohibits a sentence of imprisonment running consecutively to a sentence from which a prisoner has been released. The sentence for the new offence will take into account the aggravating feature that it was committed on licence. However, it must be commensurate with the new offence and cannot be artificially inflated with a view to ensuring that the offender serves a period in custody additional to the recall period (which will be an unknown quantity in most cases);[23] this is so even if the new sentence will, in consequence, add nothing to the period actually served.

[22] *R v Ali* (1998) 2 Cr App R 123
[23] *R v Costello* [2010] EWCA Crim 371

Circumstance	Approach
Offender subject to a s.116 return to custody The powers under s.116 Powers of Criminal Court (Sentencing) Act 2000 remain available where the offender: • has been released from a sentence of less than 12 months;[24] • committed his offence before 4 April 2005 and is released from a sentence of less than 4 years;[25] • committed his offence before 4 April 2005 and is released from a sentence of over 4 years following a Parole Board recommendation, or after serving two-thirds of his sentence under section 33(b) Criminal Justice Act 1991.[26]	The period of return under s.116 can either be ordered to be served before or concurrently with the sentence for the new offence. In either case the period of return shall be disregarded in determining the appropriate length of the new sentence.
Offender sentenced to a determinate term and subject to an existing suspended sentence order	Where an offender commits an additional offence during the operational period of a suspended sentence and the court orders the suspended sentence to be activated, the additional sentence will generally be consecutive to the activated suspended sentence, as it will arise out of unrelated facts.

[9]

SG3-12 Extended Sentences for Public Protection [10]

Circumstance	Approach
Extended sentences — using multiple offences to calculate the requisite determinate term	In the case of extended sentences imposed under the Criminal Justice Act 2003, providing there is at least one specified offence, the threshold requirement under s.227(2B) Criminal Justice Act 2003 is reached if the total determinate sentence for all offences (specified or not) would be four years or more. The extended sentence should be passed either for one specified offence or concurrently on a number of them. Ordinarily either a concurrent determinate sentence or no separate penalty will be appropriate to the remaining offences.[27] The extension period is such as the court considers necessary for the purpose of protecting members of the public from serious harm caused by the offender committing further specified offences.[28] The extension period must not exceed five years (or eight for a sexual offence). The whole aggregate term must not exceed the statutory maximum. The custodial period must be adjusted for totality in the same way as determinate sentences would be. The extension period is measured by the need for protection and therefore does not require adjustment.

24 Section 116 of the Powers of Criminal Courts (Sentencing) Act 2000 was repealed by section 332 of the Criminal Justice Act 2003 and Part 7 of Schedule 37. However, the effect of the saving in paragraph 29 of Schedule 2 to the Commencement No.8 and Transitional and Savings Provisions Order 2005 was that section 116 continued to apply where the earlier sentence was imposed for an offence committed before 4 April 2005, or was for a term of less than 12 months.

25 ibid

26 ibid. The Criminal Justice & Immigration Act 2008 contains a further transitional provision. Paragraph 4 of Schedule 26 inserts an exclusion into section 116 which prevents prisoners released under section 33(1A) of the 1991 Act (i.e. eligible discretionary conditional release prisoners, who are released automatically at ½ point of their sentence, rather than on a recommendation from the Parole Board) from being returned to prison under section 116.

27 *R v Pinnell* [2010] EWCA Crim 2848

28 *R v Cornelius* [2002] EWCA Crim 138

Circumstance	Approach
Imposing multiple indeterminate sentences on the same occasion and using multiple offences to calculate the minimum term for an indeterminate sentence	Indeterminate sentences should start on the date of their imposition and so should generally be ordered to run concurrently. If any offence is a serious and specified one and it appears that the defendant is dangerous within the meaning of the dangerousness provisions of the Criminal Justice Act 2003 then: a) first assess the notional determinate term for all offences (serious, specified or otherwise), adjusting for totality in the usual way;[29] b) ascertain whether the total determinate term would be four years or more, or the offender has previously been convicted of a Schedule 15A offence; if so an indeterminate sentence may be passed; and c) the indeterminate sentence should generally be passed concurrently on all serious specific offences, but there may be some circumstances in which it suffices to pass it on a single such offence.
Indeterminate sentence (where the offender is already serving an existing determinate sentence)	It is generally undesirable to order an indeterminate sentence to be served consecutively to any other period of imprisonment on the basis that indeterminate sentences should start on their imposition.[30] The court should instead order the sentence to run concurrently but can adjust the minimum term for the new offence to reflect half of any period still remaining to be served under the existing sentence (to take account of the early release provisions for determinate sentences). The court should then review the minimum term to ensure that the total sentence is just and proportionate.
Indeterminate sentence (where the offender is already serving an existing indeterminate sentence)	It is generally undesirable to order an indeterminate sentence to be served consecutively to any other period of imprisonment on the basis that indeterminate sentences should start on their imposition. However, where necessary the court can order an indeterminate sentence to run consecutively to an indeterminate sentence passed on an earlier occasion.[31] The second sentence will commence on the expiration of the minimum term of the original sentence and the offender will become eligible for a parole review after serving both minimum terms.[32] The court should consider the length of the aggregate minimum terms that must be served before the offender will be eligible for consideration by the Parole Board. If this is not just and proportionate, the court can adjust the minimum term.
Ordering a determinate sentence to run consecutively to an indeterminate sentence	The court can order a determinate sentence to run consecutively to an indeterminate sentence. The determinate sentence will commence on the expiry of the minimum term of the indeterminate sentence and the offender will become eligible for a parole review after serving half of the determinate sentence.[33] The court should consider the total sentence that the offender will serve before becoming eligible for consideration for release. If this is not just and proportionate, the court can reduce the length of the determinate sentence, or alternatively, can order the second sentence to be served concurrently.

29 *R v Rahuel Delucca* [2010] EWCA Crim 710
30 *R v O'Brien* [2006] EWCA Crim 1741
31 *R v Hills* [2008] EWCA Crim 1871; *R v Ashes* [2007] EWCA Crim 1848
32 Crime (Sentences) Act 1997, s. 28(1B)
33 ibid, s. 28

SG3-14 Specific applications — Non-custodial sentences [12]

Multiple Fines for Non-Imprisonable Offences

Circumstance	Approach
Offender convicted of more than one offence where a fine is appropriate	The total fine is inevitably cumulative. The court should determine the fine for each individual offence based on the seriousness of the offence[34] and taking into account the circumstances of the case including the financial circumstances of the offender so far as they are known, or appear, to the court.[35] The court should add up the fines for each offence and consider if they are just and proportionate. If the aggregate total is not just and proportionate the court should consider how to reach a just and proportionate fine. There are a number of ways in which this can be achieved. *For example:* • where an offender is to be fined for two or more offences that arose out of the same incident or where there are multiple offences of a repetitive kind, especially when committed against the same person, it will often be appropriate to impose for the most serious offence a fine which reflects the totality of the offending where this can be achieved within the maximum penalty for that offence. No separate penalty should be imposed for the other offences; • where an offender is to be fined for two or more offences that arose out of different incidents, it will often be appropriate to impose a separate fine for each of the offences. The court should add up the fines for each offence and consider if they are just and proportionate. If the aggregate amount is not just and proportionate the court should consider whether all of the fines can be proportionately reduced. Separate fines should then be passed. Where separate fines are passed, the court must be careful to ensure that there is no double-counting.[36] Where compensation is being ordered, that will need to be attributed to the relevant offence as will any necessary ancillary orders.
Multiple offences attracting fines — crossing the community threshold	If the offences being dealt with are all imprisonable, then the community threshold can be crossed by reason of multiple offending, when it would not be crossed for a single offence.[37] However, if the offences are non-imprisonable (e.g. driving without insurance) the threshold cannot be crossed.[38]

[34] Criminal Justice Act 2003, s. 164(2)
[35] ibid, s. 164(3)
[36] *R v Pointon* [2008] EWCA Crim 513
[37] Criminal Justice Act 2003, s. 148(1)
[38] ibid, s. 150A (in force since 14 July 2008) restricts the power to make a community order by limiting it to cases where the offence is punishable with imprisonment

[13] FINES IN COMBINATION WITH OTHER SENTENCES SG3-15

Circumstance	Approach
A fine may be imposed in addition to any other penalty for the same offence except:	• a hospital order;[39] • a discharge;[40] • a sentence fixed by law[41] (minimum sentences, EPP, IPP); • a minimum term imposed under s.110(2) or s.111(2) of the Powers of Criminal Courts (Sentencing) Act 2000;[42] • a life sentence imposed under s.225(2) Criminal Justice Act 2003 or a sentence of detention for life for an offender under 18 under s.226(2) Criminal Justice Act 2003.[43]
Fines and determinate custodial sentences	A fine should not generally be imposed in combination with a custodial sentence because of the effect of imprisonment on the means of the defendant. However, exceptionally, it may be appropriate to impose a fine in addition to a custodial sentence where: • the sentence is suspended; • a confiscation order is not contemplated; and • there is no obvious victim to whom compensation can be awarded; and • the offender has, or will have, resources from which a fine can be paid.[44]

[14] COMMUNITY ORDERS SG3-16

Circumstance	Approach
Multiple offences attracting community orders – crossing the custody threshold	If the offences are all imprisonable and none of the individual sentences merit a custodial sentence, the custody threshold can be crossed by reason of multiple offending.[45] If the custody threshold has been passed, the court should refer to the offence ranges in sentencing guidelines for the offences and to the general principles.
Multiple offences, where one offence would merit immediate custody and one offence would merit a community order	A community order should not be ordered to run consecutively to or concurrently with a custodial sentence. Instead the court should generally impose one custodial sentence that is aggravated appropriately by the presence of the associated offence(s). The alternative option is to impose no separate penalty for the offence of lesser seriousness.

39 Mental Health Act 1983, s. 37(8)
40 *R v McClelland* [1951] 1 All ER 557
41 Criminal Justice Act 2003, s. 163
42 ibid
43 ibid
44 [This footnote refers to guidance that has been superseded.]
45 Criminal Justice Act 2003, s. 148(1)

Circumstance	Approach
Offender convicted of more than one offence where a community order is appropriate	A community order is a composite package rather than an accumulation of sentences attached to individual counts. The court should generally impose a single community order that reflects the overall criminality of the offending behaviour. Where it is necessary to impose more than one community order, these should be ordered to run concurrently and for ease of administration, each of the orders should be identical.
Offender convicted of an offence while serving a community order	The power to deal with the offender depends on his being convicted whilst the order is still in force;[46] it does not arise where the order has expired, even if the additional offence was committed whilst it was still current. If an offender, in respect of whom a community order made by a magistrates' court is in force, is convicted by a magistrates' court of an additional offence, the magistrates' court should ordinarily revoke the previous community order and sentence afresh for both the original and the additional offence. Where an offender, in respect of whom a community order made by a Crown Court is in force, is convicted by a magistrates' court, the magistrates' court may, and ordinarily should, commit the offender to the Crown Court, in order to allow the Crown Court to re-sentence for the original offence and the additional offence. The sentencing court should consider the overall seriousness of the offending behaviour taking into account the additional offence and the original offence. The court should consider whether the combination of associated offences is sufficiently serious to justify a custodial sentence. If the court does not consider that custody is necessary, it should impose a single community order that reflects the overall totality of criminality. The court must take into account the extent to which the offender complied with the requirements of the previous order.

[14]

SG3-17 Disqualifications from Driving [15]

Circumstance	Approach
Offender convicted of two or more obligatory disqualification offences (s. 34(1) Road Traffic Offender Act 1988)	The court must impose an order of disqualification for each offence unless for special reasons it does not disqualify the offender.[47] All orders of disqualification imposed by the court on the same date take effect immediately and cannot be ordered to run consecutively to one another. The court should take into account all offences when determining the disqualification periods and should generally impose like periods for each offence.

[46] Criminal Justice Act 2003, sched. 8, paras. 21–23
[47] Road Traffic Offender Act 1988, s. 34(1)

[15]

Circumstance	Approach
Offender convicted of two or more offences involving either: a) discretionary disqualification and obligatory endorsement from driving; or b) obligatory disqualification but the court for special reasons does not disqualify the offender and the penalty points to be taken into account number 12 or more (ss. 28 and 35 Road Traffic Offender Act 1988)	Where an offender is convicted on the same occasion of more than one offence to which s. 35(1) Road Traffic Offender Act 1988 applies, only one disqualification shall be imposed on him.[48] However, the court must take into account all offences when determining the disqualification period. For the purposes of appeal, any disqualification imposed shall be treated as an order made on conviction of each of the offences.[49]
Other combinations involving two or more offences involving discretionary disqualification	As orders of disqualification take effect immediately, it is generally desirable for the court to impose a single disqualification order that reflects the overall criminality of the offending behaviour.

[16]

Compensation Orders

SG3-18

Circumstance	Approach
Global compensation orders	The court should not fix a global compensation figure unless the offences were committed against the same victim.[50] Where there are competing claims for limited funds, the total compensation available should normally be apportioned on a pro rata basis.[51]

The court may combine a compensation order with any other form of order.

Compensation orders and fines	Priority is given to the imposition of a compensation order over a fine.[52] This does not affect sentences other than fines. This means that the fine should be reduced or, if necessary, dispensed with altogether, to enable the compensation to be paid.
Compensation orders and confiscation orders	A compensation order can be combined with a confiscation order where the amount that may be realised is sufficient. If such an order is made, priority should be given to compensation.[53]
Compensation orders and community orders	A compensation order can be combined with a community order.
Compensation orders and suspended sentence orders	A compensation order can be combined with a suspended sentence order.[54]
Compensation orders and custody	A compensation order can be combined with a sentence of immediate custody where the offender is clearly able to pay or has good prospects of employment on his release from custody.

48 ibid, s. 34(3)
49 ibid
50 Powers of Criminal Courts (Sentencing) Act 2000, s. 130(12)
51 *R v Mitchell* [2001] Crim LR 239
52 Powers of Criminal Courts (Sentencing) Act 2000, s. 118(5)
53 *R v Warton* [1976] Crim LR 520
54 *R v Miller* [1976] Crim LR 694

PART 4 REDUCTION IN SENTENCE FOR A GUILTY PLEA

SG4-1

Definitive Guideline

Effective from 1 June 2017

Nothing in this guideline affects the duty of the parties to progress cases (including the service of material) and identify any issues in dispute in compliance with the Criminal Procedure Rules and Criminal Practice Directions. [3]

Section 144 of the Criminal Justice Act 2003 provides:

(1) In determining what sentence to pass on an offender who has pleaded guilty to an offence[55] in proceedings before that court or another court, a court must take into account:
  - (a) the stage in the proceedings for the offence at which the offender indicated his intention to plead guilty, and
  - (b) the circumstances in which this indication was given.

SG4-2

A. Applicability of Guideline [4]

The Sentencing Council issues this definitive guideline in accordance with section 120 of the Coroners and Justice Act 2009.

Section 125(1) of the Coroners and Justice Act 2009 provides that when sentencing offences committed after 6 April 2010:

> Every court—
> (a) must, in sentencing an offender, follow any sentencing guidelines which are relevant to the offender's case, and
> (b) must, in exercising any other function relating to the sentencing of offenders, follow any sentencing guidelines which are relevant to the exercise of the function,
>
> unless the court is satisfied that it would be contrary to the interests of justice to do so.

This guideline applies regardless of the date of the offence to all individual offenders aged 18 and older and to organisations in cases where the first hearing is on or after 1 June 2017. The guideline applies equally in magistrates' courts and the Crown Court.

Guidance on reductions in sentence for a guilty plea for under 18s is contained in the Sentencing Council *Overarching Principles – Sentencing Children and Young People* guideline to which sentencers should refer.

SG4-3

B. Key Principles [5]

The purpose of this guideline is to encourage those who are going to plead guilty to do so as early in the court process as possible. Nothing in the guideline should be used to put pressure on a defendant to plead guilty.

Although a guilty person is entitled not to admit the offence and to put the prosecution to proof of its case, an acceptance of guilt:

a) normally reduces the impact of the crime upon victims;
b) saves victims and witnesses from having to testify; and
c) is in the public interest in that it saves public time and money on investigations and trials.

A guilty plea produces greater benefits the earlier the plea is indicated. In order to maximise the above benefits and to provide an incentive to those who are guilty to indicate a guilty plea as early as possible, this guideline makes a clear distinction between a reduction in the sentence available at the first stage of the proceedings and a reduction in the sentence available at a later stage of the proceedings.

The purpose of reducing the sentence for a guilty plea is to yield the benefits described above. The guilty plea should be considered by the court to be independent of the offender's personal mitigation.

[55] 'Offence' includes breach of an order where this constitutes a separate criminal offence but not breach of terms of a sentence or licence

[5] • Factors such as admissions at interview, co-operation with the investigation and demonstrations of remorse should **not** be taken into account in determining the level of reduction. Rather, they should be considered separately and prior to any guilty plea reduction, as potential mitigating factors.
• The benefits apply regardless of the strength of the evidence against an offender. The strength of the evidence should **not** be taken into account when determining the level of reduction.
• The guideline applies only to the punitive elements of the sentence and has no impact on ancillary orders including orders of disqualification from driving.

C. The Approach SG4-4

Stage 1: Determine the appropriate sentence for the offence(s) in accordance with any offence specific sentencing guideline.
Stage 2: Determine the level of reduction for a guilty plea in accordance with this guideline.
Stage 3: State the amount of that reduction.
Stage 4: Apply the reduction to the appropriate sentence.
Stage 5: Follow any further steps in the offence specific guideline to determine the final sentence.

D. Determining the Level of Reduction SG4-5

The maximum level of reduction in sentence for a guilty plea is one-third

D1. Plea indicated at the first stage of the proceedings

Where a guilty plea is indicated at the first stage of proceedings a reduction of **one-third** should be made (subject to the exceptions in section F). The first stage will normally be the first hearing at which a plea or indication of plea is sought and recorded by the court.[56]

D2. Plea indicated after the first stage of proceedings – maximum one quarter – sliding scale of reduction thereafter

After the first stage of the proceedings the maximum level of reduction is **one-quarter** (subject to the exceptions in section F).

The reduction should be decreased from **one-quarter** to a maximum of **one-tenth** on the first day of trial having regard to the time when the guilty plea is first indicated to the court relative to the progress of the case and the trial date (subject to the exceptions in section F). The reduction should normally be decreased further, even to zero, if the guilty plea is entered during the course of the trial.

For the purposes of this guideline a trial will be deemed to have started when pre-recorded cross-examination has begun.

[6] **E. Applying the Reduction** SG4-6

E1. Imposing one type of sentence rather than another

The reduction in sentence for a guilty plea can be taken into account by imposing one type of sentence rather than another; for example:

• by reducing a custodial sentence to a community sentence, or
• by reducing a community sentence to a fine.

Where a court has imposed one sentence rather than another to reflect the guilty plea there should normally be no further reduction on account of the guilty plea. Where, however, the less severe type of sentence is justified by other factors, the appropriate reduction for the plea should be applied in the normal way.

E2. More than one summary offence

When dealing with more than one summary offence, the aggregate sentence is limited to a maximum of six months. Allowing for a reduction for each guilty plea, consecutive sentences might result in the imposition of the maximum six month sentence. Where this is the case, the court **may** make a modest *additional* reduction to the *overall* sentence to reflect the benefits derived from the guilty pleas.

E3. Keeping an either way case in the magistrates' court to reflect a guilty plea

Reducing a custodial sentence to reflect a guilty plea may enable a magistrates' court to retain jurisdiction of an either way offence rather than committing the case for sentence to the Crown Court.

[56] In cases where (in accordance with the Criminal Procedure Rules) a defendant is given the opportunity to enter a guilty plea without attending a court hearing, doing so within the required time limits will constitute a plea at the first stage of proceedings.

In such cases a magistrates' court should apply the appropriate reduction to the sentence for the offence(s) arrived at in accordance with any offence specific sentencing guideline and if the resulting sentence is then within its jurisdiction it should go on to sentence. [6]

SG4-7 F. Exceptions [7]

F1. Further information, assistance or advice necessary before indicating plea

Where the sentencing court is satisfied that there were particular circumstances which significantly reduced the defendant's ability to understand what was alleged or otherwise made it unreasonable to expect the defendant to indicate a guilty plea **sooner than was done**, a reduction of one-third should still be made.

In considering whether this exception applies, sentencers should distinguish between cases in which it is necessary to receive advice and/or have sight of evidence in order to understand whether the defendant is in fact and law guilty of the offence(s) charged, and cases in which a defendant merely delays guilty plea(s) in order to assess the strength of the prosecution evidence and the prospects of conviction or acquittal.

F2. Newton Hearings and special reasons hearings

In circumstances where an offender's version of events is rejected at a Newton hearing[57] or special reasons hearing[58], the reduction which would have been available at the stage of proceedings the plea was indicated should normally be halved. Where witnesses are called during such a hearing, it may be appropriate further to decrease the reduction.

F3. Offender convicted of a lesser or different offence

If an offender is convicted of a lesser or different offence from that originally charged, and has earlier made an unequivocal indication of a guilty plea to this lesser or different offence to the prosecution and the court, the court should give the level of reduction that is appropriate to the stage in the proceedings at which this indication of plea (to the lesser or different offence) was made taking into account any other of these exceptions that apply. In the Crown Court where the offered plea is a permissible alternative on the indictment as charged, the offender will not be treated as having made an unequivocal indication unless the offender has entered that plea.

F4. Minimum sentence under section 51A of the Firearms Act 1968

There can be no reduction for a guilty plea if the effect of doing so would be to reduce the length of sentence below the required minimum term.

F5. Appropriate custodial sentences for persons aged 18 or over when convicted under the Prevention of Crime Act 1953 and Criminal Justice Act 1988 and prescribed custodial sentences under the Power of Criminal Courts (Sentencing) Act 2000

In circumstances where:

- an *appropriate* custodial sentence of at least six months falls to be imposed on a person aged 18 or over who has been convicted under sections 1 or 1A of the Prevention of Crime Act 1953; or sections 139, 139AA or 139A of the Criminal Justice Act 1988 (certain possession of knives or offensive weapon offences) **or**
- a *prescribed* custodial sentence falls to be imposed under section 110 of the Powers of Criminal Courts (Sentencing) Act 2000 (drug trafficking offences) or section 111 of the Powers of Criminal Courts (Sentencing) Act 2000 (burglary offences), the court may impose any sentence in accordance with this guideline which is not less than **80 per cent** of the *appropriate* or *prescribed* custodial period.[59]

[57] A Newton hearing is held when an offender pleads guilty but disputes the case as put forward by the prosecution and the dispute would make a difference to the sentence. The judge will normally hear evidence from witnesses to decide which version of the disputed facts to base the sentence on.

[58] A special reasons hearing occurs when an offender is convicted of an offence carrying mandatory licence endorsement or disqualification from driving and seeks to persuade the court that there are extenuating circumstances relating to the offence that the court should take into account by reducing or avoiding endorsement or disqualification. This may involve calling witnesses to give evidence.

[59] In accordance with s. 144(2) and (3) of the Criminal Justice Act 2003

[8] **MANDATORY LIFE SENTENCES FOR MURDER** **SG4-8**

Murder is the most serious criminal offence and the sentence prescribed is different from all other sentences. By law, the sentence for murder is imprisonment (detention) for life and an offender will remain subject to the sentence for the rest of his life.

Given the special characteristic of the offence of murder and the unique statutory provision in Schedule 21 of the Criminal Justice Act 2003 of starting points for the minimum term to be served by an offender, careful consideration has to be given to the extent of any reduction for a guilty plea and to the need to ensure that the minimum term properly reflects the seriousness of the offence. Whilst the general principles continue to apply (both that a guilty plea should be encouraged and that the extent of any reduction should reduce if the indication of plea is later than the first stage of the proceedings) the process of determining the level of reduction will be different.

Determining the level of reduction

Whereas a court should consider the fact that an offender has pleaded guilty to murder when deciding whether it is appropriate to order a whole life term, where a court determines that there should be a whole life minimum term, there will be no reduction for a guilty plea.

In other circumstances:

- the court will weigh carefully the overall length of the minimum term taking into account other reductions for which the offender may be eligible so as to avoid a combination leading to an inappropriately short sentence;
- where it is appropriate to reduce the minimum term having regard to a plea of guilty, the reduction will not exceed one-sixth and will never exceed five years;
- the maximum reduction of one-sixth or five years (whichever is less) should only be given when a guilty plea has been indicated at the first stage of the proceedings. Lesser reductions should be given for guilty pleas after that point, with a maximum of one-twentieth being given for a guilty plea on the day of trial.

The exceptions outlined at F1 and F2 above, apply to murder cases.

[9] **Appendix 1** **SG4-9**

Flowchart illustrating reductions for either way offences (offences that can be tried in a magistrates' court or the Crown Court)

This flowchart is provided as an illustration of the operation of the guideline as at 1 June 2017.

It does not form part of the guideline.

The reductions and timings are subject to the exceptions set out in the guideline

[9]

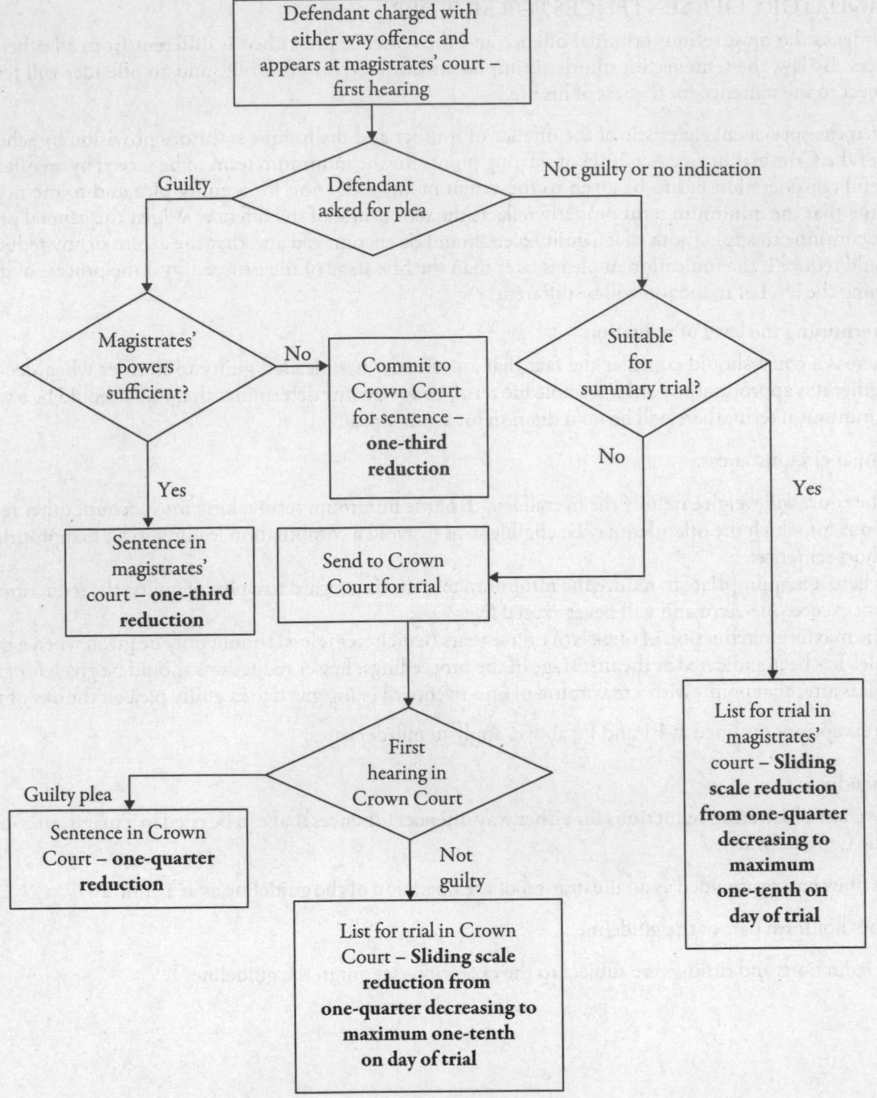

SG4-10 Appendix 2 [10]

Flowchart illustrating reductions for summary only offences (offences that can be tried only in a magistrates' court)

This flowchart is provided as an illustration of the operation of the guideline as at 1 June 2017.

It does not form part of the guideline.

The reductions and timings are subject to the exceptions set out in the guideline

[10]

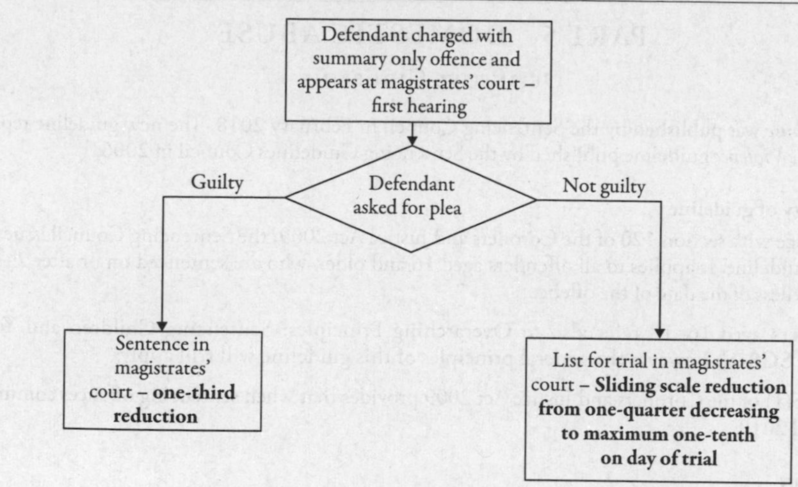

[11] **Appendix 3** SG4-11

Flowchart illustrating reductions for indictable only offences (offences that can be tried only in the Crown Court excluding murder)

This flowchart is provided as an illustration of the operation of the guideline as at 1 June 2017.

It does not form part of the guideline.

The reductions and timings are subject to the exceptions set out in the guideline

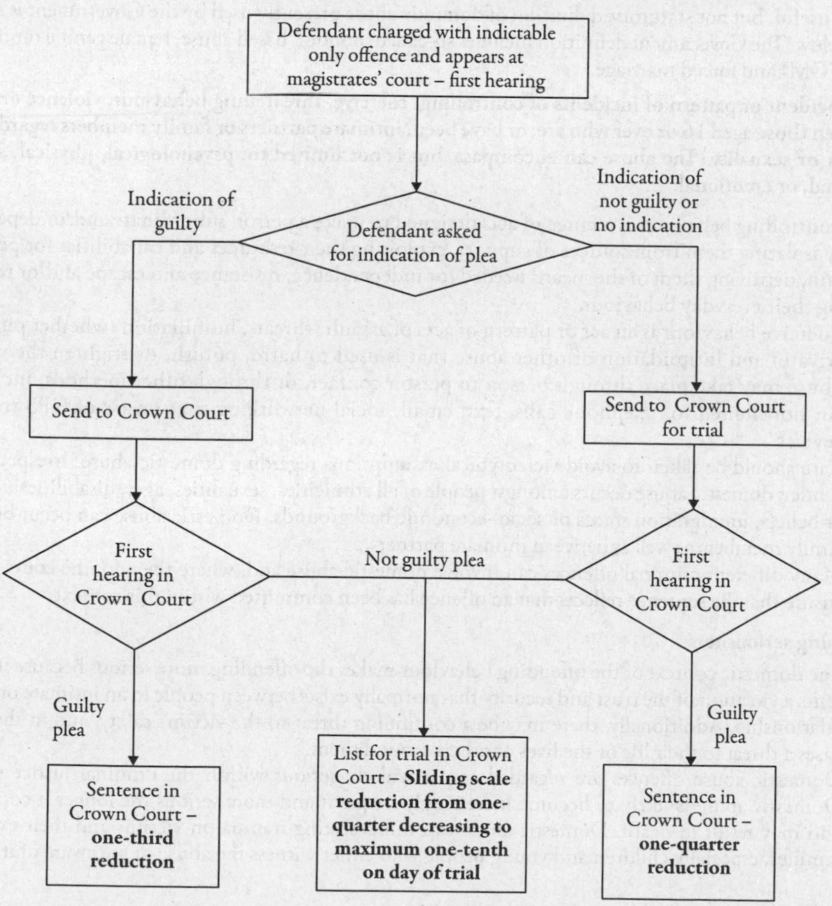

Sentencing Guidelines

PART 5 DOMESTIC ABUSE

SG5-1 DEFINITIVE GUIDELINE

Domestic Abuse was published by the Sentencing Council in February 2018. The new guideline replaces the *Domestic Violence* guideline published by the Sentencing Guidelines Council in 2006.

SG5-2 Applicability of guideline [2]

In accordance with section 120 of the Coroners and Justice Act 2009, the Sentencing Council issues this definitive guideline. It applies to all offenders aged 16 and older, who are sentenced on or after 24 May 2018, regardless of the date of the offence.

For offenders aged 16–18 refer also to Overarching Principles: Sentencing Children and Young People [see **SG8-1**]; however the general principles of this guideline will still apply.

Section 125(1) of the Coroners and Justice Act 2009 provides that when sentencing offences committed after 6 April 2010:

> Every court –
> (a) must, in sentencing an offender, follow any sentencing guidelines which are relevant to the offender's case, and
> (b) must, in exercising any other function relating to the sentencing of offenders, follow any sentencing guidelines which are relevant to the exercise of the function.
> unless the court is satisfied that it would be contrary to the interests of justice to do so.

SG5-3 Scope of the guideline

1. This guideline identifies the principles relevant to the sentencing of cases involving domestic abuse. There is no specific offence of domestic abuse. It is a general term describing a range of violent and/or controlling or coercive behaviour.
2. A useful, but not statutory, definition of domestic abuse presently used by the Government is set out below. The Government definition includes so-called 'honour' based abuse, female genital mutilation (FGM) and forced marriage.

Any incident or pattern of incidents of controlling, coercive, threatening behaviour, violence or abuse between those aged 16 or over who are, or have been, intimate partners or family members regardless of gender or sexuality. The abuse can encompass, but is not limited to: psychological, physical, sexual, financial, or emotional.

3. Controlling behaviour is a range of acts designed to make a person subordinate and/or dependent by isolating them from sources of support, exploiting their resources and capabilities for personal gain, depriving them of the means needed for independence, resistance and escape and/or regulating their everyday behaviour.
4. Coercive behaviour is an act or pattern of acts of assault, threats, humiliation (whether public or private) and intimidation or other abuse that is used to harm, punish, or frighten the victim. Abuse may take place through person to person contact, or through other methods, including but not limited to, telephone calls, text, email, social networking sites or use of GPS tracking devices.
5. Care should be taken to avoid stereotypical assumptions regarding domestic abuse. Irrespective of [3] gender, domestic abuse occurs amongst people of all ethnicities, sexualities, ages, disabilities, religion or beliefs, immigration status or socio–economic backgrounds. Domestic abuse can occur between family members as well as between intimate partners.
6. Many different criminal offences can involve domestic abuse and, where they do, the court should ensure that the sentence reflects that an offence has been committed within this context.

SG5-4 Assessing seriousness

7. The domestic context of the offending behaviour makes the offending more serious because it represents a violation of the trust and security that normally exists between people in an intimate or family relationship. Additionally, there may be a continuing threat to the victim's safety, and in the worst cases a threat to their life or the lives of others around them.
8. Domestic abuse offences are regarded as particularly serious within the criminal justice system. Domestic abuse is likely to become increasingly frequent and more serious the longer it continues, and may result in death. Domestic abuse can inflict lasting trauma on victims and their extended families, especially children and young people who either witness the abuse or are aware of it having

[3] occurred. Domestic abuse is rarely a one-off incident and it is the cumulative and interlinked physical, psychological, sexual, emotional or financial abuse that has a particularly damaging effect on the victims and those around them.

9. Cases in which the victim has withdrawn from the prosecution do not indicate a lack of seriousness and no inference should be made regarding the lack of involvement of the victim in a case.

Aggravating and mitigating factors SG5-5

The following list of non-exhaustive aggravating and mitigating factors are of **particular relevance to offences committed in a domestic context**, and should be considered alongside offence specific factors.

Aggravating Factors

- Abuse of trust and abuse of power
- Victim is particularly vulnerable (*all victims of domestic abuse are potentially vulnerable due to the nature of the abuse, but some victims of domestic abuse may be more vulnerable than others, and not all vulnerabilities are immediately apparent*)
- Steps taken to prevent the victim reporting an incident
- Steps taken to prevent the victim obtaining assistance
- Victim forced to leave home, or steps have to be taken to exclude the offender from the home to ensure the victim's safety
- Impact on children (children can be adversely impacted by both direct and indirect exposure to domestic abuse)
- Using contact arrangements with a child to instigate an offence
- A proven history of violence or threats by the offender in a domestic context
- A history of disobedience to court orders (*such as, but not limited to, Domestic Violence Protection Orders, non-molestation orders, restraining orders*)

[4] *Mitigating Factors*

- Positive good character – *as a general principle of sentencing, a court will take account of an offender's positive good character. However, it is recognised that one of the factors that can allow domestic abuse to continue unnoticed for lengthy periods is the ability of the perpetrator to have a public and a private face. In respect of offences committed within a domestic context, an offender's good character in relation to conduct outside these offences should generally be of no relevance where there is a proven pattern of behaviour*
- Evidence of genuine recognition of the need for change, and evidence of obtaining help or treatment to effect that change

Other factors influencing sentence SG5-6

The following points of principle should be considered by a court when imposing sentence for any offences committed in a domestic context:

10. A sentence imposed for an offence committed within a domestic context should be determined by the seriousness of the offence, not by **any** expressed wishes of the victim. There are a number of reasons why it may be particularly important that this principle is observed within this context:
    - The court is sentencing on behalf of the wider public
    - No victim is responsible for the sentence imposed
    - There is a risk that a plea for mercy made by a victim will be induced by threats made by, or by a fear of, the offender
    - The risk of such threats will be increased if it is generally believed that the severity of the sentence may be affected by the wishes of the victim.
11. Provocation is no mitigation to an offence within a domestic context, except in rare circumstances.
12. The offender or the victim may ask the court to consider the interests of any children by imposing a less severe sentence. The court should consider not only the effect on the children if the relationship is disrupted but also the likely effect of any further incidents of domestic abuse. The court should take great care with such requests, as the sentence should primarily be determined by the seriousness of the offence.
13. Offences involving serious violence, or where the emotional/psychological harm caused is severe, will warrant a custodial sentence in the majority of cases.
14. Some offences will be specified offences for the purposes of the dangerous offender provisions.[60] In such circumstances, consideration will need to be given to whether there is significant risk of serious

[60] Criminal Justice Act 2003 (as amended) sections 224, 229

harm to members of the public by the commission of further specified offences. The 'public' includes family members and if this test is met, the court will be required to impose a life sentence, or an extended sentence in appropriate cases. [4]

15. Passing the custody threshold does not mean that a custodial sentence should be deemed inevitable. Where the custody threshold is only just crossed, the court will wish to consider whether the better option is instead to impose a community order, including a requirement to attend an accredited domestic abuse programme or domestic abuse specific intervention. Such an option will normally only be appropriate where the court is satisfied that the offender genuinely intends to reform his or her behaviour and that there is a real prospect of rehabilitation being successful. [5]
16. The court should also consider whether it is appropriate to make a restraining order, and if doing so, should ensure that it has all relevant up to date information. The court may also wish to consider making other orders, such as a European protection order, sexual harm prevention order, criminal behaviour order (this is not an exhaustive list). Further details for restraining orders are set out below.

SG5-7 Restraining order

17. Where an offender is convicted of any offence, the court may make a restraining order (Protection from Harassment Act 1997, section 5).
18. Orders can be made on the initiative of the court; the views of the victim should be sought, but their consent is not required.
19. The order may prohibit the offender from doing anything for the purpose of protecting the victim of the offence, or any other person mentioned in the order, from further conduct which amounts to harassment or will cause a fear of violence.
20. If the parties are to continue or resume a relationship, courts may consider a prohibition within the restraining order not to molest the victim (as opposed to a prohibition on contacting the victim).
21. The order may have effect for a specified period or until further order.
22. A court before which a person is acquitted of an offence may make a restraining order if the court considers that it is necessary to protect a person from harassment by the defendant (Protection from Harassment Act 1997, section 5A).

SG5-8 Victim personal statements

23. The absence of a Victim Personal Statement (VPS) should not be taken to indicate the absence of harm. A court should consider, where available, a VPS which will help it assess the immediate and possible long-term effects of the offence on the victim (and any children, where relevant) as well as the harm caused, whether physical or psychological

PART 6 OVERARCHING PRINCIPLES: ASSAULTS ON CHILDREN AND CRUELTY TO A CHILD

Replaced by Child Cruelty Definitive Guideline. See SG20-1. **SG6-1**

PART 7 OVERARCHING PRINCIPLES: SENTENCING YOUTHS

SG7-1 Replaced by Sentencing Children and Young People: Overarching Principles and Offence Specific Guidelines for Sexual Offences and Robbery Definitive Guideline. See **SG8-1**.

PART 8 SENTENCING CHILDREN AND YOUNG PEOPLE: OVERARCHING PRINCIPLES AND OFFENCE SPECIFIC GUIDELINES FOR SEXUAL OFFENCES AND ROBBERY SG8-1

[2] **Applicability** SG8-2
Effective from 1 June 2017

The Sentencing Council issues this definitive guideline in accordance with section 120 of the Coroners and Justice Act 2009.

It applies to all children or young people, who are sentenced on or after 1 June 2017, regardless of the date of the offence.

Section 125(1) of the Coroners and Justice Act 2009 provides that when sentencing offences committed after 6 April 2010:

Every court –

(a) must, in sentencing an offender, follow any sentencing guidelines which are relevant to the offender's case, and
(b) must, in exercising any other function relating to the sentencing of offenders, follow any sentencing guidelines which are relevant to the exercise of the function, unless the court is satisfied that it would be contrary to the interests of justice to do so.

Guidance for sentencing children and young people set out in the 2006 robbery guideline and the 2007 sexual offences guideline, both produced by the Sentencing Guidelines Council, are replaced by this guideline.

Guilty Plea Section Only SG8-3

Section 144 of the Criminal Justice Act 2003 provides:

(1) *In determining what sentence to pass on an offender who has pleaded guilty to an offence*[61]
In proceedings before that court or another court, a court must take into account:

(a) the stage in the proceedings for the offence at which the offender indicated his intention to plead guilty, and
(b) the circumstances in which this indication was given.

This section of the guideline applies regardless of the date of the offence to all children or young people where the **first hearing** is on or after 1 June 2017. It applies equally in youth courts, magistrates' courts and the Crown Court.

[4] Overarching Principles – Sentencing Children and Young People SG8-4

SECTION ONE: General approach

Sentencing principles

1.1 When sentencing children or young people (those aged under 18 at the date of the finding of guilt) a court must[62] have regard to:
- the principal aim of the youth justice system (to prevent offending by children and young people);[63] and
- the welfare of the child or young person.[64]

1.2 While the seriousness of the offence will be the starting point, the approach to sentencing should be individualistic and focused on the child or young person, as opposed to offence focused. For a child or young person the sentence should focus on rehabilitation where possible. A court should also consider the effect the sentence is likely to have on the child or young person (both positive and negative) as well as any underlying factors contributing to the offending behaviour.

1.3 Domestic and international laws dictate that a custodial sentence should always be a measure of last resort for children and young people and statute provides that a custodial sentence may only be imposed when the offence is so serious that no other sanction is appropriate (see section six for more information on custodial sentences).

---

[61] Offence' includes breach of an order where this constitutes a separate criminal offence but not breach of terms of a sentence or licence.

[62] This section does not apply when imposing a mandatory life sentence, when imposing a statutory minimum custodial sentence, when imposing detention for life under the dangerous offender provisions or when making certain orders under the Mental Health Act 1983

[63] s.37(1) Crime and Disorder Act 1998

[64] s.44(1) Children and Young Persons Act 1933

1.4 It is important to avoid 'criminalising' children and young people unnecessarily; the primary purpose of the youth justice system is to encourage children and young people to take responsibility for their own actions and promote re-integration into society rather than to punish. Restorative justice disposals may be of particular value for children and young people as they can encourage them to take responsibility for their actions and understand the impact their offence may have had on others. [4]

1.5 It is important to bear in mind any factors that may diminish the culpability of a child or young person. Children and young people are not fully developed and they have not attained full maturity. As such, this can impact on their decision making and risk taking behaviour. It is important to consider the extent to which the child or young person has been acting impulsively and whether their conduct has been affected by inexperience, emotional volatility or negative influences. They may not fully appreciate the effect their actions can have on other people and may not be capable of fully understanding the distress and pain they cause to the victims of their crimes. Children and young people are also likely to be susceptible to peer pressure and other external influences and changes taking place during adolescence can lead to experimentation, resulting in criminal behaviour. When considering a child or young person's age their emotional and developmental age is of at least equal importance to their chronological age (if not greater).

1.6 For these reasons, children and young people are likely to benefit from being given an opportunity to address their behaviour and may be receptive to changing their conduct. They should, if possible, be given the opportunity to learn from their mistakes without undue penalisation or stigma, especially as a court sanction might have a significant effect on the prospects and opportunities of the [5]
child or young person and hinder their re-integration into society.

1.7 Offending by a child or young person is often a phase which passes fairly rapidly and so the sentence should not result in the alienation of the child or young person from society if that can be avoided.

1.8 The impact of punishment is likely to be felt more heavily by a child or young person in comparison to an adult as any sentence will seem longer due to their young age. In addition penal interventions may interfere with a child or young person's education and this should be considered by a court at sentencing.

1.9 Any restriction on liberty must be commensurate with the seriousness of the offence. In considering the seriousness of any offence, the court must consider the child or young person's culpability in committing the offence and any harm which the offence caused, was intended to cause or might foreseeably have caused.[65]

1.10 Section 142 of the Criminal Justice Act 2003 sets out the purposes of sentencing for offenders who are over 18 on the date of conviction. That Act was amended in 2008 to add section 142A which sets out the purposes of sentencing for children and young people, subject to a commencement order being made. The difference between the purposes of sentencing for those under and over 18 is that section 142A does not include as a purpose of sentencing 'the reduction of crime (including its reduction by deterrence)'. Section 142A has not been brought into effect. Unless and until that happens, deterrence can be a factor in sentencing children and young people although normally it should be restricted to serious offences and can, and often will, be outweighed by considerations of the child or young person's welfare.

For more information on assessing the seriousness of the offence see section four.

Welfare

1.11 The statutory obligation to have regard to the welfare of a child or young person includes the obligation to secure proper provision for education and training,[66] to remove the child or young person from undesirable surroundings where appropriate[67] and the need to choose the best option for the child or young person taking account of the circumstances of the offence.

1.12 **In having regard to the welfare of the child or young person, a court should ensure that it is alert to:**

- **any mental health problems or learning difficulties/disabilities;**
- **any experiences of brain injury or traumatic life experience (including exposure to drug and alcohol abuse) and the developmental impact this may have had;**
- **any speech and language difficulties and the effect this may have on the ability of the child or young person (or any accompanying adult) to communicate with the court, to understand the sanction imposed or to fulfil the obligations resulting from that sanction;**
- **the vulnerability of children and young people to self harm, particularly within a** custodial [6]
environment; and
- **the effect on children and young people of experiences of loss and neglect and/or abuse.**

[65] s.143(1) Criminal Justice Act 2003
[66] s. 44 Children and Young Persons Act 1933
[67] ibid.

[6] 1.13 Factors regularly present in the background of children and young people that come before the court include deprived homes, poor parental employment records, low educational attainment, early experience of offending by other family members, experience of abuse and/or neglect, negative influences from peer associates and the misuse of drugs and/or alcohol.

1.14 The court should always seek to ensure that it has access to information about how best to identify and respond to these factors and, where necessary, that a proper assessment has taken place in order to enable the most appropriate sentence to be imposed.

1.15 The court should consider the reasons why, on some occasions, a child or young person may conduct themselves inappropriately in court (e.g. due to nervousness, a lack of understanding of the system, a belief that they will be discriminated against, peer pressure to behave in a certain way because of others present, a lack of maturity etc) and take this into account.

1.16 Evidence shows that looked after children and young people are over-represented in the criminal justice system.[68] When dealing with a child or young person who is looked after the court should also bear in mind the additional complex vulnerabilities that are likely to be present in their background. For example, looked after children and young people may have no or little contact with their family and/or friends, they may have special educational needs and/or emotional and behavioural problems, they may be heavily exposed to peers who have committed crime and they are likely to have accessed the care system as a result of abuse, neglect or parental absence due to bereavement, imprisonment or desertion. The court should also bear in mind that the level of parental-type support that a looked after child or young person receives throughout the criminal justice process may vary, and may be limited. For example, while parents are required to attend court hearings, this is not the case for social workers responsible for looked after children and young people. In some instances a looked after child or young person (including those placed in foster homes and independent accommodation, as well as in care homes) may be before the court for a low level offence that the police would not have been involved in, if it had occurred in an ordinary family setting.

1.17 For looked after children and young people who have committed an offence that crosses the custody threshold sentencers will need to consider any impact a custodial sentence may have on their leaving care rights and whether this impact is proportionate to the seriousness of the offence. For other young people who are in the process of leaving care or have recently left care then sentencers should bear in mind any effect this often difficult transition may have had on the young person's behaviour.

1.18 There is also evidence to suggest that black and minority ethnic children and young people are over-represented in the youth justice system.[69] The factors contributing to this are complex. One factor

[7] is that a significant proportion of looked after children and young people are from a black and minority ethnic background.[70] A further factor may be the experience of such children and young people in terms of discrimination and negative experiences of authority. When having regard to the welfare of the child or young person to be sentenced, the particular factors which arise in the case of black and minority ethnic children and young people need to be taken into account.

1.19 The requirement to have regard to the welfare of a child or young person is subject to the obligation to impose only those restrictions on liberty that are commensurate with the seriousness of the offence; accordingly, a court should not impose greater restrictions because of other factors in the child or young person's life.

1.20 When considering a child or young person who may be particularly vulnerable, sentencers should consider which available disposal is best able to support the child or young person and which disposals could potentially exacerbate any underlying issues. This is particularly important when considering custodial sentences as there are concerns about the effect on vulnerable children and young people of being in closed conditions, with significant risks of self harm, including suicide.

1.21 The vulnerability factors that are often present in the background of children and young people should also be considered in light of the offending behaviour itself. Although they do not alone cause offending behaviour – there are many children and young people who have experienced these circumstances but do not commit crime – there is a correlation and any response to criminal activity amongst children and young people will need to recognise the presence of such factors in order to be effective.

[68] Department for Education (2014) Outcomes for Children Looked After by Local Authorities in England, as at 31 March 2014. Statistical First Release 49/2014. [accessed via: https://www.gov.uk/government/statistics/outcomes-for-children-looked-after-by-local-authorities]

[69] https://www.gov.uk/government/uploads/system/uploads/attachment_data/file/568680/bame-disproportionality-in-the-cjs.pdf

[70] https://www.gov.uk/government/statistics/children-looked-after-in-england-including-adoption-2015-to-2016 (National table, figure B1)

These principles do not undermine the fact that the sentence should reflect the seriousness of the offence. Further guidance on assessing the seriousness of an offence can be found at section four. [7]

SG8-5 SECTION TWO: **Allocation**

(See also the allocation charts below when reading this section.)

2.1 **Subject to the exceptions noted below, cases involving children and young people should be tried in the youth court.** It is the court which is best designed to meet their specific needs. A trial in the Crown Court with the inevitably greater formality and greatly increased number of people involved (including a jury and the public) should be reserved for the most serious cases.[71] The welfare principles in this guideline apply to all cases, including those tried or sentenced in the Crown Court.

This section covers the exceptions to this requirement.[72]

2.2 A child or young person must always appear in the Crown Court for trial if:

- charged with homicide;
- charged with a firearms offence subject to a mandatory minimum sentence of three years (and is over 16 years of age at the time of the offence); or
- notice has been given to the court (under section 51B or 51C of the Crime and Disorder Act 1998) in a serious or complex fraud or child case. [8]

Dangerousness

2.3 A case should be sent to the Crown Court for trial if the offence charged is a specified offence[73] **and** it seems to the court that if found guilty the child or young person would meet the criteria for a sentence under the dangerous offender provisions.

2.4 A sentence under the dangerous offender provisions can only be imposed if:

- the child or young person is found guilty of a specified violent or sexual offence; **and**
- the court is of the opinion that there is a significant risk to the public of serious harm caused by the child or young person committing further specified offences; **and**
- a custodial term of at least four years would be imposed for the offence.

2.5 A 'significant risk' is more than a mere possibility of occurrence. The assessment of dangerousness should take into account all the available information relating to the circumstances of the offence and **may** also take into account any information regarding previous patterns of behavior relating to this offence and any other relevant information relating to the child or young person. In making this assessment it will be essential to obtain a pre-sentence report.

2.6 Children and young people may change and develop within a shorter time than adults and this factor, along with their level of maturity, may be highly relevant when assessing probable future conduct and whether it may cause a significant risk of serious harm.[74]

2.7 In anything but the most serious cases it may be impossible for the court to form a view as to whether the child or young person would meet the criteria of the dangerous offender provisions without greater knowledge of the circumstances of the offence and the child or young person. In those circumstances jurisdiction for the case should be retained in the youth court. If, following a guilty plea or a finding of guilt, the dangerousness criteria appear to be met then the child or young person should be committed **for sentence.**

Grave crimes

2.8 Where a child or young person is before the court for an offence to which section 91(1) of the Powers of Criminal Courts (Sentencing) Act 2000 applies and the court considers that it ought to be possible to sentence them to more than two years' detention if found guilty of the offence, then they should be sent to the Crown Court. The test to be applied by the court is whether there is a **real prospect** that a sentence in excess of two years' detention will be imposed.

2.9 An offence comes within section 91 where:

- it is punishable with 14 years' imprisonment or more for an adult (but is not a sentence fixed by law);
- it is an offence of sexual assault, a child sex offence committed by a child or young person, sexual activity with a child family member or inciting a child family member to engage in sexual activity; or

---

[71] R on the application of *H, A and O v Southampton Youth Court* [2004] EWHC 2912 Admin

[72] s. 24 Magistrates' Courts Act 1980

[73] As listed in the Criminal Justice Act 2003 Sch. 15

[74] *R v Lang* [2005] EWCA Crim 2864, [2006] 1 WLR 2509

[9] • it is one of a number of specified offences in relation to firearms, ammunition and weapons which are subject to a minimum term but, in respect of which, a court has found exceptional circumstances justifying a lesser sentence.

2.10 Before deciding whether to send the case to the Crown Court or retain jurisdiction in the youth court, the court should hear submissions from the prosecution and defence. As there is now a power to commit grave crimes for sentence[75] the court should no longer take the prosecution case at its highest when deciding whether to retain jurisdiction.[76] In most cases it is likely to be impossible to decide whether there is a real prospect that a sentence in excess of two years' detention will be imposed without knowing more about the facts of the case and the circumstances of the child or young person. In those circumstances the youth court should retain jurisdiction and commit for sentence if it is of the view, having heard more about the facts and the circumstances of the child or young person, that its powers of sentence are insufficient.

Where the court decides that the case is suitable to be dealt with in the youth court it must warn the child or young person that all available sentencing options remain open and, if found guilty, the child or young person may be committed to the Crown Court for sentence.

Children and young people should only be sent for trial or committed for sentence to the Crown Court when charged with or found guilty of an offence of such gravity that a custodial sentence substantially exceeding two years is a realistic possibility. For children aged 10 or 11, and children/young people aged 12–14 who are not persistent offenders, the court should take into account the normal prohibition on imposing custodial sentences.

Charged alongside an adult

2.11 The proper venue for the trial of any child or young person is normally the youth court. Subject to statutory restrictions, that remains the case where a child or young person is jointly charged with an adult. If the adult is sent for trial to the Crown Court, the court should conclude that the child or young person must be tried separately in the youth court unless it is in the interests of justice for the child or young person and the adult to be tried jointly.

2.12 Examples of factors that should be considered when deciding whether to send the child or young person to the Crown Court (rather than having a trial in the youth court) include:

- whether separate trials will cause injustice to witnesses or to the case as a whole (consideration should be given to the provisions of sections 27 and 28 of the Youth Justice and Criminal Evidence Act 1999);
- the age of the child or young person; the younger the child or young person, the greater the desirability that the child or young person be tried in the youth court;
- the age gap between the child or young person and the adult; a substantial gap in age militates in favour of the child or young person being tried in the youth court;
- the lack of maturity of the child or young person;
- the relative culpability of the child or young person compared with the adult and whether the alleged role played by the child or young person was minor; and/or
- the lack of previous findings of guilt on the part of the child or young person.

[10] 2.13 The court should bear in mind that the youth court now has a general power to commit for sentence (as discussed at paragraph 2.9); in appropriate cases this will permit a sentence to be imposed by the same court on adults and children and young people who have been tried separately.

2.14 The court should follow the plea before venue procedure (see flowcharts on pages 11–13) prior to considering whether it is in the interests of justice for the child or young person and the adult to be tried jointly.

Remittal from the Crown Court for sentence

2.15 If a child or young person is found guilty before the Crown Court of an offence other than homicide the court must remit the case to the youth court, unless it would be undesirable to do so.[77] In considering whether remittal is undesirable a court should balance the need for expertise in the sentencing of children and young people with the benefits of the sentence being imposed by the court which determined guilt.

2.16 Particular attention should be given to children and young people who are appearing before the Crown Court only because they have been charged with an adult offender; referral orders are generally not available in the Crown Court but may be the most appropriate sentence.

---

[75] s. 3(b) Powers of Criminal Courts (Sentencing) Act 2000, (as amended)

[76] *R (DPP) v South Tyneside Youth Court* [2015] EWHC 1455 (Admin)

[77] s. 8 Powers of Criminal Courts (Sentencing) Act 2000

Child or young person charged alone or with other children and young people [11]

(This is intended to be a reference tool only; for full guidance on allocation, particularly for grave crimes, please see [above])

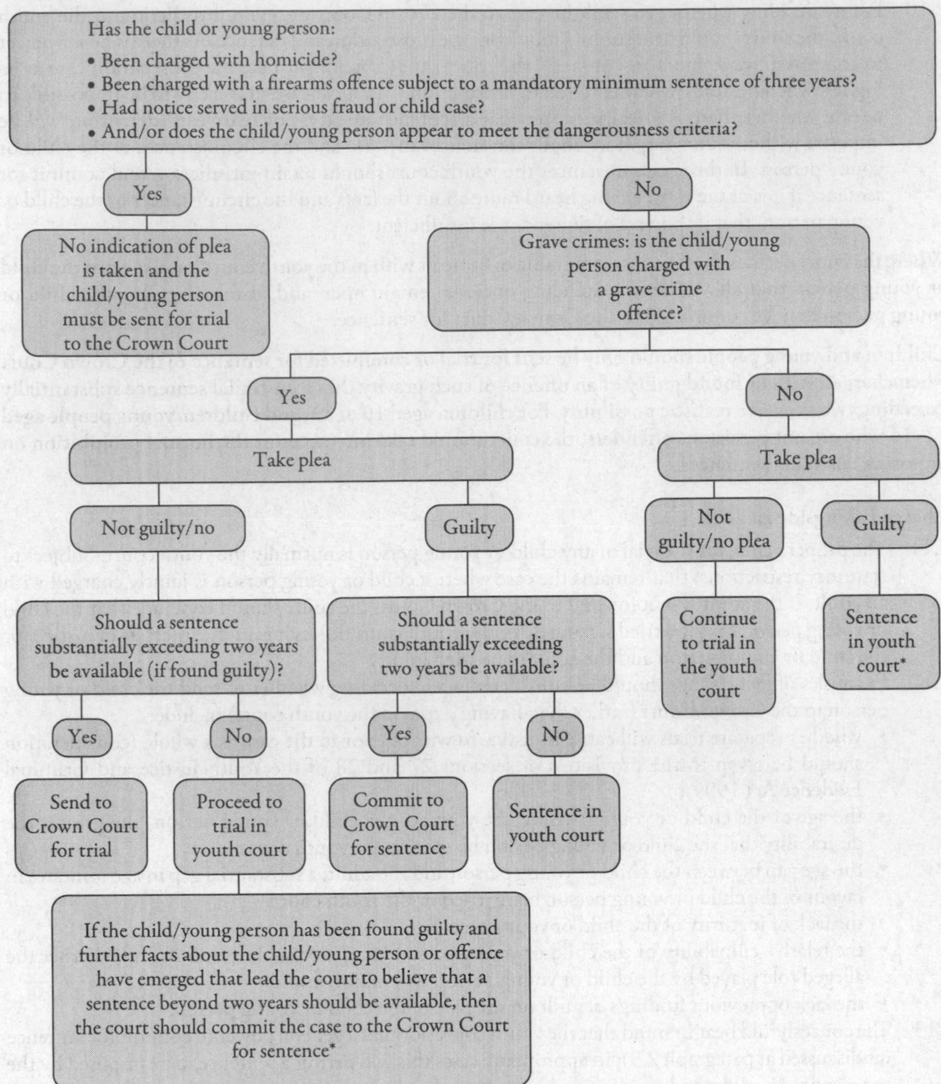
Has the child or young person:
• Been charged with homicide?
• Been charged with a firearms offence subject to a mandatory minimum sentence of three years?
• Had notice served in serious fraud or child case?
• And/or does the child/young person appear to meet the dangerousness criteria?
Yes
No
No indication of plea is taken and the child/young person must be sent for trial to the Crown Court
Grave crimes: is the child/young person charged with a grave crime offence?
Yes
No
Take plea
Take plea
Not guilty/no
Guilty
Not guilty/no plea
Guilty
Should a sentence substantially exceeding two years be available (if found guilty)?
Should a sentence substantially exceeding two years be available?
Continue to trial in the youth court
Sentence in youth court*
Yes
No
Yes
No
Send to Crown Court for trial
Proceed to trial in youth court
Commit to Crown Court for sentence
Sentence in youth court
If the child/young person has been found guilty and further facts about the child/young person or offence have emerged that lead the court to believe that a sentence beyond two years should be available, then the court should commit the case to the Crown Court for sentence*

*If the dangerousness provisions appear to be satisfied the court must commit for sentence

[12] **Child or young person and adult charged as co-defendants where the adult is charged with an indictable only offence (or an offence where notice is given to the court under s. 51B or s. 51C Crime & Disorder Act 1998)**

(This is intended to be a reference tool only; for full guidance on allocation, particularly for grave crimes, please see [above])

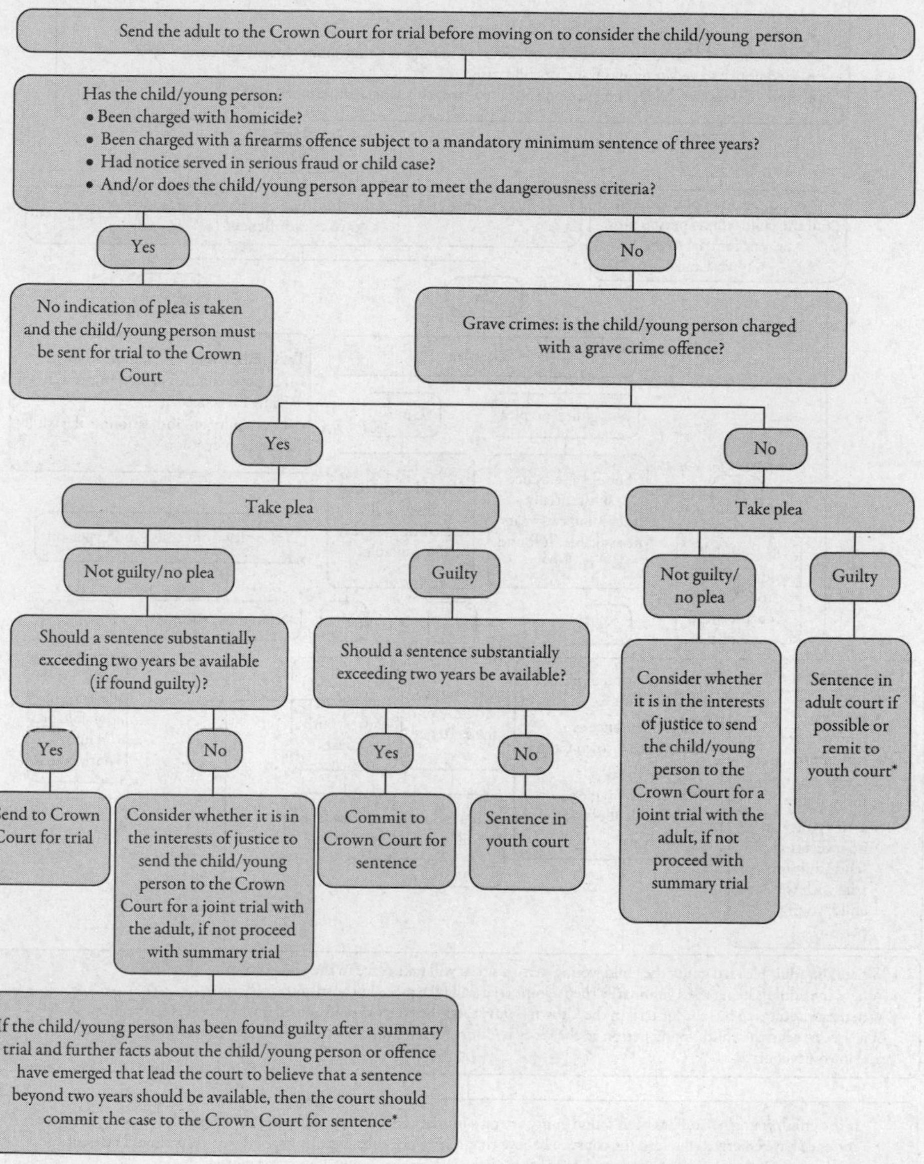
Send the adult to the Crown Court for trial before moving on to consider the child/young person
Has the child/young person:
• Been charged with homicide?
• Been charged with a firearms offence subject to a mandatory minimum sentence of three years?
• Had notice served in serious fraud or child case?
• And/or does the child/young person appear to meet the dangerousness criteria?
Yes
No
No indication of plea is taken and the child/young person must be sent for trial to the Crown Court
Grave crimes: is the child/young person charged with a grave crime offence?
Yes
No
Take plea
Take plea
Not guilty/no plea
Guilty
Not guilty/ no plea
Guilty
Should a sentence substantially exceeding two years be available (if found guilty)?
Should a sentence substantially exceeding two years be available?
Consider whether it is in the interests of justice to send the child/young person to the Crown Court for a joint trial with the adult, if not proceed with summary trial
Sentence in adult court if possible or remit to youth court*
Yes
No
Yes
No
Send to Crown Court for trial
Consider whether it is in the interests of justice to send the child/young person to the Crown Court for a joint trial with the adult, if not proceed with summary trial
Commit to Crown Court for sentence
Sentence in youth court
If the child/young person has been found guilty after a summary trial and further facts about the child/young person or offence have emerged that lead the court to believe that a sentence beyond two years should be available, then the court should commit the case to the Crown Court for sentence*

* If the dangerousness provisions appear to be satisfied the court must commit for sentence

Sentencing Guidelines

Child or young person and adult charged as co-defendants where the adult is charged with either way offence [13]

(This is intended to be a reference tool only; for full guidance on allocation, particularly for grave crimes, please see [above].)

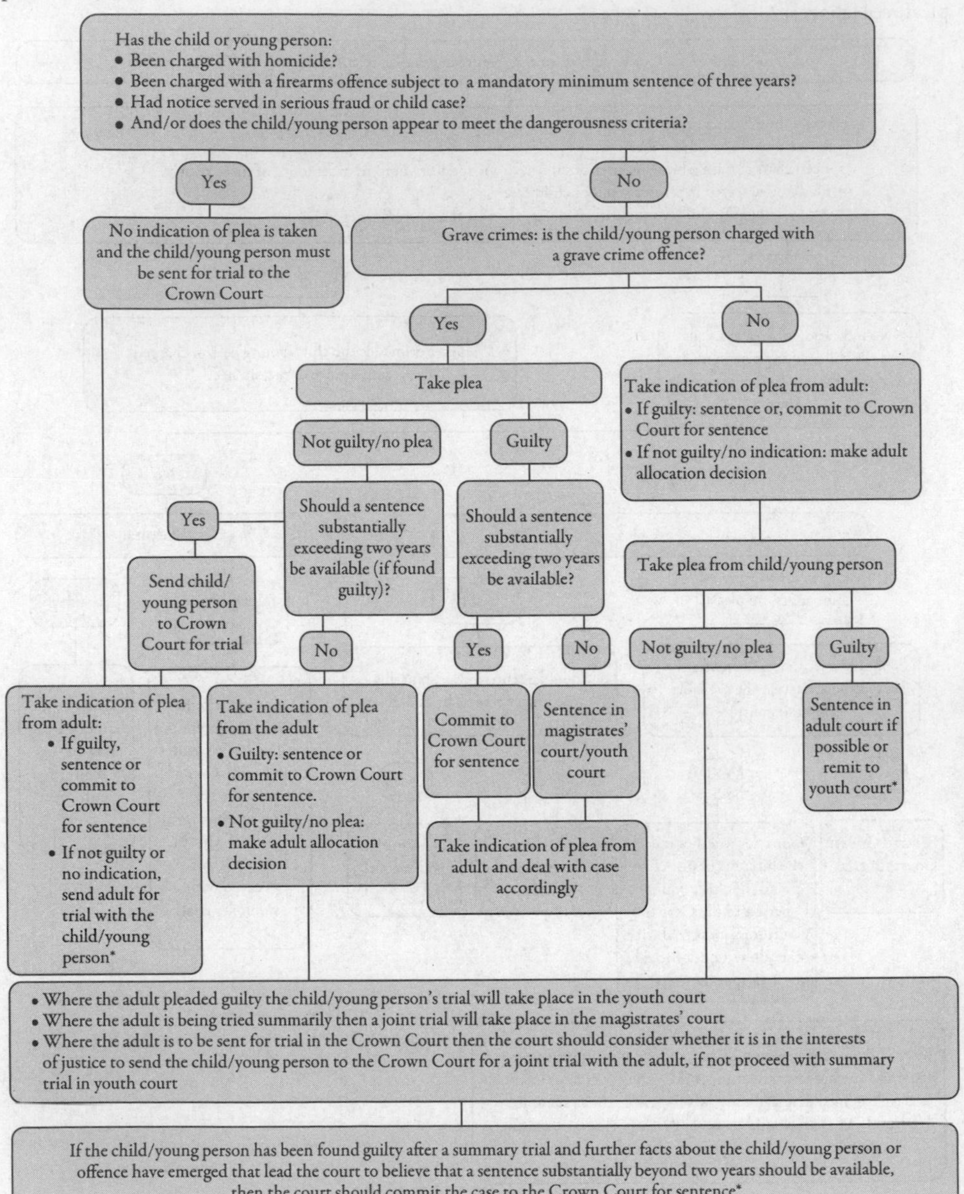

Has the child or young person:
• Been charged with homicide?
• Been charged with a firearms offence subject to a mandatory minimum sentence of three years?
• Had notice served in serious fraud or child case?
• And/or does the child/young person appear to meet the dangerousness criteria?
Yes
No
No indication of plea is taken and the child/young person must be sent for trial to the Crown Court
Grave crimes: is the child/young person charged with a grave crime offence?
Yes
No
Take plea
Take indication of plea from adult:
• If guilty: sentence or, commit to Crown Court for sentence
• If not guilty/no indication: make adult allocation decision
Not guilty/no plea
Guilty
Yes
Should a sentence substantially exceeding two years be available (if found guilty)?
Should a sentence substantially exceeding two years be available?
Take plea from child/young person
Send child/young person to Crown Court for trial
No
Yes
No
Not guilty/no plea
Guilty
Take indication of plea from adult:
• If guilty, sentence or commit to Crown Court for sentence
• If not guilty or no indication, send adult for trial with the child/young person*
Take indication of plea from the adult
• Guilty: sentence or commit to Crown Court for sentence.
• Not guilty/no plea: make adult allocation decision
Commit to Crown Court for sentence
Sentence in magistrates' court/youth court
Sentence in adult court if possible or remit to youth court*
Take indication of plea from adult and deal with case accordingly
• Where the adult pleaded guilty the child/young person's trial will take place in the youth court
• Where the adult is being tried summarily then a joint trial will take place in the magistrates' court
• Where the adult is to be sent for trial in the Crown Court then the court should consider whether it is in the interests of justice to send the child/young person to the Crown Court for a joint trial with the adult, if not proceed with summary trial in youth court
If the child/young person has been found guilty after a summary trial and further facts about the child/young person or offence have emerged that lead the court to believe that a sentence substantially beyond two years should be available, then the court should commit the case to the Crown Court for sentence*

*If the dangerousness provisions appear to be satisfied the court must commit for sentence

[14] SECTION THREE: Parental responsibilities SG8-6

3.1 For any child or young person aged under 16 appearing before court there is a statutory requirement that parents/guardians attend during all stages of proceedings, unless the court is satisfied that this would be unreasonable having regard to the circumstances of the case.[78] The court may also enforce this requirement for a young person aged 16 and above if it deems it desirable to do so.

3.2 Although this requirement can cause a delay in the case before the court it is important it is adhered to. If a court does find exception to proceed in the absence of a responsible adult then extra care must be taken to ensure the outcomes are clearly communicated to and understood by the child or young person.

3.3 In addition to this responsibility there are also orders that can be imposed on parents. If the child or young person is aged under 16 then the court has a duty to make a **parental bind over** or impose a **parenting order**, if it would be desirable in the interest of preventing the commission of further offences.[79] There is a discretionary power to make these orders where the young person is aged 16 or 17. If the court chooses not to impose a parental bind over or parenting order it must state its reasons for not doing so in open court. In most circumstances a parenting order is likely to be more appropriate than a parental bind over.

3.4 A court cannot make a bind over alongside a referral order. If the court makes a referral order the duty on the court to impose a parenting order in respect of a child or young person under 16 years old is replaced by a discretion.[80]

SECTION FOUR: Determining the sentence SG8-7

4.1 In determining the sentence, the key elements to consider are:

- the principal aim of the youth justice system (to prevent re-offending by children and young people);
- the welfare of the child or young person;
- the age of the child or young person (chronological, developmental and emotional);
- the seriousness of the offence;
- the likelihood of further offences being committed; and
- the extent of harm likely to result from those further offences.

The seriousness of the offence

(This applies to all offences; when offence specific guidance for children and young people is available this should be referred to.)

4.2 The seriousness of the offence is the starting point for determining the appropriate sentence; the sentence imposed and any restriction on liberty must be commensurate with the seriousness of the offence.

[15] 4.3 The approach to sentencing children and young people should always be individualistic and the court should always have in mind the principal aims of the youth justice system.

4.4 In order to determine the seriousness of the offence the court should assess the culpability of the child or young person and the harm that was caused, intended to be caused or could foreseeably have been caused.

4.5 In assessing **culpability** the court will wish to consider the extent to which the offence was planned, the role of the child or young person (if the offence was committed as part of a group), the level of force that was used in the commission of the offence and the awareness that the child or young person had of their actions and its possible consequences. There is an expectation that in general a child or young person will be dealt with less severely than an adult offender. In part, this is because children and young people are unlikely to have the same experience and capacity as an adult to understand the effect of their actions on other people or to appreciate the pain and distress caused and because a child or young person may be less able to resist temptation, especially where peer pressure is exerted. Children and young people are inherently more vulnerable than adults due to their age and the court will need to consider any mental health problems and/or learning disabilities they may have, as well as their emotional and developmental age. Any external factors that may have affected the child or young person's behaviour should be taken into account.

4.6 In assessing **harm** the court should consider the level of physical and psychological harm caused to the victim, the degree of any loss caused to the victim and the extent of any damage caused to property. (This assessment should also include a consideration of any harm that was intended to be caused or could foreseeably have been caused in the committal of the offence.)

[78] s. 34A Children and Young Persons Act 1933
[79] s. 150 Powers of Criminal Courts (Sentencing) Act 2000 & s. 8 Crime and Disorder Act 1998
[80] s. 9(1A) Crime and Disorder Act 1998

4.7 The court should also consider any aggravating or mitigating factors that may increase or reduce the overall seriousness of the offence. **If any of these factors are included in the definition of the committed offence they should not be taken into account when considering the relative seriousness of the offence before the court.** [15]

Aggravating factors
Statutory aggravating factors:
Previous findings of guilt, having regard to a) the **nature** of the offence to which the finding of guilt relates and its **relevance** to the current offence; and b) the **time** that has elapsed since the finding of guilt
Offence committed whilst on bail
Offence motivated by, or demonstrating hostility based on any of the following characteristics or presumed characteristics of the victim: religion, race, disability, sexual orientation or transgender identity
Other aggravating factors (non-exhaustive):
Steps taken to prevent the victim reporting or obtaining assistance
Steps taken to prevent the victim from assisting or supporting the prosecution
Victim is particularly vulnerable due to factors including but not limited to age, mental or physical disability
Restraint, detention or additional degradation of the victim
Prolonged nature of offence [16]
Attempts to conceal/dispose of evidence
Established evidence of community/wider impact
Failure to comply with current court orders
Attempt to conceal identity
Involvement of others through peer pressure, bullying, coercion or manipulation
Commission of offence whilst under the influence of alcohol or drugs
History of antagonising or bullying the victim
Deliberate humiliation of victim, including but not limited to filming of the offence, deliberately committing the offence before a group of peers with the intention of causing additional distress or circulating details/photos/videos etc of the offence on social media or within peer groups

Factors reducing seriousness or reflecting personal mitigation (non-exhaustive)
No previous findings of guilt or no relevant/recent findings of guilt
Remorse, particularly where evidenced by voluntary reparation to the victim
Good character and/or exemplary conduct
Unstable upbringing including but not limited to: time spent looked after • lack of familial presence or support • disrupted experiences in accommodation or education • exposure to drug/alcohol abuse, familial criminal behaviour or domestic abuse • victim of neglect or abuse, or exposure to neglect or abuse of others • experiences of trauma or loss
Participated in offence due to bullying, peer pressure, coercion or manipulation
Limited understanding of effect on victim
Serious medical condition requiring urgent, intensive or long-term treatment
Communication or learning disabilities or mental health concerns
In education, work or training
Particularly young or immature child or young person (where it affects their responsibility)
Determination and/or demonstration of steps taken to address addiction or offending behaviour

[16] **Age and maturity of the child or young person**

4.8 There is a statutory presumption that no child under the age of 10 can be guilty of an offence.[81]

4.9 With a child or young person, the consideration of age requires a different approach to that which would be adopted in relation to the age of an adult. Even within the category of child or young person the response of a court to an offence is likely to be very different depending on whether the child or young person is at the lower end of the age bracket, in the middle or towards the top end.

[17] 4.10 Although chronological age dictates in some instances what sentence can be imposed (see section six for more information) the developmental and emotional age of the child or young person should always be considered and it is of at least equal importance as their chronological age. It is important to consider whether the child or young person has the necessary maturity to appreciate fully the consequences of their conduct, the extent to which the child or young person has been acting on an impulsive basis and whether their conduct has been affected by inexperience, emotional volatility or negative influences.

SECTION FIVE: Guilty plea SG8-8

This section of the guideline applies regardless of the date of the offence to all children or young people where the **first hearing** is on or after 1 June 2017. It applies equally in youth courts, magistrates' courts and the Crown Court.

Key principles

5.1 The purpose of this section of the guideline is to encourage those who are going to plead guilty to do so as early in the court process as possible. Nothing in this section should be used to put pressure on a child or young person to plead guilty.

5.2 Although a guilty person is entitled not to admit the offence and to put the prosecution to proof of its case, an acceptance of guilt:

a) normally reduces the impact of the crime upon victims;
b) saves victims and witnesses from having to testify; and
c) is in the public interest in that it saves public time and money on investigations and trials.

5.3 A guilty plea produces greater benefits the earlier the plea is made. In order to maximise the above benefits and to provide an incentive to those who are guilty to indicate a guilty plea as early as possible, this section of the guideline makes a clear distinction between a reduction in the sentence available at the first stage of the proceedings and a reduction in the sentence available at a later stage of the proceedings.

5.4 The purpose of reducing the sentence for a guilty plea is to yield the benefits described above and the guilty plea should be considered by the court to be independent of the child or young person's mitigation.

- Factors such as admissions at interview, co-operation with the investigation and demonstrations of remorse should **not** be taken into account in determining the level of reduction. Rather, they should be considered separately and prior to any guilty plea reduction, as potential mitigating factors.
- The benefits apply regardless of the strength of the evidence against a child or young person.

The strength of the evidence should **not** be taken into account when determining the level of reduction.

- This section applies only to the punitive elements of the sentence and has no impact on ancillary orders including orders of disqualification from driving.

[18] **The approach**

Stage 1: Determine the appropriate sentence for the offence(s) in accordance with any offence specific sentencing guideline or using this *Overarching Principles* guideline.

Stage 2: Determine the level of reduction for a guilty plea in accordance with this guideline.

Stage 3: State the amount of that reduction.

Stage 4: Apply the reduction to the appropriate sentence.

Stage 5: Follow any further steps in the offence specific guideline to determine the final sentence.

Nothing in this guideline affects the duty of the parties to progress cases (including the service of material) and identify any issues in dispute in compliance with the Criminal Procedure Rules and Criminal Practice Directions.

[81] s. 50 Children and Young Persons Act 1933

Determining the level of reduction [18]

The maximum level of reduction for a guilty plea is one-third.

5.5 Plea indicated at the first stage of the proceedings

Where a guilty plea is indicated at the first stage of proceedings a reduction of **one-third** should be made (subject to the exceptions below). The first stage will normally be the first hearing in the magistrates' or youth court at which a plea is sought and recorded by the court.[82]

5.6 Plea indicated after the first stage of proceedings – maximum one quarter – sliding scale of reduction thereafter

After the first stage of the proceedings the maximum level of reduction is **one-quarter** (subject to the exceptions below).

5.7 The reduction should be decreased from **one-quarter** to a maximum of **one-tenth** on the first day of trial having regard to the time when the guilty plea is first indicated relative to the progress of the case and the trial date (subject to the exceptions below). The reduction should normally be decreased further, even to zero, if the guilty plea is entered during the course of the trial.

5.8 For the purposes of this guideline a trial will be deemed to have started when pre-recorded cross-examination has begun.

Applying the reduction

Detention and training orders

5.9 A detention and training order (DTO) can only be imposed for the periods prescribed – 4, 6, 8, 10, 12, 18 or 24 months. If the reduction in sentence for a guilty plea results in a sentence that falls between two prescribed periods the court must impose the lesser of those two periods.

This may result in a reduction greater than a third, in order that the full reduction is given and a lawful sentence imposed.

Imposing one type of sentence rather than another [19]

5.10 The reduction in sentence for a guilty plea can be taken into account by imposing one type of sentence rather than another, for example:
- by reducing a custodial sentence to a community sentence; or
- by reducing a community sentence to a different means of disposal.

Alternatively the court could reduce the length or severity of any punitive requirements attached to a community sentence.

5.11 The court must always have regard to the principal aim of the youth justice system, which is to prevent offending by children and young people. It is, therefore, important that the court ensures that any sentence imposed is an effective disposal.

5.12 Where a court has imposed one sentence rather than another to reflect the guilty plea there should normally be no further reduction on account of the guilty plea. Where, however, the less severe type of sentence is justified by other factors, the appropriate reduction for the plea should be applied in the normal way.

More than one summary offence

5.13 When dealing with more than one summary offence, the aggregate sentence is limited to a maximum of six months. Allowing for a reduction for each guilty plea, consecutive sentences might result in the imposition of the maximum six month sentence. Where this is the case, the court **may** make a modest *additional* reduction to the overall sentence to reflect the benefits derived from the guilty plea.

Sentencing up to 24 months DTO for offences committed by children and young people

5.14 A DTO of up to 24 months may be imposed on a child or young person if the offence is one which, but for the plea, would have attracted a sentence of detention in excess of 24 months under section 91 of the Powers of Criminal Courts (Sentencing) Act 2000.

[82] In cases where (in accordance with the Criminal Procedure Rules) a child/young person is given the opportunity to enter a guilty plea without attending a court hearing, doing so within the required time limits will constitute a plea at the first stage of proceedings.

[19] **Exceptions**

Referral order

5.15 As a referral order is a sentence that is only available upon pleading guilty there should be no further reduction of the sentence to reflect the guilty plea.

Further information, assistance or advice necessary before indicating plea

5.16 Where the sentencing court is satisfied that there were particular circumstances which significantly reduced the child or young person's ability to understand what was alleged, or otherwise made it unreasonable to expect the child or young person to indicate a guilty plea **sooner than was done**, a reduction of one-third should still be made.

5.17 In considering whether this exception applies, sentencers should distinguish between cases in which it is necessary to receive advice and/or have sight of evidence in order to understand whether
[20] the child or young person is, in fact and law, guilty of the offence(s) charged, and cases in which a child or young person merely delays guilty plea(s) in order to assess the strength of the prosecution evidence and the prospects of a finding of guilt or acquittal.

Newton hearings and special reasons hearings

5.18 In circumstances where a child or young person's version of events is rejected at a Newton hearing[83] or special reasons hearing,[84] the reduction which would have been available at the stage of proceedings the plea was indicated should normally be halved. Where witnesses are called during such a hearing, it may be appropriate further to decrease the reduction.

Child or young person found guilty of a lesser or different offence

5.19 If a child or young person is found guilty of a lesser or different offence from that originally charged, and has earlier made an unequivocal indication of a guilty plea to this lesser or different offence to the prosecution and the court, the court should give the level of reduction that is appropriate to the stage in the proceedings at which this indication of plea (to the lesser or different offence) was made taking into account any other of these exceptions that apply. In the Crown Court where the offered plea is a permissible alternative on the indictment as charged, the child or young person will not be treated as having made an unequivocal indication unless the defendant has entered that plea.

Minimum sentence under section 51A of the Firearms Act 1968

5.20 There can be no reduction for a guilty plea if the effect of doing so would be to reduce the length of sentence below the required minimum term.

Appropriate custodial sentences for young persons aged at least 16 but under 18 when found guilty under the Prevention of Crime Act 1953 and Criminal Justice Act 1988

5.21 In circumstances where an appropriate custodial sentence of a DTO of at least four months falls to be imposed on a young person who is aged at least 16 but under 18, who has been found guilty under sections 1 or 1A of the Prevention of Crime Act 1953; or section 139, 139AA or 139A of the Criminal Justice Act 1988 (certain possession of knives or offensive weapon offences) the court may impose any sentence that it considers appropriate, having taken into consideration the general principles set out above.

Mandatory life sentences for murder

5.22 Murder is the most serious criminal offence and the sentence prescribed is different from all other sentences. By law, the sentence for murder is detention for life and the child or young person will remain subject to the sentence for the rest of their life.

5.23 Given the special characteristic of the offence of murder and the unique statutory provision in
[21] Schedule 21 of the Criminal Justice Act 2003 of starting points for the minimum term to be served by a child or young person, careful consideration has to be given to the extent of any reduction for a guilty plea and to the need to ensure that the minimum term properly reflects the seriousness of the offence.

[83] A Newton hearing is held when a child/young person pleads guilty but disputes the case as put forward by the prosecution and the dispute would make a difference to the sentence. The judge will normally hear evidence from witnesses to decide which version of the disputed facts to base the sentence on.

[84] A special reasons hearing occurs when a child/young person is found guilty of an offence carrying a mandatory licence endorsement or disqualification from driving and seeks to persuade the court that there are extenuating circumstances relating to the offence that the court should take into account by reducing or avoiding endorsement or disqualification. This may involve calling witnesses to give evidence

5.24 Whilst the general principles continue to apply (both that a guilty plea should be encouraged and that the extent of any reduction should reduce if the indication of plea is later than the first stage of the proceedings) the process of determining the level of reduction will be different. [21]

Determining the level of reduction

5.25 In other circumstances:
- the court will weigh carefully the overall length of the minimum term taking into account other reductions for which the child or young person may be eligible so as to avoid a combination leading to an inappropriately short sentence;
- where it is appropriate to reduce the minimum term having regard to a plea of guilty, the reduction will not exceed one-sixth and will never exceed five years; and
- the maximum reduction of one-sixth or five years (whichever is less) should only be given when a guilty plea has been indicated at the first stage of the proceedings. Lesser reductions should be given for guilty pleas after that point, with a maximum of one-twentieth being given for a guilty plea on the day of trial.

The exceptions outlined at 5.16–5.18 apply to murder cases.

SG8-9 **SECTION SIX: Available sentences**

Crossing a significant age threshold between commission of offence and sentence

6.1 There will be occasions when an increase in the age of a child or young person will result in the maximum sentence on the date of the *finding of guilt* being greater than that available on the date on which the offence was *committed* (primarily turning 12, 15 or 18 years old).

6.2 In such situations the court should take as its starting point the sentence likely to have been imposed on the date at which the offence was committed. This includes young people who attain the age of 18 between the *commission* and *the finding of guilt of the offence* [85] but when this occurs the purpose of sentencing adult offenders[86] has to be taken into account, which is:
- the punishment of offenders;
- the reduction of crime (including its reduction by deterrence);
- the reform and rehabilitation of offenders;
- the protection of the public; and
- the making of reparation by offenders to persons affected by their offences.

6.3 When any significant age threshold is passed it will rarely be appropriate that a more severe sentence than the maximum that the court could have imposed at the time the offence was committed should be imposed. However, a sentence at or close to that maximum may be appropriate.

Persistent offenders [22]

6.4 Some sentences can only be imposed on children and young people if they are deemed a persistent offender. A child or young person **must** be classed as such for one of the following to be imposed:
- a youth rehabilitation order (YRO) with intensive supervision and surveillance when aged under 15;
- a YRO with fostering when aged under 15; and
- a detention and training order (DTO) when aged 12–14.

6.5 The term persistent offender is not defined in statute but has been considered by the Court of Appeal. In general it is expected that the child or young person would have had previous contact with authority as a result of criminal behaviour. This includes previous findings of guilt as well as admissions of guilt such as restorative justice disposals and conditional cautions.

6.6 A child or young person who has committed one previous offence cannot reasonably be classed as a persistent offender, and a child or young person who has committed two or more previous offences should not necessarily be assumed to be one. To determine if the behavior is persistent the nature of the previous offences and the lapse of time between the offences would need to be considered.[87]

6.7 If there have been three findings of guilt in the past 12 months for imprisonable offences of a comparable nature (or the child or young person has been made the subject of orders as detailed above in relation to an imprisonable offence) then the court could certainly justify classing the child or young person as a persistent offender.

[85] *R v Ghafoor* [2002] EWCA Crim 1857, [2003] 1 Cr App R (S) 428
[86] s. 142 Criminal Justice Act 2003
[87] *R v M* [2008] EWCA Crim 3329

[22] 6.8 When a child or young person is being sentenced in a single appearance for a series of separate, comparable offences committed over a short space of time then the court could justifiably consider the child or young person to be a persistent offender, despite the fact that there may be no previous findings of guilt.[88] In these cases the court should consider whether the child or young person has had prior opportunity to address their offending behavior before imposing one of the optional sentences available for persistent offenders only; if the court determines that the child or young person has not had an opportunity to address their behaviour and believes that an alternative sentence has a reasonable prospect of preventing re-offending then this alternative sentence should be imposed.

6.9 The court may also wish to consider any evidence of a reduction in the level of offending when taking into account previous offending behaviour. Children and young people may be unlikely to desist from committing crime in a clear cut manner but there may be changes in patterns of criminal behaviour (e.g. committing fewer and/or less serious offences or there being longer lengths of time between offences) that indicate that the child or young person is attempting to desist from crime.

6.10 Even where a child or young person is found to be a persistent offender, a court is not obliged to impose one of the optional sentences. The approach should still be individualistic and all other considerations still apply. **Custodial sentences must be a last resort for all children and young**

[23] **people** and there is an expectation that they will be particularly rare for children and young people aged 14 or under.

Sentences available by age:

	Age of child or young person			
Sentence	**10–11**	**12–14**	**15–17**	**Rehabilitation period**
Absolute or conditional discharge or reparation order	✓	✓	✓	Absolute discharge and reparation: spent on day of sentence Conditional discharge: spent on last day of the period of discharge
Financial order	✓	✓	✓	Spent 6 months after the finding of guilt
Referral order	✓	✓	✓	Spent on day of completion
Youth rehabilitation order (YRO)	✓	✓	✓	Spent 6 months after the last day the order is to have effect
YRO with intensive supervision and surveillance or fostering	x	✓ For persistent offenders only	✓	Spent 6 months after the last day the order is to have effect
Detention and training order	x	✓ For persistent offenders only	✓	6 months or under: spent 18 months after the sentence is completed (including supervision period) More than 6 months: spent 24 months after the sentence is completed (including supervision period)
s. 91 PCC(S) Act detention (grave crime)	✓	✓	✓	More than 6 months – 30 months: spent 24 months after sentence completed (including licence period) More than 30 months – 48 months: spent 42 months after sentence completed (including licence period) More than 48 months: never spent
Extended sentence of detention*	✓	✓	✓	Never spent

* If found guilty of a specified violent or sexual offence and the court is of the opinion that there is a significant risk to the public of serious harm caused by the child or young person committing further specified offences.

[88] *R v S* [2000] 1 Cr App R (S)18

6.11 Some sentences have longer rehabilitation periods than others, for example referral orders are spent on the last day on which the order is to have effect.[89] Sentences can also have varying impacts on the future of children and young people; for example absolute or conditional discharges are not deemed to be treated as convictions other than for the purposes of criminal proceedings[90] and therefore may have a lesser impact on the child or young person's future prospects than other sentences. The length of the rehabilitation periods and any likely effects on the child or young person's future prospects should be taken into account when considering if the sentence is commensurate to the seriousness of the offence. [23]

Breaches and the commission of further offences during the period of an order

6.12 If a child or young person is found guilty of breaching an order, or commits a further offence during the period of an order, the court will have various options available depending upon the nature of the order (**see Appendix one**). The primary aim of the court should be to encourage compliance and seek to support the rehabilitation of the child or young person.

Absolute or conditional discharge and reparation orders [24]

6.13 An absolute discharge is appropriate in the least serious cases when, despite a finding of guilt, the court considers that no punishment should be imposed.

6.14 A conditional discharge is appropriate when, despite a finding of guilt, the offence is not serious enough to warrant an immediate punishment. The fixed period of conditional discharge must not exceed three years. Unless exceptional circumstances are found, a conditional discharge cannot be imposed if the child or young person has received one of the following in the previous 24 months: two or more cautions; or a conditional caution followed by a caution.[91]

6.15 A reparation order can require a child or young person to make reparation to the victim of the offence, where a victim wishes it, or to the community as a whole. Before making an order the court must consider a written report from a relevant authority, e.g. a youth offending team (YOT), and the order must be commensurate with the seriousness of the offence.

6.16 If the court has the power to make a reparation order but chooses not to do so, it must give its reasons.

Financial order

6.17 The court may impose a fine for any offence (unless the criteria for a mandatory referral order are met). In accordance with statutory requirements, where financial orders are being considered, priority must be given to compensation orders and, when an order for costs is to be made alongside a fine, the amount of the cost must not exceed the amount of the fine. If the child or young person is under 16 then the court has a duty to order parents or guardians to pay the fine; if the young person is 16 or over this duty is discretionary. In practice, many children and young people will have limited financial resources and the court will need to determine whether imposing a fine will be the most effective disposal.

6.18 A court should bear in mind that children and young people may have money that is specifically required for travel costs to school, college or apprenticeships and lunch expenses.

Referral orders

6.19 A referral order is the mandatory sentence in a youth court or magistrates' court for most children and young people who have committed an offence for the first time and have pleaded guilty to an imprisonable offence. Exceptions are for offences where a sentence is fixed by law or if the court deems a custodial sentence, an absolute or conditional discharge or a hospital order to be more appropriate.

6.20 A discretionary referral order can also be imposed for any offence where there has been a plea of guilty regardless of previous offending history. It should be remembered that they are not community orders and in general terms may be regarded as orders which fall between community disposals and fines. However, bearing in mind that the principal aim of the youth justice system is to prevent children and young people offending, second or subsequent referral orders should be considered in those cases where:

(a) the offence is not serious enough for a YRO but the child or young person does appear to require some intervention OR [25]

[89] s. 139 Legal Aid, Sentencing and Punishment of Offenders Act 2012
[90] s. 14 (1) Powers of Criminal Courts (Sentencing) Act 2000
[91] s. 66ZB Crime & Disorder Act 1998

[25] (b) the offence is serious enough for a YRO but it is felt that a referral order would be the best way to prevent further offending (as an example, this may be because the child or young person has responded well in the past to such an order and the offence now before the court is dissimilar to that for which a referral order was previously imposed).

Referral orders are the main sentence for delivering restorative justice and all panel members are trained Restorative Conference Facilitators; as such they can be an effective sentence in encouraging children and young people to take responsibility for their actions and understand the effect their offence may have had on their victim.

6.21 In cases where children or young people have offended for the first time and have pleaded guilty to committing an offence which is on the cusp of the custody threshold, YOTs should be encouraged to convene a Youth Offender Panel prior to sentence (sometimes referred to as a 'pseudo-panel' or 'pre-panel') where the child or young person is asked to attend before a panel and agree an intensive contract. If that contract is placed before the sentencing youth court, the court can then decide whether it is sufficient to move below custody on this occasion. The proposed contract is not something the court can alter in any way; the court will still have to make a decision between referral order and custody but can do so on the basis that if it makes a referral order it can have confidence in what that will entail in the particular case.

6.22 The court determines the length of the order but a Referral Order Panel determines the requirements of the order.

Offence seriousness	Suggested length of referral order
Low	• 3–5 months
Medium	• 5–7 months
High	• 7–9 months
Very high	• 10–12 months

The YOT may propose certain requirements and the length of these requirements may not correspond to the above table; if the court feels these requirements will best achieve the aims of the youth justice system then they may still be imposed.

Youth rehabilitation orders (YRO)

6.23 A YRO is a community sentence within which a court may include one or more requirements designed to provide for punishment, protection of the public, reducing re-offending and reparation.

6.24 When imposing a YRO, the court must fix a period within which the requirements of the order are to be completed; this must not be more than three years from the date on which the order comes into effect.

6.25 The offence must be 'serious enough' in order to impose a YRO, but it does not need to be an imprisonable offence. Even if an offence is deemed 'serious enough' the court is not obliged to make a YRO.

[26] 6.26 The requirements included within the order (and the subsequent restriction on liberty) and the length of the order must be proportionate to the seriousness of the offence and suitable for the child or young person. The court should take care to ensure that the requirements imposed are not too onerous so as to make breach of the order almost inevitable.

6.27 The available requirements within a YRO are:

- activity requirement (maximum 90 days);
- supervision requirement;
- unpaid work requirement (between 40 and 240 hours);*
- programme requirement;
- attendance centre requirement (maximum 12 hours for children aged 10–13, between 12 and 24 hours for young people aged 14 or 15 and between 12 and 36 hours for young people aged 16 or over (all ages refer to age at date of the finding of guilt));
- prohibited activity requirement;
- curfew requirement (maximum 12 months and between 2 and 16 hours a day);
- exclusion requirement (maximum 3 months);
- electronic monitoring requirement;
- residence requirement;*

- local authority residence requirement (maximum 6 months but not for any period after young person attains age of 18); [26]
- fostering requirement (maximum 12 months but not for any period after young person attains age of 18);**
- mental health treatment requirement;
- drug treatment requirement (with or without drug testing);
- intoxicating substance requirement;
- education requirement; and
- intensive supervision and surveillance requirement.**

* These requirements are only available for young people aged 16 or 17 years old on the date of the finding of guilt.

** These requirements can only be imposed if the offence is an imprisonable one AND the custody threshold has been passed. For children and young people aged under 15 they must be deemed a persistent offender.

Many of the above requirements have additional restrictions. Always consult your legal adviser before imposing a YRO.

6.28 When determining the nature and extent of the requirements the court should primarily consider the likelihood of the child or young person re-offending and the risk of the child or young person causing serious harm. A higher risk of re-offending does not in itself justify a greater restriction on liberty than is warranted by the seriousness of the offence; any requirements should still be commensurate with the seriousness of the offence and regard must still be had for the welfare of the child or young person.

6.29 The YOT will assess this as part of their report and recommend an intervention level to the court for consideration. It is possible for the court to ask the YOT to consider a particular requirement.

[27]

	Child or Young person profile	Requirements of order [92]
Standard	Low likelihood of re-offending and a low risk of serious harm	Primarily seek to repair harm caused through, for example: • reparation; • unpaid work; • supervision; and/or • attendance centre.
Enhanced	Medium likelihood of re-offending or a medium risk of serious harm	Seek to repair harm caused and to enable help or change through, for example: • supervision; • reparation; • requirement to address behaviour e.g. drug treatment, offending behaviour programme, education programme; and/or • a combination of the above.
Intensive	High likelihood of re-offending or a very high risk of serious harm	Seek to ensure the control of and enable help or change for the child or young person through, for example: • supervision; • reparation; • requirement to address behaviour; • requirement to monitor or restrict movement, e.g. prohibited activity, curfew, exclusion or electronic monitoring; and/or • a combination of the above.

6.30 If a child or young person is assessed as presenting a high risk of re-offending or of causing serious harm but the offence that was committed is of relatively low seriousness then the appropriate requirements are likely to be primarily rehabilitative or for the protection of the public.

[92] The examples provided here are not exclusive; the YOT will make recommendations based upon their assessment of the young offender which may vary from some of the examples given.

[27] 6.31 Likewise if a child or young person is assessed as presenting a low risk of re-offending or of causing serious harm but the offence was of relatively high seriousness then the appropriate requirements are likely to be primarily punitive.

Orders with intensive supervision and surveillance or with fostering

6.32 An intensive supervision and surveillance requirement and a fostering requirement are both community alternatives to custody.

6.33 The offence must be punishable by imprisonment, cross the custody threshold and a custodial sentence must be merited before one of these requirements can be imposed.

6.34 An order of this nature may only be imposed on a child or young person aged below 15 (at the time of the finding of guilt) if they are a persistent offender.

With intensive supervision and surveillance:

6.35 An order of this nature must include an extended activity requirement of between 90 and 180 days, a supervision requirement and a curfew requirement. Where appropriate, a YRO with intensive supervision and surveillance may also include additional requirements (other than a fostering requirement), although the order as a whole must comply with the obligation that the requirements must be those most suitable for the child or young person and that any restrictions on liberty are commensurate with the seriousness of the offence.

[28] 6.36 When imposing such an order, the court must ensure that the requirements are not so onerous as to make the likelihood of breach almost inevitable.

With fostering:

6.37 Where a fostering requirement is included within a YRO, it will require the child or young person to reside with a local authority foster parent for a specified period that must not exceed 12 months.

6.38 In order to impose this requirement the court must be satisfied that the behaviour which constituted the offence was due to a significant extent to the circumstances in which the child or young person was living, and that the imposition of fostering requirement would assist in the child or young person's rehabilitation. It is likely that other rights will be engaged (such as those under Article 8 of the European Convention on Human Rights)[93] and any interference with such rights must be proportionate.

6.39 The court must consult the child or young person's parent or guardian (unless impracticable) and the local authority before including this requirement. It can only be included if the child or young person was legally represented in court when consideration was being given to imposing such a requirement unless the child or young person, having had the opportunity to do so, did not apply for representation or that right was withdrawn because of the child or young person's conduct. **This requirement may be included only where the court has been notified that arrangements are available in the area of the relevant authority.**

6.40 A YRO with a fostering requirement must include a supervision requirement and can include other requirements when appropriate (except an intensive supervision and surveillance requirement). The order as a whole must comply with the obligation that the requirements must be those most suitable for the child or young person and that any restrictions on liberty are commensurate with the seriousness of the offence.

6.41 It is unlikely that the statutory criteria[94] will be met in many cases; where they are met and the court is considering making an order, care should be taken to ensure that there is a well developed plan for the care and support of the child or young person throughout the period of the order and following conclusion of the order. The court will need to be provided with sufficient information, including proposals for education and training during the order and plans for the child or young person on completion of the order.

Custodial sentences

A custodial sentence should always be used as a last resort. If offence specific guidelines for children and young people are available then the court should consult them in the first instance to assess whether custody is the most appropriate disposal.

[93] Right to respect for family and private life

[94] See paragraphs 5.28–5.30

The available custodial sentences for children and young people are: [29]

Youth Court	Crown Court
• 4 months; • 6 months; • 8 months; • 10 months; • 12 months; • 18 months; or • 24 months.	• Detention and training order (the same periods are available as in the youth court) • Long-term detention (under section 91 of the Powers of Criminal Courts (Sentencing) Act 2000) • Extended sentence of detention or detention for life (if dangerousness criteria are met) • Detention at Her Majesty's pleasure (for offences of murder)

6.42 Under both domestic and international law, a custodial sentence must only be imposed as a '**measure of last resort**;' statute provides that such a sentence may be imposed only where an offence is 'so serious that neither a fine alone nor a community sentence can be justified'.[95] If a custodial sentence is imposed, a court must state its reasons for being satisfied that the offence is so serious that no other sanction would be appropriate and, in particular, why a YRO with intensive supervision and surveillance or fostering could not be justified.

6.43 The term of a custodial sentence must be the shortest commensurate with the seriousness of the offence; any case that warrants a DTO of less than four months must result in a non-custodial sentence. The court should take account of the circumstances, age and maturity of the child or young person.

6.44 In determining whether an offence has crossed the custody threshold the court will need to assess the seriousness of the offence, in particular the level of harm that was caused, or was likely to have been caused, by the offence. The risk of serious harm in the future must also be assessed. The pre-sentence report will assess this criterion and must be considered before a custodial sentence is imposed. A custodial sentence is most likely to be unavoidable where it is necessary to protect the public from serious harm.

6.45 Only if the court is satisfied that the offence crosses the custody threshold, and that no other sentence is appropriate, the court may, as a preliminary consideration, consult the equivalent adult guideline in order to decide upon the appropriate length of the sentence.

6.46 When considering the relevant adult guideline, the court **may** feel it appropriate to apply a sentence broadly within the region of half to two thirds of the adult sentence for those aged 15–17 and allow a greater reduction for those aged under 15. This is only a rough guide and must not be applied mechanistically. In most cases when considering the appropriate reduction from the adult sentence the **emotional and developmental age and maturity of the child or young person is of at least equal importance as their chronological age**.

6.47 The individual factors relating to the offence and the child or young person are of the greatest importance and may present good reason to impose a sentence outside of this range. The court should bear in mind the negative effects a short custodial sentence can have; short sentences disrupt education and/or training and family relationships and support which are crucial stabilising factors to prevent re-offending.

6.48 There is an expectation that custodial sentences will be particularly rare for a child or young person [30] aged 14 or under. If custody is imposed, it should be for a shorter length of time than that which a young person aged 15–17 would receive if found guilty of the same offence. For a child or young person aged 14 or under the sentence should normally be imposed in a youth court (except in cases of homicide or when the dangerous offender criteria are met).

6.49 The welfare of the child or young person must be considered when imposing any sentence but is especially important when a custodial sentence is being considered. A custodial sentence could have a significant effect on the prospects and opportunities of the child or young person and a child or young person is likely to be more susceptible than an adult to the contaminating influences that can be expected within a custodial setting. There is a high reconviction rate for children and young people that have had custodial sentences and there have been many studies profiling the effect on vulnerable children and young people, particularly the risk of self harm and suicide and so it is of utmost importance that custody is a last resort.

[95] s. 152(2) Criminal Justice Act 2003

[30] **Detention and training order (DTO)**

6.50 A court can only impose a DTO if the child or young person is legally represented unless they have refused to apply for legal aid or it has been withdrawn as a result of their conduct.

6.51 If it is determined that the offence is of such seriousness that a custodial sentence is unavoidable then the length of this sentence must be considered on an individual basis. The court must take into account the chronological age of the child or young person, as well as their maturity, emotional and developmental age and other relevant factors, such as their mental health or any learning disabilities.

6.52 A DTO cannot be imposed on any child under the age of 12 at the time of the finding of guilt and is only applicable to children aged 12–14 if they are deemed to be a persistent offender. (See section on persistent offenders on page 22.)

6.53 A DTO can be made only for the periods prescribed – 4, 6, 8, 10, 12, 18 or 24 months. Any time spent on remand in custody or on bail subject to a qualifying curfew condition should be taken into account when calculating the length of the order. The accepted approach is to double the time spent on remand before deciding the appropriate period of detention, in order to ensure that the regime is in line with that applied to adult offenders.[96] After doubling the time spent on remand the court should then adopt the nearest prescribed period available for a DTO.

Long-term detention

6.54 A child or young person may be sentenced by the Crown Court to long-term detention under section 91 of the Powers of Criminal Courts (Sentencing) Act 2000 if found guilty of a grave crime and neither a community order nor a DTO is suitable.

6.55 These cases may be sent for trial to the Crown Court or committed for sentence only[97] (see section two for further information).

[31] 6.56 It is possible that, following a guilty plea, a two year detention order may be appropriate as opposed to a sentence of section 91 detention, to account for the reduction.

Dangerous offenders

6.57 If a child or young person is found to be a dangerous offender they can be sentenced to **extended detention** or **detention for life**.

6.58 A sentence of extended detention may be imposed only where the appropriate custodial term would be 4 years or more. The extension period must not exceed 5 years in the case of a specified violent offence and 8 years in the case of a specified sexual offence. The term of the extended sentence of detention must not exceed the maximum term of imprisonment for an adult offender convicted of that offence.

6.59 A sentence of detention for life should be used as a last resort when an extended sentence is not able to provide the level of public protection that is necessary. In order to determine this, the court should consider the following factors in the order given:

- the seriousness of the offence;
- the child or young person's previous findings of guilt;
- the level of danger posed to the public and whether there is a reliable estimate of the length of time the child or young person will remain a danger; and
- the alternative sentences available.

The court is required to set a minimum term which must be served in custody before parole can be considered.

Detention at Her Majesty's pleasure

6.60 This is the mandatory sentence for any child or young person found guilty of committing a murder. The starting point for the minimum term is 12 years.

[32] **APPENDIX ONE: Breach of orders** **SG8-10**

Breach of a conditional discharge

7.1 If a child or young person commits an offence during the period of conditional discharge then the court has the power to re-sentence the original offence. The child or young person should be dealt with on the basis of their current age and not the age at the time of the finding of guilt and the court can deal with the original offence(s) in any way which it could have if the child or young person had just been found guilty.

7.2 There is no requirement to re-sentence; if a court deems it appropriate to do so they can sentence the child or young person for the new offence and leave the conditional discharge in place. If the

96 *R v Eagles* [2006] EWCA Crim 2368

97 s. 3(b) Powers of Criminal Courts (Sentencing) Act 2000, (as amended)

order was made by the Crown Court then the youth court can commit the child or young person in custody or release them on bail until they can be brought or appear before the Crown Court. The court shall also send to the Crown Court a memorandum of conviction. [32]

7.3 If the offender is convicted of committing a new offence after attaining the age of 18 but during the period of a conditional discharge made by a youth court then they may be re-sentenced for the original offence by the convicting adult magistrates' court. If the adult magistrates' court decides to take no action then the youth court that imposed the conditional discharge may summon the offender for the breach to be dealt with.

Breach of a reparation order

7.4 If it is proved to the appropriate court that the child or young person has failed to comply with any requirement of a reparation order that is currently in force then the court can:
- order the child or young person to pay a fine not exceeding £1,000; or
- revoke the order and re-sentence the child or young person in any way which they could have been dealt with for that offence.

If re-sentencing the child or young person the court must take into account the extent to which the child or young person has complied with the requirements of this order.

7.5 If the order was made by the Crown Court then the youth court can commit the child or young person in custody or release them on bail until they can be brought or appear before the Crown Court.

7.6 The child or young person or a Youth Offending Team (YOT) officer can also apply for the order to be revoked or amended but any new provisions must be ones that the court would have been able to include when the original reparation order was given. There is no power to re-sentence in this situation as the child or young person has not been found to be in breach of requirements.

Even when an offender has attained the age of 18 breach of a reparation order must be dealt with in the youth court.

Breach of a referral order (referral back to court) [33]

7.7 If a child or young person is found to have breached the conditions of their referral order the court can revoke the referral order and re-sentence the child or young person using the range of sentencing options (other than a referral order) that would have been available to the court that originally sentenced them. If the court chooses not to revoke the referral order then it is possible to:
- allow the referral order to continue with the existing contract;
- extend the length of the referral order up to a maximum of 12 months (in total); or
- impose a fine up to a maximum of £2,500.

7.8 If an offender has attained the age of 18 by the first court hearing then breach proceedings must be dealt with by the adult magistrates' court. If the court chooses to revoke the order then its powers are limited to those available to the court at the time of the original sentence.

Commission of further offences whilst on a referral order

7.9 The court has the power to extend a referral order in respect of additional or further offences. This applies to not only a first referral order but also to any subsequent referral orders. Any period of extension must not exceed the total 12 month limit for a referral order.

7.10 If the court chooses not to extend the existing referral order or impose a discharge they have the power to impose a new referral order (where the discretionary referral order conditions are satisfied) in respect of the new offences only. This order can remain or run alongside the new order or the court may direct that the contract under the new order is not to take effect until the earlier order is revoked or discharged. Alternatively, the court may impose an absolute or conditional discharge.

7.11 If the court sentences in any other way they have a discretionary power to revoke the referral order. Where an order is revoked, if it appears to be in the interests of justice, the court may deal with the original offence(s) in any way that the original court could have done, but may not make a new referral order. Where the referral contract has taken effect, the court shall have regard to the extent of the child or young person's compliance with the terms of the contract.

Breach of a youth rehabilitation order (YRO)

7.12 Where a child or young person is in breach of a YRO the following options are available to the court:
- take no action and allow the order to continue in its original form;
- impose a fine (up to £2,500)(and allow the order to continue in its original form);
- amend the terms of the order; or
- revoke the order and re-sentence the child or young person.

[33] 7.13 If the terms of the order are amended the new requirements must be capable of being complied with before the expiry of the overall period. The court may impose any requirement that it could have imposed when making the order and this may be in addition to, or in substitution for, any requirements contained in the order. If the YRO did not contain an unpaid work requirement and
[34] the court includes such a requirement using this power, the minimum period of unpaid work is 20 hours; this will give greater flexibility when responding to less serious breaches or where there are significant other requirements to be complied with.

7.14 A court may not amend the terms of a YRO that did not include an extended activity requirement or a fostering requirement by inserting them at this stage; should these requirements be considered appropriate following breach, the child or young person must be re-sentenced and the original YRO revoked.

7.15 A court must ensure that it has sufficient information to enable it to understand why the order has been breached and should be satisfied that the YOT and other local authority services have taken all steps necessary to ensure that the child or young person has been given appropriate opportunity and the support necessary for compliance. This is particularly important if the court is considering imposing a custodial sentence as a result of the breach.

7.16 Where the failure arises primarily from non-compliance with reporting or other similar obligations and a sanction is necessary, the most appropriate response is likely to be the inclusion of (or increase in) a primarily punitive requirement such as the curfew requirement, unpaid work, the exclusion requirement and the prohibited activity requirement or the imposition of a fine. However, continuing failure to comply with the order is likely to lead to revocation of the order and re-sentencing for the original offence.

7.17 Where the child or young person has 'wilfully and persistently' failed to comply with the order, and the court proposes to sentence again for the offence(s) in respect of which the order was made, additional powers are available.

A child or young person will almost certainly be considered to have 'wilfully and persistently' breached a YRO where there have been three breaches that have demonstrated a lack of willingness to comply with the order that have resulted in an appearance before court.

7.18 The additional powers available to the court when re-sentencing a child or young person who has 'wilfully and persistently' breached their order are:

- the making of a YRO with intensive supervision and surveillance even though the offence is non-imprisonable;
- a custodial sentence if the YRO that is breached is one with an intensive supervision and surveillance requirement, which was imposed for an offence that was imprisonable; and
- the imposition of a DTO for four months for breach of a YRO with intensive supervision and surveillance which was imposed following wilful and persistent breach of an order made for a non-imprisonable offence.

The primary objective when sentencing for breach of a YRO is to ensure that the child or young person completes the requirements imposed by the court.

7.19 If an offender has attained the age of 18 by the first court hearing then breach proceedings must be dealt with by the adult magistrates' court. If the court chooses to revoke the order then its powers are limited to those available to the court at the time of the original sentence.

[35] **Commission of further offences during a YRO**

7.20 If a child or young person commits an offence whilst subject to a YRO the court can impose any sentence for the new matter, but can only impose a new YRO if they revoke the existing order. Where the court revokes the original order they may re-sentence that matter at the same time as sentencing the new offence.

Breach of a detention and training order (DTO)

7.21 If a child or young person is found to have breached a supervision requirement after release from custody then the court may:

- impose a further period of custody of up to three months or the length of time from the date the breach was committed until the end of the order, **whichever is shorter;**
- impose a further period of supervision of up to three months or the length of time from the date the breach was committed until the end of the order, **whichever is shorter;**
- impose a fine of up to £1,000; or
- take no action.

Even if the offender has attained the age of 18 proceedings for breach of the supervision requirements must be dealt with in the youth court.

Commission of further offences during a DTO [35]

7.22 If a child or young person is found guilty of a further imprisonable offence committed during the currency of the order then the court can impose a further period of detention. This period of detention cannot exceed the period between the date of the new offence and the date of when the original order would have expired.

7.23 This period can be served consecutively or concurrently with any sentence imposed for the new offence and this period should not be taken into account when determining the appropriate length of the sentence for the new offence.

SG8-11

Sexual Offences Guideline [36]

Sentencing a child or young person for sexual offences involves a number of different considerations from adults. The primary difference is the age and level of maturity. Children and young people are less emotionally developed than adults; offending can arise through inappropriate sexual experimentation; gang or peer group pressure to engage in sexual activity; or a lack of understanding regarding consent, exploitation, coercion and appropriate sexual behaviour.

Below is a non-exhaustive list of factors that illustrate the type of background factors that may have played a part in leading a child or young person to commit an offence of this kind.

- Victim of neglect or abuse (sexual, physical or emotional) or has witnessed the neglect or abuse of another.
- Exposure to pornography or materials which are age inappropriate.
- Involvement in gangs.
- Associated with child sexual exploitation.
- Unstable living or educational arrangements.
- Communication or learning disabilities or mental health concerns.
- Part of a peer group, school or neighbourhood where harmful sexual norms and attitudes go unchallenged.
- A trigger event such as the death of a close relative or a family breakdown.

This guideline should be read alongside the Overarching Principles – Sentencing Children and Young People definitive guideline which provides comprehensive guidance on the sentencing principles and welfare considerations that the court should have in mind when sentencing children and young people.

The first step in determining the sentence is to assess the seriousness of the offence. This assessment is made by considering the nature of the offence and any aggravating and mitigating factors relating to the offence itself. **The fact that a sentence threshold is crossed does not necessarily mean that that sentence should be imposed.**

STEP ONE Offence Seriousness – Nature of the offence [37]

The boxes below give **examples** of the type of culpability and harm factors that may indicate that a particular threshold of sentence has been crossed.

A non-custodial sentence* may be the most suitable disposal where one or more of the following factors apply:
Any form of non-penetrative sexual activity
Any form of sexual activity (including penetration) without coercion, exploitation or pressure except where there is a significant disparity in age or maturity
Minimal psychological or physical harm caused to the victim

A custodial sentence or youth rehabilitation order with intensive supervision and surveillance* or fostering* may be justified where one or more of the following factors apply:
Any penetrative activity involving coercion, exploitation or pressure
Use or threats of violence against the victim or someone known to the victim
Prolonged detention/sustained incident
Severe psychological or physical harm caused to the victim

* Where the child or young person appears in the magistrates' court, and the conditions for a compulsory referral order apply, a referral order must be imposed unless the court is considering imposing a discharge, hospital order or custody.

STEP TWO Offence Seriousness – Aggravating and mitigating factors [38]

To complete the assessment of seriousness the court should consider the aggravating and mitigating factors relevant to the offence.

[38]

Aggravating factors
Statutory aggravating factors:
Previous findings of guilt, having regard to a) the **nature** of the offence to which the finding of guilt relates and its relevance to the current offence; and b) the time that has elapsed since the finding of guilt
Offence committed whilst on bail
Offence motivated by, or demonstrating hostility based on any of the following characteristics or presumed characteristics of the victim: religion, race, disability, sexual orientation or transgender identity
Other aggravating factors (non-exhaustive):
Significant degree of planning
Child or young person acts together with others to commit the offence
Use of alcohol/drugs on victim to facilitate the offence
Abuse of trust
Deliberate humiliation of victim, including but not limited to filming of the offence, deliberately committing the offence before a group of peers with the intention of causing additional distress or circulating details/photos/videos etc of the offence on social media or within peer groups
Grooming
Significant disparity of age between the child or young person and the victim (measured chronologically or with reference to level of maturity) (where not taken into account at step one)
Victim is particularly vulnerable due to factors including but not limited to age, mental or physical disability
Any steps taken to prevent reporting the incident/seeking assistance
Pregnancy or STI as a consequence of offence
Blackmail
Use of weapon
Mitigating factors (non-exhaustive)
No previous findings of guilt **or** no relevant/recent findings of guilt
Good character and/or exemplary conduct
Participated in offence due to bullying, peer pressure, coercion or manipulation
Genuine belief that activity was lawful

[39] **STEP THREE Personal mitigation**

Having assessed the offence seriousness, the court should then consider the mitigation personal to the child or young person to determine whether a custodial sentence or a community sentence is necessary. The effect of personal mitigation may reduce what would otherwise be a custodial sentence to a non-custodial one, or a community sentence to a different means of disposal.

Personal mitigating factors (non-exhaustive)
Particularly young or immature child or young person (where it affects their responsibility)
Communication or learning disabilities or mental health concerns
Unstable upbringing including but not limited to:-
• time spent looked after
• lack of familial presence or support
• disrupted experiences in accommodation or education
• exposure to drug/alcohol abuse, familial criminal behaviour or domestic abuse
• exposure by others to pornography or sexually explicit materials

• victim of neglect or abuse, or exposure to neglect or abuse of others [39]
• experiences of trauma or loss
Determination and/or demonstration of steps taken to address offending behaviour
Strong prospect of rehabilitation
Child or young person in education, training or employment

STEP FOUR Reduction for guilty plea

The court should take account of any potential reduction for a guilty plea in accordance with section 144 of the Criminal Justice Act 2003 and part one, section five of the *Overarching Principles – Sentencing Children and Young People* definitive guideline.

The reduction in sentence for a guilty plea can be taken into account by imposing one type of sentence rather than another; for example:

- by reducing a custodial sentence to a community sentence; or
- by reducing a community sentence to a different means of disposal.

Alternatively the court could reduce the length or severity of any punitive requirements attached to a community sentence.

See the *Overarching Principles – Sentencing Children and Young People* definitive guideline for details of other available sentences including Referral Orders and Reparation Orders.

STEP FIVE Review the sentence [40]

The court must now review the sentence to ensure it is the most appropriate one for the child or young person. This will include an assessment of the likelihood of reoffending and the risk of causing serious harm. A report from the Youth Offending Team may assist.

See the *Overarching Principles – Sentencing Children and Young People* definitive guideline for comprehensive guidance on the sentencing principles and welfare considerations that the court should have in mind when sentencing children and young people, and for the full range of the sentences available to the court.

Referral Orders

In cases where children or young people have offended for the first time and have pleaded guilty to committing an offence which is on the cusp of the custody threshold, YOTs should be encouraged to convene a Youth Offender Panel prior to sentence (sometimes referred to as a 'pseudo-panel' or 'pre-panel') where the child or young person is asked to attend before a panel and agree an intensive contract. If that contract is placed before the sentencing youth court, the court can then decide whether it is sufficient to move below custody on this occasion. The proposed contract is not something the court can alter in any way; the court will still have to make a decision between referral order and custody but can do so on the basis that if it makes a referral order it can have confidence in what that will entail in the particular case.

The court determines the length of the order but a Referral Order Panel determines the requirements of the order.

Offence seriousness	**Suggested length of referral order**
Low	• 3–5 months
Medium	• 5–7 months
High	• 7–9 months
Very high	• 10–12 months

The YOT may propose certain requirements and the length of these requirements may not correspond to the above table; if the court feels these requirements will best achieve the aims of the youth justice system then they may still be imposed.

Youth Rehabilitation Order (YRO)

The following table sets out the different levels of intensity that are available under a Youth Rehabilitation Order. The level of intensity and the content of the order will depend upon the court's assessment of seriousness.

Requirements of order		
[40] **Standard**	Low likelihood of re-offending **and** a low risk of serious harm	Primarily seek to repair harm caused through, for example: • reparation; • unpaid work; • supervision; and/or • attendance centre.
[41] **Enhanced**	Medium likelihood of re-offending **or** a medium risk of serious harm	Seek to repair harm caused and to enable help or change through, for example: • supervision; • reparation; • requirement to address behaviour e.g. drug treatment, offending behaviour programme, education programme; and/or • a combination of the above.
Intensive	High likelihood of re-offending **or** a very high risk of serious harm	Seek to ensure the control of and enable help or change for the child or young person through, for example: • supervision; • reparation; • requirement to address behaviour; • requirement to monitor or restrict movement, e.g. prohibited activity, curfew, exclusion or electronic monitoring; and/or • a combination of the above.

YRO with Intensive Supervision and Surveillance (ISS) or YRO with Fostering

A YRO with an ISS or fostering requirement can only be imposed where the court is of the opinion that the offence has crossed the custody threshold and custody is merited.

The YRO with ISS includes an extended activity requirement, a supervision requirement and curfew. The YRO with fostering requires the child or young person to reside with a local authority foster parent for a specified period of up to 12 months.

Custodial Sentences

If a custodial sentence is imposed, the court must state its reasons for being satisfied that the offence is so serious that no other sanction would be appropriate and, in particular, why a YRO with ISS or fostering could not be justified.

Where a custodial sentence is **unavoidable** the length of custody imposed must be the shortest commensurate with the seriousness of the offence. The court may want to consider the equivalent adult guideline in order to determine the appropriate length of the sentence.

If considering the adult guideline, the court may feel it appropriate to apply a sentence broadly within the region of half to two thirds of the appropriate adult sentence for those aged 15–17 and allow a greater reduction for those aged under 15. This is only a rough guide and must not be applied mechanistically. The individual factors relating to the offence and the child or young person are of the greatest importance and may present good reason to impose a sentence outside of this range.

[42] Robbery Guideline SG8-12

This guideline should be read alongside the *Overarching Principles – Sentencing Children and Young People* definitive guideline which provides comprehensive guidance on the sentencing principles and welfare considerations that the court should have in mind when sentencing children and young people.

The first step in determining the sentence is to assess the seriousness of the offence. This assessment is made by considering the nature of the offence and any aggravating and mitigating factors relating to the offence itself. **The fact that a sentence threshold is crossed does not necessarily mean that that sentence should be imposed.**

STEP ONE Offence Seriousness – Nature of the offence

The boxes below give **examples** of the type of culpability and harm factors that may indicate that a particular threshold of sentence has been crossed.

A non-custodial sentence* may be the most suitable disposal where one or more of the following factors apply:
Threat or use of minimal force
Little or no physical or psychological harm caused to the victim
Involved through coercion, intimidation or exploitation

[42]

A custodial sentence or youth rehabilitation order with intensive supervision and surveillance* or fostering* may be justified where one or more of the following factors apply:
Use of very significant force
Threat or use of a bladed article, firearm or imitation firearm (where produced)
Significant physical or psychological harm caused to the victim

* Where the child or young person appears in the magistrates' court, and the conditions for a compulsory referral order apply, a referral order must be imposed unless the court is considering imposing a discharge, hospital order or custody.

STEP TWO Offence Seriousness – Aggravating and mitigating factors [43]

To complete the assessment of seriousness the court should consider the aggravating and mitigating factors relevant to the offence.

Aggravating factors
Statutory aggravating factors:
Previous findings of guilt, having regard to a) the **nature** of the offence to which the finding of guilt relates and its **relevance** to the current offence; and b) the **time** that has elapsed since the finding of guilt
Offence committed whilst on bail
Offence motivated by, or demonstrating hostility based on any of the following characteristics or presumed characteristics of the victim: religion, race, disability, sexual orientation or transgender identity
Other aggravating factors (non-exhaustive):
Significant degree of planning
Deliberate humiliation of victim, including but not limited to filming of the offence, deliberately committing the offence before a group of peers with the intention of causing additional distress or circulating details/photos/videos etc of the offence on social media or within peer groups
Threat or use of a weapon other than a bladed article, firearm or imitation firearm (whether produced or not)
Threat to use a bladed article, firearm or imitation firearm (not produced)
Victim is particularly vulnerable due to factors including but not limited to age, mental or physical disability
A leading role where offending is part of a group
Attempt to conceal identity (for example, wearing a balaclava or hood)
Any steps taken to prevent reporting the incident/seeking assistance
High value goods or sums targeted or obtained (includes economic, personal or sentimental)
Restraint, detention or additional degradation of the victim
Mitigating factors (non-exhaustive)
No previous findings of guilt or no relevant/recent findings of guilt
Good character and/or exemplary conduct
Participated in offence due to bullying, peer pressure, coercion or manipulation
Remorse, particularly where evidenced by voluntary reparation to the victim
Little or no planning

[44] **STEP THREE Personal mitigation**

Having assessed the offence seriousness, the court should then consider the mitigation personal to the child or young person to determine whether a custodial sentence or a community sentence is necessary. The effect of personal mitigation may reduce what would otherwise be a custodial sentence to a non-custodial one, or a community sentence to a different means of disposal.

Personal mitigating factors (non-exhaustive)
Particularly young or immature child or young person (where it affects their responsibility)
Communication or learning disabilities or mental health concerns
Unstable upbringing including but not limited to:
• time spent looked after
• lack of familial presence or support
• disrupted experiences in accommodation or education
• exposure to drug/alcohol abuse, familial criminal behaviour or domestic abuse
• victim of neglect or abuse, or exposure to neglect or abuse of others
• experiences of trauma or loss
Determination and/or demonstration of steps taken to address offending behaviour
Child or young person in education, training or employment

STEP FOUR Reduction for guilty plea

The court should take account of any potential reduction for a guilty plea in accordance with section 144 of the Criminal Justice Act 2003 and part one, section five of the *Overarching Principles – Sentencing Children and Young People* definitive guideline.

The reduction in sentence for a guilty plea can be taken into account by imposing one type of sentence rather than another; for example:

- by reducing a custodial sentence to a community sentence; or
- by reducing a community sentence to a different means of disposal.

Alternatively the court could reduce the length or severity of any punitive requirements attached to a community sentence.

See the *Overarching Principles – Sentencing Children and Young People* definitive guideline for details of other available sentences including Referral Orders and Reparation Orders.

[45] **STEP FIVE Review the sentence**

The court must now review the sentence to ensure it is the most appropriate one for the child or young person. This will include an assessment of the likelihood of reoffending and the risk of causing serious harm. A report from the Youth Offending Team may assist.

See the *Overarching Principles – Sentencing Children and Young People* definitive guideline for comprehensive guidance on the sentencing principles and welfare considerations that the court should have in mind when sentencing children and young people, and for the full range of the sentences available to the court.

Referral Orders

In cases where children or young people have offended for the first time and have pleaded guilty to committing an offence which is on the cusp of the custody threshold, YOTs should be encouraged to convene a Youth Offender Panel prior to sentence (sometimes referred to as a 'pseudo-panel' or 'pre-panel') where the child or young person is asked to attend before a panel and agree an intensive contract. If that contract is placed before the sentencing youth court, the court can then decide whether it is sufficient to move below custody on this occasion. The proposed contract is not something the court can alter in any way; the court will still have to make a decision between referral order and custody but can do so on the basis that if it makes a referral order it can have confidence in what that will entail in the particular case. The court determines the length of the order but a Referral Order Panel determines the requirements of the order.

[45]

Offence seriousness	Suggested length of referral order
Low	• 3–5 months
Medium	• 5–7 months
High	• 7–9 months
Very high	• 10–12 months

The YOT may propose certain requirements and the length of these requirements may not correspond to the above table; if the court feels these requirements will best achieve the aims of the youth justice system then they may still be imposed.

Youth Rehabilitation Order (YRO)

The following table sets out the different levels of intensity that are available under a YRO. The level of intensity and the content of the order will depend upon the court's assessment of seriousness.

Requirements of order		
Standard	Low likelihood of re-offending and a low risk of serious harm	Primarily seek to repair harm caused through, for example: • reparation; • unpaid work; • supervision; and/or • attendance centre.
Enhanced	Medium likelihood of re-offending **or** a medium risk of serious harm	Seek to repair harm caused and to enable help or change through, for example: supervision; reparation; requirement to address behaviour e.g. drug treatment, offending behaviour programme, education programme; and/or a combination of the above.
Intensive	High likelihood of re-offending **or** a very high risk of serious harm	Seek to ensure the control of and enable help or change for the child or young person through, for example: supervision; reparation; requirement to address behaviour; requirement to monitor or restrict movement, e.g. prohibited activity, curfew, exclusion or electronic monitoring; and/or a combination of the above.

[46]

YRO with Intensive Supervision and Surveillance (ISS) or YRO with fostering

A YRO with an ISS or fostering requirement can only be imposed where the court is of the opinion that the offence has crossed the custody threshold, and custody is merited.

The YRO with ISS includes an extended activity requirement, a supervision requirement and curfew.

The YRO with fostering requires the child or young person to reside with a local authority foster parent for a specified period of up to 12 months.

Custodial Sentences

If a custodial sentence is imposed, the court must state its reasons for being satisfied that the offence is so serious that no other sanction would be appropriate and, in particular, why a YRO with ISS or fostering could not be justified.

Where a custodial sentence is **unavoidable** the length of custody imposed must be the shortest commensurate with the seriousness of the offence. The court may want to consider the equivalent adult guideline in order to determine the appropriate length of the sentence.

If considering the adult guideline, the court may feel it appropriate to apply a sentence broadly within the region of half to two thirds of the appropriate adult sentence for those aged 15–17 and allow a greater reduction for those aged under 15. This is only a rough guide and must not be applied mechanistically. The individual factors relating to the offence and the child or young person are of the greatest importance and may present good reason to impose a sentence outside of this range.

PART 9 IMPOSITION OF COMMUNITY AND CUSTODIAL SENTENCES

Definitive Guideline SG9-1

[2] **Applicability of Guideline**

In accordance with section 120 of the Coroners and Justice Act 2009, the Sentencing Council issues this definitive guideline. It applies to all offenders aged 18 and older, who are sentenced on or after 1 February 2017, regardless of the date of the offence (subject to requirement(s) being applicable).

Section 125(1) of the Coroners and Justice Act 2009 provides that when sentencing offences committed after 6 April 2010:

Every court—
(a) must, in sentencing an offender, follow any sentencing guidelines which are relevant to the offender's case, and
(b) must, in exercising any other function relating to the sentencing of offenders, follow any sentencing guidelines which are relevant to the exercise of the function,
unless the court is satisfied that it would be contrary to the interests of justice to do so.

This guideline applies only to offenders aged 18 and older. General principles to be considered in the sentencing of youths are in the Sentencing Guidelines Council's definitive guideline, *Sentencing Children and Young People: Overarching Principles* [see SG8-1].

[3] Imposition of Community Orders SG9-2

General Principles SG9-3

Community orders can fulfil all of the purposes of sentencing. In particular, they can have the effect of restricting the offender's liberty while providing punishment in the community, rehabilitation for the offender, and/or ensuring that the offender engages in reparative activities.

A community order must not be imposed unless the offence is 'serious enough to warrant such a sentence'.[98] Where an offender is being sentenced for a non-imprisonable offence, there is no power to make a community order.[99]

Sentencers must consider all available disposals at the time of sentence; even where the threshold for a community sentence has been passed, a fine or discharge may be an appropriate penalty. In particular, a Band D fine may be an appropriate alternative to a community order.

The court must ensure that the restriction on the offender's liberty is commensurate with the seriousness of the offence[100] and that the requirements imposed are the most suitable for the offender.[101]

Sentences should not necessarily escalate from one community order range to the next on each sentencing occasion. The decision as to the appropriate range of community order should be based upon the seriousness of the new offence(s) (which will take into account any previous convictions).

Save in exceptional circumstances at least one requirement must be imposed for the purpose of punishment and/or a fine imposed in addition to the community order.[102] It is a matter for the court to decide which requirements amount to a punishment in each case.

[4] **Community Order Levels** SG9-4

The seriousness of the offence should be the initial factor in determining which requirements to include in a community order. Offence-specific guidelines refer to three sentencing levels within the community order band based on offence seriousness (low, medium and high).

The culpability and harm present in the offence(s) should be considered to identify which of the three sentencing levels within the community order band (low, medium and high) is appropriate.

See below for **non-exhaustive** examples of requirements that might be appropriate in each.

98 s.148(1) Criminal Justice Act 2003
99 s.150A Criminal Justice Act 2003 nb: s.151(2) conferring powers in other circumstances is NOT in force
100 s.148(2)(b) ibid
101 s.148(2)(a) ibid
102 s.177(2A) and (2B) ibid

At least one requirement **MUST** be imposed for the purpose of punishment and/or a fine imposed in addition to the community order unless there are exceptional circumstances which relate to the offence or the offender that would make it unjust in all the circumstances to do so.[103] [4]

A full list of requirements, including those aimed at offender rehabilitation, is available below.

Low	Medium	High
Offences only just cross community order threshold, where the seriousness of the offence or the nature of the offender's record means that a discharge or fine is inappropriate	Offences that obviously fall within the community order band	Offences only just fall below the custody threshold or the custody threshold is crossed but a community order is more appropriate
In general, only one requirement will be appropriate and the length may be curtailed if additional requirements are necessary		More intensive sentences which combine two or more requirements may be appropriate
Suitable requirements might include: • Any appropriate rehabilitative requirement(s) • 40–80 hours of unpaid work • Curfew requirement within the lowest range (for example up to 16 hours per day for a few weeks) • Exclusion requirement, for a few months • Prohibited activity requirement • Attendance centre requirement (where available)	Suitable requirements might include: • Any appropriate rehabilitative requirement(s) • Greater number of hours of unpaid work (for example 80–150 hours) • Curfew requirement within the middle range (for example up to 16 hours for 2–3 months) • Exclusion requirement lasting in the region of 6 months • Prohibited activity requirement	Suitable requirements might include: • Any appropriate rehabilitative requirement(s) • 150–300 hours of unpaid work • Curfew requirement within the middle range (for example up to 16 hours for 2–3 months) • Exclusion order lasting in the region of 12 months
* If order does not contain a punitive requirement, suggested fine levels are indicated below:		
BAND A FINE	BAND B FINE	BAND C FINE

SG9-5 Specific considerations in determining requirements [5]

i) Where two or more requirements are included, they must be compatible with one another and must not be excessive.
ii) Any requirement must not conflict with an offender's religious beliefs or with the requirements of any other order to which they may be subject. Interference with an offender's attendance at work or educational establishment should also be avoided.
iii) The particular requirements imposed must be suitable for the individual offender and will be influenced by a range of factors, including:
   - the stated purpose(s) of the sentence;
   - the risk of re-offending;
   - the ability of the offender to comply;
   - the availability of the requirements in the local area.

SG9-6 Requirements

Community orders consist of one or more of the following requirements:

- **unpaid work requirement** (40–300 hours to be completed within 12 months)
- **rehabilitation activity requirement** (RAR's provide flexibility for responsible officers in managing an offender's rehabilitation post sentence. The court does not prescribe the activities to be included but will specify the maximum number of activity days the offender must complete. The responsible officer will decide the activities to be undertaken. Where appropriate this requirement should be made in addition to, and not in place of, other requirements. Sentencers should ensure the activity length of a RAR is suitable and proportionate).

[103] s.177 (2A) and (2B) Criminal Justice Act 2003

[5]
- **programme requirement** (specify the number of days)
- **prohibited activity requirement** (must consult National Probation Service)
- **curfew requirement** (2–16 hours in any 24 hours; maximum term 12 months; must consider those likely to be affected; see note on electronic monitoring below)
- **exclusion requirement** (from a specified place/places; maximum period 2 years: may be continuous or only during specified periods; see note on electronic monitoring below)
- **residence requirement** (to reside at a place specified or as directed by the responsible officer)
- **foreign travel prohibition requirement** (not to exceed 12 months)
- **mental health treatment requirement** (may be residential/non-residential; must be by/under the direction of a registered medical practitioner or chartered psychologist. The court must be satisfied: (a) that the mental condition of the offender is such as requires and may be susceptible to treatment but is not such as to warrant the making of a hospital or guardianship order; (b) that arrangements for treatment have been made; (c) that the offender has expressed willingness to comply).
- **drug rehabilitation requirement** (the court must be satisfied that the offender is dependent on or has a propensity to misuse drugs which requires or is susceptible to treatment. The offender must consent to the order. Treatment can be residential or non-residential, and reviews must be attended by the offender (subject to application for amendment) at intervals of not less than a month (discretionary on requirements of up to 12 months, mandatory on requirements of over 12 months))
- **alcohol treatment requirement** (residential or non-residential; must have offender's consent; court must be satisfied that the offender is dependent on alcohol and that the dependency is susceptible to treatment)
- **alcohol abstinence and monitoring requirement** (where available)
- **attendance centre requirement** (12–36 hours. Only available for offenders under 25).

[6] **Pre-sentence reports** SG9-7

In many cases, a pre-sentence report will be pivotal in helping the court decide whether to impose a community order and, if so, whether particular requirements or combinations of requirements are suitable for an individual offender. Whenever the court reaches the provisional view that a community order may be appropriate, it should request a pre-sentence report (whether written or verbal) unless the court is of the opinion that a report is unnecessary in all the circumstances of the case. It may be helpful to indicate to the National Probation Service the court's preliminary opinion as to which of the three sentencing ranges is relevant and the purpose(s) of sentencing that the package of requirements is expected to fulfil. Ideally a pre-sentence report should be completed on the same day to avoid adjourning the case. If an adjournment cannot be avoided, the information should be provided to the National Probation Service in written form and a copy retained on the court file for the benefit of the sentencing court. **However, the court must make clear to the offender that all sentencing options remain open including, in appropriate cases, committal for sentence to the Crown Court.**

Electronic monitoring SG9-8

The court must impose an electronic monitoring requirement where it makes a community order with a curfew or exclusion requirement save where:[104]

- there is a person (other than the offender) without whose co-operation it will not be practicable to secure the monitoring and that person does not consent;[105] and/or
- electronic monitoring is unavailable and/or impractical;[106] and/or
- in the particular circumstances of the case, it considers it inappropriate to do so.[107]

The court may impose electronic monitoring in all other cases. Electronic monitoring should be used with the primary purpose of promoting and monitoring compliance with other requirements, in circumstances where the punishment of the offender and/or the need to safeguard the public and prevent re-offending are the most important concerns.

104 s.177(3) Criminal Justice Act 2003
105 s.215(2) ibid
106 s.218(4) ibid
107 s.177(3)(b) ibid

SG9-9

Imposition of Custodial Sentences [7]

The approach to the imposition of a custodial sentence should be as follows:

1) Has the custody threshold been passed?

- A custodial sentence must not be imposed unless the offence or the combination of the offence and one or more offences associated with it was so serious that neither a fine alone nor a community sentence can be justified for the offence.
- There is no general definition of where the custody threshold lies. The circumstances of the individual offence and the factors assessed by offence-specific guidelines will determine whether an offence is so serious that neither a fine alone nor a community sentence can be justified. Where no offence specific guideline is available to determine seriousness, the harm caused by the offence, the culpability of the offender and any previous convictions will be relevant to the assessment.
- The clear intention of the threshold test is to reserve prison as a punishment for the most serious offences.

2) Is it unavoidable that a sentence of imprisonment be imposed?

- Passing the custody threshold does not mean that a custodial sentence should be deemed inevitable. Custody should not be imposed where a community order could provide sufficient restriction on an offender's liberty (by way of punishment) while addressing the rehabilitation of the offender to prevent future crime.
- For offenders on the cusp of custody, imprisonment should not be imposed where there would be an impact on dependants which would make a custodial sentence disproportionate to achieving the aims of sentencing.

3) What is the shortest term commensurate with the seriousness of the offence?

- In considering this the court must NOT consider any licence or post sentence supervision requirements which may subsequently be imposed upon the offender's release.

4) Can the sentence be suspended?

- A suspended sentence MUST NOT be imposed as a more severe form of community order. **A suspended sentence is a custodial sentence. Sentencers should be clear that they would impose an immediate custodial sentence if the power to suspend were not available.** If not, a non-custodial sentence should be imposed.

The following factors should be weighed in considering whether it is possible to suspend the sentence: [8]

Factors indicating that it would not be appropriate to suspend a custodial sentence	Factors indicating that it may be appropriate to suspend a custodial sentence
Offender presents a risk/danger to the public	Realistic prospect of rehabilitation
Appropriate punishment can only be achieved by immediate custody	Strong personal mitigation
History of poor compliance with court orders	Immediate custody will result in significant harmful impact upon others

The imposition of a custodial sentence is both punishment and a deterrent. To ensure that the overall terms of the suspended sentence are commensurate with offence seriousness, care must be taken to ensure requirements imposed are not excessive. A court wishing to impose onerous or intensive requirements should reconsider whether a community sentence might be more appropriate.

SG9-10 **Pre-sentence report**

Whenever the court reaches the provisional view that:

- the custody threshold has been passed; and, if so
- the length of imprisonment which represents the shortest term commensurate with the seriousness of the offence;

the court should obtain a pre-sentence report, whether verbal or written, unless the court considers a report to be unnecessary. Ideally a pre-sentence report should be completed on the same day to avoid adjourning the case.

Magistrates: Consult your legal adviser before deciding to sentence to custody without a pre-sentence report.

SG9-11

Suspended Sentences: General Guidance [9]

i) The guidance regarding pre-sentence reports applies if suspending custody.
ii) If the court imposes a term of imprisonment of between 14 days and 2 years (subject to magistrates' courts sentencing powers), it may suspend the sentence for between 6 months and 2 years (the

[9] 'operational period'). The time for which a sentence is suspended should reflect the length of the sentence; up to 12 months might normally be appropriate for a suspended sentence of up to 6 months.

iii) Where the court imposes two or more sentences to be served consecutively, the court may suspend the sentence where the aggregate of the terms is between 14 days and 2 years (subject to magistrates' courts sentencing powers).

iv) When the court suspends a sentence, it may impose one or more requirements for the offender to undertake in the community. The requirements are identical to those available for community orders above.

v) A custodial sentence that is suspended should be for the same term that would have applied if the sentence was to be served immediately.

[10] ## Sentencing Decision Flowchart SG9-12

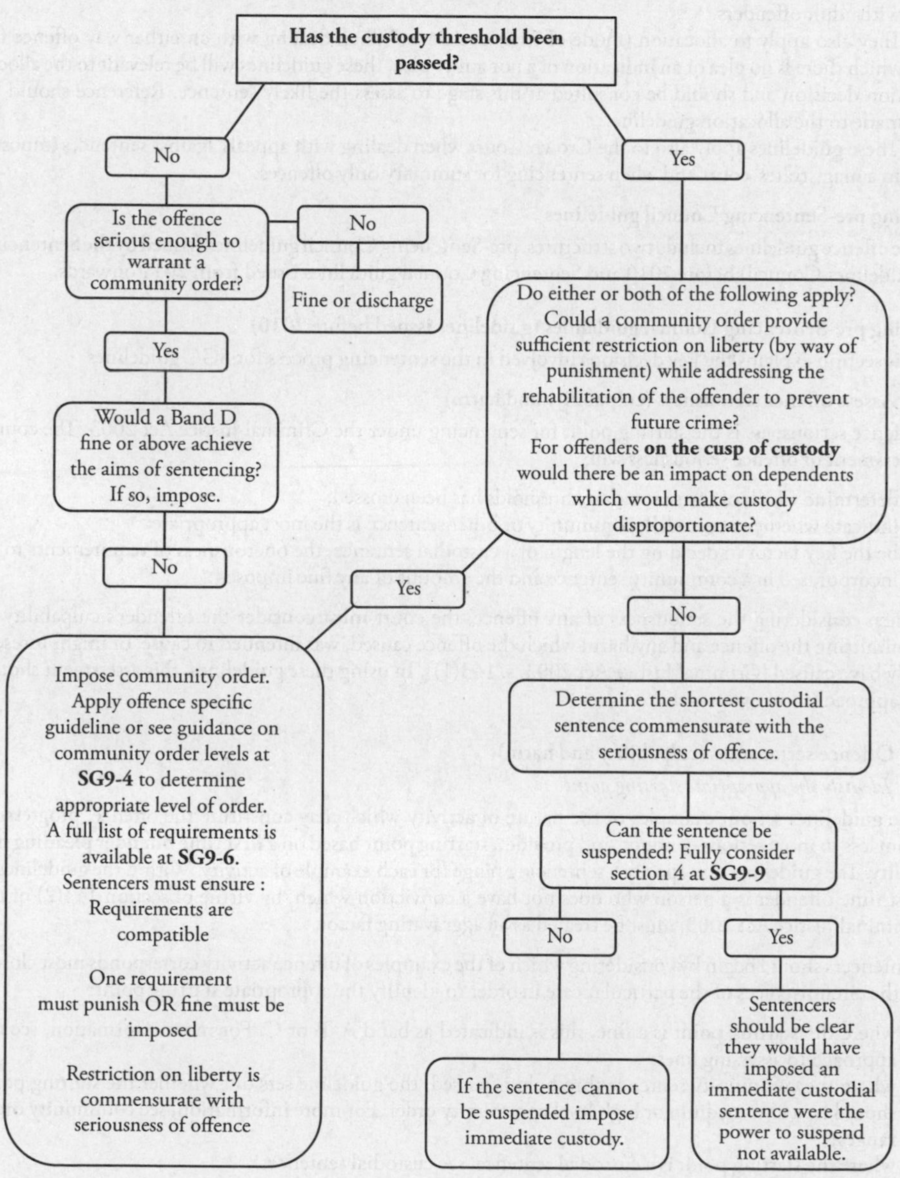
SENTENCING
Has the custody threshold been passed?
No
Yes
Is the offence serious enough to warrant a community order?
No
Fine or discharge
Yes
Would a Band D fine or above achieve the aims of sentencing? If so, impose.
No
Impose community order. Apply offence specific guideline or see guidance on community order levels at SG9-4 to determine appropriate level of order. A full list of requirements is available at SG9-6.
Sentencers must ensure :
Requirements are compatible
One requirement must punish OR fine must be imposed
Restriction on liberty is commensurate with seriousness of offence
Do either or both of the following apply? Could a community order provide sufficient restriction on liberty (by way of punishment) while addressing the rehabilitation of the offender to prevent future crime? For offenders on the cusp of custody would there be an impact on dependents which would make custody disproportionate?
Yes
No
Determine the shortest custodial sentence commensurate with the seriousness of offence.
Can the sentence be suspended? Fully consider section 4 at SG9-9
No
Yes
If the sentence cannot be suspended impose immediate custody.
Sentencers should be clear they would have imposed an immediate custodial sentence were the power to suspend not available.

PART 10 MAGISTRATES' COURT SENTENCING GUIDELINES

SG10-1 **Following these guidelines** [13]

When sentencing offences committed after 6 April 2010, every court is under a statutory obligation to follow any relevant Sentencing Council guideline unless it would be contrary to the interests of justice to do so (Coroners and Justice Act 2009, s.125(1)). If a court imposes a sentence outside the range indicated in an offence specific guideline, it is obliged to state its reasons for doing so (Criminal Justice Act 2003, s.174(2)(a)).

SG10-2 **When to use these guidelines**

- These guidelines apply to sentencing in a magistrates' court whatever the composition of the court. They cover offences for which sentences are frequently imposed in a magistrates' court when dealing with adult offenders.
- They also apply to allocation (mode of trial) decisions. When dealing with an either way offence for which there is no plea or an indication of a not guilty plea, these guidelines will be relevant to the allocation decision and should be consulted at this stage to assess the likely sentence. Reference should be made to the allocation guideline.
- These guidelines apply also to the Crown Court when dealing with appeals against sentences imposed in a magistrates' court and when sentencing for summary only offences.

SG10-3 **Using pre-Sentencing Council guidelines** [14]

The offence guidelines include two structures: pre-Sentencing Council guidelines (issued by the Sentencing Guidelines Council) before 2010 and Sentencing Council guidelines issued from 2011 onwards.

SG10-4 **Using pre-Sentencing Council guidelines (guidelines issued before 2010)**

This section explains the key decisions involved in the sentencing process for SGC guidelines.

SG10-5 **1. Assess offence seriousness (culpability and harm)**

Offence seriousness is the starting point for sentencing under the Criminal Justice Act 2003. The court's assessment of offence seriousness will:

- determine which of the sentencing thresholds has been crossed;
- indicate whether a custodial, community or other sentence is the most appropriate;
- be the key factor in deciding the length of a custodial sentence, the onerousness of requirements to be incorporated in a community sentence and the amount of any fine imposed.

When considering the seriousness of any offence, the court must consider the offender's culpability in committing the offence and any harm which the offence caused, was intended to cause, or might foreseeably have caused (Criminal Justice Act 2003, s. 143(1)). In using these guidelines, this assessment should be approached in two stages.

SG10-6 **2. Offence seriousness (culpability and harm)**

A. Identify the appropriate starting point

The guidelines set out examples of the nature of activity which may constitute the offence, progressing from less to more serious conduct, and provide a starting point based on a **first time offender pleading not guilty**. The guidelines also specify a sentencing range for each example of activity. Within the guidelines, a first time offender is a person who does not have a conviction which, by virtue of section 143(2) of the Criminal Justice Act 2003, must be treated as an aggravating factor.

Sentencers should begin by considering which of the examples of offence activity corresponds most closely to the circumstances of the particular case in order to identify the appropriate starting point:

- where the starting point is a fine, this is indicated as band A, B or C. For more information, see the approach to assessing fines;
- where the community sentence threshold is passed, the guideline sets out whether the starting point should be a low, medium or high level community order. For more information, see community order ranges; [15]
- where the starting point is a custodial sentence, see custodial sentences.

The Council's definitive guideline *Overarching Principles: Seriousness*, published 16 December 2004, identifies four levels of culpability for sentencing purposes (intention, recklessness, knowledge

[15] and negligence). The starting points in the individual offence guidelines assume that culpability is at the highest level applicable to the offence (often, but not always, intention). Where a lower level of culpability is present, this should be taken into account.

2. Offence seriousness (culpability and harm) **SG10-7**

B. Consider the effect of aggravating and mitigating factors

Once the starting point has been identified, the court can add to or reduce this to reflect any aggravating or mitigating factors that impact on the culpability of the offender and/or harm caused by the offence to reach a provisional sentence. Any factors contained in the description of the activity used to reach the starting point must not be counted again. The range is the bracket into which the provisional sentence will normally fall after having regard to factors which aggravate or mitigate the seriousness of the offence. However:

- the court is not precluded from going outside the range where the facts justify it;
- previous convictions which aggravate the seriousness of the current offence may take the provisional sentence beyond the range, especially where there are significant other aggravating factors present.

In addition, where an offender is being sentenced for multiple offences, the court's assessment of the totality of the offending may result in a sentence above the range indicated for the individual offences, including a sentence of a different type. See the definitive guideline on *Offences Taken into Consideration and Totality* for more information. The guidelines identify aggravating and mitigating factors which may be particularly relevant to each individual offence. These include some factors drawn from the general list of aggravating and mitigating factors in the Council's definitive guideline (see 'seriousness' link above). In each case, sentencers should have regard to the full list, which includes the factors that, by statute, make an offence more serious:

- offence committed while on bail for other offences;
- offence was racially or religiously aggravated;
- offence was motivated by, or demonstrates, hostility based on the victim's sexual orientation (or presumed sexual orientation);
- offence was motivated by, or demonstrates, hostility based on the victim being (or being presumed to be) transgender;
- [16] offence was motivated by, or demonstrates, hostility based on the victim's disability (or presumed disability);
- offender has previous convictions that the court considers can reasonably be treated as aggravating factors having regard to their relevance to the current offence and the time that has elapsed since conviction.

While the lists in the offence guidelines and other material referenced above, aim to identify the most common aggravating and mitigating factors, they are not intended to be exhaustive. Sentencers should always consider whether there are any other factors that make the offence more or less serious.

3. Form a preliminary view of the appropriate sentence, then consider offender mitigation **SG10-8**

When the court has reached a provisional sentence based on its assessment of offence seriousness, it should take into account matters of offender mitigation. The Council guideline *Overarching Principles: Seriousness* states that the issue of remorse should be taken into account at this point along with other mitigating features such as admissions to the police in interview.

4. Consider a reduction for a guilty plea **SG10-9**

*For cases where the first hearing is **before 1 June 2017***

The Council guideline *Reduction in Sentence for a Guilty Plea*, revised 2007, states that the punitive elements of the sentence should be reduced to recognise an offender's guilty plea. The reduction has no impact on sentencing decisions in relation to ancillary orders, including disqualification. The level of the reduction should reflect the stage at which the offender indicated a willingness to admit guilt and will be gauged on a sliding scale, ranging from a recommended one third (where the guilty plea was entered at the first reasonable opportunity), reducing to a recommended one quarter (where a trial date has been set) and to a recommended one tenth (for a guilty plea entered at the 'door of the court' or after the trial has begun). There is a presumption that the recommended reduction will be given unless there are good reasons for a lower amount. The application of the reduction may affect the type, as well as the severity, of the sentence. It may also take the sentence below the range in some cases. The court must state that it has reduced a sentence to reflect a guilty plea (Criminal Justice Act 2003, s.174(2)(d)). It should usually indicate what the sentence would have been if there had been no reduction as a result of the plea.

For cases where the first hearing is on or after 1 June 2017 [16]
Refer to the new Sentencing Council Reduction in Sentence for a Guilty Plea guideline.

SG10-10 **5. Consider ancillary orders, including compensation** [17]

Ancillary orders of particular relevance to individual offences are identified in the relevant guidelines. The court must always consider making a compensation order where the offending has resulted in personal injury, loss or damage (Powers of Criminal Courts (Sentencing) Act 2000, s. 130(1)). The court is required to give reasons if it decides not to make such an order (Powers of Criminal Courts (Sentencing) Act 2000, s. 130(3)).

SG10-11 **6. Decide sentence Give reasons**

Review the total sentence to ensure that it is proportional to the offending behaviour and properly balanced. Sentencers must state reasons for the sentence passed in every case, including for any ancillary orders imposed (Criminal Justice Act 2003, s. 174(1)). It is particularly important to identify any aggravating or mitigating factors, or matters of offender mitigation, that have resulted in a sentence more or less severe than the suggested starting point. If a court imposes a sentence of a different kind or outside the range indicated in the guidelines, it must state its reasons for doing so (Criminal Justice Act 2003, s. 174(2)(a)). The court should also give its reasons for not making an order that has been canvassed before it or that it might have been expected to make.

Where there is no guideline for an offence, it may assist in determining sentence to consider the starting points and ranges indicated for offences that are of a similar level of seriousness.

SG10-12 **Using Sentencing Council guidelines** [18]

The offence guidelines include two structures: pre-Sentencing Council guidelines (issued by the Sentencing Guidelines Council) before 2010 and Sentencing Council guidelines issued from 2011 onwards.

Using Sentencing Council guidelines (guidelines effective from 2011 onwards)

This section of the user guide explains the key decisions involved in the sentencing process for Sentencing Council guidelines.

SG10-13 **STEP ONE: Determining the offence category**

The decision making process includes a two-step approach to assessing seriousness. The first step is to determine the offence category by means of an assessment of the offender's culpability and the harm caused, or intended, by reference only to the factors set out at step one in each guideline. The contents are tailored for each offence and comprise the principal factual elements of the offence.

SG10-14 **STEP TWO: Starting point and category range**

The guidelines provide a starting point which applies to all offenders irrespective of plea or previous convictions. The guidelines also specify a category range for each offence category. The guidelines provide non-exhaustive lists of aggravating and mitigating factors relating to the context of the offence and to the offender. Sentencers should identify whether any combination of these, or other relevant factors, should result in an upward or downward adjustment from the starting point. In some cases, it may be appropriate to move outside the identified category range when reaching a provisional sentence.

SG10-15 **FURTHER STEPS**

Having reached a provisional sentence, there are a number of further steps within the guidelines. These steps are clearly set out within each guideline and are tailored specifically for each offence in order to ensure that only the most appropriate guidance is included within each offence specific guideline. The further steps include:

- reduction for assistance to the prosecution;
- reduction for guilty pleas (courts should refer to the *Reduction in Sentence for a Guilty Plea* guideline);
- where an offender is being sentenced for multiple offences – the court's assessment of the totality of the offending may result in a sentence above the range indicated for the individual offences, including a sentence of a different type (for more information, refer to the *Offences Taken into Consideration and Totality* guideline);
- compensation orders and/or ancillary orders appropriate to the case; and
- give reasons for, and explain the effect of, the sentence.

Where there is no guideline for an offence, it may assist in determining sentence to consider the starting points and ranges indicated for offences that are of a similar level of seriousness. [19]

SG10-16 **List of aggravating and mitigating factors** [20]

[Not reproduced here: see SG2-4

OFFENCES SG10-17

[21] ## ALCOHOL SALE OFFENCES SG10-18

Licensing Act 2003, s.141 (sale of alcohol to drunk person); s.146 (sale of alcohol to children); s.147 (allowing sale of alcohol to children)

Effective from: 24 April 2017

Triable only summarily
Maximum: Level 3 fine (s. 141); Unlimited fine (ss. 146 and 147)
Offence range: Conditional Discharge–Band C fine

Note

This guideline may also be relevant when sentencing offences under s. 147A of the Licensing Act 2003, persistently selling alcohol to children, which is committed if, on three or more different occasions within a period of three consecutive months, alcohol is unlawfully sold on the same premises to a person under 18. The offence is summary only and the maximum penalty is an unlimited fine. The court should refer to the sentencing approach in this guideline, adjusting the starting points and ranges bearing in mind the increased seriousness of this offence.

[22] **STEP ONE Determining the offence category**

Category 1	Higher culpability **and** greater harm
Category 2	Higher culpability **and** lesser harm **or** lower culpability **and** greater harm
Category 3	Lower culpability **and** lesser harm

The Court should determine the offence category using the table below.

The court should determine the offender's culpability and the harm caused with reference **only** to the factors below.

Where an offence does not fall squarely into a category, individual factors may require a degree of weighting before making an overall assessment and determining the appropriate offence category.

CULPABILITY demonstrated by one or more of the following:

Factors indicating higher culpability
- No attempt made to establish age
- Sale for consumption by group of intoxicated persons
- Sale intended for consumption by a child or young person
- Offender in management position (or equivalent)
- Evidence of failure to police the sale of alcohol

Factors indicating lower culpability
- Offender deceived by false identification
- Evidence of substantial effort to police the sale of alcohol
- Offender acting under direction

HARM demonstrated by one or more of the following:
Factors indicating greater harm
- Supply to younger child/children
- Supply causes or contributes to antisocial behaviour
- Large quantity of alcohol supplied

Factors indicating lesser harm
- All other cases

[23] **STEP TWO Starting point and category range**

Having determined the category at step one, the court should use the starting point to reach a sentence within the appropriate category range in the table below. The starting point applies to all offenders irrespective of plea or previous convictions.

Sentencing Guidelines

Offence Category	Starting Point	Range
Category 1	Band C fine	Band B fine – Band C fine
Category 2	Band B fine	Band A fine – Band C fine
Category 3	Band A fine	Conditional discharge – Band B fine

[23]

Note: refer to fines for **offence committed for 'commercial' purposes**

For band ranges, see **SG10-129**

The court should then consider adjustment for any aggravating or mitigating factors. The following is a **non-exhaustive** list of additional factual elements providing the context of the offence and factors relating to the offender. Identify whether any combination of these, or other relevant factors, should result in an upward or downward adjustment from the sentence arrived at so far.

Factors increasing seriousness

Statutory aggravating factors:

- Previous convictions, having regard to a) the **nature** of the offence to which the conviction relates and its **relevance** to the current offence; and b) the **time** that has elapsed since the conviction
- Offence committed whilst on bail
- Offence motivated by, or demonstrating hostility based on any of the following characteristics or presumed characteristics of the victim: religion, race, disability, sexual orientation or transgender identity

Other aggravating factors:

- Failure to comply with current court orders
- Offence committed on licence or post sentence supervision

Factors reducing seriousness or reflecting personal mitigation

- No previous convictions **or** no relevant/recent convictions
- Offence committed as the result of substantial intimidation

STEP THREE **Consider any factors which indicate a reduction, such as assistance to the prosecution** [24]

The court should take into account sections 73 and 74 of the Serious Organised Crime and Police Act 2005 (assistance by defendants: reduction or review of sentence) and any other rule of law by virtue of which an offender may receive a discounted sentence in consequence of assistance given (or offered) to the prosecutor or investigator.

STEP FOUR **Reduction for guilty pleas**

The court should take account of any potential reduction for a guilty plea in accordance with section 144 of the Criminal Justice Act 2003 and the ***Guilty Plea*** guideline.

STEP FIVE **Totality principle**

If sentencing an offender for more than one offence, or where the offender is already serving a sentence, consider whether the total sentence is just and proportionate to the overall offending behaviour in accordance with the ***Offences Taken into Consideration and Totality*** guideline.

STEP SIX **Compensation and ancillary orders**

In all cases, the court should consider whether to make **compensation** and/or other **ancillary orders** including **deprivation** and/or **forfeiture or suspension of personal liquor licence.**

STEP SEVEN **Reasons**

Section 174 of the Criminal Justice Act 2003 imposes a duty to give reasons for, and explain the effect of, the sentence.

SG10-19 Animal Cruelty [25]

Animal Welfare Act 2006, s.4 (unnecessary suffering), s.8 (fighting etc), s.9 (breach of duty of person responsible for animal to ensure welfare)

Effective from: 24 April 2017
Triable only summarily
Maximum: Unlimited fine and/or 6 months
Offence range: Band A fine–26 weeks' custody

[26] **STEP ONE Determining the offence category**

The court should determine culpability and harm caused with reference **only** to the factors below. Where an offence does not fall squarely into a category, individual factors may require a degree of weighting before making an overall assessment and determining the appropriate offence category.

CULPABILITY demonstrated by one or more of the following:

Factors indicating high culpability

- Deliberate or gratuitous attempt to cause suffering
- Prolonged or deliberate ill treatment or neglect
- Ill treatment in a commercial context
- A leading role in illegal activity

Factors indicating medium culpability

- All cases not falling into high or low culpability

Factors indicating low culpability

- Well intentioned but incompetent care
- Mental disorder or learning disability, where linked to the commission of the offence

HARM demonstrated by one or more of the following:

Factors indicating greater harm

- Death or serious injury/harm to animal
- High level of suffering caused

Factors indicating lesser harm

- All other cases

STEP TWO Starting point and category range

Having determined the category at step one, the court should use the corresponding starting point to reach a sentence within the category range below. The starting point applies to all offenders irrespective of plea or previous convictions.

A case of particular gravity, reflected by multiple features of culpability in step one, could merit upward adjustment from the starting point before further adjustment for aggravating or mitigating features, set out below.

	High culpability	**Medium culpability**	**Low culpability**
Greater harm	**Starting point** 18 weeks' custody	**Starting point** Medium level community order	**Starting point** Band C fine
	Category range 12–26 weeks' custody	**Category range** Low level community order – High level community order	**Category range** Band B fine – Low level community order
Lesser harm	**Starting point** High level community order	**Starting point** Low level community order	**Starting point** Band B fine
	Category range Low level community order – 12 weeks' custody	**Category range** Band C fine – Medium level community order	**Category range** Band A fine – B and C fine

For band ranges, see **SG10-129**

For the imposition of community orders, including the community orders table, see Imposition of Community and Custodial Sentences **SG9-2–SG9-8**

For the imposition of custodial sentences see Imposition of Community and Custodial Sentences **SG9-9–SG9-12**

[27] The court should then consider further adjustment for any aggravating or mitigating factors. The following is a **non-exhaustive** list of additional factual elements providing the context of the offence and factors relating to the offender. Identify whether any combination of these, or other relevant factors, should result in an upward or downward adjustment from the sentence arrived at so far.

Sentencing Guidelines

Factors increasing seriousness [27]

Statutory aggravating factors:

- Previous convictions, having regard to a) the **nature** of the offence to which the conviction relates and its **relevance** to the current offence; and b) the **time** that has elapsed since the conviction
- Offence committed whilst on bail
- Offence motivated by, or demonstrating hostility based on any of the following characteristics or presumed characteristics of the owner/keeper of the animal: religion, race, disability, sexual orientation or transgender identity

Other aggravating factors:

- Distress caused to owner where not responsible for the offence
- Failure to comply with current court orders
- Offence committed on licence or post sentence supervision
- Use of weapon
- Allowing person of insufficient experience or training to have care of animal(s)
- Use of technology to publicise or promote cruelty
- Ignores warning/professional advice/declines to obtain professional advice
- Use of another animal to inflict death or injury
- Offender in position of responsibility
- Animal requires significant intervention to recover
- Animal being used in public service or as an assistance dog

Factors reducing seriousness or reflecting personal mitigation

- No previous convictions **or** no relevant/recent convictions
- Remorse
- Good character and/or exemplary conduct
- Serious medical condition requiring urgent, intensive or long-term treatment
- Age and/or lack of maturity where it affects the responsibility of the offender
- Mental disorder or learning disability, where not linked to the commission of the offence
- Sole or primary carer for dependent relatives
- Offender has been given an inappropriate level of trust or responsibility
- Voluntary surrender of animals to authorities
- Cooperation with the investigation
- Isolated incident

STEP THREE Consider any factors which indicate a reduction, such as assistance to the prosecution [28]

The court should take into account sections 73 and 74 of the Serious Organised Crime and Police Act 2005 (assistance by defendants: reduction or review of sentence) and any other rule of law by virtue of which an offender may receive a discounted sentence in consequence of assistance given (or offered) to the prosecutor or investigator.

STEP FOUR Reduction for guilty pleas

The court should take account of any potential reduction for a guilty plea in accordance with section 144 of the Criminal Justice Act 2003 and the ***Guilty Plea*** guideline.

STEP FIVE Totality principle

If sentencing an offender for more than one offence, or where the offender is already serving a sentence, consider whether the total sentence is just and proportionate to the overall offending behaviour in accordance with the ***Offences Taken into Consideration and Totality*** guideline.

STEP SIX Compensation and ancillary orders

In all cases, the court should consider whether to make **compensation** and/or other **ancillary orders** including **deprivation of ownership** and **disqualification of ownership of animals.**

STEP SEVEN Reasons

Section 174 of the Criminal Justice Act 2003 imposes a duty to give reasons for, and explain the effect of, the sentence.

STEP EIGHT Consideration for time spent on bail

The court must consider whether to give credit for time spent on bail in accordance with section 240A of the Criminal Justice Act 2003.

[30]

ANTI-SOCIAL BEHAVIOUR ORDER, BREACH OF

SG10-20

Factors to take into consideration

This guideline and accompanying notes are taken from the Sentencing Guidelines Council's definitive guideline *Breach of an Anti-Social Behaviour Order*, published 9 December 2008 [see SG17-1].

Key factors

(a) An ASBO may be breached in a very wide range of circumstances and may involve one or more terms not being complied with. The examples given below are intended to illustrate how the scale of the conduct that led to the breach, taken as a whole, might come within the three levels of seriousness:
- No harm caused or intended—in the absence of intimidation or the causing of fear of violence, breaches involving being drunk or begging may be at this level, as may prohibited use of public transport or entry into a prohibited area, where there is no evidence that harassment, alarm or distress was caused or intended.
- Lesser degree of harm intended or likely—examples may include lesser degrees of threats or intimidation, the use of seriously abusive language, or causing more than minor damage to property.
- Serious harm caused or intended—breach at this level of seriousness will involve the use of violence, significant threats or intimidation or the targeting of individuals or groups of people in a manner that leads to a fear of violence.

(b) The suggested starting points are based on the assumption that the offender had the highest level of culpability.

(c) In the most serious cases, involving repeat offending and a breach causing serious harassment together with the presence of several aggravating factors, such as the use of violence, a sentence beyond the highest range will be justified.

(d) When imposing a community order, the court must ensure that the requirements imposed are proportionate to the seriousness of the breach, compatible with each other, and also with the prohibitions of the ASBO if the latter is to remain in force. Even where the threshold for a custodial sentence is crossed, a custodial sentence is not inevitable.

(e) An offender may be sentenced for more than one offence of breach, which occurred on different days. While consecutive sentences may be imposed in such cases, the overall sentence should reflect the totality principle.

[31]

Crime and Disorder Act 1988, s.1(10)

Triable either way
Maximum when tried summarily: Level 5 fine and/or 6 months
Maximum when tried on indictment: 5 years

Note: A conditional discharge is not available as a sentence for this offence

Offence seriousness (culpability and harm)

A. Identify the appropriate starting point

Starting points based on first time offender* pleading not guilty

Examples of nature of activity	Starting point	Range
Breach where no harassment, alarm or distress was caused or intended	**Low level community order**	**Band B fine–medium level community order**
Breach involving a lesser degree of actual or intended harassment, alarm or distress than in the box below, or where such harm would have been likely had the offender not been apprehended	**6 weeks' custody**	**Medium level community order–26 weeks' custody**
Breach involving serious actual or intended harassment, alarm or distress	**26 weeks' custody**	**Custody threshold–Crown Court**

* *For the purposes of this guideline a 'first time offender' is one who does not have a previous conviction for breach of an ASBO*

Offence seriousness (culpability and harm) [31]

B. Consider the effect of aggravating and mitigating factors (other than those within examples above)

Common aggravating and mitigating factors are identified [elsewhere]—the following may be particularly relevant but these lists are not exhaustive.

Factors indicating higher culpability	Factors indicating lower culpability
1. Offender has a history of disobedience to court orders 2. Breach was committed immediately or shortly after the order was made 3. Breach was committed subsequent to earlier breach proceedings arising from the same order 4. Targeting of a person the order was made to protect or a witness in the original proceedings	1. Breach occurred after a long period of compliance 2. The prohibition(s) breached was not fully understood, especially where an interim order was made without notice

[Sets out the standard sequential sentencing procedure.]

SG10-21 ARSON (CRIMINAL DAMAGE BY FIRE) [29]

Criminal Damage Act 1971, s. 1

Triable either way
Maximum when tried summarily: Level 5 fine and/or 6 months
Maximum when tried on indictment: Life

Where offence committed in domestic context, refer [below] for guidance.

Offence seriousness (culpability and harm)

A. Identify the appropriate starting point

Starting points based on first time offender pleading not guilty

Examples of nature of activity	Starting point	Range
Minor damage by fire	High level community order	Medium level community order–12 weeks' custody
Moderate damage by fire	12 weeks' custody	6–26 weeks' custody
Significant damage by fire	Crown Court	Crown Court

Offence seriousness (culpability and harm)

B. Consider the effect of aggravating and mitigating factors (other than those within examples above)

Common aggravating and mitigating factors are identified [elsewhere]—the following may be particularly relevant but these lists are not exhaustive

Factors indicating higher culpability	Factor indicating lower culpability
1. Revenge attack **Factors indicating greater degree of harm** 1. Damage to emergency equipment 2. Damage to public amenity 3. Significant public or private fear caused e.g. in domestic context	1. Damage caused recklessly

[Sets out the standard sequential sentencing procedure.]

[29] ## Assault Occasioning Actual Bodily Harm SG10-22

[Not reproduced here: see SG12-19.]

Assault with Intent to Resist Arrest SG10-23

[Not reproduced here: see SG12-22.]

Assault on a Police Constable in Execution of his Duty SG10-24

[Not reproduced here: see SG12-25.]

[32] ## Bail, Failure to Surrender SG10-25

Factors to take into consideration

This guideline and accompanying notes are taken from the Sentencing Guidelines Council's definitive guideline *Fail to Surrender to Bail*, published 29 November 2007 [see SG16-1]

Key factors

(a) Whilst the approach to sentencing should generally be the same whether the offender failed to surrender to a court or to a police station *and* whether the offence is contrary to ss. 6(1) or 6(2), the court must examine all the relevant circumstances.

(b) The following factors may be relevant when assessing the harm caused by the offence:
- Where an offender fails to appear for a first court hearing but attends shortly afterwards, the only harm caused is likely to be the financial cost to the system. Where a case could not have proceeded even if the offender had surrendered to bail, this should be taken into account.
- Where an offender appears for trial on the wrong day but enters a late guilty plea enabling the case to be disposed of to some degree at least, the harm caused by the delay may be offset by the benefits stemming from the change of plea.
- The most serious harm is likely to result when an offender fails to appear for trial, especially if this results in witnesses being sent away. Where it has been possible to conclude proceedings in the absence of the offender, this may be relevant to the assessment of harm caused.
- The level of harm is likely to be assessed as high where an offender fails to appear for sentence and is also seen to be flouting the authority of the court, such as where the avoidance of sentence results in the consequential avoidance of ancillary orders such as disqualification from driving, the payment of compensation or registration as a sex offender. This may increase the level of harm whenever the offender continues to present a risk to public safety.
- Whilst the seriousness of the original offence does not of itself aggravate or mitigate the seriousness of the offence of failing to surrender, the circumstances surrounding the original offence may be relevant in assessing the harm arising from the Bail Act offence.
- The circumstances in which bail to return to a police station is granted are less formal than the grant of court bail and the history of the individual case should be examined. There may be less culpability where bail has been enlarged on a number of occasions and less harm if court proceedings are not significantly delayed.

(c) Where the failure to surrender to custody was 'deliberate':
- at or near the bottom of the sentencing range will be cases where the offender gave no thought at all to the consequences, or other mitigating factors are present, and the degree of delay or interference with the progress of the case was not significant in all the circumstances;
- at or near the top of the range will be cases where aggravating factors 1, 2 or 4 [below] are present if there is also a significant delay and/or interference with the progress of the case.

(d) A previous conviction that is likely to be 'relevant' for the purposes of this offence is one which demonstrates failure to comply with an order of a court.

(e) Acquittal of the original offence does not automatically mitigate the Bail Act offence.

(f) The fact that an offender has a disorganised or chaotic lifestyle should not normally be treated as offence mitigation, but may be regarded as offender mitigation depending on the particular facts.

(g) A misunderstanding which does not amount to a defence may be a mitigating factor whereas a mistake on the part of the offender is his or her own responsibility.

(h) Where an offender has literacy or language difficulties, these may be mitigation (where they do not amount to a defence) where potential problems were not identified and/or appropriate steps were not taken to mitigate the risk in the circumstances as known at the time that bail was granted.

(i) An offender's position as the sole or primary carer of dependent relatives may be offender mitigation when it is the reason why the offender failed to surrender to custody. [32]
(j) The sentence for this offence should usually be in addition to any sentence for the original offence. Where custodial sentences are being imposed for a Bail Act offence and the original offence at the same time, the normal approach should be for the sentences to be consecutive. The length of any custodial sentence imposed must be commensurate with the seriousness of the offence(s).
(k) If an offence is serious enough to justify the imposition of a community order, a curfew requirement with an electronic monitoring requirement may be particularly appropriate—see [below].

[Guidelines] [33]

Bail Act 1976, ss. 6(1) and 6(2)

Triable either way
Maximum when tried summarily: Level 5 fine and/or 3 months
Maximum when tried on indictment: 12 months

In certain circumstances, a magistrates' court may commit to the Crown Court for sentence. *Consult your legal adviser for guidance.*

Offence seriousness (culpability and harm)

A. Identify the appropriate starting point
Starting points based on first time offender pleading not guilty

Examples of nature of activity	Starting point	Range
Surrenders late on day but case proceeds as planned	Band A fine	Band A fine–Band B fine
Negligent or non-deliberate failure to attend causing delay and/or interference with the administration of justice	Band C fine	Band B fine–medium level community order
Deliberate failure to attend causing delay and/or interference with the administration of justice	14 days' custody	Low level community order–10 weeks' custody

B. Consider the effect of aggravating and mitigating factors (other than those within examples above)
Common aggravating and mitigating factors are identified [elsewhere]—the following may be particularly relevant but these lists are not exhaustive

Factors indicating higher culpability	Factors indicating lower culpability
1. Serious attempts to evade justice 2. Determined attempt seriously to undermine the course of justice 3. Previous relevant convictions and/or breach of court orders or police bail	Where not amounting to a defence: 1. Misunderstanding 2. Failure to comprehend bail significance or requirements 3. Caring responsibilities
Factor indicating greater degree of harm	**Factor indicating lesser degree of harm**
4. Lengthy absence	4. Prompt voluntary surrender

[Sets out the standard sequential sentencing procedure.]

In appropriate cases, a magistrates' court may impose one day's detention: Magistrates' Courts Act 1980, s. 135

SG10-26 Benefit Fraud

[Not reproduced here: see SG26-21.]

SG10-27 Bladed Articles and Offensive Weapons – Possession

[Not reproduced here: see SG14-3 for the new guideline effective from 1 June 2018. Sets out the standard sequential sentencing procedure.]

SG10-28 Bladed Articles and Offensive Weapons – Threats

[Not reproduced here: see SG14-13 for the new guideline effective from 1 June 2018. Sets out the standard sequential sentencing procedure.]

[33] **Bladed Articles and Offensive Weapons (Possession and Threats) – Children and Young People** SG10-29

[Not reproduced here: see **SG14-23** for the new guideline effective from 1 June 2018.]

Bribery SG10-30

[Not reproduced here: see **SG26-29**.]

Burglary: Domestic Burglary SG10-31

[Not reproduced here: see **SG19-13**.]

Burglary: Non-Domestic Burglary SG10-32

[Not reproduced here: see **SG19-18**.]

Common Assault SG10-33

[Not reproduced here: see **SG12-28**.]

[38] **Communication Network Offences** SG10-34

Communications Act 2003, ss. 127(1) and 127(2)

Effective from: 24 April 2017

Triable only summarily
Maximum: Unlimited fine and/or 6 months
Offence range: Band A fine–15 weeks' custody

STEP ONE Determining the offence category
The Court should determine the offence category using the table below.

Category 1	Higher culpability **and** greater harm
Category 2	Higher culpability **and** lesser harm **or** lower culpability **and** greater harm
Category 3	Lower culpability **and** lesser harm

The court should determine the offender's culpability and the harm caused with reference **only** to the factors below. Where an offence does not fall squarely into a category, individual factors may require a degree of weighting before making an overall assessment and determining the appropriate offence category.

CULPABILITY demonstrated by one or more of the following:

Factors indicating higher culpability

- Targeting of a vulnerable victim
- Targeting offending (in terms of timing or location) to maximise effect
- Use of threats (including blackmail)
- Threat to disclose intimate material or sexually explicit images
- Campaign demonstrated by multiple calls and/or wide distribution
- False calls to emergency services
- Offence motivated by, or demonstrating, hostility based on any of the following characteristics or presumed characteristics of the victim(s): religion, race, disability, sexual orientation or transgender identity

Factors indicating lower culpability

- All other cases

HARM demonstrated by one or more of the following:

Factors indicating greater harm

- Substantial distress or fear to victim(s) **or** moderate impact on several victims
- Major disruption

Factors indicating lesser harm

- All other cases

STEP TWO Starting point and category range [39]

Having determined the category at step one, the court should use the corresponding starting point to reach a sentence within the category range in the table below. The starting point applies to all offenders irrespective of plea or previous convictions.

Offence Category	Starting Point	Range
Category 1	9 weeks' custody	High level community order – 15 weeks' custody
Category 2	Medium level community order	Low level community order – High level community order
Category 3	Band B fine	Band A fine – Band C fine

For band ranges, see **SG10-129**

For the imposition of community orders, including the community orders table, see Imposition of Community and Custodial Sentences **SG9-2–SG9-8**

For the imposition of custodial sentences see Imposition of Community and Custodial Sentences **SG9-9–SG9-12**

STEP THREE Consider any factors which indicate a reduction, such as assistance to the prosecution [40]

The court should take into account sections 73 and 74 of the Serious Organised Crime and Police Act 2005 (assistance by defendants: reduction or review of sentence) and any other rule of law by virtue of which an offender may receive a discounted sentence in consequence of assistance given (or offered) to the prosecutor or investigator.

STEP FOUR Reduction for guilty pleas

The court should take account of any potential reduction for a guilty plea in accordance with section 144 of the Criminal Justice Act 2003 and the ***Guilty Plea*** guideline.

STEP FIVE Totality principle

If sentencing an offender for more than one offence, or where the offender is already serving a sentence, consider whether the total sentence is just and proportionate to the overall offending behaviour in accordance with the ***Offences Taken into Consideration and Totality*** guideline.

STEP SIX Compensation and ancillary orders

In all cases, the court should consider whether to make **compensation** and/or other **ancillary orders** including **restraining orders.**

STEP SEVEN Reasons

Section 174 of the Criminal Justice Act 2003 imposes a duty to give reasons for, and explain the effect of, the sentence.

STEP EIGHT Consideration for time spent on bail

The court must consider whether to give credit for time spent on bail in accordance with section 240A of the Criminal Justice Act 2003.

SG10-35 COMMUNITY ORDER, BREACH OF [41]

Criminal Justice Act 2003, sch. 8

These notes are taken from the Sentencing Guidelines Council's definitive guideline *New Sentences: Criminal Justice Act 2003*, published 16 December 2004[108]

Options in breach proceedings:

When dealing with breaches of community orders for offences committed after 4 April 2005, the court must either:

- amend the terms of the original order so as to impose more onerous requirements. The court may extend the duration of particular requirements within the order, but it cannot extend the overall length of the original order; or
- revoke the original order and proceed to sentence for the original offence. Where an offender has wilfully and persistently failed to comply with an order made in respect of an offence that is not punishable by imprisonment, the court can impose up to six months' custody.

[108] Criminal Justice Act 2003, sch. 8, para. 9(1)(c)

[41] **Approach:**

- having decided that a community order is commensurate with the seriousness of the offence, the primary objective when sentencing for breach of requirements is to ensure that those requirements are completed;
- a court sentencing for breach must take account of the extent to which the offender has complied with the requirements of the original order, the reasons for the breach, and the point at which the breach has occurred;
- if increasing the onerousness of requirements, sentencers should take account of the offender's ability to comply and should avoid precipitating further breach by overloading the offender with too many or conflicting requirements;
- there may be cases where the court will need to consider re-sentencing to a differently constructed community order in order to secure compliance with the purposes of the original sentence, perhaps where there has already been partial compliance or where events since the sentence was imposed have shown that a different course of action is likely to be effective;
- where available, custody should be the last resort, reserved for those cases of deliberate and repeated breach where all reasonable efforts to ensure that the offender complies have failed.

Where the original order was made by the Crown Court, breach proceedings must be commenced in that court unless the order provided that any failure to comply with its requirements may be dealt with in a magistrates' court.

Corporate Offenders: Fraud, Bribery and Money Laundering SG10-36

[Not reproduced here: see SG26-33.]

[43]

Criminal Damage (other than by Fire) SG10-37
Racially or Religiously Aggravated Criminal Damage

Criminal Damage Act 1971, s. 1(1)

Crime and Disorder Act 1998, s. 30

Criminal damage: triable only summarily if value involved does not exceed £5,000:
Maximum: Level 4 fine and/or 3 months
Triable either way if value involved exceeds £5,000:
Maximum when tried summarily: Level 5 fine and/or 6 months
Maximum when tried on indictment: 10 years

Racially or religiously aggravated criminal damage: triable either way
Maximum when tried summarily: Level 5 fine and/or 6 months
Maximum when tried on indictment: 14 years
Where offence committed in domestic context, refer [below] for guidance

Offence seriousness (culpability and harm)

A. Identify the appropriate starting point
Starting points based on first time offender pleading not guilty

Examples of nature of activity	Starting point	Range
Minor damage e.g. breaking small window; small amount of graffiti	Band B fine	Conditional discharge–band C fine
Moderate damage e.g. breaking large plate-glass or shop window; widespread graffiti	Low level community order	Band C fine–medium level community order
Significant damage up to £5,000 e.g. damage caused as part of a spree	High level community order	Medium level community order–12 weeks' custody
Damage between £5,000 and £10,000	12 weeks' custody	6–26 weeks' custody
Damage over £10,000	Crown Court	Crown Court

B. Consider the effect of aggravating and mitigating factors (other than those within examples above) [43]

Common aggravating and mitigating factors are identified [elsewhere]—the following may be particularly relevant but these lists are not exhaustive

Factors indicating higher culpability	Factors indicating lower culpability
1. Revenge attack 2. Targeting vulnerable victim	1. Damage caused recklessly 2. Provocation
Factors indicating greater degree of harm 1. Damage to emergency equipment 2. Damage to public amenity 3. Significant public or private fear caused e.g. in domestic context	

[Sets out the standard sequential sentencing procedure. Notes that 'If offender charged and convicted of the racially or religiously aggravated offence, increase the sentence to reflect this element']

SG10-38 Cruelty to a Child Factors to take into consideration [44]

This guideline and accompanying notes are taken from the Sentencing Council's definitive guideline *Child Cruelty*, effective date 1 January 2019 [see **SG20-3–SG20-14**].

Key factors

(a) The same starting point and sentencing range is proposed for offences which might fall into the four categories (assault; ill-treatment or neglect; abandonment; and failure to protect). These are designed to take into account the fact that the victim is particularly vulnerable, assuming an abuse of trust or power and the likelihood of psychological harm, and designed to reflect the seriousness with which society as a whole regards these offences.

(b) As noted above, the starting points have been calculated to reflect the likelihood of psychological harm and this cannot be treated as an aggravating factor. Where there is an especially serious physical or psychological effect on the victim, even if unintended, this should increase sentence.

(c) The normal sentencing starting point for an offence of child cruelty should be a custodial sentence. The length of that sentence will be influenced by the circumstances in which the offence took place.

(d) However, in considering whether a custodial sentence is the most appropriate disposal, the court should take into account any available information concerning the future care of the child.

(e) Where the offender is the sole or primary carer of the victim or other dependants, this potentially should be taken into account for sentencing purposes, regardless of whether the offender is male or female. In such cases, an immediate custodial sentence may not be appropriate.

(f) The most relevant areas of personal mitigation are likely to be:
- Mental illness/depression
- Inability to cope with the pressures of parenthood
- Lack of support
- Sleep deprivation
- Offender dominated by an abusive or stronger partner
- Extreme behavioural difficulties in the child, often coupled with a lack of support
- Inability to secure assistance or support services in spite of every effort having been made by the offender.

Some of the factors identified above, in particular sleep deprivation, lack of support and an inability to cope, could be regarded as an inherent part of caring for children, especially when a child is very young and could be put forward as mitigation by most carers charged with an offence of child cruelty. It follows that, before being accepted as mitigation, there must be evidence that these factors were present to a high degree and had an identifiable and significant impact on the offender's behaviour.

[Guidelines] [45]

Children and Young Persons Act 1933, s. 1(1)

Triable either way
Maximum when tried summarily: Level 5 fine and/or 6 months
Maximum when tried on indictment: 10 years

[45] **Offence seriousness (culpability and harm)**

A. Identify the appropriate starting point

Starting points based on first time offender pleading not guilty

Examples of nature of activity	Starting point	Range
(i) Short term neglect or ill-treatment (ii) Single incident of short-term abandonment (iii) Failure to protect a child from any of the above	12 weeks' custody	Low level community order–26 weeks' custody
(i) Assault(s) resulting in injuries consistent with ABH (ii) More than one incident of neglect or ill-treatment (but not amounting to long-term behaviour) (iii) Single incident of long-term abandonment OR regular incidents of short-term abandonment (the longer the period of long-term abandonment or the greater the number of incidents of short-term abandonment, the more serious the offence) (iv) Failure to protect a child from any of the above	Crown Court	26 weeks' custody–Crown Court
(i) Series of assaults (ii) Protracted neglect or ill-treatment (iii) Serious cruelty over a period of time (iv) Failure to protect a child from any of the above	Crown Court	Crown Court

B. Consider the effect of aggravating and mitigating factors (other than those within examples above)

Common aggravating and mitigating factors are identified [elsewhere]—the following may be particularly relevant but these lists are not exhaustive

1. Targeting one particular child from the family 2. Sadistic behaviour 3. Threats to prevent the victim from reporting the offence 4. Deliberate concealment of the victim from the authorities 5. Failure to seek medical help	1. Seeking medical help or bringing the situation to the notice of the authorities

[Sets out the standard sequential sentencing procedure.]

Dangerous Dogs Act Offences and Related Offences SG10-39

[Not reproduced here: see SG21-1.]

[46] Drugs—Class A—Fail to Attend/Remain for Initial Assessment SG10-40

Drugs Act 2005, s. 12

Effective from: 24 April 2017

Triable only summarily
Maximum: Level 4 fine and/or 3 months
Offence range: Band A fine–High level community order

STEP ONE Determining the offence category

The Court should determine the offence category using the table below.

Category 1	Higher culpability and greater harm
Category 2	Higher culpability **and** lesser harm **or** lower culpability **and** greater harm
Category 3	Lower culpability **and** lesser harm

The court should determine the offender's culpability and the harm caused with reference **only** to the factors below. Where an offence does not fall squarely into a category, individual factors may require a degree of weighting before making an overall assessment and determining the appropriate offence category.

CULPABILITY demonstrated by one or more of the following: [46]

Factor indicating higher culpability

- Deliberate failure to attend/remain

Factor indicating lower culpability

- All other cases

HARM demonstrated by one or more of the following:

Factor indicating greater harm

- Aggressive, abusive or disruptive behaviour

Factor indicating lesser harm

- All other cases

STEP TWO Starting point and category range [47]

Having determined the category at step one, the court should use the corresponding starting point to reach a sentence within the category range in the table below. The starting point applies to all offenders irrespective of plea or previous convictions.

Offence Category	Starting Point	Range
Category 1	Medium level community order	Low level community order – High level community order
Category 2	Band C fine	Band B fine – Low level community order
Category 3	Band B fine	Band A fine – Band C fine

For band ranges, see **SG10-129**

For the imposition of community orders, including the community orders table, see Imposition of Community and Custodial Sentences **SG9-2–SG9-8**

The court should then consider further adjustment for any aggravating or mitigating factors. The following is a **non-exhaustive** list of additional factual elements providing the context of the offence and factors relating to the offender. Identify whether any combination of these, or other relevant factors, should result in an upward or downward adjustment from the sentence arrived at so far.

Factors increasing seriousness

Statutory aggravating factors:

- Previous convictions, having regard to a) the **nature** of the offence to which the conviction relates and its **relevance** to the current offence; and b) the **time** that has elapsed since the conviction
- Offence committed whilst on bail
- Offence motivated by, or demonstrating hostility based on any of the following characteristics or presumed characteristics of the victim: religion, race, disability, sexual orientation or transgender identity

Other aggravating factors:

- Failure to comply with current court orders
- Offence committed on licence or post sentence supervision
- Offender's actions result in a waste of resources

Factors reducing seriousness or reflecting personal mitigation

- No previous convictions **or** no relevant/recent convictions
- Remorse
- Good character and/or exemplary conduct
- Serious medical condition requiring urgent, intensive or long-term treatment
- Age and/or lack of maturity where it affects the responsibility of the offender
- Mental disorder or learning disability
- Sole or primary carer for dependent relatives
- Determination and/or demonstration of steps having been taken to address addiction or offending behaviour
- Attempts made to re-arrange appointments

[48] **STEP THREE Consider any factors which indicate a reduction, such as assistance to the prosecution**

The court should take into account sections 73 and 74 of the Serious Organised Crime and Police Act 2005 (assistance by defendants: reduction or review of sentence) and any other rule of law by virtue of which an offender may receive a discounted sentence in consequence of assistance given (or offered) to the prosecutor or investigator.

STEP FOUR Reduction for guilty pleas

The court should take account of any potential reduction for a guilty plea in accordance with section 144 of the Criminal Justice Act 2003 and the ***Guilty Plea*** guideline.

STEP FIVE Totality principle

If sentencing an offender for more than one offence, or where the offender is already serving a sentence, consider whether the total sentence is just and proportionate to the overall offending behaviour in accordance with the ***Offences Taken into Consideration and Totality*** guideline.

STEP SIX Consider ancillary orders

In all cases, the court should consider whether to make **compensation** and/or other **ancillary orders.**

STEP SEVEN Reasons

Section 174 of the Criminal Justice Act 2003 imposes a duty to give reasons for, and explain the effect of, the sentence.

[50] ## DRUGS—CLASS A—FAIL/REFUSE TO PROVIDE A SAMPLE SG10-41

Police and Criminal Evidence Act 1984, s. 63B

Effective from: 24 April 2017

Triable only summarily
Maximum: Level 4 fine and/or 3 months
Offence range: Band A fine–High level community order

STEP ONE Determining the offence category

The Court should determine the offence category using the table below.

Category 1	Higher culpability and greater harm
Category 2	Higher culpability **and** lesser harm **or** lower culpability **and** greater harm
Category 3	Lower culpability **and** lesser harm

The court should determine the offender's culpability and the harm caused with reference **only** to the factors below. Where an offence does not fall squarely into a category, individual factors may require a degree of weighting before making an overall assessment and determining the appropriate offence category.

CULPABILITY demonstrated by one or more of the following:

Factors indicating higher culpability

- Deliberate refusal

Factors indicating lower culpability

- All other cases

HARM demonstrated by one or more of the following:

Factors indicating greater harm

- Aggressive, abusive or disruptive behaviour

Factors indicating lesser harm

- All other cases

[51] **STEP TWO Starting point and category range**

Having determined the category at step one, the court should use the starting point to reach a sentence within the appropriate category range in the table below. The starting point applies to all offenders irrespective of plea or previous convictions.

Offence Category	Starting Point	Range
Category 1	Medium level community order	Low level community order – High level community order
Category 2	Band C fine	Band B fine – Low level community order
Category 3	Band B fine	Band A fine – Band C fine

[51]

For band ranges, see **SG10-129**

For the imposition of community orders, including the community orders table, see Imposition of Community and Custodial Sentences **SG9-2–SG9-8**

The court should then consider adjustment for any aggravating or mitigating factors. The following is a **non-exhaustive** list of additional factual elements providing the context of the offence and factors relating to the offender. Identify whether any combination of these, or other relevant factors, should result in an upward or downward adjustment from the sentence arrived at so far.

Factors increasing seriousness

Statutory aggravating factors:

- Previous convictions, having regard to a) the **nature** of the offence to which the conviction relates and its **relevance** to the current offence; and b) the **time** that has elapsed since the conviction
- Offence committed whilst on bail
- Offence motivated by, or demonstrating hostility based on any of the following characteristics or presumed characteristics of the victim: religion, race, disability, sexual orientation or transgender identity

Other aggravating factors:

- Failure to comply with current court orders
- Offence committed on licence or post sentence supervision
- Offender's actions result in a waste of resources

Factors reducing seriousness or reflecting personal mitigation

- No previous convictions **or** no relevant/recent convictions
- Remorse
- Good character and/or exemplary conduct
- Serious medical condition requiring urgent, intensive or long-term treatment
- Age and/or lack of maturity where it affects the responsibility of the offender
- Mental disorder or learning disability
- Sole or primary carer for dependent relatives
- Determination and/or demonstration of steps having been taken to address addiction or offending behaviour

STEP THREE Consider any factors which indicate a reduction, such as assistance to the prosecution [52]

The court should take into account sections 73 and 74 of the Serious Organised Crime and Police Act 2005 (assistance by defendants: reduction or review of sentence) and any other rule of law by virtue of which an offender may receive a discounted sentence in consequence of assistance given (or offered) to the prosecutor or investigator.

STEP FOUR Reduction for guilty pleas

The court should take account of any potential reduction for a guilty plea in accordance with section 144 of the Criminal Justice Act 2003 and the ***Guilty Plea*** guideline.

STEP FIVE Totality principle

If sentencing an offender for more than one offence, or where the offender is already serving a sentence, consider whether the total sentence is just and proportionate to the overall offending behaviour in accordance with the ***Offences Taken into Consideration and Totality*** guideline.

STEP SIX Consider ancillary orders

In all cases, the court should consider whether to make **compensation** and/or other **ancillary orders.**

STEP SEVEN Reasons

Section 174 of the Criminal Justice Act 2003 imposes a duty to give reasons for, and explain the effect of, the sentence.

[52] **Drugs—Fraudulent Evasion of a Prohibition by Bringing into or Taking Out of the UK a Controlled Drug** SG10-42

[Not reproduced here: see **SG23-2**.]

Drugs—Supplying or Offering to Supply a Controlled Drug SG10-43

[Not reproduced here: see **SG23-12**.]

Production of a Controlled Drug SG10-44

[Not reproduced here: see **SG23-17**.]

Cultivation of Cannabis Plant SG10-45

[Not reproduced here: see **SG23-18**.]

Permitting Premises to be Used SG10-46

[Not reproduced here: see **SG23-23**.]

Possession of a Controlled Drug SG10-47

[Not reproduced here: see **SG23-28**.]

[54] **Drunk and Disorderly in a Public Place** SG10-48

Criminal Justice Act 1967, s. 91

Effective from: 24 April 2017

Triable only summarily
Maximum: Level 3 fine
Offence range: Conditional discharge–Band C fine

[55] **STEPS 1 and 2 Determining the offence seriousness**

The starting point applies to all offenders irrespective of plea or previous convictions.

Starting Point	Range
Band A fine	Conditional discharge – Band C fine

For band ranges, see **SG10-129**

The court should then consider adjustment for any aggravating or mitigating factors. The following is a **non-exhaustive** list of additional factual elements providing the context of the offence and factors relating to the offender. Identify whether any combination of these, or other relevant factors, should result in an upward or downward adjustment from the sentence arrived at so far.

Factors increasing seriousness

Statutory aggravating factors:

- Previous convictions, having regard to a) the **nature** of the offence to which the conviction relates and its **relevance** to the current offence; and b) the **time** that has elapsed since the conviction
- Offence committed whilst on bail
- Offence motivated by, or demonstrating hostility based on any of the following characteristics or presumed characteristics of the victim: religion, race, disability, sexual orientation or transgender identity

Other aggravating factors:

- Substantial disturbance caused
- Offence ties up disproportionate police resource
- Disregard of earlier warning regarding conduct
- Failure to comply with current court orders
- Offence committed on licence or post sentence supervision
- Location of the offence
- Timing of the offence
- Offence committed against those working in the public sector or providing a service to the public
- Presence of others including, especially children or vulnerable people

Factors reducing seriousness or reflecting personal mitigation [55]

- Minimal disturbance caused
- No previous convictions **or** no relevant/recent convictions
- Remorse
- Good character and/or exemplary conduct
- Age and/or lack of maturity where it affects the responsibility of the offender
- Mental disorder or learning disability

STEP 3 Consider any factors which indicate a reduction, such as assistance to the prosecution [56]

The court should take into account sections 73 and 74 of the Serious Organised Crime and Police Act 2005 (assistance by defendants: reduction or review of sentence) and any other rule of law by virtue of which an offender may receive a discounted sentence in consequence of assistance given (or offered) to the prosecutor or investigator.

STEP 4 Reduction for guilty pleas

The court should take account of any potential reduction for a guilty plea in accordance with section 144 of the Criminal Justice Act 2003 and the ***Guilty Plea*** guideline.

STEP 5 Totality principle

If sentencing an offender for more than one offence, or where the offender is already serving a sentence, consider whether the total sentence is just and proportionate to the overall offending behaviour in accordance with the ***Offences Taken into Consideration and Totality*** guideline.

STEP 6 Compensation and ancillary orders

In all cases, the court should consider whether to make **compensation** and/or other **ancillary orders**, including a **football banning order** (where appropriate).

STEP 7 Reasons

Section 174 of the Criminal Justice Act 2003 imposes a duty to give reasons for, and explain the effect of, the sentence.

SG10-49 ELECTRICITY, ABSTRACT/USE WITHOUT AUTHORITY

[Not reproduced here: see **SG32-23**.]

SG10-50 ENVIRONMENTAL OFFENCES

[Not reproduced here: see **SG24-1**.]

SG10-51 EXPLOITATION OF PROSTITUTION

[Not reproduced here: see **SG31-90**.]

SG10-52 EXPOSURE

[Not reproduced here: see **SG31-134**.]

SG10-53 FIREARM, CARRYING IN PUBLIC PLACE [57]

Firearms Act 1968, s. 19

Triable either way (but triable only summarily if the firearm is an air weapon):
Maximum when tried summarily: Level 5 fine and/or 6 months
Maximum when tried on indictment: 7 years (12 months for imitation firearms)

Offence seriousness (culpability and harm)

[57] *A. Identify the appropriate starting point*

Starting points based on first time offender pleading not guilty

Examples of nature of activity	Starting point	Range
Carrying an unloaded air weapon	Low level community order	Band B fine–medium level community order
Carrying loaded air weapon/ imitation firearm/unloaded shot gun without ammunition	High level community order	Medium level community order–26 weeks' custody (air weapon) Medium level community order to Crown Court (imitation firearm, unloaded shot gun)
Carrying loaded shot gun/ carrying shot gun or any other firearm together with ammunition for it	Crown Court	Crown Court

B. Consider the effect of aggravating and mitigating factors (other than those within examples above)

Common aggravating and mitigating factors are identified [elsewhere]—the following may be particularly relevant but these lists are not exhaustive

Factors indicating higher culpability	Factors indicating lower culpability
1. Brandishing the firearm 2. Carrying firearm in a busy place 3. Planned illegal use **Factors indicating greater degree of harm** 1. Person or people put in fear 2. Offender participating in violent incident	1. Firearm not in sight 2. No intention to use firearm 3. Firearm to be used for lawful purpose (not amounting to a defence)

[Sets out the standard sequential sentencing procedure, ancillary orders to be considered include compensation, forfeiture or suspension of personal liquor licence and football banning order (where appropriate).]

[58]

Football Related Offences SG10-54

Criminal Justice and Public Order Act 1994: s. 166 (unauthorised sale or attempted sale of tickets); Football Offences Act 1991: s. 2 (throwing missile); s. 3 (indecent or racist chanting); s. 4 (going onto prohibited areas); Sporting Events (Control of Alcohol etc.) Act 1985: s. 2(1) (possession of alcohol whilst entering or trying to enter ground); s. 2(2) (being drunk in, or whilst trying to enter, ground).

Effective from: 24 April 2017

Triable only summarily

Maximum:

Level 2 fine (being drunk in ground)

Level 3 fine (throwing missile; indecent or racist chanting; going onto prohibited areas) Unlimited fine (unauthorised sale of tickets)

Level 3 fine and/or 3 months (possession of alcohol)

Offence range:

Conditional discharge–High level community order (possession of alcohol)

Conditional discharge–Band C fine (all other offences)

[59] **STEP ONE Determining the offence category**

The Court should determine the offence category using the table below.

Category 1	Higher culpability **and** greater harm
Category 2	Higher culpability **and** lesser harm **or** lower culpability **and** greater harm
Category 3	Lower culpability **and** lesser harm

The court should determine the offender's culpability and the harm caused with reference **only** to the factors below. Where an offence does not fall squarely into a category, individual factors may require a degree of weighting before making an overall assessment and determining the appropriate offence category. [59]

CULPABILITY demonstrated by one or more of the following:

Factors indicating higher culpability

- Deliberate or flagrant action
- Disregard of warnings
- Commercial operation
- Inciting others
- (Possession of) Large quantity of alcohol
- Targeted abuse

Factors indicating lower culpability

- All other cases

HARM demonstrated by one or more of the following:

Factor indicating greater harm

- Distress or alarm caused
- Actual injury or risk of injury
- Significant financial loss to others

Factors indicating lesser harm

- All other cases

STEP TWO Starting point and category range [60]

Having determined the category at step one, the court should use the starting point to reach a sentence within the appropriate category range in the table below. The starting point applies to all offenders irrespective of plea or previous convictions.

Offence Category	Starting Point	Range
Category 1	Band C fine	Band C fine
Category 2	Band B fine	Band A fine – Band C fine
Category 3	Band A fine	Conditional discharge – Band B fine

Possession of alcohol only

Offence Category	Starting Point	Range
Category 1	Band C fine	Band C fine – High level community order
Category 2	Band B fine	Band A fine – B and C fine
Category 3	Band A fine	Conditional discharge – Band B fine

For band ranges, see **SG10-129**

For the imposition of community orders, including the community orders table, see Imposition of Community and Custodial Sentences **SG9-2–SG9-8**

The court should then consider adjustment for any aggravating or mitigating factors. The following is a **non-exhaustive** list of additional factual elements providing the context of the offence and factors relating to the offender. Identify whether any combination of these, or other relevant factors, should result in an upward or downward adjustment from the sentence arrived at so far.

Factors increasing seriousness

Statutory aggravating factors:

- Previous convictions, having regard to a) the **nature** of the offence to which the conviction relates and its **relevance** to the current offence; and b) the **time** that has elapsed since the conviction
- Offence committed whilst on bail
- Offence motivated by, or demonstrating hostility based on any of the following characteristics or presumed characteristics: religion, race, disability, sexual orientation or transgender identity

[60] *Other aggravating factors:*

- Presence of children
- Offence committed on licence or post sentence supervision

Factors reducing seriousness or reflecting personal mitigation

- Remorse
- Admissions to police in interview
- Ready co-operation with authorities
- Minimal disturbance caused
- No previous convictions **or** no relevant/recent convictions
- Good character and/or exemplary conduct
- Age and/or lack of maturity where it affects the responsibility of the offender
- Mental disorder or learning disability

[61] **STEP THREE Consider any factors which indicate a reduction, such as assistance to the prosecution**

The court should take into account sections 73 and 74 of the Serious Organised Crime and Police Act 2005 (assistance by defendants: reduction or review of sentence) and any other rule of law by virtue of which an offender may receive a discounted sentence in consequence of assistance given (or offered) to the prosecutor or investigator.

STEP FOUR Reduction for guilty pleas

The court should take account of any potential reduction for a guilty plea in accordance with section 144 of the Criminal Justice Act 2003 and the ***Guilty Plea*** guideline.

STEP FIVE Totality principle

If sentencing an offender for more than one offence, or where the offender is already serving a sentence, consider whether the total sentence is just and proportionate to the overall offending behaviour in accordance with the ***Offences Taken into Consideration and Totality*** guideline.

STEP SIX Compensation and ancillary orders

In all cases, the court should consider whether to make **compensation** and/or other **ancillary orders,** including a **football banning order.**

STEP SEVEN Reasons

Section 174 of the Criminal Justice Act 2003 imposes a duty to give reasons for, and explain the effect of, the sentence.

FRAUD SG10-55

[Not reproduced here: see **SG26-1.**]

GOING EQUIPPED, FOR THEFT SG10-56

[Not reproduced here: see **SG33-19.**]

GRIEVOUS BODILY HARM/UNLAWFUL WOUNDING & RACIALLY OR RELIGIOUSLY AGGRAVATED GRIEVOUS BODILY HARM/UNLAWFUL WOUNDING SG10-57

[Not reproduced here: see **SG12-13.**]

HANDLING STOLEN GOODS SG10-58

[Not reproduced here: see **SG33-15.**]

[63] HARASSMENT—PUTTING PEOPLE IN FEAR OF VIOLENCE RACIALLY OR RELIGIOUSLY AGGRAVATED HARASSMENT—PUTTING PEOPLE IN FEAR OF VIOLENCE SG10-59

Protection from Harassment Act 1997, s. 4
Crime and Disorder Act 1998, s. 32

Harassment: triable either way
Maximum when tried summarily: Level 5 fine and/or 6 months

Maximum when tried on indictment: 5 years [63]

Racially or religiously aggravated harassment: triable either way
Maximum when tried summarily: Level 5 fine and/or 6 months
Maximum when tried on indictment: 7 years

Where offence committed in domestic context, refer [below] for guidance

Offence seriousness (culpability and harm)

A. Identify the appropriate starting point

Starting points based on first time offender pleading not guilty

Examples of nature of activity	Starting point	Range
A pattern of two or more incidents of unwanted contact	6 weeks' custody	High level community order–18 weeks' custody
Deliberate threats, persistent action over a longer period; or Intention to cause fear of violence	18 weeks' custody	12 weeks' custody– Crown Court
Sexual threats, vulnerable person targeted	Crown Court	Crown Court

B. Consider the effect of aggravating and mitigating factors (other than those within examples above)

Common aggravating and mitigating factors are identified [elsewhere]—the following may be particularly relevant but these lists are not exhaustive

Factors indicating higher culpability	Factors indicating lower culpability
1. Planning 2. Offender ignores obvious distress 3. Offender involves others 4. Using contact arrangements with a child to instigate offence **Factors indicating greater degree of harm** 1. Victim needs medical help/counselling 2. Action over long period 3. Children frightened 4. Use or distribution of photographs	1. Limited understanding of effect on victim 2. Initial provocation

[Sets out the standard sequential sentencing procedure. Notes that 'If offender charged and convicted of the racially or religiously aggravated offence, increase the sentence to reflect this element'.] [64]

SG10-60

Harassment (Without Violence) [65]

Racially or Religiously Aggravated Harassment (Non Violent)

Protection from Harassment Act 1997, s. 2
Crime and Disorder Act 1998, s. 32

Harassment: triable only summarily
Maximum: Level 5 fine and/or 6 months

Racially or religiously aggravated harassment: triable either way
Maximum when tried summarily: Level 5 fine and/or 6 months
Maximum when tried on indictment: 2 years

Where offence committed in domestic context, refer [below] for guidance

Offence seriousness (culpability and harm)

A. Identify the appropriate starting point

Examples of nature of activity	Starting point	Range
Small number of incidents	Medium level community order	Band C fine–high level community order
Constant contact at night, trying to come into workplace or home, involving others	6 weeks' custody	Medium level community order–12 weeks' custody
Threatening violence, taking personal photographs, sending offensive material	18 weeks' custody	12–26 weeks' custody

Starting points based on first time offender pleading not guilty

[65] *B. Consider the effect of aggravating and mitigating factors (other than those within examples above)*

Common aggravating and mitigating factors are identified [elsewhere]—the following may be particularly relevant but these lists are not exhaustive

Factors indicating higher culpability	Factors indicating lower culpability
1. Planning 2. Offender ignores obvious distress 3. Offender involves others 4. Using contact arrangements with a child to instigate offence **Factors indicating greater degree of harm** 1. Victim needs medical help/counselling 2. Action over long period 3. Children frightened 4. Use or distribution of photographs	1. Limited understanding of effect on victim 2. Initial provocation

[Sets out the standard sequential sentencing procedure. Notes that 'If offender charged and convicted of the racially or religiously aggravated offence, increase the sentence to reflect this element'.]

[66] Identity Documents—Possess False/Another's/Improperly Obtained SG10-61

Identity Cards Act 2006, s. 25(5)
(possession of a false identity document (as defined in s. 26—includes a passport))

Triable either way
Maximum when tried summarily: Level 5 fine and/or 6 months
Maximum when tried on indictment: 2 years (s. 25(5))

Note: possession of a false identity document with the intention of using it is an indictable-only offence (Identity Cards Act 2006, s. 25(1)). The maximum penalty is 10 years' imprisonment.

Offence seriousness (culpability and harm)

A. Identify the appropriate starting point

Starting points based on first time offender pleading not guilty

B. Consider the effect of aggravating and mitigating factors (other than those within examples above)

Examples of nature of activity	Starting point	Range
Single document possessed	Medium level community order	Band C fine–high level community order
Small number of documents, no evidence of dealing	12 weeks' custody	6 weeks' custody–Crown Court
Considerable number of documents possessed, evidence of involvement in larger operation	Crown Court	Crown Court

Common aggravating and mitigating factors are identified [elsewhere]—the following may be particularly relevant but these lists are not exhaustive

[Sets out the standard sequential sentencing procedure.]

Factors indicating higher culpability	Factor indicating lower culpability
1. Clear knowledge that documents false 2. Number of documents possessed (where not in offence descriptions above) **Factors indicating greater degree of harm** 1. Group activity 2. Potential impact of use (where not in offence descriptions above)	1. Genuine mistake or ignorance

Indecent Photographs of Children [, Possession of] SG10-62

[Not reproduced here: see **SG31-86**.]

Inflicting Grievous Bodily Harm/Unlawful Wounding SG10-63

[Not reproduced here: see **SG12-13**.]

SG10-64 **KEEPING A BROTHEL USED FOR PROSTITUTION** [66]

[Not reproduced here: see SG31-94.]

SG10-65 **MAKING OFF WITHOUT PAYMENT**

[Not reproduced here: see SG33-27.]

SG10-66 **MONEY LAUNDERING**

[Not reproduced here: see SG26-25.]

SG10-67 **OBSTRUCT/RESIST A POLICE CONSTABLE IN EXECUTION OF DUTY** [67]

Police Act 1996, s. 89(2)

Effective from: 24 April 2017

Triable only summarily
Maximum: Level 3 fine and/or one month
Offence range: Conditional Discharge–Medium level community order

STEP ONE Determining the offence category

The Court should determine the offence category using the table below.

Category 1	Higher culpability and greater harm
Category 2	Higher culpability **and** lesser harm **or** lower culpability **and** greater harm
Category 3	Lower culpability **and** lesser harm

The court should determine the offender's culpability and the harm caused with reference **only** to the factors below. Where an offence does not fall squarely into a category, individual factors may require a degree of weighting before making an overall assessment and determining the appropriate offence category.

CULPABILITY demonstrated by one or more of the following:

Factors indicating higher culpability
- Deliberate obstruction or interference
- Use of force, aggression or intimidation
- Group action

Factors indicating lower culpability
- All other cases

HARM demonstrated by one or more of the following:

Factors indicating greater harm
- Offender's actions significantly increase risk to officer or other(s)
- Offender's actions result in a suspect avoiding arrest
- Offender's actions result in a significant waste of resources

Factors indicating lesser harm
- All other cases

STEP TWO Starting point and category range [68]

Having determined the category at step one, the court should use the corresponding starting point to reach a sentence within the category range below. The starting point applies to all offenders irrespective of plea or previous convictions.

Offence Category	Starting Point	Range
Category 1	Low level community order	Band C fine – Medium level community order
Category 2	Band B fine	Band A fine – Band C fine
Category 3	Band A fine	Conditional discharge – Band B fine

For band ranges, see **SG10-129**

[68] For the imposition of community orders, including the community orders table, see Imposition of Community and Custodial Sentences **SG9-2–SG9-8**

The court should then consider adjustment for any aggravating or mitigating factors. The following is a **non-exhaustive** list of additional factual elements providing the context of the offence and factors relating to the offender. Identify whether any combination of these, or other relevant factors, should result in an upward or downward adjustment from the sentence arrived at so far.

Factors increasing seriousness

Statutory aggravating factors:

- Previous convictions, having regard to a) the **nature** of the offence to which the conviction relates and its **relevance** to the current offence; and b) the **time** that has elapsed since the conviction
- Offence committed whilst on bail
- Offence motivated by, or demonstrating hostility based on any of the following characteristics or presumed characteristics of the victim: religion, race, disability, sexual orientation or transgender identity

Other aggravating factors:

- Failure to comply with current court orders
- Offence committed on licence or post sentence supervision
- Blame wrongly placed on others
- Injury caused to an officer/another
- Giving false details

Factors reducing seriousness or reflecting personal mitigation

- No previous convictions **or** no relevant/recent convictions
- Remorse
- Brief incident
- Acting under direction or coercion of another
- Genuinely held belief if coming to the aid of another, that the other was suffering severe medical difficulty
- Good character and/or exemplary conduct
- Serious medical condition requiring urgent, intensive or long-term treatment
- Age and/or lack of maturity where it affects the responsibility of the offender
- Mental disorder or learning disability
- Sole or primary carer for dependent relatives

[69] **STEP THREE Consider any factors which indicate a reduction, such as assistance to the prosecution**

The court should take into account sections 73 and 74 of the Serious Organised Crime and Police Act 2005 (assistance by defendants: reduction or review of sentence) and any other rule of law by virtue of which an offender may receive a discounted sentence in consequence of assistance given (or offered) to the prosecutor or investigator.

STEP FOUR Reduction for guilty pleas

The court should take account of any potential reduction for a guilty plea in accordance with section 144 of the Criminal Justice Act 2003 and the ***Guilty Plea*** guideline.

STEP FIVE Totality principle

If sentencing an offender for more than one offence, or where the offender is already serving a sentence, consider whether the total sentence is just and proportionate to the overall offending behaviour in accordance with the ***Offences Taken into Consideration and Totality*** guideline.

STEP SIX Compensation and ancillary orders

In all cases, the court should consider whether to make **compensation** and/or other **ancillary orders.**

STEP SEVEN Reasons

Section 174 of the Criminal Justice Act 2003 imposes a duty to give reasons for, and explain the effect of, the sentence.

POSSESSING, MAKING OR SUPPLYING ARTICLES FOR FRAUD **SG10-68**

[Not reproduced here: see **SG26-13.**]

SG10-69 **PROTECTIVE ORDER, BREACH OF** [71]

Factors to take into consideration

This guideline and accompanying notes are taken from the Sentencing Guidelines Council's definitive guideline *Breach of a Protective Order*, published 7 December 2006 [see **SG18-1**].

Aims of sentencing

(a) The main aim of sentencing for breach of a protective order (which would have been imposed to protect a victim from future harm) should be to achieve future compliance with that order.

(b) The court will need to assess the level of risk posed by the offender. Willingness to undergo treatment or accept help may influence sentence.

Key factors

(i) The nature of the conduct that caused the breach of the order. In particular, whether the contact was direct or indirect, although it is important to recognise that indirect contact is capable of causing significant harm or anxiety.

(ii) There may be exceptional cases where the nature of the breach is particularly serious but has not been dealt with by a separate offence being charged. In these cases the risk posed by the offender and the nature of the breach will be particularly significant in determining the response.

(iii) The nature of the original conduct or offence is relevant in so far as it allows a judgement to be made on the level of harm caused to the victim by the breach, and the extent to which that harm was intended.

(iv) The sentence following a breach is for the breach alone and must avoid punishing the offender again for the offence or conduct as a result of which the order was made.

(v) It is likely that all breaches of protective orders will pass the threshold for a community sentence. Custody is the starting point where violence is used. Non-violent conduct may also cross the custody threshold where a high degree of harm or anxiety has been caused.

(vi) Where an order was made in civil proceedings, its purpose may have been to cause the subject of the order to modify behaviour rather than to imply that the conduct was especially serious. If so, it is likely to be disproportionate to impose a custodial sentence if the breach of the order did not involve threats or violence.

(vii) In some cases where a breach might result in a short custodial sentence but the court is satisfied that the offender genuinely intends to reform his or her behaviour and there is a real prospect of rehabilitation, the court may consider it appropriate to impose a sentence that will allow this. This may mean imposing a suspended sentence order or a community order (where appropriate with a requirement to attend an accredited domestic violence programme).

[Guidelines] [72]

Protection from Harassment Act 1997, s. 5(5) (breach of restraining order)
Family Law Act 1996, s. 42A (breach of non-molestation order)

Triable either way
Maximum when tried summarily: Level 5 fine and/or 6 months
Maximum when tried on indictment: 5 years

Where the conduct is particularly serious, it would normally be charged as a separate offence. These starting points are based on the premise that the activity has either been prosecuted separately as an offence or is not of a character sufficient to justify prosecution of it as an offence in its own right.

Where offence committed in domestic context, refer [below] for guidance

Offence seriousness (culpability and harm)

A. Identify the appropriate starting point

Starting points based on first time offender pleading not guilty

[72]

Examples of nature of activity	Starting point	Range
Single breach involving no/minimal direct contact	**Low level community order**	**Band C fine–medium level community order**
More than one breach involving no/minimal contact or some direct contact	**Medium level community order**	**Low level community order–high level community order**
Single breach involving some violence and/or significant physical or psychological harm to the victim	**18 weeks' custody**	**13–26 weeks' custody**
More than one breach involving some violence and/or significant physical or psychological harm to the victim	**Crown Court**	**26 weeks' custody–Crown Court**
Breach (whether one or more) involving significant physical violence and significant physical or psychological harm to the victim	**Crown Court**	**Crown Court**

B. Consider the effect of aggravating and mitigating factors (other than those within examples above)

Common aggravating and mitigating factors are identified [elsewhere]—the following may be particularly relevant but these lists are not exhaustive

Factors indicating higher culpability	**Factors indicating greater degree of harm**
1. Proven history of violence or threats by the offender 2. Using contact arrangements with a child to instigate offence 3. Offence is a further breach, following earlier breach proceedings 4. Offender has history of disobedience to court orders 5. Breach committed immediately or shortly after order made	1. Victim is particularly vulnerable 2. Impact on children 3. Victim is forced to leave home **Factors indicating lower culpability** 1. Breach occurred after long period of compliance 2. Victim initiated contact

[Sets out the standard sequential sentencing procedure.]

[73]

Public Order Act, s. 2—Violent Disorder SG10-70

Public Order Act 1986, s. 2

Triable either way
Maximum when tried summarily: Level 5 fine and/or 6 months
Maximum when tried on indictment: 5 years

Offence seriousness (culpability and harm)

A. Identify the appropriate starting point

Starting points based on first time offender pleading not guilty

These offences should normally be dealt with in the Crown Court. However, there may be rare cases involving minor violence or threats of violence leading to no or minor injury, with few people involved and no weapon or missiles, in which a custodial sentence within the jurisdiction of a magistrates' court may be appropriate.

[74]

Public Order Act, s. 3—Affray SG10-71

Public Order Act 1986, s. 3

Triable either way
Maximum when tried summarily: Level 5 fine and/or 6 months
Maximum when tried on indictment: 3 years

Offence seriousness (culpability and harm) [74]

A. Identify the appropriate starting point

Starting points based on first time offender pleading not guilty

Examples of nature of activity	Starting point	Range
Brief offence involving low-level violence, no substantial fear created	**Low level community order**	**Band C fine–medium level community order**
Degree of fighting or violence that causes substantial fear	**High level community order**	**Medium level community order–12 weeks' custody**
Fight involving a weapon/throwing objects, or conduct causing risk of serious injury	**18 weeks' custody**	**12 weeks' custody–Crown Court**

B. Consider the effect of aggravating and mitigating factors (other than those within examples above)

Common aggravating and mitigating factors are identified [elsewhere]—the following may be particularly relevant but these lists are not exhaustive

Factors indicating higher culpability	Factors indicating lower culpability
1. Group action 2. Threats 3. Lengthy incident **Factors indicating greater degree of harm** 1. Vulnerable person(s) present 2. Injuries caused 3. Damage to property	1. Did not start the trouble 2. Provocation 3. Stopped as soon as police arrived

[Sets out the standard sequential sentencing procedure and mentions the need to consider a football banning order.]

SG10-72 PUBLIC ORDER ACT, S. 4—THREATENING BEHAVIOUR—FEAR OR PROVOCATION OF VIOLENCE RACIALLY OR RELIGIOUSLY AGGRAVATED THREATENING BEHAVIOUR [75]

Public Order Act 1986, s. 4

Crime and Disorder Act 1998, s. 31

Threatening behaviour: triable only summarily
Maximum: Level 5 fine and/or 6 months

Racially or religiously aggravated threatening behaviour: triable either way
Maximum when tried summarily: Level 5 fine and/or 6 months
Maximum when tried on indictment: 2 years
Where offence committed in domestic context, refer [below] for guidance

Offence seriousness (culpability and harm)

A. Identify the appropriate starting point

Starting points based on first time offender pleading not guilty

Examples of nature of activity	Starting point	Range
Fear or threat of low level immediate unlawful violence such as push, shove or spit	**Low level community order**	**Band B fine–medium level community order**
Fear or threat of medium level immediate unlawful violence such as punch	**High level community order**	**Low level community order–12 weeks' custody**
Fear or threat of high level immediate unlawful violence such as use of weapon; missile thrown; gang involvement	**12 weeks' custody**	**6–26 weeks' custody**

[75] *B. Consider the effect of aggravating and mitigating factors (other than those within examples above)*
Common aggravating and mitigating factors are identified [elsewhere]—the following may be particularly relevant but these lists are not exhaustive

Factors indicating higher culpability	Factors indicating lower culpability
1. Planning 2. Offender deliberately isolates victim 3. Group action 4. Threat directed at victim because of job 5. History of antagonism towards victim **Factors indicating greater degree of harm** 1. Offence committed at school, hospital or other place where vulnerable persons may be present 2. Offence committed on enclosed premises such as public transport 3. Vulnerable victim(s) 4. Victim needs medical help/counselling	1. Impulsive action 2. Short duration 3. Provocation

[Sets out the standard sequential sentencing procedure and mentions the need to consider a football banning order. Notes that 'If offender charged and convicted of the racially or religiously aggravated offence, increase the sentence to reflect this element'.]

[76] Public Order Act, s. 4A—Disorderly Behaviour with Intent to Cause Harassment, Alarm or Distress SG10-73

Racially or Religiously Aggravated Disorderly Behaviour with Intent to Cause Harassment, Alarm or Distress

Public Order Act 1986, s. 4A
Crime and Disorder Act 1998, s. 31

Disorderly behaviour with intent to cause harassment, alarm or distress: triable only summarily
Maximum: Level 5 fine and/or 6 months

Racially or religiously aggravated disorderly behaviour with intent to cause harassment etc.: triable either way
Maximum when tried summarily: Level 5 fine and/or 6 months
Maximum when tried on indictment: 2 years

Offence seriousness (culpability and harm)

A. Identify the appropriate starting point

Starting points based on first time offender pleading not guilty

Examples of nature of activity	Starting point	Range
Threats, abuse or insults made more than once but on same occasion against the same person e.g. while following down the street	Band C fine	Band B fine–low level community order
Group action or deliberately planned action against targeted victim	Medium level community order	Low level community order–12 weeks' custody
Weapon brandished or used or threats against vulnerable victim—course of conduct over longer period	12 weeks' custody	High level community order–26 weeks' custody

B. Consider the effect of aggravating and mitigating factors (other than those within examples above)
Common aggravating and mitigating factors are identified [elsewhere]—the following may be particularly relevant but these lists are not exhaustive

Factors indicating higher culpability	Factors indicating lower culpability
1. High degree of planning 2. Offender deliberately isolates victim **Factors indicating greater degree of harm** 1. Offence committed in vicinity of victim's home 2. Large number of people in vicinity 3. Actual or potential escalation into violence 4. Particularly serious impact on victim	1. Very short period 2. Provocation

[76]

[Sets out the standard sequential sentencing procedure and mentions the need to consider a football banning order. Notes that 'If offender charged and convicted of the racially or religiously aggravated offence, increase the sentence to reflect this element'.]

SG10-74 Public Order Act, s. 5—Disorderly Behaviour (Harassment, Alarm or Distress) Racially or Religiously Aggravated Disorderly Behaviour [77]

Public Order Act 1986, s. 5
Crime and Disorder Act 1998, s. 31

Disorderly behaviour: triable only summarily
Maximum: Level 3 fine

Racially or religiously aggravated disorderly behaviour: triable only summarily
Maximum: Level 4 fine

Offence seriousness (culpability and harm)

A. Identify the appropriate starting point

Starting points based on first time offender pleading not guilty

Examples of nature of activity	Starting point	Range
Shouting, causing disturbance for some minutes	**Band A fine**	**Conditional discharge to band B fine**
Substantial disturbance caused	**Band B fine**	**Band A fine to band C fine**

B. Consider the effect of aggravating and mitigating factors (other than those within examples above)
Common aggravating and mitigating factors are identified [elsewhere]—the following may be particularly relevant but these lists are not exhaustive

Factors indicating higher culpability	Factors indicating lower culpability
1. Group action 2. Lengthy incident **Factors indicating greater degree of harm** 1. Vulnerable person(s) present 2. Offence committed at school, hospital or other place where vulnerable persons may be present 3. Victim providing public service	1. Stopped as soon as police arrived 2. Brief/minor incident 3. Provocation

[Sets out the standard sequential sentencing procedure and mentions the need to consider a football banning order. Notes that 'If offender charged and convicted of the racially or religiously aggravated offence, increase the sentence to reflect this element'.]

[78] RAILWAY FARE EVASION SG10-75

Regulation of Railways Act 1889, s. 5(3) (travelling on railway without paying fare, with intent to avoid payment); s. 5(1) (failing to produce ticket)

Effective from: 24 April 2017

Triable only summarily
Maximum:
Level 2 fine (s. 5(1) failing to produce ticket)
Level 3 fine and/or 3 months (s. 5(3) travelling on railway with intent to avoid payment)

Offence range:
Conditional Discharge–Band C fine (s. 5(1))
Conditional Discharge–Low level community order (s. 5(3))

[79] **STEP ONE Determining the offence category**

The Court should determine the offence category using the table below.

Category	Description
Category 1	Higher culpability **and** greater harm
Category 2	Higher culpability **and** lesser harm **or** lower culpability **and** greater harm
Category 3	Lower culpability **and** lesser harm

The court should determine the offender's culpability and the harm caused with reference **only** to the factors below. Where an offence does not fall squarely into a category, individual factors may require a degree of weighting before making an overall assessment and determining the appropriate offence category.

CULPABILITY demonstrated by one or more of the following:

Factors indicating higher culpability

- Aggressive, abusive or disruptive behaviour

Factors indicating lower culpability

- All other cases

HARM demonstrated by one or more of the following:

Factors indicating greater harm

- High revenue loss

Factors indicating lesser harm

- All other cases

STEP TWO Starting point and category range

Having determined the category at step one, the court should use the corresponding starting point to reach a sentence within the category range below. The starting point applies to all offenders irrespective of plea or previous convictions.

Travelling on railway without paying fare, with intent

Offence Category	Starting Point	Range
Category 1	Band C fine	Band B fine – Low level community order
Category 2	Band B fine	Band A fine – Band C fine
Category 3	Band A fine	Conditional discharge – Band B fine

Sentencing Guidelines

Failing to produce a ticket [79]

Offence Category	Starting Point	Range
Category 1	Band B fine	Band B fine – Band C fine
Category 2	Band A fine	Band A fine – Band B fine
Category 3	Band A fine	Conditional discharge – Band B fine

For band ranges, see SG**10-129**

For the imposition of community orders, including the community orders table, see Imposition of Community and Custodial Sentences **SG9-2–SG9-8**

The court should then consider adjustment for any aggravating or mitigating factors. The following is a **non-exhaustive** list of additional factual elements providing the context of the offence and factors relating to the offender. Identify whether any combination of these, or other relevant factors, should result in an upward or downward adjustment from the sentence arrived at so far. [80]

Factors increasing seriousness

Statutory aggravating factors:

- Previous convictions, having regard to a) the **nature** of the offence to which the conviction relates and its **relevance** to the current offence; and b) the **time** that has elapsed since the conviction
- Offence committed whilst on bail
- Offence motivated by, or demonstrating hostility based on any of the following characteristics or presumed characteristics of the victim: religion, race, disability, sexual orientation or transgender identity

Other aggravating factors:

- Offender has avoided paying any of the fare
- Offender produces incorrect ticket or document to pass as legitimate fare payer
- Failure to comply with current court orders
- Abuse to staff
- Offence committed on licence or post sentence supervision

Factors reducing seriousness or reflecting personal mitigation

- No previous convictions **or** no relevant/recent convictions
- Remorse
- Good character and/or exemplary conduct
- Serious medical condition requiring urgent, intensive or long-term treatment
- Age and/or lack of maturity where it affects the responsibility of the offender
- Mental disorder or learning disability
- Sole or primary carer for dependent relatives

STEP THREE Consider any factors which indicate a reduction, such as assistance to the prosecution [81]

The court should take into account sections 73 and 74 of the Serious Organised Crime and Police Act 2005 (assistance by defendants: reduction or review of sentence) and any other rule of law by virtue of which an offender may receive a discounted sentence in consequence of assistance given (or offered) to the prosecutor or investigator.

STEP FOUR Reduction for guilty pleas

The court should take account of any potential reduction for a guilty plea in accordance with section 144 of the Criminal Justice Act 2003 and the ***Guilty Plea*** guideline.

STEP FIVE Totality principle

If sentencing an offender for more than one offence, or where the offender is already serving a sentence, consider whether the total sentence is just and proportionate to the overall offending behaviour in accordance with the ***Offences Taken into Consideration and Totality*** guideline.

STEP SIX Compensation and ancillary orders

In all cases, the court should consider whether to make **compensation** and/or other **ancillary orders.**

STEP SEVEN Reasons

Section 174 of the Criminal Justice Act 2003 imposes a duty to give reasons for, and explain the effect of, the sentence.

[81] **Revenue Fraud** **SG10-76**

[Not reproduced here: see SG26-17.]

[82] **School Non-attendance** **SG10-77**

Education Act 1996, s. 444(1) (parent fails to secure regular attendance at school of registered pupil); s. 444(1A) (Parent knowingly fails to secure regular attendance at school of registered pupil)

Effective from: 24 April 2017

Triable only summarily
Maximum:
Level 3 fine (s. 444(1) parent fails to secure regular attendance at school);
Level 4 fine and/or 3 months (s. 444(1A) parent knowingly fails to secure regular attendance at school)

Offence range:
Conditional discharge–Band C fine (s. 444(1))
Band A fine–High level community order (s. 444(1A))

STEP ONE Determining the offence seriousness

The Court should determine the offence category using the table below.

Category 1	Higher culpability and greater harm
Category 2	Higher culpability **and** lesser harm **or** lower culpability **and** greater harm
Category 3	Lower culpability **and** lesser harm

The court should determine the offender's culpability and the harm caused with reference only to the factors below. Where an offence does not fall squarely into a category, individual factors may require a degree of weighting before making an overall assessment and determining the appropriate offence category.

CULPABILITY demonstrated by one or more of the following:

Factors indicating higher culpability

- Refusal/failure to engage with guidance and support offered
- Threats to teachers and/or officials
- Parent encouraging non attendance

Factors indicating lower culpability

- Genuine efforts to ensure attendance
- Parent concerned by child's allegations of bullying
- Parent put in fear of violence and/or threats from the child

HARM demonstrated by one or more of the following:

Factors indicating greater harm

- Significant and lengthy period of education missed
- Adverse influence on other children of the family

Factors indicating lesser harm

- All other cases

[83] **STEP TWO Starting point and category range**

Having determined the category at step one, the court should use the corresponding starting point to reach a sentence within the category range below. The starting point applies to all offenders irrespective of plea or previous convictions.

s. 444(1A) (Parent knowingly fails to secure regular attendance at school of registered pupil)

Offence Category	Starting Point	Range
Category 1	Medium level community order	Low level community order – High level community order
Category 2	Band C fine	Band B fine – Low level community order
Category 3	Band B fine	Band A fine – Band C fine

Sentencing Guidelines

s. 444(1) (parent fails to secure regular attendance at school of registered pupil) [83]

Offence Category	Starting Point	Range
Category 1	Band C fine	Band B fine – Band C fine
Category 2	Band B fine	Band A fine – Band B fine
Category 3	Band A fine	Conditional Discharge – Band B fine

For band ranges, see **SG10-129**

For the imposition of community orders, including the community orders table, see Imposition of Community and Custodial Sentences **SG9-2–SG9-8**

The court should then consider adjustment for any aggravating or mitigating factors. The following is a **non-exhaustive** list of additional factual elements providing the context of the offence and factors relating to the offender. Identify whether any combination of these, or other relevant factors, should result in an upward or downward adjustment from the sentence arrived at so far.

Factors increasing seriousness

Statutory aggravating factors:

- Previous convictions, having regard to a) the **nature** of the offence to which the conviction relates and its **relevance** to the current offence; and b) the **time** that has elapsed since the conviction
- Offence committed whilst on bail

Other aggravating factors:

- Failure to comply with current court orders
- Offence committed on licence or post sentence supervision

Factors reducing seriousness or reflecting personal mitigation

- No previous convictions **or** no relevant/recent convictions
- Remorse
- Good character and/or exemplary conduct
- Serious medical condition requiring urgent, intensive or long-term treatment
- Age and/or lack of maturity where it affects the responsibility of the offender
- Mental disorder or learning disability (of offender)
- Parent unaware of child's whereabouts
- Previously good attendance

STEP THREE Consider any factors which indicate a reduction, such as assistance to the prosecution [84]

The court should take into account sections 73 and 74 of the Serious Organised Crime and Police Act 2005 (assistance by defendants: reduction or review of sentence) and any other rule of law by virtue of which an offender may receive a discounted sentence in consequence of assistance given (or offered) to the prosecutor or investigator.

STEP FOUR Reduction for guilty pleas

The court should take account of any potential reduction for a guilty plea in accordance with section 144 of the Criminal Justice Act 2003 and the ***Guilty Plea*** guideline.

STEP FIVE Totality principle

If sentencing an offender for more than one offence, or where the offender is already serving a sentence, consider whether the total sentence is just and proportionate to the overall offending behaviour in accordance with the ***Offences Taken into Consideration and Totality*** guideline.

STEP SIX Compensation and ancillary orders

In all cases, the court should consider whether to make **compensation** and/or other **ancillary orders** including **parenting orders.**

STEP SEVEN Reasons

Section 174 of the Criminal Justice Act 2003 imposes a duty to give reasons for, and explain the effect of, the sentence.

[87] **SEX OFFENDERS REGISTER—FAIL TO COMPLY WITH NOTIFICATION REQUIREMENTS** SG10-78

Sexual Offences Act 2003, s. 91(1)(a) (fail to comply with notification requirements); s. 91(1)(b) (supply false information)

Triable either way
Maximum when tried summarily: Level 5 fine and/or 6 months
Maximum when tried on indictment: 5 years

Offence seriousness (culpability and harm)

A. Identify the appropriate starting point

Starting points based on first time offender pleading not guilty

Examples of nature of activity	Starting point	Range
Negligent or inadvertent failure to comply with requirements	**Medium level community order**	**Band C fine–high level community order**
Deliberate failure to comply with requirements OR Supply of information known to be false	**6 weeks' custody**	**High level community order–26 weeks' custody**
Conduct as described in box above AND Long period of non-compliance OR Attempts to avoid detection	**18 weeks' custody**	**6 weeks' custody–Crown Court**

B. Consider the effect of aggravating and mitigating factors (other than those within examples above)

Common aggravating and mitigating factors are identified [elsewhere]—the following may be particularly relevant but these lists are not exhaustive

Factor indicating higher culpability	Factor indicating lower culpability
1. Long period of non-compliance (where not in the examples above)	1. Genuine misunderstanding
Factor indicating greater degree of harm 1. Alarm or distress caused to victim 2. Particularly serious original offence	

[Sets out the standard sequential sentencing procedure.]

Note:
An offender convicted of this offence will always have at least one relevant previous conviction for the offence that resulted in the notification requirements being imposed. The starting points and ranges take this into account; any other previous convictions should be considered in the usual way.

[88] **SEXUAL ACTIVITY IN A PUBLIC LAVATORY** SG10-79

Sexual Offences Act 2003, s. 71

Effective from: 24 April 2017

Triable only summarily
Maximum: Unlimited fine and/or 6 months
Offence range: Band A fine–High level community order

STEP ONE Determining the offence category

The Court should determine the offence category using the table below.

Category 1	Higher culpability **and** greater harm
Category 2	Higher culpability **and** lesser harm **or** lower culpability **and** greater harm
Category 3	Lower culpability **and** lesser harm

The court should determine the offender's culpability and the harm caused with reference **only** to the factors below. Where an offence does not fall squarely into a category, individual factors may require a degree of weighting before making an overall assessment and determining the appropriate offence category.

Sentencing Guidelines

CULPABILITY demonstrated by one or more of the following: [88]

Factors indicating higher culpability

- Intimidating behaviour/threats of violence to member(s) of the public
- Blatant behaviour

Factors indicating lower culpability

- All other cases

HARM demonstrated by one or more of the following:

Factors indicating greater harm

- Distress suffered by members of the public
- Children or young persons present

Factors indicating lesser harm

- All other cases

STEP TWO Starting point and category range [89]

Having determined the category at step one, the court should use the starting point to reach a sentence within the appropriate category range in the table below. The starting point applies to all offenders irrespective of plea or previous convictions.

Offence Category	Starting Point	Range
Category 1	Low level community order	Band C fine – High level community order
Category 2	Band C fine	Band B fine – Low level community order
Category 3	Band B fine	Band A fine – Band C fine

Persistent offending of this nature may justify an upward adjustment outside the category range and may cross the community threshold even though the offence otherwise warrants a lesser sentence.

For band ranges, see **SG10-129**

For the imposition of community orders, including the community orders table, see Imposition of Community and Custodial Sentences **SG9-2–SG9-8**

The court should then consider adjustment for any aggravating or mitigating factors. The following is a **non-exhaustive** list of additional factual elements providing the context of the offence and factors relating to the offender. Identify whether any combination of these, or other relevant factors, should result in an upward or downward adjustment from the sentence arrived at so far.

Factors increasing seriousness

Statutory aggravating factors:

- Previous convictions, having regard to a) the **nature** of the offence to which the conviction relates and its **relevance** to the current offence; and b) the **time** that has elapsed since the conviction
- Offence committed whilst on bail

Other aggravating factors:

- Failure to comply with current court orders
- Offence committed on licence or post sentence supervision
- Offences taken into consideration
- Location
- Presence of children
- Established evidence of community/wider impact

Factors reducing seriousness or reflecting personal mitigation

- No previous convictions **or** no relevant/recent convictions
- Remorse
- Good character and/or exemplary conduct
- Serious medical condition requiring urgent, intensive or long-term treatment
- Age and/or lack of maturity where it affects the responsibility of the offender
- Mental disorder or learning disability

[90] **STEP THREE Consider any factors which indicate a reduction, such as assistance to the prosecution**

The court should take into account sections 73 and 74 of the Serious Organised Crime and Police Act 2005 (assistance by defendants: reduction or review of sentence) and any other rule of law by virtue of which an offender may receive a discounted sentence in consequence of assistance given (or offered) to the prosecutor or investigator.

STEP FOUR Reduction for guilty pleas

The court should take account of any potential reduction for a guilty plea in accordance with section 144 of the Criminal Justice Act 2003 and the ***Guilty Plea*** guideline.

STEP FIVE Totality principle

If sentencing an offender for more than one offence, or where the offender is already serving a sentence, consider whether the total sentence is just and proportionate to the overall offending behaviour in accordance with the ***Offences Taken into Consideration and Totality*** guideline.

STEP SIX Compensation and ancillary orders

In all cases, the court should consider whether to make **compensation** and/or other **ancillary orders.**

STEP SEVEN Reasons

Section 174 of the Criminal Justice Act 2003 imposes a duty to give reasons for, and explain the effect of, the sentence.

Sexual Assault SG10-80

[Not reproduced here: see **SG31-17**.]

Sexual Assault of a Child Under 13 SG10-81

[Not reproduced here: see **SG31-50**.]

[92]

Taxi Touting/Soliciting for Hire SG10-82

Criminal Justice and Public Order Act 1994, s. 167

Effective from: 24 April 2017

Triable only summarily
Maximum: Level 4 fine
Offence range: Conditional Discharge–Band C fine

STEP ONE Determining the offence category

The Court should determine the offence category using the table below.

Category 1	Higher culpability **and** greater harm
Category 2	Higher culpability **and** lesser harm **or** lower culpability **and** greater harm
Category 3	Lower culpability **and** lesser harm

The court should determine the offender's culpability and the harm caused with reference **only** to the factors below. Where an offence does not fall squarely into a category, individual factors may require a degree of weighting before making an overall assessment and determining the appropriate offence category.

CULPABILITY demonstrated by one or more of the following:

Factors indicating higher culpability

- Targeting of vulnerable/unsuspecting victim(s) (including tourists)
- Commercial business/large scale operation
- Offender not licensed to drive
- Positive step(s) taken to deceive

Factors indicating lower culpability

- All other cases

HARM demonstrated by one or more of the following:

Factors indicating greater harm

- Passenger safety compromised by vehicle condition
- Passenger(s) overcharged

Factors indicating lesser harm

- All other cases

STEP TWO Starting point and category range [93]

Having determined the category at step one, the court should use the starting point to reach a sentence within the appropriate category range in the table below. The starting point applies to all offenders irrespective of plea or previous convictions.

Offence Category	Starting Point	Range
Category 1	Band C fine	Band B fine – Band C fine and disqualification 6–12 months
Category 2	Band B fine	Band A fine – Band B fine and consider disqualification 3–6 months
Category 3	Band A fine	Conditional discharge – Band A fine and consider disqualification 1–3 months

Note: refer to fines for **offence committed for 'commercial' purposes**

For band ranges, see **SG10-129**

The court should then consider adjustment for any aggravating or mitigating factors. The following is a **non-exhaustive** list of additional factual elements providing the context of the offence and factors relating to the offender. Identify whether any combination of these, or other relevant factors, should result in an upward or downward adjustment from the sentence arrived at so far.

Factors increasing seriousness

Statutory aggravating factors:

- Previous convictions, having regard to a) the **nature** of the offence to which the conviction relates and its **relevance** to the current offence; and b) the **time** that has elapsed since the conviction
- Offence committed whilst on bail

Other aggravating factors:

- Failure to comply with current court orders
- Offence committed on licence or post sentence supervision
- PHV licence refused/ ineligible

Factors reducing seriousness or reflecting personal mitigation

- No previous convictions **or** no relevant/recent convictions
- Remorse
- Good character and/or exemplary conduct
- Mental disorder or learning disability
- Sole or primary carer for dependent relatives

STEP THREE Consider any factors which indicate a reduction, such as assistance to the prosecution [94]

The court should take into account sections 73 and 74 of the Serious Organised Crime and Police Act 2005 (assistance by defendants: reduction or review of sentence) and any other rule of law by virtue of which an offender may receive a discounted sentence in consequence of assistance given (or offered) to the prosecutor or investigator.

STEP FOUR Reduction for guilty pleas

The court should take account of any potential reduction for a guilty plea in accordance with section 144 of the Criminal Justice Act 2003 and the ***Guilty Plea*** guideline.

STEP FIVE Totality principle

If sentencing an offender for more than one offence, or where the offender is already serving a sentence, consider whether the total sentence is just and proportionate to the overall offending behaviour in accordance with the ***Offences Taken into Consideration and Totality*** guideline.

STEP SIX Compensation and ancillary orders

In all cases, the court should consider whether to make **compensation** and/or other **ancillary orders,** including **disqualification from driving** and the **deprivation of a vehicle.**

[94] **STEP SEVEN Reasons**

Section 174 of the Criminal Justice Act 2003 imposes a duty to give reasons for, and explain the effect of, the sentence.

Terrorism Offences—Collection of Terrorist Information **SG10-83**

[Not reproduced here. See **SG32-1** for the new guideline effective from 27 April 2018. For guidance on Ancillary Orders, see **SG10-151** to **SG10-172**. For guidance on community orders, see **SG9-2** to **SG9-8**. For guidance on custodial sentences, see **SG9-9**.]

Encouragement of Terrorism **SG10-84**

[Not reproduced here. See **SG32-27** for the new guideline effective from 27 April 2018. For guidance on Ancillary Orders, see **SG10-151** to **SG10-172**. For guidance on community orders, see **SG9-2** to **SG9-8**. For guidance on custodial sentences, see **SG9-9**.]

Failure to Disclose Information About Acts of Terrorism **SG10-85**

[Not reproduced here. See **SG32-67** for the new guideline effective from 27 April 2018. For guidance on Ancillary Orders, see **SG10-151** to **SG10-172**. For guidance on community orders, see **SG9-2** to **SG9-8**. For guidance on custodial sentences, see **SG9-9**.]

Funding Terrorism **SG10-86**

[Not reproduced here. See **SG32-57** for the new guideline effective from 27 April 2018. For guidance on Ancillary Orders, see **SG10-151** to **SG10-172**. For guidance on community orders, see **SG9-2** to **SG9-8**. For guidance on custodial sentences, see **SG9-9**.]

Possession for Terrorist Purposes **SG10-87**

[Not reproduced here. See **SG32-77** for the new guideline effective from 27 April 2018. For guidance on Ancillary Orders, see **SG10-151** to **SG10-172**. For guidance on custodial sentences, see **SG9-9**.]

Proscribed Organisations—Membership **SG10-88**

[Not reproduced here. See **SG32-37** for the new guideline effective from 27 April 2018. For guidance on Ancillary Orders, see **SG10-151** to **SG10-172**. For guidance on community orders, see **SG9-2** to **SG9-8**. For guidance on custodial sentences, see **SG9-9**.]

Proscribed Organisations—Support **SG10-89**

[Not reproduced here. See **SG32-47** for the new guideline effective from 27 April 2018. For guidance on Ancillary Orders, see **SG10-151** to **SG10-172**. For guidance on community orders, see **SG9-2** to **SG9-8**. For guidance on custodial sentences, see **SG9-9**.]

Theft—General Principles **SG10-90**

[The Guidelines relating to theft for magistrates' courts directly reproduce the Theft Offences Definitive Guideline as regards 'General Theft', which has effect in respect of all persons aged 18 or over who are sentenced on or after 1 February 2016: see **SG33-2**.]

Theft—Breach of Trust **SG10-91**

[The Guidelines relating to theft in breach of trust for magistrates' courts are now covered in the Theft Offences Definitive Guideline under 'General Theft', which has effect in respect of all persons aged 18 or over who are sentenced on or after 1 February 2016: see **SG33-2**.]

Theft—Breach of Trust **SG10-92**

[This Guideline is now superseded: see **SG10-91**.]

Theft—Dwelling **SG10-93**

[The Guidelines relating to theft in a dwelling for magistrates' courts are now covered in the Theft Offences Definitive Guideline under 'General Theft', which has effect in respect of all persons aged 18 or over who are sentenced on or after 1 February 2016: see **SG33-2**.]

SG10-94 **Theft—Person** [94]

[The Guidelines relating to theft from the person for magistrates' courts are now covered in the Theft Offences Definitive Guideline under 'General Theft', which has effect in respect of all persons aged 18 or over who are sentenced on or after 1 February 2016: see **SG33-2**.]

SG10-95 **Theft—Shop**

[The Guidelines relating to theft from a shop for magistrates' courts directly reproduce the Theft Offences Definitive Guideline as regards 'Theft from a shop or stall', which has effect in respect of all persons aged 18 or over who are sentenced on or after 1 February 2016: see **SG33-11**.]

SG10-96 **Threats to Kill** [96]

Offences against the Person Act 1861, s. 16

Triable either way
Maximum when tried summarily: Level 5 fine and/or 6 months
Maximum when tried on indictment: 10 years

Where offence committed in domestic context, refer [below] for guidance

Offence seriousness (culpability and harm)

A. Identify the appropriate starting point

Starting points based on first time offender pleading not guilty

Examples of nature of activity	Starting point	Range
One threat uttered in the heat of the moment, no more than fleeting impact on victim	Medium level community order	Low level community order–high level community order
Single calculated threat or victim fears that threat will be carried out	12 weeks' custody	6–26 weeks' custody
Repeated threats or visible weapon	Crown Court	Crown Court

B. Consider the effect of aggravating and mitigating factors (other than those within examples above)

Common aggravating and mitigating factors are identified [elsewhere]—the following may be particularly relevant but these lists are not exhaustive

Factors indicating higher culpability	Factor indicating lower culpability
1. Planning 2. Offender deliberately isolates victim 3. Group action 4. Threat directed at victim because of job 5. History of antagonism towards victim **Factors indicating greater degree of harm** 1. Vulnerable victim 2. Victim needs medical help/counselling	1. Provocation

[Sets out the standard sequential sentencing procedure and mentions need to consider football banning order.]

SG10-97 **Trade Mark, Unauthorised use of etc.** [97]

Trade Marks Act 1994, s. 92

Triable either way
Maximum when tried summarily: Level 5 fine and/or 6 months
Maximum when tried on indictment: 10 years

[97] **Offence seriousness (culpability and harm)**

A. Identify the appropriate starting point

Starting points based on first time offender pleading not guilty

Examples of nature of activity	Starting point	Range
Small number of counterfeit items	Band C fine	Band B fine–low level community order
Larger number of counterfeit items but no involvement in wider operation	Medium level community order, plus fine*	Low level community order–12 weeks' custody, plus fine*
High number of counterfeit items or involvement in wider operation e.g. manufacture or distribution	12 weeks' custody	6 weeks' custody–Crown Court
Central role in large-scale operation	Crown Court	Crown Court

* This may be an offence for which it is appropriate to combine a fine with a community order. Consult your legal adviser for further guidance.

B. Consider the effect of aggravating and mitigating factors (other than those within examples above)

Common aggravating and mitigating factors are identified [elsewhere]—the following may be particularly relevant but these lists are not exhaustive

Factors indicating higher culpability 1. High degree of professionalism 2. High level of profit **Factor indicating greater degree of harm** 1. Purchasers at risk of harm e.g. from counterfeit drugs	Factor indicating lower culpability 1. Mistake or ignorance about provenance of goods

[Sets out the standard sequential sentencing procedure and mentions need to consider ordering forfeiture and destruction of the goods.]

[98] ## TV Licence Payment Evasion SG10-98

Communications Act 2003, s. 363

Effective from: 24 April 2017
Triable only summarily
Maximum: Level 3 fine
Offence range: Band A fine–Band B fine

STEP ONE Determining the offence category

The Court should determine the offence category using the table below.

Category 1	Higher culpability and greater harm
Category 2	Higher culpability and lesser harm or lower culpability and greater harm
Category 3	Lower culpability and lesser harm

The court should determine the offender's culpability and the harm caused with reference **only** to the factors below. Where an offence does not fall squarely into a category, individual factors may require a degree of weighting before making an overall assessment and determining the appropriate offence category.

CULPABILITY demonstrated by one or more of the following:

Factors indicating higher culpability

- No attempt to obtain TV Licence
- Had additional subscription television service
- Attempts made to evade detection

Factors indicating lower culpability [98]

- Accidental oversight or belief licence held (eg failure of financial arrangement)
- Confusion of responsibility
- Licence immediately obtained
- Significant efforts made to be licensed

HARM demonstrated by one or more of the following:

Factor indicating greater harm

- Prolonged period without TV licence (over 6 months unlicensed use)

Factors indicating lesser harm

- Short period without television licence (under 6 months unlicensed use)

STEP TWO Starting point and category range [99]

Having determined the category at step one, the court should use the starting point to reach a sentence within the appropriate category range in the table below. The starting point applies to all offenders irrespective of plea or previous convictions.

Offence Category	Starting Point	Range
Category 1	Band B fine	Band B fine
Category 2	Band B fine	Band A fine – Band B fine
Category 3	Band A fine	Conditional discharge – Band A fine

For band ranges, see **SG10-129**

The court should then consider adjustment for any aggravating or mitigating factors. The following is a **non-exhaustive** list of additional factual elements providing the context of the offence and factors relating to the offender. Identify whether any combination of these, or other relevant factors, should result in an upward or downward adjustment from the sentence arrived at so far.

Factors increasing seriousness

Statutory aggravating factors:

- Previous convictions, having regard to a) the **nature** of the offence to which the conviction relates and its **relevance** to the current offence; and b) the **time** that has elapsed since the conviction
- Offence committed whilst on bail

Other aggravating factors:

- Failure to comply with current court orders
- Offence committed on licence or post sentence supervision

Factors reducing seriousness or reflecting personal mitigation

- No previous convictions **or** no relevant/recent convictions
- Remorse, especially if evidenced by immediate purchase of television licence
- Good character and/or exemplary conduct
- Age and/or lack of maturity where it affects the responsibility of the offender
- Mental disorder or learning disability
- Offender experiencing significant financial hardship at time of offence due to **exceptional** circumstances

STEP THREE Consider any factors which indicate a reduction, such as assistance to the prosecution [100]

The court should take into account sections 73 and 74 of the Serious Organised Crime and Police Act 2005 (assistance by defendants: reduction or review of sentence) and any other rule of law by virtue of which an offender may receive a discounted sentence in consequence of assistance given (or offered) to the prosecutor or investigator.

STEP FOUR Reduction for guilty pleas

The court should take account of any potential reduction for a guilty plea in accordance with section 144 of the Criminal Justice Act 2003 and the ***Guilty Plea*** guideline.

STEP FIVE Totality principle

If sentencing an offender for more than one offence, or where the offender is already serving a sentence, consider whether the total sentence is just and proportionate to the overall offending behaviour in accordance with the ***Offences Taken into Consideration and Totality*** guideline.

[100] **STEP SIX Compensation and ancillary orders**

In all cases, the court should consider whether to make **compensation** and/or other **ancillary orders.**

STEP SEVEN Reasons

Section 174 of the Criminal Justice Act 2003 imposes a duty to give reasons for, and explain the effect of, the sentence.

[102] VEHICLE INTERFERENCE **SG10-99**

Criminal Attempts Act 1981, s. 9

Effective from: 24 April 2017
Triable only summarily
Maximum: Level 4 fine and/or 3 months

Offence range: Band A fine–12 weeks' custody

STEP ONE Determining the offence category

The Court should determine the offence category using the table below.

Category 1	Higher culpability **and** greater harm
Category 2	Higher culpability **and** lesser harm **or** lower culpability **and** greater harm
Category 3	Lower culpability **and** lesser harm

The court should determine the offender's culpability and the harm caused with reference **only** to the factors below. Where an offence does not fall squarely into a category, individual factors may require a degree of weighting before making an overall assessment and determining the appropriate offence category.

CULPABILITY demonstrated by one or more of the following:

Factors indicating higher culpability

- Leading role where offending is part of a group activity
- Targeting of particular vehicles and/or contents
- Planning

Factors indicating lower culpability

- All other cases

HARM demonstrated by one or more of the following:

Factors indicating greater harm

- Damage caused significant financial loss, inconvenience or distress to victim
- Vehicle left in a dangerous condition

Factors indicating lesser harm

- All other cases

[103] **STEP TWO Starting point and category range**

Having determined the category at step one, the court should use the corresponding starting point to reach a sentence within the category range in the table below. The starting point applies to all offenders irrespective of plea or previous convictions.

Offence Category	Starting Point	Range
Category 1	High level community order	Medium level community order – 12 weeks' custody
Category 2	Medium level community order	Band C fine – High level community order
Category 3	Band C fine	Band A fine – Low level community order

For band ranges, see **SG10-129**

For the imposition of community orders, including the community orders table, see Imposition of Community and Custodial Sentences **SG9-2–SG9-8**

For the imposition of custodial sentences see Imposition of Community and Custodial Sentences **SG9-9–SG9-12**

Sentencing Guidelines

The court should then consider adjustment for any aggravating or mitigating factors. The following is a **non-exhaustive** list of additional factual elements providing the context of the offence and factors relating to the offender. Identify whether any combination of these, or other relevant factors, should result in an upward or downward adjustment from the sentence arrived at so far. [103]

Factors increasing seriousness

Statutory aggravating factors:

- Previous convictions, having regard to a) the **nature** of the offence to which the conviction relates and its **relevance** to the current offence; and b) the **time** that has elapsed since the conviction
- Offence committed whilst on bail

Other aggravating factors:

- Failure to comply with current court orders
- Offence committed on licence or post sentence supervision
- Part of a spree
- Offence against emergency services vehicle

Factors reducing seriousness or reflecting personal mitigation

- No previous convictions **or** no relevant/recent convictions
- Good character and/or exemplary conduct
- Age and/or lack of maturity where it affects the responsibility of the offender
- Mental disorder or learning disability
- Sole or primary carer for dependent relatives

STEP THREE Consider any factors which indicate a reduction, such as assistance to the prosecution [104]

The court should take into account sections 73 and 74 of the Serious Organised Crime and Police Act 2005 (assistance by defendants: reduction or review of sentence) and any other rule of law by virtue of which an offender may receive a discounted sentence in consequence of assistance given (or offered) to the prosecutor or investigator.

STEP FOUR Reduction for guilty pleas

The court should take account of any potential reduction for a guilty plea in accordance with section 144 of the Criminal Justice Act 2003 and the ***Guilty Plea*** guideline.

STEP FIVE Totality principle

If sentencing an offender for more than one offence, or where the offender is already serving a sentence, consider whether the total sentence is just and proportionate to the overall offending behaviour in accordance with the ***Offences Taken into Consideration and Totality*** guideline.

STEP SIX Compensation and ancillary orders

In all cases, the court should consider whether to make **compensation** and/or other **ancillary orders**, including **disqualification from driving.**

STEP SEVEN Reasons

Section 174 of the Criminal Justice Act 2003 imposes a duty to give reasons for, and explain the effect of, the sentence.

STEP EIGHT Consideration for time spent on bail

The court must consider whether to give credit for time spent on bail in accordance with section 240A of the Criminal Justice Act 2003.

SG10-100 VEHICLE LICENCE/REGISTRATION FRAUD [106]

Vehicle Excise and Registration Act 1994, s.44

Triable either way
Maximum when tried summarily: Level 5 fine
Maximum when tried on indictment: 2 years

Offence seriousness (culpability and harm)

[106] *A. Identify the appropriate starting point*

Starting points based on first time offender pleading not guilty

Examples of nature of activity	Starting point	Range
Use of unaltered licence from another vehicle	Band B fine	Band B fine
Forged licence bought for own use, or forged/altered for own use	Band C fine	Band C fine
Use of number plates from another vehicle; or Licence/number plates forged or altered for sale to another	High level community order (in Crown Court)	Medium level community order–Crown Court (Note: community order and custody available only in Crown Court)

B. Consider the effect of aggravating and mitigating factors (other than those within examples above)

Common aggravating and mitigating factors are identified [elsewhere]—the following may be particularly relevant but these lists are not exhaustive

Factors indicating higher culpability	Factors indicating lower culpability
1. LGV, PSV, taxi etc. 2. Long-term fraudulent use **Factors indicating greater degree of harm** 1. High financial gain 2. Innocent victim deceived 3. Legitimate owner inconvenienced	1. Licence/registration mark from another vehicle owned by defendant 2. Short-term use

[Sets out the standard sequential sentencing procedure and mentions the need to consider disqualification from driving and deprivation of property (including vehicle).]

[107] VEHICLE TAKING, WITHOUT CONSENT SG10-101

Theft Act 1968, s. 12

Effective from: 24 April 2017
Triable only summarily
Maximum: Unlimited fine and/or 6 months

Offence range: Band B fine–26 weeks' custody

[108] **STEP ONE Determining the offence category**

The Court should determine the offence category using the table below.

Category 1	Higher culpability **and** greater harm
Category 2	Higher culpability **and** lesser harm **or** lower culpability **and** greater harm
Category 3	Lower culpability **and** lesser harm

The court should determine the offender's culpability and the harm caused with reference only to the factors below. Where an offence does not fall squarely into a category, individual factors may require a degree of weighting before making an overall assessment and determining the appropriate offence category.

CULPABILITY demonstrated by one or more of the following:

Factors indicating higher culpability

- A leading role where offending is part of a group activity
- Involvement of others through coercion, intimidation or exploitation
- Sophisticated nature of offence/significant planning
- Abuse of position of power or trust or responsibility
- Commission of offence in association with or to further other criminal activity

Factors indicating lower culpability [108]

- Performed limited function under direction
- Involved through coercion, intimidation or exploitation
- Limited awareness or understanding of offence
- Exceeding authorised use of e.g. employer's or relative's vehicle
- Retention of hire car for short period beyond return date

HARM demonstrated by one or more of the following: Factors indicating greater harm

- Vehicle later burnt
- Vehicle belonging to elderly/disabled person
- Emergency services vehicle
- Medium to large goods vehicle
- Passengers carried
- Damage to lock/ignition
- Vehicle taken from private premises

Factors indicating lesser harm

- All other cases

STEP TWO Starting point and category range [109]

Having determined the category at step one, the court should use the appropriate starting point to reach a sentence within the category range in the table below. The starting point applies to all offenders irrespective of plea or previous convictions.

Level of seriousness	Starting Point	Range	Disqualification
Category 1	High level community order	Medium level community order – 26 weeks' custody	Consider disqualification 9 to 12 months (Extend if imposing immediate custody)
Category 2	Medium level community order	Low level community order – High level community order	Consider disqualification 5 to 8 months
Category 3	Low level community order	Band B fine – Medium level community order	Consider disqualification

For band ranges, see **SG10-129**

For the imposition of community orders, including the community orders table, see Imposition of Community and Custodial Sentences **SG9-2–SG9-8**

For the imposition of custodial sentences see Imposition of Community and Custodial Sentences **SG9-9–SG9-12**

The court should then consider further adjustment for any aggravating or mitigating factors. The following is a **non-exhaustive** list of additional factual elements providing the context of the offence and factors relating to the offender. Identify whether any combination of these, or other relevant factors, should result in an upward or downward adjustment from the sentence arrived at so far.

Factors increasing seriousness

Statutory aggravating factors:

- Previous convictions, having regard to a) the **nature** of the offence to which the conviction relates and its **relevance** to the current offence; and b) the **time** that has elapsed since the conviction
- Offence committed whilst on bail

Other aggravating factors:

- Failure to comply with current court orders
- Offence committed on licence or post sentence supervision

Factors reducing seriousness or reflecting personal mitigation

- No previous convictions or no relevant/recent convictions
- Remorse
- Good character and/or exemplary conduct
- Age and/or lack of maturity where it affects the responsibility of the offender
- Mental disorder or learning disability
- Sole or primary carer for dependent relatives
- Co-operation with the investigation

[110] **STEP THREE Consider any factors which indicate a reduction, such as assistance to the prosecution**

The court should take into account sections 73 and 74 of the Serious Organised Crime and Police Act 2005 (assistance by defendants: reduction or review of sentence) and any other rule of law by virtue of which an offender may receive a discounted sentence in consequence of assistance given (or offered) to the prosecutor or investigator.

STEP FOUR Reduction for guilty pleas

The court should take account of any potential reduction for a guilty plea in accordance with section 144 of the Criminal Justice Act 2003 and the *Guilty Plea* guideline.

STEP FIVE Totality principle

If sentencing an offender for more than one offence, or where the offender is already serving a sentence, consider whether the total sentence is just and proportionate to the overall offending behaviour in accordance with the *Offences Taken into Consideration and Totality guideline.*

STEP SIX Compensation and ancillary orders

In all cases, the court should consider whether to make **compensation** and/or other **ancillary orders**, including **disqualification from driving.**

STEP SEVEN Reasons

Section 174 of the Criminal Justice Act 2003 imposes a duty to give reasons for, and explain the effect of, the sentence.

STEP EIGHT Consideration for time spent on bail

The court must consider whether to give credit for time spent on bail in accordance with section 240A of the Criminal Justice Act 2003.

[111]

VEHICLE TAKING (AGGRAVATED) SG10-102

DAMAGE CAUSED TO PROPERTY OTHER THAN THE VEHICLE IN ACCIDENT OR DAMAGE CAUSED TO THE VEHICLE

Theft Act 1968, s. 12A(2)(c) and (d)

Triable either way (triable only summarily if damage under £5,000)
Maximum when tried summarily: Level 5 fine and/or 6 months
Maximum when tried on indictment: 2 years

- Must endorse and disqualify for at least 12 months
- Must disqualify for *at least* 2 years if offender has had two or more disqualifications for periods of 56 days or more in preceding 3 years . . .

If there is a delay in sentencing after conviction, consider interim disqualification

Offence seriousness (culpability and harm)

A. Identify the appropriate starting point

Starting points based on first time offender pleading not guilty

Examples of nature of activity	Starting point	Range
Exceeding authorised use of e.g. employer's or relative's vehicle; retention of hire car beyond return date; minor damage to taken vehicle	Medium level community order	Low level community order–high level community order
Greater damage to taken vehicle and/or moderate damage to another vehicle and/or property	High level community order	Medium level community order–12 weeks' custody
Vehicle taken as part of burglary or from private premises; severe damage	18 weeks' custody	12–26 weeks' custody (Crown Court if damage over £5,000)

B. Consider the effect of aggravating and mitigating factors (other than those within examples above) [111]

Common aggravating and mitigating factors are identified [elsewhere]—the following may be particularly relevant but these lists are not exhaustive

Factors indicating higher culpability 1. Vehicle deliberately damaged/destroyed 2. Offender under influence of alcohol/drugs **Factors indicating greater degree of harm** 1. Passenger(s) carried 2. Vehicle belonging to elderly or disabled person 3. Emergency services vehicle 4. Medium to large goods vehicle 5. Damage caused in moving traffic accident	Factors indicating lower culpability 1. Misunderstanding with owner 2. Damage resulting from actions of another (where this does not provide a defence)

[Sets out the standard sequential sentencing procedure.]

SG10-103

Vehicle Taking (Aggravated) [112]

Dangerous Driving or Accident Causing Injury

Theft Act 1968, ss. 12A(2)(a) and (b)

Triable either way
Maximum when tried summarily: Level 5 fine and/or 6 months
Maximum when tried on indictment: 2 years; 14 years if accident caused death

- Must endorse and disqualify for at least 12 months
- Must disqualify for *at least* 2 years if offender has had two or more disqualifications for periods of 56 days or more in preceding 3 years . . .

If there is a delay in sentencing after conviction, consider interim disqualification

Offence seriousness (culpability and harm)

A. Identify the appropriate starting point

Starting points based on first time offender pleading not guilty

Examples of nature of activity	Starting point	Range
Taken vehicle involved in single incident of bad driving where little or no damage or risk of personal injury	High level community order	Medium level community order–12 weeks' custody
Taken vehicle involved in incident(s) involving excessive speed or showing off, especially on busy roads or in built-up area	18 weeks' custody	12–26 weeks' custody
Taken vehicle involved in prolonged bad driving involving deliberate disregard for safety of others	Crown Court	Crown Court

B. Consider the effect of aggravating and mitigating factors (other than those within examples above)

Common aggravating and mitigating factors are identified [elsewhere]—the following may be particularly relevant but these lists are not exhaustive

Factors indicating higher culpability 1. Disregarding warnings of others 2. Evidence of alcohol or drugs 3. Carrying out other tasks while driving 4. Carrying passengers or heavy load 5. Tiredness 6. Trying to avoid arrest 7. Aggressive driving, such as driving much too close to vehicle in front, inappropriate attempts to overtake, or cutting in after overtaking	Factors indicating greater degree of harm 1. Injury to others 2. Damage to other vehicles or property

[112] [Sets out the standard sequential sentencing procedure and mentions the need to consider ordering disqualification until appropriate driving test passed.]

VOYEURISM SG10-104

[Not reproduced here: see SG31-138.]

[113] WITNESS INTIMIDATION SG10-105

Criminal Justice and Public Order Act 1994, s. 51

Triable either way
Maximum when tried summarily: 6 months or level 5 fine
Maximum when tried on indictment: 5 years

Where offence committed in domestic context, refer [below] for guidance

Offence seriousness (culpability and harm)

A. Identify the appropriate starting point

Starting points based on first time offender pleading not guilty

Examples of nature of activity	Starting point	Range
Sudden outburst in chance encounter	6 weeks' custody	Medium level community order–18 weeks' custody
Conduct amounting to a threat; staring at, approaching or following witnesses; talking about the case; trying to alter or stop evidence	18 weeks' custody	12 weeks' custody–Crown Court
Threats of violence to witnesses and/or their families; deliberately seeking out witnesses	Crown Court	Crown Court

B. Consider the effect of aggravating and mitigating factors (other than those within examples above)

Common aggravating and mitigating factors are identified [elsewhere]—the following may be particularly relevant but these lists are not exhaustive

Factors indicating higher culpability
1. Breach of bail conditions 2. Offender involves others
Factors indicating greater degree of harm
1. Detrimental impact on administration of justice 2. Contact made at or in vicinity of victim's home

[Sets out the standard sequential sentencing procedure.]

[MOTORING OFFENCES] SG10-106

[114] CARELESS DRIVING (DRIVE WITHOUT DUE CARE AND ATTENTION)

Road Traffic Act 1988, s. 3

Effective from: 24 April 2017

Triable only summarily
Maximum: Unlimited fine
Offence range: Band A fine–Band C fine

STEP ONE Determining the offence category

The Court should determine the offence category using the table below.

Category 1	Higher culpability **and** greater harm
Category 2	Higher culpability **and** lesser harm **or** lower culpability **and** greater harm
Category 3	Lower culpability **and** lesser harm

The court should determine the offender's culpability and the harm caused with reference only to the factors below. Where an offence does not fall squarely into a category, individual factors may require a degree of weighting before making an overall assessment and determining the appropriate offence category.

CULPABILITY demonstrated by one or more of the following: [114]

Factors indicating higher culpability

- Excessive speed or aggressive driving
- Carrying out other tasks while driving
- Vehicle used for the carriage of heavy goods or for the carriage of passengers for reward
- Tiredness or driving whilst unwell
- Driving contrary to medical advice (including written advice from the drug manufacturer not to drive when taking any medicine)

Factors indicating lower culpability

- All other cases

HARM demonstrated by one or more of the following:

Factors indicating greater harm

- Injury to others
- Damage to other vehicles or property
- High level of traffic or pedestrians in vicinity

Factors indicating lesser harm

- All other cases

STEP TWO Starting point and category range [115]

Having determined the category at step one, the court should use the appropriate starting point to reach a sentence within the category range in the table below. The starting point applies to all offenders irrespective of plea or previous convictions.

Level of seriousness	Starting Point	Range	Disqualification/points
Category 1	Band C fine	Band C fine	Consider disqualification **OR** 7–9 points
Category 2	Band B fine	Band B fine	5–6 points
Category 3	Band A fine	Band A fine	3–4 points

- **Must endorse and may disqualify. If no disqualification impose 3–9 points**

For band ranges, see **SG10-129**

The court should then consider further adjustment for any aggravating or mitigating factors. The following is a **non-exhaustive** list of additional factual elements providing the context of the offence and factors relating to the offender. Identify whether any combination of these, or other relevant factors, should result in an upward or downward adjustment from the sentence arrived at so far.

Factors increasing seriousness

Statutory aggravating factors:

- Previous convictions, having regard to a) the **nature** of the offence to which the conviction relates and its **relevance** to the current offence; and b) the **time** that has elapsed since the conviction
- Offence committed whilst on bail

Other aggravating factors:

- Failure to comply with current court orders
- Offence committed on licence or post sentence supervision
- Contravening a red signal at a level crossing

Factors reducing seriousness or reflecting personal mitigation

- No previous convictions **or** no relevant/recent convictions
- Remorse
- Good character and/or exemplary conduct

STEP THREE Consider any factors which indicate a reduction, such as assistance to the prosecution [116]

The court should take into account sections 73 and 74 of the Serious Organised Crime and Police Act 2005 (assistance by defendants: reduction or review of sentence) and any other rule of law by virtue of which an offender may receive a discounted sentence in consequence of assistance given (or offered) to the prosecutor or investigator.

[116] **STEP FOUR Reduction for guilty pleas**

The court should take account of any potential reduction for a guilty plea in accordance with section 144 of the Criminal Justice Act 2003 and the *Guilty Plea* guideline.

STEP FIVE Totality principle

If sentencing an offender for more than one offence, or where the offender is already serving a sentence, consider whether the total sentence is just and proportionate to the overall offending behaviour in accordance with the *Offences Taken into Consideration and Totality* guideline.

STEP SIX Compensation and ancillary orders

In all cases, the court should consider whether to make **compensation** and/or other **ancillary orders**, including **disqualification from driving.**

STEP SEVEN Reasons

Section 174 of the Criminal Justice Act 2003 imposes a duty to give reasons for, and explain the effect of, the sentence.

[118] CAUSING DEATH BY CARELESS OR INCONSIDERATE DRIVING SG10-107

This guideline and accompanying notes are taken from the Sentencing Guidelines Council's definitive guideline *Causing Death by Driving*, published 15 July 2008 [see **SG22-1**].

Factors to take into consideration

Key factors

(a) It is unavoidable that some cases will be on the borderline between *dangerous* and *careless* driving, or may involve a number of factors that significantly increase the seriousness of an offence. As a result, the guideline for this offence identifies three levels of seriousness, the range for the highest of which overlaps with ranges for the lower levels of seriousness for *causing death by dangerous driving*.

(b) The three levels of seriousness are defined by the degree of carelessness involved in the standard of driving:
- the most serious level for this offence is where the offender's driving fell *not that far short of dangerous*;
- the least serious group of offences relates to those cases where the level of culpability is low—for example in a case involving an offender who misjudges the speed of another vehicle, or turns without seeing an oncoming vehicle because of restricted visibility;
- other cases will fall into the intermediate level.

(c) Where the level of carelessness is low and there are no aggravating factors, even the fact that death was caused is not sufficient to justify a prison sentence.

(d) A fine is unlikely to be an appropriate sentence for this offence; where a non-custodial sentence is considered appropriate, this should be a community order. The nature of the requirements will be determined by the purpose identified by the court as of primary importance. Requirements most likely to be relevant include unpaid work requirement, activity requirement, programme requirement and curfew requirement.

(e) Offender mitigation particularly relevant to this offence includes conduct after the offence such as where the offender gave direct, positive, assistance at the scene of a collision to victim(s). It may also include remorse—whilst it can be expected that anyone who has caused a death by driving would be remorseful, this cannot undermine its importance for sentencing purposes. It is for the court to determine whether an expression of remorse is genuine.

(f) Where an offender has a good driving record, this is not a factor that automatically should be treated as mitigation, especially now that the presence of previous convictions is a statutory aggravating factor. However, any evidence to show that an offender has previously been an exemplary driver, for example having driven an ambulance, police vehicle, bus, taxi or similar vehicle conscientiously and without incident for many years, is a fact that the courts may well wish to take into account by way of offender mitigation. This is likely to have even greater effect where the driver is driving on public duty (for example, on ambulance, fire services or police duties) and was responding to an emergency.

(g) Disqualification of the offender from driving and endorsement of the offender's driving licence are mandatory, and the offence carries between 3 and 11 penalty points when the court finds special reasons for not imposing disqualification. There is a discretionary power to order an extended driving test/re-test where a person is convicted of this offence.

Guidelines

Road Traffic Act 1988, s. 2B [119]

Triable either way
Maximum when tried summarily: Level 5 fine and/or 6 months
Maximum when tried on indictment: 5 years

Offence seriousness (culpability and harm)

A. Identify the appropriate starting point

Starting points based on first time offender pleading not guilty

Examples of nature of activity	Starting point	Range
Careless or inconsiderate driving arising from momentary inattention with no aggravating factors	Medium level community order	Low level community order–high level community order
Other cases of careless or inconsiderate driving	Crown Court	High level community order–Crown Court
Careless or inconsiderate driving falling not far short of dangerous driving	Crown Court	Crown Court

B. Consider the effect of aggravating and mitigating factors (other than those within examples above)

Common aggravating and mitigating factors are identified [elsewhere]—the following may be particularly relevant but these lists are not exhaustive

Factors indicating higher culpability	Factors indicating lower culpability
1. Other offences committed at the same time, such as driving other than in accordance with the terms of a valid licence; driving while disqualified; driving without insurance; taking a vehicle without consent; driving a stolen vehicle 2. Previous convictions for motoring offences, particularly offences that involve bad driving 3. Irresponsible behaviour, such as failing to stop or falsely claiming that one of the victims was responsible for the collision **Factors indicating greater degree of harm** 1. More than one person was killed as a result of the offence 2. Serious injury to one or more persons in addition to the death(s)	1. Offender seriously injured in the collision 2. The victim was a close friend or relative 3. The actions of the victim or a third party contributed to the commission of the offence 4. The offender's lack of driving experience contributed significantly to the likelihood of a collision occurring and/or death resulting 5. The driving was in response to a proven and genuine emergency falling short of a defence

[Sets out the standard sequential sentencing procedure and mentions need to consider ordering disqualification and deprivation of property.]

SG10-108 CAUSING DEATH BY DRIVING: UNLICENSED, DISQUALIFIED OR UNINSURED DRIVERS [120]

Factors to take into consideration

Key factors

(a) Culpability arises from the offender driving a vehicle on a road or other public place when, by law, not allowed to do so; the offence does not involve any fault in the standard of driving.
(b) Since driving whilst disqualified is more culpable than driving whilst unlicensed or uninsured, a higher starting point is proposed when the offender was disqualified from driving at the time of the offence.
(c) Being uninsured, unlicensed or disqualified are the only determinants of seriousness for this offence, as there are no factors relating to the standard of driving. The list of aggravating factors identified is slightly different as the emphasis is on the decision to drive by an offender who is not permitted by law to do so.
(d) A fine is unlikely to be an appropriate sentence for this offence; where a non-custodial sentence is considered appropriate, this should be a community order.
(e) Where the *decision to drive was brought about by a genuine and proven emergency*, that may mitigate offence seriousness and so it is included as an additional mitigating factor.
(f) An additional mitigating factor covers those situations where an offender genuinely believed that there was valid insurance or a valid licence.

[120] (g) Offender mitigation particularly relevant to this offence includes conduct after the offence such as where the offender gave direct, positive, assistance at the scene of a collision to victim(s). It may also include remorse—whilst it can be expected that anyone who has caused a death by driving would be remorseful, this cannot undermine its importance for sentencing purposes. It is for the court to determine whether an expression of remorse is genuine.

(h) Where an offender has a good driving record, this is not a factor that automatically should be treated as mitigation, especially now that the presence of previous convictions is a statutory aggravating factor. However, any evidence to show that an offender has previously been an exemplary driver, for example having driven an ambulance, police vehicle, bus, taxi or similar vehicle conscientiously and without incident for many years, is a fact that the courts may well wish to take into account by way of offender mitigation. This is likely to have even greater effect where the driver is driving on public duty (for example, on ambulance, fire services or police duties) and was responding to an emergency.

(i) Disqualification of the offender from driving and endorsement of the offender's driving licence are mandatory, and the offence carries between 3 and 11 penalty points when the court finds special reasons for not imposing disqualification. There is a discretionary power[109] to order an extended driving test/re-test where a person is convicted of this offence.

Guidelines

[121] *Road Traffic Act 1988, s. 3ZB*

Triable either way
Maximum when tried summarily: Level 5 fine and/or 6 months
Maximum when tried on indictment: 2 years

Offence seriousness (culpability and harm)

A. Identify the appropriate starting point

Starting points based on first time offender pleading not guilty

Examples of nature of activity	**Starting point**	**Range**
The offender was unlicensed or uninsured—no aggravating factors	Medium level community order	Low level community order–high level community order
The offender was unlicensed or uninsured plus at least 1 aggravating factor from the list below	26 weeks' custody	High level community order–Crown Court
The offender was disqualified from driving **OR** The offender was unlicensed or uninsured plus 2 or more aggravating factors from the list below	Crown Court	Crown Court

B. Consider the effect of aggravating and mitigating factors (other than those within examples above)

Common aggravating and mitigating factors are identified [elsewhere]—the following may be particularly relevant but these lists are not exhaustive

Factors indicating higher culpability	**Factors indicating lower culpability**
1. Previous convictions for motoring offences, whether involving bad driving or involving an offence of the same kind that forms part of the present conviction (i.e. unlicensed, disqualified or uninsured driving) 2. Irresponsible behaviour such as failing to stop or falsely claiming that someone else was driving **Factors indicating greater degree of harm** 1. More than one person was killed as a result of the offence 2. Serious injury to one or more persons in addition to the death(s)	1. The decision to drive was brought about by a proven and genuine emergency falling short of a defence 2. The offender genuinely believed that he or she was insured or licensed to drive 3. The offender was seriously injured as a result of the collision 4. The victim was a close friend or relative

[Sets out the standard sequential sentencing procedure and mentions need to consider ordering disqualification and deprivation of property.]

[109] Road Traffic Offenders Act 1988, s. 36(4)

SG10-109

Dangerous Driving [122]

Road Traffic Act 1988, s. 2

Triable either way
Maximum when tried summarily: Level 5 fine and/or 6 months
Maximum when tried on indictment: 2 years

- Must endorse and disqualify for *at least* 12 months. Must order extended re-test
- Must disqualify for *at least* 2 years if offender has had two or more disqualifications for periods of 56 days or more in preceding 3 years. If there is a delay in sentencing after conviction, consider interim disqualification

Offence seriousness (culpability and harm)

A. Identify the appropriate starting point

Starting points based on first time offender pleading not guilty

Examples of nature of activity	Starting point	Range
Single incident where little or no damage or risk of personal injury	Medium level community order	Low level community order–high level community order Disqualify 12–15 months
Incident(s) involving excessive speed or showing off, especially on busy roads or in built-up area; OR Single incident where little or no damage or risk of personal injury but offender was disqualified driver	12 weeks' custody	High level community order–26 weeks' custody Disqualify 15–24 months
Prolonged bad driving involving deliberate disregard for safety of others; OR Incident(s) involving excessive speed or showing off, especially on busy roads or in built-up area, by disqualified driver; OR Driving as described in box above while being pursued by police	Crown Court	Crown Court

B. Consider the effect of aggravating and mitigating factors (other than those within examples above)

Common aggravating and mitigating factors are identified [elsewhere]—the following may be particularly relevant but these lists are not exhaustive

Factors indicating higher culpability	Factors indicating lower culpability
1. Disregarding warnings of others 2. Evidence of alcohol or drugs 3. Carrying out other tasks while driving 4. Carrying passengers or heavy load 5. Tiredness 6. Aggressive driving, such as driving much too close to vehicle in front, racing, inappropriate attempts to overtake, or cutting in after overtaking 7. Driving when knowingly suffering from a medical condition which significantly impairs the offender's driving skills 8. Driving a poorly maintained or dangerously loaded vehicle, especially where motivated by commercial concerns **Factors indicating greater degree of harm** 1. Injury to others 2. Damage to other vehicles or property	1. Genuine emergency 2. Speed not excessive 3. Offence due to inexperience rather than irresponsibility of driver

[Sets out the standard sequential sentencing procedure and mentions need to consider order for deprivation of property.] [123]

[124] ## Drive Whilst Disqualified SG10-110

Road Traffic Act 1988, s. 103

Effective from: 24 April 2017

Triable only summarily
Maximum: Unlimited fine and/or 6 months
Offence range: Band C fine–26 weeks' custody

STEP ONE Determining the offence category

The Court should determine the offence category using the table below.

Category 1	Higher culpability **and** greater harm
Category 2	Higher culpability **and** lesser harm **or** lower culpability **and** greater harm
Category 3	Lower culpability **and** lesser harm

The court should determine the offender's culpability and the harm caused with reference **only** to the factors below. Where an offence does not fall squarely into a category, individual factors may require a degree of weighting before making an overall assessment and determining the appropriate offence category.

CULPABILITY demonstrated by one or more of the following:

Factors indicating higher culpability

- Driving shortly after disqualification imposed
- Vehicle obtained during disqualification period
- Driving for reward

Factors indicating lower culpability

- All other cases

HARM demonstrated by one or more of the following:

Factors indicating greater harm

- Significant distance driven
- Evidence of associated bad driving

Factors indicating lesser harm

- All other cases

[125] ### STEP TWO Starting point and category range

Having determined the category at step one, the court should use the appropriate starting point to reach a sentence within the category range in the table below. The starting point applies to all offenders irrespective of plea or previous convictions.

- **Must endorse and may disqualify. If no disqualification impose 6 points**
- **Extend disqualification if imposing immediate custody**

Level of seriousness	Starting Point	Range	Penalty points/disqualification
Category 1	12 weeks' custody	High Level community order – 26 weeks' custody	Disqualify for 12–18 months beyond expiry of current ban (Extend if imposing immediate custody)
Category 2	High level community order	Medium level community order – 12 weeks' custody	Disqualify for 6–12 months beyond expiry of current ban (Extend if imposing immediate custody)
Category 3	Low level community order	Band C fine – Medium level community order	Disqualify for 3–6 months beyond expiry of current ban OR 6 points

For band ranges, see SG10-129 [125]

For the imposition of community orders, including the community orders table, see Imposition of Community and Custodial Sentences **SG9-2–SG9-8**

For the imposition of custodial sentences see Imposition of Community and Custodial Sentences **SG9-9–SG9-12**

The court should then consider further adjustment for any aggravating or mitigating factors. The following is a **non-exhaustive** list of additional factual elements providing the context of the offence and factors relating to the offender. Identify whether any combination of these, or other relevant factors, should result in an upward or downward adjustment from the sentence arrived at so far. [126]

Factors increasing seriousness

Statutory aggravating factors:

- Previous convictions, having regard to a) the **nature** of the offence to which the conviction relates and its **relevance** to the current offence; and b) the **time** that has elapsed since the conviction

Note An offender convicted of this offence will always have at least one relevant previous conviction for the offence that resulted in disqualification. The starting points and ranges take this into account; any other previous convictions should be considered in the usual way.

- Offence committed whilst on bail

Other aggravating factors:

- Failure to comply with current court orders (not including the current order for disqualification)
- Offence committed on licence or post sentence supervision
- Carrying passengers
- Giving false details

Factors reducing seriousness or reflecting personal mitigation

- No previous convictions **or** no relevant/recent convictions
- Good character and/or exemplary conduct
- Remorse
- Genuine emergency established
- Age and/or lack of maturity where it affects the responsibility of the offender
- Serious medical condition requiring urgent, intensive or long-term treatment
- Sole or primary carer for dependent relatives

STEP THREE Consider any factors which indicate a reduction, such as assistance to the prosecution [127]

The court should take into account sections 73 and 74 of the Serious Organised Crime and Police Act 2005 (assistance by defendants: reduction or review of sentence) and any other rule of law by virtue of which an offender may receive a discounted sentence in consequence of assistance given (or offered) to the prosecutor or investigator.

STEP FOUR Reduction for guilty pleas

The court should take account of any potential reduction for a guilty plea in accordance with section 144 of the Criminal Justice Act 2003 and the ***Guilty Plea*** guideline.

STEP FIVE Totality principle

If sentencing an offender for more than one offence, or where the offender is already serving a sentence, consider whether the total sentence is just and proportionate to the overall offending behaviour in accordance with the ***Offences Taken into Consideration and Totality*** guideline.

STEP SIX Compensation and ancillary orders

In all cases, the court should consider whether to make **compensation** and/or other **ancillary orders** including **disqualification from driving.**

STEP SEVEN Reasons

Section 174 of the Criminal Justice Act 2003 imposes a duty to give reasons for, and explain the effect of, the sentence.

[127] **STEP EIGHT Consideration for time spent on bail**

The court must consider whether to give credit for time spent on bail in accordance with section 240A of the Criminal Justice Act 2003.

[128]

EXCESS ALCOHOL (DRIVE/ATTEMPT TO DRIVE) SG10-111

Road Traffic Act 1988, s. 5(1)(a)

Effective from: 24 April 2017
Triable only summarily
Maximum: Unlimited fine and/or 6 months
Offence range: Band B fine–26 weeks' custody

[129] **STEPS 1 AND 2 Determining the offence seriousness**

- Must endorse and disqualify for at least 12 months
- Must disqualify for at least 2 years if offender has had two or more disqualifications for periods of 56 days or more in preceding 3 years – refer to disqualification guidance and consult your legal adviser for further guidance
- Must disqualify for at least 3 years if offender has been convicted of a relevant offence in preceding 10 years – consult your legal adviser for further guidance
- Extend disqualification if imposing immediate custody

If there is a delay in sentencing after conviction, consider interim **disqualification**

The starting point applies to all offenders irrespective of plea or previous convictions.

Level of alcohol			Starting point	Range	Disqualification	Disqual. 2nd offence in 10 years – see note above
Breath (µg)	Blood (mg)	Urine (mg)				
120–150 and above	276–345 and above	367–459 and above	12 weeks' custody	High level community order – 26 weeks' custody	29–36 months (Extend if imposing immediate custody)	**36–60 months**
90–119	207–275	275–366	Medium level community order	Low level community order – High level community order	23–28 months	**36–52 months**
60–89	138–206	184–274	Band C Fine	Band C Fine – Low level community order	17–22 months	**36–46 months**
36–59	81–137	108–183	Band C Fine	Band B Fine – Band C fine	12–16 months	**36–40 months**

Note: when considering the guidance regarding the length of disqualification in the case of a second offence, the period to be imposed in any individual case will depend on an assessment of all the relevant circumstances, including the length of time since the earlier ban was imposed and the gravity of the current offence but disqualification must be for at least three years.

For band ranges, see SG10-129

For the imposition of community orders, including the community orders table, see Imposition of Community and Custodial Sentences **SG9-2–SG9-8** [129]

For the imposition of custodial sentences see Imposition of Community and Custodial Sentences **SG9-9–SG9-12**

The court should then consider further adjustment for any aggravating or mitigating factors. The following is a **non-exhaustive** list of additional factual elements providing the context of the offence and factors relating to the offender. Identify whether any combination of these, or other relevant factors, should result in an upward or downward adjustment from the sentence arrived at so far. [130]

Factors increasing seriousness

Statutory aggravating factors:

- Previous convictions, having regard to a) the **nature** of the offence to which the conviction relates and its **relevance** to the current offence; and b) the **time** that has elapsed since the conviction
- Offence committed whilst on bail

Other aggravating factors:

- Failure to comply with current court orders
- Offence committed on licence or post sentence supervision
- LGV, HGV, PSV etc
- Poor road or weather conditions
- Carrying passengers
- Driving for hire or reward
- Evidence of unacceptable standard of driving
- Involved in accident
- High level of traffic or pedestrians in the vicinity

Factors reducing seriousness or reflecting personal mitigation

- No previous convictions **or** no relevant/recent convictions
- Genuine emergency established*
- Spiked drinks*
- Very short distance driven*
- Remorse
- Good character and/or exemplary conduct
- Serious medical condition requiring urgent, intensive or long-term treatment
- Age and/or lack of maturity where it affects the responsibility of the offender
- Mental disorder or learning disability
- Sole or primary carer for dependent relatives

* even where not amounting to special reasons

STEP 3 Consider any factors which indicate a reduction, such as assistance to the prosecution [131]

The court should take into account sections 73 and 74 of the Serious Organised Crime and Police Act 2005 (assistance by defendants: reduction or review of sentence) and any other rule of law by virtue of which an offender may receive a discounted sentence in consequence of assistance given (or offered) to the prosecutor or investigator.

STEP 4 Reduction for guilty pleas

The court should take account of any potential reduction for a guilty plea in accordance with section 144 of the Criminal Justice Act 2003 and the ***Guilty Plea*** guideline.

STEP 5 Totality principle

If sentencing an offender for more than one offence, or where the offender is already serving a sentence, consider whether the total sentence is just and proportionate to the overall offending behaviour in accordance with the ***Offences Taken into Consideration and Totality*** guideline.

STEP 6 Compensation and ancillary orders

In all cases, the court should consider whether to make **compensation** and/or other **ancillary orders** including offering a **drink/drive rehabilitation course**, **deprivation**, and /or **forfeiture or suspension of personal liquor licence.**

[131] **STEP 7 Reasons**

Section 174 of the Criminal Justice Act 2003 imposes a duty to give reasons for, and explain the effect of, the sentence.

STEP 8 Consideration for time spent on bail

The court must consider whether to give credit for time spent on bail in accordance with section 240A of the Criminal Justice Act 2003.

[132]

EXCESS ALCOHOL (IN CHARGE) SG10-112

Road Traffic Act 1988, s. 5(1)(b)

Effective from: 24 April 2017

Triable only summarily
Maximum: Level 4 fine and/or 3 months
Offence range: Band A fine–6 weeks' custody

STEPS 1 AND 2 Determining the offence seriousness

- **Must endorse and may disqualify. If no disqualification impose 10 points**
- **Extend any disqualification if imposing immediate custody**

The starting point applies to all offenders irrespective of plea or previous convictions.

Level of alcohol			Starting point	Range	Disqualification/Points
Breath (µg)	Blood (mg)	Urine (mg)			
120–150 and above	276–345 and above	367–459 and above	Medium level community order	Low level community order – 6 weeks' custody	Disqualify 6–12 months (Extend if imposing immediate custody)
90–119	207–275	275–366	Band C fine	Band C Fine – Medium level community order	Consider disqualification up to 6 months **OR** 10 points
60–89	138–206	184–274	Band B fine	Band B fine – Band C fine	Consider disqualification **OR** 10 points
36–59	81–137	108–183	Band B fine	Band A fine – Band B fine	10 points

For band ranges, see **SG10-129**

For the imposition of community orders, including the community orders table, see Imposition of Community and Custodial Sentences **SG9-2–SG9-8**

For the imposition of custodial sentences see Imposition of Community and Custodial Sentences **SG9-9–SG9-12**

[133] The court should then consider further adjustment for any aggravating or mitigating factors. The following is a **non-exhaustive** list of additional factual elements providing the context of the offence and factors relating to the offender. Identify whether any combination of these, or other relevant factors, should result in an upward or downward adjustment from the sentence arrived at so far.

Factors increasing seriousness

Statutory aggravating factors:

- Previous convictions, having regard to a) the **nature** of the offence to which the conviction relates and its **relevance** to the current offence; and b) the **time** that has elapsed since the conviction
- Offence committed whilst on bail

Other aggravating factors:

- Failure to comply with current court orders
- Offence committed on licence or post sentence supervision
- In charge of LGV, HGV, PSV etc
- High likelihood of driving
- Offering to drive for hire or reward

Factors reducing seriousness or reflecting personal mitigation [133]

- No previous convictions or no relevant/recent convictions
- Low likelihood of driving
- Spiked drinks*
- Remorse
- Good character and/or exemplary conduct
- Serious medical condition requiring urgent, intensive or long-term treatment
- Age and/or lack of maturity where it affects the responsibility of the offender
- Mental disorder or learning disability
- Sole or primary carer for dependent relatives

* even where not amounting to special reasons

STEP 3 Consider any factors which indicate a reduction, such as assistance to the prosecution [134]

The court should take into account sections 73 and 74 of the Serious Organised Crime and Police Act 2005 (assistance by defendants: reduction or review of sentence) and any other rule of law by virtue of which an offender may receive a discounted sentence in consequence of assistance given (or offered) to the prosecutor or investigator.

STEP 4 Reduction for guilty pleas

The court should take account of any potential reduction for a guilty plea in accordance with section 144 of the Criminal Justice Act 2003 and the ***Guilty Plea*** guideline.

STEP 5 Totality principle

If sentencing an offender for more than one offence, or where the offender is already serving a sentence, consider whether the total sentence is just and proportionate to the overall offending behaviour in accordance with the ***Offences Taken into Consideration and Totality*** guideline.

STEP 6 Compensation and ancillary orders

In all cases, the court should consider whether to make **compensation** and/or other **ancillary orders** including offering a **drink/drive rehabilitation course, deprivation**, and/or **forfeiture or suspension of personal liquor licence.**

STEP 7 Reasons

Section 174 of the Criminal Justice Act 2003 imposes a duty to give reasons for, and explain the effect of, the sentence.

STEP 8 Consideration for time spent on bail

The court must consider whether to give credit for time spent on bail in accordance with section 240A of the Criminal Justice Act 2003.

SG10-113

Fail to Stop/Report Road Accident [135]

Road Traffic Act 1988, s. 170(4)

Effective from: 24 April 2017

Triable only summarily
Maximum: Unlimited fine and/or 6 months
Offence range: Band A fine–26 weeks' custody

STEP 1 Determining the offence category

The Court should determine the offence category using the table below.

Category 1	Higher culpability **and** greater harm
Category 2	Higher culpability **and** lesser harm **or** lower culpability **and** greater harm
Category 3	Lower culpability **and** lesser harm

The court should determine the offender's culpability and the harm caused with reference **only** to the factors below. Where an offence does not fall squarely into a category, individual factors may require a degree of weighting before making an overall assessment and determining the appropriate offence category.

[135] **CULPABILITY demonstrated by one or more of the following:**

Factors indicating higher culpability

- Offence committed in circumstances where a request for a sample of breath, blood or urine would have been made had the offender stopped
- Offence committed by offender seeking to avoid arrest for another offence
- Offender knew or suspected that personal injury caused and/or left injured party at scene
- Giving false details

Factors indicating lower culpability

- All other cases

HARM demonstrated by one or more of the following:

Factors indicating greater harm

- Injury caused
- Significant damage

Factors indicating lesser harm

- All other cases

[136] **STEP 2 Starting point and category range**

Having determined the category at step one, the court should use the appropriate starting point to reach a sentence within the category range in the table below. The starting point applies to all offenders irrespective of plea or previous convictions.

- **Must endorse and may disqualify. If no disqualification impose 3–9 points**
- **Extend disqualification if imposing immediate custody**

Level of seriousness	Starting Point	Range	Disqualification/points
Category 1	High level community order	Low level community order – 26 weeks' custody	Disqualify 6–12 months OR 9–10 points (Extend if imposing immediate custody)
Category 2	Band C fine	Band B fine – Medium level community order	Disqualify up to 6 months OR 7–8 points
Category 3	Band B fine	Band A fine – Band C fine	5–6 points

For band ranges, see **SG10-129**

For the imposition of community orders, including the community orders table, see Imposition of Community and Custodial Sentences **SG9-2–SG9-8**

For the imposition of custodial sentences see Imposition of Community and Custodial Sentences **SG9-9–SG9-12**

The court should then consider further adjustment for any aggravating or mitigating factors. The following is a **non-exhaustive** list of additional factual elements providing the context of the offence and factors relating to the offender. Identify whether any combination of these, or other relevant factors, should result in an upward or downward adjustment from the sentence arrived at so far.

Factors increasing seriousness

Statutory aggravating factors:

- Previous convictions, having regard to a) the **nature** of the offence to which the conviction relates and its **relevance** to the current offence; and b) the **time** that has elapsed since the conviction
- Offence committed whilst on bail

Other aggravating factors:

- Little or no attempt made to comply with duty
- Evidence of bad driving
- Failure to comply with current court orders
- Offence committed on licence or post sentence supervision

Factors reducing seriousness or reflecting personal mitigation [136]

- No previous convictions or no relevant/recent convictions
- Remorse
- Good character and/or exemplary conduct
- Reasonably believed identity known
- Genuine fear of retribution
- Significant attempt made to comply with duty
- Serious medical condition requiring urgent, intensive or long-term treatment
- Age and/or lack of maturity where it affects the responsibility of the offender
- Mental disorder or learning disability
- Sole or primary carer for dependent relatives

STEP 3 Consider any factors which indicate a reduction, such as assistance to the prosecution [137]

The court should take into account sections 73 and 74 of the Serious Organised Crime and Police Act 2005 (assistance by defendants: reduction or review of sentence) and any other rule of law by virtue of which an offender may receive a discounted sentence in consequence of assistance given (or offered) to the prosecutor or investigator.

STEP 4 Reduction for guilty pleas

The court should take account of any potential reduction for a guilty plea in accordance with section 144 of the Criminal Justice Act 2003 and the ***Guilty Plea*** guideline.

STEP 5 Totality principle

If sentencing an offender for more than one offence, or where the offender is already serving a sentence, consider whether the total sentence is just and proportionate to the overall offending behaviour in accordance with the ***Offences Taken into Consideration and Totality*** guideline.

STEP 6 Compensation and ancillary orders

In all cases, the court should consider whether to make **compensation** and/or other ancillary orders, including **disqualification from driving** and **deprivation of a vehicle.**

STEP 7 Reasons

Section 174 of the Criminal Justice Act 2003 imposes a duty to give reasons for, and explain the effect of, the sentence.

STEP 8 Consideration for time spent on bail

The court must consider whether to give credit for time spent on bail in accordance with section 240A of the Criminal Justice Act 2003.

SG10-114 FAIL TO PROVIDE SPECIMEN FOR ANALYSIS (DRIVE/ATTEMPT TO DRIVE) [139]

Road Traffic Act 1988, s. 7(6)

Effective from: 24 April 2017

Triable only summarily
Maximum: Unlimited fine and/or 6 months
Offence range: Band B fine–26 weeks' custody

STEP ONE Determining the offence category

The Court should determine the offence category using the table below.

Category 1	Higher culpability **and** greater harm
Category 2	Higher culpability **and** lesser harm **or** lower culpability **and** greater harm
Category 3	Lower culpability **and** lesser harm

The court should determine the offender's culpability and the harm caused with reference **only** to the factors below. Where an offence does not fall squarely into a category, individual factors may require a degree of weighting before making an overall assessment and determining the appropriate offence category.

[139] **CULPABILITY demonstrated by one or more of the following:**

Factors indicating higher culpability

- Deliberate refusal/ failure

Factors indicating lower culpability

- All other cases

HARM demonstrated by one or more of the following:

Factors indicating greater harm

- High level of impairment

Factors indicating lesser harm

- All other cases

[140] **STEP TWO Starting point and category range**

Having determined the category at step one, the court should use the appropriate starting point to reach a sentence within the category range in the table below.

- **Must endorse and disqualify for at least 12 months**
- **Must disqualify for at least 2 years if offender has had two or more disqualifications for periods of 56 days or more in preceding 3 years – refer to the disqualification guidance and consult your legal adviser for further guidance**
- **Must disqualify for at least 3 years if offender has been convicted of a relevant offence in preceding 10 years – consult your legal adviser for further guidance**
- **Extend disqualification if imposing immediate custody**

If there is a delay in sentencing after conviction, consider interim disqualification.

The starting point applies to all offenders irrespective of plea or previous convictions.

Level of seriousness	Starting point	Range	Disqualification	Disqual. 2nd offence in 10 years
Category 1	12 weeks' custody	High level community order – 26 weeks' custody	29–36 months (Extend if imposing immediate custody)	36–60 months (Extend if imposing immediate custody
Category 2	Medium level community order	Low level community order – High level community order	17–28 months	36–52 months
Category 3	Band C fine	Band B fine – Low level community order	12–16 months	36–40 months

Note: when considering the guidance regarding the length of disqualification in the case of a second offence, the period to be imposed in any individual case will depend on an assessment of all the relevant circumstances, including the length of time since the earlier ban was imposed and the gravity of the current offence but disqualification must be for at least three years.

For band ranges, see **SG10-129**

For the imposition of community orders, including the community orders table, see Imposition of Community and Custodial Sentences **SG9-2–SG9-8**

For the imposition of custodial sentences see Imposition of Community and Custodial Sentences **SG9-9–SG9-12**

[141] The court should then consider further adjustment for any aggravating or mitigating factors. The following is a **non-exhaustive** list of additional factual elements providing the context of the offence and factors relating to the offender. Identify whether any combination of these, or other relevant factors, should result in an upward or downward adjustment from the sentence arrived at so far.

Factors increasing seriousness [141]

Statutory aggravating factors:

- Previous convictions, having regard to a) the **nature** of the offence to which the conviction relates and its **relevance** to the current offence; and b) the **time** that has elapsed since the conviction
- Offence committed whilst on bail

Other aggravating factors:

- Failure to comply with current court orders
- Offence committed on licence or post sentence supervision
- LGV, HGV PSV etc.
- Poor road or weather conditions
- Carrying passengers
- Driving for hire or reward
- Evidence of unacceptable standard of driving
- Involved in accident
- High level of traffic or pedestrians in the vicinity

Factors reducing seriousness or reflecting personal mitigation

- No previous convictions **or** no relevant/recent convictions
- Remorse
- Good character and/or exemplary conduct
- Serious medical condition requiring urgent, intensive or long-term treatment
- Age and/or lack of maturity where it affects the responsibility of the offender
- Mental disorder or learning disability
- Sole or primary carer for dependent relatives

STEP THREE Consider any factors which indicate a reduction, such as assistance to the prosecution [142]

The court should take into account sections 73 and 74 of the Serious Organised Crime and Police Act 2005 (assistance by defendants: reduction or review of sentence) and any other rule of law by virtue of which an offender may receive a discounted sentence in consequence of assistance given (or offered) to the prosecutor or investigator.

STEP FOUR Reduction for guilty pleas

The court should take account of any potential reduction for a guilty plea in accordance with section 144 of the Criminal Justice Act 2003 and the ***Guilty Plea*** guideline.

STEP FIVE Totality principle

If sentencing an offender for more than one offence, or where the offender is already serving a sentence, consider whether the total sentence is just and proportionate to the overall offending behaviour in accordance with the ***Offences Taken into Consideration and Totality*** guideline.

STEP SIX Consider ancillary orders

In all cases, the court should consider whether to make **compensation** and/or other **ancillary orders** including offering a **drink/drive rehabilitation course.**

STEP SEVEN Reasons

Section 174 of the Criminal Justice Act 2003 imposes a duty to give reasons for, and explain the effect of, the sentence.

STEP EIGHT Consideration for time spent on bail

The court must consider whether to give credit for time spent on bail in accordance with section 240A of the Criminal Justice Act 2003.

SG10-115 Fail to Provide Specimen for Analysis (In Charge) [143]

Road Traffic Act 1988, s. 7(6)

Effective from: 24 April 2017

Triable only summarily

Maximum: Level 4 fine and/or 3 months

Offence range: Band B fine–6 weeks' custody

[143] **STEP ONE Determining the offence category**

The Court should determine the offence category using the table below.

Category 1	Higher culpability **and** greater harm
Category 2	Higher culpability **and** lesser harm **or** lower culpability **and** greater harm
Category 3	Lower culpability **and** lesser harm

The court should determine the offender's culpability and the harm caused with reference **only** to the factors below. Where an offence does not fall squarely into a category, individual factors may require a degree of weighting before making an overall assessment and determining the appropriate offence category.

CULPABILITY demonstrated by one or more of the following:

Factors indicating higher culpability

- Deliberate refusal/ failure

Factors indicating lower culpability

- Honestly held belief but unreasonable excuse
- Genuine attempt to comply
- All other cases

HARM demonstrated by one or more of the following:

Factors indicating greater harm

- High level of impairment

Factors indicating lesser harm

- All other cases

[144] **STEP TWO Starting point and category range**

Having determined the category at step one, the court should use the corresponding starting point to reach a sentence within the category range below.

- **Must endorse and may disqualify. If no disqualification impose 10 points**
- **Extend any disqualification if imposing immediate custody**

The starting point applies to all offenders irrespective of plea or previous convictions.

Level of seriousness	Starting Point	Range	Disqualification/points
Category 1	Medium level community order	Low level community order – 6 weeks' custody	Disqualify 6–12 months (Extend if imposing immediate custody)
Category 2	Band C fine	Band C fine – Medium level community order	Disqualify up to 6 months **OR** 10 points
Category 3	Band B fine	Band B fine	10 points

For band ranges, see **SG10-129**

For the imposition of community orders, including the community orders table, see Imposition of Community and Custodial Sentences **SG9-2–SG9-8**

For the imposition of custodial sentences see Imposition of Community and Custodial Sentences **SG9-9–SG9-12**

The court should then consider further adjustment for any aggravating or mitigating factors. The following is a **non-exhaustive** list of additional factual elements providing the context of the offence and factors relating to the offender. Identify whether any combination of these, or other relevant factors, should result in an upward or downward adjustment from the sentence arrived at so far.

Factors increasing seriousness

Statutory aggravating factors:

- Previous convictions, having regard to a) the **nature** of the offence to which the conviction relates and its **relevance** to the current offence; and b) the **time** that has elapsed since the conviction
- Offence committed whilst on bail

Other aggravating factors: [144]

- High likelihood of driving
- Failure to comply with current court orders
- Offence committed on licence or post sentence supervision
- In charge of LGV, HGV, PSV etc.
- Offering to drive for hire or reward

Factors reducing seriousness or reflecting personal mitigation

- No previous convictions **or** no relevant/recent convictions
- Remorse
- Good character and/or exemplary conduct
- Serious medical condition requiring urgent, intensive or long-term treatment
- Age and/or lack of maturity where it affects the responsibility of the offender
- Mental disorder or learning disability
- Sole or primary carer for dependent relatives

STEP THREE **Consider any factors which indicate a reduction, such as assistance to the prosecution** [145]

The court should take into account sections 73 and 74 of the Serious Organised Crime and Police Act 2005 (assistance by defendants: reduction or review of sentence) and any other rule of law by virtue of which an offender may receive a discounted sentence in consequence of assistance given (or offered) to the prosecutor or investigator.

STEP FOUR **Reduction for guilty pleas**

The court should take account of any potential reduction for a guilty plea in accordance with section 144 of the Criminal Justice Act 2003 and the ***Guilty Plea*** guideline.

STEP FIVE **Totality principle**

If sentencing an offender for more than one offence, or where the offender is already serving a sentence, consider whether the total sentence is just and proportionate to the overall offending behaviour in accordance with the ***Offences Taken into Consideration and Totality*** guideline.

STEP SIX **Compensation and ancillary orders**

In all cases, the court should consider whether to make **compensation** and/or other **ancillary orders** including offering a **drink/drive rehabilitation course, deprivation,** and/or **forfeiture or suspension of personal liquor licence.**

STEP SEVEN **Reasons**

Section 174 of the Criminal Justice Act 2003 imposes a duty to give reasons for, and explain the effect of, the sentence.

STEP EIGHT **Consideration for time spent on bail**

The court must consider whether to give credit for time spent on bail in accordance with section 240A of the Criminal Justice Act 2003.

SG10-116 No Insurance [147]

Road Traffic Act 1988, s. 143

Effective from: 24 April 2017

Triable only summarily
Maximum: Unlimited fine
Offence range: Band B–Band C fine

STEP ONE **Determining the offence category**

The Court should determine the offence category using the table below.

Category 1	Higher culpability and greater harm
Category 2	Higher culpability and lesser harm **or** lower culpability and greater harm
Category 3	Lower culpability and lesser harm

[147] The court should determine the offender's culpability and the harm caused with reference **only** to the factors below. Where an offence does not fall squarely into a category, individual factors may require a degree of weighting before making an overall assessment and determining the appropriate offence category.

CULPABILITY demonstrated by one or more of the following:

Factors indicating higher culpability

- Never passed test
- Gave false details
- Driving LGV, HGV, PSV etc
- Driving for hire or reward
- Evidence of sustained uninsured use

Factors indicating lower culpability

- All other cases

HARM demonstrated by one or more of the following:

Factors indicating greater harm

- Involved in accident where injury caused
- Involved in accident where damage caused

Factors indicating lesser harm

- All other cases

[148] **STEP TWO Starting point and category range**

Having determined the category at step one, the court should use the appropriate starting point to reach a sentence within the category range in the table below. The starting point applies to all offenders irrespective of plea or previous convictions.

- **Must endorse and may disqualify. If no disqualification impose 6–8 points**

Level of seriousness	Starting Point	Range	Disqualification/points
Category 1	Band C fine	Band C fine	Disqualify 6–12 months
Category 2	Band C fine	Band C fine	Consider disqualification for up to 6 months OR 8 points
Category 3	Band C fine	Band B fine – Band C fine	6–8 points

For band ranges, see **SG10-129**

The court should then consider further adjustment for any aggravating or mitigating factors. The following is a **non-exhaustive** list of additional factual elements providing the context of the offence and factors relating to the offender. Identify whether any combination of these, or other relevant factors, should result in an upward or downward adjustment from the sentence arrived at so far.

Factors increasing seriousness

Statutory aggravating factors:

- Previous convictions, having regard to a) the **nature** of the offence to which the conviction relates and its **relevance** to the current offence; and b) the **time** that has elapsed since the conviction
- Offence committed whilst on bail

Other aggravating factors:

- Failure to comply with current court orders
- Offence committed on licence or post sentence supervision

Factors reducing seriousness or reflecting personal mitigation

- No previous convictions **or** no relevant/recent convictions
- Remorse
- Good character and/or exemplary conduct
- Responsibility for providing insurance rests with another (where not amounting to a defence)
- Genuine misunderstanding
- Recent failure to renew or failure to transfer vehicle details where insurance was in existence
- Vehicle not being driven

Sentencing Guidelines

STEP THREE Consider any factors which indicate a reduction, such as assistance to the prosecution [149]

The court should take into account sections 73 and 74 of the Serious Organised Crime and Police Act 2005 (assistance by defendants: reduction or review of sentence) and any other rule of law by virtue of which an offender may receive a discounted sentence in consequence of assistance given (or offered) to the prosecutor or investigator.

STEP FOUR Reduction for guilty pleas

The court should take account of any potential reduction for a guilty plea in accordance with section 144 of the Criminal Justice Act 2003 and the ***Guilty Plea*** guideline.

STEP FIVE Totality principle

If sentencing an offender for more than one offence, or where the offender is already serving a sentence, consider whether the total sentence is just and proportionate to the overall offending behaviour in accordance with the ***Offences Taken into Consideration and Totality*** guideline.

STEP SIX Compensation and ancillary orders

In all cases, the court should consider whether to make **compensation** and/or other **ancillary orders.**

STEP SEVEN Reasons

Section 174 of the Criminal Justice Act 2003 imposes a duty to give reasons for, and explain the effect of, the sentence.

SG10-117 SPEEDING [151]

Road Traffic Regulation Act 1984, s. 89(1)

Effective from: 24 April 2017
Triable only summarily
Maximum: Level 3 fine (level 4 if motorway)
Offence range: Band A fine–Band C fine

STEPS 1 AND 2 Determining the offence seriousness [152]

The starting point applies to all offenders irrespective of plea or previous convictions.

Speed limit (mph)	**Recorded speed (mph)**		
20	41 and above	31–40	21–30
30	51 and above	41–50	31–40
40	66 and above	56–65	41–55
50	76 and above	66–75	51–65
60	91 and above	81–90	61–80
70	101 and above	91–100	71–90
Sentencing range	**Band C fine**	**Band B fine**	**Band A fine**
Points/disqualification	Disqualify 7–56 days **OR** 6 points	Disqualify 7–28 days **OR** 4–6 points	3 points

- Must endorse and may disqualify. If no disqualification impose 3–6 points
- Where an offender is driving grossly in excess of the speed limit the court should consider a disqualification in excess of 56 days.

For band ranges, see **SG10-129**

The court should then consider further adjustment for any aggravating or mitigating factors. The following is a **non-exhaustive** list of additional factual elements providing the context of the offence and factors relating to the offender. Identify whether any combination of these, or other relevant factors, should result in an upward or downward adjustment from the sentence arrived at so far.

Factors increasing seriousness

Statutory aggravating factors:

- Previous convictions, having regard to a) the **nature** of the offence to which the conviction relates and its **relevance** to the current offence; and b) the **time** that has elapsed since the conviction
- Offence committed whilst on bail

[152] *Other aggravating factors:*

- Offence committed on licence or post sentence supervision
- Poor road or weather conditions
- Driving LGV, HGV, PSV etc.
- Towing caravan/trailer
- Carrying passengers or heavy load
- Driving for hire or reward
- Evidence of unacceptable standard of driving over and above speed
- Location e.g. near school
- High level of traffic or pedestrians in the vicinity

Factors reducing seriousness or reflecting personal mitigation

- No previous convictions or no relevant/recent convictions
- Good character and/or exemplary conduct
- Genuine emergency established

[153] **STEP 3 Consider any factors which indicate a reduction, such as assistance to the prosecution**

The court should take into account sections 73 and 74 of the Serious Organised Crime and Police Act 2005 (assistance by defendants: reduction or review of sentence) and any other rule of law by virtue of which an offender may receive a discounted sentence in consequence of assistance given (or offered) to the prosecutor or investigator.

STEP 4 Reduction for guilty pleas

The court should take account of any potential reduction for a guilty plea in accordance with section 144 of the Criminal Justice Act 2003 and the ***Guilty Plea*** guideline.

STEP 5 Totality principle

If sentencing an offender for more than one offence, or where the offender is already serving a sentence, consider whether the total sentence is just and proportionate to the overall offending behaviour in accordance with the ***Offences Taken into Consideration and Totality*** guideline.

STEP 6 Compensation and ancillary orders

In all cases, the court should consider whether to make **compensation** and/or other **ancillary orders.**

STEP 7 Reasons

Section 174 of the Criminal Justice Act 2003 imposes a duty to give reasons for, and explain the effect of, the sentence.

[154] **UNFIT THROUGH DRINK OR DRUGS (DRIVE/ATTEMPT TO DRIVE)** **SG10-118**

Road Traffic Act 1988, s. 4(1)

Effective from: 24 April 2017

Triable only summarily
Maximum: Unlimited fine and/or 6 months
Offence range: Band B fine–26 weeks' custody

STEP ONE Determining the offence category

The Court should determine the offence category using the table below.

Category 1	Higher culpability and greater harm
Category 2	Higher culpability **and** lesser harm **or** lower culpability **and** greater harm
Category 3	Lower culpability **and** lesser harm

The court should determine the offender's culpability and the harm caused with reference **only** to the factors below. Where an offence does not fall squarely into a category, individual factors may require a degree of weighting before making an overall assessment and determining the appropriate offence category.

CULPABILITY demonstrated by one or more of the following:

Factors indicating higher culpability

- Driving LGV, HGV or PSV etc.
- Driving for hire or reward

Sentencing Guidelines

Factors indicating lower culpability [154]

- All other cases

HARM demonstrated by one or more of the following:

Factors indicating greater harm

- High level of impairment

Factors indicating lesser harm

- All other cases

STEP TWO Starting point and category range [155]

Having determined the category at step one, the court should use the appropriate starting point to reach a sentence within the category range in the table below.

- **Must endorse and disqualify for at least 12 months**
- **Must disqualify for at least 2 years if offender has had two or more disqualifications for periods of 56 days or more in preceding 3 years – refer to the disqualification guidance and consult your legal adviser for further guidance**
- **Must disqualify for at least 3 years if offender has been convicted of a relevant offence in preceding 10 years – consult your legal adviser for further guidance**
- **Extend disqualification if imposing immediate custody**

If there is a delay in sentencing after conviction, consider interim disqualification.

The starting point applies to all offenders irrespective of plea or previous convictions

Level of seriousness	Starting point	Range	Disqualification	Disqual. 2nd offence in 10 years
Category 1	12 weeks' custody	High level community order – 26 weeks' custody	29–36 months (Extend if imposing immediate custody)	36–60 months (Extend if imposing immediate custody
Category 2	Medium level community order	Low level community order – High level community order	17–28 months	36–52 months
Category 3	Band C fine	Band B fine – Low level community order	12–16 months	36–40 months

Note: when considering the guidance regarding the length of disqualification in the case of a second offence, the period to be imposed in any individual case will depend on an assessment of all the relevant circumstances, including the length of time since the earlier ban was imposed and the gravity of the current offence but disqualification must be for at least three years.

For band ranges, see **SG10-129**

For the imposition of community orders, including the community orders table, see Imposition of Community and Custodial Sentences **SG9-2–SG9-8**

For the imposition of custodial sentences see Imposition of Community and Custodial Sentences **SG9-9–SG9-12**

The court should then consider further adjustment for any aggravating or mitigating factors. The following is a **non-exhaustive** list of additional factual elements providing the context of the offence and factors relating to the offender. Identify whether any combination of these, or other relevant factors, should result in an upward or downward adjustment from the sentence arrived at so far. [156]

Factors increasing seriousness

Statutory aggravating factors:

- Previous convictions, having regard to a) the **nature** of the offence to which the conviction relates and its **relevance** to the current offence; and b) the **time** that has elapsed since the conviction
- Offence committed whilst on bail

[156] *Other aggravating factors:*

- Failure to comply with current court orders
- Offence committed on licence or post sentence supervision
- Poor road or weather conditions
- Evidence of unacceptable standard of driving
- Involved in accident
- Carrying passengers
- High level of traffic or pedestrians in the vicinity

Factors reducing seriousness or reflecting personal mitigation

- No previous convictions **or** no relevant/recent convictions
- Remorse
- Good character and/or exemplary conduct
- Serious medical condition requiring urgent, intensive or long-term treatment
- Age and/or lack of maturity where it affects the responsibility of the offender
- Mental disorder or learning disability
- Sole or primary carer for dependent relatives

[157] **STEP THREE Consider any factors which indicate a reduction, such as assistance to the prosecution**

The court should take into account sections 73 and 74 of the Serious Organised Crime and Police Act 2005 (assistance by defendants: reduction or review of sentence) and any other rule of law by virtue of which an offender may receive a discounted sentence in consequence of assistance given (or offered) to the prosecutor or investigator.

STEP FOUR Reduction for guilty pleas

The court should take account of any potential reduction for a guilty plea in accordance with section 144 of the Criminal Justice Act 2003 and the ***Guilty Plea*** guideline.

STEP FIVE Totality principle

If sentencing an offender for more than one offence, or where the offender is already serving a sentence, consider whether the total sentence is just and proportionate to the overall offending behaviour in accordance with the ***Offences Taken into Consideration and Totality*** guideline.

STEP SIX Compensation and ancillary orders

In all cases, the court should consider whether to make **compensation** and/or other **ancillary orders** including offering a **drink/drive rehabilitation course, deprivation**, and/or **forfeiture or suspension of personal liquor licence.**

STEP SEVEN Reasons

Section 174 of the Criminal Justice Act 2003 imposes a duty to give reasons for, and explain the effect of, the sentence.

STEP EIGHT Consideration for time spent on bail

The court must consider whether to give credit for time spent on bail in accordance with section 240A of the Criminal Justice Act 2003.

[159]

UNFIT THROUGH DRINK OR DRUGS (IN CHARGE) SG10-119

Road Traffic Act 1988, s. 4(2)

Effective from: 24 April 2017

Triable only summarily
Maximum: Level 4 fine and/or 3 months
Offence range: Band B fine–12 weeks' custody

STEP ONE Determining the offence category

The Court should determine the offence category using the table below.

Category 1	Higher culpability **and** greater harm
Category 2	Higher culpability **and** lesser harm **or** lower culpability **and** greater harm
Category 3	Lower culpability **and** lesser harm

The court should determine the offender's culpability and the harm caused with reference **only** to the factors below. Where an offence does not fall squarely into a category, individual factors may require a degree of weighting before making an overall assessment and determining the appropriate offence category. [159]

CULPABILITY demonstrated by one or more of the following:

Factors indicating higher culpability

- High likelihood of driving
- In charge of LGV, HGV or PSV etc.
- Offering to drive for hire or reward

Factors indicating lower culpability

- All other cases

HARM demonstrated by one or more of the following:

Factors indicating greater harm

- High level of impairment

Factors indicating lesser harm

- All other cases

STEP TWO Starting point and category range [160]

Having determined the category at step one, the court should use the appropriate starting point to reach a sentence within the category range in the table below.

- Must endorse and may disqualify. If no disqualification impose 10 points
- Extend disqualification if imposing immediate custody

The starting point applies to all offenders irrespective of plea or previous convictions.

Level of seriousness	Starting Point	Range	Disqualification/points
Category 1	High level community order	Medium level community order – 12 weeks' custody	Consider disqualification (extend if imposing immediate custody) **OR** 10 points
Category 2	Band C fine	Band B fine – Medium level community order	Consider disqualification **OR** 10 points
Category 3	Band B fine	Band B fine	10 points

For band ranges, see **SG10-129**

For the imposition of community orders, including the community orders table, see Imposition of Community and Custodial Sentences **SG9-2–SG9-8**

For the imposition of custodial sentences see Imposition of Community and Custodial Sentences **SG9-9–SG9-12**

The court should then consider further adjustment for any aggravating or mitigating factors. The following is a **non-exhaustive** list of additional factual elements providing the context of the offence and factors relating to the offender. Identify whether any combination of these, or other relevant factors, should result in an upward or downward adjustment from the sentence arrived at so far.

Factors increasing seriousness

Statutory aggravating factors:

- Previous convictions, having regard to a) the **nature** of the offence to which the conviction relates and its **relevance** to the current offence; and b) the **time** that has elapsed since the conviction
- Offence committed whilst on bail

Other aggravating factors:

- Failure to comply with current court orders
- Offence committed on licence or post sentence supervision

Factors reducing seriousness or reflecting personal mitigation

- No previous convictions **or** no relevant/recent convictions
- Remorse

[160]
- Good character and/or exemplary conduct
- Serious medical condition requiring urgent, intensive or long-term treatment
- Age and/or lack of maturity where it affects the responsibility of the offender
- Mental disorder or learning disability
- Sole or primary carer for dependent relatives

[161] **STEP THREE Consider any factors which indicate a reduction, such as assistance to the prosecution**

The court should take into account sections 73 and 74 of the Serious Organised Crime and Police Act 2005 (assistance by defendants: reduction or review of sentence) and any other rule of law by virtue of which an offender may receive a discounted sentence in consequence of assistance given (or offered) to the prosecutor or investigator.

STEP FOUR Reduction for guilty pleas

The court should take account of any potential reduction for a guilty plea in accordance with section 144 of the Criminal Justice Act 2003 and the ***Guilty Plea*** guideline.

STEP FIVE Totality principle

If sentencing an offender for more than one offence, or where the offender is already serving a sentence, consider whether the total sentence is just and proportionate to the overall offending behaviour in accordance with the ***Offences Taken into Consideration and Totality*** guideline.

STEP SIX Compensation and ancillary orders

In all cases, the court should consider whether to make **compensation** and/or other **ancillary orders** including offering a **drink/drive rehabilitation course, deprivation,** and/or **forfeiture or suspension of personal liquor licence.**

STEP SEVEN Reasons

Section 174 of the Criminal Justice Act 2003 imposes a duty to give reasons for, and explain the effect of, the sentence.

STEP EIGHT Consideration for time spent on bail

The court must consider whether to give credit for time spent on bail in accordance with section 240A of the Criminal Justice Act 2003.

[163]

OFFENCES APPROPRIATE FOR IMPOSITION OF FINE OR DISCHARGE SG10-120

Part 1: Offences concerning the driver SG10-121

Offence	Maximum	Points	Starting point	Special considerations
Fail to co-operate with preliminary (roadside) breath test	L3	4	B	
Fail to give information of driver's identity as required	L3	6	C	For limited companies, endorsement is not available; a fine is the only available penalty
Fail to produce insurance certificate	L4	–	A	Fine per offence, not per document
Fail to produce test certificate	L3	–	A	
Drive otherwise than in accordance with licence (where could be covered)	L3	–	A	
Drive otherwise than in accordance with licence	L3	3–6	A	Aggravating factor if no licence ever held

Part 2: Offences concerning the vehicle SG10-122

* The guidelines for some of the offences below differentiate between three types of offender when the offence is committed in the course of business: driver, owner-driver and owner-company. **For owner-driver, the starting point is the same as for driver; however, the court should consider an uplift of at least 25%.**

Sentencing Guidelines

Offence	Maximum	Points	Starting point	Special considerations
No excise licence	L3 or 5 times annual duty, whichever is greater	–	A (1–3 months unpaid) B (4–6 months unpaid) C (7–12 months unpaid)	Add duty lost [163]
Fail to notify change of ownership to DVLA	L3	–	A	If offence committed in course of business: A (driver) A* (owner-driver) B (owner-company)
No test certificate	L3	–	A	If offence committed in course of business: A (driver) A* (owner-driver) B (owner-company)
Brakes defective	L4	3	B	If offence committed in course of business: B (driver) B* (owner-driver) C (owner-company) L5 if goods vehicle—see Part 5 below
Steering defective	L4	3	B	If offence committed in course of business: B (driver) B* (owner-driver) C (owner- company) L5 if goods vehicle—see Part 5 below
Tyres defective	L4	3	B	If offence committed in course of business: B (driver) B* (owner-driver) C (owner-company) L5 if goods vehicle—see Part 5 below Penalty per tyre [164]
Condition of vehicle/ accessories/Equipment involving danger of injury (Road Traffic Act 1988, s.40A)	L4	3	B	Must disqualify for at least 6 months if offender has one or more previous convictions for same offence within three years If offence committed in course of business: B (driver) B* (owner-driver) C (owner-company) L5 if goods vehicle—see Part 5 below
Exhaust defective	L3	–	A	If offence committed in course of business: A (driver) A* (owner-driver) B (owner-company)
Lights defective	L3	–	A	If offence committed in course of business: A (driver) A* (owner-driver) B (owner-company)

SG10-123 **Part 3: Offences concerning use of vehicle**

*The guidelines for some of the offences below differentiate between three types of offender when the offence is committed in the course of business: driver, owner-driver and owner-company. **For owner-driver, the starting point is the same as for driver; however, the court should consider an uplift of at least 25%.**

Offence	Maximum	Points	Starting point	Special considerations
Weight, position or distribution of load or manner in which load secured involving danger of injury (Road Traffic Act 1988, s.40A)	L4	3	B	Must disqualify for at least 6 months if offender has one or more previous convictions for same offence within three years. If offence committed in course of business: A (driver) A* (owner-driver) B (owner-company) L5 if goods vehicle—see Part 5 below

[164]

Offence	Maximum	Points	Starting point	Special considerations
Number of passengers or way carried involving danger of injury (Road Traffic Act 1988, s.40A)	L4	3	B	If offence committed in course of business: A (driver) A* (owner-driver) B (owner-company) L5 if goods vehicle—see Part 5 below
Position or manner in which load secured (not involving danger) (Road Traffic Act 1988, s.42)	L3	–	A	L4 if goods vehicle—see Part 5 below
[165] Overloading/exceeding axle weight	L5	–	A	Starting point caters for cases where the overload is up to and including 10%. Thereafter, 10% should be added to the penalty for each additional 1% of overload Penalty per axle If offence committed in course of business: A (driver) A* (owner-driver) B (owner-company) If goods vehicle—see Part 5 below
Dangerous parking	L3	3	A	
Pelican/zebra crossing contravention	L3	3	A	
Fail to comply with traffic sign (e.g. red traffic light, stop sign, double white lines, no entry sign)	L3	3	A	
Fail to comply with traffic sign (e.g. give way sign, keep left sign, temporary signs)	L3	–	A	
Fail to comply with police constable directing traffic	L3	3	A	
Fail to stop when required by police constable	L5 (mechanically propelled vehicle) L3 (cycle)	–	B	
Use of mobile telephone	L3	3	A	
Seat belt offences	L2 (adult or child in front) L2 (child in rear)	–	A	
Fail to use appropriate child car seat	L2		A	

Part 4: Motorway Offences

SG10-124

Offence	Maximum	Points	Starting point	Special considerations
Drive in reverse or wrong way on slip road	L4	3	B	
Drive in reverse or wrong way on motorway	L4	3	C	
Drive off carriageway (central reservation or hard shoulder)	L4	3	B	
Make U turn	L4	3	C	

(continued)

Sentencing Guidelines

Offence	Maximum	Points	Starting point	Special considerations
Learner driver or excluded vehicle	L4	3	B	
Stop on hard shoulder	L4	–	A	
Vehicle in prohibited lane	L4	3	A	
Walk on motorway, slip road or hard shoulder	L4	–	A	

[165]

SG10-125 Part 5: Offences re buses/goods vehicles over 3.5 tonnes (GVW) [166]

* The guidelines for these offences differentiate between three types of offender: driver; owner-driver; and owner-company. **For owner-driver, the starting point is the same as for driver; however, the court should consider an uplift of at least 25%.**

** In all cases, take safety, damage to roads and commercial gain into account. Refer [below] for approach to fines for 'commercially motivated' offences.

Offence	Maximum	Points	Starting point	Special considerations
No goods vehicle plating certificate	L3	–	A (driver) A* (owner-driver) B (owner-company)	
No goods vehicle test certificate	L4	–	B (driver) B* (owner-driver) C (owner-company)	
Brakes defective	L5	3	B (driver) B* (owner-driver) C (owner-company)	
Steering defective	L5	3	B (driver) B* (owner-driver) C (owner-company)	
Tyres defective	L5	3	B (driver) B* (owner-driver) C (owner-company)	Penalty per tyre
Exhaust emission	L4	–	B (driver) B* (owner-driver) C (owner-company)	
Condition of vehicle/ accessories/equipment involving danger of injury (Road Traffic Act 1988, s.40A)	L5	3	B (driver) B* (owner-driver) C (owner-company)	Must disqualify for at least 6 months if offender has one or more previous convictions for same offence within three years
Number of passengers or way carried involving danger of injury (Road Traffic Act 1988, s.40A)	L5	3	B (driver) B* (owner-driver) C (owner-company)	Must disqualify for at least 6 months if offender has one or more previous convictions for same offence within three years
Weight, position or distribution of load or manner in which load secured involving danger of injury (Road Traffic Act 1988, s.40A)	L5	3	B (driver) B* (owner-driver) C (owner-company)	Must disqualify for at least 6 months if offender has one or more previous convictions for same offence within three years
Position or manner in which load secured (not involving danger) (Road Traffic Act 1988, s.42)	L4	–	B (driver) B* (owner-driver) C (owner-company)	

	Offence	Maximum	Points	Starting point	Special considerations
[166]	Overloading/ exceeding axle weight	L5	–	B (driver) B* (owner-driver) C (owner-company)	Starting points cater for cases where the overload is up to and including 10%. Thereafter, 10% should be added to the penalty for each additional 1% of overload Penalty per axle
[167]	No operator's licence	L4 (PSV) L5 (Goods)	–	B (driver) B* (owner-driver) C (owner-company)	
	Speed limiter not used or incorrectly calibrated	L4	–	B (driver) B* (owner-driver) C (owner-company)	
	Tachograph not used/ not working	L5	–	B (driver) B* (owner-driver) C (owner-company)	
	Exceed permitted driving time/periods of duty	L4	–	B (driver) B* (owner-driver) C (owner-company)	
	Fail to keep/return written record sheets	L4	–	B (driver) B* (owner-driver) C (owner-company)	
	Falsify or alter records with intent to deceive	L5/2 years	–	B (driver) B* (owner-driver) C (owner-company)	Either way offence

Sentencing Guidelines

[168]

DRUG DRIVING

SG10-126

Introduction

Since the new offence came into force in March 2015 the Sentencing Council has received a large number of requests for a sentencing guideline. It has been brought to our attention that there are concerns with sentencing in this area and a risk of inconsistent practices developing.

The new offence is a strict liability offence, which is committed once the specified limit for any of 17 specified controlled drugs is exceeded. The 17 drugs include both illegal drugs and drugs that may be medically prescribed.

The limits for illegal drugs are set in line with a zero tolerance approach but ruling out accidental exposure. The limits for drugs that may be medically prescribed are set in line with a road safety risk-based approach, at levels above the normal concentrations found with therapeutic use. This is different from the approach taken when setting the limit for alcohol, where the limit was set at a level where the effect of the alcohol would be expected to have impaired a person's driving ability. **For these reasons it would be wrong to rely on the Driving with Excess Alcohol guideline when sentencing an offence under this legislation.**

Guidance Only

At present there is insufficient reliable data available from the Department for Transport upon which the Sentencing Council can devise a full guideline. For that reason, and given the number of requests for guidance that have been received, the Sentencing Council has devised the attached guidance to assist sentencers.

It is important to note that this guidance does not carry the same authority as a sentencing guideline, and sentencers are not obliged to follow it. However, it is hoped that the majority of sentencers will find it useful in assisting them to deal with these cases.

The Sentencing Council will, in due course produce a guideline with the assistance of evidence and data gathered by the Department for Transport. Any new guideline will be made subject to public consultation before it is finalised.

Drug Driving Guidance [169]

Background

The Crime and Courts Act 2013 inserted a new section 5A into the Road Traffic Act 1988 (RTA), which makes it an offence to drive, attempt to drive, or be in charge of a motor vehicle with a concentration of a specified controlled drug in the body above the specified limit. The offence came into force on 2 March 2015.

Driving or Attempting to Drive

Triable only summarily:
Maximum: Unlimited fine and/or 6 months • Must endorse and disqualify for at least 12 months • Must disqualify for at least 2 years if offender has had two or more disqualifications for periods of 56 days or more in preceding 3 years – refer to disqualification guidance and consult your legal adviser for further guidance • Must disqualify for at least 3 years if offender has been convicted ofa relevant offence in preceding 10 years – consult your legal adviser for further guidance
If there is a delay in sentencing after conviction, consider interim disqualification

- As a guide, where an offence of driving or attempting to drive has been committed and there are no factors that increase seriousness the Court should consider a starting point of a **Band C fine** [For band ranges, see **SG10-129**], and a disqualification in the region of 12–22 months. The list of factors that increase seriousness appears at page 170. Please note this is an exhaustive list and only factors that appear in the list should be considered.
- Where there are factors that increase seriousness the Court should consider increasing the sentence on the basis of the level of seriousness.
- The **community order** threshold is likely to be crossed where there is evidence of one or more factors that increase seriousness [For the imposition of community orders, including the community orders table, see Imposition of Community and Custodial Sentences **SG9-2–SG9-8**]. The Court should also consider imposing a disqualification in the region of 23–28 months.
- The **custody** threshold is likely to be crossed where there is evidence of one or more factors that increase seriousness and one or more aggravating factors (see below) [For the imposition of custodial sentences see Imposition of Community and Custodial Sentences **SG9-9–SG9-12**]. The Court should also consider imposing a disqualification in the region of 29–36 months.
- Having determined a starting point, the Court should consider additional factors that may make the offence more or less serious. A non-exhaustive list of aggravating and mitigating factors is set out below.

Factors that increase seriousness (this is an exhaustive list) [170]

- Evidence of another specified drug[110] or of alcohol in the body
- Evidence of an unacceptable standard of driving
- Driving (or in charge of) an LGV, HGV or PSV
- Driving (or in charge of) a vehicle driven for hire or reward

Aggravating and mitigating factors (these are non-exhaustive lists)

Aggravating Factors

- Previous convictions having regard to a) the **nature** of the offence to which the conviction relates and its **relevance** to the current offence; and b) the **time** that has elapsed since the conviction'
- Location e.g. near school
- Carrying passengers
- High level of traffic or pedestrians in the vicinity
- Poor road or weather conditions

[110] For these purposes, cocaine and benzoylecgonine (BZE) shall be treated as one drug as they both occur in the body as a result of cocaine use rather than poly-drug use. Similarly 6-Monoacteylmorphine and Morphine shall be treated as one drug as they both occur in the body as a result of heroin use. Finally, Diazepam and Temazepam shall be treated as one drug as they also both occur in the body as a result of Temazepam use.

[170] *Mitigating Factors*

- No previous convictions or no relevant/recent convictions
- Remorse
- Good character and/or exemplary conduct
- Age and/or lack of maturity where it affects the responsibility of the offender
- Mental disorder or learning disability
- Sole or primary carer for dependent relatives
- Very short distance driven
- Genuine emergency established

[171]

In Charge

Triable only summarily:
Maximum: Level 4 fine and/or 3 months
Must endorse and may disqualify. If no disqualification, impose 10 points

- As a guide, where an offence of being in charge has been committed but there are no factors that increase seriousness the Court should consider a starting point of a **Band B fine** [For band ranges, see **SG10-129**], and endorsing the licence with 10 penalty points. The list of factors that increase seriousness appears below. Please note this is an exhaustive list and only factors that appear in the list should be considered.
- Where there are factors that increase seriousness the Court should consider increasing the sentence on the basis of the level of seriousness.
- The **community order** threshold is likely to be crossed where there is evidence of one or more factors that increase seriousness and one or more aggravating factors (see below) [For the imposition of community orders, including the community orders table, see Imposition of Community and Custodial Sentences **SG9-2–SG9-8**]. The Court should also consider imposing a disqualification.
- Where there is evidence of one or more factors that increase seriousness and a greater number of aggravating factors (see below) the Court may consider it appropriate to impose a short **custodial** sentence of up to 12 weeks [For the imposition of custodial sentences see Imposition of Community and Custodial Sentences **SG9-9–SG9-12**]. The Court should also consider imposing a disqualification.
- Having determined a starting point, the Court should consider additional factors that may make the offence more or less serious. A non-exhaustive list of aggravating and mitigating factors is set out below.

[172]

Factors that increase seriousness – (this is an exhaustive list)

- Evidence of another specified drug[111] or of alcohol in the body
- Evidence of an unacceptable standard of driving
- Driving (or in charge of) an LGV, HGV or PSV
- Driving (or in charge of) a vehicle driven for hire or reward

Aggravating and mitigating factors (these are non-exhaustive lists)

Aggravating Factors

- Previous convictions having regard to a) the nature of the offence to which the conviction relates and its relevance to the current offence; and b) the time that has elapsed since the conviction'
- Location e.g. near school
- Carrying passengers
- High level of traffic or pedestrians in the vicinity
- Poor road or weather conditions

Mitigating Factors

- No previous convictions or no relevant/recent convictions
- Remorse
- Good character and/or exemplary conduct
- Age and/or lack of maturity where it affects the responsibility of the offender

[111] For these purposes, cocaine and benzoylecgonine (BZE) shall be treated as one drug as they both occur in the body as a result of cocaine use rather than poly-drug use. Similarly 6-Monoacteylmorphine and Morphine shall be treated as one drug as they both occur in the body as a result of heroin use. Finally, Diazepam and Temazepam shall be treated as one drug as they also both occur in the body as a result of Temazepam use.

- Mental disorder or learning disability [172]
- Sole or primary carer for dependent relatives
- Very short distance driven
- Genuine emergency established

SG10-127 **Approach to the Assessment of Fines** [423]

SG10-128 **Introduction**

1. The amount of a fine must reflect the *seriousness* of the offence.[112]
2. The court must also take into account the *financial circumstances* of the offender; this applies whether it has the effect of increasing or reducing the fine.[113]
3. The aim is for the fine to have an equal impact on offenders with different financial circumstances; it should be a hardship but should not force the offender below a reasonable 'subsistence' level. Normally a fine should be of an amount that is capable of being paid within 12 months though there may be exceptions to this.
4. The guidance below aims to establish a clear, consistent and principled approach to the assessment of fines that will apply fairly in the majority of cases. However, it is impossible to anticipate every situation that may be encountered and in each case the court will need to exercise its judgement to ensure that the fine properly reflects the *seriousness of the offence* and takes into account the *financial circumstances* of the offender.

SG10-129 **Fine bands**

5. For the purpose of the offence guidelines, a fine is based on one of three bands (A, B or C). The selection of the relevant fine band, and the position of the individual offence within that band, is determined by the seriousness of the offence. In some cases fine bands D–F may be used even where the community or custody threshold have been passed.

	Starting point	Range
Fine Band A	50% of relevant weekly income	25–75% of relevant weekly income
Fine Band B	100% of relevant weekly income	75–125% of relevant weekly income
Fine Band C	150% of relevant weekly income	125–175% of relevant weekly income
Fine Band D	250% of relevant weekly income	200–300% of relevant weekly income
Fine Band E	400% of relevant weekly income	300–500% of relevant weekly income
Fine Band F	600% of relevant weekly income	500–700% of relevant weekly income

6. For an explanation of the meaning of starting point and range, both generally and in relation to fines, see [SG10-6].

SG10-130 **Definition of relevant weekly income**

7. The *seriousness* of an offence determines the choice of fine band and the position of the offence within the range for that band. The offender's *financial circumstances* are taken into account by expressing that position as a proportion of the offender's *relevant weekly income.*
8. Where
   - an offender is in receipt of income from employment or is self-employed *and*
   - that income is *more than £120 per week* after deduction of tax and national insurance (or equivalent where the offender is self-employed),

   the actual income is the *relevant weekly income.*
9. Where [424]
   - an offender's only source of income is state benefit (including where there is relatively low additional income as permitted by the benefit regulations) or
   - the offender is in receipt of income from employment or is self-employed but the amount of income after deduction of tax and national insurance is *£120 or less,*

   the *relevant weekly income is deemed to be £110.*

   Additional information about the basis for this approach is set out [at **SG10-139**].
10. In calculating relevant weekly income, no account should be taken of tax credits, housing benefit, child benefit or similar.

[112] Criminal Justice Act 2003, s. 164(2)

[113] ibid, ss. 164(1) and 164(4)

[424] **No reliable information** SG10-131

11. Where an offender has failed to provide information, or the court is not satisfied that it has been given sufficient reliable information, it is entitled to make such determination as it thinks fit regarding the financial circumstances of the offender.[114] Any determination should be clearly stated on the court records for use in any subsequent variation or enforcement proceedings. In such cases, a record should also be made of the applicable fine band and the court's assessment of the position of the offence within that band based on the seriousness of the offence.
12. Where there is no information on which a determination can be made, the court should proceed on the basis of an *assumed relevant weekly income of £440*. This is derived from national median pre-tax earnings; a gross figure is used as, in the absence of financial information from the offender, it is not possible to calculate appropriate deductions.[115]
13. Where there is some information that tends to suggest a significantly lower or higher income than the recommended £440 default sum, the court should make a determination based on that information.
14. A court is empowered to remit a fine in whole or part if the offender subsequently provides information as to means.[116] The assessment of offence seriousness and, therefore, the appropriate fine band and the position of the offence within that band is not affected by the provision of this information.

Assessment of financial circumstances SG10-132

15. While the initial consideration for the assessment of a fine is the offender's relevant weekly income, the court is required to take account of the offender's *financial circumstances* including assets more broadly. Guidance on important parts of this assessment is set out below.
16. An offender's financial circumstances may have the effect of increasing or reducing the amount of the fine; however, they are not relevant to the assessment of offence seriousness. They should be considered separately from the selection of the appropriate fine band and the court's assessment of the position of the offence within the range for that band.

Out of the ordinary expenses SG10-133

17. In deciding the proportions of relevant weekly income that are the starting points and ranges for each fine band, account has been taken of reasonable living expenses. Accordingly, no further allowance should normally be made for these. In addition, no allowance should normally be made where the offender has dependants.
18. Outgoings will be relevant to the amount of the fine only where the expenditure is *out of the ordinary* and *substantially* reduces the ability to pay a financial penalty so that the requirement to pay a fine based on the standard approach would lead to *undue* hardship.

Unusually low outgoings SG10-134

[425] 19. Where the offender's living expenses are substantially lower than would normally be expected, it may be appropriate to adjust the amount of the fine to reflect this. This may apply, for example, where an offender does not make any financial contribution towards his or her living costs.

Savings SG10-135

20. Where an offender has savings these will not normally be relevant to the assessment of the amount of a fine although they may influence the decision on time to pay.
21. However, where an offender has little or no income but has substantial savings, the court may consider it appropriate to adjust the amount of the fine to reflect this.

Household has more than one source of income SG10-136

22. Where the household of which the offender is a part has more than one source of income, the fine should normally be based on the income of the offender alone.
23. However, where the offender's part of the income is very small (or the offender is wholly dependent on the income of another), the court may have regard to the extent of the household's income and assets which will be available to meet any fine imposed on the offender.[117]

---

114 Criminal Justice Act 2003, s. 164(5)

115 This figure is a projected estimate based upon the 2012–13 Survey of Personal Incomes using economic assumptions consistent with the Office for Budget Responsibility's March 2015 economic and fiscal outlook. The latest actual figure is for 2012–13, when median pre-tax income was £404 per week (https://www.gov.uk/government/statistics/shares-of-total-income-before-and-after-tax-and-income-tax-for-percentile-groups).

116 Criminal Justice Act 2003, s. 165(2)

117 *R v Engen* [2004] EWCA Crim 1536 (CA)

SG10-137 Potential earning capacity [425]

24. Where there is reason to believe that an offender's potential earning capacity is greater than his or her current income, the court may wish to adjust the amount of the fine to reflect this.[118] This may apply, for example, where an unemployed offender states an expectation to gain paid employment within a short time. The basis for the calculation of fine should be recorded in order to ensure that there is a clear record for use in variation or enforcement proceedings.

SG10-138 High income offenders

25. Where the offender is in receipt of very high income, a fine based on a proportion of relevant weekly income may be disproportionately high when compared with the seriousness of the offence. In such cases, the court should adjust the fine to an appropriate level; as a general indication, in most cases the fine for a first time offender pleading not guilty should not exceed 75% of the maximum fine. In the case of fines which are unlimited the court should decide the appropriate level with the guidance of the legal adviser.

SG10-139 Approach to offenders on low income

26. An offender whose primary source of income is state benefit will generally receive a base level of benefit (e.g. job seekers' allowance, a relevant disability benefit or income support) and may also be eligible for supplementary benefits depending on his or her individual circumstances (such as child tax credits, housing benefit, council tax benefit and similar). In some cases these benefits may have been replaced by Universal Credit.

27. If relevant weekly income were defined as the amount of benefit received, this would usually result in higher fines being imposed on offenders with a higher level of need; in most circumstances that would not properly balance the seriousness of the offence with the financial circumstances of the offender. While it might be possible to exclude from the calculation any allowance above the basic entitlement of a single person, that could be complicated and time consuming.

28. Similar issues can arise where an offender is in receipt of a low earned income since this may trigger eligibility for means related benefits such as working tax credits and housing benefit depending on the particular circumstances. It will not always be possible to determine with any confidence whether such a person's financial circumstances are significantly different from those of a person whose primary source of income is state benefit.

29. For these reasons, a simpler and fairer approach to cases involving offenders in receipt of low income (whether primarily earned or as a result of benefit) is to identify an amount that is deemed to represent the offender's relevant weekly income. [426]

30. While a precise calculation is neither possible nor desirable, it is considered that an amount that is approximately half-way between the base rate for job seekers' allowance and the net weekly income of an adult earning the minimum wage for 30 hours per week represents a starting point that is both realistic and appropriate; this is currently £120.[119] The calculation is based on a 30 hour working week in recognition of the fact that many of those on minimum wage do not work a full 37 hour week and that lower minimum wage rates apply to younger people.

31. It is expected that this figure will remain in use until 31 March 2015. Future revisions of the guideline will update the amount in accordance with current benefit and minimum wage levels.

SG10-140 Offence committed for 'commercial' purposes

32. Some offences are committed with the intention of gaining a significant commercial benefit. These often occur where, in order to carry out an activity lawfully, a person has to comply with certain processes which may be expensive. They include, for example, 'taxi-touting' (where unauthorised persons seek to operate as taxi drivers) and 'fly-tipping' (where the cost of lawful disposal is considerable).

33. In some of these cases, a fine based on the standard approach set out above may not reflect the level of financial gain achieved or sought through the offending. Accordingly:

   a. where the offender has generated income or avoided expenditure to a level that can be calculated or estimated, the court may wish to consider that amount when determining the financial penalty;

---

[118] *R v Little* (unreported) 14 April 1976 (CA)

[119] With effect from 1 October 2014, the minimum wage is £6.50 per hour for an adult aged 21 or over. Based on a 30 hour week, this equates to approximately £189 after deductions for tax and national insurance. To ensure equivalence of approach, the level of job seekers' allowance for a single person aged 18 to 24 has been used for the purpose of calculating the mid point; this is currently £57.90.

[426] b. where it is not possible to calculate or estimate that amount, the court may wish to draw on information from the enforcing authorities about the general costs of operating within the law.

Offence committed by an organisation **SG10-141**

34. Where an offence is committed by an organisation, guidance on fines can be found in the environmental offences guideline [see **SG24-1**].
35. See the Criminal Practice Direction CPD XIII Listing Annex 3 [see **PD-122**] for directions on dealing with cases involving very large fines in the magistrates' court.[120]

Reduction for a guilty plea **SG10-142**

36. Where a guilty plea has been entered, the amount of the fine should be reduced by the appropriate proportion. Courts should refer to the *Guilty Plea* guidelines [at **SG4-1**].

[Other considerations] **SG10-143**

[427] *Maximum fines*

37. A fine must not exceed the statutory limit. Where this is expressed in terms of a 'level', the maxima are:

Level 1	£200
Level 2	£500
Level 3	£1,000
Level 4	£2,500
Level 5	unlimited[121]

See the Criminal Practice Direction XIII Listing Annex 3 [at **PD-122**] for directions on dealing with cases involving very large fines in the magistrates' court.

Multiple offences

38. Where an offender is to be fined for two or more offences that arose out of the same incident, it will often be appropriate to impose on the most serious offence a fine which reflects the totality of the offending where this can be achieved within the maximum penalty for that offence. 'No separate penalty' should be imposed for the other offences.
39. Where compensation is being ordered, that will need to be attributed to the relevant offence as will any necessary ancillary orders.

Imposition of fines with custodial sentences

40. A fine and a custodial sentence may be imposed for the same offence although there will be few circumstances in which this is appropriate, particularly where the custodial sentence is to be served immediately. One example might be where an offender has profited financially from an offence but there is no obvious victim to whom compensation can be awarded. Combining these sentences is most likely to be appropriate only where the custodial sentence is short and/or the offender clearly has, or will have, the means to pay.
41. Care must be taken to ensure that the overall sentence is proportionate to the seriousness of the offence and that better off offenders are not able to 'buy themselves out of custody'.
42. Consult your legal adviser if considering lodging fines or costs on the imposition of a custodial sentence.

Consult your legal adviser in any case in which you are considering combining a fine with a custodial sentence.

Payment

43. A fine is payable in full on the day on which it is imposed. The offender should always be asked for immediate payment when present in court and some payment on the day should be required wherever possible.
44. Where that is not possible, the court may, in certain circumstances,[122] require the offender to be detained. More commonly, a court will allow payments to be made over a period set by the court:

[120] https://www.justice.gov.uk/courts/procedure-rules/criminal/rulesmenu
[121] For offences committed after 13 March 2015. For offences committed before that date the level 5 maximum is £5,000.
[122] See section 82 of the Magistrates' Court Act for restrictions on the power to impose imprisonment on default.

a. if periodic payments are allowed, the fine should normally be payable within a maximum of 12 months; [427]

b. compensation should normally be payable within 12 months. However, in exceptional circumstances it may be appropriate to allow it to be paid over a period of up to 3 years.

45. Where fine bands D, E and F apply (see paragraph 5 above), it may be appropriate for the fine to be of an amount that is larger than can be repaid within 12 months. In such cases, the fine should normally be payable within a maximum of 18 months (band D) or 2 years (bands E and F). [428]

46. When allowing payment by *instalments payments should be set at a realistic rate taking into account the offender's disposable* income. The following approach may be useful.

Net weekly income	Starting point for weekly payment
£60	£5
£120	£10
£200	£25
£250	£30
£300	£50
£400	£80

If the offender has dependants or larger than usual commitments, the weekly payment is likely to be decreased.

47. The payment terms must be included in any collection order made in respect of the amount imposed; see below.

SG10-144 Collection orders

48. The Courts Act 2003 created a fines collection scheme which provides for greater administrative enforcement of fines. Consult your legal adviser for further guidance.

Attachment of earnings orders/applications for benefit deductions

49. Unless it would be impracticable or inappropriate to do so, the court must make an attachment of earnings or (AEO) or application for benefit deductions (ABD) whenever:

- compensation is imposed;[123] or
- the court concludes that the offender is an existing defaulter and that the existing default cannot be disregarded.[124]

50. In other cases, the court may make an AEO or ABD with the offender's consent.[125]

The court must make a collection order in every case in which a fine or compensation order is imposed unless this would be impracticable or inappropriate.[126] The collection order must state:

- the amount of the sum due, including the amount of any fine, compensation order or other sum;
- whether the court considers the offender to be an existing defaulter;
- whether an AEO or ABD has been made and information about the effect of the order;
- if the court has not made an AEO or ABD, the payment terms;
- if an AEO or ABD has been made, the reserve terms (i.e. the payment terms that will apply if the AEO or ABD fails). It will often be appropriate to set a reserve term of payment in full within 14 days.

SG10-145 Compensation [429]

1. The court *must* consider making a compensation order in any case where personal injury, loss or damage has resulted from the offence. It can either be a sentence in its own right or an ancillary order. The court must give reasons if it decides not to order compensation.[127]

123 Courts Act 2003, sch. 5, para. 7A
124 ibid, para. 8
125 ibid, para. 9
126 ibid, para.12
127 Powers of Criminal Courts (Sentencing) Act 2000, s. 130

[429] 2. There is no statutory limit on the amount of compensation that may be imposed in respect of offences for an offender aged 18 or over. Compensation may also be ordered in respect of offences taken into consideration.[128]

3. Where the personal injury, loss or damage arises from a road accident, a compensation order may be made only if there is a conviction for an offence under the Theft Act 1968, or the offender is uninsured and the Motor Insurers' Bureau will not cover the loss.

4. Subject to consideration of the victim's views (see paragraph 6 below), the court must order compensation wherever possible and should not have regard to the availability of other sources such as civil litigation or the Criminal Injuries Compensation Scheme. Any amount paid by an offender under a compensation order will generally be deducted from a subsequent civil award or payment under the Scheme to avoid double compensation.

5. Compensation may be ordered for such amount as the court considers appropriate having regard to any evidence and any representations made by the offender or prosecutor. The court must also take into account the offender's means (see also paragraphs 9–11 below).

6. Compensation should benefit, not inflict further harm on, the victim. Any financial recompense from the offender may cause distress. A victim may or may not want compensation from the offender and assumptions should not be made either way. The victim's views are properly obtained through sensitive discussion by the police or witness care unit, when it can be explained that the offender's ability to pay will ultimately determine whether, and how much, compensation is ordered and whether the compensation will be paid in one lump sum or by instalments. If the victim does not want compensation, this should be made known to the court and respected.

7. In cases where it is difficult to ascertain the full amount of the loss suffered by the victim, consideration should be given to making a compensation order for an amount representing the agreed or likely loss. Where relevant information is not immediately available, it may be appropriate to grant an adjournment for it to be obtained.

8. The court should consider two types of loss:
   - financial loss sustained as a result of the offence such as the cost of repairing damage or, in case of injury, any loss of earnings or medical expenses;
   - pain and suffering caused by the injury (including terror, shock or distress) and any loss of facility. This should be assessed in light of all factors that appear to the court to be relevant, including any medical evidence, the victim's age and personal circumstances.

9. Once the court has formed a preliminary view of the appropriate level of compensation, it must have regard to the means of the offender so far as they are known. Where the offender has little money, the order may have to be scaled down or additional time allowed to pay; the court may allow compensation to be paid over a period of up to three years in appropriate cases.

[430] 10. The fact that a custodial sentence is imposed does not, in itself, make it inappropriate to order compensation; however, it may be relevant to whether the offender has the means to satisfy the order. *Consult your legal adviser in any case where you are considering combining compensation with a custodial sentence.*

11. Where the court considers that it would be appropriate to impose a fine and a compensation order but the offender has insufficient means to pay both, priority should be given to compensation. Compensation also takes priority over the victim surcharge where the offender's means are an issue.

Suggested starting points for physical and mental injuries **SG10-146**

12. The tables below suggest starting points for compensating physical and mental injuries commonly encountered in a magistrates' court. They have been developed to be consistent with the approach in the Criminal Injuries Compensation Authority tariff (revised 2012). The CICA tariff makes no

[128] ibid, s. 131

award for minor injuries which result in short term disability; the suggested starting points for these injuries are adapted from an earlier tariff. [430]

Type of injury	Description	Suggested Starting point
Graze	Depending on size	Up to £75
Bruise	Depending on size	Up to £100
Cut: no permanent scar	Depending on size and whether stitched	£100–300
Black eye		£125
Eye	Blurred or double vision lasting up to 6 weeks Blurred or double vision lasting for 6 to 13 weeks Blurred or double vision lasting for more than 13 weeks (recovery expected)	£500 £1,000 £1,500
Brain	Concussion lasting one week	£1,500
Nose	Undisplaced fracture of nasal bone Displaced fracture requiring manipulation Deviated nasal septum requiring septoplasty	£1,000 £2,000 £2,000
Loss of non-front tooth Loss of front tooth	Depending on cosmetic effect	£750 per tooth £1,500 per tooth
Facial scar	Minor disfigurement (permanent)	£1,000
Arm	Fractured humerus, radius, ulna (substantial recovery)	£1,500
Shoulder	Dislocated (substantial recovery)	£900
Wrist	Dislocated/fractured—including scaphoid fracture (substantial recovery) Fractured—colles type (substantial recovery)	£2,400 £2,400
Sprained wrist, ankle	Disabling for up to 6 weeks Disabling for 6 to 13 weeks Disabling for more than 13 weeks	£500 £800 £1,000
Finger	Fractured finger other than index finger (substantial recovery) Fractured index finger (substantial recovery) Fractured thumb (substantial recovery)	£300 [431] £1,200 £1,750
Leg	Fractured fibula (substantial recovery) Fractured femur, tibia (substantial recovery)	£1,000 £1,800
Abdomen	Injury requiring laparotomy	£1,800
Temporary mental anxiety (including terror, shock, distress), not medically verified		£500
Disabling mental anxiety, lasting more than 6 weeks, medically verified*		£1,000
Disability mental illness, lasting up to 28 weeks, confirmed by psychiatric diagnosis*		£1,500

*mental injury is disabling if it has a substantial adverse effect on a person's ability to carry out normal day-to-day activities for the time specified (e.g. impaired work or school performance or effects on social relationships or sexual dysfunction).

13. The following table, which is also based on the Criminal Injuries Compensation Authority tariff, sets out suggested starting points for compensating physical and sexual abuse. It will be rare for cases involving this type of harm to be dealt with in a magistrates' court and it will be important to *consult your legal adviser for guidance in these situations.*

[431]

Type of injury	Description	Suggested starting point
Physical abuse of adult	Intermittent physical assaults resulting in accumulation of healed wounds, burns or scalds, but with no appreciable disfigurement	£2,000
Physical abuse of child	Isolated or intermittent assault(s) resulting in weals, hair pulled from scalp etc. Intermittent physical assaults resulting in accumulation of healed wounds, burns or scalds, but with no appreciable disfigurement	£1,000 £1,000
Sexual abuse of adult	Non-penetrative indecent physical acts over clothing Non-penetrative indecent act(s) under clothing	£1,000 £2,000
Sexual abuse of child (under 18)	Non-penetrative indecent physical act(s) over clothing Non-penetrative frequent assaults over clothing or non-penetrative indecent act under clothing Repetitive indecent acts under clothing	£1,000 £1,500 or 2,000 £3,300

[432]

PROSECUTION COSTS SG10-147

Where an offender is convicted of an offence, the court has discretion to make such order as to costs as it considers just and reasonable.[129]

The Court of Appeal has given the following guidance:[130]

i) an order for costs should never exceed the sum which, having regard to the offender's means and any other financial order imposed, he or she is able to pay and which it is reasonable to order him or her to pay;
ii) an order for costs should never exceed the sum which the prosecutor actually and reasonably incurred;
iii) the purpose of the order is to compensate the prosecutor. Where the conduct of the defence has put the prosecutor to avoidable expense, the offender may be ordered to pay some or all of that sum to the prosecutor but the offender must not be punished for exercising the right to defend himself or herself;
iv) the costs ordered to be paid should not be grossly disproportionate to any fine imposed for the offence. This principle was affirmed in *BPS Advertising Limited v London Borough of Barnet*[131] in which the Court held that, while there is no question of an arithmetical relationship, the question of costs should be viewed in the context of the maximum penalty considered by Parliament to be appropriate for the seriousness of the offence;
v) if the combined total of the proposed fine and the costs sought by the prosecutor exceeds the sum which the offender could reasonably be ordered to pay, the costs order should be reduced rather than the fine;
vi) it is for the offender to provide details of his or her financial position so as to enable the court to assess what he or she can reasonably afford to pay. If the offender fails to do so, the court is entitled to draw reasonable inferences as to means from all the circumstances of the case;
vii) if the court proposes to make any financial order against the offender, it must give him or her fair opportunity to adduce any relevant financial information and to make appropriate submissions.

Where the prosecutor is the Crown Prosecution Service, prosecution costs exclude the costs of the investigation, which are met by the police. In non-CPS cases where the costs of the investigation are incurred by the prosecutor a costs award may cover the costs of investigation as well as prosecution.[132] However, where the investigation was carried out as part of a council officer's routine duties, for which he or she would have been paid in the normal way, this is a relevant factor to be taken into account when deciding the appropriate amount of any costs order.[133]

Where the court wishes to impose costs in addition to a fine, compensation and/or the victim surcharge but the offender has insufficient resources to pay the total amount, the order of priority is:

i) compensation;
ii) victim surcharge;
iii) fine;
iv) costs.

[129] Prosecution of Offences Act 1985, s. 18
[130] *R v Northallerton Magistrates' Court, ex parte Dove* [2000] 1 Cr App R (S) 136 (CA)
[131] [2006] EWCA 3335 (Admin) QBD
[132] Further guidance is provided in the Criminal Costs Practice Direction and the Criminal Procedure Rules Part 76 see https://www.justice.gov.uk/courts/procedure-rules/criminal/rulesmenu
[133] ibid

SG10-148

Victim Surcharge

[433]

1. When sentencing for offences committed on or after 1 October 2012 a court must order the Victim Surcharge in the following ways:[134]

Disposal type	One or more offence(s) committed before 8 April 2016	One or more offence(s) committed before 28 June 2019	All offence(s) committed on or after 28 June 2019
Conditional discharge	£15	£20	£21
Fine	10 per cent of the fine value		
	£20 minimum and £120 maximum (rounded up or down to the nearest pound)	£30 minimum and £170 maximum (rounded up or down to the nearest pound)	£32 minimum and £181 maximum (rounded up or down to the nearest pound)
Community sentence	£60	£85	£90
Suspended sentence order	£80 (six months or less)	£115 (six months or less)	£122 (six months or less)
Immediate custody	*£80 (six months or less)	£115 (six months or less)	£122 (six months or less)

Offenders aged under 18 at the date of the offence

Disposal type	One or more offence(s) committed before 8 April 2016	One or more offence(s) committed before 28 June 2019	All offence(s) committed on or after 28 June 2019
Conditional discharge	£10	£15	£16
Fine, Youth Rehabilitation Order, Community Order, Referral Order	£15	£20	£21
Suspended sentence order	£20	£30	£32
Immediate custody	*£20	£30	£32

* When sentencing an offender to immediate custody for a single offence committed before 1 September 2014 or more than one offence, at least one of which was committed before 1 September 2014, no surcharge is payable. (Criminal Justice Act 2003 (Surcharge) Order 2012 as amended by Criminal Justice Act 2003 (Surcharge) (Amendment) Order 2014)

Person who is not an individual (for example, a company or other legal person)

[434]

Disposal type	One or more offence(s) committed before 8 April 2016	One or more offence(s) committed before 28 June 2019	All offence(s) committed on or after 28 June 2019
Conditional discharge	£15	£20	£21
Fine	10 per cent of the fine value with a £20 minimum and a £120 maximum (rounded up or down to the nearest pound)	10 per cent of the fine value with a £30 minimum and a £170 maximum (rounded up or down to the nearest pound)	10 per cent of the fine value with a £32 minimum and a £181 maximum (rounded up or down to the nearest pound)

Where an offender is dealt with in different ways only one surcharge (whichever attracts the higher sum) will be paid. Where there is more than one fine ordered, then the surcharge for the highest individual fine is assessed, NOT the total of all fines ordered. Where a custodial sentence is imposed the surcharge is based upon the longest individual sentence, NOT the aggregate term imposed.

Where the court dealing with an offender for more than one offence and at least one offence was committed when the offender was under 18, the surcharge should be ordered at the rate for under 18s (Criminal

[134] Criminal Justice Act 2003, s.161A; CJA 2003 (Surcharge) Order 2012; CJA 2003 (Surcharge) (Amendment) Order 2016) and CJA 2003 (Surcharge) (Amendment) Order 2019

[434] Justice Act 2003 (surcharge) Order 2012 art.5(3)). There is no victim surcharge payable when compensation is ordered as a sentence (as opposed to ancillary order).

The surcharge should not be repeated when dealing with breach of a community order, suspended sentence order or conditional discharge.

Where the offender has the means to pay the financial impositions of the court, there should be no reduction in compensation or fines whenever the surcharge is ordered. However, when the court:

- orders the offender to pay both a surcharge and compensation, but the offender is unable to pay both, the court must reduce the amount of the surcharge (if necessary to nil) (Criminal Justice Act 2003, s.161A(3)); or
- orders the offender to pay both a fine and a surcharge, the court may only reduce the fine to the extent that the offender is unable to pay both (Criminal Justice Act 2003, s.164(4A)).

Where the offender does not have sufficient means to pay the total financial penalty considered appropriate by the court, the order of priority is:

- compensation
- surcharge
- fine
- costs.

When sentencing for one or more offences any one of which was committed **after 1 April 2007 but before 1 October 2012**, a surcharge is payable only if the offender is dealt with by way of a fine, at a flat rate of £15 (Criminal Justice Act 2003 (Surcharge) Order 2012 art.7(2)).

COMMUNITY ORDERS SG10-149

See Imposition Guideline at **SG9-2**.

CUSTODIAL SENTENCES SG10-150

See Imposition Guideline at **SG9-9**.

[435]

ANCILLARY ORDERS SG10-151

There are several ancillary orders available in a magistrates' court which should be considered in appropriate cases. Annex A lists the offences in respect of which certain orders are available [not reproduced]. The individual offence guidelines above also identify ancillary orders particularly likely to be relevant to the offence. **In all cases, consult your legal adviser regarding available orders and their specific requirements and effects.**

Ancillary orders should be taken into account when assessing whether the overall penalty is commensurate with offence seriousness.

Anti-social behaviour orders SG10-152

These have now been replaced by Criminal Behaviour Orders (see below)

Binding over orders SG10-153

The court has the power to bind an individual over to keep the peace.[135]

The order is designed to prevent future misconduct and requires the individual to promise to pay a specified sum if the terms of the order are breached. Exercise of the power does not depend upon conviction.

Guidance on the making of binding over orders is set out in [CPD VII, Sentencing J: see **PD-80**]. Key principles include:

(1) before imposing the order, the court must be satisfied so that it is sure that a breach of the peace involving violence or an imminent threat of violence has occurred, or that there is a real risk of violence in the future. The court should hear evidence and the parties before making any order;
(2) the court should state its reasons for making the order;
(3) the order should identify the specific conduct or activity from which the individual must refrain, the length of the order and the amount of the recognisance;
(4) the length of the order should be proportionate to the harm sought to be avoided and should not generally exceed 12 months;
(5) when fixing the amount of the recognisance, the court should have regard to the individual's financial resources.

[135] Justices of the Peace Act 1361, Magistrates Court Act 1980, s. 115

SG10-154 **Confiscation orders** [436]

Confiscation orders under the Proceeds of Crime Act 2002 may only be made by the Crown Court.

An offender convicted of an offence in a magistrates' court must be committed to the Crown Court where this is requested by the prosecution with a view to a confiscation order being considered.[136]

If the committal is made in respect of an either way offence, the court must state whether it would have committed the offender to the Crown Court for sentencing had the issue of a confiscation order not arisen.

SG10-155 **Criminal Behaviour Orders**

A Criminal Behaviour Order (CBO) is an order which is available on conviction for any criminal offence by any criminal court, introduced by the Anti-social Behaviour, Crime and Policing Act 2014[137] with effect from 20 October 2014. It replaces the former powers of the court to make orders such as an ASBO or a drinking banning order on conviction.

A CBO is an order designed to tackle the most serious and persistent anti-social individuals where their behaviour has brought them before a criminal court. The anti-social behaviour to be addressed does not need to be connected to the criminal behaviour, or activity which led to the conviction. However, if there is no link the court will need to reflect on the reasons for making the order.

A CBO can deal with a wide range of anti-social behaviours following the offender's conviction, for example threatening violence against others in the community, or persistently being drunk and aggressive in public. However, the order should not be designed to stop reasonable, trivial or benign behaviours that have not caused, or are not likely to cause anti-social behaviour.

Any application will be made by the prosecution.[138] The majority of applications will therefore be made by the CPS, either at their own initiative, or at the request of the police. However, it may also be applied for by local councils, providing they are the prosecuting authority in the case. *The court cannot make a CBO of its own volition.*

A CBO may only be made against an offender when they have been sentenced to at least a conditional discharge for the substantive offence.[139] *A CBO cannot be made where the offender has been given an absolute discharge.*

The court may only make a CBO if it is satisfied that two conditions are met:[140]

1. The court must be satisfied, beyond reasonable doubt, that the offender has engaged in behaviour that caused, or was likely to cause, harassment, alarm or distress to one or more persons,[141] and
2. That making the order will help in preventing the offender from engaging in such behaviour.[142]

For the first condition, the burden of proof on the prosecution is to the criminal standard, beyond reasonable doubt. (There is no test of necessity as with ASBOs.)

A CBO may:

1. Prohibit the offender from doing anything described in the order ('a prohibition'), and/or
2. Require the offender to do anything described in the order ('a requirement').[143]

However, any prohibitions and/or requirements must, so far as practicable, avoid any interference with times an offender would normally work, attend school or other educational establishment and any conflict with any other court order or injunction.[144]

If the order requires the offender to do anything, then the order must specify the individual or organisation that is responsible for supervising compliance with the requirement[145] and must hear from them about both the suitability and enforceability of a requirement, before including it in the CBO.[146]

The order must be proportionate and reasonable. It will be for the court to decide the measures which are most appropriate and available to tackle the underlying cause of the anti-social behaviour.

The order should be tailored to the specific needs of each perpetrator. [437]

136 Proceeds of Crime Act 2002, s. 70
137 Anti-social Behaviour, Crime and Policing Act 2014, s. 22
138 ibid, s. 22(7)
139 ibid, s. 22(8)
140 ibid, s. 22(2)
141 ibid, s. 22(3)
142 ibid, s. 22(4)
143 ibid, s. 22(5)
144 ibid, s. 22(9)
145 ibid, s. 24(2)
146 ibid, s. 24(3)

[437] When deciding whether or not to make a CBO, the court is entitled to consider evidence submitted by the prosecution and by the offender.[147] It does not matter whether the evidence would have been admissible, or has been heard as part of the criminal proceedings in which the offender was convicted,[148] but it should be relevant to the test to be applied to the making of the order (i.e. that the offender has engaged in behaviour that caused, or was likely to cause, harassment, alarm or distress to any person, and that the court considers that making the order will assist in preventing the offender from engaging in such behaviour). This evidence could include hearsay or bad character evidence. Special measures are available for witnesses who are vulnerable and intimidated witnesses in accordance with section 16 and 17 Youth Justice and Criminal Evidence Act 1999.[149]

A CBO takes effect on the day it is made,[150] unless the offender is already subject to an existing CBO, in which case it may take effect on the day in which the previous order expires.[151] The order must specify the period for which it has effect.[152] In the case of an adult, the order must be for a fixed period of not less than two years or it may be an indefinite period, so that it is made until further order.[153] An order may specify different periods for which particular prohibitions or requirements have effect within the order.[154]

The court can impose an *interim order* in cases where the offender is convicted but the court is adjourning the hearing of the application for a CBO,[155] before or after sentence for the offence. The offender need not be sentenced to be made subject to an interim order.[156] The court can make an interim order if the court thinks it is just to do so. An interim order can be made until final hearing or further order.[157] When making an interim order the court has the same powers as if it were making a final order.[158]

It is likely that the hearing for a CBO will take place at the same time as the sentencing for the criminal case. For adult offenders, there is no formal consultation requirement. However, in order to ensure that applications are made appropriately and efficiently, there is an expectation that any relevant agencies will have been consulted so that the prosecution have the relevant information to decide whether to make an order or not and if so, in what terms. The prosecution should be prepared to deal with an application on the date of hearing.

The court may deal with the application for a CBO at the same time as it imposes sentence for the offence. Alternatively, the court may sentence the offender for the criminal offence and adjourn the application for a CBO to a later date.[159] However, the court cannot hear an application once sentence has taken place, unless the application was made by the prosecution before sentence was concluded, as an application cannot be made retrospectively.

If the offender does not appear at an adjourned hearing for a CBO, the court may further adjourn the proceedings, issue a warrant for the offender's arrest, or hear the proceedings in the offender's absence.[160] To issue a warrant for the offender's arrest, the court must be satisfied that the offender has been given adequate notice of the time and place for the hearing.[161] To proceed in the offender's absence, the court
438] must be satisfied that the offender has been given adequate notice of the time and place for the hearing and been told if they do not attend, the court may hear the application in their absence.[162]

Further guidance is provided by the Home Office in *Anti-social Behaviour, Crime and Policing Act 2014: Reform of anti-social behaviour powers; Statutory guidance for frontline professionals.* July 2014.[163]

Deprivation orders **SG10-156**

The court has the power to deprive an offender of property used for the purpose of committing or facilitating the commission of an offence, whether or not it deals with the offender in any other way.[164]

Before making the order, the court must have regard to the value of the property and the likely financial and other effects on the offender.

147 ibid, s. 23(1)
148 ibid, s. 23(2)
149 ibid, s. 31
150 ibid, s. 25(1)
151 ibid, s. 25(2)
152 ibid, s. 25(3)
153 ibid, s. 25(5)
154 ibid, s. 25(6)
155 ibid, s. 26(1)
156 ibid, s. 26(3)
157 ibid, s. 26(2)
158 ibid, s. 26(4)
159 ibid, s. 26(3)
160 ibid, s. 23(4)
161 ibid, s. 23(5)
162 ibid, s. 23(6)
163 www.gov.uk/government/uploads/system/uploads/attachment_data/file/332839/StatutoryGuidanceFrontline.pdf
164 Powers of Criminal Courts (Sentencing) Act 2000, s. 143

Without limiting the circumstances in which the court may exercise the power, a vehicle is deemed to have been used for the purpose of committing the offence where the offence is punishable by imprisonment and consists of: [438]

(1) driving, attempting to drive, or being in charge of a motor vehicle;
(2) failing to provide a specimen; or
(3) failing to stop and/or report an accident.[165]

SG10-157 **Deprivation of ownership of animal**

Where an offender convicted of one of the following offences under the Animal Welfare Act 2006 is the owner of an animal in relation to which the offence is committed, the court may make an order depriving him or her of ownership of the animal and for its disposal:[166]

(1) causing unnecessary suffering (s. 4);
(2) mutilation (s. 5);
(3) docking of dogs' tails (ss. 6(1) and 6(2));
(4) fighting etc. (s. 8);
(5) breach of duty to ensure welfare (s. 9);
(6) breach of disqualification order (s. 36(9)).

The court is required to give reasons if it decides not to make such an order.

Deprivation of ownership may be ordered instead of or in addition to dealing with the offender in any other way.

SG10-158 **Destruction orders and contingent destruction orders for dogs** [439]

See the Dangerous Dogs Guideline at [SG21-1]....

SG10-159 **Disqualification from ownership of animals**

Where an offender is convicted of one of the following offences under the Animal Welfare Act 2006, the court may disqualify him or her from owning or keeping animals, dealing in animals, and/or transporting animals:[167]

(1) causing unnecessary suffering (s. 4);
(2) mutilation (s. 5);
(3) docking of dogs' tails (ss. 6(1) and 6(2));
(4) administration of poisons etc. (s. 7);
(5) fighting etc. (s. 8);
(6) breach of duty to ensure welfare (s. 9);
(7) breach of licensing or registration requirements (s. 13(6));
(8) breach of disqualification order (s. 36(9)).

The court is required to give reasons if it decides not to make such an order.

The court may specify a period during which an offender may not apply for termination of the order under section 43 of the Animal Welfare Act 2006; if no period is specified, an offender may not apply for termination of the order until one year after the order was made.

Disqualification may be imposed instead of or in addition to dealing with the offender in any other way.

SG10-160 **Disqualification from driving — general power**

The court may disqualify any person convicted of an offence from driving for such period as it thinks fit.[168] This may be instead of or in addition to dealing with the offender in any other way.

The section does not require the offence to be connected to the use of a vehicle. The Court of Appeal has held that the power is available as part of the overall punitive element of a sentence, and the only restrictions on the exercise of the power are those in the statutory provision.[169]

SG10-161 **Disqualification of company directors**

The Company Directors Disqualification Act 1986 empowers the court to disqualify an offender from being a director or taking part in the promotion, formation or management of a company for up to five years.

---

165 ibid, ss. 143(6) and 143(7)
166 Animal Welfare Act 2006, s. 33
167 ibid, s. 34
168 Powers of Criminal Courts (Sentencing) Act 2000, s. 146
169 *R v Cliff* [2004] EWCA Crim 3139

[439] An order may be made in two situations:

(1) where an offender has been convicted of an indictable offence in connection with the promotion, formation, management, liquidation or striking off of a company;[170] or
(2) where an offender has been convicted of an offence involving a failure to file documents with, or give notice to, the registrar of companies. If the offence is triable only summarily, disqualification can be ordered only where the offender has been the subject of three default orders or convictions in the preceding five years.[171]

[440] **Exclusion orders** SG10-162

The court may make an exclusion order where an offender has been convicted of an offence committed on licensed premises involving the use or threat of violence.

The order prohibits the offender from entering *specified* licensed premises without the consent of the licensee. The term of the order must be between three months and two years.

Football banning orders SG10-163

The court must make a football banning order where an offender has been convicted of a relevant offence and it is satisfied that there are reasonable grounds to believe that making a banning order would help to prevent violence or disorder.[172] If the court is not so satisfied, it must state that fact and give its reasons.

Relevant offences are those set out in schedule 1 [to] the Football Spectators Act 1989 …

The order requires the offender to report to a police station within five days, may require the offender to surrender his or her passport, and may impose requirements on the offender in relation to any regulated football matches.

Where the order is imposed in addition to a sentence of immediate imprisonment, the term of the order must be between six and ten years. In other cases, the term of the order must be between three and five years.

[441] **Forfeiture and destruction of drugs** SG10-164

Where an offender is convicted of an offence under the Misuse of Drugs Act 1971, the court may order forfeiture and destruction of anything shown to the satisfaction of the court to relate to the offence.[173]

Forfeiture and destruction of weapons orders SG10-165

A court convicting a person of possession of an offensive weapon may make an order for the forfeiture or disposal of the weapon (Prevention of Crime Act 1953, s1(2))

See also deprivation orders [at **SG10-156**].

Forfeiture and destruction of goods bearing unauthorised trade mark SG10-166

Where the court is satisfied that an offence under section 92 of the Trade Marks Act 1994 has been committed, it must (on the application of a person who has come into possession of the goods in connection with the investigation or prosecution of the offence) order forfeiture of the goods.[174]

If it considers it appropriate, instead of ordering destruction of the goods, the court may direct that they be released to a specified person on condition that the offending sign is erased, removed or obliterated.

Forfeiture or suspension of liquor licence SG10-167

Where an offender who holds a personal licence to supply alcohol is charged with a 'relevant offence', he or she is required to produce the licence to the court, or inform the court of its existence, no later than his or her first appearance.[175]

'Relevant offences' are listed in schedule 4 [to] the Licensing Act 2003 …

Where the offender is convicted, the court may order forfeiture of the licence or suspend it for up to six months.[176] When deciding whether to order forfeiture or suspension, the court may take account of the offender's previous convictions for 'relevant offences'.[177]

170 Company Directors Disqualification Act 1988, s. 2
171 ibid, s. 5
172 Football Spectators Act 1989, s. 14A
173 Misuse of Drugs Act 1971, s. 27(1)
174 Trade Marks Act 1994, s. 97
175 Licensing Act 2003, s. 128(1)
176 ibid, s. 129(2)
177 ibid, s. 129(3)

Whether or not forfeiture or suspension is ordered, the court is required to notify the licensing authority of the offender's conviction and the sentence imposed. [441]

SG10-168 **Parenting orders**

The court may make a parenting order where an offender has been convicted of an offence under section 444 of the Education Act 1996 (failing to secure regular attendance at school) and the court is satisfied that the order would be desirable in the interests of preventing the commission of any further offence under that section.[178]

The order may impose such requirements that the court considers desirable in the interests of preventing the commission of a further offence under section 444.

A requirement to attend a counselling or guidance programme may be included only if the offender has been the subject of a parenting order on a previous occasion.

The term of the order must not exceed 12 months.

SG10-169 **Restitution orders**

Where goods have been stolen and an offender is convicted of any offence with reference to theft of those goods, the court may make a restitution order.[179]

The court may:

(1) order anyone in possession or control of the stolen goods to restore them to the victim;
(2) on the application of the victim, order that goods directly or indirectly representing the stolen goods (as being the proceeds of any disposal or realisation of the stolen goods) be transferred to the victim; or
(3) order that a sum not exceeding the value of the stolen goods be paid to the victim out of any money taken out of the offender's possession on his or her apprehension.

SG10-170 **Restraining orders** [442]

Where an offender is convicted of any offence, the court may make a restraining order.[180]

The order may prohibit the offender from doing anything for the purpose of protecting the victim of the offence, or any other person mentioned in the order, from further conduct which amounts to harassment or will cause a fear of violence.

The order may have effect for a specified period or until further order.

A court before which a person is *acquitted* of an offence may make a restraining order if the court considers that it is necessary to protect a person from harassment by the defendant.[181] *Consult your legal adviser for guidance.*

SG10-171 **Sexual harm prevention orders**

Orders can be made in relation to a person who has been convicted, found not guilty by reason of insanity or found to be under a disability and to have done the act charged, or cautioned etc. for an offence listed in either Schedule 3 or Schedule 5 to the Sexual Offences Act 2003 either in the UK or overseas (see Annex A [not reproduced]). This includes offenders whose convictions etc. pre-date the commencement of the 2003 Act.

No application is necessary for the court to make a SHPO at the point of sentence although the prosecutor may wish to invite the court to consider making an order in appropriate cases. The court may ask pre-sentence report writers to consider the suitability of a SHPO on a non-prejudicial basis.

In order to make a SHPO, the court must be satisfied that the offender presents a risk of sexual harm to the public (or particular members of the public) and that an order is necessary to protect against this risk. The details of the offence are likely to be a key factor in the court's decision, together with the offender's previous convictions and the assessment of risk presented by the national probation service in any pre-sentence report. The court may take into consideration the range of other options available to it in respect of protecting the public. The court may want to consider:

1. would an order minimise the risk of harm to the public or to any particular members of the public?
2. is it proportionate?
3. can it be policed effectively?

178 Crime and Disorder Act 1998, s. 8
179 Powers of Criminal Courts (Sentencing) Act 2000, s. 148
180 Protection from Harassment Act 1997, s. 5
181 ibid, s. 5A

[442] The only prohibitions which can be imposed by a SHPO are those which are necessary for the purpose of protecting the public from sexual harm from the defendant. These can, however, be wide ranging. An order may, for example, prohibit someone from undertaking certain forms of employment such as acting as a home tutor to children. It may also prohibit the offender from engaging in particular activities on the internet. The decision of the Court of Appeal in *R v Smith and Others* [2011] EWCA Crim 1772 reinforces the need for the terms of a SHPO to be tailored to the exact requirements of the case. SHPOs may be used to limit and manage internet use by an offender, where it is considered proportionate and necessary to do so. The behaviour prohibited by the order might well be considered unproblematic if exhibited by another member of the public — it is the offender's previous offending behaviour and subsequent demonstration that they may pose a risk of further such behaviour, which will make them eligible for an order.

The order may include only negative prohibitions; there is no power to impose positive obligations. The order may have effect for a fixed period (not less than five years) or until further order. *Consult your legal adviser for guidance.*

Sexual offences prevention orders **SG10-172**

These have now been replaced by Sexual Harm Prevention Orders. A Sexual Offences Prevention Order may only be made if the order was applied for before 8 March 2015. *Consult your legal adviser for guidance.*

[443]

Deferred Sentences **SG10-173**

The court is empowered to defer passing sentence for up to six months.[182] The court may impose any conditions during the period of deferment that it considers appropriate. These could be specific requirements as set out in the provisions for community sentences, restorative justice activities[183] or requirements that are drawn more widely. The purpose of deferment is to enable the court to have regard to the offender's conduct after conviction or any change in his or her circumstances, including the extent to which the offender has complied with any requirements imposed by the court.

Three conditions must be satisfied before sentence can be deferred:

1) the offender must consent (and in the case of restorative justice activities the other participants must consent);[184]
2) the offender must undertake to comply with requirements imposed by the court; and
3) the court must be satisfied that deferment is in the interests of justice.

Deferred sentences will be appropriate in very limited circumstances:

- deferred sentences will be appropriate in very limited circumstances;
- deferred sentences are likely to be relevant predominantly in a small group of cases close to either the community or custodial sentence threshold where, should the offender be prepared to adapt his behaviour in a way clearly specified by the sentencer, the court may be prepared to impose a lesser sentence;
- sentencers should impose specific and measurable conditions that do not involve a serious restriction on liberty;
- the court should give a clear indication of the type of sentence it would have imposed if it had decided not to defer;
- the court should also ensure that the offender understands the consequences of failure to comply with the court's wishes during the deferment period.

If the offender fails to comply with any requirement imposed in connection with the deferment, or commits another offence, he or she can be brought back to court before the end of the deferment period and the court can proceed to sentence.

[444]

Offences Committed in a Domestic Context **SG10-174**

See Overarching Principles: Domestic Abuse [at **SG5-1**]

182 Powers of Criminal Courts (Sentencing) Act 2000, s. 1 as amended by Criminal Justice Act 2003, s. 278 and sch. 23, para. 1
183 ibid, s. 1ZA as inserted by the Crime and Courts Act 2013, s. 44, sch. 16, Pt 2, para. 5
184 ibid, s.1ZA(3)

Sentencing Guidelines

SG10-175 Hate Crime[185] [446]

SG10-176 Racial or religious aggravation—statutory provisions

1. Sections 29 to 32 of the Crime and Disorder Act 1998 create specific racially or religiously aggravated offences, which have higher maximum penalties than the non-aggravated versions of those offences. The individual offence guidelines indicate whether there is a specifically aggravated form of the offence.
2. An offence is racially or religiously aggravated for the purposes of sections 29–32 of the Act if the offender demonstrates hostility towards the victim based on his or her membership (or presumed membership) of a racial or religious group, or if the offence is (wholly or partly) motivated by racial or religious hostility.
3. For all other offences, section 145 of the Criminal Justice Act 2003 provides that the court must regard racial or religious aggravation as an aggravating factor.
4. The court should not treat an offence as racially or religiously aggravated for the purposes of section 145 where a racially or religiously aggravated form of the offence was charged but resulted in an acquittal. The court should not normally treat an offence as racially or religiously aggravated if a racially or religiously aggravated form of the offence was available but was not charged. *Consult your legal adviser for further guidance in these situations.*

SG10-177 Aggravation related to disability, sexual orientation or transgender identity—statutory provisions

5. Under section 146 of the Criminal Justice Act 2003, the court must treat as an aggravating factor the fact that:
   - an offender demonstrated hostility towards the victim based on his or her disability, sexual orientation or transgender identity (or presumed disability, sexual orientation or transgender identity); or
   - the offence was (wholly or partly) motivated by hostility towards persons who have a particular disability, who are of a particular sexual orientation or who are transgender.

SG10-178 Approach to sentencing

6. A court should not conclude that offending involved aggravation related to race, religion, disability, sexual orientation or transgender identity without first putting the offender on notice and allowing him or her to challenge the allegation.
7. When sentencing any offence where such aggravation is found to be present, the following approach should be followed. This applies both to the specific racially or religiously aggravated offences under the Crime and Disorder Act 1998 and to offences which are regarded as aggravated under section 145 or 146 of the Criminal Justice Act 2003:
   - sentencers should first determine the appropriate sentence, leaving aside the element of aggravation related to race, religion, disability, sexual orientation or transgender identity but taking into account all other aggravating or mitigating factors;
   - the sentence should then be increased to take account of the aggravation related to race, religion, disability, sexual orientation or transgender identity;
   - the increase may mean that a more onerous penalty of the same type is appropriate, or that the threshold for a more severe type of sentence is passed;
   - the sentencer must state in open court that the offence was aggravated by reason of race, religion, disability, sexual orientation or transgender identity; [447]
   - the sentencer should state what the sentence would have been without that element of aggravation.
8. The extent to which the sentence is increased will depend on the seriousness of the aggravation. The following factors could be taken as indicating a high level of aggravation:

SG10-179 Offender's intention

- The element of aggravation based on race, religion, disability, sexual orientation or transgender identity was planned
- The offence was part of a pattern of offending by the offender
- The offender was a member of, or was associated with, a group promoting hostility based on race, religion, disability, sexual orientation or transgender identity
- The incident was deliberately set up to be offensive or humiliating to the victim or to the group of which the victim is a member

[185] In respect of the guidance in paragraphs 5–9 below, courts must treat transgender identity as an aggravating factor under section 146 of the Criminal Justice Act 2003 only upon implementation of section 65 of the Legal Aid, Sentencing and Punishment of Offenders Act 2012

[447] **Impact on the victim or others** SG10-180

- The offence was committed in the victim's home
- The victim was providing a service to the public
- The timing or location of the offence was calculated to maximise the harm or distress it caused
- The expressions of hostility were repeated or prolonged
- The offence caused fear and distress throughout a local community or more widely
- The offence caused particular distress to the victim and/or the victim's family.

9. At the lower end of the scale, the aggravation may be regarded as less serious if:
   - It was limited in scope or duration
   - The offence was not motivated by hostility on the basis of race, religion, disability, sexual orientation or transgender identity, and the element of hostility or abuse was minor or incidental
10. In these guidelines, the specific racially or religiously aggravated offences under the Crime and Disorder Act 1998 are addressed on the same page as the 'basic offence'; the starting points and ranges indicated on the guideline relate to the 'basic' (i.e. non-aggravated) offence. The increase for the element of racial or religious aggravation may result in a sentence above the range; *this will not constitute a departure from the guideline for which reasons must be given.*

Environmental/Health and Safety Offences SG10-181

[Omitted.]

[448] Road Traffic Offences – Disqualification SG10-182

Obligatory disqualification SG10-183

1. Some offences carry obligatory disqualification for a minimum of 12 months.[186] The minimum period is automatically increased where there have been certain previous convictions and disqualifications.
2. An offender must be disqualified for at least two years if he or she has been disqualified two or more times for a period of at least 56 days in the three years preceding the commission of the offence.[187] The following disqualifications are to be disregarded for the purposes of this provision:
   - interim disqualification;
   - disqualification where vehicle used for the purpose of crime;
   - disqualification for stealing or taking a vehicle or going equipped to steal or take a vehicle.
3. An offender must be disqualified for *at least three years* if he or she is convicted of one of the following offences *and* has within the ten years preceding the commission of the offence been convicted of any of these offences:[188]
   - causing death by careless driving when under the influence of drink or drugs;
   - driving or attempting to drive while unfit;
   - driving or attempting to drive with excess alcohol;
   - failing to provide a specimen (drive/attempting to drive).
4. The individual offence guidelines above indicate whether disqualification is mandatory for the offence and the applicable minimum period. Consult your legal adviser for further guidance.

Special Reasons

5. The period of disqualification may be reduced or avoided if there are special reasons.[189] These must relate to the offence; circumstances peculiar to the offender cannot constitute special reasons.[190] The Court of Appeal has established that, to constitute a special reason, a matter must:[191]
   - be a mitigating or extenuating circumstance;
   - not amount in law to a defence to the charge;
   - be directly connected with the commission of the offence;
   - be one which the court ought properly to take into consideration when imposing sentence.

186 Road Traffic Offenders Act 1988, s. 34
187 ibid., s. 34(4)
188 ibid., s. 34(3)
189 ibid., s. 34(1)
190 *Whittal v Kirby* [1946] 2 All ER 552 (CA)
191 *R v Wickens* (1958) 42 Cr App R 436 (CA)

Consult your legal adviser for further guidance on special reasons applications.

'Totting up' disqualification [449]

6. Disqualification for a *minimum* of six months must be ordered if an offender incurs 12 penalty points or more within a three-year period.[192] The minimum period may be automatically increased if the offender has been disqualified within the preceding three years. Totting up disqualifications, unlike other disqualifications, erase all penalty points.
7. The period of a totting up disqualification can be reduced or avoided for exceptional hardship or other mitigating circumstances. No account is to be taken of hardship that is not exceptional hardship or circumstances alleged to make the offence not serious. Any circumstances taken into account in the preceding three years to reduce or avoid a totting disqualification must be disregarded.[193]
8. *Consult your legal adviser for further guidance on exceptional hardship applications.*

Discretionary disqualification

9. Whenever an offender is convicted of an endorsable offence or of taking a vehicle without consent, the court has a discretionary power to disqualify instead of imposing penalty points. The individual offence guidelines above indicate whether the offence is endorsable and the number or range of penalty points it carries.
10. The number of variable points or the period of disqualification should reflect the seriousness of the offence. Some of the individual offence guidelines above include penalty points and/or periods of disqualification in the sentence starting points and ranges; however, the court is not precluded from sentencing outside the range where the facts justify it. Where a disqualification is for less than 56 days, there are some differences in effect compared with disqualification for a longer period; in particular, the licence will automatically come back into effect at the end of the disqualification period (instead of requiring application by the driver) and the disqualification is not taken into account for the purpose of increasing subsequent obligatory periods of disqualification.[194]
11. In some cases in which the court is considering discretionary disqualification the offender may already have sufficient penalty points on his or her licence that he or she would be liable to a 'totting up' disqualification if further points were imposed. In these circumstances, the court should impose penalty points rather than discretionary disqualification so that the minimum totting up disqualification period applies (see paragraph 6 above).

Disqualification until a test is passed

12. Where an offender is convicted of dangerous driving, the court must order disqualification until an extended driving test is passed.
13. The court has discretion to disqualify until a test is passed where an offender is convicted of any endorsable offence.[195] Where disqualification is obligatory, the extended test applies. In other cases, it will be the ordinary test.
14. An offender disqualified as a 'totter' under the penalty points provisions may also be ordered to re-take a driving test; in this case, the extended test applies.
15. The discretion to order a re-test is likely to be exercised where there is evidence of inexperience, incompetence or infirmity, or the disqualification period is lengthy (that is, the offender is going to be 'off the road' for a considerable time).

Reduced period of disqualification for completion of rehabilitation course [450]

16. Where an offender is disqualified for 12 months or more in respect of an alcohol-related driving offence, the court may order that the period of disqualification will be reduced if the offender satisfactorily completes an approved rehabilitation course.[196]
17. Before offering an offender the opportunity to attend a course, the court must be satisfied that an approved course is available and must inform the offender of the effect of the order, the fees that the offender is required to pay, and when he or she must pay them.
18. The court should also explain that the offender may be required to satisfy the Secretary of State that he or she does not have a drink problem and is fit to drive before the offender's licence will be returned at the end of the disqualification period.[197]

---

192 Road Traffic Offenders Act 1988, s. 35
193 ibid.
194 ibid, ss. 34(4), 35(2), 37(1A)
195 ibid, s. 36(4)
196 Road Traffic Offenders Act 1988, s. 34A
197 Road Traffic Act 1988

[450] 19. In general, a court should consider offering the opportunity to attend a course to all offenders convicted of a relevant offence for the first time. The court should be willing to consider offering an offender the opportunity to attend a second course where it considers there are good reasons. It will not usually be appropriate to give an offender the opportunity to attend a third course.

20. The reduction must be at least three months but cannot be more than one quarter of the total period of disqualification:
- a period of 12 months disqualification must be reduced to nine months;
- in other cases, a reduction of one week should be made for every month of the disqualification so that, for example, a disqualification of 24 months will be reduced by 24 weeks.

21. When it makes the order, the court must specify a date for completion of the course which is at least two months before the end of the reduced period of disqualification.

Disqualification in the offender's absence

22. When considering disqualification in absence the starting point should be that disqualification in absence should be imposed if there is no reason to believe the defendant is not aware of the proceedings, and after the statutory notice has been served pursuant to section 11(4) of the Magistrates' Courts Act 1980 where appropriate. Disqualification should not be imposed in absence where there is evidence that the defendant has an acceptable reason for not attending or where there are reasons to believe it would be contrary to the interests of justice to do so.

New drivers

23. Drivers who incur six points or more during the two-year probationary period after passing the driving test will have their licence revoked automatically by the Secretary of State; they will be able to drive only after application for a provisional licence pending the passing of a further test.[198]

24. An offender liable for an endorsement which will cause the licence to be revoked under the new drivers' provisions may ask the court to disqualify rather than impose points. This will avoid the requirement to take a further test. Generally, this would be inappropriate since it would circumvent the clear intention of Parliament.

[451] *Extension period of disqualification from driving where a custodial sentence is also imposed*

25. Where a court imposes disqualification in addition to a custodial sentence or a detention and training order, the court must extend the disqualification period by one half of the custodial sentence or detention or training order to take into account the period the offender will spend in custody. This will avoid a driving ban expiring, or being significantly diminished, during the period the offender is in custody (s. 35a Criminal Justice and Courts Act, 2015). Periods of time spent on remand or subject to an electronically monitored curfew do not apply.

26. Where a rehabilitation course is completed, any extension period is disregarded when reducing the ban.

27. For example where a court imposes a 6 month custodial sentence and a disqualification period of 12 months, the ban will be extended to 15 months. Where a rehabilitation course is completed, the reduction will remain at a maximum of 3 months.

[452] Out of Court Disposals SG10-184

1. There are several alternatives to formal charges available to police and CPS when dealing with adults, including cannabis and khat warnings, penalty notices for disorder, community resolution, simple cautions and conditional cautions.

Cannabis or khat warning

2. A cannabis or khat warning may be given where the offender is found in possession of a small amount of cannabis or khat consistent with personal use and the offender admits the elements of the offence. The drug is confiscated and a record of the warning will be made on local systems. The warning is not a conviction and should not be regarded as an aggravating factor when sentencing for subsequent offences.

Simple caution

3. A simple caution may be issued where there is evidence that the offender has committed an offence, the offender admits to the offence, and the offender agrees to being given the caution.

198 Road Traffic (New Drivers) Act 1995

4. When sentencing an offender who has received a simple caution on a previous occasion: [452]
   - the simple caution is not a previous conviction and, therefore, is not a statutory aggravating factor;
   - however, the caution will form part of the offender's criminal record and if the caution is recent and is relevant to the current offence it may be considered to be an aggravating factor.

SG10-185 *Conditional Cautions*

5. A conditional caution[199] requires an offender to comply with conditions, as an alternative to prosecution. The conditions that can be attached must be rehabilitative, reparative and/or a financial penalty. (If the offender is a 'relevant foreign offender' — that is someone without permission to enter or stay in the UK, conditions can be offered that have the object of effecting departure from and preventing return to the UK.) Before the caution can be given, the offender must admit the offence and consent to the conditions.
6. When sentencing an offender who has received a conditional caution in respect of an earlier offence:
   - a conditional caution is not a previous conviction and, therefore, is not a statutory aggravating factor;
   - however, if the conditional caution is recent and is relevant to the current offence it may be considered to be an aggravating factor;
   - the offender's response to the caution may properly influence the court's assessment of the offender's suitability for a particular sentence, so long as it remains within the limits established by the seriousness of the current offence.

Approach to sentencing for offence for which offender was cautioned but failed to comply with conditions

7. If the offender fails, without reasonable cause, to comply with the conditional caution, he or she may be prosecuted for the original offence. When sentencing in such a case:
   - the offender's non-compliance with the conditional caution does not increase the seriousness of the original offence and must not be regarded as an aggravating factor;
   - the offender's non-compliance may be relevant to selection of the type of sentence. For example, it may indicate that it is inappropriate to include certain requirements as part of a community order. The circumstances of the offender's failure to satisfy the conditions, and any partial compliance, will be relevant to this assessment.

SG10-186 *Penalty notices—fixed penalty notices and penalty notices for disorder* [453]

8. Penalty notices may be issued as an alternative to prosecution in respect of a range of offences. Unlike conditional cautions, an admission of guilt is not a prerequisite to issuing a penalty notice.
9. An offender who is issued with a penalty notice may nevertheless be prosecuted for the offence if he or she:
   - asks to be tried for the offence;
   - fails to pay the penalty within the period stipulated in the notice and the prosecutor decides to proceed with charges.[200]
10. When sentencing in cases in which a penalty notice was available:
    - the fact that the offender did not take advantage of the penalty (whether that was by requesting a hearing or failing to pay within the specified timeframe) does not increase the seriousness of the offence and must not be regarded as an aggravating factor. The appropriate sentence must be determined in accordance with the sentencing principles set out above (including the amount of any fine, which must take an offender's financial circumstances into account), disregarding the availability of the penalty;
    - where a penalty notice was not offered or taken up for reasons unconnected with the offence itself, such as administrative difficulties outside the control of the offender, the starting point should be a fine equivalent to the amount of the penalty and no order of costs should be imposed. The offender should not be disadvantaged by the unavailability of the penalty notice in these circumstances. A list of offences for which penalty notices are available, and the amount of the penalty, is set out in Annex B.
11. Where an offender has had previous penalty notice(s), the fact that an offender has previously been issued with a penalty notice does not increase the seriousness of the current offence and must not be regarded as an aggravating factor. It may, however, properly influence the court's assessment of the

[199] Criminal Justice Act 2003, s. 22

[200] In some cases of non-payment, the penalty is automatically registered and enforceable as a fine without need for recourse to the courts. This procedure applies to penalty notices for disorder and fixed penalty notices issued in respect of certain road traffic offences but not to fixed penalty notices issued for most other criminal offences.

[453] offender's suitability for a particular sentence, so long as it remains within the limits established by the seriousness of the current offence.

Community Resolution SG10-187

12. Community resolution is an informal non-statutory disposal used for dealing with less serious crime and anti-social behaviour where the offender accepts responsibility. The views of the victim (where there is one) are taken into account in reaching an informal agreement between the parties which can involve restorative justice techniques.
13. When sentencing an offender who has received a community resolution for an earlier offence:
    - A community resolution is not a conviction and is therefore not a statutory aggravating factor, but if recent and relevant to the offence it may be considered to be an aggravating factor.

[454]

VICTIM PERSONAL STATEMENTS SG10-188

A victim personal statement (VPS) gives victims a formal opportunity to say how a crime has affected them. Where the victim has chosen to make such a statement, a court should consider and take it into account prior to passing sentence.

[CPD VII, Sentencing F: see **PD-76**] emphasises that:

- evidence of the effects of an offence on the victim must be in the form of a witness statement under section 9 of the Criminal Justice Act 1967 or an expert's report;
- the statement must be served on the defence prior to sentence;
- except where inferences can properly be drawn from the nature of or circumstances surrounding the offence, the court must not make assumptions unsupported by evidence about the effects of an offence on the victim;
- at the discretion of the court the VPS may also be read aloud in whole or in part or it may be summarised. If it is to be read aloud the court should also determine who should do so. In making these decisions the court should take into account the victim's preferences, and follow them unless there is a good reason not to do so (for example, inadmissible or potentially harmful content). Court hearings should not be adjourned solely to allow the victim to attend court to read the VPS;
- the court must pass what it judges to be the appropriate sentence having regard to the circumstances of the offence and the offender, taking into account, so far as the court considers it appropriate, the consequences to the victim;
- the opinions of the victim or the victim's close relatives as to what the sentence should be are not relevant.

See also the guidance [at **SG10-145**] particularly with reference to the victim's views as to any compensation order that may be imposed.

Prevalence and community impact statements SG10-189

Taken from the Sentencing Guidelines Council's definitive guideline *Overarching Principles: Seriousness*.

The seriousness of an individual case should be judged on its own dimensions of harm and culpability rather than as part of a collective social harm.

However, there may be exceptional local circumstances that arise which may lead a court to decide that prevalence should influence sentencing levels. The pivotal issue in such cases will be the harm being caused to the community. It is essential that sentencers both have supporting evidence from an external source (for example a community impact statement compiled by the police) to justify claims that a particular crime is prevalent in their area and are satisfied that there is a compelling need to treat the offence more seriously than elsewhere. A community impact statement is a document providing information to the court about the impact of offences on the community.

The key factor in determining whether sentencing levels should be enhanced in response to prevalence will be the level of harm being caused in the locality. Enhanced sentences should be exceptional and in response to exceptional circumstances. Sentencers must sentence within the sentencing guidelines once the prevalence has been addressed.

[455]

ANNEX A: AVAILABILITY OF ANCILLARY ORDERS SG10-190

[Annex A consists of a list of offences covered in the MCSG for which particular ancillary orders are available and is omitted. For guidance on the various available ancillary orders, see the relevant material in the main work.]

Annex B [Offences for which Penalty Notices are Available] [459]

SG10-191 **Penalty notices for disorder**

Offence	Legislation	Amount
Criminal damage (where damage under £500 in value, and not normally where damage over £300)	Criminal Damage Act 1971, s.1	£90
Disorderly behaviour	Public Order Act 1986, s.5	£90
Drunk and disorderly	Criminal Justice Act 1967, s.91	£90
Sale of alcohol to drunk person on relevant premises (not including off-licenses)	Licensing Act 2003, s.141	£90
Sale of alcohol to person under 18 (staff only; licensees should be subject of a summons)	Licensing Act 2003, s.146	£90
Theft from a shop (where goods under £200 in value, and not normally where goods over £100)	Theft Act 1968, s.1	£90

SG10-192 **Fixed penalty notices**

Offence	Legislation	Amount	Penalty points
Careless driving	Road Traffic Act 1988, s. 3	£100	3
Brakes, steering or tyres defective	Road Traffic Act 1988, s.41A	£200	3
Breach of other construction and use requirements	Road Traffic Act 1988, s.42	£100 or £200	–
Driving other than in accordance with licence	Road Traffic Act 1988, s.87(1)	£100	3
Failing to comply with police officer signal	Road Traffic Act 1988, s.35	£100	3
Failing to comply with traffic sign	Road Traffic Act 1988, s.36	£100	3
Failing to supply details of driver's identity	Road Traffic Act 1988, s.172	£200	6
No insurance	Road Traffic Act 1988, s.143	£300	6
No test certificate	Road Traffic Act 1988, s.47	£100	–
Overloading/exceeding axle weight	Road Traffic Act 1988, s.41B	£100 to £300	–
Pelican/zebra crossing contravention	Road Traffic Regulation Act 1984, s.25(5)	£100	3
Railway fare evasion (where penalty notice scheme in operation by train operator)	Railways (Penalty Fares) Regulations 1994	£20 or twice the full single fare to next stop, whichever is greater	–
Seat belt offences	Road Traffic Act 1988, s.14 and s. 15(2) or 15(4)	£100	–
School non-attendance	Education Act 1996, s.444(1)	£60 if paid within 21 days; £120 if paid within 28 days	–
Speeding	Road Traffic Regulation Act 1984, s.89(1)	£100	3
Using hand-held mobile phone while driving	Road Traffic Act 1988, s.41D	£100	3
Using vehicle in dangerous condition	Road Traffic Act 1988, s.40A	£100	3

PART 11 ARSON AND CRIMINAL DAMAGE

Arson (criminal damage by fire) SG11-1

Applicability

Criminal Damage Act 1971, s.1

Effective from: 1 October 2019

This is a serious specified offence for the purposes of section 224 of the Criminal Justice Act 2003.

Triable either way
Maximum when tried summarily: Level 5 fine and/or 6 months' custody
Maximum when tried on indictment: Life
Offence range: Discharge – 8 years' custody

Where offence committed in domestic context, refer to **Overarching principles – domestic abuse** [SG5-1–SG5-8]

In accordance with section 120 of the Coroners and Justice Act 2009, the Sentencing Council issues this definitive guideline. It applies to all offenders aged 18 and older, who are sentenced on or after the effective date of this guideline, regardless of the date of the offence (subject to requirement(s) being applicable).

Section 125(1) of the Coroners and Justice Act 2009 provides that when sentencing offences committed after 6 April 2010:

'Every court –
a. must, in sentencing an offender, follow any sentencing guidelines which are relevant to the offender's case, and
b. must, in exercising any other function relating to the sentencing of offenders, follow any sentencing guidelines which are relevant to the exercise of the function,

unless the court is satisfied that it would be contrary to the interests of justice to do so.'

This guideline applies only to offenders aged 18 and older. General principles to be considered in the sentencing of children and young people are in the Sentencing Guidelines Council's definitive guideline, **Overarching Principles – Sentencing Children and Young People** [SG8-1–SG8-12]

Courts should consider requesting a report from: liaison and diversion services, a medical practitioner, or where it is necessary, ordering a psychiatric report, to ascertain both whether the offence is linked to a mental disorder or learning disability (to assist in the assessment of culpability) and whether any mental health disposal should be considered.

STEP 1 Determining the offence category SG11-2

The court should determine the offence category with reference only to the factors in the tables below. In order to determine the category the court should assess **culpability** and **harm.**

The level of **culpability** is determined by weighing up all the factors of the case. **Where there are characteristics present which fall under different levels of culpability, the court should balance these characteristics to reach a fair assessment of the offender's culpability.**

Culpability demonstrated by one or more of the following
A – High culpability • High degree of planning or premeditation • Revenge attack • Use of accelerant • Intention to cause very serious damage to property • Intention to create a high risk of injury to persons

B – Medium culpability
• Some planning • Recklessness as to whether very serious damage caused to property • Recklessness as to whether serious injury caused to persons • Other cases that fall between categories A and C because: o Factors are present in A and C which balance each other out **and/or** o The offender's culpability falls between the factors described in A and C
C – Lesser culpability
• Little or no planning; offence committed on impulse • Recklessness as to whether some damage to property caused • Offender's responsibility substantially reduced by mental disorder or learning disability • Involved through coercion, intimidation or exploitation

Harm	
The level of harm is assessed by weighing up all the factors of the case.	
Category 1	• Serious physical and/or psychological harm caused • Serious consequential economic or social impact of offence • High value of damage caused
Category 2	• Harm that falls between categories 1 and 3
Category 3	• No or minimal physical and/or psychological harm caused • Low value of damage caused

SG11-3 **STEP 2 Starting point and category range**

Having determined the category at step one, the court should use the corresponding starting point to reach a sentence within the category range below. The starting point applies to all offenders irrespective of plea or previous convictions.

Where the offender is dependent on or has a propensity to misuse drugs or alcohol, which **is linked to the offending**, a community order with a drug rehabilitation requirement under section 209, or an alcohol treatment requirement under section 212 of the Criminal Justice Act 2003 may be a proper alternative to a short or moderate custodial sentence.

Where the offender suffers from a medical condition that is susceptible to treatment but does not warrant detention under a hospital order, a community order with a mental health treatment requirement under section 207 of the Criminal Justice Act 2003 may be a proper alternative to a short or moderate custodial sentence.

In exceptional cases within category 1A, sentences of above 8 years may be appropriate.

	Culpability		
Harm	A	B	C
Category 1	**Starting point** 4 years' custody	**Starting point** 1 year 6 months' custody	**Starting point** 9 months' custody
	Category range 2 – 8 years' custody	**Category range** 9 months – 3 years' custody	**Category range** 6 months – 1 year 6 months' custody
Category 2	**Starting point** 2 years' custody	**Starting point** 9 months' custody	**Starting point** High level community order
	Category range 1 – 4 years' custody	**Category range** 6 months – 1 year 6 months' custody	**Category range** Medium level community order – 9 months' custody
Category 3	**Starting point** 1 year's custody	**Starting point** High level community order	**Starting point** Low level community order
	Category range 6 months – 2 years' custody	**Category range** Medium level Community order – 9 months' custody	**Category range** Discharge – High level community order

For the imposition of community orders, including the community orders table, see Imposition of Community and Custodial Sentences at **SG9-2–SG9-8**.

For the imposition of custodial sentences, see Imposition of Community and Custodial Sentences at SG9-9–SG9-12.

The court should then consider any adjustment for any aggravating or mitigating factors. Below is a **non-exhaustive** list of additional factual elements providing the context of the offence and factors relating to the offender.

Identify whether any combination of these, or other relevant factors, should result in an upward or downward adjustment from the starting point.

Factors increasing seriousness
Statutory aggravating factors • Previous convictions, having regard to a) the **nature** of the offence to which the conviction relates and its **relevance** to the current offence; and b) the **time** that has elapsed since the conviction • Offence committed whilst on bail • Offence motivated by, or demonstrating hostility based on any of the following characteristics or presumed characteristics of the victim: religion, race, disability, sexual orientation, or transgender identity
Other aggravating factors • Commission of offence whilst under the influence of alcohol or drugs • Offence committed for financial gain • Offence committed to conceal other offences • Victim is particularly vulnerable • Offence committed within a domestic context • Fire set in or near a public amenity • Damage caused to heritage and/or cultural assets • Significant impact on emergency services or resources • Established evidence of community/wider impact • Failure to comply with current court orders • Offence committed on licence or post sentence supervision • Offences taken into consideration
Factors reducing seriousness or reflecting personal mitigation
• No previous convictions **or** no relevant/recent convictions • Steps taken to minimise the effect of the fire or summon assistance • Remorse • Good character and/or exemplary conduct • Serious medical condition requiring urgent, intensive or long-term treatment • Age and/or lack of maturity • Mental disorder or learning disability (where not taken into account at step one) • Sole or primary carer for dependent relatives • Determination and/or demonstration of steps having been taken to address addiction or offending behaviour

STEP 3 Consider any factors which indicate a reduction, such as assistance to the prosecution **SG11-4**

The court should take into account sections 73 and 74 of the Serious Organised Crime and Police Act 2005 (assistance by defendants: reduction or review of sentence) and any other rule of law by virtue of which an offender may receive a discounted sentence in consequence of assistance given (or offered) to the prosecutor or investigator.

STEP 4 Reduction for guilty pleas **SG11-5**

The court should take account of any potential reduction for a guilty plea in accordance with section 144 of the Criminal Justice Act 2003 and the guideline for Reduction in Sentence for a Guilty Plea (where first hearing is on or after 1 June 2017, or first hearing before 1 June 2017).

STEP 5 Dangerousness **SG11-6**

The court should consider whether having regard to the criteria contained in Chapter 15 of Part 12 of the Criminal Justice Act 2003 it would be appropriate to impose a life sentence (section 225) or an extended sentence (section 226A). When sentencing offenders to a life sentence under these provisions the notional determinate sentence should be used as the basis for the setting of a minimum term.

SG11-7 **STEP 6 Totality principle**

If sentencing an offender for more than one offence, or where the offender is already serving a sentence, consider whether the total sentence is just and proportionate to the overall offending behaviour in accordance with the **Totality** guideline [see **SG3-7** ***et seq.***].

SG11-8 **STEP 7 Compensation and ancillary orders**

In all cases, the court must consider whether to make a **compensation order** and/or other **ancillary orders**.

Compensation order

The court should consider compensation orders in all cases where personal injury, loss or damage has resulted from the offence. The court must give reasons if it decides not to award compensation in such cases.

SG11-9 **STEP 8 Reasons**

Section 174 of the Criminal Justice Act 2003 imposes a duty to give reasons for, and explain the effect of, the sentence.

SG11-10 **STEP 9 Consideration for time spent on bail (tagged curfew)**

The court must consider whether to give credit for time spent on bail in accordance with section 240A of the Criminal Justice Act 2003.

SG11-11 Criminal damage (other than by fire) value exceeding £5,000/ Racially or religiously aggravated criminal damage—

Crime and Disorder Act 1998, s.30, Criminal Damage Act 1971, s.1(1)

Effective from: 1 October 2019

Criminal damage (other than by fire) value exceeding £5,000, Criminal Damage Act 1971, s.1(1)

Triable either way
Maximum: 10 years' custody
Offence range: Discharge – 4 years' custody

> Note:
>
> Where an offence of criminal damage is added to the indictment at the Crown Court the statutory maximum sentence is 10 years' custody regardless of the value of the damage. In such cases where the value does not exceed £5,000 regard should also be had to the not exceeding £5000 guideline.

Racially or religiously aggravated criminal damage, Crime and Disorder Act 1998, s.30
Triable either way
Maximum: 14 years' custody

Where offence committed in domestic context, refer to **Overarching principles – domestic abuse** [see **SG5-1** ***et seq.***].

SG11-12 **STEP 1 Determining the offence category**

The court should determine the offence category with reference only to the factors in the tables below. In order to determine the category the court should assess **culpability** and **harm.**

The level of **culpability** is determined by weighing up all the factors of the case. **Where there are characteristics present which fall under different levels of culpability, the court should balance these characteristics to reach a fair assessment of the offender's culpability.**

Culpability demonstrated by one or more of the following
A – High culpability • High degree of planning or premeditation • Revenge attack • Intention to cause very serious damage to property • Intention to create a high risk of injury to persons
B – Medium culpability • Some planning • Recklessness as to whether very serious damage caused to property • Recklessness as to whether serious injury caused to persons • Other cases that fall between categories A and C because: o Factors are present in A and C which balance each other out **and/or** o The offender's culpability falls between the factors described in A and C
C – Lesser culpability • Little or no planning; offence committed on impulse • Recklessness as to whether some damage to property caused • Offender's responsibility substantially reduced by mental disorder or learning disability • Involved through coercion, intimidation or exploitation

Harm

The level of harm is assessed by weighing up all the factors of the case.

Category 1	• Serious distress caused • Serious consequential economic or social impact of offence • High value of damage
Category 2	• Harm that falls between categories 1 and 3
Category 3	• No or minimal distress caused • Low value damage

STEP 2 Starting point and category range

SG11-13

Having determined the category at step one, the court should use the corresponding starting point to reach a sentence within the category range below. The starting point applies to all offenders irrespective of plea or previous convictions.

Where the offender is dependent on or has a propensity to misuse drugs or alcohol, which **is linked to the offending**, a community order with a drug rehabilitation requirement under section 209, or an alcohol treatment requirement under section 212 of the Criminal Justice Act 2003 may be a proper alternative to a short or moderate custodial sentence.

Where the offender suffers from a medical condition that is susceptible to treatment but does not warrant detention under a hospital order, a community order with a mental health treatment requirement under section 207 of the Criminal Justice Act 2003 may be a proper alternative to a short or moderate custodial sentence.

Maximum: 10 years' custody (basic offence)

	Culpability		
Harm	**A**	**B**	**C**
Category 1	**Starting point** 1 year 6 months' custody	**Starting point** 6 months' custody	**Starting point** High level community order
	Category range 6 months – 4 years' custody	**Category range** High level community order – 1 year 6 months' custody	**Category range** Medium level community order – 9 months' custody
Category 2	**Starting point** 6 months' custody	**Starting point** High level community order	**Starting point** Low level community order
	Category range High level community order – 1 year 6 months' custody	**Category range** Medium level community order – 9 months' custody	**Category range** Band C fine – High level community order

Category 3	**Starting point** High level community order	**Starting point** Low level community order	**Starting point** Band B fine
	Category range Medium level community order – 9 months' custody	**Category range** Band C fine – High level community order	**Category range** Discharge – Low level community order

For band ranges, see **SG10-129**.

For the imposition of community orders, including the community orders table, see Imposition of Community and Custodial Sentences at **SG9-2–SG9-8**.

For the imposition of custodial sentences, see Imposition of Community and Custodial Sentences at **SG9-9–SG9-12**.

The court should then consider any adjustment for any aggravating or mitigating factors. Below is a **non-exhaustive** list of additional factual elements providing the context of the offence and factors relating to the offender.

Identify whether any combination of these, or other relevant factors, should result in an upward or downward adjustment from the starting point.

Factors increasing seriousness
Statutory aggravating factors • Previous convictions, having regard to a) the **nature** of the offence to which the conviction relates and its **relevance** to the current offence; and b) the **time** that has elapsed since the conviction • Offence committed whilst on bail • Offence motivated by, or demonstrating hostility based on any of the following characteristics or presumed characteristics of the victim: disability, sexual orientation, or transgender identity
Other aggravating factors • Damaged items of great value to the victim (whether economic, commercial, sentimental or personal value) • Commission of offence whilst under the influence of alcohol or drugs • Victim is particularly vulnerable • Offence committed in a domestic context • Damage caused to heritage and/or cultural assets • Significant impact on emergency services or resources • Established evidence of community/wider impact • Failure to comply with current court orders • Offence committed on licence or post sentence supervision • Offences taken into consideration
Factors reducing seriousness or reflecting personal mitigation
• No previous convictions **or** no relevant/recent convictions • Remorse • Good character and/or exemplary conduct • Serious medical condition requiring urgent, intensive or long-term treatment • Age and/or lack of maturity • Mental disorder or learning disability (where not taken into account at step one) • Sole or primary carer for dependent relatives • Determination and/or demonstration of steps having been taken to address addiction or offending behaviour

SG11-14 Racially or Religiously Aggravated Criminal Damage Offences Only

Having determined the category of the basic offence to identify the sentence of a non-aggravated offence, the court should now consider the level of racial or religious aggravation involved and apply an appropriate uplift to the sentence in accordance with the guidance below. The following is a list of factors which the court should consider to determine the level of aggravation. Where there are characteristics present which fall under different levels of aggravation, the court should balance these to reach a fair assessment of the level of aggravation present in the offence.

Maximum sentence for the aggravated offence on indictment is 14 years' custody (maximum for the basic offence is 10 years' custody)

Care should be taken to avoid double counting factors already taken into account in assessing the level of harm at step one

High level of racial or religious aggravation	Sentence uplift
Racial or religious aggravation was the predominant motivation for the offence. Offender was a member of, or was associated with, a group promoting hostility based on race or religion. Aggravated nature of the offence caused severe distress to the victim or the victim's family (**over and above the distress already considered at step one**). Aggravated nature of the offence caused serious fear and distress throughout local community or more widely.	Increase the length of custodial sentence if already considered for the basic offence or consider a custodial sentence, if not already considered for the basic offence.
Medium level of racial or religious aggravation	**Sentence uplift**
Racial or religious aggravation formed a significant proportion of the offence as a whole. Aggravated nature of the offence caused some distress to the victim or the victim's family (**over and above the distress already considered at step one**). Aggravated nature of the offence caused some fear and distress throughout local community or more widely.	Consider a significantly more onerous penalty of the same type or consider a more severe type of sentence than for the basic offence.
Low level of racial or religious aggravation	**Sentence uplift**
Aggravated element formed a minimal part of the offence as a whole. Aggravated nature of the offence caused minimal or no distress to the victim or the victim's family (**over and above the distress already considered at step one**).	Consider a more onerous penalty of the same type identified for the basic offence.

Magistrates may find that, although the appropriate sentence for the basic offence would be within their powers, the appropriate increase for the aggravated offence would result in a sentence in excess of their powers. If so, they must commit for sentence to the Crown Court.

The sentencer should state in open court that the offence was aggravated by reason of race or religion, and should also state what the sentence would have been without that element of aggravation.

STEP 3 Consider any factors which indicate a reduction, such as assistance to the prosecution SG11-15

The court should take into account sections 73 and 74 of the Serious Organised Crime and Police Act 2005 (assistance by defendants: reduction or review of sentence) and any other rule of law by virtue of which an offender may receive a discounted sentence in consequence of assistance given (or offered) to the prosecutor or investigator.

STEP 4 Reduction for guilty pleas SG11-16

The court should take account of any potential reduction for a guilty plea in accordance with section 144 of the Criminal Justice Act 2003 and the guideline for Reduction in Sentence for a Guilty Plea (where **first hearing is on or after 1 June 2017**, or **first hearing before 1 June 2017**).

STEP 5 Totality principle SG11-17

If sentencing an offender for more than one offence, or where the offender is already serving a sentence, consider whether the total sentence is just and proportionate to the overall offending behaviour in accordance with the Totality guideline [see SG3-7 *et seq.*].

STEP 6 Compensation and ancillary orders SG11-18

In all cases, the court must consider whether to make a **compensation order** and/or other **ancillary orders**.

Compensation order

The court should consider compensation orders in all cases where personal injury, loss or damage has resulted from the offence. The court must give reasons if it decides not to award compensation in such cases.

SG11-19 STEP 7 **Reasons**

Section 174 of the Criminal Justice Act 2003 imposes a duty to give reasons for, and explain the effect of, the sentence.

SG11-20 STEP 8 **Consideration for time spent on bail (tagged curfew)**

The court must consider whether to give credit for time spent on bail in accordance with section 240A of the Criminal Justice Act 2003.

SG11-21

Criminal Damage (Other than by fire) Value not Exceeding £5,000/ Racially or Religiously Aggravated Criminal Damage

Crime and Disorder Act 1998, s.30, Criminal Damage Act 1971, s.1(1)

Effective from: 1 October 2019

Criminal damage (other than by fire) value not exceeding £5,000, Criminal Damage Act 1971, s.1(1)

Triable only summarily
Maximum: Level 4 fine and/or 3 months' custody
Offence range: Discharge – 3 months' custody
Note:

Where an offence of criminal damage is added to the indictment at the Crown Court the statutory maximum sentence is 10 years' custody regardless of the value of the damage. In such cases where the value does not exceed £5,000, the exceeding £5,000 guideline should be used but regard should also be had to this guideline.
Racially or religiously aggravated criminal damage, Crime and Disorder Act 1998, s.30

Triable either way
Maximum: 14 years' custody

Where offence committed in domestic context, refer to <u>**Overarching principles – domestic abuse**</u>.

<u>**User guide for this offence**</u>

In accordance with section 120 of the Coroners and Justice Act 2009, the Sentencing Council issues this definitive guideline. It applies to all offenders aged 18 and older, who are sentenced on or after the effective date of this guideline, regardless of the date of the offence (subject to requirement(s) being applicable).

Section 125(1) of the Coroners and Justice Act 2009 provides that when sentencing offences committed after 6 April 2010:

'Every court –
a. must, in sentencing an offender, follow any sentencing guidelines which are relevant to the offender's case, and
b. must, in exercising any other function relating to the sentencing of offenders, follow any sentencing guidelines which are relevant to the exercise of the function,
unless the court is satisfied that it would be contrary to the interests of justice to do so.'

This guideline applies only to offenders aged 18 and older. General principles to be considered in the sentencing of children and young people are in the Sentencing Guidelines Council's definitive guideline, <u>**Overarching Principles – Sentencing Children and Young People**</u> [see SG8-1 *et seq.*].

STEP 1 **Determining the offence category**

SG11-22 The court should determine the offence category with reference only to the factors in the tables below. In order to determine the category the court should assess **culpability** and **harm**.

The level of **culpability** is determined by weighing up all the factors of the case. **Where there are characteristics present which fall under different levels of culpability, the court should balance these characteristics to reach a fair assessment of the offender's culpability.**

Culpability demonstrated by one or more of the following:
A – High culpability • High degree of planning or premeditation • Revenge attack • Intention to cause very serious damage to property • Intention to create a high risk of injury to persons
B – Medium culpability • Some planning • Recklessness as to whether very serious damage caused to property • Recklessness as to whether serious injury caused to persons • Other cases that fall between categories A and C because: o Factors are present in A and C which balance each other out **and/or** o The offender's culpability falls between the factors described in A and C
C – Lesser culpability • Little or no planning; offence committed on impulse • Recklessness as to whether some damage to property caused • Offender's responsibility substantially reduced by mental disorder or learning disability • Involved through coercion, intimidation or exploitation

Harm	
The level of harm is assessed by weighing up all the factors of the case.	
Category 1	• Serious distress caused • Serious consequential economic or social impact of offence • High value of damage
Category 2	• All other cases

STEP 2 Starting point and category range SG11-23

Having determined the category at step one, the court should use the corresponding starting point to reach a sentence within the category range below. The starting point applies to all offenders irrespective of plea or previous convictions.

Where the offender is dependent on or has a propensity to misuse drugs or alcohol, which **is linked to the offending,** a community order with a drug rehabilitation requirement under section 209, or an alcohol treatment requirement under section 212 of the Criminal Justice Act 2003 may be a proper alternative to a short or moderate custodial sentence.

Where the offender suffers from a medical condition that is susceptible to treatment but does not warrant detention under a hospital order, a community order with a mental health treatment requirement under section 207 of the Criminal Justice Act 2003 may be a proper alternative to a short or moderate custodial sentence.

Maximum Level 4 fine and/or 3 months custody (basic offence)

	Culpability		
Harm	A	B	C
Category 1	**Starting point** High level community order	**Starting point** Low level community order	**Starting point** Band B fine
	Category range Medium level community order – 3 months' custody	**Category range** Band C fine – High level community order	**Category range** Discharge – Low level community order
Category 2	**Starting point** Low level community order	**Starting point** Band B fine	**Starting point** Band A fine
	Category range Band C fine – High level community order	**Category range** Discharge – Low level community order	**Category range** Discharge – Band B fine

For band ranges, see **SG10-129**.

For the imposition of community orders, including the community orders table, see Imposition of Community and Custodial Sentences at **SG9-2–SG9-8**.

For the imposition of custodial sentences, see Imposition of Community and Custodial Sentences at **SG9-9–SG9-12**.

The court should then consider any adjustment for any aggravating or mitigating factors. Below is a **non-exhaustive** list of additional factual elements providing the context of the offence and factors relating to the offender.

Identify whether any combination of these, or other relevant factors, should result in an upward or downward adjustment from the starting point.

Factors increasing seriousness
Statutory aggravating factors • Previous convictions, having regard to a) the **nature** of the offence to which the conviction relates and its **relevance** to the current offence; and b) the **time** that has elapsed since the conviction • Offence committed whilst on bail • Offence motivated by, or demonstrating hostility based on any of the following characteristics or presumed characteristics of the victim: disability, sexual orientation, or transgender identity
Other aggravating factors • Damaged items of great value to the victim (whether economic, commercial, sentimental or personal value) • Commission of offence whilst under the influence of alcohol or drugs • Victim is particularly vulnerable • Offence committed within a domestic context • Damage caused to heritage and/or cultural assets • Significant impact on emergency services or resources • Established evidence of community/wider impact • Failure to comply with current court orders • Offence committed on licence or post sentence supervision • Offences taken into consideration
Factors reducing seriousness or reflecting personal mitigation
• No previous convictions or no relevant/recent convictions • Remorse • Good character and/or exemplary conduct • Serious medical condition requiring urgent, intensive or long-term treatment • Age and/or lack of maturity • Mental Disorder or learning disability (where not taken into account at step one) • Sole or primary carer for dependent relative • Determination and/or demonstration of steps having been taken to address addiction or offending behaviour

SG11-24 Racially or Religiously Aggravated Criminal Damage Offences Only

Having determined the category of the basic offence to identify the sentence of a non-aggravated offence, the court should now consider the level of racial or religious aggravation involved and apply an appropriate uplift to the sentence in accordance with the guidance below. The following is a list of factors which the court should consider to determine the level of aggravation. Where there are characteristics present which fall under different levels of aggravation, the court should balance these to reach a fair assessment of the level of aggravation present in the offence.

Maximum sentence for the aggravated offence on indictment is 14 years' custody (maximum for the basic offence is 10 years' custody).

Care should be taken to avoid double counting factors already taken into account in assessing the level of harm at step one.

High level of racial or religious aggravation	Sentence uplift
Racial or religious aggravation was the predominant motivation for the offence. Offender was a member of, or was associated with, a group promoting hostility based on race or religion. Aggravated nature of the offence caused severe distress to the victim or the victim's family (**over and above the distress already considered at step one**). Aggravated nature of the offence caused serious fear and distress throughout local community or more widely.	Increase the length of custodial sentence if already considered for the basic offence or consider a custodial sentence, if not already considered for the basic offence.
Medium level of racial or religious aggravation	**Sentence uplift**
Racial or religious aggravation formed a significant proportion of the offence as a whole. Aggravated nature of the offence caused some distress to the victim or the victim's family (**over and above the distress already considered at step one**). Aggravated nature of the offence caused some fear and distress throughout local community or more widely.	Consider a significantly more onerous penalty of the same type **or consider** a more severe type of sentence than for the basic offence.
Low level of racial or religious aggravation	**Sentence uplift**
Aggravated element formed a minimal part of the offence as a whole. Aggravated nature of the offence caused minimal or no distress to the victim or the victim's family (**over and above the distress already considered at step one**).	Consider a more onerous penalty of the same type identified for the basic offence.

Magistrates may find that, although the appropriate sentence for the basic offence would be within their powers, the appropriate increase for the aggravated offence would result in a sentence in excess of their powers. If so, they must commit for sentence to the Crown Court.

The sentencer should state in open court that the offence was aggravated by reason of race or religion, and should also state what the sentence would have been without that element of aggravation.

STEP 3 Consider any factors which indicate a reduction, such as assistance to the prosecution **SG11-25**

The court should take into account sections 73 and 74 of the Serious Organised Crime and Police Act 2005 (assistance by defendants: reduction or review of sentence) and any other rule of law by virtue of which an offender may receive a discounted sentence in consequence of assistance given (or offered) to the prosecutor or investigator.

STEP 4 Reduction for guilty pleas **SG11-26**

The court should take account of any potential reduction for a guilty plea in accordance with section 144 of the Criminal Justice Act 2003 and the guideline for Reduction in Sentence for a Guilty Plea (where **first hearing is on or after 1 June 2017**, or **first hearing before 1 June 2017**).

STEP 5 Totality principle **SG11-27**

If sentencing an offender for more than one offence, or where the offender is already serving a sentence, consider whether the total sentence is just and proportionate to the overall offending behaviour in accordance with the **Totality** guideline [see SG3-7 *et seq*.].

STEP 6 Compensation and ancillary orders **SG11-28**

In all cases, the court must consider whether to make a **compensation order** and/or other **ancillary orders**.

Compensation order

The court should consider compensation orders in all cases where personal injury, loss or damage has resulted from the offence. The court must give reasons if it decides not to award compensation in such cases.

SG11-29 **STEP 7 Reasons**

Section 174 of the Criminal Justice Act 2003 imposes a duty to give reasons for, and explain the effect of, the sentence.

SG11-30 **STEP 8 Consideration for time spent on bail (tagged curfew)**

The court must consider whether to give credit for time spent on bail in accordance with section 240A of the Criminal Justice Act 2003.

SG11-31

Criminal Damage/Arson with Intent to Endanger Life or Reckless as to Whether life Endangered

Criminal Damage Act 1971, s.1(2)

Effective from: 1 October 2019

This is a serious specified offence for the purposes of section 224 of the Criminal Justice Act 2003.

Triable only on indictment
Maximum: Life imprisonment
Offence range: High level community order – 12 years' custody

Where offence committed in domestic context, refer to **Overarching principles – domestic abuse**.

User guide for this offence

In accordance with section 120 of the Coroners and Justice Act 2009, the Sentencing Council issues this definitive guideline. It applies to all offenders aged 18 and older, who are sentenced on or after the effective date of this guideline, regardless of the date of the offence (subject to requirement(s) being applicable).

Section 125(1) of the Coroners and Justice Act 2009 provides that when sentencing offences committed after 6 April 2010:

'Every court –

a. must, in sentencing an offender, follow any sentencing guidelines which are relevant to the offender's case, and

b. must, in exercising any other function relating to the sentencing of offenders, follow any sentencing guidelines which are relevant to the exercise of the function,

unless the court is satisfied that it would be contrary to the interests of justice to do so.'

This guideline applies only to offenders aged 18 and older. General principles to be considered in the sentencing of children and young people are in the Sentencing Guidelines Council's definitive guideline, **Overarching Principles – Sentencing Children and Young People**. [see **SG8-1** ***et seq.***]

Courts should consider requesting a report from: liaison and diversion services, a medical practitioner, or where it is necessary, ordering a psychiatric report, to ascertain both whether the offence is linked to a mental disorder or learning disability (to assist in the assessment of culpability) and whether any mental health disposal should be considered.

SG11-32 **STEP 1 Determining the offence category**

The court should determine the offence category with reference only to the factors in the tables below. In order to determine the category the court should assess **culpability** and **harm**.

Within this guideline culpability is fixed: culpability A is for intent, culpability B is for recklessness.	
Culpability A	• Offender intended to endanger life
Culpability B	• Offender was reckless as to whether life was endangered

Harm The level of harm is assessed by weighing up all the factors of the case.
Category 1 • Very serious physical and/or psychological harm caused • High risk of very serious physical and/or psychological harm • Serious consequential economic or social impact of offence caused • Very high value of damage caused
Category 2 • Significant physical and/or psychological harm caused • Significant risk of serious physical and/or psychological harm • Significant value of damage caused • All other harm that falls between categories 1 and 3
Category 3 • No or minimal physical and/or psychological harm caused • Low risk of serious physical and/or psychological harm • Low value of damage caused

STEP 2 Starting point and category range SG11-33

Having determined the category at step one, the court should use the corresponding starting point to reach a sentence within the category range below. The starting point applies to all offenders irrespective of plea or previous convictions.

Where the offender is dependent on or has a propensity to misuse drugs or alcohol, which **is linked to the offending**, a community order with a drug rehabilitation requirement under section 209, or an alcohol treatment requirement under section 212 of the Criminal Justice Act 2003 may be a proper alternative to a short or moderate custodial sentence.

Where the offender suffers from a medical condition that is susceptible to treatment but does not warrant detention under a hospital order, a community order with a mental health treatment requirement under section 207 of the Criminal Justice Act 2003 may be a proper alternative to a short or moderate custodial sentence.

In exceptional cases within category 1A, sentences of above 12 years may be appropriate.

Harm	Culpability	
	A	B
Category 1	**Starting point** 8 years' custody	**Starting point** 6 years' custody
	Category range 5 years – 12 years' custody	**Category range** 4 years – 10 years' custody
Category 2	**Starting point** 6 years' custody	**Starting point** 4 years' custody
	Category range 4 – 8 years' custody	**Category range** 2 – 6 years' custody
Category 3	**Starting point** 2 years' custody	**Starting point** 1 year's custody
	Category range 6 months – 4 years' custody	**Category range** High level community order – 2 years 6 months' custody

For the imposition of community orders, including the community orders table, see Imposition of Community and Custodial Sentences at **SG9-2–SG9-8**.

For the imposition of custodial sentences, see Imposition of Community and Custodial Sentences at SG9-9–SG9-12.

The court should then consider any adjustment for any aggravating or mitigating factors. Below is a **non-exhaustive** list of additional factual elements providing the context of the offence and factors relating to the offender.

Identify whether any combination of these, or other relevant factors, should result in an upward or downward adjustment from the starting point.

Care should be taken to avoid double counting factors already taken into account in assessing the level of harm at step one

Factors increasing seriousness
Statutory aggravating factors • Previous convictions, having regard to a) the **nature** of the offence to which the conviction relates and its **relevance** to the current offence; and b) the **time** that has elapsed since the conviction • Offence committed whilst on bail • Offence motivated by, or demonstrating hostility based on any of the following characteristics or presumed characteristics of the victim: religion, race, disability, sexual orientation, or transgender identity
Other aggravating factors • Commission of offence whilst under the influence of alcohol or drugs • Revenge attack • Significant degree of planning or premeditation • Use of accelerant • Fire set in or near a public amenity • Victim is particularly vulnerable • Offence committed within a domestic context • Damage caused to heritage and/or cultural assets • Multiple people endangered • Significant impact on emergency services or resources • Established evidence of community/wider impact • Failure to comply with current court orders • Offence committed on licence or post sentence supervision • Offences taken into consideration
Factors reducing seriousness or reflecting personal mitigation
• No previous convictions or no relevant/recent convictions • Offender's responsibility substantially reduced by mental disorder or learning disability • Lack of premeditation • Involved through coercion, intimidation or exploitation • Remorse • Good character and/or exemplary conduct • Serious medical condition requiring urgent, intensive or long-term treatment • Age and/or lack of maturity • Sole or primary carer for dependent relatives • Determination and/or demonstration of steps having been taken to address addiction or offending behaviour

SG11-34 STEP 3 **Consider any factors which indicate a reduction, such as assistance to the prosecution**

The court should take into account sections 73 and 74 of the Serious Organised Crime and Police Act 2005 (assistance by defendants: reduction or review of sentence) and any other rule of law by virtue of which an offender may receive a discounted sentence in consequence of assistance given (or offered) to the prosecutor or investigator.

SG11-35 STEP 4 **Reduction for guilty pleas**

The court should take account of any potential reduction for a guilty plea in accordance with section 144 of the Criminal Justice Act 2003 and the guideline for Reduction in Sentence for a Guilty Plea (where **first hearing is on or after 1 June 2017**, or **first hearing before 1 June 2017**).

SG11-36 STEP 5 **Dangerousness**

The court should consider whether having regard to the criteria contained in Chapter 15 of Part 12 of the Criminal Justice Act 2003 it would be appropriate to impose a life sentence (section 225) or an extended sentence (section 226A). When sentencing offenders to a life sentence under these provisions the notional determinate sentence should be used as the basis for the setting of a minimum term.

STEP 6 Totality principle SG11-37

If sentencing an offender for more than one offence, or where the offender is already serving a sentence, consider whether the total sentence is just and proportionate to the overall offending behaviour in accordance with the **Totality** guideline [see SG3-7 *et seq.*].

STEP 7 Compensation and ancillary orders SG11-38

In all cases, the court must consider whether to make a **compensation order** and/or other **ancillary orders**.

Compensation order

The court should consider compensation orders in all cases where personal injury, loss or damage has resulted from the offence. The court must give reasons if it decides not to award compensation in such cases.

STEP 8 Reasons SG11-39

Section 174 of the Criminal Justice Act 2003 imposes a duty to give reasons for, and explain the effect of, the sentence.

STEP 9 Consideration for time spent on bail (tagged curfew) SG11-40

The court must consider whether to give credit for time spent on bail in accordance with section 240A of the Criminal Justice Act 2003.

Threats to Destroy or Damage Property SG11-41

Criminal Damage Act 1971, s.2

Effective from: 1 October 2019

Triable either way
Maximum: 10 years' custody
Offence range: Discharge – 4 years' custody
Where offence committed in domestic context, refer to **Overarching principles – domestic abuse**.

User guide for this offence

In accordance with section 120 of the Coroners and Justice Act 2009, the Sentencing Council issues this definitive guideline. It applies to all offenders aged 18 and older, who are sentenced on or after the effective date of this guideline, regardless of the date of the offence (subject to requirement(s) being applicable).

Section 125(1) of the Coroners and Justice Act 2009 provides that when sentencing offences committed after 6 April 2010:

'Every court –

a. must, in sentencing an offender, follow any sentencing guidelines which are relevant to the offender's case, and
b. must, in exercising any other function relating to the sentencing of offenders, follow any sentencing guidelines which are relevant to the exercise of the function,

unless the court is satisfied that it would be contrary to the interests of justice to do so.'

This guideline applies only to offenders aged 18 and older. General principles to be considered in the sentencing of children and young people are in the Sentencing Guidelines Council's definitive guideline, **Overarching Principles – Sentencing Children and Young People** [see SG8-1 *et seq.*].

In cases of threats to cause damage by fire, courts should consider requesting a report from: liaison and diversion services, a medical practitioner, or where it is necessary, ordering a psychiatric report, to ascertain both whether the offence is linked to a mental disorder or learning disability (to assist in the assessment of culpability) and whether any mental health disposal should be considered.

STEP 1 Determining the offence category SG11-42

The court should determine the offence category with reference only to the factors in the tables below. In order to determine the category the court should assess **culpability** and **harm.**

The level of **culpability** is determined by weighing up all the factors of the case. **Where there are characteristics present which fall under different levels of culpability, the court should balance these characteristics to reach a fair assessment of the offender's culpability.**

Culpability demonstrated by one or more of the following
A – High culpability • Significant planning or premeditation • Offence motivated by revenge • Offence committed to intimidate, coerce or control • Threat to burn or bomb property
B – Medium culpability Cases that fall between categories A and C because: • Factors are present in A and C which balance each other out **and/or** • The offender's culpability falls between the factors described in A and C
C – Lesser culpability • Little or no planning; offence committed on impulse • Offender's responsibility substantially reduced by mental disorder or learning disability • Involved through coercion, intimidation or exploitation

Harm The level of harm is assessed by weighing up all the factors of the case.	
Category 1	• Serious distress caused to the victim • Serious disruption/inconvenience caused to others • High level of consequential financial harm and inconvenience caused to the victim
Category 2	• Harm that falls between categories 1 and 3
Category 3	• No or minimal distress caused to the victim

Where the offender is dependent on or has a propensity to misuse drugs or alcohol, which **is linked to the offending**, a community order with a drug rehabilitation requirement under section 209, or an alcohol treatment requirement under section 212 of the Criminal Justice Act 2003 may be a proper alternative to a short or moderate custodial sentence.

Where the offender suffers from a medical condition that is susceptible to treatment but does not warrant detention under a hospital order, a community order with a mental health treatment requirement under section 207 of the Criminal Justice Act 2003 may be a proper alternative to a short or moderate custodial sentence.

STEP 2 Starting point and category range

SG11-43 Having determined the category at step one, the court should use the corresponding starting point to reach a sentence within the category range below. The starting point applies to all offenders irrespective of plea or previous convictions.

Harm	Culpability		
	A	B	C
Category 1	**Starting point** 1 year 6 months' custody	**Starting point** 6 months' custody	**Starting point** High level community order
	Category range 6 months – 4 years' custody	**Category range** High level community order – 1 year 6 months' custody	**Category range** Medium level community order – 9 months' custody
Category 2	**Starting point** 6 months' custody	**Starting point** High level community order	**Starting point** Low level community order
	Category range High level community order – 1 year 6 months' custody	**Category range** Medium level community order – 9 months' custody	**Category range** Band C fine – High level community order
Category 3	**Starting point** High level community order	**Starting point** Low level community order	**Starting point** Band B fine
	Category range Medium level community order – 9 months' custody	**Category range** Band C fine – High level community order	**Category range** Discharge – Low level community order

For band ranges, see **SG10-129**.

For the imposition of community orders, including the community orders table, see Imposition of Community and Custodial Sentences at **SG9-2–SG9-8**.

For the imposition of custodial sentences, see Imposition of Community and Custodial Sentences at **SG9-9–SG9-12**.

The court should then consider any adjustment for any aggravating or mitigating factors. Below is a **non-exhaustive** list of additional factual elements providing the context of the offence and factors relating to the offender.

Identify whether any combination of these, or other relevant factors, should result in an upward or downward adjustment from the starting point.

Factors increasing seriousness
Statutory aggravating factors • Previous convictions, having regard to a) the **nature** of the offence to which the conviction relates and its **relevance** to the current offence; and b) the **time** that has elapsed since the conviction • Offence committed whilst on bail • Offence motivated by, or demonstrating hostility based on any of the following characteristics or presumed characteristics of the victim: religion, race, disability, sexual orientation, or transgender identity
Other aggravating factors • Commission of offence whilst under the influence of alcohol or drugs • Victim is particularly vulnerable • Offence committed in a domestic context • Threats made in the presence of children • Considerable damage threatened • Damage threatened to heritage and/or cultural assets • Established evidence of community/wider impact • Failure to comply with current court orders • Offence committed on licence or post sentence supervision • Offences taken into consideration
Factors reducing seriousness or reflecting personal mitigation
• No previous convictions **or** no relevant/recent convictions • Remorse • Good character and/or exemplary conduct • Serious medical condition requiring urgent, intensive or long-term treatment • Age and/or lack of maturity • Mental disorder or learning disability (where not taken into account at step one) • Sole or primary carer for dependent relatives • Determination and/or demonstration of steps having been taken to address addiction or offending behaviour

STEP 3 Consider any factors which indicate a reduction, such as assistance to the prosecution **SG11-44**

The court should take into account sections 73 and 74 of the Serious Organised Crime and Police Act 2005 (assistance by defendants: reduction or review of sentence) and any other rule of law by virtue of which an offender may receive a discounted sentence in consequence of assistance given (or offered) to the prosecutor or investigator.

STEP 4 Reduction for guilty pleas **SG11-45**

The court should take account of any potential reduction for a guilty plea in accordance with section 144 of the Criminal Justice Act 2003 and the guideline for Reduction in Sentence for a Guilty Plea (where **first hearing is on or after 1 June 2017**, or **first hearing before 1 June 2017**).

STEP 5 Totality principle **SG11-46**

If sentencing an offender for more than one offence, or where the offender is already serving a sentence, consider whether the total sentence is just and proportionate to the overall offending behaviour in accordance with the **Totality** guideline [see **SG3-7** ***et seq.***].

STEP 6 Compensation and ancillary orders **SG11-47**

In all cases, the court must consider whether to make a **compensation order** and/or other **ancillary orders**.

Compensation order

The court should consider compensation orders in all cases where personal injury, loss or damage has resulted from the offence. The court must give reasons if it decides not to award compensation in such cases.

SG11-48 STEP 7 **Reasons**

Section 174 of the Criminal Justice Act 2003 imposes a duty to give reasons for, and explain the effect of, the sentence.

SG11-49 STEP 8 **Consideration for time spent on bail (tagged curfew)**

The court must consider whether to give credit for time spent on bail in accordance with section 240A of the Criminal Justice Act 2003.

PART 12 ASSAULT

Definitive Guideline

[2] **Applicability of Guideline** SG12-1

In accordance with section 120 of the Coroners and Justice Act 2009, the Sentencing Council issues this definitive guideline. It applies to all offenders aged 18 and older, who are sentenced on or after 13 June 2011, regardless of the date of the offence.

Section 125(1) of the Coroners and Justice Act 2009 provides that when sentencing offences committed after 6 April 2010:

Every court—
(a) must, in sentencing an offender, follow any sentencing guideline which is relevant to the offender's case, and
(b) must, in exercising any other function relating to the sentencing of offenders, follow any sentencing guidelines which are relevant to the exercise of the function,

unless the court is satisfied that it would be contrary to the interests of justice to do so.

This guideline applies only to offenders aged 18 and older. General principles to be considered in the sentencing of youths are in the Sentencing Guidelines Council's definitive guideline, *Sentencing Children and Young People: Overarching Principles* [see SG8-1].

Structure, ranges and starting points SG12-2

For the purposes of section 125(3)–(4) of the Coroners and Justice Act 2009, the guideline specifies *offence ranges*—the range of sentences appropriate for each type of offence. Within each offence, the Council has specified three *categories* which reflect varying degrees of seriousness. The offence range is split into *category ranges*—sentences appropriate for each level of seriousness. The Council has also identified a starting point within each category.

Starting points define the position within a category range from which to start calculating the provisional sentence. **Starting points apply to all offences within the corresponding category and are applicable to all offenders in all cases irrespective of plea or previous convictions.** Once the starting point is established the court should consider further aggravating and mitigating factors and previous convictions so as to adjust the sentence within the range. Credit for a guilty plea is taken into consideration only at step 4 in the process, after the appropriate sentence has been identified.

Information on community orders and fine bands is [available at SG9-2 and SG10-129].

[3] **Causing Grievous Bodily Harm with Intent to do Grievous Bodily Harm/ Wounding with Intent to do Grievous Bodily Harm** SG12-3

Offences against the Person Act 1861 (section 18)

This is a serious specified offence for the purposes of section 224 of the Criminal Justice Act 2003

Triable only on indictment

Maximum: Life imprisonment

Offence range: 3–16 years' custody

[4] **STEP ONE Determining the offence category** SG12-4

The court should determine the offence category using the table below.

Category 1	Greater harm (serious injury must normally be present) **and** higher culpability
Category 2	Greater harm (serious injury must normally be present) **and** lower culpability; **or** lesser harm **and** higher culpability
Category 3	Lesser harm **and** lower culpability

The court should determine the offender's culpability and the harm caused, or intended, by reference only to the factors below (as demonstrated by the presence of one or more). These factors comprise the principal factual elements of the offence and should determine the category. [4]

Factors indicating greater harm	Factors indicating lesser harm
Injury (which includes disease transmission and/or psychological harm) which is serious in the context of the offence (must normally be present) Victim is particularly vulnerable because of personal circumstances Sustained or repeated assault on the same victim	Injury which is less serious in the context of the offence
Factors indicating higher culpability	**Factors indicating lower culpability**
Statutory aggravating factors: Offence racially or religiously aggravated Offence motivated by, or demonstrating, hostility to the victim based on his or her sexual orientation (or presumed sexual orientation) Offence motivated by, or demonstrating, hostility to the victim based on the victim's disability (or presumed disability) *Other aggravating factors:* A significant degree of premeditation Use of weapon or weapon equivalent (for example, shod foot, headbutting, use of acid, use of animal) Intention to commit more serious harm than actually resulted from the offence Deliberately causes more harm than is necessary for commission of offence Deliberate targeting of vulnerable victim Leading role in group or gang Offence motivated by, or demonstrating, hostility based on the victim's age, sex, gender identity (or presumed gender identity)	Subordinate role in a group or gang A greater degree of provocation than normally expected Lack of premeditation Mental disorder or learning disability, where linked to commission of the offence Excessive self defence

SG12-5 **STEP TWO Starting point and category range** [5]

Having determined the category, the court should use the corresponding starting points to reach a sentence within the category range below. The starting point applies to all offenders irrespective of plea or previous convictions. A case of particular gravity, reflected by multiple features of culpability in step one, could merit upward adjustment from the starting point before further adjustment for aggravating or mitigating features, set out below.

Offence category	Starting Point (*Applicable to all Offenders*)	Category Range (*Applicable to all Offenders*)
Category 1	**12 years' custody**	**9–16 years' custody**
Category 2	**6 years' custody**	**5–9 years' custody**
Category 3	**4 years' custody**	**3–5 years' custody**

The table below contains a non-exhaustive list of additional factual elements providing the context of the offence and factors relating to the offender. Identify whether any combination of these, or other relevant factors, should result in an upward or downward adjustment from the starting point. In some cases, having considered these factors, it may be appropriate to move outside the identified category range.

Factors increasing seriousness	Factors reducing seriousness or reflecting personal mitigation
Statutory aggravating factors: Previous convictions, having regard to a) the nature of the offence to which the conviction relates and its relevance to the current offence; and b) the time that has elapsed since the conviction Offence committed whilst on bail Offence was committed against an emergency worker acting in the exercise of functions as such a worker *Other aggravating factors include:* Location of the offence Timing of the offence Ongoing effect upon the victim Offence committed against those working in the public sector or providing a service to the public Presence of others including relatives, especially children or partner of the victim Gratuitous degradation of victim	No previous convictions or no relevant/recent convictions Single blow Remorse Good character and/or exemplary conduct Determination, and/or demonstration of steps taken to address addiction or offending behaviour Serious medical conditions requiring urgent, intensive or long-term treatment Isolated incident Age and/or lack of maturity where it affects the responsibility of the offender

[5]

In domestic violence cases, victim forced to leave their home Failure to comply with current court orders Offence committed whilst on licence An attempt to conceal or dispose of evidence Failure to respond to warnings or concerns expressed by others about the offender's behaviour Commission of offence whilst under the influence of alcohol or drugs Abuse of power and/or position of trust Exploiting contact arrangements with a child to commit an offence Previous violence or threats to the same victim Established evidence of community impact Any steps taken to prevent the victim reporting an incident, obtaining assistance and/or from assisting or supporting the prosecution Offences taken into consideration (TICs)	Lapse of time since the offence where this is not the fault of the offender Mental disorder or learning disability, where not linked to the commission of the offence Sole or primary carer for dependent relatives

[6] **STEP THREE Consider any other factors which indicate a reduction, such as assistance to the prosecution** **SG12-6**

The court should take into account sections 73 and 74 of the Serious Organised Crime and Police Act 2005 (assistance by defendants: reduction or review of sentence) and any other rule of law by virtue of which an offender may receive a discounted sentence in consequence of assistance given (or offered) to the prosecutor or investigator.

STEP FOUR Reduction for Guilty Pleas **SG12-7**

The court should take account of any potential reduction for a guilty plea in accordance with section 144 of the Criminal Justice Act 2003 and the *Guilty Plea* guideline.

STEP FIVE Dangerousness **SG12-8**

Causing grievous bodily harm with intent to do grievous bodily harm/wounding with intent to do grievous bodily harm is a serious offence within the meaning of Chapter 5 of the Criminal Justice Act 2003 and at this stage the court should consider whether having regard to the criteria contained in that Chapter it would be appropriate to award a life sentence, imprisonment for public protection or an extended sentence. Where offenders meet the dangerousness criteria, the notional determinate sentence should be used as the basis for the setting of a minimum term.

STEP SIX Totality Principle **SG12-9**

If sentencing an offender for more than one offence, or where the offender is already serving a sentence, consider whether the total sentence is just and proportionate to the offending behaviour.

STEP SEVEN Compensation and ancillary orders **SG12-10**

In all cases, the court should consider whether to make compensation and/or other ancillary orders.

STEP EIGHT Reasons **SG12-11**

Section 174 of the Criminal Justice Act 2003 imposes a duty to give reasons for, and explain the effect of, the sentence.

STEP NINE Consideration for remand time **SG12-12**

Sentencers should take into consideration any remand time served in relation to the final sentence. The court should consider whether to give credit for time spent on remand in custody or on bail in accordance with sections 240 and 240A of the Criminal Justice Act 2003.

[7] **INFLICTING GRIEVOUS BODILY HARM/UNLAWFUL WOUNDING** **SG12-13**

Offences against the Person Act 1861 (section 20)

RACIALLY/RELIGIOUSLY AGGRAVATED GBH/UNLAWFUL WOUNDING

Crime and Disorder Act 1998 (section 29)

These are specified offences for the purposes of section 224 of the Criminal Justice Act 2003

Triable either way

Maximum (section 20): 5 years

Maximum (section 29): 7 years

Offence range: Community order–4 years' custody

SG12-14 **STEP ONE Determining the offence category** [8]

Category 1	Greater harm (serious injury must normally be present) **and** higher culpability
Category 2	Greater harm (serious injury must normally be present) **and** lower culpability; **or** lesser harm **and** higher culpability
Category 3	Lesser harm **and** lower culpability

The court should determine the offender's culpability and the harm caused, or intended, by reference only to the factors below (as demonstrated by the presence of one or more). These factors comprise the principal factual elements of the offence and should determine the category.

Factors indicating greater harm Injury (which includes disease transmission and/or psychological harm) which is serious in the context of the offence (must normally be present) Victim is particularly vulnerable because of personal circumstances Sustained or repeated assault on the same victim	**Factors indicating lesser harm** Injury which is less serious in the context of the offence
Factors indicating higher culpability *Statutory aggravating factors:* Offence motivated by, or demonstrating, hostility to the victim based on his or her sexual orientation (or presumed sexual orientation) Offence motivated by, or demonstrating, hostility to the victim based on the victim's disability (or presumed disability) *Other aggravating factors:* A significant degree of premeditation Use of weapon or weapon equivalent (for example, shod foot, headbutting, use of acid, use of animal) Intention to commit more serious harm than actually resulted from the offence Deliberately causes more harm than is necessary for commission of offence Deliberate targeting of vulnerable victim Leading role in group or gang Offence motivated by, or demonstrating, hostility based on the victim's age, sex, gender identity (or presumed gender identity)	**Factors indicating lower culpability** Subordinate role in group or gang A greater degree of provocation than normally expected Lack of premeditation Mental disorder or learning disability, where linked to commission of the offence Excessive self defence

SG12-15 **STEP TWO Starting Point and Category Range**

Having determined the category, the court should use the corresponding starting points to reach a sentence within the category range below. The starting point applies to all offenders irrespective of plea or previous convictions. A case of particular gravity, reflected by multiple features of culpability in step one, could merit upward adjustment from the starting point before further adjustment for aggravating or mitigating features, set out below.

Offence Category	Starting Point (*Applicable to all offenders*)	Category Range (*Applicable to all offenders*)
Category 1	3 years' custody	2 years 6 months'–4 years' custody
Category 2	1 year 6 months' custody	1–3 years' custody
Category 3	High level community order	Low level community order–51 weeks' custody

The table below contains a **non-exhaustive** list of additional factual elements providing the context of the offence and factors relating to the offender. Identify whether any combination of these, or other relevant factors, should result in an upward or downward adjustment from the starting point. In some cases, having considered these factors, it may be appropriate to move outside the identified category range. [9]

When sentencing **category 3 offences**, the court should also consider the custody threshold as follows:

- Has the custody threshold been passed?
- If so, is it unavoidable that a custodial sentence be imposed?
- If so, can that sentence be suspended?

[9]

Factors increasing seriousness	Factors reducing seriousness or reflecting personal mitigation
Statutory aggravating factors: Previous convictions, having regard to a) the nature of the offence to which the conviction relates and its relevance to the current offence; and b) the time that has elapsed since the conviction Offence committed whilst on bail Offence was committed against an emergency worker acting in the exercise of functions as such a worker *Other aggravating factors include:* Location of the offence Timing of the offence Ongoing effect upon the victim Offence committed against those working in the public sector or providing a service to the public Presence of others including relatives, especially children or partner of the victim Gratuitous degradation of victim In domestic violence cases, victim forced to leave their home Failure to comply with current court orders Offence committed whilst on licence An attempt to conceal or dispose of evidence Failure to respond to warnings or concerns expressed by others about the offender's behaviour Commission of offence whilst under the influence of alcohol or drugs Abuse of power and/or position of trust Exploiting contact arrangements with a child to commit an offence Previous violence or threats to the same victim Established evidence of community impact Any steps taken to prevent the victim reporting an incident, obtaining assistance and/or from assisting or supporting the proscecution Offences taken into consideration (TICs)	No previous convictions or no relevant/recent convictions Single blow Remorse Good character and/or exemplary conduct Determination and/or demonstration of steps taken to address addiction or offending behaviour Serious medical conditions requiring urgent, intensive or long-term treatment Isolated incident Age and/or lack of maturity where it affects the responsibility of the offender Lapse of time since the offence where this is not the fault of the offender Mental disorder or learning disability, where **not** linked to the commission of the offence Sole or primary carer for dependent relatives

Section 29 offences only: The court should determine the appropriate sentence for the offence without taking account of the element of aggravation and then make an addition to the sentence, considering the level of aggravation involved. It may be appropriate to move outside the identified category range, taking into account the increased statutory maximum.

[10] **STEP THREE Consider any other factors which indicate a reduction, such as assistance to the prosecution** SG12-16

The court should take into account sections 73 and 74 of the Serious Organised Crime and Police Act 2005 (assistance by defendants: reduction or review of sentence) and any other rule of law by virtue of which an offender may receive a discounted sentence in consequence of assistance given (or offered) to the prosecutor or investigator.

STEP FOUR Reduction for guilty pleas SG12-17

The court should take account of any potential reduction for a guilty plea in accordance with section 144 of the Criminal Justice Act 2003 and the *Guilty Plea* guideline.

STEP FIVE Dangerousness SG12-18

Inflicting grievous bodily harm/Unlawful wounding and racially/religiously aggravated GBH/Unlawful wounding are specified offences within the meaning of Chapter 5 of the Criminal Justice Act 2003 and at this stage the court should consider whether having regard to the criteria contained in that Chapter it would be appropriate to award an extended sentence.

[Steps Six to Nine are almost identical to those which apply for causing grievous bodily harm with intent: see **SG12-3** ***et seq.***]

Sentencing Guidelines

SG12-19 Assault Occasioning Actual Bodily Harm [11]

Offences against the Person Act 1861 (section 47)

Racially/Religiously Aggravated ABH

Crime and Disorder Act 1998 (section 29)

These are specified offences for the purposes of section 224 of the Criminal Justice Act 2003

Triable either way

Maximum (section 47): 5 years' custody

Maximum (section 29): 7 years' custody

Offence range: Fine–3 years' custody

SG12-20 STEP ONE Determining the offence category [12]

The court should determine the offence category using the table below.

Category 1	Greater harm (serious injury must normally be present) **and** higher culpability
Category 2	Greater harm (serious injury must normally be present) **and** lower culpability; **or** lesser harm **and** higher culpability
Category 3	Lesser harm **and** lower culpability

The court should determine the offender's culpability and the harm caused, or intended, by reference **only** to the factors identified in the table below (as demonstrated by the presence of one or more). These factors comprise the principal factual elements of the offence and should determine the category.

Factors indicating greater harm Injury (which includes disease transmission and/or psychological harm) which is serious in the context the offence (must normally be present) Victim is particularly vulnerable because of personal circumstances Sustained or repeated assault on the same victim	**Factors indicating lesser harm** Injury which is less serious in the context of the offence
Factors indicating higher culpability *Statutory aggravating factors:* Offence motivated by, or demonstrating, hostility to the victim based on his or her sexual orientation (or presumed sexual orientation) Offence motivated by, or demonstrating, hostility to the victim based on the victim's disability (or presumed disability) *Other aggravating factors:* A significant degree of premeditation Use of weapon or weapon equivalent (for example, shod foot, headbutting, use of acid, use of animal) Intention to commit more serious harm than actually resulted from the offence Deliberately causes more harm than is necessary for commission of offence Deliberate targeting of vulnerable victim Leading role in group or gang Offence motivated by, or demonstrating, hostility based on the victim's age, sex, gender identity (or presumed gender identity)	**Factors indicating lower culpability** Subordinate role in a group or gang A greater degree of provocation than normally expected Lack of premeditation Mental disorder or learning disability, where linked to commission of the offence Excessive self defence

SG12-21 STEP TWO Starting Point and Category Range

Having determined the category, the court should use the corresponding starting points to reach a sentence within the category range below. The starting point applies to all offenders irrespective of plea or previous convictions. A case of particular gravity, reflected by multiple features of culpability in step one, could merit upward adjustment from the starting point before further adjustment for aggravating or mitigating features, set out below.

[12]

Offence category	Starting Point (*Applicable to all offenders*)	Category Range (*Applicable to all offenders*)
Category 1	1 year 6 months' custody	1–3 years' custody
Category 2	26 weeks' custody	Low level community order–51 weeks' custody
Category 3	Medium level community order	Band A fine–High level community order

[13] The table below contains a **non-exhaustive** list of additional factual elements providing the context of the offence and factors relating to the offender. Identify whether any combination of these, or other relevant factors, should result in an upward or downward adjustment from the starting point. In some cases, having considered these factors, it may be appropriate to move outside the identified category range.

When sentencing **category 2** offences, the court should also consider the custody threshold as follows:

- Has the custody threshold been passed?
- If so, is it unavoidable that a custodial sentence be imposed?
- If so, can that sentence be suspended?

When sentencing **category 3** offences, the court should also consider the community order threshold as follows:

- Has the community order threshold been passed?

Factors increasing seriousness	Factors reducing seriousness or reflecting personal mitigation
Statutory aggravating factors: Previous convictions, having regard to a) the nature of the offence to which the conviction relates and its relevance to the current offence; and b) the time that has elapsed since the conviction Offence committed whilst on bail Offence was committed against an emergency worker acting in the exercise of functions as such a worker *Other aggravating factors include:* Location of the offence Timing of the offence Ongoing effect upon the victim Offence committed against those working in the public sector or providing a service to the public Presence of others including relatives, especially children or partner of the victim Gratuitous degradation of victim In domestic violence cases, victim forced to leave their home Failure to comply with current court orders Offence committed whilst on licence An attempt to conceal or dispose of evidence Failure to respond to warnings or concerns expressed by others about the offender's behaviour Commission of offence whilst under the influence of alcohol or drugs Abuse of power and/or position of trust Exploiting contact arrangements with a child to commit an offence Established evidence of community impact Any steps taken to prevent the victim reporting an incident, obtaining assistance and/or from assisting or supporting the prosecution Offences taken into consideration (TICs)	No previous convictions or no relevant/recent convictions Single blow Remorse Good character and/or exemplary conduct Determination and/or demonstration of steps taken to address addiction or offending behaviour Serious medical conditions requiring urgent, intensive or long-term treatment Isolated incident Age and/or lack of maturity where it affects the responsibility of the offender Lapse of time since the offence where this is not the fault of the offender Mental disorder or learning disability, where not linked to the commission of the offence Sole or primary carer for dependent relatives

Section 29 offences only: The court should determine the appropriate sentence for the offence without taking account of the element of aggravation and then make an addition to the sentence, considering the level of aggravation involved. It may be appropriate to move outside the identified category range, taking into account the increased statutory maximum.

[14] [Steps Three to Nine are almost identical to those for inflicting grievous bodily harm: see **SG12-3** ***et seq.***]

SG12-22 ASSAULT WITH INTENT TO RESIST ARREST [15]

Offences against the Person Act 1861 (section 38)

This is a specified offence for the purposes of section 224 of the Criminal Justice Act 2003

Triable either way

Maximum 2 years' custody

Offence range: Fine–51 weeks' custody

SG12-23 STEP ONE Determining the offence category [16]

The court should determine the offence category using the table below.

Category 1	Greater harm **and** higher culpability
Category 2	Greater harm **and** lower culpability; **or** lesser harm **and** higher culpability
Category 3	Lesser harm **and** lower culpability

The court should determine the offender's culpability and the harm caused, or intended, by reference **only** to the factors identified in the table below (as demonstrated by the presence of one or more). These factors comprise the principal factual elements of the offence and should determine the category.

Factors indicating greater harm Sustained or repeated assault on the same victim **Factors indicating higher culpability** *Statutory aggravating factors:* Offence racially or religiously aggravated Offence motivated by, or demonstrating, hostility to the victim based on his or her sexual orientation (or presumed sexual orientation) Offence motivated by, or demonstrating, hostility to the victim based on the victim's disability (or presumed disability) *Other aggravating factors:* A significant degree of premeditation Use of weapon or weapon equivalent (for example, shod foot, headbutting, use of acid, use of animal) Intention to commit more serious harm than actually resulted from the offence Deliberately causes more harm than is necessary for commission of offence Leading role in group or gang Offence motivated by, or demonstrating, hostility based on the victim's age, sex, gender identity (or presumed gender identity)	**Factors indicating lesser harm** Injury which is less serious in the context of the offence **Factors indicating lower culpability** Subordinate role in group or gang Lack of premeditation Mental disorder or learning disability, where linked to commission of the offence

SG12-24 STEP TWO Starting Point and Category Range [17]

Having determined the category, the court should use the corresponding starting points to reach a sentence within the category range below. The starting point applies to all offenders irrespective of plea or previous convictions. A case of particular gravity, reflected by multiple features of culpability in step one, could merit upward adjustment from the starting point before further adjustment for aggravating or mitigating features, set out below.

Offence Category	Starting Point (*Applicable to all offenders*)	Category Range (*Applicable to all offenders*)
Category 1	**26 weeks' custody**	**12 weeks'–51 weeks' custody**
Category 2	**Medium level community order**	**Low level community order–High level community order**
Category 3	**Band B fine**	**Band A fine–Band C fine**

[17] The table below contains a **non-exhaustive** list of additional factual elements providing the context of the offence and factors relating to the offender. Identify whether any combination of these, or other relevant factors, should result in an upward or downward adjustment from the starting point. In some cases, having considered these factors, it may be appropriate to move outside the identified category range.

When sentencing **category 1** offences, the court should consider whether the sentence can be suspended.

Factors increasing seriousness	**Factors reducing seriousness or reflecting personal mitigation**
Statutory aggravating factors: Previous convictions, having regard to a) the nature of the offence to which the conviction relates and its relevance to the current offence; and b) the time that has elapsed since the conviction Offence committed whilst on bail *Other aggravating factors include:* Location of the offence Timing of the offence Ongoing effect upon the victim Gratuitous degradation of victim Failure to comply with current court orders Offence committed whilst on licence An attempt to conceal or dispose of evidence Failure to respond to warnings or concerns expressed by others about the offender's behaviour Commission of offence whilst under the influence of alcohol or drugs Established evidence of community impact Any steps taken to prevent the victim reporting an incident, obtaining assistance and/or from assisting or supporting the prosecution Offences taken into consideration (TICs)	No previous convictions **or** no relevant/recent convictions Single blow Remorse Good character and/or exemplary conduct Determination and/or demonstration of steps taken to address addiction or offending behaviour Serious medical conditions requiring urgent, intensive or long-term treatment Isolated incident Age and/or lack of maturity where it affects the responsibility of the offender Lapse of time since the offence where this is not the fault of the offender Mental disorder or learning disability, where **not** linked to the commission of the offence Sole or primary carer for dependent relatives

[18] [Steps Three to Nine are almost identical to those for inflicting grievous bodily harm: see **SG12-3** ***et seq.***]

[19] Assault on a Police Constable in Execution of his Duty SG12-25

Police Act 1996 (section 89)

Triable only summarily

Maximum: 26 weeks' custody

Offence range: Fine–26 weeks' custody

[20] STEP ONE Determining the offence category SG12-26

The court should determine the offence category using the table below.

Category 1	Greater harm **and** higher culpability
Category 2	Greater harm **and** lower culpability; **or** lesser harm **and** higher culpability
Category 3	Lesser harm **and** lower culpability

The court should determine the offender's culpability and the harm caused, or intended, by reference **only** to the factors below (as demonstrated by the presence of one or more). These factors comprise the principal factual elements of the offence and should determine the category.

Factors indicating greater harm Sustained or repeated assault on the same victim **Factors indicating higher culpability**	**Factors indicating lesser harm** Injury which is less serious in the context of the offence [20]
Statutory aggravating factors: Offence racially or religiously aggravated Offence motivated by, or demonstrating, hostility to the victim based on his or her sexual orientation (or presumed sexual orientation) Offence motivated by, or demonstrating, hostility to the victim based on the victim's disability (or presumed disability)	**Factors indicating lower culpability** Subordinate role in group or gang Lack of premeditation Mental disorder or learning disability, where linked to commission of the offence
Other aggravating factors: A significant degree of premeditation Use of weapon or weapon equivalent (for example, shod foot, headbutting, use of acid, use of animal) Intention to commit more serious harm than actually resulted from the offence Deliberately causes more harm than is necessary for commission of offence Leading role in group or gang Offence motivated by, or demonstrating, hostility based on the victim's age, sex, gender identity (or presumed gender identity)	

SG12-27 STEP TWO **Starting point and category range** [21]

Having determined the category, the court should use the corresponding starting points to reach a sentence within the category range below. The starting point applies to all offenders irrespective of plea or previous convictions. A case of particular gravity, reflected by multiple features of culpability in step one, could merit upward adjustment from the starting point before further adjustment for aggravating or mitigating features, set out below.

Offence Category	Starting Point (*Applicable to all offenders*)	Category Range (*Applicable to all offenders*)
Category 1	**12 weeks' custody**	**Low level community order–26 weeks' custody**
Category 2	**Medium level community order**	**Low level community order–High level community order**
Category 3	**Band B fine**	**Band A fine–Band C fine**

The table below contains a **non-exhaustive** list of additional factual elements providing the context of the offence and factors relating to the offender. Identify whether any combination of these, or other relevant factors, should result in an upward or downward adjustment from the starting point. In some cases, having considered these factors, it may be appropriate to move outside the identified category range.

When sentencing **category 1** offences, the court should also consider the custody threshold as follows:

- Has the custody threshold been passed?
- If so, is it unavoidable that a custodial sentence be imposed?
- If so, can that sentence be suspended?

[21]

Factors increasing seriousness	Factors reducing seriousness or reflecting personal mitigation
Statutory aggravating factors: Previous convictions, having regard to a) the nature of the offence to which the conviction relates and its relevance to the current offence; and b) the time that has elapsed since the conviction Offence committed whilst on bail *Other aggravating factors include:* Location of the offence Timing of the offence Ongoing effect upon the victim Gratuitous degradation of victim Failure to comply with current court orders Offence committed whilst on licence An attempt to conceal or dispose of evidence Failure to respond to warnings or concerns expressed by others about the offender's behaviour Commission of offence whilst under the influence of alcohol or drugs Established evidence of community impact Any steps taken to prevent the victim reporting an incident, obtaining assistance and/or from assisting or supporting the prosecution Offences taken into consideration (TICs)	No previous convictions **or** no relevant/recent convictions Single blow Remorse Good character and/or exemplary conduct Determination and/or demonstration of steps taken to address addiction or offending behaviour Serious medical conditions requiring urgent, intensive or long-term treatment Isolated incident Age and/or lack of maturity where it affects the responsibility of the defendant Mental disorder or learning disability, where **not** linked to the commission of the offence Sole or primary carer for dependent relatives

[22] [Steps Three to Eight are almost identical to those for inflicting grievous bodily harm (see **SG12-3** ***et seq***) but with the omission of Step Five (Dangerousness).]

[23]

COMMON ASSAULT SG12-28

Criminal Justice Act 1988 (section 39)

RACIALLY/RELIGIOUSLY AGGRAVATED COMMON ASSAULT

Crime and Disorder Act 1998 (section 29)

Racially/religiously aggravated assault is a specified offence for the purposes of section 224 of the Criminal Justice Act 2003

Triable only summarily

Maximum (section 39): 26 weeks' custody

Triable either way

Maximum (section 29): 2 years' custody

Offence range: Discharge–26 weeks' custody

[24] **STEP ONE Determining the Offence Category** SG12-29

The court should determine the offence category using the table below.

Category 1	Greater harm (injury or fear of injury must normally be present) **and** higher culpability
Category 2	Greater harm (injury or fear of injury must normally be present) **and** lower culpability; **or** lesser harm **and** higher culpability
Category 3	Lesser harm **and** lower culpability

The court should determine the offender's culpability and the harm caused, or intended, by reference **only** to the factors below (as demonstrated by the presence of one or more). These factors comprise the principal factual elements of the offence and should determine the category. [24]

Factors indicating greater harm	Factors indicating lesser harm
Injury or fear of injury which is serious in the context of the offence (must normally be present) Victim is particularly vulnerable because of personal circumstances Sustained or repeated assault on the same victim	Injury which is less serious in the context of the offence
Factors indicating higher culpability *Statutory aggravating factors:* Offence motivated by, or demonstrating, hostility to the victim based on his or her sexual orientation (or presumed sexual orientation) Offence motivated by, or demonstrating, hostility to the victim based on the victim's disability (or presumed disability) *Other aggravating factors:* A significant degree of premeditation Threatened or actual use of weapon or weapon equivalent (for example, shod foot, headbutting, use of acid, use of animal) Intention to commit more serious harm than actually resulted from the offence Deliberately causes more harm than is necessary for commission of offence Deliberate targeting of vulnerable victim Leading role in group or gang Offence motivated by, or demonstrating, hostility based on the victim's age, sex, gender identity (or presumed gender identity)	**Factors indicating lower culpability** Subordinate role in group or gang A greater degree of provocation than normally expected Lack of premeditation Mental disorder or learning disability, where linked to commission of the offence Excessive self defence

SG12-30 STEP TWO **Starting point and category range**

Having determined the category, the court should use the corresponding starting points to reach a sentence within the category range below. The starting point applies to all offenders irrespective of plea or previous convictions. A case of particular gravity, reflected by multiple features of culpability in step one, could merit upward adjustment from the starting point before further adjustment for aggravating or mitigating features, set out below.

Offence Category	Starting Point (*Applicable to all offenders*)	Category Range (*Applicable to all offenders*)
Category 1	**High level community order**	**Low level community order–26 weeks' custody**
Category 2	**Medium level community order**	**Band A fine–High level community order**
Category 3	**Band A fine**	**Discharge–Band C fine**

The table below contains a **non-exhaustive** list of additional factual elements providing the context of the offence and factors relating to the offender. Identify whether any combination of these, or other relevant factors, should result in an upward or downward adjustment from the starting point. In some cases, having considered these factors, it may be appropriate to move outside the identified category range. [25]

When sentencing **category 1** offences, the court should also consider the custody threshold as follows:

- Has the custody threshold been passed?
- If so, is it unavoidable that a custodial sentence be imposed?
- If so, can that sentence be suspended?

When sentencing **category 2** offences, the court should also consider the community order threshold as follows:

- Has the community order threshold been passed?

[25]

Factors increasing seriousness	Factors reducing seriousness or reflecting personal mitigation
Statutory aggravating factors: Previous convictions, having regard to a) the nature of the offence to which the conviction relates and its relevance to the current offence; and b) the time that has elapsed since the conviction Offence committed whilst on bail *Other aggravating factors include:* Location of the offence Timing of the offence Ongoing effect upon the victim Offence committed against those working in the public sector or providing a service to the public Presence of others including relatives, especially children or partner of the victim Gratuitous degradation of victim In domestic violence cases, victim forced to leave their home Failure to comply with current court orders Offence committed whilst on licence An attempt to conceal or dispose of evidence Failure to respond to warnings or concerns expressed by others about the offender's behaviour Commission of offence whilst under the influence of alcohol or drugs Abuse of power and/or position of trust Exploiting contact arrangements with a child to commit an offence Established evidence of community impact Any steps taken to prevent the victim reporting an incident, obtaining assistance and/or from assisting or supporting the prosecution Offences taken into consideration (TICs)	No previous convictions or no relevant/recent convictions Single blow Remorse Good character and/or exemplary conduct Determination and/or demonstration of steps taken to address addiction or offending behaviour Serious medical conditions requiring urgent, intensive or long-term treatment Isolated incident Age and/or lack of maturity where it affects the responsibility of the offender Lapse of time since the offence where this is not the fault of the offender Mental disorder or learning disability, where **not** linked to the commission of the offence Sole or primary carer for dependent relatives

Section 29 offences only: The court should determine the appropriate sentence for the offence without taking account of the element of aggravation and then make an addition to the sentence, considering the level of aggravation involved. It may be appropriate to move outside the identified category range, taking into account the increased statutory maximum.

[26] [Steps Three to Nine are almost identical to those for inflicting grievous bodily harm: see SG12-3 *et seq.*]

[27]

Annex: Fine Bands and Community Orders SG12-31

[The tables set out here are also set out in the Magistrates' Court Sentencing Guidelines, which include further guidance on fines and community orders: see SG10-129 and SG9-2.]

PART 13 ATTEMPTED MURDER

Definitive Guideline

SG13-1 ... This guideline applies to the sentencing of offenders convicted of any of the offences dealt with herein who are sentenced on or after 27 July 2009. [1]

This guideline applies only to the sentencing of offenders aged 18 and older. The legislative provisions relating to the sentencing of youths are different; the younger the age, the greater the difference. A separate guideline setting out general principles relating to the sentencing of youths is planned.

...

SG13-2 **Introduction** [3]

1. This guideline covers the single offence of attempted murder. The Council has published a separate definitive guideline for offences of assault which do not result in the death of the victim.[201]
2. There are critical differences between murder and attempted murder; not only is the intended result not achieved but also, for attempted murder, there must have been an intention to kill whereas a charge of murder may arise where the intention was to inflict grievous bodily harm. These differences are reflected in the approach set out below which supersedes previous guidance from the Court of Appeal in *Ford*[202] and other judgments.

SG13-3 **A. Assessing seriousness**

(i) Culpability and harm

3. The culpability of the offender is the initial factor in determining the seriousness of an offence. It is an essential element of the offence of attempted murder that the offender had an intention to kill; accordingly an offender convicted of this offence will have demonstrated a high level of culpability. Even so, the precise level of culpability will vary in line with the circumstances of the offence and whether the offence was planned or spontaneous. The use of a weapon may influence this assessment.
4. In common with all offences against the person, this offence has the potential to contain an imbalance between culpability and harm.[203]
5. Where the degree of harm actually caused to the victim of an attempted murder is negligible, it is inevitable that this will impact on the overall assessment of offence seriousness.
6. However, although the degree of (or lack of) physical or psychological harm suffered by a victim may generally influence sentence, the statutory definition of harm encompasses not only the harm actually caused by an offence but also any harm that the offence was intended to cause or might foreseeably have caused; since the offence can only be committed where there is an intention to kill, an offence of attempted murder will always involve, in principle, the most serious level of harm.

(ii) Aggravating and mitigating factors [4]

7. The most serious offences of attempted murder will include those which encompass the factors set out in schedule 21 to the Criminal Justice Act 2003, paragraphs 4 and 5 that, had the offence been murder, would make the seriousness of the offence 'exceptionally high' or 'particularly high'. [See E3.2 in the main work.]
8. The particular facts of the offence will identify the appropriate level. In all cases, the aggravating and mitigating factors that will influence the identification of the provisional sentence within the range follow those set out in schedule 21 with suitable adjustments. These factors are included in the guideline [below].
9. The *Seriousness* guideline[204] sets out aggravating and mitigating factors that are applicable to a wide range of cases; [see **SG2-1**]. Some are already reflected in the factors referred to above. Care needs to be taken to ensure that there is no double counting where an essential element of the offence charged might, in other circumstances, be an aggravating factor. An additional statutory aggravating factor has been introduced by the Counter-Terrorism Act 2008 for prescribed offences which include attempted murder.[205]
10. This guideline is not intended to provide for an offence found to be based on a genuine belief that the murder would have been an act of mercy. Whilst the approach to assessing the seriousness of the

---

201 *Assault and other offences against the person*, published 20 February 2008, www.sentencing-guidelines.gov.uk
202 [2005] EWCA Crim 1358
203 See *Overarching Principles: Seriousness*, para. 1.17, published 16 December 2004, www.sentencing-guidelines.gov.uk
204 *Overarching Principles: Seriousness*, paras. 1.20–1.27 published on 16 December 2004; www.sentencing-guidelines.gov.uk
205 Section 30 and schedule 2. If a court determines that the offence has a terrorist connection, it must treat that as an aggravating factor, and state in open court that the offence was so aggravated.

[4] offence may be similar, there are likely to be other factors present (relating to the offence and the offender) that would have to be taken into account and reflected in the sentence.

B. Ancillary orders SG13-4

Compensation orders

11. A court must consider making a compensation order in respect of any personal injury, loss or damage occasioned. There is no limit to the amount of compensation that may be awarded in the Crown Court.

[5] **C. Sentencing ranges and starting points** SG13-5

12. Typically, a guideline will apply to an offence that can be committed in a variety of circumstances with different levels of seriousness. The starting points and ranges are based upon an adult '*first time offender*' who has been **convicted after a trial**. Within the guidelines, a '*first time offender*' is a person who does not have a conviction which, by virtue of section 143(2) of the Criminal Justice Act 2003, must be treated as an aggravating factor.
13. As an aid to consistency of approach, the guideline describes a number of levels or types of activity which would fall within the broad definition of the offence.
14. The expected approach is for a court to identify the description that most nearly matches the particular facts of the offence for which sentence is being imposed. This will identify a **starting point** from which the sentencer can depart to reflect aggravating or mitigating factors affecting the seriousness of the offence (beyond those contained within the column describing the nature of the offence) to reach a **provisional sentence.**
15. The **sentencing range** is the bracket into which the provisional sentence will normally fall after having regard to factors which aggravate or mitigate the seriousness of the offence. The particular circumstances may, however, make it appropriate that the provisional sentence falls outside the range.
16. Where the offender has previous convictions which aggravate the seriousness of the current offence, that may take the provisional sentence beyond the range given particularly where there are significant other aggravating factors present.
17. Once the provisional sentence has been identified by reference to those factors affecting the seriousness of the offence, the court will take into account any relevant factors of personal mitigation, which may take the sentence below the range given.
18. Where there has been a guilty plea, any reduction attributable to that plea will be applied to the sentence at this stage. This reduction may take the sentence below the range provided.
19. A court must give its reasons for imposing a sentence of a different kind or outside the range provided in the guidelines.

[6] **D. Factors to take into consideration** SG13-6

1. Attempted murder is a serious offence for the purposes of the provisions in the Criminal Justice Act 2003[206] for dealing with dangerous offenders. When sentencing an offender convicted of this offence, in many circumstances a court may need to consider imposing a discretionary life sentence or one of the sentences for public protection prescribed in the Act.
2. The starting points and ranges are based upon a first time adult offender convicted after a trial (see paragraphs 12–19 above). They will be relevant when imposing a determinate sentence and when fixing any minimum term that may be necessary. When setting the minimum term to be served within an indeterminate sentence, in accordance with normal practice that term will usually be half the equivalent determinate sentence.[207]
3. Attempted murder requires an intention to kill. Accordingly, an offender convicted of this offence will have demonstrated a high level of culpability. Even so, the precise level of culpability will vary in line with the circumstances of the offence and whether the offence was planned or spontaneous. The use of a weapon may influence this assessment.
4. The level of injury or harm sustained by the victim as well as any harm that the offence was intended to cause or might foreseeably have caused, must be taken into account and reflected in the sentence imposed.
5. The degree of harm will vary greatly. Where there is low harm and high culpability, culpability is more significant.[208] Even in cases where a low level of injury (or no injury) has been caused, an offence of attempted murder will be extremely serious.
6. The most serious offences will include those which encompass the factors set out in schedule 21 to the Criminal Justice Act 2003, paragraphs 4 and 5 that, had the offence been murder, would make the seriousness of the offence 'exceptionally high' or 'particularly high': see [E3.2 in the main work].

[206] Sections 224–230 as amended
[207] *R v Szczerba* [2002] 2 Cr App R (S) 86
[208] *Overarching Principles: Seriousness*, para. 1.19, published on 16 December 2004; www.sentencing.guidelines.gov.uk

7. The particular facts of the offence will identify the appropriate level. In all cases, the aggravating and mitigating factors that will influence the identification of the provisional sentence within the range follow those set out in schedule 21 with suitable adjustments. This guideline is not intended to provide for an offence found to be based on a genuine belief that the murder would have been an act of mercy. [6]
8. When assessing the seriousness of an offence, the court should also refer to the list of general aggravating and mitigating factors in the Council guideline on *Seriousness* (see [SG2-1]). Care should be taken to ensure there is no double counting where an essential element of the offence charged might, in other circumstances, be an aggravating factor.

SG13-7 Attempted Murder [7]

Criminal Attempts Act 1981 (section 1(1))

THIS IS A SERIOUS OFFENCE FOR THE PURPOSES OF SECTION 224 CRIMINAL JUSTICE ACT 2003

Maximum penalty: Life imprisonment

Nature of offence	Starting point	Sentencing range
Level 1 *The most serious offences including those which (if the charge had been murder) would come within para. 4 or para. 5 of schedule 21 to the Criminal Justice Act 2003*		
• Serious and long term physical or psychological harm	30 years' custody	27–35 years' custody
• Some physical or psychological harm	20 years' custody	17–25 years' custody
• Little or no physical or psychological harm	15 years' custody	12–20 years' custody
Level 2 *Other planned attempt to kill*		
• Serious and long term physical or psychological harm	20 years' custody	17–25 years' custody
• Some physical or psychological harm	15 years' custody	12–20 years' custody
• Little or no physical or psychological harm	10 years' custody	7–15 years' custody
Level 3 *Other spontaneous attempt to kill*		
• Serious and long term physical or psychological harm	15 years' custody	12–20 years' custody
• Some physical or psychological harm	12 years' custody	9–17 years' custody
• Little or no physical or psychological harm	9 years' custody	6–14 years' custody

Specific aggravating factors	Specific mitigating factors
(a) the fact that the victim was particularly vulnerable, for example, because of age or disability (b) mental or physical suffering inflicted on the victim (c) the abuse of a position of trust (d) the use of duress or threats against another person to facilitate the commission of the offence (e) the fact that the victim was providing a public service or performing a public duty	(a) the fact that the offender suffered from any mental disorder or mental disability which lowered his degree of culpability (b) the fact that the offender was provoked (for example, by prolonged stress) (c) the fact that the offender acted to any extent in self-defence (d) the age of the offender

The presence of one or more aggravating features will indicate a more severe sentence within the suggested range and, if the aggravating feature(s) are exceptionally serious, the case will move up to the next level.

SG13-8 [Annex A is an extract from the CJA 2003, sch. 21. It is not reproduced here. For the relevant text, see E3.4 in the main work. [8]

Annex B reproduces the elements indicating higher culpability, a more than usually serious degree of harm and lower culpability and factors which may be relevant personal mitigation from the Council guideline *Overarching Principles: Seriousness*. See SG2-1 for the full guideline.] [9]

PART 14 BLADED ARTICLES AND OFFENSIVE WEAPONS

Definitive Guideline SG14-1

[2] **Applicability** SG14-2

Effective from 1 June 2018

The Sentencing Council issues this definitive guideline in accordance with section 120 of the Coroners and Justice Act 2009.

The guidelines on pages 3 to 14 [SG14-3–SG14-21] apply to all offenders aged 18 and older, who are sentenced on or after 1 June 2018, regardless of the date of the offence.

The guideline on pages 15 to 21 [SG14-22–SG14-30] applies to all children or young people, who are sentenced on or after 1 June 2018, regardless of the date of the offence.

Section 125(1) of the Coroners and Justice Act 2009 provides that when sentencing offences committed after 6 April 2010:

Every court –

(a) must, in sentencing an offender, follow any sentencing guidelines which are relevant to the offender's case, and

(b) must, in exercising any other function relating to the sentencing of offenders, follow any sentencing guidelines which are relevant to the exercise of the function,

unless the court is satisfied that it would be contrary to the interests of justice to do so.

[3]

Bladed Articles and Offensive Weapons – Possession SG14-3

Possession of an offensive weapon in a public place
Prevention of Crime Act 1953 (section 1(1))

Possession of an article with blade/point in a public place
Criminal Justice Act 1988 (section 139(1))

Possession of an offensive weapon on school premises
Criminal Justice Act 1988 (section 139A(2))

Possession of an article with blade/point on school premises
Criminal Justice Act 1988 (section 139A(1))

Unauthorised possession in prison of a knife or offensive weapon
Prison Act 1952 (section 40CA)

Triable either way

Maximum: 4 years' custody

Offence range: Fine–2 years 6 months' custody

This guideline applies only to offenders aged 18 and older.

[4] This offence is subject to statutory minimum sentencing provisons.

See STEP THREE for further details.

STEP ONE Determining the offence category SG14-4

The court should determine the offence category with reference only to the factors listed in the tables below. In order to determine the category, the court should assess **culpability** and **harm**.

The court should weigh all the factors set out below in determining the offender's culpability.

Where there are characteristics present which fall under different levels of culpability, the court should balance these characteristics to reach a fair assessment of the offender's culpability.

Culpability demonstrated by one or more of the following:	
A	• Possession of a bladed article • Possession of a highly dangerous weapon* • Offence motivated by, or demonstrating hostility based on any of the following characteristics or presumed characteristics of the victim: religion, race, disability, sexual orientation or transgender identity
B	• Possession of weapon (other than a bladed article or a highly dangerous weapon) – used to threaten or cause fear
C	• Possession of weapon (other than a bladed article or a highly dangerous weapon) – not used to threaten or cause fear
D	• Possession of weapon falls just short of reasonable excuse

[4]

*NB an offensive weapon is defined in legislation as 'any article made or adapted for use for causing injury, or is intended by the person having it with him for such use'. A highly dangerous weapon is, therefore, a weapon, including a corrosive substance (such as acid), whose dangerous nature must be substantially above and beyond this. The court must determine whether the weapon is highly dangerous on the facts and circumstances of the case.

Harm The court should consider the factors set out below to determine the level of harm that has been caused or was risked	
Category 1	• Offence committed at a school or other place where vulnerable people are likely to be present • Offence committed in prison • Offence committed in circumstances where there is a risk of serious disorder • Serious alarm/distress
Category 2	• All other cases

SG14-5 **STEP TWO Starting point and category range** [5]

Having determined the category at step one, the court should use the corresponding starting point to reach a sentence within the category range below. The starting point applies to all offenders irrespective of plea or previous convictions. A case of particular gravity, reflected by multiple features of culpability or harm in step one, could merit upward adjustment from the starting point before further adjustment for aggravating or mitigating features, set out on the next page.

	Culpability			
Harm	**A**	**B**	**C**	**D**
Category 1	**Starting point** 1 year 6 months' custody	**Starting point** 9 months' custody	**Starting point** 3 months' custody	**Starting point** High level community order
	Category range 1–2 years 6 months' custody	**Category range** 6 months'–1 year 6 months' custody	**Category range** High level community order–6 months' custody	**Category range** Medium level community order–3 months' custody
Category 2	**Starting point** 6 months' custody	**Starting point** High level community order	**Starting point** Medium level community order	**Starting point** Low level community order
	Category range 3 months'–1 year's custody	**Category range** Medium level community order–6 months' custody	**Category range** Low level community order–High level community order	**Category range** Band C fine–Medium level community order

The table below contains a non-exhaustive list of additional factual elements providing the context of the offence and factors relating to the offender. Identify whether any combination of these, or other relevant factors, should result in an upward or downward adjustment from the sentence arrived at so far. In [6]

[6] particular, relevant recent convictions are likely to result in an upward adjustment. In some cases, having considered these factors, it may be appropriate to move outside the identified category range.

Factors increasing seriousness
Statutory aggravating factors: Previous convictions, having regard to a) the **nature** of the offence to which the conviction relates and its **relevance** to the current offence; and b) the **time** that has elapsed since the conviction (unless the convictions will be relevant for the purposes of the statutory minimum sentencing provisions – see step three) Offence committed whilst on bail
Other aggravating factors: Offence was committed as part of a group or gang Attempts to conceal identity Commission of offence whilst under the influence of alcohol or drugs Attempts to conceal/dispose of evidence Failure to comply with current court orders Offence committed on licence or post sentence supervision Offences taken into consideration Failure to respond to warnings about behaviour

Factors reducing seriousness or reflecting personal mitigation
No previous convictions **or** no relevant/recent convictions Good character and/or exemplary conduct Serious medical condition requiring urgent, intensive or long-term treatment Age and/or lack of maturity where it affects the responsibility of the offender Mental disorder or learning disability Sole or primary carer for dependent relatives Co-operation with the police

[7] **STEP THREE Minimum Terms – second or further relevant offence** **SG14-6**

When sentencing the offences of:

- possession of an offensive weapon in a public place;
- possession of an article with a blade/point in a public place;
- possession of an offensive weapon on school premises; and
- possession of an article with blade/point on school premises

a court must impose a sentence of at least 6 months' imprisonment where this is a second or further relevant offence **unless the court is of the opinion that there are particular circumstances relating to the offence, the previous offence or the offender which make it unjust to do so in all the circumstances.**

A 'relevant offence' includes those offences listed above and the following offences:

- threatening with an offensive weapon in a public place;
- threatening with an article with a blade/point in a public place;
- threatening with an article with a blade/point on school premises; and
- threatening with an offensive weapon on school premises.

Unjust in all of the circumstances

In considering whether a statutory minimum sentence would be 'unjust in all of the circumstances' the court must have regard to the particular circumstances of the offence and the offender. If the circumstances of the offence, the previous offence or the offender make it unjust to impose the statutory minimum sentence then the court **must impose either a shorter custodial sentence than the statutory minimum provides or an alternative sentence.**

The offence:

Having reached this stage of the guideline the court should have made a provisional assessment of the seriousness of the current offence. In addition, the court must consider the seriousness of the previous offence(s) and the period of time that has elapsed between offences. Where the seriousness of the combined offences is such that it falls far below the custody threshold, or where there has been a significant period of time between the offences, the court may consider it unjust to impose the statutory minimum sentence.

The offender: [7]

The court should consider the following factors to determine whether it would be unjust to impose the statutory minimum sentence;

- any strong personal mitigation;
- whether there is a realistic prospect of rehabilitation;
- whether custody will result in significant impact on others.

SG14-7 STEP FOUR **Consider any factors which indicate a reduction for assistance to the prosecution** [8]

The court should take into account sections 73 and 74 of the Serious Organised Crime and Police Act 2005 (assistance by defendants: reduction or review of sentence) and any other rule of law by virtue of which an offender may receive a discounted sentence in consequence of assistance given (or offered) to the prosecutor or investigator.

SG14-8 STEP FIVE **Reduction for guilty pleas**

The court should take account of any potential reduction for a guilty plea in accordance with section 144 of the Criminal Justice Act 2003 and the Guilty Plea guideline. Where a statutory minimum sentence has been imposed, the court must ensure that any reduction for a guilty plea does not reduce the sentence to less than 80 per cent of the statutory minimum.

SG14-9 STEP SIX **Totality principle**

If sentencing an offender for more than one offence, or where the offender is already serving a sentence, consider whether the total sentence is just and proportionate to the overall offending behaviour in accordance with the Offences Taken into Consideration and Totality guideline.

SG14-10 STEP SEVEN **Ancillary orders**

In all cases the court should consider whether to make ancillary orders.

SG14-11 STEP EIGHT **Reasons**

Section 174 of the Criminal Justice Act 2003 imposes a duty to give reasons for, and explain the effect of, the sentence.

SG14-12 STEP NINE **Consideration for time spent on bail**

The court must consider whether to give credit for time spent on bail in accordance with section 240A of the Criminal Justice Act 2003.

SG14-13 BLADED ARTICLES AND OFFENSIVE WEAPONS – THREATS [9]

Threatening with an offensive weapon in a public place
Prevention of Crime Act 1953 (section 1A)

Threatening with an article with blade/point in a public place
Criminal Justice Act 1988 (section 139AA(1))

Threatening with an article with blade/point or offensive weapon on school premises Criminal Justice Act 1988 (section 139AA(1))

Triable either way

Maximum: 4 years' custody

Offence range: 6 months' custody–3 years' custody

This offence is subject to statutory minimum sentencing provisions. [10]

See STEP THREE for further details.

SG14-14 STEP ONE **Determining the offence category**

The court should determine the offence category with reference **only** to the factors listed in the tables below. In order to determine the category, the court should assess **culpability and harm.**

The court should weigh all the factors set out below in determining the offender's culpability.

Where there are characteristics present which fall under different levels of culpability, the court should balance these characteristics to reach a fair assessment of the offender's culpability.

[10]

Culpability demonstrated by one or more of the following:	
A – Higher culpability:	• Offence committed using a bladed article • Offence committed using a highly dangerous weapon* • Offence motivated by, or demonstrating hostility based on any of the following characteristics ore presumed characteristics of the victim: religion, race, disability, sexual orientation or transgender identity • Significant degree of planning or premeditation
B – Lower culpability:	• All other cases

*NB an offensive weapon is defined in legislation as 'any article made or adapted for use for causing injury, or is intended by the person having it with him for such use'. A highly dangerous weapon is, therefore, a weapon, including a corrosive substance (such as acid), whose dangerous nature must be substantially above and beyond this. The court must determine whether the weapon is highly dangerous on the facts and circumstances of the case

Harm The court should consider the factors set out below to determine the level of harm that has been caused or was intended to be caused to the victim.	
Category 1	• Offence committed at a school or other place where vulnerable people are likely to be present • Offence committed in prison • Offence committed in circumstances where there is a risk of serious disorder • Serious alarm/distress caused to the victim • Prolonged incident
Category 2	•All other cases

[11] **STEP TWO Starting point and category range** **SG14-15**

Having determined the category at step one, the court should use the corresponding starting point to reach a sentence within the category range below. The starting point applies to all offenders irrespective of plea or previous convictions. A case of particular gravity, reflected by multiple features of culpability or harm in step one, could merit upward adjustment from the starting point before further adjustment for aggravating or mitigating features, set out on the next page.

	Culpability	
Harm	**A**	**B**
Category 1	**Starting point** 2 years' custody	**Starting point** 1 year 6 months' custody
	Category range 1 year 6 months'–3 years' custody	**Category range** 1–2 years' custody
Category 2	**Starting point** 15 months' custody	**Starting point** 6 months' custody
	Category range 9 months'–2 years' custody	**Category range** 6 months'–1 year 6 months' custody

[12] The table below contains a **non-exhaustive** list of additional factual elements providing the context of the offence and factors relating to the offender. Identify whether any combination of these, or other relevant factors, should result in an upward or downward adjustment from the sentence arrived at so far. In particular, relevant recent convictions are likely to result in an upward adjustment. In some cases, having considered these factors, it may be appropriate to move outside the identified category range.

[12]

Factors increasing seriousness
Statutory aggravating factors: Previous convictions, having regard to a) the **nature** of the offence to which the conviction relates and its **relevance** to the current offence; and b) the **time** that has elapsed since the conviction Offence committed whilst on bail *Other aggravating factors:* Victim is targeted due to a vulnerability (or a perceived vulnerability) Offence was committed as part of a group or gang Attempts to conceal identity Commission of offence whilst under the influence of alcohol or drugs Attempts to conceal/dispose of evidence Offence committed against those working in the public sector or providing a service to the public Steps taken to prevent the victim reporting or obtaining assistance and/or from assisting or supporting the prosecution Failure to comply with current court orders Offence committed on licence or post sentence supervision Offences taken into consideration Failure to respond to warnings about behaviour

Factors reducing seriousness or reflecting personal mitigation
No previous convictions **or** no relevant/recent convictions Good character and/or exemplary conduct Serious medical condition requiring urgent, intensive or long-term treatment Age and/or lack of maturity where it affects the responsibility of the offender Mental disorder or learning disability (where not linked to the commission of the offence) Little or no planning Sole or primary carer for dependent relatives Co-operation with the police

SG14-16 **STEP THREE Minimum Terms** [13]

When sentencing these offences a court must impose a sentence of at least 6 months imprisonment unless the court is of the opinion that there are particular circumstances relating to the offence or the offender which make it unjust to do so in all the circumstances.

Unjust in all of the circumstances

In considering whether a statutory minimum sentence would be 'unjust in all of the circumstances' the court must have regard to the particular circumstances of the offence and the offender. If the circumstances of the offence or the offender make it unjust to impose the statutory minimum sentence then the court **must impose either a shorter custodial sentence than the statutory minimum provides or an alternative sentence.**

The offence:

Having reached this stage of the guideline the court should have made a provisional assessment of the seriousness of the offence. Where the court has determined that the offence seriousness falls far below the custodial threshold the court may consider it unjust to impose the statutory minimum sentence.

The offender:

The court should consider the following factors to determine whether it would be unjust to impose the statutory minimum sentence;

- any strong personal mitigation;
- whether there is a realistic prospect of rehabilitation;
- whether custody will result in significant impact on others.

SG14-17 **STEP FOUR Consider any factors which indicate a reduction for assistance to the prosecution**

The court should take into account sections 73 and 74 of the Serious Organised Crime and Police Act 2005 (assistance by defendants: reduction or review of sentence) and any other rule of law by virtue of which an offender may receive a discounted sentence in consequence of assistance given (or offered) to the prosecutor or investigator.

[13] **STEP FIVE Reduction for guilty pleas** SG14-18

The court should take account of any potential reduction for a guilty plea in accordance with section 144 of the Criminal Justice Act 2003 and the Guilty Plea guideline.

Where a statutory minimum sentence has been imposed, the court must ensure that any reduction for a guilty plea does not reduce the sentence to less than 80 per cent of the statutory minimum.

[14] **STEP SIX Totality principle** SG14-19

If sentencing an offender for more than one offence, or where the offender is already serving a sentence, consider whether the total sentence is just and proportionate to the overall offending behaviour in accordance with the Offences Taken into Consideration and Totality guideline.

STEP SEVEN Ancillary Orders SG14-20

In all cases the court should consider whether to make ancillary orders.

STEP EIGHT Reasons SG14-21

Section 174 of the Criminal Justice Act 2003 imposes a duty to give reasons for, and explain the effect of, the sentence.

STEP NINE Consideration for time spent on bail SG14-22

The court must consider whether to give credit for time spent on bail in accordance with section 240A of the Criminal Justice Act 2003.

[15]

BLADED ARTICLES AND OFFENSIVE WEAPONS (POSSESSION AND THREATS) – CHILDREN AND YOUNG PEOPLE SG14-23

This guideline should be read alongside the *Overarching Principles- Sentencing Children and Young People* definitive guideline which provides comprehensive guidance on the sentencing principles and welfare considerations that the court should have in mind when sentencing children and young people.

The offence is subject to statutory minimum sentencing provisions. See STEP FIVE for further details.

The first step in determining the sentence is to assess the seriousness of the offence. This assessment is made by considering the nature of the offence and any aggravating and mitigating factors relating to the offence itself. **The fact that a sentence threshold is crossed does not necessarily mean that that sentence should be imposed.**

STEP ONE Offence Seriousness – Nature of the offence SG14-24

The boxes below give examples of the type of culpability and harm factors that may indicate that a particular threshold of sentence has been crossed.

A non-custodial sentence* may be the most suitable disposal where one or more of the following factors apply:
Possession of weapon falls just short of reasonable excuse
No/minimal risk of weapon being used to threaten or cause harm
Fleeting incident and no/minimal distress

A custodial sentence or youth rehabilitation order with intensive supervision and surveillance* or fostering* may be justified where one or more of the following factors apply:
Possession of a bladed article whether produced or not
Possession of a highly dangerous weapon† whether produced or not
Offence motivated by, or demonstrating hostility based on any of the following characteristics or presumed characteristics of the victim: religion, race, disability, sexual orientation or transgender identity
Prolonged incident and serious alarm/distress
Offence committed at a school or other place where vulnerable people may be present

[16] *Where the child or young person appears in the magistrates' court, and the conditions for a compulsory referral order apply, a referral order must be imposed unless the court is considering imposing a discharge, hospital order or custody.

†N B an offensive weapon is defined in legislation as 'any article made or adapted for use for causing injury, or is intended by the person having it with him for such use'. A highly dangerous weapon is, therefore, a weapon, including a corrosive substance (such as acid), whose dangerous nature must be substantially above and beyond this. The court must determine whether the weapon is highly dangerous on the facts and circumstances of the case.

SG14-25 **STEP TWO Offence Seriousness – Aggravating and mitigating factors** [16]

To complete the assessment of seriousness the court should consider the aggravating and mitigating factors relevant to the offence.

Aggravating factors
Statutory aggravating factors: Previous findings of guilt, having regard to a) the **nature** of the offence to which the finding of guilt relates and its **relevance** to the current offence; and b) the **time** that has elapsed since the finding of guilt (unless the convictions will be relevant for the purposes of the statutory minimum sentencing provisions – see step five) Offence committed whilst on bail *Other aggravating factors (non-exhaustive):* Significant degree of planning /premeditation Deliberate humiliation of victim, including but not limited to filming of the offence, deliberately committing the offence before a group of peers with the intent of causing additional distress or circulating details/photos/ videos etc of the offence on social media or within peer groups Victim is particularly vulnerable due to factors including but not limited to age, mental or physical disability Offence was committed as part of a group or gang Attempts to conceal identity Steps taken to prevent reporting the incident/seeking assistance Commission of offence whilst under the influence of alcohol or drugs Offence committed against those working in the public sector or providing a service to the public

Mitigating factors (non-exhaustive)
No findings of guilt **or** no relevant/recent findings of guilt Good character and/or exemplary conduct Participated in offence due to bullying, peer pressure, coercion or manipulation Little or no planning Co-operation with the police

SG14-26 **STEP THREE Personal Mitigation** [17]

Having assessed the offence seriousness the court should then consider the mitigation personal to the child or young person to determine whether a custodial sentence or a community sentence is necessary. The effect of personal mitigation may reduce what would otherwise be a custodial sentence to a non-custodial one or a community sentence to a different means of disposal.

Personal mitigating factors (non-exhaustive)
Particularly young or immature child or young person (where it affects their responsibility) Communication or learning disabilities or mental health concerns Unstable upbringing including but not limited to:- • time spent looked after • lack of familial presence or support • disrupted experiences in accommodation or education • exposure to drug/alcohol abuse, familial criminal behaviour or domestic abuse • victim of neglect or abuse, or exposure to neglect or abuse of others • experiences of trauma or loss Determination and/or demonstration of steps taken to address offending behaviour Child or young person in education, training or employment

SG14-27 **STEP FOUR Reduction for guilty pleas**

The court should take account of any potential reduction for a guilty plea in accordance with section 144 of the Criminal Justice Act 2003 and part one, section five of the Overarching Principles – Sentencing Children and Young People definitive guideline.

The reduction in sentence for a guilty plea can be taken into account by imposing one type of sentence rather than another; for example:

- by reducing a custodial sentence to a community sentence, or
- by reducing a community sentence to a different means of disposal.

[17] Alternatively the court could reduce the length or severity of any punitive requirements attached to a community sentence.

See the Overarching Principles – Sentencing Children and Young People definitive guideline for details of other available sentences including Referral Orders and Reparation Orders.

[18] **STEP FIVE Statutory minimum sentencing provisions** **SG14-28**

The following provisions apply to those young people who were aged 16 or over on the date of the offence[209]

Threatening with Bladed Articles or Offensive Weapons

When sentencing these offences a court must impose a sentence of at least 4 months Detention and Training Order unless the court is of the opinion that there are particular circumstances relating to the offence, the previous offence or the young person which make it unjust to do so in all the circumstances.

Possession of Bladed Articles or Offensive Weapons

When sentencing the offences of:

- possession of an offensive weapon in a public place;
- possession of an article with a blade/point in a public place;
- possession of an offensive weapon on school premises; and
- possession of an article with blade/point on school premises a court must impose a sentence of at least 4 months' Detention and Training Order where this is a second or further relevant offence unless the court is of the opinion that there are particular circumstances relating to the offence, any previous relevant offence or the young person which make it unjust to do so in all the circumstances.

A 'relevant offence' includes those offences listed above and the following offences:

- threatening with an offensive weapon in a public place;
- threatening with an article with a blade/point in a public place;
- threatening with an article with a blade/point on school premises; and
- threatening with an offensive weapon on school premises.

[19] **Unjust in all of the circumstances**

In considering whether a statutory minimum sentence would be 'unjust in all of the circumstances' the court must have regard to the particular circumstances of the offence, any relevant previous offence and the young person. If the circumstances make it unjust to impose the statutory minimum sentence then the court must impose an alternative sentence.

The offence:

Having reached this stage of the guideline the court should have made a provisional assessment of the seriousness of the offence. Where the court has determined that the offence seriousness falls far below the custody threshold the court may consider it unjust to impose the statutory minimum sentence.

Where the court is considering a statutory minimum sentence as a result of a second or further relevant offence, consideration should be given to the seriousness of the previous offence(s) and the period of time that has elapsed between offending. Where the seriousness of the combined offences is such that it falls far below the custody threshold, or where there has been a significant period of time between the offences, the court may consider it unjust to impose the statutory minimum sentence.

The young person:

The statutory obligation to have regard to the welfare of a young person includes the obligation to secure proper provision for education and training, to remove the young person from undesirable surroundings where appropriate, and the need to choose the best option for the young person taking account of the circumstances of the offence.

In having regard to the welfare of the young person, a court should ensure that it considers:

- any mental health problems or learning difficulties/disabilities;

[209] The age of the young person at the date of the earlier offence(s) is irrelevant

- any experiences of brain injury or traumatic life experience (including exposure to drug and alcohol abuse) and the developmental impact this may have had; [19]
- any speech and language difficulties and the effect this may have on the ability of the young person (or any accompanying adult) to communicate with the court, to understand the sanction imposed or to fulfil the obligations resulting from that sanction;
- the vulnerability of young people to self harm, particularly within a custodial environment; and
- the effect on young people of experiences of loss and neglect and/or abuse.

In certain cases the concerns about the welfare of the young person may be so significant that the court considers it unjust to impose the statutory minimum sentence.

SG14-29 STEP SIX **Review the sentence** [20]

The court must now review the sentence to ensure it is the most appropriate one for the child or young person. This will include an assessment of the likelihood of reoffending and the risk of causing serious harm. A report from the Youth Offending Team may assist.

See the Overarching Principles – Sentencing Children and Young People definitive guideline for comprehensive guidance on the sentencing principles and welfare considerations that the court should have in mind when sentencing children and young people, and for the full range of sentences available to the court.

Referral Orders

In cases where children or young people have offended for the first time and have pleaded guilty to committing an offence which is on the cusp of the custody threshold, youth offending teams (YOT) should be encouraged to convene a Youth Offender Panel prior to sentence (sometimes referred to as a "pseudo-panel" or "pre-panel") where the child or young person is asked to attend before a panel and agree an intensive contract. If that contract is placed before the sentencing youth court, the court can then decide whether it is sufficient to move below custody on this occasion. The proposed contract is not something the court can alter in any way; the court will still have to make a decision between referral order and custody but can do so on the basis that if it makes a referral order it can have confidence in what that will entail in the particular case.

The court determines the length of the order but a Referral Order Panel determines the requirements of the order.

Offence seriousness	Suggested length of referral order
Low	3–5 months
Medium	5–7 months
High	7–9 months
Very high	10–12 months

The YOT may propose certain requirements and the length of these requirements may not correspond to the above table; if the court feels these requirements will best achieve the aims of the youth justice system then they may still be imposed.

Youth Rehabilitation Order (YRO) [21]

The following table sets out the different levels of intensity that are available under a Youth Rehabilitation Order. The level of intensity and the content of the order will depend upon the court's assessment of seriousness.

Requirements of order		
Standard	Low likelihood of re-offending **and** a low risk of serious harm	Primarily seek to repair harm caused through, for example: • reparation; • unpaid work; • supervision; and/or • attendance centre.
Enhanced	Medium likelihood of re-offending **or** a medium risk of serious harm	Seek to repair harm caused and to enable help or change through, for example: • supervision; • reparation; • requirement to address behaviour e.g. drug treatment, offending behaviour programme, education programme; and/or • a combination of the above

[21]

Requirements of order		
Intensive	High likelihood of re-offending **or** a very high risk of serious harm	Seek to ensure the control of and enable help or change for the child or young person through, for example: • supervision; • reparation; • requirement to address behaviour; • requirement to monitor or restrict movement, e.g. prohibited activity, curfew, exclusion or electronic monitoring; and/or • a combination of the above

YRO with Intensive Supervision and Surveillance (ISS) or YRO with fostering

A YRO with an ISS or fostering requirement can only be imposed where the court is of the opinion that the offence has crossed the custody threshold and custody is merited.

The YRO with ISS includes an extended activity requirement, a supervision requirement and curfew. The YRO with fostering requires the child or young person to reside with a local authority foster parent for a specified period of up to 12 months.

Custodial Sentences

If a custodial sentence is imposed, the court must state its reasons for being satisfied that the offence is so serious that no other sanction would be appropriate and, in particular, why a YRO with ISS or fostering could not be justified.

Where a custodial sentence is unavoidable the length of custody imposed must be the shortest commensurate with the seriousness of the offence. The court may want to consider the equivalent adult guideline in order to determine the appropriate length of the sentence.

If considering the adult guideline, the court may feel it appropriate to apply a sentence broadly within the region of half to two thirds of the appropriate adult sentence for those aged 15–17 and allow a greater reduction for those aged under 15. This is only a rough guide and must not be applied mechanistically. The individual factors relating to the offence and the child or young person are of the greatest importance and may present good reason to impose a sentence outside of this range.

[22] ANNEX: FINE BANDS AND COMMUNITY ORDERS SG14-30

Fine Bands

In this guideline, fines are expressed as one of three fine bands (A, B, C).

Fine Band	**Starting point** (applicable to all offenders)	**Category range** (applicable to all offenders)
Band A	50% of relevant weekly income	25–75% of relevant weekly income
Band B	100% of relevant weekly income	75–125% of relevant weekly income
Band C	150% of relevant weekly income	125–175% of relevant weekly income

[23] **Community Orders**

In this guideline, community sentences are expressed as one of three levels (low, medium and high).

An illustrative description of examples of requirements that might be appropriate for each level is provided below. Where two or more requirements are ordered, they must be compatible with each other. Save in exceptional circumstances, the court must impose at least one requirement for the purpose of punishment, or combine the community order with a fine, or both (see section 177 Criminal Justice Act 2003).

The Magistrates' Court Sentencing Guidelines includes further guidance on fines. The table set out here is also set out in the Imposition of Community and Custodial Sentences Guideline, which includes further guidance on community orders: see **SG9-4**.

PART 15 BREACH OFFENCES

SG15-1 DEFINITIVE GUIDELINE [2]

Applicability of guideline

In accordance with section 120 of the Coroners and Justice Act 2009, the Sentencing Council issues this definitive guideline. It applies to all offenders aged 18 and older, who are sentenced on or after 1 October 2018, regardless of the date of the offence.

Section 125(1) Coroners and Justice Act 2009 provides that when sentencing offences committed after 6 April 2010:

Every court –
(a) must, in sentencing an offender, follow any sentencing guidelines which are relevant to the offender's case, and
(b) must, in exercising any other function relating to the sentencing of offenders, follow any sentencing guidelines which are relevant to the exercise of the function, unless the court is satisfied that it would be contrary to the interests of justice to do so.

This guideline applies only to offenders aged 18 and older.

SG15-2 **Structure, ranges and starting points**

For the purposes of section 125(3)–(4) of the Coroners and Justice Act 2009, the guideline specifies offence ranges – the range of sentences appropriate for each type of offence. Within each offence, the Council has specified a number of categories which reflect varying degrees of seriousness. The offence range is split into category ranges – sentences appropriate for each level of seriousness. The Council has also identified a starting point within each category.

Starting points define the position within a category range from which to start calculating the provisional sentence. The court should consider further features of the offence or the offender that warrant adjustment of the sentence within the range, including the aggravating and mitigating factors set out at step two. Starting points and ranges apply to all offenders, whether they have pleaded guilty or been convicted after trial.

Credit for a guilty plea is taken into consideration only at step four in the decision making process, after the appropriate sentence has been identified.

Information on community orders is set out in the annex at [SG15-50].

SG15-3 BREACH OF A COMMUNITY ORDER [3]

SG15-4 *Criminal Justice Act 2003 (Schedule 8)*

SG15-5 **Breach of community order by failing to comply with requirements** [4]

The court must take into account the extent to which the offender has complied with the requirements of the community order when imposing a penalty.

In assessing the level of compliance with the order the court should consider:

i) the overall attitude and engagement with the order as well as the proportion of elements completed;
ii) the impact of any completed or partially completed requirements on the offender's behaviour;
iii) the proximity of breach to imposition of order; and
iv) evidence of circumstances or offender characteristics, such as disability, mental health issues or learning difficulties which have impeded offender's compliance with the order.

Overall compliance with order	**Penalty**
Wilful and persistent non-compliance	Revoke the order and re-sentence imposing custodial sentence (even where the offence seriousness did not originally merit custody)
Low level of compliance	Revoke the order and re-sentence original offence **OR** Add curfew requirement 20–30 days* **OR** 30–50 hours additional unpaid work/extend length of order/add additional requirement(s) **OR** Band C fine

[4]

Overall compliance with order	Penalty
Medium level of compliance	Revoke the order and resentence original offence **OR** Add curfew requirement 10–20 days* **OR** 20–30 hours additional unpaid work/extend length of order/add additional requirement(s) **OR** Band B fine
High level of compliance	Add curfew requirement 6–10 days* **OR** 10–20 hours additional unpaid work/extend length of order/add additional requirement(s) **OR** Band A fine

* curfew days do not have to be consecutive and may be distributed over particular periods, for example at weekends, as the court deems appropriate. The period of the curfew should not exceed the duration of the community order and cannot be for longer than 12 months.

[5] **Technical guidance** SG15-6

a) If imposing more onerous requirements the length of the order may be extended up to 3 years or six months longer than the previous length, which ever is longer (but only once).
b) If imposing unpaid work as a more onerous requirement and an unpaid work requirement was not previously included, the minimum number of hours that can be imposed is 20.
c) The maximum fine that can be imposed is £2,500.
d) If re-sentencing, a suspended sentence **MUST NOT** be imposed as a more severe alternative to a community order. A suspended sentence may only be imposed if it is fully intended that the offender serve a custodial sentence in accordance with the Imposition of Community and Custodial Sentences guideline.
e) Where the order was imposed by the Crown Court, magistrates should consider their sentencing powers in dealing with a breach. Where the judge imposing the order reserved any breach proceedings commit the breach for sentence.

Powers of the court following a subsequent conviction SG15-7

A conviction for a further offence does not constitute a breach of a community order. However, in such a situation, the court should consider the following guidance from the ***Offences Taken into Consideration and Totality*** guideline:[210]

Offender convicted of an offence while serving a community order

The power to deal with the offender depends on his being convicted whilst the order is still in force; it does not arise where the order has expired, even if the additional offence was committed whilst it was still current.

If an offender, in respect of whom a community order made by a magistrates' court is in force, is convicted by a magistrates' court of an additional offence, the magistrates' court should ordinarily revoke the previous community order and sentence afresh for both the original and the additional offence.

Where an offender, in respect of whom a community order made by a Crown Court is in force, is convicted by a magistrates' court, the magistrates' court may, and ordinarily should, commit the offender to the Crown Court, in order to allow the Crown Court to re-sentence for the original offence and the additional offence.

The sentencing court should consider the overall seriousness of the offending behaviour taking into account the additional offence and the original offence. The court should consider whether the combination of associated offences is sufficiently serious to justify a custodial sentence.

If the court does not consider that custody is necessary, it should impose a single community order that reflects the overall totality of criminality. The court must take into account the extent to which the offender complied with the requirements of the previous order.

[210] https://www.sentencingcouncil.org.uk/wp-content/uploads/Definitive_guideline_TICs__totality_Final_web.pdf p.14

SG15-8 ## Breach of a Suspended Sentence Order [7]

SG15-9 *Criminal Justice Act 2003 (Schedule 12)*

SG15-10 **Breach of a suspended sentence order** [8]

1) Conviction for further offence committed during operational period of order

The court must activate the custodial sentence unless it would be unjust in all the circumstances to do so. The predominant factor in determining whether activation is unjust relates to the level of compliance with the suspended sentence order and the facts/nature of any new offence. **These factors are already provided for in the penalties below which are determined by the nature of the new offence and level of compliance, but permit a reduction to the custodial term for relevant completed or partially completed requirements where appropriate.**

The facts/nature of the new offence is the primary consideration in assessing the action to be taken on the breach.

Where the breach is in the second or third category below, the prior level of compliance is also relevant. In assessing the level of compliance with the order the court should consider:

i) the overall attitude and engagement with the order as well as the proportion of elements completed;
ii) the impact of any completed or partially completed requirements on the offender's behaviour;
iii) the proximity of breach to imposition of order; and
iv) evidence of circumstances or offender characteristics, such as disability, mental health issues or learning difficulties which have impeded offender's compliance with the order.

Breach involves	**Penalty**
Multiple and/or more serious new offence(s) committed	Full activation of original custodial term
New offence similar in type and gravity to offence for which suspended sentence order imposed and: a) No/low level of compliance with suspended sentence order **OR** b) Medium or High level of compliance with suspended sentence order	Full activation of original custodial term Activate sentence but apply appropriate reduction* to original custodial term taking into consideration any unpaid work or curfew requirements completed
New offence less serious than original offence but requires a custodial sentence and: a) No/low level of compliance with suspended sentence order **OR** b) Medium or high level of compliance with suspended sentence order	Full activation of original custodial term Activate sentence but apply appropriate reduction* to original custodial term taking into consideration any unpaid work or curfew requirements completed
New offence does not require custodial sentence	Activate sentence but apply reduction* to original custodial term taking into consideration any unpaid work or curfew requirements completed **OR** Impose more onerous requirement(s) and/or extend supervision period and/ or extend operational period and/or impose fine

*It is for the court dealing with the breach to identify the appropriate proportionate reduction depending on the extent of any compliance with the requirements specified

SG15-11 **Unjust in all the circumstances** [9]

The court dealing with the breach should remember that the court imposing the original sentence determined that a custodial sentence was appropriate in the original case.

In determining if there are other factors which would cause activation to be unjust, the court may consider all factors including:

- any strong personal mitigation;
- whether there is a realistic prospect of rehabilitation;
- whether immediate custody will result in significant impact on others.

[9] Only new and exceptional factors/circumstances not present at the time the suspended sentence order was imposed should be taken into account.

In cases where the court considers that it would be unjust to order the custodial sentence to take effect, it must state its reasons and it must deal with the offender in one of the following ways:

(a) impose a fine not exceeding £2,500; OR
(b) extend the operational period (to a maximum of two years from date of original sentence); OR
(c) if the SSO imposes community requirements, do one or more of:
 (i) impose more onerous community requirements;
 (ii) extend the supervision period (to a maximum of two years from date of original sentence);
 (iii) extend the operational period (to a maximum of two years from date of original sentence).

[10] 2) Failure to comply with a community requirement during the supervision period of the order

The court must activate the custodial sentence unless it would be unjust in all the circumstances to do so. The predominant factor in determining whether activation is unjust relates to the level of compliance with the suspended sentence order. This factor is already provided for in the penalties below which are determined by the level of compliance, but permit a reduction to the custodial term for relevant completed or partially completed requirements where appropriate.

The court must take into account the extent to which the offender has complied with the suspended sentence order when imposing a sentence.

In assessing the level of compliance with the order the court should consider:

i) the overall attitude and engagement with the order as well as the proportion of elements completed;
ii) the impact of any completed or partially completed requirements on the offender's behaviour; and
iii) the proximity of breach to imposition of order; and
iv) evidence of circumstances or offender characteristics, such as disability, mental health issues or learning difficulties which have impeded offender's compliance with the order.

Breach involves	Penalty
No/low level of compliance	Full activation of original custodial term
Medium level of compliance	Activate sentence but apply reduction* to original custodial term taking into consideration any unpaid work or curfew requirements completed
High level of compliance	Activate sentence but apply reduction* to original custodial term taking into consideration any unpaid work or curfew requirements completed OR Impose more onerous requirement(s) and/or extend supervision period and/ or extend operational period and/or impose fine

*It is for the court dealing with the breach to identify the appropriate proportionate reduction depending on the extent of any compliance with the requirements specified

[11] **Unjust in all the circumstances** SG15-12

The court dealing with the breach should remember that the court imposing the original sentence determined that a custodial sentence was appropriate in the original case.

In determining if there are other factors which would cause activation to be unjust, the court may consider all factors including:

- any strong personal mitigation;
- whether there is a realistic prospect of rehabilitation;
- whether immediate custody will result in significant impact on others.

Only new and exceptional factors/circumstances not present at the time the suspended sentence order was imposed should be taken into account.

In cases where the court considers that it would be unjust to order the custodial sentence to take effect, it must state its reasons and it must deal with the offender in one of the following ways:

(a) impose a fine not exceeding £2,500; OR
(b) extend the operational period (to a maximum of two years from date of original sentence); OR

(c) if the SSO imposes community requirements, do one or more of: [11]
 (i) impose more onerous community requirements;
 (ii) extend the supervision period (to a maximum of two years from date of original sentence);
 (iii) extend the operational period (to a maximum of two years from date of original sentence).

SG15-13 BREACH OF POST-SENTENCE SUPERVISION [13]

SG15-14 *Criminal Justice Act 2003 (section 256AC and Schedule 19A)*

SG15-15 **Breach of post-sentence supervision** [14]

Where the court determines a penalty is appropriate for a breach of a post sentence supervision requirement it must take into account the extent to which the offender has complied with all of the requirements of the post-sentence supervision or supervision default order when imposing a penalty.

In assessing the level of compliance with the order the court should consider:

i) the offender's overall attitude and engagement with the order as well as the proportion of elements completed;
ii) the impact of any completed or partially completed requirements on the offender's behaviour;
iii) the proximity of the breach to the imposition of the order; and
iv) evidence of circumstances or offender characteristics, such as disability, mental health issues or learning difficulties which have impeded offender's compliance with the order.

Level of Compliance	Penalty
Low	Up to 7 days' committal to custody **OR** Supervision default order in range of 30–40 hours unpaid work **OR** 8–12 hour curfew for minimum of 20 days
Medium	Supervision default order in range of 20–30 hours unpaid work **OR** 4–8 hour curfew for minimum of 20 days **OR** Band B fine
High	Band A fine

Breach of supervision default order

Level of Compliance	Penalty
Low	Revoke supervision default order and order up to 14 days' committal to custody
Medium	Revoke supervision default order and impose new order in range of 40–60 hours unpaid work **OR** 8–16 hour curfew for minimum of 20 days
High	Band B fine

i) A supervision default order must include either:

an unpaid work requirement of between 20 hours–60 hours

OR

a curfew requirement for between 2–16 hours for a minimum of 20 days and no longer than the end of the post sentence supervision period.

ii) The maximum fine which can be imposed is £1,000.

SG15-16 FAILURE TO SURRENDER TO BAIL [15]

Bail Act 1976 (section 6)

Triable either way
Maximum: 12 months' custody
Offence range: Discharge–26 weeks' custody

[16] **STEP ONE Determining the offence category** SG15-17

The court should determine the offence category with reference only to the factors listed in the tables below. In order to determine the category the court should assess **culpability** and **harm.**

Culpability	
A	**Failure to surrender represents deliberate attempt to evade or delay justice**
B	**Cases falling between categories A and C**
C	**Reason for failure to surrender just short of reasonable cause**

Harm

The level of **harm** is determined by weighing up all the factors of the case to determine the harm that has been caused or was intended to be caused.

Category 1	Failure to attend Crown Court hearing results in substantial delay and/or interference with the administration of justice
Category 2	Failure to attend magistrates' court hearing results in substantial delay and/or interference with the administration of justice*
Category 3	Cases in either the magistrates' court or Crown Court not in categories 1 and 2

* In particularly serious cases where the failure to attend is in the magistrates' court and the consequences of the delay have a severe impact on victim(s) and /or witness(es) warranting a sentence outside of the powers of the magistrates' court, the case should be committed to the Crown Court pursuant to section 6(6)(a) of the Bail Act 1976 and the Crown Court should sentence the case according to the range in Category A1.

[17] **STEP TWO Starting point and category range** SG15-18

Having determined the category at step one, the court should use the corresponding starting point to reach a sentence within the category range from the appropriate sentence table below. The starting point applies to all offenders irrespective of plea or previous convictions.

Where a custodial sentence is available within the category range and the substantive offence attracts a custodial sentence, a consecutive custodial sentence should normally be imposed for the failure to surrender offence.

	Culpability		
Harm	**A**	**B**	**C**
Category 1	**Starting point** 6 weeks' custody	**Starting point** 21 days' custody	**Starting point** Medium level community order*
	Category range 28 days'–26 weeks' custody[1]	**Category range** High level community order*–13 weeks' custody	**Category range** Low level community order*–6 weeks' custody
Category 2	**Starting point** 21 days' custody	**Starting point** Medium level community order*	**Starting point** Band B fine
	Category range High level community order*–13 weeks' custody	**Category range** Band B fine–6 weeks' custody	**Category range** Band A fine–Low level community order*
Category 3	**Starting point** 14 days' custody	**Starting point** Band C fine	**Starting point** Band A fine
	Category range Low level community order*–6 weeks' custody	**Category range** Band A fine–Medium level community order*	**Category range** Discharge–Band B fine

Maximum sentence in magistrates' court – 3 months' imprisonment
Maximum sentence in Crown Court – 12 months' imprisonment
* To include a curfew and/or unpaid work requirement only
[1] In A1 cases which are particularly serious and where the consequences of the delay have a severe impact on victim(s) and /or witness(es), a sentence in excess of the specified range may be appropriate.

Sentencing Guidelines

The table below contains a **non-exhaustive** list of additional factual elements providing the context of the offence and factors relating to the offender. Identify whether any combination of these, or other relevant factors, should result in an upward or downward adjustment from the starting point. In some cases, having considered these factors, it may be appropriate to move outside the identified category range. [18]

Factors increasing seriousness
Statutory aggravating factor:
Previous convictions, having regard to a) the **nature** of the offence to which the conviction relates and its **relevance** to the current offence; and b) the **time** that has elapsed since the conviction ***Other aggravating factors:*** History of breach of court orders or police bail Distress to victim(s) and /or witness(es) Offence committed on licence or while subject to post sentence supervision

Factors reducing seriousness or reflecting personal mitigation
Genuine misunderstanding of bail or requirements Prompt voluntary surrender Sole or primary carer for dependent relatives

SG15-19 STEP THREE **Consider any factors which indicate a reduction for assistance to the prosecution** [19]

The court should take into account sections 73 and 74 of the Serious Organised Crime and Police Act 2005 (assistance by defendants: reduction or review of sentence) and any other rule of law by virtue of which an offender may receive a discounted sentence in consequence of assistance given (or offered) to the prosecutor or investigator.

SG15-20 STEP FOUR **Reduction for guilty pleas**

The court should take account of any reduction for a guilty plea in accordance with section 144 of the Criminal Justice Act 2003 and the *Guilty Plea* guideline.

SG15-21 STEP FIVE **Totality principle**

If sentencing an offender for more than one offence, or where the offender is already serving a sentence, consider whether the total sentence is just and proportionate to the overall offending behaviour in accordance with the *Offences Taken into Consideration and Totality* guideline.

SG15-22 STEP SIX **Ancillary orders**

In all cases the court should consider whether to make compensation and/or ancillary orders.

SG15-23 STEP SEVEN **Reasons**

Section 174 of the Criminal Justice Act 2003 imposes a duty to give reasons for, and explain the effect of, the sentence.

SG15-24 STEP EIGHT **Consideration for time spent on bail**

The court must consider whether to give credit for time spent on bail in accordance with section 240A of the Criminal Justice Act 2003.

SG15-25 Breach of a Protective Order (Restraining and Non-Molestation Orders) [21]

Restraining orders: Protections from Harassment Act 1997 (section 5(5) and (5A))

Non-molestation orders: Family Law Act 1996 (section 42A)

Triable either way
Maximum: 5 years' custody
Offence range: Fine–4 years' custody

[22] **STEP ONE Determining the offence category** SG15-26

The court should determine the offence category with reference only to the factors listed in the tables below. In order to determine the category the court should assess **culpability** and **harm.**

Culpability

In assessing culpability, the court should consider the intention and motivation of the offender in committing any breach.

A	• Very serious and/or persistent breach
B	• Deliberate breach falling between A and C
C	• Minor breach • Breach just short of reasonable excuse

Harm

The level of harm is determined by weighing up all the factors of the case to determine the harm that has been caused or was intended to be caused.

Category 1	Breach causes **very** serious harm or distress
Category 2	Cases falling between categories 1 and 3
Category 3	Breach causes little or no harm or distress*

* where a breach is committed in the context of a background of domestic abuse, the sentencer should take care not to underestimate the harm which may be present in a breach

[23] **STEP TWO Starting point and category range** SG15-27

Having determined the category at step one, the court should use the corresponding starting point to reach a sentence within the category range from the appropriate sentence table below. The starting point applies to all offenders irrespective of plea or previous convictions.

	Culpability		
Harm	**A**	**B**	**C**
Category 1	**Starting point** 2 years' custody	**Starting point** 1 year's custody	**Starting point** 12 weeks' custody
	Category range 1–4 years' custody	**Category range** High level community order–2 years' custody	**Category range** Medium level community order–1 year's custody
Category 2	**Starting point** 1 year's custody	**Starting point** 12 weeks' custody	**Starting point** High level community order
	Category range High level community order–2 years' custody	**Category range** Medium level community order–1 year's custody	**Category range** Low level community order–26 weeks' custody
Category 3	**Starting point** 12 weeks' custody	**Starting point** High level community order	**Starting point** Low level community order
	Category range Medium level community order–1 year's custody	**Category range** Low level community order–26 weeks' custody	**Category range** Band B fine–High level community order

The table above refers to single offences. Where there are multiple offences consecutive sentences may be appropriate – please refer to the ***Offences Taken Into Consideration and Totality*** guideline.

[24] The table below contains a non-exhaustive list of additional factual elements providing the context of the offence and factors relating to the offender. Identify whether any combination of these, or other relevant factors, should result in an upward or downward adjustment from the starting point. In some cases, having considered these factors, it may be appropriate to move outside the identified category range.

Factors increasing seriousness
Statutory aggravating factors: Previous convictions, having regard to a) the **nature** of the offence to which the conviction relates and its **relevance** to the current offence; and b) the **time** that has elapsed since the conviction Offence committed whilst on bail ***Other aggravating factors:*** Breach committed shortly after order made History of disobedience to court orders (where not already taken into account as a previous conviction) Breach involves a further offence (where not separately prosecuted) Using contact arrangements with a child/children to instigate offence and/or proven history of violence or threats by offender Breach results in victim or protected person being forced to leave their home Impact upon children or family members Victim or protected subject of order breached is particularly vulnerable Offender takes steps to prevent victim or subject harmed by breach from reporting an incident or seeking assistance Offence committed on licence or while subject to post sentence supervision

[24]

Factors reducing seriousness or reflecting personal mitigation
Breach committed after long period of compliance Prompt voluntary surrender/admission of breach or failure Age and/or lack of maturity where it affects the responsibility of the offender Mental disorder or learning disability where linked to the commission of the offence Sole or primary carer for dependent relatives Contact not initiated by offender – a careful examination of all the circumstances is required before weight is given to this factor

SG15-28 STEPS THREE TO EIGHT [25]

[These are in the same terms as those applicable to failure to surrender to bail: see **SG15-16 *et seq*.**]

SG15-29 [27]

Breach of a Criminal Behaviour Order (Also Applicable to Breach of an Anti-Social Behaviour Order)

Anti-Social Behaviour, Crime and Policing Act 2014 (section 30)

Triable either way
Maximum: 5 years' custody
Offence range: Fine–4 years' custody

SG15-30 STEP ONE **Determining the offence category** [28]

The court should determine the offence category with reference only to the factors listed in the tables below. In order to determine the category the court should assess **culpability** and **harm.**

Culpability

In assessing culpability, the court should consider the intention and motivation of the offender in committing any breach.

A	• Very serious and/or persistent breach
B	• Deliberate breach falling between A and C
C	• Minor breach • Breach just short of reasonable excuse

[28] **Harm**

The level of harm is determined by weighing up all the factors of the case to determine the harm that has been caused or was at risk of being caused.

In assessing any risk of harm posed by the breach, consideration should be given to the original offence(s) or activity for which the order was imposed and the circumstances in which the breach arose.

Category 1	• Breach causes very serious harm or distress • Breach demonstrates a continuing risk of serious criminal and/or anti-social behaviour
Category 2	• Cases falling between categories 1 and 3
Category 3	• Breach causes little or no harm or distress • Breach demonstrates a continuing risk of minor criminal and/or anti-social behaviour

[29] **STEP TWO Starting point and category range** **SG15-31**

Having determined the category at step one, the court should use the corresponding starting point to reach a sentence within the category range from the appropriate sentence table below. The starting point applies to all offenders irrespective of plea or previous convictions.

	Culpability		
Harm	**A**	**B**	**C**
Category 1	**Starting point** 2 years' custody	**Starting point** 1 year's custody	**Starting point** 12 weeks' custody
	Category range 1–4 years' custody	**Category range** High level community order–2 years' custody	**Category range** Medium level community order–1 year's custody
Category 2	**Starting point** 1 year's custody	**Starting point** 12 weeks' custody	**Starting point** High level community order
	Category range High level community order–2 years' custody	**Category range** Medium level community order–1 year's custody	**Category range** Low level community order–26 weeks' custody
Category 3	**Starting point** 12 weeks' custody	**Starting point** High level community order	**Starting point** Low level community order
	Category range Medium level community order–1 year's custody	**Category range** Low level community order–26 weeks' custody	**Category range** Band B fine–High level community order

NOTE: A Conditional Discharge **MAY NOT** be imposed for breach of a criminal behaviour order.

[30] The table below contains a **non-exhaustive** list of additional factual elements providing the context of the offence and factors relating to the offender. Identify whether any combination of these, or other relevant factors, should result in an upward or downward adjustment from the starting point. In some cases, having considered these factors, it may be appropriate to move outside the identified category range.

Factors increasing seriousness
Statutory aggravating factors: Previous convictions, having regard to a) the **nature** of the offence to which the conviction relates and its **relevance** to the current offence; and b) the **time** that has elapsed since the conviction Offence committed whilst on bail ***Other aggravating factors:*** Offence is a further breach, following earlier breach proceedings Breach committed shortly after order made History of disobedience of court orders or orders imposed by local authorities

Breach constitutes a further offence (where not separately prosecuted) Targeting of a person the order was made to protect or a witness in the original proceedings Victim or protected subject of order breached is particularly vulnerable due to age, disability, culture, religion, language, or other factors Offence committed on licence or while subject to post sentence supervision

[30]

Factors reducing seriousness or reflecting personal mitigation
Genuine misunderstanding of terms of order Breach committed after long period of compliance Prompt voluntary surrender/admission of breach or failure Age and/or lack of maturity where it affects the responsibility of the offender Mental disorder or learning disability where linked to the commission of the offence Sole or primary carer for dependent relatives

SG15-32 STEPS THREE TO EIGHT [31]

[These are in the same terms as those applicable to failure to surrender to bail: see **SG15-16** ***et seq.***]

SG15-33 BREACH OF A SEXUAL HARM PREVENTION ORDER (ALSO APPLICABLE TO BREACH OF A SEXUAL OFFENCES PREVENTION ORDER AND TO BREACH OF A FOREIGN TRAVEL ORDER) [33]

Sexual Offences Act 2003 (section 103I)

Triable either way
Maximum: 5 years' custody
Offence range Fine–4 years and 6 months' custody

SG15-34 STEP ONE **Determining the offence category** [34]

The court should determine the offence category with reference only to the factors listed in the tables below. In order to determine the category the court should assess **culpability** and **harm.**

Culpability

In assessing culpability, the court should consider the **intention** and **motivation** of the offender in committing any breach.

A	• Very serious and/or persistent breach
B	• Deliberate breach falling between A and C
C	• Minor breach • Breach just short of reasonable excuse

Harm

The level of **harm** is determined by weighing up all the factors of the case to determine the harm that has been caused or was at risk of being caused.

In assessing any risk of harm posed by the breach, consideration should be given to the original offence(s) or activity for which the order was imposed and the circumstances in which the breach arose.

Category 1	Breach causes or risks very serious harm or distress
Category 2	Cases falling between categories 1 and 3
Category 3	Breach causes or risks little or no harm or distress

[35] **STEP TWO Starting point and category range** **SG15-35**

Having determined the category at step one, the court should use the corresponding starting point to reach a sentence within the category range from the appropriate sentence table below. The starting point applies to all offenders irrespective of plea or previous convictions.

Harm	Culpability		
	A	B	C
Category 1	**Starting point** 3 years' custody	**Starting point** 2 years' custody	**Starting point** 1 year's custody
	Category range 2–4 years 6 months' custody	**Category range** 36 weeks–3 years' custody	**Category range** High level community order–2 years' custody
Category 2	**Starting point** 2 years' custody	**Starting point** 1 year's custody	**Starting point** High level community order
	Category range 36 weeks–3 years' custody	**Category range** High level community order–2 years' custody	**Category range** Medium level community order–26 weeks' custody
Category 3	**Starting point** 1 year's custody	**Starting point** 26 weeks' custody	**Starting point** Medium level community order
	Category range High level community order–2 years' custody	**Category range** Medium level community order–36 weeks' custody	**Category range** Band B fine–High level community order

[36] The table below contains a **non-exhaustive** list of additional factual elements providing the context of the offence and factors relating to the offender. Identify whether any combination of these, or other relevant factors, should result in an upward or downward adjustment from the starting point. In some cases, having considered these factors, it may be appropriate to move outside the identified category range.

Factors increasing seriousness
Statutory aggravating factors:
Previous convictions, having regard to a) the **nature** of the offence to which the conviction relates and its **relevance** to the current offence; and b) the **time** that has elapsed since the conviction
Offence committed whilst on bail
Other aggravating factors:
Breach committed shortly after order made
History of disobedience of court orders or orders imposed by local authorities
Breach constitutes a further offence (where not separately prosecuted)
Targeting of particular individual the order was made to protect
Victim or protected subject of order breached is particularly vulnerable
Offender takes steps to prevent victim or subject harmed by breach from reporting an incident or seeking assistance
Offence committed on licence or while subject to post sentence supervision

Factors reducing seriousness or reflecting personal mitigation
Breach committed after long period of compliance
Prompt voluntary surrender/admission of breach or failure
Age and/or lack of maturity where it affects the responsibility of the offender
Mental disorder or learning disability where linked to the commission of the offence
Sole or primary carer for dependent relatives

SG15-36 **STEPS THREE TO EIGHT** [37]

[These are in the same terms as those applicable to failure to surrender to bail: see **SG15-16** ***et seq.***]

SG15-37 **FAIL TO COMPLY WITH NOTIFICATION REQUIREMENTS** [39]

Sexual Offences Act 2003 (section 91)

Triable either way
Maximum: 5 years' custody
Offence range: Fine–4 years' custody

SG15-38 **STEP ONE Determining the offence category** [40]

The court should determine the offence category with reference only to the factors listed in the tables below. In order to determine the category the court should assess **culpability** and **harm.**

Culpability

In assessing culpability, the court should consider the **intention** and **motivation** of the offender in committing any breach.

A	• Determined attempts to avoid detection • Long period of non compliance
B	• Deliberate failure to comply with requirement
C	• Minor breach • Breach just short of reasonable excuse

Harm

The level of **harm** is determined by weighing up all the factors of the case to determine the harm that has been caused or was at risk of being caused.

In assessing any risk of harm posed by the breach, consideration should be given to the original offence(s) or activity for which the order was imposed and the circumstances in which the breach arose.

Category 1	Breach causes or risks very serious harm or distress
Category 2	Cases falling between categories 1 and 3
Category 3	Breach causes or risks little or no harm or distress

SG15-39 **STEP TWO Starting point and category range** [41]

Having determined the category at step one, the court should use the corresponding starting point to reach a sentence within the category range from the appropriate sentence table below. The starting point applies to all offenders irrespective of plea or previous convictions.

	Culpability		
Harm	**A**	**B**	**C**
Category 1	**Starting point** 2 years' custody	**Starting point** 1 year's custody	**Starting point** 36 weeks' custody
	Category range 1 year's–4 years' custody	**Category range** 26 weeks'–2 years' custody	**Category range** 26 weeks'–1 year 6 months' custody
Category 2	**Starting point** 1 year's custody	**Starting point** 36 weeks' custody	**Starting point** High level community order
	Category range 26 weeks'–2 years' custody	**Category range** 26 weeks'–1 year 6 months' custody	**Category range** Medium level community order–36 weeks' custody
Category 3	**Starting point** 36 weeks' custody	**Starting point** High level community order	**Starting point** Low level community order
	Category range 26 weeks'–1 year 6 months' custody	**Category range** Medium level community order–36 weeks' custody	**Category range** Band B fine–Medium level community order

[42] The table below contains a non-exhaustive list of additional factual elements providing the context of the offence and factors relating to the offender. Identify whether any combination of these, or other relevant factors, should result in an upward or downward adjustment from the starting point. In some cases, having considered these factors, it may be appropriate to move outside the identified category range.

Factors increasing seriousness
Statutory aggravating factors: Previous convictions, having regard to a) the **nature** of the offence to which the conviction relates and its **relevance** to the current offence; and b) the **time** that has elapsed since the conviction Offence committed whilst on bail ***Other aggravating factors:*** Breach committed shortly after order made History of disobedience of court orders or orders imposed by local authorities Breach constitutes a further offence (where not separately prosecuted) Offence committed on licence or while subject to post sentence supervision

Factors reducing seriousness or reflecting personal mitigation
Breach committed after long period of compliance Prompt voluntary surrender/admission of breach or failure Age and/or lack of maturity where it affects the responsibility of the offender Mental disorder or learning disability where linked to the commission of the offence Sole or primary carer for dependent relatives

[43] **STEPS THREE TO EIGHT** SG15-40

[These are in the same terms as those applicable to failure to surrender to bail: see **SG15-16 *et seq*.**]

[45] **BREACH OF DISQUALIFICATION FROM ACTING AS A DIRECTOR** SG15-41

Company Directors Disqualification Act 1986 (section 13)

Triable either way
Maximum: 2 years' custody
Offence range: Discharge–1 year and 6 months' custody

[46] **STEP ONE Determining the offence category** SG15-42

The court should determine the offence category with reference only to the factors listed in the tables below. In order to determine the category the court should assess **culpability and harm.**

Culpability

A	• Breach involves deceit/dishonesty in relation to actual role within company • Breach involves deliberate concealment of disqualified status
B	• All other cases

Harm

The level of **harm** is determined by weighing up all the factors of the case to determine the harm that has been caused or was at risk of being caused.

In assessing any risk of harm posed by the breach, consideration should be given to the original offence(s) or activity for which the order was imposed and the circumstances in which the breach arose.

Sentencing Guidelines

Category 1	Breach results in significant risk of or actual serious financial loss **OR** Breach results in significant risk of or actual serious non-financial harm to company/organisation or others	[46]
Category 2	Cases falling between categories 1 and 3	
Category 3	Breach results in very low risk of or little or no harm (financial or non-financial) to company/organisation or others	

SG15-43 STEP TWO **Starting point and category range** [47]

Having determined the category at step one, the court should use the corresponding starting point to reach a sentence within the category range from the appropriate sentence table below. The starting point applies to all offenders irrespective of plea or previous convictions. The court should then consider further adjustment within the category range for aggravating or mitigating features.

	Culpability	
Harm	**A**	**B**
Category 1	**Starting point** 1 year's custody **Category range** 26 weeks–1 year 6 months' custody	**Starting point** 12 weeks' custody **Category range** High level community order–36 weeks' custody
Category 2	**Starting point** 26 weeks' custody **Category range** 12 weeks'–36 weeks' custody	**Starting point** High level community order **Category range** Medium level community order–26 weeks' custody
Category 3	**Starting point** 12 weeks' custody **Category range** Medium level community order–26 weeks' custody	**Starting point** Medium level community order **Category range** Band C Fine–High level community order

The table below contains a **non-exhaustive** list of additional factual elements providing the context of the offence and factors relating to the offender. Identify whether any combination of these, or other relevant factors, should result in an upward or downward adjustment from the starting point. In some cases, having considered these factors, it may be appropriate to move outside the identified category range. [48]

Factors increasing seriousness
Statutory aggravating factors: Previous convictions, having regard to a) the **nature** of the offence to which the conviction relates and its **relevance** to the current offence; and b) the **time** that has elapsed since the conviction Offence committed whilst on bail ***Other aggravating factors:*** Breach committed shortly after order made Breach continued after warnings received Breach is continued over a sustained period of time Breach involves acting as a director in multiple companies Breach motivated by personal gain Offence committed on licence or while subject to post sentence supervision

[48]

Factors reducing seriousness or reflecting personal mitigation
Breach not motivated by personal gain Breach committed after long period of compliance Genuine misunderstanding of terms of disqualification Evidence of voluntary reparation/compensation made to those suffering loss Breach activity minimal or committed for short duration Age and/or lack of maturity where it affects the responsibility of the offender Mental disorder or learning disability where linked to the commission of the offence Sole or primary carer for dependent relatives

[49] **STEPS THREE TO EIGHT** SG15-44

[These are in the same terms as those applicable to failure to surrender to bail: see **SG15-16** ***et seq.***]

[51] Breach of Disqualification from Keeping an Animal SG15-45

Animal Welfare Act 2006 (section 32)

Triable either way
Maximum: 6 months' custody
Offence range: Discharge–26 weeks' custody

[52] **STEP ONE Determining the offence category** SG15-46

The court should determine the offence category with reference only to the factors listed in the tables below. In order to determine the category the court should assess **culpability** and **harm.**

Culpability

A	Serious and/or persistent breach
B	All other cases

Harm

The level of **harm** is determined by weighing up all the factors of the case to determine the harm that has been caused or was at risk of being caused.

In assessing any risk of harm posed by the breach, consideration should be given to the original offence(s) or activity for which the order was imposed and the circumstances in which the breach arose.

Category 1	• Breach causes or risks death or very serious harm or suffering to animal(s) • Breach results in risk of or actual serious harm to individual(s)
Category 2	• Cases falling between categories 1 and 3
Category 3	• Breach causes or risks little or no harm or suffering to animal(s) • Breach results in very low risk of or little or no harm to individual(s)

[53] **STEP TWO Starting point and category range** SG15-47

Having determined the category at step one, the court should use the corresponding starting point to reach a sentence within the category range from the appropriate sentence table below. The starting point applies to all offenders irrespective of plea or previous convictions. The court should then consider further adjustment within the category range for aggravating or mitigating features.

[53]

	Culpability	
Harm	A	B
Category 1	**Starting point** 16 weeks' custody **Category range** 6 weeks'–26 weeks' custody	**Starting point** 8 weeks' custody **Category range** Medium level community order–16 weeks' custody
Category 2	**Starting point** 8 weeks' custody **Category range** Medium level community order–16 weeks' custody	**Starting point** Medium level community order **Category range** Band C Fine–High level community order
Category 3	**Starting point** Medium level community order **Category range** Band C Fine–High level community order	**Starting point** Band A Fine **Category range** Discharge–Band B Fine

The table below contains a **non-exhaustive** list of additional factual elements providing the context of the offence and factors relating to the offender. Identify whether any combination of these, or other relevant factors, should result in an upward or downward adjustment from the starting point. In some cases, having considered these factors, it may be appropriate to move outside the identified category range. [54]

Factors increasing seriousness
Statutory aggravating factors: Previous convictions, having regard to a) the **nature** of the offence to which the conviction relates and its **relevance** to the current offence; and b) the **time** that has elapsed since the conviction Offence committed whilst on bail ***Other aggravating factors:*** Breach committed shortly after order made History of disobedience to court orders Breach conducted in commercial context Breach involves deceit regarding ownership of/responsibility for animal Breach motivated by personal gain Offence committed on licence or while subject to post sentence supervision

Factors reducing seriousness or reflecting personal mitigation
Breach committed after long period of compliance Genuine misunderstanding of terms of order Prompt voluntary surrender/admission of breach or failure Age and/or lack of maturity where it affects the responsibility of the offender Mental disorder or learning disability where linked to the commission of the offence Sole or primary carer for dependent relatives

SG15-48 STEPS THREE TO EIGHT [55]

[These are in the same terms as those applicable to failure to surrender to bail: see **SG15-16** ***et seq.***]

SG15-49

Other Breach Offences

[56]

Where an offence is not covered by a sentencing guideline a court is also entitled to use, and may be assisted by, a guideline for an analogous offence subject to differences in the elements of the offences and the statutory maxima.

[56] In sentencing the breach offences below, the court should refer to the sentencing approach in step one of the guideline for breach of a criminal behaviour order to determine culpability and harm, and determine an appropriate sentence bearing in mind the maximum penalty for the offence.

Offence	Mode of Trial	Maximum Sentence
Breach of football banning order (section 14J Football Spectators Act 1989	Triable summarily only	A person guilty of an offence under this section is liable on summary conviction to imprisonment for a term not exceeding six months, or a fine not exceeding level 5 on the standard scale, or both.
Failure to comply with dispersal order Part 3 Anti-social Behaviour, Crime and Policing Act 2014 (Requires a person committing, or likely to commit ASB to leave an area for up to 48 hours.)	Triable summarily only	A person guilty of an offence under subsection (1) (Failure to move on) is liable on summary conviction – to imprisonment for a period not exceeding 3 months, or to a fine not exceeding level 4 on the standard scale. A person guilty of an offence under subsection (3) (Failure to hand over items) is liable on summary conviction to a fine not exceeding level 2 on the standard scale.
Community protection notice Part 4, Chapter 1 Anti-social Behaviour, Crime and Policing Act 2014 (Stops a person, business or organisation committing ASB which spoils the community's quality of life.)	Triable summarily only	A person guilty of an offence under this section is liable on summary conviction — to a fine not exceeding level 4 on the standard scale, in the case of an individual; to a fine of up to £20,000, in the case of a body. (If dealt with by way of fixed penalty, a fixed penalty notice of up to £100.)
Breach of public spaces protection order Part 4, Chapter 2 Anti-social Behaviour, Crime and Policing Act 2014 (Stops people committing ASB in a particular public place.)	Triable summarily only	A person guilty of an offence under this section is liable on summary conviction to a fine not exceeding level 3 on the standard scale. (If dealt with by way of fixed penalty, a fixed penalty notice of up to £100.)
Closure Power Part 4, Chapter 3 Anti-social Behaviour, Crime and Policing Act 2014 (Allows the police or local council to close premises where ASB is being committed, or is likely to be committed.)	Triable summarily only	A person guilty of obstructing a person acting under section 79 or 85(1) is liable on summary conviction — (a) to imprisonment for a period not exceeding 3 months, or (b) to a fine A person who is guilty of remaining on or entering premises in contravention of a closure order is liable on summary conviction — (a) to imprisonment for a period not exceeding 6 months, or (b) to a fine, or to both.

[57]

ANNEX: FINE BANDS AND COMMUNITY ORDERS SG15-50

Fine Bands

In this guideline, fines are expressed as one of three fine bands (A, B, C).

Fine Band	**Starting point** (applicable to all offenders)	**Category range** (applicable to all offenders)
Band A	50% of relevant weekly income	25–75% of relevant weekly income
Band B	100% of relevant weekly income	75–125% of relevant weekly income
Band C	150% of relevant weekly income	125–175% of relevant weekly income

SG15-51 **Community Orders** [58]

In this guideline, community sentences are expressed as one of three levels (low, medium and high).

An illustrative description of examples of requirements that might be appropriate for each level is provided below. Where two or more requirements are ordered, they must be compatible with each other. Save in exceptional circumstances, the court must impose at least one requirement for the purpose of punishment, or combine the community order with a fine, or both (see section 177 Criminal Justice Act 2003).

Low	**Medium**	**High**
Offences only just cross community order threshold, where the seriousness of the offence or the nature of the offender's record means that a discharge or fine is inappropriate	Offences that obviously fall within the community order band	Offences only just fall below the custody threshold or the custody threshold is crossed but a community order is more appropriate in the circumstances
In general, only one requirement will be appropriate and the length may be curtailed if additional requirements are necessary		More intensive sentences which combine two or more requirements may be appropriate
Suitable requirements might include: • Any appropriate rehabilitative requirement(s) • 40–80 hours of unpaid work • Curfew requirement within the lowest range (for example up to 16 hours per day for a few weeks) • Exclusion requirement, for a few months • Prohibited activity requirement • Attendance centre requirement (where available)	Suitable requirements might include: • Any appropriate rehabilitative requirement(s) • Greater number of hours of unpaid work (for example 80–150 hours) • Curfew requirement within the middle range (for example up to 16 hours for 2–3 months) • Exclusion requirement lasting in the region of 6 months • Prohibited activity requirement	Suitable requirements might include: • Any appropriate rehabilitative requirement(s) • 150–300 hours of unpaid work • Curfew requirement within the middle range for 16 hours for 4–12 months • Exclusion order lasting in the region of 12 months
* If order does not contain a punitive requirement, suggested fine levels are indicated below:		
BAND A FINE	BAND B FINE	BAND C FINE

The Magistrates' Court Sentencing Guidelines includes further guidance on fines. The table above is also set out in the *Imposition of Community and Custodial Sentences* guideline which includes further guidance on community orders.

PART 16 BAIL, FAIL TO SURRENDER TO

[1] DEFINITIVE GUIDELINE SG16-1

Foreword

This guideline applies to the sentencing of offenders convicted of failing to surrender to bail who are sentenced on or after **10 December 2007**. Bail Act offences are committed in significant numbers each year and are a major cause of disruption, delay and unnecessary cost for the criminal justice system. A prime objective of courts is to bring criminal proceedings to a conclusion as soon as practicable, and a rigorous and consistent response when offenders fail to answer bail is needed to help achieve this. This, in turn, may help to discourage future offending. Where it is not possible to dispose of the original offence, sentencing for a Bail Act offence should normally be undertaken separately and carried out as soon as appropriate in light of the circumstances of an individual case.

When a Bail Act offence has been committed, the sentence must be commensurate with the seriousness of the offence and must take into account both the reason why the offender failed to surrender and the degree of harm intended or caused. For these purposes, 'harm' is not only that caused to individual victims and witnesses but includes the consequential effect on police and court resources and the wider negative impact on public confidence in the criminal justice system.

As the considerations for offences committed by youths will differ markedly from those relevant for adult offenders, this guideline relates to the sentencing of adult offenders only.

[3] FAIL TO SURRENDER TO BAIL SG16-2

A. Statutory provision

1. [Sets out the Bail Act 1976, s. 6 (see **D7.134** in the main work.)]
2. An offence under subsection (1) or (2) is punishable either on summary conviction or, in the Crown Court, as if it were a criminal contempt of court. The maximum sentence in a magistrates' court is 3 months imprisonment.[211] If the matter is committed to the Crown Court for sentence, or dealt with there, the maximum sentence is 12 months custody and the sentence is subject to the usual appellate procedures.[212]

B. Assessing Seriousness SG16-3

3. When assessing the seriousness of an offence, the court must consider the offender's culpability and any harm which the offence caused, was intended to cause or might foreseeably have caused.[213]
4. In assessing **culpability**, a court will need to consider whether the failure to surrender was intended to cause harm and, if so, what level of harm. In assessing **harm**, a court will need to consider to what extent the failure to surrender impeded the course of justice. When applied to Bail Act offences, 'harm' includes not only the harm caused to individual victims and witnesses but the consequential drain on police and court resources and the wider negative impact on public confidence in the criminal justice system.
5. The same *approach* to sentencing should be adopted whether the offence is committed contrary to section 6(1) or to section 6(2). However, the offence contrary to section 6(2) requires that there had been a reasonable excuse not to attend on the original date and so the degree of harm arising from the failure to attend as soon as reasonably practicable after that date is likely to be less. Accordingly, the seriousness of the offence is likely to be less also.

[4] ***(i) Culpability***

6. The obligation on a person who is granted bail is to surrender to custody at the court or the police station as required. The assessment of culpability requires consideration of the immediate reason why the defendant failed to appear. This can range from forgetfulness (comparable to the category of culpability described as 'negligence' in the Council guideline on seriousness[214]) or fear of the outcome of

[211] Police and Justice Act 2006, section 34 amends various sections of the Criminal Justice Act 2003 so that this maximum sentence is not affected by the general provisions relating to custodial sentences of less than 12 months when in force.
[212] Administration of Justice Act 1960, s. 13
[213] Criminal Justice Act 2003, s. 143(1)
[214] *Overarching Principles: Seriousness*, page 4, www.sentencing-guidelines.gov.uk

the hearing through to a deliberate act. Where the failure to surrender was deliberate, it will be relevant whether it was designed to disrupt the system to the defendant's advantage or whether the defendant simply gave no thought at all to the consequences. [4]

(ii) Harm

7. Some degree of harm, even if only a minor delay or inconvenience to the authorities, will always be caused when a defendant fails to surrender. The degree of harm *actually* caused will vary considerably depending on the particular circumstances of the offence. The harm that the offence might foreseeably have caused[215] must also be taken into account.
8. **Failure to surrender to a court** for any reason (whether bail is granted by the police or by a court) inevitably delays justice. Potentially, it will result in additional distress to victims and witnesses. It will almost always waste public money in the form of court time and the resources of the prosecution, the police and the defence.
   (a) Where a defendant fails to appear for a first court hearing but attends shortly afterwards, the only harm caused is likely to be the financial cost to the system. Procedural delays may also be caused by the prosecution, the defence or the Courts Service at various stages of the process and, where a case could not have proceeded even if the defendant had surrendered to bail, this should be taken into account when assessing the harm actually caused.
   (b) Where a defendant appears for trial on the wrong day but enters a late guilty plea enabling the case to be disposed of to some degree at least (albeit with some delay and disruption), the harm caused by the delay may be offset by the benefits stemming from the change of plea.
   (c) The most serious harm is likely to result when a defendant fails to appear for trial, especially if this results in witnesses being sent away. A lengthy aborted trial in the Crown Court will be more harmful than a short hearing in a magistrates' court though each situation has the potential to affect public confidence in the system.
   (d) Where a court decides not to proceed to trial in the absence of the defendant (see paragraphs 34–39), interference with the course of justice may be particularly acute. Memories may become less certain with the passage of time. Victims and witnesses, many of whom find the prospect of preparing for and attending court daunting, are likely to be caused distress and/or inconvenience. They may find it more difficult to attend court on the second or subsequent occasion, to the extent that they may not even appear at all. In such circumstances the harm is very high because justice will be prevented. Victims of violent or sexual offences are particularly likely to be distressed to learn that the accused is 'at large' in defiance of the court.
   (e) The level of harm is likely to be assessed as high where an offender fails to appear for sentence and is also seen to be flouting the authority of the court, such as where the avoidance of sentence results in the consequential avoidance of ancillary orders such as disqualification from driving or from working with children or vulnerable adults, the payment of compensation or registration as a sex offender. This may increase the level of harm whenever the offender continues to present a risk to public safety. [5]
9. In general terms, the same approach to sentencing should be adopted whether the offence involves a failure to surrender to a court or to a police station since the legal obligation is the same. However, the harm that results from failure to surrender to a court will usually be greater than that resulting from failure to surrender to a police station and this will affect the assessment of the seriousness of an individual offence.
10. **Failure to surrender to a police station** results in police time being wasted and the course of justice being impeded; potentially, it can also result in victims and witnesses being distressed and concerned about their safety and the ability of the system to protect the public and deliver justice. However, the circumstances in which such bail is granted are less formal than the grant of court bail and the history of the individual case should be examined. There may be less culpability where bail has been enlarged on a number of occasions and less harm if *court* proceedings are not significantly delayed.

(iii) Nature and seriousness of original offence

11. Failure to surrender to custody is an offence in its own right and the sentence imposed should be proportionate to the seriousness of the offending behaviour itself. Where the Bail Act offence is sentenced in advance of the offence in relation to which bail was granted the assessment of seriousness will take place without reference to the seriousness of, or likely sentence for, the original offence.
12. However, the specific nature of the original offence may significantly affect the harm or likelihood of harm caused by the failure to surrender. Particular types of offence (such as violent or sexual offences) may have implications for public protection and safety and the offender's failure to surrender might cause fear and distress to witnesses.

[215] Criminal Justice Act, s. 143(1)

[5] 13. Seriousness is not reduced automatically by subsequent acquittal of the original offence. Whilst it may seem harsh that a defendant before the court for an offence of which he is not guilty should be punished for the ancillary offence of failure to surrender during the course of the prosecution of that offence, both the culpability and the likely harm—delay, distress and inconvenience to witnesses, and additional costs—are the same. Moreover, one of the most serious effects of a Bail Act offence can be that a trial cannot take place because of the failure to surrender and it will often be invidious to expect a court to identify genuinely innocent defendants.

[6] *(iv) Aggravating and mitigating factors*

14. Since 'recent and relevant' previous convictions aggravate the seriousness of an offence,[216] defendants who repeatedly fail to attend court are likely to receive more severe sentences.
15. The period of time for which a defendant absconds is also likely to influence the court when considering sentence. Whilst being absent for a long period of time will aggravate an offence, the fact that a defendant arrives at court only a few days, or even only a few hours, late, is not a factor that will necessarily mitigate sentence; in many cases, the harm will already have been done (for example, the trial may have been put back, witnesses may have been inconvenienced and there may be an increased likelihood that witnesses will fail to attend at a future hearing).
16. Leaving the jurisdiction is an aggravating factor as are other actions designed to avoid the jurisdiction of the court such as changing identity and appearance.
17. **The following aggravating factors are particularly relevant to an offence of failing to surrender to bail:**
    - repeat offending;
    - offender's absence causes a lengthy delay to the administration of justice;
    - determined attempt to avoid the jurisdiction of the court.
18. Prompt voluntary surrender might mitigate sentence where it saves police time in tracing and arresting an offender. It may also be an indication of remorse. This must be weighed against the degree of harm caused by the offence, which may still be significant. Surrender initiated by the offender merits consideration as a mitigating factor. Surrender in response to follow up action has no significance.
19. The fact that an offender has a disorganised or chaotic lifestyle, which may be due to a dependency on drugs or alcohol, does not of itself reduce the seriousness of the offence. Depending on the particular facts, it may be regarded as personal mitigation.
20. A misunderstanding (which does not amount to a defence) may be a mitigating factor but must be differentiated from a mistake on the part of the defendant, where the error must be regarded as his or her own responsibility.[217]
21. Where an offender has literacy or language difficulties, steps should normally be taken by the police or the court to address this when bail is granted. Such difficulties may be mitigation (where they do not amount to a defence but contribute to the offender failing to surrender to bail) where potential problems were not identified and/or appropriate steps were not taken to mitigate the risk in the circumstances as known at the time that bail is granted.

[7] 22. An offender's position as the sole or primary carer of dependant relatives may be personal mitigation when it is the reason why the offender has failed to surrender to custody.

23. **The following mitigating factors are particularly relevant to an offence of failing to surrender:**
    - prompt voluntary surrender;

    and, where they are not sufficient to amount to a defence:
    - misunderstanding;
    - a failure to comprehend the requirements or significance of bail;
    - caring responsibilities.

C. Procedural issues SG16-4

(i) When to sentence

24. The key principle is that a court should *deal* with a defendant who fails to surrender *as soon as is practicable* even if the trial or other hearing for the offence that led to the grant of bail is adjourned.[218] The following factors are relevant to the decision as to what is practicable:
    - when the proceedings in respect of which bail was granted are expected to conclude;
    - the seriousness of the offence for which the defendant is already being prosecuted;
    - the type of penalty that might be imposed for the breach of bail and for the original offence;
    - any other relevant circumstances.

216 ibid, s. 143(2)
217 See, for example, *Laidlaw v Atkinson* Queen's Bench Division CO/275/86
218 See Consolidated Criminal Practice Direction last revised April 2007—www.hmcourtsservice.gov.uk/cms/pds.htm

25. Whether or not the defendant is guilty of a Bail Act offence should be determined as soon as possible. It will be central to the issue of whether bail should now be granted or refused. Even where the offence is denied, a trial is normally short; it should be held on the first appearance after arrest or surrender, unless an adjournment is necessary (for example, for the defence to obtain medical evidence). [7]
26. When there is a plea or finding of guilt, sentence should be imposed *as soon as practicable*. The point at which it becomes possible to sentence an offence and the point at which it is practicable to do so will vary widely from case to case; a decision about timing is best made according to individual circumstances.
27. A key relevant circumstance is whether the substantive offence is to be adjourned, either for a pre-sentence report or for trial, and whether the remand is to be on bail or in custody.
28. Where the defendant is remanded in custody, the sentencing options for the Bail Act offence are limited. [8]
29. Where the defendant is to regain his or her liberty, there is the possibility of a noncustodial sentence. A community order, including an electronically monitored curfew requirement and, perhaps, a supervision requirement or an activity requirement may be helpful in ensuring attendance at future court hearings.
30. In more serious cases in which the custody threshold has been passed, a suspended sentence order could serve the same purpose.
31. These factors support sentencing without delay or with a short delay for a presentence report. On the other hand, there will be occasions when it is more appropriate that all outstanding matters should be dealt with on one sentencing occasion. This may be where the totality of offending may affect sentence type (for example where two or more offences together pass the custody threshold, but individually do not) or where the harm caused by the failure to surrender cannot be assessed at an early stage (for example, where witnesses may no longer be available).
32. A magistrates' court will be constrained by the maximum sentence available. In certain circumstances, Bail Act offences that would normally be dealt with in a magistrates' court may be committed to the Crown Court to be dealt with.[219]

(ii) Consecutive and concurrent custodial sentences

33. Where a custodial sentence is imposed for the original offence and a custodial sentence is also deemed appropriate for a Bail Act offence, a court should normally impose a consecutive sentence. However, a concurrent sentence will be appropriate where otherwise the overall sentence would be disproportionate to the combined seriousness of the offences.

(iii) Conducting trials in the absence of the defendant

34. A defendant has a duty to surrender to bail and a right to be present at his or her trial. However, where a defendant is absent voluntarily, having breached the duty to surrender, a court may proceed to hear a case in the defendant's absence. In a magistrates' court this is a statutory power.[220] While some sentences may be imposed in a defendant's absence, it is not possible to impose a custodial sentence or a community order, and it is undesirable to impose a disqualification from driving.
35. The Consolidated Criminal Practice Direction[221] reinforces the encouragement to courts to proceed in absence and identifies factors to be taken into account before so doing which include:
    - the conduct of the defendant;
    - the disadvantage to the defendant;
    - the public interest;
    - the effect of any delay; and
    - whether the attendance of the defendant could be secured at a later hearing.
36. Additional factors for a magistrates' court to consider include: [9]
    - there is less risk of either a magistrate or a district judge drawing an impermissible inference from a defendant's absence than would be the case with a jury; and
    - in a magistrates' court the finder of fact may ask questions and test the evidence of prosecution witnesses.
37. The overriding concern of the court is to ensure that a trial conducted in the absence of the defendant is as fair as circumstances permit and, in particular, that the defendant's rights under Article 6 of the European Convention on Human Rights (ECHR)[222] are not infringed.

[219] Bail Act 1976, s. 6(6)
[220] Magistrates' Courts Act 1980, s. 11
[221] Last revised April 2007—www.hmcourts-service.gov.uk/cms/pds.htm
[222] Right to a fair trial

[9] 38. Proceeding to trial in the absence of the defendant may reduce the harm arising from a Bail Act offence. When considering the degree to which this should influence sentence, it must be borne in mind that the position in a magistrates' court is different from that in the Crown Court. An appeal against conviction from a magistrates' court can result in a re-hearing, whereas that is not the case after a jury trial. There is also the discretionary power under section 142 of the Magistrates' Courts Act 1980 to set aside a conviction and order a re-hearing in a magistrates' court. If an application to set aside a conviction is successful, witnesses will be required to give evidence again at a later date. It will be relevant to an assessment of harm whether either of those provisions has been used.

39. Where it has proved possible to proceed to trial or conclude proceedings in the absence of the defendant, this should have no bearing on *culpability* for a Bail Act offence as the intention of the defendant remains unchanged. It may, however, be relevant to the assessment of *harm* as this may have been reduced or avoided because of the decision to proceed in absence.

[10] **D. Sentencing ranges and starting points** SG16-5

(i) This guideline applies to a first time offender who has been convicted after a trial. A first time offender is a person who does not have a conviction which, by virtue of section 143(2) of the Criminal Justice Act 2003, must be treated as an aggravating factor.

(ii) The guideline establishes levels of seriousness based upon both offender culpability and the resulting consequences. These are set out in the column headed 'nature of failure and harm'.

(iii) A court will identify the description that most nearly matches the particular facts of the offence and this will identify a starting point from which the sentencer can depart to reflect any aggravating or mitigating factors affecting the *seriousness of the offence* to reach a provisional sentence.

(iv) The sentencing range is the bracket into which the provisional sentence will normally fall. The particular circumstances may, however, make it appropriate that the provisional sentence falls outside the range.

(v) Where the offender has previous convictions which aggravate the seriousness of the current offence, that may take the provisional sentence beyond the range given particularly where there are significant other aggravating factors present.

(vi) Once the provisional sentence has been identified by reference to those factors affecting the seriousness of the offence, the court will take into account any relevant factors of personal mitigation, which may take the sentence beyond the range given.

(vii) Where there has been a guilty plea, any reduction attributable to that plea will be applied to the sentence at this stage. Again, this reduction may take the sentence below the range provided.

(viii) A court must give its reasons for imposing a sentence of a different kind or outside the range provided in the guidelines.[223]

[11] **The Decision Making Process**

[Sets out the standard sequential decision making process: identify starting point, consider aggravating factors, consider mitigating factors, apply reduction for guilty plea, review in light of the totality principle and give reasons.]

[12] **E. Factors to take into consideration** SG16-6

1. Whilst the approach to sentencing should generally be the same whether the defendant failed to surrender to a court or to a police station and whether the offence is contrary to section 6(1) or 6(2), the court must examine all the relevant circumstances.
2. Whilst the seriousness of the original offence does not of itself aggravate or mitigate the seriousness of the offence of failing to surrender, the circumstances surrounding the original offence may be relevant in assessing the harm arising from this offence.
3. Where it has proved possible to conclude proceedings in the absence of the defendant, this may be relevant to the assessment of harm caused.
4. Where the failure to surrender to custody was 'deliberate':
   - at or near the bottom of the range will be cases where the defendant gave no thought at all to the consequences, or other mitigating factors are present, and the degree of delay or interference with the progress of the case was not significant in all the circumstances;
   - at or near the top of the range will be cases where any of aggravating factors 1–3 are present if there is also a significant delay and/or interference with the progress of the case.
5. Only the most common aggravating and mitigating factors specifically relevant to Bail Act offences are included in the guideline. When assessing the seriousness of an offence, the courts must always have regard to the full list of aggravating and mitigating factors in the Council guideline on Seriousness.[224]

Sentencing Guidelines

223 Criminal Justice Act 2003, s. 174(2)(a)

224 *Overarching Principles: Seriousness*, pages 6–7, published 16 December 2004, www.sentencing-guidelines.gov.uk

6. A previous conviction that is likely to be 'relevant' for the purposes of this offence is one which demonstrates failure to comply with an order of a court. [12]
7. Acquittal of the original offence does not automatically mitigate this offence.
8. The fact that an offender has a disorganised or chaotic lifestyle should not normally be treated as mitigation of the offence, but may be regarded as personal mitigation depending on the particular facts of a case.
9. Once the provisional sentence has been identified by reference to factors affecting the seriousness of the offence, the court will take into account any relevant factors of personal mitigation, and any reduction where a guilty plea was entered.[225]
10. The sentence for this offence should normally be in addition to any sentence for the original offence. Where custodial sentences are being imposed for a Bail Act offence and the original offence at the same time, the normal approach should be for the sentences to be consecutive. The length of any custodial sentence imposed must be commensurate with the seriousness of the offence(s).[226]
11. If an offence is serious enough to justify imposition of a community order, a curfew requirement with an electronic monitoring requirement may be a particularly appropriate part of such an order in any of the three sentencing ranges.
12. Power exists for magistrates' courts to impose one day's detention in appropriate cases.[227]

SG16-7 Bail Act 1976, ss. 6(1) & 6(2) [13]

Maximum penalty: 12 months imprisonment in the Crown Court
3 months imprisonment in a magistrates' court

The following starting points and sentencing ranges are for a first time offender aged 18 or over who pleaded not guilty. They should be applied as set out above.

Nature of failure & harm	Starting point	Sentencing range
Deliberate failure to attend causing delay and/or interference with the administration of justice. *The type and degree of harm actually caused will affect where in the range the case falls. See guidance …*	**14 days' custody**	*Crown Court* **Community order (medium)– 40 weeks' custody** *Magistrates' court* **Community order (low)–10 weeks' custody**
Negligent or non-deliberate failure to attend causing delay and/or interference with the administration of justice	**Fine**	**Fine–Community order (medium)**
Surrenders late on day but case proceeds as planned	**Fine**	**Fine**

Additional aggravating factors	Additional mitigating factors
1. Lengthy absence 2. Serious attempts to evade justice 3. Determined attempt seriously to undermine the course of justice 4. Previous relevant convictions and/or repeated breach of court orders or police bail	1. Prompt voluntary surrender *When not amounting to a defence* 2. Misunderstanding 3. A failure to comprehend bail significance or requirements 4. Caring responsibilities [see para. 22 for further detail]

225 Reduction in sentence for a guilty plea (revised), published July 2007, www.sentencing-guidelines.gov.uk
226 Criminal Justice Act 2003, s. 152(2)
227 Magistrates' Courts Act 1980, s. 135

[1] # PART 17 ANTI-SOCIAL BEHAVIOUR ORDERS, BREACH OF

… This guideline applies to the sentencing of offenders convicted of breaching an anti-social behaviour order (ASBO) who are sentenced on or after 5 January 2009. SG17-1

The Council has previously set out the approach to dealing with breaches of orders in its guidelines on New Sentences: Criminal Justice Act 2003 and Breach of Protective Orders. The main aim of sentencing for breach of a court order is to achieve the purpose of the order; in the case of an ASBO that is to protect the public from behaviour that is likely to cause harassment, alarm or distress.

Any perception that the courts do not treat seriously a failure to comply with a court order can undermine public confidence and is therefore an important additional consideration.

Since the ability of a court to deal appropriately with an order that has been breached depends on how it was made, Annex A to the guideline summarises the key principles and considerations applicable to the making of an ASBO.

This guideline applies to the sentencing of adult and young offenders. It is recognised that a large proportion of orders are imposed on persons under 18 years of age. Although the sentencing framework for youths is very different from that for adults, and a guideline for sentencing young offenders will follow in due course, the Council considered that sentencers would find it helpful to have guiding principles for sentencing young offenders for breach of an ASBO …

[2] **A. Statutory provision** SG17-2

1. [Sets out the CDA 1998, s. 1(10).]
2. Where a person is convicted of an offence of breach of an anti-social behaviour order (ASBO), it is not open to the court to make an order discharging the offender conditionally.[228]

B. Introduction SG17-3

3. An ASBO is a preventative order that can be made in either civil or criminal proceedings; its aim is to protect the public from behaviour that causes, or is likely to cause, harassment, alarm or distress. An order may be made on application to a magistrates' court, on conviction, or in conjunction with other proceedings in the County Court.
4. Since the ability of a court to deal appropriately with an order that has been breached depends on how it was made, Annex A summarises the key principles and considerations applicable to the making of an ASBO.
5. This guideline relates to the sentencing of both adult and young offenders. As the sentencing framework that applies to offenders aged under 18 is significantly different from that for older offenders, the guidance for young offenders is in the form of principles particularly regarding the circumstances in which a custodial sentence might be justified. The maximum penalty in the case of a young offender is detention for 24 months.
6. Breach of this type of order is different from breach of a community order or failure to surrender to custody because it has the potential to affect a community or the public at large in a way that causes direct harm.

The main aim of sentencing for breach of a court order is to achieve the purpose of the order. Therefore, the sentence for breach of an ASBO should primarily reflect the harassment, alarm or distress involved; the fact that it constituted breach of a court order is a secondary consideration.

C. Assessing seriousness SG17-4

7. The sentence for breach of an ASBO must be commensurate with the seriousness of the offence; that is determined by assessing the culpability of the offender and any harm which the offence caused, was intended to cause or might foreseeably have caused.[229]

[3] 8. A community sentence can be imposed only if a court considers that the offence is serious enough to justify it,[230] and a custodial sentence can be imposed only if a court considers that a community

[228] Crime and Disorder Act 1998, s. 1(11)
[229] Criminal Justice Act 2003, s. 143(1)
[230] ibid, s. 148(1)

sentence or a fine alone cannot be justified in view of the seriousness of the offence.[231] The Council has published a definitive guideline on seriousness that guides sentencers through the process of determining whether the respective sentencing thresholds have been crossed.[232] [3]

9. A wide range of prohibitions can be attached to an order; consequently the degree of harm resulting from a breach will vary greatly and may be experienced by the wider community as well as by individuals.
10. In order properly to assess the seriousness of a breach of an ASBO, a court needs to be aware of the purpose of the order and the context in which it was made. A breach may be of one or more prohibitions in an order; the approach to sentencing is based on an assessment of the seriousness of the harm arising from the breach (or intended by the offender) rather than the number of prohibitions not complied with.

(i) Culpability and harm

11. When a court is considering the seriousness of breach of an order such as an ASBO, it will need to consider two aspects of culpability:
    (a) **The degree to which the offender intended to breach the order.**
    Culpability is variable and an offender may have:
    - intended the breach;
    - been reckless as to whether the order was breached;
    - been aware of the risk of breach; or
    - been unaware of this risk due to an incomplete understanding of the terms of the order.

    (b) **The degree to which the offender intended to cause the harm that resulted (or could have resulted).**
    Culpability will be higher where the offender foresaw the harm likely to be caused by the breach and will be at its highest where such harm was intended.
12. There are also two dimensions to the harm involved in breach of an ASBO:
    (a) the breach may itself cause harassment, alarm or distress, which can reduce the quality of life in a community.
    (b) breach of an ASBO contravenes an order of the court, and this can undermine public confidence in the effective administration of justice.
13. The assessment of the seriousness of an individual offence must take into account not only the harm actually caused by an offence but also any harm that was intended or might foreseeably have been caused.[233]
14. The test of foreseeability is objective[234] but as the prohibitions imposed must have been considered by a court to be necessary to prevent anti-social behaviour, some degree of harm must always be foreseeable whenever an order is breached. Where a breach causes harm that was not readily foreseeable, the level of culpability should carry more weight than harm when assessing offence seriousness.[235] [4]

(ii) Relevance of the originating conduct

15. The **original conduct** that led to the making of an order is a relevant consideration in so far as it indicates the level of harm caused and whether this was intended.[236]
16. High culpability and/or harm may be indicated if the breach continues a pattern of behaviour against an identifiable victim. Conversely, where there is little connection between the breach and the behaviour that the order was aimed at, this may indicate a less serious offence.
17. The court should examine the prohibitions of the order itself (particularly those in older orders which may have been made without the benefit of the guidance summarised in Annex A), their necessity and reasonableness in all the circumstances.[237]

(iii) Breach of an interim order

18. Breach of an interim order or a final order is equally serious and the same approach to sentencing should be taken.
19. Sentence for a breach of an interim order should be imposed as soon as possible. If the hearing regarding the final order can be brought forward, this should be done so that the two issues can be considered together. However, sentencing for the breach of the interim order should not be delayed for this purpose.

---

231 ibid, s. 152(2)
232 *Overarching Principles: Seriousness*, published 16 December 2004, www.sentencing-guidelines.gov.uk
233 Criminal Justice Act 2003, s. 143(1)
234 Harm must have been foreseeable by 'a reasonable person'
235 *Overarching Principles: Seriousness*, published 16 December 2004, www.sentencing-guidelines.gov.uk
236 *Breach of a Protective Order*, published 7 December 2006, www.sentencing-guidelines.gov.uk
237 Where appropriate, an application may be made separately for the order to be varied: Crime and Disorder Act 1998, s. 1(8) or 1CA. See also the Magistrates' Courts (Anti-Social Behaviour Orders) Rules 2002. Where the subject/offender is aged under 18, Practice Direction (Magistrates' Courts: Anti-Social Behaviour Orders: Composition of Benches) [2006] 1 AER 886 provides for the constitution of the court.

[4] 20. Where an interim order is breached the court should consider the extent to which an urgent need for specific interim prohibitions was demonstrated, or if the interim order was sought principally to obtain additional time to prepare a case for the full hearing.[238]

21. Where an interim order has been made without notice to the subject, the order does not take effect until it has been served. If doubts arise about the extent to which the subject has understood the prohibitions but the defence of reasonable excuse is not made out, a lack of understanding of the terms of the order may still mitigate the seriousness of the offence through reducing culpability.

[5] **(iv) A breach that also constitutes another criminal offence**

22. Whether one offence or two has been charged, the sentence should reflect all relevant aspects of the offence so that, provided the facts are not in issue, the result should be the same.[239]
   (a) if the substantive offence only has been charged, the fact that it constitutes breach of an ASBO should be treated as an aggravating factor;
   (b) if breach of the order only has been charged, the sentence should reflect the full circumstances of the breach, which will include the conduct that could have been charged as a substantive offence.

23. Where breach of an ASBO also constitutes another offence with a lower maximum penalty than that for breach of the order, this penalty is an element to be considered in the interests of proportionality, although the court is not limited by it when sentencing an adult or youth for breach.

(v) Aggravating and mitigating factors

24. The Council guideline *Overarching Principles: Seriousness* identifies a number of factors that might increase or mitigate the seriousness of an offence. For ease of reference, the factors are set out in Annex B.

(vi) Personal mitigation

25. Offender mitigation is particularly relevant to breach of an ASBO as compliance with the order depends on the ability to understand its terms and make rational decisions in relation to these. Sentence may be mitigated where:
   - the offender has a lower level of understanding due to mental health issues or learning difficulties;
   - the offender was acting under the influence of an older or more experienced offender; or
   - there has been compliance with an Individual Support Order or Intervention Order imposed when the ASBO was made.

[6] **D. Sentencing guideline—Adult offenders** **SG17-5**

Sentencing ranges and starting points

1. This guideline applies to a *'first time offender'* who has been **convicted after a trial.** In common with other proceedings based on breach of a court order,[240] it is likely that an offender in breach of an ASBO will have previous convictions. That has been taken into account in determining the starting points and ranges. Therefore, within this guideline, a 'first time offender' is a person who does not have a conviction for breach of an ASBO rather than the usual approach which is based on the existence of any conviction which, by virtue of section 143(2) of the Criminal Justice Act 2003, must be treated as an aggravating factor.
2. As an aid to consistency of approach, the guideline describes a number of types of activity which would fall within the broad definition of the offence. These are set out in a column headed 'Nature of failure & harm'.
3. The expected approach is for a court to identify the description that most nearly matches the particular facts of the offence for which sentence is being imposed. This will identify a starting point from which the sentencer can depart to reflect aggravating or mitigating factors affecting the seriousness of the offence (beyond those contained within the column describing the nature of the failure or of the harm) to reach a **provisional sentence.**
4. The **sentencing range** is the bracket into which the provisional sentence will normally fall after having regard to factors which aggravate or mitigate the seriousness of the offence. The particular circumstances may, however, make it appropriate that the provisional sentence falls outside the range.

[238] A report commissioned by the YJB concluded that there may be grounds for interim ASBOs only where there is an urgent need for specific prohibitions: Aikta-Reena Solanki, Tim Bateman, Gwyneth Boswell and Emily Hill, Anti-social Behaviour Orders, YJB (2006).

[239] *Breach of a Protective Order*, published 7 December 2006, www.sentencing-guidelines.gov.uk

[240] For example, failing to surrender to bail

5. Where the offender has previous convictions which aggravate the seriousness of the current offence, that may take the provisional sentence beyond the range given particularly where there are significant other aggravating factors present. [6]
6. Once the provisional sentence has been identified by reference to those factors affecting the seriousness of the offence, the court will take into account any relevant factors of personal mitigation, which may take the sentence beyond the range given.
7. Where there has been a guilty plea, any reduction attributable to that plea will be applied to the sentence at this stage. Again, this reduction may take the sentence below the range provided.
8. A court must give its reasons for imposing a sentence of a different kind or outside the range provided in the guidelines.[241]

The decision making process [7]

[Sets out the standard sequential decision making process: identify starting point, consider aggravating factors, consider mitigating factors, apply reduction for guilty plea, consider ancillary orders, review in light of the totality principle and give reasons.]

Factors to take into consideration [8]

1. The starting points and sentencing ranges are for a *'first time offender'* who pleaded not guilty. In this guideline, a *'first time offender'* is one who does not have a previous conviction for breach of an ASBO.
2. Where a court determines that there are other convictions which it is reasonable to treat as a factor aggravating the seriousness of the breach,[242] that factor will be taken into account at stage 2 of the sentencing process set out on page 7.
3. An ASBO may be breached in a wide range of circumstances and may involve one or more prohibitions not being complied with. The examples given below are intended to illustrate how the scale of the conduct that led to the breach, taken as a whole, might come within the three levels of seriousness:
   - Serious harm caused or intended—breach at this level of seriousness will involve the use of violence, significant threats or intimidation or the targeting of individuals or groups of people in a manner that leads to a fear of violence.
   - Lesser degree of harm intended or likely—examples may include lesser degrees of threats or intimidation, the use of seriously abusive language, or causing more than minor damage to property.
   - No harm caused or intended—in the absence of intimidation or the causing of fear of violence, breaches involving being drunk or begging may be at this level, as may prohibited use of public transport or entry into a prohibited area, where there is no evidence that harassment, alarm or distress was caused or intended.
4. The suggested starting points are based on the assumption that the offender had the highest level of culpability.
5. Aggravating and mitigating factors specifically relevant to sentencing for breach of an ASBO are included in the guideline. Care needs to be taken to ensure that there is no double counting where an element of the breach determines the level of seriousness where it might in other circumstances be an aggravating factor. When assessing the seriousness of an offence, the court must always refer to the full list of aggravating and mitigating factors in the Council guideline on Seriousness (see Annex B).[243]
6. In the most serious cases, involving repeat offending and a breach causing serious harassment together with the presence of several aggravating factors, such as the use of violence, a sentence beyond the highest range will be justified.
7. Once the provisional sentence has been identified by reference to factors affecting the seriousness of the offence, the court will take into account any relevant factors of personal mitigation (see paragraph 25 above), and, in accordance with the Council guideline[244] consider reducing the sentence where a guilty plea was entered.
8. When imposing a community order, the court must ensure that the requirements imposed are proportionate to the seriousness of the breach, compatible with each other,[245] and also with the prohibitions of the ASBO if the latter is to remain in force. Even where the threshold for a custodial sentence is crossed, a custodial sentence is not inevitable.[246]

---

241 Criminal Justice Act 2003, s. 174(2)(a)
242 In accordance with Criminal Justice Act 2003, s. 143(2)
243 *Overarching Principles: Seriousness*, published 16 December 2004, www.sentencing-guidelines.gov.uk
244 *Reduction in Sentence for a Guilty Plea*, published 20 July 2007, www.sentencing-guidelines.gov.uk
245 *New Sentences: Criminal Justice Act 2003*, published 16 December 2004, www.sentencing-guidelines.gov.uk
246 ibid

[9] 9. An offender may be sentenced for more than one offence of breach, which occurred on different days. While consecutive sentences may be imposed in such cases, the overall sentence should reflect the totality principle.

Breach of an Anti-social Behaviour Order SG17-6

Crime and Disorder Act 1998 (section 1(10))

Maximum Penalty: 5 years' imprisonment

Note: A conditional discharge is not available as a sentence for this offence

Nature of failure & harm	Starting point	Sentencing range
Serious harassment, alarm or distress has been caused or where such harm was intended	26 weeks' custody	Custody threshold–2 years' custody
Lesser degree of harassment, alarm or distress, where such harm was intended, or where it would have been likely if the offender had not been apprehended	6 weeks' custody	Community Order (MEDIUM)–26 weeks' custody
No harassment, alarm or distress was actually caused by the breach and none was intended by the offender	Community Order (LOW)	Fine Band B–Community Order (MEDIUM)

Aggravating factors	Mitigating factors
1. Offender has a history of disobedience to court orders. 2. Breach was committed immediately or shortly after the order was made. 3. Breach was committed subsequent to earlier breach proceedings arising from the same order. 4. Targeting of a person the order was made to protect or a witness in the original proceedings.	1. Breach occurred after a long period of compliance. 2. The prohibition(s) breached was not fully understood, especially where an interim order was made without notice.

[10] **E. Sentencing principles: Young Offenders** SG17-7

1. The approach to assessing the seriousness of a breach outlined above at paragraphs 7 to 25 applies equally to youths. A court must impose a community or custodial sentence only if such a sentence is warranted by the seriousness of the offence and no lesser sentence can be justified.
2. When sentencing a young offender, the normal approach is for the penalty to reflect both the reduction in culpability (for example, due to a lesser ability to foresee the consequences of actions) and the more onerous effects of punishments on education and personal development in comparison with an adult offender.
3. The sentencing framework that applies to offenders aged under 18 is significantly different from that for adult offenders and key principles are set out in Annex C. The maximum penalty for this offence when committed by a young offender is a 24 month detention and training order (DTO). With the exception of a conditional discharge,[247] the full range of disposals of the youth court is available, and these are also outlined in Annex C.[248]
4. In most cases of breach by a young offender convicted after a trial, the appropriate sentence will be a community sentence.[249] Within the sentence(s) available, a range of requirements can be attached; the court will consider the seriousness of the breach, which requirement(s) will best prevent further offending and the individual circumstances of the offender.
5. The court must ensure that the requirements imposed are compatible both with each other and with the prohibitions of the ASBO if the latter is to remain in force, and that the combination of both is not so onerous as to make further breaches likely.

[247] Crime and Disorder Act 1998, s. 1(11) and s. 1C(9)

[248] If the young offender has also been charged with a grave crime under section 91 Powers of Criminal Courts (Sentencing) Act 2000, the case may be committed to the Crown Court. Similarly, where the young offender is committed to the Crown Court for sentence under the dangerous offender provisions.

[249] Though see paragraph 7 below

6. The particular stage of intellectual or emotional maturity of the individual (which may not correspond with actual age) will also influence sentence. A young offender is likely to perceive a particular time period as being longer in comparison with an adult, and this may be of relevance when considering how much time has elapsed between imposition and breach of the order. [10]
7. The principles to be followed when sentencing a youth for breach of an ASBO are as follows: [11]

'First time offender'[250] **pleading guilty:** the court[251] must make a referral order unless it imposes an absolute discharge, a custodial sentence or a hospital order;
In all other cases:

(i) in some less serious cases, such as where the breach has not involved any harassment, alarm or distress, a fine may be appropriate if it will be paid by the offender, or otherwise a reparation order;
(ii) in most cases, the appropriate sentence will be a community sentence;
(iii) the custody threshold should be set at a significantly higher level than the threshold applicable to adult offenders;
(iv) the custody threshold usually will not be crossed unless the breach involved serious harassment, alarm or distress through either the use of violence, threats or intimidation or the targeting of individuals/groups in a manner that led to a fear of violence;
(v) exceptionally, the custody threshold may also be crossed where a youth is being sentenced for more than one offence of breach (committed on separate occasions within a short period) involving a lesser but substantial degree of harassment, alarm or distress;
(vi) even where the custody threshold is crossed, the court should normally impose a community sentence in preference to a DTO, as custody should be used only as a measure of last resort; and
(vii) where the court considers a custodial sentence to be unavoidable, the starting point for sentencing should be 4 months detention, with a range of up to 12 months. Where a youth is being sentenced for more than one breach involving serious harassment, alarm or distress, sentence may go beyond that range.

Aggravating and mitigating factors [12]

8. As with adult offenders, factors that are likely to aggravate an offence of breach of an anti-social behaviour order are:
   - history of disobedience of court orders;
   - the breach was committed immediately or shortly after the order was made;
   - the breach was committed subsequent to earlier breach proceedings arising from the same order;
   - targeting of a person the order was made to protect or of a witness in the original proceedings.
9. Factors that are likely to mitigate the seriousness of the breach are:
   - the breach occurred after a long period of compliance;
   - the prohibition(s) breached was not fully understood, especially where an interim order was made without notice.

Personal mitigation

10. Offender mitigation is particularly relevant to breach of an ASBO as compliance with the order depends on the ability to understand its terms and make rational decisions in relation to these. Sentence may be mitigated where:
    - the offender has a lower level of understanding due to mental health issues or learning difficulties;
    - the offender was acting under the influence of an older or more experienced offender; or
    - there has been compliance with an Individual Support Order or Intervention Order imposed when the ASBO was made.
11. Other offender mitigating factors that may be particularly relevant to young offenders include peer pressure and a lack of parental support.

[250] For the purpose of this requirement, a 'first time offender' is an offender who has never been convicted by or before a court in the United Kingdom of any offence other than the offence and any connected offence, or been bound over in criminal proceedings; Powers of Criminal Court (Sentencing) Act 2000, s. 17(1)(b) and (c)
[251] A referral order may be made by a youth court or other magistrates' court; Powers of Criminal Courts (Sentencing) Act 2000, s. 16(1)

PART 18 PROTECTIVE ORDER, BREACH OF

Definitive Guideline SG18-1

[1] **Foreword**

… This guideline applies to offenders convicted of breach of an order who are sentenced on or after 18 December 2006.

This guideline deals specifically with the sentencing of offenders who have breached either a restraining order imposed in order to prevent future conduct causing harassment or fear of violence, or a non-molestation order which prohibits a person from molesting another person.

It highlights the particular factors that courts should take into account when dealing with the criminal offence of breaching an order and includes starting points based on the different types of activity which can constitute a breach. It also identifies relevant aggravating and mitigating factors.

…

[3] **A. Statutory Provisions** SG18-2

1.1 For the purposes of this guideline, two protective orders are considered:

(i) Restraining Order

1.2 It is an offence contrary to the Protection from Harassment Act 1997 to behave in a way which a person knows (or ought to know) causes someone else harassment (section 2) or fear of violence (section 4). When imposing sentence on an offender, a court may also impose a restraining order to prevent future conduct causing harassment or fear of violence.

1.3 An offence under these provisions may have occurred in a domestic context or may have occurred in other contexts. The Domestic Violence, Crime and Victims Act 2004 provides for such orders also to be made on conviction for any offence or following acquittal.[252]

1.4 It is an offence contrary to section 5(5) of the Act to fail to comply with the restraining order without reasonable excuse. That offence is punishable with a maximum of five years' imprisonment.

(ii) Non-Molestation Order

1.5 Section 42 of the Family Law Act 1996 provides that, during family proceedings, a court may make a non-molestation order containing either or both of the following provisions:

(a) *provision prohibiting a person ('the respondent') from molesting another person who is associated with the respondent;*

(b) *provision prohibiting the respondent from molesting a relevant child.*

1.6 Section 1 of the Domestic Violence, Crime and Victims Act 2004[253] inserts a new section 42A into the 1996 Act. Section 42A(1) will provide that it is an offence to fail to comply with the order without reasonable excuse. That offence is punishable with a maximum of five years imprisonment.

1.7 In addition, breach of a non-molestation order may be dealt with as a contempt of court.

B. Sentencing for Breach SG18-3

2.1 The facts that constitute a breach of a protective order may or may not also constitute a substantive offence. Where they do constitute a substantive offence, it is desirable that the substantive offence and the breach of the order should be charged as separate counts. Where necessary, consecutive sentences should be considered to reflect the seriousness of the counts and achieve the appropriate totality.

[4] 2.2 Sometimes, however, only the substantive offence or only the breach of the order will be charged. The basic principle is that the sentence should reflect all relevant aspects of the offence so that, provided the facts are not in issue, the result should be the same, regardless of whether one count or two has been charged. For example:

(i) **if the substantive offence only has been charged, the fact that it constitutes breach of a protective order should be treated as an aggravating factor;**

(ii) **if breach of the protective order only has been charged, the sentence should reflect the nature of the breach, namely, the conduct that amounts to the substantive offence, aggravated by the fact that it is also breach of an order.**

252 When in force, section 12 of the 2004 Act amends section 5 of the 1997 Act and inserts a new section 5A to that Act.

253 When in force.

2.3 If breach of a protective order has been charged where no substantive offence was involved, the sentence should reflect the circumstances of the breach, including whether it was an isolated breach, or part of a course of conduct in breach of the order; whether it was planned or unpre-meditated; and any consequences of the breach, including psychiatric injury or distress to the person protected by the order. [4]

SG18-4 C. Factors Influencing Sentencing

3.1 **In order to ensure that a protective order achieves the purpose it is intended for—protecting the victim from harm—it is important that the terms of the order are necessary and proportionate.**

3.2 The circumstances leading to the making of one of the protective orders will vary widely. Whilst a restraining order will be made in criminal proceedings, it will almost certainly result from offences of markedly different levels of seriousness or even acquittal. A nonmolestation order will have been made in civil proceedings and, again, may follow a wide variety of conduct by the subject of the order.

3.3 **In all cases the order will have been made to protect an individual from harm and action in response to breach should have as its primary aim the importance of ensuring that the order is complied with and that it achieves the protection that it was intended to achieve.**

3.4 **When sentencing for a breach of an order, the main aim should be to achieve future compliance with that order where that is realistic.**

The nature and context of the originating conduct or offence

3.5 The nature of the original conduct or offence is relevant in so far as it allows a judgement to be made on the level of harm caused to the victim by the breach and the extent to which that harm was intended by the offender.

3.6 If the original offence was serious, conduct which breaches the order might have a severe effect on the victim where in other contexts such conduct might appear minor. Even indirect contact, such as telephone calls, can cause significant harm or anxiety for a victim.

3.7 However, sentence following a breach is for the breach alone and must avoid punishing the offender again for the offence or conduct as a result of which the order was made.

The nature and context of the conduct that caused the breach [5]

3.8 **The protective orders are designed to protect a victim. When dealing with a breach, a court will need to consider the extent to which the conduct amounting to breach put the victim at risk of harm.**

3.9 There may be exceptional cases where the nature of the breach is particularly serious but has not been dealt with by a separate offence being charged. In these cases, the risk posed by the offender and the nature of the breach will be particularly significant in determining the response. Where the order is breached by the use of physical violence, the starting point should normally be a custodial sentence.

3.10 Non-violent behaviour and/or indirect contact can also cause (or be intended to cause) a high degree of harm and anxiety. In such circumstances, it is likely that the custody threshold will have been crossed.

3.11 Where an order was made in civil proceedings, its purpose may have been to cause the subject of the order to modify behaviour rather than to imply that the conduct was especially serious. If so, it is likely to be disproportionate to impose a custodial sentence for a breach of the order if the breach did not involve threats or violence.

3.12 In some cases where a breach might result in a short custodial sentence but the court is satisfied that the offender genuinely intends to reform his or her behaviour and there is a real prospect of rehabilitation, the court may consider it appropriate to impose a sentence that will allow this. This may mean imposing a suspended sentence order or a community order (where appropriate with a requirement to attend an accredited domestic violence programme).

3.13 **Breach of a protective order will generally be more serious than breach of a conditional discharge.** Not only is a breach of a protective order an offence in its own right but it also undermines a specific prohibition imposed by the court. Breach of a conditional discharge amounts to an offender failing to take a chance that has been provided by the court.

SG18-5 D. Aggravating and Mitigating Factors

4.1 Many of the aggravating factors which apply to an offence of violence in a domestic context will apply also to an offence arising from breach of a protective order.

[5] *Aggravating Factors*

(i) Victim is particularly vulnerable

4.2 For cultural, religious, language, financial or any other reasons, some victims may be more vulnerable than others. This vulnerability means that the terms of a protective order are particularly important and a violation of those terms will warrant a higher penalty than usual.

4.3 Age, disability or the fact that the victim was pregnant or had recently given birth at the time of the offence may make a victim particularly vulnerable.

4.4 Any steps taken to prevent the victim reporting an incident or obtaining assistance will usually aggravate the offence.

[6] *(ii) Impact on children*

4.5 If a protective order is imposed in order to protect children, either solely or in addition to another victim, then a breach of that order will generally be more serious.[254]

(iii) A proven history of violence or threats by the offender

4.6 Of necessity, a breach of a protective order will not be the first time an offender has caused fear or harassment towards a victim. However, the offence will be more serious if the breach is part of a series of prolonged violence or harassment towards the victim or the offender has a history of disobedience to court orders.

4.7 Where an offender has previously been convicted of an offence involving domestic violence, either against the same or a different person, or has been convicted for a breach of an order, this is likely to be a statutory aggravating factor.[255]

(iv) Using contact arrangements with a child to instigate an offence

4.8 An offence will be aggravated where an offender exploits contact arrangements with a child in order to commit an offence.

(v) Victim is forced to leave home

4.9 A breach will be aggravated if, as a consequence, the victim is forced to leave home.

(vi) Additional aggravating factors

4.10 In addition to the factors listed above, the following will aggravate a breach of an order:

- the offence is a further breach, following earlier breach proceedings;
- the breach was committed immediately or shortly after the order was made.

Mitigating Factors

(i) Breach was committed after a long period of compliance

4.11 If the court is satisfied that the offender has complied with a protective order for a substantial period before a breach is committed, the court should take this into account when imposing sentence for the breach. The history of the relationship and the specific nature of the contact will be relevant in determining its significance as a mitigating factor.

(ii) Victim initiated contact

4.12 If the conditions of an order are breached following contact from the victim, this should be considered as mitigation. It is important to consider the history of the relationship and the specific nature of the contact in determining its significance as a mitigating factor.

4.13 Nonetheless it is important for the court to make clear that it is the responsibility of the offender and not the victim to ensure that the order is complied with.

[7] **E. Factors to take into Consideration** **SG18-6**

Aims of sentencing

(a) When sentencing for a breach of a protective order (which would have been imposed to protect a victim from further harm), the main aim should be to achieve future compliance with that order.

(b) A court will need to assess the level of risk posed by the offender. If the offender requires treatment or assistance for mental health or other issues, willingness to undergo treatment or accept help may influence sentence.

[254] The definition of 'harm' in section 31(9) of the Children Act 1989 as amended by section 120 of the Adoption and Children Act 2002 includes 'impairment suffered from seeing or hearing the ill-treatment of another'.

[255] Criminal Justice Act 2003, s. 143(2)

1. Key Factors [7]

(a) The nature of the conduct that caused the breach of the order, in particular, whether the contact was direct or indirect, although it is important to recognise that indirect contact is capable of causing significant harm or anxiety.
(b) **There may be exceptional cases where the nature of the breach is particularly serious but has not been dealt with by a separate offence being charged. In these cases the risk posed by the offender and the nature of the breach will be particularly significant in determining the response.**
(c) The nature of the original conduct or offence is relevant to sentencing for the breach in so far as it allows a judgement to be made on the level of harm caused to the victim by the breach, and the extent to which that harm was intended by the offender.
(d) The sentence following a breach is for the breach alone and must avoid punishing the offender again for the offence or conduct as a result of which the order was made.
(e) Where violence is used to breach a restraining order or a molestation order, custody is the starting point for sentence.
(f) Non-violent conduct in breach may cross the custody threshold where a high degree of harm or anxiety has been caused to the victim.
(g) Where an order was made in civil proceedings, its purpose may have been to cause the subject of the order to modify behaviour rather than to imply that the conduct was especially serious. If so, it is likely to be disproportionate to impose a custodial sentence for a breach of the order if the breach did not involve threats or violence.
(h) In some cases where a breach might result in a short custodial sentence but the court is satisfied that the offender genuinely intends to reform his or her behaviour and there is a real prospect of rehabilitation, the court may consider it appropriate to impose a sentence that will allow this. This may mean imposing a suspended sentence order or a community order (where appropriate with a requirement to attend an accredited domestic violence programme).
(i) While, in principle, consecutive sentences may be imposed for each breach of which the offender is convicted, the overall sentence should reflect the totality principle.

2. General [8]

(a) Breach of a protective order should be considered more serious than a breach of a conditional discharge.
(b) The principle of reduction in sentence for a guilty plea should be applied as set out in the Council guideline *Reduction in Sentence for a Guilty Plea*.

3. Non-custodial sentences

(a) It is likely that all breaches of protective orders will pass the threshold for a community sentence. The reference in the starting points to medium and low range community orders refers to the Council guideline *New Sentences: Criminal Justice Act 2003* paragraphs 1.1.18–1.1.32.
(b) In accordance with general principle, the fact that the seriousness of an offence crosses a particular threshold does not preclude the court from imposing another type of sentence of a lower level where appropriate.

SG18-7 BREACH of a PROTECTIVE ORDER [9]

Breach of a Restraining Order
Section 5(5) Protection from Harassment Act 1997

Breach of a Non-Molestation Order
*Section 42A Family Law Act 1996**

Maximum Penalty: **5 years' imprisonment**

Where the conduct is particularly serious, it would normally be charged as a separate offence. These starting points are based on the premise that the activity has either been prosecuted separately as an offence or is not of a character sufficient to justify prosecution of it as an offence in its own right.

[9]

Nature of activity	Starting points
	Custodial Sentence
Breach (whether one or more) involving significant physical violence and significant physical or psychological harm to the victim.	More than 12 months The length of the custodial sentence imposed will depend on the nature and seriousness of the breach(es).
More than one breach involving some violence and/or significant physical or psychological harm to the victim.	26–39 weeks' custody [Medium/High Custody Plus order]*
Single breach involving some violence and/or significant physical or psychological harm to the victim.	13–26 weeks' custody [Low/Medium Custody Plus order]**
	Non-Custodial Sentence
More than one breach involving no/minimal contact or some direct contact.	MEDIUM range community order
Single breach involving no/minimal direct contact.	LOW range community order

Additional aggravating factors	Additional mitigating factors
1. Victim is particularly vulnerable. 2. Impact on children. 3. A proven history of violence or threats by the offender. 4. Using contact arrangements with a child to instigate an offence. 5. Victim is forced to leave home. 6. Offence is a further breach, following earlier breach proceedings. 7. Offender has a history of disobedience to court orders. 8. Breach was committed immediately or shortly after the order was made.	1. Breach occurred after a long period of compliance. 2. Victim initiated contact.

*When in force.

**When the relevant provisions of the Criminal Justice Act 2003 are in force.

PART 19 BURGLARY OFFENCES

SG19-1

Definitive Guideline

Applicability of Guideline [2]

In accordance with section 120 of the Coroners and Justice Act 2009, the Sentencing Council issues this definitive guideline. It applies to all offenders aged 18 and older, who are sentenced on or after 16 January 2012, regardless of the date of the offence.

Section 125(1) of the Coroners and Justice Act 2009 provides that when sentencing offences committed after 6 April 2010:

Every court —

(a) must, in sentencing an offender, follow any sentencing guideline which is relevant to the offender's case, and

(b) must, in exercising any other function relating to the sentencing of offenders, follow any sentencing guidelines which are relevant to the exercise of the function,

unless the court is satisfied that it would be contrary to the interests of justice to do so.

This guideline applies only to offenders aged 18 and older. General principles to be considered in the sentencing of youths are in the Sentencing Guidelines Council's definitive guideline, *Sentencing Children and Young People: Overarching Principles* [see **SG8-1**].

SG19-2 **Structure, ranges and starting points**

For the purposes of section 125(3)–(4) Coroners and Justice Act 2009, the guideline specifies offence ranges — the range of sentences appropriate for each type of offence. Within each offence, the Council has specified three categories which reflect varying degrees of seriousness. The offence range is split into category ranges — sentences appropriate for each level of seriousness. The Council has also identified a starting point within each category.

Starting points define the position within a category range from which to start calculating the provisional sentence. As in the Sentencing Council's Assault Definitive Guideline, this guideline adopts an offence based starting point. **Starting points apply to all offences within the corresponding category and are applicable to all offenders, in all cases.** Once the starting point is established, the court should consider further aggravating and mitigating factors and previous convictions so as to adjust the sentence within the range. Starting points and ranges apply to all offenders, whether they have pleaded guilty or been convicted after trial. Credit for a guilty plea is taken into consideration only at step four in the decision making process, after the appropriate sentence has been identified.

Information on community orders and fine bands is set out in the annex [not reproduced: see **SG10-129** and **SG9-2**].

SG19-3

Aggravated Burglary [3]

Theft Act 1968 (section 10)

This is a serious specified offence for the purposes of section 224 of the Criminal Justice Act 2003

Triable only on indictment
Maximum: Life imprisonment

Offence range: 1–13 years' custody

SG19-4 **STEP ONE Determining the offence category** [4]

Category 1	Greater harm **and** higher culpability
Category 2	Greater harm **and** lower culpability **or** lesser harm **and** higher culpability
Category 3	Lesser harm **and** lower culpability

The court should determine the offence category using the table below.

The court should determine culpability and harm caused or intended, by reference only to the factors below, which comprise the principal factual elements of the offence. Where an offence does not fall squarely into a category, individual factors may require a degree of weighting before making an overall assessment and determining the appropriate offence category.

[4]

Factors indicating greater harm	Factors indicating higher culpability
Theft of/damage to property causing a significant degree of loss to the victim (whether economic, commercial, sentimental or personal value) Soiling, ransacking or vandalism of property Victim at home or on the premises (or returns) while offender present Significant physical or psychological injury or other significant trauma to the victim Violence used or threatened against victim, particularly involving a weapon Context of general public disorder **Factors indicating lesser harm** No physical or psychological injury or other significant trauma to the victim No violence used or threatened and a weapon is not produced	Victim or premises deliberately targeted (for example, due to vulnerability or hostility based on disability, race, sexual orientation) A significant degree of planning or organisation Equipped for burglary (for example, implements carried and/or use of vehicle) Weapon present on entry Member of a group or gang **Factors indicating lower culpability** Offender exploited by others Mental disorder or learning disability, where linked to the commission of the offence

STEP TWO Starting point and category range

SG19-5

Having determined the category, the court should use the corresponding starting points to reach a sentence within the category range below. The starting point applies to all offenders irrespective of plea or previous convictions. A case of particular gravity, reflected by multiple features of culpability or harm in step 1, could merit upward adjustment from the starting point before further adjustment for aggravating or mitigating features, set out below.

[5]

Offence Category	Starting Point (*Applicable to all offenders*)	Category Range (*Applicable to all offenders*)
Category 1	10 years' custody	9–13 years' custody
Category 2	6 years' custody	4–9 years' custody
Category 3	2 years' custody	1–4 years' custody

The table below contains a **non-exhaustive** list of additional factual elements providing the context of the offence and factors relating to the offender. Identify whether any combination of these, or other relevant factors, should result in an upward or downward adjustment from the starting point. **In particular, relevant recent convictions are likely to result in an upward adjustment.** In some cases, having considered these factors, it may be appropriate to move outside the identified category range.

Factors increasing seriousness	Factors reducing seriousness or reflecting personal mitigation
Statutory aggravating factors: Previous convictions, having regard to a) the nature of the offence to which the conviction relates and its relevance to the current offence; and b) the time that has elapsed since the conviction Offence committed whilst on bail *Other aggravating factors include:* Child at home (or returns home) when offence committed Offence committed at night Abuse of power and/or position of trust Gratuitous degradation of victim Any steps taken to prevent the victim reporting the incident or obtaining assistance and/or from assisting or supporting the prosecution Victim compelled to leave their home (in particular victims of domestic violence) Established evidence of community impact Commission of offence whilst under the influence of alcohol or drugs Failure to comply with current court orders Offence committed whilst on licence Offences Taken Into Consideration (TICs)	Subordinate role in a group or gang Injuries caused recklessly Nothing stolen or only property of very low value to the victim (whether economic, commercial, sentimental or personal) Offender has made voluntary reparation to the victim No previous convictions or no relevant/recent convictions Remorse Good character and/or exemplary conduct Determination, and/or demonstration of steps taken to address addiction or offending behaviour Serious medical conditions requiring urgent, intensive or long-term treatment Age and/or lack of maturity where it affects the responsibility of the offender Lapse of time since the offence where this is not the fault of the offender Mental disorder or learning disability, where not linked to the commission of the offence Sole or primary carer for dependent relatives

SG19-6 **STEP THREE Consider any factors which indicate a reduction, such as assistance to the prosecution** [6]

The court should take into account sections 73 and 74 of the Serious Organised Crime and Police Act 2005 (assistance by defendants: reduction or review of sentence) and any other rule of law by virtue of which an offender may receive a discounted sentence in consequence of assistance given (or offered) to the prosecutor or investigator.

SG19-7 **STEP FOUR Reduction for guilty pleas**

The court should take account of any potential reduction for a guilty plea in accordance with section 144 of the Criminal Justice Act 2003 and the *Guilty Plea* guideline.

SG19-8 **STEP FIVE Dangerousness**

An aggravated burglary is a serious specified offence within the meaning of chapter 5 of the Criminal Justice Act 2003 and at this stage the court should consider whether having regard to the criteria contained in that chapter it would be appropriate to award a life sentence, imprisonment for public protection or an extended sentence. Where offenders meet the dangerousness criteria, the notional determinate sentence should be used as the basis for the setting of a minimum term.

SG19-9 **STEP SIX Totality principle**

If sentencing an offender for more than one offence, or where the offender is already serving a sentence, consider whether the total sentence is just and proportionate to the offending behaviour.

SG19-10 **STEP SEVEN Compensation and ancillary orders**

In all cases, courts should consider whether to make compensation and/or other ancillary orders.

SG19-11 **STEP EIGHT Reasons**

Section 174 of the Criminal Justice Act 2003 imposes a duty to give reasons for, and explain the effect of, the sentence.

SG19-12 **STEP NINE Consideration for remand time**

Sentencers should take into consideration any remand time served in relation to the final sentence at this final step. The court should consider whether to give credit for time spent on remand in custody or on bail in accordance with sections 240 and 240A of the Criminal Justice Act 2003.

SG19-13 DOMESTIC BURGLARY [7]

Theft Act 1968 (section 9)

This is a serious specified offence for the purposes of section 224 Criminal Justice Act 2003 if it was committed with intent to:

(a) inflict grievous bodily harm on a person, or
(b) do unlawful damage to a building or anything in it.

Triable either way

Maximum when tried summarily: Level 5 fine and/or 26 weeks' custody
Maximum when tried on indictment: 14 years' custody

Offence range: Community order–6 years' custody

Where sentencing an offender for a qualifying third domestic burglary, the court must apply Section 111 of the Powers of the Criminal Courts (Sentencing) Act 2000 and impose a custodial term of at least three years, unless it is satisfied that there are particular circumstances which relate to any of the offences or to the offender which would make it unjust to do so.

SG19-14 **STEP ONE Determining the offence category** [8]

The court should determine the offence category using the table below.

Category 1	Greater harm **and** higher culpability
Category 2	Greater harm **and** lower culpability **or** lesser harm **and** higher culpability
Category 3	Lesser harm **and** lower culpability

The court should determine culpability and harm caused or intended, by reference **only** to the factors below, which comprise the principal factual elements of the offence. Where an offence does not fall squarely into a category, individual factors may require a degree of weighting before making an overall assessment and determining the appropriate offence category.

[8]

Factors indicating greater harm	Factors indicating higher culpability
Theft of/damage to property causing a significant degree of loss to the victim (whether economic, sentimental or personal value) Soiling, ransacking or vandalism of property Occupier at home (or returns home) while offender present Trauma to the victim, beyond the normal inevitable consequence of intrusion and theft Violence used or threatened against victim Context of general public disorder **Factors indicating lesser harm** Nothing stolen or only property of very low value to the victim (whether economic, sentimental or personal) Limited damage or disturbance to property	Victim or premises deliberately targeted (for example, due to vulnerability or hostility based on disability, race, sexual orientation) A significant degree of planning or organisation Knife or other weapon carried (where not charged separately) Equipped for burglary (for example, implements carried and/or use of vehicle) Member of a group or gang **Factors indicating lower culpability** Offence committed on impulse, with limited intrusion into property Offender exploited by others Mental disorder or learning disability, where linked to the commission of the offence

STEP TWO Starting point and category range **SG19-15**

Having determined the category, the court should use the corresponding starting points to reach a sentence within the category range below. The starting point applies to all offenders irrespective of plea or previous convictions.

Where the defendant is dependent on or has a propensity to misuse drugs and there is sufficient prospect of success, a community order with a drug rehabilitation requirement under section 209 of the Criminal Justice Act 2003 may be a proper alternative to a short or moderate custodial sentence.

[9]

Offence Category	Starting Point (*Applicable to all offenders*)	Category Range (*Applicable to all Offenders*)
Category 1	3 years' custody	2–6 years' custody
Category 2	1 year's custody	High level community order–2 years' custody
Category 3	High level Community Order	Low level community order–26 weeks' custody

A case of particular gravity, reflected by multiple features of culpability or harm in step 1, could merit upward adjustment from the starting point before further adjustment for aggravating or mitigating features, set out below.

The table below contains a non-exhaustive list of additional factual elements providing the context of the offence and factors relating to the offender. Identify whether any combination of these, or other relevant factors, should result in an upward or downward adjustment from the starting point. **In particular, relevant recent convictions are likely to result in an upward adjustment**. In some cases, having considered these factors, it may be appropriate to move outside the identified category range.

When sentencing **category 2 or 3** offences, the court should also consider the custody threshold as follows:

- Has the custody threshold been passed?
- If so, is it unavoidable that a custodial sentence be imposed?
- If so, can that sentence be suspended?

Factors increasing seriousness	Factors reducing seriousness or reflecting personal mitigation
Statutory aggravating factors: Previous convictions, having regard to a) the nature of the offence to which the conviction relates and its relevance to the current offence; and b) the time that has elapsed since the conviction* Offence committed whilst on bail *Other aggravating factors include*: Child at home (or returns home) when offence committed Offence committed at night Gratuitous degradation of the victim Any steps taken to prevent the victim reporting the incident or obtaining assistance and/or from assisting or supporting the prosecution Victim compelled to leave their home (in particular victims of domestic violence) Established evidence of community impact Commission of offence whilst under the influence of alcohol or drugs Failure to comply with current court orders Offence committed whilst on licence Offences Taken Into Consideration (TICs)	Offender has made voluntary reparation to the victim Subordinate role in a group or gang No previous convictions or no relevant/recent convictions Remorse Good character and/or exemplary conduct Determination, and/or demonstration of steps taken to address addiction or offending behaviour Serious medical conditions requiring urgent, intensive or long-term treatment Age and/or lack of maturity where it affects the responsibility of the offender Lapse of time since the offence where this is not the fault of the offender Mental disorder or learning disability, where not linked to the commission of the offence Sole or primary carer for dependent relatives

* Where sentencing an offender for a qualifying **third domestic burglary**, the court must apply section 111 of the Powers of the Criminal Courts (Sentencing) Act 2000 and impose a custodial term of at least three years, unless it is satisfied that there are particular circumstances which relate to any of the offences or to the offender which would make it unjust to do so. [9]

SG19-16 **STEP THREE Consider any factors which indicate a reduction, such as assistance to the prosecution** [10]

The court should take into account sections 73 and 74 of the Serious Organised Crime and Police Act 2005 (assistance by defendants: reduction or review of sentence) and any other rule of law by virtue of which an offender may receive a discounted sentence in consequence of assistance given (or offered) to the prosecutor or investigator.

SG19-17 **STEP FOUR Reduction for guilty pleas**

The court should take account of any potential reduction for a guilty plea in accordance with section 144 of the Criminal Justice Act 2003 and the *Guilty Plea* guideline.

Where a minimum mandatory sentence is imposed under section 111 Powers of Criminal Courts (Sentencing) Act, the discount for an early guilty plea must not exceed 20 per cent.

[Steps Five to Nine are identical to those for aggravated burglary: see **SG19-3**.]

SG19-18 [11]

Non-domestic Burglary

Theft Act 1968 (section 9)

This is a serious specified offence for the purposes of section 224 Criminal Justice Act 2003 if it was committed with intent to:

(a) inflict grievous bodily harm on a person, or
(b) do unlawful damage to a building or anything in it.

Triable either way

Maximum when tried summarily: Level 5 fine and/or 26 weeks' custody
Maximum when tried on indictment: 10 years' custody

Offence range: Fine–5 years' custody

SG19-19 **STEP ONE Determining the offence category** [12]

The court should determine the offence category using the table below.

Category 1	Greater harm **and** higher culpability
Category 2	Greater harm **and** lower culpability **or** lesser harm **and** higher culpability
Category 3	Lesser harm **and** lower culpability

The court should determine culpability and harm caused or intended, by reference only to the factors below, which comprise the principal factual elements of the offence. Where an offence does not fall squarely into a category, individual factors may require a degree of weighting before making an overall assessment and determining the appropriate offence category.

Factors indicating greater harm Theft of/damage to property causing a significant degree of loss to the victim (whether economic, commercial or personal value) Soiling, ransacking or vandalism of property Victim on the premises (or returns) while offender present Trauma to the victim, beyond the normal inevitable consequence of intrusion and theft Violence used or threatened against victim Context of general public disorder	**Factors indicating higher culpability** Premises or victim deliberately targeted (to include pharmacy or doctor's surgery and targeting due to vulnerability of victim or hostility based on disability, race, sexual orientation and so forth) A significant degree of planning or organisation Knife or other weapon carried (where not charged separately) Equipped for burglary (for example, implements carried and/or use of vehicle) Member of a group or gang
Factors indicating lesser harm Nothing stolen or only property of very low value to the victim (whether economic, commercial or personal) Limited damage or disturbance to property	**Factors indicating lower culpability** Offence committed on impulse, with limited intrusion into property Offender exploited by others Mental disorder or learning disability, where linked to the commission of the offence

[12] **STEP TWO Starting point and category range** **SG19-20**

Having determined the category, the court should use the corresponding starting points to reach a sentence within the category range below. The starting point applies to all offenders irrespective of plea or previous convictions.

Where the defendant is dependent on or has a propensity to misuse drugs and there is sufficient prospect of success, a community order with a drug rehabilitation requirement under section 209 of the Criminal Justice Act 2003 may be a proper alternative to a short or moderate custodial sentence.

A case of particular gravity, reflected by multiple features of culpability or harm in step 1, could merit upward adjustment from the starting point before further adjustment for aggravating or mitigating features, set out [below].

[13]

Offence Category	Starting Point (*Applicable to all offenders*)	Category Range (*Applicable to all Offenders*)
Category 1	2 years' custody	1–5 years' custody
Category 2	18 weeks' custody	Low level community order–51 weeks' custody
Category 3	Medium level community order	Band B fine–18 weeks' custody

The table below contains a non-exhaustive list of additional factual elements providing the context of the offence and factors relating to the offender. Identify whether any combination of these, or other relevant factors, should result in an upward or downward adjustment from the starting point. **In particular, relevant recent convictions are likely to result in an upward adjustment.** In some cases, having considered these factors, it may be appropriate to move outside the identified category range.

When sentencing **category 2 or 3** offences, the court should also consider the custody threshold as follows:

- Has the custody threshold been passed?
- If so, is it unavoidable that a custodial sentence be imposed?
- If so, can that sentence be suspended?

When sentencing **category 3** offences, the court should also consider the community order threshold as follows:

- Has the community order threshold been passed?

Factors increasing seriousness	**Factors reducing seriousness or reflecting personal mitigation**
Statutory aggravating factors: Previous convictions, having regard to a) the nature of the offence to which the conviction relates and its relevance to the current offence; and b) the time that has elapsed since the conviction Offence committed whilst on bail *Other aggravating factors include*: Offence committed at night, particularly where staff present or likely to be present Abuse of a position of trust Gratuitous degradation of the victim Any steps taken to prevent the victim reporting the incident or obtaining assistance and/or from assisting or supporting the prosecution Established evidence of community impact Commission of offence whilst under the influence of alcohol or drugs Failure to comply with current court orders Offence committed whilst on licence Offences Taken Into Consideration (TICs)	Offender has made voluntary reparation to the victim Subordinate role in a group or gang No previous convictions or no relevant/recent convictions Remorse Good character and/or exemplary conduct Determination, and/or demonstration of steps taken to address addiction or offending behaviour Serious medical conditions requiring urgent, intensive or long-term treatment Age and/or lack of maturity where it affects the responsibility of the offender Lapse of time since the offence where this is not the fault of the offender Mental disorder or learning disability, where not linked to the commission of the offence Sole or primary carer for dependent relatives

[14] [Steps Three to Nine are identical to those for domestic burglary: see **SG19-13**.] **SG19-21**

[15] ## Annex: Fine Bands and Community Orders **SG19-22**

[The tables set out here are also set out in the Magistrates' Court Sentencing Guidelines, which include further guidance on fines and community orders: see **SG10-129** and **SG9-2**.]

PART 20 CHILD CRUELTY

SG20-1 ## Definitive Guideline

Applicability of guideline [2]

[Omitted: See **SG19-1** for identical text save that this guideline has effect from 1 January 2019]

SG20-2 **Structure, ranges and starting points**

For the purposes of sections 125(3)–(4) of the Coroners and Justice Act 2009, the guideline specifies offence ranges – the range of sentences appropriate for each type of offence. Within each offence, the Council has specified a number of categories which reflect varying degrees of seriousness. The offence range is split into category ranges – sentences appropriate for each level of seriousness. The Council has also identified a starting point within each category.

Starting points define the position within a category range from which to start calculating the provisional sentence. The court should consider further features of the offence or the offender that warrant adjustment of the sentence within the range, including the aggravating and mitigating factors set out at step two. Starting points and ranges apply to all offenders, whether they have pleaded guilty or been convicted after trial. Credit for a guilty plea is taken into consideration only at step four in the decision making process, after the appropriate sentence has been identified.

Information on community orders is set out in the annex at **SG20-37**.

SG20-3 ## Cruelty to a Child – Assault and Ill Treatment, Abandonment, Neglect, and Failure to Protect [3]

Children and Young Persons Act 1933 (section 1(1))

Triable either way

Maximum: 10 years' custody

Offence range: Community order–8 years' custody

This is a specified offence for the purposes of section 226A (extended sentence for certain violent or sexual offences) of the Criminal Justice Act 2003

SG20-4 **STEP ONE Determining the offence category** [4]

The court should determine the offence category with reference **only** to the factors listed in the tables below. In order to determine the category the court should assess **culpability** and **harm.**

The court should weigh all the factors set out below in determining the offender's culpability.

Where there are characteristics present which fall under different levels of culpability, the court should balance these characteristics to reach a fair assessment of the offender's culpability.

Culpability demonstrated by one or more of the following:
A – High culpability: • Prolonged and/or multiple incidents of serious cruelty, including serious neglect • Gratuitous degradation of victim and/or sadistic behaviour • Use of very significant force • Use of a weapon • Deliberate disregard for the welfare of the victim • Failure to take any steps to protect the victim from offences in which the above factors are present • Offender with professional responsibility for the victim (where linked to the commission of the offence)
B – Medium culpability: • Use of significant force • Prolonged and/or multiple incidents of cruelty, including neglect • Limited steps taken to protect victim in cases with category A factors present • Other cases falling between A and C because: ° Factors in both high and lesser categories are present which balance each other out; and/or ° The offender's culpability falls between the factors as described in high and lesser culpability

[4]

C – Lesser culpability:
- Offender's responsibility substantially reduced by mental disorder or learning disability or lack of maturity
- Offender is victim of domestic abuse, including coercion and/or intimidation (where linked to the commission of the offence)
- Steps taken to protect victim but fell just short of what could reasonably be expected
- Momentary or brief lapse in judgment including in cases of neglect
- Use of some force or failure to protect the victim from an incident involving some force
- Low level of neglect

[5]

Harm

The court should consider the factors set out below to determine the level of harm that has been caused or was intended to be caused to the victim.

Psychological, developmental or emotional harm

A finding that the psychological, developmental or emotional harm is serious may be based on a clinical diagnosis but the court may make such a finding based on other evidence from or on behalf of the victim that serious psychological, developmental or emotional harm exists. It is important to be clear that the absence of such a finding does not imply that the psychological, developmental or emotional harm suffered by the victim is minor or trivial.

Category 1	• Serious psychological, developmental, and/or emotional harm • Serious physical harm (including illnesses contracted due to neglect)
Category 2	• Cases falling between categories 1 and 3 • A high likelihood of category 1 harm being caused
Category 3	• Little or no psychological, developmental, and/or emotional harm • Little or no physical harm

STEP TWO Starting point and category range SG20-5

Having determined the category at step one, the court should use the corresponding starting point to reach a sentence within the category range below. The starting point applies to all offenders irrespective of plea or previous convictions.

Where a case does not fall squarely within a category, adjustment from the starting point may be required before adjustment for aggravating or mitigating features.

	Culpability		
Harm	**A**	**B**	**C**
Category 1	**Starting point** 6 years' custody	**Starting point** 3 years' custody	**Starting point** 1 year's custody
	Category range 4–8 years' custody	**Category range** 2–6 years' custody	**Category range** High level community order–2 years 6 months' custody
Category 2	**Starting point** 3 years' custody	**Starting point** 1 year's custody	**Starting point** High level community order
	Category range 2–6 years' custody	**Category range** High level community order –2 years 6 months' custody	**Category range** Medium level community order–1 year's custody
Category 3	**Starting point** 1 year's custody	**Starting point** High level community order	**Starting point** Medium level community order
	Category range High level community order –2 years 6 months' custody	**Category range** Medium level community order–1 year's custody	**Category range** Low level community order–6 months' custody

SG20-6 The table below contains a **non-exhaustive** list of additional factual elements providing the context of the offence and factors relating to the offender. Identify whether any combination of these, or other relevant factors, should result in an upward or downward adjustment from the sentence arrived at so far. In particular, relevant recent convictions are likely to result in an upward adjustment. In some cases, having considered these factors, it may be appropriate to move outside the identified category range. [6]

Factors increasing seriousness
Statutory aggravating factors: Previous convictions, having regard to a) the **nature** of the offence to which the conviction relates and its **relevance** to the current offence; and b) the **time** that has elapsed since the conviction Offence committed whilst on bail
Other aggravating factors: Failure to seek medical help (where not taken into account at step one) Commission of offence whilst under the influence of alcohol or drugs Deliberate concealment and/or covering up of the offence Blame wrongly placed on others Failure to respond to interventions or warnings about behaviour Threats to prevent reporting of the offence Failure to comply with current court orders Offence committed on licence or post sentence supervision Offences taken into consideration Offence committed in the presence of another child
Factors reducing seriousness or reflecting personal mitigation
No previous convictions or no relevant/recent convictions Remorse Determination and demonstration of steps having been taken to address addiction or offending behaviour, including co-operation with agencies working for the welfare of the victim Sole or primary carer for dependent relatives (see step five for further guidance on parental responsibilities) Good character and/or exemplary conduct (where previous good character/exemplary conduct has been used to facilitate or conceal the offence, this should not normally constitute mitigation and such conduct may constitute aggravation) Serious medical condition requiring urgent, intensive or long-term treatment Mental disorder, learning disability or lack of maturity (where not taken into account at step one) Co-operation with the investigation

SG20-7 **STEP THREE Consider any factors which indicate a reduction for assistance to the prosecution** [7]

The court should take into account sections 73 and 74 of the Serious Organised Crime and Police Act 2005 (assistance by defendants: reduction or review of sentence) and any other rule of law by virtue of which an offender may receive a discounted sentence in consequence of assistance given (or offered) to the prosecutor or investigator.

SG20-8 **STEP FOUR Reduction for guilty pleas**

The court should take account of any potential reduction for a guilty plea in accordance with section 144 of the Criminal Justice Act 2003 and the Guilty Plea guideline.

SG20-9 **STEP FIVE Parental responsibilities of sole or primary carers**

In the majority of child cruelty cases the offender will have parental responsibility for the victim.

[7] When considering whether to impose custody the court should step back and review whether this sentence will be in the best interests of the victim (as well as other children in the offender's care). This must be balanced with the seriousness of the offence and all sentencing options remain open to the court but careful consideration should be given to the effect that a custodial sentence could have on the family life of the victim and whether this is proportionate to the seriousness of the offence. This may be of particular relevance in lower culpability cases or where the offender has otherwise been a loving and capable parent/carer.

Where custody is unavoidable consideration of the impact on the offender's children may be relevant to the length of the sentence imposed. For more serious offences where a substantial period of custody is appropriate, this consideration will carry less weight.

STEP SIX Dangerousness SG20-10

The court should consider whether having regard to the criteria contained in Chapter 5 of Part 12 of the Criminal Justice Act 2003 it would be appropriate to impose an extended sentence (section 226A).

STEP SEVEN Totality principle SG20-11

If sentencing an offender for more than one offence, or where the offender is already serving a sentence, consider whether the total sentence is just and proportionate to the overall offending behaviour in accordance with the Offences Taken into Consideration and Totality guideline.

STEP EIGHT Ancillary orders SG20-12

In all cases the court should consider whether to make ancillary orders.

[8] **STEP NINE Reasons** SG20-13

Section 174 of the Criminal Justice Act 2003 imposes a duty to give reasons for, and explain the effect of, the sentence.

STEP TEN Consideration for time spent on bail (tagged curfew) SG20-14

The court must consider whether to give credit for time spent on bail in accordance with section 240A of the Criminal Justice Act 2003.

[9] Causing or Allowing a Child to Suffer Serious Physical Harm SG20-15

Domestic Violence, Crime and Victims Act 2004 (section 5)

Indictable only

Maximum: 10 years' custody

Offence range: Community order–9 years' custody

Causing or Allowing a Child to Die SG20-16

Domestic Violence, Crime and Victims Act 2004 (section 5)

Indictable only

Maximum: 14 years' custody

Offence range: 1 year's custody–14 years' custody

These are specified offences for the purposes of section 226A (extended sentence for certain violent or sexual offences) of the Criminal Justice Act 2003

This guideline applies only when the victim of the offence is aged 15 or under.

[10] **STEP ONE Determining the offence category** SG20-17

The court should determine the offence category with reference **only** to the factors listed in the tables below. In order to determine the category, the court should assess **culpability** and **harm.**

The court should weigh all the factors set out below in determining the offender's culpability.

Where there are characteristics present which fall under different levels of culpability, the court should balance these characteristics to reach a fair assessment of the offender's culpability. [10]

Culpability demonstrated by one or more of the following:
A – High culpability: • Prolonged and/or multiple incidents of serious cruelty, including serious neglect • Gratuitous degradation of victim and/or sadistic behaviour • Use of very significant force • Use of a weapon • Deliberate disregard for the welfare of the victim • Failure to take any steps to protect the victim from offences in which the above factors are present • Offender with professional responsibility for the victim (where linked to the commission of the offence)
B – Medium culpability: • Use of significant force • Prolonged and/or multiple incidents of cruelty, including neglect • Limited steps taken to protect victim in cases with category A factors present • Other cases falling between A and C because: ° Factors in both high and lesser categories are present which balance each other out; and/or ° The offender's culpability falls between the factors as described in high and lesser culpability
C – Lesser culpability: • Offender's responsibility substantially reduced by mental disorder or learning disability or lack of maturity • Offender is victim of domestic abuse, including coercion and/or intimidation (where linked to the commission of the offence) • Steps taken to protect victim but fell just short of what could reasonably be expected • Momentary or brief lapse in judgment including in cases of neglect • Use of some force or failure to protect the victim from an incident involving some force • Low level of neglect

[11]

Harm	
The court should consider the factors set out below to determine the level of harm that has been caused or was intended to be caused to the victim.	
Psychological, developmental or emotional harm A finding that the psychological, developmental or emotional harm is serious may be based on a clinical diagnosis but the court may make such a finding based on other evidence from or on behalf of the victim that serious psychological, developmental or emotional harm exists. It is important to be clear that the absence of such a finding does not imply that the psychological/ developmental harm suffered by the victim is minor or trivial.	
Category 1	• Death
Category 2	• Serious physical harm which has a substantial and/or long term effect • Serious psychological, developmental and/or emotional harm • Significantly reduced life expectancy • A progressive, permanent or irreversible condition
Category 3	• Serious physical harm that does not fall into category 2

SG20-18 STEP TWO **Starting point and category range**

Having determined the category at step one, the court should use the corresponding starting point to reach a sentence within the category range below. The starting point applies to all offenders irrespective of plea or previous convictions.

Where a case does not fall squarely within a category, adjustment from the starting point may be required before adjustment for aggravating or mitigating features.

[11]

Harm	Culpability A	B	C
Category 1	**Starting point** 9 years' custody	**Starting point** 5 years' custody	**Starting point** 2 years' custody
	Category range 7–14 years' custody	**Category range** 3–8 years' custody	**Category range** 1–4 years' custody
Category 2	**Starting point** 7 years' custody	**Starting point** 3 years' custody	**Starting point** 1 year 6 months' custody
	Category range 5–9 years' custody	**Category range** 1 year 6 months–6 years' custody	**Category range** 6 months–3 years' custody
Category 3	**Starting point** 3 years' custody	**Starting point** 1 year 6 months' custody	**Starting point** 9 months' custody
	Category range 1 year 6 months–6 years' custody	**Category range** 6 months–3 years' custody	**Category range** High level community order –2 years' custody

[12] The table below contains a **non-exhaustive** list of additional factual elements providing the context of the offence and factors relating to the offender. Identify whether any combination of these, or other relevant factors, should result in an upward or downward adjustment from the sentence arrived at so far. In particular, relevant recent convictions are likely to result in an upward adjustment. In some cases, having considered these factors, it may be appropriate to move outside the identified category range.

Factors increasing seriousness
Statutory aggravating factors: Previous convictions, having regard to a) the nature of the offence to which the conviction relates and its relevance to the current offence; and b) the time that has elapsed since the conviction
Offence committed whilst on bail
Other aggravating factors: Failure to seek medical help (where not taken into account at step one) Prolonged suffering prior to death Commission of offence whilst under the influence of alcohol or drugs Deliberate concealment and/or covering up of the offence Blame wrongly placed on others Failure to respond to interventions or warnings about behaviour Threats to prevent reporting of the offence Failure to comply with current court orders Offence committed on licence or post sentence supervision Offences taken into consideration Offence committed in the presence of another child
Factors reducing seriousness or reflecting personal mitigation
No previous convictions **or** no relevant/recent convictions Remorse Determination and demonstration of steps having been taken to address addiction or offending behaviour, including co-operation with agencies working for the welfare of the victim Sole or primary carer for dependent relatives (**see step five for further guidance on parental responsibilities**) Good character and/or exemplary conduct (where previous good character/exemplary conduct has been used to facilitate or conceal the offence, this should not normally constitute mitigation and such conduct may constitute aggravation) Serious medical condition requiring urgent, intensive or long-term treatment Mental disorder, learning disability or lack of maturity (where not taken into account at step one) Co-operation with the investigation

SG20-19 **STEP THREE Consider any factors which indicate a reduction for assistance to the prosecution** [13]

The court should take into account sections 73 and 74 of the Serious Organised Crime and Police Act 2005 (assistance by defendants: reduction or review of sentence) and any other rule of law by virtue of which an offender may receive a discounted sentence in consequence of assistance given (or offered) to the prosecutor or investigator.

SG20-20 **STEP FOUR Reduction for guilty pleas**

The court should take account of any potential reduction for a guilty plea in accordance with section 144 of the Criminal Justice Act 2003 and the Guilty Plea guideline.

SG20-21 **STEP FIVE Parental responsibilities of sole or primary carers**

In the majority of child cruelty cases the offender will have parental responsibility for the victim.

When considering whether to impose custody the court should step back and review whether this sentence will be in the best interests of the victim (as well as other children in the offender's care). This must be balanced with the seriousness of the offence and all sentencing options remain open to the court but careful consideration should be given to the effect that a custodial sentence could have on the family life of the victim and whether this is proportionate to the seriousness of the offence. This may be of particular relevance in lower culpability cases or where the offender has otherwise been a loving and capable parent/carer.

Where custody is unavoidable consideration of the impact on the offender's children may be relevant to the length of the sentence imposed. For more serious offences where a substantial period of custody is appropriate, this consideration will carry less weight.

SG20-22 **STEP SIX Dangerousness**

The court should consider whether having regard to the criteria contained in Chapter 5 of Part 12 of the Criminal Justice Act 2003 it would be appropriate to impose an extended sentence (section 226A).

SG20-23 **STEP SEVEN Totality principle**

If sentencing an offender for more than one offence, or where the offender is already serving a sentence, consider whether the total sentence is just and proportionate to the overall offending behaviour in accordance with the Offences Taken into Consideration and Totality guideline.

SG20-24 **STEP EIGHT Ancillary orders**

In all cases the court should consider whether to make ancillary orders.

SG20-25 **STEP NINE Reasons** [14]

Section 174 of the Criminal Justice Act 2003 imposes a duty to give reasons for, and explain the effect of, the sentence.

SG20-26 **STEP TEN Consideration for time spent on bail (tagged curfew)**

The court must consider whether to give credit for time spent on bail in accordance with section 240A of the Criminal Justice Act 2003.

SG20-27 Failing to Protect Girl from Risk of Genital Mutilation [15]

Female Genital Mutilation Act 2003 (section 3A)

Indictable only

Maximum: 7 years' custody

Offence range: Community order–6 years' custody

[16]

SG20-28 **STEP ONE Determining the offence category**

The court should determine the offence category with reference **only** to the factors listed in the tables below. In order to determine the category, the court should assess **culpability and harm.**

The court should weigh all the factors set out below in determining the offender's culpability.

[16] **Where there are characteristics present which fall under different levels of culpability, the court should balance these characteristics to reach a fair assessment of the offender's culpability.**

Culpability demonstrated by one or more of the following:
A – High culpability: • Child was the subject of an FGM Protection Order • Failure to respond to interventions or warnings including, but not limited to, those from medical professionals/social services • Involving others through coercion, intimidation or exploitation • Failure to take any steps to protect the victim from the FGM offence
B – Medium culpability: • Limited steps taken to protect the victim from the FGM offence • Other cases falling between A and C because: ° Factors in both high and lesser categories are present which balance each other out; and/or ° The offender's culpability falls between the factors as described in high and lesser culpability
C – Lesser culpability: • Steps taken to protect the victim but fell just short of what could reasonably be expected • Offender is victim of domestic abuse (where linked to commission of the offence) • Offender subjected to coercion, intimidation or exploitation • Offender's responsibility substantially reduced by mental disorder or learning disability

Harm	
The court should consider the factors set out below to determine the level of harm that has been caused to the victim. **Psychological harm** A finding that the psychological harm is serious may be based on a clinical diagnosis but the court may make such a finding based on other evidence from or on behalf of the victim that serious psychological harm exists. It is important to be clear that the absence of such a finding does not imply that the harm suffered by the victim is minor or trivial.	
Category 1	• Serious physical or psychological harm which has a substantial or long-term effect
Category 2	• Harm which does not fall into category 1

[17] **STEP TWO Starting point and category range** **SG20-29**

Having determined the category at step one, the court should use the corresponding starting point to reach a sentence within the category range below. The starting point applies to all offenders irrespective of plea or previous convictions.

Where a case does not fall squarely within a category, adjustment from the starting point may be required before adjustment for aggravating or mitigating features.

	Culpability		
Harm	**A**	**B**	**C**
Category 1	**Starting point** 5 years' custody	**Starting point** 3 years' custody	**Starting point** 1 year's custody
	Category range 3–6 years' custody	**Category range** 2–4 years' custody	**Category range** High level community order–3 years' custody
Category 2	**Starting point** 3 years' custody	**Starting point** 1 year's custody	**Starting point** High level community order
	Category range 2–4 years' custody	**Category range** High level community order–2 years' custody	**Category range** Low level community order –1 year's custody

Sentencing Guidelines

The table below contains a **non-exhaustive** list of additional factual elements providing the context of the offence and factors relating to the offender. Identify whether any combination of these, or other relevant factors, should result in an upward or downward adjustment from the sentence arrived at so far. In particular, relevant recent convictions are likely to result in an upward adjustment. In some cases, having considered these factors, it may be appropriate to move outside the identified category range. [18]

Factors increasing seriousness
Statutory aggravating factors: Previous convictions, having regard to a) the nature of the offence to which the conviction relates and its relevance to the current offence; and b) the time that has elapsed since the conviction Offence committed whilst on bail
Other aggravating factors: Failure to seek medical help when necessary Deliberate concealment and/or covering up of the offence Blame wrongly placed on others Threats to prevent reporting of the offence Failure to comply with current court orders (where not taken into account at step one) Offence committed on licence or post sentence supervision Offences taken into consideration
Factors reducing seriousness or reflecting personal mitigation
No previous convictions **or** no relevant/recent convictions Remorse Offender particularly isolated with limited access to support Appropriate medical care sought for victim Sole or primary carer for dependent relatives **(see step five for further guidance on parental responsibilities)** Good character and/or exemplary conduct Serious medical condition requiring urgent, intensive or long-term treatment Age and/or lack of maturity Mental disorder or learning disability (where not taken into account at step one) Co-operation with the investigation

SG20-30 **STEP THREE Consider any factors which indicate a reduction for assistance to the prosecution** [19]

The court should take into account sections 73 and 74 of the Serious Organised Crime and Police Act 2005 (assistance by defendants: reduction or review of sentence) and any other rule of law by virtue of which an offender may receive a discounted sentence in consequence of assistance given (or offered) to the prosecutor or investigator.

SG20-31 **STEP FOUR Reduction for guilty pleas**

The court should take account of any potential reduction for a guilty plea in accordance with section 144 of the Criminal Justice Act 2003 and the Guilty Plea guideline.

SG20-32 **STEP FIVE Parental responsibilities of sole or primary carers**

In the majority of child cruelty cases the offender will have parental responsibility for the victim.

When considering whether to impose custody the court should step back and review whether this sentence will be in the best interests of the victim (as well as other children in the offender's care). This must be balanced with the seriousness of the offence and all sentencing options remain open to the court but careful consideration should be given to the effect that a custodial sentence could have on the family life of the victim and whether this is proportionate to the seriousness of the offence. This may be of particular relevance in lower culpability cases or where the offender has otherwise been a loving and capable parent/carer.

Where custody is unavoidable consideration of the impact on the offender's children may be relevant to the length of the sentence imposed. For more serious offences where a substantial period of custody is appropriate, this consideration will carry less weight.

[19] **STEP SIX Totality principle** SG20-33

If sentencing an offender for more than one offence, or where the offender is already serving a sentence, consider whether the total sentence is just and proportionate to the overall offending behaviour in accordance with the Offences Taken into Consideration and Totality guideline.

STEP SEVEN Ancillary orders SG20-34

In all cases the court should consider whether to make ancillary orders.

STEP EIGHT Reasons SG20-35

Section 174 of the Criminal Justice Act 2003 imposes a duty to give reasons for, and explain the effect of, the sentence.

[20] **STEP NINE Consideration for time spent on bail (tagged curfew)** SG20-36

The court must consider whether to give credit for time spent on bail in accordance with section 240A of the Criminal Justice Act 2003.

[21]

ANNEX: COMMUNITY ORDERS SG20-37

In this guideline, community sentences are expressed as one of three levels (low, medium or high). An illustrative description of examples of requirements that might be appropriate for each level is provided below.

Where two or more requirements are ordered, they must be compatible with each other. Save in exceptional circumstances, the court must impose at least one requirement for the purpose of punishment, or combine the community order with a fine, or both (see section 177 Criminal Justice Act 2003).

Low	Medium	High
Offences only just cross community order threshold, where the seriousness of the offence or the nature of the offender's record means that a discharge or fine is inappropriate	Offences obviously fall within the community order band	Offences only just fall below the custody threshold or the custody threshold is crossed but a community order is more appropriate in the circumstances
In general, only one requirement will be appropriate and the length may be curtailed if additional requirements are necessary		More intensive sentences which combine two or more requirements may be appropriate
Suitable requirements might include: • Any appropriate rehabilitative requirement(s) • 40–80 hours of unpaid work • Curfew requirement within the lowest range (for example up to 16 hours per day for a few weeks) • Exclusion requirement, for a few months • Prohibited activity requirement • Attendance centre requirement (where available)	Suitable requirements might include: • Any appropriate rehabilitative requirement(s) • Greater number of hours of unpaid work (for example 80–150 hours) • Curfew requirement within the middle range (for example up to 16 hours for 2–3 months) • Exclusion requirement lasting in the region of 6 months • Prohibited activity requirement	Suitable requirements might include: • Any appropriate rehabilitative requirement(s) • 150–300 hours of unpaid work • Curfew requirement up to 16 hours per day for 4–12 months • Exclusion order lasting in the region of 12 months

The table above is also set out in the Imposition of Community and Custodial Sentences Guideline [see SG9-4] which includes further guidance on community orders.

PART 21 DANGEROUS DOG OFFENCES

SG21-1 DEFINITIVE GUIDELINE

Applicability of guideline [2]
[Omitted: See **SG19-1** for identical text save that this guideline has effect from 1 July 2016.]

Structure, ranges and starting points
[Omitted: See **SG19-2** for identical text.]

SG21-2 OWNER OR PERSON IN CHARGE OF A DOG DANGEROUSLY OUT OF CONTROL IN ANY PLACE IN ENGLAND OR WALES (WHETHER OR NOT A PUBLIC PLACE) WHERE DEATH IS CAUSED [3]

Dangerous Dogs Act 1991 (section 3(1))

Triable either way
Maximum: 14 years' custody

Offence range: High level community order–14 years' custody

SG21-3 STEP ONE Determining the offence category [4]

In order to determine the category the court should assess **culpability** and **harm**. The court should determine the offence category with reference only to the factors in the tables below.

The level of culpability is determined by weighing up all the factors of the case. **Where there are characteristics present which fall under different levels of culpability, the court should balance these characteristics to reach a fair assessment of the offender's culpability.**

Culpability demonstrated by one or more of the following:
A – High culpability Dog used as a weapon or to intimidate people Dog known to be prohibited Dog trained to be aggressive Offender disqualified from owning a dog, or failed to respond to official warnings, or to comply with orders concerning the dog
B – Medium culpability All other cases where characteristics for categories A or C are not present, and in particular: Failure to respond to warnings or concerns expressed by others about the dog's behaviour Failure to act on prior knowledge of the dog's aggressive behaviour Lack of safety or control measures taken in situations where an incident could reasonably have been foreseen Failure to intervene in the incident (where it would have been reasonable to do so) Ill treatment or failure to ensure welfare needs of the dog (where connected to the offence and where not charged separately)
C – Lesser culpability Attempts made to regain control of the dog and/or intervene Provocation of the dog without fault of the offender Evidence of safety or control measures having been taken Incident could not have reasonably been foreseen by the offender Momentary lapse of control/attention

Harm
There is no variation in the level of harm caused, as by definition the harm involved in an offence where a death is caused is always of the utmost seriousness.

SG21-4 STEP TWO Starting point and category range [5]

Having determined the category at step one, the court should use the corresponding starting points to reach a sentence within the category range below. The starting point applies to all offenders irrespective of plea or previous convictions.

[5]

High culpability	Starting point 8 years' custody	Category range 6–14 years' custody
Medium culpability	Starting point 4 years' custody	Category range 2–7 years' custody
Lesser culpability	Starting point 1 year's custody	Category range High level community order–2 years' custody

The table is for single offences. Concurrent sentences reflecting the overall criminality of offending will ordinarily be appropriate where offences arise out of the same incident or facts: please refer to the *Offences Taken into Consideration* and *Totality* guideline [see SG3-1 and SG3-7].

The court should then consider any adjustment for any aggravating or mitigating factors. [Below] is a **non-exhaustive** list of additional factual elements providing the context of the offence and factors relating to the offender.

Identify whether any combination of these, or other relevant factors, should result in an upward or downward adjustment from the starting point.

[6]

Factors increasing seriousness
Statutory aggravating factors: Previous convictions, having regard to a) the **nature** of the offence to which the conviction relates and its **relevance** to the current offence; and b) the **time** that has elapsed since the conviction Offence committed whilst on bail Offence motivated by, or demonstrating hostility based on any of the following characteristics or presumed characteristics of the victim: religion, race, disability, sexual orientation or transgender identity
Other aggravating factors Victim is a child or otherwise vulnerable because of personal circumstances Location of the offence Sustained or repeated attack Significant ongoing effect on witness(es) to the attack Serious injury caused to others (where not charged separately) Allowing person insufficiently experienced or trained, to be in charge of the dog Lack or loss of control of the dog due to influence of alcohol or drugs Offence committed against those working in the public sector or providing a service to the public Injury to other animals Established evidence of community/wider impact Failure to comply with current court orders (except where taken into account in assessing culpability) Offence committed on licence Offences taken into consideration
Factors reducing seriousness or reflecting personal mitigation
No previous convictions **or** no relevant/recent convictions No previous complaints against, or incidents involving, the dog Evidence of responsible ownership Remorse Good character and/or exemplary conduct Serious medical conditions requiring urgent, intensive or long-term treatment Age and/or lack of maturity where it affects the responsibility of the offender Mental disorder or learning disability Sole or primary carer for dependent relatives Determination and/or demonstration of steps taken to address offending behaviour

[7] **STEP THREE Consider any factors which indicate a reduction, such as assistance to the prosecution** **SG21-5**

The court should take into account sections 73 and 74 of the Serious Organised Crime and Police Act 2005 (assistance by defendants: reduction or review of sentence) and any other rule of law by virtue of which an offender may receive a discounted sentence in consequence of assistance given (or offered) to the prosecutor or investigator.

STEP FOUR Reduction for guilty pleas **SG21-6**

The court should take account of any potential reduction for a guilty plea in accordance with section 144 of the Criminal Justice Act 2003 and the guideline for *Reduction in Sentence for a Guilty Plea* (where first hearing is **on or after 1 June 2017**, or first hearing **before 1 June 2017**). [see **SG4-1**].

SG21-7 **STEP FIVE Totality principle** [7]

If sentencing an offender for more than one offence, or where the offender is already serving a sentence, consider whether the total sentence is just and proportionate to the overall offending behaviour in accordance with the *Totality* guideline [see SG3-1 and SG3-7].

SG21-8 **STEP SIX Compensation and ancillary orders**

In all cases, the court should consider whether to make a compensation order and/or other ancillary orders.

Compensation order

The court should consider compensation orders in all cases where personal injury, loss or damage has resulted from the offence. The court must give reasons if it decides not to award compensation in such cases.

Other ancillary orders available include:

Disqualification from having a dog

The court **may** disqualify the offender from having custody of a dog. The test the court should consider is whether the offender is a fit and proper person to have custody of a dog.

Destruction order/contingent destruction order

In any case where the offender is not the owner of the dog, the owner must be given an opportunity to be present and make representations to the court.

If the dog is a prohibited dog refer to the guideline for possession of a prohibited dog in relation to destruction/contingent destruction orders.

The court **shall** make a destruction order unless the court is satisfied that the dog would not constitute a danger to public safety. [8]

In reaching a decision, the court should consider the relevant circumstances which **must** include:

- the temperament of the dog and its past behaviour;
- whether the owner of the dog, or the person for the time being in charge of it is a fit and proper person to be in charge of the dog;

and **may** include:

- other relevant circumstances.

If the court is satisfied that the dog would not constitute a danger to public safety and the dog is not prohibited, it **may** make a contingent destruction order requiring the dog to be kept under proper control. A contingent destruction order may specify the measures to be taken by the owner for keeping the dog under proper control, which include:

- muzzling;
- keeping on a lead;
- neutering in appropriate cases; and
- excluding it from a specified place.

Where the court makes a destruction order, it **may** appoint a person to undertake destruction and order the offender to pay what it determines to be the reasonable expenses of destroying the dog and of keeping it pending its destruction.

Fit and proper person

In determining whether a person is a fit and proper person to be in charge of a dog the following non-exhaustive factors may be relevant:

- any relevant previous convictions, cautions or penalty notices;
- the nature and suitability of the premises that the dog is to be kept at by the person;
- where the police have released the dog pending the court's decision whether the person has breached conditions imposed by the police; and
- any relevant previous breaches of court orders.

SG21-9 **STEP SEVEN Reasons**

Section 174 of the Criminal Justice Act 2003 imposes a duty to give reasons for, and explain the effect of, the sentence.

[8] **STEP EIGHT Consideration for time spent on bail** SG21-10

The court should consider whether to give credit for time spent on bail in accordance with section 240A of the Criminal Justice Act 2003.

[9] OWNER OR PERSON IN CHARGE OF A DOG DANGEROUSLY OUT OF CONTROL IN ANY PLACE IN ENGLAND OR WALES (WHETHER OR NOT A PUBLIC PLACE) WHERE A PERSON IS INJURED SG21-11

Dangerous Dogs Act 1991 (section 3(1))

Triable either way

Maximum: 5 years' custody

Offence range: Discharge–4 years' custody

[10] **STEP ONE Determining the offence category** SG21-12

In order to determine the category the court should assess **culpability** and **harm**. The court should determine the offence category with reference only to the factors in the tables below.

[The factors affecting *culpability* are identical to those set out at **SG21-3**; those affecting harm are set out below.]

HARM	
The level of harm is assessed by weighing up all the factors of the case.	
Category 1	Serious injury (which includes disease transmission) Serious psychological harm
Category 2	Harm that falls between categories 1 and 3
Category 3	Minor injury and no significant psychological harm

[11] **STEP TWO Starting point and category range** SG21-13

Having determined the category at step one, the court should use the corresponding starting points to reach a sentence within the category range below. The starting point applies to all offenders irrespective of plea or previous convictions.

	Culpability		
Harm	A	B	C
Category 1	**Starting point** 3 years' custody	**Starting point** 1 year 6 months' custody	**Starting point** High level community order
	Category range 2 years 6 months'–4 years' custody	**Category range** 6 months'–2 years 6 months' custody	**Category range** Medium level community order–6 months' custody
Category 2	**Starting point** 2 years' custody	**Starting point** 6 months' custody	**Starting point** Band C fine
	Category range 1 year–3 years' custody	**Category range** Medium level community order–1 year's custody	**Category range** Band B fine–High level community order
Category 3	**Starting point** 6 months' custody	**Starting point** Low level community	**Starting point** Band B fine order
	Category range High level community order–1 year 6 months' custody	**Category range** Band C fine–6 months' custody	**Category range** Discharge–Band C fine

The table is for single offences. Concurrent sentences reflecting the overall criminality of offending will ordinarily be appropriate where offences arise out of the same incident or facts: please refer to the *Totality* guideline [see SG3-1 and SG3-7].

Sentencing Guidelines

The court should then consider any adjustment for any aggravating or mitigating factors. [At **SG21-4** and see below] is a **non-exhaustive** list of additional factual elements providing the context of the offence and factors relating to the offender. [11]

Identify whether any combination of these, or other relevant factors, should result in an upward or downward adjustment from the starting point.

[The Factors increasing seriousness and the Factors reducing seriousness or reflecting personal mitigation are the same as those listed at **SG21-4** bar one additional factor reducing seriousness, namely 'Isolated incident'.]

SG21-14 [Steps Three to Eight are identical to those applicable where death is caused (see **SG21-5**).] [13–14]

SG21-15 OWNER OR PERSON IN CHARGE OF A DOG DANGEROUSLY OUT OF CONTROL IN ANY PLACE IN ENGLAND OR WALES (WHETHER OR NOT A PUBLIC PLACE) WHERE AN ASSISTANCE DOG IS INJURED OR KILLED [15]

Dangerous Dogs Act 1991 (section 3(1))

Triable either way

Maximum: 3 years' custody

Offence range: Discharge–2 years' 6 months' custody

SG21-16 STEP ONE **Determining the offence category** [16]

In order to determine the category the court should assess **culpability** and **harm**. The court should determine the offence category with reference only to the factors in the tables below.

[The factors affecting *culpability* are identical to those set out at **SG21-3**, but one additional matter is listed as demonstrating High culpability, namely 'Offence motivated by, or demonstrating hostility to the victim (assisted person) based on the victim's disability (or presumed disability)'; those affecting Harm are set out below.]

HARM	
The level of harm is assessed by weighing up all the factors of the case.	
Category 1	Fatality or serious injury to an assistance dog and/or
	Serious impact on the assisted person (whether psychological or other harm caused by the offence)
Category 2	Harm that falls between categories 1 and 3
Category 3	Minor injury to assistance dog and impact of the offence on the assisted person is limited

SG21-17 STEP TWO **Starting point and category range** [17]

Having determined the category at step one, the court should use the corresponding starting point to reach a sentence within the category range below. The starting point applies to all offenders irrespective of plea or previous convictions.

[17]

Harm	Culpability A	B	C
Category 1	**Starting point** 2 years' custody	**Starting point** 9 months' custody	**Starting point** Medium level community order
	Category range 1 year–2 years 6 months' custody	**Category range** Medium level community order–1 year's custody	**Category range** Low level community order–High level community order
Category 2	**Starting point** 1 years' custody	**Starting point** High level community order	**Starting point** Band B fine
	Category range 6 months'–1 year 6 months' custody	**Category range** Low level community order–6 months' custody	**Category range** Band A fine–Low level community order
Category range 3	**Starting point** High level community order	**Starting point** Band C fine	**Starting point** Band A fine
	Category range Medium level community order–6 months' custody	**Category range** Band B fine–High level community order	**Category range** Discharge–Band B fine

The court should then consider any adjustment for any aggravating or mitigating factors. [Below] is a **non-exhaustive** list of additional factual elements providing the context of the offence and factors relating to the offender.

Identify whether any combination of these, or other relevant factors, should result in an upward or downward adjustment from the starting point.

[18]

Factors increasing seriousness
Statutory aggravating factors: Previous convictions, having regard to a) the **nature** of the offence to which the conviction relates and its **relevance** to the current offence; and b) the **time** that has elapsed since the conviction Offence committed whilst on bail Offence motivated by, or demonstrating hostility based on any of the following characteristics or presumed characteristics of the victim: religion, race, sexual orientation or transgender identity
Other aggravating factors: Location of the offence Sustained or repeated attack Significant ongoing effect on witness(es) to the attack Allowing person insufficiently experienced or trained, to be in charge of the dog Lack or loss of control of the dog due to influence of alcohol or drugs Offence committed against those working in the public sector or providing a service to the public Injury to other animals Cost of retraining an assistance dog Established evidence of community/wider impact Failure to comply with current court orders (except where taken into account in assessing culpability) Offence committed on licence Offences taken into consideration
Factors reducing seriousness or reflecting personal mitigation
No previous convictions or no relevant/recent convictions Isolated incident No previous complaints against, or incidents involving the dog Evidence of responsible ownership Remorse Good character and/or exemplary conduct Serious medical condition requiring urgent, intensive or long-term treatment Age and/or lack of maturity where it affects the responsibility of the offender Mental disorder or learning disability Sole or primary carer for dependent relatives Determination and/or demonstration of steps having been taken to address offending behaviour

[Steps Three to Eight are identical to those applicable where death is caused (see SG21-5).] **SG21-18**

SG21-19 Owner or Person in Charge of a Dog Dangerously Out of Control in any Place in England or Wales (whether or not a Public Place) [21]

Dangerous Dogs Act 1991 (section 3(1))

Triable only summarily

Maximum: 6 months' custody

Offence range: Discharge–6 months' custody

SG21-20 STEP ONE **Determining the offence category** [22]

In order to determine the category the court should assess **culpability** and **harm**. The court should determine the offence category with reference only to the factors in the tables below.

The level of culpability is determined by weighing up all the factors of the case. **Where there are characteristics present which fall under different levels of culpability, the court should balance these characteristics to reach a fair assessment of the offender's culpability.**

Culpability demonstrated by one or more of the following:
A – Higher culpability
Dog used as a weapon or to intimidate people Dog known to be prohibited Dog trained to be aggressive Offender disqualified from owning a dog, or failed to respond to official warnings, or to comply with orders concerning the dog
B – Lower culpability
Attempts made to regain control of the dog and/or intervene Provocation of dog without fault of the offender Evidence of safety or control measures having been taken Incident could not have reasonably been foreseen by the offender Momentary lapse of control/attention

Harm **The level of harm is assessed by weighing up all the factors of the case.**	
Greater harm	Presence of children or others who are vulnerable because of personal circumstances
	Injury to other animals
Lesser harm	Low risk to the public

SG21-21 STEP TWO **Starting point and category range** [23]

Having determined the category at step one, the court should use the corresponding starting point to reach a sentence within the category range below. The starting point applies to all offenders irrespective of plea or previous convictions.

	Culpability	
Harm	**A**	**B**
Greater harm	**Starting point** Medium level community order	**Starting point** Band B fine
	Category range Band C fine–6 months' custody	**Category range** Band A fine–Band C fine
Lesser harm	**Starting point** Band C fine	**Starting point** Band A fine
	Category range Band B fine–Low level community order	**Category range** Discharge–Band B fine

The court should then consider any adjustment for any aggravating or mitigating factors. [Below] is a **non-exhaustive** list of additional factual elements providing the context of the offence and factors relating to the offender.

Identify whether any combination of these, or other relevant factors, should result in an upward or downward adjustment from the starting point.

[24]

Factors increasing seriousness
Statutory aggravating factors: Previous convictions, having regard to a) the **nature** of the offence to which the conviction relates and its **relevance** to the current offence; and b) the **time** that has elapsed since the conviction Offence committed whilst on bail Offence motivated by, or demonstrating hostility based on any of the following characteristics or presumed characteristics of the victim: religion, race, disability, sexual orientation or transgender identity
Other aggravating factors: Location of the offence Significant ongoing effect on the victim and/or others Failing to take adequate precautions to prevent the dog from escaping Allowing person insufficiently experienced or trained, to be in charge of the dog Ill treatment or failure to ensure welfare needs of the dog (where connected to the offence and where not charged separately) Lack or loss of control of the dog due to influence of alcohol or drugs Offence committed against those working in the public sector or providing a service to the public Established evidence of community/wider impact Failure to comply with current court orders (unless this has already been taken into account in assessing culpability) Offence committed on licence Offences taken into consideration
Factors reducing seriousness or reflecting personal mitigation
[These are identical to those listed in relation to an attack on an assistance dog (see SG21-17).]

25–26] [Steps Three to Eight are similar to those applicable where death or injury is caused following an attack by a dog (see **SG21-5**). However, in Step Six, instead of the duty on the court to make a destruction order unless it is satisfied that the dog would not constitute a danger to public safety the requirement is as follows: **SG21-22**

> If the dog is not prohibited and the court is satisfied that the dog would constitute a danger to public safety the court **may** make a destruction order.

[27]

Possession of a Prohibited Dog **SG21-23**

Dangerous Dogs Act 1991 (section 1(7))

Breeding, Selling, Exchanging or Advertising a Prohibited Dog

Dangerous Dogs Act 1991 (section 1(7))

Triable only summarily

Maximum: 6 months' custody

Offence range: Discharge–6 months' custody

[28] **STEP ONE Determining the offence category** **SG21-24**

In order to determine the category the court should assess **culpability** and **harm.** The court should determine the offence category with reference only to the factors in the tables below.

The level of culpability is determined by weighing up all the factors of the case. **Where there are characteristics present which fall under different levels of culpability, the court should balance these characteristics to reach a fair assessment of the offender's culpability.**

Culpability demonstrated by one or more of the following:
A – Higher culpability: Possessing a dog known to be prohibited Breeding from a dog known to be prohibited Selling, exchanging or advertising a dog known to be prohibited Offence committed for gain Dog used to threaten or intimidate Permitting fighting Training and/or possession of paraphernalia for dog fighting
B – Lower culpability: All other cases

Sentencing Guidelines

Harm The level of harm is assessed by weighing up all the factors of the case.	
Greater harm	High risk to the public and/or animals
Lesser harm	Low risk to the public and/or animals

[28]

SG21-25 **STEP TWO Starting point and category range** [29]

Having determined the category at step one, the court should use the corresponding starting point to reach a sentence within the category range below. The starting point applies to all offenders irrespective of plea or previous convictions.

	Culpability	
Harm	**A**	**B**
Greater harm	**Starting point** Medium level community order	**Starting point** Band B fine
	Category range Band C fine–6 months' custody	**Category range** Band A fine–Low level community order
Lesser harm	**Starting point** Band C fine	**Starting point** Band A fine
	Category range Band B fine–Medium level community order	**Category range** Discharge–Band B fine

The court should then consider any adjustment for any aggravating or mitigating factors. Below is a **non-exhaustive** list of additional factual elements providing the context of the offence and factors relating to the offender. [30]

Identify whether any combination of these, or other relevant factors, should result in an upward or downward adjustment from the starting point.

Factors increasing seriousness
Statutory aggravating factors: Previous convictions, having regard to a) the **nature** of the offence to which the conviction relates and its **relevance** to the current offence; and b) the **time** that has elapsed since the conviction Offence committed whilst on bail
Other aggravating factors: Presence of children or others who are vulnerable because of personal circumstances Ill treatment or failure to ensure welfare needs of the dog (where connected to the offence and where not charged separately) Established evidence of community/wider impact Failure to comply with current court orders Offence committed on licence Offences taken into consideration
Factors reducing seriousness or reflecting personal mitigation
No previous convictions or no relevant/recent convictions Unaware that dog was prohibited type despite reasonable efforts to identify type Evidence of safety or control measures having been taken by owner Prosecution results from owner notification Evidence of responsible ownership Remorse Good character and/or exemplary conduct Serious medical condition requiring urgent, intensive or long-term treatment Age and/or lack of maturity where it affects the responsibility of the offender Mental disorder or learning disability Sole or primary carer for dependent relatives Determination and/or demonstration of steps having been taken to address offending behaviour Lapse of time since the offence where this is not the fault of the offender

[31] [Steps Three to Five, Seven and Eight are identical to those applicable where death or injury is caused by virtue of an attack by a dog (see **SG21-5**). Step Six is set out below.] **SG21-26**

STEP SIX Compensation and ancillary orders **SG21-27**

In all cases, the court must consider whether to make a compensation order and/or other ancillary orders.

Compensation order

The court should consider compensation orders in all cases where personal injury, loss or damage has resulted from the offence. The court must give reasons if it decides not to award compensation in such cases.

Other ancillary orders available include:

Disqualification from having a dog

The court may disqualify the offender from having custody of a dog for such period as it thinks fit. The test the court should consider is whether the offender is a fit and proper person to have custody of a dog.

Destruction order/contingent destruction order

In any case where the offender is not the owner of the dog, the owner must be given an opportunity to be present and make representations to the court.

The court **shall** make a destruction order unless the court is satisfied that the dog would not constitute a danger to public safety.

[32] In reaching a decision, the court should consider the relevant circumstances which **must** include:

- the temperament of the dog and its past behaviour;
- whether the owner of the dog, or the person for the time being in charge of it is a fit and proper person to be in charge of the dog;

and **may** include:

- other relevant circumstances.

If the court is satisfied that the dog would not constitute a danger to public safety, it **shall** make a contingent destruction order requiring that the dog be exempted from the prohibition on possession or custody within the requisite period.

Where the court makes a destruction order, it **may** appoint a person to undertake destruction and order the offender to pay what it determines to be the reasonable expenses of destroying the dog and keeping it pending its destruction.

Fit and proper person

In determining whether a person is a fit and proper person to be in charge of a dog the following non-exhaustive factors may be relevant:

- any relevant previous convictions, cautions or penalty notices;
- the nature and suitability of the premises that the dog is to be kept at by the person;
- where the police have released the dog pending the court's decision whether the person has breached conditions imposed by the police; and
- any relevant previous breaches of court orders.

Note: the court must be satisfied that the person who is assessed by the court as a fit and proper person can demonstrate that they are the owner or the person ordinarily in charge of that dog at the time the court is considering whether the dog is a danger to public safety. Someone who has previously not been in charge of the dog should not be considered for this assessment because it is an offence under the Dangerous Dogs Act 1991 to make a gift of a prohibited dog.

[33]

ANNEX: FINE BANDS AND COMMUNITY ORDERS **SG21-28**

[The tables set out here are also set out in the Magistrates' Court Sentencing Guidelines, which include further guidance on fines and community orders: see **SG10-129** and **SG9-2**.]

PART 22 DEATH BY DRIVING, CAUSING

SG22-1

Definitive Guideline

Foreword

... This guideline applies to the sentencing of offenders convicted of any of the offences dealt with herein who are sentenced on or after **4 August 2008**. [1]

This guideline applies only to the sentencing of offenders aged 18 and older. The legislative provisions relating to the sentencing of youths are different; the younger the age, the greater the difference. A separate guideline setting out general principles relating to the sentencing of youths is planned.

...

SG22-2 **Introduction** [2]

1. This guideline applies to the four offences of *causing death by dangerous driving, causing death by driving under the influence of alcohol or drugs, causing death by careless driving and causing death by driving: unlicensed, disqualified or uninsured drivers.*
2. The Crown Prosecution Service's *Policy for Prosecuting Cases of Bad Driving* sets out the approach for prosecutors when considering the appropriate charge based on an assessment of the standard of the offender's driving. This has been taken into account when formulating this guideline. Annex A sets out the statutory definitions for dangerous, careless and inconsiderate driving together with examples of the types of driving behaviour likely to result in the charge of one offence rather than another.
3. Because the principal harm done by these offences (the death of a person) is an element of the offence, the factor that primarily determines the starting point for sentence is the culpability of the offender. Accordingly, for all offences other than *causing death by driving: unlicensed, disqualified or uninsured drivers*, the central feature should be an evaluation of the quality of the driving involved and the degree of danger that it foreseeably created. These guidelines draw a distinction between those factors of an offence that are intrinsic to the quality of driving (referred to as 'determinants of seriousness') and those which, while they aggravate the offence, are not.
4. The levels of seriousness in the guidelines for those offences based on dangerous or careless driving alone have been determined by reference *only* to determinants of seriousness. Aggravating factors will have the effect of either increasing the starting point within the sentencing range provided or, in certain circumstances, of moving the offence up to the next sentencing range. The outcome will depend on both the number of aggravating factors present and the potency of those factors. Thus, the same outcome could follow from the presence of one particularly bad aggravating factor or two or more less serious factors.
5. The determinants of seriousness likely to be relevant in relation to *causing death by careless driving under the influence* are both the degree of carelessness and the level of intoxication. The guideline sets out an approach to assessing both those aspects but giving greater weight to the degree of intoxication since Parliament has provided for a maximum of 14 years' imprisonment rather than the maximum of 5 years where the death is caused by careless driving only.
6. Since there will be no allegation of bad driving, the guideline for *causing death by driving; unlicensed, disqualified or uninsured drivers* links the assessment of offender culpability to the nature of the prohibition on the offender's driving and includes a list of factors that may aggravate an offence.
7. The degree to which an aggravating factor is present (and its interaction with any other aggravating and mitigating factors) will be immensely variable and the court is best placed to judge the appropriate impact on sentence. Clear identification of those factors relating to the standard of driving as the initial determinants of offence seriousness is intended to assist the adoption of a common approach.

SG22-3 **A. Assessing seriousness** [3]

(i) Determinants of seriousness

8. There are five factors that may be regarded as determinants of offence seriousness, each of which can be demonstrated in a number of ways. Common examples of each of the determinants are set out below and key issues are discussed in the text that follows ...

   Examples of the determinants are:
   - *Awareness of risk*
     (a) a prolonged, persistent and deliberate course of very bad driving

[3]
- *Effect of alcohol or drugs*
  - (b) consumption of alcohol above the legal limit
  - (c) consumption of alcohol at or below the legal limit where this impaired the offender's ability to drive
  - (d) failure to supply a specimen for analysis
  - (e) consumption of illegal drugs, where this impaired the offender's ability to drive
  - (f) consumption of legal drugs or medication where this impaired the offender's ability to drive (including legal medication known to cause drowsiness) where the driver knew, or should have known, about the likelihood of impairment
- *Inappropriate speed of vehicle*
  - (g) greatly excessive speed; racing; competitive driving against another vehicle
  - (h) driving above the speed limit
  - (i) driving at a speed that is inappropriate for the prevailing road or weather conditions
  - (j) driving a PSV, HGV or other goods vehicle at a speed that is inappropriate either because of the nature of the vehicle or its load, especially when carrying passengers
- *Seriously culpable behaviour of offender*
  - (k) aggressive driving (such as driving much too close to the vehicle in front, persistent inappropriate attempts to overtake, or cutting in after overtaking)
  - (l) driving while using a hand-held mobile phone
  - (m) driving whilst the driver's attention is avoidably distracted, for example by reading or adjusting the controls of electronic equipment such as a radio, hands-free mobile phone or satellite navigation equipment
  - (n) driving when knowingly suffering from a medical or physical condition that significantly impairs the offender's driving skills, including failure to take prescribed medication
  - (o) driving when knowingly deprived of adequate sleep or rest, especially where commercial concerns had a bearing on the commission of the offence
  - (p) driving a poorly maintained or dangerously loaded vehicle, especially where commercial concerns had a bearing on the commission of the offence
- *Victim*
  - (q) failing to have proper regard to vulnerable road users

[4] 9. Issues relating to the determinants of seriousness are considered below.

(a) Alcohol/drugs

10. For those offences where the presence of alcohol or drugs is not an element of the offence, where there is sufficient evidence of driving impairment attributable to alcohol or drugs, the consumption of alcohol or drugs prior to driving will make an offence more serious. Where the drugs were legally purchased or prescribed, the offence will only be regarded as more serious if the offender knew or should have known that the drugs were likely to impair driving ability.
11. Unless inherent in the offence or charged separately, failure to provide a specimen for analysis (or to allow a blood specimen taken without consent to be analysed) should be regarded as a determinant of offence seriousness.
12. Where it is established to the satisfaction of the court that an offender had consumed alcohol or drugs unwittingly before driving, that may be regarded as a mitigating factor. However, consideration should be given to the circumstances in which the offender decided to drive or continue to drive when driving ability was impaired.

(b) Avoidable distractions

13. A distinction has been drawn between **ordinary** avoidable distractions and those that are more significant because they divert the attention of the driver for longer periods or to a greater extent; in this guideline these are referred to as a **gross** avoidable distraction. The guideline for causing *death by dangerous driving* provides for a gross avoidable distraction to place the offence in a higher level of seriousness.
14. Any avoidable distraction will make an offence more serious but the degree to which an offender's driving will be impaired will vary. Where the reaction to the distraction is significant, it may be the factor that determines whether the offence is based on *dangerous* driving or on *careless* driving; in those circumstances, care must be taken to avoid 'double counting'.
15. Using a hand-held mobile phone when driving is, in itself, an unlawful act; the fact that an offender was avoidably distracted by using a hand-held mobile phone when a causing death by driving offence was committed will always make an offence more serious. Reading or composing text messages *over a*

period of time will be a gross avoidable distraction and is likely to result in an offence of causing death by dangerous driving being in a higher level of seriousness. [4]

16. Where it is proved that an offender was briefly distracted by reading a text message or adjusting a hands-free set or its controls at the time of the collision, this would be on a par with consulting a map or adjusting a radio or satellite navigation equipment, activities that would be considered an avoidable distraction.

(c) Vulnerable road users

17. Cyclists, motorbike riders, horse riders, pedestrians and those working in the road are vulnerable road users and a driver is expected to take extra care when driving near them. Driving too close to a bike or horse; allowing a vehicle to mount the pavement; driving into a cycle lane; and driving without the care needed in the vicinity of a pedestrian crossing, hospital, school or residential home, are all examples of factors that should be taken into account when determining the seriousness of an offence. See paragraph 24 below for the approach where the actions of another person contributed to the collision.
18. The fact that the victim of a causing death by driving offence was a particularly vulnerable road user is a factor that should be taken into account when determining the seriousness of an offence. [5]

(ii) Aggravating and mitigating factors

(a) More than one person killed

19. The seriousness of any offence included in these guidelines will generally be greater where more than one person is killed since it is inevitable that the degree of harm will be greater. In relation to the assessment of culpability, whilst there will be circumstances in which a driver could reasonably anticipate the possible death of more than one person (for example, the driver of a vehicle with passengers (whether that is a bus, taxi or private car) or a person driving badly in an area where there are many people), there will be many circumstances where the driver could not anticipate the number of people who would be killed.
20. The greater obligation on those responsible for driving other people is not an element essential to the quality of the driving and so has not been included amongst the determinants of seriousness that affect the choice of sentencing range. In practical terms, separate charges are likely to be brought in relation to each death caused. Although concurrent sentences are likely to be imposed (in recognition of the fact that the charges relate to one episode of offending behaviour), each individual sentence is likely to be higher because the offence is aggravated by the fact that more than one death has been caused.
21. Where more than one person is killed, that will aggravate the seriousness of the offence because of the increase in harm. Where the number of people killed is high *and* that was reasonably foreseeable, the number of deaths is likely to provide sufficient justification for moving an offence into the next highest sentencing band.

(b) Effect on offender

22. Injury to the offender may be a mitigating factor when the offender has suffered very serious injuries. In most circumstances, the weighting it is given will be dictated by the circumstances of the offence and the effect should bear a direct relationship to the extent to which the offender's driving was at fault—the greater the fault, the less the effect on mitigation; this distinction will be of particular relevance where an offence did not involve any fault in the offender's standard of driving.
23. Where one or more of the victims was in a close personal or family relationship with the offender, this may be a mitigating factor. In line with the approach where the offender is very seriously injured, the degree to which the relationship influences the sentence should be linked to offender culpability in relation to the commission of the offence; mitigation for this reason is likely to have less effect where the culpability of the driver is particularly high.

(c) Actions of others

24. Where the actions of the victim or a third party contributed to the commission of an offence, this should be acknowledged and taken into account as a mitigating factor.

(d) Offender's age/lack of driving experience [6]

25. The Council guideline *Overarching Principles: Seriousness* [see **SG2-1**] includes a generic mitigating factor '*youth or age, where it affects the responsibility of the individual defendant*'. There is a great deal of difference between recklessness or irresponsibility—which may be due to youth—and inexperience in dealing with prevailing conditions or an unexpected or unusual situation that presents itself—which may be present regardless of the age of the offender. The fact that an offender's lack of driving experience contributed to the commission of an offence should be treated as a mitigating factor; in this regard, the age of the offender is not relevant.

[6] *(iii) Personal mitigation*

(a) Good driving record

26. This is not a factor that automatically should be treated as a mitigating factor, especially now that the presence of previous convictions is a statutory aggravating factor. However, any evidence to show that an offender has previously been an exemplary driver, for example having driven an ambulance, police vehicle, bus, taxi or similar vehicle conscientiously and without incident for many years, is a fact that the courts may well wish to take into account by way of personal mitigation. This is likely to have even greater effect where the driver is driving on public duty (for example, on ambulance, fire services or police duties) and was responding to an emergency.

(b) Conduct after the offence

—Giving assistance at the scene

27. There may be many reasons why an offender does not offer help to the victims at the scene—the offender may be injured, traumatised by shock, afraid of causing further injury or simply have no idea what action to take—and it would be inappropriate to assess the offence as more serious on this ground (and so increase the level of sentence). However, where an offender gave direct, positive, assistance to victim(s) at the scene of a collision, this should be regarded as personal mitigation.

—Remorse

28. Whilst it can be expected that anyone who has caused death by driving would be expected to feel remorseful, this cannot undermine its importance for sentencing purposes. Remorse is identified as personal mitigation in [*Overarching Principles: Seriousness*: see SG2-1] and the Council can see no reason for it to be treated differently for this group of offences. It is for the court to determine whether an expression of remorse is genuine; where it is, this should be taken into account as personal mitigation.

(c) Summary

29. Evidence that an offender is normally a careful and conscientious driver, giving direct, positive assistance to a victim and genuine remorse may be taken into account as personal mitigation and may justify a reduction in sentence.

[7] **B. Ancillary orders** SG22-4

(i) Disqualification for driving

30. For each offence, disqualification is a mandatory part of the sentence (subject to the usual (very limited) exceptions), and therefore an important element of the overall punishment for the offence. In addition, an order that the disqualification continues until the offender passes an extended driving test order is compulsory[256] for those convicted of causing death by dangerous driving or by careless driving when under the influence, and discretionary[257] in relation to the two other offences.

31. Any disqualification is effective from the date on which it is imposed. When ordering disqualification from driving, the duration of the order should allow for the length of any custodial period in order to ensure that the disqualification has the desired impact. In principle, the minimum period of disqualification should either equate to the length of the custodial sentence imposed (in the knowledge that the offender is likely to be released having served half of that term), or the relevant statutory minimum disqualification period, whichever results in the longer period of disqualification.

(ii) Deprivation order

32. A general sentencing power exists which enables courts to deprive an offender of property used for the purposes of committing an offence.[258] A vehicle used to commit an offence included in this guideline can be regarded as being used for the purposes of committing the offence.

[8] **C. Sentencing ranges and starting points** SG22-5

1. Typically, a guideline will apply to an offence that can be committed in a variety of circumstances with different levels of seriousness. It will apply to a first-time offender who has been convicted after a trial. Within the guidelines, a first-time offender is a person who does not have a conviction which, by virtue of section 143(2) of the CJA 2003, must be treated as an aggravating factor.
2. As an aid to consistency of approach, the guidelines describe a number of types of activity which would fall within the broad definition of the offence. These are set out in a column headed 'Type/nature of activity'.

[256] Road Traffic Offenders Act 1988, s. 36(1)
[257] ibid, s. 36(4)
[258] Powers of Criminal Courts (Sentencing) Act 2000, s. 143

3. The expected approach is for a court to identify the description that most nearly matches the particular facts of the offence for which sentence is being imposed. This will identify a starting point from which the sentencer can depart to reflect aggravating or mitigating factors affecting the seriousness of the offence (beyond those contained within the column describing the type or nature of offence activity) to reach a provisional sentence. [8]
4. The *sentencing range* is the bracket into which the provisional sentence will normally fall after having regard to factors which aggravate or mitigate the seriousness of the offence. The particular circumstances may, however, make it appropriate that the provisional sentence falls outside the range.
5. Where the offender has previous convictions which aggravate the seriousness of the current offence, that may take the provisional sentence beyond the range given, particularly where there are significant other aggravating factors present.
6. Once the provisional sentence has been identified by reference to those factors affecting the seriousness of the offence, the court will take into account any relevant factors of personal mitigation, which may take the sentence outside the range indicated in the guideline.
7. Where there has been a guilty plea, any reduction attributable to that plea will be applied to the sentence at this stage. This reduction may take the sentence below the range provided.
8. A court must give its reasons for imposing a sentence of a different kind or outside the range provided in the guidelines.[259]

The decision making process [9]

The process set out below is intended to show that the sentencing approach for offences of causing death by driving is fluid and requires the structured exercise of discretion.

[Sets out the standard decision making process: identify dangerous offenders, identify starting point, consider aggravating factors, consider mitigating factors, apply reduction for guilty plea, consider ancillary orders, review in light of totality principle and give reasons.]

SG22-6 **D. Offence guidelines** [10]

Causing death by dangerous driving

Factors to take into consideration

1. The following guideline applies to a 'first-time offender' aged 18 or over convicted after trial (see . . . above), who has not been assessed as a dangerous offender requiring a sentence under ss. 224–228 Criminal Justice Act 2003 (as amended).
2. When assessing the seriousness of any offence, the court must always refer to the full list of aggravating and mitigating factors in the Council guideline on Seriousness[260] as well as those set out in the adjacent table as being particularly relevant to this type of offending behaviour.
3. **Levels of seriousness**

The 3 levels are distinguished by factors related predominantly to the standard of driving; the general description of the degree of risk is complemented by examples of the type of bad driving arising. The presence of aggravating factors or combinations of a small number of determinants of seriousness will increase the starting point within the range. Where there is a larger group of determinants of seriousness and/or aggravating factors, this may justify moving the starting point to the next level.

Level 1—The most serious offences encompassing driving that involved a deliberate decision to ignore (or a flagrant disregard for) the rules of the road and an apparent disregard for the great danger being caused to others. Such offences are likely to be characterised by:

- *A prolonged, persistent and deliberate course of very bad driving AND/OR*
- *Consumption of substantial amounts of alcohol or drugs leading to gross impairment AND/OR*
- *A group of determinants of seriousness which in isolation or smaller number would place the offence in level 2*

Level 1 is that for which the increase in maximum penalty was aimed primarily. Where an offence involves both of the determinants of seriousness identified, particularly if accompanied by aggravating factors such as multiple deaths or injuries, or a very bad driving record, this may move an offence towards the top of the sentencing range.

Level 2—This is driving that created a substantial risk of danger and is likely to be characterised by:

- *Greatly excessive speed, racing or competitive driving against another driver OR*
- *Gross avoidable distraction such as reading or composing text messages over a period of time OR*

---

259 Criminal Justice Act 2003, s. 174(2)(a)

260 *Overarching Principles: Seriousness*, published 16 December 2004, www.sentencing-guidelines.gov.uk

[10] • *Driving whilst ability to drive is impaired as a result of consumption of alcohol or drugs, failing to take prescribed medication or as a result of a known medical condition OR*
• *A group of determinants of seriousness which in isolation or smaller number would place the offence in level 3*

Level 3 — This is driving that created a significant risk of danger and is likely to be characterised by:

• *Driving above the speed limit/at a speed that is inappropriate for the prevailing conditions OR*
• *Driving when knowingly deprived of adequate sleep or rest or knowing that the vehicle has a dangerous defect or is poorly maintained or is dangerously loaded OR*
• *A brief but obvious danger arising from a seriously dangerous manoeuvre OR*
• *Driving whilst avoidably distracted OR*
• *Failing to have proper regard to vulnerable road users*

The starting point and range overlap with Level 2 is to allow the breadth of discretion necessary to accommodate circumstances where there are significant aggravating factors.

4. Sentencers should take into account relevant matters of personal mitigation; see in particular guidance on **good driving record, giving assistance at the scene and remorse** ... above.

[11]

Causing Death by Dangerous Driving SG22-7

Road Traffic Act 1988 (section 1)

This is a serious offence for the purposes of section 224 Criminal Justice Act 2003

Maximum penalty: 14 years' imprisonment;
minimum disqualification of 2 years with compulsory extended re-test

Nature of offence	Starting point	Sentencing range
Level 1 The most serious offences encompassing driving that involved a deliberate decision to ignore (or a flagrant disregard for) the rules of the road and an apparent disregard for the great danger being caused to others	8 years' custody	7–14 years' custody
Level 2 Driving that created a *substantial* risk of danger	5 years' custody	4–7 years' custody
Level 3 Driving that created a *significant* risk of danger *[Where the driving is markedly less culpable than for this level, reference should be made to the starting point and range for the most serious level of causing death by careless driving]*	3 years' custody	2–5 years' custody

Additional aggravating factors	Additional mitigating factors
1. Previous convictions for motoring offences, particularly offences that involve bad driving or the consumption of excessive alcohol or drugs before driving 2. More than one person killed as a result of the offence 3. Serious injury to one or more victims, in addition to the death(s) 4. Disregard of warnings 5. Other offences committed at the same time, such as driving other than in accordance with the terms of a valid licence; driving while disqualified; driving without insurance; taking a vehicle without consent; driving a stolen vehicle 6. The offender's irresponsible behaviour such as failing to stop, falsely claiming that one of the victims was responsible for the collision, or trying to throw the victim off the car by swerving in order to escape 7. Driving off in an attempt to avoid detection or apprehension	1. Alcohol or drugs consumed unwittingly 2. Offender was seriously injured in the collision 3. The victim was a close friend or relative 4. Actions of the victim or a third party contributed significantly to the likelihood of a collision occurring and/or death resulting 5. The offender's lack of driving experience contributed to the commission of the offence 6. The driving was in response to a proven and genuine emergency falling short of a defence

SG22-8 **Causing death by careless driving when under the influence of drink or drugs or having failed without reasonable excuse either to provide a specimen for analysis or to permit the analysis of a blood sample** [12]

Factors to take into consideration

1. The following guideline applies to a 'first-time offender' aged 18 or over convicted after trial (see . . . above), who has not been assessed as a dangerous offender requiring a sentence under ss. 224–228 Criminal Justice Act 2003 (as amended).
2. When assessing the seriousness of any offence, the court must always refer to the full list of aggravating and mitigating factors in the Council guideline on Seriousness[261] as well as those set out in the adjacent table as being particularly relevant to this type of offending behaviour.
3. This offence can be committed through:
   (i) being unfit to drive through drink or drugs;
   (ii) having consumed so much alcohol as to be over the prescribed limit;
   (iii) failing without reasonable excuse to provide a specimen for analysis within the timescale allowed; or
   (iv) failing without reasonable excuse to permit the analysis of a blood sample taken when incapable of giving consent.
4. In comparison with *causing death by dangerous driving*, the level of culpability in the actual manner of driving is lower but that culpability is increased in all cases by the fact that the offender has driven after consuming drugs or an excessive amount of alcohol. Accordingly, there is considerable parity in the levels of seriousness with the deliberate decision to drive after consuming alcohol or drugs aggravating the *careless* standard of driving onto a par with *dangerous* driving.
5. The fact that the offender was under the influence of drink or drugs is an inherent element of this offence. For discussion on the significance of driving after having consumed drink or drugs, see . . . above.
6. The guideline is based both on the level of alcohol or drug consumption and on the degree of carelessness.
7. The increase in sentence is more marked where there is an increase in the level of intoxication than where there is an increase in the degree of carelessness reflecting the 14 year imprisonment maximum for this offence compared with a 5 year maximum for causing death by careless or inconsiderate driving alone.
8. A refusal to supply a specimen for analysis may be a calculated step by an offender to avoid prosecution for driving when having consumed in excess of the prescribed amount of alcohol, with a view to seeking to persuade the court that the amount consumed was relatively small. A court is entitled to draw adverse inferences from a refusal to supply a specimen without reasonable excuse and should treat with caution any attempt to persuade the court that only a limited amount of alcohol had been consumed.[262] The three levels of seriousness where the offence has been committed in this way derive from the classification in the Magistrates' Court Sentencing Guidelines.
9. Sentencers should take into account relevant matters of personal mitigation; see in particular guidance on **good driving record, giving assistance at the scene** and **remorse** . . . above.

SG22-9 Causing Death by Careless Driving when Under the Influence of Drink or Drugs or having Failed either to Provide a Specimen for Analysis or to Permit Analysis of a Blood Sample [13]

Road Traffic Act 1988 (section 3A)

This is a serious offence for the purposes of section 224 Criminal Justice Act 2003

Maximum penalty: 14 years' imprisonment;
minimum disqualification of 2 years with compulsory extended re-test

[261] *Overarching Principles: Seriousness*, published 16 December 2004, www.sentencing-guidelines.gov.uk

[262] *Attorney-General's Reference No. 21 of 2000* [2001] 1 Cr App R (S) 173

[13]

The legal limit of alcohol is 35 µg breath (80 mg in blood and 107 mg in urine)	Careless/inconsiderate driving arising from momentary inattention with no aggravating factors	Other cases of careless/ inconsiderate driving	Careless/inconsiderate driving falling not far short of dangerousness
71 µ or above of alcohol/high quantity of drugs OR deliberate non-provision of specimen where evidence of serious impairment	**Starting point:** 6 years' custody **Sentencing range:** 5–10 years' custody	**Starting point:** 7 years' custody **Sentencing range:** 6–12 years' custody	**Starting point:** 8 years' custody **Sentencing range:** 7–14 years' custody
51–70 µg of alcohol/moderate quantity of drugs OR deliberate non-provision of specimen	**Starting point:** 4 years' custody **Sentencing range:** 3–7 years' custody	**Starting point:** 5 years' custody **Sentencing range:** 4–8 years' custody	**Starting point:** 6 years' custody **Sentencing range:** 5–9 years' custody
35–50 µg of alcohol/minimum quantity of drugs OR test refused because of honestly held but unreasonable belief	**Starting point:** 18 months' custody **Sentencing range:** 26 weeks'–4 years' custody	**Starting point:** 3 years' custody **Sentencing range:** 2–5 years' custody	**Starting point:** 4 years' custody **Sentencing range:** 3–6 years' custody

Additional aggravating factors	Additional mitigating factors
1. Other offences committed at the same time, such as driving other than in accordance with the terms of a valid licence; driving while disqualified; driving without insurance; taking a vehicle without consent; driving a stolen vehicle 2. Previous convictions for motoring offences, particularly offences that involve bad driving or the consumption of excessive alcohol before driving 3. More than one person was killed as a result of the offence 4. Serious injury to one or more persons in addition to the death(s) 5. Irresponsible behaviour such as failing to stop or falsely claiming that one of the victims was responsible for the collision	1. Alcohol or drugs consumed unwittingly 2. Offender was seriously injured in the collision 3. The victim was a close friend or relative 4. The actions of the victim or a third party contributed significantly to the likelihood of a collision occurring and/or death resulting 5. The driving was in response to a proven and genuine emergency falling short of a defence

[14] **Causing death by careless or inconsiderate driving** SG22-10

Factors to take into consideration

1. The following guideline applies to a 'first-time offender' aged 18 or over convicted after trial (see . . . above), who has not been assessed as a dangerous offender requiring a sentence under ss. 224–228 Criminal Justice Act 2003 (as amended).
2. When assessing the seriousness of any offence, the court must always refer to the full list of aggravating and mitigating factors in the Council guideline on Seriousness[263] as well as those set out in the adjacent table as being particularly relevant to this type of offending behaviour.
3. The maximum penalty on indictment is 5 years' imprisonment. The offence is triable either way and, in a magistrates' court, statute provides that the maximum sentence is 12 months imprisonment; this will be revised to 6 months imprisonment until such time as the statutory provisions increasing the sentencing powers of a magistrates' court are implemented.[264]

[263] *Overarching Principles: Seriousness*, published 16 December 2004, www.sentencing-guidelines.gov.uk
[264] Criminal Justice Act 2003, ss. 154(1) and 282; Road Safety Act 2006, s. 61(5)

4. Disqualification of the offender from driving and endorsement of the offender's driving licence are mandatory, and the offence carries between 3 and 11 penalty points when the court finds special reasons for not imposing disqualification. There is a discretionary power[265] to order an extended driving test where a person is convicted of this offence. [14]
5. Since the maximum sentence has been set at 5 years' imprisonment, the sentence ranges are generally lower for this offence than for the offences of *causing death by dangerous driving* or *causing death by careless driving under the influence*, for which the maximum sentence is 14 years' imprisonment. However, it is unavoidable that some cases will be on the borderline between *dangerous* and *careless* driving, or may involve a number of factors that significantly increase the seriousness of an offence. As a result, the guideline for this offence identifies three levels of seriousness, the range for the highest of which overlaps with ranges for the lowest level of seriousness for *causing death by dangerous driving*.
6. The three levels of seriousness are defined by the degree of carelessness involved in the standard of driving. The most serious level for this offence is where the offender's driving fell *not that far short of dangerous*. The least serious group of offences relates to those cases where the level of culpability is low—for example in a case involving an offender who misjudges the speed of another vehicle, or turns without seeing an oncoming vehicle because of restricted visibility. Other cases will fall into the intermediate level.
7. The starting point for the most serious offence of *causing death by careless driving* is lower than that for the least serious offence of *causing death by dangerous driving* in recognition of the different standards of driving behaviour. However, the range still leaves scope, within the 5 year maximum, to impose longer sentences where the case is particularly serious.
8. Where the level of carelessness is low and there are no aggravating factors, even the fact that death was caused is not sufficient to justify a prison sentence. [15]
9. A fine is unlikely to be an appropriate sentence for this offence; where a non-custodial sentence is considered appropriate, this should be a community order. The nature of the requirements will be determined by the purpose[266] identified by the court as of primary importance. Requirements most likely to be relevant include unpaid work requirement, activity requirement, programme requirement and curfew requirement.
10. Sentencers should take into account relevant matters of personal mitigation; see in particular guidance on **good driving record, giving assistance at the scene** and **remorse** . . . above.

SG22-11

Causing Death by Careless or Inconsiderate Driving

Road Traffic Act 1988 (section 2B)

Maximum penalty: 5 years' imprisonment;
minimum disqualification of 12 months, discretionary re-test

Nature of offence	Starting point	Sentencing range
Careless or inconsiderate driving falling not far short of dangerous driving	15 months' custody	36 weeks'–3 years' custody
Other cases of careless or inconsiderate driving	36 weeks' custody	Community order (HIGH)–2 years' custody
Careless or inconsiderate driving arising from momentary inattention with no aggravating factors	Community order (MEDIUM)	Community order (LOW)–Community order (HIGH)

265 Road Traffic Offenders Act 1988, s. 36(4)
266 Criminal Justice Act 2003, s. 142(1)

[15]

Additional aggravating factors	Additional mitigating factors
1. Other offences committed at the same time, such as driving other than in accordance with the terms of a valid licence; driving while disqualified; driving without insurance; taking a vehicle without consent; driving a stolen vehicle 2. Previous convictions for motoring offences, particularly offences that involve bad driving 3. More than one person was killed as a result of the offence 4. Serious injury to one or more persons in addition to the death(s) 5. Irresponsible behaviour, such as failing to stop or falsely claiming that one of the victims was responsible for the collision	1. Offender was seriously injured in the collision 2. The victim was a close friend or relative 3. The actions of the victim or a third party contributed to the commission of the offence 4. The offender's lack of driving experience contributed significantly to the likelihood of a collision occurring and/or death resulting 5. The driving was in response to a proven and genuine emergency falling short of a defence

[16] **Causing death by driving: unlicensed, disqualified or uninsured drivers** **SG22-12**

Factors to take into consideration

1. The following guideline applies to a 'first-time offender' aged 18 or over convicted after trial (see ... above), who has not been assessed as a dangerous offender requiring a sentence under ss. 224–228 Criminal Justice Act 2003 (as amended).
2. When assessing the seriousness of any offence, the court must always refer to the full list of aggravating and mitigating factors in the Council guideline on Seriousness[267] as well as those set out in the adjacent table as being particularly relevant to this type of offending behaviour.
3. This offence has a maximum penalty of 2 years' imprisonment and is triable either way. In a magistrates' court, statute provides that the maximum sentence is 12 months imprisonment; this will be revised to 6 months imprisonment until such time as the statutory provisions increasing the sentencing powers of a magistrates' court are implemented.[268]
4. Disqualification of the offender from driving and endorsement of the offender's driving licence are mandatory, and the offence carries between 3 and 11 penalty points when the court finds special reasons for not imposing disqualification. There is a discretionary power[269] to order an extended driving test where a person is convicted of this offence.
5. Culpability arises from the offender driving a vehicle on a road or other public place when, by law, not allowed to do so; the offence does not require proof of any fault in the standard of driving.
6. Because of the significantly lower maximum penalty, the sentencing ranges are considerably lower than for the other three offences covered in this guideline; many cases may be sentenced in a magistrates' court, particularly where there is an early guilty plea.
7. A fine is unlikely to be an appropriate sentence for this offence; where a noncustodial sentence is considered appropriate, this should be a community order.
8. Since driving whilst disqualified is more culpable than driving whilst unlicensed or uninsured, a higher starting point is proposed when the offender was disqualified from driving at the time of the offence.
9. Being uninsured, unlicensed or disqualified are the only determinants of seriousness for this offence, as there are no factors relating to the standard of driving. The list of aggravating factors identified is slightly different as the emphasis is on the decision to drive by an offender who is not permitted by law to do so.

[17] 10. In some cases, the extreme circumstances that led an offender to drive whilst unlicensed, disqualified or uninsured may result in a successful defence of 'duress of circumstances'.[270] In less extreme circumstances, where the *decision to drive was brought about by a genuine and proven emergency*, that may mitigate offence seriousness and so it is included as an additional mitigating factor.

---

[267] *Overarching Principles: Seriousness*, published 16 December 2004, www.sentencing-guidelines.gov.uk

[268] Criminal Justice Act 2003, ss. 154(1) and 282; Road Safety Act 2006, s. 61(5)

[269] Road Traffic Offenders Act 1988, s. 36(4)

[270] In *DPP v Mullally* [2006] EWHC 3448 (Admin) the Divisional Court held that the defence of necessity must be strictly controlled and that it must be proved that the actions of the defendant were reasonable in the given circumstances. See also *Hasan* [2005] UKHL 22

11. A driver may hold a reasonable belief in relation to the validity of insurance (for example having just missed a renewal date or relied on a third party to make an application) and also the validity of a licence (for example incorrectly believing that a licence covered a particular category of vehicle). In light of this, an additional mitigating factor covers those situations where an offender genuinely believed that there was valid insurance or a valid licence. [17]
12. Sentencers should take into account relevant matters of personal mitigation; see in particular guidance on **good driving record, giving assistance at the scene** and **remorse** . . . above.

SG22-13 Causing Death by Driving: Unlicensed, Disqualified or Uninsured Drivers

Road Traffic Act 1988 (section 3ZB)

Maximum penalty: 2 years' imprisonment;
minimum disqualification of 12 months, discretionary re-test

Nature of offence	Starting point	Sentencing range
The offender was disqualified from driving **OR** The offender was unlicensed or uninsured plus 2 or more aggravating factors from the list below	12 months' custody	36 weeks'–2 years' custody
The offender was unlicensed or uninsured plus at least 1 aggravating factor from the list below	26 weeks' custody	Community order (HIGH)–36 weeks' custody
The offender was unlicensed or uninsured—no aggravating factors	Community order (MEDIUM)	Community order (LOW)–Community order (HIGH)

Additional aggravating factors	Additional mitigating factors
1. Previous convictions for motoring offences, whether involving bad driving or involving an offence of the same kind that forms part of the present conviction (i.e. unlicensed, disqualified or uninsured driving) 2. More than one person was killed as a result of the offence 3. Serious injury to one or more persons in addition to the death(s) 4. Irresponsible behaviour such as failing to stop or falsely claiming that someone else was driving	1. The decision to drive was brought about by a proven and genuine emergency falling short of a defence 2. The offender genuinely believed that he or she was insured or licensed to drive 3. The offender was seriously injured as a result of the collision 4. The victim was a close friend or relative

SG22-14 Annex A: Dangerous and Careless Driving [18]

Statutory definitions and examples

[Omitted—see the relevant material in part C]

PART 23 DRUG OFFENCES

Definitive Guideline

SG23-1

[2] **Applicability of Guideline**

[Omitted: See **SG19-1** for identical text save that this guideline has effect from 27 February 2012.]

Structure, ranges and starting points

[Omitted: See **SG19-2** for identical text.]

[3] ## Fraudulent Evasion of a Prohibition by Bringing Into or Taking Out of the UK a Controlled Drug

SG23-2

Misuse of Drugs Act 1971 (section 3)

Customs and Excise Management Act 1979 (section 170(2))

Triable either way unless the defendant could receive the minimum sentence of seven years for a third drug trafficking offence under section 110 Powers of Criminal Courts (Sentencing) Act 2000 in which case the offence is triable only on indictment.

Class A

Maximum: Life imprisonment

Offence range: 3 years 6 months'–16 years' custody

A Class A offence is a drug trafficking offence for the purpose of imposing a minimum sentence under section 110 Powers of Criminal Courts (Sentencing) Act 2000

Class B

Maximum: 14 years' custody and/or unlimited fine

Offence range: 12 weeks'–10 years' custody

Class C

Maximum: 14 years' custody and/or unlimited fine

Offence range: Community order–8 years' custody

[4] **STEP ONE Determining the offence category**

SG23-3

The court should determine the offender's culpability (role) and the harm caused (quantity) with reference to the tables below.

In assessing culpability, the sentencer should weigh up all the factors of the case to determine role. Where there are characteristics present which fall under different role categories, the court should balance these characteristics to reach a fair assessment of the offender's culpability.

In assessing harm, quantity is determined by the weight of the product. Purity is not taken into account at step 1 but is dealt with at step 2.

Where the operation is on the most serious and commercial scale, involving a quantity of drugs significantly higher than category 1, sentences of 20 years and above may be appropriate, depending on the role of the offender.

Culpability demonstrated by offender's role	Category of harm
One or more of these characteristics may demonstrate the offender's role. These lists are not exhaustive.	Indicative quantity of drug concerned (upon which the starting point is based):
LEADING role: • Directing or organising buying and selling on a commercial scale; • Substantial links to, and influence on, others in a chain; • Close links to original source; • Expectation of substantial financial gain; • Uses business as cover; • Abuses a position of trust or responsibility.	**Category 1:** • Heroin, cocaine — 5kg; • Ecstasy — 10,000 tablets; • LSD — 250,000 squares; • Amphetamine — 20kg; • Cannabis — 200kg; • Ketamine — 5kg. **Category 2:** • Heroin, cocaine — 1kg; • Ecstasy — 2,000 tablets; • LSD — 25,000 squares; • Amphetamine — 4kg; • Cannabis — 40kg; • Ketamine — 1kg
SIGNIFICANT role: • Operational or management function within a chain; • Involves others in the operation whether by pressure, influence, intimidation or reward; • Motivated by financial or other advantage, whether or not operating alone; • Some awareness and understanding of scale of operation. **LESSER role:** • Performs a limited function under direction; • Engaged by pressure, coercion, intimidation; • Involvement through naivety/exploitation; • No influence on those above in a chain; • Very little, if any, awareness or understanding of the scale of operation; • If own operation, solely for own use (considering reasonableness of account in all the circumstances).	**Category 3:** • Heroin, cocaine — 150g; • Ecstasy — 300 tablets; • LSD — 2,500 squares; • Amphetamine — 750g; • Cannabis — 6kg; • Ketamine — 150g. **Category 4:** • Heroin, cocaine — 5g; • Ecstasy — 20 tablets; • LSD — 170 squares; • Amphetamine — 20g; • Cannabis — 100g; • Ketamine — 5g.

[4]

SG23-4 STEP TWO Starting point and category range [5]

Having determined the category, the court should use the corresponding starting point to reach a sentence within the category range below. The starting point applies to all offenders irrespective of plea or previous convictions. The court should then consider further adjustment within the category range for aggravating or mitigating features, set out [at SG23-5]. In cases where the offender is regarded as being at the very top of the 'leading' role it may be justifiable for the court to depart from the guideline.

Where the defendant is dependent on or has a propensity to misuse drugs and there is sufficient prospect of success, a community order with a drug rehabilitation requirement under section 209 of the Criminal Justice Act 2003 can be a proper alternative to a short or moderate length custodial sentence.

For class A cases, section 110 of the Powers of Criminal Courts (Sentencing) Act 2000 provides that a court should impose a minimum sentence of at least seven years' imprisonment for a third class A trafficking offence except where the court is of the opinion that there are particular circumstances which (a) relate to any of the offences or to the offender; and (b) would make it unjust to do so in all the circumstances.

[5]

CLASS A	Leading role	Significant role	Lesser role
Category 1	**Starting point** 14 years' custody	**Starting point** 10 years' custody	**Starting point** 8 years' custody
	Category range 12–16 years' custody	**Category range** 9–12 years' custody	**Category range** 6–9 years' custody
Category 2	**Starting point** 11 years' custody	**Starting point** 8 years' custody	**Starting point** 6 years' custody
	Category range 9–13 years' custody	**Category range** 6 years 6 months'–10 years' custody	**Category range** 5–7 years' custody
Category 3	**Starting point** 8 years 6 months' custody	**Starting point** 6 years' custody	**Starting point** 4 years 6 months' custody
	Category range 6 years 6 months'–10 years' custody	**Category range** 5–7 years' custody	**Category range** 3 years 6 months'–5 years' custody
Category 4	Where the quantity falls below the indicative amount set out for category 4 [at SG23-3], first identify the role for the importation offence, then refer to the starting point and ranges for possession or supply offences, depending on intent. Where the quantity is significantly larger than the indicative amounts for category 4 but below category 3 amounts, refer to the category 3 ranges above.		

[6]

CLASS B	Leading role	Significant role	Lesser role
Category 1	**Starting point** 8 years' custody	**Starting point** 5 years 6 months' custody	**Starting point** 4 years' custody
	Category range 7–10 years' custody	**Category range** 5–7 years' custody	**Category range** 2 years 6 months'–5 years' custody
Category 2	**Starting point** 6 years' custody	**Starting point** 4 years' custody	**Starting point** 2 years' custody
	Category range 4 years 6 months'–8 years' custody	**Category range** 2 years 6 months'–5 years' custody	**Category range** 18 months'–3 years' custody
Category 3	**Starting point** 4 years' custody	**Starting point** 2 years' custody	**Starting point** 1 years' custody
	Category range 2 years 6 months'–5 years' custody	**Category range** 18 months'–3 years' custody	**Category range** 12 weeks'–18 months' custody
Category 4	Where the quantity falls below the indicative amount set out for category 4 [at SG23-3], first identify the role for the importation offence, then refer to the starting point and ranges for possession or supply offences, depending on intent. Where the quantity is significantly larger than the indicative amounts for category 4 but below category 3 amounts, refer to the category 3 ranges above.		

CLASS C	Leading role	Significant role	Lesser role
Category 1	**Starting point** 5 years' custody	**Starting point** 3 years' custody	**Starting point** 18 months' custody
	Category range 4–8 years' custody	**Category range** 2–5 years' custody	**Category range** 1–3 years' custody
Category 2	**Starting point** 3 years 6 months' custody	**Starting point** 18 months' custody	**Starting point** 26 weeks' custody
	Category range 2 years'–5 years' custody	**Category range** 1–3 years' custody	**Category range** 12 weeks'–18 months' custody
Category 3	**Starting point** 18 months' custody	**Starting point** 26 weeks' custody	**Starting point** High level community order
	Category range 1–3 years' custody	**Category range** 12 weeks'–18 months' custody	**Category range** Medium level community order–12 weeks' custody
Category 4	Where the quantity falls below the indicative amount set out for category 4 [at SG23-3], first identify the role for the importation offence, then refer to the starting point and ranges for possession or supply offences, depending on intent. Where the quantity is significantly larger than the indicative amounts for category 4 but below category 3 amounts, refer to the category 3 ranges above.		

[6]

SG23-5 The table below contains a **non-exhaustive** list of additional factual elements providing the context of the offence and factors relating to the offender. Identify whether any combination of these, or other relevant factors, should result in an upward or downward adjustment from the starting point. In some cases, having considered these factors, it may be appropriate to move outside the identified category range. [7]

For appropriate **class C** ranges, consider the custody threshold as follows:

- Has the custody threshold been passed?
- If so, is it unavoidable that a custodial sentence be imposed?
- If so, can that sentence be suspended?

Factors increasing seriousness	Factors reducing seriousness or reflecting personal mitigation
Statutory aggravating factors: Previous convictions, having regard to a) nature of the offence to which conviction relates and relevance to current offence; and b) time elapsed since conviction (see [italicised text at SG23-14] if third drug trafficking conviction) Offender used or permitted a person under 18 to deliver a controlled drug to a third person Offence committed on bail *Other aggravating factors include:* Sophisticated nature of concealment and/or attempts to avoid detection Attempts to conceal or dispose of evidence, where not charged separately Exposure of others to more than usual danger, for example drugs cut with harmful substances Presence of weapon, where not charged separately High purity Failure to comply with current court orders Offence committed on licence	Lack of sophistication as to nature of concealment Involvement due to pressure, intimidation or coercion falling short of duress, except where already taken into account at step 1 Mistaken belief of the offender regarding the type of drug, taking into account the reasonableness of such belief in all the circumstances Isolated incident Low purity No previous convictions or no relevant or recent convictions Offender's vulnerability was exploited Remorse Good character and/or exemplary conduct Determination and/or demonstration of steps having been taken to address addiction or offending behaviour Serious medical conditions requiring urgent, intensive or long-term treatment Age and/or lack of maturity where it affects the responsibility of the offender Mental disorder or learning disability Sole or primary carer for dependent relatives

[8] **STEP THREE Consider any factors which indicate a reduction, such as assistance to the prosecution** SG23-6

The court should take into account sections 73 and 74 of the Serious Organised Crime and Police Act 2005 (assistance by defendants: reduction or review of sentence) and any other rule of law by virtue of which an offender may receive a discounted sentence in consequence of assistance given (or offered) to the prosecutor or investigator.

STEP FOUR Reduction for guilty pleas SG23-7

The court should take account of any potential reduction for a guilty plea in accordance with section 144 of the Criminal Justice Act 2003 and the *Guilty Plea* guideline [see **SG4-1**].

For class A offences, where a minimum mandatory sentence is imposed under section 110 Powers of Criminal Courts (Sentencing) Act, the discount for an early guilty plea must not exceed 20 per cent.

STEP FIVE Totality principle SG23-8

If sentencing an offender for more than one offence, or where the offender is already serving a sentence, consider whether the total sentence is just and proportionate to the offending behaviour.

STEP SIX Confiscation and ancillary orders SG23-9

In all cases, the court is required to consider confiscation where the Crown invokes the process or where the court considers it appropriate. It should also consider whether to make ancillary orders.

STEP SEVEN Reasons SG23-10

Section 174 of the Criminal Justice Act 2003 imposes a duty to give reasons for, and explain the effect of, the sentence.

STEP EIGHT Consideration for remand time SG23-11

Sentencers should take into consideration any remand time served in relation to the final sentence at this final step. The court should consider whether to give credit for time spent on remand in custody or on bail in accordance with sections 240 and 240A of the Criminal Justice Act 2003.

[9] ## Supplying or Offering to Supply a Controlled Drug SG23-12

Misuse of Drugs Act 1971 (section 4(3))

Possession of a Controlled Drug with Intent to Supply it to Another

Misuse of Drugs Act 1971 (section 5(3))

Triable either way unless the defendant could receive the minimum sentence of seven years for a third drug trafficking offence under section 110 Powers of Criminal Courts (Sentencing) Act 2000 in which case the offence is triable only on indictment.

Class A
Maximum: Life imprisonment

Offence range: Community order–16 years' custody

A class A offence is a drug trafficking offence for the purpose of imposing a minimum sentence under section 110 Powers of Criminal Courts (Sentencing) Act 2000

Class B
Maximum: 14 years' custody and/or unlimited fine

Offence range: Fine–10 years' custody

Class C
Maximum: 14 years' custody and/or unlimited fine

Offence range: Fine–8 years' custody

[10] **STEP ONE Determining the offence category** SG23-13

The court should determine the offender's culpability (role) and the harm caused (quantity/type of offender) with reference to the tables below.

In assessing culpability, the sentencer should weigh up all the factors of the case to determine role. Where there are characteristics present which fall under different role categories, the court should balance these characteristics to reach a fair assessment of the offender's culpability. [10]

In assessing harm, quantity is determined by the weight of the product. Purity is not taken into account at step 1 but is dealt with at step 2. Where the offence is street dealing or supply of drugs in prison by a prison employee, the quantity of the product is less indicative of the harm caused and therefore the starting point is not based on quantity.

Where the operation is on the most serious and commercial scale, involving a quantity of drugs significantly higher than category 1, sentences of 20 years and above may be appropriate, depending on the role of the offender.

[11]

Culpability demonstrated by offender's role One or more of these characteristics may demonstrate the offender's role. These lists are not exhaustive.	**Category of harm** Indicative quantity of drug concerned (upon which the starting point is based):
LEADING role: • Directing or organising buying and selling on a commercial scale; • Substantial links to, and influence on, others in a chain; • Close links to original source; • Expectation of substantial financial gain; • Uses business as cover; • Abuses a position of trust or responsibility, for example prison employee, medical professional.	**Category 1** • Heroin, cocaine — 5kg; • Ecstasy — 10,000 tablets; • LSD — 250,000 squares; • Amphetamine — 20kg; • Cannabis — 200kg; • Ketamine — 5kg. **Category 2** • Heroin, cocaine — 1kg; • Ecstasy — 2,000 tablets; • LSD — 25,000 squares; • Amphetamine — 4kg; • Cannabis — 40kg; • Ketamine — 1kg.
SIGNIFICANT role: • Operational or management function within a chain; • Involves others in the operation whether by pressure, influence, intimidation or reward; • Motivated by financial or other advantage, whether or not operating alone; • Some awareness and understanding of scale of operation; • Supply, other than by a person in position of responsibility, to a prisoner for gain without coercion. **LESSER role:** • Performs a limited function under direction; • Engaged by pressure, coercion, intimidation; • Involvement through naivety/exploitation; • No influence on those above in a chain; • Very little, if any, awareness or understanding of the scale of operation; • If own operation, absence of financial gain, for example joint purchase for no profit, or sharing minimal quantity between peers on non-commercial basis.	**Category 3** Where the offence is selling direct to users [footnote indicates that this includes test purchase officers] ('street-dealing'), the starting point is not based on a quantity OR Where the offence is supply of drugs in prison by a prison employee, the starting point is not based on a quantity — see [italicised text above]. OR • Heroin, cocaine — 150g; • Ecstasy — 300 tablets; • LSD — 2,500 squares; • Amphetamine — 750g; • Cannabis — 6kg; • Ketamine — 150g. **Category 4** • Heroin, cocaine — 5g; • Ecstasy — 20 tablets; • LSD — 170 squares; • Amphetamine — 20g; • Cannabis — 100g; • Ketamine — 5g; OR Where the offence is selling directly to users [footnote indicates that this includes test purchase officers] ('street-dealing'), the starting point is not based on quantity — go to category 3.

[12] **STEP TWO Starting point and category range** **SG23-14**

Having determined the category, the court should use the corresponding starting point to reach a sentence within the category range below. The starting point applies to all offenders irrespective of plea or previous convictions. The court should then consider further adjustment within the category range for aggravating or mitigating features, set out [at **SG23-15**]. In cases where the offender is regarded as being at the very top of the 'leading' role it may be justifiable for the court to depart from the guideline.

Where the defendant is dependent on or has a propensity to misuse drugs and there is sufficient prospect of success, a community order with a drug rehabilitation requirement under section 209 of the Criminal Justice Act 2003 can be a proper alternative to a short or moderate length custodial sentence.

For class A cases, section 110 of the Powers of Criminal Courts (Sentencing) Act 2000 provides that a court should impose a minimum sentence of at least seven years' imprisonment for a third class A trafficking offence except where the court is of the opinion that there are particular circumstances which (a) relate to any of the offences or to the offender; and (b) would make it unjust to do so in all the circumstances.

CLASS A	Leading role	Significant role	Lesser role
Category 1	**Starting point** 14 years' custody	**Starting point** 10 years' custody	**Starting point** 7 years' custody
	Category range 12–16 years' custody	**Category range** 9–12 years' custody	**Category range** 6–9 years' custody
Category 2	**Starting point** 11 years' custody	**Starting point** 8 years' custody	**Starting point** 5 years' custody
	Category range 9–13 years' custody	**Category range** 6 years 6 months'–10 years' custody	**Category range** 3 years 6 months'–7 years' custody
Category 3	**Starting point** 8 years 6 months' custody	**Starting point** 4 years 6 months' custody	**Starting point** 3 years' custody
	Category range 6 years 6 months'–10 years' custody	**Category range** 3 years 6 months'–7 years' custody	**Category range** 2–4 years 6 months' custody
Category 4	**Starting point** 5 years 6 months' custody	**Starting point** 3 years 6 months' custody	**Starting point** 18 months' custody
	Category range 4 years 6 months'–7 years 6 months' custody	**Category range** 2–5 years' custody	**Category range** High level community order–3 years' custody

[13]

CLASS B	Leading role	Significant role	Lesser role
Category 1	**Starting point** 8 years' custody	**Starting point** 5 years 6 months' custody	**Starting point** 3 years' custody
	Category range 7–10 years' custody	**Category range** 5–7 years' custody	**Category range** 2 years 6 months'–5 years' custody
Category 2	**Starting point** 6 years' custody	**Starting point** 4 years' custody	**Starting point** 1 years' custody
	Category range 4 years 6 months'–8 years' custody	**Category range** 2 years 6 months'–5 years' custody	**Category range** 26 weeks'–3 years' custody
Category 3	**Starting point** 4 years' custody	**Starting point** 1 year's custody	**Starting point** High level community order
	Category range 2 years 6 months'–5 years' custody	**Category range** 26 weeks'–3 years' custody	**Category range** Low level community order–26 weeks' custody

CLASS B	Leading role	Significant role	Lesser role
Category 4	**Starting point** 18 months' custody	**Starting point** High level community order	**Starting point** Low level community order
	Category range 26 weeks'–3 years' custody	**Category range** Medium level community order–26 weeks' custody	**Category range** Band B fine–medium level community order

[13]

CLASS C	Leading role	Significant role	Lesser role
Category 1	**Starting point** 5 years' custody	**Starting point** 3 years' custody	**Starting point** 18 months' custody
	Category range 4–8 years' custody	**Category range** 2–5 years' custody	**Category range** 1–3 years' custody
Category 2	**Starting point** 3 years 6 months' custody	**Starting point** 18 months' custody	**Starting point** 26 weeks' custody
	Category range 2 years'–5 years' custody	**Category range** 1–3 years' custody	**Category range** 12 weeks–18 months' custody
Category 3	**Starting point** 18 months' custody	**Starting point** 26 weeks' custody	**Starting point** High level community order
	Category range 1–3 years' custody	**Category range** 12 weeks'–18 months' custody	**Category range** Low level community order–12 weeks' custody
Category 4	**Starting point** 26 weeks' custody	**Starting point** High level community order	**Starting point** Low level community order
	Category range High level community order–18 months' custody	**Category range** Low level community order–12 weeks' custody	**Category range** Band A fine–medium level community order

SG23-15 The table below contains a **non-exhaustive** list of additional factual elements providing the context of the offence and factors relating to the offender. Identify whether any combination of these, or other relevant factors, should result in an upward or downward adjustment from the starting point. In some cases, having considered these factors, it may be appropriate to move outside the identified category range. [14]

For appropriate **class B** and **C** ranges, consider the custody threshold as follows:

- Has the custody threshold been passed?
- If so, is it unavoidable that a custodial sentence be imposed?
- If so, can that sentence be suspended?

For appropriate **class B** and **C** ranges, the court should also consider the community threshold as follows:

- Has the community threshold been passed?

[14]

Factors increasing seriousness	Factors reducing seriousness or reflecting personal mitigation
Statutory aggravating factors: Previous convictions, having regard to a) nature of the offence to which conviction relates and relevance to current offence; and b) time elapsed since conviction (see [italicised text at **SG23-20**] if third drug trafficking conviction) Offender used or permitted a person under 18 to deliver a controlled drug to a third person Offender 18 or over supplies or offers to supply a drug on, or in the vicinity of, school premises either when school in use as such or at a time between one hour before and one hour after they are to be used Offence committed on bail *Other aggravating factors include:* Targeting of any premises intended to locate vulnerable individuals or supply to such individuals and/or supply to those under 18 Exposure of others to more than usual danger, for example drugs cut with harmful substances Attempts to conceal or dispose of evidence, where not charged separately Presence of others, especially children and/or non-users Presence of weapon, where not charged separately Charged as importation of a very small amount High purity Failure to comply with current court orders Offence committed on licence Established evidence of community impact	Involvement due to pressure, intimidation or coercion falling short of duress, except where already taken into account at step 1 Supply only of drug to which offender addicted Mistaken belief of the offender regarding the type of drug, taking into account the reasonableness of such belief in all the circumstances Isolated incident Low purity No previous convictions or no relevant or recent convictions Offender's vulnerability was exploited Remorse Good character and/or exemplary conduct Determination and/or demonstration of steps having been taken to address addiction or offending behaviour Serious medical conditions requiring urgent, intensive or long-term treatment Age and/or lack of maturity where it affects the responsibility of the offender Mental disorder or learning disability Sole or primary carer for dependent relatives

[15] [Steps Three to Eight are identical to those applicable to Fraudulent evasion of a prohibition by bringing into or taking out of the UK a controlled drug: see **SG23-6**.] **SG23-16**

[17]

Production of a Controlled Drug **SG23-17**

Misuse of Drugs Act 1971 (section 4(2)(a) or (b))

Triable either way unless the defendant could receive the minimum sentence of seven years for a third drug trafficking offence under section 110 Powers of Criminal Courts (Sentencing) Act 2000 in which case the offence is triable only on indictment.

Class A

Maximum: Life imprisonment

Offence range: Community order–16 years' custody

A class A offence is a drug trafficking offence for the purpose of imposing a minimum sentence under section 110 Powers of Criminal Courts (Sentencing) Act 2000

Class B

Maximum: 14 years' custody

Offence range: Discharge–10 years' custody

Class C

Maximum: 14 years' custody

Offence range: Discharge–8 years' custody

SG23-18

CULTIVATION OF CANNABIS PLANT [17]

Misuse of Drugs Act 1971 (section 6(2))

Maximum: 14 years' custody

Offence range: Discharge–10 years' custody

SG23-19

STEP ONE Determining the offence category [18]

The court should determine the offender's culpability (role) and the harm caused (output or potential output) with reference to the tables below.

In assessing culpability, the sentencer should weigh up all of the factors of the case to determine role. Where there are characteristics present which fall under different role categories, the court should balance these characteristics to reach a fair assessment of the offender's culpability.

In assessing harm, output or potential output is determined by the weight of the product or number of plants/ scale of operation. For production offences, purity is not taken into account at step 1 but is dealt with at step 2.

Where the operation is on the most serious and commercial scale, involving a quantity of drugs significantly higher than category 1, sentences of 20 years and above may be appropriate, depending on the role of the offender.

Culpability demonstrated by offender's role One or more of these characteristics may demonstrate the offender's role. These lists are not exhaustive.	**Category of harm** Indicative quantity of drug concerned (upon which the starting point is based):
LEADING role: • Directing or organising buying and selling on a commercial scale; • Substantial links to, and influence on, others in a chain; • Expectation of substantial financial gain; • Uses business as cover; • Abuses a position of trust or responsibility	**Category 1** • Heroin, cocaine — 5kg; • Ecstasy — 10,000 tablets; • LSD — 250,000 squares; • Amphetamine — 20kg; • Cannabis — operation capable of producing industrial quantities for commercial use; • Ketamine — 5kg.
SIGNIFICANT role: • Operational or management function within a chain; • Involves others in the operation whether by pressure, influence, intimidation or reward; • Motivated by financial or other advantage, whether or not operating alone; • Some awareness and understanding of scale of operation;	**Category 2** • Heroin, cocaine — 1kg; • Ecstasy — 2,000 tablets; • LSD — 25,000 squares; • Amphetamine — 4kg; • Cannabis — operation capable of producing significant quantities for commercial use; • Ketamine — 1kg.
LESSER role: • Performs a limited function under direction; • Engaged by pressure, coercion, intimidation; • Involvement through naivety/exploitation; • No influence on those above in a chain; • Very little, if any, awareness or understanding of the scale of operation; • If own operation, solely for own use (considering reasonableness of account in all the circumstances).	**Category 3** • Heroin, cocaine — 150g; • Ecstasy — 300 tablets; • LSD — 2,500 squares; • Amphetamine — 750g; • Cannabis — 28 plants; [footnote indicates 'With assumed yield of 40g per plant'] • Ketamine — 150g.
	Category 4 • Heroin, cocaine — 5g; • Ecstasy — 20 tablets; • LSD — 170 squares; • Amphetamine — 20g; • Cannabis — 9 plants (domestic operation); [footnote indicates 'With assumed yield of 40g per plant'] • Ketamine — 5g.

SG23-20

STEP TWO Starting point and category range [19]

Having determined the category, the court should use the corresponding starting point to reach a sentence within the category range below. The starting point applies to all offenders irrespective of plea or previous convictions. The court should then consider further adjustment within the category range for aggravating or mitigating features, set out [at **SG23-21**]. In cases where the offender is regarded as being at the very top of the 'leading' role it may be justifiable for the court to depart from the guideline.

[19] Where the defendant is dependent on or has a propensity to misuse drugs and there is sufficient prospect of success, a community order with a drug rehabilitation requirement under section 209 of the Criminal Justice Act 2003 can be a proper alternative to a short or moderate length custodial sentence.

For class A cases, section 110 of the Powers of Criminal Courts (Sentencing) Act 2000 provides that a court should impose a minimum sentence of at least seven years' imprisonment for a third class A trafficking offence except where the court is of the opinion that there are particular circumstances which (a) relate to any of the offences or to the offender; and (b) would make it unjust to do so in all the circumstances.

CLASS A	Leading role	Significant role	Lesser role
Category 1	**Starting point** 14 years' custody	**Starting point** 10 years' custody	**Starting point** 7 years' custody
	Category range 12–16 years' custody	**Category range** 9–12 years' custody	**Category range** 6–9 years' custody
Category 2	**Starting point** 11 years' custody	**Starting point** 8 years' custody	**Starting point** 5 years' custody
	Category range 9–13 years' custody	**Category range** 6 years 6 months'–10 years' custody	**Category range** 3 years 6 months'–7 years' custody
Category 3	**Starting point** 8 years 6 months' custody	**Starting point** 5 years' custody	**Starting point** 3 years 6 months' custody
	Category range 6 years 6 months'–10 years' custody	**Category range** 3 years 6 months'–7 years' custody	**Category range** 2–5 years' custody
Category 4	**Starting point** 5 years 6 months' custody	**Starting point** 3 years 6 months' custody	**Starting point** 18 months' custody
	Category range 4 years 6 months'–7 years 6 months' custody	**Category range** 2–5 years' custody	**Category range** High level community order–3 years' custody

[20]

CLASS B	Leading role	Significant role	Lesser role
Category 1	**Starting point** 8 years' custody	**Starting point** 5 years 6 months' custody	**Starting point** 3 years' custody
	Category range 7–10 years' custody	**Category range** 5–7 years' custody	**Category range** 2 years 6 months'–5 years' custody
Category 2	**Starting point** 6 years' custody	**Starting point** 4 years' custody	**Starting point** 1 years' custody
	Category range 4 years 6 months'–8 years' custody	**Category range** 2 years 6 months'–5 years' custody	**Category range** 26 weeks'–3 years' custody
Category 3	**Starting point** 4 years' custody	**Starting point** 1 year's custody	**Starting point** High level community order
	Category range 2 years 6 months'–5 years' custody	**Category range** 26 weeks'–3 years' custody	**Category range** Low level community order–26 weeks' custody
Category 4	**Starting point** 1 years' custody	**Starting point** High level community order	**Starting point** Band C fine
	Category range High level community order–3 years' custody	**Category range** Medium level community order–26 weeks' custody	**Category range** Discharge–medium level community order

CLASS C	Leading role	Significant role	Lesser role
Category 1	**Starting point** 5 years' custody	**Starting point** 3 years' custody	**Starting point** 18 months' custody
	Category range 4–8 years' custody	**Category range** 2–5 years' custody	**Category range** 1–3 years' custody

CLASS C	Leading role	Significant role	Lesser role
Category 2	**Starting point** 3 years 6 months' custody	**Starting point** 18 months' custody	**Starting point** 26 weeks' custody
	Category range 2–5 years' custody	**Category range** 1–3 years' custody	**Category range** High level community order–18 months' custody
Category 3	**Starting point** 18 months' custody	**Starting point** 26 weeks' custody	**Starting point** High level community order
	Category range 1–3 years' custody	**Category range** High level community order–18 months' custody	**Category range** Low level community order–12 weeks' custody
Category 4	**Starting point** 26 weeks' custody	**Starting point** High level community order	**Starting point** Band C fine
	Category range High level community order–18 months' custody	**Category range** Low level community order–12 weeks' custody	**Category range** Discharge–medium level community order

[20]

SG23-21 The table below contains a **non-exhaustive** list of additional factual elements providing the context of the offence and factors relating to the offender. Identify whether any combination of these, or other relevant factors, should result in an upward or downward adjustment from the starting point. In some cases, having considered these factors, it may be appropriate to move outside the identified category range. [21]

Where appropriate, consider the custody threshold as follows:

- Has the custody threshold been passed?
- If so, is it unavoidable that a custodial sentence be imposed?
- If so, can that sentence be suspended?

Where appropriate, the court should also consider the community threshold as follows:

- Has the community threshold been passed?

Factors increasing seriousness	**Factors reducing seriousness or reflecting personal mitigation**
Statutory aggravating factors: Previous convictions, having regard to a) nature of the offence to which conviction relates and relevance to current offence; and b) time elapsed since conviction (see [italicised text at **SG23-20**] if third drug trafficking conviction) Offence committed on bail *Other aggravating factors include:* Nature of any likely supply Level of any profit element Use of premises accompanied by unlawful access to electricity/other utility supply of others Ongoing/large scale operation as evidenced by presence and nature of specialist equipment Exposure of others to more than usual danger, for example drugs cut with harmful substances Attempts to conceal or dispose of evidence, where not charged separately Presence of others, especially children and/or non-users Presence of weapon, where not charged separately High purity or high potential yield Failure to comply with current court orders Offence committed on licence Established evidence of community impact	Involvement due to pressure, intimidation or coercion falling short of duress, except where already taken into account at step 1 Isolated incident Low purity No previous convictions **or** no relevant or recent convictions Offender's vulnerability was exploited Remorse Good character and/or exemplary conduct Determination and/or demonstration of steps having been taken to address addiction or offending behaviour Serious medical conditions requiring urgent, intensive or long-term treatment Age and/or lack of maturity where it affects the responsibility of the offender Mental disorder or learning disability Sole or primary carer for dependent relatives

[22] [Steps Three to Eight are identical to those applicable to Fraudulent evasion of a prohibition by bringing into or taking out of the UK a controlled drug: see SG23-6.] **SG23-22**

[23] **SG23-23**

Permitting Premises to be Used

Misuse of Drugs Act 1971 (section 8)

Triable either way unless the defendant could receive the minimum sentence of seven years for a third drug trafficking offence under section 110 Powers of Criminal Courts (Sentencing) Act 2000 in which case the offence is triable only on indictment.

Class A

Maximum: 14 years' custody

Offence range: Community order–4 years' custody

A class A offence is a drug trafficking offence for the purpose of imposing a minimum sentence under section 110 Powers of Criminal Courts (Sentencing) Act 2000

Class B

Maximum: 14 years' custody

Offence range: Fine–18 months' custody

Class C

Maximum: 14 years' custody

Offence range: Discharge–26 weeks' custody

[24] **STEP ONE Determining the offence category** **SG23-24**

The court should determine the offender's culpability and the harm caused (extent of the activity and/or the quantity of drugs) with reference to the table below.

In assessing harm, quantity is determined by the weight of the product. Purity is not taken into account at step 1 but is dealt with at step 2

Category 1	Higher culpability **and** greater harm
Category 2	Lower culpability **and** greater harm; **or** higher culpability **and** lesser harm
Category 3	Lower culpability **and** lesser harm

Factors indicating culpability (non-exhaustive)	Factors indicating harm (non-exhaustive)
Higher culpability: Permits premises to be used primarily for drug activity, for example crack house Permits use in expectation of substantial financial gain Uses legitimate business premises to aid and/or conceal illegal activity, for example public house or club *Lower culpability*: Permits use for limited or no financial gain No active role in any supply taking place Involvement through naivety	*Greater harm*: Regular drug-related activity Higher quantity of drugs, for example: Heroin, cocaine — more than 5g; Cannabis — more than 50g. *Lesser harm:* Infrequent drug-related activity Lower quantity of drugs, for example: Heroin, cocaine — up to 5g; Cannabis — up to 50g.

[25] **STEP TWO Starting point and category range** **SG23-25**

Having determined the category, the court should use the table below to identify the corresponding starting point to reach a sentence within the category range. The starting point applies to all offenders irrespective of plea or previous convictions. The court should then consider further adjustment within the category range for aggravating or mitigating features, set out [at SG23-26].

Where the defendant is dependent on or has a propensity to misuse drugs and there is sufficient prospect of success, a community order with a drug rehabilitation requirement under section 209 of the Criminal Justice Act 2003 can be a proper alternative to a short or moderate length custodial sentence. [25]

For class A cases, section 110 of the Powers of Criminal Courts (Sentencing) Act 2000 provides that a court should impose a minimum sentence of at least seven years' imprisonment for a third class A trafficking offence except where the court is of the opinion that there are particular circumstances which (a) relate to any of the offences or to the offender; and (b) would make it unjust to do so in all the circumstances.

Class A

Offence category	Starting point (*applicable to all offenders*)	Category range (*applicable to all Offenders*)
Category 1	2 years 6 months' custody	18 months'–4 years' custody
Category 2	36 weeks' custody	High level community order–18 months' custody
Category 3	Medium level community order	Low level community order–high level community order

Class B

Offence category	Starting point (*applicable to all offenders*)	Category range (*applicable to all Offenders*)
Category 1	1 year's custody	26 weeks'–18 months' custody
Category 2	High level community order	Low level community order–26 weeks' custody
Category 3	Band C fine	Band A fine–low level community order

Class C

Offence category	Starting point (*applicable to all offenders*)	Category range (*applicable to all Offenders*)
Category 1	12 weeks' custody	High level community order–26 weeks' custody [footnote indicates that 'when tried summarily, the maximum penalty is 12 weeks' custody']
Category 2	Low level community order	Band C fine–high level community order
Category 3	Band A fine	Discharge–Band C fine

SG23-26 The table below contains a **non-exhaustive** list of additional factual elements providing the context of the offence and factors relating to the offender. Identify whether any combination of these, or other relevant factors, should result in an upward or downward adjustment from the starting point. In some cases, having considered these factors, it may be appropriate to move outside the identified category range. [26]

Where appropriate, consider the custody threshold as follows:

- Has the custody threshold been passed?
- If so, is it unavoidable that a custodial sentence be imposed?
- If so, can that sentence be suspended?

Where appropriate, the court should also consider the community threshold as follows:

- Has the community threshold been passed?

[26]

Factors increasing seriousness	Factors reducing seriousness or reflecting personal mitigation
Statutory aggravating factors: Previous convictions, having regard to a) nature of the offence to which conviction relates and relevance to current offence; and b) time elapsed since conviction (see [italicised text at S23-25] if third drug trafficking conviction) Offence committed on bail *Other aggravating factors include:* Length of time over which premises used for drug activity Volume of drug activity permitted Premises adapted to facilitate drug activity Location of premises, for example proximity to school Attempts to conceal or dispose of evidence, where not charged separately Presence of others, especially children and/or non-users High purity Presence of weapons, where not charged separately Failure to comply with current court orders Offence committed on licence Established evidence of community impact	Involvement due to pressure, intimidation or coercion falling short of duress Isolated incident Low purity No previous convictions **or** no relevant or recent convictions Offender's vulnerability was exploited Remorse Good character and/or exemplary conduct Determination and/or demonstration of steps having been taken to address addiction or offending behaviour Serious medical conditions requiring urgent, intensive or long-term treatment Age and/or lack of maturity where it affects the responsibility of the offender Mental disorder or learning disability Sole or primary carer for dependent relatives

[27] [Steps Three to Eight are identical to those applicable to Fraudulent evasion of a prohibition by bringing into or taking out of the UK a controlled drug: see SG23-6.] **SG23-27**

[29]

Possession of a Controlled Drug **SG23-28**

Misuse of Drugs Act 1971 (section 5(2))

Triable either way

Class A

Maximum: 7 years' custody

Offence range: Fine–51 weeks' custody

Class B

Maximum: 5 years' custody

Offence range: Discharge–26 weeks' custody

Class C

Maximum: 2 years' custody

Offence range: Discharge–Community order

[30] **STEP ONE Determining the offence category** **SG23-29**

The court should identify the offence category based on the class of drug involved.

Category 1	Class A drug
Category 2	Class B drug
Category 3	Class C drug

STEP TWO Starting point and category range **SG23-30**

The court should use the table below to identify the corresponding starting point. The starting point applies to all offenders irrespective of plea or previous convictions. The court should then consider further adjustment within the category range for aggravating or mitigating features, set out [at **SG23-31**]. [30]

Where the defendant is dependent on or has a propensity to misuse drugs and there is sufficient prospect of success, a community order with a drug rehabilitation requirement under section 209 of the Criminal Justice Act 2003 can be a proper alternative to a short or moderate length custodial sentence.

Offence category	**Starting point** (*applicable to all offenders*)	**Category range** (*applicable to all offenders*)
Category 1 (class A)	Band C fine	Band A fine–51 weeks' custody
Category 2 (class B)	Band B fine	Discharge–26 weeks' custody
Category 3 (class C)	Band A fine	Discharge–medium level community order

SG23-31 The table below contains a **non-exhaustive** list of additional factual elements providing the context of the offence and factors relating to the offender. Identify whether any combination of these, or other relevant factors, should result in an upward or downward adjustment from the starting point. **In particular, possession of drugs in prison is likely to result in an upward adjustment**. In some cases, having considered these factors, it may be appropriate to move outside the identified category range. [31]

Where appropriate, consider the custody threshold as follows:

- Has the custody threshold been passed?
- If so, is it unavoidable that a custodial sentence be imposed?
- If so, can that sentence be suspended?

Where appropriate, the court should also consider the community threshold as follows:

- Has the community threshold been passed?

Factors increasing seriousness	**Factors reducing seriousness or reflecting personal mitigation**
Statutory aggravating factors: Previous convictions, having regard to a) nature of the offence to which conviction relates and relevance to current offence; and b) time elapsed since conviction Offence committed on bail *Other aggravating factors include:* Possession of drug in prison Presence of others, especially children and/or non-users Possession of drug in a school or licensed premises Failure to comply with current court orders Offence committed on licence Attempts to conceal or dispose of evidence, where not charged separately Charged as importation of a very small amount Established evidence of community impact	No previous convictions **or** no relevant or recent convictions Remorse Good character and/or exemplary conduct Offender is using cannabis to help with a diagnosed medical condition Determination and/or demonstration of steps having been taken to address addiction or offending behaviour Serious medical conditions requiring urgent, intensive or long-term treatment Isolated incident Age and/or lack of maturity where it affects the responsibility of the offender Mental disorder or learning disability Sole or primary carer for dependent relatives

SG23-32 [Steps Three to Eight are similar to those applicable to Fraudulent evasion of a prohibition by bringing into or taking out of the UK a controlled drug (see **SG23-6**) but the reference at Step Four to minimum mandatory sentences does not apply and Step Six merely states 'In all cases, the court should consider whether to make ancillary orders'.] [32]

SG23-33 ANNEX: FINE BANDS AND COMMUNITY ORDERS [33]

[The tables set out here are also set out in the Magistrates' Court Sentencing Guidelines, which includes further guidance on fines and community orders: see **SG10-129** and **SG9-2**.]

PART 24 ENVIRONMENTAL OFFENCES

Definitive Guideline SG24-1

[2] **Applicability of guideline**

[Omitted: See SG19-1 for identical text save that this guideline has effect from 1 July 2014.]

This guideline applies only to individual offenders aged 18 and older or organisations. General principles to be considered in the sentencing of youths are in the Sentencing Guidelines Council's definitive guideline, *Sentencing Children and Young People: Overarching Principles* [see SG8-1].

Structure, ranges and starting points

[Omitted: See SG19-2]

[3] ## Organisations SG24-2

Unauthorised or harmful deposit, treatment or disposal etc. of waste

Illegal discharges to air, land and water

Environmental Protection Act 1990 (section 33)

Environmental Permitting (England and Wales) Regulations 2010 (regulations 12 and 38(1), (2) and (3))

Also relevant, with adjustments, to certain related offences (see [SG24-17])

Triable either way

Maximum: when tried on indictment: unlimited fine
when tried summarily: £50,000 fine

Offence range: £100 fine–£3 million fine

Use this guideline when the offender is an organisation. If the offender is an individual, please refer to the guideline for individuals.

Confiscation

Committal to the Crown Court for sentence is mandatory if confiscation (see step two) is to be considered: Proceeds of Crime Act 2002 section 70. In such cases magistrates should state whether they would otherwise have committed for sentence.

Financial orders must be considered in this order: (1) compensation, (2) confiscation, and (3) fine (see Proceeds of Crime Act 2002 section 13).

[4] **STEP ONE Compensation** SG24-3

The court must consider making a compensation order requiring the offender to pay compensation for any personal injury, loss or damage resulting from the offence in such an amount as the court considers appropriate, having regard to the evidence and to the means of the offender.

Where the means of the offender are limited, priority should be given to the payment of compensation over payment of any other financial penalty.

Reasons should be given if a compensation order is not made.

(See section 130 Powers of Criminal Courts (Sentencing) Act 2000)

STEP TWO Confiscation (Crown Court only) SG24-4

Confiscation must be considered if either the Crown asks for it or the court thinks that it may be appropriate. Confiscation must be dealt with before any other fine or financial order (except compensation).

(See sections 6 and 13 Proceeds of Crime Act 2002)

SG24-5 STEP THREE **Determining the offence category** [5]

The court should determine the offence category using only the culpability and harm factors in the tables below. The culpability and harm categories are on a sliding scale; there is inevitable overlap between the factors described in adjacent categories. Where an offence does not fall squarely into a category, individual factors may require a degree of weighting before making an overall assessment and determining the appropriate offence category.

SG24-6 Dealing with a **risk of harm** involves consideration of both the likelihood of harm occurring and the extent of it if it does. Risk of harm is less serious than the same actual harm. Where the offence has caused risk of harm but no (or less) actual harm the normal approach is to move down to the next category of harm. This may not be appropriate if either the likelihood or extent of potential harm is particularly high.

Culpability	Harm	
Deliberate Intentional breach of or flagrant disregard for the law by person(s) whose position of responsibility in the organisation is such that their acts/omissions can properly be attributed to the organisation; **OR** deliberate failure by organisation to put in place and to enforce such systems as could reasonably be expected in all the circumstances to avoid commission of the offence.	Category 1	• Polluting material of a dangerous nature, for example, hazardous chemicals or sharp objects • Major adverse effect or damage to air or water quality, amenity value, or property • Polluting material was noxious, widespread or pervasive with long-lasting effects on human health or quality of life, animal health or flora • Major costs incurred through clean-up, site restoration or animal rehabilitation • Major interference with, prevention or undermining of other lawful activities or regulatory regime due to offence
Reckless Actual foresight of, or wilful blindness to, risk of offending but risk nevertheless taken by person(s) whose position of responsibility in the organisation is such that their acts/omissions can properly be attributed to the organisation; **OR** reckless failure by organisation to put in place and to enforce such systems as could reasonably be expected in all the circumstances to avoid commission of the offence.	Category 2	• Significant adverse effect or damage to air or water quality, amenity value, or property • Significant adverse effect on human health or quality of life, animal health or flora • Significant costs incurred through clean-up, site restoration or animal rehabilitation • Significant interference with or undermining of other lawful activities or regulatory regime due to offence • Risk of category 1 harm
Negligent Failure by the organisation as a whole to take reasonable care to put in place and enforce proper systems for avoiding commission of the offence.	Category 3	• Minor, localised adverse effect or damage to air or water quality, amenity value, or property • Minor adverse effect on human health or quality of life, animal health or flora • Low costs incurred through clean-up, site restoration or animal rehabilitation • Limited interference with or undermining of other lawful activities or regulatory regime due to offence • Risk of category 2 harm
Low or no culpability Offence committed with little or no fault on the part of the organisation as a whole, for example by accident or the act of a rogue employee and despite the presence and due enforcement of all reasonably required preventive measures, or where such proper preventive measures were unforeseeably overcome by exceptional events.	Category 4	• Risk of category 3 harm

[6] **STEP FOUR Starting point and category range** SG24-7

Having determined the category, the court should refer to the tables [below]. There are four tables of starting points and ranges: one for large organisations, one for medium organisations, one for small organisations and one for micro-organisations. The court should refer to the table that relates to the size of the offending organisation.

The court should use the corresponding starting point to reach a sentence within the category range. The court should then consider further adjustment within the category range for aggravating and mitigating features, set out [below].

General principles to follow in setting a fine

The court should determine the appropriate level of fine in accordance with section 164 of the Criminal Justice Act 2003, which requires that the fine must reflect the seriousness of the offence and the court to take into account the financial circumstances of the offender.

The level of fine should reflect the extent to which the offender fell below the required standard. The fine should meet, in a fair and proportionate way, the objectives of punishment, deterrence and the removal of gain derived through the commission of the offence; it should not be cheaper to offend than to take the appropriate precautions.

Obtaining financial information

Offenders which are companies, partnerships or bodies delivering a public or charitable service, are expected to provide comprehensive accounts for the last three years, to enable the court to make an accurate assessment of its financial status. In the absence of such disclosure, or where the court is not satisfied that it has been given sufficient reliable information, the court will be entitled to draw reasonable inferences as to the offender's means from evidence it has heard and from all the circumstances of the case.

Normally, only information relating to the organisation before the court will be relevant, unless it is demonstrated to the court that the resources of a linked organisation are available and can properly be taken into account.

1. *For companies*: annual accounts. Particular attention should be paid to turnover; profit before tax; directors' remuneration, loan accounts and pension provision; and assets as disclosed by the balance sheet. Most companies are required to file audited accounts at Companies House. **Failure to produce relevant recent accounts on request may properly lead to the conclusion that the company can pay any appropriate fine.**
2. *For partnerships*: annual accounts. Particular attention should be paid to turnover; profit before tax; partners' drawings, loan accounts and pension provision; assets as above. Limited Liability Partnerships (LLPs) may be required to file audited accounts with Companies House. **If adequate accounts are not produced on request, see paragraph 1.**
3. *For local authorities, fire authorities and similar public bodies*: the Annual Revenue Budget ('ARB') is the equivalent of turnover and the best indication of the size of the defendant organisation. It is unlikely to be necessary to analyse specific expenditure or reserves (where relevant) unless inappropriate expenditure is suggested.

[7] 4. *For health trusts*: the independent regulator of NHS Foundation Trusts is Monitor. It publishes quarterly reports and annual figures for the financial strength and stability of trusts from which the annual income can be seen, available via **www.monitor-nhsft.gov.uk**. Detailed analysis of expenditure or reserves is unlikely to be called for.
5. *For charities*: it will be appropriate to inspect annual audited accounts. Detailed analysis of expenditure or reserves is unlikely to be called for unless there is a suggestion of unusual or unnecessary expenditure.

At step four, the court will be required to focus on the organisation's annual turnover or equivalent to reach a starting point for a fine. At step six, the court may be required to refer to the other financial factors listed above to ensure that the proposed fine is proportionate.

Very large organisations
Where a defendant company's turnover or equivalent very greatly exceeds the threshold for large companies, it may be necessary to move outside the suggested range to achieve a proportionate sentence.

Sentencing Guidelines

Large — Turnover or equivalent: £50 million and over. [7]

Large	Starting Point	Range
Deliberate		
Category 1	£1,000,000	£450,000–£3,000,000
Category 2	£500,000	£180,000–£1,250,000
Category 3	£180,000	£100,000–£450,000
Category 4	£100,000	£55,000–£250,000
Reckless		
Category 1	£550,000	£250,000–£1,500,000
Category 2	£250,000	£100,000–£650,000
Category 3	£100,000	£60,000–£250,000
Category 4	£60,000	£35,000–£160,000
Negligent		
Category 1	£300,000	£140,000–£750,000
Category 2	£140,000	£60,000–£350,000
Category 3	£60,000	£35,000–£150,000
Category 4	£35,000	£22,000–£100,000
Low / No culpability		
Category 1	£50,000	£25,000–£130,000
Category 2	£25,000	£14,000–£70,000
Category 3	£14,000	£10,000–£40,000
Category 4	£10,000	£7,000–£25,000

Medium — Turnover or equivalent: between £10 million and £50 million. [8]

Medium	Starting Point	Range
Deliberate		
Category 1	£400,000	£170,000–£1,000,000
Category 2	£170,000	£70,000–£450,000
Category 3	£70,000	£40,000–£180,000
Category 4	£40,000	£22,000–£100,000
Reckless		
Category 1	£220,000	£100,000–£500,000
Category 2	£100,000	£40,000–£250,000
Category 3	£40,000	£24,000–£100,000
Category 4	£24,000	£14,000–£60,000
Negligent		
Category 1	£120,000	£55,000–£300,000
Category 2	£55,000	£25,000–£140,000
Category 3	£25,000	£14,000–£60,000
Category 4	£14,000	£8,000–£35,000

[8]

Medium	Starting Point	Range
Low / No culpability		
Category 1	£20,000	£10,000–£50,000
Category 2	£10,000	£5,500–£25,000
Category 3	£5,000	£3,500–£14,000
Category 4	£3,000	£2,500–£10,000

[9] **Small** — Turnover or equivalent: between £2 million and £10 million.

Small	Starting Point	Range
Deliberate		
Category 1	£100,000	£45,000–£400,000
Category 2	£45,000	£17,000–£170,000
Category 3	£17,000	£10,000–£70,000
Category 4	£10,000	£5,000–£40,000
Reckless		
Category 1	£55,000	£24,000–£220,000
Category 2	£24,000	£10,000–£100,000
Category 3	£10,000	£5,000–£40,000
Category 4	£5,000	£3,000–£24,000
Negligent		
Category 1	£30,000	£13,000–£120,000
Category 2	£13,000	£6,000–£55,000
Category 3	£6,000	£3,000–£23,000
Category 4	£3,000	£1,500–£14,000
Low / No culpability		
Category 1	£5,000	£2,500–£20,000
Category 2	£2,500	£1,000–£10,000
Category 3	£1,000	£700–£5,000
Category 4	£700	£400–£3,500

[10] **Micro** — Turnover or equivalent: not more than £2 million.

Micro	Starting Point	Range
Deliberate		
Category 1	£50,000	£9,000–£95,000
Category 2	£22,000	£3,000–£45,000
Category 3	£9,000	£2,000–£17,000
Category 4	£5,000	£1,000–£10,000
Reckless		
Category 1	£30,000	£3,000–£55,000
Category 2	£12,000	£1,500–£24,000

Micro	Starting Point	Range
Category 3	£5,000	£1,000–£10,000
Category 4	£3,000	£500–£5,500
Negligent		
Category 1	£15,000	£1,500–£30,000
Category 2	£6,500	£1,000–£13,000
Category 3	£2,500	£500–£5,500
Category 4	£1,400	£350–£3,000
Low / No culpability		
Category 1	£2,500	£500–£5,000
Category 2	£1,000	£350–£2,400
Category 3	£400	£175–£1,000
Category 4	£200	£100–£700

[10]

The table below contains a **non-exhaustive** list of factual elements providing the context of the offence and factors relating to the offender. Identify whether any combination of these, or other relevant factors, should result in an upward or downward adjustment from the starting point. **In particular, relevant recent convictions and/or a history of non-compliance are likely to result in a substantial upward adjustment.** In some cases, having considered these factors, it may be appropriate to move outside the identified category range. [11]

Factors increasing seriousness	Factors reducing seriousness or reflecting mitigation
Statutory aggravating factors: Previous convictions, having regard to a) the nature of the offence to which the conviction relates and its relevance to the current offence; and b) the time that has elapsed since the conviction *Other aggravating factors include:* History of non-compliance with warnings by regulator Location of the offence, for example, near housing, schools, livestock or environmentally sensitive sites Repeated incidents of offending or offending over an extended period of time, where not charged separately Deliberate concealment of illegal nature of activity Ignoring risks identified by employees or others Established evidence of wider/community impact Breach of any order Offence committed for financial gain Obstruction of justice	No previous convictions **or** no relevant/recent convictions Evidence of steps taken to remedy problem Remorse Compensation paid voluntarily to remedy harm caused One-off event not commercially motivated Little or no financial gain Effective compliance and ethics programme Self-reporting, co-operation and acceptance of responsibility Good character and/or exemplary conduct

SG24-8 STEPS FIVE to SEVEN [12]

The court should now 'step back' and, using the factors set out in steps five, six and seven, review whether the sentence as a whole meets, in a fair way, the objectives of punishment, deterrence and removal of gain derived through the commission of the offence. At steps five to seven, the court may increase or reduce the proposed fine reached at step four, if necessary moving outside the range.

SG24-9 STEP FIVE **Ensure that the combination of financial orders (compensation, confiscation if appropriate, and fine) removes any economic benefit derived from the offending**

[12] The court should remove any economic benefit the offender has derived through the commission of the offence including:

- avoided costs;
- operating savings;
- any gain made as a direct result of the offence.

Where the offender is fined, the amount of economic benefit derived from the offence should normally be added to the fine arrived at in step four. If a confiscation order is made, in considering economic benefit, the court should avoid double recovery.

Economic benefit will not always be an identifiable feature of a case. For example, in some water pollution cases there may be strict liability but very little obvious gain. However, even in these cases there may be some avoidance of cost, for example alarms not installed and maintained, inadequate funding or security measures not installed. Any costs avoided will be considered as economic benefit.

Where it is not possible to calculate or estimate the economic benefit, the court may wish to draw on information from the enforcing authorities about the general costs of operating within the law.

STEP SIX Check whether the proposed fine based on turnover is proportionate to the means of the offender SG24-10

The combination of financial orders must be sufficiently substantial to have a real economic impact which will bring home to both management and shareholders the need to improve regulatory compliance. Whether the fine will have the effect of putting the offender out of business will be relevant; in some bad cases this may be an acceptable consequence.

It will be necessary to examine the financial circumstances of the organisation in the round. If an organisation has a small profit margin relative to its turnover, downward adjustment may be needed. If it has a large profit margin, upward adjustment may be needed.

In considering the ability of the offending organisation to pay any financial penalty, the court can take into account the power to allow time for payment or to order that the amount be paid in instalments.

[13] STEP SEVEN Consider other factors that may warrant adjustment of the proposed fine SG24-11

The court should consider any further factors that are relevant to ensuring that the proposed fine is proportionate having regard to the means of the offender and the seriousness of the offence.

Where the fine will fall on public or charitable bodies, the fine should normally be substantially reduced if the offending organisation is able to demonstrate the proposed fine would have a significant impact on the provision of their services.

The non-exhaustive list below contains additional factual elements the court should consider in deciding whether an increase or reduction to the proposed fine is required:

- fine impairs offender's ability to make restitution to victims;
- impact of fine on offender's ability to improve conditions in the organisation to comply with the law;
- impact of fine on employment of staff, service users, customers and local economy.

STEP EIGHT Consider any factors which indicate a reduction, such as assistance to the prosecution SG24-12

The court should take into account sections 73 and 74 of the Serious Organised Crime and Police Act 2005 (assistance by defendants: reduction or review of sentence) and any other rule of law by virtue of which an offender may receive a discounted sentence in consequence of assistance given (or offered) to the prosecutor or investigator.

STEP NINE Reduction for guilty pleas SG24-13

The court should take account of any potential reduction for a guilty plea in accordance with section 144 of the Criminal Justice Act 2003 and the *Guilty Plea* guideline.

STEP TEN Ancillary orders SG24-14

In all cases, the court must consider whether to make ancillary orders. These may include:

Forfeiture of vehicle [13]

The court may order the forfeiture of a vehicle used in or for the purposes of the commission of the offence in accordance with section 33C of the Environmental Protection Act 1990.

Deprivation of property

Where section 33C of the Environmental Protection Act 1990 does not apply, the court may order the offender be deprived of property used to commit crime or intended for that purpose in accordance with section 143 of the Powers of Criminal Courts (Sentencing) Act 2000. In considering whether to make an order under section 143, the court must have regard to the value of the property and the likely effects on the offender of making the order taken together with any other order the court makes.

Remediation

Where an offender is convicted of an offence under regulation 38(1), (2) or (3) of the Environmental Permitting (England and Wales) Regulations 2010, a court may order the offender to take steps to remedy the cause of the offence within a specified period in accordance with regulation 44 of the Environmental Permitting (England and Wales) Regulations 2010.

SG24-15 STEP ELEVEN **Totality principle** [14]

If sentencing an offender for more than one offence, or where the offender is already serving a sentence, consider whether the total sentence is just and proportionate to the offending behaviour.

SG24-16 STEP TWELVE **Reasons**

Section 174 of the Criminal Justice Act 2003 imposes a duty to give reasons for, and explain the effect of, the sentence.

SG24-17 **Other environmental offences**

In sentencing other relevant and analogous environmental offences, the court should refer to the sentencing approach in steps one to three and five to seven of the guideline, **adjusting the starting points and ranges bearing in mind the statutory maxima** for those offences. An indicative list of such offences is set out below.

Offence	Mode of trial	Statutory maxima
Section 1 Control of Pollution (Amendment) Act 1989 — transporting controlled waste without registering	Triable summarily only	• level 5 fine
Section 34 Environmental Protection Act 1990 — breach of duty of care	Triable either way	• when tried on indictment: unlimited fine • when tried summarily: level 5 fine
Section 80 Environmental Protection Act 1990 — breach of an abatement notice	Triable summarily only	• where the offence is committed on industrial, trade or business premises: £20,000 fine • where the offence is committed on non-industrial etc. premises: level 5 fine with a further fine of an amount equal to one-tenth of that level for each day on which the offence continues after the conviction
Section 111 Water Industry Act 1991 — restrictions on use of public sewers	Triable either way	• when tried on indictment: imprisonment for a term not exceeding two years or a fine or both • when tried summarily: a fine not exceeding the statutory maximum and a further fine not exceeding £50 for each day on which the offence continues after conviction
Offences under the Transfrontier Shipment of Waste Regulations 2007	Triable either way	• when tried on indictment: a fine or two years' imprisonment or both • when tried summarily: a fine not exceeding the statutory maximum or three months' imprisonment or both

[15] INDIVIDUALS SG24-18

Unauthorised or harmful deposit, treatment or disposal etc. of waste

Illegal discharges to air, land and water

Environmental Protection Act 1990 (section 33)

Environmental Permitting (England and Wales) Regulations 2010 (regulations 12 and 38(1), (2) and (3))

Also relevant, with adjustments, to certain related offences (see [SG24-17])

Triable either way

Maximum: when tried on indictment: unlimited fine and/or 5 years' custody
when tried summarily: £50,000 fine and/or 6 months' custody

Offence range: conditional discharge–3 years' custody

Use this guideline when the offender is an individual. If the offender is an organisation, please refer to the guideline for organisations.

Confiscation
Committal to the Crown Court for sentence is mandatory if confiscation (see step two) is to be considered: Proceeds of Crime Act 2002 section 70. In such cases magistrates should state whether they would otherwise have committed for sentence.
If a fine is imposed, the financial orders must be considered in this order: (1) compensation, (2) confiscation, and (3) fine (see Proceeds of Crime Act 2002 section 13).

[16] **STEP ONE Compensation** SG24-19

The court must consider making a compensation order requiring the offender to pay compensation for any personal injury, loss or damage resulting from the offence in such an amount as the court considers appropriate, having regard to the evidence and to the means of the offender.

Where the means of the offender are limited, priority should be given to the payment of compensation over payment of any other financial penalty.

Reasons should be given if a compensation order is not made.

(See section 130 Powers of Criminal Courts (Sentencing) Act 2000)

STEP TWO Confiscation (Crown Court only) SG24-20

Confiscation must be considered if either the Crown asks for it or the court thinks that it may be appropriate. Confiscation must be dealt with before any other fine or financial order (except compensation).

(See sections 6 and 13 Proceeds of Crime Act 2002)

[17] **STEP THREE Determining the offence category** SG24-21

The court should determine the offence category using only the culpability and harm factors in the tables below. The culpability and harm categories are on a sliding scale; there is inevitable overlap between the factors described in adjacent categories. Where an offence does not fall squarely into a category, individual factors may require a degree of weighting before making an overall assessment and determining the appropriate offence category.

Dealing with a **risk of harm** involves consideration of both the likelihood of harm occurring and the extent of it if it does. Risk of harm is less serious than the same actual harm. Where the offence has caused risk of harm but no (or less) actual harm the normal approach is to move down to the next category of harm. This may not be appropriate if either the likelihood or extent of potential harm is particularly high.

Culpability	Harm		[17]
Deliberate Where the offender intentionally breached, or flagrantly disregarded, the law **Reckless** Actual foresight of, or wilful blindness to, risk of offending but risk nevertheless taken **Negligent** Offence committed through act or omission which a person exercising reasonable care would not commit **Low or no culpability** Offence committed with little or no fault, for example by genuine accident despite the presence of proper preventive measures, or where such proper preventive measures were unforeseeably overcome by exceptional events	Category 1	• Polluting material of a dangerous nature, for example, hazardous chemicals or sharp objects • Major adverse effect or damage to air or water quality, amenity value, or property • Polluting material was noxious, widespread or pervasive with long-lasting effects on human health or quality of life, animal health, or flora • Major costs incurred through clean-up, site restoration or animal rehabilitation • Major interference with, prevention or undermining of other lawful activities or regulatory regime due to offence	
	Category 2	• Significant adverse effect or damage to air or water quality, amenity value, or property • Significant adverse effect on human health or quality of life, animal health or flora • Significant costs incurred through clean-up, site restoration or animal rehabilitation • Significant interference with or undermining of other lawful activities or regulatory regime due to offence • Risk of category 1 harm	
	Category 3	• Minor, localised adverse effect or damage to air or water quality, amenity value, or property • Minor adverse effect on human health or quality of life, animal health or flora • Low costs incurred through clean-up, site restoration or animal rehabilitation • Limited interference with or undermining of other lawful activities or regulatory regime due to offence • Risk of category 2 harm	
	Category 4	• Risk of category 3 harm	

SG24-22 STEP FOUR Starting point and category range [18]

Having determined the category, the court should refer to the starting points [not reproduced here] to reach a sentence within the category range. The court should then consider further adjustment within the category range for aggravating and mitigating features, [not reproduced here].

General principles to follow in setting a fine

The court should determine the appropriate level of fine in accordance with section 164 of the Criminal Justice Act 2003, which requires that the fine must reflect the seriousness of the offence and the court to take into account the financial circumstances of the offender.

The level of fine should reflect the extent to which the offender fell below the required standard. The fine should meet, in a fair and proportionate way, the objectives of punishment, deterrence and the removal of gain derived through the commission of the offence; it should not be cheaper to offend than to take the appropriate precautions.

Obtaining financial information

In setting a fine, the court may conclude that the offender is able to pay any fine imposed unless the offender has supplied any financial information to the contrary. It is for the offender to disclose to the court such data relevant to their financial position as will enable it to assess what they can reasonably afford to pay. If necessary, the court may compel the disclosure of an individual offender's financial circumstances pursuant to section 162 of the Criminal Justice Act 2003. **In the absence of such disclosure, or where the court is not satisfied that it has been given sufficient reliable information, the court will be entitled to draw reasonable inferences as to the offender's means from evidence it has heard and from all the circumstances of the case.**

[19] *Starting points and ranges*

Where the range includes a potential sentence of custody, the court should consider the custody threshold as follows:

- Has the custody threshold been passed?
- If so, is it unavoidable that a custodial sentence be imposed?
- If so, can that sentence be suspended?

Where the range includes a potential sentence of a community order, the court should consider the community order threshold as follows:

- Has the community order threshold been passed?

However, even where the community order threshold has been passed, a fine will normally be the most appropriate disposal. Where confiscation is not applied for, consider, if wishing to remove any economic benefit derived through the commission of the offence, combining a fine with a community order.

Offence category	Starting Point	Range
Deliberate		
Category 1	18 months' custody	1–3 years' custody
Category 2	1 year's custody	26 weeks'–18 months' custody
Category 3	Band F fine	Band E fine or medium level community order– 26 weeks' custody
Category 4	Band E fine	Band D fine or low level community order–B and E fine
Reckless		
Category 1	26 weeks' custody	Band F fine or high level community order– 12 months' custody
Category 2	Band F fine	Band E fine or medium level community order– 26 weeks' custody
Category 3	Band E fine	Band D fine or low level community order–Band E fine
Category 4	Band D fine	Band C fine–Band D fine
Negligent		
Category 1	Band F fine	Band E fine or medium level community order– 26 weeks' custody
Category 2	Band E fine	Band D fine or low level community order–Band E fine
Category 3	Band D fine	Band C fine–Band D fine
Category 4	Band C fine	Band B fine–Band C fine
Low / No culpability		
Category 1	Band D fine	Band C fine–Band D fine
Category 2	Band C fine	Band B fine–Band C fine
Category 3	Band B fine	Band A fine–Band B fine
Category 4	Band A fine	Conditional discharge–Band A fine

[20] The table below contains a **non-exhaustive** list of factual elements providing the context of the offence and factors relating to the offender. Identify whether any combination of these, or other relevant factors, should result in an upward or downward adjustment from the starting point. **In particular, relevant recent convictions and/or a history of non-compliance are likely to result in a substantial upward adjustment.** In some cases, having considered these factors, it may be appropriate to move outside the identified category range.

Factors increasing seriousness	Factors reducing seriousness or reflecting mitigation
Statutory aggravating factors: Previous convictions, having regard to a) the nature of the offence to which the conviction relates and its relevance to the current offence; and b) the time that has elapsed since the conviction Offence committed whilst on bail *Other aggravating factors include:* History of non-compliance with warnings by regulator Location of the offence, for example, near housing, schools, livestock or environmentally sensitive sites Repeated incidents of offending or offending over an extended period of time, where not charged separately Deliberate concealment of illegal nature of activity Ignoring risks identified by employees or others Established evidence of wider/community impact Breach of any order Offence committed for financial gain Obstruction of justice Offence committed whilst on licence	No previous convictions or no relevant/recent convictions Remorse Compensation paid voluntarily to remedy harm caused Evidence of steps taken to remedy problem One-off event not commercially motivated Little or no financial gain Self-reporting, co-operation and acceptance of responsibility Good character and/or exemplary conduct Mental disorder or learning disability, where linked to the commission of the offence Serious medical conditions requiring urgent, intensive or long-term treatment Age and/or lack of maturity where it affects the responsibility of the offender Sole or primary carer for dependent relatives

[20]

SG24-23 STEPS FIVE and SIX [21]

Where the sentence is or includes a fine, the court should 'step back' and, using the factors set out in steps five and six, **review whether the sentence as a whole meets, in a fair way, the objectives of punishment, deterrence and removal of gain derived through the commission of the offence.** At steps five and six, the court may increase or reduce the proposed fine reached at step four, if necessary moving outside the range.

SG24-24 STEP FIVE **Ensure that the combination of financial orders (compensation, confiscation if appropriate, and fine) removes any economic benefit derived from the offending**

The court should remove any economic benefit the offender has derived through the commission of the offence including:

- avoided costs;
- operating savings;
- any gain made as a direct result of the offence.

Where the offender is fined, the amount of economic benefit derived from the offence should normally be added to the fine arrived at in step four. If a confiscation order is made, in considering economic benefit, the court should avoid double recovery.

Economic benefit will not always be an identifiable feature of a case. For example, in some water pollution cases there may be strict liability but very little obvious gain. However, even in these cases there may be some avoidance of cost, for example alarms not installed and maintained, inadequate funding or security measures not installed. Any costs avoided will be considered as economic benefit.

Where it is not possible to calculate or estimate the economic benefit derived from the offence, the court may wish to draw on information from the enforcing authorities about the general costs of operating within the law.

SG24-25 STEP SIX **Consider other factors that may warrant adjustment of the proposed fine**

The court should consider any further factors that are relevant to ensuring that the proposed fine is proportionate having regard to the means of the offender and the seriousness of the offence.

The **non-exhaustive** list below contains additional factual elements the court should consider in deciding whether an increase or reduction to the proposed fine is required:

- fine impairs offender's ability to make restitution to victims;
- impact of fine on offender's ability to improve conditions to comply with the law;
- impact of fine on employment of staff, service users, customers and local economy.

[22] **STEP SEVEN Consider any factors which indicate a reduction, such as assistance to the prosecution** SG24-26

The court should take into account sections 73 and 74 of the Serious Organised Crime and Police Act 2005 (assistance by defendants: reduction or review of sentence) and any other rule of law by virtue of which an offender may receive a discounted sentence in consequence of assistance given (or offered) to the prosecutor or investigator.

STEP EIGHT Reduction for guilty pleas SG24-27

The court should take account of any potential reduction for a guilty plea in accordance with section 144 of the Criminal Justice Act 2003 and the *Guilty Plea* guideline.

STEP NINE Ancillary orders SG24-28

In all cases, the court must consider whether to make ancillary orders. These may include:

Disqualification of director

An offender may be disqualified from being a director of a company in accordance with section 2 of the Company Directors Disqualification Act 1986. The maximum period of disqualification is 15 years (Crown Court) or 5 years (magistrates' court).

Disqualification from driving

The court may order disqualification from driving where a vehicle has been used in connection with the commission of the offence (section 147 of the Powers of Criminal Courts (Sentencing) Act 2000).

The court may disqualify an offender from driving on conviction for any offence either in addition to any other sentence or instead of any other sentence (section 146 of the Powers of Criminal Courts (Sentencing) Act 2000).

The court should inform the offender of its intention to disqualify and hear representations.

Forfeiture of vehicle

The court may order the forfeiture of a vehicle used in or for the purposes of the commission of the offence in accordance with section 33C of the Environmental Protection Act 1990.

Deprivation of property

Where section 33C of the Environmental Protection Act 1990 does not apply, the court may order the offender to be deprived of property used to commit crime or intended for that purpose in accordance with section 143 of the Powers of Criminal Courts (Sentencing) Act 2000. In considering whether to make an order under section 143, the court must have regard to the value of the property and the likely effects on the offender of making the order taken together with any other order the court makes.

Remediation

Where an offender is convicted of an offence under regulation 38(1), (2) or (3) of the Environmental Permitting (England and Wales) Regulations 2010, a court may order the offender to take steps to remedy the cause of the offence within a specified period in accordance with regulation 44 of the Environmental Permitting (England and Wales) Regulations 2010.

[23] **STEP TEN Totality principle** SG24-29

If sentencing an offender for more than one offence, or where the offender is already serving a sentence, consider whether the total sentence is just and proportionate to the offending behaviour.

STEP ELEVEN Reasons SG24-30

Section 174 of the Criminal Justice Act 2003 imposes a duty to give reasons for, and explain the effect of, the sentence.

STEP TWELVE Consideration for time spent on bail SG24-31

The court must consider whether to give credit for time spent on bail in accordance with section 240A of the Criminal Justice Act 2003.

Other environmental offences SG24-32

In sentencing other relevant and analogous environmental offences, the court should refer to the sentencing approach in steps one to three and five and six of the guideline, **adjusting the starting points and ranges bearing in mind the statutory maxima** for those offences. An indicative list of such offences is set out [at SG24-17 — **the list is identical for organisations and individuals**].

[24] ## Annex: Fine Bands and Community Orders SG24-33

[The tables set out here are also set out in the Magistrates' Court Sentencing Guidelines, which include further guidance on fines and community orders: see **SG10-129** and **SG9-2**.]

PART 25 MANSLAUGHTER

Definitive Guideline

SG25-1 **Applicability of Guideline** [2]

The Sentencing Council issues this definitive guideline in accordance with section 120 of the Coroners and Justice Act 2009.

It applies to all offenders aged 18 and older, who are sentenced on or after **1 November 2018**, regardless of the date of the offence.

Section 125(1) of the Coroners and Justice Act 2009 provides that when sentencing offences committed after 6 April 2010:

> Every court –
> (a) must, in sentencing an offender, follow any sentencing guidelines which are relevant to the offender's case, and
> (b) must, in exercising any other function relating to the sentencing of offenders, follow any sentencing guidelines which are relevant to the exercise of the function,
>
> unless the court is satisfied that it would be contrary to the interests of justice to do so.

This guideline applies only to individual offenders aged 18 and older.

When sentencing those under 18 refer to the general principles in the Sentencing Council definitive guideline: Sentencing Children and Young People, Overarching Principles (Part 8) .

When sentencing organisations for the offence of corporate manslaughter refer to the Sentencing Council Corporate Manslaughter definitive guideline (Part 25).

SG25-2 **Structure, ranges and starting points**

For the purposes of section 125(3)–(4) of the Coroners and Justice Act 2009, the guideline specifies offence ranges – the range of sentences appropriate for each type of offence. Within each offence, the Council has specified a number of categories which reflect varying degrees of seriousness. The offence range is split into category ranges – sentences appropriate for each level of seriousness. The Council has also identified a starting point within each category.

Starting points define the position within a category range from which to start calculating the provisional sentence. The court should consider further features of the offence or the offender that warrant adjustment of the sentence within the range, including the aggravating and mitigating factors set out at step two. Starting points and ranges apply to all offenders, whether they have pleaded guilty or been convicted after trial.

Credit for a guilty plea is taken into consideration only at step four (step seven for manslaughter by reason of diminished responsibility) in the decision making process, after the appropriate sentence has been identified.

SG25-3

Unlawful Act Manslaughter [4]

Common law

Triable only on indictment

Maximum: Life imprisonment

Offence range: 1–24 years' custody

This is a serious specified offence for the purposes of sections 224 and 225(2) (life sentences for serious offences) of the Criminal Justice Act 2003.

This is an offence listed in Part 1 of Schedule 15B for the purposes of section 224A (life sentence for a second listed offence) and section 226A (extended sentence for certain violent or sexual offences) of the Criminal Justice Act 2003.

The type of manslaughter (and thereby the appropriate guideline) should have been identified prior to sentence. If there is any dispute or uncertainty about the type of manslaughter that applies the judge should give clear reasons for the basis of sentence.

[4] **STEP ONE Determining the offence category** SG25-4

Culpability

- **The characteristics set out below are indications of the level of culpability that may attach to the offender's conduct; the court should balance these characteristics to reach a fair assessment of the offender's overall culpability in the context of the circumstances of the offence.**
- **The court should avoid an overly mechanistic application of these factors.**

A – Very high culpability	Very high culpability may be indicated by: • the extreme character of one or more culpability B factors and /or • a combination of culpability B factors
B – Factors indicating high culpability	Death was caused in the course of an unlawful act which involved an intention by the offender to cause harm falling just short of GBH
	Death was caused in the course of an unlawful act which carried a high risk of death or GBH which was or ought to have been obvious to the offender
	Death was caused in the course of committing or escaping from a serious offence in which the offender played more than a minor role
	Concealment, destruction, defilement or dismemberment of the body (where not separately charged)
C – Factors indicating medium culpability	Cases falling between high and lower **including but not limited to** • where death was caused in the course of an unlawful act which involved an intention by the offender to cause harm (or recklessness as to whether harm would be caused) that falls between high and lower culpability • where death was caused in the course of committing or escaping from a less serious offence but in which the offender played more than a minor role
D – Factors indicating lower culpability	Death was caused in the course of an unlawful act • which was in defence of self or other(s) (where not amounting to a defence) OR • where there was no intention by the offender to cause any harm **and** no obvious risk of anything more than minor harm OR • in which the offender played a minor role
	The offender's responsibility was substantially reduced by mental disorder, learning disability or lack of maturity

Harm

For all cases of manslaughter the harm caused will inevitably be of the utmost seriousness. The loss of life is taken into account in the sentencing levels at step two.

[5] **STEP TWO Starting point and category range** SG25-5

Having determined the category at step one, the court should use the corresponding starting point to reach a sentence within the category range below. The starting point applies to all offenders irrespective of plea or previous convictions.

- **Where a case does not fall squarely within a category, adjustment from the starting point may be required before adjustment for aggravating or mitigating features.**

Culpability			
A	B	C	D
Starting point 18 years' custody	**Starting point** 12 years' custody	**Starting point** 6 years' custody	**Starting point** 2 years' custody
Category range 11–24 years' custody	**Category range** 8–16 years' custody	**Category range** 3–9 years' custody	**Category range** 1–4 years' custody

Note: The table is for a single offence of manslaughter resulting in a single fatality. Where another offence or offences arise out of the same incident or facts, concurrent sentences **reflecting the overall criminality** of offending will ordinarily be appropriate: please refer to the *Offences Taken into Consideration and Totality guideline* (Part 3) and step six of this guideline. [5]

There follows a **non-exhaustive** list of additional elements providing the context of the offence and factors relating to the offender. Identify whether a combination of these or other relevant factors should result in any upward or downward adjustment from the sentence arrived at so far.

Care should be taken to avoid double counting factors already taken into account in assessing culpability [6]

Factors increasing seriousness
Statutory aggravating factors: Previous convictions, having regard to a) the **nature** of the offence to which the conviction relates and its **relevance** to the current offence; and b) the **time** that has elapsed since the conviction (See step five for a consideration of dangerousness) Offence committed whilst on bail Offence motivated by, or demonstrating hostility based on any of the following characteristics or presumed characteristics of the victim: religion, race, disability, sexual orientation or transgender identity Offence was committed against an emergency worker acting in the exercise of functions as such a worker
Other aggravating factors: History of violence or abuse towards victim by offender Involvement of other(s) through coercion, intimidation or exploitation Significant mental or physical suffering caused to the deceased Victim particularly vulnerable due to age or disability Victim was providing a public service or performing a public duty at the time of the offence Commission of offence whilst under the influence of alcohol or drugs Persistence of violence Offence involved use of a weapon Other(s) put at risk of harm by the offending Leading role in group Death occurred in the context of an offence which was planned or premeditated Offence committed in the presence of children Actions after the event (including but not limited to attempts to cover up/conceal evidence) Blame wrongly placed on other(s) Abuse of a position of trust Offence committed on licence or post sentence supervision or while subject to court order(s)

[7]

Factors reducing seriousness or reflecting personal mitigation
No previous convictions **or** no relevant/recent convictions Remorse Attempts to assist the victim History of significant violence or abuse towards the offender by the victim Lack of premeditation Good character and/or exemplary conduct Serious medical conditions requiring urgent, intensive or long-term treatment Mental disorder or learning disability Age and/or lack of maturity Sole or primary carer for dependent relatives

SG25-6 STEP THREE **Consider any factors which indicate a reduction for assistance to the prosecution** [8]

The court should take into account sections 73 and 74 of the Serious Organised Crime and Police Act 2005 (assistance by defendants: reduction or review of sentence) and any other rule of law by virtue of

[8] which an offender may receive a discounted sentence in consequence of assistance given (or offered) to the prosecutor or investigator.

STEP FOUR Reduction for guilty pleas SG25-7

The court should take account of any potential reduction for a guilty plea in accordance with section 144 of the Criminal Justice Act 2003 and the Guilty Plea guideline.

STEP FIVE Dangerousness SG25-8

The court should consider whether having regard to the criteria contained in Chapter 5 of Part 12 of the Criminal Justice Act 2003 it would be appropriate to impose a life sentence (section 224A or section 225) or an extended sentence (section 226A). When sentencing offenders to a life sentence under these provisions, the notional determinate sentence should be used as the basis for the setting of a minimum term.

STEP SIX Totality principle SG25-9

If sentencing an offender for more than one offence, or where the offender is already serving a sentence, consider whether the total sentence is just and proportionate to the overall offending behaviour in accordance with the Offences Taken into Consideration and Totality guideline.

STEP SEVEN Compensation and ancillary orders SG25-10

In all cases the court should consider whether to make compensation and/or other ancillary orders.

STEP EIGHT Reasons SG25-11

Section 174 of the Criminal Justice Act 2003 imposes a duty to give reasons for, and explain the effect of, the sentence.

STEP NINE Consideration for time spent on bail (tagged curfew) SG25-12

The court must consider whether to give credit for time spent on bail in accordance with section 240A of the Criminal Justice Act 2003.

[10]

GROSS NEGLIGENCE MANSLAUGHTER SG25-13

Common law

Triable only on indictment

Maximum: Life imprisonment

Offence range: 1–18 years' custody

This is a serious specified offence for the purposes of sections 224 and 225(2) (life sentences for serious offences) of the Criminal Justice Act 2003.

This is an offence listed in Part 1 of Schedule 15B for the purposes of section 224A (life sentence for a second listed offence) and section 226A (extended sentence for certain violent or sexual offences) of the Criminal Justice Act 2003.

The type of manslaughter (and thereby the appropriate guideline) should have been identified prior to sentence. If there is any dispute or uncertainty about the type of manslaughter that applies the judge should give clear reasons for the basis of sentence.

STEP ONE Determining the offence category SG25-14

Culpability

- **The characteristics set out below are indications of the level of culpability that may attach to the offender's conduct; the court should balance these characteristics to reach a fair assessment of the offender's overall culpability in the context of the circumstances of the offence.**
- **The court should avoid an overly mechanistic application of these factors particularly in cases to which they do not readily apply.**

A – Very high culpability	Very high culpability **may** be indicated by: • the extreme character of one or more culpability B factors and /or • a combination of culpability B factors	[10]
B – Factors indicating high culpability	The offender continued or repeated the negligent conduct in the face of the obvious suffering caused to the deceased by that conduct	
	The negligent conduct was in the context of other serious criminality	
	The offence was particularly serious because the offender showed a blatant disregard for a very high risk of death resulting from the negligent conduct	
	The negligent conduct was motivated by financial gain (or avoidance of cost)	
	The offender was in a leading role if acting with others in the offending	
	Concealment, destruction, defilement or dismemberment of the body (where not separately charged)	
C – Factors indicating medium culpability	Cases falling between high and lower because • factors are present in high and lower which balance each other out **and/or** • the offender's culpability falls between the factors as described in high and lower	
D – Factors indicating lower culpability	The negligent conduct was a lapse in the offender's otherwise satisfactory standard of care	
	The offender was in a lesser or subordinate role if acting with others in the offending	
	The offender's responsibility was substantially reduced by mental disorder, learning disability or lack of maturity	

Harm

For all cases of manslaughter the harm caused will inevitably be of the utmost seriousness. The loss of life is taken into account in the sentencing levels at step two.

SG25-15 STEP TWO **Starting point and category range** [11]

Having determined the category at step one, the court should use the corresponding starting point to reach a sentence within the category range below. The starting point applies to all offenders irrespective of plea or previous convictions.

- Where a case does not fall squarely within a category, adjustment from the starting point may be required before adjustment for aggravating or mitigating features.

Culpability			
A	**B**	**C**	**D**
Starting point 12 years' custody	**Starting point** 8 years' custody	**Starting point** 4 years' custody	**Starting point** 2 years' custody
Category range 10–18 years' custody	**Category range** 6–12 years' custody	**Category range** 3–7 years' custody	**Category range** 1–4 years' custody

Where the offender's acts or omissions would also constitute another offence, the sentencer should have regard to any guideline relevant to the other offence to ensure that the sentence for manslaughter does not fall below what would be imposed under that guideline.

Note: The table is for a single offence of manslaughter resulting in a single fatality. Where another offence or offences arise out of the same incident or facts, concurrent sentences **reflecting the overall criminality** of offending will ordinarily be appropriate: please refer to the *Offences Taken into Consideration and Totality* guideline (Part 3) and step six of this guideline.

There follows a **non-exhaustive** list of additional elements providing the context of the offence and factors relating to the offender. Identify whether a combination of these or other relevant factors should result in any upward or downward adjustment from the sentence arrived at so far.

[12] **Care should be taken to avoid double counting factors already taken into account in assessing culpability**

Factors increasing seriousness
Statutory aggravating factors: Previous convictions, having regard to a) the **nature** of the offence to which the conviction relates and its **relevance** to the current offence; and b) the **time** that has elapsed since the conviction (See step five for a consideration of dangerousness) Offence committed whilst on bail Offence motivated by, or demonstrating hostility based on any of the following characteristics or presumed characteristics of the victim: religion, race, disability, sexual orientation or transgender identity
Other aggravating factors: History of violence or abuse towards victim by offender Involvement of others through coercion, intimidation or exploitation Significant mental or physical suffering caused to the deceased Offender ignored previous warnings Commission of offence whilst under the influence of alcohol or drugs Offence involved use of a weapon Other(s) put at risk of harm by the offending Actions after the event (including but not limited to attempts to cover up/conceal evidence) Investigation has been hindered and/or other(s) have suffered as a result of being falsely blamed by the offender Offence committed on licence or post sentence supervision or while subject to court order(s)

[13]

Factors reducing seriousness or reflecting personal mitigation
No previous convictions or no relevant/recent convictions Remorse Attempts to assist the victim Self-reporting and/or co-operation with the investigation For reasons beyond the offender's control, the offender lacked the necessary expertise, equipment, support or training which contributed to the negligent conduct For reasons beyond the offender's control, the offender was subject to stress or pressure (including from competing or complex demands) which related to and contributed to the negligent conduct For reasons beyond the offender's control, the negligent conduct occurred in circumstances where there was reduced scope for exercising usual care and competence The negligent conduct was compounded by the actions or omissions of others beyond the offender's control Good character and/or exemplary conduct Serious medical conditions requiring urgent, intensive or long-term treatment Mental disorder or learning disability Age and/or lack of maturity Sole or primary carer for dependent relatives

[14] **STEP THREE Consider any factors which indicate a reduction for assistance to the prosecution** **SG25-16**

The court should take into account sections 73 and 74 of the Serious Organised Crime and Police Act 2005 (assistance by defendants: reduction or review of sentence) and any other rule of law by virtue of which an offender may receive a discounted sentence in consequence of assistance given (or offered) to the prosecutor or investigator.

STEP FOUR Reduction for guilty pleas **SG25-17**

The court should take account of any potential reduction for a guilty plea in accordance with section 144 of the Criminal Justice Act 2003 and the Guilty Plea guideline.

STEP FIVE Dangerousness **SG25-18**

The court should consider whether having regard to the criteria contained in Chapter 5 of Part 12 of the Criminal Justice Act 2003 it would be appropriate to impose a life sentence (section 224A or section 225) or an extended sentence (section 226A). When sentencing offenders to a life sentence under these provisions, the notional determinate sentence should be used as the basis for the setting of a minimum term.

SG25-19 **STEP SIX Totality principle** [14]

If sentencing an offender for more than one offence, or where the offender is already serving a sentence, consider whether the total sentence is just and proportionate to the overall offending behaviour in accordance with the Offences Taken into Consideration and Totality guideline.

SG25-20 **STEP SEVEN Compensation and ancillary orders**

In all cases the court should consider whether to make compensation and/or other ancillary orders.

In appropriate cases an offender may be disqualified from being a director of a company in accordance with section 2 of the Company Directors Disqualification Act 1986. The maximum period of disqualification is 15 years.

SG25-21 **STEP EIGHT Reasons**

Section 174 of the Criminal Justice Act 2003 imposes a duty to give reasons for, and explain the effect of, the sentence.

SG25-22 **STEP NINE Consideration for time spent on bail (tagged curfew)**

The court must consider whether to give credit for time spent on bail in accordance with section 240A of the Criminal Justice Act 2003.

SG25-23 MANSLAUGHTER BY REASON OF LOSS OF CONTROL [15]

Common Law and Coroners and Justice Act 2009 (sections 54 and 55)

Triable only on indictment

Maximum: Life imprisonment

Offence range: 3–20 years' custody

This is a serious specified offence for the purposes of sections 224 and 225(2) (life sentences for serious offences) of the Criminal Justice Act 2003.

This is an offence listed in Part 1 of Schedule 15B for the purposes of section 224A (life sentence for a second listed offence) and section 226A (extended sentence for certain violent or sexual offences) of the Criminal Justice Act 2003.

The type of manslaughter (and thereby the appropriate guideline) should have been identified prior to sentence. If there is any dispute or uncertainty about the type of manslaughter that applies the judge should give clear reasons for the basis of sentence.

SG25-24 **STEP ONE Determining the offence category** [16]

Culpability

- **The characteristics set out below are indications of the level of culpability that may attach to the offender's conduct; the court should balance these characteristics to reach a fair assessment of the offender's overall culpability in the context of the circumstances of the offence.**
- **The court should avoid an overly mechanistic application of these factors.**

A – High culpability	• Planning of criminal activity (including the carrying of a weapon) before the loss of control • Offence committed in the context of other serious criminal activity • Use of a firearm (whether or not taken to the scene) • Loss of self-control in circumstances which only just met the criteria for a qualifying trigger • Concealment, destruction, defilement or dismemberment of the body (where not separately charged)
B – Medium culpability	Cases falling between high and lower because: • factors are present in high and lower which balance each other out **and/or** • the offender's culpability falls between the factors as described in high and lower
C – Lower culpability	• Qualifying trigger represented a very high degree of provocation

[16] **Harm**

For all cases of manslaughter the harm caused will inevitably be of the utmost seriousness. The loss of life is taken into account in the sentencing levels at step two.

[17] **STEP TWO Starting point and category range** **SG25-25**

Having determined the category at step one, the court should use the corresponding starting point to reach a sentence within the category range below. The starting point applies to all offenders irrespective of plea or previous convictions.

- Where a case does not fall squarely within a category, adjustment from the starting point may be required before adjustment for aggravating or mitigating features.

Culpability		
A	**B**	**C**
Starting point 14 years' custody	**Starting point** 8 years' custody	**Starting point** 5 years' custody
Category range 10–20 years' custody	**Category range** 5–12 years' custody	**Category range** 3–6 years' custody

Note: The table is for a single offence of manslaughter resulting in a single fatality. Where another offence or offences arise out of the same incident or facts, concurrent sentences **reflecting the overall criminality** of offending will ordinarily be appropriate: please refer to the *Offences Taken into Consideration and Totality* guideline (Part 3) and step six of this guideline.

There follows a **non-exhaustive** list of additional elements providing the context of the offence and factors relating to the offender. Identify whether a combination of these or other relevant factors should result in any upward or downward adjustment from the sentence arrived at so far.

[18] **Care should be taken to avoid double counting factors already taken into account in assessing culpability or in the finding of a qualifying trigger**

Factors increasing seriousness
Statutory aggravating factors: Previous convictions, having regard to a) the **nature** of the offence to which the conviction relates and its **relevance** to the current offence; and b) the **time** that has elapsed since the conviction (See step five for a consideration of dangerousness) Offence committed whilst on bail Offence motivated by, or demonstrating hostility based on any of the following characteristics or presumed characteristics of the victim: religion, race, disability, sexual orientation or transgender identity Offence was committed against an emergency worker acting in the exercise of functions as such a worker
Other aggravating factors:
History of violence or abuse towards victim by offender Involvement of other(s) through coercion, intimidation or exploitation Significant mental or physical suffering caused to the deceased Victim was providing a public service or performing a public duty at the time of the offence Commission of offence whilst under the influence of alcohol or drugs Persistence of violence Offence involved use of a weapon Other(s) put at risk of harm by the offending Actions after the event (including but not limited to attempts to cover up/conceal evidence) Offence committed on licence or post sentence supervision or while subject to court order(s)
Factors reducing seriousness or reflecting personal mitigation
No previous convictions **or** no relevant/recent convictions Remorse Intention to cause serious bodily harm rather than to kill History of significant violence or abuse towards the offender by the victim Violence initiated by the victim Good character and/or exemplary conduct Serious medical conditions requiring urgent, intensive or long-term treatment Mental disorder or learning disability Age and/or lack of maturity Sole or primary carer for dependent relatives

SG25-26 **STEP THREE Consider any factors which indicate a reduction for assistance to the prosecution** [19]

The court should take into account sections 73 and 74 of the Serious Organised Crime and Police Act 2005 (assistance by defendants: reduction or review of sentence) and any other rule of law by virtue of which an offender may receive a discounted sentence in consequence of assistance given (or offered) to the prosecutor or investigator.

SG25-27 **STEP FOUR Reduction for guilty pleas**

The court should take account of any potential reduction for a guilty plea in accordance with section 144 of the Criminal Justice Act 2003 and the Guilty Plea guideline.

SG25-28 **STEP FIVE Dangerousness**

The court should consider whether having regard to the criteria contained in Chapter 5 of Part 12 of the Criminal Justice Act 2003 it would be appropriate to impose a life sentence (section 224A or section 225) or an extended sentence (section 226A). When sentencing offenders to a life sentence under these provisions, the notional determinate sentence should be used as the basis for the setting of a minimum term.

SG25-29 **STEP SIX Totality principle**

If sentencing an offender for more than one offence, or where the offender is already serving a sentence, consider whether the total sentence is just and proportionate to the overall offending behaviour in accordance with the Offences Taken into Consideration and Totality guideline.

SG25-30 **STEP SEVEN Compensation and ancillary orders**

In all cases the court should consider whether to make compensation and/or other ancillary orders.

SG25-31 **STEP EIGHT Reasons**

Section 174 of the Criminal Justice Act 2003 imposes a duty to give reasons for, and explain the effect of, the sentence.

SG25-32 **STEP NINE Consideration for time spent on bail (tagged curfew)**

The court must consider whether to give credit for time spent on bail in accordance with section 240A of the Criminal Justice Act 2003.

SG25-33 MANSLAUGHTER BY REASON OF DIMINISHED RESPONSIBILITY [21]

Common Law and Homicide Act 1957 (section 2)

Triable only on indictment

Maximum: Life imprisonment

Offence range: 3–40 years' custody

This is a serious specified offence for the purposes of sections 224 and 225(2) (life sentences for serious offences) of the Criminal Justice Act 2003.

This is an offence listed in Part 1 of Schedule 15B for the purposes of section 224A (life sentence for a second listed offence) and section 226A (extended sentence for certain violent or sexual offences) of the Criminal Justice Act 2003.

The type of manslaughter (and thereby the appropriate guideline) should have been identified prior to sentence. If there is any dispute or uncertainty about the type of manslaughter that applies the judge should give clear reasons for the basis of sentence.

SG25-34 **STEP ONE Assessing the degree of responsibility retained: high, medium or lower** [22]

- A conviction for manslaughter by reason of diminished responsibility necessarily means that the offender's ability to understand the nature of the conduct, form a rational judgment and/or exercise self-control was substantially impaired.
- The court should determine what level of responsibility the offender **retained:**
  - High;
  - Medium; or
  - Lower
- The court should consider the extent to which the offender's responsibility was diminished by the mental disorder **at the time of the offence** with reference to the medical evidence and all the relevant information available to the court.

[22] • The degree to which the offender's actions or omissions contributed to the seriousness of the mental disorder at the time of the offence may be a relevant consideration. For example:
  - where an offender exacerbates the mental disorder by voluntarily abusing drugs or alcohol or by voluntarily failing to seek or follow medical advice this may increase responsibility. In considering the extent to which the offender's behaviour was voluntary, the extent to which a mental disorder has an impact on the offender's ability to exercise self-control or to engage with medical services will be relevant.
• The degree to which the mental disorder was undiagnosed and/or untreated may be a relevant consideration. For example:
  - where an offender has sought help but not received appropriate treatment this may reduce responsibility.

Harm

For all cases of manslaughter the harm caused will inevitably be of the utmost seriousness. The loss of life is taken into account in the sentencing levels at step two.

[23] **STEP TWO Starting point and category range** **SG25-35**

Having determined the level of responsibility retained at step one, the court should use the corresponding starting point to reach a sentence within the category range below. The starting point applies to all offenders irrespective of plea or previous convictions.

Level of responsibility retained		
High	**Medium**	**Lower**
Starting point 24 years' custody	**Starting point** 15 years' custody	**Starting point** 7 year's custody
Category range 15–40 years' custody	**Category range** 10–25 years' custody	**Category range** 3–12 years' custody

Note: The table is for a single offence of manslaughter resulting in a single fatality. Where another offence or offences arise out of the same incident or facts concurrent sentences **reflecting the overall criminality** of offending will ordinarily be appropriate: please refer to the *Offences Taken into Consideration and Totality guideline* (Part 3) and step eight of this guideline.

There follows a **non-exhaustive** list of additional factual elements providing the context of the offence and factors relating to the offender. Identify whether a combination of these or other relevant factors should result in any upward or downward adjustment from the sentence arrived at so far.

[24] **Care should be taken to avoid double counting factors already taken into account in assessing the level of responsibility retained**

Factors increasing seriousness
Statutory aggravating factors: Previous convictions, having regard to a) the **nature** of the offence to which the conviction relates and its **relevance** to the current offence; and b) the **time** that has elapsed since the conviction (See step three for a consideration of dangerousness) Offence committed whilst on bail Offence motivated by, or demonstrating hostility based on any of the following characteristics or presumed characteristics of the victim: religion, race, disability, sexual orientation or transgender identity Offence was committed against an emergency worker acting in the exercise of functions as such a worker
Other aggravating factors:
History of violence or abuse towards victim by offender Involvement of other(s) through coercion, intimidation or exploitation Significant mental or physical suffering caused to the deceased Victim particularly vulnerable due to age or disability Victim was providing a public service or performing a public duty at the time of the offence Commission of offence whilst under the influence of alcohol or drugs (the extent to which a mental disorder has an effect on offender's ability to make informed judgments or exercise self-control will be a relevant consideration in deciding how much weight to attach to this factor) Asignificant degree of planning or premeditation Offence involved use of a weapon Other(s) put at risk of harm by the offending Actions after the event (including but not limited to attempts to cover up/conceal evidence) Concealment, destruction, defilement or dismemberment of the body Blame wrongly placed on other(s) Offence committed on licence or post sentence supervision or while subject to court order(s)

Factors reducing seriousness or reflecting personal mitigation
No previous convictions **or** no relevant/recent convictions
Remorse
Intention to cause serious bodily harm rather than to kill
History of significant violence or abuse towards the offender by the victim
Lack of premeditation
The offender acted in self-defence or in fear of violence (where not amounting to a defence)
The offender made genuine and sustained attempts to seek help for the mental disorder
Belief by the offender that the killing was an act of mercy
Good character and/or exemplary conduct
Serious medical conditions requiring urgent, intensive or long-term treatment
Age and/or lack of maturity
Sole or primary carer for dependent relatives

[25]

SG25-36 STEP THREE **Consideration of dangerousness**

The court should then go on to consider whether having regard to the criteria contained in Chapter 5 of part 12 of the Criminal Justice Act 2003 it would be appropriate to impose a **life sentence** (section 224A or section 225) or an **extended sentence** (section 226A).

- When sentencing to a life sentence the notional determinate term (identified at step two above) should be used as the basis for setting the minimum term.

SG25-37 STEP FOUR **Consideration of mental health disposals (Mental Health Act 1983)** [26]

Where:

(i) the evidence of medical practitioners suggests that the offender is currently suffering from a mental disorder,
(ii) treatment is available, and
(iii) the court considers that a hospital order (with or without a restriction) may be an appropriate way of dealing with the case,

the court should consider **all sentencing options** including a section 45A direction and consider the importance of a penal element in the sentence taking into account the level of responsibility assessed at step one.

Section 45A hospital and limitation direction

a. Before a hospital order is made under section 37 (with or without a restriction order under section 41), consider whether the mental disorder can appropriately be dealt with by custody with a hospital and limitation direction under section 45A. In deciding whether a section 45A direction is appropriate the court should bear in mind that the limitation direction will cease to have effect at the automatic release date of a determinate sentence.
b. If a penal element is appropriate and the mental disorder can appropriately be dealt with by a direction under section 45A, then the judge should make such a direction. (Not available for a person under the age of 21 at the time of conviction).

Section 37 hospital order and section 41 restriction order

c. If a section 45A direction is not appropriate the court must then consider (assuming the conditions in section 37(2)(a) are satisfied) whether the matters referred to in section 37(2)(b) would make a hospital order (with or without a restriction order under section 41) the most suitable disposal. The court should explain why a penal element is not appropriate.

SG25-38 STEP FIVE IN ALL CASES **Consider factors that may warrant an adjustment to the sentence**

Cases of manslaughter by reason of diminished responsibility vary considerably on the facts of the offence and on the circumstances of the offender.

- The court should review whether the sentence as a whole meets the objectives of punishment, rehabilitation and protection of the public in a fair and proportionate way.
- Relevant factors will include the psychiatric evidence and the regime on release.
- An adjustment may require a departure from the sentence range identified at step two above.

SG25-39 STEP SIX **Consider any factors which indicate a reduction for assistance to the prosecution**

The court should take into account sections 73 and 74 of the Serious Organised Crime and Police Act 2005 (assistance by defendants: reduction or review of sentence) and any other rule of law by virtue of which an offender may receive a discounted sentence in consequence of assistance given (or offered) to the prosecutor or investigator.

[27] **STEP SEVEN Reduction for guilty pleas** SG25-40

The court should take account of any potential reduction for a guilty plea in accordance with section 144 of the Criminal Justice Act 2003 and the Guilty Plea guideline. Note: the limitations on reductions for murder do not apply to manslaughter.

STEP EIGHT Totality principle SG25-41

If sentencing an offender for more than one offence, or where the offender is already serving a sentence, consider whether the total sentence is just and proportionate to the overall offending behaviour in accordance with the Offences Taken into Consideration and Totality guideline.

STEP NINE Compensation and ancillary orders SG25-42

In all cases the court should consider whether to make compensation and/or other ancillary orders.

STEP TEN Reasons SG25-43

Section 174 of the Criminal Justice Act 2003 imposes a duty to give reasons for, and explain the effect of, the sentence.

STEP ELEVEN Consideration for time spent on bail (tagged curfew) SG25-44

The court must consider whether to give credit for time spent on bail in accordance with section 240A of the Criminal Justice Act 2003.

PART 26 FRAUD, BRIBERY AND MONEY LAUNDERING OFFENCES

SG26-1 DEFINITIVE GUIDELINE [4]

Effective from 1 October 2014

SG26-2 **Applicability of Guideline**
[Omitted: See SG19-1]

SG26-3 **Structure, ranges and starting points**
[Omitted: See SG19-2]

SG26-4 FRAUD [5]

Fraud by false representation, fraud by failing to disclose information, fraud by abuse of position
Fraud Act 2006 (section 1)
Triable either way

Conspiracy to defraud
Common law
Triable on indictment only

Maximum: 10 years' custody
Offence range: Discharge–8 years' custody

False accounting
Theft Act 1968 (section 17)
Triable either way

Maximum: 7 years' custody
Offence range: Discharge–6 years and 6 months' custody

SG26-5 STEP ONE **Determining the offence category** [6]

The court should determine the offence category with reference to the tables below. In order to determine the category the court should assess **culpability** and **harm.**

The level of **culpability** is determined by weighing up all the factors of the case to determine the offender's role and the extent to which the offending was planned and the sophistication with which it was carried out.

Culpability demonstrated by one or more of the following:
A — High culpability
A leading role where offending is part of a group activity
Involvement of others through pressure, influence
Abuse of position of power or trust or responsibility
Sophisticated nature of offence/significant planning
Fraudulent activity conducted over sustained period of time
Large number of victims
Deliberately targeting victim on basis of vulnerability
B — Medium culpability
Other cases that fall between categories A or C because: – Factors are present in A and C which balance each other out **and/or** – The offender's culpability falls between the factors as described in A and C A significant role where offending is part of a group activity

[6]

Culpability demonstrated by one or more of the following:
C — Lesser culpability
Involved through coercion, intimidation or exploitation
Not motivated by personal gain
Peripheral role in organised fraud
Opportunistic 'one-off' offence; very little or no planning
Limited awareness or understanding of the extent of fraudulent activity

Where there are characteristics present which fall under different levels of culpability, the court should balance these characteristics to reach a fair assessment of the offender's culpability.

[7] **Harm** is initially assessed by the actual, intended or risked loss as may arise from the offence.

The values in the table below are to be used for **actual** or **intended** loss only.

Intended loss relates to offences where circumstances prevent the actual loss that is intended to be caused by the fraudulent activity.

Risk of loss (for instance in mortgage frauds) involves consideration of both the likelihood of harm occurring and the extent of it if it does. Risk of loss is less serious than actual or intended loss. Where the offence has caused risk of loss but no (or much less) actual loss the normal approach is to move down to the corresponding point in the next category. This may not be appropriate if either the likelihood or extent of risked loss is particularly high.

Harm A — Loss caused or intended		
Category 1	£500,000 or more	Starting point based on £1 million
Category 2	£100,000–£500,000 **or** Risk of category 1 harm	Starting point based on £300,000
Category 3	£20,000–£100,000 **or** Risk of category 2 harm	Starting point based on £50,000
Category 4	£5,000–£20,000 **or** Risk of category 3 harm	Starting point based on £12,500
Category 5	Less than £5,000 **or** Risk of category 4 harm	Starting point based on £2,500
Risk of category 5 harm, move down the range within the category		

Harm B — Victim impact demonstrated by one or more of the following:
The court should then take into account the level of harm caused to the victim(s) or others to determine whether it warrants the sentence being moved up to the corresponding point in the next category or further up the range of the initial category.
High impact — move up a category; if in category 1 move up the range
Serious detrimental effect on the victim whether financial or otherwise, for example substantial damage to credit rating
Victim particularly vulnerable (due to factors including but not limited to their age, financial circumstances, mental capacity)
Medium impact — move upwards within the category range
Considerable detrimental effect on the victim whether financial or otherwise
Lesser impact — no adjustment
Some detrimental impact on victim, whether financial or otherwise

SG26-6 **STEP TWO Starting point and category range** [8]

Having determined the category at step one, the court should use the appropriate starting point (as adjusted in accordance with step one above) to reach a sentence within the category range in the table below. The starting point applies to all offenders irrespective of plea or previous convictions.

Where the value is larger or smaller than the amount on which the starting point is based, this should lead to upward or downward adjustment as appropriate.

Where the value greatly exceeds the amount of the starting point in category 1, it may be appropriate to move outside the identified range.

TABLE 1 Section 1 Fraud Act 2006 conspiracy to defraud

Maximum: 10 years' custody

	Culpability		
Harm	**A**	**B**	**C**
Category 1 £500,000 or more	**Starting point** 7 years' custody	**Starting point** 5 years' custody	**Starting point** 3 years' custody
Starting point based on £1 million	**Category range** 5–8 years' custody	**Category range** 3–6 years' custody	**Category range** 18 months'–4 years' custody
Category 2 £100,000–£500,000	**Starting point** 5 years' custody	**Starting point** 3 years' custody	**Starting point** 18 months' custody
Starting point based on £300,000	**Category range** 3–6 years' custody	**Category range** 18 months'–4 years' custody	**Category range** 26 weeks'–3 years' custody
Category 3 £20,000–£100,000	**Starting point** 3 years' custody	**Starting point** 18 months' custody	**Starting point** 26 weeks' custody
Starting point based on £50,000	**Category range** 18 months'–4 years' custody	**Category range** 26 weeks'–3 years' custody	**Category range** Medium level community order–1 year's custody
Category 4 £5,000–£20,000	**Starting point** 18 months' custody	**Starting point** 26 weeks' custody	**Starting point** Medium level community order
Starting point based on £12,500	**Category range** 26 weeks'–3 years' custody	**Category range** Medium level community order –1 year's custody	**Category range** Band B fine–High level community order
Category 5 Less than £5,000	**Starting point** 36 weeks' custody	**Starting point** Medium level community order	**Starting point** Band B fine
Starting point based on £2,500	**Category range** High level community order–1 year's custody	**Category range** Band B fine–26 weeks' custody	**Category range** Discharge–Medium level community order

[9] **TABLE 2 Section 17 Theft Act 1968: False Accounting**

Maximum: 7 years' custody

	Culpability		
Harm	**A**	**B**	**C**
Category 1 £500,000 or more	**Starting point** 5 years 6 months' custody	**Starting point** 4 years' custody	**Starting point** 2 years 6 months' custody
Starting point based on £1 million	**Category range** 4 years'–6 years 6 months' custody	**Category range** 2 years 6 months'–5 years' custody	**Category range** 15 months'–3 years 6 months' custody
Category 2 £100,000–£500,000	**Starting point** 4 years' custody	**Starting point** 2 years 6 months' custody	**Starting point** 15 months' custody
Starting point based on £300,000	**Category range** 2 years 6 months'–5 years' custody	**Category range** 15 months'–3 years 6 months' custody	**Category range** 26 weeks'–2 years 6 months' custody
Category 3 £20,000–£100,000	**Starting point** 2 years 6 months' custody	**Starting point** 15 months' custody	**Starting point** High level community order
Starting point based on £50,000	**Category range** 15 months'–3 years 6 months' custody	**Category range** High level community order–2 years 6 months' custody	**Category range** Low level community order–36 weeks' custody
Category 4 £5,000–£20,000	**Starting point** 15 months' custody	**Starting point** High level community order	**Starting point** Low level community order
Starting point based on £12,500	**Category range** High level community order–2 years 6 months' custody	**Category range** Low level community order–36 weeks' custody	**Category range** Band B fine–Medium level community order
Category 5 Less than £5,000	**Starting point** 26 weeks' custody	**Starting point** Low level community order	**Starting point** Band B fine
Starting point based on £2,500	**Category range** Medium level community order–36 weeks' custody	**Category range** Band B fine–Medium level community order	**Category range** Discharge–Low level community order

[10] The table below contains a non-exhaustive list of additional factual elements providing the context of the offence and factors relating to the offender.

Identify whether any combination of these or other relevant factors should result in an upward or downward adjustment from the sentence arrived at so far.

Consecutive sentences for multiple offences may be appropriate where large sums are involved.

Sentencing Guidelines

Factors increasing seriousness	Factors reducing seriousness or reflecting personal mitigation
Statutory aggravating factors: Previous convictions, having regard to a) the nature of the offence to which the conviction relates and its relevance to the current offence; and b) the time that has elapsed since the conviction Offence committed whilst on bail *Other aggravating factors:* Steps taken to prevent the victim reporting or obtaining assistance and/or from assisting or supporting the prosecution Attempts to conceal/dispose of evidence Established evidence of community/wider impact Failure to comply with current court orders Offence committed on licence Offences taken into consideration Failure to respond to warnings about behaviour Offences committed across borders Blame wrongly placed on others	No previous convictions or no relevant/recent convictions Remorse Good character and/or exemplary conduct Little or no prospect of success Serious medical conditions requiring urgent, intensive or long-term treatment Age and/or lack of maturity where it affects the responsibility of the offender Lapse of time since apprehension where this does not arise from the conduct of the offender Mental disorder or learning disability Sole or primary carer for dependent relatives Offender co-operated with investigation, made early admissions and/or voluntarily reported offending Determination and/or demonstration of steps having been taken to address addiction or offending behaviour Activity originally legitimate

[10]

SG26-7 **STEP THREE Consider any factors which indicate a reduction, such as assistance to the prosecution** [11]

The court should take into account sections 73 and 74 of the Serious Organised Crime and Police Act 2005 (assistance by defendants: reduction or review of sentence) and any other rule of law by virtue of which an offender may receive a discounted sentence in consequence of assistance given (or offered) to the prosecutor or investigator.

SG26-8 **STEP FOUR Reduction for guilty pleas**

The court should take account of any potential reduction for a guilty plea in accordance with section 144 of the Criminal Justice Act 2003 and the *Guilty Plea* guideline.

SG26-9 **STEP FIVE Totality principle**

If sentencing an offender for more than one offence, or where the offender is already serving a sentence, consider whether the total sentence is just and proportionate to the overall offending behaviour.

SG26-10 **STEP SIX Confiscation, compensation and ancillary orders**

The court must proceed with a view to making a confiscation order if it is asked to do so by the prosecutor or if the court believes it is appropriate for it to do so.

Where the offence has resulted in loss or damage the court must consider whether to make a compensation order.

If the court makes both a confiscation order and an order for compensation and the court believes the offender will not have sufficient means to satisfy both orders in full, the court must direct that the compensation be paid out of sums recovered under the confiscation order (section 13 of the Proceeds of Crime Act 2002).

The court may also consider whether to make ancillary orders. These may include a deprivation order, a financial reporting order, a serious crime prevention order and disqualification from acting as a company director.

SG26-11 **STEP SEVEN Reasons**

Section 174 of the Criminal Justice Act 2003 imposes a duty to give reasons for, and explain the effect of, the sentence.

[11] **STEP EIGHT Consideration for time spent on bail** **SG26-12**

The court must consider whether to give credit for time spent on bail in accordance with section 240A of the Criminal Justice Act 2003.

[13] POSSESSING, MAKING OR SUPPLYING ARTICLES FOR USE IN FRAUD **SG26-13**

Possession of articles for use in frauds
Fraud Act 2006 (section 6)
Triable either way
Maximum: 5 years' custody
Offence range: Band A fine–3 years' custody

Making or supplying articles for use in frauds
Fraud Act 2006 (section 7)
Triable either way
Maximum: 10 years' custody
Offence range: Band C fine–7 years' custody

[14] **STEP ONE Determining the offence category** **SG26-14**

The court should determine the offence category with reference to the tables below. In order to determine the category the court should assess **culpability** and **harm.**

The level of **culpability** is determined by weighing up all the factors of the case to determine the offender's role and the extent to which the offending was planned and the sophistication with which it was carried out.

Culpability demonstrated by one or more of the following:
A — High culpability
A leading role where offending is part of a group activity Involvement of others through pressure, influence Abuse of position of power or trust or responsibility Sophisticated nature of offence/significant planning Fraudulent activity conducted over sustained period of time Articles deliberately designed to target victims on basis of vulnerability
B — Medium culpability
Other cases that fall between categories A or C because: – Factors are present in A and C which balance each other out **and/or** – The offender's culpability falls between the factors as described in A and C A significant role where offending is part of a group activity
C — Lesser culpability
Performed limited function under direction Involved through coercion, intimidation or exploitation Not motivated by personal gain Opportunistic 'one-off' offence; very little or no planning Limited awareness or understanding of extent of fraudulent activity

Where there are characteristics present which fall under different levels of culpability, the court should balance these characteristics to reach a fair assessment of the offender's culpability.

Sentencing Guidelines

Harm	[14]
This guideline refers to preparatory offences where no substantive fraud has been committed. The level of harm is determined by weighing up all the factors of the case to determine the harm that would be caused if the article(s) were used to commit a substantive offence.	
Greater harm	
Large number of articles created/supplied/in possession Article(s) have potential to facilitate fraudulent acts affecting large number of victims Article(s) have potential to facilitate fraudulent acts involving significant sums Use of third party identities Offender making considerable gain as result of the offence	
Lesser harm	
All other offences	

SG26-15 STEP TWO Starting point and category range [15]

Having determined the category at step one, the court should use the appropriate starting point to reach a sentence within the category range in the table below. The starting point applies to all offenders irrespective of plea or previous convictions.

Section 6 Fraud Act 2006: Possessing articles for use in fraud

Maximum: 5 years' custody

	Culpability		
Harm	**A**	**B**	**C**
Greater	**Starting point** 18 months' custody	**Starting point** 36 weeks' custody	**Starting point** High level community order .
	Category range 36 weeks' custody–3 years' custody	**Category range** High level community order–2 years' custody	**Category range** Medium level community order–26 weeks' custody
Lesser	**Starting point** 26 weeks' custody	**Starting point** Medium level community order	**Starting point** Band B fine
	Category range High level community order–18 months' custody	**Category range** Low level community order–26 weeks' custody	**Category range** Band A fine–Medium level community order

Section 7 Fraud Act 2006: Making or adapting or supplying articles for use in fraud

Maximum: 10 years' custody

	Culpability		
Harm	**A**	**B**	**C**
Greater	**Starting point** 4 years 6 months' custody	**Starting point** 2 years 6 months' custody	**Starting point** 1 year's custody
	Category range 3–7 years' custody	**Category range** 18 months'–5 years' custody	**Category range** High level community order–3 years' custody
Lesser	**Starting point** 2 years' custody	**Starting point** 36 weeks' custody	**Starting point** Medium level community order
	Category range 26 weeks'–4 years' custody	**Category range** Low level community order–2 years' custody	**Category range** Band C fine–26 weeks' custody

[16] The table below contains a non-exhaustive list of additional factual elements providing the context of the offence and factors relating to the offender.

Identify whether any combination of these or other relevant factors should result in an upward or downward adjustment from the starting point

Consecutive sentences for multiple offences may be appropriate where large sums are involved.

Factors increasing seriousness	**Factors reducing seriousness or reflecting personal mitigation**
Statutory aggravating factors: Previous convictions, having regard to a) the nature of the offence to which the conviction relates and its relevance to the current offence; and b) the time that has elapsed since the conviction Offence committed whilst on bail *Other aggravating factors:* Steps taken to prevent the victim reporting or obtaining assistance and/or from assisting or supporting the prosecution Attempts to conceal/dispose of evidence Established evidence of community/wider impact Failure to comply with current court orders Offence committed on licence Offences taken into consideration Failure to respond to warnings about behaviour Offences committed across borders Blame wrongly placed on others	No previous convictions or no relevant/recent convictions Remorse Good character and/or exemplary conduct Little or no prospect of success Serious medical conditions requiring urgent, intensive or long-term treatment Age and/or lack of maturity where it affects the responsibility of the offender Lapse of time since apprehension where this does not arise from the conduct of the offender Mental disorder or learning disability Sole or primary carer for dependent relatives Offender co-operated with investigation, made early admissions and/or voluntarily reported offending Determination and/or demonstration of steps having been taken to address addiction or offending behaviour Activity originally legitimate

[17] **STEPS THREE to EIGHT** **SG26-16**

[These are identical to those set out at **SG26-7** ***et seq.***]

[19] REVENUE FRAUD **SG26-17**

Fraud

Conspiracy to defraud (common law)
Triable on indictment only
Fraud Act 2006 (section 1)
Triable either way

Maximum: 10 years' custody
Offence range: Low level community order–8 years' custody

False accounting

Theft Act 1968 (section 17)

Fraudulent evasion of VAT; False statement for VAT purposes; Conduct amounting to an offence

Value Added Tax Act 1994 (section 72)

Fraudulent evasion of income tax

Taxes Management Act 1970 (section 106A)

Fraudulent evasion of excise duty; Improper importation of goods [19]

Customs and Excise Management Act 1979 (sections 50, 170 and 170B)
Triable either way
Maximum: 7 years' custody
Offence range: Band C fine–6 years and 6 months' custody

Fraud

Cheat the public revenue (common law)
Triable on indictment only
Maximum: Life imprisonment
Offence range: 3–17 years' custody

SG26-18 STEP ONE **Determining the offence category** [20]

The court should determine the offence category with reference to the tables below. In order to determine the category the court should assess **culpability** and **harm.**

The level of **culpability** is determined by weighing up all the factors of the case to determine the offender's role and the extent to which the offending was planned and the sophistication with which it was carried out.	Harm — Gain/intended gain to offender or loss/ intended loss to HMRC
Culpability demonstrated by one or more of the following:	**Category 1** £50 million or more Starting point based on £80 million
A — High culpability	**Category 2** £10 million–£50 million Starting point based on £30 million
A leading role where offending is part of a group activity	**Category 3** £2 million–£10 million Starting point based on £5 million
Involvement of others through pressure/influence	**Category 4** £500,000–£2 million Starting point based on £1 million
Abuse of position of power or trust or responsibility	**Category 5** £100,000–£500,000 Starting point based on £300,000
Sophisticated nature of offence/significant planning	**Category 6** £20,000–£100,000 Starting point based on £50,000
Fraudulent activity conducted over sustained period of time	**Category 7** Less than £20,000 Starting point based on £12,500
B — Medium culpability	
Other cases that fall between categories A or C because: – Factors are present in A and C which balance each other out **and/or** – The offender's culpability falls between the factors as described in A and C	
A significant role where offending is part of a group activity	
C — Lesser culpability	
Involved through coercion, intimidation or exploitation	
Not motivated by personal gain	
Opportunistic 'one-off' offence; very little or no planning	
Performed limited function under direction	
Limited awareness or understanding of extent of fraudulent activity	

[20] **Where there are characteristics present which fall under different levels of culpability, the court should balance these characteristics to reach a fair assessment of the offender's culpability**

[21] **STEP TWO Starting point and category range** **SG26-19**

Having determined the category at step one, the court should use the appropriate starting point to reach a sentence within the category range in the table below. The starting point applies to all offenders irrespective of plea or previous convictions.

Where the value is larger or smaller than the amount on which the starting point is based, this should lead to upward or downward adjustment as appropriate.

Where the value greatly exceeds the amount of the starting point in category 1, it may be appropriate to move outside the identified range.

TABLE 1 Section 1 Fraud Act 2006: Conspiracy to defraud (common law)

Maximum: 10 years' custody

For offences where the value of the fraud is over £2 million refer to the corresponding category in Table 3 subject to the maximum sentence of 10 years for this offence.

	Culpability		
Harm	A	B	C
Category 4 £500,000–£2 million	**Starting point** 7 years' custody	**Starting point** 5 years' custody	**Starting point** 3 years' custody
Starting point based on £1 million	**Category range** 5–8 years' custody	**Category range** 3–6 years' custody	**Category range** 18 months'–4 years' custody
Category 5 £100,000–£500,000	**Starting point** 5 years' custody	**Starting point** 3 years' custody	**Starting point** 18 months' custody
Starting point based on £300,000	**Category range** 3–6 years' custody	**Category range** 18 months'–4 years' custody	**Category range** 26 weeks'–3 years' custody
Category 6 £20,000–£100,000	**Starting point** 3 years' custody	**Starting point** 18 months' custody	**Starting point** 26 weeks' custody
Starting point based on £50,000	**Category range** 18 months'–4 years' custody	**Category range** 26 weeks'–3 years' custody	**Category range** Medium level community order–1 year's custody
Category 7 Less than £20,000	**Starting point** 18 months' custody	**Starting point** 36 weeks' custody	**Starting point** Medium level community order
Starting point based on £12,500	**Category range** 36 weeks'–3 years' custody	**Category range** Medium level community order–18 months' custody	**Category range** Low level community order–High level community order

TABLE 2 Section 17 Theft Act 1968: False Accounting [22]

Section 72(1) Value Added Tax Act 1994: Fraudulent evasion of VAT

Section 72(3) Valued Added Tax Act 1994: False statement for VAT purposes

Section 72(8) Value Added Tax Act 1994: Conduct amounting to an offence

Section 106(a) Taxes Management Act 1970: Fraudulent evasion of income tax

Section 170(1)(a)(i), (ii), (b), 170(2)(a), 170B Customs and Excise Management Act 1979: Fraudulent evasion of excise duty

Section 50(1)(a), (2) Customs and Excise Management Act 1979: Improper importation of goods

Maximum: 7 years' custody

	Culpability		
Harm	**A**	**B**	**C**
Category 4 £500,000–£2 million	**Starting point** 5 years 6 months' custody	**Starting point** 4 years' custody	**Starting point** 2 years 6 months' custody
Starting point based on £1 million	**Category range** 4 years'–6 years 6 months' custody	**Category range** 2 years 6 months'–5 years' custody	**Category range** 15 months'–3 years 6 months' custody
Category 5 £100,000–£500,000	**Starting point** 4 years' custody	**Starting point** 2 years 6 months' custody	**Starting point** 15 months' custody
Starting point based on £300,000	**Category range** 2 years 6 months'–5 years' custody	**Category range** 15 months'–3 years 6 months' custody	**Category range** 26 weeks'–2 years 6 months' custody
Category 6 £20,000–£100,000	Starting point 2 years 6 months' custody	**Starting point** 15 months' custody	**Starting point** High level community order
Starting point based on £50,000	Category range 15 months'–3 years 6 months' custody	**Category range** High level community order–2 years 6 months' custody	**Category range** Low level community order–36 weeks' custody
Category 7 Less than £20,000	**Starting point** 15 months' custody	**Starting point** 26 weeks' custody	**Starting point** Medium level community order
Starting point based on £12,500	**Category range** 26 weeks'–2 years 6 months' custody	**Category range** Medium level community order–15 months' custody	**Category range** Band C fine–High level community order

[23] **TABLE 3 Cheat the Revenue (common law)**

Maximum: Life imprisonmentWhere the offending is on the most serious scale, involving sums significantly higher than the starting point in category 1, sentences of 15 years and above may be appropriate depending on the role of the offender. In cases involving sums below £2 million the court should refer to Table 1.

	Culpability		
Harm	**A**	**B**	**C**
Category 1 £50 million or more	**Starting point** 12 years' custody	**Starting point** 8 years' custody	**Starting point** 6 years' custody
Starting point based on £80 million	**Category range** 10–17 years' custody	**Category range** 7–12 years' custody	**Category range** 4–8 years' custody
Category 2 £10 million–£50 million	**Starting point** 10 years' custody	**Starting point** 7 years' custody	**Starting point** 5 years' custody
Starting point based on £30 million	**Category range** 8–13 years' custody	**Category range** 5–9 years' custody	**Category range** 3–6 years' custody
Category 3 £2 million–£10 million	**Starting point** 8 years' custody	**Starting point** 6 years' custody	**Starting point** 4 years' custody
Starting point based on £5 million	**Category range** 6–10 years' custody	**Category range** 4–7 years' custody	**Category range** 3–5 years' custody

[24] The table below contains a non-exhaustive list of additional factual elements providing the context of the offence and factors relating to the offender.

Identify whether any combination of these or other relevant factors should result in any further upward or downward adjustment from the starting point.

Consecutive sentences for multiple offences may be appropriate where large sums are involved.

Factors increasing seriousness	**Factors reducing seriousness or reflecting personal mitigation**
Statutory aggravating factors: Previous convictions, having regard to a) the nature of the offence to which the conviction relates and its relevance to the current offence; and b) the time that has elapsed since the conviction Offence committed whilst on bail *Other aggravating factors:* Involves multiple frauds Number of false declarations Attempts to conceal/dispose of evidence Failure to comply with current court orders Offence committed on licence	No previous convictions **or** no relevant/recent convictions Remorse Good character and/or exemplary conduct Little or no prospect of success Serious medical condition requiring urgent, intensive or long term treatment Age and/or lack of maturity where it affects the responsibility of the offender Lapse of time since apprehension where this does not arise from the conduct of the offender Mental disorder or learning disability Sole or primary carer for dependent relatives

Offences taken into consideration Failure to respond to warnings about behaviour Blame wrongly placed on others Damage to third party (for example as a result of identity theft) Dealing with goods with an additional health risk Disposing of goods to under age purchasers	Offender co-operated with investigation, made early admissions and/or voluntarily reported offending Determination and/or demonstration of steps having been taken to address addiction or offending behaviour Activity originally legitimate

[24]

SG26-20 **STEPS THREE to EIGHT** [25]

[These are identical to those set out at **SG26-7** *et seq*.]

SG26-21 **BENEFIT FRAUD** [27]

Dishonest representations for obtaining benefit etc
Social Security Administration Act 1992 (section 111A)

Tax Credit fraud
Tax Credits Act 2002 (section 35)

False accounting
Theft Act 1968 (section 17)
Triable either way
Maximum: 7 years' custody
Offence range: Discharge–6 years 6 months' custody

False representations for obtaining benefit etc
Social Security Administration Act 1992 (section 112)
Triable summarily only
Maximum: Level 5 fine and/or 3 months' custody
Offence range: Discharge–12 weeks' custody

Fraud by false representation, fraud by failing to disclose information, fraud by abuse of position
Fraud Act 2006 (section 1)
Triable either way

Conspiracy to defraud
Common law
Triable on indictment only
Maximum: 10 years' custody
Offence range: Discharge–8 years' custody

SG26-22 STEP ONE **Determining the offence category** [28]

The court should determine the offence category with reference to the tables below. In order to determine the category the court should assess **culpability** and **harm**.

[28]

The level of **culpability** is determined by weighing up all the factors of the case to determine the offender's role and the extent to which the offending was planned and the sophistication with which it was carried out.	**Harm — Amount obtained or intended to be obtained**
Culpability demonstrated by one or more of the following:	**Category 1** £500,000–£2 million Starting point based on £1 million
A — High culpability	**Category 2** £100,000–£500,000 Starting point based on £300,000
A leading role where offending is part of a group activity	**Category 3** £50,000–£100,000 Starting point based on £75,000
Involvement of others through pressure/influence	**Category 4** £10,000–£50,000 Starting point based on £30,000
Abuse of position of power or trust or responsibility	**Category 5** £2,500–£10,000 Starting point based on £5,000
Sophisticated nature of offence/significant planning	**Category 6** Less than £2,500 Starting point based on £1,000
B — Medium culpability	
Other cases that fall between categories A or C because: – Factors are present in A and C which balance each other out **and/or** – The offender's culpability falls between the factors as described in A and C	
Claim not fraudulent from the outset	
A significant role where offending is part of a group activity	
C — Lesser culpability	
Involved through coercion, intimidation or exploitation	
Performed limited function under direction	

Where there are characteristics present which fall under different levels of culpability, the court should balance these characteristics to reach a fair assessment of the offender's culpability. **SG26-23**

[29] **STEP TWO Starting point and category range**

Having determined the category at step one, the court should use the appropriate starting point to reach a sentence within the category range in the table below. The starting point applies to all offenders irrespective of plea or previous convictions.

Where the value is larger or smaller than the amount on which the starting point is based, this should lead to upward or downward adjustment as appropriate.

Where the value greatly exceeds the amount of the starting point in category 1, it may be appropriate to move outside the identified range.

TABLE 1 Section 111A Social Security Administration Act 1992: Dishonest representations to obtain benefit etc [29]

Section 35 Tax Credits Act 2002: Tax Credit fraud

Section 17 Theft Act 1968: False accounting

Maximum: 7 years' custody

	Culpability		
Harm	**A**	**B**	**C**
Category 1 £500,000 or more	**Starting point** 5 years 6 months' custody	**Starting point** 4 years' custody	**Starting point** 2 years 6 months' custody
Starting point based on £1 million	**Category range** 4 years'–6 years 6 months' custody	**Category range** 2 years 6 months'– 5 years' custody	**Category range** 15 months'–3 years 6 months' custody
Category 2 £100,000–£500,000	**Starting point** 4 years' custody	**Starting point** 2 years 6 months' custody	**Starting point** 1 year's custody
Starting point based on £300,000	**Category range** 2 years 6 months'– 5 years' custody	**Category range** 15 months'–3 years 6 months' custody	**Category range** 26 weeks'–2 years 6 months' custody
Category 3 £50,000–£100,000	**Starting point** 2 years 6 months' custody	**Starting point** 1 year's custody	**Starting point** 26 weeks' custody
Starting point based on £75,000	**Category range** 2 years'–3 years 6 months' custody	**Category range** 26 weeks'–2 years 6 months' custody	**Category range** High level community order–36 weeks' custody
Category 4 £10,000–£50,000	**Starting point** 18 months' custody	**Starting point** 36 weeks' custody	**Starting point** Medium level community order
Starting point based on £30,000	**Category range** 36 weeks'–2 years 6 months' custody	**Category range** Medium level community order–21 months' custody	**Category range** Low level community order–26 weeks' custody
Category 5 £2,500–£10,000	**Starting point** 36 weeks' custody	**Starting point** Medium level community order	**Starting point** Low level community order
Starting point based on £5,000	**Category range** Medium level community order–18 months' custody	**Category range** Low level community order–26 weeks' custody	**Category range** Band B fine–Medium level community order
Category 6 Less than £2,500	**Starting point** Medium level community order	**Starting point** Low level community order	**Starting point** Band A fine
Starting point based on £1,000	**Category range** Low level community order–26 weeks' custody	**Category range** Band A fine–Medium level community order	**Category range** Discharge–Band B fine

[30] **TABLE 2 Section 112 Social Security Administration Act 1992: False representations for obtaining benefit etc**

Maximum: Level 5 fine and/or 3 months' custody

	Culpability		
Harm	A	B	C
Category 5 Above £2,500	**Starting point** High level community order	**Starting point** Medium level community order	**Starting point** Low level community order
Starting point based on £5,000	**Category range** Medium level community order–12 weeks' custody	**Category range** Band B fine–High level community order	**Category range** Band A fine–Medium level community order
Category 6 Less than £2,500	**Starting point** Medium level community order	**Starting point** Band B fine	**Starting point** Band A fine
Starting point based on £1,000	**Category range** Low level community order–High level community order	**Category range** Band A fine–Band C fine	**Category range** Discharge–Band B fine

[31] **TABLE 3 Section 1 Fraud Act 2006**

Conspiracy to defraud (common law)

Maximum: 10 years' custody

	Culpability		
Harm	**A**	**B**	**C**
Category 1 £500,000 or more	**Starting point** 7 years' custody	**Starting point** 5 years' custody	**Starting point** 3 years' custody
Starting point based on £1 million	**Category range** 5–8 years' custody	**Category range** 3–6 years' custody	**Category range** 18 months'–4 years' custody
Category 2 £100,000–£500,000	**Starting point** 5 years' custody	**Starting point** 3 years' custody	**Starting point** 15 months' custody
Starting point based on £300,000	**Category range** 3–6 years' custody	**Category range** 18 months'–4 years' custody	**Category range** 26 weeks'–3 years' custody
Category 3 £50,000–£100,000	**Starting point** 3 years' custody	**Starting point** 15 months' custody	**Starting point** 36 weeks' custody
Starting point based on £75,000	**Category range** 2 years 6 months'– 4 years' custody	**Category range** 36 weeks'–3 years' custody	**Category range** 26 weeks'–1 year's custody
Category 4 £10,000–£50,000	**Starting point** 21 months' custody	**Starting point** 1 year's custody	**Starting point** High level community order
Starting point based on £30,000	**Category range** 1 year's–3 years' custody	**Category range** High level community order–2 years' custody	**Category range** Low level community order–26 weeks' custody

	Culpability		
Harm	**A**	**B**	**C**
Category 5 £2,500–£10,000	**Starting point** 1 year's custody	**Starting point** High level community order	**Starting point** Medium level community order
Starting point based on £5,000	**Category range** High level community order–2 years' custody	**Category range** Low level community order–26 weeks' custody	**Category range** Band C fine–High level community order
Category 6 Less than £2,500	**Starting point** High level community order	**Starting point** Low level community order	**Starting point** Band B fine
Starting point based on £1,000	**Category range** Low level community order–26 weeks' custody	**Category range** Band B fine–Medium level community order	**Category range** Discharge–Band C fine

[31]

The table below contains a non-exhaustive list of additional factual elements providing the context of the offence and factors relating to the offender. [32]

Identify whether any combination of these or other relevant factors should result in any further upward or downward adjustment from the starting point.

Consecutive sentences for multiple offences may be appropriate where large sums are involved.

Factors increasing seriousness	**Factors reducing seriousness or reflecting personal mitigation**
Statutory aggravating factors: Previous convictions, having regard to a) the nature of the offence to which the conviction relates and its relevance to the current offence; and b) the time that has elapsed since the conviction Offence committed whilst on bail *Other aggravating factors:* Claim fraudulent from the outset Proceeds of fraud funded lavish lifestyle Length of time over which the offending was committed Number of false declarations Attempts to conceal/dispose of evidence Failure to comply with current court orders Offence committed on licence Offences taken into consideration Failure to respond to warnings about behaviour Blame wrongly placed on others Damage to third party (for example as a result of identity theft)	No previous convictions or no relevant/recent convictions Remorse Good character and/or exemplary conduct Serious medical condition requiring urgent, intensive or long term treatment Legitimate entitlement to benefits not claimed Little or no prospect of success Age and/or lack of maturity where it affects the responsibility of the offender Lapse of time since apprehension where this does not arise from the conduct of the offender Mental disorder or learning disability Sole or primary carer for dependent relatives Offender co-operated with investigation, made early admissions and/or voluntarily reported offending Determination and/or demonstration of steps having been taken to address addiction or offending behaviour Offender experiencing significant financial hardship or pressure at time fraud was committed due to **exceptional** circumstances

[34] **STEPS THREE to EIGHT** SG26-24

[These are identical to those set out at SG26-7 *et seq.*]

[35] MONEY LAUNDERING SG26-25

Concealing/disguising/converting/transferring/removing criminal property from England & Wales
Proceeds of Crime Act 2002 (section 327)

Entering into arrangements concerning criminal property
Proceeds of Crime Act 2002 (section 328)

Acquisition, use and possession of criminal property
Proceeds of Crime Act 2002 (section 329)

Triable either way
Maximum: 14 years' custody
Offence range: Band B fine–13 years' imprisonment

[36] **STEP ONE Determining the offence category** SG26-26

The court should determine the offence category with reference to the tables below. In order to determine the category the court should assess **culpability** and **harm.**

The level of **culpability** is determined by weighing up all the factors of the case to determine the offender's role and the extent to which the offending was planned and the sophistication with which it was carried out.	**Harm A**
Culpability demonstrated by one or more of the following:	Harm is initially assessed by the value of the money laundered.
A — High culpability	**Category 1** £10 million or more Starting point based on £30 million
A leading role where offending is part of a group activity	**Category 2** £2 million–£10 million Starting point based on £5 million
Involvement of others through pressure, influence	**Category 3** £500,000–£2 million Starting point based on £1 million
Abuse of position of power or trust or responsibility	**Category 4** £100,000–£500,000 Starting point based on £300,000
Sophisticated nature of offence/significant planning	**Category 5** £10,000–£100,000 Starting point based on £50,000
Criminal activity conducted over sustained period of time	**Category 6** Less than £10,000 Starting point based on £5,000
B — Medium culpability Other cases that fall between categories A or C because: – Factors are present in A and C which balance each other out **and/or** – The offender's culpability falls between the factors as described in A and C	**Harm B** Money laundering is an integral component of much serious criminality. **To complete the assessment of harm, the court should take into account the level of harm associated with the underlying offence to determine whether it warrants upward adjustment of the starting point within the range, or in appropriate cases, outside the range.** Where it is possible to identify the underlying offence, regard should be given to the relevant sentencing levels for that offence.
A significant role where offending is part of a group activity	
C — Lesser culpability	
Performed limited function under direction	
Involved through coercion, intimidation or exploitation	
Not motivated by personal gain	
Opportunistic 'one-off' offence; very little or no planning	
Limited awareness or understanding of extent of criminal activity	

Sentencing Guidelines

Where there are characteristics present which fall under different levels of culpability, the court should balance these characteristics to reach a fair assessment of the offender's culpability. [36]

SG26-27 **STEP TWO Starting point and category range** [37]

Having determined the category at step one, the court should use the appropriate starting point (as adjusted in accordance with step one above) to reach a sentence within the category range in the table below. The starting point applies to all offenders irrespective of plea or previous convictions.

Where the value is larger or smaller than the amount on which the starting point is based, this should lead to upward or downward adjustment as appropriate.

Where the value greatly exceeds the amount of the starting point in category 1, it may be appropriate to move outside the identified range.

Section 327 Proceeds of Crime Act 2002: Concealing/disguising/converting/transferring/removing criminal property from England & Wales

Section 328 Proceeds of Crime Act 2002: Entering into arrangements concerning criminal property

Section 329 Proceeds of Crime Act 2002: Acquisition, use and possession of criminal property

Maximum: 14 years' custody

	Culpability		
Harm	A	B	C
Category 1 £10 million or more	**Starting point** 10 years' custody	**Starting point** 7 years' custody	**Starting point** 4 years' custody
Starting point based on £30 million	**Category range** 8–13 years' custody	**Category range** 5–10 years' custody	**Category range** 3–6 years' custody
Category 2 £2 million–£10 million	**Starting point** 8 years' custody	**Starting point** 6 years' custody	**Starting point** 3 years 6 months' custody
Starting point based on £5 million	**Category range** 6–9 years' custody	**Category range** 3 years 6 months'–7 years' custody	**Category range** 2–5 years' custody
Category 3 £500,000–£2 million	**Starting point** 7 years' custody	**Starting point** 5 years' custody	**Starting point** 3 years' custody
Starting point based on £1 million	**Category range** 5–8 years' custody	**Category range** 3–6 years' custody	**Category range** 18 months'–4 years' custody
Category 4 £100,000–£500,000	**Starting point** 5 years' custody	**Starting point** 3 years' custody	**Starting point** 18 months' custody
Starting point based on £300,000	**Category range** 3–6 years' custody	**Category range** 18 months'–4 years' custody	**Category range** 26 weeks'–3 years' custody
Category 5 £10,000–£100,000	**Starting point** 3 years' custody	**Starting point** 18 months' custody	**Starting point** 26 weeks' custody
Starting point based on £50,000	**Category range** 18 months'–4 years' custody	**Category range** 26 weeks'–3 years' custody	**Category range** Medium level community order–1 year's custody
Category 6 Less than £10,000	**Starting point** 1 year's custody	**Starting point** High level community order	**Starting point** Low level community order
Starting point based on £5,000	**Category range** 26 weeks'–2 years' custody	**Category range** Low level community order–1 year's custody	**Category range** Band B fine–Medium level community order

[38] The table below contains a non-exhaustive list of additional factual elements providing the context of the offence and factors relating to the offender.

Identify whether any combination of these or other relevant factors should result in an upward or downward adjustment of the sentence arrived at thus far.

Consecutive sentences for multiple offences may be appropriate where large sums are involved.

Factors increasing seriousness	**Factors reducing seriousness or reflecting personal mitigation**
Statutory aggravating factors: Previous convictions, having regard to a) the nature of the offence to which the conviction relates and its relevance to the current offence; and b) the time that has elapsed since the conviction Offence committed whilst on bail *Other aggravating factors:* Attempts to conceal/dispose of evidence Established evidence of community/wider impact Failure to comply with current court orders Offence committed on licence Offences taken into consideration Failure to respond to warnings about behaviour Offences committed across borders Blame wrongly placed on others Damage to third party for example loss of employment to legitimate employees	No previous convictions **or** no relevant/recent convictions Remorse Little or no prospect of success Good character and/or exemplary conduct Serious medical conditions requiring urgent, intensive or long-term treatment Age and/or lack of maturity where it affects the responsibility of the offender Lapse of time since apprehension where this does not arise from the conduct of the offender Mental disorder or learning disability Sole or primary carer for dependent relatives Offender co-operated with investigation, made early admissions and/or voluntarily reported offending Determination and/or demonstration of steps having been taken to address addiction or offending behaviour Activity originally legitimate

[39] **STEPS THREE to EIGHT** SG26-28

[These are identical to those set out at SG26-7 *et seq.*]

[41] BRIBERY SG26-29

Bribing another person

Bribery Act 2010 (section 1)

Being bribed

Bribery Act 2010 (section 2)

Bribery of foreign public officials

Bribery Act 2010 (section 6)

Triable either way
Maximum: 10 years' custody
Offence range: Discharge–8 years' custody

Sentencing Guidelines

SG26-30 **STEP ONE Determining the offence category** [42]

The court should determine the offence category with reference to the tables below. In order to determine the category the court should assess **culpability** and **harm.**

The level of **culpability** is determined by weighing up all the factors of the case to determine the offender's role and the extent to which the offending was planned and the sophistication with which it was carried out.	**Harm** is assessed in relation to any impact caused by the offending (whether to identifiable victims or in a wider context) and the actual or intended gain to the offender.	
Culpability demonstrated by one or more of the following:	Harm demonstrated by one or more of the following factors:	
A — High culpability	**Category 1**	• Serious detrimental effect on individuals (for example by provision of substandard goods or services resulting from the corrupt behaviour) • Serious environmental impact • Serious undermining of the proper function of local or national government, business or public services • Substantial actual or intended financial gain to offender or another or loss caused to others
A leading role where offending is part of a group activity	**Category 2**	• Significant detrimental effect on individuals • Significant environmental impact • Significant undermining of the proper function of local or national government, business or public services • Significant actual or intended financial gain to offender or another or loss caused to others • Risk of category 1 harm
Involvement of others through pressure, influence	**Category 3**	• Limited detrimental impact on individuals, the environment, government, business or public services • Risk of category 2 harm
Abuse of position of significant power or trust or responsibility	**Category 4**	• Risk of category 3 harm
Intended corruption (directly or indirectly) of a senior official performing a public function	**Risk of harm** involves consideration of both the likelihood of harm occurring and the extent of it if it does. Risk of harm is less serious than the same actual harm. Where the offence has caused risk of harm but no (or much less) actual harm, the normal approach is to move to the next category of harm down. This may not be appropriate if either the likelihood or extent of potential harm is particularly high.	
Intended corruption (directly or indirectly) of a law enforcement officer		
Sophisticated nature of offence/significant planning		
Offending conducted over sustained period of time		
Motivated by expectation of substantial financial, commercial or political gain		

[42]

B — Medium culpability
Other cases that fall between categories A or C because: – Factors are present in A and C which balance each other out **and/or** – The offender's culpability falls between the factors as described in A and C
A significant role where offending is part of a group activity
C — Lesser culpability
Involved through coercion, intimidation or exploitation
Not motivated by personal gain
Peripheral role in organised activity
Opportunistic 'one-off' offence; very little or no planning
Limited awareness or understanding of extent of corrupt activity

Where there are characteristics present which fall under different levels of culpability, the court should balance these characteristics to reach a fair assessment of the offender's culpability. SG26-31

[43] **STEP TWO Starting point and category range**

Having determined the category at step one, the court should use the corresponding starting point to reach a sentence within the category range below. The starting point applies to all offenders irrespective of plea or previous convictions.

Section 1 Bribery Act 2010: Bribing another person

Section 2 Bribery Act 2010: Being bribed

Section 6 Bribery Act 2010: Bribery of foreign public officials

Maximum: 10 years' custody

	Culpability		
Harm	**A**	**B**	**C**
Category 1	**Starting point** 7 years' custody	**Starting point** 5 years' custody	**Starting point** 3 years' custody
	Category range 5–8 years' custody	**Category range** 3–6 years' custody	**Category range** 18 months'–4 years' custody
Category 2	**Starting point** 5 years' custody	**Starting point** 3 years' custody	**Starting point** 18 months' custody
	Category range 3–6 years' custody	**Category range** 18 months'–4 years' custody	**Category range** 26 weeks'–3 years' custody
Category 3	**Starting point** 3 years' custody	**Starting point** 18 months' custody	**Starting point** 26 weeks' custody
	Category range 18 months'–4 years' custody	**Category range** 26 weeks'–3 years' custody	**Category range** Medium level community order–1 year's custody
Category 4	**Starting point** 18 months' custody	**Starting point** 26 weeks' custody	**Starting point** Medium level community order
	Category range 26 weeks'–3 years' custody	**Category range** Medium level community order–1 year's custody	**Category range** Band B fine–High level community order

The table below contains a non-exhaustive list of additional factual elements providing the context of the offence and factors relating to the offender. [44]

Identify whether any combination of these or other relevant factors should result in an upward or downward adjustment from the starting point.

Consecutive sentences for multiple offences may be appropriate where large sums are involved.

Factors increasing seriousness	**Factors reducing seriousness or reflecting personal mitigation**
Statutory aggravating factors: Previous convictions, having regard to a) the nature of the offence to which the conviction relates and its relevance to the current offence; and b) the time that has elapsed since the conviction Offence committed whilst on bail *Other aggravating factors:* Steps taken to prevent victims reporting or obtaining assistance and/or from assisting or supporting the prosecution Attempts to conceal/dispose of evidence Established evidence of community/wider impact Failure to comply with current court orders Offence committed on licence Offences taken into consideration Failure to respond to warnings about behaviour Offences committed across borders Blame wrongly placed on others Pressure exerted on another party Offence committed to facilitate other criminal activity	No previous convictions or no relevant/recent convictions Remorse Good character and/or exemplary conduct Little or no prospect of success Serious medical conditions requiring urgent, intensive or long-term treatment Age and/or lack of maturity where it affects the responsibility of the offender Lapse of time since apprehension where this does not arise from the conduct of the offender Mental disorder or learning disability Sole or primary carer for dependent relatives Offender co-operated with investigation, made early admissions and/or voluntarily reported offending

SG26-32 STEPS THREE to EIGHT [45]

[These are identical to those set out at **SG26-7** ***et seq.***]

SG26-33 CORPORATE OFFENDERS: FRAUD, BRIBERY, AND MONEY LAUNDERING [47]

Fraud
Conspiracy to defraud (common law)
Cheat the public revenue (common law)
Triable only on indictment

Fraud Act 2006 (sections 1, 6 and 7)
Theft Act 1968 (section 17)
Value Added Tax Act 1994 (section 72)
Customs and Excise Management Act 1979 (section 170)
Triable either way

Bribery
Bribery Act 2010 (sections 1, 2, 6 and 7)
Triable either way

[47] **Money laundering**
Proceeds of Crime Act 2002 (sections 327, 328 and 329)
Triable either way
Maximum: Unlimited fine

Most cases of corporate offending in this area are likely to merit allocation for trial to the Crown Court.

Committal for sentence is mandatory if confiscation (see step two) is to be considered. (Proceeds of Crime Act 2002 section 70).

[48] **STEP ONE Compensation** SG26-34

The court must consider making a compensation order requiring the offender to pay compensation for any personal injury, loss or damage resulting from the offence in such an amount as the court considers appropriate, having regard to the evidence and to the means of the offender.

Where the means of the offender are limited, priority should be given to the payment of compensation over payment of any other financial penalty.

Reasons should be given if a compensation order is not made.

(See section 130 Powers of Criminal Courts (Sentencing) Act 2000)

STEP TWO Confiscation SG26-35

Confiscation must be considered if either the Crown asks for it or the court thinks that it may be appropriate.

Confiscation must be dealt with before, and taken into account when assessing, any other fine or financial order (except compensation).

(See Proceeds of Crime Act 2002 sections 6 and 13)

[49] **STEP THREE Determining the offence category** SG26-36

Culpability	**Harm**	
The sentencer should weigh up all the factors of the case to determine culpability. **Where there are characteristics present which fall under different categories, the court should balance these characteristics to reach a fair assessment of the offender's culpability.** Culpability demonstrated by the offending corporation's role and motivation. May be demonstrated by one or more of the following non-exhaustive characteristics.	Harm is represented by a financial sum calculated by reference to the table below **Amount obtained or intended to be obtained (or loss avoided or intended to be avoided)**	
A — High culpability	**Fraud**	For offences of fraud, conspiracy to defraud, cheating the Revenue and fraudulent evasion of duty or VAT, harm will normally be the actual or intended gross gain to the offender.
Corporation plays a leading role in organised, planned unlawful activity (whether acting alone or with others)	**Bribery**	For offences under the Bribery Act the appropriate figure will normally be the gross profit from the contract obtained, retained or sought as a result of the offending. An alternative measure for offences under section 7 may be the likely cost avoided by failing to put in place appropriate measures to prevent bribery.
Wilful obstruction of detection (for example destruction of evidence, misleading investigators, suborning employees)	**Money laundering**	For offences of money laundering the appropriate figure will normally be the amount laundered or, alternatively, the likely cost avoided by failing to put in place an effective anti-money laundering programme if this is higher.

Sentencing Guidelines

Culpability	Harm [49]
Involving others through pressure or coercion (for example employees or suppliers)	**General** Where the actual or intended gain cannot be established, the appropriate measure will be the amount that the court considers was likely to be achieved in all the circumstances. In the absence of sufficient evidence of the amount that was likely to be obtained, 10–20 per cent of the relevant revenue (for instance between 10 and 20 per cent of the worldwide revenue derived from the product or business area to which the offence relates for the period of the offending) **may** be an appropriate measure. There may be large cases of fraud or bribery in which the true harm is to commerce or markets generally. That may justify adopting a harm figure beyond the normal measures here set out.
Targeting of vulnerable victims or a large number of victims	
Corruption of local or national government officials or ministers	
Corruption of officials performing a law enforcement role	
Abuse of dominant market position or position of trust or responsibility	
Offending committed over a sustained period of time	
Culture of wilful disregard of commission of offences by employees or agents with no effort to put effective systems in place (section 7 Bribery Act only)	
B — Medium culpability	
Corporation plays a significant role in unlawful activity organised by others	
Activity not unlawful from the outset	
Corporation reckless in making false statement (section 72 VAT Act 1994)	
Other cases that fall between categories A or C because: – Factors are present in A and C which balance each other out **and/or** – The offender's culpability falls between the factors as described in A and C	
C — Lesser culpability	
Corporation plays a minor, peripheral role in unlawful activity organised by others	
Some effort made to put bribery prevention measures in place but insufficient to amount to a defence (section 7 Bribery Act only)	
SG26-37 Involvement through coercion, intimidation or exploitation	

STEP FOUR Starting point and category range [50]

Having determined the culpability level at step three, the court should use the table below to determine the starting point within the category range below. The starting point applies to all offenders irrespective of plea or previous convictions.

The harm figure at step three is multiplied by the relevant percentage figure representing culpability.

	Culpability Level		
	A	**B**	**C**
Harm figure multiplier	**Starting point** 300%	**Starting point** 200%	**Starting point** 100%
	Category range 250% to 400%	**Category range** 100% to 300%	**Category range** 20% to 150%

Having determined the appropriate starting point, the court should then consider adjustment within the category range for aggravating or mitigating features. In some cases, having considered these factors, it may be appropriate to move outside the identified category range. (See below for a **non-exhaustive** list of aggravating and mitigating factors.)

[50]

Factors increasing seriousness	Factors reducing seriousness or reflecting mitigation
Previous relevant convictions or subject to previous relevant civil or regulatory enforcement action Corporation or subsidiary set up to commit fraudulent activity Fraudulent activity endemic within corporation Attempts made to conceal misconduct Substantial harm (whether financial or otherwise) suffered by victims of offending or by third parties affected by offending Risk of harm greater than actual or intended harm (for example in banking/credit fraud) Substantial harm caused to integrity or confidence of markets Substantial harm caused to integrity of local or national governments Serious nature of underlying criminal activity (money laundering offences) Offence committed across borders or jurisdictions	No previous relevant convictions or previous relevant civil or regulatory enforcement action Victims voluntarily reimbursed/compensated No actual loss to victims Corporation co-operated with investigation, made early admissions and/or voluntarily reported offending Offending committed under previous director(s)/ manager(s) Little or no actual gain to corporation from offending

[51] **General principles to follow in setting a fine**

The court should determine the appropriate level of fine in accordance with section 164 of the Criminal Justice Act 2003, which requires that the fine must reflect the seriousness of the offence and requires the court to take into account the financial circumstances of the offender.

Obtaining financial information

Companies and bodies delivering public or charitable services

Where the offender is a company or a body which delivers a public or charitable service, it is expected to provide comprehensive accounts for the last three years, to enable the court to make an accurate assessment of its financial status. In the absence of such disclosure, or where the court is not satisfied that it has been given sufficient reliable information, the court will be entitled to draw reasonable inferences as to the offender's means from evidence it has heard and from all the circumstances of the case.

1. *For companies*: annual accounts. Particular attention should be paid to turnover; profit before tax; directors' remuneration, loan accounts and pension provision; and assets as disclosed by the balance sheet. Most companies are required to file audited accounts at Companies House. Failure to produce relevant recent accounts on request may properly lead to the conclusion that the company can pay any appropriate fine.
2. *For partnerships*: annual accounts. Particular attention should be paid to turnover; profit before tax; partners' drawings, loan accounts and pension provision; assets as above. Limited liability partnerships (LLPs) may be required to file audited accounts with Companies House. If adequate accounts are not produced on request, see paragraph 1.
3. *For local authorities, fire authorities and similar public bodies*: the Annual Revenue Budget ('ARB') is the equivalent of turnover and the best indication of the size of the defendant organisation. It is unlikely to be necessary to analyse specific expenditure or reserves unless inappropriate expenditure is suggested.
4. *For health trusts*: the independent regulator of NHS Foundation Trusts is Monitor. It publishes quarterly reports and annual figures for the financial strength and stability of trusts from which the annual income can be seen, available via www.monitor-nhsft.gov.uk. Detailed analysis of expenditure or reserves is unlikely to be called for.
5. *For charities*: it will be appropriate to inspect annual audited accounts. Detailed analysis of expenditure or reserves is unlikely to be called for unless there is a suggestion of unusual or unnecessary expenditure.

[52] **STEP FIVE Adjustment of fine** **SG26-38**

Having arrived at a fine level, the court should consider whether there are any further factors which indicate an adjustment in the level of the fine. The court should 'step back' and consider the overall effect of its orders. The combination of orders made, compensation, confiscation and fine ought to achieve:

- the removal of all gain
- appropriate additional punishment, and
- deterrence

The fine may be adjusted to ensure that these objectives are met in a fair way. The court should consider any further factors relevant to the setting of the level of the fine to ensure that the fine is proportionate, having regard to the size and financial position of the offending organisation and the seriousness of the offence. [52]

The fine must be substantial enough to have a real economic impact which will bring home to both management and shareholders the need to operate within the law. Whether the fine will have the effect of putting the offender out of business will be relevant; in some bad cases this may be an acceptable consequence.

In considering the ability of the offending organisation to pay any financial penalty the court can take into account the power to allow time for payment or to order that the amount be paid in instalments.

The court should consider whether the level of fine would otherwise cause unacceptable harm to third parties. In doing so the court should bear in mind that the payment of any compensation determined at step one should take priority over the payment of any fine.

The table below contains a **non-exhaustive** list of additional factual elements for the court to consider. The Court should identify whether any combination of these, or other relevant factors, should result in a proportionate increase or reduction in the level of fine.

SG26-39 STEP SIX **Consider any factors which would indicate a reduction, such as assistance to the prosecution** [53]

Factors to consider in adjusting the level of fine
Fine fulfils the objectives of punishment, deterrence and removal of gain
The value, worth or available means of the offender
Fine impairs offender's ability to make restitution to victims
Impact of fine on offender's ability to implement effective compliance programmes
Impact of fine on employment of staff, service users, customers and local economy (but not shareholders)
Impact of fine on performance of public or charitable function

The court should take into account sections 73 and 74 of the Serious Organised Crime and Police Act 2005 (assistance by defendants: reduction or review of sentence) and any other rule of law by virtue of which an offender may receive a discounted sentence in consequence of assistance given (or offered) to the prosecutor or investigator.

SG26-40 STEP SEVEN **Reduction for guilty pleas**

The court should take into account any potential reduction for a guilty plea in accordance with section 144 of the Criminal Justice Act 2003 and the *Guilty Plea* guideline.

SG26-41 STEP EIGHT **Ancillary Orders**

In all cases the court must consider whether to make any ancillary orders.

SG26-42 STEP NINE **Totality principle**

If sentencing an offender for more than one offence, consider whether the total sentence is just and proportionate to the offending behaviour.

SG26-43 STEP TEN **Reasons**

Section 174 of the Criminal Justice Act 2003 imposes a duty to give reasons for, and explain the effect of, the sentence.

PART 27 INTIMIDATORY OFFENCES

Definitive Guideline SG27-1

[4] **Applicability of guideline**

The Sentencing Council issues this definitive guideline in accordance with section 120 of the Coroners and Justice Act 2009.

The guidelines apply to all offenders aged 18 and older, who are sentenced on or after 1 October 2018, regardless of the date of the offence.

Section 125(1) of the Coroners and Justice Act 2009 provides that when sentencing offences committed after 6 April 2010:

Every court —
(a) must, in sentencing an offender, follow any sentencing guidelines which are relevant to the offender's case, and
(b) must, in exercising any other function relating to the sentencing of offenders, follow any sentencing guidelines which are relevant to the exercise of the function,
unless the court is satisfied that it would be contrary to the interests of justice to do so.

Structure, ranges and starting points SG27-2

For the purposes of section 125(3)–(4) of the Coroners and Justice Act 2009, the guideline specifies offence ranges – the range of sentences appropriate for each type of offence. Within each offence, the Council has specified a number of categories which reflect varying degrees of seriousness. The offence range is split into category ranges – sentences appropriate for each level of seriousness. The Council has also identified a starting point within each category.

Starting points define the position within a category range from which to start calculating the provisional sentence. The court should consider further features of the offence or the offender that warrant adjustment of the sentence within the range, including the aggravating and mitigating factors set out at step two. Starting points and ranges apply to all offenders, whether they have pleaded guilty or been convicted after trial. Credit for a guilty plea is taken into consideration only at step four in the decision making process, after the appropriate sentence has been identified.

Information on community orders and fine bands is set out in the annex at [SG27-48]. SG27-3

[5]

Harassment SG27-4

(putting people in fear of violence) Protection from Harassment Act 1997 (section 4)

Stalking SG27-5

(involving fear of violence or serious alarm or distress) Protection from Harassment Act 1997 (section 4A)

Triable either way Maximum: 10 years' custody
Offence range: Fine–8 years' custody

Racially or religiously aggravated harassment SG27-6

(putting people in fear of violence) Crime and Disorder Act 1998 (section 32(1)(b))

Racially or religiously aggravated stalking

(involving fear of violence or serious alarm or distress) Crime and Disorder Act 1998 (section 32(1)(b))

Triable either way
Maximum: 14 years' custody

The racially or religiously aggravated offence is a specified offence for the purposes of Section 226A (extended sentence for certain violent or sexual offences) of the Criminal Justice Act 2003

Where offence committed in a domestic context, also refer to the *Overarching principles: Domestic abuse* guideline

SG27-7 **STEP ONE Determining the offence category** [6]

The court should determine the offence category with reference only to the factors in the tables below. In order to determine the category the court should assess **culpability** and **harm.**

The level of **culpability** is determined by weighing up all the factors of the case. **Where there are characteristics present which fall under different levels of culpability, the court should balance these characteristics to reach a fair assessment of the offender's culpability.**

Culpability demonstrated by one or more of the following:	
A	**Very high culpability** — the extreme nature of one or more culpability B factors or the extreme culpability indicated by a combination of culpability B factors may elevate to category A.
B	**High culpability:** • Conduct intended to maximise fear or distress • High degree of planning and/or sophisticated offence • Persistent action over a prolonged period • Offence motivated by, or demonstrating, hostility based on any of the following characteristics or presumed characteristics of the victim: age, sex, disability, sexual orientation or transgender identity
C	**Medium culpability:** Cases that fall between categories B and D, and in particular: • Conduct intended to cause some fear or distress • Some planning • Scope and duration of offence that falls between categories B and D
D	**Lesser culpability:** • Offender's responsibility substantially reduced by mental disorder or learning disability • Conduct unlikely to cause significant fear or distress • Little or no planning • Offence was limited in scope and duration

Harm The level of harm is assessed by weighing up all the factors of the case.	
Category 1	• Very serious distress caused to the victim • Significant psychological harm caused to the victim • Victim caused to make considerable changes to lifestyle to avoid contact
Category 2	Harm that falls between categories 1 and 3, and in particular: • Some distress caused to the victim • Some psychological harm caused to the victim • Victim caused to make some changes to lifestyle to avoid contact
Category 3	• Limited distress or harm caused to the victim

Where offence committed in a domestic context, also refer to the *Overarching principles: Domestic abuse* guideline

SG27-8 **STEP TWO Starting point and category range** [7]

Having determined the category at step one, the court should use the corresponding starting point to reach a sentence within the category range below. The starting point applies to all offenders irrespective of plea or previous convictions.

Sentencers should consider whether to ask for psychiatric reports in order to assist in the appropriate sentencing (hospital orders, or mental health treatment requirements) of certain offenders to whom this consideration may be relevant.

Maximum: 10 years' custody (basic offence)

[7]

Harm	Culpability A	B	C	D
Category 1	**Starting point** 5 years' custody	**Starting point** 2 years 6 months' custody	**Starting point** 36 weeks' custody	**Starting point** 12 weeks' custody
	Category range 3 years 6 months'–8 years' custody	**Category range** 1–4 years' custody	**Category range** 12 weeks–1 year 6 months' custody	**Category range** High level community order–36 weeks' custody
Category 2	**Starting point** 2 years 6 months' custody	**Starting point** 36 weeks' custody	**Starting point** 12 weeks' custody	**Starting point** High level community order
	Category range 1–4 years' custody	**Category range** 12 weeks'–1 year 6 months' custody	**Category range** High level community order–36 weeks' custody	**Category range** Low level community order–12 weeks' custody
Category 3	**Starting point** 36 weeks' custody	**Starting point** 12 weeks' custody	**Starting point** High level community order	**Starting point** Low level community order
	Category range 12 weeks'–1 year 6 months' custody	**Category range** High level community order–36 weeks' custody	**Category range** Low level community order–12 weeks' custody	**Category range** Band C fine–High level community order

Where offence committed in a domestic context, also refer to the *Overarching principles: Domestic abuse* guideline

[8] The court should then consider any adjustment for any aggravating or mitigating factors. Below is a **non-exhaustive** list of additional factual elements providing the context of the offence and factors relating to the offender.

Identify whether any combination of these, or other relevant factors, should result in an upward or downward adjustment from the starting point.

Factors increasing seriousness
Statutory aggravating factors:
Previous convictions, having regard to a) the **nature** of the offence to which the conviction relates and its **relevance** to the current offence; and b) the **time** that has elapsed since the conviction Offence committed whilst on bail
Other aggravating factors:
Using a position of trust to facilitate the offence Victim is particularly vulnerable (not all vulnerabilities are immediately apparent) Grossly violent or offensive material sent Impact of offence on others, particularly children Exploiting contact arrangements with a child to commit the offence Offence committed against those working in the public sector or providing a service to the public Failure to comply with current court orders Offence committed on licence or post sentence supervision Offences taken into consideration

Factors reducing seriousness or reflecting personal mitigation
No previous convictions **or** no relevant/recent convictions Remorse Good character and/or exemplary conduct Serious medical condition requiring urgent, intensive or long-term treatment Age and/or lack of maturity Mental disorder or learning disability (where not taken into account at step one) Sole or primary carer for dependent relatives Determination and/or demonstration of steps having been taken to address offending behaviour

[8]

Where offence committed in a domestic context, also refer to the *Overarching principles: Domestic abuse* guideline

SG27-9 Racially or Religiously Aggravated Harassment/Stalking Offences [9]

Having determined the category of the basic offence to identify the sentence of a non-aggravated offence, the court should now consider the level of racial or religious aggravation involved and apply an appropriate uplift to the sentence in accordance with the guidance below. The following is a list of factors which the court should consider to determine the level of aggravation. Where there are characteristics present which fall under different levels of aggravation, the court should balance these to reach a fair assessment of the level of aggravation present in the offence.

Maximum sentence for the aggravated offence on indictment is 14 years' custody (maximum for the basic offence is 10 years' custody)

HIGH LEVEL OF RACIAL OR RELIGIOUS AGGRAVATION	SENTENCE UPLIFT
• Racial or religious aggravation was the predominant motivation for the offence. • Offender was a member of, or was associated with, a group promoting hostility based on race or religion (where linked to the commission of the offence). • Aggravated nature of the offence caused severe distress to the victim or the victim's family (over and above the distress already considered at step one). • Aggravated nature of the offence caused serious fear and distress throughout local community or more widely.	Increase the length of custodial sentence if already considered for the basic offence or consider a custodial sentence, if not already considered for the basic offence.
MEDIUM LEVEL OF RACIAL OR RELIGIOUS AGGRAVATION	**SENTENCE UPLIFT**
• Racial or religious aggravation formed a significant proportion of the offence as a whole. • Aggravated nature of the offence caused some distress to the victim or the victim's family (over and above the distress already considered at step one). • Aggravated nature of the offence caused some fear and distress throughout local community or more widely.	Consider a significantly more onerous penalty of the same type or consider a more severe type of sentence than for the basic offence.
LOW LEVEL OF RACIAL OR RELIGIOUS AGGRAVATION	**SENTENCE UPLIFT**
• Aggravated element formed a minimal part of the offence as a whole. • Aggravated nature of the offence caused minimal or no distress to the victim or the victim's family (over and above the distress already considered at step one).	Consider a more onerous penalty of the same type identified for the basic offence.

Magistrates may find that, although the appropriate sentence for the basic offence would be within their powers, the appropriate increase for the aggravated offence would result in a sentence in excess of their powers. If so, they must commit for sentence to the Crown Court.

The sentencer should state in open court that the offence was aggravated by reason of race or religion, and should also state what the sentence would have been without that element of aggravation.

[9] **Where offence committed in a domestic context, also refer to the *Overarching principles: Domestic abuse* guideline**

[10] **STEP THREE Consider any factors which indicate a reduction for assistance to the prosecution** SG27-10

The court should take into account sections 73 and 74 of the Serious Organised Crime and Police Act 2005 (assistance by defendants: reduction or review of sentence) and any other rule of law by virtue of which an offender may receive a discounted sentence in consequence of assistance given (or offered) to the prosecutor or investigator.

STEP FOUR Reduction for guilty pleas SG27-11

The court should take account of any potential reduction for a guilty plea in accordance with section 144 of the Criminal Justice Act 2003 and the Guilty Plea guideline.

STEP FIVE Dangerousness SG27-12

The court should consider whether having regard to the criteria contained in Chapter 5 of Part 12 of the Criminal Justice Act 2003 it would be appropriate to impose an extended sentence (section 226A).

STEP SIX Totality principle SG27-13

If sentencing an offender for more than one offence, or where the offender is already serving a sentence, consider whether the total sentence is just and proportionate to the overall offending behaviour in accordance with the Offences Taken into Consideration and Totality guideline.

Where offence committed in a domestic context, also refer to the *Overarching principles: Domestic abuse* guideline

[11] **STEP SEVEN Compensation and ancillary orders** SG27-14

In all cases, the court must consider whether to make a compensation order and/or other ancillary orders.

Compensation order

The court should consider compensation orders in all cases where personal injury, loss or damage has resulted from the offence. The court must give reasons if it decides not to award compensation in such cases.

Other ancillary orders available include:

Restraining order

Where an offender is convicted of any offence, the court may make a restraining order (section 5 of the Protection from Harassment Act 1997).

The order may prohibit the offender from doing anything for the purpose of protecting the victim of the offence, or any other person mentioned in the order, from further conduct which amounts to harassment or will cause a fear of violence.

The order may have effect for a specified period or until further order.

STEP EIGHT Reasons SG27-15

Section 174 of the Criminal Justice Act 2003 imposes a duty to give reasons for, and explain the effect of, the sentence.

STEP NINE Consideration for time spent on bail (tagged curfew) SG27-16

The court must consider whether to give credit for time spent on bail in accordance with section 240A of the Criminal Justice Act 2003.

Where offence committed in a domestic context, also refer to the *Overarching principles: Domestic abuse* guideline

[13] HARASSMENT SG27-17

Protection from Harassment Act 1997 (section 2)

STALKING SG27-18

Protection from Harassment Act 1997 (section 2A)

Triable only summarily
Maximum: 6 months' custody
Offence range: Discharge–26 weeks' custody

SG27-19 **RACIALLY OR RELIGIOUSLY AGGRAVATED HARASSMENT** [13]

Crime and Disorder Act 1998 (section 32(1)(a))

SG27-20 **RACIALLY OR RELIGIOUSLY AGGRAVATED STALKING**

Crime and Disorder Act 1998 (section 32(1)(a))

Triable either way
Maximum: 2 years' custody

Where offence committed in a domestic context, also refer to the *Overarching principles: Domestic abuse* guideline

SG27-21 STEP ONE **Determining the offence category** [14]

The court should determine the offence category with reference only to the factors in the tables below. In order to determine the category the court should assess **culpability** and **harm.**

The level of **culpability** is determined by weighing up all the factors of the case. **Where there are characteristics present which fall under different levels of culpability, the court should balance these characteristics to reach a fair assessment of the offender's culpability.**

Culpability demonstrated by one or more of the following:	
A	**High culpability:** • Conduct intended to maximise fear or distress • High degree of planning and/or sophisticated offence • Persistent action over a prolonged period • Threat of serious violence • Offence motivated by, or demonstrating hostility based on any of the following characteristics or presumed characteristics of the victim: age, sex, disability, sexual orientation or transgender identity
B	**Medium culpability:** Cases that fall between categories A and C, in particular: • Conduct intended to cause some fear or distress • Some planning • Threat of some violence • Scope and duration of offence that falls between categories A and C
C	**Lesser culpability:** • Offender's responsibility substantially reduced by mental disorder or learning disability • Little or no planning • Offence was limited in scope and duration

Harm The level of harm is assessed by weighing up all the factors of the case.	
Category 1	• Very serious distress caused to the victim • Significant psychological harm caused to the victim • Victim caused to make considerable changes to lifestyle to avoid contact
Category 2	Harm that falls between categories 1 and 3, and in particular: • Some distress caused to the victim • Some psychological harm caused to the victim • Victim caused to make some changes to lifestyle to avoid contact
Category 3	• Limited distress or harm caused to the victim

Where offence committed in a domestic context, also refer to the *Overarching principles: Domestic abuse* guideline

[15] **STEP TWO Starting point and category range** SG27-22

Having determined the category at step one, the court should use the corresponding starting point to reach a sentence within the category range below. The starting point applies to all offenders irrespective of plea or previous convictions.

Maximum 6 months' custody (basic offence)

	Culpability		
Harm	**A**	**B**	**C**
Category 1	**Starting point** 12 weeks' custody	**Starting point** High level community order	**Starting point** Medium level community order
	Category range High level community order–26 weeks' custody	**Category range** Medium level community order–16 weeks' custody	**Category range** Low level community order–12 weeks' custody
Category 2	**Starting point** High level community order	**Starting point** Medium level community order	**Starting point** Low level community order
	Category range Medium level community order–16 weeks' custody	**Category range** Low level community order–12 weeks' custody	**Category range** Band B fine–Medium level community order
Category 3	**Starting point** Medium level community order	**Starting point** Low level community order	**Starting point** Band B fine
	Category range Low level community order–12 weeks' custody	**Category range** Band B fine–Medium level community order	**Category range** Discharge–Low level community order

Where offence committed in a domestic context, also refer to the *Overarching principles: Domestic abuse* guideline

[16] The court should then consider any adjustment for any aggravating or mitigating factors. Below is a **non-exhaustive** list of additional factual elements providing the context of the offence and factors relating to the offender.

Identify whether any combination of these, or other relevant factors, should result in an upward or downward adjustment from the starting point.

Factors increasing seriousness
Statutory aggravating factors: Previous convictions, having regard to a) the **nature** of the offence to which the conviction relates and its **relevance** to the current offence; and b) the **time** that has elapsed since the conviction Offence committed whilst on bail ***Other aggravating factors:*** Using a position of trust to facilitate the offence Victim is particularly vulnerable (not all vulnerabilities are immediately apparent) Grossly violent or offensive material sent Impact of offence on others, particularly children Exploiting contact arrangements with a child to commit the offence Offence committed against those working in the public sector or providing a service to the public Failure to comply with current court orders Offence committed on licence or post sentence supervision Offences taken into consideration

Factors reducing seriousness or reflecting personal mitigation
No previous convictions or no relevant/recent convictions Remorse Good character and/or exemplary conduct Serious medical condition requiring urgent, intensive or long-term treatment Age and/or lack of maturity Mental disorder or learning disability (where not taken into account at step one) Sole or primary carer for dependent relatives Determination and/or demonstration of steps having been taken to address offending behaviour

[16]

Where offence committed in a domestic context, also refer to the *Overarching principles: Domestic abuse* guideline

SG27-23 RACIALLY OR RELIGIOUSLY AGGRAVATED HARASSMENT/STALKING OFFENCES ONLY [17]

[This follows the same terms as those applicable to Harassment (putting people in fear of violence) Protection from Harassment Act 1997 (section 4) and Stalking (involving fear of violence or serious alarm or distress) Protection from Harassment Act 1997 (section 4A): see **SG-27-4** ***et seq.***]

SG27-24 STEP THREE **Consider any factors which indicate a reduction for assistance to the prosecution** [18]

The court should take into account sections 73 and 74 of the Serious Organised Crime and Police Act 2005 (assistance by defendants: reduction or review of sentence) and any other rule of law by virtue of which an offender may receive a discounted sentence in consequence of assistance given (or offered) to the prosecutor or investigator.

SG27-25 STEP FOUR **Reduction for guilty pleas**

The court should take account of any potential reduction for a guilty plea in accordance with section 144 of the Criminal Justice Act 2003 and the Guilty Plea guideline.

SG27-26 STEP FIVE **Totality principle**

If sentencing an offender for more than one offence, or where the offender is already serving a sentence, consider whether the total sentence is just and proportionate to the overall offending behaviour in accordance with the Offences Taken into Consideration and Totality guideline.

SG27-27 STEP SIX **Compensation and ancillary orders**

In all cases, the court must consider whether to make a compensation order and/or other ancillary orders.

Compensation order

The court should consider compensation orders in all cases where personal injury, loss or damage has resulted from the offence. The court must give reasons if it decides not to award compensation in such cases.

Other ancillary orders available include:

Restraining order

Where an offender is convicted of any offence, the court may make a restraining order (section 5 of the Protection from Harassment Act 1997).

The order may prohibit the offender from doing anything for the purpose of protecting the victim of the offence, or any other person mentioned in the order, from further conduct which amounts to harassment or will cause a fear of violence.

The order may have effect for a specified period or until further order.

SG27-28 STEP SEVEN **Reasons** [19]

Section 174 of the Criminal Justice Act 2003 imposes a duty to give reasons for, and explain the effect of, the sentence.

SG27-29 STEP EIGHT **Consideration for time spent on bail (tagged curfew)**

The court must consider whether to give credit for time spent on bail in accordance with section 240A of the Criminal Justice Act 2003.

[20] **Where offence committed in a domestic context, also refer to the *Overarching principles: Domestic abuse* guideline**

[21] ## Disclosing Private Sexual Images SG27-30

Criminal Justice and Courts Act 2015 (section 33)

Triable either way
Maximum: 2 years' custody
Offence range: Discharge–1 year 6 months' custody

Where offence committed in a domestic context, also refer to the *Overarching principles: Domestic abuse* guideline

[22] ### STEP ONE Determining the offence category SG27-31

The court should determine the offence category with reference only to the factors in the tables below. In order to determine the category the court should assess **culpability** and **harm.**

The level of **culpability** is determined by weighing up all the factors of the case. **Where there are characteristics present which fall under different levels of culpability, the court should balance these characteristics to reach a fair assessment of the offender's culpability.**

Culpability demonstrated by one or more of the following:	
A – Higher culpability	• Conduct intended to maximise distress and/or humiliation • Images circulated widely/publically • Significant planning and/or sophisticated offence • Repeated efforts to keep images available for viewing
B – Medium culpability	• Some planning • Scope and duration that falls between categories A and C • All other cases that fall between categories A and C
C – Lesser culpability	• Offender's responsibility substantially reduced by mental disorder or learning disability • Little or no planning • Conduct intended to cause limited distress and/or humiliation • Offence was limited in scope and duration

Harm The level of harm is assessed by weighing up all the factors of the case.	
Category 1	• Very serious distress caused to the victim • Significant psychological harm caused to the victim • Offence has a considerable practical impact on the victim
Category 2	Harm that falls between categories 1 and 3, and in particular: • Some distress caused to the victim • Some psychological harm caused to the victim • Offence has some practical impact on the victim
Category 3	• Limited distress or harm caused to the victim

Where offence committed in a domestic context, also refer to the *Overarching principles: Domestic abuse* guideline

[23] ### STEP TWO Starting point and category range SG27-32

Having determined the category at step one, the court should use the corresponding starting point to reach a sentence within the category range below. The starting point applies to all offenders irrespective of plea or previous convictions.

Sentencing Guidelines

	Culpability			[23]
Harm	**A**	**B**	**C**	
Category 1	**Starting point** 1 year's custody	**Starting point** 26 weeks' custody	**Starting point** 12 weeks' custody	
	Category range 26 weeks'–1 year 6 months' custody	**Category range** 12 weeks'–1 year's custody	**Category range** High level community order–26 weeks' custody	
Category 2	**Starting point** 26 weeks' custody	**Starting point** 12 weeks' custody	**Starting point** High level community order	
	Category range 12 weeks'–1 year's custody	**Category range** High level community order–26 weeks' custody	**Category range** Low level community order–12 weeks' custody	
Category 3	**Starting point** 12 weeks' custody	**Starting point** High level community order	**Starting point** Low level community order	
	Category range High level community order–26 weeks' custody	**Category range** Low level community order–12 weeks' custody	**Category range** Discharge–High level community order	

Where offence committed in a domestic context, also refer to the *Overarching principles: Domestic abuse* guideline

The court should then consider any adjustment for any aggravating or mitigating factors. Below is a **non-exhaustive** list of additional factual elements providing the context of the offence and factors relating to the offender. [24]

Identify whether any combination of these, or other relevant factors, should result in an upward or downward adjustment from the starting point.

Factors increasing seriousness
Statutory aggravating factors:
Previous convictions, having regard to a) the **nature** of the offence to which the conviction relates and its **relevance** to the current offence; and b) the **time** that has elapsed since the conviction Offence committed whilst on bail Offence motivated by, or demonstrating hostility based on any of the following characteristics or presumed characteristics of the victim: religion, race, disability, sexual orientation, or transgender identity
Other aggravating factors:
Impact of offence on others, particularly children Victim is particularly vulnerable (not all vulnerabilities are immediately apparent) Failure to comply with current court orders Offence committed on licence or post sentence supervision Offences taken into consideration

Factors reducing seriousness or reflecting personal mitigation
No previous convictions **or** no relevant/recent convictions Offender took steps to limit circulation of images Remorse Good character and/or exemplary conduct Serious medical condition requiring urgent, intensive or long-term treatment Age and/or lack of maturity Mental disorder or learning disability (where not taken into account at step one) Sole or primary carer for dependent relatives Determination and/or demonstration of steps having been taken to address offending behaviour

[24] **Where offence committed in a domestic context, also refer to the *Overarching principles: Domestic abuse* guideline**

[25]–[26] STEPS THREE TO EIGHT SG27-33

[These are in the same terms as those applicable to Harassment: Protection from Harassment Act 1997 (section 2) and Stalking: Protection from Harassment Act 1997 (section 2A): see SG27-17 *et seq*.]

[27] ## Controlling or Coercive Behaviour in an Intimate or Family Relationship SG27-34

Serious Crime Act 2015 (section 76)

Triable either way

Maximum: 5 years' custody
Offence range: Community order–4 years' custody

Where offence committed in a domestic context, also refer to the *Overarching principles: Domestic abuse* guideline

[28] STEP ONE **Determining the offence category** SG27-35

The court should determine the offence category with reference only to the factors in the tables below. In order to determine the category the court should assess **culpability** and **harm.**

The level of **culpability** is determined by weighing up all the factors of the case. **Where there are characteristics present which fall under different levels of culpability, the court should balance these characteristics to reach a fair assessment of the offender's culpability.**

Culpability demonstrated by one or more of the following:	
A – Higher culpability	• Conduct intended to maximise fear or distress • Persistent action over a prolonged period • Use of multiple methods of controlling or coercive behaviour • Sophisticated offence • Conduct intended to humiliate and degrade the victim
B – Medium culpability	• Conduct intended to cause some fear or distress • Scope and duration of offence that falls between categories A and C • All other cases that fall between categories A and C
C – Lesser culpability	• Offender's responsibility substantially reduced by mental disorder or learning disability • Offence was limited in scope and duration

Harm The level of harm is assessed by weighing up all the factors of the case.	
Category 1	• Fear of violence on many occasions • Very serious alarm or distress which has a substantial adverse effect on the victim • Significant psychological harm
Category 2	• Fear of violence on at least two occasions • Serious alarm or distress which has a substantial adverse effect on the victim

[29] STEP TWO **Starting point and category range** SG27-36

Having determined the category at step one, the court should use the corresponding starting point to reach a sentence within the category range below. The starting point applies to all offenders irrespective of plea or previous convictions.

	Culpability			[29]
Harm	A	B	C	
Category 1	**Starting point** 2 years 6 months' custody	**Starting point** 1 year's custody	Starting point 26 weeks' custody	
	Category range 1–4 years' custody	**Category range** 26 weeks'–2 years 6 months' custody	**Category range** High level community order–1 year's custody	
Category 2	**Starting point** 1 year's custody	**Starting point** 26 weeks' custody	**Starting point** Medium level community order	
	Category range 26 weeks'–2 years 6 months' custody	**Category range** High level community order–1 year's custody	**Category range** Low level community order–26 weeks' custody	

The court should then consider any adjustment for any aggravating or mitigating factors. Below is a **non-exhaustive** list of additional factual elements providing the context of the offence and factors relating to the offender. [30]

Identify whether any combination of these, or other relevant factors, should result in an upward or downward adjustment from the starting point

Factors increasing seriousness
Statutory aggravating factors: Previous convictions, having regard to a) the **nature** of the offence to which the conviction relates and its **relevance** to the current offence; and b) the **time** that has elapsed since the conviction Offence committed whilst on bail Offence motivated by, or demonstrating hostility based on any of the following characteristics or presumed characteristics of the victim: religion, race, disability, sexual orientation, or transgender identity ***Other aggravating factors:*** Steps taken to prevent the victim reporting an incident Steps taken to prevent the victim obtaining assistance A proven history of violence or threats by the offender in a domestic context Impact of offence on others particularly children Exploiting contact arrangements with a child to commit the offence Victim is particularly vulnerable (not all vulnerabilities are immediately apparent) Victim left in debt, destitute or homeless Failure to comply with current court orders Offence committed on licence or post sentence supervision Offences taken into consideration

Factors reducing seriousness or reflecting personal mitigation
No previous convictions **or** no relevant/recent convictions Remorse Good character and/or exemplary conduct Serious medical condition requiring urgent, intensive or long-term treatment Age and/or lack of maturity Mental disorder or learning disability (where not taken into account at step one) Sole or primary carer for dependent relatives Determination and/or demonstration of steps having been taken to address offending behaviour

[31]–[32] **STEPS THREE TO EIGHT** SG27-37

[These are in the same terms as those applicable to Harassment: Protection from Harassment Act 1997 (section 2) and Stalking: Protection from Harassment Act 1997 (section 2A): see **SG-27-17** ***et seq***.]

[33] **THREATS TO KILL** SG27-38

Offences Against the Person Act 1861 (section 16)

Triable either way
Maximum: 10 years' custody

Offence range: Community order–7 years' custody

This is a specified offence for the purposes of section 226A (extended sentence for certain violent or sexual offences) of the Criminal Justice Act 2003

Where offence committed in a domestic context, also refer to the *Overarching principles: Domestic abuse* guideline

[34] **STEP ONE Determining the offence category** SG27-39

The court should determine the offence category with reference only to the factors in the tables below. In order to determine the category the court should assess **culpability** and **harm.**

The level of **culpability** is determined by weighing up all the factors of the case. **Where there are characteristics present which fall under different levels of culpability, the court should balance these characteristics to reach a fair assessment of the offender's culpability.**

Culpability demonstrated by one or more of the following:	
A – Higher culpability	• Significant planning and/or sophisticated offence • Visible weapon • Threat(s) made in the presence of children • History of and/or campaign of violence towards the victim • Threat(s) with significant violence
B – Medium culpability	**Cases that fall between categories A and C because:** • Factors are present in A and C which balance each other out and/or • The offender's culpability falls between the factors described in A and C
C – Lesser culpability	• Offender's responsibility substantially reduced by mental disorder or learning disability • Offence was limited in scope and duration

Harm The level of harm is assessed by weighing up all the factors of the case.	
Category 1	• Very serious distress caused to the victim • Significant psychological harm caused to the victim • Offence has a considerable practical impact on the victim
Category 2	**Harm that falls between categories 1 and 3, and in particular:** • Some distress caused to the victim • Some psychological harm caused to the victim • Offence has some practical impact on the victim
Category 3	• Little or no distress or harm caused to the victim

Where offence committed in a domestic context, also refer to the *Overarching principles: Domestic abuse* guideline

SG27-40 **STEP TWO Starting point and category range** [34]

Having determined the category at step one, the court should use the corresponding starting point to reach a sentence within the category range below. The starting point applies to all offenders irrespective of plea or previous convictions.

	Culpability		
Harm	**A**	**B**	**C**
Category 1	**Starting point** 4 years' custody	**Starting point** 2 years' custody	**Starting point** 1 year's custody
	Category range 2–7 years' custody	**Category range** 1–4 years' custody	**Category range** 26 weeks'–2 years 6 months' custody
Category 2	**Starting point** 2 years' custody	**Starting point** 1 year's custody	**Starting point** 26 weeks' custody
	Category range 1–4 years' custody	**Category range** 26 weeks'–2 years 6 months' custody	**Category range** High level community order–1 year's custody
Category 3	**Starting point** 1 year's custody	**Starting point** 26 weeks' custody	**Starting point** Medium level community order
	Category range 26 weeks'–2 years 6 months' custody	**Category range** High level community order–1 year's custody	**Category range** Low level community order–High level community order

Where offence committed in a domestic context, also refer to the *Overarching principles: Domestic abuse* guideline

The court should then consider any adjustment for any aggravating or mitigating factors. Below is a **non-exhaustive** list of additional factual elements providing the context of the offence and factors relating to the offender. [35]

Identify whether any combination of these, or other relevant factors, should result in an upward or downward adjustment from the starting point

Factors increasing seriousness
Statutory aggravating factors: Previous convictions, having regard to a) the **nature** of the offence to which the conviction relates and its **relevance** to the current offence; and b) the **time** that has elapsed since the conviction Offence committed whilst on bail Offence motivated by, or demonstrating hostility based on any of the following characteristics or presumed characteristics of the victim: religion, race, disability, sexual orientation, or transgender identity Offence was committed against an emergency worker acting in the exercise of functions as such a worker
Other aggravating factors: Offence committed against those working in the public sector or providing a service to the public Impact of offence on others, particularly children Victim is particularly vulnerable (not all vulnerabilities are immediately apparent) Failure to comply with current court orders Offence committed on licence or post sentence supervision Offences taken into consideration

Factors reducing seriousness or reflecting personal mitigation
No previous convictions **or** no relevant/recent convictions Remorse Good character and/or exemplary conduct Serious medical condition requiring urgent, intensive or long-term treatment Age and/or lack of maturity Mental disorder or learning disability (where not taken into account at step one) Sole or primary carer for dependent relatives Determination and/or demonstration of steps having been taken to address offending behaviour

[35] **Where offence committed in a domestic context, also refer to the *Overarching principles: Domestic abuse* guideline**

[37] **STEP THREE Consider any factors which indicate a reduction, such as assistance to the prosecution** SG27-41

The court should take into account sections 73 and 74 of the Serious Organised Crime and Police Act 2005 (assistance by defendants: reduction or review of sentence) and any other rule of law by virtue of which an offender may receive a discounted sentence in consequence of assistance given (or offered) to the prosecutor or investigator.

STEP FOUR Reduction for guilty pleas SG27-42

The court should take account of any potential reduction for a guilty plea in accordance with section 144 of the Criminal Justice Act 2003 and the Guilty Plea guideline.

STEP FIVE Dangerousness SG27-43

The court should consider whether having regard to the criteria contained in Chapter 5 of Part 12 of the Criminal Justice Act 2003 it would be appropriate to impose an extended sentence (section 226A).

STEP SIX Totality principle SG27-44

If sentencing an offender for more than one offence, or where the offender is already serving a sentence, consider whether the total sentence is just and proportionate to the overall offending behaviour in accordance with the Offences Taken into Consideration and Totality guideline.

[38] **STEP SEVEN Compensation and ancillary orders** SG27-45

In all cases, the court must consider whether to make a compensation order and/or other ancillary orders.

Compensation order

The court should consider compensation orders in all cases where personal injury, loss or damage has resulted from the offence. The court must give reasons if it decides not to award compensation in such cases.

Other ancillary orders available include:

Restraining order

Where an offender is convicted of any offence, the court may make a restraining order (section 5 of the Protection from Harassment Act 1997).

The order may prohibit the offender from doing anything for the purpose of protecting the victim of the offence, or any other person mentioned in the order, from further conduct which amounts to harassment or will cause a fear of violence.

The order may have effect for a specified period or until further order.

STEP EIGHT Reasons SG27-46

Section 174 of the Criminal Justice Act 2003 imposes a duty to give reasons for, and explain the effect of, the sentence.

STEP NINE SG27-47

Consideration for time spent on bail (tagged curfew) The court must consider whether to give credit for time spent on bail in accordance with section 240A of the Criminal Justice Act 2003.

Where offence committed in a domestic context, also refer to the *Overarching principles: Domestic abuse* guideline

[40] ANNEX: FINE BANDS AND COMMUNITY ORDERS SG27-48

Fine Bands

In this guideline, fines are expressed as one of three fine bands (A, B, C).

Fine Band	**Starting point** (applicable to all offenders)	**Category range** (applicable to all offenders)
Band A	50% of relevant weekly income	25–75% of relevant weekly income
Band B	100% of relevant weekly income	75–125% of relevant weekly income
Band C	150% of relevant weekly income	125–175% of relevant weekly income

SG27-49 Community Orders [41]

In this guideline, community sentences are expressed as one of three levels (low, medium and high).

An illustrative description of examples of requirements that might be appropriate for each level is provided below. Where two or more requirements are ordered, they must be compatible with each other. Save in exceptional circumstances, the court must impose at least one requirement for the purpose of punishment, or combine the community order with a fine, or both (see section 177 Criminal Justice Act 2003).

Low	Medium	High
Offences only just cross community order threshold, where the seriousness of the offence or the nature of the offender's record means that a discharge or fine is inappropriate	Offences that obviously fall within the community order band	Offences only just fall below the custody threshold or the custody threshold is crossed but a community order is more appropriate in the circumstances
In general, only one requirement will be appropriate and the length may be curtailed if additional requirements are necessary		More intensive sentences which combine two or more requirements may be appropriate
Suitable requirements might include: • Any appropriate rehabilitative requirement(s) • 40–80 hours of unpaid work • Curfew requirement within the lowest range (for example up to 16 hours per day for a few weeks) • Exclusion requirement, for a few months • Prohibited activity requirement • Attendance centre requirement (where available)	Suitable requirements might include: • Any appropriate rehabilitative requirement(s) • Greater number of hours of unpaid work (for example 80–150 hours) • Curfew requirement within the middle range (for example up to 16 hours for 2–3 months) • Exclusion requirement lasting in the region of 6 months • Prohibited activity requirement	Suitable requirements might include: • Any appropriate rehabilitative requirement(s) • 150–300 hours of unpaid work • Curfew requirement within the middle range for 16 hours for 4–12 months • Exclusion order lasting in the region of 12 months
* If order does not contain a punitive requirement, suggested fine levels are indicated below:		
BAND A FINE	BAND B FINE	BAND C FINE

The Magistrates' Court Sentencing Guidelines includes further guidance on fines. The table above is also set out in the *Imposition of Community and Custodial Sentences* guideline which includes further guidance on community orders.

PART 28 CORPORATE MANSLAUGHTER

Definitive Guideline SG28-1

[This is an excerpt from the definitive guideline 'Health and Safety Offences, Corporate Manslaughter and Food Safety and Hygiene Offences'.]

Applicability of guidelines
[Omitted: See SG19-1 for identical text save that this guideline has effect from 1 February 2016.]

[21] Corporate Manslaughter SG28-2

Corporate Manslaughter and Corporate Homicide Act 2007 (section 1)

Triable only on indictment

Maximum: unlimited fine

Offence range: £180,000 fine–£20 million fine

[22] **STEP ONE Determining the seriousness of the offence** SG28-3

By definition, the **harm** and **culpability** involved in corporate manslaughter will be very serious. Every case will involve death and corporate fault at a high level. The court should assess factors affecting the seriousness of the offence within this context by asking:

(a) How foreseeable was serious injury?

Usually, the more foreseeable a serious injury was, the graver the offence. Failure to heed warnings or advice from the authorities, employees or others or to respond appropriately to 'near misses' arising in similar circumstances may be factors indicating greater foreseeability of serious injury.

[22] *(b) How far short of the appropriate standard did the offender fall?*

Where an offender falls far short of the appropriate standard, the level of culpability is likely to be high. Lack of adherence to recognised standards in the industry or the inadequacy of training, supervision and reporting arrangements may be relevant factors to consider.

(c) How common is this kind of breach in this organisation?

How widespread was the non-compliance? Was it isolated in extent or, for example, indicative of a systematic departure from good practice across the offender's operations or representative of systemic failings? Widespread non-compliance is likely to indicate a more serious offence.

(d) Was there more than one death, or a high risk of further deaths, or serious personal injury in addition to death?

The greater the number of deaths, very serious personal injuries or people put at high risk of death, the more serious the offence.

Offence Category A: Where answers to questions (a)–(d) indicate a high level of harm or culpability within the context of offence.

Offence Category B: Where answers to questions (a)–(d) indicate a lower level of culpability.

[23] **STEP TWO Starting point and category range** SG28-4

Having determined the offence category, the court should identify the relevant table for the offender [below]. There are tables for different sized organisations.

At step two, the court is required to focus on the organisation's annual turnover or equivalent to reach a starting point for a fine. The court should then consider further adjustment within the category range for aggravating and mitigating features.

At step three, the court may be required to refer to other financial factors listed below to ensure that the proposed fine is proportionate.

Obtaining financial information

The offender is expected to provide comprehensive accounts for the last three years, to enable the court to make an accurate assessment of its financial status. In the absence of such disclosure, or where the court is not satisfied that it has been given sufficient reliable information, the court will be entitled to draw reasonable inferences as to the offender's means from evidence it has heard and from all the circumstances of the case, **which may include the inference that the offender can pay any fine**. [23]

Normally, only information relating to the organisation before the court will be relevant, unless it is demonstrated to the court that the resources of a linked organisation are available and can properly be taken into account.

1. *For companies*: annual accounts. Particular attention should be paid to turnover; profit before tax; directors' remuneration, loan accounts and pension provision; and assets as disclosed by the balance sheet. Most companies are required to file audited accounts at Companies House. **Failure to produce relevant recent accounts on request may properly lead to the conclusion that the company can pay any appropriate fine.**
2. *For partnerships*: annual accounts. Particular attention should be paid to turnover; profit before tax; partners' drawings, loan accounts and pension provision; assets as above. Limited liability partnerships (LLPs) may be required to file audited accounts with Companies House. **If adequate accounts are not produced on request, see paragraph 1.**
3. *For local authorities, fire authorities and similar public bodies*: the Annual Revenue Budget ('ARB') is the equivalent of turnover and the best indication of the size of the organisation. It is unlikely to be necessary to analyse specific expenditure or reserves (where relevant) unless inappropriate expenditure is suggested.
4. *For health trusts*: the independent regulator of NHS Foundation Trusts is Monitor. It publishes quarterly reports and annual figures for the financial strength and stability of trusts from which the annual income can be seen, available via **www.monitor-nhsft.gov.uk**. Detailed analysis of expenditure or reserves is unlikely to be called for.
5. *For charities*: it will be appropriate to inspect annual audited accounts. Detailed analysis of expenditure or reserves is unlikely to be called for unless there is a suggestion of unusual or unnecessary expenditure.

Very large organisation [24]
Where an offending organisation's turnover or equivalent very greatly exceeds the threshold for large organisations, it may be necessary to move outside the suggested range to achieve a proportionate sentence.

Large organisation — Turnover more than £50 million

Offence category	Starting point	Category range
A	£7,500,000	£4,800,000 — £20,000,000
B	£5,000,000	£3,000,000 — £12,500,000

Medium organisation — Turnover £10 million to £50 million

Offence category	Starting point	Category range
A	£3,000,000	£1,800,000 — £7,500,000
B	£2,000,000	£1,200,000 — £5,000,000

Small organisation — Turnover £10 million to £50 million

Offence category	Starting point	Category range
A	£800,000	£540,000 — £2,800,000
B	£540,000	£350,000 — £2,000,000

Micro organisation — Turnover up to £2 million

Offence category	Starting point	Category range
A	£450,000	£270,000 — £800,000
B	£300,000	£180,000 — £540,000

[25] The table below contains a **non-exhaustive** list of factual elements providing the context of the offence and factors relating to the offender. Identify whether any combination of these, or other relevant factors, should result in an upward or downward adjustment from the starting point.

Factors increasing seriousness	Factors reducing seriousness or reflecting mitigation
Statutory aggravating factor: Previous convictions, having regard to a) the nature of the offence to which the conviction relates and its relevance to the current offence; and b) the time that has elapsed since the conviction *Other aggravating factors include*: Cost-cutting at the expense of safety Deliberate concealment of illegal nature of activity Breach of any court order Obstruction of justice Poor health and safety record Falsification of documentation or licences Deliberate failure to obtain or comply with relevant licences in order to avoid scrutiny by authorities Offender exploited vulnerable victims	No previous convictions or no relevant/recent convictions Evidence of steps taken to remedy problem High level of co-operation with the investigation, beyond that which will always be expected Good health and safety record Effective health and safety procedures in place Self-reporting, co-operation and acceptance of responsibility Other events beyond the responsibility of the offender contributed to the death (**however**, actions of victims are unlikely to be considered contributory events. Offenders are required to protect workers or others who are neglectful of their own safety in a way which is reasonably foreseeable)

STEPS THREE AND FOUR SG28-5

The court should 'step back', review and, if necessary, adjust the initial fine based on turnover to **ensure that it fulfils the objectives of sentencing** for these offences. The court may adjust the fine upwards or downwards, including outside the range.

STEP THREE **Check whether the proposed fine based on turnover is proportionate to the overall means of the offender** SG28-6

General principles to follow in setting a fine

The court should finalise the appropriate level of fine in accordance with section 164 of the Criminal Justice Act 2003, which requires that the fine must reflect the seriousness of the offence and requires the court to take into account the financial circumstances of the offender.

Fines cannot and do not attempt to value a human life in money. The fine should meet the objectives of punishment, the reduction of offending through deterrence and removal of gain derived through the commission of the offence. The fine **must be sufficiently substantial to have a real economic impact which will bring home to management and shareholders the need to achieve a safe environment for workers and members of the public affected by their activities.**

[26] *Review of the fine based on turnover*

The court should 'step back', review and, if necessary, adjust the initial fine reached at step two to **ensure that it fulfils the general principles** set out above. The court may adjust the fine upwards or downwards including outside of the range.

The court should examine the financial circumstances of the offender in the round to assess the economic realities of the organisation and the most efficacious way of giving effect to the purposes of sentencing.

In finalising the sentence, the court should have regard to the following factors:

- The profitability of an organisation will be a relevant factor. If an organisation has a small profit margin relative to its turnover, downward adjustment may be needed. If it has a large profit margin, upward adjustment may be needed.
- Any quantifiable economic benefit derived from the offence, including through avoided costs or operating savings, should normally be added to the fine arrived at in step two. Where this is not readily available, the court may draw on information available from enforcing authorities and others about general costs of operating within the law.
- Whether the fine will have the effect of putting the offender out of business will be relevant; in some cases this may be an acceptable consequence.

In considering the ability of the offending organisation to pay any financial penalty, the court can take into account the **power to allow time for payment or to order that the amount be paid in instalments**, if necessary over a number of years. [26]

SG28-7 STEP FOUR **Consider other factors that may warrant adjustment of the proposed fine**

The court should consider any wider impacts of the fine within the organisation or on innocent third parties; such as (but not limited to):

- impact of the fine on offender's ability to improve conditions in the organisation to comply with the law;
- impact of the fine on employment of staff, service users, customers and local economy (but not shareholders or directors).

Where the fine will fall on public or charitable bodies, the fine should normally be substantially reduced if the offending organisation is able to demonstrate the proposed fine would have a significant impact on the provision of their services.

SG28-8 STEP FIVE **Consider any factors which indicate a reduction, such as assistance to the prosecution** [27]

The court should take into account sections 73 and 74 of the Serious Organised Crime and Police Act 2005 (assistance by defendants: reduction or review of sentence) and any other rule of law by virtue of which an offender may receive a discounted sentence in consequence of assistance given (or offered) to the prosecutor or investigator.

SG28-9 STEP SIX **Reduction for guilty pleas**

The court should take account of any potential reduction for a guilty plea in accordance with section 144 of the Criminal Justice Act 2003 and the *Guilty Plea* guideline.

SG28-10 STEP SEVEN **Compensation and ancillary orders**

In all cases, the court must consider whether to make ancillary orders. These may include:

Publicity Orders

(Section 10 Corporate Manslaughter and Corporate Homicide Act 2007)

A publicity order should ordinarily be imposed in a case of corporate manslaughter. It may require publication in a specified manner of:

a) the fact of conviction;
b) specified particulars of the offence;
c) the amount of any fine;
d) the terms of any remedial order.

The object of a publicity order is deterrence and punishment.

(i) The order should specify with particularity the matters to be published in accordance with section 10(1). Special care should be taken with the terms of the particulars of the offence committed.
(ii) The order should normally specify the place where public announcement is to be made, and consideration should be given to indicating the size of any notice or advertisement required. It should ordinarily contain a provision designed to ensure that the conviction becomes known to shareholders in the case of companies and local people in the case of public bodies. Consideration should be given to requiring a statement on the offender's website. A newspaper announcement may be unnecessary if the proceedings are certain to receive news coverage in any event, but if an order requires publication in a newspaper it should specify the paper, the form of announcement to be made and the number of insertions required.
(iii) The prosecution should provide the court in advance of the sentencing hearing, and should serve on the offender, a draft of the form of order suggested and the judge should personally endorse the final form of the order.
(iv) Consideration should be given to stipulating in the order that any comment placed by the offender alongside the required announcement should be separated from it and clearly identified as such.

A publicity order is part of the penalty. Any exceptional cost of compliance should be considered in fixing the fine. It is not, however, necessary to fix the fine first and then deduct the cost of compliance.

[28] *Remediation*

(Section 9 Corporate Manslaughter and Corporate Homicide Act 2007)

An offender ought by the time of sentencing to have remedied any specific failings involved in the offence and if it has not, will be deprived of significant mitigation.

If, however, it has not, a remedial order should be considered if it can be made sufficiently specific to be enforceable. The prosecution is required by section 9(2) Corporate Manslaughter and Corporate Homicide Act 2007 to give notice of the form of any such order sought, which can only be made on its application. The judge should personally endorse the final form of such an order.

The cost of compliance with such an order should not ordinarily be taken into account in fixing the fine; the order requires only what should already have been done.

Compensation

Where the offence has resulted in loss or damage, the court must consider whether to make a compensation order. The assessment of compensation in cases involving death or serious injury will usually be complex and will ordinarily be covered by insurance. In the great majority of cases the court should conclude that compensation should be dealt with in the civil courts, and should say that no order is made for that reason.

If compensation is awarded, priority should be given to the payment of compensation over payment of any other financial penalty where the means of the offender are limited.

Where the offender does not have sufficient means to pay the total financial penalty considered appropriate by the court, compensation and fine take priority over prosecution costs.

STEP EIGHT **Totality principle** **SG28-11**

If sentencing an offender for more than one offence, consider whether the total sentence is just and proportionate to the offending behaviour in accordance with the *Offences Taken Into Consideration* and *Totality* guideline.

STEP NINE **Reasons** **SG28-12**

Section 174 of the Criminal Justice Act 2003 imposes a duty to give reasons for, and explain the effect of, the sentence.

PART 29 MANSLAUGHTER BY REASON OF PROVOCATION

SG29-1 **Replaced by Manslaughter Definitive Guideline, see SG-25-1.**

PART 30 ROBBERY

Definitive Guideline SG30-1

[2] **Applicability of Guideline**

... [This guideline] applies to all offenders aged 18 and older, who are sentenced on or after 1 April 2016, regardless of the date of the offence.

[This definitive guideline was issued by the Sentencing Council in 2016. For the guideline for young people sentenced on or after 1 June 2017, see **SG8-12**.]

...

Structure, ranges and starting points SG30-2

For the purposes of section 125(3)–(4) of the Coroners and Justice Act 2009, the guideline specifies *offence ranges* – the range of sentences appropriate for each type of offence. Within each offence, the Council has specified a number of *categories* which reflect varying degrees of seriousness. The offence range is split into *category ranges* – sentences appropriate for each level of seriousness. The Council has also identified a starting point within each category.

Starting points define the position within a category range from which to start calculating the provisional sentence. The court should consider further features of the offence or the offender that warrant adjustment of the sentence within the range, including the aggravating and mitigating factors set out at step two. Starting points and ranges apply to all offenders, whether they have pleaded guilty or been convicted after trial. Credit for a guilty plea is taken into consideration only at step four in the decision making process, after the appropriate sentence has been identified.

[3] Robbery – street and less sophisticated commercial SG30-3

Theft Act 1968 (section 8(1))

This is a serious specified offence for the purposes of section 224 of the Criminal Justice Act 2003.

Triable only on indictment
Maximum: Life imprisonment

Offence range: Community order–12 years' custody

This guideline applies only to offenders aged 18 and older.

Street/less sophisticated commercial robbery refers to robberies committed in public places, including those committed in taxis or on public transport. It also refers to unsophisticated robberies within commercial premises or targeting commercial goods or money.

There is relevant guidance for sentencing young offenders within the *Sentencing Children and Young People: Overarching Principles and Offence Specific Guidelines for Sexual Offences and Robbery* guideline at SG8-1 *et seq* and particularly SG8-12 *et seq*.

[4] **STEP ONE Determining the offence category** SG30-4

The court should determine the offence category with reference **only** to the factors listed in the tables below. In order to determine the category the court should assess **culpability and harm.**

The court should weigh all the factors set out below in determining the offender's culpability.

Where there are characteristics present which fall under different levels of culpability, the court should balance these characteristics to reach a fair assessment of the offender's culpability.

Culpability demonstrated by one or more of the following:		[4]
A – High culpability	• Use of a weapon to inflict violence • Production of a bladed article or firearm or imitation firearm to threaten violence • Use of very significant force in the commission of the offence • Offence motivated by, or demonstrating hostility based on any of the following characteristics or presumed characteristics of the victim: religion, race, disability, sexual orientation or transgender identity	
B – Medium Culpability	• Production of a weapon other than a bladed article or firearm or imitation firearm to threaten violence • Threat of violence by any weapon (but which is not produced) • Other cases that fall between categories A or C because: – Factors are present in A and C which balance each other out **and/or** – The offender's culpability falls between the factors as described in A and C	
C – Lesser culpability	• Involved through coercion, intimidation or exploitation • Threat or use of minimal force • Mental disability or learning disability where linked to the commission of the offence	

Harm The court should consider the factors set out below to determine the level of harm that has been caused or was intended to be caused to the victim.	
Category 1	• Serious physical and/or psychological harm caused to the victim • Serious detrimental effect on the business
Category 2	• Other cases where characteristics for categories 1 or 3 are not present
Category 3	• No/minimal physical or psychological harm caused to the victim • No/minimal detrimental effect on the business

SG30-5

STEP TWO Starting point and category range [5]

Having determined the category at step one, the court should use the corresponding starting point to reach a sentence within the category range below. The starting point applies to all offenders irrespective of plea or previous convictions. A case of particular gravity, reflected by multiple features of culpability or harm in step one, could merit upward adjustment from the starting point before further adjustment for aggravating or mitigating features, set out [below].

Consecutive sentences for multiple offences may be appropriate – please refer to the *Offences Taken into Consideration* and *Totality* guideline [see SG3-1 and SG3-7].

	Culpability		
Harm	**A**	**B**	**C**
Category 1	**Starting point** 8 years' custody	**Starting point** 5 years' custody	**Starting point** 4 years' custody
	Category range 7–12 years' custody	**Category range** 4–8 years' custody	**Category range** 3–6 years' custody
Category 2	**Starting point** 5 years' custody	**Starting point** 4 years' custody	**Starting point** 2 years' custody
	Category range 4–8 years' custody	**Category range** 3–6 years' custody	**Category range** 1–4 years' custody
Category 3	**Starting point** 4 years' custody	**Starting point** 2 years' custody	**Starting point** 1 year's custody
	Category range 3–6 years' custody	**Category range** 1–4 years' custody	**Category range** High level community order–3 years' custody

The table [below] contains a **non-exhaustive** list of additional factual elements providing the context of the offence and factors relating to the offender. Identify whether any combination of these, or other relevant factors, should result in an upward or downward adjustment from the sentence arrived at so far. In particular, relevant recent convictions are likely to result in an upward adjustment. In some cases, having considered these factors, it may be appropriate to move outside the identified category range.

[6]

Factors increasing seriousness

Statutory aggravating factors

- Previous convictions, having regard to a) the **nature** of the offence to which the conviction relates and its **relevance** to the current offence; and b) the **time** that has elapsed since the conviction
- Offence committed whilst on bail

Other aggravating factors

- High value goods or sums targeted or obtained (whether economic, personal or sentimental)
- Victim is targeted due to a vulnerability (or a perceived vulnerability)
- Significant planning
- Steps taken to prevent the victim reporting or obtaining assistance and/or from assisting or supporting the prosecution
- Prolonged nature of event
- Restraint, detention or additional degradation of the victim
- A leading role where offending is part of a group activity
- Involvement of others through coercion, intimidation or exploitation
- Location of the offence (including cases where the location of the offence is the victim's residence)
- Timing of the offence
- Attempt to conceal identity (for example, wearing a balaclava or hood)
- Commission of offence whilst under the influence of alcohol or drugs
- Attempts to conceal/dispose of evidence
- Established evidence of community/wider impact
- Failure to comply with current court orders
- Offence committed on licence
- Offences taken into consideration
- Failure to respond to warnings about behaviour

Factors reducing seriousness or reflecting personal mitigation

- No previous convictions or no relevant/recent convictions
- Remorse, particularly where evidenced by voluntary reparation to the victim
- Good character and/or exemplary conduct
- Serious medical condition requiring urgent, intensive or long-term treatment
- Age and/or lack of maturity where it affects the responsibility of the offender
- Mental disorder or learning disability (where not linked to the commission of the offence)
- Little or no planning
- Sole or primary carer for dependent relatives
- Determination and/or demonstration of steps having been taken to address addiction or offending behaviour

[7] **STEP THREE Consider any factors which indicate a reduction for assistance to the prosecution** SG30-6

The court should take into account sections 73 and 74 of the Serious Organised Crime and Police Act 2005 (assistance by defendants: reduction or review of sentence) and any other rule of law by virtue of which an offender may receive a discounted sentence in consequence of assistance given (or offered) to the prosecutor or investigator.

STEP FOUR Reduction for guilty pleas SG30-7

The court should take account of any potential reduction for a guilty plea in accordance with section 144 of the Criminal Justice Act 2003 and the *Guilty Plea* guideline [see SG4-1].

STEP FIVE Dangerousness SG30-8

The court should consider whether having regard to the criteria contained in Chapter 5 of Part 12 of the Criminal Justice Act 2003 it would be appropriate to impose a life sentence (section 224A or section 225) or an extended sentence (section 226A). When sentencing offenders to a life sentence under these provisions, the notional determinate sentence should be used as the basis for the setting of a minimum term.

STEP SIX Totality principle SG30-9

If sentencing an offender for more than one offence, or where the offender is already serving a sentence, consider whether the total sentence is just and proportionate to the overall offending behaviour in accordance with the *Offences Taken into Consideration* and *Totality* guideline [see SG3-1 and SG3-7].

SG30-10 **STEP SEVEN Compensation and ancillary orders** [7]

In all cases the court should consider whether to make compensation and/or other ancillary orders.

Where the offence involves a firearm, an imitation firearm or an offensive weapon the court may consider the criteria in section 19 of the Serious Crime Act 2007 for the imposition of a Serious Crime Prevention Order.

SG30-11 **STEP EIGHT Reasons**

Section 174 of the Criminal Justice Act 2003 imposes a duty to give reasons for, and explain the effect of, the sentence.

SG30-12 **STEP NINE Consideration for time spent on bail**

The court must consider whether to give credit for time spent on bail in accordance with section 240A of the Criminal Justice Act 2003.

SG30-13

Robbery – professionally planned commercial [9]

Theft Act 1968 (section 8(1))

This is a serious specified offence for the purposes of section 224 of the Criminal Justice Act 2003.

Triable only on indictment
Maximum: Life imprisonment

Offence range: 18 months'–20 years' custody

This guideline applies only to offenders aged 18 and older.

Professionally planned commercial robbery refers to robberies involving a significant degree of planning, sophistication or organisation.

SG30-14 **STEP ONE Determining the offence category** [10]

The court should determine the offence category with reference **only** to the factors listed in the tables below. In order to determine the category the court should assess **culpability** and **harm.**

The court should weigh all the factors set out below in determining the offender's culpability.

Where there are characteristics present which fall under different levels of culpability, the court should balance these characteristics to reach a fair assessment of the offender's culpability.

Culpability demonstrated by one or more of the following:	
A – High culpability	• Use of a weapon to inflict violence • Production of a bladed article or firearm or imitation firearm to threaten violence • Use of very significant force in the commission of the offence • A leading role where offending is part of a group activity • Offence motivated by, or demonstrating hostility based on any of the following characteristics or presumed characteristics of the victim: religion, race, disability, sexual orientation or transgender identity • Abuse of position
B – Medium culpability	• Production of a weapon other than a bladed article or firearm or imitation firearm to threaten violence • Threat of violence by any weapon (but which is not produced) • A significant role where offending is part of a group activity • Other cases that fall between categories A or C because: – Factors are present in A and C which balance each other out **and/or** – The offender's culpability falls between the factors as described in A and C
C – Lesser culpability	• Performed limited function under direction • Involved through coercion, intimidation or exploitation • Threat or use of minimal force • Mental disability or learning disability where linked to the commission of the offence

[10]

Harm	
The level of **harm** is determined by weighing up all the factors of the case to determine the harm that has been caused or was intended to be caused to the victim. The victim relates both to the commercial organisation that has been robbed and any individual(s) who has suffered the use or threat of force during the commission of the offence.	
Category 1	• Serious physical and/or psychological harm caused to the victim • Serious detrimental effect on the business • Very high value goods or sums targeted or obtained (whether economic, personal or sentimental)
Category 2	• Other cases where characteristics for categories 1 or 3 are not present
Category 3	• No/minimal physical or psychological harm caused to the victim • No/minimal detrimental effect on the business • Low value goods or sums targeted or obtained (whether economic, personal or sentimental)

[11] **STEP TWO Starting point and category range** **SG30-15**

Having determined the category at step one, the court should use the corresponding starting point to reach a sentence within the category range below. The starting point applies to all offenders irrespective of plea or previous convictions. A case of particular gravity, reflected by multiple features of high culpability or harm in step one, could merit upward adjustment from the starting point before further adjustment for aggravating or mitigating features, set out [below].

Consecutive sentences for multiple offences may be appropriate particularly where exceptionally high levels of harm have been caused, please refer to the *Offences Taken into Consideration* and *Totality* guideline [see SG3-1 and SG3-7].

Where multiple offences or a single conspiracy to commit multiple offences of particular severity have taken place sentences in excess of 20 years may be appropriate.

Culpability			
Harm	**A**	**B**	**C**
Category 1	**Starting point** 16 years' custody **Category range** 12–20 years' custody	**Starting point** 9 years' custody **Category range** 7–14 years' custody	**Starting point** 5 years' custody **Category range** 4–8 years' custody
Category 2	**Starting point** 9 years' custody **Category range** 7–14 years' custody	**Starting point** 5 years' custody **Category range** 4–8 years' custody	**Starting point** 3 years' custody **Category range** 2–5 years' custody
Category 3	**Starting point** 5 years' custody **Category range** 4–8 years' custody	**Starting point** 3 years' custody **Category range** 2–5 years' custody	**Starting point** 2 years' custody **Category range** 18 months'–4 years' custody

The table [below] contains a **non-exhaustive** list of additional factual elements providing the context of the offence and factors relating to the offender. Identify whether any combination of these, or other relevant factors, should result in an upward or downward adjustment from the sentence arrived at so far. In particular, relevant recent convictions are likely to result in an upward adjustment. In some cases, having considered these factors, it may be appropriate to move outside the identified category range.

Factors increasing seriousness
Statutory aggravating factors • Previous convictions, having regard to a) the **nature** of the offence to which the conviction relates and its **relevance** to the current offence; and b) the **time** that has elapsed since the conviction • Offence committed whilst on bail *Other aggravating factors* • Victim is targeted due to a vulnerability (or a perceived vulnerability) • Steps taken to prevent the victim reporting or obtaining assistance and/or from assisting or supporting the prosecution • Prolonged nature of attack • Restraint, detention or additional degradation of the victim • Involvement of others through coercion, intimidation or exploitation • Location of the offence (including cases where the location of the offence is the victim's residence) • Timing of the offence • Attempt to conceal identity (for example, wearing a balaclava or hood) • Commission of offence whilst under the influence of alcohol or drugs • Attempts to conceal/dispose of evidence • Established evidence of community/wider impact • Failure to comply with current court orders • Offence committed on licence • Offences taken into consideration • Failure to respond to warnings about behaviour

[12]

Factors reducing seriousness or reflecting personal mitigation
• No previous convictions **or** no relevant/recent convictions • Remorse, particularly where evidenced by voluntary reparation to the victim • Good character and/or exemplary conduct • Serious medical condition requiring urgent, intensive or long-term treatment • Age and/or lack of maturity where it affects the responsibility of the offender • Mental disorder or learning disability (where not linked to the commission of the offence) • Sole or primary carer for dependent relatives • Determination and/or demonstration of steps having been taken to address addiction or offending behaviour

SG30-16 STEPS THREE TO NINE [13]

[These are identical to those that apply in respect of street and less sophisticated commercial robbery: see SG30-6.]

SG30-17 ROBBERY – DWELLING [15]

Theft Act 1968 (section 8(1))

This is a serious specified offence for the purposes of section 224 of the Criminal Justice Act 2003.

Triable only on indictment
Maximum: Life imprisonment
Offence range: 1 year's custody–16 years' custody

This guideline applies only to offenders aged 18 and older.

SG30-18 STEP ONE **Determining the offence category** [16]

The court should determine the offence category with reference **only** to the factors listed in the tables below. In order to determine the category the court should assess **culpability** and **harm.**

The court should weigh all the factors set out below in determining the offender's culpability.

Where there are characteristics present which fall under different levels of culpability, the court should balance these characteristics to reach a fair assessment of the offender's culpability.

[16]

Culpability demonstrated by one or more of the following:	
A – High culpability	• Use of a weapon to inflict violence • Production of a bladed article or firearm or imitation firearm to threaten violence • Use of very significant force in the commission of the offence • Sophisticated organised nature of offence • A leading role where offending is part of a group activity • Offence motivated by, or demonstrating hostility based on any of the following characteristics or presumed characteristics of the victim: religion, race, disability, sexual orientation or transgender identity • Abuse of position
B – Medium culpability	• Production of a weapon other than a bladed article or firearm or imitation firearm to threaten violence • Threat of violence by any weapon (but which is not produced) • A significant role where offending is part of a group activity • Other cases that fall between categories A or C because: – Factors are present in A and C which balance each other out **and/or** – The offender's culpability falls between the factors as described in A and C
C – Lesser culpability	• Performed limited function under direction • Involved through coercion, intimidation or exploitation • Threat or use of minimal force • Very little or no planning • Mental disability or learning disability where linked to the commission of the offence

Harm The court should weigh up all the factors set out below to determine the harm that has been caused or was intended to be caused to the victim.	
Category 1	• Serious physical and/or psychological harm caused to the victim • Very high value goods or sums targeted or obtained (whether economic, sentimental or personal) • Soiling, ransacking or vandalism of property
Category 2	• Other cases where characteristics for categories 1 or 3 are not present
Category 3	• No/minimal physical or psychological harm caused to the victim • Low value goods or sums targeted or obtained (whether economic, personal or sentimental) • Limited damage or disturbance to property

SG30-19

[17] **STEP TWO Starting point and category range**

Having determined the category at step one, the court should use the corresponding starting point to reach a sentence within the category range below. The starting point applies to all offenders irrespective of plea or previous convictions. A case of particular gravity, reflected by multiple features of culpability or harm in step one, could merit upward adjustment from the starting point before further adjustment for aggravating or mitigating features, set out [below].

Consecutive sentences for multiple offences may be appropriate particularly where exceptionally high levels of harm have been caused – please refer to the *Offences Taken into Consideration* and *Totality* guideline [see SG3-1 and SG3-7].

In a case of particular gravity, reflected by extremely serious violence, a sentence in excess of 13 years may be appropriate.

	Culpability		
Harm	**A**	**B**	**C**
Category 1	**Starting point** 13 years' custody **Category range** 10–16 years' custody	**Starting point** 8 years' custody **Category range** 6–10 years' custody	**Starting point** 5 years' custody **Category range** 4–8 years' custody
Category 2	**Starting point** 8 years' custody **Category range** 6–10 years' custody	**Starting point** 5 years' custody **Category range** 4–8 years' custody	**Starting point** 3 years' custody **Category range** 2–5 years' custody

Category 3	**Starting point** 5 years' custody **Category range** 4–8 years' custody	**Starting point** 3 years' custody **Category range** 2–5 years' custody	**Starting point** 18 months' custody **Category range** 1–3 years' custody

The table [below] contains a **non-exhaustive** list of additional factual elements providing the context of the offence and factors relating to the offender. Identify whether any combination of these, or other relevant factors, should result in an upward or downward adjustment from the sentence arrived at so far. In particular, relevant recent convictions are likely to result in an upward adjustment. In some cases, having considered these factors, it may be appropriate to move outside the identified category range.

[18]

Factors increasing seriousness
Statutory aggravating factors • Previous convictions, having regard to a) the nature of the offence to which the conviction relates and its **relevance** to the current offence; and b) the **time** that has elapsed since the conviction • Offence committed whilst on bail *Other aggravating factors* • Victim is targeted due to a vulnerability (or a perceived vulnerability) • Steps taken to prevent the victim reporting or obtaining assistance and/or from assisting or supporting the prosecution • Prolonged nature of event • Restraint, detention or additional degradation of the victim • Involvement of others through coercion, intimidation or exploitation • Timing of the offence • Attempt to conceal identity (for example, wearing a balaclava or hood) • Commission of offence whilst under the influence of alcohol or drugs • Attempts to conceal/dispose of evidence • Child or vulnerable person at home (or returns home) when offence committed • Victim compelled to leave their home • Established evidence of community/wider impact • Failure to comply with current court orders • Offence committed on licence • Offences taken into consideration • Failure to respond to warnings about behaviour

SG30-20

Factors reducing seriousness or reflecting personal mitigation
• No previous convictions or no relevant/recent convictions • Remorse, particularly where evidenced by voluntary reparation to the victim • Good character and/or exemplary conduct • Serious medical condition requiring urgent, intensive or long-term treatment • Age and/or lack of maturity where it affects the responsibility of the offender • Mental disorder or learning disability (where not linked to the commission of the offence) • Sole or primary carer for dependent relatives • Determination and/or demonstration of steps having been taken to address addiction or offending behaviour

STEPS THREE TO NINE

[These are identical to those that apply in respect of street and less sophisticated commercial robbery: see SG30-6.]

PART 31 SEXUAL OFFENCES

[7] DEFINITIVE GUIDELINE SG31-1

Applicability of guideline

In accordance with section 120 of the Coroners and Justice Act 2009, the Sentencing Council issues this definitive guideline. It applies to all offenders aged 18 and older, who are sentenced on or after 1 April 2014.

. . .

This guideline applies only to offenders aged 18 and older. There is relevant guidance for sentencing young offenders within the *Overarching Principles and Offence Specific Guidelines for Sexual Offences and Robbery* guideline at **SG8-1** ***et seq*** and particularly **SG8-11** ***et seq.***

Structure, ranges and starting points SG31-2

For the purposes of section 125(3)–(4) of the Coroners and Justice Act 2009, the guideline specifies *offence ranges*—the range of sentences appropriate for each type of offence. Within each offence, the Council has specified different *categories* which reflect varying degrees of seriousness. The offence range is split into *category ranges*—sentences appropriate for each level of seriousness. The Council has also identified a starting point within each category.

Starting points define the position within a category range from which to start calculating the provisional sentence. **Starting points apply to all offences within the corresponding category and are applicable to all offenders, in all cases.** Once the starting point is established, the court should consider further aggravating and mitigating factors and previous convictions so as to adjust the sentence within the range. Starting points and ranges apply to all offenders, whether they have pleaded guilty or been convicted after trial. Credit for a guilty plea is taken into consideration only at step four in the decision making process, after the appropriate sentence has been identified.

Information on ancillary orders is set out at Annex A [see **SG31-156**]. Information on historic offences is set out at annexes B and C on [see **SG31-157** and **SG31-158**].

Information on community orders and fine bands is set out at Annex D [not reproduced here but see **SG10-129** and **SG9-2**].

[9] RAPE SG31-3

Sexual Offences Act 2003 (section 1)

[For rape of a child under 13, see **SG31-28**.]

Triable only on indictment

Maximum: Life imprisonment
Offence range: 4–19 years' custody

This is a serious specified offence for the purposes of sections 224 and 225(2) (life sentence for serious offences) of the Criminal Justice Act 2003.

For offences committed on or after 3 December 2012, this is an offence listed in Part 1 of Schedule 15B for the purposes of sections 224A (life sentence for second listed offence) of the Criminal Justice Act 2003.

For convictions on or after 3 December 2012 (irrespective of the date of commission of the offence), this is a specified offence for the purposes of section 226A (extended sentence for certain violent or sexual offences) of the Criminal Justice Act 2003.

[10] **STEP ONE Determining the offence category** SG31-4

The court should determine which categories of harm and culpability the offence falls into by reference **only** to the tables below.

Offences may be of such severity, for example involving a campaign of rape, that sentences of 20 years and above may be appropriate.

Sentencing Guidelines

Harm		[10]
Category 1	• The extreme nature of one or more category 2 factors or the extreme impact caused by a combination of category 2 factors may elevate to category 1	
Category 2	• Severe psychological or physical harm • Pregnancy or STI as a consequence of offence • Additional degradation/humiliation • Abduction • Prolonged detention/sustained incident • Violence or threats of violence (beyond that which is inherent in the offence) • Forced/uninvited entry into victim's home • Victim is particularly vulnerable due to personal circumstances*	
Category 3	Factor(s) in categories 1 and 2 not present	

* For children under 13 please refer to the guideline [at SG31-28].

Culpability	
A	B
• Significant degree of planning • Offender acts together with others to commit the offence • Use of alcohol/drugs on victim to facilitate the offence • Abuse of trust • Previous violence against victim • Offence committed in course of burglary • Recording of the offence • Commercial exploitation and/or motivation • Offence racially or religiously aggravated • Offence motivated by, or demonstrating, hostility to the victim based on his or her sexual orientation (or presumed sexual orientation) or transgender identity (or presumed transgender identity) • Offence motivated by, or demonstrating, hostility to the victim based on his or her disability (or presumed disability)	Factor(s) in category A not present

SG31-5 **STEP TWO Starting point and category range**

Having determined the category, the court should use the corresponding starting points to reach a sentence within the category range below. The starting point applies to all offenders irrespective of plea or previous convictions. Having determined the starting point, step two allows further adjustment for aggravating or mitigating features set out below.

A case of particular gravity, reflected by multiple features of culpability or harm in step one, could merit upward adjustment from the starting point before further adjustment for aggravating or mitigating features, set out below.

	A	B	[11]
Category 1	**Starting point** 15 years' custody **Category range** 13–19 years' custody	**Starting point** 12 years' custody **Category range** 10–15 years' custody	
Category 2	**Starting point** 10 years' custody **Category range** 9–13 years' custody	**Starting point** 8 years' custody **Category range** 7–9 years' custody	
Category 3	**Starting point** 7 years' custody **Category range** 6–9 years' custody	**Starting point** 5 years' custody **Category range** 4–7 years' custody	

[11] The table below contains a **non-exhaustive** list of additional factual elements providing the context of the offence and factors relating to the offender. Identify whether any combination of these, or other relevant factors, should result in an upward or downward adjustment from the starting point. **In particular, relevant recent convictions are likely to result in an upward adjustment.** In some cases, having considered these factors, it may be appropriate to move outside the identified category range.

Aggravating factors
Statutory aggravating factors • Previous convictions, having regard to a) the nature of the offence to which the conviction relates and its relevance to the current offence; and b) the time that has elapsed since the conviction • Offence committed whilst on bail
Other aggravating factors • Specific targeting of a particularly vulnerable victim • Ejaculation (where not taken into account at step one) • Blackmail or other threats made (where not taken into account at step one) • Location of offence • Timing of offence • Use of weapon or other item to frighten or injure • Victim compelled to leave their home (including victims of domestic violence) • Failure to comply with current court orders • Offence committed whilst on licence • Exploiting contact arrangements with a child to commit an offence • Presence of others, especially children • Any steps taken to prevent the victim reporting an incident, obtaining assistance and/or from assisting or supporting the prosecution • Attempts to dispose of or conceal evidence • Commission of offence whilst under the influence of alcohol or drugs

Mitigating factors
• No previous convictions **or** no relevant/recent convictions • Remorse • Previous good character and/or exemplary conduct* • Age and/or lack of maturity where it affects the responsibility of the offender • Mental disorder or learning disability, particularly where linked to the commission of the offence

* Previous good character/exemplary conduct is different from having no previous convictions. The more serious the offence, the less the weight which should normally be attributed to this factor. Where previous good character/exemplary conduct has been used to facilitate the offence, this mitigation should not normally be allowed and such conduct may constitute an aggravating factor.

In the context of this offence, previous good character/exemplary conduct should not normally be given any significant weight and will not normally justify a reduction in what would otherwise be the appropriate sentence.

[12] **STEP THREE Consider any factors which indicate a reduction, such as assistance to the prosecution** **SG31-6**

The court should take into account sections 73 and 74 of the Serious Organised Crime and Police Act 2005 (assistance by defendants: reduction or review of sentence) and any other rule of law by virtue of which an offender may receive a discounted sentence in consequence of assistance given (or offered) to the prosecutor or investigator.

STEP FOUR Reduction for guilty pleas **SG31-7**

The court should take account of any potential reduction for a guilty plea in accordance with section 144 of the Criminal Justice Act 2003 and the *Guilty Plea* guideline.

SG31-8 **STEP FIVE Dangerousness** [12]

The court should consider whether having regard to the criteria contained in Chapter 5 of Part 12 of the Criminal Justice Act 2003 it would be appropriate to award a life sentence (section 224A or section 225(2)) or an extended sentence (section 226A). When sentencing offenders to a life sentence under these provisions, the notional determinate sentence should be used as the basis for the setting of a minimum term.

SG31-9 **STEP SIX Totality principle**

If sentencing an offender for more than one offence, or where the offender is already serving a sentence, consider whether the total sentence is just and proportionate to the offending behaviour.

SG31-10 **STEP SEVEN Ancillary orders**

The court must consider whether to make any ancillary orders. The court must also consider what other requirements or provisions may *automatically* apply. Further information is included at Annex A [see **SG31-156**].

SG31-11 **STEP EIGHT Reasons**

Section 174 of the Criminal Justice Act 2003 imposes a duty to give reasons for, and explain the effect of, the sentence.

SG31-12 **STEP NINE Consideration for time spent on bail**

The court must consider whether to give credit for time spent on bail in accordance with section 240A of the Criminal Justice Act 2003.

SG31-13 [13]

Assault by Penetration

Sexual Offences Act 2003 (section 2)

Triable only on indictment

Maximum: Life imprisonment

Offence range: Community order–19 years' custody

[Repeats information as to the CJA 2003, ss. 224, 225(2), 224A and 226A which is set out at **SG31-3**.]

SG31-14 **STEP ONE Determining the offence category** [14]

The court should determine which categories of harm and culpability the offence falls into by reference **only** to the tables below.

Harm	
Category 1	• The extreme nature of one or more category 2 factors or the extreme impact caused by a combination of category 2 factors **may** elevate to category 1
Category 2	• Severe psychological or physical harm • Penetration using large or dangerous object(s) • Additional degradation/humiliation • Abduction • Prolonged detention/sustained incident • Violence or threats of violence (beyond that which is inherent in the offence) • Forced/uninvited entry into victim's home • Victim is particularly vulnerable due to personal circumstances*
Category 3	Factor(s) in categories 1 and 2 not present

* For children under 13 please refer to the guideline [at **SG31-39**].

[14]

Culpability	
A	B
• Significant degree of planning • Offender acts together with others to commit the offence • Use of alcohol/drugs on victim to facilitate the offence • Abuse of trust • Previous violence against victim • Offence committed in course of burglary • Recording of the offence • Commercial exploitation and/or motivation • Offence racially or religiously aggravated • Offence motivated by, or demonstrating, hostility to the victim based on his or her sexual orientation (or presumed sexual orientation) or transgender identity (or presumed transgender identity) • Offence motivated by, or demonstrating, hostility to the victim based on his or her disability (or presumed disability)	Factor(s) in category A not present

STEP TWO Starting point and category range SG31-15

Having determined the category, the court should use the corresponding starting points to reach a sentence within the category range below. The starting point applies to all offenders irrespective of plea or previous convictions.

Having determined the starting point, step two allows further adjustment for aggravating or mitigating features, set out below.

A case of particular gravity, reflected by multiple features of culpability or harm in step one, could merit upward adjustment from the starting point before further adjustment for aggravating or mitigating features, set out below.

Where there is a sufficient prospect of rehabilitation, a community order with a sex offender treatment programme requirement under section 202 of the Criminal Justice Act 2003 can be a proper alternative to a short or moderate length custodial sentence.

[15]

	A	B
Category 1	**Starting point** 15 years' custody **Category range** 13–19 years' custody	**Starting point** 12 years' custody **Category range** 10–15 years' custody
Category 2	**Starting point** 8 years' custody **Category range** 5–13 years' custody	**Starting point** 6 years' custody **Category range** 4–9 years' custody
Category 3	**Starting point** 4 years' custody **Category range** 2–6 years' custody	**Starting point** 2 years' custody **Category range** High level community order–4 years' custody

The table below contains a **non-exhaustive** list of additional factual elements providing the context of the offence and factors relating to the offender. Identify whether any combination of these, or other relevant factors, should result in an upward or downward adjustment from the starting point. **In particular, relevant recent convictions are likely to result in an upward adjustment.** In some cases, having considered these factors, it may be appropriate to move outside the identified category range.

When sentencing appropriate **category 3** offences, the court should also consider the custody threshold as follows:

- Has the custody threshold been passed?
- If so, is it unavoidable that a custodial sentence be imposed?
- If so, can that sentence be suspended?

Aggravating factors
Statutory aggravating factors
• Previous convictions, having regard to a) the nature of the offence to which the conviction relates and its relevance to the current offence; and b) the time that has elapsed since the conviction • Offence committed whilst on bail
Other aggravating factors
• Specific targeting of a particularly vulnerable victim • Blackmail or other threats made (where not taken into account at step one) • Location of offence • Timing of offence • Use of weapon or other item to frighten or injure • Victim compelled to leave their home (including victims of domestic violence) • Failure to comply with current court orders • Offence committed whilst on licence • Exploiting contact arrangements with a child to commit an offence • Presence of others, especially children • Any steps taken to prevent the victim reporting an incident, obtaining assistance and/or from assisting or supporting the prosecution • Attempts to dispose of or conceal evidence • Commission of offence whilst under the influence of alcohol or drugs

[15]

Mitigating factors
• No previous convictions or no relevant/recent convictions • Remorse • Previous good character and/or exemplary conduct* • Age and/or lack of maturity where it affects the responsibility of the offender • Mental disorder or learning disability, particularly where linked to the commission of the offence

*[Repeats note as to distinction between previous good character/exemplary conduct and having no previous convictions and how to deal with them in respect of the offence: see SG31-5 for the full text.]

SG31-16 STEPS THREE TO NINE [16]

[These are in the same terms as those applicable to rape: see **SG31-6** ***et seq.***]

SG31-17 Sexual Assault [17]

Sexual Offences Act 2003 (section 3)

Triable either way

Maximum: 10 years' custody

Offence range: Community order–7 years' custody

For convictions on or after 3 December 2012 (irrespective of the date of commission of the offence), this is a specified offence for the purposes of section 226A (extended sentence for certain violent or sexual offences) of the Criminal Justice Act 2003.

SG31-18 STEP ONE Determining the offence category [18]

The court should determine which categories of harm and culpability the offence falls into by reference **only** to the tables below.

Harm	
Category 1	• Severe psychological or physical harm • Abduction • Violence or threats of violence • Forced/uninvited entry into victim's home
Category 2	• Touching of naked genitalia or naked breasts • Prolonged detention/sustained incident • Additional degradation/humiliation • Victim is particularly vulnerable due to personal circumstances*
Category 3	Factor(s) in categories 1 and 2 not present

* For children under 13 please refer to the guideline [at **SG31-50**].

[18]

Culpability	
A	B
• Significant degree of planning • Offender acts together with others to commit the offence • Use of alcohol/drugs on victim to facilitate the offence • Abuse of trust • Previous violence against victim • Offence committed in course of burglary • Recording of offence • Commercial exploitation and/or motivation • Offence racially or religiously aggravated • Offence motivated by, or demonstrating, hostility to the victim based on his or her sexual orientation (or presumed sexual orientation) or transgender identity (or presumed transgender identity) • Offence motivated by, or demonstrating, hostility to the victim based on his or her disability (or presumed disability)	Factor(s) in category A not present

STEP TWO Starting point and category range SG31-19

Having determined the category, the court should use the corresponding starting points to reach a sentence within the category range below. The starting point applies to all offenders irrespective of plea or previous convictions. Having determined the starting point, step two allows further adjustment for aggravating or mitigating features, set out below.

A case of particular gravity, reflected by multiple features of culpability or harm in step one, could merit upward adjustment from the starting point before further adjustment for aggravating or mitigating features, set out below.

Where there is a sufficient prospect of rehabilitation, a community order with a sex offender treatment programme requirement under section 202 of the Criminal Justice Act 2003 can be a proper alternative to a short or moderate length custodial sentence.

[19]

	A	B
Category 1	**Starting point** 4 years' custody **Category range** 3–7 years' custody	**Starting point** 2 years 6 months' custody **Category range** 2–4 years' custody
Category 2	**Starting point** 2 years' custody **Category range** 1–4 years' custody	**Starting point** 1 year's custody **Category range** High level community order–2 years' custody
Category 3	**Starting point** 26 weeks' custody **Category range** High level community order–1 year's custody	**Starting point** High level community order **Category range** Medium level community order–26 weeks' custody

The table below contains a **non-exhaustive** list of additional factual elements providing the context of the offence and factors relating to the offender. Identify whether any combination of these, or other relevant factors, should result in an upward or downward adjustment from the starting point. **In particular, relevant recent convictions are likely to result in an upward adjustment.** In some cases, having considered these factors, it may be appropriate to move outside the identified category range.

When sentencing appropriate **category 2 or 3 offences**, the court should also consider the custody threshold as follows:

- Has the custody threshold been passed?
- If so, is it unavoidable that a custodial sentence be imposed?
- If so, can that sentence be suspended?

Aggravating factors
Statutory aggravating factors • Previous convictions, having regard to a) the nature of the offence to which the conviction relates and its relevance to the current offence; and b) the time that has elapsed since the conviction • Offence committed whilst on bail • Offence was committed against an emergency worker acting in the exercise of functions as such a worker
Other aggravating factors • Specific targeting of a particularly vulnerable victim • Blackmail or other threats made (where not taken into account at step one) • Location of offence • Timing of offence • Use of weapon or other item to frighten or injure • Victim compelled to leave their home (including victims of domestic violence) • Failure to comply with current court orders • Offence committed whilst on licence • Exploiting contact arrangements with a child to commit an offence • Presence of others, especially children • Any steps taken to prevent the victim reporting an incident, obtaining assistance and/or from assisting or supporting the prosecution • Attempts to dispose of or conceal evidence • Commission of offence whilst under the influence of alcohol or drugs

[19]

Mitigating factors
• No previous convictions **or** no relevant/recent convictions • Remorse • Previous good character and/or exemplary conduct* • Age and/or lack of maturity where it affects the responsibility of the offender • Mental disorder or learning disability, particularly where linked to the commission of the offence • Demonstration of steps taken to address offending behaviour

* Previous good character/exemplary conduct is different from having no previous convictions. The more serious the offence, the less the weight which should normally be attributed to this factor. Where previous good character/exemplary conduct has been used to facilitate the offence, this mitigation should not normally be allowed and such conduct may constitute an aggravating factor.

SG31-20 STEP THREE **Consider any factors which indicate a reduction, such as assistance to the prosecution** [20]

The court should take into account sections 73 and 74 of the Serious Organised Crime and Police Act 2005 (assistance by defendants: reduction or review of sentence) and any other rule of law by virtue of which an offender may receive a discounted sentence in consequence of assistance given (or offered) to the prosecutor or investigator.

SG31-21 STEP FOUR **Reduction for guilty pleas**

The court should take account of any potential reduction for a guilty plea in accordance with section 144 of the Criminal Justice Act 2003 and the *Guilty Plea* guideline.

SG31-22 STEP FIVE **Dangerousness**

The court should consider whether having regard to the criteria contained in Chapter 5 of Part 12 of the Criminal Justice Act 2003 it would be appropriate to award an extended sentence (section 226A).

SG31-23 STEPS SIX TO NINE

[These are in the same terms as those applicable to rape: see **SG31-6** ***et seq.***]

SG31-24 CAUSING A PERSON TO ENGAGE IN SEXUAL ACTIVITY WITHOUT CONSENT [21]

Sexual Offences Act 2003 (section 4)

Triable only on indictment (if penetration involved)

• otherwise, triable either way

Maximum: Life imprisonment (if penetration involved)

• otherwise, 10 years

Offence range: Community order–7 years' custody (if no penetration involved) / 19 years' custody (if penetration involved)

[Repeats information as to the CJA 2003, ss. 224, 225(2), 224A and 226A which is set out at **SG31-3**.]

SG31-25 STEP ONE **Determining the offence category** [22]

The court should determine which categories of harm and culpability the offence falls into by reference **only** to the tables below.

[22]

Harm	
Category 1	• The extreme nature of one or more category 2 factors or the extreme impact caused by a combination of category 2 factors **may** elevate to category 1
Category 2	• Severe psychological or physical harm • Penetration using large or dangerous object(s) • Pregnancy or STI as a consequence of offence • Additional degradation/humiliation • Abduction • Prolonged detention/sustained incident • Violence or threats of violence • Forced/uninvited entry into victim's home • Victim is particularly vulnerable due to personal circumstances*
Category 3	Factor(s) in categories 1 and 2 not present

*For children under 13 please refer to the guideline [at **SG31-57**].

Culpability	
A	B
• Significant degree of planning • Offender acts together with others to commit the offence • Use of alcohol/drugs on victim to facilitate the offence • Abuse of trust • Previous violence against victim • Offence committed in course of burglary • Recording of the offence • Commercial exploitation and/or motivation • Offence racially or religiously aggravated • Offence motivated by, or demonstrating, hostility to the victim based on his or her sexual orientation (or presumed sexual orientation) or transgender identity (or presumed transgender identity) • Offence motivated by, or demonstrating, hostility to the victim based on his or her disability (or presumed disability)	Factor(s) in category A not present

STEP TWO Starting point and category range **SG31-26**

Having determined the category, the court should use the corresponding starting points to reach a sentence within the category range below. The starting point applies to all offenders irrespective of plea or previous convictions.

Having determined the starting point, step two allows further adjustment for aggravating or mitigating features, set out below.

A case of particular gravity, reflected by multiple features of culpability or harm in step one, could merit upward adjustment from the starting point before further adjustment for aggravating or mitigating features, set out below.

Where there is a sufficient prospect of rehabilitation, a community order with a sex offender treatment programme requirement under section 202 of the Criminal Justice Act 2003 can be a proper alternative to a short or moderate length custodial sentence.

[23] **Where offence involved penetration**

	A	B
Category 1	**Starting point** 15 years' custody **Category range** 13–19 years' custody	**Starting point** 12 years' custody **Category range** 10–15 years' custody
Category 2	**Starting point** 8 years' custody **Category range** 5–13 years' custody	**Starting point** 6 years' custody **Category range** 4–9 years' custody
Category 3	**Starting point** 4 years' custody **Category range** 2–6 years' custody	**Starting point** 2 years' custody **Category range** High level community order–4 years' custody

Where offence did not involve penetration [23]

	A	B
Category 1	**Starting point** 4 years' custody **Category range** 3–7 years' custody	**Starting point** 2 years 6 months' custody **Category range** 2–4 years' custody
Category 2	**Starting point** 2 years' custody **Category range** 1–4 years' custody	**Starting point** 1 year's custody **Category range** High level community order–2 years' custody
Category 3	**Starting point** 26 weeks' custody **Category range** High level community order–1 year's custody	**Starting point** High level community order **Category range** Medium level community order–26 weeks' custody

The table below contains a **non-exhaustive** list of additional factual elements providing the context of the offence and factors relating to the offender. Identify whether any combination of these, or other relevant factors, should result in an upward or downward adjustment from the starting point. **In particular, relevant recent convictions are likely to result in an upward adjustment.** In some cases, having considered these factors, it may be appropriate to move outside the identified category range. [24]

When sentencing appropriate **category 2 or 3** offences, the court should also consider the custody threshold as follows:

- Has the custody threshold been passed?
- If so, is it unavoidable that a custodial sentence be imposed?
- If so, can that sentence be suspended?

Aggravating factors
Statutory aggravating factors • Previous convictions, having regard to a) the nature of the offence to which the conviction relates and its relevance to the current offence; and b) the time that has elapsed since the conviction • Offence committed whilst on bail
Other aggravating factors • Specific targeting of a particularly vulnerable victim • Ejaculation (where not taken into account at step one) • Blackmail or other threats made (where not taken into account at step one) • Location of offence • Timing of offence • Use of weapon or other item to frighten or injure • Victim compelled to leave their home (including victims of domestic violence) • Failure to comply with current court orders • Offence committed whilst on licence • Exploiting contact arrangements with a child to commit an offence • Presence of others, especially children • Any steps taken to prevent the victim reporting an incident, obtaining assistance and/or from assisting or supporting the prosecution • Attempts to dispose of or conceal evidence • Commission of offence whilst under the influence of alcohol or drugs

[24]

Mitigating factors
• No previous convictions **or** no relevant/recent convictions • Remorse • Previous good character and/or exemplary conduct* • Age and/or lack of maturity where it affects the responsibility of the offender • Mental disorder or learning disability, particularly where linked to the commission of the offence

* [Repeats note as to distinction between previous good character/exemplary conduct and having no previous convictions and how to deal with them in respect of the offence: see **SG31-5** for the full text.]

[25] **STEPS THREE TO NINE** **SG31-27**

[These are in the same terms as those applicable to rape: see **SG31-6** ***et seq.***]

[27] **SG31-28**

RAPE OF A CHILD UNDER 13

Sexual Offences Act 2003 (section 5)

Triable only on indictment

Maximum: Life imprisonment

Offence range: 6–19 years' custody

This is a serious specified offence for the purposes of sections 224 and 225(2) (life sentences for serious offences) of the Criminal Justice Act 2003.

For offences committed on or after 3 December 2012, this is an offence listed in Part 1 of Schedule 15B for the purposes of section 224A (life sentence for second listed offence) of the Criminal Justice Act 2003.

For convictions on or after 3 December 2012 (irrespective of the date of commission of the offence), this is a specified offence for the purposes of section 226A (extended sentence for certain violent or sexual offences) of the Criminal Justice Act 2003.

For convictions on or after 13 April 2015 (irrespective of the date of commission of the offence) this is an offence listed in Schedule 18A for the purposes of section 236A (special custodial sentence for certain offenders of particular concern) of the Criminal Justice Act 2003.

[28] **STEP ONE Determining the offence category** **SG31-29**

The court should determine which categories of harm and culpability the offence falls into by reference **only** to the tables below.

Offences may be of such severity, for example involving a campaign of rape, that sentences of 20 years and above may be appropriate.

When dealing with the statutory offence of rape of a child under 13, the court may be faced with a wide range of offending behaviour.

Sentencers should have particular regard to the fact that these offences are not only committed through force or fear of force but may include exploitative behaviour towards a child which should be considered to indicate high culpability.

This guideline is designed to deal with the majority of offending behaviour which deserves a significant custodial sentence; the starting points and ranges reflect the fact that such offending merits such an approach. There may also be **exceptional** cases, where a lengthy community order with a requirement to participate in a sex offender treatment programme may be the best way of changing the offender's behaviour and of protecting the public by preventing any repetition of the offence. This guideline may not be appropriate where the sentencer is satisfied that on the available evidence, and in the absence of exploitation, a young or particularly immature defendant genuinely believed, on reasonable grounds, that the victim was aged 16 or over and that they were engaging in lawful sexual activity.

Sentencers are reminded that if sentencing outside the guideline they must be satisfied that it would be contrary to the interests of justice to follow the guideline.

Harm		[29]
Category 1	• The extreme nature of one or more category 2 factors or the extreme impact caused by a combination of category 2 factors **may** elevate to category 1	
Category 2	• Severe psychological or physical harm • Pregnancy or STI as a consequence of offence • Additional degradation/humiliation • Abduction • Prolonged detention /sustained incident • Violence or threats of violence • Forced/uninvited entry into victim's home • Child is particularly vulnerable due to extreme youth and/or personal circumstances	
Category 3	Factor(s) in categories 1 and 2 not present	

Culpability	
A	B
• Significant degree of planning • Offender acts together with others to commit the offence • Use of alcohol/drugs on victim to facilitate the offence • Grooming behaviour used against victim • Abuse of trust • Previous violence against victim • Offence committed in course of burglary • Sexual images of victim recorded, retained, solicited or shared • Deliberate isolation of victim • Commercial exploitation and/or motivation • Offence racially or religiously aggravated • Offence motivated by, or demonstrating, hostility to the victim based on his or her sexual orientation (or presumed sexual orientation) or transgender identity (or presumed transgender identity) • Offence motivated by, or demonstrating, hostility to the victim based on his or her disability (or presumed disability)	Factor(s) in category A not present

SG31-30 STEP TWO **Starting point and category range** [30]

Having determined the category, the court should use the corresponding starting points to reach a sentence within the category range below. The starting point applies to all offenders irrespective of plea or previous convictions. Having determined the starting point, step two allows further adjustment for aggravating or mitigating features, set out below.

A case of particular gravity, reflected by multiple features of culpability or harm in step one, could merit upward adjustment from the starting point before further adjustment for aggravating or mitigating features, set out below.

Sentencers should also note the wording set out at step one which may be applicable in exceptional cases.

	A	B
Category 1	**Starting point** 16 years' custody **Category range** 13–19 years' custody	**Starting point** 13 years' custody **Category range** 11–17 years' custody
Category 2	**Starting point** 13 years' custody **Category range** 11–17 years' custody	**Starting point** 10 years' custody **Category range** 8–13 years' custody
Category 3	**Starting point** 10 years' custody **Category range** 8–13 years' custody	**Starting point** 8 years' custody **Category range** 6–11 years' custody

The table below contains a **non-exhaustive** list of additional factual elements providing the context of the offence and factors relating to the offender. Identify whether any combination of these, or other relevant factors, should result in an upward or downward adjustment from the starting point. **In particular, relevant recent convictions are likely to result in an upward adjustment.** In some cases, having considered these factors, it may be appropriate to move outside the identified category range. [31]

[31]

Aggravating factors
Statutory aggravating factors
• Previous convictions, having regard to a) the nature of the offence to which the conviction relates and its relevance to the current offence; and b) the time that has elapsed since the conviction • Offence committed whilst on bail *Other aggravating factors* • Specific targeting of a particularly vulnerable child • Ejaculation (where not taken into account at step one) • Blackmail or other threats made (where not taken into account at step one) • Location of offence • Timing of offence • Use of weapon or other item to frighten or injure • Victim compelled to leave their home, school, etc • Failure to comply with current court orders • Offence committed whilst on licence • Exploiting contact arrangements with a child to commit an offence • Presence of others, especially other children • Any steps taken to prevent the victim reporting an incident, obtaining assistance and/or from assisting or supporting the prosecution • Attempts to dispose of or conceal evidence • Commission of offence whilst offender under the influence of alcohol or drugs • Victim encouraged to recruit others

Mitigating factors
• No previous convictions **or** no relevant/recent convictions • Remorse • Previous good character and/or exemplary conduct* • Age and/or lack of maturity where it affects the responsibility of the offender • Mental disorder or learning disability, particularly where linked to the commission of the offence

* [Repeats note as to distinction between previous good character/exemplary conduct and having no previous convictions and how to deal with them in respect of the offence: see SG31-5 for the full text.]

[32] **STEP THREE Consider any factors which indicate a reduction, such as assistance to the prosecution** **SG31-31**

The court should take into account sections 73 and 74 of the Serious Organised Crime and Police Act 2005 (assistance by defendants: reduction or review of sentence) and any other rule of law by virtue of which an offender may receive a discounted sentence in consequence of assistance given (or offered) to the prosecutor or investigator.

STEP FOUR Reduction for guilty pleas **SG31-32**

The court should take account of any potential reduction for a guilty plea in accordance with section 144 of the Criminal Justice Act 2003 and the guideline for Reduction in Sentence for a Guilty Plea (where first hearing is on or after 1 June 2017, or first hearing before 1 June 2017).

STEP FIVE Dangerousness **SG31-33**

The court should consider whether having regard to the criteria contained in Chapter 5 of Part 12 of the Criminal Justice Act 2003 it would be appropriate to award a life sentence (section 224A or section 225(2)) or an extended sentence (section 226A). When sentencing offenders to a life sentence under these provisions, the notional determinate sentence should be used as the basis for the setting of a minimum term.

STEP SIX Special Custodial Sentence for certain offenders of particular concern (section 236A) **SG31-34**

Where the Court does not impose a sentence of imprisonment for life or an extended sentence, but does impose a period of imprisonment, the term of the sentence must be equal to the aggregate of the appropriate custodial term and a further period of one year for which the offender is to be subject to a licence. [Step added 20/11/2018].

STEP SEVEN Totality principle **SG31-35**

If sentencing an offender for more than one offence, or where the offender is already serving a sentence, consider whether the total sentence is just and proportionate to the offending behaviour. See *Totality* guideline.

STEP EIGHT Ancillary orders **SG31-36**

The court must consider whether to make any ancillary orders. The court must also consider what other requirements or provisions may *automatically* apply. Further information is included at Annex A [see SG31-156].

STEP NINE Reasons **SG31-37**

Section 174 of the Criminal Justice Act 2003 imposes a duty to give reasons for, and explain the effect of, the sentence.

SG31-38 **STEP TEN Consideration for time spent on bail** [32]

The court must consider whether to give credit for time spent on bail in accordance with section 240A of the Criminal Justice Act 2003.

SG31-39 ASSAULT OF A CHILD UNDER 13 BY PENETRATION [33]

Sexual Offences Act 2003 (section 6)

Triable only on indictment

Maximum: Life imprisonment

Offence range: 2–19 years' custody

This is a serious specified offence for the purposes of sections 224 and 225(2) (life sentences for serious offences) of the Criminal Justice Act 2003.

For offences committed on or after 3 December 2012, this is an offence listed in Part 1 of Schedule 15B for the purposes of section 224A (life sentence for second listed offence) of the Criminal Justice Act 2003.

For convictions on or after 3 December 2012 (irrespective of the date of commission of the offence), this is a specified offence for the purposes of section 226A (extended sentence for certain violent or sexual offences) of the Criminal Justice Act 2003.

For convictions on or after 13 April 2015 (irrespective of the date of commission of the offence) this is an offence listed in Schedule 18A for the purposes of section 236A (special custodial sentence for certain offenders of particular concern) of the Criminal Justice Act 2003.

SG31-40 **STEP ONE Determining the offence category** [34]

The court should determine which categories of harm and culpability the offence falls into by reference **only** to the tables below.

Harm	
Category 1	The extreme nature of one or more category 2 factors or the extreme impact caused by a combination of category 2 factors **may** elevate to category 1
Category 2	• Severe psychological or physical harm • Penetration using large or dangerous object(s) • Additional degradation/humiliation • Abduction • Prolonged detention /sustained incident • Violence or threats of violence • Forced/uninvited entry into victim's home • Child is particularly vulnerable due to extreme youth and/or personal circumstances
Category 3	Factor(s) in categories 1 and 2 not present

Culpability	
A	B
• Significant degree of planning • Offender acts together with others to commit the offence • Use of alcohol/drugs on victim to facilitate the offence • Grooming behaviour used against victim • Abuse of trust • Previous violence against victim • Offence committed in course of burglary • Sexual images of victim recorded, retained, solicited or shared • Deliberate isolation of victim • Commercial exploitation and/or motivation • Offence racially or religiously aggravated • Offence motivated by, or demonstrating, hostility to the victim based on his or her sexual orientation (or presumed sexual orientation) or transgender identity (or presumed transgender identity) • Offence motivated by, or demonstrating, hostility to the victim based on his or her disability (or presumed disability)	Factor(s) in category A not present

[34] **STEP TWO Starting point and category range** **SG31-41**

Having determined the category, the court should use the corresponding starting points to reach a sentence within the category range below. The starting point applies to all offenders irrespective of plea or previous convictions. Having determined the starting point, step two allows further adjustment for aggravating or mitigating features, set out below.

A case of particular gravity, reflected by multiple features of culpability or harm in step one, could merit upward adjustment from the starting point before further adjustment for aggravating or mitigating features, set out below.

	A	B
Category 1	**Starting point** 16 years' custody **Category range** 13–19 years' custody	**Starting point** 13 years' custody **Category range** 11–17 years' custody
Category 2	**Starting point** 11 years' custody **Category range** 7–15 years' custody	**Starting point** 8 years' custody **Category range** 5–13 years' custody
Category 3	**Starting point** 6 years' custody **Category range** 4–9 years' custody	**Starting point** 4 years' custody **Category range** 2–6 years' custody

[35] The table below contains a **non-exhaustive** list of additional factual elements providing the context of the offence and factors relating to the offender. Identify whether any combination of these, or other relevant factors, should result in an upward or downward adjustment from the starting point. **In particular, relevant recent convictions are likely to result in an upward adjustment.** In some cases, having considered these factors, it may be appropriate to move outside the identified category range.

Aggravating factors
Statutory aggravating factors • Previous convictions, having regard to a) the nature of the offence to which the conviction relates and its relevance to the current offence; and b) the time that has elapsed since the conviction • Offence committed whilst on bail
Other aggravating factors • Specific targeting of a particularly vulnerable child • Blackmail or other threats made (where not taken into account at step one) • Location of offence • Timing of offence • Use of weapon or other item to frighten or injure • Victim compelled to leave their home, school etc • Failure to comply with current court orders • Offence committed whilst on licence • Exploiting contact arrangements with a child to commit an offence • Presence of others, especially other children • Any steps taken to prevent the victim reporting an incident, obtaining assistance and/or from assisting or supporting the prosecution • Attempts to dispose of or conceal evidence • Commission of offence whilst under the influence of alcohol or drugs • Victim encouraged to recruit others

Mitigating factors
• No previous convictions **or** no relevant/recent convictions • Remorse • Previous good character and/or exemplary conduct* • Age and/or lack of maturity where it affects the responsibility of the offender • Mental disorder or learning disability, particularly where linked to the commission of the offence

*[Repeats note as to distinction between previous good character/exemplary conduct and having no previous convictions and how to deal with them in respect of the offence: see **SG31-5** for the full text.]

Sentencing Guidelines

SG31-42 **STEP THREE Consider any factors which indicate a reduction, such as assistance to the prosecution** [36]

The court should take into account sections 73 and 74 of the Serious Organised Crime and Police Act 2005 (assistance by defendants: reduction or review of sentence) and any other rule of law by virtue of which an offender may receive a discounted sentence in consequence of assistance given (or offered) to the prosecutor or investigator.

SG31-43 **STEP FOUR Reduction for guilty pleas**

The court should take account of any potential reduction for a guilty plea in accordance with section 144 of the Criminal Justice Act 2003 and the guideline for Reduction in Sentence for a Guilty Plea (where first hearing is on or after 1 June 2017, or first hearing before 1 June 2017).

SG31-44 **STEP FIVE Dangerousness**

The court should consider whether having regard to the criteria contained in Chapter 5 of Part 12 of the Criminal Justice Act 2003 it would be appropriate to award a life sentence (section 224A or section 225(2)) or an extended sentence (section 226A). When sentencing offenders to a life sentence under these provisions, the notional determinate sentence should be used as the basis for the setting of a minimum term.

SG31-45 **STEP SIX Special Custodial Sentence for certain offenders of particular concern (section 236A)**

Where the Court does not impose a sentence of imprisonment for life or an extended sentence, but does impose a period of imprisonment, the term of the sentence must be equal to the aggregate of the appropriate custodial term and a further period of one year for which the offender is to be subject to a licence. [Step added 20/11/2018].

SG31-46 **STEP SEVEN Totality principle**

If sentencing an offender for more than one offence, or where the offender is already serving a sentence, consider whether the total sentence is just and proportionate to the offending behaviour. See *Totality* guideline.

SG31-47 **STEP EIGHT Ancillary orders**

The court must consider whether to make any ancillary orders. The court must also consider what other requirements or provisions may *automatically* apply. Further information is included at Annex A [see **SG31-156**].

SG31-48 **STEP NINE Reasons**

Section 174 of the Criminal Justice Act 2003 imposes a duty to give reasons for, and explain the effect of, the sentence.

SG31-49 **STEP TEN Consideration for time spent on bail**

The court must consider whether to give credit for time spent on bail in accordance with section 240A of the Criminal Justice Act 2003.

SG31-50

SEXUAL ASSAULT OF A CHILD UNDER 13 [37]

Sexual Offences Act 2003 (section 7)

Triable either way

Maximum: 14 years' custody

Offence range: Community order–9 years' custody

For offences committed on or after 3 December 2012, this is an offence listed in Part 1 of Schedule 15B for the purposes of section 224A (life sentence for second listed offence) of the Criminal Justice Act 2003.

For convictions on or after 3 December 2012 (irrespective of the date of commission of the offence), this is a specified offence for the purposes of section 226A (extended sentence for certain violent or sexual offences) of the Criminal Justice Act 2003.

SG31-51 **STEP ONE Determining the offence category** [38]

The court should determine which categories of harm and culpability the offence falls into by reference **only** to the tables below.

Harm	
Category 1	• Severe psychological or physical harm • Abduction • Violence or threats of violence • Forced/uninvited entry into victim's home

[38]

Harm	
Category 2	• Touching of naked genitalia or naked breast area • Prolonged detention/sustained incident • Additional degradation/humiliation • Child is particularly vulnerable due to extreme youth and/or personal circumstances
Category 3	Factor(s) in categories 1 and 2 not present

Culpability	
A	B
• Significant degree of planning • Offender acts together with others to commit the offence • Use of alcohol/drugs on victim to facilitate the offence • Grooming behaviour used against victim • Abuse of trust • Previous violence against victim • Offence committed in course of burglary • Sexual images of victim recorded, retained, solicited or shared • Deliberate isolation of victim • Commercial exploitation and/or motivation • Offence racially or religiously aggravated • Offence motivated by, or demonstrating, hostility to the victim based on his or her sexual orientation (or presumed sexual orientation) or transgender identity (or presumed transgender identity) • Offence motivated by, or demonstrating, hostility to the victim based on his or her disability (or presumed disability)	Factor(s) in category A not present

STEP TWO Starting point and category range **SG31-52**

Having determined the category, the court should use the corresponding starting points to reach a sentence within the category range below. The starting point applies to all offenders irrespective of plea or previous convictions. Having determined the starting point, step two allows further adjustment for aggravating or mitigating features, set out below.

A case of particular gravity, reflected by multiple features of culpability or harm in step one, could merit upward adjustment from the starting point before further adjustment for aggravating or mitigating features, set out below.

Where there is a sufficient prospect of rehabilitation, a community order with a sex offender treatment programme requirement under section 202 of the Criminal Justice Act 2003 can be a proper alternative to a short or moderate length custodial sentence.

[39]

	A	B
Category 1	**Starting point** 6 years' custody **Category range** 4–9 years' custody	**Starting point** 4 years' custody **Category range** 3–7 years' custody
Category 2	**Starting point** 4 years' custody **Category range** 3–7 years' custody	**Starting point** 2 years' custody **Category range** 1–4 years' custody
	A	B
Category 3	**Starting point** 1 year's custody **Category range** 26 weeks'– 2 years' custody	**Starting point** 26 weeks' custody **Category range** High level community order–1 year's custody

The table below contains a **non-exhaustive** list of additional factual elements providing the context of the offence and factors relating to the offender. Identify whether any combination of these, or other relevant factors, should result in an upward or downward adjustment from the starting point. **In particular, relevant recent convictions are likely to result in an upward adjustment.** In some cases, having considered these factors, it may be appropriate to move outside the identified category range.

Aggravating factors [39]
Statutory aggravating factors • Previous convictions, having regard to a) the nature of the offence to which the conviction relates and its relevance to the current offence; and b) the time that has elapsed since the conviction • Offence committed whilst on bail *Other aggravating factors* • Specific targeting of a particularly vulnerable child • Blackmail or other threats made (where not taken into account at step one) • Location of offence • Timing of offence • Use of weapon or other item to frighten or injure • Victim compelled to leave their home, school, etc • Failure to comply with current court orders • Offence committed whilst on licence • Exploiting contact arrangements with a child to commit an offence • Presence of others, especially other children • Any steps taken to prevent the victim reporting an incident, obtaining assistance and/or from assisting or supporting the prosecution • Attempts to dispose of or conceal evidence • Commission of offence whilst under the influence of alcohol or drugs • Victim encouraged to recruit others

Mitigating factors
• No previous convictions **or** no relevant/recent convictions • Remorse • Previous good character and/or exemplary conduct* • Age and/or lack of maturity where it affects the responsibility of the offender • Mental disorder or learning disability, particularly where linked to the commission of the offence

*[Repeats note as to distinction between previous good character/exemplary conduct and having no previous convictions and how to deal with them in respect of the offence: see **SG31-5** for the full text.]

SG31-53 STEP THREE **Consider any factors which indicate a reduction, such as assistance to the prosecution** [40]

The court should take into account sections 73 and 74 of the Serious Organised Crime and Police Act 2005 (assistance by defendants: reduction or review of sentence) and any other rule of law by virtue of which an offender may receive a discounted sentence in consequence of assistance given (or offered) to the prosecutor or investigator.

SG31-54 STEP FOUR **Reduction for guilty pleas**

The court should take account of any potential reduction for a guilty plea in accordance with section 144 of the Criminal Justice Act 2003 and the *Guilty Plea* guideline.

SG31-55 STEP FIVE **Dangerousness**

The court should consider whether having regard to the criteria contained in Chapter 5 of Part 12 of the Criminal Justice Act 2003 it would be appropriate to award a life sentence (section 224A) or an extended sentence (section 226A). When sentencing offenders to a life sentence under these provisions, the notional determinate sentence should be used as the basis for the setting of a minimum term.

SG31-56 STEPS SIX TO NINE

[These are in the same terms as those applicable to rape: see **SG31-6** ***et seq.***]

SG31-57 Causing or Inciting a Child Under 13 to Engage in Sexual Activity [41]

Sexual Offences Act 2003 (section 8)

Triable only on indictment (if penetration involved)

• otherwise, triable either way

Maximum: Life imprisonment (if penetration involved)

• otherwise, 14 years' custody

Offence range: 1–17 years' custody

[Repeats information as to the CJA 2003, ss. 224, 225(2), 224A and 226A, which is set out at **SG31-3**.]

[42] **STEP ONE Determining the offence category** SG31-58

The court should determine which categories of harm and culpability the offence falls into by reference **only** to the tables below.

Harm	
Category 1	• The extreme nature of one or more category 2 factors or the extreme impact caused by a combination of category 2 factors may elevate to category 1
Category 2	• Severe psychological or physical harm • Penetration of vagina or anus (using body or object) by, or of, victim • Penile penetration of mouth by, or of, victim • Additional degradation/humiliation • Abduction • Prolonged detention/sustained incident • Violence or threats of violence • Forced/uninvited entry into victim's home • Child is particularly vulnerable due to extreme youth and/or personal circumstances
Category 3	Factor(s) in categories 1 and 2 not present

Culpability	
A	B
• Significant degree of planning • Offender acts together with others to commit the offence • Use of alcohol/drugs on victim to facilitate the offence • Grooming behaviour used against victim • Abuse of trust • Previous violence against victim • Offence committed in course of burglary • Sexual images of victim recorded, retained, solicited or shared • Deliberate isolation of victim • Commercial exploitation and/or motivation • Offence racially or religiously aggravated • Offence motivated by, or demonstrating hostility to the victim based on his or her sexual orientation (or presumed sexual orientation) or transgender identity (or presumed transgender identity) • Offence motivated by, or demonstrating, hostility to the victim based on his or her disability (or presumed disability)	Factor(s) in category A not present

STEP TWO Starting point and category range SG31-59

Having determined the category, the court should use the corresponding starting points to reach a sentence within the category range below. The starting point applies to all offenders irrespective of plea or previous convictions. Having determined the starting point, step two allows further adjustment for aggravating or mitigating features, set out below.

A case of particular gravity, reflected by multiple features of culpability or harm in step one, could merit upward adjustment from the starting point before further adjustment for aggravating or mitigating features, set out below.

[43]

	A	B
Category 1	**Starting point** 13 years' custody **Category range** 11–17 years' custody	**Starting point** 11 years' custody **Category range** 10–15 years' custody
Category 2	**Starting point** 8 years' custody **Category range** 5–10 years' custody	**Starting point** 6 years' custody **Category range** 3–9 years' custody
Category 3	**Starting point** 5 years' custody **Category range** 3–8 years' custody	**Starting point** 2 years' custody **Category range** 1–4 years' custody

The table below contains a **non-exhaustive** list of additional factual elements providing the context of the offence and factors relating to the offender. Identify whether any combination of these, or other relevant factors, should result in an upward or downward adjustment from the starting point. **In particular, relevant recent convictions are likely to result in an upward adjustment.** In some cases, having considered these factors, it may be appropriate to move outside the identified category range. [43]

Aggravating factors
Statutory aggravating factors • Previous convictions, having regard to a) the nature of the offence to which the conviction relates and its relevance to the current offence; and b) the time that has elapsed since the conviction • Offence committed whilst on bail
Other aggravating factors • Specific targeting of a particularly vulnerable child • Ejaculation (where not taken into account at step one) • Blackmail or other threats made (where not taken into account at step one) • Pregnancy or STI as a consequence of offence • Location of offence • Timing of offence • Use of weapon or other item to frighten or injure • Victim compelled to leave their home, school, etc • Failure to comply with current court orders • Offence committed whilst on licence • Exploiting contact arrangements with a child to commit an offence • Presence of others, especially other children • Any steps taken to prevent the victim reporting an incident, obtaining assistance and/or from assisting or supporting the prosecution • Attempts to dispose of or conceal evidence • Commission of offence whilst offender under the influence of alcohol or drugs • Victim encouraged to recruit others

Mitigating factors
• No previous convictions **or** no relevant/recent convictions • Remorse • Previous good character and/or exemplary conduct* • Age and/or lack of maturity where it affects the responsibility of the offender • Mental disorder or learning disability, particularly where linked to the commission of the offence • Sexual activity was incited but no activity took place because the offender voluntarily desisted or intervened to prevent it

*[Repeats note as to distinction between previous good character/exemplary conduct and having no previous convictions and how to deal with them in respect of the offence: see SG31-5 for the full text.]

SG31-60 STEPS THREE TO NINE [44]

[These are in the same terms as those applicable to rape: see **SG31-6 *et seq.***]

SG31-61 SEXUAL ACTIVITY WITH A CHILD [45]

Sexual Offences Act 2003 (section 9)

CAUSING OR INCITING A CHILD TO ENGAGE IN SEXUAL ACTIVITY

Sexual Offences Act 2003 (section 10)

Triable only on indictment (if penetration involved)

• otherwise, triable either way

Maximum: 14 years' custody

Offence range: Community order–10 years' custody

[Repeats information as to the CJA 2003, ss. 224A and 226A, which is set out at **SG31-50.**]

Arranging or facilitating the commission of a child offence (section 14 of the Sexual Offences Act 2003—[see SG31-73])
The starting points and ranges in this guideline are also applicable to offences of arranging or facilitating the commission of a child offence. In such cases, the level of harm should be determined by reference to the type of activity arranged or facilitated. Sentences commensurate with the applicable starting point and range will ordinarily be appropriate. For offences involving significant commercial exploitation and/or an international element, it may, in the interests of justice, be appropriate to increase a sentence to a point above the category range. In exceptional cases, such as where a vulnerable offender performed a limited role, having been coerced or exploited by others, sentences below the starting point and range may be appropriate.

[46] **STEP ONE Determining the offence category** SG31-62

The court should determine which categories of harm and culpability the offence falls into by reference **only** to the tables below.

This guideline also applies to offences committed remotely/online

Harm	
Category 1	• Penetration of vagina or anus (using body or object) • Penile penetration of mouth In either case by, or of, the victim
Category 2	Touching, or exposure, of naked genitalia or naked breasts by, or of, the victim
Category 3	Other sexual activity

Culpability	
A	B
• Significant degree of planning • Offender acts together with others to commit the offence • Use of alcohol/drugs on victim to facilitate the offence • Grooming behaviour used against victim • Abuse of trust • Use of threats (including blackmail) • Sexual images of victim recorded, retained, solicited or shared • Specific targeting of a particularly vulnerable child • Offender lied about age • Significant disparity in age • Commercial exploitation and/or motivation • Offence racially or religiously aggravated • Offence motivated by, or demonstrating, hostility to the victim based on his or her sexual orientation (or presumed sexual orientation) or transgender identity (or presumed transgender identity) • Offence motivated by, or demonstrating, hostility to the victim based on his or her disability (or presumed disability)	Factor(s) in category A not present

[47] **STEP TWO Starting point and category range** SG31-63

Having determined the category, the court should use the corresponding starting points to reach a sentence within the category range below. The starting point applies to all offenders irrespective of plea or previous convictions. Having determined the starting point, step two allows further adjustment for aggravating or mitigating features, set out below.

A case of particular gravity, reflected by multiple features of culpability or harm in step one, could merit upward adjustment from the starting point before further adjustment for aggravating or mitigating features, set out below.

Where there is a sufficient prospect of rehabilitation, a community order with a sex offender treatment programme requirement under section 202 of the Criminal Justice Act 2003 can be a proper alternative to a short or moderate length custodial sentence.

	A	B
Category 1	**Starting point** 5 years' custody **Category range** 4–10 years' custody	**Starting point** 1 year's custody **Category range** High level community order–2 years' custody
Category 2	**Starting point** 3 years' custody **Category range** 2–6 years' custody	**Starting point** 26 weeks' custody **Category range** High level community order–1 year's custody
Category 3	**Starting point** 26 weeks' custody **Category range** High level community order–3 years' custody	**Starting point** Medium level community order **Category range** Low level community order–High level community order

[48] The table below contains a **non-exhaustive** list of additional factual elements providing the context of the offence and factors relating to the offender. Identify whether any combination of these, or other relevant

factors, should result in an upward or downward adjustment from the starting point. **In particular, relevant recent convictions are likely to result in an upward adjustment.** In some cases, having considered these factors, it may be appropriate to move outside the identified category range. [48]

When sentencing appropriate **category 2 or 3 offences**, the court should also consider the custody threshold as follows:

- Has the custody threshold been passed?
- If so, is it unavoidable that a custodial sentence be imposed?
- If so, can that sentence be suspended?

Aggravating factors
Statutory aggravating factors • Previous convictions, having regard to a) the nature of the offence to which the conviction relates and its relevance to the current offence; and b) the time that has elapsed since the conviction • Offence committed whilst on bail *Other aggravating factors* • Severe psychological or physical harm • Ejaculation • Pregnancy or STI as a consequence of offence • Location of offence • Timing of offence • Victim compelled to leave their home, school, etc • Failure to comply with current court orders • Offence committed whilst on licence • Exploiting contact arrangements with a child to commit an offence • Presence of others, especially other children • Any steps taken to prevent the victim reporting an incident, obtaining assistance and/or from assisting or supporting the prosecution • Attempts to dispose of or conceal evidence • Failure of offender to respond to previous warnings • Commission of offence whilst under the influence of alcohol or drugs • Victim encouraged to recruit others • Period over which offence committed

Mitigating factors
• No previous convictions or no relevant/recent convictions • Remorse • Previous good character and/or exemplary conduct* • Age and/or lack of maturity where it affects the responsibility of the offender • Mental disorder or learning disability, particularly where linked to the commission of the offence • Sexual activity was incited but no activity took place because the offender voluntarily desisted or intervened to prevent it

*[Repeats note as to distinction between previous good character/exemplary conduct and having no previous convictions and how to deal with them in respect of the offence: see SG31-5 for the full text.]

SG31-64 STEPS THREE TO NINE [49]

[These are in the same terms as those applicable to sexual assault of a child under 13: see **SG31-53 *et seq.***]

SG31-65 Sexual Activity with a Child Family Member [51]

Sexual Offences Act 2003 (section 25)

Inciting a Child Family Member to Engage in Sexual Activity

Sexual Offences Act 2003 (section 26)

Triable only on indictment (if penetration involved)

- otherwise, triable either way

Maximum: 14 years' custody

Offence range: Community order–10 years' custody

[Repeats information as to the CJA 2003, ss. 224A and 226A, which is set out at **SG31-50**.]

[52] **STEP ONE Determining the offence category** SG31-66

The court should determine which categories of harm and culpability the offence falls into by reference **only** to the tables below. This offence involves those who have a family relationship with the victim and it should be assumed that the greater the abuse of trust within this relationship the more grave the offence.

Harm	
Category 1	• Penetration of vagina or anus (using body or object) • Penile penetration of mouth In either case by, or of, the victim
Category 2	Touching of naked genitalia or naked breasts by, or of, the victim
Category 3	Other sexual activity

Culpability	
A	B
• Significant degree of planning • Offender acts together with others to commit the offence • Use of alcohol/drugs on victim to facilitate the offence • Grooming behaviour used against victim • Use of threats (including blackmail) • Sexual images of victim recorded, retained, solicited or shared • Specific targeting of a particularly vulnerable child • Significant disparity in age • Commercial exploitation and/or motivation • Offence racially or religiously aggravated • Offence motivated by, or demonstrating, hostility to the victim based on his or her sexual orientation (or presumed sexual orientation) or transgender identity (or presumed transgender identity) • Offence motivated by, or demonstrating, hostility to the victim based on his or her disability (or presumed disability)	Factor(s) in category A not present

[53] **STEP TWO Starting point and category range** SG31-67

Having determined the category, the court should use the corresponding starting points to reach a sentence within the category range below. The starting point applies to all offenders irrespective of plea or previous convictions. Having determined the starting point, step two allows further adjustment for aggravating or mitigating features, set out below.

A case of particular gravity, reflected by multiple features of culpability or harm in step one, could merit upward adjustment from the starting point before further adjustment for aggravating or mitigating features, set out below.

Where there is a sufficient prospect of rehabilitation, a community order with a sex offender treatment programme requirement under section 202 of the Criminal Justice Act 2003 can be a proper alternative to a short or moderate length custodial sentence.

	A	B
Category 1	**Starting point** 6 years' custody **Category range** 4–10 years' custody	**Starting point** 3 years 6 months' custody **Category range** 2 years 6 months'–5 years' custody
Category 2	**Starting point** 4 years' custody **Category range** 2–6 years' custody	**Starting point** 18 months' custody **Category range** 26 weeks'–2 years 6 months' custody
Category 3	**Starting point** 1 year's custody **Category range** High level community order–3 years' custody	**Starting point** Medium level community order **Category range** Low level community order–High level community order

[54] The table below contains a **non-exhaustive** list of additional factual elements providing the context of the offence and factors relating to the offender. Identify whether any combination of these, or other relevant factors, should result in an upward or downward adjustment from the starting point. **In particular, relevant recent convictions are likely to result in an upward adjustment.** In some cases, having considered these factors, it may be appropriate to move outside the identified category range.

When sentencing appropriate **category 3 offences**, the court should also consider the custody threshold as follows: [54]

- Has the custody threshold been passed?
- If so, is it unavoidable that a custodial sentence be imposed?
- If so, can that sentence be suspended?

Aggravating factors
Statutory aggravating factors • Previous convictions, having regard to a) the nature of the offence to which the conviction relates and its relevance to the current offence; and b) the time that has elapsed since the conviction • Offence committed whilst on bail *Other aggravating factors* • Severe psychological or physical harm • Ejaculation • Pregnancy or STI as a consequence of offence • Location of offence • Timing of offence • Victim compelled to leave their home, school, etc • Failure to comply with current court orders • Offence committed whilst on licence • Exploiting contact arrangements with a child to commit an offence • Presence of others, especially other children • Any steps taken to prevent the victim reporting an incident, obtaining assistance and/or from assisting or supporting the prosecution • Attempts to dispose of or conceal evidence • Failure of offender to respond to previous warnings • Commission of offence whilst under the influence of alcohol or drugs • Victim encouraged to recruit others • Period over which offence committed

Mitigating factors
• No previous convictions **or** no relevant/recent convictions • Remorse • Previous good character and/or exemplary conduct* • Age and/or lack of maturity where it affects the responsibility of the offender • Mental disorder or learning disability, particularly where linked to the commission of the offence • Sexual activity was incited but no activity took place because the offender voluntarily desisted or intervened to prevent it

*[Repeats note as to distinction between previous good character/exemplary conduct and having no previous convictions and how to deal with them in respect of the offence: see **SG31-5** for the full text.]

SG31-68 STEPS THREE TO NINE [55]

[These are in the same terms as those applicable to sexual assault of a child under 13: see **SG31.53** ***et seq.***]

SG31-69 Engaging in Sexual Activity in the Presence of a Child [57]

Sexual Offences Act 2003 (section 11)

Causing a Child to Watch a Sexual Act

Sexual Offences Act 2003 (section 12)

Triable either way

Maximum: 10 years' custody

Offence range: Community order–6 years' custody

[Repeats information as to the CJA 2003, ss. 224A and 226A, which is set out at **SG31-50.**]

Arranging or facilitating the commission of a child offence (section 14 of the Sexual Offences Act 2003—guidance [at SG31-73])
The starting points and ranges in this guideline are also applicable to offences of arranging or facilitating the commission of a child offence. In such cases, the level of harm should be determined by reference to the type of activity arranged or facilitated. Sentences commensurate with the applicable starting point and range will ordinarily be appropriate. For offences involving significant commercial exploitation and/or an international element, it may, in the interests of justice, be appropriate to increase a sentence to a point above the category range. In exceptional cases, such as where a vulnerable offender performed a limited role, having been coerced or exploited by others, sentences below the starting point and range may be appropriate.

[58] **STEP ONE Determining the offence category** SG31-70

The court should determine which categories of harm and culpability the offence falls into by reference **only** to the tables below.

Harm	
Category 1	• Causing victim to view extreme pornography • Causing victim to view indecent/prohibited images of children • Engaging in, or causing a victim to view live, sexual activity involving sadism/violence/sexual activity with an animal/a child
Category 2	Engaging in, or causing a victim to view images of or view live, sexual activity involving: • penetration of vagina or anus (using body or object) • penile penetration of the mouth • masturbation
Category 3	Factor(s) in categories 1 and 2 not present

Culpability	
A	B
• Significant degree of planning • Offender acts together with others in order to commit the offence • Use of alcohol/drugs on victim to facilitate the offence • Grooming behaviour used against victim • Abuse of trust • Use of threats (including blackmail) • Specific targeting of a particularly vulnerable child • Significant disparity in age • Commercial exploitation and/or motivation • Offence racially or religiously aggravated • Offence motivated by, or demonstrating, hostility to the victim based on his or her sexual orientation (or presumed sexual orientation) or transgender identity (or presumed transgender identity) • Offence motivated by, or demonstrating, hostility to the victim based on his or her disability (or presumed disability)	Factor(s) in category A not present

STEP TWO Starting point and category range SG31-71

Having determined the category, the court should use the corresponding starting points to reach a sentence within the category range below. The starting point applies to all offenders irrespective of plea or previous convictions. Having determined the starting point, step two allows further adjustment for aggravating or mitigating features, set out below.

A case of particular gravity, reflected by multiple features of culpability or harm in step one, could merit upward adjustment from the starting point before further adjustment for aggravating or mitigating features, set out below.

Where there is a sufficient prospect of rehabilitation, a community order with a sex offender treatment programme requirement under section 202 of the Criminal Justice Act 2003 can be a proper alternative to a short or moderate length custodial sentence.

[59]

	A	B
Category 1	**Starting point** 4 years' custody **Category range** 3–6 years' custody	**Starting point** 2 years' custody **Category range** 1–3 years' custody
Category 2	**Starting point** 2 years' custody **Category range** 1–3 years' custody	**Starting point** 1 year's custody **Category range** High level community order–18 months' custody
Category 3	**Starting point** 26 weeks' custody **Category range** High level community order–1 year's custody	**Starting point** Medium level community order **Category range** Low level community order–Medium level community order

The table below contains a **non-exhaustive** list of additional factual elements providing the context of the offence and factors relating to the offender. Identify whether any combination of these, or other relevant factors, should result in an upward or downward adjustment from the starting point. **In particular, relevant recent convictions are likely to result in an upward adjustment.** In some cases, having considered these factors, it may be appropriate to move outside the identified category range. [59]

When sentencing appropriate **category 2 or 3 offences**, the court should also consider the custody threshold as follows:

- has the custody threshold been passed?
- if so, is it unavoidable that a custodial sentence be imposed?
- if so, can that sentence be suspended?

Aggravating factors
Statutory aggravating factors • Previous convictions, having regard to a) the nature of the offence to which the conviction relates and its relevance to the current offence; and b) the time that has elapsed since the conviction • Offence committed whilst on bail
Other aggravating factors • Location of offence • Timing of offence • Victim compelled to leave their home, school, etc • Failure to comply with current court orders • Offence committed whilst on licence • Exploiting contact arrangements with a child to commit an offence • Presence of others, especially other children • Any steps taken to prevent the victim reporting an incident, obtaining assistance and/or from assisting or supporting the prosecution • Attempts to dispose of or conceal evidence • Failure of offender to respond to previous warnings • Commission of offence whilst offender under the influence of alcohol or drugs • Victim encouraged to recruit others
Mitigating factors
• No previous convictions **or** no relevant/recent convictions • Remorse • Previous good character and/or exemplary conduct* • Age and/or lack of maturity where it affects the responsibility of the offender • Mental disorder or learning disability, particularly where linked to the commission of the offence • Demonstration of steps taken to address offending behaviour

*[Repeats note as to distinction between previous good character/exemplary conduct and having no previous convictions and how to deal with them in respect of the offence: see **SG31-19** for the full text.]

SG31-72 STEPS THREE TO NINE [60]

[These are in the same terms as those applicable to sexual assault of a child under 13: see **SG31-53 *et seq.***]

SG31-73 ARRANGING OR FACILITATING THE COMMISSION OF A CHILD SEX OFFENCE [61]

Sexual Offences Act 2003 (section 14)

Triable either way

Maximum: 14 years' custody

[Repeats information as to the CJA 2003, ss. 224A and 226A, which is set out at **SG31-50**.]

Sentencers should refer to the guideline for the applicable, substantive offence of arranging or facilitating under sections 9 to 12. See [SG31-64 et seq.]. The level of harm should be determined by reference to the type of activity arranged or facilitated. Sentences commensurate with the applicable starting point and range will ordinarily be appropriate. For offences involving significant commercial exploitation and/or an international element, it may, in the interests of justice, be appropriate to increase a sentence to a point above the category range. In exceptional cases, such as where a vulnerable offender performed a limited role, having been coerced or exploited by others, sentences below the starting point and range may be appropriate.

[63] MEETING A CHILD FOLLOWING SEXUAL GROOMING SG31-74

Sexual Offences Act 2003 (section 15)

Triable either way

Maximum: 10 years' custody

Offence range: 1–7 years' custody

[Repeats information as to the CJA 2003, ss. 224A and 226A, which is set out at **SG31-50**.]

[64] **STEP ONE Determining the offence category** SG31-75

The court should determine the offence category using the table below.

Category 1	Raised harm **and** raised culpability
Category 2	Raised harm **or** raised culpability
Category 3	Grooming **without** raised harm or culpability factors present

The court should determine culpability and harm caused or intended, by reference **only** to the factors below, which comprise the principal factual elements of the offence. Where an offence does not fall squarely into a category, individual factors may require a degree of weighting before making an overall assessment and determining the appropriate offence category.

Factors indicating raised harm
• Continued contact despite victim's attempts to terminate contact • Sexual images exchanged • Victim exposed to extreme sexual content for example, extreme pornography • Child is particularly vulnerable due to personal circumstances

Factors indicating raised culpability
• Offender acts together with others to commit the offence • Communication indicates penetrative sexual activity is intended • Offender lied about age/persona • Use of threats (including blackmail), gifts or bribes • Abuse of trust • Specific targeting of a particularly vulnerable child • Abduction/detention • Commercial exploitation and/or motivation • Offence racially or religiously aggravated • Offence motivated by, or demonstrating, hostility to the victim based on his or her sexual orientation (or presumed sexual orientation) or transgender identity (or presumed transgender identity) • Offence motivated by, or demonstrating, hostility to the victim based on his or her disability (or presumed disability)

[65] **STEP TWO Starting point and category range** SG31-76

Having determined the category, the court should use the corresponding starting points to reach a sentence within the category range below. The starting point applies to all offenders irrespective of plea or previous convictions. Having determined the starting point, step two allows further adjustment for aggravating or mitigating features, set out below.

A case of particular gravity, reflected by multiple features of culpability or harm in step one, could merit upward adjustment from the starting point before further adjustment for aggravating or mitigating features, set out below.

Category 1	**Starting point** 4 years' custody **Category range** 3–7 years' custody
Category 2	**Starting point** 2 years' custody **Category range** 1–4 years' custody
Category 3	**Starting point** 18 months' custody **Category range** 1 year–2 years 6 months' custody

The table below contains a **non-exhaustive** list of additional factual elements providing the context of the offence and factors relating to the offender. Identify whether any combination of these, or other relevant factors, should result in an upward or downward adjustment from the starting point. **In particular, relevant recent convictions are likely to result in an upward adjustment.** In some cases, having considered these factors, it may be appropriate to move outside the identified category range. [65]

Aggravating factors
Statutory aggravating factors • Previous convictions, having regard to a) the nature of the offence to which the conviction relates and its relevance to the current offence; and b) the time that has elapsed since the conviction • Offence committed whilst on bail *Other aggravating factors* • Failure to comply with current court orders • Offence committed whilst on licence • Any steps taken to prevent the victim reporting an incident, obtaining assistance and/or from assisting or supporting the prosecution • Attempts to dispose of or conceal evidence • Victim encouraged to recruit others

Mitigating factors
• No previous convictions **or** no relevant/recent convictions • Remorse • Previous good character and/or exemplary conduct* • Age and/or lack of maturity where it affects the responsibility of the offender • Mental disorder or learning disability, particularly where linked to the commission of the offence • Demonstration of steps taken to address offending behaviour

*[Repeats note as to distinction between previous good character/exemplary conduct and having no previous convictions and how to deal with them in respect of the offence: see **SG31-19** for the full text.]

SG31-77 STEPS THREE TO NINE [66]

[These are in the same terms as those applicable to sexual assault of a child under 13: see **SG31-53 *et seq.***]

SG31-78 ## Abuse of Position of Trust: Sexual Activity with a Child [67]

Sexual Offences Act 2003 (section 16)

Abuse of Position of Trust: Causing or Inciting a Child to Engage in Sexual Activity

Sexual Offences Act 2003 (section 17)

Triable either way

Maximum: 5 years' custody

Offence range: Community order–2 years' custody

[Repeats information as to the CJA 2003, s. 226A which is set out at **SG31-17**.]

SG31-79 STEP ONE **Determining the offence category** [68]

The court should determine which categories of harm and culpability the offence falls into by reference **only** to the tables below.

This guideline also applies to offences committed remotely/online

Harm	
Category 1	• Penetration of vagina or anus (using body or object) • Penile penetration of mouth In either case by, or of, the victim
Category 2	• Touching, or exposure, of naked genitalia or naked breasts by, or of, the victim
Category 3	Factor(s) in categories 1 and 2 not present

[68]

Culpability	
A	B
• Significant degree of planning • Offender acts together with others to commit the offence • Use of alcohol/drugs on victim to facilitate the offence • Grooming behaviour used against victim • Use of threats (including blackmail) • Sexual images of victim recorded, retained, solicited or shared • Specific targeting of a particularly vulnerable child • Commercial exploitation and/or motivation • Offence racially or religiously aggravated • Offence motivated by, or demonstrating, hostility to the victim based on his or her sexual orientation (or presumed sexual orientation) or transgender identity (or presumed transgender identity) • Offence motivated by, or demonstrating, hostility to the victim based on his or her disability (or presumed disability)	Factor(s) in category A not present

STEP TWO Starting point and category range SG31-80

Having determined the category, the court should use the corresponding starting points to reach a sentence within the category range below. The starting point applies to all offenders irrespective of plea or previous convictions. Having determined the starting point, step two allows further adjustment for aggravating or mitigating features, set out below.

A case of particular gravity, reflected by multiple features of culpability or harm in step one, could merit upward adjustment from the starting point before further adjustment for aggravating or mitigating features, set out below.

Where there is a sufficient prospect of rehabilitation, a community order with a sex offender treatment programme requirement under section 202 of the Criminal Justice Act 2003 can be a proper alternative to a short or moderate length custodial sentence.

[69]

	A	B
Category 1	**Starting point** 18 months' custody **Category range** 1–2 years' custody	**Starting point** 1 year's custody **Category range** 26 weeks'–18 months' custody
Category 2	**Starting point** 1 year's custody **Category range** 26 weeks'–18 months' custody	**Starting point** 26 weeks' custody **Category range** High level community order–1 year's custody
Category 3	**Starting point** 26 weeks' custody **Category range** High level community order–1 year's custody	**Starting point** Medium level community order **Category range** Low level community order–High level community order

The table below contains a **non-exhaustive** list of additional factual elements providing the context of the offence and factors relating to the offender. Identify whether any combination of these, or other relevant factors, should result in an upward or downward adjustment from the starting point. **In particular, relevant recent convictions are likely to result in an upward adjustment.** In some cases, having considered these factors, it may be appropriate to move outside the identified category range.

When sentencing appropriate **category 2 or 3 offences,** the court should also consider the custody threshold as follows:

- Has the custody threshold been passed?
- If so, is it unavoidable that a custodial sentence be imposed?
- If so, can that sentence be suspended?

Aggravating factors
Statutory aggravating factors • Previous convictions, having regard to a) the nature of the offence to which the conviction relates and its relevance to the current offence; and b) the time that has elapsed since the conviction • Offence committed whilst on bail *Other aggravating factors* • Ejaculation • Pregnancy or STI as a consequence of offence • Location of offence • Timing of offence • Victim compelled to leave their home, school, etc • Failure to comply with current court orders • Offence committed whilst on licence • Presence of others, especially other children • Any steps taken to prevent the victim reporting an incident, obtaining assistance and/or from assisting or supporting the prosecution • Attempts to dispose of or conceal evidence • Failure of offender to respond to previous warnings • Commission of offence whilst under the influence of alcohol or drugs • Victim encouraged to recruit others

[69]

Mitigating factors
• No previous convictions or no relevant/recent convictions • Remorse • Previous good character and/or exemplary conduct* • Age and/or lack of maturity where it affects the responsibility of the offender • Mental disorder or learning disability, particularly where linked to the commission of the offence • Sexual activity was incited but no activity took place because the offender voluntarily desisted or intervened to prevent it • Demonstration of steps taken to address offending behaviour

*[Repeats note as to distinction between previous good character/exemplary conduct and having no previous convictions and how to deal with them in respect of the offence: see **SG31-19** for the full text.]

SG31-81 STEPS THREE TO NINE [70]

[These are in the same terms as those applicable to sexual assault: see **SG31-20** ***et seq.***]

SG31-82 ABUSE OF POSITION OF TRUST: SEXUAL ACTIVITY IN THE PRESENCE OF A CHILD [71]

Sexual Offences Act 2003 (section 18)

ABUSE OF POSITION OF TRUST: CAUSING A CHILD TO WATCH A SEXUAL ACT

Sexual Offences Act 2003 (section 19)

Triable either way

Maximum: 5 years' custody

Offence range: Community order–2 years' custody

[Repeats information as to the CJA 2003, s. 226A, which is set out at **SG31-17**.]

SG31-83 STEP ONE **Determining the offence category** [72]

The court should determine which categories of harm and culpability the offence falls into by reference only to the tables below.

[72]

Harm	
Category 1	• Causing victim to view extreme pornography • Causing victim to view indecent/prohibited images of children • Engaging in, or causing a victim to view live, sexual activity involving sadism/violence/sexual activity with an animal/a child
Category 2	Engaging in, or causing a victim to view images of or view live, sexual activity involving: • penetration of vagina or anus (using body or object) • penile penetration of mouth • masturbation
Category 3	Factor(s) in categories 1 and 2 not present

Culpability	
A	B
• Significant degree of planning • Offender acts together with others to commit the offence • Use of alcohol/drugs on victim to facilitate the offence • Grooming behaviour used against victim • Use of threats (including blackmail) • Specific targeting of a particularly vulnerable child • Commercial exploitation and/or motivation • Offence racially or religiously aggravated • Offence motivated by, or demonstrating, hostility to the victim based on his or her sexual orientation (or presumed sexual orientation) or transgender identity (or presumed transgender identity) • Offence motivated by, or demonstrating, hostility to the victim based on his or her disability (or presumed disability)	Factor(s) in category A not present

STEP TWO Starting point and category range SG31-84

Having determined the category, the court should use the corresponding starting points to reach a sentence within the category range below. The starting point applies to all offenders irrespective of plea or previous convictions. Having determined the starting point, step two allows further adjustment for aggravating or mitigating features, set out below.

A case of particular gravity, reflected by multiple features of culpability or harm in step one, could merit upward adjustment from the starting point before further adjustment for aggravating or mitigating features, set out below.

Where there is a sufficient prospect of rehabilitation, a community order with a sex offender treatment programme requirement under section 202 of the Criminal Justice Act 2003 can be a proper alternative to a short or moderate length custodial sentence.

[73]

	A	B
Category 1	**Starting point** 18 months' custody **Category range** 1–2 years' custody	**Starting point** 1 year's custody **Category range** 26 weeks'–18 months' custody
Category 2	**Starting point** 1 year's custody **Category range** 26 weeks'–18 months' custody	**Starting point** 26 weeks' custody **Category range** High level community order–1 year's custody
Category 3	**Starting point** 26 weeks' custody **Category range** High level community order–1 year's custody	**Starting point** Medium level community order **Category range** Low level community order–High level community order

The table below contains a **non-exhaustive** list of additional factual elements providing the context of the offence and factors relating to the offender. Identify whether any combination of these, or other relevant factors, should result in an upward or downward adjustment from the starting point. **In particular, relevant recent convictions are likely to result in an upward adjustment.** In some cases, having considered these factors, it may be appropriate to move outside the identified category range. [73]

When sentencing appropriate **category 2 or 3 offences**, the court should also consider the custody threshold as follows:

- Has the custody threshold been passed?
- If so, is it unavoidable that a custodial sentence be imposed?
- If so, can that sentence be suspended?

Aggravating factors
Statutory aggravating factors • Previous convictions, having regard to a) the nature of the offence to which the conviction relates and its relevance to the current offence; and b) the time that has elapsed since the conviction • Offence committed whilst on bail *Other aggravating factors* • Location of offence • Timing of offence • Victim compelled to leave their home, school, etc • Failure to comply with current court orders • Offence committed whilst on licence • Presence of others, especially other children • Any steps taken to prevent the victim reporting an incident, obtaining assistance and/or from assisting or supporting the prosecution • Attempts to dispose of or conceal evidence • Failure of offender to respond to previous warnings • Commission of offence whilst under the influence of alcohol or drugs • Victim encouraged to recruit others

Mitigating factors
• No previous convictions **or** no relevant/recent convictions • Remorse • Previous good character and/or exemplary conduct* • Age and/or lack of maturity where it affects the responsibility of the offender • Mental disorder or learning disability, particularly where linked to the commission of the offence • Demonstration of steps taken to address offending behaviour

*[Repeats note as to distinction between previous good character/exemplary conduct and having no previous convictions and how to deal with them in respect of the offence: see **SG31-19** for the full text.]

SG31-85 STEPS THREE TO NINE [74]

[These are in the same terms as those applicable to sexual assault: see **SG31-20 *et seq.***]

SG31-86 POSSESSION OF INDECENT PHOTOGRAPH OF CHILD [75]

Criminal Justice Act 1988 (section 160)

Triable either way

Maximum: 5 years' custody

Offence range: Community order–3 years' custody

INDECENT PHOTOGRAPHS OF CHILDREN

Protection of Children Act 1978 (section 1)

Triable either way

Maximum: 10 years' custody

Offence range: Community order–9 years' custody

[Repeats information as to the CJA 2003, ss. 224A and 226A, which is set out at **SG31-50.**]

[76] **STEP ONE Determining the offence category** SG31-87

The court should determine the offence category using the table below.

	Possession	Distribution*	Production**
Category A	Possession of images involving penetrative sexual activity Possession of images involving sexual activity with an animal or sadism	Sharing images involving penetrative sexual activity Sharing images involving sexual activity with an animal or sadism	Creating images involving penetrative sexual activity Creating images involving sexual activity with an animal or sadism
Category B	Possession of images involving non-penetrative sexual activity	Sharing of images involving non-penetrative sexual activity	Creating images involving non-penetrative sexual activity
Category C	Possession of other indecent images not falling within categories A or B	Sharing of other indecent images not falling within categories A or B	Creating other indecent images not falling within categories A or B

* Distribution includes possession with a view to distributing or sharing images.

** Production includes the taking or making of any image at source for instance the original image. Making an image by simple downloading should be treated as possession for the purposes of sentencing.

In most cases the intrinsic character of the most serious of the offending images will initially determine the appropriate category. If, however, the most serious images are unrepresentative of the offender's conduct a lower category may be appropriate. A lower category will not, however, be appropriate if the offender has produced or taken (for example photographed) images of a higher category.

[77] **STEP TWO Starting point and category range** SG31-88

Having determined the category, the court should use the corresponding starting points to reach a sentence within the category range below. The starting point applies to all offenders irrespective of plea or previous convictions. Having determined the starting point, step two allows further adjustment for aggravating or mitigating features, set out below.

Where there is a sufficient prospect of rehabilitation, a community order with a sex offender treatment programme requirement under section 202 of the Criminal Justice Act 2003 can be a proper alternative to a short or moderate length custodial sentence.

	Possession	Distribution	Production
Category A	**Starting point** 1 year's custody **Category range** 26 weeks–3 years' custody	**Starting point** 3 years' custody **Category range** 2–5 years' custody	**Starting point** 6 years' custody **Category range** 4–9 years' custody
Category B	**Starting point** 26 weeks' custody **Category range** High level community order–18 months' custody	**Starting point** 1 year's custody **Category range** 26 weeks–2 years' custody	**Starting point** 2 years' custody **Category range** 1–4 years' custody
Category C	**Starting point** High level community order **Category range** Medium level community order–26 weeks' custody	**Starting point** 13 weeks' custody **Category range** High level community order–26 weeks' custody	**Starting point** 18 months' custody **Category range** 1–3 years' custody

[78] The table below contains a **non-exhaustive** list of additional factual elements providing the context of the offence and factors relating to the offender. Identify whether any combination of these, or other relevant factors, should result in an upward or downward adjustment from the starting point. **In particular, relevant recent convictions are likely to result in an upward adjustment.** In some cases, having considered these factors, it may be appropriate to move outside the identified category range.

When sentencing appropriate **category 2 or 3 offences**, the court should also consider the custody threshold as follows:

- Has the custody threshold been passed?
- If so, is it unavoidable that a custodial sentence be imposed?
- If so, can that sentence be suspended?

Aggravating factors
Statutory aggravating factors • Previous convictions, having regard to a) the nature of the offence to which the conviction relates and its relevance to the current offence; and b) the time that has elapsed since the conviction • Offence committed whilst on bail *Other aggravating factors* • Failure to comply with current court orders • Offence committed whilst on licence • Age and/or vulnerability of the child depicted* • Discernable pain or distress suffered by child depicted • Period over which images were possessed, distributed or produced • High volume of images possessed, distributed or produced • Placing images where there is the potential for a high volume of viewers • Collection includes moving images • Attempts to dispose of or conceal evidence • Abuse of trust • Child depicted known to the offender • Active involvement in a network or process that facilitates or commissions the creation or sharing of indecent images of children • Commercial exploitation and/or motivation • Deliberate or systematic searching for images portraying young children, category A images or the portrayal of familial sexual abuse • Large number of different victims • Child depicted intoxicated or drugged

[78]

*Age and/or vulnerability of the child should be given significant weight. In cases where the actual age of the victim is difficult to determine sentencers should consider the development of the child (infant, pre-pubescent, post-pubescent)

Mitigating factors
• No previous convictions **or** no relevant/recent convictions • Remorse • Previous good character and/or exemplary conduct* • Age and/or lack of maturity where it affects the responsibility of the offender • Mental disorder or learning disability, particularly where linked to the commission of the offence • Demonstration of steps taken to address offending behaviour

*[Repeats note as to distinction between previous good character/exemplary conduct and having no previous convictions and how to deal with them in respect of the offence: see **SG31-19** for the full text.]

SG31-89 STEPS THREE TO NINE [79]

[These are in the same terms as those applicable to sexual assault of a child under 13: see **SG31-53** ***et seq***.]

SG31-90 CAUSING OR INCITING PROSTITUTION FOR GAIN [81]

Sexual Offences Act 2003 (section 52)

CONTROLLING PROSTITUTION FOR GAIN

Sexual Offences Act 2003 (section 53)

Triable either way

Maximum: 7 years' custody

Offence range: Community order–6 years' custody

[Repeats information as to the CJA 2003, s. 226A which is set out at **SG31-17**.]

The terms 'prostitute' and 'prostitution' are used in this guideline in accordance with the statutory language contained in the Sexual Offences Act 2003.

SG31-91 STEP ONE **Determining the offence category** [82]

The court should determine which categories of harm and culpability the offence falls into by reference **only** to the tables below.

[82]

Harm	
Category 1	• Abduction/detention • Violence or threats of violence • Sustained and systematic psychological abuse • Individual(s) forced or coerced to participate in unsafe/degrading sexual activity • Individual(s) forced or coerced into seeing many 'customers' • Individual(s) forced/coerced/deceived into prostitution
Category 2	Factor(s) in category 1 not present

Culpability		
A	B	C
• Causing, inciting or controlling prostitution on significant commercial basis • Expectation of significant financial or other gain • Abuse of trust • Exploitation of those known to be trafficked • Significant involvement in limiting the freedom of prostitute(s) • Grooming of individual(s) to enter prostitution including through cultivation of a dependency on drugs or alcohol	• Close involvement with prostitute(s) for example control of finances, choice of clients, working conditions, etc (where offender's involvement is not as a result of coercion)	• Performs limited function under direction • Close involvement but engaged by coercion/intimidation/exploitation

STEP TWO Starting point and category range SG31-92

Having determined the category, the court should use the corresponding starting points to reach a sentence within the category range below. The starting point applies to all offenders irrespective of plea or previous convictions. Having determined the starting point, step two allows further adjustment for aggravating or mitigating features, set out below.

A case of particular gravity, reflected by multiple features of culpability or harm in step one, could merit upward adjustment from the starting point before further adjustment for aggravating or mitigating features, set out below.

Where there is a sufficient prospect of rehabilitation, a community order with a sex offender treatment programme requirement under section 202 of the Criminal Justice Act 2003 can be a proper alternative to a short or moderate length custodial sentence.

[83]

	A	B	C
Category 1	**Starting point** 4 years' custody **Category range** 3–6 years' custody	**Starting point** 2 years 6 months' custody **Category range** 2–4 years' custody	**Starting point** 1 year's custody **Category range** 26 weeks'–2 years' custody
Category 2	**Starting point** 2 years' 6 months' custody **Category range** 2–5 years' custody	**Starting point** 1 year's custody **Category range** High level community order–2 years' custody	**Starting point** Medium level community Order **Category range** Low level community order–High level community order

The table below contains a **non-exhaustive** list of additional factual elements providing the context of the offence and factors relating to the offender. Identify whether any combination of these, or other relevant factors, should result in an upward or downward adjustment from the starting point. **In particular, relevant recent convictions are likely to result in an upward adjustment.** In some cases, having considered these factors, it may be appropriate to move outside the identified category range.

When sentencing appropriate **category 2 offences**, the court should also consider the custody threshold as follows: [83]

- Has the custody threshold been passed?
- If so, is it unavoidable that a custodial sentence be imposed?
- If so, can that sentence be suspended?

Aggravating factors
Statutory aggravating factors • Previous convictions, having regard to a) the nature of the offence to which the conviction relates and its relevance to the current offence; and b) the time that has elapsed since the conviction • Offence committed whilst on bail *Other aggravating factors* • Failure to comply with current court orders • Offence committed whilst on licence • Deliberate isolation of prostitute(s) • Threats made to expose prostitute(s) to the authorities (for example, immigration or police), family/friends or others • Harm threatened against the family/friends of prostitute(s) • Passport/identity documents removed • Prostitute(s) prevented from seeking medical treatment • Food withheld • Earnings withheld/kept by offender or evidence of excessive wage reduction or debt bondage, inflated travel or living expenses or unreasonable interest rates • Any steps taken to prevent the reporting of an incident, obtaining assistance and/or from assisting or supporting the prosecution • Attempts to dispose of or conceal evidence • Prostitute(s) forced or coerced into pornography • Timescale over which operation has been run

Mitigating factors
• No previous convictions or no relevant/recent convictions • Remorse • Previous good character and/or exemplary conduct* • Age and/or lack of maturity where it affects the responsibility of the offender • Mental disorder or learning disability, particularly where linked to the commission of the offence • Demonstration of steps taken to address offending behaviour

*[Repeats note as to distinction between previous good character/exemplary conduct and having no previous convictions and how to deal with them in respect of the offence: see **SG31-19** for the full text.]

SG31-93 STEPS THREE TO NINE [84]

[These are in the same terms as those applicable to sexual assault: see **SG31-20**.]

SG31-94 KEEPING A BROTHEL USED FOR PROSTITUTION [85]

Sexual Offences Act 1956 (section 33A)

Triable either way

Maximum: 7 years' custody

Offence range: Community order–6 years' custody

The terms 'prostitute' and 'prostitution' are used in this guideline in accordance with the statutory language contained in the Sexual Offences Act 2003.

SG31-95 STEP ONE **Determining the offence category** [86]

The court should determine which categories of harm and culpability the offence falls into by reference **only** to the tables below.

[86]

Harm	
Category 1	• Under 18 year olds working in brothel • Abduction/detention • Violence or threats of violence • Sustained and systematic psychological abuse • Those working in brothel forced or coerced to participate in unsafe/degrading sexual activity • Those working in brothel forced or coerced into seeing many 'customers' • Those working in brothel forced/coerced/deceived into prostitution • Established evidence of community impact
Category 2	Factor(s) in category 1 not present

Culpability		
A	B	C
• Keeping brothel on significant commercial basis • Involvement in keeping a number of brothels • Expectation of significant financial or other gain • Abuse of trust • Exploitation of those known to be trafficked • Significant involvement in limiting freedom of those working in brothel • Grooming of a person to work in the brothel including through cultivation of a dependency on drugs or alcohol	• Keeping/managing premises • Close involvement with those working in brothel e.g. control of finances, choice of clients, working conditions, etc. (where offender's involvement is not as a result of coercion)	• Performs limited function under direction • Close involvement but engaged by coercion/ intimidation/ exploitation

Sentencing Guidelines

STEP TWO Starting point and category range SG31-96

Having determined the category, the court should use the corresponding starting points to reach a sentence within the category range below. The starting point applies to all offenders irrespective of plea or previous convictions. Having determined the starting point, step two allows further adjustment for aggravating or mitigating features, set out below.

A case of particular gravity, reflected by multiple features of culpability or harm in step one, could merit upward adjustment from the starting point before further adjustment for aggravating or mitigating features, set out below.

Where there is a sufficient prospect of rehabilitation, a community order with a sex offender treatment programme requirement under section 202 of the Criminal Justice Act 2003 can be a proper alternative to a short or moderate length custodial sentence.

[87]

	A	B	C
Category 1	**Starting point** 5 years' custody **Category range** 3–6 years' custody	**Starting point** 3 years' custody **Category range** 2–5 years' custody	**Starting point** 1 year's custody **Category range** High level community order–18 months' custody
Category 2	**Starting point** 3 years' custody **Category range** 2–5 years' custody	**Starting point** 12 months' custody **Category range** 26 weeks'–2 years' custody	**Starting point** Medium level community order **Category range** Low level community order–High level community order

The table below contains a **non-exhaustive** list of additional factual elements providing the context of the offence and factors relating to the offender. Identify whether any combination of these, or other relevant factors, should result in an upward or downward adjustment from the starting point. **In particular, relevant recent convictions are likely to result in an upward adjustment.** In some cases, having considered these factors, it may be appropriate to move outside the identified category range.

When sentencing appropriate **category 1 offences**, the court should also consider the custody threshold as follows: [87]

- Has the custody threshold been passed?
- If so, is it unavoidable that a custodial sentence be imposed?
- If so, can that sentence be suspended?

Aggravating factors
Statutory aggravating factors • Previous convictions, having regard to a) the nature of the offence to which the conviction relates and its relevance to the current offence; and b) the time that has elapsed since the conviction • Offence committed whilst on bail *Other aggravating factors* • Failure to comply with current court orders • Offence committed whilst on licence • Deliberate isolation of those working in brothel • Threats made to expose those working in brothel to the authorities (for example, immigration or police), family/friends or others • Harm threatened against the family/friends of those working in brothel • Passport/identity documents removed • Those working in brothel prevented from seeking medical treatment • Food withheld • Those working in brothel passed around by offender and moved to other brothels • Earnings of those working in brothel withheld/kept by offender or evidence of excessive wage reduction or debt bondage, inflated travel or living expenses or unreasonable interest rates • Any steps taken to prevent those working in brothel reporting an incident, obtaining assistance and/or from assisting or supporting the prosecution • Attempts to dispose of or conceal evidence • Those working in brothel forced or coerced into pornography • Timescale over which operation has been run

Mitigating factors
• No previous convictions **or** no relevant/recent convictions • Remorse • Previous good character and/or exemplary conduct* • Age and/or lack of maturity where it affects the responsibility of the offender • Mental disorder or learning disability, particularly where linked to the commission of the offence • Demonstration of steps taken to address offending behaviour

*[Repeats note as to distinction between previous good character/exemplary conduct and having no previous convictions and how to deal with them in respect of the offence: see SG31-19 for the full text.]

SG31-97 STEPS THREE TO EIGHT [88]

[These are the same as those applicable to rape (see **SG31-6** ***et seq***) but with the omission of the step relating to dangerousness.]

SG31-98 CAUSING OR INCITING SEXUAL EXPLOITATION OF A CHILD [89]

Sexual Offences Act 2003 (section 48)

CONTROLLING A CHILD IN RELATION TO SEXUAL EXPLOITATION

Sexual Offences Act 2003 (section 49)

[89] **ARRANGING OR FACILITATING SEXUAL EXPLOITATION OF A CHILD**

Sexual Offences Act 2003 (section 50)

Triable either way

Maximum: 14 years' custody

Offence range:		
	Victim aged under 13	1–13 years' custody
	Victim aged 13–15	26 weeks'–11 years' custody
	Victim aged 16–17	Community order–7 years' custody

[Repeats information as to the CJA 2003, ss. 224A and 226A which is set out at SG31-50.]

[90] **STEP ONE Determining the offence category** SG31-99

The court should determine which categories of harm and culpability the offence falls into by reference **only** to the tables below.

For offences that involve wide scale commercial and/or international activity sentences above the category range may be appropriate.

Harm	
Category 1	• Victims involved in penetrative sexual activity • Abduction/detention • Violence or threats of violence • Sustained and systematic psychological abuse • Victim(s) participated in unsafe/degrading sexual activity beyond that which is inherent in the offence • Victim(s) passed around by the offender to other 'customers' and/or moved to other brothels
Category 2	Factor(s) in category 1 not present

Culpability		
A	B	C
• Directing or organising sexual exploitation of a child on significant commercial basis • Expectation of significant financial or other gain • Abuse of trust • Exploitation of victim(s) known to be trafficked • Significant involvement in limiting the freedom of the victim(s) • Grooming of a victim for sexual exploitation including through cultivation of a dependency on drugs or alcohol	• Close involvement with inciting, controlling, arranging or facilitating sexual exploitation (where offender's involvement is not as a result of coercion)	• Performs limited function under direction • Close involvement but engaged by coercion/ intimidation / exploitation

[91] **STEP TWO Starting point and category range** SG31-100

Having determined the category, the court should use the corresponding starting points to reach a sentence within the category range below. The starting point applies to all offenders irrespective of plea or previous convictions. Having determined the starting point, step two allows further adjustment for aggravating or mitigating features, set out below.

A case of particular gravity, reflected by multiple features of culpability or harm in step one, could merit upward adjustment from the starting point before further adjustment for aggravating or mitigating features, set out below. [91]

Where there is a sufficient prospect of rehabilitation, a community order with a sex offender treatment programme requirement under section 202 of the Criminal Justice Act 2003 can be a proper alternative to a short or moderate length custodial sentence.

		A	B	C
Category 1	U13	**Starting point** 10 years' custody **Category range** 8–13 years' custody	**Starting point** 8 years' custody **Category range** 6–11 years' custody	**Starting point** 5 years' custody **Category range** 2–6 years' custody
	13–15	**Starting point** 8 years' custody **Category range** 6–11 years' custody	**Starting point** 5 years' custody **Category range** 4–8 years' custody	**Starting point** 2 years 6 months' custody **Category range** 1–4 years' custody
	16–17	**Starting point** 4 years' custody **Category range** 3–7 years' custody	**Starting point** 2 years' custody **Category range** 1–4 years' custody	**Starting point** 1 year's custody **Category range** 26 weeks'–2 years' custody
Category 2	U13	**Starting point** 8 years' custody **Category range** 6–11 years' custody	**Starting point** 6 years' custody **Category range** 4–9 years' custody	**Starting point** 2 years' custody **Category range** 1–4 years' custody
	13–15	**Starting point** 6 years' custody **Category range** 4–9 years' custody	**Starting point** 3 years' custody **Category range** 2–5 years' custody	**Starting point** 1 year's custody **Category range** 26 weeks'–2 years' custody
	16–17	**Starting point** 3 years' custody **Category range** 2–5 years' custody	**Starting point** 1 year's custody **Category range** 26 weeks'–2 years' custody	**Starting point** 26 weeks' custody **Category range** High level community order–1 year's custody

The table below contains a **non-exhaustive** list of additional factual elements providing the context of the offence and factors relating to the offender. Identify whether any combination of these, or other relevant factors, should result in an upward or downward adjustment from the starting point. **In particular, relevant recent convictions are likely to result in an upward adjustment.** In some cases, having considered these factors, it may be appropriate to move outside the identified category range. [92]

When sentencing appropriate **category 2 offences**, the court should also consider the custody threshold as follows:

- Has the custody threshold been passed?
- If so, is it unavoidable that a custodial sentence be imposed?
- If so, can that sentence be suspended?

[92]

Aggravating factors

Statutory aggravating factors
- Previous convictions, having regard to a) the nature of the offence to which the conviction relates and its relevance to the current offence; and b) the time that has elapsed since the conviction
- Offence committed whilst on bail

Other aggravating factors
- Failure to comply with current court orders
- Offence committed whilst on licence
- Deliberate isolation of victim(s)
- Vulnerability of victim(s)
- Threats made to expose victim(s) to the authorities (for example immigration or police), family/friends or others
- Harm threatened against the family/friends of victim(s)
- Passport/identity documents removed
- Victim(s) prevented from seeking medical treatment
- Victim(s) prevented from attending school
- Food withheld
- Earnings withheld/kept by offender or evidence of excessive wage reduction or debt bondage, inflated travel or living expenses or unreasonable interest rates
- Any steps taken to prevent the victim reporting an incident, obtaining assistance and/or from assisting or supporting the prosecution
- Attempts to dispose of or conceal evidence
- Timescale over which the operation has been run

Mitigating factors
- No previous convictions or no relevant/recent convictions
- Remorse
- Previous good character and/or exemplary conduct*
- Age and/or lack of maturity where it affects the responsibility of the offender
- Mental disorder or learning disability, particularly where linked to the commission of the offence

*[Repeats note as to distinction between previous good character/exemplary conduct and having no previous convictions and how to deal with them in respect of the offence: see SG31-5 for the full text.]

[93] **STEPS THREE TO NINE** **SG31-101**

[These are in the same terms as those applicable to sexual assault of a child under 13: see **SG31-53** ***et seq.***]

[95] **PAYING FOR THE SEXUAL SERVICES OF A CHILD** **SG31-102**

Sexual Offences Act 2003 (section 47)

Triable only on indictment (if involving penetration against victim under 16)—otherwise triable either way

Maximum:	Victim under 13 (penetrative)	Life imprisonment
	Victim under 13 (non-penetrative)	14 years' custody
	Victim aged 13–15	14 years' custody
	Victim aged 16–17	7 years' custody
Offence range:	Victim aged 16–17	Community order–5 years' custody

This guideline should only be used where the victim is aged 16 or 17 years old. If the victim is under 13 please refer to the guidelines for rape of a child under 13, assault by penetration of a child under 13, sexual assault of a child under 13 or causing or inciting a child under 13 to engage in sexual activity, depending on the activity involved in the offence.

If the victim is aged 13–15 please refer to the sexual activity with a child guideline.

[Repeats information as to the CJA 2003, s. 226A, which is set out at **SG31-17**.]

Sentencing Guidelines

SG31-103 **STEP ONE Determining the offence category** [96]

The court should determine which categories of harm and culpability the offence falls into by reference **only** to the tables below.

This guideline should only be used where the victim was aged 16 or 17 years old.

Harm	
Category 1	• Penetration of vagina or anus (using body or object) by, or of, the victim • Penile penetration of mouth by, or of, the victim • Violence or threats of violence • Victim subjected to unsafe/degrading sexual activity (beyond that which is inherent in the offence)
Category 2	• Touching of naked genitalia or naked breasts by, or of, the victim
Category 3	• Other sexual activity

Culpability	
A	**B**
• Abduction/detention • Sexual images of victim recorded, retained, solicited or shared • Offender acts together with others to commit the offence • Use of alcohol/drugs on victim • Abuse of trust • Previous violence against victim • Sexual images of victim recorded, retained, solicited or shared • Blackmail or other threats made (including to expose victim to the authorities, family/friends or others) • Offender aware that he has a sexually transmitted disease • Offender aware victim has been trafficked	Factor(s) in category A not present

SG31-104 **STEP TWO Starting point and category range**

Having determined the category, the court should use the corresponding starting points to reach a sentence within the category range below **for victims aged 16 or 17**. The starting point applies to all offenders irrespective of plea or previous convictions. Having determined the starting point, step two allows further adjustment for aggravating or mitigating features, set out below.

A case of particular gravity, reflected by multiple features of culpability in step one, could merit upward adjustment from the starting point before further adjustment for aggravating or mitigating features, set out below.

Where there is a sufficient prospect of rehabilitation, a community order with a sex offender treatment programme requirement under section 202 of the Criminal Justice Act 2003 can be a proper alternative to a short or moderate length custodial sentence. [97]

	A	B
Category 1	**Starting point** 4 years' custody **Category range** 2–5 years' custody	**Starting point** 2 years' custody **Category range** 1–4 years' custody
Category 2	**Starting point** 3 years' custody **Category range** 1–4 years' custody	**Starting point** 1 year's custody **Category range** 26 weeks'–2 years' custody
Category 3	**Starting point** 1 year's custody **Category range** 26 weeks'–2 years' custody	**Starting point** 26 weeks' custody **Category range** High level community order–1 year's custody

[97] The table below contains a **non-exhaustive** list of additional factual elements providing the context of the offence and factors relating to the offender. Identify whether any combination of these, or other relevant factors, should result in an upward or downward adjustment from the starting point. **In particular, relevant recent convictions are likely to result in an upward adjustment.** In some cases, having considered these factors, it may be appropriate to move outside the identified category range.

When sentencing appropriate **category 3 offences**, the court should also consider the custody threshold as follows:

- Has the custody threshold been passed?
- If so, is it unavoidable that a custodial sentence be imposed?
- If so, can that sentence be suspended?

Aggravating factors
Statutory aggravating factors • Previous convictions, having regard to a) the nature of the offence to which the conviction relates and its relevance to the current offence; and b) the time that has elapsed since the conviction • Offence committed whilst on bail *Other aggravating factors* • Ejaculation • Failure to comply with current court orders • Offence committed whilst on licence • Any steps taken to prevent the victim reporting an incident, obtaining assistance and/or from assisting or supporting the prosecution • Attempts to dispose of or conceal evidence

Mitigating factors
• No previous convictions or no relevant/recent convictions • Remorse • Previous good character and/or exemplary conduct* • Age and/or lack of maturity where it affects the responsibility of the offender • Mental disorder or learning disability, particularly where linked to the commission of the offence • Demonstration of steps taken to address offending behaviour

*[Repeats note as to distinction between previous good character/exemplary conduct and having no previous convictions and how to deal with them in respect of the offence: see SG31-19 for the full text.]

[98] STEPS THREE TO NINE SG31-105

[These are in the same terms as those applicable to sexual assault: see **SG31-20** *et seq.*]

[99] Trafficking People for Sexual Exploitation SG31-106

Sexual Offences Act 2003 (sections 59A)

(This guideline also applies to offences, committed before 6 April 2013, of trafficking into/within/out of the UK for sexual exploitation contrary to sections 57 to 59 of the Sexual Offences Act 2003)

Triable either way

Maximum: 14 years' custody

Offence range: Community order–12 years' custody

[Repeats information as to the CJA 2003, s. 226A, which is set out at **SG31-17**.]

The term 'prostitution' is used in this guideline in accordance with the statutory language contained in the Sexual Offences Act 2003.

Sentencing Guidelines

Interim explanatory guidance pending the production of a full guideline for Modern Slavery [99]

* Section 59A of the Sexual Offences Act 2003 (SOA) has now been repealed by Schedule 5, paragraph 5 of the Modern Slavery Act 2015 (MSA). However, section 59A SOA remains in force for those offences committed wholly or partly before 31 July 2015.

Sentencers may consider that this is an appropriate guideline to follow when sentencing cases of sexual exploitation prosecuted under section 2 of the MSA. However, it is important to note that although the either way offence in section 2 of the MSA is in some ways similar to the SOA offence the maximum penalty for the MSA offence is life imprisonment. In addition the following provisions apply to the offence under the MSA:

- This is a specified offence for the purposes of sections 224 and 225(2) (life sentence for serious offences) of the Criminal Justice Act 2003.
- It is listed in Part 1 of Schedule 15B for the purposes of Section 224A (life sentence for second listed offence) of the Criminal Justice Act 2003.
- This is a specified offence for the purposes of section 226A (extended sentence for certain violent or sexual offences) of the Criminal Justice Act 2003.

Sentencers seeking to rely on this guideline when sentencing offenders under the MSA may, therefore, need to adjust the starting point and ranges bearing in mind the increased statutory maximum.

SG31-107 STEP ONE **Determining the offence category** [100]

The court should determine which categories of harm and culpability the offence falls into by reference **only** to the tables below.

Harm	
Category 1	• Abduction/detention • Violence or threats of violence • Sustained and systematic psychological abuse • Victim(s) under 18 • Victim(s) forced or coerced to participate in unsafe/degrading sexual activity • Victim(s) forced/coerced into prostitution • Victim(s) tricked/deceived as to purpose of visit
Category 2	• Factor(s) in category 1 not present

Culpability		
A	**B**	**C**
• Directing or organising trafficking on significant commercial basis • Expectation of significant financial or other gain • Significant influence over others in trafficking organisation/hierarchy • Abuse of trust	• Operational or management function within hierarchy • Involves others in operation whether by coercion/ intimidation/exploitation or reward (and offender's involvement is not as a result of coercion)	• Performs limited function under direction • Close involvement but engaged by coercion/ intimidation/exploitation

SG31-108 STEP TWO **Starting point and category range**

Having determined the category of harm and culpability, the court should use the corresponding starting points to reach a sentence within the category range below. The starting point applies to all offenders irrespective of plea or previous convictions. Having determined the starting point, step two allows further adjustment for aggravating or mitigating features, set out below.

A case of particular gravity, reflected by multiple features of culpability or harm in step one, could merit upward adjustment from the starting point before further adjustment for aggravating or mitigating features, set out below.

Where there is a sufficient prospect of rehabilitation, a community order with a sex offender treatment programme requirement under section 202 of the Criminal Justice Act 2003 can be a proper alternative to a short or moderate length custodial sentence.

[101]

	A	B	C
Category 1	**Starting point** 8 years' custody **Category range** 6–2 years' custody	**Starting point** 6 years' custody **Category range** 4–8 years' custody	**Starting point** 18 months' custody **Category range** 26 weeks'–2 years' custody
Category 2	**Starting point** 6 years' custody **Category range** 4–8 years' custody	**Starting point** 4 years' custody **Category range** 2–6 years' custody	**Starting point** 26 weeks' custody **Category range** High level community order–18 months' custody

The table below contains a **non-exhaustive** list of additional factual elements providing the context of the offence and factors relating to the offender. Identify whether any combination of these, or other relevant factors, should result in an upward or downward adjustment from the starting point. **In particular, relevant recent convictions are likely to result in an upward adjustment.** In some cases, having considered these factors, it may be appropriate to move outside the identified category range.

When sentencing appropriate **category 2 offences**, the court should also consider the custody threshold as follows:

- Has the custody threshold been passed?
- If so, is it unavoidable that a custodial sentence be imposed?
- If so, can that sentence be suspended?

Aggravating factors
Statutory aggravating factors • Previous convictions, having regard to a) the nature of the offence to which the conviction relates and its relevance to the current offence; and b) the time that has elapsed since the conviction • Offence committed whilst on bail *Other aggravating factors* • Failure to comply with current court orders • Offence committed whilst on licence • Deliberate isolation of victim(s) • Children of victim(s) left in home country due to trafficking • Threats made to expose victim(s) to the authorities (for example immigration or police), family/friends or others • Harm threatened against the family/friends of victim • Exploitation of victim(s) from particularly vulnerable backgrounds • Victim(s) previously trafficked/sold/passed around • Passport/identity documents removed • Victim(s) prevented from seeking medical treatment • Food withheld • Use of drugs/alcohol or other substance to secure victim's compliance • Earnings of victim(s) withheld/kept by offender or evidence of excessive wage reduction, debt bondage, inflated travel or living expenses, unreasonable interest rates • Any steps taken to prevent the victim reporting an incident, obtaining assistance and/or from assisting or supporting the prosecution • Attempts to dispose of or conceal evidence • Timescale over which operation has been run

Mitigating factors
• No previous convictions **or** no relevant/recent convictions • Remorse • Previous good character and/or exemplary conduct* • Age and/or lack of maturity where it affects the responsibility of the offender • Mental disorder or learning disability, particularly where linked to the commission of the offence

*[Repeats note as to distinction between previous good character/exemplary conduct and having no previous convictions and how to deal with them in respect of the offence: see **SG31-5** for the full text.]

SG31-109 STEPS THREE TO NINE [102]

[These are in the same terms as those applicable to sexual assault: see **SG31-20** ***et seq.***]

SG31-110 SEXUAL ACTIVITY WITH A PERSON WITH A MENTAL DISORDER IMPEDING CHOICE [103]

Sexual Offences Act 2003 (section 30)

CAUSING OR INCITING A PERSON, WITH A MENTAL DISORDER IMPEDING CHOICE, TO ENGAGE IN SEXUAL ACTIVITY

Sexual Offences Act 2003 (section 31)

Triable only on indictment (if penetration involved)

- otherwise, triable either way

Maximum: Life imprisonment (if penetration involved)

- otherwise, 14 years' custody

Offence range: Community order–19 years' custody

[Repeats information as to the CJA 2003, ss. 224, 225(2), 224A and 226A, which is set out at **SG31-3**.]

SG31-111 STEP ONE **Determining the offence category** [104]

The court should determine which categories of harm and culpability the offence falls into by reference **only** to the tables below.

Harm	
Category 1	• The extreme nature of one or more category 2 factors or the extreme impact caused by a combination of category 2 factors **may** elevate to category 1
Category 2	• Severe psychological or physical harm • Pregnancy or STI as a consequence of offence • Additional degradation/humiliation • Abduction • Prolonged detention /sustained incident • Violence or threats of violence • Forced/uninvited entry into victim's home or residence
Category 3	Factor(s) in categories 1 and 2 not present

Culpability	
A	B
• Significant degree of planning • Offender acts together with others to commit the offence • Use of alcohol/drugs on victim to facilitate the offence • Grooming behaviour used against victim • Abuse of trust • Previous violence against victim • Offence committed in course of burglary • Sexual images of victim recorded, retained, solicited or shared • Deliberate isolation of victim • Commercial exploitation and/or motivation • Offence racially or religiously aggravated • Offence motivated by, or demonstrating, hostility to the victim based on his or her sexual orientation (or presumed sexual orientation) or transgender identity (or presumed transgender identity) • Offence motivated by, or demonstrating, hostility to the victim based on the victim's disability (or presumed disability)	Factor(s) in category A not present

[105] **STEP TWO Starting point and category range** SG31-112

Having determined the category of harm and culpability, the court should use the corresponding starting points to reach a sentence within the category range below. The starting point applies to all offenders irrespective of plea or previous convictions. Having determined the starting point, step two allows further adjustment for aggravating or mitigating features, set out below.

A case of particular gravity, reflected by multiple features of culpability or harm in step one, could merit upward adjustment from the starting point before further adjustment for aggravating or mitigating features, set out below.

Where there is a sufficient prospect of rehabilitation, a community order with a sex offender treatment programme requirement under section 202 of the Criminal Justice Act 2003 can be a proper alternative to a short or moderate length custodial sentence.

Where offence involved penetration

	A	B
Category 1	**Starting point** 16 years' custody **Category range** 13–19 years' custody	**Starting point** 13 years' custody **Category range** 11–17 years' custody
Category 2	**Starting point** 13 years' custody **Category range** 11–17 years' custody	**Starting point** 10 years' custody **Category range** 8–13 years' custody
Category 3	**Starting point** 10 years' custody **Category range** 8–13 years' custody	**Starting point** 8 years' custody **Category range** 6–11 years' custody

Where offence did not involve penetration

	A	B
Category 1	**Starting point** 6 years' custody **Category range** 4–9 years' custody	**Starting point** 4 years' custody **Category range** 3–7 years' custody
Category 2	**Starting point** 4 years' custody **Category range** 3–7 years' custody	**Starting point** 2 years' custody **Category range** 1–4 years' custody
Category 3	**Starting point** 1 year's custody **Category range** 26 weeks'– 2 years' custody	**Starting point** 26 weeks' custody **Category range** High level community order– 1 year's custody

[106] The table below contains a **non-exhaustive** list of additional factual elements providing the context of the offence and factors relating to the offender. Identify whether any combination of these, or other relevant factors, should result in an upward or downward adjustment from the starting point. **In particular, relevant recent convictions are likely to result in an upward adjustment.** In some cases, having considered these factors, it may be appropriate to move outside the identified category range.

When appropriate, the court should also consider the custody threshold as follows:

- Has the custody threshold been passed?
- If so, is it unavoidable that a custodial sentence be imposed?
- If so, can that sentence be suspended?

Aggravating factors
Statutory aggravating factors • Previous convictions, having regard to a) the nature of the offence to which the conviction relates and its relevance to the current offence; and b) the time that has elapsed since the conviction • Offence committed whilst on bail
Other aggravating factors • Ejaculation (where not taken into account at step one) • Blackmail or other threats made (where not taken into account at step one) • Location of offence • Timing of offence • Use of weapon or other item to frighten or injure • Victim compelled to leave their home or institution (including victims of domestic violence) • Failure to comply with current court orders • Offence committed whilst on licence • Presence of others, especially children • Any steps taken to prevent the victim reporting an incident, obtaining assistance and/or from assisting or supporting the prosecution • Attempts to dispose of or conceal evidence • Commission of offence whilst under the influence of alcohol or drugs

[106]

Mitigating factors
• No previous convictions **or** no relevant/recent convictions • Remorse • Previous good character and/or exemplary conduct* • Age and/or lack of maturity where it affects the responsibility of the offender • Mental disorder or learning disability, particularly where linked to the commission of the offence • Sexual activity was incited but no activity took place because the offender voluntarily desisted or intervened to prevent it

*[Repeats note as to distinction between previous good character/exemplary conduct and having no previous convictions and how to deal with them in respect of the offence: see **SG31-5** for the full text.]

SG31-113 STEPS THREE TO NINE [107]

[These are in the same terms as those applicable to rape: see **SG31-6 *et seq*.**]

SG31-114 ENGAGING IN SEXUAL ACTIVITY IN THE PRESENCE OF A PERSON WITH MENTAL DISORDER IMPEDING CHOICE [109]

Sexual Offences Act 2003 (section 32)

CAUSING A PERSON, WITH MENTAL DISORDER IMPEDING CHOICE, TO WATCH A SEXUAL ACT

Sexual Offences Act 2003 (section 33)

Triable either way

Maximum: 10 years' custody

Offence range: Community order–6 years' custody

[Repeats information as to the CJA 2003, s. 226A which is set out at **SG31-17**.]

SG31-115 STEP ONE **Determining the offence category** [110]

The court should determine which categories of harm and culpability the offence falls into by reference **only** to the tables below.

[110]

Harm	
Category 1	• Causing victim to view extreme pornography • Causing victim to view indecent/prohibited images of children • Engaging in, or causing a victim to view live, sexual activity involving sadism/violence/ sexual activity with an animal/a child
Category 2	Engaging in, or causing a victim to view images of or view live, sexual activity involving: • penetration of vagina or anus (using body or object) • penile penetration of mouth • masturbation
Category 3	Factor(s) in categories 1 and 2 not present

Culpability	
A	B
• Significant degree of planning • Offender acts together with others in order to commit the offence • Use of alcohol/drugs on victim to facilitate the offence • Grooming behaviour used against victim • Abuse of trust • Use of threats (including blackmail) • Commercial exploitation and/or motivation • Offence racially or religiously aggravated • Offence motivated by, or demonstrating, hostility to the victim based on his or her sexual orientation (or presumed sexual orientation) or transgender identity (or presumed transgender identity) • Offence motivated by, or demonstrating, hostility to the victim based on his or her disability (or presumed disability)	Factor(s) in category A not present

STEP TWO Starting point and category range SG31-116

Having determined the category of harm and culpability, the court should use the corresponding starting points to reach a sentence within the category range below. The starting point applies to all offenders irrespective of plea or previous convictions.

Having determined the starting point, step two allows further adjustment for aggravating or mitigating features, set out below.

A case of particular gravity, reflected by multiple features of culpability or harm in step one, could merit upward adjustment from the starting point before further adjustment for aggravating or mitigating features, set out below.

Where there is a sufficient prospect of rehabilitation, a community order with a sex offender treatment programme requirement under section 202 of the Criminal Justice Act 2003 can be a proper alternative to a short or moderate length custodial sentence.

[111]

	A	B
Category 1	**Starting point** 4 years' custody **Category range** 3–6 years' custody	**Starting point** 2 years' custody **Category range** 1–3 years' custody
Category 2	**Starting point** 2 years' custody **Category range** 1–3 years' custody	**Starting point** 1 year's custody **Category range** High level community order–18 months' custody
Category 3	**Starting point** 26 weeks' custody **Category range** High level community order–1 year's custody	**Starting point** Medium level community order **Category range** Low level community order–Medium level community order

The table below contains a **non-exhaustive** list of additional factual elements providing the context of the offence and factors relating to the offender. Identify whether any combination of these, or other relevant factors, should result in an upward or downward adjustment from the starting point. **In particular, relevant recent convictions are likely to result in an upward adjustment.** In some cases, having considered these factors, it may be appropriate to move outside the identified category range. [111]

When sentencing appropriate **category 2 or 3 offences**, the court should also consider the custody threshold as follows:

- Has the custody threshold been passed?
- If so, is it unavoidable that a custodial sentence be imposed?
- If so, can that sentence be suspended?

Aggravating factors
Statutory aggravating factors • Previous convictions, having regard to a) the nature of the offence to which the conviction relates and its relevance to the current offence; and b) the time that has elapsed since the conviction • Offence committed whilst on bail *Other aggravating factors* • Location of offence • Timing of offence • Failure to comply with current court orders • Offence committed whilst on licence • Any steps taken to prevent the victim reporting an incident, obtaining assistance and/or from assisting or supporting the prosecution • Attempts to dispose of or conceal evidence • Commission of offence whilst under the influence of alcohol or drugs

Mitigating factors
• No previous convictions **or** no relevant/recent convictions • Remorse • Previous good character and/or exemplary conduct* • Age and/or lack of maturity where it affects the responsibility of the offender • Mental disorder or learning disability, particularly where linked to the commission of the offence • Demonstration of steps taken to address offending behaviour

*[Repeats note as to distinction between previous good character/exemplary conduct and having no previous convictions and how to deal with them in respect of the offence: see **SG31-19** for the full text.]

SG31-117 STEPS THREE TO NINE [112]

[These are in the same terms as those applicable to sexual assault: see **SG31-20** ***et seq.***]

SG31-118 INDUCEMENT, THREAT OR DECEPTION TO PROCURE SEXUAL ACTIVITY WITH A PERSON WITH A MENTAL DISORDER [113]

Sexual Offences Act 2003 (section 34)

CAUSING A PERSON WITH A MENTAL DISORDER TO ENGAGE IN OR AGREE TO ENGAGE IN SEXUAL ACTIVITY BY INDUCEMENT, THREAT OR DECEPTION

Sexual Offences Act 2003 (section 35)

Triable only on indictment (if penetration involved); otherwise triable either way

Maximum: Life imprisonment (if penetration involved); otherwise 14 years' custody

Offence range: Community order–10 years' custody

[Repeats information as to the CJA 2003, ss. 224, 225(2), 224A and 226A, which is set out at **SG31-3**.]

[114] **STEP ONE Determining the offence category** SG31-119

The court should determine which categories of harm and culpability the offence falls into by reference **only** to the tables below.

This guideline also applies to offences committed remotely/online.

Harm	
Category 1	• Penetration of vagina or anus (using body or object) • Penile penetration of mouth In either case by, or of, the victim
Category 2	Touching, or exposure, of naked genitalia or naked breasts by, or of, the victim
Category 3	Other sexual activity

Culpability	
A	B
• Significant degree of planning • Offender acts together with others to commit the offence • Use of alcohol/drugs on victim to facilitate the offence • Abuse of trust • Sexual images of victim recorded, retained, solicited or shared • Commercial exploitation and/or motivation • Offence racially or religiously aggravated • Offence motivated by, or demonstrating, hostility to the victim based on his or her sexual orientation (or presumed sexual orientation) or transgender identity (or presumed transgender identity) • Offence motivated by, or demonstrating, hostility to the victim based on his or her disability (or presumed disability)	Factor(s) in category A not present

STEP TWO Starting point and category range SG31-120

Having determined the category of harm and culpability, the court should use the corresponding starting points to reach a sentence within the category range below. The starting point applies to all offenders irrespective of plea or previous convictions. Having determined the starting point, step two allows further adjustment for aggravating or mitigating features, set out below.

A case of particular gravity, reflected by multiple features of culpability or harm in step one, could merit upward adjustment from the starting point before further adjustment for aggravating or mitigating features, set out below.

Where there is a sufficient prospect of rehabilitation, a community order with a sex offender treatment programme requirement under section 202 of the Criminal Justice Act 2003 can be a proper alternative to a short or moderate length custodial sentence.

[115]

	A	B
Category 1	**Starting point** 5 years' custody **Category range** 4–10 years' custody	**Starting point** 1 year's custody **Category range** High level community order–2 years' custody
Category 2	**Starting point** 3 years' custody **Category range** 2–6 years' custody	**Starting point** 26 weeks' custody **Category range** High level community order–1 year's custody
Category 3	**Starting point** 26 weeks' custody **Category range** High level community order–3 years' custody	**Starting point** Medium level community order **Category range** Low level community order–High level community order

Sentencing Guidelines

The table below contains a **non-exhaustive** list of additional factual elements providing the context of the offence and factors relating to the offender. Identify whether any combination of these, or other relevant factors, should result in an upward or downward adjustment from the starting point. **In particular, relevant recent convictions are likely to result in an upward adjustment.** In some cases, having considered these factors, it may be appropriate to move outside the identified category range. [115]

When sentencing appropriate **category 2 or 3 offences**, the court should also consider the custody threshold as follows:

- Has the custody threshold been passed?
- If so, is it unavoidable that a custodial sentence be imposed?
- If so, can that sentence be suspended?

Aggravating factors
Statutory aggravating factors • Previous convictions, having regard to a) the nature of the offence to which the conviction relates and its relevance to the current offence; and b) the time that has elapsed since the conviction • Offence committed whilst on bail *Other aggravating factors* • Severe psychological or physical harm • Ejaculation • Pregnancy or STI as a consequence of offence • Location of offence • Timing of offence • Victim compelled to leave their home or institution (including victims of domestic violence) • Failure to comply with current court orders • Offence committed whilst on licence • Any steps taken to prevent the victim reporting an incident, obtaining assistance and/or from assisting or supporting the prosecution • Attempts to dispose of or conceal evidence • Commission of offence whilst under the influence of alcohol or drugs

Mitigating factors
• No previous convictions **or** no relevant/recent convictions • Remorse • Previous good character and/or exemplary conduct* • Age and/or lack of maturity where it affects the responsibility of the offender • Mental disorder or learning disability, particularly where linked to the commission of the offence

*[Repeats note as to distinction between previous good character/exemplary conduct and having no previous convictions and how to deal with them in respect of the offence: see **SG31-5** for the full text.]

SG31-121 STEPS THREE TO NINE [116]

[These are in the same terms as those applicable to rape: see **SG31-6 *et seq*.**]

SG31-122 Engaging in Sexual Activity in the Presence, Procured by Inducement, Threat or Deception, of a Person with a Mental Disorder [117]

Sexual Offences Act 2003 (section 36)

Causing a Person with a Mental Disorder to Watch a Sexual Act by Inducement, Threat or Deception

Sexual Offences Act 2003 (section 37)

Triable either way

Maximum: 10 years' custody

Offence range: Community order–6 years' custody

[Repeats information as to the CJA 2003, s. 226A, which is set out at **SG31-17**.]

[118] **STEP ONE Determining the offence category** SG31-123

The court should determine which categories of harm and culpability the offence falls into by reference only to the tables below.

Harm	
Category 1	• Causing victim to view extreme pornography • Causing victim to view indecent/prohibited images of children • Engaging in, or causing a victim to view live, sexual activity involving sadism/violence/sexual activity with an animal/a child
Category 2	Engaging in, or causing a victim to view images of or view live, sexual activity involving: • penetration of vagina or anus (using body or object) • penile penetration of mouth • masturbation
Category 3	Factor(s) in categories 1 and 2 not present

Culpability	
A	B
• Significant degree of planning • Offender acts together with others in order to commit the offence • Use of alcohol/drugs on victim to facilitate the offence • Abuse of trust • Commercial exploitation and/or motivation • Offence racially or religiously aggravated • Offence motivated by, or demonstrating, hostility to the victim based on his or her sexual orientation (or presumed sexual orientation) or transgender identity (or presumed transgender identity) • Offence motivated by, or demonstrating, hostility to the victim based on his or her disability (or presumed disability)	Factor(s) in category A not present

STEP TWO Starting point and category range SG31-124

Having determined the category of harm and culpability, the court should use the corresponding starting points to reach a sentence within the category range below. The starting point applies to all offenders irrespective of plea or previous convictions. Having determined the starting point, step two allows further adjustment for aggravating or mitigating features, set out below.

A case of particular gravity, reflected by multiple features of culpability or harm in step one, could merit upward adjustment from the starting point before further adjustment for aggravating or mitigating features, set out below.

Where there is a sufficient prospect of rehabilitation, a community order with a sex offender treatment programme requirement under section 202 of the Criminal Justice Act 2003 can be a proper alternative to a short or moderate length custodial sentence.

[119]

	A	B
Category 1	**Starting point** 4 years' custody **Category range** 3–6 years' custody	**Starting point** 2 years' custody **Category range** 1–3 years' custody
Category 2	**Starting point** 2 years' custody **Category range** 1–3 years' custody	**Starting point** 1 year's custody **Category range** High level community order–18 months' custody
Category 3	**Starting point** 26 weeks' custody **Category range** High level community order–1 year's custody	**Starting point** Medium level community order **Category range** Low level community order–Medium level community order

The table below contains a **non-exhaustive** list of additional factual elements providing the context of the offence and factors relating to the offender. Identify whether any combination of these, or other relevant factors, should result in an upward or downward adjustment from the starting point. **In particular, relevant recent convictions are likely to result in an upward adjustment.** In some cases, having considered these factors, it may be appropriate to move outside the identified category range. [119]

When sentencing appropriate **category 2 or 3 offences**, the court should also consider the custody threshold as follows:

- Has the custody threshold been passed?
- If so, is it unavoidable that a custodial sentence be imposed?
- If so, can that sentence be suspended?

Aggravating factors
Statutory aggravating factors • Previous convictions, having regard to a) the nature of the offence to which the conviction relates and its relevance to the current offence; and b) the time that has elapsed since the conviction • Offence committed whilst on bail *Other aggravating factors* • Location of offence • Timing of offence • Failure to comply with current court orders • Offence committed whilst on licence • Any steps taken to prevent the victim reporting an incident, obtaining assistance and/or from assisting or supporting the prosecution • Attempts to dispose of or conceal evidence • Commission of offence whilst under the influence of alcohol or drugs

Mitigating factors
• No previous convictions **or** no relevant/recent convictions • Remorse • Previous good character and/or exemplary conduct* • Age and/or lack of maturity where it affects the responsibility of the offender • Mental disorder or learning disability, particularly where linked to the commission of the offence • Demonstration of steps taken to address offending behaviour

*[Repeats note as to distinction between previous good character/exemplary conduct and having no previous convictions and how to deal with them in respect of the offence: see **SG31-19** for the full text.]

SG31-125 STEPS THREE TO NINE [120]

[These are in the same terms as those applicable to sexual assault: see **SG31-20** ***et seq***.]

SG31-126 Care Workers: Sexual Activity with a Person with a Mental Disorder [121]

Sexual Offences Act 2003 (section 38)

Care Workers: Causing or Inciting Sexual Activity

Sexual Offences Act 2003 (section 39)

Triable only on indictment (if penetration involved); otherwise triable either way

Maximum: 14 years' custody (if penetration involved); otherwise 10 years' custody

Offence range: Community order–10 years' custody

[Repeats information as to the CJA 2003, s. 226A, which is set out at **SG31-17.**]

SG31-127 STEP ONE **Determining the offence category** [122]

The court should determine which categories of harm and culpability the offence falls into by reference **only** to the tables below.

This guideline also applies to offences committed remotely/online.

[122]

Harm	
Category 1	• Penetration of vagina or anus (using body or object) • Penile penetration of mouth In either case by, or of, the victim
Category 2	• Touching, or exposure, of naked genitalia or naked breasts by, or of, the victim
Category 3	Factor(s) in categories 1 and 2 not present

Culpability	
A	B
• Significant degree of planning • Offender acts together with others to commit the offence • Use of alcohol/drugs on victim to facilitate the offence • Grooming behaviour used against victim • Use of threats (including blackmail) • Sexual images of victim recorded, retained, solicited or shared • Commercial exploitation and/or motivation • Offence racially or religiously aggravated • Offence motivated by, or demonstrating, hostility to the victim based on his or her sexual orientation (or presumed sexual orientation) or transgender identity (or presumed transgender identity) • Offence motivated by, or demonstrating, hostility to the victim based on his or her disability (or presumed disability)	Factor(s) in category A not present

STEP TWO Starting point and category range SG31-128

Having determined the category of harm and culpability, the court should use the corresponding starting points to reach a sentence within the category range below. The starting point applies to all offenders irrespective of plea or previous convictions. Having determined the starting point, step two allows further adjustment for aggravating or mitigating features, set out below.

A case of particular gravity, reflected by multiple features of culpability or harm in step one, could merit upward adjustment from the starting point before further adjustment for aggravating or mitigating features, set out below.

Where there is a sufficient prospect of rehabilitation, a community order with a sex offender treatment programme requirement under section 202 of the Criminal Justice Act 2003 can be a proper alternative to a short or moderate length custodial sentence.

[123]

	A	B
Category 1	**Starting point** 5 years' custody **Category range** 4–10 years' custody	**Starting point** 18 months' custody **Category range** 1–2 years' custody
Category 2	**Starting point** 3 year's custody **Category range** 2–6 years' custody	**Starting point** 26 weeks' custody **Category range** Medium level community order–1 year's custody
Category 3	**Starting point** 26 weeks' custody **Category range** High level community order–3 years' custody	**Starting point** Medium level community order **Category range** Low level community order–High level community order

The table below contains a **non-exhaustive** list of additional factual elements providing the context of the offence and factors relating to the offender. Identify whether any combination of these, or other relevant factors, should result in an upward or downward adjustment from the starting point. **In particular, relevant recent convictions are likely to result in an upward adjustment.** In some cases, having considered these factors, it may be appropriate to move outside the identified category range.

When sentencing appropriate **category 2 or 3 offences**, the court should also consider the custody threshold as follows: [123]

- Has the custody threshold been passed?
- If so, is it unavoidable that a custodial sentence be imposed?
- If so, can that sentence be suspended?

Aggravating factors
Statutory aggravating factors • Previous convictions, having regard to a) the nature of the offence to which the conviction relates and its relevance to the current offence; and b) the time that has elapsed since the conviction • Offence committed whilst on bail *Other aggravating factors* • Ejaculation • Pregnancy or STI as a consequence of offence • Location of offence • Timing of offence • Victim compelled to leave their home or institution (including victims of domestic violence) • Failure to comply with current court orders • Offence committed whilst on licence • Any steps taken to prevent the victim reporting an incident, obtaining assistance and/or from assisting or supporting the prosecution • Attempts to dispose of or conceal evidence • Failure of offender to respond to previous warnings • Commission of offence whilst under the influence of alcohol or drugs

Mitigating factors
• No previous convictions or no relevant/recent convictions • Remorse • Previous good character and/or exemplary conduct* • Age and/or lack of maturity where it affects the responsibility of the offender • Mental disorder or learning disability, particularly where linked to the commission of the offence • Sexual activity was incited but no activity took place because the offender voluntarily desisted or intervened to prevent it

*[Repeats note as to distinction between previous good character/exemplary conduct and having no previous convictions and how to deal with them in respect of the offence: see **SG31-5** for the full text.]

SG31-129 STEPS THREE TO NINE [124]

[These are in the same terms as those applicable to sexual assault: see **SG31-20 *et seq*.**]

SG31-130 Care Workers: Sexual Activity in the Presence of a person with a Mental Disorder [125]

Sexual Offences Act 2003 (section 40)

Care Workers: Causing a Person with a Mental Disorder to Watch a Sexual Act

Sexual Offences Act 2003 (section 41)

Triable either way

Maximum: 7 years' custody

Offence range: Community order–2 years' custody

[Repeats information as to the CJA 2003, s. 226A, which is set out at **SG31-17**.]

[126] **STEP ONE Determining the offence category** SG31-131

The court should determine which categories of harm and culpability the offence falls into by reference **only** to the tables below.

Harm	
Category 1	• Causing victim to view extreme pornography • Causing victim to view indecent/prohibited images of children • Engaging in, or causing a victim to view live, sexual activity involving sadism/violence/ sexual activity with an animal/a child
Category 2	Engaging in, or causing a victim to view images of or view live, sexual activity involving: • penetration of vagina or anus (using body or object) • penile penetration of mouth • masturbation
Category 3	Factor(s) in categories 1 and 2 not present

Culpability	
A	B
• Significant degree of planning • Offender acts together with others to commit the offence • Use of alcohol/drugs on victim to facilitate the offence • Grooming behaviour used against victim • Use of threats (including blackmail) • Commercial exploitation and/or motivation • Offence racially or religiously aggravated • Offence motivated by, or demonstrating, hostility to the victim based on his or her sexual orientation (or presumed sexual orientation) or transgender identity (or presumed transgender identity) • Offence motivated by, or demonstrating, hostility to the victim based on his or her disability (or presumed disability)	Factor(s) in category A not present

STEP TWO Starting point and category range SG31-132

Having determined the category of harm and culpability, the court should use the corresponding starting points to reach a sentence within the category range below. The starting point applies to all offenders irrespective of plea or previous convictions. Having determined the starting point, step two allows further adjustment for aggravating or mitigating features, set out below.

A case of particular gravity, reflected by multiple features of culpability or harm in step one, could merit upward adjustment from the starting point before further adjustment for aggravating or mitigating features, set out below.

Where there is a sufficient prospect of rehabilitation, a community order with a sex offender treatment programme requirement under section 202 of the Criminal Justice Act 2003 can be a proper alternative to a short or moderate length custodial sentence.

[127]

	A	B
Category 1	**Starting point** 18 months' custody **Category range** 1–2 years' custody	**Starting point** 1 year's custody **Category range** 26 weeks'–18 months' custody
Category 2	**Starting point** 1 year's custody **Category range** 26 weeks'–18 months' custody	**Starting point** 26 weeks' custody **Category range** High level community order–1 year's custody
Category 3	**Starting point** 26 weeks' custody **Category range** High level community order–1 year's custody	**Starting point** Medium level community order **Category range** Low level community order–High level community order

The table below contains a **non-exhaustive** list of additional factual elements providing the context of the offence and factors relating to the offender. Identify whether any combination of these, or other relevant factors, should result in an upward or downward adjustment from the starting point. **In particular, relevant recent convictions are likely to result in an upward adjustment.** In some cases, having considered these factors, it may be appropriate to move outside the identified category range. [127]

When sentencing appropriate **category 2 or 3 offences**, the court should also consider the custody threshold as follows:

- Has the custody threshold been passed?
- If so, is it unavoidable that a custodial sentence be imposed?
- If so, can that sentence be suspended?

Aggravating factors
Statutory aggravating factors • Previous convictions, having regard to a) the nature of the offence to which the conviction relates and its relevance to the current offence; and b) the time that has elapsed since the conviction • Offence committed whilst on bail *Other aggravating factors* • Location of offence • Timing of offence • Failure to comply with current court orders • Offence committed whilst on licence • Any steps taken to prevent the victim reporting an incident, obtaining assistance and/or from assisting or supporting the prosecution • Attempts to dispose of or conceal evidence • Failure of offender to respond to previous warnings • Commission of offence whilst under the influence of alcohol or drugs

Mitigating factors
• No previous convictions **or** no relevant/recent convictions • Remorse • Previous good character and/or exemplary conduct* • Age and/or lack of maturity where it affects the responsibility of the offender • Mental disorder or learning disability, particularly where linked to the commission of the offence • Demonstration of steps taken to address offending behaviour

*[Repeats note as to distinction between previous good character/exemplary conduct and having no previous convictions and how to deal with them in respect of the offence: see **SG31-19** for the full text.]

SG31-133 STEPS THREE TO NINE [128]

[These are in the same terms as those applicable to sexual assault: see **SG31-20** ***et seq***.]

SG31-134 EXPOSURE [129]

Sexual Offences Act 2003 (section 66)

Triable either way

Maximum: 2 years' custody

Offence range: Fine–1 year's custody

[Repeats information as to the CJA 2003, s. 226A, which is set out at **SG31-17**.]

SG31-135 STEP ONE **Determining the offence category** [130]

The court should determine the offence category using the table below.

Category 1	Raised harm **and** raised culpability
Category 2	Raised harm **or** raised culpability
Category 3	Exposure **without** raised harm or culpability factors present

[130] The court should determine culpability and harm caused or intended, by reference **only** to the factors below, which comprise the principal factual elements of the offence. Where an offence does not fall squarely into a category, individual factors may require a degree of weighting before making an overall assessment and determining the appropriate offence category.

Factors indicating raised harm
• Victim followed/pursued • Offender masturbated

Factors indicating raised culpability
• Specific or previous targeting of a particularly vulnerable victim • Abuse of trust • Use of threats (including blackmail) • Offence racially or religiously aggravated • Offence motivated by, or demonstrating, hostility to the victim based on his or her sexual orientation (or presumed sexual orientation) or transgender identity (or presumed transgender identity) • Offence motivated by, or demonstrating, hostility to the victim based on his or her disability (or presumed disability)

STEP TWO Starting point and category range SG31-136

Having determined the category, the court should use the corresponding starting points to reach a sentence within the category range below. The starting point applies to all offenders irrespective of plea or previous convictions. Having determined the starting point, step two allows further adjustment for aggravating or mitigating features, set out below.

A case of particular gravity, reflected by multiple features of culpability or harm in step one, could merit upward adjustment from the starting point before further adjustment for aggravating or mitigating features, set out below.

Where there is a sufficient prospect of rehabilitation, a community order with a sex offender treatment programme requirement under section 202 of the Criminal Justice Act 2003 can be a proper alternative to a short or moderate length custodial sentence.

[131]

Category 1	**Starting point** 26 weeks' custody **Category range** 12 weeks'–1 year's custody
Category 2	**Starting point** High level community order **Category range** Medium level community order–26 weeks' custody
Category 3	**Starting point** Medium level community order **Category range** Band A fine–High level community order

The table below contains a **non-exhaustive** list of additional factual elements providing the context of the offence and factors relating to the offender. Identify whether any combination of these, or other relevant factors, should result in an upward or downward adjustment from the starting point. **In particular, relevant recent convictions are likely to result in an upward adjustment.** In some cases, having considered these factors, it may be appropriate to move outside the identified category range.

When sentencing **category 2 offences**, the court should also consider the custody threshold as follows:

- Has the custody threshold been passed?
- If so, is it unavoidable that a custodial sentence be imposed?
- If so, can that sentence be suspended?

When sentencing **category 3 offences**, the court should also consider the community order threshold as follows: [131]

- Has the community order threshold been passed?

Aggravating factors
Statutory aggravating factors • Previous convictions, having regard to a) the nature of the offence to which the conviction relates and its relevance to the current offence; and b) the time that has elapsed since the conviction • Offence committed whilst on bail
Other aggravating factors • Location of the offence • Timing of the offence • Any steps taken to prevent the victim reporting an incident, obtaining assistance and/or from assisting or supporting the prosecution • Failure to comply with current court orders • Offence committed whilst on licence • Commission of offence whilst under the influence of alcohol or drugs • Presence of others, especially children

Mitigating factors
• No previous convictions **or** no relevant/recent convictions • Remorse • Previous good character and/or exemplary conduct* • Age and/or lack of maturity where it affects the responsibility of the offender • Mental disorder or learning disability, particularly where linked to the commission of the offence • Demonstration of steps taken to address offending behaviour

*[Repeats note as to distinction between previous good character/exemplary conduct and having no previous convictions and how to deal with them in respect of the offence: see **SG31-19** for the full text.]

SG31-137 STEPS THREE TO NINE [132]

[These are in the same terms as those applicable to sexual assault: see **SG31-20 *et seq.***]

SG31-138 VOYEURISM [133]

Sexual Offences Act 2003 (section 67)

Triable either way

Maximum: 2 years' custody

Offence range: Fine–18 months' custody

[Repeats information as to the CJA 2003, s. 226A, which is set out at **SG31-17**.]

SG31-139 STEP ONE **Determining the offence category** [134]

The court should determine the offence category using the table below.

Category 1	Raised harm **and** raised culpability
Category 2	Raised harm **or** raised culpability
Category 3	Voyeurism **without** raised harm or culpability factors present

The court should determine culpability and harm caused or intended, by reference **only** to the factors below, which comprise the principal factual elements of the offence. Where an offence does not fall squarely into a category, individual factors may require a degree of weighting before making an overall assessment and determining the appropriate offence category.

[134]

Factors indicating raised harm
• Image(s) available to be viewed by others • Victim observed or recorded in their own home or residence

Factors indicating raised culpability
• Significant degree of planning • Image(s) recorded • Abuse of trust • Specific or previous targeting of a particularly vulnerable victim • Commercial exploitation and/or motivation • Offence racially or religiously aggravated • Offence motivated by, or demonstrating, hostility to the victim based on his or her sexual orientation (or presumed sexual orientation) or transgender identity (or presumed transgender identity) • Offence motivated by, or demonstrating, hostility to the victim based on his or her disability (or presumed disability)

STEP TWO Starting point and category range SG31-140

Having determined the category, the court should use the corresponding starting points to reach a sentence within the category range below. The starting point applies to all offenders irrespective of plea or previous convictions. Having determined the starting point, step two allows further adjustment for aggravating or mitigating features, set out below.

A case of particular gravity, reflected by multiple features of culpability or harm in step one, could merit upward adjustment from the starting point before further adjustment for aggravating or mitigating features, set out below.

Where there is a sufficient prospect of rehabilitation, a community order with a sex offender treatment programme requirement under section 202 of the Criminal Justice Act 2003 can be a proper alternative to a short or moderate length custodial sentence.

[135]

Category 1	**Starting point** 26 weeks' custody **Category range** 12 weeks'–18 months' custody
Category 2	**Starting point** High level community order **Category range** Medium level community order–26 weeks' custody
Category 3	**Starting point** Medium level community order **Category range** Band A fine–High level community order

The table below contains a **non-exhaustive** list of additional factual elements providing the context of the offence and factors relating to the offender. Identify whether any combination of these, or other relevant factors, should result in an upward or downward adjustment from the starting point. **In particular, relevant recent convictions are likely to result in an upward adjustment.** In some cases, having considered these factors, it may be appropriate to move outside the identified category range.

When sentencing **category 2 offences**, the court should also consider the custody threshold as follows:

- Has the custody threshold been passed?
- If so, is it unavoidable that a custodial sentence be imposed?
- If so, can that sentence be suspended?

When sentencing **category 3 offences**, the court should also consider the community order threshold as follows:

- Has the community order threshold been passed?

Aggravating factors
Statutory aggravating factors • Previous convictions, having regard to a) the nature of the offence to which the conviction relates and its relevance to the current offence; and b) the time that has elapsed since the conviction • Offence committed whilst on bail *Other aggravating factors* • Location of offence • Timing of offence • Failure to comply with current court orders • Offence committed whilst on licence • Distribution of images, whether or not for gain • Placing images where there is the potential for a high volume of viewers • Period over which victim observed • Period over which images were made or distributed • Any steps taken to prevent victim reporting an incident, obtaining assistance and/or from assisting or supporting the prosecution • Attempts to dispose of or conceal evidence

[135]

Mitigating factors
• No previous convictions **or** no relevant/recent convictions • Remorse • Previous good character and/or exemplary conduct* • Age and/or lack of maturity where it affects the responsibility of the offender • Mental disorder or learning disability, particularly where linked to the commission of the offence • Demonstration of steps taken to address offending behaviour

*[Repeats note as to distinction between previous good character/exemplary conduct and having no previous convictions and how to deal with them in respect of the offence: see **SG31-19** for the full text.]

SG31-141 STEPS THREE TO NINE [136]

[These are in the same terms as those applicable to sexual assault: see **SG31-20**.]

SG31-142 Sex with an Adult Relative: Penetration [137]

Sexual Offences Act 2003 (section 64)

Sex with an Adult Relative: Consenting to Penetration

Sexual Offences Act 2003 (section 65)

Triable either way

Maximum: 2 years' custody

Offence range: Fine–2 years' custody

[Repeats information as to the CJA 2003, s. 226A, which is set out at **SG31-17**.]

SG31-143 STEP ONE **Determining the offence category** [138]

The court should determine the offence category using the table below.

Category 1	Raised harm **and** raised culpability
Category 2	Raised harm **or** raised culpability
Category 3	Sex with an adult relative **without** raised harm or culpability factors present

The court should determine culpability and harm caused or intended, by reference **only** to the factors below, which comprise the principal factual elements of the offence. Where an offence does not fall squarely into a category, individual factors may require a degree of weighting before making an overall assessment and determining the appropriate offence category.

[138]

Factors indicating raised harm
• Victim is particularly vulnerable due to personal circumstances • Child conceived

Factors indicating raised culpability
• Grooming behaviour used against victim • Use of threats (including blackmail)

STEP TWO Starting point and category range SG31-144

Having determined the category, the court should use the corresponding starting points to reach a sentence within the category range below. The starting point applies to all offenders irrespective of plea or previous convictions. Having determined the starting point, step two allows further adjustment for aggravating or mitigating features, set out below.

A case of particular gravity, reflected by multiple features of culpability or harm in step one, could merit upward adjustment from the starting point before further adjustment for aggravating or mitigating features, set out below.

Where there is a sufficient prospect of rehabilitation, a community order with a sex offender treatment programme requirement under section 202 of the Criminal Justice Act 2003 can be a proper alternative to a short or moderate length custodial sentence.

[139]

Category 1	**Starting point** 1 year's custody **Category range** 26 weeks'–2 years' custody
Category 2	**Starting point** High level community order **Category range** Medium level community order– 1 year's custody
Category 3	**Starting point** Medium level community order **Category range** Band A fine–High level community order

The table below contains a **non-exhaustive** list of additional factual elements providing the context of the offence and factors relating to the offender. Identify whether any combination of these, or other relevant factors, should result in an upward or downward adjustment from the starting point. **In particular, relevant recent convictions are likely to result in an upward adjustment.** In some cases, having considered these factors, it may be appropriate to move outside the identified category range.

When sentencing **category 2 offences**, the court should also consider the custody threshold as follows:

- Has the custody threshold been passed?
- If so, is it unavoidable that a custodial sentence be imposed?
- If so, can that sentence be suspended?

When sentencing **category 3 offences**, the court should also consider the community order threshold as follows:

- Has the community order threshold been passed?

Aggravating factors
Statutory aggravating factors • Previous convictions, having regard to a) the nature of the offence to which the conviction relates and its relevance to the current offence; and b) the time that has elapsed since the conviction • Offence committed whilst on bail

Sentencing Guidelines

Aggravating factors
Other aggravating factors • Failure to comply with current court orders • Offence committed whilst on licence • Failure of offender to respond to previous warnings • Any steps taken to prevent reporting an incident, obtaining assistance and/or from assisting or supporting the prosecution • Attempts to dispose of or conceal evidence

[139]

Mitigating factors
• No previous convictions or no relevant/recent convictions • Remorse • Previous good character and/or exemplary conduct* • Age and/or lack of maturity where it affects the responsibility of the offender • Mental disorder or learning disability, particularly where linked to the commission of the offence • Demonstration of steps taken to address offending behaviour

*[Repeats note as to distinction between previous good character/exemplary conduct and having no previous convictions and how to deal with them in respect of the offence: see **SG31-19** for the full text.]

SG31-145 STEPS THREE TO NINE [140]

[These are in the same terms as those applicable to sexual assault: see **SG31-20** ***et seq.***]

SG31-146 ADMINISTERING A SUBSTANCE WITH INTENT [141]

Sexual Offences Act 2003 (section 61)

Triable either way

Maximum: 10 years' custody

Offence range: 1–9 years' custody

[Repeats information as to the CJA 2003, s. 226A, which is set out at **SG31-17**.]

SG31-147 STEP ONE **Determining the offence category** [142]

The court should determine the offence category using the table below.

Category 1	Raised harm **and** raised culpability
Category 2	Raised harm **or** raised culpability
Category 3	Administering a substance with intent **without** raised harm or culpability factors present

The court should determine culpability and harm caused or intended, by reference **only** to the factors below, which comprise the principal factual elements of the offence. Where an offence does not fall squarely into a category, individual factors may require a degree of weighting before making an overall assessment and determining the appropriate offence category. Where no substantive sexual offence has been committed the main consideration for the court will be the offender's conduct as a whole including, but not exclusively, the offender's intention.

Factors indicating raised harm
• Severe psychological or physical harm • Prolonged detention/sustained incident • Additional degradation/humiliation

[142]

Factors indicating raised culpability
• Significant degree of planning • Specific targeting of a particularly vulnerable victim • Intended sexual offence carries a statutory maximum of life • Abuse of trust • Recording of offence • Offender acts together with others to commit the offence • Commercial exploitation and/or motivation • Offence racially or religiously aggravated • Offence motivated by, or demonstrating, hostility to the victim based on his or her sexual orientation (or presumed sexual orientation) or transgender identity (or presumed transgender identity) • Offence motivated by, or demonstrating, hostility to the victim based on his or her disability (or presumed disability)

[143] **STEP TWO Starting point and category range** SG31-148

Having determined the category, the court should use the corresponding starting points to reach a sentence within the category range below. The starting point applies to all offenders irrespective of plea or previous convictions. Having determined the starting point, step two allows further adjustment for aggravating or mitigating features, set out below.

A case of particular gravity, reflected by multiple features of culpability or harm in step one, could merit upward adjustment from the starting point before further adjustment for aggravating or mitigating features, set out below.

Category 1	**Starting point** 6 years' custody **Category range** 4–9 years' custody
Category 2	**Starting point** 4 years' custody **Category range** 3–7 years' custody
Category 3	**Starting point** 2 years' custody **Category range** 1–5 years' custody

The table below contains a **non-exhaustive** list of additional factual elements providing the context of the offence and factors relating to the offender. Identify whether any combination of these, or other relevant factors, should result in an upward or downward adjustment from the starting point. **In particular, relevant recent convictions are likely to result in an upward adjustment.** In some cases, having considered these factors, it may be appropriate to move outside the identified category range.

Aggravating factors
Statutory aggravating factors • Previous convictions, having regard to a) the nature of the offence to which the conviction relates and its relevance to the current offence; and b) the time that has elapsed since the conviction • Offence committed whilst on bail *Other aggravating factors* • Location of offence • Timing of offence • Any steps taken to prevent reporting an incident, obtaining assistance and/or from assisting or supporting the prosecution • Attempts to dispose of or conceal evidence • Failure to comply with current court orders • Offence committed whilst on licence

Sentencing Guidelines

Mitigating factors
• No previous convictions or no relevant/recent convictions • Remorse • Previous good character and/or exemplary conduct* • Age and/or lack of maturity where it affects the responsibility of the offender • Mental disorder or learning disability, particularly where linked to the commission of the offence • Demonstration of steps taken to address offending behaviour

[143]

*[Repeats note as to distinction between previous good character/exemplary conduct and having no previous convictions and how to deal with them in respect of the offence: see **SG31-19** for the full text.]

SG31-149 STEPS THREE TO NINE [144]

[These are in the same terms as those applicable to sexual assault: see **SG31-20** ***et seq.***]

SG31-150 COMMITTING AN OFFENCE WITH INTENT TO COMMIT A SEXUAL OFFENCE [145]

Sexual Offences Act 2003 (section 62)

Triable only on indictment (if kidnapping or false imprisonment committed)

• otherwise, triable either way

Maximum: Life imprisonment (if kidnapping or false imprisonment committed)

• otherwise, 10 years

[Repeats information as to the CJA 2003, ss. 224, 225(2), 224A and 226A which is set out at **SG31-3**.]

The starting point and range should be commensurate with that for the preliminary offence actually committed, but with an enhancement to reflect the intention to commit a sexual offence.

The enhancement will vary depending on the nature and seriousness of the intended sexual offence, but 2 years is suggested as a suitable enhancement where the intent was to commit rape or assault by penetration.

SG31-151 TRESPASS WITH INTENT TO COMMIT A SEXUAL OFFENCE [147]

Sexual Offences Act 2003 (section 63)

Triable either way

Maximum: 10 years' custody

Offence range: 1–9 years' custody

[Repeats information as to the CJA 2003, s. 226A, which is set out at **SG31-17**.]

SG31-152 STEP ONE **Determining the offence category** [148]

The court should determine the offence category using the table below.

Category 1	Raised harm **and** raised culpability
Category 2	Raised harm **or** raised culpability
Category 3	Trespass with intent to commit a sexual offence **without** raised harm or culpability factors present

The court should determine culpability and harm caused or intended, by reference **only** to the factors below, which comprise the principal factual elements of the offence. Where an offence does not fall squarely into a category, individual factors may require a degree of weighting before making an overall assessment and determining the appropriate offence category. Where no substantive sexual offence has been committed the main consideration for the court will be the offender's conduct as a whole including, but not exclusively, the offender's intention.

Factors indicating raised harm
• Prolonged detention/sustained incident • Additional degradation/humiliation • Offence committed in victim's home

[148]

Factors indicating raised culpability
• Significant degree of planning • Specific targeting of a particularly vulnerable victim • Intended sexual offence attracts a statutory maximum of life imprisonment • Possession of weapon or other item to frighten or injure • Abuse of trust • Offender acts together with others to commit the offence • Commercial exploitation and/or motivation • Offence racially or religiously aggravated • Offence motivated by, or demonstrating, hostility to the victim based on his or her sexual orientation (or presumed sexual orientation) or transgender identity (or presumed transgender identity) • Offence motivated by, or demonstrating, hostility to the victim based on his or her disability (or presumed disability)

[149] **STEP TWO Starting point and category range** **SG31-153**

Having determined the category, the court should use the corresponding starting points to reach a sentence within the category range below. The starting point applies to all offenders irrespective of plea or previous convictions. Having determined the starting point, step two allows further adjustment for aggravating or mitigating features, set out below.

A case of particular gravity, reflected by multiple features of culpability or harm in step one, could merit upward adjustment from the starting point before further adjustment for aggravating or mitigating features, set out below.

Category 1	**Starting point** 6 years' custody **Category range** 4–9 years' custody
Category 2	**Starting point** 4 years' custody **Category range** 3–7 years' custody
Category 3	**Starting point** 2 years' custody **Category range** 1–5 years' custody

The table below contains a **non-exhaustive** list of additional factual elements providing the context of the offence and factors relating to the offender. Identify whether any combination of these, or other relevant factors, should result in an upward or downward adjustment from the starting point. **In particular, relevant recent convictions are likely to result in an upward adjustment.** In some cases, having considered these factors, it may be appropriate to move outside the identified category range.

Aggravating factors
Statutory aggravating factors • Previous convictions, having regard to a) the nature of the offence to which the conviction relates and its relevance to the current offence; and b) the time that has elapsed since the conviction • Offence committed whilst on bail *Other aggravating factors* • Location of offence • Timing of offence • Any steps taken to prevent reporting an incident, obtaining assistance and/or from assisting or supporting the prosecution • Attempts to dispose of or conceal evidence • Failure to comply with current court orders • Offence committed whilst on licence

Mitigating factors
• No previous convictions or no relevant/recent convictions • Remorse • Previous good character and/or exemplary conduct* • Age and/or lack of maturity where it affects the responsibility of the offender • Mental disorder or learning disability, particularly where linked to the commission of the offence • Demonstration of steps taken to address offending behaviour

[149]

*[Repeats note as to distinction between previous good character/exemplary conduct and having no previous convictions and how to deal with them in respect of the offence: see **SG31-19** for the full text.]

SG31-154 STEPS THREE TO NINE [150]

[These are in the same terms as those applicable to sexual assault: see **SG31-20** ***et seq.***]

SG31-155 Child Sex Offences Committed by Children or Young Persons (Sections 9–12) (Offender Under 18) [151]

Sexual Offences Act 2003 (section 13)

Sexual Activity with a Child Family Member (Offender Under 18)

Sexual Offences Act 2003 (section 25)

Inciting a Child Family Member to Engage in Sexual Activity (Offender Under 18)

Sexual Offences Act 2003 (section 26)

Triable either way

Maximum: 5 years' custody

These are 'grave crimes' for the purposes of section 91 of the Powers of Criminal Courts (Sentencing) Act 2000.

[Repeats information as to the CJA 2003, s. 226A which is set out at **SG31-17**.]

*Definitive guidelines for the sentencing of offenders under 18 years old are **not** included.*

When sentencing offenders under 18, a court must in particular follow:

- *Sentencing Children and Young People: Overarching Principles* [see **SG8-1**].
- *Sentencing Children and Young People: Sexual Offences* [see **SG8-11**].

and have regard to:

- *the principal aim of the young justice system (to prevent offending by children and young people); and the welfare of young offenders.*

SG31-156 Annex A – Ancillary Orders [153]

This summary of the key provisions is correct as at the date of publication but will be subject to subsequent changes in law. If necessary, seek legal advice.

Ancillary order	Statutory reference
Compensation The court must consider making a compensation order in any case in which personal injury, loss or damage has resulted from the offence. The court must give reasons if it decides not to make an order in such cases.	Section 130 of the Powers of Criminal Courts (Sentencing) Act 2000

[153]

Ancillary order	Statutory reference
Confiscation A confiscation order may be made by the Crown Court in circumstances in which the offender has obtained a financial benefit as a result of, or in connection with, his criminal conduct.	Section 6 and Schedule 2 of the Proceeds of Crime Act 2002
Deprivation of property The court may order the offender is deprived of property used for the purpose of committing, or facilitating the commission of, any offence, or intended for that purpose.	Section 143 of the Powers of Criminal Courts (Sentencing) Act 2000
Disqualification from working with children From 17 June 2013 courts no longer have the power to disqualify offenders from working with children pursuant to the Criminal Justice and Court Services Act 2000.	Schedule 10 of the Safeguarding Vulnerable Groups Act 2006 Safeguarding Vulnerable Groups Act 2006 (Commencement No. 8 and Saving) Order 2012 (SI 2012/2231) Protection of Freedoms Act 2012 (Commencement No. 6) Order 2013 (SI 2013/1180)
Restraining order Following a conviction *or an acquittal*, a court may make a restraining order for the purpose of protecting the victim or another person from harassment or a fear of violence.	Sections 5 and 5A of the Protection from Harassment Act 1997
Serious crime prevention order (SCPO) An SCPO may be made by the Crown Court in respect of qualifying offenders, if the court is satisfied such an order would protect the public by preventing, restricting or disrupting the involvement of the offender in serious crime.	Section 19 and Schedule 1 of the Serious Crime Act 2007
Sexual offences prevention order (SOPO) A SOPO may be made against qualifying offenders if the court is satisfied such an order is necessary to protect the public or any particular member of the public from serious sexual harm from the offender. The terms of the SOPO must be proportionate to the objective of protecting the public and consistent with the sentence and other ancillary orders, conditions and requirements to which the offender is subject.	Section 104 and Schedules 3 and 5 of the Sexual Offences Act 2003
[154] **Slavery and Trafficking Prevention Orders** A court may make a slavery and trafficking prevention order against an offender convicted of a slavery or human trafficking offence, if satisfied that • there is a risk that the offender may commit a slavery or human trafficking offence, and • it is necessary to make the order for the purpose of protecting persons generally, or particular persons, from the physical or psychological harm which would be likely to occur if the offender committed such an offence	Section 14 of the Modern Slavery Act 2015

Automatic orders on conviction

The following requirements or provisions are **not** part of the sentence imposed by the court but apply automatically by operation of law. The role of the court is to inform the offender of the applicable requirements and/or prohibition.

Requirement or provision	Statutory reference
Notification requirements A relevant offender automatically becomes subject to notification requirements, obliging him to notify the police of specified information for a specified period. The court should inform the offender accordingly. *The operation of the notification requirement is not a relevant consideration in determining the sentence for the offence.*	Sections 80 to 88 and Schedule 3 of the Sexual Offences Act 2003

Requirement or provision	Statutory reference
Protection for children and vulnerable adults A statutory scheme pursuant to which offenders *will* or *may* be barred from regulated activity relating to children or vulnerable adults, with or without the right to make representations, depending on the offence. The court should inform the offender accordingly.	Section 2 and Schedule 3 of the Safeguarding Vulnerable Groups Act 2006 Safeguarding Vulnerable Groups Act 2006 (Prescribed Criteria and Miscellaneous Provisions) Regulations 2009 (SI 2009/37) (as amended)

[154]

[155]

SG31-157 ANNEX B – APPROACH TO SENTENCING OF HISTORIC SEXUAL OFFENCES

Details of the principal offences are set out in the table at Annex C [at SG31-158].

When sentencing sexual offences under the Sexual Offences Act 1956, or other legislation pre-dating the 2003 Act, the court should apply the following principles:[271]

1. The offender must be sentenced in accordance with the sentencing regime applicable at the *date of sentence*. Under the Criminal Justice Act 2003[272] the court must have regard to the statutory purposes of sentencing and must base the sentencing exercise on its assessment of the seriousness of the offence.
2. The sentence is limited to the maximum sentence available at the *date of the commission of the offence*. If the maximum sentence has been reduced, the lower maximum will be applicable.
3. The court should have regard to any applicable sentencing guidelines for equivalent offences under the Sexual Offences Act 2003. Where the offence, if committed on the day on which the offender was convicted, would have constituted an offence contrary to section 5 or section 6 of the Sexual Offences Act 2003, section of the 236A Criminal Justice Act (special custodial sentence for certain offenders of particular concern) applies [added 22/11/2018].
4. The seriousness of the offence, assessed by the culpability of the offender and the harm caused or intended, is the main consideration for the court. The court should not seek to establish the likely sentence had the offender been convicted shortly after the date of the offence.
5. When assessing the culpability of the offender, the court should have regard to relevant culpability factors set out in any applicable guideline.
6. The court must assess carefully the harm done to the victim based on the facts available to it, having regard to relevant harm factors set out in any applicable guideline. Consideration of the circumstances which brought the offence to light will be of importance.
7. The court must consider the relevance of the passage of time carefully as it has the potential to aggravate or mitigate the seriousness of the offence. It will be an aggravating factor where the offender has continued to commit sexual offences against the victim or others or has continued to prevent the victim reporting the offence.
8. Where there is an absence of further offending over a long period of time, especially combined with evidence of good character, this may be treated by the court as a mitigating factor. However, as with offences dealt with under the Sexual Offences Act 2003, previous good character/exemplary conduct is different from having no previous convictions. The more serious the offence, the less the weight which should normally be attributed to this factor. Where previous good character/exemplary conduct has been used to facilitate the offence, this mitigation should not normally be allowed and such conduct may constitute an aggravating factor.
9. If the offender was very young and immature at the time of the offence, depending on the circumstances of the offence, this may be regarded as personal mitigation.
10. If the offender made admissions at the time of the offence that were not investigated this is likely to be regarded as personal mitigation. Even greater mitigation is available to the offender who reported himself to the police and/or made early admissions.
11. A reduction for an early guilty plea should be made in the usual manner.

[271] *R v H and others* [2011] EWCA Crim 2753
[272] Section 143

[157]

Annex C – Historic Offences

SG31-158

Offence (Sexual Offences Act 1956 unless stated otherwise)	Effective dates	Maximum
Rape and assault offences		
Rape (section 1)	1 January 1957–30 April 2004	Life
Buggery with a person or animal (section 12)	1 January 1957–30 April 2004 (from 3 November 1994 non-consensual acts of buggery were defined as rape)	Life
Indecent assault on a woman (section 14)	1 January 1957–30 April 2004	1 January 1957–1 July 1960: 2 years 2 July 1960–15 September 1985: 2 years or 5 years if victim under 13 and age stated on indictment 16 September 1985 onwards: 10 years
Indecent assault upon a man (section 15)	1 January 1957–30 April 2004	10 years
Offences against children		
Sexual intercourse with a girl under 13 (section 5)	1 January 1957–30 April 2004	Life
Incest by a male person (section 10)	1 January 1957–30 April 2004	Life if victim under 13; otherwise 7 years
Incest by a female person (section 11)	1 January 1957–30 April 2004	7 years
Indecency between men (section 13)	1 January 1957–30 April 2004	1 January 1957–2 November 1994: 2 years 3 November 1994 onwards: Male offender over 21 with male under age of consent: 5 years Otherwise: 2 years
Indecency with a child (section 1 of the Indecency with Children Act 1960)	2 July 1960–30 April 2004	1 July 1960–30 September 1997: 2 years 1 October 1997 onwards: 10 years *Note: on 11 January 2001 the age definition of a child increased from 14 to 16.*
Incitement of a girl under 16 to commit incest (section 54 of the Criminal Law Act 1977)	8 September 1977–30 April 2004	2 years
Abuse of position of trust (section 3 of the Sexual Offences (Amendment) Act 2000)	8 January 2001–30 April 2004	5 years
[158] **Indecent images**		
Taking indecent photographs of a child (section 1 of the Protection of Children Act 1978)	20 August 1978–present	20 August 1978–10 January 2001: 3 years 11 January 2001 onwards: 10 years
Possession of indecent photographs of a child (section 160 of the Criminal Justice Act 1988)	29 September 1988–present	29 September 1988–10 January 2001: 6 months 11 January 2001 onwards: 5 years

[158]

Offence (Sexual Offences Act 1956 unless stated otherwise)	Effective dates	Maximum
Exploitation offences		
Procurement of woman by threats (section 2) Procurement by false pretences (section 3) Causing prostitution of women (section 22) Procuration of girl under 21 for unlawful sexual intercourse in any part of the world (section 23) Detention in a brothel (section 24) Permitting a defective to use premises for intercourse (section 27) Causing or encouraging prostitution (etc) of a girl under 16 (section 28) Causing or encouraging prostitution of a defective (section 29)	1 January 1957–30 April 2004	2 years
Living on earnings of prostitution (section 30) Controlling a prostitute (section 31)	1 January 1957–30 April 2004	1 January 1957–15 August 1959: 2 years 16 August 1959 onwards: 7 years
Trafficking into/within/out of the UK for sexual exploitation (sections 57–59 of the Sexual Offences Act 2003)	1 May 2005–5 April 2013	14 years
[159] **Offences against those with a mental disorder**		
Intercourse with a defective (section 7) Procurement of a defective (section 9)	1 January 1957–30 April 2004	2 years
Sexual intercourse with patients (section 128 of the Mental Health Act 1956)	1 November 1960–30 April 2004	2 years
Other offences		
Administering drugs to obtain or facilitate intercourse (section 4)	1 January 1957–30 April 2004	2 years
Burglary with intent to commit rape (section 9 of the Theft Act 1968)	1 January 1969–30 April 2004	14 years if dwelling; otherwise 10 years

With thanks to Sweet & Maxwell, HHJ Rook QC and Robert Ward CBE for their kind permission to reproduce parts of *Sexual Offences Law & Practice*.

SG31-159 ANNEX D – FINE BANDS AND COMMUNITY ORDERS [160]

[The information set out here is also set out in the Magistrates' Court Sentencing Guidelines, which include further guidance on fines and community orders: see **SG10-129** and **SG10-149**.]

PART 32 TERRORISM OFFENCES SG32-1

Definitive Guideline

[4] **Applicability of guideline**

The Sentencing Council issues this definitive guideline in accordance with section 120 of the Coroners and Justice Act 2009.

The guidelines apply to all offenders aged 18 and older, who are sentenced on or after **27 April 2018**, regardless of the date of the offence.

Section 125(1) of the Coroners and Justice Act 2009 provides that when sentencing offences committed after 6 April 2010:

Every court –
(a) must, in sentencing an offender, follow any sentencing guidelines which are relevant to the offender's case, and
(b) must, in exercising any other function relating to the sentencing of offenders, follow any sentencing guidelines which are relevant to the exercise of the function, unless the court is satisfied that it would be contrary to the interests of justice to do so.

Structure, ranges and starting points SG32-2

For the purposes of section 125(3)-(4) of the Coroners and Justice Act 2009, the guideline specifies offence ranges – the range of sentences appropriate for each type of offence. Within each offence, the Council has specified a number of categories which reflect varying degrees of seriousness. The offence range is split into category ranges – sentences appropriate for each level of seriousness. The Council has also identified a starting point within each category.

Starting points define the position within a category range from which to start calculating the provisional sentence. The court should consider further features of the offence or the offender that warrant adjustment of the sentence within the range, including the aggravating and mitigating factors set out at step two. Starting points and ranges apply to all offenders, whether they have pleaded guilty or been convicted after trial. Credit for a guilty plea is taken into consideration only at step four in the decision making process, after the appropriate sentence has been identified.

Information on community orders is set out in the annex at [SG32-101].

[5]

Preparation of terrorist acts SG32-3

Terrorism Act 2006 (section 5)

This is a serious specified offence for the purposes of sections 224 and 225(2) (life sentence for serious offences) of the Criminal Justice Act 2003.

This is an offence listed in Part 1 of Schedule 15B for the purposes of sections 224A (life sentence for second listed offence) of the Criminal Justice Act 2003.

This is a specified offence for the purposes of section 226A (extended sentence for certain violent or sexual offences) of the Criminal Justice Act 2003.

This is an offence listed in Schedule 18A for the purposes of section 236A (special custodial sentence for certain offenders of particular concern) of the Criminal Justice Act 2003.

Triable only on indictment

Maximum: Life imprisonment

Offence range: 3 years' custody–Life Imprisonment (minimum term 40 years)

This guideline applies only to offenders aged 18 and older

Sentencing Guidelines

SG32-4 **STEP ONE Determining the offence category** [6]

The court should determine the offence category with reference **only** to the factors listed in the tables below. In order to determine the category the court should assess **culpability** and **harm.**

The court should weigh all the factors set out below in determining the offender's culpability. **Where there are characteristics present which fall under different levels of culpability, the court should balance these characteristics to reach a fair assessment of the offender's culpability.**

Culpability demonstrated by one or more of the following:	
A	• Acting alone, or in a leading role, in terrorist activity where preparations were complete or were so close to completion that, but for apprehension, the activity was very likely to have been carried out
B	• **Acting alone**, or in a **leading** role, in terrorist activity where preparations were advanced and, but for apprehension, the activity was likely to have been carried out • Significant role in terrorist activity where preparations were complete or were so close to completion that, but for apprehension, the activity was very likely to have been carried out • Offender has coordinated others to take part in terrorist activity, whether in the UK or abroad (where not falling within A)
C	• **Leading** role in terrorist activity where preparations were not far advanced • **Significant** role in terrorist activity where preparations were advanced and, but for apprehension, the activity was likely to have been carried out • **Lesser** role in terrorist activity where preparations were complete or were so close to completion that, but for apprehension, the activity was very likely to have been carried out • Offender acquires training or skills for purpose of terrorist activity (where not falling within A or B) • Acts of significant assistance or encouragement of other(s) (where not falling within A or B)
D	• Offender has engaged in very limited preparation for terrorist activity • Act(s) of lesser assistance or encouragement of other(s) • Other cases not falling within A, B or C

Harm Harm is assessed based on the type of harm risked and the likelihood of that harm being caused. When considering the likelihood of harm, the court should consider the viability of any plan.	
Category 1	• Multiple deaths risked and very likely to be caused
Category 2	• Multiple deaths risked but not very likely to be caused • Any death risked and very likely to be caused
Category 3	• Any death risked but not very likely to be caused • Risk of widespread or serious damage to property or economic interests • Risk of a substantial impact upon civic infrastructure • Any other cases

SG32-5 **STEP TWO Starting point and category range** [7]

Having determined the category at step one, the court should use the corresponding starting point to reach a sentence within the category range below. The starting point applies to all offenders irrespective of plea or previous convictions. A case of particular gravity, reflected by multiple features of culpability or harm in step one, could merit upward adjustment from the starting point before further adjustment for aggravating or mitigating features, set out [at SG32-6]. **Offenders committing the most serious offences are likely to be found dangerous and so the table below includes options for life sentences. However, the court should consider the dangerousness provisions in *all* cases, having regard to the criteria contained in Chapter 5 of Part 12 of the Criminal Justice Act 2003 to make the appropriate determination, before imposing either a life sentence or an extended sentence. (See STEP FIVE below).**

The court must also consider the provisions set out in section 236A Criminal Justice Act 2003 (special custodial sentence for certain offenders of particular concern). (See STEP SIX below).

[7]

Harm	Culpability A	B	C	D
Category 1	**Starting point** Life imprisonment – minimum term 35 years' custody	**Starting point** Life imprisonment – minimum term 25 years' custody	**Starting point** Life imprisonment – minimum term 15 years' custody	**Starting point** 15 years' custody
	Category range Life imprisonment – minimum term 30–40 years' custody	**Category range** Life imprisonment – minimum term 20–30 years' custody	**Category range** Life imprisonment – minimum term 10–20 years' custody	**Category range** 10–20 years' custody
Category 2	**Starting point** Life imprisonment – minimum term 25 years	**Starting point** Life imprisonment – minimum term 15 years	**Starting point** 15 years' custody	**Starting point** 8 years' custody
	Category range Life imprisonment – minimum term 20–30 years' custody	**Category range** Life imprisonment – minimum term 10–20 years' custody	**Category range** 10–20 years' custody	**Category range** 6–10 years' custody
Category 3	**Starting point** 16 years' custody	**Starting point** 12 years' custody	**Starting point** 8 years' custody	**Starting point** 4 years' custody
	Category range 12–20 years' custody	**Category range** 8–16 years' custody	**Category range** 6–10 years' custody	**Category range** 3–6 years' custody

[8] The table below contains a **non-exhaustive** list of additional factual elements providing the context of the offence and factors relating to the offender. Identify whether any combination of these, or other relevant factors, should result in an upward or downward adjustment from the sentence arrived at so far. In particular, relevant recent convictions are likely to result in an upward adjustment. In some cases, having considered these factors, it may be appropriate to move outside the identified category range. **SG32-6**

Factors increasing seriousness
Statutory aggravating factors: Previous convictions, having regard to a) the **nature** of the offence to which the conviction relates and its **relevance** to the current offence; and b) the **time** that has elapsed since the conviction Offence committed whilst on bail Offence motivated by, or demonstrating hostility based on any of the following characteristics or presumed characteristics of the victim: religion, race, disability, sexual orientation or transgender identity *(When considering this factor, sentencers should bear in mind the statutory definition of terrorism in section 1 of the Terrorism Act 2000, and should be careful to avoid double counting)*
Other aggravating factors: Recent and/or repeated possession or accessing of extremist material Communication with other extremists Deliberate use of encrypted communications or similar technologies to facilitate the commission of the offence and/or avoid or impede detection Offender attempted to disguise their identity to prevent detection Indoctrinated or encouraged others Preparation was with a view to engage in combat with UK armed forces Conduct in preparation includes the actual or planned commission of other offences, where not taken into account in step one Failure to respond to warnings Failure to comply with current court orders Offence committed on licence or Post Sentence Supervision Offence committed whilst in prison

Factors reducing seriousness or reflecting personal mitigation
No previous convictions **or** no relevant/recent convictions Good character and/or exemplary conduct Offender involved through coercion, intimidation or exploitation Clear evidence of a change of mind set prior to arrest Offender's responsibility substantially reduced by mental disorder or learning disability Age and/or lack of maturity where it affects the responsibility of the offender Sole or primary carer for dependent relatives

[8]

SG32-7 **STEP THREE Consider any factors which indicate a reduction, such as assistance to the prosecution** [9]

The court should take into account sections 73 and 74 of the Serious Organised Crime and Police Act 2005 (assistance by defendants: reduction or review of sentence) and any other rule of law by virtue of which an offender may receive a discounted sentence in consequence of assistance given (or offered) to the prosecutor or investigator.

SG32-8 **STEP FOUR Reduction for guilty plea**

The court should take account of any potential reduction for a guilty plea in accordance with section 144 of the Criminal Justice Act 2003 and the guideline for *Reduction in Sentence for a Guilty Plea* (where first hearing is **on or after 1 June 2017**, or first hearing **before 1 June 2017**).

SG32-9 **STEP FIVE Dangerousness**

The court should consider whether having regard to the criteria contained in Chapter 5 of Part 12 of the Criminal Justice Act 2003 it would be appropriate to impose a life sentence (section 224A or section 225) or an extended sentence (section 226A). When sentencing offenders to a life sentence under these provisions, the notional determinate sentence should be used as the basis for the setting of a minimum term.

SG32-10 **STEP SIX Special custodial sentence for certain offenders of particular concern (section 236A)**

Where the court does not impose a sentence of imprisonment for life or an extended sentence, but does impose a period of imprisonment, the term of the sentence must be equal to the aggregate of the appropriate custodial term and a further period of 1 year for which the offender is to be subject to a licence.

SG32-11 **STEP SEVEN Totality principle**

If sentencing an offender for more than one offence, or where the offender is already serving a sentence, consider whether the total sentence is just and proportionate to the overall offending behaviour in accordance with the *Totality* guideline.

SG32-12 **STEP EIGHT Ancillary orders**

In all cases the court should consider whether to make ancillary orders. See Additional guidance [at SG32-99].

SG32-13 **STEP NINE Reasons** [10]

Section 174 of the Criminal Justice Act 2003 imposes a duty to give reasons for, and explain the effect of, the sentence.

SG32-14 **STEP TEN Consideration for time spent on bail (tagged curfew)**

The court must consider whether to give credit for time spent on bail in accordance with section 240A of the Criminal Justice Act 2003.

SG32-15 Explosive Substances (terrorism only) [11]

Causing explosion likely to endanger life or property
Explosive Substances Act 1883 (section 2)

Attempt to cause explosion, or making or keeping explosive with intent to endanger life or property
Explosive Substances Act 1993 (section 3)

This is a serious specified offence for the purposes of sections 224 and 225(2) (life sentence for serious offences) of the Criminal Justice Act 2003.

This is an offence listed in Part 1 of Schedule 15B for the purposes of sections 224A (life sentence for second listed offence) of the Criminal Justice Act 2003.

This is a specified offence for the purposes of section 226A (extended sentence for certain violent or sexual offences) of the Criminal Justice Act 2003.

[11] This is an offence listed in Schedule 18A for the purposes of section 236A (special custodial sentence for certain offenders of particular concern) of the Criminal Justice Act 2003.

Triable only on indictment

Maximum: Life imprisonment

Offence range: 3 years' custody–Life Imprisonment (minimum term 40 years)

This guideline applies only to offenders aged 18 and older

[12] **STEP ONE Determining the offence category** SG32-16

The court should determine the offence category with reference **only** to the factors listed in the tables below. In order to determine the category, the court should assess **culpability and harm.**

The court should weigh all the factors set out below in determining the offender's culpability.

Where there are characteristics present which fall under different levels of culpability, the court should balance these characteristics to reach a fair assessment of the offender's culpability.

Culpability demonstrated by one or more of the following:	
A	• Offender caused an explosion or used, developed or was in possession of a viable explosive device • **Acting alone**, or in a **leading** role, in terrorist activity involving explosives, where preparations were complete or were so close to completion that, but for apprehension, the activity was very likely to have been carried out
B	• Offender took significant steps towards creating an explosion or developing or obtaining a viable explosive device • **Acting alone**, or in a **leading** role, in terrorist activity involving explosives where preparations were advanced and, but for apprehension, the activity was likely to have been carried out • **Significant** role in terrorist activity involving explosives where preparations were complete or were so close to completion that, but for apprehension, the activity was very likely to have been carried out
C	• **Leading** role in terrorist activity involving explosives where preparations were not far advanced • **Significant** role in terrorist activity involving explosives where preparations were advanced and, but for apprehension, the activity was likely to have been carried out • **Lesser** role in terrorist activity involving explosives where preparations were complete or were so close to completion that, but for apprehension, the activity was very likely to have been carried out • Act(s) of significant assistance or encouragement of other(s) involved in causing, developing or possessing an explosive device (where not falling within A or B)
D	• Offender took very limited steps toward creating an explosion or developing or obtaining a viable explosive device • Offender has engaged in very limited preparation of terrorist activity involving explosives • Act(s) of lesser assistance or encouragement of other(s) • Other cases not falling within A, B or C

Harm Harm is assessed based on the type of harm risked and the likelihood of that harm being caused. When considering the likelihood of harm, the court should consider the viability of any plan.	
Category 1	• Multiple deaths risked and very likely to be caused
Category 2	• Multiple deaths risked but not very likely to be caused • Any death risked and very likely to be caused
Category 3	• Any death risked but not very likely to be caused • Risk of widespread or serious damage to property or economic interests • Risk of a substantial impact upon civic infrastructure • Any other cases

[13] **STEP TWO Starting point and category range** SG32-17

Having determined the category at step one, the court should use the corresponding starting point to reach a sentence within the category range below. The starting point applies to all offenders irrespective of plea or previous convictions. A case of particular gravity, reflected by multiple features of culpability or harm in step one, could merit upward adjustment from the starting point before further adjustment for aggravating or mitigating features, set out [at **SG32-18**].

Offenders committing the most serious offences are likely to be found dangerous and so the table below includes options for life sentences. However, the court should consider the dangerousness provisions in

***all* cases, having regard to the criteria contained in Chapter 5 of Part 12 of the Criminal Justice Act 2003 to make the appropriate determination, before imposing either a life sentence or an extended sentence. (See STEP FIVE below).** [13]

The court must also consider the provisions set out in section 236A Criminal Justice Act 2003 (special custodial sentence for certain offenders of particular concern). (See STEP SIX below).

	Culpability			
Harm	**A**	**B**	**C**	**D**
Category 1	**Starting point** Life imprisonment – minimum term 35 years' custody	**Starting point** Life imprisonment – minimum term 25 years' custody	**Starting point** Life imprisonment – minimum term 15 years' custody	**Starting point** 15 years' custody
	Category range Life imprisonment – minimum term 30–40 years' custody	**Category range** Life imprisonment – minimum term 20–30 years' custody	**Category range** Life imprisonment – minimum term 10–20 years' custody	**Category range** 10–20 years' custody
Category 2	**Starting point** Life imprisonment – minimum term 25 years	**Starting point** Life imprisonment – minimum term 15 years	**Starting point** 15 years' custody	**Starting point** 8 years' custody
	Category range Life imprisonment – minimum term 20–30 years' custody	**Category range** Life imprisonment – minimum term 10–20 years' custody	**Category range** 10–20 years' custody	**Category range** 6–10 years custody
Category 3	**Starting point** 16 years' custody	**Starting point** 12 years' custody	**Starting point** 8 years' custody	**Starting point** 4 years' custody
	Category range 12–20 years' custody	**Category range** 8–16 years' custody	**Category range** 6–10 years' custody	**Category range** 3–6 years' custody

SG32-18 The table below contains a **non-exhaustive** list of additional factual elements providing the context of the offence and factors relating to the offender. Identify whether any combination of these, or other relevant factors, should result in an upward or downward adjustment from the sentence arrived at so far. In particular, relevant recent convictions are likely to result in an upward adjustment. In some cases, having considered these factors, it may be appropriate to move outside the identified category range. [14]

Factors increasing seriousness
Statutory aggravating factors: Previous convictions, having regard to a) the **nature** of the offence to which the conviction relates and its **relevance** to the current offence; and b) the **time** that has elapsed since the conviction Offence committed whilst on bail Offence motivated by, or demonstrating hostility based on any of the following characteristics or presumed characteristics of the victim: religion, race, disability, sexual orientation or transgender identity *(When considering this factor, sentencers should bear in mind the statutory definition of terrorism in section 1 of the Terrorism Act 2000, and should be careful to avoid double counting)*
Other aggravating factors: Recent and/or repeated possession or accessing of extremist material Communication with other extremists Deliberate use of encrypted communications or similar technologies to facilitate the commission of the offence and/or avoid or impede detection Offender attempted to disguise their identity to prevent detection Indoctrinated or encouraged others Conduct in preparation includes the actual or planned commission of other offences, where not taken into account in step one Failure to respond to warnings Failure to comply with current court orders Offence committed on licence or Post Sentence Supervision Offence committed whilst in prison

[14]

Factors reducing seriousness or reflecting personal mitigation
No previous convictions or no relevant/recent convictions
Good character and/or exemplary conduct
Offender involved through coercion, intimidation or exploitation
Clear evidence of a change of mind set prior to arrest
Offender's responsibility substantially reduced by mental disorder or learning disability
Age and/or lack of maturity where it affects the responsibility of the offender
Sole or primary carer for dependent relatives

[15] **STEP THREE Consider any factors which indicate a reduction, such as assistance to the prosecution** SG32-19

The court should take into account sections 73 and 74 of the Serious Organised Crime and Police Act 2005 (assistance by defendants: reduction or review of sentence) and any other rule of law by virtue of which an offender may receive a discounted sentence in consequence of assistance given (or offered) to the prosecutor or investigator.

STEP FOUR Reduction for guilty plea SG32-20

The court should take account of any potential reduction for a guilty plea in accordance with section 144 of the Criminal Justice Act 2003 and the guideline for *Reduction in Sentence for a Guilty Plea* (where first hearing is **on or after 1 June 2017**, or first hearing **before 1 June 2017**).

STEP FIVE Dangerousness SG32-21

The court should consider whether having regard to the criteria contained in Chapter 5 of Part 12 of the Criminal Justice Act 2003 it would be appropriate to award a life sentence (section 224A or section 225(2)) or an extended sentence (section 226A). When sentencing offenders to a life sentence under these provisions, the notional determinate sentence should be used as the basis for the setting of a minimum term.

STEP SIX Special custodial sentence for certain offenders of particular concern (section 236A) SG32-22

Where the court does not impose a sentence of imprisonment for life or an extended sentence, but does impose a period of imprisonment, the term of the sentence must be equal to the aggregate of the appropriate custodial term and a further period of 1 year for which the offender is to be subject to a licence.

STEP SEVEN Totality principle SG32-23

If sentencing an offender for more than one offence, or where the offender is already serving a sentence, consider whether the total sentence is just and proportionate to the overall offending behaviour in accordance with the *Totality* guideline.

STEP EIGHT Ancillary orders SG32-24

In all cases the court should consider whether to make ancillary orders. See Additional guidance [at SG32-99].

[16] **STEP NINE Reasons** SG32-25

Section 174 of the Criminal Justice Act 2003 imposes a duty to give reasons for, and explain the effect of, the sentence.

STEP TEN Consideration for time spent on bail (tagged curfew) SG32-26

The court must consider whether to give credit for time spent on bail in accordance with section 240A of the Criminal Justice Act 2003.

[17]

Encouragement of Terrorism SG32-27

Encouragement of terrorism

Terrorism Act 2006 (section 1)

Dissemination of terrorist publications

Terrorism Act 2006 (section 2)

Triable either way

Maximum: 7 years' custody

Offence range: High level community order–6 years' custody

This guideline applies only to offenders aged 18 and older

SG32-28 **STEP ONE Determining the offence category** [18]

The court should determine the offence category with reference **only** to the factors listed in the tables below. In order to determine the category, the court should assess **culpability** and **harm.**

The court should weigh all the factors set out below in determining the offender's culpability. **Where there are characteristics present which fall under different levels of culpability, the court should balance these characteristics to reach a fair assessment of the offender's culpability.**

Culpability demonstrated by one or more of the following:	
A	• Offender in position of trust, authority or influence and abuses their position to encourage others • Intended to encourage others to engage in any form of terrorist activity • Intended to provide assistance to others to engage in terrorist activity
B	•Reckless as to whether others would be encouraged or assisted to engage in terrorist activity and published statement/disseminated publication widely to a large or targeted audience (if via social media this can include both open or closed groups)
C	•Other cases where characteristics for categories A or B are not present

Harm The court should consider the factors set out below to determine the level of harm	
Category 1	• Evidence that others have acted on or been assisted by the encouragement to carry out activities endangering life • Statement or publication provides instruction for specific terrorist activity endangering life
Category 2	• Evidence that others have acted on or been assisted by the encouragement to carry out activities not endangering life • Statement or publication provides non-specific content encouraging support for terrorist activity endangering life • Statement or publication provides instruction for specific terrorist activity not endangering life
Category 3	• Statement or publication provides non-specific content encouraging support for terrorist activity not endangering life • Other cases where characteristics for categories 1 or 2 are not present

SG32-29 **STEP TWO Starting point and category range** [19]

Having determined the category at step one, the court should use the corresponding starting point to reach a sentence within the category range below. The starting point applies to all offenders irrespective of plea or previous convictions. A case of particular gravity, reflected by multiple features of culpability or harm in step one, could merit upward adjustment from the starting point before further adjustment for aggravating or mitigating features, set out [at SG32-30].

	Culpability		
Harm	**A**	**B**	**C**
Category 1	**Starting point** 5 years' custody	**Starting point** 4 years' custody	**Starting point** 3 years' custody
	Category range 4–6 years' custody	**Category range** 3–5 years' custody	**Category range** 2–4 years' custody
Category 2	**Starting point** 4 years' custody	**Starting point** 3 years' custody	**Starting point** 2 years' custody
	Category range 3–5 years' custody	**Category range** 2–4 years' custody	**Category range** 1–3 years' custody
Category 3	**Starting point** 3 years' custody	**Starting point** 2 years' custody	**Starting point** 1 year's custody
	Category range 2–4 years' custody	**Category range** 1–3 years' custody	**Category range** High level community order–2 years' custody

SG32-30 The table below contains a **non-exhaustive** list of additional factual elements providing the context of the offence and factors relating to the offender. Identify whether any combination of these, or other [20]

[20] relevant factors, should result in an upward or downward adjustment from the sentence arrived at so far. In particular, relevant recent convictions are likely to result in an upward adjustment. In some cases, having considered these factors, it may be appropriate to move outside the identified category range.

Factors increasing seriousness
Statutory aggravating factors: Previous convictions, having regard to a) the **nature** of the offence to which the conviction relates and its **relevance** to the current offence; and b) the **time** that has elapsed since the conviction Offence committed whilst on bail Offence motivated by, or demonstrating hostility based on any of the following characteristics or presumed characteristics of the victim: religion, race, disability, sexual orientation or transgender identity *(When considering this factor, sentencers should bear in mind the statutory definition of terrorism in section 1 of the Terrorism Act 2000, and should be careful to avoid double counting)*
Other aggravating factors: Specifically targeted audience (if not considered at step 1) Vulnerable/impressionable audience (if not considered at step 1) Communication with known extremists Deliberate use of encrypted communications or similar technologies to facilitate the commission of the offence and/or avoid or impede detection Significant volume of terrorist publications published or disseminated Used multiple social media platforms to reach a wider audience Offender attempted to disguise their identity to prevent detection Failure to respond to warnings Failure to comply with current court orders Offence committed on licence or Post Sentence Supervision Offence committed whilst in prison

Factors reducing seriousness or reflecting personal mitigation
No previous convictions **or** no relevant/recent convictions Good character and/or exemplary conduct Offender involved through coercion, intimidation or exploitation Clear evidence of a change of mind set prior to arrest Offender's responsibility substantially reduced by mental disorder or learning disability Age and/or lack of maturity where it affects the responsibility of the offender Sole or primary carer for dependent relatives

[21] **STEP THREE Consider any factors which indicate a reduction for assistance to the prosecution** SG32-31

The court should take into account sections 73 and 74 of the Serious Organised Crime and Police Act 2005 (assistance by defendants: reduction or review of sentence) and any other rule of law by virtue of which an offender may receive a discounted sentence in consequence of assistance given (or offered) to the prosecutor or investigator.

STEP FOUR Reduction for guilty pleas SG32-32

The court should take account of any potential reduction for a guilty plea in accordance with section 144 of the Criminal Justice Act 2003 and the guideline for *Reduction in Sentence for a Guilty Plea* (where first hearing is **on or after June 2017**, or first hearing **before 1 June 2017**).

STEP FIVE Totality principle SG32-33

If sentencing an offender for more than one offence, or where the offender is already serving a sentence, consider whether the total sentence is just and proportionate to the overall offending behaviour in accordance with the *Totality* guideline.

STEP SIX Ancillary orders SG32-34

In all cases the court should consider whether to make ancillary orders. See Additional guidance [at SG32-99].

STEP SEVEN Reasons SG32-35

Section 174 of the Criminal Justice Act 2003 imposes a duty to give reasons for, and explain the effect of, the sentence.

SG32-36 **STEP EIGHT Consideration for time spent on bail (tagged curfew)** [21]

The court must consider whether to give credit for time spent on bail in accordance with section 240A of the Criminal Justice Act 2003.

SG32-37 PROSCRIBED ORGANISATIONS [23]

Membership

Terrorism Act 2000 (section 11)

Triable either way

Maximum: 10 years' custody

Offence range: High level community order–9 years' custody

This guideline applies only to offenders aged 18 and older

SG32-38 **STEP ONE Determining the offence category** [24]

The court should determine the offence category with reference **only** to the factors listed in the tables below. In order to determine the category, the court should assess **culpability and harm.**

The court should weigh all the factors set out below in determining the offender's culpability. **Where there are characteristics present which fall under different levels of culpability, the court should balance these characteristics to reach a fair assessment of the offender's culpability.**

Culpability demonstrated by one or more of the following:	
A	• Prominent member of organisation
B	• Active (but not prominent) member of organisation
C	• All other cases

Harm

There is no variation in the level of harm caused. Membership of any organisation which is concerned in terrorism either through the commission, participation, preparation, promotion or encouragement of terrorism is inherently harmful.

SG32-39 **STEP TWO Starting point and category range**

Having determined the category at step one, the court should use the corresponding starting point to reach a sentence within the category range below. The starting point applies to all offenders irrespective of plea or previous convictions. A case of particular gravity, reflected by multiple features of culpability in step one, could merit upward adjustment from the starting point before further adjustment for aggravating or mitigating features, set out [at **SG32-40**].

	Culpability		
Harm	**A**	**B**	**C**
Category 1	**Starting point** 7 years' custody	**Starting point** 5 years' custody	**Starting point** 2 years' custody
	Category range 5–9 years' custody	**Category range** 3–7 years' custody	**Category range** High level community order–4 years' custody

SG32-40 The table below contains a non-exhaustive list of additional factual elements providing the context of the offence and factors relating to the offender. Identify whether any combination of these, or other relevant factors, should result in an upward or downward adjustment from the sentence arrived at so far. In particular, relevant recent convictions are likely to result in an upward adjustment. In some cases, having considered these factors, it may be appropriate to move outside the identified category range. [25]

[25]

Factors increasing seriousness
Statutory aggravating factors: Previous convictions, having regard to a) the **nature** of the offence to which the conviction relates and its **relevance** to the current offence; and b) the **time** that has elapsed since the conviction Offence committed whilst on bail Offence motivated by, or demonstrating hostility based on any of the following characteristics or presumed characteristics of the victim: religion, race, disability, sexual orientation or transgender identity *(When considering this factor, sentencers should bear in mind the statutory definition of terrorism in section 1 of the Terrorism Act 2000, and should be careful to avoid double counting)* *Other aggravating factors:* Length of time over which offending was committed Failure to respond to warnings Failure to comply with current court orders Offence committed on licence or Post Sentence Supervision Offence committed whilst in prison

Factors reducing seriousness or reflecting personal mitigation
Unaware that organisation was proscribed No previous convictions **or** no relevant/recent convictions Good character and/or exemplary conduct Offender involved through coercion, intimidation or exploitation Clear evidence of a change of mind set prior to arrest Offender's responsibility substantially reduced by mental disorder or learning disability Age and/or lack of maturity where it affects the responsibility of the offender Sole or primary carer for dependent relatives

[26] **STEP THREE Consider any factors which indicate a reduction for assistance to the prosecution** **SG32-41**

The court should take into account sections 73 and 74 of the Serious Organised Crime and Police Act 2005 (assistance by defendants: reduction or review of sentence) and any other rule of law by virtue of which an offender may receive a discounted sentence in consequence of assistance given (or offered) to the prosecutor or investigator.

STEP FOUR Reduction for guilty pleas **SG32-42**

The court should take account of any potential reduction for a guilty plea in accordance with section 144 of the Criminal Justice Act 2003 and the guideline for *Reduction in Sentence for a Guilty Plea* (where first hearing is **on or after 1 June 2017**, or first hearing **before 1 June 2017**).

STEP FIVE Totality principle **SG32-43**

If sentencing an offender for more than one offence, or where the offender is already serving a sentence, consider whether the total sentence is just and proportionate to the overall offending behaviour in accordance with the *Totality* guideline.

STEP SIX Ancillary orders **SG32-44**

In all cases the court should consider whether to make ancillary orders. See Additional guidance [at SG32-99].

STEP SEVEN Reasons **SG32-45**

Section 174 of the Criminal Justice Act 2003 imposes a duty to give reasons for, and explain the effect of, the sentence.

STEP EIGHT Consideration for time spent on bail (tagged curfew) **SG32-46**

The court must consider whether to give credit for time spent on bail in accordance with section 240A of the Criminal Justice Act 2003.

[27] PROSCRIBED ORGANISATIONS **SG32-47**

Support

Terrorism Act 2000 (section12)

Triable either way

Maximum: 10 years' custody

Offence range: High level community order–9 years' custody

This guideline applies only to offenders aged 18 and older

Sentencing Guidelines

SG32-48 STEP ONE **Determining the offence category** [28]

The court should determine the offence category with reference **only** to the factors listed in the tables below. In order to determine the category, the court should assess **culpability** and **harm.**

The court should weigh all the factors set out below in determining the offender's culpability. **Where there are characteristics present which fall under different levels of culpability, the court should balance these characteristics to reach a fair assessment of the offender's culpability.**

Culpability demonstrated by one or more of the following:	
A	• Offender in position of trust, authority or influence and abuses their position • Persistent efforts to gain widespread or significant support for organisation • Encourages activities intended to cause endangerment to life
B	• Arranged or played a significant part in the arrangement of a meeting/event aimed at gaining a significant support for organisation • Intended to gain widespread or significant support for organisation • Encourages activities intended to cause widespread or serious damage to property, or economic interests or substantial impact upon civic infrastructure
C	• Lesser cases where characteristics for categories A or B are not present

Harm The court should consider the factors set out below to determine the level of harm	
Category 1	• Evidence that others have acted on or been assisted by the encouragement to carry out activities endangering life • Significant support for the organisation gained or likely to be gained
Category 2	• Evidence that others have acted on or been assisted by the encouragement to carry out activities not endangering life
Category 3	• All other cases

SG32-49 STEP TWO **Starting point and category range** [29]

Having determined the category at step one, the court should use the corresponding starting point to reach a sentence within the category range below. The starting point applies to all offenders irrespective of plea or previous convictions. A case of particular gravity, reflected by multiple features of culpability or harm in step one, could merit upward adjustment from the starting point before further adjustment for aggravating or mitigating features, set out [at SG32-50].

	Culpability		
Harm	**A**	**B**	**C**
Category 1	**Starting point** 7 years' custody	**Starting point** 5 years' custody	**Starting point** 3 years' custody
	Category range 6–9 years' custody	**Category range** 4–6 years' custody	**Category range** 2–4 years' custody
Category 2	**Starting point** 6 years' custody	**Starting point** 4 years' custody	**Starting point** 2 years' custody
	Category range 5–7 years' custody	**Category range** 3–5 years' custody	**Category range** 1–3 years' custody
Category 3	**Starting point** 5 years' custody	**Starting point** 3 years' custody	**Starting point** 1 years' custody
	Category range 4–6 years' custody	**Category range** 2–4 years' custody	**Category range** High level community order–2 years' custody

SG32-50 The table below contains a **non-exhaustive** list of additional factual elements providing the context of the offence and factors relating to the offender. Identify whether any combination of these, or other relevant factors, should result in an upward or downward adjustment from the sentence arrived at so far. In particular, relevant recent convictions are likely to result in an upward adjustment. In some cases, having considered these factors, it may be appropriate to move outside the identified category range. [30]

[30]

Factors increasing seriousness
Statutory aggravating factors: Previous convictions, having regard to a) the **nature** of the offence to which the conviction relates and its **relevance** to the current offence; and b) the **time** that has elapsed since the conviction Offence committed whilst on bail Offence motivated by, or demonstrating hostility based on any of the following characteristics or presumed characteristics of the victim: religion, race, disability, sexual orientation or transgender identity *(When considering this factor, sentencers should bear in mind the statutory definition of terrorism in section 1 of the Terrorism Act 2000, and should be careful to avoid double counting)* *Other aggravating factors:* Vulnerable/impressionable audience Failure to respond to warnings Failure to comply with current court orders Offence committed on licence or Post Sentence Supervision Offence committed whilst in prison

Factors reducing seriousness or reflecting personal mitigation
No previous convictions or no relevant/recent convictions Good character and/or exemplary conduct Offender involved through coercion, intimidation or exploitation Clear evidence of a change of mind set prior to arrest Offender's responsibility substantially reduced by mental disorder or learning disability Age and/or lack of maturity where it affects the responsibility of the offender Sole or primary carer for dependent relatives

[31] **STEP THREE Consider any factors which indicate a reduction for assistance to the prosecution** SG32-51

The court should take into account sections 73 and 74 of the Serious Organised Crime and Police Act 2005 (assistance by defendants: reduction or review of sentence) and any other rule of law by virtue of which an offender may receive a discounted sentence in consequence of assistance given (or offered) to the prosecutor or investigator.

STEP FOUR Reduction for guilty pleas SG32-52

The court should take account of any potential reduction for a guilty plea in accordance with section 144 of the Criminal Justice Act 2003 and the guideline for *Reduction in Sentence for a Guilty Plea* (where first hearing is **on or after 1 June 2017**, or first hearing **before 1 June 2017**).

STEP FIVE Totality principle SG32-53

If sentencing an offender for more than one offence, or where the offender is already serving a sentence, consider whether the total sentence is just and proportionate to the overall offending behaviour in accordance with the *Totality* guideline.

STEP SIX Ancillary orders SG32-54

In all cases the court should consider whether to make ancillary orders. See Additional guidance [at SG32-99].

STEP SEVEN Reasons SG32-55

Section 174 of the Criminal Justice Act 2003 imposes a duty to give reasons for, and explain the effect of, the sentence.

STEP EIGHT Consideration for time spent on bail (tagged curfew) SG32-56

The court must consider whether to give credit for time spent on bail in accordance with section 240A of the Criminal Justice Act 2003.

[33]

FUNDING TERRORISM SG32-57

Fundraising

Terrorism Act 200 (section 15)

Use and possession [33]
Terrorism Act 2000 (section 16)

Funding arrangements
Terrorism Act 2000 (section 17)

Money laundering
Terrorism Act 2000 (section 18)

Triable either way

Maximum: 14 years' custody

Offence range: High level community order–13 years' custody

This guideline applies only to offenders aged 18 and older

SG32-58 STEP ONE **Determining the offence category** [34]

The court should determine the offence category with reference **only** to the factors listed in the tables below. In order to determine the category, the court should assess **culpability** and **harm**.

The court should weigh all the factors set out below in determining the offender's culpability.

Where there are characteristics present which fall under different levels of culpability, the court should balance these characteristics to reach a fair assessment of the offender's culpability.

Culpability demonstrated by one or more of the following:	
A	• A significant role where offending is part of a group activity • Involvement of others through pressure or influence • Abuse of position of power, trust or responsibility • Sophisticated nature of offence/significant planning • Activities took place over a sustained period of time
B	• Cases whose characteristics fall between A and C
C	• Performed limited function under direction • Very little or no planning

Harm The court should consider the factors set out below to determine the level of harm	
Category 1	• Money or property made, or likely to make, a significant contribution to furthering terrorism • Use or provision of money or property to fund or assist activities endangering life
Category 2	• Use or provision of money or property to fund or assist activities which involve a risk of widespread or serious damage to property, or economic interests or substantial impact upon civic infrastructure • All other cases whose characteristics fall between 1 and 3
Category 3	• Money or property made, or was likely to make, a minor contribution to furthering terrorism

SG32-59 STEP TWO **Starting point and category range** [35]

Having determined the category at step one, the court should use the corresponding starting point to reach a sentence within the category range below. The starting point applies to all offenders irrespective of plea or previous convictions. A case of particular gravity, reflected by multiple features of culpability or harm in step one, could merit upward adjustment from the starting point before further adjustment for aggravating or mitigating features, set out [at **SG32-60**].

[35]

Harm	Culpability A	B	C
Category 1	**Starting point** 12 years' custody	**Starting point** 9 years' custody	**Starting point** 7 years' custody
	Category range 10–13 years' custody	**Category range** 8–10 years' custody	**Category range** 6–8 years' custody
Category 2	**Starting point** 9 years' custody	**Starting point** 7 years' custody	**Starting point** 4 years' custody
	Category range 8–10 years' custody	**Category range** 6–8 years' custody	**Category range** 2–5 years' custody
Category 3	**Starting point** 7 years' custody	**Starting point** 4 years' custody	**Starting point** 2 years' custody
	Category range 6–8 years' custody	**Category range** 2–5 years' custody	**Category range** High level community order–3 years' custody

[36] The table below contains a **non-exhaustive** list of additional factual elements providing the context of the offence and factors relating to the offender. Identify whether any combination of these, or other relevant factors, should result in an upward or downward adjustment from the sentence arrived at so far. In particular, relevant recent convictions are likely to result in an upward adjustment. In some cases, having considered these factors, it may be appropriate to move outside the identified category range. **SG32-60**

Factors increasing seriousness
Statutory aggravating factors: Previous convictions, having regard to a) the **nature** of the offence to which the conviction relates and its **relevance** to the current offence; and b) the **time** that has elapsed since the conviction Offence committed whilst on bail Offence motivated by, or demonstrating hostility based on any of the following characteristics or presumed characteristics of the victim: religion, race, disability, sexual orientation or transgender identity *(When considering this factor, sentencers should bear in mind the statutory definition of terrorism in section 1 of the Terrorism Act 2000, and should be careful to avoid double counting)* *Other aggravating factors:* Deliberate use of encrypted communications or similar technologies to facilitate the commission of the offence and/or avoid or impede detection Indoctrinated or encouraged others Use or provision of false or fraudulent identification Misrepresenting nature of organisation Failure to respond to warnings Failure to comply with current court orders Offence committed on licence or Post Sentence Supervision

Factors reducing seriousness or reflecting personal mitigation
No previous convictions **or** no relevant/recent convictions Good character and/or exemplary conduct Offender involved through coercion, intimidation or exploitation Clear evidence of a change of mind set prior to arrest Offender's responsibility substantially reduced by mental disorder or learning disability Age and/or lack of maturity where it affects the responsibility of the offender Sole or primary carer for dependent relatives

[37] **STEP THREE Consider any factors which indicate a reduction for assistance to the prosecution** **SG32-61**

The court should take into account sections 73 and 74 of the Serious Organised Crime and Police Act 2005 (assistance by defendants: reduction or review of sentence) and any other rule of law by virtue of which an offender may receive a discounted sentence in consequence of assistance given (or offered) to the prosecutor or investigator.

SG32-62 **STEP FOUR Reduction for guilty pleas** [37]

The court should take account of any potential reduction for a guilty plea in accordance with section 144 of the Criminal Justice Act 2003 and the guideline for a *Reduction in Sentence for a Guilty Plea* (where first hearing is **on or after 1 June 2017**, or first hearing **before 1 June 2017**).

SG32-63 **STEP FIVE Totality principle**

If sentencing an offender for more than one offence, or where the offender is already serving a sentence, consider whether the total sentence is just and proportionate to the overall offending behaviour in accordance with the *Totality* guideline.

SG32-64 **STEP SIX Ancillary orders**

In all cases the court should consider whether to make ancillary orders. See Additional guidance [at **SG32-99**].

SG32-65 **STEP SEVEN Reasons**

Section 174 of the Criminal Justice Act 2003 imposes a duty to give reasons for, and explain the effect of, the sentence.

SG32-66 **STEP EIGHT Consideration for time spent on bail (tagged curfew)**

The court must consider whether to give credit for time spent on bail in accordance with section 240A of the Criminal Justice Act 2003.

SG32-67 FAILURE TO DISCLOSE INFORMATION ABOUT ACTS OF TERRORISM [39]

Terrorism Act 2000 (section 38B)

Triable either way

Maximum: 5 years' custody

Offence range: High level community order–4 years 6 months' custody

This guideline applies only to offenders aged 18 and older

SG32-68 **STEP ONE Determining the offence category** [40]

The court should determine the offence category with reference **only** to the factors listed in the tables below. In order to determine the category, the court should assess **culpability and harm.**

The court should weigh all the factors set out below in determining the offender's culpability.

Culpability demonstrated by one or more of the following:	
A	• Information was very significant (including, but not limited to, information which could have prevented an act of terrorism
B	• Cases whose characteristics fall between A and C
C	• Information was of low significance

Harm The court should consider the factors set out below to determine the level of harm	
Category 1	• Information related to terrorist activity endangering life • Information related to terrorist activity intended to cause widespread or serious damage to property, or economic interest or substantial impact upon civic infrastructure
Category 2	• All other cases

SG32-69 **STEP TWO Starting point and category range** [41]

Having determined the category at step one, the court should use the corresponding starting point to reach a sentence within the category range below. The starting point applies to all offenders irrespective of plea or previous convictions. A case of particular gravity, reflected by multiple features of culpability or harm in step one, could merit upward adjustment from the starting point before further adjustment for aggravating or mitigating features, set out [at **SG32-70**].

[41]

Harm	Culpability A	B	C
Category 1	**Starting point** 4 years' custody	**Starting point** 3 years' custody	**Starting point** 2 years' custody
	Category range 3–4 years 6 months' custody	**Category range** 2–4 years' custody	**Category range** 6 months–3 years' custody
Category 2	**Starting point** 3 years' custody	**Starting point** 2 years' custody	**Starting point** 1 years 6 months' custody
	Category range 2–4 years' custody	**Category range** 6 months–3 years' custody	**Category range** High level community order–2 years' custody

[42] The table below contains a **non-exhaustive** list of additional factual elements providing the context of the offence and factors relating to the offender. Identify whether any combination of these, or other relevant factors, should result in an upward or downward adjustment from the sentence arrived at so far. In particular, relevant recent convictions are likely to result in an upward adjustment. In some cases, having considered these factors, it may be appropriate to move outside the identified category range. **SG32-70**

Factors increasing seriousness
Statutory aggravating factors: Previous convictions, having regard to a) the **nature** of the offence to which the conviction relates and its **relevance** to the current offence; and b) the **time** that has elapsed since the conviction Offence committed whilst on bail Offence motivated by, or demonstrating hostility based on any of the following characteristics or presumed characteristics of the victim: religion, race, disability, sexual orientation or transgender identity *(When considering this factor, sentencers should bear in mind the statutory definition of terrorism in section 1 of the Terrorism Act 2000, and should be careful to avoid double counting)* *Other aggravating factors:* Many lives endangered Length of time over which offending was committed Failure to respond to warnings Failure to comply with current court orders Offence committed on licence or Post Sentence Supervision Offence committed whilst in prison

Factors reducing seriousness or reflecting personal mitigation
No previous convictions **or** no relevant/recent convictions Good character and/or exemplary conduct Offender involved through coercion, intimidation or exploitation Offender discloses information but not as soon as was reasonably practicable Offender's responsibility substantially reduced by mental disorder or learning disability Age and/or lack of maturity where it affects the responsibility of the offender Sole or primary carer for dependent relatives

[43] **STEP THREE Consider any factors which indicate a reduction for assistance to the prosecution** **SG32-71**

The court should take into account sections 73 and 74 of the Serious Organised Crime and Police Act 2005 (assistance by defendants: reduction or review of sentence) and any other rule of law by virtue of which an offender may receive a discounted sentence in consequence of assistance given (or offered) to the prosecutor or investigator.

STEP FOUR Reduction for guilty pleas **SG32-72**

The court should take account of any potential reduction for a guilty plea in accordance with section 144 of the Criminal Justice Act 2003 and the guideline for *Reduction in Sentence for a Guilty Plea* (where first hearing is **on or after 1 June 2017**, or first hearing **before 1 June 2017**).

STEP FIVE Totality principle **SG32-73**

If sentencing an offender for more than one offence, or where the offender is already serving a sentence, consider whether the total sentence is just and proportionate to the overall offending behaviour in accordance with the *Totality* guideline.

SG32-74 **STEP SIX Ancillary orders** [43]

In all cases the court should consider whether to make ancillary orders. See Additional guidance [at SG32-99].

SG32-75 **STEP SEVEN Reasons**

Section 174 of the Criminal Justice Act 2003 imposes a duty to give reasons for, and explain the effect of, the sentence.

SG32-76 **STEP EIGHT Consideration for time spent on bail (tagged curfew)**

The court must consider whether to give credit for time spent on bail in accordance with section 240A of the Criminal Justice Act 2003.

SG32-77

Possession for Terrorist Purposes [45]

Terrorism Act 2000 (section 57)

This is a serious specified offence for the purposes of sections 224 and 225(2) (life sentence for serious offences) of the Criminal Justice Act 2003.

This is an offence listed in Part 1 of Schedule 15B for the purposes of sections 224A (life sentence for second listed offence) of the Criminal Justice Act 2003.

This is a specified offence for the purposes of sections 226A (extended sentence for certain violent or sexual offences) of the Criminal Justice Act 2003.

This is an offence listed in Schedule 18A for the purposes of section236A (special custodial sentence for certain offenders of particular concern) of the Criminal Justice Act 2003.

Triable either way

Maximum: 15 years' custody

Offence range: 1–14 years' custody

This guideline applies only to offenders aged 18 and older

SG32-78 **STEP ONE Determining the offence category** [46]

The court should determine the offence category with reference **only** to the factors listed in the tables below. In order to determine the category, the court should assess **culpability and harm.**

The court should weigh all the factors set out below in determining the offender's culpability.

Where there are characteristics present which fall under different levels of culpability, the court should balance these characteristics to reach a fair assessment of the offender's culpability.

Culpability demonstrated by one or more of the following:	
A	• Possession of article(s) indicates that the offender's preparations for terrorist activity are complete or almost complete • Offender is a significant participant in the commission, preparation or instigation of an act of terrorism
B	• Cases whose characteristics fall between A and C
C	• Possession of article(s) indicates that offender has engaged in limited preparation toward terrorist activity • Offender is of limited assistance or encouragement to others who are preparing for terrorist activity

Harm Harm is assessed based on the type of harm risked and the likelihood of that harm being caused	
Category 1	• Article(s) had potential to facilitate an offence endangering life **and harm is very likely to be caused**
Category 2	• Article(s) had potential to facilitate an offence endangering life **but harm is not very likely to be caused** • Article(s) had potential to facilitate an offence causing widespread or serious damage to property, or economic interest or substantial upon civic infrastructure
Category 3	• All other cases

[47] **STEP TWO Starting point and category range** SG32-79

Having determined the category at step one, the court should use the corresponding starting point to reach a sentence within the category range below. The starting point applies to all offenders irrespective of plea or previous convictions. A case of particular gravity, reflected by multiple features of culpability or harm in step one, could merit upward adjustment from the starting point before further adjustment for aggravating or mitigating features, set out [at **SG32-80**].

	Culpability		
Harm	**A**	**B**	**C**
Category 1	**Starting point** 12 years' custody	**Starting point** 7 years' custody	**Starting point** 4 years' custody
	Category range 9–14 years' custody	**Category range** 6–9 years' custody	**Category range** 3–6 years' custody
Category 2	**Starting point** 8 years' custody	**Starting point** 6 years' custody	**Starting point** 3 years' custody
	Category range 7–9 years' custody	**Category range** 4–7 years' custody	**Category range** 2–4 years' custody
Category 3	**Starting point** 6 years' custody	**Starting point** 4 years' custody	**Starting point** 2 years' custody
	Category range 4–7 years' custody	**Category range** 2–5 years' custody	**Category range** 1–3 years' custody

[48] The table below contains a non-exhaustive list of additional factual elements providing the context of the offence and factors relating to the offender. Identify whether any combination of these, or other relevant factors, should result in an upward or downward adjustment from the sentence arrived at so far. In particular, relevant recent convictions are likely to result in an upward adjustment. In some cases, having considered these factors, it may be appropriate to move outside the identified category range. SG32-80

Factors increasing seriousness
Statutory aggravating factors: Previous convictions, having regard to a) the **nature** of the offence to which the conviction relates and its **relevance** to the current offence; and b) the **time** that has elapsed since the conviction Offence committed whilst on bail Offence motivated by, or demonstrating hostility based on any of the following characteristics or presumed characteristics of the victim: religion, race, disability, sexual orientation or transgender identity *(When considering this factor, sentencers should bear in mind the statutory definition of terrorism in section 1 of the Terrorism Act 2000, and should be careful to avoid double counting)*
Other aggravating factors: Article has the potential to endanger many lives Length of time over which offending was committed Communication with other extremists Deliberate use of encrypted communications or similar technologies to facilitate the commission of the offence and/or avoid or impede detection Offender attempted to disguise their identity to prevent detection Indoctrinated or encouraged others Failure to respond to warnings Failure to comply with current court orders Offence committed on licence or Post Sentence Supervision Offence committed whilst in prison

Factors reducing seriousness or reflecting personal mitigation
No previous convictions **or** no relevant/recent convictions Good character and/or exemplary conduct Offender involved through coercion, intimidation or exploitation Clear evidence of a change of mind set prior to arrest Offender's responsibility substantially reduced by mental disorder or learning disability Age and/or lack of maturity where it affects the responsibility of the offender Sole or primary carer for dependent relatives

SG32-81 STEP THREE **Consider any factors which indicate a reduction for assistance to the prosecution** [49]

The court should take into account sections 73 and 74 of the Serious Organised Crime and Police Act 2005 (assistance by defendants: reduction or review of sentence) and any other rule of law by virtue of which an offender may receive a discounted sentence in consequence of assistance given (or offered) to the prosecutor or investigator.

SG32-82 STEP FOUR **Reduction for guilty pleas**

The court should take account of any potential reduction for a guilty plea in accordance with section 144 of the Criminal Justice Act 2003 and the guideline for *Reduction in Sentence for a Guilty Plea* (where first hearing is **on or after 1 June 2017**, or first hearing **before June 2017**).

SG32-83 STEP FIVE **Dangerousness**

The court should consider whether having regard to the criteria contained in Chapter 5 of Part 12 of the Criminal Justice Act 2003 it would be appropriate to impose a life sentence (section 224A or section 225) or an extended sentence (section 226A). When sentencing offenders to a life sentence under these provisions, the notional determinate sentence should be used as the basis for the setting of a minimum term.

SG32-84 STEP SIX **Special custodial sentence for certain offenders of particular concern (section 236A)**

Where the court does not impose a sentence of imprisonment for life or an extended sentence, but does impose a period of imprisonment, the term of the sentence must be equal to the aggregate of the appropriate custodial term and a further period of 1 year for which the offender is to be subject to a licence.

SG32-85 STEP SEVEN **Totality principle**

If sentencing an offender for more than one offence, or where the offender is already serving a sentence, consider whether the total sentence is just and proportionate to the overall offending behaviour in accordance with the *Totality* guideline.

SG32-86 STEP EIGHT **Ancillary orders**

In all cases the court should consider whether to make ancillary orders. See Additional guidance [at SG32-99].

SG32-87 STEP NINE **Reasons**

Section 174 of the Criminal Justice Act 2003 imposes a duty to give reasons for, and explain the effect of, the sentence.

SG32-88 STEP TEN **Consideration for time spent on bail (tagged curfew)**

The court must consider whether to give credit for time spent on bail in accordance with section 240A of the Criminal Justice Act 2003.

SG32-89 COLLECTION OF TERRORIST INFORMATION [51]

Terrorism Act 2000 (section 58)

Triable either way

Maximum: 10 years' custody

Offence range: High level community order–9 years' custody

This guideline applies only to offenders aged 18 and older

SG32-90 STEP ONE **Determining the offence category** [52]

The court should determine the offence category with reference **only** to the factors listed in the tables below. In order to determine the category, the court should assess **culpability** and **harm**.

The court should weigh all the factors set out below in determining the offender's culpability. **Where there are characteristics present which fall under different levels of culpability, the court should balance these characteristics to reach a fair assessment of the offender's culpability.**

[52]

Culpability demonstrated by one or more of the following:	
A	• Offender collected, made a record of, or was in possession of information for use in a specific terrorist act
B	• Offender collected, made a record of, or was in possession of information likely to be useful to a person committing or preparing an act of terrorism and the offender had terrorist connections or motivations • Offender repeatedly accessed extremist material (where not falling within A)
C	• Offender collected, made a record of, or was in possession of information likely to be useful to a person committing or preparing an act of terrorism but had no terrorist connections or motivations

Harm Harm is assessed based on the type of harm risked and the likelihood of that harm being caused	
Category 1	• Material provides instruction for specific terrorist activity endangering life **and harm is very likely to be caused**
Category 2	• Material provides instruction for specific terrorist activity endangering life **but harm is not very likely to be caused** • Material provides instruction for specific terrorist activity intended to cause widespread or serious damage to property, or economic interest or substantial impact upon civic infrastructure
Category 3	• All other cases

[53] **STEP TWO Starting point and category range** **SG32-91**

Having determined the category at step one, the court should use the corresponding starting point to reach a sentence within the category range below. The starting point applies to all offenders irrespective of plea or previous convictions. A case of particular gravity, reflected by multiple features of culpability or harm in step one, could merit upward adjustment from the starting point before further adjustment for aggravating or mitigating features, set out [at SG32-92].

	Culpability		
Harm	**A**	**B**	**C**
Category 1	**Starting point** 7 years' custody	**Starting point** 5 years' custody	**Starting point** 2 years' custody
	Category range 5–9 years' custody	**Category range** 3–6 years' custody	**Category range** 1–4 years' custody
Category 2	**Starting point** 6 years' custody	**Starting point** 4 years' custody	**Starting point** 1 year 6 months' custody
	Category range 4–8 years' custody	**Category range** 3–5 years' custody	**Category range** 6 months–3 years' custody
Category 3	**Starting point** 5 years' custody	**Starting point** 3 years' custody	**Starting point** 1 year's custody
	Category range 3–6 years' custody	**Category range** 2–5 years' custody	**Category range** High level community order–2 years' custody

[54] The table below contains a **non-exhaustive** list of additional factual elements providing the context of the offence and factors relating to the offender. Identify whether any combination of these, or other relevant factors, should result in an upward or downward adjustment from the sentence arrived at so far. In particular, relevant recent convictions are likely to result in an upward adjustment. In some cases, having considered these factors, it may be appropriate to move outside the identified category range. **SG32-92**

Factors increasing seriousness
Statutory aggravating factors: Previous convictions, having regard to a) the **nature** of the offence to which the conviction relates and its **relevance** to the current offence; and b) the **time** that has elapsed since the conviction Offence committed whilst on bail Offence motivated by, or demonstrating hostility based on any of the following characteristics or presumed characteristics of the victim: religion, race, disability, sexual orientation or transgender identity *(When considering this factor, sentencers should bear in mind the statutory definition of terrorism in section 1 of the Terrorism Act 2000, and should be careful to avoid double counting)* *Other aggravating factors:* Significant volume of terrorist publications Length of time over which offending was committed Deliberate use of encrypted communications or similar technologies to facilitate the commission of the offence and/or avoid or impede detection Failure to respond to warnings Failure to comply with current court orders Offence committed on licence or Post Sentence Supervision Offence committed whilst in prison

[54]

Factors reducing seriousness or reflecting personal mitigation
No previous convictions **or** no relevant/recent convictions Good character and/or exemplary conduct Offender involved through coercion, intimidation or exploitation Clear evidence of a change of mind set prior to arrest Offender's responsibility substantially reduced by mental disorder or learning disability Age and/or lack of maturity where it affects the responsibility of the offender Sole or primary carer for dependent relatives

SG32-93 **STEP THREE Consider any factors which indicate a reduction for assistance to the prosecution** [55]

The court should take into account sections 73 and 74 of the Serious Organised Crime and Police Act 2005 (assistance by defendants: reduction or review of sentence) and any other rule of law by virtue of which an offender may receive a discounted sentence in consequence of assistance given (or offered) to the prosecutor or investigator.

SG32-94 **STEP FOUR Reduction for guilty pleas**

The court should take account of any potential reduction for a guilty plea in accordance with section 144 of the Criminal Justice Act 2003 and the guideline for *Reduction in Sentence for a Guilty Plea* (where first hearing is **on or after 1 June 2017**, or first hearing **before 1 June 2017**).

SG32-95 **STEP FIVE Totality principle**

If sentencing an offender for more than one offence, or where the offender is already serving a sentence, consider whether the total sentence is just and proportionate to the overall offending behaviour in accordance with the *Totality* guideline.

SG32-96 **STEP SIX Ancillary orders**

In all cases the court should consider whether to make ancillary orders. See Additional guidance [at **SG32-99**].

SG32-97 **STEP SEVEN Reasons**

Section 174 of the Criminal Justice Act 2003 imposes a duty to give reasons for, and explain the effect of, the sentence.

SG32-98 **STEP EIGHT Consideration for time spent on bail (tagged curfew)**

The court must consider whether to give credit for time spent on bail in accordance with section 240A of the Criminal Justice Act 2003.

[57] ## Additional Guidance SG32-99

ANCILLARY ORDER	STATUTORY REFERENCE
Confiscation A confiscation order may be made by the Crown Court in circumstances in which the offender has obtained a financial benefit as a result of, or in connection with, his criminal conduct.	Section 6 and Schedule 2 of the Proceeds of Crime Act 2002
Forfeiture When sentencing for a funding offence (sections 15-18 Terrorism Act 2000), the court may order the forfeiture of money or property which the offender had possession or control of at the time of the offence	Section23 to 23B Terrorism Act 2000

Automatic Orders on Conviction SG32-100

The following requirements or provisions are not part of the sentence imposed by the court but apply automatically by operation of law. The role of the court is to inform the offender of the applicable requirements and/or prohibition.

ANCILLARY ORDER	STATUTORY REFERENCE
Notification requirements A relevant offender automatically becomes subject to notification requirements, obliging him to notify the police of specified information for a specified period. The court should inform the offender accordingly. The operation of the notification requirement is not a relevant consideration in determining the sentence for the offence.	Sections 41–53 Counter-Terrorism Act 2008

[58] **Sentencing for offences not covered by this guideline but with a terrorist connection section 30 Counter Terrorism Act 2008**

Where a court is considering the seriousness of an offence specified in Schedule 2 Counter Terrorism Act 2008, and it appears that the offence has or may have a terrorist connection, the court must determine whether that is the case. To make this determination the court may hear evidence, and must take account of any representations made by the parties.

If the court determines that the offence has a terrorist connection it **must** treat that fact as a statutory aggravating factor and state in open court that the offence was so aggravated.

Notification requirements apply to these offences.

Offences not covered by schedule 2 Counter Terrorism Act 2008

Where a court is considering the seriousness of an offence not specified in Schedule 2 Counter Terrorism Act 2008, and it appears that the offence has or may have a terrorist connection, the court should determine whether that is the case by hearing evidence where necessary.

If the court determines that the offence has a terrorist connection it **may** treat that fact as a non-statutory aggravating factor where it appears relevant and appropriate to do so.

Notification requirements do not apply to these offences.

[59] ## Annex: Community Orders SG32-101

In this guideline, community sentences are expressed as one of three levels (low, medium and high).

An illustrative description of examples of requirements that might be appropriate for each level is provided below. Where two or more requirements are ordered, they must be compatible with each other. Save in exceptional circumstances, the court must impose at least one requirement for the purpose of punishment, or combine the community order with a fine, or both (see section 177 Criminal Justice Act 2003).

Low	Medium	High
Offences only just cross community order threshold, where the seriousness of the offence or the nature of the offender's record means that a discharge or fine is inappropriate	Offences obviously fall within the community order band	Offences only just fall below the custody threshold or the custody threshold is crossed but a community order is more appropriate in the circumstances
In general, only one requirement will be appropriate and the length may be curtailed if additional requirements are necessary		More intensive sentences which combine two or more requirements may be appropriate
Suitable requirements might include: • Any appropriate rehabilitative requirement(s) • 40-80 hours of unpaid work • Curfew requirement within the lowest range (for example up to 16 hours per day for a few weeks) • Exclusion requirement, for a few months • Prohibited activity requirement • Attendance centre requirement where available	Suitable requirements might include: • Any appropriate rehabilitative requirement(s) • Greater number of hours unpaid work (for example 80-150 hours) • Curfew requirement within the middle range (for example up to 16 hours for 2-3 months) • Exclusion requirement lasting in the region of 6 months • Prohibited activity requirement	Suitable requirements might include: • Any appropriate rehabilitative requirement(s) • 150-300 hours of unpaid work • Curfew requirement up to 16 hours per day for 4-12 months • Exclusion order lasting in the region of 12 months

[59]

The table above is also set out in the *Imposition of Community and Custodial Sentences Guideline* which includes further guidance on community orders [see SG9-4].

PART 33 THEFT

Definitive Guideline SG33-1

[2] **Applicability of Guideline**

[Omitted: See SG19-1 for identical text save that this guideline has effect from 1 February 2016.]

Structure, ranges and starting points

[Omitted: See SG19-2 for identical text.]

[3]

General Theft SG33-2

Theft Act 1968 (section 1)

Including:
Theft from the person
Theft in a dwelling
Theft in breach of trust
Theft from a motor vehicle
Theft of a motor vehicle
Theft of a pedal bicycle
and all other section 1 Theft Act 1968 offences, excluding theft from a shop or stall

Triable either way
Maximum: 7 years' custody
Offence range: Discharge–6 years' custody

[4] **STEP ONE Determining the offence category** SG33-3

The court should determine the offence category with reference **only** to the factors identified in the following tables. In order to determine the category the court should assess **culpability and harm.**

The level of culpability is determined by weighing up all the factors of the case to determine the offender's role and the extent to which the offending was **planned** and the **sophistication** with which it was carried out.

CULPABILITY demonstrated by one or more of the following:
A — High culpability
A leading role where offending is part of a group activity
Involvement of others through coercion, intimidation or exploitation
Breach of a high degree of trust or responsibility
Sophisticated nature of offence/significant planning
Theft involving intimidation or the use or threat of force
Deliberately targeting victim on basis of vulnerability
B — Medium culpability
A significant role where offending is part of a group activity
Some degree of planning involved
Breach of some degree of trust or responsibility
Other cases that fall between categories A or C because:
– Factors are present in A and C which balance each other out **and/or**
– The offender's culpability falls between the factors as described in A and C
C — Lesser culpability
Performed limited function under direction
Involved through coercion, intimidation or exploitation
Little or no planning
Limited awareness or understanding of offence

CULPABILITY demonstrated by one or more of the following:

Where there are characteristics present which fall under different levels of culpability, the court should balance these characteristics to reach a fair assessment of the offender's culpability.

HARM [5]

Harm is assessed by reference to the **financial loss** that results from the theft **and any significant additional harm** suffered by the victim or others — examples of significant additional harm may include **but are not limited to:**

Items stolen were of substantial value to the loser — regardless of monetary worth
High level of inconvenience caused to the victim or others
Consequential financial harm to victim or others
Emotional distress
Fear/loss of confidence caused by the crime
Risk of or actual injury to persons or damage to property
Impact of theft on a business
Damage to heritage assets
Disruption caused to infrastructure

Intended loss should be used where actual loss has been prevented.

Category 1	Very high value goods stolen (above £100,000) **or** High value with significant additional harm to the victim or others
Category 2	High value goods stolen (£10,000 to £100,000) and no significant additional harm **or** Medium value with significant additional harm to the victim or others
Category 3	Medium value goods stolen (£500 to £10,000) **and** no significant additional harm **or** Low value with significant additional harm to the victim or others
Category 4	Low value goods stolen (up to £500) **and** Little or no significant additional harm to the victim or others

SG33-4 STEP TWO **Starting point and category range** [6]

Having determined the category at step one, the court should use the starting point to reach a sentence within the appropriate category range in the table below.

The starting point applies to all offenders irrespective of plea or previous convictions.

	Culpability		
Harm	**A**	**B**	**C**
Category 1 Adjustment should be made for any significant additional harm factors where very high value goods are stolen.	**Starting point** 3 years 6 months' custody	**Starting point** 2 years' custody	**Starting point** 1 year's custody
	Category range 2 years 6 months' — 6 years' custody	**Category range** 1–3 years–6 months' custody	**Category range** 26 weeks'–2 years' custody
Category 2	**Starting point** 2 years' custody	**Starting point** 1 year's custody	**Starting point** High level community order
	Category range 1 — 3 years 6 months' custody	**Category range** 26 weeks' — 2 years' custody	**Category range** Low level community order — 36 weeks' custody
Category 3	**Starting point** 1 year's custody	**Starting point** High level community order	**Starting point** Band C fine
	Category range 26 weeks' — 2 years' custody	**Category range** Low level community order— 36 weeks' custody	**Category range** Band B fine — Low level community order

[6]

Category 4	Culpability		
	Starting point High level community order	**Starting point** Low level community order	**Starting point** Band B fine
	Category range Medium level community order — 36 weeks' custody	**Category range** Band C fine Medium level community order	**Category range** Discharge — Band C fine

The table above refers to single offences. Where there are multiple offences, consecutive sentences may be appropriate: please refer to the *Offences Taken Into Consideration* and *Totality guideline* [see **SG3-1** and **SG3-7**].

Where multiple offences are committed in circumstances which justify consecutive sentences, and the total amount stolen is in excess of £1 million, then an aggregate sentence in excess of 7 years may be appropriate.

Where the offender is dependent on or has a propensity to misuse drugs or alcohol and there is sufficient prospect of success, a community order with a drug rehabilitation requirement under section 209, or an alcohol treatment requirement under section 212 of the Criminal Justice Act 2003 may be a proper alternative to a short or moderate custodial sentence.

Where the offender suffers from a medical condition that is susceptible to treatment but does not warrant detention under a hospital order, a community order with a mental health treatment requirement under section 207 of the Criminal Justice Act 2003 may be a proper alternative to a short or moderate custodial sentence.

[7] The court should then consider further adjustment for any aggravating or mitigating factors. The following is a **non-exhaustive** list of additional factual elements providing the context of the offence and factors relating to the offender. Identify whether any combination of these, or other relevant factors, should result in an upward or downward adjustment from the sentence arrived at so far.

Factors increasing seriousness	**Factors reducing seriousness or reflecting personal mitigation**
Statutory aggravating factors: Previous convictions, having regard to a) the **nature** of the offence to which the conviction relates and its **relevance** to the current offence; and b) the **time** that has elapsed since the conviction Offence committed whilst on bail Offence motivated by, or demonstrating hostility based on any of the following characteristics or presumed characteristics of the victim: religion, race, disability, sexual orientation or transgender identity *Other aggravating factors:* Stealing goods to order Steps taken to prevent the victim reporting or obtaining assistance and/or from assisting or supporting the prosecution Offender motivated by intention to cause harm or out of revenge Offence committed over sustained period of time Attempts to conceal/dispose of evidence Failure to comply with current court orders Offence committed on licence Offences taken into consideration Blame wrongly placed on others Established evidence of community/wider impact (for issues other than prevalence) Prevalence — see below	No previous convictions **or** no relevant/recent convictions Remorse, particularly where evidenced by voluntary reparation to the victim Good character and/or exemplary conduct Serious medical condition requiring urgent, intensive or long-term treatment Age and/or lack of maturity where it affects the responsibility of the offender Mental disorder or learning disability Sole or primary carer for dependent relatives Determination and/or demonstration of steps having been taken to address addiction or offending behaviour Inappropriate degree of trust or responsibility

Prevalence

There may be exceptional local circumstances that arise which may lead a court to decide that prevalence should influence sentencing levels. The pivotal issue in such cases will be the harm caused to the community.

It is essential that the court before taking account of prevalence:

- has supporting evidence from an external source, for example, Community Impact Statements, to justify claims that a particular crime is prevalent in their area, and is causing particular harm in that community, and
- is satisfied that there is a compelling need to treat the offence more seriously than elsewhere.

SG33-5 **STEP THREE Consider any factors which indicate a reduction, such as assistance to the prosecution** [8]

The court should take into account sections 73 and 74 of the Serious Organised Crime and Police Act 2005 (assistance by defendants: reduction or review of sentence) and any other rule of law by virtue of which an offender may receive a discounted sentence in consequence of assistance given (or offered) to the prosecutor or investigator.

SG33-6 **STEP FOUR Reduction for guilty pleas**

The court should take account of any potential reduction for a guilty plea in accordance with section 144 of the Criminal Justice Act 2003 and the *Guilty Plea* guideline [see **SG4-1**].

SG33-7 **STEP FIVE Totality principle**

If sentencing an offender for more than one offence, or where the offender is already serving a sentence, consider whether the total sentence is just and proportionate to the overall offending behaviour in accordance with the *Offences Taken into Consideration* and *Totality* guideline [see **SG3-1** and **SG3-7**].

SG33-8 **STEP SIX Confiscation, compensation and ancillary orders**

The court must proceed with a view to making a confiscation order if it is asked to do so by the prosecutor or if the court believes it is appropriate for it to do so.

Where the offence has resulted in loss or damage the court must consider whether to make a compensation order.

If the court makes both a confiscation order and an order for compensation and the court believes the offender will not have sufficient means to satisfy both orders in full, the court must direct that the compensation be paid out of sums recovered under the confiscation order (section 13 of the Proceeds of Crime Act 2002).

The court may also consider whether to make ancillary orders. These may include a deprivation order, or a restitution order.

SG33-9 **STEP SEVEN Reasons**

Section 174 of the Criminal Justice Act 2003 imposes a duty to give reasons for, and explain the effect of, the sentence.

SG33-10 **STEP EIGHT Consideration for time spent on bail**

The court must consider whether to give credit for time spent on bail in accordance with section 240A of the Criminal Justice Act 2003.

SG33-11 THEFT FROM A SHOP OR STALL [9]

Theft Act 1968 (section 1)

Triable either way

Maximum: 7 years' custody

(except for an offence of low-value shoplifting which is treated as a summary only offence in accordance with section 22A of the Magistrates' Courts Act 1980 where the maximum is 6 months' custody).

Offence range: Discharge–3 years' custody

SG33-12 **STEP ONE Determining the offence category** [10]

The court should determine the offence category with reference **only** to the factors identified in the following tables. In order to determine the category the court should assess **culpability and harm.**

The level of culpability is determined by weighing up all the factors of the case to determine the offender's role and the extent to which the offending was **planned** and the **sophistication** with which it was carried out.

[10]

CULPABILITY demonstrated by one or more of the following:
A — High culpability
A leading role where offending is part of a group activity Involvement of others through coercion, intimidation or exploitation Sophisticated nature of offence/significant planning Significant use or threat of force Offender subject to a banning order from the relevant store Child accompanying offender is actively used to **facilitate** the offence (not merely present when offence is committed)
B — Medium culpability
A significant role where offending is part of a group activity Some degree of planning involved Limited use or threat of force All other cases where characteristics for categories A or C are not present
C — Lesser culpability
Performed limited function under direction Involved through coercion, intimidation or exploitation Little or no planning Mental disorder/learning disability where linked to commission of the offence

Where there are characteristics present which fall under different levels of culpability, the court should balance these characteristics to reach a fair assessment of the offender's culpability.

[11] **HARM**

Harm is assessed by reference to the **financial loss** that results from the theft **and any significant additional harm** suffered by the victim—examples of significant additional harm may include **but are not limited to:**

Emotional distress Damage to property Effect on business A greater impact on the victim due to the size or type of their business A particularly vulnerable victim

Intended loss should be used where actual loss has been prevented.

Category 1	High value goods stolen (above £1,000) **or** Medium value with significant additional harm to the victim
Category 2	Medium value goods stolen (£200 to £1,000) **and** no significant additional harm **or** Low value with significant additional harm to the victim
Category 3	Low value goods stolen (up to £200) **and** Little or no significant additional harm to the victim

SG33-13 **STEP TWO Starting point and category range** [12]

Having determined the category at step one, the court should use the starting point to reach a sentence within the appropriate category range in the table below.

The starting point applies to all offenders irrespective of plea or previous convictions.

	Culpability		
Harm	**A**	**B**	**C**
Category 1 Where the value greatly exceeds £1,000 it may be appropriate to move outside the identified range. Adjustment should be made for any significant additional harm where high value goods are stolen.	**Starting point** 26 weeks' custody	**Starting point** Medium level community order	**Starting point** Band C fine
	Category range 12 weeks' — 3 years' custody	**Category range** Low level community order — 26 weeks' custody	**Category range** Band B fine — Low level community order
Category 2	**Starting point** 12 weeks' custody	**Starting point** Low level community order	**Starting point** Band B fine
	Category range High level community order — 26 weeks' custody	**Category range** Band C fine — Medium level community order	**Category range** Band A fine — Band C fine
Category 3	**Starting point** High level community order	**Starting point** Band C fine	**Starting point** Band A fine
	Category range Low level community order — 12 weeks' custody	**Category range** Band B fine — Low level community order	**Category range** Discharge — Band B fine

Consecutive sentences for multiple offences may be appropriate—please refer to the *Offences Taken Into Consideration* and *Totality* guideline [see **SG3-1** and **SG3-7**].

Previous diversionary work with an offender does not preclude the court from considering this type of sentencing option again if appropriate.

Where the offender is dependent on or has a propensity to misuse drugs or alcohol and there is sufficient prospect of success, a community order with a drug rehabilitation requirement under section 209, or an alcohol treatment requirement under section 212 of the Criminal Justice Act 2003 may be a proper alternative to a short or moderate custodial sentence.

Where the offender suffers from a medical condition that is susceptible to treatment but does not warrant detention under a hospital order, a community order with a mental health treatment requirement under section 207 of the Criminal Justice Act 2003 may be a proper alternative to a short or moderate custodial sentence.

The court should then consider further adjustment for any aggravating or mitigating factors. The following is a **non-exhaustive** list of additional factual elements providing the context of the offence and factors relating to the offender. Identify whether any combination of these, or other relevant factors, should result in an upward or downward adjustment from the sentence arrived at so far. [13]

[13]

Factors increasing seriousness	Factors reducing seriousness or reflecting personal mitigation
Statutory aggravating factors: Previous convictions, having regard to a) the **nature** of the offence to which the conviction relates and its **relevance** to the current offence; and b) the time that has elapsed since the conviction Relevant recent convictions **may** justify an upward adjustment, including outside the category range. In cases involving significant persistent offending, the community and custodial thresholds may be crossed even though the offence otherwise warrants a lesser sentence. Any custodial sentence must be kept to the necessary minimum Offence committed whilst on bail Offence motivated by, or demonstrating hostility based on any of the following characteristics or presumed characteristics of the victim: religion, race, disability, sexual orientation or transgender identity *Other aggravating factors:* Stealing goods to order Steps taken to prevent the victim reporting or obtaining assistance and/or from assisting or supporting the prosecution Attempts to conceal/dispose of evidence Offender motivated by intention to cause harm or out of revenge Failure to comply with current court orders Offence committed on licence Offences taken into consideration Established evidence of community/wider impact (for issues other than prevalence) Prevalence — see below	No previous convictions or no relevant/recent convictions Remorse, particularly where evidenced by voluntary reparation to the victim Good character and/or exemplary conduct Serious medical condition requiring urgent, intensive or long-term treatment Age and/or lack of maturity where it affects the responsibility of the offender Mental disorder or learning disability (where not linked to the commission of the offence) Sole or primary carer for dependent relatives Determination and/or demonstration of steps having been taken to address addiction or offending behaviour Offender experiencing **exceptional** financial hardship

Prevalence

There may be exceptional local circumstances that arise which may lead a court to decide that prevalence should influence sentencing levels. The pivotal issue in such cases will be the harm caused to the community. It is essential that the court before taking account of prevalence:

- has supporting evidence from an external source, for example, Community Impact Statements, to justify claims that a particular crime is prevalent in their area, and is causing particular harm in that community, and
- is satisfied that there is a compelling need to treat the offence more seriously than elsewhere.

[14] [Steps Three to Eight are identical to those applicable to General Theft: see **SG33-5**.] **SG33-14**

[15] HANDLING STOLEN GOODS **SG33-15**

Theft Act 1968 (section 22)

Triable either way

Maximum: 14 years' custody

Offence range: Discharge–8 years' custody

[16] **STEP ONE Determining the offence category** **SG33-16**

The court should determine the offence category with reference **only** to the factors identified in the following tables. In order to determine the category the court should assess **culpability** and **harm.**

The level of culpability is determined by weighing up all the factors of the case to determine the offender's role and the extent to which the offending was **planned** and the **sophistication** with which it was carried out.

CULPABILITY demonstrated by one or more of the following:
A — High culpability
A leading role where offending is part of a group activity Involvement of others through coercion, intimidation or exploitation Abuse of position of power or trust or responsibility Professional and sophisticated offence Advance knowledge of the primary offence Possession of very recently stolen goods from a domestic burglary or robbery
B — Medium culpability
A significant role where offending is part of a group activity Offender acquires goods for resale Other cases that fall between categories A or C because: – Factors are present in A and C which balance each other out **and/or** – The offender's culpability falls between the factors as described in A and C
C — Lesser culpability
Performed limited function under direction Involved through coercion, intimidation or exploitation Little or no planning Limited awareness or understanding of offence Goods acquired for offender's personal use

[16]

Where there are characteristics present which fall under different levels of culpability, the court should balance these characteristics to reach a fair assessment of the offender's culpability.

HARM [17]

Harm is assessed by reference to the **financial value** (to the loser) of the handled goods **and any significant additional harm** associated with the underlying offence on the victim or others — examples of additional harm may include **but are not limited to:**

Property stolen from a domestic burglary or a robbery (unless this has already been taken into account in assessing culpability)
Items stolen were of substantial value to the loser, regardless of monetary worth
Metal theft causing disruption to infrastructure
Damage to heritage assets

Category	
Category 1	Very high value goods stolen (above £100,000) **or** High value with significant additional harm to the victim or others
Category 2	High value goods stolen (£10,000 to £100,000) and no significant additional harm **or** Medium value with significant additional harm to the victim or others
Category 3	Medium value goods stolen (£1,000 to £10,000) and no significant additional harm **or** Low value with significant additional harm to the victim or others
Category 4	Low value goods stolen (up to £1,000) **and** Little or no significant additional harm to the victim or others

SG33-17 STEP TWO **Starting point and category range** [18]

Having determined the category at step one, the court should use the starting point to reach a sentence within the appropriate category range in the table below.

The starting point applies to all offenders irrespective of plea or previous convictions.

[18]

Harm	Culpability A	B	C
Category 1 Where the value greatly exceeds £100,000, it may be appropriate to move outside the identified range. Adjustment should be made for any significant additional harm where very high value stolen goods are handled	**Starting point** 5 years' custody	**Starting point** 3 years' custody	**Starting point** 1 year's custody
	Category range 3 — 8 years' custody	**Category range** 1 year 6 months' — 4 years' custody	**Category range** 26 weeks' — 1 year 6 months' custody
Category 2	**Starting point** 3 years' custody	**Starting point** 1 year's custody	**Starting point** High level community order
	Category range 1 year 6 months' — 4 years' custody	**Category range** 26 weeks' — 1 year 6 months' custody	**Category range** Low level community order — 26 weeks' custody
Category 3	**Starting point** 1 year's custody	**Starting point** High level community order	**Starting point** Band C fine
	Category range 26 weeks' — 2 years' custody	**Category range** Low level community order — 26 weeks' custody	**Category range** Band B fine — Low level community order
Category 4	**Starting point** High level community order	**Starting point** Low level community order	**Starting point** Band B fine
	Category range Medium level community order — 26 weeks' custody	**Category range** Band C fine — High level community order	**Category range** Discharge — Band C fine

Consecutive sentences for multiple offences may be appropriate — please refer to the *Offences Taken Into Consideration* and *Totality* guideline [see **SG3-1** and **SG3-7**].

[19] The court should then consider further adjustment for any aggravating or mitigating factors. The following is a **non-exhaustive** list of additional factual elements providing the context of the offence and factors relating to the offender. Identify whether any combination of these, or other relevant factors, should result in an upward or downward adjustment from the starting point.

Factors increasing seriousness	Factors reducing seriousness or reflecting personal mitigation
Statutory aggravating factors: Previous convictions, having regard to a) the **nature** of the offence to which the conviction relates and its **relevance** to the current offence; and b) the **time** that has elapsed since the conviction Offence committed whilst on bail *Other aggravating factors:* Seriousness of the underlying offence, for example, armed robbery Deliberate destruction, disposal or defacing of stolen property Damage to a third party Failure to comply with current court orders Offence committed on licence Offences taken into consideration Established evidence of community/wider impact	No previous convictions **or** no relevant/recent convictions Good character and/or exemplary conduct Serious medical condition requiring urgent, intensive or long-term treatment Age and/or lack of maturity where it affects the responsibility of the offender Mental disorder or learning disability Sole or primary carer for dependent relatives Determination and/or demonstration of steps having been taken to address addiction or offending behaviour

SG33-18 [Steps Three to Eight are identical to those applicable to General Theft: see SG33-5.] [20]

SG33-19 Going Equipped for Theft or Burglary [21]

Theft Act 1968 (section 25)

Triable either way
Maximum: 3 years' custody
Offence range: Discharge–18 months' custody

SG33-20 STEP ONE Determining the offence category [22]

The court should determine the offence category with reference **only** to the factors identified in the following tables. In order to determine the category the court should assess **culpability** and **harm**.

The level of culpability is determined by weighing up all the factors of the case to determine the offender's role and the extent to which the offending was **planned** and the **sophistication** with which it was carried out.

CULPABILITY demonstrated by one or more of the following
A — High culpability
A leading role where offending is part of a group activity Involvement of others through coercion, intimidation or exploitation Significant steps taken to conceal identity and/or avoid detection Sophisticated nature of offence/significant planning Offender equipped for robbery or domestic burglary
B — Medium culpability
A significant role where offending is part of a group activity Other cases that fall between categories A or C because: – Factors are present in A and C which balance each other out **and/or** – The offender's culpability falls between the factors as described in A and C
C — Lesser culpability
Involved through coercion, intimidation or exploitation Limited awareness or understanding of offence Little or no planning

Where there are characteristics present which fall under different levels of culpability, the court should balance these characteristics to reach a fair assessment of the offender's culpability.

Harm

This guideline refers to preparatory offences where no theft has been committed. The level of harm is determined by weighing up all the factors of the case to determine the harm that would be caused if the item(s) were used to commit a substantive offence.

Greater harm

Greater harm
Possession of item(s) which have the potential to facilitate an offence affecting a large number of victims
Possession of item(s) which have the potential to facilitate an offence involving high value items

Lesser harm

Lesser harm
All other cases

SG33-21 STEP TWO Starting point and category range [23]

Having determined the category at step one, the court should use the starting point to reach a sentence within the appropriate category range in the table below.

[23] The starting point applies to all offenders irrespective of plea or previous convictions.

Harm	Culpability		
	A	B	C
Greater	**Starting point** 1 year's custody	**Starting point** 18 weeks' custody	**Starting point** Medium level community order
	Category range 26 weeks' — 1 year 6 months' custody	**Category range** High level community order — 36 weeks' custody	**Category range** Low level community order — High level community order
Lesser	**Starting point** 26 weeks' custody	**Starting point** High level community order	**Starting point** Band C fine
	Category range 12 weeks' — 36 weeks' custody	**Category range** Medium level community order — 12 weeks' custody	**Category range** Discharge — Medium level community order

Consecutive sentences for multiple offences may be appropriate — please refer to the *Offences Taken Into Consideration* and *Totality* guideline [see **SG3-1** and **SG3-7**].

The court should then consider further adjustment for any aggravating or mitigating factors. The following is a **non-exhaustive** list of additional factual elements providing the context of the offence and factors relating to the offender. Identify whether any combination of these, or other relevant factors, should result in an upward or downward adjustment from the starting point.

Factors increasing seriousness	**Factors reducing seriousness or reflecting personal mitigation**
Statutory aggravating factors: Previous convictions, having regard to a) the **nature** of the offence to which the conviction relates and its **relevance** to the current offence; and b) the **time** that has elapsed since the conviction Offence committed whilst on bail *Other aggravating factors:* Attempts to conceal/dispose of evidence Established evidence of community/wider impact Failure to comply with current court orders Offence committed on licence Offences taken into consideration	No previous convictions **or** no relevant/recent convictions Good character and/or exemplary conduct Serious medical condition requiring urgent, intensive or long-term treatment Age and/or lack of maturity where it affects the responsibility of the offender Mental disorder or learning disability Sole or primary carer for dependent relatives Determination and/or demonstration of steps having been taken to address addiction or offending behaviour

[24] [Steps Three to Eight are identical to those applicable to General Theft: see SG33-5.] **SG33-22**

[25] ABSTRACTING ELECTRICITY **SG33-23**

Theft Act 1968 (section 13)

Triable either way
Maximum: 5 years' custody
Offence range: Discharge–1 year's custody

[26] STEP ONE **Determining the offence category** **SG33-24**

The court should determine the offence category with reference **only** to the factors identified in the following tables. In order to determine the category the court should assess **culpability** and **harm**.

The level of culpability is determined by weighing up all the factors of the case to determine the offender's role and the extent to which the offending was **planned** and the **sophistication** with which it was carried out.

CULPABILITY demonstrated by one or more of the following:	[26]

CULPABILITY demonstrated by one or more of the following:
A — High culpability
A leading role where offending is part of a group activity Involvement of others through coercion, intimidation or exploitation Sophisticated nature of offence/significant planning Abuse of position of power or trust or responsibility Commission of offence in association with or to further other criminal activity
B — Medium culpability
A significant role where offending is part of a group activity Other cases that fall between categories A or C because: – Factors are present in A and C which balance each other out **and/or** – The offender's culpability falls between the factors as described in A and C
C — Lesser culpability
Performed limited function under direction Involved through coercion, intimidation or exploitation Limited awareness or understanding of offence

Where there are characteristics present which fall under different levels of culpability, the court should balance these characteristics to reach a fair assessment of the offender's culpability.

HARM

The level of harm is assessed by weighing up all the factors of the case to determine the level of harm caused.

Greater harm

A significant risk of, or actual injury to persons or damage to property Significant volume of electricity extracted as evidenced by length of time of offending and/or advanced type of illegal process used

Lesser harm

All other cases

SG33-25 **STEP TWO Starting point and category range** [27]

Having determined the category at step one, the court should use the starting point to reach a sentence within the appropriate category range in the table below.

The starting point applies to all offenders irrespective of plea or previous convictions.

	Culpability		
Harm	A	B	C
Greater	**Starting point** 12 weeks' custody	**Starting point** Medium level community order	**Starting point** Band C fine
	Category range High level community order — 1 year's custody	**Category range** Low level community order — 12 weeks' custody	**Category range** Band B fine — Low level community order
Lesser	**Starting point** High level community order	**Starting point** Low level community order	**Starting point** Band A fine
	Category range Medium level community order — 12 weeks' custody	**Category range** Band C fine — Medium level community order	**Category range** Discharge — Band C fine

[27] The court should then consider further adjustment for any aggravating or mitigating factors. The table below contains a **non-exhaustive** list of additional factual elements providing the context of the offence and factors relating to the offender.

Identify whether any combination of these, or other relevant factors, should result in an upward or downward adjustment from the starting point.

Factors increasing seriousness	**Factors reducing seriousness or reflecting personal mitigation**
Statutory aggravating factors: Previous convictions, having regard to a) the **nature** of the offence to which the conviction relates and its **relevance** to the current offence; and b) the **time** that has elapsed since the conviction Offence committed whilst on bail *Other aggravating factors:* Electricity abstracted from another person's property Attempts to conceal/dispose of evidence Failure to comply with current court orders Offence committed on licence Offences taken into consideration Blame wrongly placed on others Established evidence of community/wider impact	No previous convictions **or** no relevant/recent convictions Good character and/or exemplary conduct Serious medical condition requiring urgent, intensive or long-term treatment Age and/or lack of maturity where it affects the responsibility of the offender Mental disorder or learning disability Sole or primary carer for dependent relatives Determination and/or demonstration of steps having been taken to address addiction or offending behaviour

[28] [Steps Three to Eight are identical to those applicable to General Theft: see SG33-5.] **SG33-26**

[29] **SG33-27**

Making Off without Payment

Theft Act 1978 (section 3)

Triable either way
Maximum: 2 years' custody
Offence range: Discharge–36 weeks' custody

[30] **STEP ONE Determining the offence category** **SG33-28**

The court should determine the offence category with reference **only** to the factors identified in the following tables. In order to determine the category the court should assess **culpability** and **harm.**

The level of culpability is determined by weighing up all the factors of the case to determine the offender's role and the extent to which the offending was **planned** and the **sophistication** with which it was carried out.

CULPABILITY demonstrated by one or more of the following
A — High culpability
A leading role where offending is part of a group activity
Involvement of others through coercion, intimidation or exploitation
Sophisticated nature of offence/significant planning
Offence involving intimidation or the use or threat of force
Deliberately targeting victim on basis of vulnerability
B — Medium culpability
A significant role where offending is part of a group activity
Some degree of planning involved
Other cases that fall between categories A or C because:
– Factors are present in A and C which balance each other out **and/or**
– The offender's culpability falls between the factors as described in A and C
C — Lesser culpability
Performed limited function under direction
Involved through coercion, intimidation or exploitation
Little or no planning
Limited awareness or understanding of offence

Where there are characteristics present which fall under different levels of culpability, the court should balance these characteristics to reach a fair assessment of the offender's culpability. [30]

HARM [31]

Harm is assessed by reference to the **actual loss** that results from the offence **and any significant additional harm** suffered by the victim — examples of additional harm may include **but are not limited to:**

A high level of inconvenience caused to the victim
Emotional distress
Fear/loss of confidence caused by the crime
A greater impact on the victim due to the size or type of their business

Category 1	Goods or services obtained above £200 or Goods/services up to £200 with significant additional harm to the victim
Category 2	Goods or services obtained up to £200 and Little or no significant additional harm to the victim

SG33-29 STEP TWO **Starting point and category range** [32]

Having determined the category at step one, the court should use the starting point to reach a sentence within the appropriate category range in the table below.

The starting point applies to all offenders irrespective of plea or previous convictions.

	Culpability		
Harm	**A**	**B**	**C**
Category 1 Where the value greatly exceeds £200, it may be appropriate to move outside the identified range. Adjustment should be made for any significant additional harm for offences above £200.	**Starting point** 12 weeks' custody	**Starting point** Low level community order	**Starting point** Band B fine
	Category range High level community order — 36 weeks' custody	**Category range** Band C fine — High level community order	**Category range** Band A fine — Low level community order
Category 2	**Starting point** Medium level community order	**Starting point** Band C fine	**Starting point** Band A fine
	Category range Low level community order — 12 weeks' custody	**Category range** Band B fine — Low level community order	**Category range** Discharge — Band B fine

Consecutive sentences for multiple offences may be appropriate — please refer to the *Offences Taken Into Consideration* and *Totality* guideline [see **SG3-1** and **SG3-7**].

The court should then consider further adjustment for any aggravating or mitigating factors. The following list is a **non-exhaustive** list of additional factual elements providing the context of the offence and factors relating to the offender. [33]

Identify whether any combination of these, or other relevant factors, should result in an upward or downward adjustment from the starting point.

[33]

Factors increasing seriousness	Factors reducing seriousness or reflecting personal mitigation
Statutory aggravating factors: Previous convictions, having regard to a) the **nature** of the offence to which the conviction relates and its **relevance** to the current offence; and b) the **time** that has elapsed since the conviction Offence committed whilst on bail Offence motivated by, or demonstrating hostility based on any of the following characteristics or presumed characteristics of the victim: religion, race, disability, sexual orientation or transgender identity *Other aggravating factors:* Steps taken to prevent the victim reporting or obtaining assistance and/or from assisting or supporting the prosecution Attempts to conceal/dispose of evidence Failure to comply with current court orders Offence committed on licence Offences taken into consideration Established evidence of community/wider impact	No previous convictions **or** no relevant/recent convictions Remorse, particularly where evidenced by voluntary reparation to the victim Good character and/or exemplary conduct Serious medical condition requiring urgent, intensive or long-term treatment Age and/or lack of maturity where it affects the responsibility of the offender Mental disorder or learning disability Sole or primary carer for dependent relatives Determination and/or demonstration of steps having been taken to address addiction or offending behaviour

[34] [Steps Three to Eight are identical to those applicable to General Theft: see SG33-5.] **SG33-30**

[35] ANNEX **SG33-31**

[The tables set out here are also set out in the Magistrates' Court Sentencing Guidelines, which include further guidance on fines and community orders: see **SG10-129** and **SG9-2**.]

Index

Abandonment of a child SG20-3–SG20-14
Absconding R-336, R-339
Absence, trials in PD-29, PD-32
Abstraction of electricity SG10-49, SG33-23–SG33-36
Abuse of position
  benefit fraud SG-473
  causing a child to watch a sexual act SG31-82–SG31-85
  causing or inciting a child to engage in sexual activity SG31-78–SG31-81
  fraud SG26-4, SG26-21
  online/remotely, offences committed SG31-79
  trust, position of SG31-78–SG31-85
Abuse of process, stay of proceedings for PD-5, R-26
Account monitoring orders (AMOs) R-526, R-526A, R-532, R-532A
Accounts R-378
Acquittals R-259, R-268–R-274, R-385
Actual bodily harm, assault occasioning SG10-22, SG12-19–SG12-21
  racial or religious aggravation SG12-19–SG12-21
Administering a substance with intent SG31-146–SG31-149
Admission, evidence by R-232, R-256
Adult relatives, sex with SG31-142–SG31-145
Advance information *see* Initial details of prosecution case (advance information)
Affray SG10-71
Aggravated vehicle taking SG10-102–SG10-103
Aggravating factors *see also* Racially or religiously aggravated offences
  burglary SG19-3
  children SG6-1
  criminal damage SG11-13, SG11-33, SG11-43
  disabilities, persons with SG10-177
  domestic abuse SG5-5
  first time offenders SG10-6
  harassment SG27-9–SG27-17
  protective orders, breach of SG18-5
  seriousness SG2-5, SG10-6–SG10-7
  sexual orientation SG10-7, SG10-177
  starting points and category range SG10-14
  transgender identity SG10-7, SG10-177–SG10-180
  vehicle taking SG10-102–SG10-103
Air weapons, carrying SG10-53
Alcohol offences *see also* Drink-driving offences
  drunk and disorderly in a public place SG10-48
  football ground, possession whilst entering or trying to enter SG10-54
  liquor licences, forfeiture or suspension of SG-158
  magistrates' courts SG10-17
  motoring offences SG10-111, SG10-112
  racial or religious aggravation SG11-13
  sale offences SG12-13
Allocation decisions R-75–R-90
  committal for sentence SG1-1
  guidelines SG10-2
  juveniles SG1-1, SG8-5
  magistrates' courts PD-79–PD-80, R-84–R-90
  special measures directions PD-45
  venue for trial SG1-1
Ammunition SG10-53
Ancillary orders SG10-15, SG-151–SG-172, SG10-188, SG10-189
  animals
    deprivation of ownership SG-157
    destruction orders SG-158
    disqualification from ownership SG10-159, SG15-44–SG15-47
  anti-social behaviour orders (ASBOs) SG-152
  automatic orders on conviction SG31-156
  availability SG10-189
  binding over orders SG-153
  children, protection of SG31-156
  corporate manslaughter SG28-10
  criminal behaviour orders (CBOs) SG-152, SG-155
  deprivation orders SG-156, SG-157
  destruction orders
    dogs, contingent destruction orders for SG-158
    trade marks, unauthorised SG-166
    weapons orders, destruction of SG-165
  directors, disqualification of SG10-161, SG24-6
  disqualification
    animals, ownership of SG10-159
    children, working with SG31-156
    directors SG10-161, SG24-6
    driving, from SG10-160
  drinking banning orders SG10-162
  driving, disqualification from SG10-160
  drugs, forfeiture and destruction of SG10-164
  environmental crimes SG24-12, SG24-28
  exclusion orders SG10-163
  football banning orders SG10-164
  forfeiture SG10-164–SG10-166
  fraud SG26-10
  guilty pleas SG10-10
  liquor licences, forfeiture or suspension of SG10-167
  magistrates' courts SG10-151–SG10-172, SG10-189
  notification requirements SG31-156
  parenting orders SG10-168
  reasons SG10-10–SG10-11
  restitution orders SG10-169
  restraining orders SG31-156
  restraint orders R-365–R-371
  robbery SG30-10
  serious crime prevention orders (SCPOs) SG31-156
  sexual harm prevention orders (SOPOs) SG10-171
  sexual offences prevention orders (SOPOs) SG10-122, SG10-172
  slavery and trafficking prevention orders (STPOs) SG31-156

Ancillary orders (*cont.*)
table SG31-156
theft SG33-5
trade marks, forfeiture and destruction of goods bearing unauthorised SG10-166
vulnerable persons, protection of SG31-156
Animals *see also* Dangerous dog offences
cruelty SG10-19
deprivation of ownership SG10-157
disqualification from ownership SG10-159, SG15-44–SG15-47
magistrates' courts SG10-19
Anonymity R-466, R-559, R-559A *see also* Investigation anonymity orders; Witness anonymity orders
Anti-social behaviour orders (ASBOs) R-304, SG10-20
adult offenders SG17-5
another criminal offence, breach that may constitute SG17-4
breach SG15-28–SG15-31, SG17-1–SG17-7
decision-making process SG17-5
interim orders SG17-4
juveniles SG17-7
magistrates' courts SG10-20
originating conduct, relevance of SG17-4
Appeals PD-90–PD-98 *see also* Confiscation and related proceedings, appeals in; Court of Appeal; Crown Court, appeals to; High Court, appeals to
bail PD-35, R-128–R-129, R-490, R-633–R-637
case management R-16–R-17
certification of fitness to appeal PD-35
conviction, against PD-90–PD-98, R-437–R-450
costs R-499, R-504
custody time limits R-140
extradition PD-103–PD-104, R-626–R-636
fines R-295
fingerprints etc., retention of R-555, R-555A
fitness to appeal, certification of PD-35
foreign driving disqualification, appeals against recognition of R-291
investigation anonymity orders R-559, R-559A
jury service R-263–R-267
lenient sentences R-460–R-465
Proceeds of Crime Act 2002 R-467–R-486
reporting restrictions R-451–R-459
road traffic penalties R-291
sentences, appeals against R-437–R-449
special measures directions PD-9
Supreme Court R-487–R-490
Arranging or facilitating sexual exploitation of a child SG31-98–SG31-101
Arranging or facilitating the commission of a child sex offence SG31-51, SG31-73
Arrest
assault with intent to resist arrest SG10-23, SG12-22–SG12-24
extradition R-614, R-616–R-617, R-619–R-621
magistrates' courts SG10-23
provisional arrest R-619–R-621
warrants R-114–R-120, R-613–R-616
closed, warrants issued when court office is R-120
execution R-118
extradition R-613–R-617, R-619
information to be included R-117
payment, warrants that cease to have effect on R-119
terms R-115
Arson SG10-21, SG11-1–SG11-10
life or reckless as to whether life endangered, intent to endanger SG11-31–SG11-40
Assault SG12-1–SG12-30 *see also* Assaults on children/cruelty to a child; Sexual assault
actual bodily harm, occasioning SG10-22, SG12-19
arrest, assault with intent to resist or prevent SG10-23, SG12-22–SG12-24
common assault SG10-133, SG12-28–SG12-31
grievous bodily harm SG10-157, SG10-63, SG12-3–SG12-13
police constable in the execution of his duty, on a SG12-25–SG12-27
racially/religiously aggravated assault SG10-33, SG10-37, SG10-57, SG10-63, SG12-13–SG12-19, SG12-28
wounding SG10-57, SG10-63, SG12-13
Assaults on children/cruelty to a child SG6-1, SG10-38, SG20-1–SG20-27
abandonment SG20-3–SG-20-14
die, causing or allowing a child to SG20-16–SG20-26
failure to protect SG20-3–SG20-14
female genital mutilation (FGM), failure to protect a girl from SG20-27–SG20-36
forms of cruelty SG12-19
ill-treatment SG20-3–SG20-14
nature of activities SG10-47
overarching principles SG6-1
parental responsibilities of sole or primary carers SG20-9, SG20-21, SG20-32
primary care responsibilities, offenders with SG6–1
psychological harm SG6-1
serious physical harm, causing or allowing a child to suffer SG20-15
victims, adverse effects of sentence on SG6–1
Assistance, giving or withholding R-285
Attachment of earnings orders SG10-140
Attempts
explosives SG31-15–SG31-26
murder SG13-1–SG13-8
Attendance at court R-238, R-425, R-436, R-447, R-458, R-465
Audio recording of interviews PD-39

Bad character evidence PD-50, R-205–R-210
applications R-206–R-207
content of applications or notices R-206
defendants R-208
expert evidence PD-47
non-defendants R-207
notice R-208
spent convictions PD-50
variation of requirements R-210
Bail PD-28–PD-35, R-121–R-137
absence, trials in PD-29, PD-32
accommodation or support requirements R-133
appeals PD-35, R-128–R-129, R-131–R-132, R-490, R-632–R-637

case management PD-3
charge, extension before R-140–R-142
conditions R-136
conduct of proceedings PD-30
Court of Appeal R-444–R-446
court officers, duties of R-124
Crown Court PD-35, R-128
custody time limits R-122
electronic monitoring R-132
estreatment of recognisances PD-33
EU member states
conditions to be enforced in another R-136
enforcement of measures imposed in another member state R-137
exercise of court's powers R-122, R-140
extension of period R-141
failure to answer/surrender PD-29–PD-30, SG10-25, SG15-16–SG15-23, SG16-1–SG16-7
absence of defendant, conducting trials in SG16-4
consecutive and concurrent custodial sentences SG16-4
decision-making process SG16-6
factors taken into consideration SG16-6
magistrates' courts SG10-25
procedural issues SG16-4
seriousness SG16-3
fitness to appeal, certification of PD-35
forfeiture of sureties PD-33, R-135, R-446
information from defendant, application to withhold R-142
initiating proceedings PD-30
justices' legal adviser, duties of R-123
magistrates' courts PD-32, R-123, R-126, R-128
Crown Court, appeals to R-128
justices' legal adviser, duties of R-123
reconsideration of bail R-126
trials PD-32
murder cases R-130
not guilty pleas PD-3
notice of applications R-127
penalties for failure to surrender PD-30
police bail
initiation of proceedings PD-30
reconsideration by magistrates of R-126
pre-charge bail, extension of R-141–R-142
prosecutors
appeals R-129
representations R-125
reconsideration by magistrates' courts R-126
remands in bail or in custody, relationship between Bail Act offences and further PD-31
residence, condition of R-131
robbery SG30-12
sending for trial, before PD-28
sentencing for Bail Act offences PD-30
support requirements R-133
Supreme Court R-485
sureties/recognizances PD-33, R-134–R-135, R-446
timing of disposal PD-30
trial, bail during PD-34
trials on indictment PD-32
Behaviour orders *see* Criminal behaviour orders (CBOs)
Benefit fraud SG10-26, SG26-21–SG26-23
conspiracy to defraud SG26-21–SG26-23
dishonest representations SG26-21
false accounting SG26-21
false representations SG26-21, SG26-23
personal mitigation SG26-23
tax credits SG26-21, SG26-23
Binding over orders PD-82, SG10-153
Bladed articles and offensive weapons SG10-27–SG10-29, SG14-1–SG14-30
custodial sentences SG14-29
fine bands SG14-30
forfeiture and destruction of weapons orders SG10-165
juveniles SG10-29, SG14-22–SG14-29
custodial sentences SG14-29
referral orders SG14-29
welfare of offenders SG14-28
youth rehabilitation orders (YROs) SG14-29
minimum terms SG14-6, SG14-16, SG14-28
possession SG10-27–SG10-29, SG14-3, SG14-22–SG14-29
public place, threatening with an offensive weapon in a SG14-13
referral orders SG14-29
second or further offences SG14-6
threats SG10-28, SG10-29, SG14-13–SG14-29
youth rehabilitation orders (YROs) SG14-29
Brakes SG10-122, SG10-125
Breach
anti-social behaviour orders (ASBOs) SG17-1–SG17-7
community orders R-313–R-316, SG10-38
deferred prosecution agreements R-104
juveniles SG8-9, SG8-10
list of offences SG15-48
non-molestation orders SG18-2
protective orders SG10-69, SG18-2–SG18-6
restraining order SG18-2
Breath tests, failure to cooperate with preliminary SG10-121
Bribery SG10-30, SG26-1–SG26-3, SG26-29–SG26-43
another person, bribing a SG26-29, SG26-31
being bribed SG26-29, SG26-31
corporate crime SG10-36, SG26-33–SG26-43
foreign public officials SG26-29, SG26-31
Brothel used for prostitution, keeping a SG10-64, SG31-94–SG31-97
Bundles PD-18, PD-108
Burglary SG19-1–SG19-22
aggravated burglary SG19-3
buildings other than dwellings SG10-32, SG19-18
community orders SG19-22
domestic burglary SG10-31, SG19-13–SG19-17, SG19-13
dwellings SG10-31, SG19-13
fine bands SG19-22
going equipped SG10-56, SG33-19–SG33-22
non-domestic burglary SG10-32, SG19-18–SG19-21
Buses, motoring offences by SG10-125

Cannabis and cannabis resin
cultivation of plants SG10-45, SG23-18–SG23-22
out of court disposals SG10-183
warnings SG10-183
Care workers
causing a person with a mental disorder to watch a sexual act SG31-130–SG31-133
causing or inciting sexual activity SG31-126–SG31-130
sexual activity in the presence of a person with a mental disorder SG31-130–SG31-133
sexual activity with a person with a mental disorder SG31-126–SG31-130
Careless driving (driving without due care and attention) SG10-106–SG10-107, SG22-8–SG22-10
Careless or inconsiderate driving SG10-107, SG22-10
Careless or inconsiderate driving, causing death by SG10-107
Carriageways, driving off SG10-124
Case management R-7–R-33 *see also* Directions
abuse of process PD-5
appeals PD-90, R-16–R-17
bail PD-3
case progression and trial progression PD-3, R-15
case progression officers and their duties R-10
compliance hearings PD-3
conduct of trials or appeals R-17
Court of Appeal R-404
court officers, duty of R-18
Crown Court
appeals PD-90
preparation for trial in PD-3, PD-5, R-19–R-32
custody, defendants in PD-3
devolution issues PD-10
duty of the court R-8
Effective Trial Monitoring form, completion of PD-3
evidence, pagination and indexing of served PD-4
extradition R-627
further case management hearings PD-3
general matters PD-3–PD-15
guilty pleas in Crown Court PD-3
indexing of served evidence PD-4
live links PD-15, R-8
magistrates' courts PD-3, R-33
organised crime cases PD-127
pagination and indexing of served evidence PD-4
parties, duty of R-9
Plea and Trial Preparation Hearing (PTPH) PD-3
preparation and progression of cases R-15, R-19–R-33
readiness for trial or appeal R-16
security of prisoners at court PD-13–PD-14
special measures for vulnerable witnesses PD-6–PD-9, PD-15
telephone facilities PR-15, R-8
terrorism cases PD-126
time limits, variation of R-13
vary requirements, court's power to R-14
vulnerable people in the courts PD-6–PD-9
Wales and Welsh language PD-10–PD-12
witness anonymity orders PD-44
Case progression in magistrates' court PD-3
Case stated R-398–R-402
justices' legal advisers, duty of R-401
preparation R-400
variation of court's powers R-402
Causing a child to watch a sexual act SG31-69–SG31-72, SG31-82–SG31-85
Causing a person to engage in sexual activity without consent SG31-24–SG31-27
Causing a person with a mental disorder impeding choice to watch a sexual act SG31-114–SG31-117
Causing a person with a mental disorder to engage in or agree to engage in sexual activity by inducement, threat or deception SG31-118–SG31-121
Causing a person with a mental disorder to watch a sexual act by inducement, threat or deception SG31-122–SG31-125
Causing death by careless driving under the influence of drink or drugs SG22-8
Causing death by careless or inconsiderate driving SG10-107, SG22-10
Causing death by dangerous driving SG22-6
Causing death by driving SG22-1–SG22-12
Causing grievous bodily harm with intent to do GBH/wounding with intent to do GBH SG12-3–SG12-12
Causing or inciting a child to engage in sexual activity SG31-51–SG31-64, SG31-78–SG31-81
abuse of a position of trust SG31-78–SG31-81
remotely/online, offences committed SG31-51, SG31-79
Causing or inciting a person with a mental disorder impeding choice to engage in sexual activity SG31-110–SG31-113
Causing or inciting prostitution for gain SG31-90–SG31-93
Causing or inciting sexual exploitation of a child SG31-98–SG31-101
Cautions
conditional SG10-184
failure to comply SG10-184
CBOs *see* Criminal behaviour orders (CBOs)
Central funds, costs out of R-497
Chambers, business in R-351
Character evidence PD-50, R-205–R-210 *see also* Bad character evidence
Charities
corporate crime SG28-4
financial information, obtaining SG24-6, SG26-37, SG28-4
Cheating the public revenue SG26-17–SG26-20
Child sex offences *see also* Familial sex offences
13, children under
assault SG10-81, SG31-39–SG31-56
causing or inciting a child to engage in sexual activity SG31-57–SG31-59
penetration, assault by SG31-39–SG31-50
rape of a child under 13 SG31-28–SG31-31
abuse of a position of trust SG31-78–SG31-85
adult relatives, sex with SG31-142–SG31-145
arranging or facilitating sexual exploitation of a child SG31-98–SG31-101
arranging or facilitating the commission of a child sex offence SG31-51, SG31-69, SG31-73

assault of a child under 13 SG10-81, SG31-39–SG31-50
causing a child to watch a sexual act SG31-69–SG31-72, SG31-82–SG31-85
causing or inciting a child to engage in sexual activity SG31-57–SG31-64
13 years, child under SG31-57–SG31-60
abuse of a position of trust SG31-78–SG31-81
causing or inciting a child under 13 to engage in sexual activity SG31-57–SG31-60
causing or inciting sexual exploitation of a child SG31-98–SG31-101
children or young persons, committed by SG31-155
consent to penetration SG31-142–SG31-145
controlling a child in relation to sexual exploitation SG31-98–SG31-101
engaging in sexual activity in presence of a child SG31-69–SG31-72
grooming, meeting a child following sexual SG31-74–SG31-77
inciting a child family member to engage in sexual activity SG31-65–SG31-68
inciting a child family member to engage in sexual activity (offender under 18) SG31-155
indecent photographs of children SG10-62, SG31-86–SG31-89
Internet SG31-51, SG31-63, SG31-79
juveniles SG30-155
online/remotely, offences committed SG31-53, SG31-79
paying for the sexual services of a child SG31-102–SG31-105
penetration SG31-142–SG31-145
photographs, indecent SG10-62, SG31-86–SG31-89
prostitution or pornography SG10-62, SG31-86–SG31-89, SG31-98–SG31-101
arranging or facilitating sexual exploitation of a child SG31-98–SG31-101
controlling a child in relation to sexual exploitation SG31-98–SG31-101
indecent photographs of children SG10-62, SG31-86–SG31-89
paying for the sexual services of a child SG31-102–SG31-105
rape of a child under 13 SG31-28–SG31-31
remotely/online, offences committed SG31-51, SG31-79
sexual activity in the presence of a child SG31-82–SG31-85
sexual activity with a child
causing or inciting a child to engage in sexual activity SG31-71–SG31-73
family members, inciting child SG31-65–SG31-68
watch a sexual act, causing a child to SG31-69–SG31-72
Children and young persons *see also* Child sex offences; Juveniles
13, assault of a child under SG10-81, SG31-39–SG31-50
abandonment SG20-3–SG20-14
assault SG20-3–SG20-14
car seats, failure to use child SG10-123
cruelty SG6-1, SG10-38, SG20-1–SG20-37
die, causing or allowing a child to SG20-16–SG20-26
disqualification from working with children SG31-156
failure to protect SG20-3–SG20-14
female genital mutilation (FGM), failure to protect a girl from SG20-27–SG20-36
ill-treatment SG20-3–SG20-14
intermediaries PD-8
parental responsibilities of sole or primary carers SG20-9, SG20-21, SG20-32
serious physical harm, causing or allowing a child to suffer SG20-15
special measures directions R-173
witnesses PD-8, PD-40, PD-45, PD-46, R-173
Citation of authorities PD-113–PD-115
Hansard PD-115
neutral citation PD-114
Committal for sentence PD-83, R-284, SG2-1, SG9-7, SG10-154, SG21-25
Committing an offence with intent to commit a sexual offence SG31-150
Common assault SG10-33, SG12-28
Communication network offences SG10-34
Community and other orders R-313–R-316, SG3-16, SG9-1–SG9-3, SG12-301
amendment R-313–R-316
applicability of SGs SG9-1
breach R-314–R-316, SG10-35
burglary SG19-22
communication network offences SG10-34
compatibility of requirements SG9-5
dangerous dogs SG21-28
defendants or affected persons, applications by R-315
electronic monitoring R-132, SG9-8
environmental crimes SG24-22, SG24-33
fines as an alternative SG9-3
general principles SG9-3
illustrations SG15-50
imposition of orders SG9-3–SG9-8
levels SG9-4
high SG9-4
low SG9-4
medium SG9-4
list of requirements SG9-6
magistrates' court SG10-149
notice R-277
orders, conflict with other SG9-5
pre-sentence reports SG9-7
ranges SG10-149
requirements, onerousness of SG10-5
religious beliefs, conflict with SG9-5
responsible officers or supervisors, applications by R-314, R-316
revocation R-313–R-316
seriousness of offences SG9-3–SG9-4
threshold SG2-6, SG9-3–SG9-4
totality principle SG3-10, SG3-16
Community impact statements PD-80, SG10-188
Community orders *see* Community and other orders
Community resolution SG10-186

Companies *see* Corporate crime
Compensation orders **SG10-9, SG10-15, SG10-145, SG13-4**
combined orders **SG24-9, SG24-44**
companies **SG26-34**
confiscation orders **R-335, R-339–R-340**
Criminal Injuries Compensation Scheme **SG10-145–SG10-146**
custodial sentences are imposed, where **SG10-145**
environmental offences **SG24-3, SG24-9, SG24-19, SG24-24**
fines **SG10-145**
magistrates' courts **SG10-145–SG10-147**
mandatory, where orders are **SG10-145**
means of offenders **SG10-145**
personal injuries from road accidents **SG10-145**
robbery **SG30-10**
theft **SG33-5**
totality principle **SG3-18**
Victim Surcharge **SG15-10**
victims, view of **SG10-145**
Compliance hearings **PD-3**
Concealing/disguising/converting/transferring/removing property from England & Wales **SG26-25**
Concurrent and consecutive sentences **PD-77**
Conditional discharges **PD-82**
Confidentiality **PD-18, PD-44, R-161**
Confiscation and related proceedings **R-317–R-385**
see also Confiscation and related proceedings, appeals in
absconders **R-336, R-339**
acquittals in drug trafficking cases, compensation after **R-385**
available amount **R-332–R-333**
banks or building societies, payment of money in **R-340**
closed, where court office is **R-319**
combined orders **SG24-9, SG24-24**
committal for sentencing **SG10-154**
compensation **R-235, R-338–R-339, R-385**
compliance orders, applications for **R-330**
contempt proceedings **R-386**
corporate crime **SG26-35**
default, increase in term of imprisonment in cases of **R-337, R-384**
detention
appeals **R-347**
extend period, applications to **R-345–R-346**
vary or discharge orders for extended detention, applications to **R-346**
discharge **R-334, R-383**
drug trafficking **R-380–R-385**
environmental offences **SG24-2, SG24-4, SG24-9, SG24-20, SG24-24**
held or detained in satisfaction of confiscation orders, payment of money **R-340**
imprisonment, applications for increase in terms of **R-337, R-384**
inadequacy of available amount, variation due to **R-333**
international co-operation **R-613**
material available, applications to Crown Court to discharge or vary orders to make **R-383**
Northern Ireland orders, applications for registration of **R-320**
postponement **R-381, R-588**
receivership proceedings **R-348–R-366, R-372–R-379**
reconsideration, applications for **R-331**
register of orders **R-322**
registration, applications to vary or set aside **R-322**
restraint proceedings **R-348–R-371**
revised assessments **R-382**
Scottish orders, applications for registration of **R-320**
searches **R-344**
seized property **R-341–R-342, R-344**
service of documents **R-326–R-327**
certificates **R-327**
outside the jurisdiction **R-327**
statements in connection with proceedings **R-331, R-380**
statements of truth **R-323**
surplus proceeds, directions about **R-343**
theft **SG33-5**
time, calculation of **R-318**
variation **R-333, R-335, R-383**
witness statements for other purposes, use of **R-324**
Confiscation and related proceedings, appeals in **R-467–R-486**
abandonment of appeal **R-479, R-483**
amendment of appeal **R-479, R-483**
compliance, appeals about **R-480–R-486**
Court of Appeal **R-467–R-486**
examination of witnesses by court **R-469**
exhibits **R-470**
extension of time **R-467**
full court, determinations by **R-473**
information from court of trial, Registrar's power to require **R-471**
interest in property, appeals by persons with **R-477–R-479**
notice of appeal **R-477, R-481**
notice of determination **R-474**
permission to appeal **R-480, R-485**
conditions **R-485**
setting aside **R-485**
prosecutor, appeals by **R-477–R-479**
receivership orders **R-480–R-486**
record of proceedings **R-475**
respondent's notice **R-478, R-482**
restraint orders **R-480–R-486**
single judges, hearings by **R-472**
stay of proceedings **R-484**
striking out notices **R-485**
Supreme Court, appeals to **R-476**
transcripts **R-475**
witnesses **R-469**
Consent
adult relatives, sex with **SG31-142–SG31-145**
causing a person to engage in sexual activity without consent **SG31-24–SG31-27**
extradition proceedings, dealing with other offences in **R-641**
penetration, to **SG31-142–SG31-145**
receivership proceedings **R-358**
restraint proceedings **R-358**

Conspiracy to defraud SG26-4, SG26-6, SG26-19, SG26-21, SG26-23
Contempt of court R-582–R-598
access to documents R-568, R-568A
adjourn, magistrates' powers to R-597
assistance given or withheld, applications to review sentences due to R-285
confiscation proceedings R-386
credibility and consistency of makers of written statements/other hearsay R-596
cross-examination of makers of written statements or other hearsay R-595
discharge orders for imprisonment, applications to R-582
electronic data, orders for access to R-581
enquiries R-588–R-589
exercise of court's powers R-580
failure to comply with orders R-590–R-598
hearsay R-592, R-596
investigation orders R-519, R-519A, R-568, R-590
juries PD-69
magistrates' courts PD-103, R-598
obstruction and disruption R-586–R-589
postponement of enquiries R-588
procedure on hearings R-591
restraint orders R-386
retention or return of property R-552, R-552A
reviews after temporary detention R-587
sentences due to assistance given or withheld, applications to review R-285
suspension of imprisonment, notice of R-581
variation R-598
wasted costs R-502
witness statements R-592–R-593, R-595
Controlling a child in relation to sexual exploitation SG31-98–SG31-101
Controlling or coercive behaviour in an intimate or family relationship SG27-34–SG27-37
Controlling prostitution for gain SG31-90–SG31-93
Convictions
appeals PD-90–PD-98, R-437–R-451
costs R-498
jury, without a R-259
procedure R-260
setting aside R-244
spent convictions PD-50
Corporate crime *see also* Corporate manslaughter
annual accounts SG26-37
bribery SG10-36, SG26-33–SG26-43
compensation orders SG10-145, SG26-34
confiscation orders SG26-35
directors, disqualification of SG10-161, SG24-6
fines SG26-37–SG26-38
fraud SG10-36, SG26-33–SG26-43
magistrates' courts SG10-36
money laundering SG10-36, SG10-166, SG26-33–SG26-43
Victim Surcharge SG10-148
Corporate liability *see* Corporate crime; Corporate manslaughter
Corporate manslaughter SG28-1–SG28-12
confiscation orders SG26-36
financial information SG27-4, SG27-10
fine, level of SG28-4–SG28-12
adjustment SG28-7
financial information, obtaining SG26-37, SG28-4
general principles SG28-37
turnover SG28-6
remedial orders SG28-10
size and nature of organisation SG28-4
Costs PD-100, R-494–R-507
appeals R-499, R-506
assessments R-364, R-504–R-507
costs judges, appeal to R-505
re-assessment R-504
central funds R-497
conviction, on R-498
extension of time, applications for R-507
High Court judge, appeal to R-506
legal representatives, costs against a R-502
magistrates' courts R-244, SG10-147
one party to another, payment by R-498–R-502
orders R-363, R-495
prosecution costs, guidance on SG10-147
receivership orders R-363–R-366
restraint proceedings R-363–R-366
sentences R-498
third parties, against R-503
time for compliance R-365
unnecessary or improper acts, resulting from R-501
variation R-244, R-496
wasted costs R-502
Court of Appeal R-403–R-486
abandonment of appeals R-415–R-416, R-479, R-483
adverse to the prosecution, appeals against rulings which are R-426–R-436
amendment of appeals R-479, R-483
anonymity of defendants on references of point of law R-465
attend hearings, right to R-425, R-436, R-447, R-459, R-465
bail R-444–R-446
conditions R-445–R-446
recognizances, forfeiture of R-446
retrials R-445–R-446
case management R-404
conditions of leave R-485
confiscation proceedings R-467–R-486
convictions PD-90–PD-98, R-437–R-449
copies of documents for appeals or reference, Registrar's duty to provide R-413
Criminal Appeal Office Summaries PD-98
Criminal Cases Review Commission R-440
Crown court officers, duty of R-410
decisions to appeal R-427
declarations of incompatibility R-414
documentary exhibits, supply of R-470
evidence R-443, R-458
exhibits R-412, R-470
expediting appeals R-430
extension of time limits R-406, R-467
fitness for appeal, certificates of R-440
form of appeal notices R-420, R-429, R-439, R-453, R-462
full court, determinations by R-473

Court of Appeal (*cont.*)
ground of appeals
abandonment **R-416**
notices **PD-94**
hearings **R-408–R-409, R-425, R-436, R-447, R-459, R-465, R-486**
hospital, directions on re-admission to **R-449**
indictment **R-98**
information, registrar's power to require **R-471**
judges, powers of **R-433, R-434**
lenient sentences, appeals against **R-458–R-465**
listing **PD-93**
loss of time **PD-96**
notice **PD-92, PD-94–PD-95**
confiscation **R-477–R-479**
determinations, of **R-474**
form of notice **R-420, R-429, R-440**
grounds of appeal **PD-94**
hearings and decisions **R-409, R-419–R-420**
respondents **PD-95, R-422, R-432, R-442, R-456, R-463, R-478, R-482**
restraint or receivership orders **R-481–R-482**
service **R-419, R-428, R-438, R-452, R-461**
striking out **R-485**
variation **R-464**
withdrawal **R-464**
opposition, abandonment of **R-416**
permission/leave **R-421, R-462, R-480, R-485**
points of law, appeals on **R-460–R-466**
preparatory hearings **R-418–R-425**
Proceeds of Crime Act 2002 **R-467–R-475**
public access restrictions **R-451–R-459**
public interest rulings **R-433**
receivership orders **R-480–R-486**
record of proceedings **R-475**
refusal of applications, renewal after **R-407**
renewal of applications **R-407, R-424, R-435, R-456**
re-opening appeals **R-417**
reporting restrictions **R-451–R-459**
restraint orders **R-480–R-486**
retrials **R-270–R-274, R-445–R-446, R-450**
sentencing **PD-90–PD-98, R-437–R-449**
service of notices **R-419, R-428, R-438, R-452, R-461**
single judges **R-472**
skeleton arguments **PD-97, PD-113**
stay of proceedings **R-484**
striking out **R-485**
Supreme Court, appeals to **R-476, R-487–R-490**
transcripts **R-411, R-475**
variation **R-405, R-448**
witnesses, examination of **R-469**
Court office is closed, procedure where **R-319**
Court officers
duties **R-18, R-109, R-124, R-183, R-262, R-410, R-613, R-638**
service of documents **R-513, R-513A**
Court records **R-51–R-56**
access to information **PD-18, R-54–R-56**
case materials, custody of **R-53**
confidential documents **PD-18**
Crown Court, recording and transcription of proceedings in **R-52**
duty to make records **R-51**
exhibits **PD-18**
jury bundles **PD-18**
medical certificates, issue of **PD-19**
parties of information or documents from records or case materials, supply of **R-54**
prohibitions against provision of information **PD-18**
public, supply to the **R-55**
reporters, supply to **PD-18, R-55**
table of considerations likely to arise **PD-18**
transcripts **PD-18**
witness statements of witnesses who give oral evidence **PD-18**
written certificates or extracts, supply of **PD-19, R-56**
written decisions **PD-18**
Criminal behaviour orders (CBOs) **R-302–R-312**
ASBOs, replacement of **SG10-152, SG10-155**
breach **SG15-28–SG15-31**
cross-examination of makers of hearsay statements **R-308**
definition **SG10-155**
European protection orders (EPOs) **R-310–R-311**
evidence to assist the court **R-305**
general rules **R-303**
hearsay **R-306–R-310**
credibility and consistency **R-309**
cross-examination **R-308**
notice **R-307**
notice of terms **R-304**
revocation **R-306**
special rules **R-304–R-305**
variation **R-306, R-312**
Criminal Cases Review Commission (CCRC) **R-392, R-437–R-439, R-441, R-442**
Criminal damage **SG10-21, SG10-37, SG11-11–SG11-23**
£5000, value exceeding **SG11-11–SG11-13**
£5000, value not exceeding **SG11-21–SG11-30**
aggravating factors **SG11-11–SG11-13, SG11-21–SG11-30, SG11-33, SG11-43**
life or reckless as to whether life endangered, intent to endanger **SG11-31–SG11-40**
racial or religious aggravation **SG10-37, SG11-11–SG11-13, SG11-21–SG11-30**
threats to destroy or damage property **SG11-41-SG11-49**
Criminal Injuries Compensation Scheme (CICS) **SG10-145–SG10-146**
Criminal Practice Directions (CPDs) **PD-1–PD-127**
access to information held by the court **PD-18**
allocation **PD-24, PD-119**
appeals **PD-90–PD-98**
bad character evidence **PD-50**
bail **PD-28–PD-35**
case management **PD-3–PD-15, PD-126–PD-127**
citation of authorities **PD-112–PD-115**
Consolidated Criminal Practice Direction, replacement of **PD-1**
contempt of court **PD-103**
costs **PD-100**
court dress **PD-110**
Court of Appeal, appeals against conviction and sentence in **PD-90–PD-98**

Court of Justice, preliminary references to PD-99
Criminal Procedure Rules, relationship with PD-1
cross-examination advocates PD-52
Crown Court
allocation of business PD-120
appeals PD-100
referral of cases PD-117
trial and sentence in PD-56
custody time-limits PD-28–PD-35, PD-121
defendants' right to give or not give evidence PD-71
disclosure of unused material PD-36
dress in court PD-110
entry into force PD-1
expert evidence PD-47–PD-49
extradition PD-104–PD-109
fines PD-125
forms PD-16
general application PD-110–PD-115
general matters PD-1, PD-2, PD-18–PD-19, PD-22–PD-23
Hansard, citation of PD-115
indictment PD-26–PD-27
settling the PD-26
voluntary bills of indictment PD-27
information, access to PD-18–PD-19
initial details of the prosecution case PD-24
investigation orders and warrants PD-101
judges
authorisation of PD-119
magistrates, deployment in PD-123
judgments
copies PD-112–PD-113
preparation PD-114
juries PD-58–PD-72
listing PD-116–PD-122
classification PD-117
judicial responsibility PD-116
other than trials, listing of hearings PD-121
referral of cases in Crown Court to resident judge and presiding judges PD-118
magistrates' courts
deployment of judiciary PD-123
trial and sentence PD-53–PD-54, PD-123, PD-125
very large fines PD-125
medical certificates, issue of PD-19
mode of trial (allocation) PD-25
modes of address and titles of judges and magistrates PD-111
notes in court, taking PD-23
open justice PD-70
organised crime cases, case management of PD-127
overriding objective PD-2
preliminary proceedings PD-20–PD-27
preliminary references PD-100
records, access to PD-18–PD-19
reporting restrictions PD-20–PD-21
sending for trial PD-25
sentencing PD-73–PD-88
sexual behaviour, evidence of complainant's previous PD-51
sexual offences in Youth Court PD-124
skeleton arguments PD-112–PD-113
special measures directions PD-41–PD-46
spent convictions PD-50
terrorism cases, case management of PD-126
transfer of cases PD-121
witness summonses, warrants and orders PD-40
written witness statements PD-37–PD-39
Youth Court, sexual offences in PD-124
Criminal Procedure Rules (CrimPR) R-1–R-641
acquittals for serious offences, retrials after R-268–R-274
Acts of Parliament, references to R-6
adverse to the prosecution, appeals against rulings which are R-426–R-436
allocation R-75–R-90
appeals
case stated R-398–R-402
Court of Appeal R-403–R-490
Crown Court, to R-387–R-397
Supreme Court, to R-487–R-490
application and understanding of rules R-4–R-6
arrest, warrants for R-114–R-120
bad character evidence R-205–R-210
bail R-121–R-137, R-140–R-142
case management R-7–R-32
case stated R-398–R-402
community and other orders, breach, revocation and amendment of R-313–R-316
confiscation and related proceedings R-317–R-386, R-467–R-486
contempt of court R-582–R-598
convictions or sentence, appeals against R-437–R-450
costs R-494–R-507
Court of Appeal R-402–R-490
confiscation and related proceedings R-467–R-486
convictions or sentence, appeals against R-437–R-450
lenient sentences R-460–R-466
point of law, references on R-455–R-466
preparatory hearings, appeals against P-418–R-425
prosecution, rulings adverse to the R-426–R-436
reporting or public access restrictions R-451–R-459
Supreme Court, appeals to R-487–R-490
Court of Justice, preliminary references to R-491–R-493
court records R-51–R-56
criminal behaviour orders (CBOs) after verdicts or findings R-303–R-313
cross-examination by defendants in person, restrictions on R-219–R-226
Crown Court R-245–R-274, R-387–R-397
appeals R-387–R-397
juries R-263–R-267
trial and sentence R-245–R-262
custody time limits R-121–R-124, R-138–R-139
deferred prosecution agreements R-100–R-110
definitions R-5
detention, warrants for R-116–R-120
disclosure R-71–R-74, R-143–R-151
discontinuance R-111–R-113

Criminal Procedure Rules (CrimPR) (*cont.*)
drugs and confiscation proceedings **R-380–R-385**
expert evidence **R-190–R-199**
extradition **R-610–R-641**
fines and orders for payment, enforcement of **R-292–R-301**
forms **R-48–R-50**
hearsay **R-200–R-204**
imprisonment, warrants for **R-116–R-120**
indictment **R-91–R-99**
initial details of prosecution case **R-71–R-74**
international cooperation **R-599–R-618**
investigation orders and warrants **R-511–R-581, R-511A–R-578A**
juries **R-263–R-267**
legal representatives **R-508–R-510**
legislation, references to **R-6**
lenient sentences, appeals against **R-460–R-465**
magistrates' court
starting a prosecution in a **R-67–R-70**
trial and sentence **R-227–R-244**
overriding objective **R-1–R-3**
points of law, appeals against **R-460–R-466**
preliminary references **R-491–R-494**
preparatory hearings, appeals against **P-418–R-425**
prosecution, rulings adverse to the **R-426–R-436**
public access restrictions **R-451–R-459**
receivership proceedings **R-348–R-366, R-372–R-379**
records **R-51–R-56**
reporting etc restrictions **R-57–R-66, R-451–R-459**
representatives and supporters **R-508–R-510**
restraint proceedings **R-348–R-371**
retrials for acquittals for serious offences **R-268–R-274**
road traffic penalties **R-286–R-291**
seizure and detention proceedings **R-344–R-347**
sending for trial **R-75–R-90**
sentencing
appeals against sentence **R-437–R-450**
community and other orders, breach, revocation and amendment of **R-313–R-316**
special cases, in **R-275–R-285**
service of documents **R-35–R-47**
sexual behaviour, evidence of complainant's previous **R-211–R-218**
special measures **R-164–R-189**
starting prosecutions **R-67–R-70**
statutory instruments, references to **R-6**
Supreme Court, appeals or references to **R-487–R-490**
vary requirements, court's power to **R-14**
warrants for arrest, detention or imprisonment **R-114–R-116**
when the Rules apply **R-4**
witnesses **R-152–R-189**
expert evidence **R-190–R-199**
special measures **R-164–R-189**
statements **R-152–R-155**
summonses, warrants and orders **R-156–R-163**
Cross-examination **R-219–R-226, R-308, R-595**
advocates, provisional appointment of **PD-52**
appointment of advocates **R-220**
case papers, supply of, **PD-52**
contempt of court **R-595**
discharge prohibition imposed by court, application to, **R-223**
exercise of court's powers **R-221**
hearsay **R-308, R-595**
information withheld from other party, applications containing, **R-224**
pre-recording **PD-45–PD-46**
prohibit cross-examination, applications to **R-221–R-226**
representations in response **R-225**
restrictions on cross-examination by defendants **R-219–R-226**
sexual behaviour, evidence of previous **PD-51, R-215**
vary requirements, court's power to **R-226**
Crown Court **R-245–R-366, R-387–R-397** *see also* Crown Court, appeals to; Juries; Preparation for trial in the Crown Court; Sending for trial to Crown Court
abuse of process, applications for stay for **PD-5**
acquittal without a jury **R-259**
admission, evidence by **R-257**
case management **PD-3, PD-5, R-19–R-32**
compliance hearings **PD-3**
further hearings **PD-3**
Constitution **R-397**
convictions
jury, without a **R-259**
procedure after **R-260**
court officers, duty of **R-262**
Criminal Cases Review Commission **R-392**
documents, provision of **R-261**
evidence **R-247, R-255–R-257**
fitness to plead **R-254**
general powers and requirements **R-246**
guilty pleas **PD-3, PD-73, R-87, R-248–R-249**
juries **PD-93**
juveniles **R-87**
magistrates' courts **R-128**
not guilty pleas **R-84, R-253**
Plea and Trial Preparation Hearings **PD-3**
pleas **PD-3, PD-73, R-82–R-86, R-248, R-253**
adult defendants **R-83–R-85**
guilty pleas **R-83**
not guilty pleas **R-84**
requests **R-82**
preparation for trial and case progression **PD-3, PD-5, R-19–R-32**
procedure, applications for ruling on **R-247**
prosecutor's application for Crown Court trial **R-86**
questions of law, applications for ruling on **R-247**
recording and transcription of proceedings **R-52**
security arrangements **PD-14**
sentences **PD-56, R-245–R-262, SG10-2**
stay of proceedings **PD-5**
summary offences **SG10-2**
summing up **R-258**
summons, applications for **R-273**
trials, **PD-56, R-245–R-262**
urgent applications **PD-14**
verdicts **R-258**

warrants, applications for R-273
Welsh language PD-12
witnesses R-255–R-256
Crown Court, appeals to R-387–R-397, SG10-2
abandonment of appeals R-395
case management information, supply of PD-90
Constitution of Crown Court R-397
Criminal Cases Review Commission R-392
exhibits, duty of persons keeping R-391
form of notice R-389
hearings and decisions R-394
information, provision of PD-90–PD-91
magistrates' courts
information, supply of PD-91
officers, duties of R-390
notice R-388–R-389
preparation for appeals R-393
reasons PD-90
respondent's notice R-384–R-385
service of notice R-388
variation R-396
Cruelty
animals SG10-19
children SG6-1, SG10-38
Cultivation of cannabis SG10-45, SG23-18–SG23-22
Curfews R-132
Culpability SG2-3, SG2-5, SG10-5–SG10-7
Custodial sentences SG9-9–SG9-12
applicability of SGs SG9-1
bladed articles and offensive weapons SG14-29
communication network offences SG10-34
compensation orders SG10-145
concurrent and consecutive sentences SG3-9
confiscation proceedings, default in R-337
contempt of court R-581–R-582
discharge orders R-582
driving, disqualification from SG10-183
extended sentences for public protection SG3-12
extension period of disqualification SG10-183
fines SG9-3
flowchart SG10-12
guidance SG10-150
guilty pleas SG4-7
imposition of sentences SG9-9–SG9-10
intermittent custody SG2-6
life imprisonment PD-84–PD-85, SG4-8–SG4-9,
magistrates' courts SG10-150
murder, mandatory life sentences for SG4-8–SG4-9
pre-sentence reports SG9-10, SG10-150
protective orders SG18-6
seriousness threshold SG2-6, SG10-5
shortest period commensurate with seriousness of offence SG9-9
suspended sentences SG9-11, SG10-150
terrorists, special custodial sentences for SG32-10, SG32-22, SG32-84
threshold SG9-9, SG9-12, SG10-5
warrants for imprisonment R-114, R-116–R-120
Custody time limits R-138–R-139
appeals R-139
court officers, duties of R-124
exercise of court's powers R-122
extension, applications for R-138
justices' legal adviser, duties of R-123
listing PD-121
sending for trial, before PD-28
Customer information orders (CIOs) R-525, R-525A, R-531, R-531A
Dangerous conditions of vehicles/ accessories SG10-125
Dangerous dog offences SG21-2–SG21-28
assistance dog is injured or killed, owner of person in charge of dog where SG21-15–SG21-18
breeding, selling, exchanging or advertising a prohibited dog SG21-23–SG21-28
community orders SG21-28
dangerously out of control, owner or person in charge of dog SG21-19–SG21-22
death is caused, owner or person in charge of dog where SG21-3–SG21-11
destruction/contingent destruction orders SG10-158, SG21-11
disqualification from having a dog SG21-11
fines SG21-17
fit and proper persons SG21-11
guilty pleas SG21-11
injury is caused, owner or person in charge of dog where SG21-12–SG21-14
magistrates' courts SG10-39
prohibited dog, possession of a SG21-23–SG21-28
seriousness SG21-5, SG21-21, SG21-25
Dangerous driving SG10-103, SG10-109, SG22-6
Death by driving, causing SG22-1–SG22-12
age of offenders SG22-3
alcohol/drugs SG22-3
assistance at the scene, giving SG22-3
avoidable distractions SG22-3
awareness of risk SG22-3
careless or inconsiderate driving SG10-107, SG22-8–SG22-10
dangerous driving SG22-6
deprivation orders SG22-5
disqualification from driving SG22-4
drink or drugs, death by careless driving under the influence of SG22-8
effect on offenders SG22-3
experience, lack of driving SG22-3
factors to take into consideration SG22-6
good driving record SG22-3
more than one person killed SG22-3
others, actions of SG22-3
remorse SG22-3
speeding SG10-117, SG22-3
unlicensed, disqualified or uninsured drivers SG10-108, SG22-12
vulnerable road users SG22-3
Death by careless driving under the influence of drink or drugs, causing SG22-8
Death by careless or inconsiderate driving, causing SG10-107, SG22-10
Death by dangerous driving, causing SG22-6
Declarations of incompatibility R-414, R-637
Defence trial advocates, identity of R-25
Deferred prosecution agreements R-100–R-110
approve proposals, applications to R-102
breach of agreement, applications on R-104
court officers, duty of R-109

Deferred prosecution agreements (*cont.*)
discontinue prosecution, notice to **R-107**
exercise of court's powers **R-101**
postponement of publication of information by the prosecutor, applications for **R-108**
suspension of prosecution, application to lift **R-106**
terms, application to approve **R-103**
variations **R-105, R-110**
Deferred sentences **SG10-173**
Deprivation orders **SG10-152, SG10-156, SG10-157, SG24-12, SG24-28**
Destruction orders
dogs, contingent destruction orders for **SG10-158**
drugs **SG10-164**
trade marks, unauthorised **SG10-166**
weapons orders, destruction of **SG10-165**
Detention *see also* Custodial sentences; Custody time limits
appeals, detention pending **R-489, R-635**
case progression in magistrates' court **PD-3**
confiscation proceedings **R-345–R-347**
detention and training orders (DTOs) **SG8-9, SG8-10**
hospital, detention in **R-283, R-449**
juveniles **SG8-9, SG8-10**
seizure and detention proceedings **R-344–R-347**
temporary detention, reviews after **R-587**
warrants, for **R-114, R-116–R-120**
Detention and training orders (DTOs) **SG8-9, SG8-10**
Devolution issues **PD-10**
Die, causing or allowing a child to **SG20-16–SG20-26**
Diminished responsibility **SG25-33–SG25-44**
Directions *see also* Criminal Practice Directions (CPDs); Live link directions; Special measures directions
evidence **R-177–R-180**
extradition **PD-107, PD-109**
intermediaries **PD-8**
Leveson Review **PD-67**
medical reports, commissioning **R-34, R-282**
service of documents **R-47**
variation **R-12**
Directors' disqualification orders **SG10-161, SG15-40–SG15-43, SG24-28**
Disabilities, persons with **SG10-177–SG10-180**
Discharges
absolute discharges **SG8-9, SG8-10**
appropriate offences for discharge **SG10-120–SG10-144**
conditional discharges **PD-82, SG2-7, SG8-9**
motoring offences **SG10-120–SG10-125**
Disclosure **R-143–R-151**
benefit fraud **SG26-21**
defence **R-146–R-149**
failure to disclose information **SG26-21**
fraud **SG26-4**
further information orders **R-523, R-523A, R-530, R-530A**
orders **R-523, R-523A, R-530, R-530A**
proceeds of crime **R-530, R-530A**
prosecution **R-144–R-145, R-147**
public interest rulings **R-145, R-148**
receivership orders **R-356, R-361**
restraint proceedings **R-356, R-361**
terrorism **R-523, R-523A, SG32-26–SG32-76**
unauthorised use **R-150**
unused material **PD-36**
use of disclosed materials **R-149–R-150**
vary requirements, court's power to **R-151**
witness anonymity orders **PD-44**
Discontinuance **R-107, R-111–R-113, R-633**
Discrimination, aggravation relating to **SG10-177** *see also* Racially or religiously aggravated offences
Disorderly behaviour with intent to cause harassment, alarm or distress **SG10-73, SG10-74**
Disqualification from driving
absence, in offenders' **SG10-183**
custodial sentences, imposition of **SG10-183**
death by driving, causing **SG22-4**
discretionary disqualification **SG10-183**
driving whilst disqualified **SG10-110**
environmental crimes **SG24-28**
foreign driving disqualification, appeals against recognition of **R-291**
magistrates' courts **SG10-110**
new drivers **SG10-183**
obligatory disqualification **R-287, SG10-183**
rehabilitation course, completion of **SG10-183**
representations **R-286**
special reasons **SG10-183**
tests, passing of extended driving **SG10-183**
totting up **SG10-183**
unlicensed, disqualified or uninsured drivers **SG10-108, SG22-12**
use of a vehicle, no requirement for link with **SG10-160**
Disqualification orders *see also* Disqualification from driving
animals **SG10-159, SG15-44–SG15-47, SG21-4**
dangerous dogs **SG21-4, SG21-11**
directors **SG10-161, SG15-40–SG15-43, SG24-6**
suspension **R-280, R-443**
Distress **R-348**
Document exchange (DX), service by **R-39**
Documents, provision of **R-261, R-564–R-568, R-564A–R-568A**
Dogs *see* Dangerous dog offences
Domestic abuse **SG5-1–SG5-8, SG10-174**
coercive behaviour, definition of **SG5-3, SG10-174**
controlling behaviour, definition of **SG5-3, SG10-174**
custodial sentences **SG10-174**
definition **SG10-174**
factors taken into consideration **SG5-6**
female genital mutilation **SG10-174**
forced marriages **SG10-174**
'honour' based violence **SG10-174**
magistrates' courts sentencing guidelines **SG10-174–SG10-175**
provocation **SG10-174**
restraining orders **SG5-7**
victim personal statements **SG5-8**
Dress in court **PD-110**
Drink-driving offences
breath tests, failure to cooperate with preliminary **SG10-121**

death by careless driving under the influence of drink or drugs, causing SG22-8
driving/attempting to drive SG10-118, SG10-126
excess alcohol, driving/attempting to drive with SG10-111
failure to provide specimen for analysis SG10-114–SG10-115
in charge with excess alcohol SG10-112
magistrates' courts SG10-111–SG10-112, SG10-118–SG10-119
unfit through drink or drugs SG10-118, SG10-126
Driving offences *see* Motoring offences; Road traffic offences
Drug driving
driving or attempted to drive SG10-126
in charge SG10-126
prescription drugs SG10-126
sentencing guidance SG10-126
Drugs and drug-related offences SG22-1–SG23-33
acquittals, compensation in cases of R-385
administering a substance with intent SG31-146–SG31-149
cannabis SG10-45, SG10-183
cultivation SG10-45, SG23-18–SG23-22
out of court disposals SG6-1
warnings SG10-183
confiscation orders R-380–R-385
cultivating cannabis SG10-45, SG23-18–SG23-22
death by careless driving under the influence of drink or drugs, causing SG22-8
destruction SG10-164
failure to attend/remain for initial assessments SG10-40
forfeiture SG10-164
fraudulent evasion of prohibition by bringing into or taking out of UK a controlled drug SG10-42, SG23-18–SG23-22
intent to supply SG10-46, SG23-12–SG23-16
khat warnings SG10-183
magistrates' courts SG10-40–SG10-45, SG10-47
motoring offences SG10-119–SG10-120, SG10-126, SG22-8
out of court disposals SG6-1
possession SG23-28–SG23-33
premises to be used, permitting SG10-46, SG23-23–SG23-27
production of controlled drugs SG10-44, SG23-17
racial or religious aggravation SG11-13
samples, failure or refusal to provide SG10-41
supplying or offering to supply SG10-43, SG10-46, SG23-12–SG23-16
unfit through drink or drugs, driving/attempting to drive whilst SG10-118–SG10-119, SG10-126
warnings SG10-183
Drunk and disorderly in a public place SG10-48
Due care and attention, driving without SG10-106–SG10-107, SG22-8–SG22-10
DVLA, failure to notify change of ownership to SG10-125

Education, non-attendance at school and SG10-77
Effective Trial Monitoring form, completion of PD-3
Either way offences, flowchart on SG4-9
Electricity, abstraction of SG10-49, SG33-23–SG33-26
Electronic communications PD-22, R-40, R-65, R-93, R-267 *see also* Electronic data, orders for access to
Electronic data, orders for access to R-573A–R-578A, R-576–R-581
applications R-573A–R-577A, R-576–R-580
contempt of court R-578A, R-581
Crime (Overseas Production Orders) Act 2019 R-573A–R-578A, R-576–R-581
exercise of court's power R-574A, R-577
information withheld from respondents or other persons, applications containing R-577A, R-580
overseas production orders R-573A–R-578A, R-576–R-581
revocation, applications for R-576A, R-579
variation, applications for R-576A, R-579
Electronic means, service by R-40
Electronic monitoring (tagging) R-132, SG9-8
Engaging in sexual activity in the presence of a child SG31-69–SG31-72
Engaging in sexual activity in the presence of a person with mental disorder impeding choice SG31-114–SG31-117
Engaging in sexual activity in the presence, procured by inducement, threat or deception, of a person with a mental disorder SG31-122–SG31-125
Entry, powers of R-522, R-522A, R-529, R-529A
Environmental crimes SG10-50, SG24-1–SG24-33
air, land and water, illegal discharges to SG24-2–SG24-33
annual accounts SG24-6
charities, obtaining financial information from SG24-6
companies, obtaining financial information from SG24-6
compensation orders SG24-3, SG24-9, SG24-19, SG24-24
confiscation orders SG24-2, SG24-4, SG24-9, SG24-20, SG24-24
deprivation of property SG24-12, SG24-28
directors, disqualification from SG24-28
driving, disqualification from SG24-28
economic benefit, removal of SG24-9
financial information, obtaining SG24-6, SG24-22
financial orders, combinations of SG24-9, SG24-24
fines SG10-141, SG24-2–SG24-32
adjustments SG24-11–SG24-12, SG24-25–SG24-28
bands SG24-33
combined orders SG24-9, SG24-24
financial information, obtaining SG24-6, SG24-22
general principles SG24-6, SG24-22
organisations SG24-6
proportionality SG24-10
reductions SG24-12, SG24-25
turnover SG24-6, SG24-10
forfeiture of vehicles SG24-12
health trusts, obtaining financial information from SG24-6
individuals SG24-18–SG24-33

Environmental crimes (*cont.*)
local authorities, fire authorities, and similar public bodies, obtaining financial information from SG24-6
magistrates' courts SG10-50, SG10-183
organisations SG24-2–SG24-17
other environmental offences SG24-17
partnerships, obtaining financial information from SG24-6
remediation SG24-12, SG24-28
unauthorised or harmful deposit, treatment or disposal etc of waste SG24-2–SG24-33
very large organisations, fining SG24-6
Estreatment of recognisances PD-33
EU law
bail R-136–R-137
European investigation orders (EIOs) R-616–R-618
European protection orders (EPOs) R-310–R-311
fines R-301
preliminary references to Court of Justice PD-99, R-492–R-493
European Convention on Human Rights (ECHR) *see also* Particular rights
declarations of incompatibility R-414, R-637
European investigation orders (EIOs) R-612–R-615
live links R-613
oral evidence, receipt of R-612
production orders R-617–R-618
revocation R-615
search warrants R-617–R-618
variation R-615
European protection orders (EPOs) R-310–R-311
Evasion *see also* Tax fraud
railway fares SG10-75
TV licence payment SG10-98
Evidence *see also* Character evidence; Disclosure; Exhibits; Expert evidence; Hearsay; Witnesses
admission, by R-232, R-257
audio recorded interviews, of PD-39
case management PD-4
Court of Appeal R-443, R-458
criminal behaviour orders (CBOs) R-305
Criminal Cases Review Commission (CCRC) R-392
Crown Court PD-90, R-247, R-256–R-257, R-387–R-397
directions R-177–R-180
extradition R-624
international cooperation R-612
juries PD-68, PD-71
magistrates' courts R-230–R-232
pagination and indexing of served evidence PD-4
receivership proceedings R-352
restraint proceedings R-352
video recorded evidence in chief PD-38
video recorded interviews PD-39, PD-43
watching video recorded interviews at different times from jury PD-43
written statements PD-37
Excess alcohol, driving/attempting to drive with SG10-11
Excise duty
driving without excise licence SG10-125
fraudulent evasion SG26-17, SG26-19
Exclusion orders SG10-162
Exhausts SG10-125, SG10-128
Exhibits PD-18, R-155, R-391, R-412, R-469
Expert evidence PD-47–PD-49, R-191–R-199
bad character evidence PD-47
content of reports R-193
declarations of truth PD-48
directions, failure to comply with R-191
duty to the court R-191
instructions to single joint experts R-197
introduction of expert evidence R-192
pre-hearing discussions PD-49, R-195
reports PD-48, R-194
service of reports, experts to be informed of R-194
single joint experts R-197
statements of understanding PD-48
variation of requirements R-199
Explanation orders R-524, R-524A
Explosive substances SG32-15–SG32-26
attempts to cause explosions SG32-15–SG32-26
causing explosion likely to endanger life SG32-15–SG32-26
making or keeping explosives with intent to endanger life SG32-15–SG32-26
Exposure SG10-52, SG31-134–SG31-137
Extradition PD-104–PD-128, R-610–R-641
abridgement of time PD-107
adjournments PD-107
appeals PD-104–PD-105, R-626–R-636
amendments to notices PD-105
consent, by PD-105, R-633
disposal of applications PD-105
early termination R-633
expedition PD-104–PD-105
form of notice R-629
hearings R-632
management of appeals PD-104–PD-105
permission, renewing applications for R-631
reopening determination of appeals PD-107, R-636
respondent's notice R-630
service of notice R-628
Supreme Court R-623–R-635
arrangement of extradition hearings R-621
arrest
issue of warrants R-617
preliminary hearings after arrest R-614, R-620
provisional arrest R-619–R-621
warrants R-616–R-617, R-619
bundles PD-108
case management in High Court R-627
categories of offences PD-104
consent to deal with other offences R-641
court officers, duties of R-610, R-638
court papers PD-108
declarations of incompatibility R-637
defendant, meaning of R-610
directions
discharge, ancillary to a PD-107
non-compliance PD-109
variation PD-107
discharge
directions ancillary to a discharge PD-107

requests withdrawn, where R-623
time limits, failure to comply with R-625
warrants withdrawn, where R-616
evidence R-624
exercise of court's powers R-612
extension of time PD-107
fees, payment of High Court R-640
further extradition, consent to R-641
hearings R-614–R-612, R-621–R-622, R-625
High Court PD-105, R-626–R-640
interpreters PD-105
investigation warrants R-542A
legal representatives PD-106–PD-107
live links PD-105
magistrates' courts R-612–R-613
points of law of general public importance, applications to certify PD-107
post-extradition proceedings R-641
preliminary hearings R-614, R-618, R-620
presenting officer, meaning of R-610
production orders R-533, R-533A
provisional arrest R-619–R-621
representation orders PD-106
requests withdrawn, discharge where R-623
skeleton arguments PD-108
Supreme Court
applications for permission to appeal R-637
detention pending appeal R-635
time limits
extension or abridgment of time PD-107
failure to comply with R-625
warrants
arrest R-625, R-628, R-633, R-638
provisional arrest warrants R-619–R-620
withdrawal R-633
withdrawal R-622
Extended sentences for public protection SG3-12

Failure to protect SG20-3–SG-20-14
Failure to provide specimens for analysis
driving/attempting to drive SG10-114
in charge SG10-115
Failure to stop/report road accidents SG10-113
Failure to stop when required SG10-123
False accounting SG24-4, SG26-6–SG26-12, SG26-17, SG26-19, SG26-21, SG26-23
False representations/statements SG26-4, SG26-17, SG26-19, SG26-21, SG26-23
Familial sex offences
adult relatives, sex with SG31-142–SG31-145
inciting a child family member to engage in sexual activity SG31-65–SG31-68, SG31-155
inciting a child family member to engage in sexual activity (offender under 18) SG31-155
juveniles SG31-155
penetration, consenting to SG31-142–SG31-145
sexual activity with a child family member (offender under 18) SG31-155
Fatal accidents *see* Death by driving, causing
Female genital mutilation (FGM) SG10-174, SG20-27–SG20-36
Financial information, obtaining SG24-6, SG24–22, SG26-37, SG28-4

Fines R-292–R-301
adjustments SG24-11–SG24-12, SG24-25–SG24-28
amount SG10-5, SG10-127–SG10-145
appeals against decisions of fines officers R-295
appropriate offences for discharge SG10-120–SG10-144
assessment SG10-127–SG10-145
attachment of earnings orders SG10-144
bands SG6-1, SG10-129, SG14-30, SG15-49, SG19-22, SG21-28, SG23-33, SG31-159
benefits, persons on SG10-139, SG10-144
bladed articles and offensive weapons SG14-30
burglary SG19-18
collection orders SG10-144
combined orders SG24-9, SG24-24
commercial purposes, offences committed for SG10-140
community orders SG9-3
compensation orders SG10-145
corporations
corporate manslaughter SG28-4–SG28-12
fraud SG26-37–SG26-38
courts charges, remission of R-296
custodial sentences SG10-143
dangerous dog offences SG21-17
enforcement R-292–R-301, SG10-144
environmental offences SG10-141, SG24-6, SG24-9–SG24-17, SG24-22–SG24-28, SG24-33
European Union member states, financial penalties imposed in other R-301
expenses, out of the ordinary SG10-133
financial circumstances, assessment of SG10-132
financial information, obtaining SG-6, SG24-22, SG26-37, SG28-4
fixed penalty notices, claims to avoid fines after R-289, R-297
high income offenders SG10-138
information, where no SG10-131
juveniles SG8-9
low income, approach to offenders on SG10-139, SG10-145
low outgoings, unusually SG10-134
magistrates' court PD-125, SG10-120–SG10-144, SG31-159
maximum fines SG10-143
more than one source of income, households with SG10-136
motoring/road traffic offences R-289, SG10-120–SG10-125
multiple offences SG10-143
organisation, offences committed by an SG10-141, SG24-6
payment, time for SG10-143
potential earning capacity SG10-138
proportionality SG24-10
receipts, duty to give R-294
reduction of fines R-296, SG10-142, SG24-12, SG24-25
sale of goods taken under warrants R-300
savings SG10-134
starting point, identification of appropriate SG10-6
state benefits, persons on SG10-139, SG10-144

Fines (*cont.*)
totality principle **SG3-14–SG3-15**
turnover of companies **SG24-6, SG24-10, SG28-6**
variation **R-296**
very large organisations **SG24-6**
Victim Surcharge **SG10-148**
warrants of control
dispute resolution, applications for **R-300**
extension of time, applications for **R-299**
information to be included **R-298**
weekly income, definition of relevant **SG10-130**
Fingerprints **R-542–R-555, R-542A–R-555A**
appeals **R-555, R-555A**
exercise of court's powers **R-553, R-553A**
extend period, application to **R-554, R-554A**
investigation orders **R-552–R-555, R-552A–R-555A**
retention **R-552–R-555, R-552A–R-555A**
Firearms
carrying in public place **SG10-53**
carrying loaded air weapon/imitation firearm/unloaded shot gun without ammunition **SG10-53**
carrying loaded shot gun/carrying shot gun or any other firearm together with ammunition for it **SG10-53**
carrying unloaded air weapon **SG10-53**
guilty pleas **SG4-7**
juveniles **SG8-8**
minimum sentences **SG4-7, SG8-8**
First time offenders **SG10-6**
Fitness to plead **R-254**
Fixed penalty notices (FPNs)
disorder, penalty notices for (PNDs) **SG10-191**
fines, statutory declarations to avoid **R-289, R-297**
magistrates' courts **SG10-190–SG10-192**
Football-related offences
alcohol whilst entering or trying to enter ground, possession of **SG10-54**
banning orders **SG10-163**
drunk in, or whilst trying to enter ground, being **SG10-54**
guilty pleas, reductions for **SG10-54**
indecent or racist chanting **SG10-54**
magistrates' courts **SG10-54**
prohibited areas, going onto **SG10-54**
throwing missiles **SG10-54**
tickets, unauthorised sale or attempted sale of **SG10-54**
Forced marriages **SG10-174**
Foreign travel orders, breach of **SG15-32–SG15-35**
Foreseeability **SG10-5**
Forfeiture
ancillary orders **SG10-165–SG10-166**
drugs **SG10-164**
international co-operation **R-609**
liquor licences, forfeiture or suspension of **SG10-167**
orders **SG10-156–SG10-159**
overseas forfeiture orders **R-609**
receivership proceedings **R-348**
sound recordings **R-66**
sureties **PD-33, R-136, R-446**
trade marks, unauthorised **SG10-166**
vehicles **SG24-12**
weapons **SG10-165**
Forms
electronic means, applications by **R-48**
Effective Trial Monitoring form, completion of **PD-3**
extradition **R-629**
general matters **PD-16**
signatures **R-50**
Welsh, forms in **R-49**
witness summons **R-159**
FPNs *see* Fixed penalty notices (FPNs)
Fraud **SG10-55, SG26-2–SG26-28**
abuse of position **SG26-4, SG26-21**
benefit fraud **SG10-26, SG26-21–SG26-23**
cheating the revenue **SG26-19**
conspiracy to defraud **SG26-4, SG26-6, SG26-19, SG26-21, SG26-23**
corporate crime **SG10-36, SG26-33–SG26-43**
disclose information, failure to **SG26-15**
drug, evasion of prohibition by bringing in or taking out of UK a controlled **SG10-42, SG23-2–SG23-6**
excise duty, evasion of **SG26-17, SG26-19**
false accounting **SG26-4, SG26-6–SG26-12, SG26-19, SG26-21, SG26-23**
false representations, fraud by **SG26-4**
income tax, evasion of **SG26-17**
magistrates' courts **SG10-55, SG10-69, SG10-100**
possessing, making or supplying articles for use in fraud **SG10-68, SG26-13–SG26-16**
revenue fraud **SG10-76, SG26-17–SG26-20**
social security benefit fraud **SG10-26, SG26-21–SG26-23**
statutory offences **SG26-1**
VAT frauds **SG26-17, SG26-19**
vehicle licence/registration fraud **SG10-100**
victims, impact on **SG26-5**
Freezing orders **R-608**
Further information orders **R-523, R-523A, R-530, R-530A**
Further offences
bladed articles and offensive weapons **SG14-6**
juveniles **SG8-9, SG8-10**
referral orders **SG8-9**

Going equipped for theft or burglary **SG10-56, SG33-19–SG33–22**
Goods vehicles **SG10-125**
Grievous bodily harm (GBH) **SG10-57, SG10-63**
causing grievous bodily harm with intent to do GBH/wounding with intent to do GBH **SG12-3**
inflicting grievous bodily harm **SG12-13**
magistrates' courts **SG10-57**
racially or religiously aggravated GBH **SG10-57, SG10-63, SG12-13**
Grooming, meeting a child following sexual **SG31-74–SG31-77**
Gross negligence manslaughter **SG25-13–SG25-22**
Ground rules hearings **PD-8, PD-45–PD-46, PD-51**
Guardians **R-283**
Guilty pleas *see also* Guilty pleas, reduction in sentences for

absent, procedure where party is, R-238
adult defendants R-83
communication network offences SG10-34
convicts, procedure where court, R-237
corporate manslaughter SG28-9
Crown Court PD-73, R-83
documents, provision of, R-239
facts to be stated PD-76
juveniles SG8-3, SG8-8, SG19-22
magistrates' courts PD-3, R-83, R-233–R-239
murder SG4-8
procedure R-233, R-248
reduction SG2-5
robbery SG8-8, SG30-7
sexual offenders SG8-8
single justice procedure, special rules for, R-235
theft SG33-5
vacate, applications to R-249
withdrawal R-236
written pleas, special rules for, R-234
Guilty pleas, reduction in sentences for SG4-1–SG4-11, SG10-15
ancillary orders SG10-9
application of reduction SG4-6
approach SG4-4
assistance or advice necessary before indicating pleas SG4-7
custodial sentences SG4-7
determination of level SG4-5, SG4-8
either way offences
flowchart SG4-9
magistrates' courts, keeping in SG4-6
exceptions SG4-7
firearms, minimum sentences relating to SG4-7
flowcharts SG4-9–SG4-11
further information before indicating pleas SG4-7
imposing one type of sentence rather than another SG4-6
indication of plea after first stage of proceedings SG4-5
indictable offences, flowchart on SG4-11
June 1, 2017, cases where first hearing is before SG10-9
June 1, 2017, cases where first hearing is on or after SG10-9
juveniles SG8-8
key principles SG4-3
lesser or different offences, offenders convicted of SG4-7
mandatory life sentences for murder SG4-8–SG4-9
Newton hearings SG4-7
robbery SG30-7
special reasons hearings SG4-7
summary offences SG4-6, SG4-10
flowchart SG4-10
more than one SG4-6
Handling stolen goods SG10-58, SG33-15–SG33-18
Hansard PD-115
Harassment
aggravated offences SG27-9–SG27-17
disorderly behaviour SG10-73, SG10-74
harassment, alarm or distress SG10-73, SG10-74
magistrates' courts SG10-59, SG10-69
non-molestation orders, breach of SG10-69
protective orders, breach of SG10-69
putting people in fear of violence SG10-59, SG10-60
racially or religiously aggravated harassment SG10-59, SG10-70, SG27-19, SG27-23–SG27-29
restraining orders, breach of SG10-69
stalking SG27-18–SG27-29
violence, without SG10-60
Hard shoulder on motorways SG10-124
Harm SG10-6–SG10-7
Hate crime
disability, aggravation relating to SG–259
magistrates' courts SG10-176–SG10-180
intention of offenders SG10–179
racial or religious aggravation SG10–177
sexual orientation, aggravation relating to SG10–177
transgender identity, aggravation relating to SG–259
victim or others, impact on SG–161
Health and safety offences SG10-181
Health authorities, obtaining financial information on SG26-37
Health trusts SG24-6, SG25-37, SG28-4
Hearings
compliance hearings PD-3
extradition R-615, R-620–R-621
High Court, appeals to R-632
Plea and Trial Preparation Hearings (PTPHs) PD-3
preliminary hearings PD-3, R-611, R-620
private hearings R-62–R-64
Hearsay R-200–R-204
contempt of court R-592, R-6023
credibility and consistency R-309, R-596
criminal behaviour orders (CBOs) R-307–R-310
cross-examination R-308, R-595
notice R-201, R-307, R-594
opposition to evidence R-202
receivership orders R-355
restraint proceedings R-355
unopposed evidence R-203
variation R-204, R-312
Her Majesty's pleasure, detention at SG8-9
High Court, appeals to R-626–R-640
case management R-627
constitution of High Court R-639
court officers, duties of R-638
declarations of incompatibility with Convention rights R-637
detention pending appeal, determination of R-635
discharge of defendant R-635
discontinuance R-633
exercise of High Court's powers R-626
extradition PD-105, R-626–R-640
fees, payment of R-640
hearings R-632
notice
form of notice R-629
respondents R-630
service R-628
permission
renewal of applications R-631
Supreme Court, appeals to R-634

High Court, appeals to (*cont.*)
reopening the determination of an appeal **R-636**
service of notice **R-628**
Supreme Court
detention pending appeal, determination of **R-635**
discharge of defendant **R-635**
permission, applications for **R-636**
Historical sexual offences **SG31-157–SG31-158**
principles **SG31-158**
table **SG31-158**
HM Revenue & Customs *see* Revenue offences
Homicide *see also* Corporate manslaughter; Murder
careless driving under the influence of drink or drugs, causing death by **SG22-8**
careless or inconsiderate driving, causing death by **SG10-107, SG22-10**
dangerous driving, causing death by **SG22-6**
driving, causing death by **SG22-1–SG22-12**
'Honour' based violence **SG10-174**
Hospital, detention in **R-34, R-283, R-449**

Identity documents, possessing false/another's/ improperly obtained **SG10-61**
Ignorance of proceedings, statutory declaration of **R-243**
Ill-treatment of children **SG20-3–SG20-14**
Imitation firearms without ammunition, carrying loaded **SG10-53**
Impact Statements for Business (ISB) **PD-81**
Imprisonment *see* Custodial sentences
In charge
drug driving **SG10-126**
excess alcohol, driving with **SG10-112**
Incest *see* Familial sex offences
Inciting a child family member to engage in sexual activity **SG31-65–SG31-68, SG31-155**
Income tax fraud **SG26-17–SG26-20**
Indecent or racist chanting at football matches **SG10-54**
Indecent photographs of children **SG10-62, SG31-86–SG31-89**
Indication of sentence, applications for **PD-75, R-29**
Indictable offences, flowchart on **SG4-11**
Indictment **R-91–R-99**
amendments **PD-26**
appeals **R-93**
arraigning the defendant **R-30**
content **PD-26**
Court of Appeal, service at direction of **R-93**
deferred prosecution agreements **R-96**
draft indictments **PD-26, R-93–R-99**
electronically, draft indictments generated **PD-26, R-93**
form and content **R-99**
general rules **R-92**
High Court's permission to serve draft indictment **R-95, R-99**
joint and separate trials **PD-26**
jury trials and then by judge alone, multiple offending tried by **PD-26**
multiple offending **PD-26**
preferring the indictment **PD-26**
preliminary proceedings **PD-26–PD-27**
preparation **PD-26**
printing **PD-26**
prosecutor, draft indictment served by **PD-26**
reinstitution of proceedings, service by prosecutor on **R-97**
sending for trial to Crown Court **R-93–R-94**
service **R-94–R-95, R-97–R-99**
settling the indictment **PD-26**
signature **PD-26**
voluntary bills **PD-274**
Inducement, threat or deception to procure sexual activity with a person with a person with a mental disorder **SG31-118–SG31-121**
Inflicting grievous bodily harm/unlawful wounding **SG12-13-SG12-18**
racial and religious aggravation **SG12-13–SG12-18**
Information *see also* Initial details of prosecution case (advance information)
bail, applications to withhold information from defendants applying for **R-142**
court records **PD-18, R-51–R-56**
customer information orders (CIOs) **R-525, R-525A, R-531, R-531A**
further information orders **R-523, R-523A, R-530, R-530A**
juries **PD-58, R-264**
magistrates' courts **PD-91, R-68–R-69**
special measures directions **R-175**
terrorism **R-521–R-526, R-521A–R-526A, SG10-83, SG32-89–SG32-99**
withheld from another party, application containing information **R-175**
Initial details of prosecution case (advance information) **R-71–R-74**
content of initial details **R-73**
provision of details **R-72**
record of defendants **PD-24**
Inspection of documents **R-356**
Insurance **SG10-116, SG10-121**
Intention **SG10-6**
Interference with a vehicle **SG10-99**
Intermediaries **PD-8, R-170, R-449**
18, witnesses and defendants under **PD-8**
assessments **PD-8**
attendance at ground rules hearings **PD-8**
defendants **PD-8**
ineffective directions **PD-8**
photographs of court facilities **PD-8**
role and functions **PD-8**
witnesses, prosecution and defence **PD-8**
International co-operation **R-609–R-611**
assistance abroad, requests for **R-601**
confiscation orders **R-611**
European investigation orders (EIOs), giving effect to **R-612**
forfeiture orders **R-609**
freezing orders **R-608**
interpreters where television or telephone links **R-604**
notice
requests for assistance abroad, supply of copy of notices for **R-601**
service out of jurisdiction **R-596**
oral evidence, receipt of **R-612**
overseas records **R-607**

persons entitled to appear and take part R-602
public access, prohibition of R-602
records of proceedings to hear evidence before nominated courts R-605
requests for assistance abroad, supply of copy of notices for R-601
restraint orders R-610
service out of the jurisdiction
notice to accompany process R-600
proof R-600
telephone links R-606
television links R-605–R-606
translations R-596
Internet
child sex offences SG31-51, SG31-63, SG31-79
communication network offences SG10-34
Interpreters PD-12, PD-105, R-32, R-604
Intimidation
intimidatory offences SG27-1–SG27-49
witnesses SG10-105
Intoxication *see* Drink-driving offences
Investigation anonymity orders R-556–R-560, R-556A–R-560A
Investigation of crime *see also* Investigation orders; Investigation warrants
access to documents R-564–R-568, R-564A–R-568A
applications R-566, R-566A
contempt of court R-568, R-568A
exercise of court's powers R-565, R-565A
withheld from respondents or other persons, information R-567, R-567A
anonymity orders R-556–R-560, R-556A–R-560A
extradition R-542, R-542A
Proceeds of Crime Act 2002 R-527–R-533, R-527A–R-533A, R-542, R-542A, R-569–R-571, R-569A–R-572A
warrants R-542, R-542A
Investigation orders PD-101, R-511–R-563, R-511A–R-563A
account monitoring orders R-532, R-532A
anonymity orders R-556–R-560, R-556A–R-560A
applicant, definition of R-512, R-512A
applications R-516–R-518, R-516A–R-518A
approval orders R-561–R-563, R-561A–R-563A
approval for authorisation or notice, application for R-563, R-563A
exercise of powers R-562, R-562A
contempt of court R-519, R-519A, R-568, R-568A, R-590
court, definition of R-512, R-512A
court officers, documents served on R-513, R-513A
customer information orders R-531, R-531A
discharge R-518, R-518A
disclosure orders R-530, R-530A
European investigation orders (EIOs) R-612–R-615
exercise of court's powers R-515, R-515A
extradition R-533, R-533A, R-543, R-543A
fingerprints etc, orders for retention of R-552–R-555, R-552A–R-555A
further information orders R-530, R-530A
proceeds of crime R-527–R-532, R-527A–R-532A, R-542, R-542A
production orders R-520, R-520A, R-528, R-528A
respondent, definition of R-512, R-512A
retention or return of property, orders for R-545–R-551, R-545A–R-551A
service on court officers R-513, R-513A
terrorism R-521–R-526, R-521A–R-526A, R-541, R-541A
variation R-518, R-518A
withheld from respondents or other persons, applications containing R-517, R-517A
Investigation warrants R-511–R-513, R-511A–R-513A, R-534–R-544, R-534A–R-544A
applications R-536, R-536A, R-538–R-564, R-538A–R-564A
court officers, documents served on R-513, R-513A
exercise of court's powers R-535, R-535A
extradition R-543, R-543A
information to be included R-537, R-537A
proceeds of crime R-542, R-542A
Joining of applications R-349
Joint or separate trials, applications for R-27–R-28
Judges
Court of Appeal R-423, R-434
costs R-506
Crown Court cases, referral of PD-118
listing PD-119
magistrates' courts PD-123
single judges, hearings by R-472
summing up R-258
Judgments
Court of Appeal and High Court judgments, availability of PD-112–PD-113
preparation PD-114
Juries PD-58–PD-72, R-263–R-267
appeals against jury service R-263–R-267
bundles PD-18
connections to case or parties, PD-61
closing speeches, PD-67
contempt in the face of the court PD-69
conviction or acquittal without a jury R-259
Crown Court R-87
deliberations PD-69
directions PD-67, R-258
discharging jurors PD-65, R-251
effective panel, ensuring an PD-63
electronic communication devices, surrender of PD-69, R-267
eligibility PD-60
English language ability PD-60
evidence, defendant's right to give or not give, PD-71
excusal by court R-263–R-264
exhibits and evidence in retirement, access to PD-68
identification of the issues in the case PD-56
information, provision of PD-58, R-265
irregularities PD-69
long trials, assessment of availability for PD-61, R-266
majority verdicts PD-72
number PD-69
oaths or affirmations PD-62

Juries (*cont.*)
objections **R-252**
open justice **PD-70**
personal reasons, discharge for **PD-65**
police officers, prison officers or employees of prosecuting agencies **PD-60**
postponement, refusal of **R-264**
precautionary measures before swearing **PD-61**
preliminary instructions to jurors **PD-64**
preliminary matters **PD-59**
professional and public service commitments **PD-60**
record-keeping **PD-67**
selection **R-250**
summing up **PD-67, R-258**
swearing in **PD-62**
verdicts **PD-67, PD-72, R-258**
views **PD-66**
Welsh language **PD-12**
written materials **PD-67**
Justices' legal advisers **R-123**
Juveniles **SG8-2–SG9-1** *see also* Youth rehabilitation orders (YROs)
absolute or conditional discharges **SG8-9, SG8-10**
adults, children tried with **SG1-1, SG8-5**
age
available sentences by age **SG8-9**
maturity **SG8-7**
threshold between commission and sentence, crossing a significant **SG8-9**
allocation **SG8-5**
alone, charged **SG8-5**
ASBOs **SG12-301**
bladed articles and offensive weapons **SG10-29, SG14-22–SG14-29**
breaches **SG8-9, SG8-10**
child sex offences, commission of **SG31-155**
Crown Court **SG8-5**
custodial sentences **SG8-8, SG14-29**
dangerous offenders **SG8-4, SG8-9**
detention and training orders (DTOs) **SG8-9, SG8-10**
breach **SG8-10**
further offences, commission of **SG8-10**
either way offences **SG8-5**
financial orders/fines **SG8-9**
firearms offences, minimum sentences for **SG8-8**
flowcharts **SG8-5**
further offences, commission of **SG8-9, SG8-10**
grave crimes **SG8-5**
guilty pleas **SG8-3, SG8-8**
Her Majesty's Pleasure, detention at **SG8-9**
indictable offences **SG8-5**
jointly charged with adults **SG1-1, SG8-5**
lesser or different offence, where juvenile found guilty of **SG8-8**
live links **PD-15**
long-term detention **SG8-9**
minimum sentences
firearms **SG8-8**
more than one summary offence **SG8-8**
murder, mandatory life sentences for **SG8-8**
Newton hearings **SG8-8**
other children and young people, charged with **SG8-5**
overarching principles **SG8-2–SG8-10**
parenting orders **SG10-168**
parents and guardians, enforcing responsibilities of **SG8-6**
persistent offenders **SG8-9**
referral orders **SG8-9, SG8-10, SG14-29, SG31-147**
remittal from Crown Court **SG8-5**
reparation orders **SG8-9, SG8-10**
robbery **SG8-2–SG8-12**
sentencing **SG7-1**
sexual offences **SG31-155**
special reasons hearings **SG8-8**
summary offence, more than one **SG8-8**
Victim Surcharge **SG10-148**
welfare of offenders **SG8-4, SG14-28**

Khat warnings **SG10-183**
Knives *see* Bladed articles and offensive weapons
Knowledge **SG8-4**

Lanes, driving in prohibited **SG10-124**
Lavatory, sexual activity in a public **SG10-79**
Learner drivers **SG10-124**
Legal aid **R-510**
Legal representatives **R-508–R-510**
advocates, provisional appointment of **PD-52**
change legal representatives, applications to **R-510**
costs **R-502**
defence trial advocates, identity of **R-25**
extradition **PD-106–PD-107**
functions of representatives **R-508**
legal aid **R-510**
notice of appointment **R-509**
provisional assessment **R-220**
representation orders **PD-106**
service **R-44**
supporters, functions of **R-508**
Lenient sentences, appeals against **R-460–R-465**
attend hearing, right to **R-465**
form of notice of reference **R-462**
permission, applications for **R-461–R-462, R-464**
respondent's notice **R-464**
service of notices **R-461**
variation or withdrawal of notice **R-464**
Licence, driving otherwise than in accordance with **SG10-121**
Life or reckless as to whether life endangered, intent to endanger
arson **SG11-31–SG11-40**
criminal damage **SG11-31–SG11-40**
explosives **SG32-15–SG32-26**
Life imprisonment **PD-84–PD-85, SG4-8–SG4-9**
Lights **SG10-122, SG10-125**
Liquor licences, forfeiture or suspension of **SG10-167**
Listing
allocation of business within Crown Court **PD-120**
authorisation of judges **PD-119**
classification **PD-117**
Court of Appeal **PD-93**
custody time limits **PD-121**
hearings other than trials **PD-122**
judicial responsibility **PD-116**
pre-recorded evidence **PD-45**

referral of Crown Court cases to resident judge and presiding judge **PD-118**
special measures directions **PD-45**
transfer of cases **PD-121**
Welsh language **PD-12**
Live link directions **PD-42, R-186–R-189**
absence of defendants **PD-15**
applications **R-187–R-188**
case management **PD-15, R-8**
conduct of participants **PD-15**
content of applications **R-187**
discharge **R-189**
effective participation **PD-15**
European investigation orders (EIOs) **R-613**
exercise of court's powers **R-186**
extradition **PD-105**
juveniles **PD-15**
not require, where live links **PD-15**
open justice **PD-158**
pre-trial hearings **PD-15**
record of proceedings **PD-15**
representations in response **R-189**
sentence, passing **PD-15**
Live text-based forms of communication from court, use of
fair and accurate reporting, purpose of **PD-22**
notes, taking **PD-23**
photography, restrictions on **PD-22**
Local authorities **SG24-6, SG26-37, SG28-4**
Loss of control **SG25-23–SG25-32**

Magistrates' courts **R-226–R-243, SG10-1–SG10-191**
absence of parties **R-237**
adjourn, power to **R-597**
admission, evidence by **R-231**
aggravated vehicle taking **SG10-102–SG10-103**
alcohol sale offences **SG10-17**
allocation **PD-79, R-78, R-82–R-88**
ancillary orders **SG10-151–SG10-172, SG10-189**
anti-social behaviour orders, breach of **SG10-20**
animal cruelty **SG10-19**
arrest **SG10-23**
arson **SG10-21**
bail **PD-32, R-123, R-126, R-128, SG10-25**
case management **PD-33**
case progression and trial **PD-3**
child, cruelty to a **SG10-38**
communication network offences **SG10-34**
community orders **SG10-35, SG10-149**
compensation orders **SG10-145–SG10-147**
compliance hearings **PD-3**
conduct of hearings **PD-3**
contempt of court **R-598, PD-103**
conviction, procedure after **R-236**
corporate offenders **SG10-36**
costs **R-243, SG10-147**
court officers, duty of **R-79, R-242, R-390, R-638**
Crown Court **PD-3, R-128**
custodial sentences **SG10-150**
custody, defendants in **PD-3**
dangerous dogs **SG10-39**
deferred sentences **SG10-173**
documents, provision of **R-239**
domestic context, offences committed in a **SG10-174–SG10-175**
drink-driving **SG10-111–SG10-112, SG10-118–SG10-119**
drug offences **SG10-40–SG10-45, SG10-47**
drunk and disorderly in a public place **SG10-48**
environmental crimes **SG10-50, SG10-181**
evidence **R-230–R-232**
exposure **SG10-52**
extradition **R-612–R-616**
fines **PD-125, SG10-120–SG10-124, SG31-159**
firearms in a public place, carrying **SG10-53**
fixed penalty notices **SG10-190–SG10-192**
football related offences **SG10-54**
fraud **SG10-55, SG10-69, SG10-100**
further case management hearings **PD-3**
grievous bodily harm/unlawful wounding **SG10-57**
guilty pleas **PD-3, R-83, R-233–R-239**
harassment **SG10-59, SG10-60, SG10-69**
hate crime **SG10-176–SG-180**
identity documents, possession of false/another's/ improperly obtained **SG10-61**
ignorance of proceedings, declarations of, **R-243**
information **SG10-7, R-68–R-69**
initial details of the prosecution case **PD-24, R-71–R-74**
content **R-73**
records of defendants, consideration of **PD-24**
use **R-74**
issues in case, identification of **PD-54**
judiciary, deployment of **PD-123**
justices' legal advisers, duty of **PD-53, R-123, R-241, R-401**
money laundering **SG10-66**
motoring/road traffic offences **SG10-106–SG10-144, SG10-182–SG10-183**
not guilty pleas **PD-3, R-84, R-229**
obstruct/resist a police constable in execution of duty **SG-67**
out of court disposals **SG10-183–SG10-186**
place of trial **R-240**
Plea and Trial Preparation Hearings (PTPHs) **PD-3**
pleas
adult defendants **R-83–R-85**
guilty pleas **R-83**
not guilty pleas **R-84**
requests **R-82**
police bail, reconsideration of **R-126**
powers, exercise of **PD-3, PD-80**
preliminary proceedings **PD-24**
pre-recorded evidence **PD-45**
preparation for trial **PD-33**
pre-trial hearings **PD-3, R-33**
prosecution costs **SG-147**
prostitution, exploitation of **SG10-51**
public order **SG10-70–SG10-74**
racially or religiously aggravated criminal damage **SG10-37**
racially or religiously aggravated harassment **SG10-59, SG10-60**
railway fare evasion **SG10-75**
records of defendants, consideration of **PD-24**
requisitions **R-70**

Magistrates' courts (*cont.*)
school non-attendance **SG10-77**
security arrangements **PD-14**
sending for trial to Crown Court **PD-3, R-74–R-80**
sentences **PD-53–PD-54, R-227–R-244**
setting aside convictions, **R-244**
sex offenders register, failure to comply with notification requirements in relation to **SG10-78**
sexual activity in a public lavatory **SG10-79**
starting prosecutions **R-67–R-70**
summonses or charges **R-68–R-70**
allegations of offences **R-69**
applications **R-68**
taxi touting/soliciting for hire **SG10-82**
terrorism **SG10-83–SG10-89**
theft **SG10-90–SG10-95**
threats **SG10-96**
threats to kill **SG10-96**
trade marks, unauthorised use etc of **SG10-97**
trials **PD-53–PD-54, R-227–R-244**
TV licence payment, evasion of **SG10-98**
urgent applications **PD-14**
vehicle licence/registration fraud **SG10-100**
vehicles, interference with **SG10-99**
vehicles without consent, taking **SG10-101, SG10-102**
victim personal statements **SG10-187–SG10-189**
witness intimidation **SG10-105**
warrants **R-70**
witnesses
in person **R-230**
writing **R-231**
written charges **R-68–R-69**
written evidence **R-231**
Making off without payment **SG10-65, SG33-27–SG33-30**
Mandatory life sentences for murder **SG4-8–SG4-9**
Manslaughter **SG25-1–SG25-44** *see also* Provocation, manslaughter by reason of
diminished responsibility **SG25-33–SG25-44**
gross negligence manslaughter **SG25-13–SG25-22**
loss of control **SG25-23–SG-32**
unlawful act manslaughter **SG25-3–SG25-12**
Marriages, forced **SG10-174**
Media *see* Reporting etc restrictions
Medical reports
commissioning, preparation and consideration of reports **PD-16, PD-89, R-34, R-282**
directions **R-34, R-282**
funding **PD-16, PD-89**
purposes other than sentencing, for **R-34**
remand in custody **PD-16, PD-89**
sentencing **R-282**
timetable **PD-16**
Meeting a child following sexual grooming **SG31-74–SG31-77**
Memory, refreshing **PD-43**
Mental disorders *see* Insanity; Mental disorders, sex offences against persons with; Mental Health Act patients
Mental disorders, sex offences against persons with
care workers **SG31-126–SG31-133**
causing a person with a mental disorder to engage in or agree to engage in sexual activity by inducement, threat or deception **SG31-118–SG31-121**
causing a person with a mental disorder to watch a sexual act **SG31-114–SG31-117, SG31-122–SG31-125, SG31-130–SG31-133**
causing or inciting a person with a mental disorder impeding choice to engage in sexual activity **SG31-110–SG31-113**
engaging in sexual activity in the presence of a person with mental disorder impeding choice **SG31-114–SG31-117**
engaging in sexual activity in the presence, procured by inducement, threat or deception, of a person with a mental disorder **SG31-122–SG31-125**
inducement, threat or deception, causing a person with a mental disorder to watch a sexual act by **SG31-122–SG31-125**
sexual activity with a person with a mental disorder **SG31-110–SG31-113, SG31-126–SG31-130**
Missiles, throwing **SG10-54**
Mitigation **SG2-5, SG10-7, SG10-14**
Mobile telephones, use while driving of **SG10-123**
Mode of trial *see* Allocation decisions
Modes of address **PD-111**
Money laundering **SG26-1–SG26-3, SG26-25–SG26-28**
concealing/disguising/converting/transferring/removing property from England & Wales **SG26-25**
corporate crime **SG10-36, SG10-66, SG26-33–SG26-43**
explosive substances **SG32-57–SG32-66**
magistrates' courts **SG10-166**
Motoring offences *see also* Death by driving, causing; Disqualification from driving; Drink-driving offences; Road traffic offences
aggravated vehicle-taking **SG10-102–SG10-103**
buses **SG10-125**
careless driving **SG10-106–SG10-107, SG22-8–SG22-10**
change of ownership to DVLA, failure to notify **SG10-122**
child car seat, failure to use **SG10-123**
dangerous condition of vehicle/accessories **SG10-125**
dangerous driving **SG10-103, SG10-109, SG22-6**
dangerous parking **SG10-123**
discharge, offences suitable for **SG10-120–SG10-125**
driver offences **SG10-121**
drug driving **SG10-126**
due care and attention, driving without **SG10-106**
excise licences, where there are no **SG10-122**
fines or discharge offences **SG10-120–SG10-125**
goods vehicles **SG10-125**
identity, failure to give information of **SG10-121**
injury, accidents causing **SG10-103**
insurance
failure to produce certificate **SG10-121**
no insurance, where **SG10-116**

licence, driving otherwise than in accordance with SG10-121
magistrates' courts SG10-106–SG10-144
mobile telephones, use while driving of SG10-123
motorway offences SG10-124
number of passengers SG10-123, SG10-125
overloading SG10-124, SG10-125
parking SG10-123
pelican/zebra crossings, contravention of SG10-123
police constables directing traffic, failure to comply with SG10-123
seat belt offences SG10-123
securing of loads SG10-123, SG10-125
speeding SG10-117
stop/report road accidents, failure to SG10-113
stop when required, failure to SG10-123
tachographs SG10-113
test certificates
failure to produce SG10-121
no certificate, where SG10-122
traffic directions, failure to comply with SG10-123
traffic signs, failure to comply with SG10-123
use of vehicle offences SG10-123
weight and loading SG10-123, SG10-125
Motorway offences
carriageway, driving off SG10-124
excluded vehicles SG10-124
hard shoulder, stopping on the SG10-124
lanes, driving in prohibited SG10-124
learner drivers SG10-124
motorway, driving in reverse or wrong way on SG10-124
reverse or the wrong way, driving in SG10-124
slip roads, driving in reverse or the wrong way on SG10-124
U turns SG10-124
walking on motorways, slip roads or hard shoulders SG10-124
Multiple offences SG10-7, SG10-15
Murder
attempted SG13-1–SG13-8
bail R-130
guilty pleas SG4-8–SG4-9
life imprisonment SG4-8–SG4-9

Negligence SG10-6
Neutral citation PD-115
New drivers SG10-183
Newton hearings SG4-7, SG8-8
Non-attendance at school SG10-77
Non-molestation orders SG10-69, SG15-23–SG15-37, SG18-1–SG18-7
Northern Ireland, confiscation proceedings in R-320
Not guilty pleas PD-3, R-84, R-228, R-253, SG10-6
Notes in court, taking PD-23
Notification requirements SG15-36–SG15-39, SG31-156

Oaths or affirmations PD-62
Obstructing/resisting a police constable in execution of duty SG10-67
Offensive weapons *see* Bladed articles and offensive weapons
Omissions R-359
Open justice PD-70, PD-158 *see also* Reporting restrictions
Organised crime cases, case management of PD-127
Out of court disposals SG10-183–SG10-186
cannabis or khat warnings SG10-183
community resolution SG10-186
conditional cautions SG10-184
fixed penalty notices (FPNs) SG10-180
penalty notices for disorder (PNDs) SG10-180
simple cautions SG10-183
Overloading SG10-124, SG10-125
Overriding objective PD-2, R-1–R-3
Overseas production orders R-576–R-581
Overseas forfeiture orders R-609

PACE codes of practice PD-39
Parents
enforcing responsibilities SG8-6
parenting orders SG10-168
Parking, dangerous SG10-123
Partnerships SG24-6, SG26-37, SG28-4
Passengers, number of SG10-123, SG10-125
Paying for the sexual services of a child SG31-102–SG31-105
Pelican/zebra crossings, contravention of SG10-123
Penalty notices *see* Fixed penalty notices (FPNs)
Penetration, assault by SG31-13–SG31-16, SG31-142–SG31-145
Penetration, assault of a child under 13 by SG30-39–SG30-50
Persistent offenders SG8-9
Photographs
court facilities PD-8
indecent photographs of children SG10-62, SG31-86–SG31-89
restrictions in court PD-22
Plea and Trial Preparation Hearings (PTPHs) PD-3, PD-45
Pleas *see also* Guilty pleas
adult defendants R-82–R-84
Crown Court PD-3, PD-73, R-82–R-86, R-248, R-253
magistrates' courts R-82–R-86
not guilty pleas PD-3, R-84, R-229, R-253, SG10-6
Plea and Trial Preparation Hearings (PTPHs) PD-3, PD-45
requests for pleas R-82
unfitness to plead R-254
Police *see also* Investigation of crime
assault SG10-24, SG12-25
assault on a police constable in the execution of his duty SG10-24, SG12-25
bail PD-30, R-126
interviews, recording of PD-39
juries PD-60
obstructing/resisting a constable in execution of duty SG10-67
stop when required, failure to SG10-123
traffic directions, failure to comply with SG10-123
Pornography
indecent photographs of children SG10-62, SG31-86–SG31-89

Possession
bladed articles and offensive weapons SG10-27–SG10-29, SG14-3, SG14-22–SG14-29
drugs SG23-12–SG23-14, SG23-16, SG23-28–SG23-33
explosive substances SG32-57–SG32-66
fraud SG26-13–SG26-16
identity documents, false/another's/improperly obtained SG10-61
indecent photographs of children SG10-62, SG31-86–SG31-89
offensive weapons SG10-27–SG10-29
Practice Directions *see* Criminal Practice Directions (CPDs)
Preliminary rulings to the Court of Justice PD-99, R-491–R-493
Preparation for trial in the Crown Court PD-3, R-19–R-32
abuse of process, applications to stay for R-26
arraigning the defendant on the indictment R-30
defence trial advocates, identity of R-25
indictment, amendment of R-28
joint or separate trials, applications for R-27–R-28
non-jury trials containing information withheld from defendant R-22
place of trial R-31
preparatory hearings PD-12, PD-20–PD-23, R-20–R-32, R-418–R-425
applications R-21–R-23, R-26, R-29
commencement R-24
joint or separate trials, applications for R-27–R-28
representations R-23
pre-recorded evidence PD-45
pre-trial hearings, general rules for R-19
security arrangements PD-14
sending for trial PD-25
sentence, indication of R-29
Welsh language, use of R-32
Preparatory hearings
applications R-21–R-23, R-26, R-29
commencement R-24
Court of Appeal R-418–R-425
Crown Court R-20–R-32
joint or separate trials, applications for R-27–R-28
reporting restrictions PD-20–PD-23
representations R-23
Welsh language PD-12
Pre-recording of cross-examination and re-examination PD-45–PD-46
applications PD-45
Court of Appeal guidance PD-45
first hearing in magistrates' court PD-45
ground rules hearings PD-45–PD-46
listing and allocation PD-45
Plea and Trial Preparation Hearings (PTPH) PD-45
preparation for trial PD-45
reporting restrictions and media access PD-45
special measures directions PD-45
Pre-sentence reports SG9-7, SG9-10, SG10-150
Presumption of innocence PD-2
Prevalence SG2-7, SG10-188, SG33-4
Previous convictions SG10-7
Primary care responsibilities, offenders with SG6-1
Prison *see* Custodial sentences
Private hearings R-62–R-64
Private sexual images, disclosing SG27-30–SG27-33
Proceeds of Crime Act 2002
account monitoring orders R-531, R-531A
appeals R-467–R-486
closed, where court office is R-319
Court of Appeal R-467–R-486
customer information orders R-531, R-531A
disclosure orders R-530, R-530A
entry, powers of R-529, R-529A
further information orders R-529, R-529A
investigations R-527–R-533, R-527A–R-533A, R-542, R-542A, R-569–R-572, R-569A–R-572A
moratorium period, orders for extension of R-569–R-572, R-569A–R-572A
production orders R-528, R-528A
Production orders R-520, R-520A, R-522, R-522A, R-528, R-528A
electronic data, orders for access to R-576–R-581, R-573A–R-578A
European investigation orders (EIOs) R-614–R-615
extradition R-533, R-533A
overseas production orders R-576–R-581, R-573A–R-578A
terrorism R-522, R-522A
Proportionality SG10-11
Proscribed organisations SG32-37–SG32-56
membership SG10-88, SG32-37–SG32-346
supporting SG10-89, SG32-47–SG32-56
Prosecution *see also* Deferred prosecution agreements
appeals against rulings adverse to the prosecution R-245–R-436
assisting the prosecution SG10-15
costs SG10-147
disclosure R-144–R-145, R-148
discontinuance R-107, R-111–R-113, R-633
draft indictments, service of PD-26
starting prosecutions R-67–R-70
Prostitution
arranging or facilitating sexual exploitation of a child SG31-98–SG31-101
brothel used for prostitution, keeping a SG10-64, SG31-94–SG31-97
causing or inciting sexual exploitation of a child SG31-98–SG31-111
causing or inciting prostitution for gain SG10-51, SG31-90–SG31-93
child, paying for the sexual services of a SG31-102–SG31-105
controlling a child in relation to sexual exploitation SG31-98–SG31-101
controlling prostitution for gain SG10-151, SG31-90–SG31-93
magistrates' courts SG10-151
Protective orders, breach of SG10-69, SG18-1–SG18-7
custodial sentences SG10-69, SG18-1–SG18-6
non-molestation orders SG10-69, SG15-23–SG15-37, SG18-1–SG18-7

restraining orders SG10-69, SG15-23–SG15-37, SG18-1–SG18-7
Provocation, manslaughter by reason of SG10-174, SG29-1
Psychological harm SG6-1
Public access restrictions R-60–R-66
Court of Appeal R-451–R-459
electronic communications R-65
forfeiture of unauthorised sound recordings R-66
international co-operation R-602
private hearings R-62–R-64
removal R-61
representations in response R-63
sound recordings R-65–R-66
variation R-61
Public bodies SG24-6, SG26-37, SG28-4
Public funding R-510
Public interest R-145, R-148, R-433
Public order offences
affray SG10-71
disorderly behaviour SG10-72–SG10-73
drunk and disorderly in public place SG10-48
fear or provocation of violence SG10-72
harassment, alarm or distress
disorderly behaviour SG10-72, SG10-74
intent to cause SG10-72
magistrates' courts SG10-70–SG10-74
racially/religiously aggravated disorderly behaviour SG10-74
racially/religiously aggravated threatening behaviour SG10-72
violent disorder SG10-70
Public places
drunk and disorderly in SG10-48
firearms, carrying SG10-53
threatening with an offensive weapon SG14-13
Public protection, extended sentences for SG3-12
Publicity orders SG28-10

Questions of law, applications for ruling on R-247

Racially or religiously aggravated offences SG11-11–SG11-30
actual bodily harm, assault occasioning SG10-22, SG12-19–SG12-21
assault SG10-33, SG10-37, SG10-57, SG10-63, SG12-13–SG12-19, SG12-28
common assault SG10-33, SG12-28
criminal damage SG10-37, SG11-11–SG11-13
£5000, value exceeding SG11-11–SG11-13
£5000, value not exceeding SG11-21–SG11-30
drugs or alcohol, misuse of SG11-13
grievous bodily harm SG10-57, SG10-63, SG12-13–SG12-18
harassment SG10-50, SG10-73, SG10-74, SG10-159
hate crime SG10-177–SG10-180
public order SG10-72
seriousness SG10-7
stalking SG27-20–SG27-29
statutory provisions SG10-176
threatening behaviour SG10-172
wounding SG10-57, SG10-63, SG-143
Racist chanting at football matches SG10-54
Railway fare evasion SG10-75
Rape SG31-3–SG31-12
13, child under SG31-38–SG31-31
campaigns of rape SG31-4, SG31-30
Reasons
ancillary orders SG10-10–SG10-11
bad character evidence R-209
sentencing R-275
sexual behaviour, evidence of previous R-213
special measures directions R-167
Receivership proceedings R-344–R-365, R-372–R-379
accounts R-378
chambers, business in R-351
conferral of powers R-373
confiscation proceedings R-348–R-366, R-372–R-379, R-480–R-486
consent orders R-358
control of goods, taking R-348
costs R-363–R-366
assessment R-364
rules, application of R-366
time for compliance R-365
court documents R-357–R-362
Court of Appeal R-480–R-486
discharge R-374
disclosure R-356, R-361
distress and forfeiture R-348
enforcement receivers
applications, for R-372–R-373
appointment R-372
conferral of powers R-373
evidence, court's power to control R-372
forfeiture R-348
hearsay R-355
inspection of documents R-356
joining of applications R-349
management receivers
applications, for R-372–R-373
appointment R-372
conferral of powers R-373
non-compliance by receivers R-379
omissions R-359
preparation of documents R-362
remuneration R-377
security R-376
slips R-359
summons R-354
sums in the hands of receivers R-375
supply of documents from court records R-360
variation R-374
witnesses R-353–R-354
writing, applications to be dealt with in R-350
Recklessness SG10-6
Recording interviews
audio recording PD-39
memory refreshing and watching at different time from juror PD-43
video recording PD-39, PD-43
Records *see* Court records
Reductions PD-73, PD-76, SG4-1–SG4-11
Re-examination, pre-recording of PD-45–PD-46
Referral orders SG8-9, SG8-10, SG14-29, SG31-147
Religiously aggravated offences *see* Racially or religiously aggravated offences

Remands PD-31, PD-89
Remedial orders SG28-10
Reparation orders SG8-9, SG8-10
Reporting etc. restrictions R-57–R-66
access restrictions R-60
appeals
advance notice R-454
Court of Appeal R-451–R-459
form of notice R-453
respondent's notice R-456
service of notice R-452
attend hearing, right to R-459
electronic communications PD-22, R-65–R-66
evidence, right to introduce R-458
exercise of court's powers R-58
fair and accurate reporting, use of live text-based forms of communication for PD-22
forfeiture of unauthorised sound recordings R-66
general matters PD-22
live text-based communication, use of PD-22
notes in court, taking PD-23
preliminary proceedings PD-20–PD-23
pre-recorded evidence PD-45
private, trials in R-62, R-64
public access, restricting R-454–R-455
removal of restrictions R-61
renewal of applications R-457
representations in response R-63
retrials for acquittals for serious offences R-270
sound recordings R-65–R-66
preliminary proceedings PD-20–PD-21
unofficial PD-20
special measures directions PD-45
Twitter PD-22
variation R-61
Representation orders PD-106
Representatives *see* Legal representatives
Requisitions R-70
Resist arrest, assault with intent to SG10-23, SG12-22
Restitution orders R-281, SG10-169
Restraining orders R-317–R-328, SG15-23–SG15-37, SG18-1–SG18-7
acquittals SG10-170
ancillary orders R-367–R-371
contempt of court R-386
Court of Appeal R-480–R-486
discharge R-369–R-371
domestic abuse SG5-7
forfeiture R-348
harassment SG10-69
international co-operation R-610
variation R-369–R-370
Restraint proceedings R-348–R-371
ancillary orders, applications for R-367–R-371
appeals R-480–R-486
applications R-367–R-368
chambers, business in R-351
consent orders R-358
contempt of court R-386
control of goods, taking R-348
costs R-363–R-366
assessment R-364
rules, application of R-366
time for compliance R-365
court documents R-357–R-362
discharge R-369–R-371
disclosure R-356, R-361
evidence R-352
hearsay R-355
inspection of documents R-356
joining of applications R-349
omissions R-359
preparation of documents R-362
slips R-359
summons R-354
supply of documents from court records R-360
variation R-369–R-370
witnesses R-353–R-354
writing, applications to be dealt with in R-350
Restraints in court, use of PD-13
Retention or return of property R-545–R-551, R-545A–R-551A
applications R-547–R-548, R-547A–R-548A
contempt of court R-551, R-551A
exercise of court's powers R-546, R-546A
information withheld from other party, applications containing R-550, R-550A
Police (Property) Act 1897, applications for orders under R-547, R-547A
representations in response R-550, R-550A
Retrials after acquittal R-268–R-274
certificates, application for R-269
Court of Appeal, applications to R-270–R-274
Crown Court for summons or warrants, application to R-273
reporting restrictions R-270
respondent's notice R-272
summons or warrants, application for R-273
Retrials for acquittals for serious offences R-268–R-274
certificates, application for R-269
Court of Appeal
full court, determination by R-473
procedure R-274
quash acquittal, to R-269
notice R-272
quash acquittals, applications to R-270
respondent's notice R-272
summons or warrants, application to Crown Court for R-273
Revenue offences
fraud SG10-76, SG26-17–SG26-20
VAT fraud SG26-17, SG26-19
Reverse or the wrong way, driving in SG10-124
Road traffic offences R-286–R-291 *see also* Disqualification from driving; individual offences; Motoring offences
appeals R-291
compensation orders SG-145
courses or programme certificate decisions, declarations about R-290
endorsements
information to be supplied R-288
representations R-286
fines R-289
fixed penalty notices, statutory declarations to avoid fines after R-289
foreign driving disqualification, appeals against recognition of R-290

information R-288
magistrates' courts SG10-182–SG10-183
penalties R-286–R-291
personal injuries SG10-145
Robbery SG30-1–SG30-20
commercial robbery SG30-3–SG30-20
dwellings, robberies in SG30-17–SG30-20
juveniles SG30-147
overarching principles and guidelines SG30-147
professionally planned commercial robberies SG30-13–SG30-16
reasons SG30-11
reductions SG30-6–SG30-7
referral orders SG30-147
street or less sophisticated robbery SG30-3–SG30-12
structure, ranges and starting points SG30-2, SG30-5, SG30-14–SG30-15, SG30-18–SG30-19
totality principle SG30-9

Samples *see* Specimens/samples
Schools, non-attendance at SG10-77
Scotland, confiscation proceedings in R-162
Searches
confiscation proceedings R-344
European investigation orders (EIOs) R-614–R-615
Seat belt offences SG10-123
Securing of loads SG10-123, SG10-125
Security arrangements at court PD-13–PD-14
additional security measures PD-13
armed police presence, procedure for application for PD-14
Crown Court, applications to PD-14
designated court centres PD-14
emergency situations PD-14
high-risk prisoners giving evidence from witness box PD-13
magistrates' court, applications to PD-14
preparatory work prior to applications PD-14
restraints, applications for use of approved PD-13
Royal Courts of Justice, armed police presence in PD-15
urgent applications PD-14
Seizure R-341–R-347
appeals R-342
approval, applications for R-344
detention proceedings R-344–R-347
extend detention period, applications to R-345–R-346
realise seized property, applications to R-341–R-342
search, applications to R-344
surplus proceedings, applications for directions about R-342
Sending for trial to Crown Court R-75–R-90
allocation PD-25, R-80–R-88
bail PD-28
case management PD-3
court officers, duties of R-79
custody time limits PD-28
dismissal, applications for R-90
exercise of powers R-76
guilty pleas PD-3
indictment R-93–R-94
initial procedure after sending R-89–R-90
justices legal advisers, duties of R-78
magistrates' courts PD-3, R-75–R-81
matters to be specified R-77
mode of trial PD-25
preliminary proceedings PD-24
prosecutor's notice requiring Crown Court trial R-80
service of prosecution evidence R-89
without allocation to Crown Court, sending R-80–R-81
Sentencing *see under* individual sentences; Sentencing Guidelines; Sentencing procedure
Sentencing Guidelines SG4-1–SG33-31 *see also under* Specific offences
aggravating factors SG10-6–SG10-7, SG10-11, SG10-14
allocation decisions SG1-1, SG10-2
ancillary orders SG10-10, SG10-15, SG10-151–SG10-171, SG10-189
category
determination of offence SG10-13
range SG10-14
community orders SG9-1, SG9-2–SG9-8, SG10-149
breach SG10-35
compensation orders SG10-15, SG10-145–SG10-146
costs SG10-147–SG10-148
Crown Court SG10-2
culpability SG2-3, SG2-5, SG10-5–SG10-7
custodial sentences SG9-1, SG9-9–SG9-12, SG10-5, SG10-150
deferred sentences SG10-173
fines SG10-6, SG10-127–SG10-144
first time offenders SG10-6
fixed penalty notices (FPNs) SG10-190
further steps SG10-15
guilty pleas, reduction for SG4-1–SG4-11, SG10-9, SG10-15
harm SG10-6–SG10-7
intention SG10-6
juveniles SG7-1, SG8-2–SG8-12
knowledge SG10-6
magistrates' courts SG10-1–SG10-191
mitigation SG10-7–SG10-8, SG10-11, SG10-14
multiple offences SG10-7, SG10-15
negligence SG10-6
not guilty pleas SG10-6
obligation to follow guidelines SG10-1
offence activities SG10-6
overarching principles SG2-1–SG2-7, SG5-1–SG5-8, SG6-1
pre-Sentencing Council Guidelines, using SG10-3–SG10-4, SG10-12
proportionality SG10-11
protective orders, breach of SG10-69, SG18-1–SG18-6
provisional sentences SG10-7–SG10-8, SG10-14–SG10-15
racially or religiously aggravated offences
criminal damage SG10-37

Sentencing Guidelines (*cont.*)
disorderly behaviour **SG10-73, SG10-74**
grievous bodily harm **SG10-57**
harassment, alarm or distress **SG10-73**
threatening behaviour **SG10-72**
reasons for departing from guidelines, obligation to provide reasons **SG10-1, SG10-11**
recklessness **SG10-6**
seriousness **SG2-1–SG2-7, SG10-5–SG10-8, SG10–15**
starting points **SG10-6–SG10-7, SG10-14**
taken into consideration, offences **SG3-1–SG3-6**
totality principle **SG3-7–SG3-18, SG10-15**
use of guidelines **SG10-2, SG10-12**
victim personal statements **SG10-187–SG10-188**
Sentencing procedure **PD-73–PD-88, R-275–R-284**
see also Totality principle in sentencing
appeals **PD-90–PD-98, R-437–R-449**
assistance given or withheld, applications to review sentence because **R-285**
binding over orders **PD-82**
businesses, impact statements for **PD-81**
committal for sentence **PD-83, R-283, SG21-25, SG2-1, SG9-7, SG10-154**
compensation etc orders, variation or discharge of **R-279**
community impact statements **PD-80**
community sentences, **R-276**
concurrent and consecutive sentences **PD-77**
conditional discharges **PD-82**
discharge **R-279**
disqualification, applications to remove, revoke or suspend **R-280**
factual basis, determination of **PD-74**
families bereaved by homicide and other criminal conduct **PD-79**
financial information required **PD-88**
flowchart **SG9-12**
guardianship, information to be supplied on admission to **R-283**
guilty pleas, reduction for **PD-73, PD-76**
hospital, information to be supplied on admission to **R-283**
indication of sentence, applications for **PD-75, R-29**
lenient sentences, appeals against **R-460–R-465**
life sentences, imposition of **PD-84–PD-85**
live links **PD-15**
mandatory life sentences **PD-85**
medical reports, commissioning **R-282**
minimum term in open court, procedure for announcing **PD-87**
notification requirements **R-277**
reasons, provision of **R-275**
restitution orders in theft cases **R-281**
seriousness **SG2-1–SG2-7**
special cases **R-275–R-284**
suspension **R-280**
transitional arrangements **PD-86**
variation **R-278–R-279**
victim personal statements **PD-78**
Serious crime prevention orders (SCPOs) **SG31-156**
Serious physical harm, causing or allowing a child to suffer **SG20-15**
Seriousness, overarching principle of **SG2-2–SG2-7, SG10–15**
aggravating factors **SG2-5, SG10-7**
community sentences threshold **SG2-6, SG9-3–SG9-4**
culpability **SG2-3, SG2-5, SG10-5–SG10-7**
custody threshold **SG2-6, SG10-5**
foreseeability **SG10-5**
guilty pleas, reduction for **SG2-5**
harm **SG2-4–SG2-5, SG10-6–SG10-7**
mitigation **SG2-5, SG10-7–SG10-8**
prevalence **SG2-7**
previous convictions **SG10-7**
racially or religiously aggravated offences **SG10-7**
sexual orientation, hostility based on **SG10-7**
thresholds **SG2-6, SG10-5**
transgender identity, hostility based on **SG10-7**
Service of documents **R-35–R-47, R-513A**
confiscation proceedings **R-326–R-327**
Court of Appeal **R-419, R-428, R-438, R-452, R-461**
court officers, on **R-513, R-513A**
Crown Court appeals **R-388**
custody, persons in **R-42**
date of service **R-45**
directions **R-47**
document exchange (DX), by **R-39**
electronic means, by **R-40**
handing over documents, by **R-37**
High Court, appeals to **R-628**
indictment **R-91, R-93–R-95, R-97–R-99**
international co-operation **R-600–R-601**
leaving documents, by **R-38**
legal representative, documents that may not be served on a **R-44**
methods **R-36–R-44**
notice to accompany process served out of jurisdiction **R-596**
other methods other than described/specified, service by **R-43**
outside the jurisdiction **R-325, R-596–R-600**
post, by **R-38**
Proceeds of Crime Act 2002 **R-317–R-326**
process **R-600**
proof of service **R-46**
sending for trial to Crown Court **R-89**
specified methods, documents which must be served by **R-41**
witness summons **R-159**
Sex Offenders Register, failure to comply with notification requirements of **SG10-78**
Sexual assault **SG31-17–SG31-20**
13, children under **SG10-81, SG31-39–SG31-56**
magistrates' courts **SG10-80, SG10-81**
penetration, assault by **SG31-6–SG31-16, SG31-39–SG31-50**
Sexual behaviour, evidence of complainant's previous **R-211–R-217**
applications for permission to introduce evidence or cross-examination **R-214**
cross-examination **PD-51, R-214**
decisions and reasons **R-213**
exercise of court's powers **R-212**
grounds rules hearings (GRHs) **PD-51**

late applications PD-51
reasons for decisions R-213
replies to applications R-215
special measures directions, applications for R-216–R-217
vary requirements, court's power to R-218
Sexual harm prevention orders (SHPOs) SG10-171, SG10-172, SG15-32–SG15-35
Sexual offences SG31-4–SG31-6 *see also* Child sex offences; Mental disorders, sex offences against persons with; Prostitution; Sexual assault
causing a person to engage in sexual activity without consent SG31-24–SG31-27
causing or inciting sexual activity SG31-126–SG31-130
children or young persons, offences committed by SG8-2–SG8-9, SG-155
committing an offence with intent to commit a sexual offence SG31-150
evidence PD-51
exposure SG10-52, SG31-134–SG31-137
historical sexual offences SG31-157–SG31-158
notification requirements SG15-36–SG15-39, SG31-156
previous sexual behaviour, evidence of complainant's R-211–R-217
private sexual images, disclosing SG27-30–SG27-33
public lavatory, sexual activity in a SG10-79
rape SG31-3–SG31-6, SG31-28–SG31-31
13, child under SG31-28–SG31-31
campaigns of rape SG31-4, SG31-30
sexual activity in a public lavatory SG10-79
sexual harm prevention orders (SHPOs) SG10-171, SG10-172
sexual offences prevention orders SG10-172, SG31-156
trafficking SG31-106–SG31-109
trespass with intent to commit a sexual offence SG31-151–SG31-154
voyeurism SG10-104, SG31-138
youth court PD-124
Sexual offences prevention orders (SOPOs) SG10-172, SG31-156
Sexual orientation, aggravation relating to SG10-7, SG10-177–SG10-180
Shoplifting SG10-95, SG33-11–SG33-14
Shot guns, carrying SG10-53
Skeleton arguments PD-97, PD-108, PD-113
Slavery and trafficking prevention orders (STPOs) SG31-156
Slip roads SG10-124
Slips R-359
Social security
fines SG10-139, SG10-144
fraud SG10-26, SG26-21–SG26-23
Sound recordings R-65–R-66
Special measures directions PD-41–PD-46, R-164–R-189 *see also* Live link directions
allocation PD-45
anonymity PD-44, R-181–R-185
appeal hearings, at PD-9
applications PD-45, R-166, R-173–R-175, R-178–R-179, R-216–R-217
before trial, sentencing or appeal PD-9
case management PD-6–PD-9, PD–15
children and young witnesses PD-45, PD-46
content of applications R-173–R-175, R-178
custody of documents R-169
decisions and reasons R-167
defendants' evidence directions R-177–R-180
discharge R-174, R-179
exercise of court's powers R-171, R-177
general rules R-166–R-170
ground rules for questioning PD-7
ground rules hearings (GRHs) PD-45–PD-46
information withheld from another party, applications containing R-175
intermediaries PD-8, R-170
listing PD-45
media access PD-45
memory, refreshing PD-43
photographs of court facilities PD-8
preparation for trial PD-45
pre-recording of cross-examination and re-examination PD-45
public access PD-45
reasons R-167
recording of cross-examination and re-examination PD-45
reporting restrictions PD-45
representations in response R-176, R-180
sentencing hearings, at PD-9
trial, at PD-9
variation of requirements R-168, R-174, R-179
visually recorded interviews PD-43
watching at a different time from trial court PD-43
withheld from another party, applications containing information R-175
witness, definition of R-165
young witnesses R-172
Special reasons hearings SG4-7
Specimens/samples
drink-driving SG10-114–SG10-115
drugs SG10-41
failure or refusal to provide SG10-41
failure to provide for analysis SG10-114–SG10-115
Speeding SG10-117, SG22-3
Spent convictions PD-50
Stalking SG27-18–SG27-29
racially or religiously aggravated stalking SG27-20–SG27-29
Statements of truth R-323
Stay of proceedings PD-5, R-26, R-484
Steering SG10-122, SG10-125
Stop/report road accidents, failure to SG10-113
Stop when required, failure to SG10-123
Striking out notices R-485
Summary offences, flowchart on SG4-10
Summary trials *see* Magistrates' courts
Summing-up PD-67, R-258
Summonses R-68–R-70, R-273, R-354
Supply or offering to supply drugs SG10-43, SG10-46, SG30-25–SG30-29
Supreme Court, appeals or references to R-487–R-490
bail R-490
confiscation proceedings R-476
Court of Appeal R-476, R-487–R-490

Supreme Court, appeals or references to (*cont.*)
detention pending appeal R-489, R-635
discharge of defendants R-635
extradition R-634–R-635
High Court, appeals to R-634–R-637
permission R-488, R-634
Sureties/recognizances
bail PD-33, R-134–R-135, R-446
forfeiture PD-33, R-135, R-446
Suspended sentences R-276, SG9-11, SG10-150

Tachographs SG10-125
Tagging R-132, SG9-8
Taken into consideration offences (tics) SG3-1–SG3-6
Taking vehicles without consent SG10-103
Tax credit fraud SG26-21, SG26-23
Tax fraud SG26-17–SG26-20
cheating the public revenue SG26-17–SG26-20
income tax SG26-17–SG26-20
VAT frauds SG26-17–SG26-20
Taxis, touting/soliciting for hire by SG10-82
Telephone facilities PD-15, R-8, R-598
Television links R-604
Terrorism R-516–R-521, R-516A–R-521A, SG32-1–SG32-101
account monitoring orders R-526, R-526A
additional guidance SG32-99
case management PD-126
collection of terrorist information SG10-83, SG32-89–SG32-99
ancillary orders SG32-99–SG32-100
automatic orders on conviction SG32-100
community orders SG32-101
custodial offences SG32-10, SG32-22
customer information orders R-525, R-525A
dangerousness SG32-9, SG32-21, SG32-83
definitive guideline SG32-1–SG32-101
disclosure
failure to disclose information SG10-85, SG32-67–SG32-76
orders R-523, R-523A
dissemination of terrorist publications SG32-27–SG32-36
encouragement of terrorism SG10-84, SG32-27–SG32-36
entry, powers of R-522, R-522A
explanation orders R-524, R-524A
explosive substances SG32-15–SG32-26
attempts to cause explosions SG32-15–SG32-26
causing explosion likely to endanger life SG32-15–SG32-26
making or keeping explosives with intent to endanger life SG32-15–SG32-26
funding terrorism SG10-86, SG32-57–SG32-66
fundraising SG32-57–SG32-66
money laundering SG32-57–SG32-66
use and possession SG32-57–SG32-66
further information orders R-523, R-523A
investigation orders R-521–R-526, R-521A–R-526A, R-541, R-541A
magistrates' courts SG10-83–SG10-90
notification requirements SG32-100
possession for terrorist purposes SG32-77–SG32-88
preparation of terrorist acts SG32-3–SG32-14
production orders R-522, R-522A
proscribed organisations SG32-37–SG32-56
membership SG10-88, SG32-37–SG32-46
supporting SG10-89, SG32-47–SG32-56
special custodial sentences for certain offenders of particular concern SG32-10, SG32-22, SG32-84
Test certificates SG10-121–SG10-122
Theft SG33-1–SG33-26
abstraction/use of electricity without authority SG10-49, SG33-23–SG33-25
ancillary orders SG33-5
breach of trust SG10-91–SG10-92
diversionary work SG33-13
dwellings, in SG10-93
general principles SG10-90
general theft SG33-2–SG33-4
going equipped for theft or burglary SG10-56, SG33-19–SG33-22
guilty pleas SG33-5
handling stolen goods SG10-58, SG33-15–SG33-18
harm SG10-57, SG33-3, SG33-12
magistrates' courts SG10-90–SG10-95
person, from the SG10-94
prevalence SG33-4
restitution orders R-281
seriousness SG33-4, SG33-13
shoplifting SG10-95, SG33-11–SG33-14
stalls, from SG33-11–SG33-14
vehicle taking (aggravated) SG10-102
vehicle taking without consent SG10-103
Threats
bladed articles and offensive weapons SG10-28, SG10-29, SG14-13–SG14-29
criminal damage SG11-41–SG11-49
fear or provocation of violence SG10-72
kill, threats to SG10-96, SG27-37–SG27-49
magistrates' courts SG10-96
mental disorder, sexual offences against persons with a SG31-118–SG31-125
racial or religious aggravation SG10-72
sexual activity by inducement, threat or deception, causing a person with a mental disorder to engage in or agree to engage in SG31-118–SG31-122
Throwing missiles SG10-54
Tickets, unauthorised sale or attempted sale of SG10-54
Time limits *see* Custody time limits
Totality principle in sentencing SG3-7–SG3-18, SG10-15
aggravating factors SG10-7
community orders SG3-10, SG3-16
compensation orders SG3-18
concurrent and consecutive sentences SG3-9–SG3-10
custodial sentences
determinate SG3-11
specific application SG3-11
disqualification from driving SG3-17
extended sentences for public protection SG3-12
fines
combined with other sentences SG3-15

multiple fines, for non-imprisonable offences SG3-14
general principles SG3-8
indeterminate sentences SG3-13
mitigation SG10-7
public protection sentences SG3-12
Trade marks, unauthorised SG10-97, SG10-166
Traffic directions, failure to comply with SG10-123
Traffic signs, failure to comply with SG10-123
Trafficking people SG31-106–SG31-109
interim guidance SG31-106
Modern Slavery Act 2015 SG31-106
sexual exploitation SG31-106–SG31-109
slavery and trafficking prevention orders (STPOs) SG31-156
Transcripts PD-18, R-475
Transgender identity SG10-7, SG10-177–SG10-180
Translations R-596
Trespass with intent to commit a sexual offence SG31-151–SG31-154
TV licence payment evasion SG10-98
Tyres SG10-122, SG10-125

U turns SG10-124
Unfit through drink or drugs, driving/attempting to drive whilst SG10-118–SG10-119
Unlawful act manslaughter SG25-3–SG25-12
Unlawful wounding SG10-57, SG10-63, SG12-13
Unlicensed, disqualified or uninsured drivers, death caused by SG10-108, SG22-12
Urgent applications PD-14

VAT fraud SG26-17–SG26-20
Vehicle taking (aggravated) SG10-103–SG10-104
Vehicle taking without consent SG10-104
Vehicles *see also* Motoring offences; Road traffic offences
aggravated vehicle taking SG10-103–SG10-104
dangerous condition of vehicle/ accessories SG10-122, SG10-125
forfeiture SG24-12
interference with vehicle SG10-99
licence/registration fraud SG10-100
Venue for trial SG1-1
Verdicts PD-67, R-258
Victim personal statements (VPSs) PD-78, SG10-187–SG10-188
community impact statements SG10-188
domestic abuse SG5-8
prevalence SG10-188
Victims *see also* Compensation orders; Victim personal statements (VPSs)
assault, effect of SG6-1
fraud SG26-5
hate crime, impact of SG10-180
homicide and other criminal conduct, families bereaved by PD-79
provocation SG28-12
Victim Surcharge SG10-145, SG10-148
Video recording
evidence in chief PD-43
interviews PD-39, PD-43
juries, watching at different times from PD-43
PACE codes of practice PD-39
Views PD-66
Violent disorder SG10-70
Visually recorded interviews PD-43
Voluntary bills of indictment PD-27
Voyeurism SG10-104, SG31-138–SG31-141
Vulnerable persons *see also* Vulnerable people in court
ancillary orders SG31-156
road users SG22-3
Vulnerable people in court PD-6–PD-9 *see also* Special measures directions
before trial, sentencing or appeal PD-9
ground rules hearings to plan questioning PD-7
photographs of court facilities PD-8
trial, sentencing or appeal hearing, during PD-9

Wales and Welsh language PD-10–PD-12
applications for evidence to be given in Welsh PD-11
Crown Court PD-12, R-32
devolution issues PD-10
forms R-49
interpreters PD-12, R-32
jurors PD-12
liaison judges, role of PD-12
listing PD-12
preliminary and plea and case management hearings PD-12
use in court PD-12, R-32
witnesses PD-12
Walking on motorways, slip roads or hard shoulders SG10-124
Warnings on cannabis, informal SG10-183
Warrants *see also* Investigation warrants; Warrants for arrest, detention or imprisonment
European investigation orders (EIOs) R-614–R-615
fines R-298–R-300
magistrates' courts R-68
search warrants R-614–R-615
Warrants for arrest, detention or imprisonment R-114–R-120, R-616–R-619
cease to have effect on payment, warrants which R-119
closed, issued when court office is R-120
Crown Court, applications to R-273
execution R-118
extradition R-615–R-620, R-625, R-628, R-633, R-638
information to be included R-117
provisional warrants R-619–R-620
terms R-115–R-116
Wasted costs R-502
Watch a sexual act, causing a child to SG31-69–SG31-72, SG31-82–SG31-85
Weapons SG10-165, SG27-12 *see also* Bladed articles and offensive weapons; Firearms
Weight and loading of vehicles SG10-123, SG10-125
Welfare benefit fraud SG26-21, SG26-23
Welsh *see* Wales and Welsh language
Witness anonymity orders R-181–R-185
applications PD-44
case management PD-44
conduct of applications R-182
confidential information, retention of PD-44

Witness anonymity orders (*cont.*)
content of applications **R-182**
determination of applications **PD-44**
Director of Public Prosecutions, duty of court officers to notify **R-183**
discharge **PD-44, R-184**
disclosure of prosecution material pending applications **PD-44**
exercise of court's powers **R-181**
representations in response **R-185**
responses to applications **PD-44**
service of evidence **PD-44**
variation **PD-44, R-184**
Witness statements **R-152–R-155**
audio recorded interviews **PD-39**
composite statements **PD-37**
confiscation proceedings **R-324**
contempt of court **R-592–R-593, R-595**
contents **R-153, R-592–R-593**
Crown Court **R-256**
editing single statements **PD-37**
evidence, written statements in **PD-37, R-155**
exhibits, references to **R-154**
oral evidence, witnesses who give **PD-18**
Proceeds of Crime Act 2002 **R-324**
video recorded evidence in chief **PD-38**
video recorded interviews **PD-39**
written statements **R-152–R-155**
Witness summons, warrants and orders **R-156–R-163**
applications **R-158**
children subject to current family proceedings **PD-40**
confidentiality **R-161**
documents, applications for summons to produce **R-160–R-161**
form **R-159**
issue with or without a hearing **R-157**
relevance **R-161**
service **R-159**
special rules **R-160**
variation of requirements **R-163**
wards of court **PD-40**
withdrawal, applications for **R-162**
Witnesses *see also* Cross-examination; Special measures directions; Witness statements
anonymity orders **R-181–R-185, R-466**
child witnesses **PD-8, PD-40, PD-45, PD-46, R-172**
confiscation proceedings **R-469**
Court of Appeal **R-469**
Crown Court **R-255–R-256**
definition **R-165**
European investigation orders (EIOs) **R-612–R-613**
examination of witnesses by court **R-469**
high-risk prisoners giving evidence from witness box **PD-13**
intimidation **SG10-105**
magistrates' courts **R-230–R-231**
memory, refreshing **PD-43**
receivership orders **R-353–R-355**
restraint proceedings **R-353–R-354**
security arrangements **PD-13**
summons, warrants and orders **R-156–R-163**
Welsh language **PD-12**
Wounding
intent, wounding with **SG12-3–SG12-18**
magistrates' courts **SG10-57**
racially or religiously aggravated wounding **SG10-57, SG10-63, SG12-3**
unlawful wounding **SG10-57, SG10-63, SG12-3**

Young persons *see* Children and young persons; Juveniles
Youth rehabilitation orders (YROs) **SG8-9–SG8-10**
bladed articles and offensive weapons **SG14-29**
breaches **SG8-10**
fostering **SG8-9, SG8-12, SG14-29**
further offences, commission of **SG8-10**
nature and extent of requirements **SG8-9**
supervision and surveillance, intensive **SG8-9, SG8-12, SG14-29**
wilful and persistent breaches **SG8-10**